000779

Printed in the United States of America
Library of Congress Catalog Card Number: 72–149978

ISBN: 0-13-392316-9

10 9 8 7 6 5 4 3 2 1

Prentice-Hall International, Inc., *London*
Prentice-Hall of Australia, Pty. Ltd., *Sydney*
Prentice-Hall of Canada, Ltd., *Toronto*
Prentice-Hall of India Private Limited, *New Delhi*
Prentice-Hall of Japan, Inc., *Tokyo*

3rd Edition

A
History
of
United States
Foreign
Policy

Julius W. Pratt

PRENTICE-HALL, INC., Englewood Cliffs, N.J.

To My Former Students—
Young Men and Women of a Dozen College Generations

Contents

Maps

A Note on Documentation

In general, bibliographical data for every book cited in the foot-notes are given as part of its first citation in any chapter. The following works, however, are cited so frequently that it seems best to give full citations once and for all by reference here to the Bibliographical Essay, and to cite them hereafter only by the short forms indicated:

Bemis, *Latin American Policy*—Samuel F. Bemis, *The Latin American Policy of the United States.* See p. 569.

Documents on American Foreign Relations. See p. 564.

Foreign Relations—*Papers Relating to the Foreign Relations of the United States.* See p. 564.

Hull, *Memoirs*—*The Memoirs of Cordell Hull.* See p. 581.

Miller, *Treaties*—Hunter Miller, ed., *Treaties and Other International Acts of the United States of America.* See p. 564.

Perkins, *History of the Monroe Doctrine*—Dexter Perkins, *A History of the Monroe Doctrine.* See p. 568.

Pratt, *Cordell Hull*—Julius W. Pratt, *Cordell Hull,* 2 vols. (Vols. XII and XIII of *The American Secretaries of State and Their Diplomacy*). See p. 566.

U.S. in World Affairs—*The United States in World Affairs.* See p. 588.

Preface

The crisis-packed years since the second edition of this book appeared in 1965 have necessitated expansion of the narrative by the addition of two new chapters—a second chapter on the Western Hemisphere and an entire chapter on the war in Indochina—as well as the supplementing or revision of other chapters dealing with recent events. Minor revisions and condensations in earlier parts of the book have been effected for the purpose of holding its growth in length to a minimum. Other revisions take cognizance of the conclusions of recent scholarship. In a Bibliographical Essay, substituted for the former chapter bibliographies, I have tried to provide improved guidance for further reading. Readers who have followed the course of events of the last six years, especially in Southeast Asia, will not be surprised to find that the concluding chapter betrays less optimism about America's role in the world than characterized previous editions.

As in earlier editions, but to a still greater degree, I am indebted to the authors of numerous books, monographs, and scholarly articles whose contributions I have undertaken to acknowledge in footnotes and in the Bibliographical Essay. To former colleagues and secretaries, to librarians, critics, and others, whose assistance I acknowledged in the prefaces to previous editions, I reiterate my expression of appreciation. For assistance on this third edition special thanks are due to the librarians of the Buffalo and Erie County Public Library for invariably helpful and friendly service and to my former colleague, Professor Selig Adler, who read critically and perspicaciously several of the new or revised chapters, but who is hereby absolved from responsibility for any errors of fact or interpretation therein. As in earlier editions, the collaboration of my wife, Louisa, as typist, researcher, and critic, has been so vital that only her protest restrains me from naming her as co-author. My sister, Marjorie L. Pratt, has made cheerful and invaluable contributions to the infrastructure of authorship.

Julius W. Pratt

International relations began when two states first existed side by side or in such close proximity as to make the behavior of one the concern of the other. They will continue until some process of federation or conquest unites the world under a single sovereignty, or until the human race perishes or reverts to a primitive condition in which nations and nationalism will be no more.

The foreign policy of any nation comprises the objectives that it seeks in its international relations and the means and the methods by which it pursues them. In the study of a nation's foreign policy, therefore, it is of basic importance to know what the nation's objectives are in its relations with its neighbors.

(1) First and foremost, any nation must seek to assure its own security—its ability to repel threatened attacks from without and to protect its own existence and well-being. There have been a few happy periods in the world's history when certain favorably situated nations have not had to concern themselves with security problems, but such periods have been the exception. In general, international society has engaged in a continual struggle for existence in which each national entity, in order to hope for survival, has had to look to its fitness for the competition.

The quest for security takes many forms. One of the commonest is the attempt to obtain defensible frontiers—a seacoast, a mountain barrier, a river difficult to cross. The pushing of dangerous neighbors back behind such frontiers is a familiar phenomenon in the international struggle. If the boundary coincides with a formidable natural barrier, it may provide mutual security to both parties. If one party holds a "bridgehead" beyond the barrier, it endangers the other's security. Development of the airplane and the ballistic missile as weapons has obviously robbed natural barriers of much of their significance, though a wide ocean between one and one's enemy is still an element of defensive strength.

Nations that feel insecure because of the insufficiency of natural barriers or the presence of powerful rivals, or both, have customarily sought to bolster their security by political means. They have made alliances or formed friendships; they have undertaken to

1

The Aims of Foreign Policy

divide or isolate or destroy their enemies or potential enemies. They have, of course, built up their military and naval and air armaments and have sought dependable access to sources of strategic materials—ship timber and "naval stores" in the day of wooden fighting ships; iron, coal, petroleum, bauxite, wolfram, tin, rubber, manganese, uranium, and a score of other commodities in this age of machines and atomic energy.

(2) Acquisition of new territory, often sought for reasons of security, may also be pursued for less compelling motives—dynastic, historic, ethnic, or economic. Royal families were wont to attempt the enlargement of their dominions for their own glorification. The recovery of lands once possessed but lost by conquest has been a frequent objective of foreign policy in the modern world. Often, too, this historic motive has blended with an ethnic one, the uniting or reuniting of ethnically or linguistically similar populations under the same sovereignty, or the acquisition of territory to which a surplus population may migrate without changing its allegiance. Instances of expansion for economic motives will readily come to the mind of the history student—expansion for the acquisition of iron ore deposits, farm lands, harbors, and the mouths and navigable courses of rivers.

(3) Economic motives have determined other objectives of foreign policy. Negotiations have been conducted, treaties have been made, and wars have been fought to promote trade, to break down commercial barriers, to protect traders and their ships in peace and in war, and to open the doors to, and eventually to safeguard, investments in foreign lands. In all these matters, too, each nation has undertaken to guard its nationals and their property against discrimination—to assure to them all the privileges accorded to the nationals and the property of the "most favored nation."

(4) Ideological objectives, although less common than most of those just mentioned, have produced some of the bitterest conflicts in the history of international relations. In earlier centuries such ideologies were most likely to be religious, and their enthusiastic votaries at times embarked upon aggressive careers aimed, if not at the extermination, at least at the conquest and conversion, of neighboring nations which knew not "the truth." The Jews Moses led from Egypt destroyed or subdued, in the name of Jehovah, the tribes they found dwelling in the Promised Land. Saracens and Turks, inspired by Mohammed's gospel, carried the Crescent across Africa and into Europe at both Gibraltar and the Bosporus. Even Christian nations, Protestant and Catholic, fought each other in the name of their religion. In more recent times the ideologies that nations have sought to project upon their neighbors have usually been political, or economic and social. The French armies of 1793 carried their ideals of "liberty, equality, and fraternity" to most of Western Europe. The armies and the "fifth columns" of Hitler and Stalin were dedicated to the spread of more sinister systems, whereas the nations of the West rallied to the defense of democracy. In the years since World War II, as never before in modern times, ideological differences have dominated international relations and shaped foreign policies.

(5) It is not to be understood from the foregoing paragraphs that international relations are always unfriendly or that the foreign policies of one nation are invariably designed to do injury to others. Although a national foreign policy is necessarily dictated by national self-interest, an enlightened self-interest will often see the national welfare as dependent upon the well-being of neighbor states. Boundaries may be adjusted to mutual advantage; lowering of trade barriers may conduce to the common prosperity; limitation of armaments may contribute to mutual security; agreements to settle controversies peacefully may inure to both the security and the prosperity of all parties; "collective security" agreements, still in the experimental stage, may (it is hoped) produce the happy state of affairs that the term implies; the friendly exchange of ideas, in mutual respect, will enrich civilization on both sides of the border. The century that began with Waterloo and ended with Sarajevo—the century in which the

United States came to maturity—was a period in which the foreign policies of the great powers seemed more and more to be pursuing these enlightened objectives.

Foreign Policy Objectives of the United States

If the United States grew to maturity in a happy era, it nevertheless passed its infancy amid scenes of turmoil and violence. Emerging as a nation from the throes of one major European war, it enjoyed a scant ten years of peace before the opening of another, which lasted more than two decades. Small in numbers, poor in liquid wealth, weak in military power, the United States had perforce, in those years of international disorder, to direct much of its attention to its own security. In the long run, the European wars of a century and three-quarters ago worked to the advantage of the United States. This is a fact that is clear enough to students of history today: it was less clear to Washington, John Adams, Jefferson, Madison, and Monroe, the Presidents who piloted the young nation through those perilous years. They had sufficient cause to worry over threats to the security and the vital interests of the United States.

But American foreign policy antedated Washington's presidency. It began before independence was won, and a secure independence was its first objective. This and other broad objectives of American foreign policy may be listed as follows:

1. To secure independence with satisfactory boundaries—boundaries that would contribute to the national security.
2. To extend those boundaries in the interest of security, navigation and commerce, space for a growing population, and the spread of democracy.
3. To promote and protect the rights and interests of American citizens in commerce with, and investments in, foreign lands; to safeguard trade on the high seas, in peace and in war; and, as a special application of this aim in

the nineteenth century, to open the Far East to American trade and American influence.
4. To preserve neutrality and peace—to keep out of the wars of Europe (and Asia) as long as nonparticipation is compatible with preservation of American security and vital interests—and to devise means for the peaceful settlement of all international controversies.
5. To prevent the powers of Europe from further colonizing in the western hemisphere and from interfering in the affairs of the United States and of the Americas in general. In the twentieth century this has involved the maintenance or the restoration of the "balance of power" in Europe, even by the throwing of American weight into the scales. In the 1940's and thereafter, the effort to protect the Americas from the spread of totalitarianism in its Nazi and Communist forms involved a struggle to protect all Western civilization from the same peril. The peril was sometimes exaggerated, and the resulting apprehension led the United States, on some occasions, to questionable intervention in the affairs of other states.
6. To these fairly specific objectives of American foreign policy may be added one more general and pervasive—a humanitarian desire to do good in the world; to spread Christianity and democracy, to put an end to the slave trade, to halt the massacres or persecutions of racial and religious minorities, to relieve the victims of flood, fire, earthquake, famine, and civil war, to raise standards of living in backward countries. Such humanitarian activities have been, for the most part, the work of private individuals and nongovernmental organizations. Until recently, they have not been among the main objectives of American foreign policy. Yet they have, from time to time, deeply influenced that policy—upon occasion with important consequences. After World War II, the government itself entered the international campaign against poverty, ignorance, and disease as a means of combating Communism.

The Tools of Foreign Policy

The United States, like most other powers, has always sought to attain the objectives of its foreign policy by peaceful negotiation, by the processes of diplomacy. When these means have failed, and when the objectives aimed at have seemed of sufficiently vital importance to the responsible leaders, it has, like other powers, resorted to the use of force—to war. Neither the tools of diplomacy nor the tools of force can be suddenly improvised for use in crises. They must be kept in a state of greater or less readiness for use. The success of a nation's foreign policy will depend, in part at least, upon the efficiency and the readiness of the instruments with which that policy is pursued. The next chapter, therefore, will examine the diplomatic instruments and procedures which the United States has utilized for the attainment of its foreign policy objectives, and will consider briefly the relationship of military policy to diplomacy.

The United States, like other peacefully inclined nations, has always sought to attain the objectives of its foreign policy through the tools of diplomacy, that is, through friendly, or at least peaceful, negotiation. Only when, in the opinion of its responsible officials, such measures have failed to safeguard its vital interests or to avert threats to its security, has it resorted to the use of force.

The machinery of diplomacy, simple and inexpensive in George Washington's day, had become complex and costly a century and a half later. The change, indeed, was comparable to that from the scythe and flail with which Washington's contemporaries harvested their wheat to the farm combine of 1970. But in Washington's day no less than in Nixon's, the conduct of foreign relations required a twofold organization, a directing office at home and agents of that office abroad. Today these branches are known respectively as the Department of State and the Foreign Service.

2

The Instruments and Procedures of Foreign Policy

The Department of State

The Department of State (or State Department, as it is popularly called) was a creation of the First Congress under the Constitution in 1789. It had been preceded by a Department of Foreign Affairs (1781–1789), a Committee (of Congress) of Foreign Affairs (1777–1781), and a Committee (also of Congress) of Secret Correspondence (1775–1777). From the opening of the American Revolution in 1775 to the inauguration of the new government under the Constitution fourteen years later, Congress [1] alone exercised authority in the name of the United States. There was no separate executive branch, and the Committee, or Department, of Foreign Affairs served as an agent of Congress, which gave directions and made final decisions. The Constitution, which provided for the executive and judicial branches of the government, placed the direction of foreign relations in the hands of the President as head of the executive branch.

1. The Second Continental Congress until 1781; thereafter, the Congress under the Articles of Confederation.

The President was empowered to make appointments, to receive foreign ambassadors and ministers, and to conclude treaties with foreign governments. Congress, however, as the legislative branch of the new government, retained important checks upon the President's direction of foreign affairs. The President's appointments to office, diplomatic or other, had to be confirmed by the Senate. The same body, by a two-thirds vote of the members present, had to approve treaties before they could become effective. Congress as a whole held the purse strings and thus could give or withhold the funds necessary to the execution of a foreign policy. To Congress belonged the power to declare war, though the President was made commander in chief of the armed forces. Congress, through its committees, could also investigate the activities of the executive, though it was early established that in the field of foreign relations the President might withhold from Congress documents whose publication would be "incompatible with the public interest."

Since no one expected the President himself to be able to give adequate time to the management of foreign policy, the First Congress provided by law for a department under the President to have charge of that branch of executive business. Called at first, like its predecessor under the old government, a Department of Foreign Affairs, it was soon renamed the Department of State, a name held to be more suitable because of the assignment to the department of certain domestic functions, such as relations with the states, the keeping and publication of laws of Congress, and the like.

Under President Washington, the Department of State consisted of the Secretary of State, a chief clerk, three ordinary clerks, and a translator—a total of six persons. For a century or more, the department grew slowly in size and complexity. A reorganization in 1833 apportioned the work of the department among eight divisions or bureaus, topped by a chief clerk and the Secretary. In 1870 the number of bureaus was increased to 13; two assistant secretaries had meanwhile been added, but even then the entire personnel of the department numbered only 53. This modest number of employees had grown to 202 by 1909. Rapid expansion accompanied both world wars. State Department personnel numbered 963 in 1938, 2,755 in 1943, and 5,905 in 1948 (this figure fell to 5,522 in 1963). Thus, although the population of the United States had increased less than forty-fivefold (1790 to 1960), the number of persons in the State Department, occupied chiefly with the conduct of foreign relations, had grown nine hundredfold.

Occasional reorganizations of the department accompanied its growth in size, "usually," according to one authority, "producing more confusion as a result of trying to achieve more order." [2] Such major reorganizations were effected in 1909, 1944 (two in one year), and 1947–1948. Further changes were made upon the recommendation of the Commission on Organization of the Executive Branch of the Government, headed by ex-President Herbert Hoover. As reorganized in 1949 and 1950 under President Truman, and still further under subsequent Presidents, the top personnel of the department, as of July 1, 1969, comprised the Secretary, two Under Secretaries, two Deputy Under Secretaries (one for administration and one for economic affairs), a counselor, a legal adviser, the chairman of the Policy Planning Council, a director of international scientific and technological affairs, a director of intelligence and research, an administrator of the Bureau of Security and Consular Affairs, the United States representative to the Council of the Organization of American States, and ten assistant secretaries. Five of the assistant secretaries headed geographic bureaus dealing with African Affairs, East Asian and Pacific Affairs, European Affairs, Inter-American Affairs, and Near Eastern and South Asian Affairs. In these five geographic bureaus were stationed the experts in politics, economics, intelligence, and other aspects of the respective areas. Other assistant secretaries

2. J. L. McCamy, *The Administration of American Foreign Affairs* (New York: Alfred A. Knopf, Inc., 1950), p. 48.

headed the bureaus or offices of Congressional Relations, International Organization, Economic Affairs, Educational and Cultural Affairs, and Public Affairs.[3]

A semiautonomous agency within the State Department was the Agency for International Development (AID). Successor to several earlier agencies bearing different names, the AID was responsible for carrying out nonmilitary foreign assistance programs. In the program for Latin America under the Alliance for Progress, it shared responsibility with the Bureau of Inter-American Affairs. Also sheltered under the broad State Department roof was the Peace Corps. Detached from the department but partly subject to its supervision was the United States Information Agency (USIA), successor to the Office of War Information (OWI) established during World War II. Its best known activity was the "Voice of America," which broadcast American news and ideas to foreign lands in over forty languages. The agency also maintained over a hundred offices and libraries abroad, under the supervision of the diplomatic chiefs of mission in the countries concerned, and used films and the press or other media of communication. Its purpose was to explain American principles, aims, and activities to audiences behind the "iron curtain" as well as in friendly and unaligned countries.[4]

The Foreign Service

The formation and direction of foreign policy, under the President, are functions of the State Department. The implementation of that policy is shared between the State Department and the Foreign Service, the body of officers who represent the United States in foreign

countries. Such officers also contribute to the formation of foreign policy through the information they convey in regard to situations and attitudes in the countries to which they are accredited.

The Foreign Service comprises diplomatic and consular personnel. The diplomatic mission of one government in the capital of another country is the agency through which the two governments conduct business. The chief of the mission is the direct representative of his government to that of the foreign country. Since early in the nineteenth century, the grades of chiefs of mission have been standardized by international agreement. The officer of highest rank is an ambassador. In a day when most governments were headed by kings or queens, an ambassador was the representative of the sovereign. In the United States, he is the representative of the President. An ambassador's place of residence and official business is called an embassy.

Ranking below an ambassador is—or was—a minister, who, in the days alluded to, represented the foreign office rather than the sovereign. A minister's official residence was called a legation.

Whether a particular diplomatic mission was given the rank of an embassy or a legation—whether its chief was an ambassador or a minister—formerly depended upon the importance that the two governments attached to their mutual relations. During the first century of its existence, the United States maintained only legations abroad, and, reciprocally, foreign governments kept only legations in the American capital. In 1893, Congress provided for the elevation of several of the more important legations to embassies on a reciprocal basis. Thereafter, embassies gradually replaced legations until 1966, when the last American legations (those in Bulgaria and Hungary) became embassies. The change was indicative of the growing importance that the United States attached to its foreign relations. (The rank of career minister—close to the top in the Foreign Service—was still retained, but if such an officer became a chief of mission he was designated an ambassador.)

3. *U.S. Government Organization Manual, 1969–70.* Revised July 1, 1969 (Washington, D.C.: Government Printing Office [1969]), pp. 77–94.
4. William Barnes and John Heath Morgan, *The Foreign Service of the United States: Origins, Development, and Functions* (Washington, D.C.: Department of State [1961]), pp. 285–90; E. W. Barrett, *Truth Is Our Weapon* (New York: Funk & Wagnalls, 1953), chaps. 5, 6.

A chargé d'affaires ad interim is a diplomatic officer of lower rank left in charge of an embassy or legation in the absence of the ambassador or minister and acting for the time being as chief of mission. Below chiefs of mission are lesser diplomatic officers and employees—counselors, secretaries, political and economic officers, attachés, and so forth—the number in each case depending upon the importance of the mission and the volume of the business that it transacts.

The diplomatic officer is the spokesman for his government in its intercourse with the government of the foreign country. The consular officer, or consul, to use the simplest term,[5] is an official guardian in foreign ports of the welfare and interests of the citizens of the country he represents. It is to the nearest United States consul that Americans in trouble in foreign lands normally make their first appeal for aid. It is from consuls that reports on business openings in foreign countries are expected. The consul performs a multitude of duties with reference to trade, shipping, execution of legal documents, the granting of immigration visas, and the like. "In him," writes one authority, "are amalgamated the functions of the secretary of a chamber of commerce, a justice of the peace, a notary public, a commissioner of immigration and naturalization, a Veteran's Administration official, a reporter and information analyst, a local negotiator, a shipping official, a postmaster, and a treasury agent." [6]

Since it is important that a consular official be within reach wherever American citizens or American interests are significant in number or amount, it is customary to maintain consular establishments in some large seaports or commercial cities in addition to that at the seat of government. Thus, whereas there will be but a single American diplomatic establishment in a foreign country, American consulates in the same jurisdiction are limited in number only by the desires of the United States and the willingness of the foreign government to grant exequaturs (official documents of recognition) to American appointees. In 1968 the United States maintained 117 diplomatic and 135 consular missions abroad.[7]

The work of American consuls in any one foreign country is usually supervised and coordinated by a consul general and is under the general authority of the American ambassador or minister in that country.

History of the Foreign Service

The United States instituted both its diplomatic and consular services very early. Informal diplomatic representation began in 1776 when Benjamin Franklin reached Paris in his quest for French recognition of the United States. That representation became formal upon the granting of recognition in 1778. Other Americans represented the United States diplomatically in the Netherlands, Prussia, Spain, and England during the Revolution or the period of the Confederation. Consular representation, too, began as early as 1780, when Congress sent a consul to France. Under the Constitution, Congress provided for the establishment of a diplomatic service in 1790 and a separate consular service in 1792.

Although possession of suitable qualifications was perhaps never completely lost sight of in the making of diplomatic and consular appointments, for many years after the rise of the spoils system in American politics such appointments were customarily distributed as political plums to deserving members of the party in power. Occasionally they were used to recognize or reward distinguished literary achievement, as in the cases of Nathaniel Hawthorne (consul at Liverpool, 1853–1857), Washington Irving (secretary of legation at

---

5. The grades of consular officers are consul general, consul, vice consul (a grade now discontinued by the United States), and consular agent.

6. Elmer Plischke, *Conduct of American Diplomacy* (New York: D. Van Nostrand Company, 1950), p. 243.

7. W. W. Blancké, *The Foreign Service of the United States* (New York: Frederick A. Praeger, Inc., 1969), p. 33.

London, 1829–1832, minister to Spain, 1842–1846), and James Russell Lowell (minister to Spain and to Great Britain, 1877–1885). Between 1885 and 1915, however, the consular service and positions in the diplomatic service below the grade of minister were gradually removed from the "spoils system" and placed on a merit basis as to appointments, promotion, and tenure.

The Rogers Act of 1924 combined the diplomatic and consular services into a single Foreign Service, the members of which might be called upon to serve in either diplomatic or consular posts. It classified Foreign Service officers into nine classes, with career ministers at the top, and reaffirmed the requirement that appointments and promotions be based upon merit. Under the Rogers Act as amended to 1969, Foreign Service officers were graded in ten classes. Appointment to Class VIII (the lowest class) after written and oral examinations was probationary. Thereafter promotion was dependent upon the quality of the officer's record as judged by an impartial board. An officer who advanced to Class I was eligible for appointment as counselor of embassy or as consul general. Above Class I were the grades of career minister and (since 1955) career ambassador. A career minister was eligible for appointment as chief of mission with rank of minister or ambassador. Promotion to the grade of career ambassador came only as recognition of long and "exceptionally distinguished service to the Government." The President was left free to select chiefs of mission from among distinguished Foreign Service officers or to base such appointments, as in earlier days, upon political service or distinction outside the field of diplomacy. An ambassador in an important post, such as London, was often burdened with expenses that exceeded his salary and allowances; hence these posts were often assigned to men with substantial private incomes.

As reorganized by legislation subsequent to the Rogers Act (notably the Foreign Service Act of 1946), the Foreign Service included three categories in addition to chiefs of mission and Foreign Service officers. Foreign Service Reserve officers were specialists in other fields (economics, for example) given temporary appointments in the Foreign Service. Since 1968, such appointments may be made permanent in selected cases. Foreign Service Staff officers and employees embraced accountants, clerks, typists, translators, guards, couriers, and the like; they were American citizens and were appointed by the Secretary of State without examination. Alien employees, performing many of the same services as members of the staff group, constituted the third category.

Integration of State Department and Foreign Service

State Department and Foreign Service were manned by distinct and noninterchangeable corps of employees. Permanent members of the State Department staff were members of the Classified Civil Service, administered by the Civil Service Commission. Foreign Service officers and employees were under a separate system with its own examinations and rules of promotion. State Department officers and employees served, as a rule, only in the United States. Foreign Service officers from time to time occupied responsible posts in the State Department but never lost their identity as Foreign Service personnel. This dualism promoted friction and jealousy. It produced, so critics maintained, a State Department personnel ill-informed about foreign countries and a Foreign Service personnel that had lost touch with America.

One of the important proposals of the Commission on Organization of the Executive Branch of the Government (Hoover Commission) in 1949 called for the amalgamation of the two bodies of personnel, "over a short period of years into a single foreign affairs service obligated to serve at home or overseas and constituting a safeguarded career group administered separately from the general Civil Service." The proposed amalgamation would include all State Department personnel below the rank of assistant secretary and all Foreign

Service personnel below the rank of minister, with the exception of aliens, unskilled labor categories, and certain technical personnel needed only in Washington.

The proposal for amalgamation, though approved by the administration, encountered foot-dragging, chiefly on the part of the Foreign Service, and not until further study and recommendation by another committee, headed by President Henry M. Wriston of Brown University, was amalgamation—now termed "integration"—actually achieved. The process began in 1954, and by 1957, 1,525 persons had been transferred to the Foreign Service officer category, 631 from the State Department's Civil Service group, 802 from the Foreign Service Staff Corps, 69 from the Foreign Service Reserve, and 23 from Civil Service positions in other Federal agencies. State Department officers not "integrated" were, on the whole, those whose duties necessitated continuity of service in Washington. Some others declined transfer because of reluctance to take up duties abroad. In the Foreign Service Staff Corps remained the personnel holding the less responsible positions. There were now over 3,400 Foreign Service officers qualified and obligated to serve either in Washington or abroad. That figure remained almost unchanged in 1968. All branches of the Foreign Service, including reserve and staff officers and employees, then totaled just over 11,000. In addition there were some 12,900 aliens, known as Foreign Service local employees, serving American missions in foreign countries.

The Foreign Service had lost its semi-autonomous position and had been brought under the authority of the Secretary of State, though the Director General of the Foreign Service, holder of an office created in 1946, played "the major operational role in Foreign Service recruitment, training, placement, counseling, evaluation, discipline, and retirement." [8]

8. Barnes and Morgan, *Foreign Service*, pp. 280–83; Blancké, *Foreign Service*, pp. 32–34, 78.

Other Agencies of Foreign Policy

If it was true in the early years of the Republic that the State Department alone, under the President, was responsible for the country's foreign relations, that simple situation has long since ceased to exist. The task force that studied the administration of foreign relations for the Hoover Commission found within the executive branch of the government at least forty-six "departments, agencies, commissions, boards, and interdepartmental councils," the work of which "involves some aspects of the conduct of foreign affairs." The integration of the work of these numerous agencies into a unified foreign policy had become a major problem. Ultimately the President must make decisions on questions of first importance, but most interagency conflicts or contradictions must be resolved at lower levels. The most important and widely used device for such coordination was the interdepartmental committee. The task force found thirty-three such committees operating in the field of foreign affairs, some created by law, others by executive order or interdepartmental agreement.

Of special importance among such committees was the National Security Council, created by the National Security Act of 1947. As later modified (up to 1969), it comprised the President, the Vice-President, the Secretaries of State and Defense, and the Director of the Office of Emergency Preparedness. A Special Assistant to the President for National Security Affairs (who in some instances rivaled or even exceeded the Secretary of State in influence) and an Executive Secretary served as officials of the Council; the Joint Chiefs of Staff (the military heads of Army, Navy, and Air Force) were the principal military advisers to the President and the National Security Council. [9]

It is obvious from the composition of the

9. *U.S. Government Organization Manual, 1969–70*, p. 61.

National Security Council that it is designed to promote harmony between foreign policy on the one hand and the military and material means to support that policy on the other. The Council has advisory powers only; the President must make the decisions.

The act that created the National Security Council also created and placed under its direction the Central Intelligence Agency (CIA). This top-secret agency had as its stated purpose "coordinating the intelligence activities of the several Government departments and agencies in the interest of national security," but, rightly or wrongly, its name came to be associated with undercover anti-Communist operations, both military and subversive, in many parts of the world.[10]

The proliferation of agencies in Washington with interests in foreign affairs was, of course, paralleled abroad, where in 1968 only 20 percent of persons representing the United States were under the direct supervision of the Secretary of State. Several attempts have been made to bring all such activities under centralized control. In 1965 a bill to create a government-wide foreign affairs establishment passed the House of Representatives but failed in the Senate. In the following year, President Johnson designated the Secretary of State "director" of all overseas operations affecting one or more government departments, military operations excluded. The Secretary would exercise this authority through a new committee, the Senior Interdepartmental Group (SIG), having an under secretary of state as chairman.[11] "If the new system works," wrote Max Frankel in the *New York Times,* "it will make the State Department instead of the White House, as often in the past, the main arena of policy debate." [12] The trend under the next administration, however, was in the opposite direction.

10. David Wise and Thomas B. Ross, *The Invisible Government* (New York: Random House, Inc., 1964).
11. Blancké, *Foreign Service,* pp. 244–46; *Department of State Bulletin,* 54 (March 28, 1966), 506–9.
12. *New York Times,* March 5, 1966.

The Channels of Diplomacy

Although much influence over American foreign policy has found its way into other hands, the State Department still remains the normal channel for communications and negotiations between the government of the United States and other governments. In times of crisis, it is true, the President himself may communicate directly with the heads of other governments in person, by letter or telegram, or by telephone. The most notable modern instance of this type of diplomacy is found in the relations of Franklin D. Roosevelt and Winston Churchill, who made frequent use of all the means of communication enumerated. The two of them also met twice with Stalin and once with Chiang Kai-shek, the heads of other allied governments in World War II. In earlier years, President Herbert Hoover had conferred with Prime Minister Ramsay MacDonald "on a log by the Rapidan," and Woodrow Wilson had met with the British, French, and Italian Premiers at the Paris Peace Conference. Other instances of presidential diplomacy were Franklin Roosevelt's plea for peace to the Japanese Emperor on the eve of Pearl Harbor and an appeal by President Taft to the Prince Regent of China in behalf of would-be American investors in Chinese railroads. Usually, however, official communications from one head of state or government to another have been limited to such ceremonial messages as letters of condolence and congratulation or appointments of ambassadors. A President may occasionally hold an important conference with the minister or ambassador of another country or may himself draft diplomatic notes to be signed by the Secretary of State, as Wilson sometimes did; but a President who trusts his Secretary of State customarily leaves such responsibilities to him.

The Secretary of State can follow any one of three courses in communicating with his opposite number, the Foreign Minister of another government. He may confer with him directly, in person or by other means. Such direct exchanges were almost unknown until very recent times. He may communicate through an "instruction"[13] to the American chief of mission at the foreign capital, who then calls upon the Foreign Minister and either leaves with him a copy of the "instruction" or informs him of its substance. Thirdly, he may confer in person or by letter with the chief of mission of the foreign government in Washington, who then reports to the Foreign Minister at home. Which of these last two channels is followed in any given case depends upon the subject of discussion and the personalities and personal relationships of the people concerned.

It follows from what has just been said that important negotiations, often resulting in treaties, may be carried on equally well in Washington or in the foreign capital. Thus, to take a few instances, the Jay Treaty with Great Britain of 1794 was drawn up in London, the Clayton-Bulwer Treaty of 1850, in Washington; the Louisiana Purchase was negotiated in Paris, the Florida and Alaska Purchases, in Washington, and the Mexican cessions of 1848 and 1853, in or near Mexico City.

Important negotiations are occasionally conducted not through any of the regular official channels that have been described, but through confidential agents of the President, serving without diplomatic commissions and often bypassing the State Department. Presidents Wilson and Franklin D. Roosevelt were addicted more than others to the employment of such special agents. Thus, Colonel Edward M. House went to Europe on several delicate missions for Wilson, and Harry Hopkins performed similar services for Roosevelt. After Roosevelt's death, President Truman sent Hopkins on a final mission to Moscow, where he secured from Stalin, what seemed then, important concessions in regard to the proposed United Nations Charter and the government of Poland.

13. Outgoing communications from the State Department to its missions abroad are called "instructions"; those incoming are "dispatches."

How Treaties Are Made and Ratified

Agreements between states may take the form of treaties (or conventions), executive agreements, or simple legislation (acts or joint resolutions of Congress).

The time-honored form of international agreement, legally binding upon all parties, is the treaty or convention. The distinction between the two is one in name only, though agreements on matters of prime importance, such as the making of peace or the transfer of territory, are almost always called treaties. What is said here about treaties applies equally to conventions. Before a treaty becomes effective, five steps must be achieved: (1) negotiation and signing by agents (such as the Secretary of State and the ambassador of the other country) duly commissioned by their governments to perform that function; (2) legislative approval; (3) ratification; (4) exchange of ratifications; (5) proclamation.

Several of these steps require some clarification. Legislative approval, in the United States, means the giving by the Senate of its "advice and consent" by a vote of at least two-thirds of the senators present. The Senate may give its advice and consent in a simple affirmative vote; it may amend the treaty before doing so; or it may attach interpretations or reservations to the treaty, giving its understanding of what the treaty means or of the limits of the obligations assumed under it by the United States. If the Senate amends the treaty, the consent of the other party to the amendment must be secured. If the Senate attaches reservations or interpretations, it may or may not require that the other party agree to these before the treaty becomes binding on the United States. Ordinarily it does not make this requirement.

It is to be emphasized here that, popular opinion and phraseology to the contrary notwithstanding, the Senate does not "ratify" treaties. It merely gives its advice and consent in favor of the treaty. Ratification is an executive act, performed by the President after the

Senate has consented. The President, however, is not required to ratify a treaty that the Senate has approved. If he objects to an amendment or reservation made by the Senate, or if he has merely changed his mind about the desirability of the treaty or the need for it, he is under no obligation to ratify. If he fails to do so, the treaty simply dies. To take one hypothetical illustration, if the Senate, in March 1920, had given its advice and consent to the Treaty of Versailles with the Lodge Reservations attached,[14] it seems almost certain that President Wilson would have refused to ratify it, so strong was his disapproval of the reservations.

When a treaty has been ratified by the executives of both governments, following whatever form of legislative approval their constitutions require, copies of the instruments of ratification [15] are exchanged by the two governments, and the heads of states (in the United States, the President) then proclaim the treaty to be in effect.

Treaties may be multilateral instead of bilateral. In that event, the treaty will specify whether ratification by all or by a certain number of the parties shall be necessary to make it binding on those that have ratified. It will also designate the capital at which ratifications are to be deposited. A treaty may be perpetual—that is, without any time limit for its duration or stipulation of procedure for its abrogation. Such a treaty, ideally speaking, can be set aside only by the consent of all parties to it. Only after intermittent negotiations over a twenty-year period did the United States secure British consent to the abrogation of the Clayton-Bulwer Treaty, which blocked American ambitions for an American-controlled isthmian canal. Unilateral abrogation is always possible but is analogous to breaking a contract and may present the other party with a valid grievance. On the other hand, a treaty may be limited to a specified period, or

it may provide that either party may terminate it by giving notice, usually six months or a year in advance, of its intention to do so. Thus, the treaty of 1818 for joint occupation of Oregon by Great Britain and the United States set a ten-year limit on that arrangement; the treaty of 1827, continuing the joint occupation, permitted either government to terminate it by giving a year's notice. Treaties ceding territory are, by their nature, perpetual.

Other Forms of International Agreement

The required two-thirds majority in the Senate has, in a number of important instances, proved an insurmountable obstacle to the approval of treaties desired by the executive. Two means of circumventing this requirement have been utilized more and more frequently in recent times. These two means are the executive agreement and legislation.

Executive agreements, between the President and the executive head of another government, may be made with or without prior authorization by Congress. The Reciprocal Trade Agreements Act of 1934 empowered the President to make executive agreements with other governments providing reciprocally for the lowering of duties (within limits set by Congress) on the products of each country when imported into the other. This was a means of avoiding not only the two-thirds rule but the logrolling that had always obstructed attempts to lower duties by treaty or legislation. Over forty reciprocal trade agreements were made under the authority conferred by this act and extended by subsequent enactments. Since Congress had authorized them in advance, their legality was assured.

Of a quite different character were certain executive agreements made by the President upon his own responsibility, in circumstances when Senate approval was doubtful or when prolonged debate in Senate or Congress might defeat the objectives of the agreements. Notable among such agreements was FDR's destroyer-bases trade of September 2, 1940—a transaction far more important than many

14. See Chapter 29.
15. See Plischke, *American Diplomacy,* pp. 476–78, for specimens of Senate resolution of advice and consent, instrument of ratification, deposit of ratification, and presidential proclamation of treaty.

treaties—by which the United States turned over to Great Britain fifty old destroyers in exchange for the right to establish bases on British territory in the Western Hemisphere. Of similar character were the later agreements with the Danish minister in Washington and the Icelandic government by which the United States in 1941 undertook to garrison and defend Greenland and Iceland for the duration of the war. All of these agreements, unlike certain of those later made at Yalta, were promptly reported to Congress by President Roosevelt. Senate approval was not requested. Whether it could have been obtained is doubtful. In any event, an attempt to secure it would have resulted in long delay at a time when immediate action was deemed necessary. When a president acts in this way, he of course runs the risk that Congress may repudiate his action.

Criticism of certain of President Roosevelt's executive agreements, especially those made at Yalta, led to an attempt to limit the power of the President in this respect. A proposed amendment to the Constitution, sponsored by Senator John W. Bricker of Ohio, would have subjected all such agreements to regulation by Congress and would also have placed restrictions on the treaty-making power, specifying that the Federal government could not exercise through treaties powers not clearly assigned to it in the Constitution. The Bricker Amendment and proposed substitutes for it were defeated in the Senate in February 1954.

Legislation by act or joint resolution of Congress is another substitute for treaty-making, the advantage being that such legislation requires a bare majority in each house of Congress instead of the two-thirds majority in the Senate required for treaties. Such legislation presupposes some parallel action by the other party to the agreement. Early instances of such action by joint resolution were the annexations of Texas and Hawaii. In each of these cases, action by treaty had first been tried and laid aside when the two-thirds majority in the Senate proved unattainable. In 1911 President Taft made an executive agreement with Canada for reciprocal lowering of tariffs, to be carried out by concurrent legislation by Congress and the Canadian Parliament. Congress passed the necessary legislation, but the agreement failed to receive Canadian approval. A more modern instance was the passage by Congress, April 3, 1948, of the Foreign Assistance Act, which set in motion the Marshall Plan for aid to Western Europe in the rehabilitation of its war-shattered economy.

The Growing Power of Congress— and of the President

Mention of the Foreign Assistance Act calls attention to the growing authority exercised by Congress over American foreign policy. Since passage of the Lend-Lease Act in 1941, American foreign policy has included a large element of material assistance to allies and friends—first, aid in winning the war; then aid in economic recovery; still later, aid in rearming to resist the march of Russian Communism, and aid in promoting the economic development of backward nations. In whatever form such aid is agreed upon—treaty, law, or executive agreement—eventually it costs money, and money must be appropriated by Congress. Without the support of Congress, therefore, many aspects of current foreign policy simply cannot be carried out. In the words of one authority: "When money talks as loudly and as often as it does in United States foreign relations since 1940, Congress is an everpresent participant in the making of foreign policy." [16]

But if Congress can tie the hands of the President in many foreign policy programs, Presidents of the post-World War II era were charged repeatedly with assuming powers that rightly belonged to Congress. Indeed, there was growing concern, in Congress and out, over the assertion by the President, in the nuclear age, of the "inherent power" to take

16. McCamy, *Administration of Foreign Affairs*, p. 336.

the country into war in defiance of the constitutional grant to Congress of the exclusive power to "declare war." [17] Criticism of what seemed to many a dangerous presidential encroachment on the power of Congress began when President Truman decided, on his own responsibility, to send American troops to fight in Korea. It heightened, especially in the Senate Committee on Foreign Relations, when President Johnson sent American troops into the war in Vietnam, after securing the loosely worded Tonkin Gulf Resolution from Congress. The criticism reached a climax when President Nixon ordered the invasion of Cambodia by United States ground forces on April 30, 1970.[18] To concede to one man the power to make such fateful decisions was, said the critics, both plainly contrary to the Constitution and perilous to the nation's existence. What was needed was a new War Powers Act, clearly defining the line between the powers of the President and those of the Congress.[19] In the absence of such a statute, or of a clearly thought out plan for one, the best that Congress could do was to pass stopgap measures like the Cooper-Church amendment, forbidding the President to return United States troops to Cambodia after their withdrawal without specific authorization by Congress.[20]

Arms as an Adjunct to Diplomacy

When a nation fails to gain its ends by diplomacy, it must either forgo them for the time being or, if they are sufficiently important, seek to gain them by force. "War," said the Prussian military authority, Karl von Clausewitz, "is a mere continuation of policy by other means." Actual war, if successful, may

achieve what diplomacy has failed to achieve. A capacity to make war and a recognized willingness to wage it may support diplomacy: the opposing government may make concessions, or refrain from contemplated aggression, rather than face armed conflict. Thus adequate preparation for war may attain national ends without actual resort to arms. Military weakness, on the other hand, or a real or supposed unwillingness to fight in defense of vital national interests, may invite aggression and drive a reluctant nation into war despite an initial hesitation.

In surveying the history of American foreign relations, therefore, we may well ask what part military preparedness and military policy have played in the success or failure of American diplomacy. Have the means and the willingness to make war contributed to diplomatic successes? Or has military unpreparedness, physical or moral, been a contributing factor to situations that resulted in war? Before attempting to answer these questions, it will be useful to glance briefly at the development of American policy in the matter of military and naval preparedness. During the first century of national existence, the military and naval power maintained in peacetime was insignificant vis-à-vis any formidable opponent. Geographical isolation, together with the balance of power in Europe, seemed during most of that period to safeguard the nation against any serious threat of attack from overseas. Its immediate neighbors were weak and unaggressive. The nation, for its first few decades, was poor, and armaments were expensive. It was natural, then, that despite the contrary advice of President Washington and others, Congress should choose to rely upon a diminutive Regular Army, poorly trained state militia, and, in time of actual war, initially untrained volunteers. The Navy in the same period, except when temporarily built up during the Civil War, comprised only a few light vessels adapted to coast defense or to attacks upon an enemy's commerce.

Somewhat paradoxically, it was in this same period, at least from the 1840's to the end of the century, that the American public, and

---

17. The case for the president's right to make war as commander in chief of the armed forces is presented by L. C. Meeker in "The Legality of United States Participation in the Defense of Viet-Nam," *Department of State Bulletin,* 54 (March 28, 1966), 474–89.
18. For the Korean, Tonkin Gulf, and Cambodian incidents, see Chapters 44, 46.
19. See M. J. Pusey, *The Way We Go to War* (Boston: Houghton Mifflin Company, 1969), esp. chap. 10.
20. See Chapter 46.

often the American government, displayed a jingoist attitude in times of controversy with other powers. The other parties to such controversies, therefore, had to consider not only the armed forces ready for action, but also the nation's substantial latent military capacity.

The 1890's brought the beginning of a change in policy, seen first in the Navy. Influenced by the writings of the naval historian and philosopher, A. T. Mahan,[21] the United States then began the building of a fighting fleet, on the same lines as the major European navies. The Regular Army was usefully reorganized in the early 1900's; the organized militia (National Guard) was coordinated with the Regular Army in organization, equipment, and discipline. Both were greatly expanded during the First and Second World Wars and supplemented by conscription (selective service). A separate Air Force was created in 1947, and the three services were "unified" under a single Department of Defense. At the end of World War II, however, as after all its previous wars, the United States acted on the assumption that, except for the Navy, only token forces were necessary in peacetime. Demobilization began immediately, and by 1948 the strength of the armed forces had dropped from a wartime peak of over 12,000,000 personnel to about 1,350,000.

A revolutionary change in military policy was soon to take place, but before considering that change, it is proper here to attempt to answer the questions posed earlier.

First, were there occasions when both military force, whether adequate or not, and an evident disposition to use it, helped to achieve diplomatic success without war? There were several such instances. At the climax of the Oregon controversy in 1846, the firm stand taken by President Polk, backed by the popular slogan, "Fifty-four forty or fight!" almost certainly conduced to a British retreat, despite the insignificant size of the American Army and Navy. The availability of military power, a residue from the Civil War, was valuable to

Secretary of State Seward in persuading the French to withdraw from Mexico in 1867. President Theodore Roosevelt's display of naval power in Pacific waters in 1908 was a prelude to a generally satisfactory agreement with Japan—the Root-Takahira agreement. Finally—to take an instance from the period after the revolutionary change in policy alluded to above—President Kennedy's proclaimed readiness to use force, nuclear force if necessary, to rid Cuba of Russian ballistic missiles in October 1962, induced Nikita Khrushchev to yield, thereby possibly preventing nuclear war.

Our second question, necessarily speculative, may be phrased thus: Might any of the foreign wars in which the United States has been engaged have been avoided by the possession of larger military or naval forces?

A better state of preparedness would hardly have obviated the war with Mexico or that with Spain. American demands in each case collided with national pride and sensitivity that probably would not have given way before the threat of force, no matter how overwhelming. In the controversies preceding the War of 1812, on the other hand, the United States would have found its cause greatly strengthened by the possession of substantial military and naval force and a reputation for being willing to use it. It was Admiral Mahan's opinion that an American squadron of ten or twelve ships-of-the-line would have been sufficient to exact from Great Britain concessions that would have made war unnecessary.[22]

In the controversy over German use of the submarine, which involved the United States in the First World War, Germany was not deterred by the formidable naval power of the United States. Since the British Navy already commanded the surface of the sea, addition of the American fleet to the British would not have materially altered the situation. American military power, as distinct from naval, was not ready to be thrown into the scale and could not be ready for a year or more. In the

21. A. T. Mahan, *The Influence of Sea Power upon History, 1660–1783* (Boston: Little, Brown and Company, 1890).

22. A. T. Mahan, *Sea Power in Its Relations to the War of 1812,* 2 vols. (Boston: Little, Brown and Company, 1905), 2: 212.

meantime, Germany expected to win the war. A dozen American army divisions, ready for quick mobilization, might well have restrained the German government from challenging the United States with the submarine.

American diplomacy vis-à-vis Germany, Italy, and Japan (1936–1941) was handicapped by a wholly inadequate Army and Air Force, a Navy designed for one ocean when two were at stake, and a neutrality policy that told the world the United States would have no part in "other people's wars." It is at least arguable that a more adequate force and a less pacifist disposition on the part of the United States (particularly if shared by Great Britain and France) would have checked aggression in its infancy, both east and west, and thus have made World War II unnecessary.

Such a policy of preparedness, the United States eventually came to believe, would be necessary to prevent World War III. By 1948 many Americans were convinced that the Soviet Union was bent upon a program of Communist expansion that could be checked only by force or the threat of force. Now, for the first time in its history, the United States realized the necessity of permanent peacetime preparedness. While American diplomats contracted defensive alliances with over forty other nations of the non-Communist world, the United States began a slow rebuilding of the strength of its own armed forces, and those of its allies, all greatly depleted since 1945. By 1951 it had taken measures for keeping its ground and air forces at a peacetime level sufficient for meeting sudden emergencies.

In the Eisenhower era (1953–1961), emphasis shifted sharply to atomic and nuclear weapons, to be discharged from airplanes or (increasingly after the first Russian Sputnik in 1957) to be propelled halfway around the globe by ballistic missiles.

Eisenhower's Secretary of State, John Foster Dulles, in 1954 proclaimed the doctrine of "massive retaliation." A future attack on United States forces or an ally of the United States would, he hinted, be repelled, not as in the long drawn out, muddy fight in Korea, but by dropping nuclear bombs on the enemy centers responsible for the aggression. In other words, Communist aggression in Indochina or Berlin might mean atomic bombs on Peking or Moscow. This threat, it was supposed, would deter the opponent from making any aggressive move. The doctrine served as an excuse for a reduction in American ground and tactical air forces—a measure of economy.[23]

The doctrine of "massive retaliation" overlooked the fact that this was a game that two could play. As the Soviet Union developed similar capabilities in the production and delivery of nuclear weapons, the American deterrent lost much of its credibility. Would the United States respond to a Communist thrust at an ally—for example an encroachment on West Berlin—by commencing a suicidal exchange of nuclear weapons with Moscow? To many the answer seemed doubtful. President Charles de Gaulle of France, for example, contended that the United States would not risk its own existence to protect Europe. In order to provide a more credible deterrent against piecemeal Communist aggression and thereby to give better support to diplomacy—the Kennedy administration (1961–1963) undertook a build-up of the conventional forces whose strength had been sacrificed in obeisance to the dogma of "massive retaliation." Under subsequent administrations, the United States and its NATO allies devised a system of "flexible response." According to this plan, the response to a hypothetical Russian local aggression in Europe would begin with conventional weapons and progress, so far as necessary, from these to local use of tactical (low-yield) nuclear weapons and only as a last resort, to all-out nuclear attack on the Soviet Union. Knowledge of this plan, it was hoped, would restore credibility to the U.S.-NATO deterrent.

23. J. F. Dulles, "Policy for Security and Peace," *Foreign Affairs,* 32 (April 1954), 353–64; *New York Times,* January 13, 1954.

3

The Diplomacy of the Revolution

The disruption of the British Empire in the 1770's was one of the fateful events of modern history. Had British statesmanship then been capable of the levels of wisdom it attained in the next century, a British-American, or American-British, Commonwealth of Nations might have guided the world along paths of peaceful development with little to fear from a Wilhelm II, a Hitler, or a Stalin. Such a might-have-been is a fascinating subject of speculation. The student of history must deal with facts.

The facts are that a shortsighted British policy, bent upon holding the colonies in subordination, drove them instead to complete independence. New taxes, new assertions of imperial authority, new devices for enforcing old commercial restrictions, new interferences with the acquisition of western lands, harsh measures of punishment when the new exactions were resisted—all combined to provoke the colonial population to revolt. The measures undertaken were not ill-intentioned. They were designed, with some degree of justice, to require the colonies to share the cost of imperial defense and imperial administration. But the colonies had come to think of themselves as self-governing entities, as having "dominion status," to use a term of later origin, and they refused to have their duties prescribed for them by Parliament and King. Parliament and King were unwilling to accept such a novel theory of empire. Great Britain, consequently, found herself involved in war not only with her colonies but eventually with most of Europe, too. The war, though not wholly disastrous to British arms, deprived Great Britain of the most valuable of her colonial possessions and cast her down from the pinnacle of power that she had attained by the Peace of Paris of 1763.

The initial aim of armed revolt was not independence but a restoration and recognition of what the colonials held to be their rights as British subjects. They professed to have been content with their status under British policy prior to 1763. That the colonies turned to independence in the second year of the struggle was the consequence partly of the British government's spurning of compromise and its adoption, instead, of severe repressive measures; partly of a dawning realization of the advantages that might accrue from independence. No one set forth the arguments for independence so persuasively as a recent immigrant from England named Thomas Paine, who published the pamphlet *Common Sense* in Philadelphia in January 1776. Among Paine's arguments, two were significant for the future foreign policy of the United States. Independence, said Paine, would free the former colonies from being dragged at the heels of England into European wars in which they had no concern.[1] A declaration of independence would improve their chances of securing foreign aid.

The Quest for Foreign Aid

Greatly inferior to the mother country in numbers, in wealth, in industry, in military and naval power, the colonies, as their wiser leaders saw from the beginning, could hardly hope for decisive military success unless aided by one of the major European powers. Months before deciding upon independence, Congress had set up a secret committee to make contact with friends abroad and this committee had sent to Paris a secret agent in the guise of a merchant to seek supplies and credit. The agent, Silas Deane of Connecticut, arriving in Paris in July 1776, soon found that the French government was disposed to give secret assistance to England's revolting colonies. French ministers, in fact, had been on the lookout since 1763 for an opportunity to weaken and humiliate France's victorious rival, Great Britain. That opportunity had now arrived. So thought the celebrated French playwright and amateur diplomat, Caron de Beaumarchais, who had already been in contact with another colonial agent, Arthur Lee, in London; and so too believed the Comte de Vergennes, French Foreign Minister. Vergennes and Beaumarchais

were able to persuade King Louis XVI that aid to the colonies was in the French interest.

As yet, however, France was not willing to avow openly her friendship for the colonies or to give material aid except in secret. This was managed through the creation by Beaumarchais of a fictitious commercial firm, Rodrigue Hortalez et Compagnie, through which were channeled gunpowder and other essential supplies from the French arsenals to the armies of George Washington. Spain, too, was persuaded by France to give aid through this channel and by other means. All in all, measured in the dollars of that day, France contributed to the American cause nearly $2,000,000 in subsidies and over $6,350,000 in loans; Spain approximately $400,000 and $250,000 in subsidies and loans respectively.[2]

The French Alliance

These arrangements for secret "lend-lease" had been instituted before Deane's arrival in Paris. After the Declaration of Independence, Congress sent to France the most widely known, most admired, and most persuasive American of his day, Benjamin Franklin. In Paris he joined Deane and also Arthur Lee, who had come from London, to form a three-man American commission. As secretary, the commission employed a Dr. Edward Bancroft, a native of Massachusetts and a friend of Franklin. Bancroft was secretly in the pay of the British government, to which he faithfully reported the work of the commission and its relations with the French ministers. Arthur Lee was convinced of Bancroft's treachery but could not shake Franklin's and Deane's faith in their employee.

The principal purpose of Franklin's mission was to secure from the French government official recognition of the United States as an independent nation. Recognition could be accomplished by the signing of a treaty between

---

1. Of the four intercolonial wars, the European origin of the first three was attested by the names given them in America: King William's War, Queen Anne's War, King George's War. The fourth, on the other hand, was of colonial origin, as its name in America—the French and Indian War—suggests.

2. These figures are slightly simplified from those given in S. F. Bemis, *The Diplomacy of the American Revolution* (New York: Appleton-Century-Crofts, 1935), p. 93.

France and the United States, and Franklin brought with him to Paris a draft of a proposed treaty of amity and commerce, which had been prepared by a committee of Congress and which embodied the liberal commercial principles that Congress hoped to see adopted not only by France but by the entire trading world. This "Plan of 1776," as it has been called, was to serve for many years as the goal of American commercial policy.[3]

Though friendly to the United States, Vergennes was unwilling to grant formal recognition, thus risking war with England, until the Americans could offer some evidence of their ability to do their share in winning the war. Quite understandably, he did not wish to involve France in a war for a losing cause. Such evidence was not forthcoming until December 1777, when news arrived that General Burgoyne's British army, thrusting down from Montreal into New York, had been forced to surrender to General Gates at Saratoga. This was what Vergennes had been waiting for; he tried to enlist Spain in the cause and when Spain procrastinated, resolved that France should proceed without her. On December 17, the American commissioners were informed that France would grant recognition and make a treaty with the United States, and on February 6, 1778, a treaty of amity and commerce and a treaty of alliance were signed in Paris, the latter to take effect if Great Britain went to war with France because of the former.

Vergennes had hastened to take this action because of fear that if he did not, England would effect a reconciliation with her former colonies. Burgoyne's surrender had produced a sensation in England and led the ministry to offer liberal terms of settlement to the Americans. In March, Parliament passed a series of bills repealing all the legislation enacted since 1763 of which the colonists had complained. In April, a commission headed by the Earl of Carlisle was dispatched to America, empowered to offer to Congress virtually everything it had claimed, independence alone excepted, if the former colonies would lay down their arms and resume their allegiance to the British

Crown. The right to control their own taxation, to elect their governors and other officials formerly appointed, to be represented in Parliament if they so desired, to continue Congress as an American legislature; release from quitrents, assurance that their colonial charters would not be altered without their consent, full pardon for all who had engaged in rebellion—these terms of the offer indicate how far Great Britain was willing to go to save her empire from disruption. In effect she was offering "dominion status" to America.[4]

Had such an offer been made at any time prior to the Declaration of Independence, perhaps at any time prior to Burgoyne's surrender, it would have been accepted and the thirteen states would have become the first British dominion. Now the offer came too late. With recognition and the promise of an alliance and open aid from France, independence seemed assured, and there was no turning back. Congress ratified the treaties with France without even stopping to parley with the Carlisle Commission.

The treaty of amity and commerce placed each nation on a most-favored-nation basis[5] with reference to the other and embodied practically unaltered the liberal principles of the "Plan of 1776"—principles which would protect the interest of either signatory that might chance to be neutral when the other was at war. The treaty of alliance was to go into effect if France should become embroiled in the existing war against Great Britain. Its object was "to maintain effectually the liberty, Sovereignty, and independence absolute and unlimited" of the United States. France renounced forever any designs upon Bermuda or upon any parts of the continent of North America which before the Treaty of Paris of 1763 or by virtue of that treaty had belonged to Great Britain or the former British colonies. She reserved the right to possess herself of any

3. See Chapter 5 for the "Plan of 1776."

4. The Royal Instructions to the Peace Commission of 1778 are conveniently printed in S. E. Morison, ed., *Sources and Documents Illustrating the American Revolution, 1764–1788* (Oxford: The Clarendon Press, 1923), pp. 186–203.

5. See p. 30 for discussion of the most-favored-nation relationship.

of the British West Indian colonies. The United States, on the other hand, was free to conquer and hold Bermuda or any of Great Britain's mainland possessions. Neither party should make a separate peace with Great Britain nor lay down its arms until American independence was won. Each signatory guaranteed to the other the American possessions which it then held and with which it might emerge from the war. France, in addition, undertook to guarantee the liberty, sovereignty, and independence of the United States.

The treaty just described constituted the only "entangling alliance" in which the United States participated until the middle of the twentieth century. It was to cause serious embarrassment before it was set aside in 1800,[6] but in the winning of independence it was indispensable. A French army under General Rochambeau was sent to America, and French fleets under Admirals d'Estaing and de Grasse operated off the American coast. The importance of French aid is pointed up by the reflection that in the final scene of the Revolution, at Yorktown, Cornwallis' British army was caught between a French fleet and an allied army, of which two-thirds were also French.

Spain and the Revolution

Spain, though bound to France by a dynastic alliance, the "Family Compact," and though giving secret aid to the United States, hung back from entering the war for over a year after France had become a belligerent. There were advantages that Spain might gain from a successful war with England: the recovery of Gibraltar (lost in 1713) and of Florida (lost in 1763). Gibraltar, the more valuable of these, the Spanish court hoped to regain peaceably, as a reward for mediating between Great Britain and France. Only when Great Britain declined the proffered service did Spain sign a definite alliance with France (Convention of Aranjuez, April 12, 1779) and declare war against Great Britain (June 21, 1779). The Franco-American treaty of alliance had re-

served for Spain the right to become a member, but Spain declined to sign it or to make any kind of treaty with the United States. A colonial power herself, Spain naturally hesitated to give formal acknowledgment to a rebellion of the colonies of Great Britain. John Jay spent many bitter months in Madrid asking in vain for recognition. Even an offer to waive the American claim of right to navigate the Mississippi River could not persuade the Spanish government to recognize the young republic. By the Convention of Aranjuez, France and Spain agreed that neither would make peace till Spain had recovered Gibraltar. Since the United States had promised not to make peace without France, it could not, if all treaty engagements were observed, make peace till Gibraltar was restored to Spain.

In America, Spanish interests ran counter to those of the United States. The United States desired the Mississippi River as its western boundary and the right of navigating the river through Spanish territory to the Gulf of Mexico. Spain, anxious to monopolize as far as might be the navigation and commerce of both river and gulf, was unwilling to concede to the Americans either the use of the river or a foothold on its eastern bank. If the Spanish had their way, the western boundary of the United States would be fixed as near as possible to the summit of the Appalachians.

The bargaining position of Spain was strengthened by the daring and vigor of Bernardo de Galvez, the young governor of Louisiana. Within less than two years after Spain's entry into the war, he had routed the British out of all of West Florida, from Natchez on the north to Pensacola on the east. He had established Spain's claim to a cession of Florida at the end of the war and to full control of the lower Mississippi.

A Pawn in the European Chess Game

In order to win independence the United States had found it necessary to involve itself in the international rivalries and politics of Europe. Those same rivalries and politics, however, threatened to terminate the war with

6. See Chapter 5.

American independence still unwon. Spain, having entered the war reluctantly, soon grew tired of it. In 1780 the Spanish government received a British mission, come to discuss peace terms. For America, the Spanish ministers proposed a long truce between Great Britain and her "colonies," without specific recognition of independence and with a division of territory on the basis of *uti possidetis,* or retention by each party of the areas then occupied. This would have left the British in control of Maine, the northern frontier, New York City, Long Island, and the principal seaports south of Virginia.

Vergennes disapproved these Anglo-Spanish conversations, which violated the Convention of Aranjuez. He was willing to listen, however, to proposals for mediation from the Czarina Catherine II of Russia and the Austrian Emperor, Joseph II, which would have had much the same effect in America. John Adams, who had been named American peace commissioner and came from the Hague to Paris at Vergennes' behest, rejected the proposal out of hand when Vergennes laid it before him. No truce, he said, till all British troops were withdrawn from the United States; no negotiation with England without guarantees that American sovereignty and independence would be respected. But in America, Congress was more easily persuaded than was Adams. Under pressure (and in some instances monetary persuasion) from La Luzerne, the French minister, Congress on June 15, 1781, drew up new instructions to its prospective peace commissioners in Europe. Not only were they directed to accept the mediation of the Czarina and the Emperor; they were to place themselves in the hands of the French ministers, "to undertake nothing in the negotiations for peace or truce without their knowledge and concurrence," and ultimately to be governed "by their advice and opinion." It was perhaps fortunate for the United States that the British government rejected the proposal for mediation.[7]

Great Britain in Difficulty

The surrender of Cornwallis to Washington and Rochambeau at Yorktown, October 19, 1781, was the climax of Great Britain's misfortunes. She was now at war, or on the verge of war, with most of the western world. To the list of her open enemies she herself had added the Netherlands, forcing them into war rather than permit continuance of their neutral trade with France. The Baltic countries, Russia, Denmark, and Sweden, had in 1780 organized themselves into a League of Armed Neutrality for the purpose of protecting their commerce against what they considered the illegitimate exactions of the British Navy; and they had been joined by Prussia, the Emperor (of the Holy Roman Empire), the Kingdom of the Two Sicilies, and even Portugal, Great Britain's traditional ally. There was little that the British could hope to gain by prolonging the war.

In February 1782, following receipt of the news of the disaster at Yorktown, the British House of Commons resolved that the war ought to be terminated. In March, the ministry of Lord North, whose policies had precipitated the American conflict, resigned, and a new ministry headed by the Marquis of Rockingham took office. The Earl of Shelburne, as Secretary of State for the Southern Department, initiated peace talks by sending Richard Oswald, a Scot, to confer with the American representatives in Paris. After Rockingham's death in July 1782, Shelburne became Prime Minister but continued to guide negotiations with the United States. This was fortunate, for Shelburne was an advocate of a generous peace, which might result in recapturing for Great Britain the bulk of American trade and at some future day, perhaps, tempt the United States back into some sort of imperial federation.

---

7. In the subsequent peace negotiations in Paris, the offer of mediation was accepted as a matter of form by the European belligerents. The representatives of the Czarina and the Emperor signed the treaties, nothing more. In the negotiations between the United States and Great Britain they took not even a nominal part.

The American Congress named five peace commissioners, of whom three actually handled the negotiations. Franklin was in Paris when the talks began. John Jay, who had been vainly seeking recognition and a treaty in Madrid, arrived in June 1782. John Adams, who had secured recognition and a loan from the Netherlands, reached Paris in October. Henry Laurens was on hand in time to sign the treaty. Thomas Jefferson, the fifth of those named by Congress, declined to serve. Most of the work was done by Franklin and Jay, with Adams giving valuable aid toward the close of the negotiations.

The Stakes of Diplomacy

The American commissioners had three principal objectives: (1) recognition of independence, which was now assured; (2) the widest boundaries obtainable; (3) retention of the inshore fishing privileges on the coasts of British North America which the colonials had enjoyed as British subjects. The British government was ready to recognize American independence and to act generously on the other American demands. It hoped in turn to secure from the United States (1) provision for the payment of the pre-Revolutionary debts of American planters and others to British creditors, and (2) an agreement to compensate the Loyalists (Americans who had sided with Great Britain in the struggle) for the lands and other property that had been seized by the states in which they lived.

Of the American demands the most controversial was that concerning boundaries, for American claims on this point involved not only adjustments with Great Britain but disputes with Spain—disputes in which Vergennes chose to support his Spanish rather than his American ally.

In their more sanguine moments, Benjamin Franklin and other American leaders dreamed of including in their confederacy the whole of British North America and certain of the outlying islands. Such hopes had no chance of fulfillment. What the United States Congress laid claim to as a matter of right was the entire western country between the Appalachian Mountains and the Mississippi River, extending from the thirty-first parallel on the south to a northern line drawn from the St. Lawrence River at north latitude 45° to Lake Nipissing (the southwestern boundary of Quebec before 1774) and thence to the source of the Mississippi. These claims, based chiefly upon the sea-to-sea clauses in certain colonial charters, had never been taken seriously by the British government, which in the years since 1763 had acted upon the theory that the western lands still belonged to the Crown. The campaigns of George Rogers Clark during the war had done little to strengthen American claims to the country north of the Ohio River.[8]

South of the Ohio River, American settlements in central Kentucky and eastern and central Tennessee gave the United States a solid basis for claiming those areas, but farther south it was the Spanish, not the Americans, who had driven the British out. The Spanish held the east bank of the Mississippi as far north as Natchez; they hoped, as was previously noted, to deny the Americans access to the Mississippi and to draw the boundary as near as possible to the Appalachian watershed. In this endeavor they had French support.

In the summer of 1779, Congress had taken the first step toward peace negotiations by naming John Adams commissioner for that purpose. In instructions prepared for him (August 14, 1779), it had proposed boundaries including the entire area claimed by the states from the mountains to the Mississippi. It had added that although it was "of the utmost importance to the peace and Commerce

8. J. A. James, in his *Life of George Rogers Clark* (Chicago: University of Chicago Press, 1928), maintains that Clark's military exploits played an important part in inducing the British to surrender the Northwest to the United States. This thesis has not been widely accepted. On the other side see C. W. Alvord, "Virginia and the West; an Interpretation," 1782," *Western Pennsylvania Historical Magazine,* 17 *Mississippi Valley Historical Review,* 3 (1916), 19–38; R. C. Downes, "Indian War on the Upper Ohio, 1779– (1934), 93–115.

of the United States that Canada and Nova Scotia should be ceded" and that equal rights in the fisheries should be guaranteed, a desire to terminate the war had led Congress to refrain from making the acquisition of these objects an ultimatum. Subsequently, under stress of military necessity and pressure from the French minister, Congress had modified those demands. In the new instructions of June 15, 1781, it insisted only upon independence and the preservation of the treaties with France as indispensable conditions. With regard to boundaries, the commissioners were to regard the earlier instructions as indicating "the desires and expectations of Congress," but were not to adhere to them if they presented an obstacle to peace. The task of the commissioners was to get as much as they could of the terms proposed two years earlier. In this they did very well.

The Peace Negotiations

The first obstacles encountered by the Americans were erected by the Spanish and French, not by the British. When John Jay arrived in Paris, suspicious of both Spain and France after his futile mission in Madrid, he found disturbing confirmation of his distrust. Conversations with the Spanish ambassador in Paris and with a spokesman for Vergennes showed that the Spanish, with French support, were bent upon excluding the United States from the Mississippi Valley.

French support of Spanish claims impaired the confidential relations between Vergennes and the American commissioners. Vergennes had previously agreed that the American and French negotiations should proceed separately but at equal pace and with the understanding that neither settlement should become effective without the other. Franklin and Jay now proceeded to negotiate their own preliminary terms with the British, neglecting, with considerable justification, to make those "most candid and confidential communications" to the French ministers enjoined upon them by their instructions of June 15, 1781. In negotiating

their settlement with Great Britain, they simply disregarded Spanish claims in the western country north of the 31st parallel, assuming (as did the British) that that country was still Great Britain's to dispose of.

In informal talks with Oswald, Franklin had already sketched what, as an American, he considered the "necessary" and the "advisable" terms of a lasting peace. Among "necessary" terms he included, after independence and withdrawal of troops, "a confinement of the boundaries of Canada" to what they had been before the Quebec Act (i.e., the St. Lawrence-Nipissing line), "if not to a still more contracted state," and the retention of fishing privileges. Among "advisable" terms which might be expected to contribute to a permanent reconciliation, he mentioned indemnification by Great Britain of those persons who had been ruined through the devastations of war, acknowledgment of error expressed in an act of Parliament or in some other public document, admission of American ships and trade to British and Irish ports upon the same terms as those of Britain, and "giving up every part of Canada."

A delay in the negotiations now ensued, first because Oswald had no formal commission as an agent of the British government, and after his commission arrived, August 8, because it failed to authorize him to recognize the independence of the United States as a preliminary to negotiation, but on the contrary empowered him to treat with representatives of "colonies" of Great Britain. It did, however, authorize him to make recognition of independence the first article of the proposed treaty. Franklin and Jay were at first inclined to insist upon formal recognition of independence as a condition precedent to negotiation; but, becoming alarmed lest France use any further delay to their disadvantage, they agreed to accept as recognition a new commission that authorized Oswald to treat with commissioners of the United States of America. Time had been consumed, nevertheless, in this meticulous stickling for matters of form, and with the passage of time the situation was modified to the disadvantage of the United States.

On September 1, instructions were sent to Oswald to agree to terms of peace on the basis of the "necessary" terms proposed by Franklin, conceding to the United States the western country as far north as the Nipissing line, and making no stipulation for the payment of pre-war debts or the restitution of property confiscated from the Loyalists. A draft of a treaty on these terms was actually initialed by the commissioners on October 5 and referred to London. The unfortunate results of delay now became apparent. News had arrived in London of the failure of a major assault upon Gibraltar, which had been besieged for three years by Spanish and French land and sea forces. With this victory in hand, Shelburne took a firmer tone toward the United States. He not only insisted that something be done for creditors and Loyalists but made a last moment attempt to hold the Northwest, though this latter move may have been merely a gesture designed to secure concessions on the other points. "They wanted," Franklin reported, "to bring their boundary down to the Ohio and to settle the loyalists in the Illinois country. We did not choose such neighbors."

The Americans, now reinforced by Adams, insisted upon retention of the Northwest, but were ready to make concessions on this and other points. They agreed to inclusion in the treaty of articles in the interest of the Loyalists and the British creditors. They accepted the St. Croix River instead of the St. John, which Congress had originally proposed, as the northeastern boundary, thereby laying the basis of a controversy which it took sixty years to settle.[9] In the West, they dropped the Nipissing line proposal, agreeing to accept instead either of two alternatives: a line drawn due west along the 45th parallel from the St. Lawrence to the Mississippi, or a line through the middle of the St. Lawrence and the Great Lakes and thence via the Lake of the Woods to the Mississippi. The British accepted the second alternative. The preliminary treaty was signed at Paris on November 30, 1782, not to

9. See p. 43 and Chapter 10. By the October 5 draft, the exact location of the northeast boundary was to be determined by a mixed commission.

become effective until France also made peace with England.

The treaty thus signed and, in due course, ratified by the parties was less favorable to the United States in three respects than the draft initialed on October 5. It contained troublesome provisions for Loyalists and for British creditors, and the northern boundary followed the river and lake line instead of that by way of Lake Nipissing. By the latter change, the United States lost the greater and the most valuable part of the modern province of Ontario. Had Jay and Franklin been willing to treat with Oswald on the basis of his first commission, it is at least possible that they might have agreed upon Franklin's "necessary terms" early in September instead of a month later, and that Shelburne might have accepted these terms before he received news of the victory at Gibraltar.

But this is another might-have-been. What is remarkable about the treaty is that the United States got as much as it did, especially that the British surrendered title to all territory east of the Mississippi between the Great Lakes and the 31st parallel. For the explanation of this surrender, one must look neither to the legal weight of the colonial charters nor to the military victories of George Rogers Clark, but to the enlightened policy of the Earl of Shelburne. Desirous of a peace of reconciliation, he saw a means of achieving it at small cost to the Empire. The Northwest, demanded by the Americans, appeared to him to be of slight value to Great Britain. The regulation of the fur trade in that area was proving ruinously expensive to the royal treasury, and experience had seemed to show that the region was of little value without control of the mouth of the Mississippi, now more firmly than ever in the hands of Spain. Why not buy American good will at so cheap a price?

The Treaty

In detail, the principal provisions of the preliminary treaty signed on November 30, 1782, were as follows: The boundary of the United

NORTHWEST "BOUNDARY GAP"

C A N A D A

St. Lawrence R.

45°

L O U I S I A N A

U N I T E D

S T A T E S

Mississippi River

Chattahoochee R.

St. Mary's R.

31°

F L O R I D A

A t l a n t i c   O c e a n

- - - - {Boundaries of 1783 (northeast boundary as finally determined).
∧∧∧∧ 1st U.S. proposal for northern boundary.
-·-·- {2nd U.S. proposal for northern boundary.
▦ Claimed by U.S. till 1842.
▨ To be retained by Gt. Britain if she retained Florida.

**BOUNDARIES OF THE U.S.A.
UNDER TREATY OF PARIS-**
WITH ALTERNATIVE U.S. PROPOSALS

States began at the mouth of the St. Croix River on the Maine frontier, followed that river to its source and thence ran due north to the highlands dividing the St. Lawrence from the Atlantic watershed, along those highlands to the northwesternmost head of the

Connecticut River, and down that river to the 45th parallel, which it followed to the St. Lawrence. It then followed the middle of the St. Lawrence and of Lakes Ontario, Erie, and Huron and connecting waters to Lake Superior; through that lake to Long Lake and then through certain small lakes and streams to the Lake of the Woods, from the northwesternmost point of which it was to be drawn due west to the Mississippi—an impossible line, since the Mississippi rose well to the southward. It followed the Mississippi down to the 31st parallel, ran due east along that parallel to the Chattahoochee, descended that stream to its junction with the Flint, leaped thence straight to the head of the St. Mary's River, which it followed to the Atlantic. A secret article, introduced by the British but not incorporated in the final treaty, stipulated that if Great Britain retained West Florida, the northern line of that province should be, as it had been since 1764, not the 31st parallel but a line drawn east from the junction of the Yazoo with the Mississippi. The navigation of the Mississippi was to remain forever "free and open to the subjects of Great-Britain, and the citizens of the United States."

Great Britain acknowledged the independence and sovereignty of the thirteen states individually, promised to withdraw all its armies, garrisons, and fleets from their soil and waters "with all convenient speed," and conceded to American fishermen the "liberty" to ply their trade much as before in the territorial waters of British North America. The United States, on its part, made certain promises in the interest of Loyalists and British creditors. The parties agreed that creditors on either side should "meet with no lawful impediment" in the recovery of the full value of bona fide debts previously contracted. The United States agreed that there should be no further prosecutions or confiscations of property against any persons for the parts they had taken in the war, and promised that it would "earnestly recommend" to the legislatures of the states that, with certain exceptions, rights and properties of Loyalists be restored.

This preliminary treaty, minus the secret article, became the definitive treaty, signed September 3, 1783, at the same time that Great Britain made peace with her other enemies. The Floridas, with limits undefined, Great Britain ceded to Spain. Spain was not a party to the treaty between Great Britain and the United States, and hence did not consider herself bound by its provisions with respect to the navigation of the Mississippi and the southern boundary of the United States. With both Spain and Great Britain, the United States had still many difficulties to overcome before the paper stipulations of the treaty could be converted into reality.

4

Problems of
Independence

Americans soon learned that independence was no bed of roses. When the war officially ended in 1783, the new government had been recognized by France, Great Britain, the Netherlands, and Sweden. Inexperienced diplomats from the United States had wandered over Europe in vain efforts to secure recognition from Russia, Prussia, Austria, Spain, and the Grand Duke of Tuscany. In all these courts they had been coldly received. Few monarchs cared to imitate the indiscretion of Louis XVI of France, by countenancing rebellion and the institution of republican government.

A few other recognitions followed independence. In 1784 Spain finally gave in, sending Don Diego de Gardoqui as her first minister to the United States. Prussia made a treaty in 1785, Morocco in 1786. By 1787, then, the United States had commercial treaties with those two powers and with France (1778), the Netherlands (1782), and Sweden (1783). It had no commercial treaty with Great Britain until 1794, no treaty at all with Spain till 1795. The British government thought so little of the importance of the United States that though it received John Adams as minister in 1785 and maintained consular or other agents in American ports, it did not send a full-fledged minister to Philadelphia until 1791.

There were reasons for this temporary "underprivileged" status of the United States. It was an upstart nation, the product of revolution, an experiment in democracy, small in population, poor in fluid resources. But it also, under the Articles of Confederation, had a government that no foreign power need respect—a government without dependable revenue, without an army or navy, without power to coerce the governments of the thirteen individual states. Such a government was unable to fulfill its obligations under the treaty of peace. Such a government could not make promises with assurance that they would be observed, or threats with any expectation that they would be carried out. Such a government was incapable of securing equality of commercial treatment abroad. It was incapable of enforcing its sovereignty in the area assigned to it by the treaty of peace or of putting an end, by either diplomacy or force, to foreign occupation of its soil. Not until after it was replaced by the more effective government provided for by the Constitution of 1787 were any of the pressing national problems solved. Even then, their solution owed much to the involvement of France, Spain, and Great Britain in the wars of the French Revolution. Then, to quote the familiar aphorism of Professor Samuel F. Bemis, "Europe's distress became America's advantage."

Independence Disrupts Trade

Particularly inconvenient for the young nation was the lack of a commercial treaty with Great Britain. The thirteen original states of the American Union had, while they existed as colonies under the British flag, developed a flourishing merchant marine and a large and profitable commerce. Colonial shipyards turned out ships more cheaply than British. Ships built and owned in the colonies shared equally with English ships the privileges of Empire trade and protection by the Royal Navy. American tobacco, rice, indigo, wheat, flour, meat, fish, rum, furs, and lumber found markets in England, on the continent of Europe, in Africa, and in the West Indies; they were exchanged for manufactured goods, sugar and molasses, coffee, rum, slaves, and specie. The Revolution, while it lasted, disrupted large segments of this thriving commercial activity. American ships, with their cargoes, were excluded from British Empire ports and could roam the seas only at the risk of capture by British cruisers or privateers. Many American shipowners took to privateering themselves and harried British commerce even in the English Channel and the Irish Sea. The coming of peace in 1783 put an end to such warlike employment. It compelled the United States, in the exercise of its newly won independence, to seek markets for its produce, cargoes and foreign ports for its merchantmen, and protection for ships and cargoes against the piracies of North African freebooters.

Trade with the various portions of the British Empire might have gone on as before the war if the British had been willing. The American peace commissioners of 1782 were instructed to secure, if possible, for citizens of the United States, "a direct commerce to all parts of the British dominions and possessions" in return for the admission of British subjects to trade with all parts of the United States. The British government declined, at that time, to make a commercial treaty, and the House of Commons defeated a bill, introduced by William Pitt the younger, that would have admitted American ships and American commodities to British Empire ports on the same terms as British vessels and products. The British Parliament was in no mood to be generous to its former colonies—least of all to encourage a rival in the American merchant marine. American ships carrying American products were admitted to ports in the British Isles on fairly liberal terms, but, in harmony with prevalent mercantile theory, American ships, like other foreign ships, were excluded from trading with the British colonies. New England merchants missed particularly what had once been a profitable trade with the British West Indies; only gradually and at considerable risk did they succeed in reopening this trade through clandestine and illegal channels. To varying degrees, and with some exceptions, other colonial powers adhered to the same mercantilist policy of reserving trade with their colonies to their own ships.

American Commercial Principles

In this situation it became an object of American diplomacy to recapture, or find substitutes for, the markets lost as a result of independence and to assure to the languishing shipping interest the right to carry cargoes to and from those markets. In pursuing this object, the government sought to embody certain principles or ideals in treaties or agreements with other powers. The most important of these principles were the following:

1. *Equality of treatment.* American ships and cargoes should enjoy, in the ports of another power, any privileges which that power accorded to ships and cargoes of any third

party. An agreement to this effect was usually embodied in a reciprocal *most-favored-nation* clause in a treaty with the power concerned.

2. *Admission to trade with the colonies of foreign powers.* Although the United States could in no sense claim as a right a concession so contrary to mercantilist theory, it sought such admission unremittingly as a privilege considered to be of vital importance to its commercial and shipping interests.

3. *Reciprocity.* Concessions such as the lowering of tariff rates or the elimination of extra duties on commodities imported in foreign ships might be granted in return for similar concessions allowed by a foreign power.

4. The establishment of *liberal neutrality principles,* as befitted a nation with a large merchant marine and a small navy, a nation that expected to remain aloof from the strife of Europe.

Finding Ports and Markets in Europe

Access for American ships to the ports of the principal European powers (exclusive of colonial ports) on a most-favored-nation basis was not too difficult to attain. The first treaty negotiated by the United States—the treaty of amity and commerce with France of February 6, 1778—embodied the most-favored-nation principle in the following article:

> Article 2. The most Christian King, and the United States engage mutually not to grant any particular Favour to other Nations in respect of Commerce and Navigation, which shall not immediately become common to the other Party, who shall enjoy the same Favour, freely, if the Concession was freely made, or on allowing the same Compensation, if the Concession was Conditional. . . .[1]

1. The article quoted embodied the most-favored-nation principle in its conditional form—a form not in use prior to this treaty, but one that the United States continued to use, with few exceptions, until well into the twentieth century. Under such a clause, privileges extended to one power by a reciprocity treaty could not be claimed by a third power unless it granted corresponding concessions to the United States. Around 1923 the United States abandoned the

The ports of France (or such of them as were open to any foreign ships) were therefore open to the ships and cargoes of the United States. Other European ports were similarly opened to the Americans. The Netherlands signed a commercial treaty in 1782, Sweden in 1783, Prussia in 1785. All of these treaties contained most-favored-nation articles. Great Britain, as already noted, permitted American ships to bring to her shores most commodities of American production, but products of the whale fisheries were excluded, with disastrous results to the New England whaling fleets. Other nations that as yet had no commercial treaties with the upstart republic—Russia, for example, and to a less degree Spain—also welcomed American ships and their cargoes of raw materials. Into the Baltic and Mediterranean, into hitherto unfamiliar Chinese waters at Canton, into the forbidden ports of the British West Indies, Yankee ships made their way in increasing numbers, but reviving trade owed much more to individual enterprise than to assistance from the ineffectual American government.

Problems of the West

Even more serious in the long view than the problem of commerce was that of controlling the great region between the mountains and the Mississippi. The treaty of peace had assigned spacious boundaries to the United States, but American sovereignty within the boundaries was largely a legal fiction. American settlement beyond the mountains took the

conditional for the unconditional type of most-favored-nation agreement. Thereafter, if by a reciprocal trade agreement it lowered the duties on certain commodities produced by nation *A,* it was bound automatically to make similar reductions on the same commodities supplied by nations *B* and *C,* with which it had unconditional most-favored-nation treaties. B. H. Williams, *Economic Foreign Policy of the United States* (New York: McGraw-Hill Book Company, 1929), pp. 290, 298–302; U. S. Tariff Commission, *Reciprocity and Commercial Treaties* (Washington, D.C.: Government Printing Office, 1919), pp. 17–20.

form of a narrow wedge with its base stretching from Pittsburgh to the Watauga settlements in eastern Tennessee and its apex at Nashville on the Cumberland River. Within it lay the villages in the Kentucky bluegrass region and at the Falls of the Ohio (Louisville). To these should be added the old French villages on the Wabash and in the Illinois country. All told, there were perhaps 25,000 settlers between the crest of the mountains and the Mississippi. Beyond these limits, to the north, west, and south, was the country of unfriendly Indians, and the explorer or trader who penetrated the Indian barrier was likely to find himself facing garrisons of British or Spanish troops upon land within the treaty boundaries of the United States. The British army still occupied every strategic point on the Great Lakes, and Spanish soldiers held the Mississippi at Natchez and (a little later) at the sites of the future Vicksburg and Memphis; and both British and Spanish were in alliance or understanding with the Indians for the purpose of preventing the United States from taking possession of the territory assigned to it by the treaty of peace.

There was, furthermore, no assurance that the frontier settlers themselves would be firm in their allegiance to the state governments in the East or to the weak Congress that symbolized their Union. A do-nothing government could not command a vital patriotism. The frontier found its natural outlets through the Mississippi and the St. Lawrence Rivers, and the nations that controlled those watercourses exerted a powerful attraction upon the settlements on their upper waters. Frontier leaders were not always above bartering their allegiance in return for special favors from the British and Spanish governments.

Before the United States could make its actual sovereignty coextensive with its treaty boundaries, it had to accomplish three difficult tasks. It had to make sure of its hold upon the allegiance of the frontiersmen. It had to bring the Indian tribes under its control. It had to secure from England and Spain, respectively, the execution and the recognition of the terms of the Treaty of Paris. These tasks

were interrelated. Only through ousting British and Spanish from their footholds upon its soil could the United States hope to control the Indians, and only by dealing effectively with both Indians and Europeans could it bind to itself the "men of the western waters."

None of these problems proved capable of solution during the period of the Articles of Confederation. The British held seven fortified posts on United States soil, strung out from the foot of Lake Champlain to Michilimackinac at the junction of Lakes Huron and Michigan. The British excused this violation of the peace treaty by asserting that the United States had not fulfilled its obligations under the same instrument.[2] In reality, the decision to hold the posts had been taken before the treaty was formally proclaimed, obviously before the nature of the American performance under it could be known. Retention of the posts served to keep a valuable trade in furs in the hands of Canadian traders and enabled the British government to meet its obligations to Indian tribes which had been its allies during the recent war. British authorities did not hesitate to encourage these tribes, living south of the Canadian border, to resist American attempts to purchase and settle their lands. The British also showed an interest in the dissatisfaction of American frontier communities in Vermont and Kentucky, which might perhaps be willing to detach themselves from the Confederation.

The treaty of 1783 between Great Britain

2. By the terms of the treaty, the United States had agreed that British creditors should "meet with no lawful impediment" to the collection of their debts in the United States, and that Congress should "earnestly recommend" to the legislatures of the states the restoration of the rights and confiscated property of Loyalists who had not actually borne arms against the United States. It cannot be maintained that the states adhered to the spirit of these agreements, but the decision to retain the posts was arrived at before the British government could know this. "It is fruitless," writes Professor Bemis, "to attempt to attach the burden of prior infraction to either party." S. F. Bemis, *Jay's Treaty: A Study in Commerce and Diplomacy* (New Haven: Yale University Press, 1962), p. 14.

NORTHWEST
BOUNDARY
GAP →

St. Lawrence R.

Michilimackinac

Oswegatchie
Pointe au Fer
Dutchman's
Point

Oswego

Niagara

Detroit

Pittsburgh

Marietta

Cincinnati

Louisville

Lexington

Ohio R.

Nashville

Knoxville

San
Fernando

Tennessee R.

Ft. Confederacion

Los Nogales

Natchez

WEST FLORIDA

EAST FLORIDA

Mississippi River

L O U I S I A N A

A t l a n t i c   O c e a n

G u l f   o f   M e x i c o

Indian barrier state proposed
by British and Indians

Extreme Spanish territorial claims

U.S. settlements

---- U.S., Treaty of 1783
++++ Greenville Treaty line, 1795
☐ British posts until 1796
⊙ Spanish posts until 1798
● U.S. frontier towns

THE NORTHWEST AND
SOUTHWEST, 1783–1798

and the United States had fixed the southern boundary of the latter, from the Chattahoochee to the Mississippi, at the 31st parallel, had made the middle of the Mississippi the western boundary, and had declared: "The navigation of the river Mississippi, from its source to the ocean, shall forever remain free and open to the subjects of Great-Britain, and the citizens of the United States." In the contemporaneous settlement with Spain, Great Britain had ceded to that nation East and West Florida without defining their boundaries. Louisiana, embracing the region west of the Mississippi and New Orleans east of that river, had been ceded by France to Spain in 1762. After 1783, therefore, Spain hemmed in the United States on both the west and the south.

Spain was not a signatory to the treaty between Great Britain and the United States and refused to consider herself bound by its terms, either as to the southern boundary of the United States or as to the free navigation of the Mississippi. As a result of the successful campaign under Galvez in 1779–1781, Spain claimed a large area in the Southwest by right of conquest and denied the right of Great Britain to cede it to the United States. Holding both banks of the Mississippi from its mouth to far above New Orleans, Spain likewise denied the right of Great Britain to guarantee to citizens of the United States its free navigation. Spanish policy after 1783 comprised the assertion of title to a region as far north as the Tennessee and Ohio Rivers, the denial to the Americans of the use of the lower Mississippi except as a privilege granted by Spain, and the cultivation of the friendship and trade of the powerful Indian nations of the Southwest with a view to using them as a barrier against the Americans. From time to time, also, Spain intrigued with shifty leaders in the American frontier communities who appeared ready to barter their allegiance for privileges or bounties conferred by the Spanish crown.

The extreme boundary claims of Spain were apparently set up chiefly for bargaining purposes. Diego de Gardoqui, who came to New York in 1784 as the first Spanish minister to the United States, was empowered to make liberal boundary concessions and to offer substantial trading privileges in return for the consent of the United States to waive its claim to the navigation of the Mississippi. John Jay of New York, serving as Secretary for Foreign Affairs under the direction of Congress, thought the trade offer advantageous, the navigation of the Mississippi of little immediate importance. He asked Congress for authority to consent to closure of the river for a period of twenty-five or thirty years. The vote on his proposal showed a sectional cleavage. Virginia, the Carolinas, and Georgia, all with land claims extending to the Mississippi, voted against Jay's proposal. Maryland voted with her southern sisters. The seven states to the north (Delaware having no delegate in Congress) supported Jay. The majority of seven to five was sufficient to alter Jay's instructions, but any treaty that he might make would require the vote of nine states for ratification. Jay and Gardoqui continued their conversations, but there was no point in making a treaty which Congress would not approve.[3]

Failure of the Jay-Gardoqui negotiations left matters *in statu quo*. In the next year (1787), however, the Spanish authorities opened the river at the behest of Americans from the Kentucky settlements. One of these, James Wilkinson, a veteran of the Revolution, paid for the privilege by taking a secret oath of allegiance to the Spanish Crown. He also undertook to advise the Spanish upon the best means of winning over other Kentuckians. Spain made no permanent converts among the frontiersmen—Wilkinson himself was soon to

3. It has long been held that southern alarm at the possibility of seeing its interests bargained away by a northern majority resulted in southern insistence, in the Constitutional Convention of 1787, upon the requirement that treaties be approved by two-thirds of the senators present. This theory is called in question by the fact that the delegations of South Carolina and Georgia voted subsequently to substitute a majority for a two-thirds vote. M. S. McDougal and Asher Lans, *Treaties and Congressional-Executive or Presidential Agreements: Interchangeable Instruments of National Policy* (reprinted from *Yale Law Journal*, Vol. 54, Nos. 2, 3, March and June 1945), pp. 541–43.

don a United States brigadier general's uniform—and her alternative policy of building anti-American alliances with the southern Indians won no victories. But the establishment of satisfactory relations with Spain, as well as with Britain, awaited the formation of a more efficient American government.

A New Government for the United States

While Britishers and Spaniards flirted with American frontiersmen and dabbled in alliances with the Indians in their respective spheres of influence, the United States was setting up a new government that effectually overcame the deficiencies of the Articles of Confederation and soon gave the country a respectable standing among the nations of the world. The Constitution written at Philadelphia in 1787 went into effect two years later. Under it, the new government had bargaining power that the old had lacked. It could control commerce, raise revenue, create and maintain armies and navies. Treaties, both those already made and those to be made in the future, were declared to be "the supreme law of the land," overriding state enactments and even state constitutions. Separate executive and judicial departments provided all the machinery necessary for enforcement. No longer could foreign governments scorn the promises or scoff at the threats of the United States. The adoption of the Constitution inaugurated a new era in American diplomacy.

The new American government had hardly got upon its feet when it was assailed by reverberations from the strife of Europe and the necessity of deciding upon its attitude to the international struggle precipitated by the French Revolution. Should it remain neutral in this, the first European war since the young nation had attained its independence? If so, what neutral rights should it claim, and how should it enforce them? What neutral obligations should it assume? The outbreak of war in Europe confronted the administration of George Washington with a host of perplexing questions which it had to attempt to answer before it could settle those border controversies with Great Britain and Spain that were described in the last chapter.

Neutrality, or nonparticipation in the wars of other states, was destined to become one of the cornerstones of American foreign policy. Tom Paine, it will be recalled, had advanced immunity from the wars of Europe as one of the chief advantages to be gained by independence. John Adams, speaking in 1776 of the proposed negotiations with France, remarked:

> . . . we ought not to enter into any alliance with her which should entangle us in any future wars in Europe; we ought to lay it down as a first principle and a maxim never to be forgotten, to maintain an entire neutrality in all future European wars.[1]

Such neutrality became the ideal, the not always realizable ideal, of the young republic. It remained so until well into the twentieth century, when changed world conditions made the outcome of the wars of Europe a matter of intimate concern to the United States.

The Meaning of Neutrality

Neutrality, which thus became the aim, though not always the achievement, of the early leaders of the Republic, is a status that developed only in modern times, accompanying the emergence of independent and sovereign national states from feudalism and the

1. Quoted in E. M. Borchard and W. P. Lage, *Neutrality for the United States*, 2nd ed. (New Haven: Yale University Press, 1940), p. 21.

5

War in Europe Raises New and Settles Old Problems

overlordship of the Holy Roman Empire. Neutrality is the abstention by a state from the wars of its neighbors and its insulation, as far as may be, from the pains and inconveniences of those wars. Neutrality implies both rights and duties, and a state that claims the rights of a neutral must observe the obligations of a neutral. The concept of neutral obligations has changed from time to time. The Dutch authority, Hugo Grotius, writing early in the seventeenth century, held that a neutral should seek to determine which of two belligerents was in the right and then "do nothing which would further the cause of the one in the wrong, or hamper the movements of the one in the right." The Swiss, Emmeric de Vattel, a century later, laid down the rule that was to be generally accepted by the modern world, at least until after World War I. According to Vattel, the neutral should not pass judgment upon the merits of the conflict, but should treat the two belligerents with entire impartiality, the only exception being the case where the neutral was bound by treaty to furnish assistance to one belligerent.

More specifically, the government of a neutral state should give no aid of any kind to either belligerent. It must exclude belligerent armies from its territory, prevent recruiting within its jurisdiction by either belligerent, and prevent the use of its harbors or territorial waters as bases of operations by belligerent naval forces. Certain things that a neutral government must not do, it is under no obligation to prevent its citizens from doing. It need not prevent its citizens from making loans or selling supplies to belligerent governments, though if those citizens undertake to sell military supplies (contraband of war) to a belligerent or to trade with a blockaded port, they do so at their own risk, and have no claim to compensation if the ships and cargoes they have risked in such trade are seized and confiscated by the other belligerent.

In return for its observance of the duties of a neutral, the neutral state may insist upon the corresponding rights. First and foremost, it has a right to expect that the armed forces of the belligerents will not set foot upon its soil or engage in any acts of war within its harbors or territorial waters (generally, that is, within three miles of its shores). It may also expect certain immunities from belligerent interference with its property and commerce at sea. It may claim for its nationals the right to trade with either belligerent as long as the trade is in noncontraband commodities and with ports not under blockade. It may claim a right to unlimited trade with other neutrals, unless it can be shown that such trade is a subterfuge, with one of the belligerents as the real beneficiary. In such a case the other belligerent will often assert the right to interfere.

Within these very general rules there was, when the United States won its independence, room for widely varying interpretations. What commodities constituted contraband of war? Under what conditions was a port legally blockaded? Could a belligerent confiscate enemy property on a neutral ship, or neutral property on an enemy ship? Was a neutral ship free to trade between different ports of a belligerent? What circumstances, if any, justified a belligerent in interfering in trade between neutrals? To many of these questions, answers could be found in treaties between the chief maritime powers, but in time of war the belligerent whose superior navy controlled the seas—and that generally meant England— sought to enlarge the rights of belligerents and to whittle away those of neutrals, while the neutrals and the belligerents with weaker navies attempted to enlarge or at least defend neutral rights. From 1793, when France and England went to war, to 1812, the United States was in almost uninterrupted controversy over conflicting interpretations of neutral rights. Such controversies were to involve it in undeclared hostilities with France in 1798, and, in conjunction with other grievances, in the more serious conflict with England in 1812.

American Principles of Neutrality

In its exertions to secure essential French aid in the Revolution, the United States departed in some degree from John Adams' advice against an alliance with France "which should entangle us in any future wars in Europe." The treaty of alliance of February 6, 1778, looking beyond the war then in progress, bound each of the allies to guarantee to the other the American possessions that it might hold at the end of the war. To that extent only was the United States obligated to assist France in any future war. Should an enemy of France attempt to seize the French islands in the West Indies, France might justly claim the support of the United States.

The other treaty signed on the same date, the treaty of amity and commerce, embodied definitions of neutral rights as proposed by Congress in its treaty plan of 1776, which in turn followed almost word for word a commercial treaty between England and France signed at Utrecht in 1713.[2] The treaty of 1778 between the United States and France defined the privileges to be enjoyed by the ships and commerce of either during a war in which it was neutral while the other was belligerent. The ships of the neutral should be free to carry noncontraband merchandise not only to the unblockaded ports of an enemy but from one enemy port to another. Free ships were to make free goods; in other words, enemy property, noncontraband, carried on a neutral ship, was not to be liable to capture. The same was true of enemy nationals traveling on a neutral ship unless they were soldiers in enemy service. On the other hand, neutral property on an enemy ship took on the character of enemy property and was subject to confiscation. Contraband goods were defined so narrowly as to consist almost exclusively of arms and ammunition. All else was noncontraband; the noncontraband list mentioned specifically fabrics, wearing apparel, metals, food, provisions, tobacco, and naval stores. All such goods the neutral might carry freely to enemy ports, with the exception of such ports "as are at that time besieged, blocked up or invested." There was no definition of what constituted a legal blockade.

Other articles of the treaty, also contained in the proposals of 1776, allowed special privileges in the ports of the neutral to the armed ships, public and private, of the belligerent ally, while denying them to the ships of the opposing belligerent. Ships-of-war and privateers of the belligerent ally were to be free to bring their prizes into the ports of the neutral (nothing was said of any right to sell prizes or to fit out armed vessels in such ports) and to depart with them at their pleasure and without interference; but such privileges were expressly denied to the armed vessels of the opposing belligerent, which, furthermore, should not be permitted to fit out ships-of-war or privateers in the ports of the neutral.

It had been the hope of Congress, when it adopted the "Plan of 1776," to have its principles with regard to the privileges of neutral commerce incorporated in treaties with all the maritime powers. Those principles were embodied in treaties with the Netherlands (1782), Sweden (1783), Prussia (1785), and Morocco (1786).

There was one conspicuous exception to the rather general willingness of the European powers to make liberal commercial treaties with the United States. Great Britain refused to incorporate in the treaty of peace (1783) any provision for the protection of neutral trade, or even to make a commercial treaty of any kind until the mission of John Jay in 1794. Great Britain, therefore, was under no obligation to observe the principles of 1776 when she and France again went to war.[3]

The First Struggle for Neutrality

In February 1793, following the execution by the French of their King, Louis XVI, and the

---

2. The treaties with France are in the usual official collections of treaties. For the "Plan of 1776," see W. C. Ford et al., eds., *Journals of the Continental Congress,* 34 vols. (Washington, D.C.: Government Printing Office, 1904–1937), 5: 768–78. Relevant portions of these documents and of the Utrecht treaty are printed in Department of State, *Policy of the United States toward Maritime Commerce in War,* prepared by Carlton Savage, 2 vols. (Washington, D.C.: Government Printing Office, 1934–1936), 1: 132–40.

3. Russia also declined to make a treaty with the United States at this time, but in a declaration of 1780, the Russian government had adopted the main principles of the plan of 1776.

withdrawal from Paris of the British ambassador, the French Republic declared war upon Great Britain. France was already at war with her neighbors on the continent. The opening of the English phase of the war launched the conflict upon the sea and brought it to the shores of the United States.

Could the United States remain neutral? American popular sympathy was strong for France—the ally in the recent war and now the exemplar of republicanism and democracy in monarchical and aristocratic Europe. "Jacobin Clubs," patterned after those in France, were organized among the American populace, and their members addressed one another as "citizen" and "citizeness" after the current French fashion. But, aside from popular sentiment, the United States had treaty obligations to France—an obligation under certain circumstances to protect French possessions in America, an obligation to allow French naval vessels and privateers privileges denied to the ships of Great Britain. To these forces pulling the United States toward France was added a British policy of ruthless interference with American trade at sea and consistent opposition to American interests on the frontier. To drift into war with England would be easy, and a war with England, when the United States was barely getting on its feet under the new Constitution, was certain to be disastrous economically and disruptive politically.

President Washington and his advisers were fully aware of the perils of the situation. Anticipating the arrival of the first minister of the French Republic, the young and exuberant Edmond Genêt, Washington submitted a group of thirteen questions to the members of his cabinet—Thomas Jefferson, Secretary of State; Alexander Hamilton, Secretary of the Treasury; Henry Knox, Secretary of War; and Edmund Randolph, Attorney General—and requested their opinions. The essence of the questions can be summarized in three: (1) Shall the President issue a proclamation of neutrality as between France and her enemies? (2) Are the treaties made with the French government of Louis XVI still binding upon the United States, now that that government has been overthrown and the King sent to the guillotine? (3) Shall Genêt be received as the minister of the French Republic?

Of historic importance were the answers to these questions returned by Jefferson and Hamilton—Knox siding with Hamilton and Randolph with Jefferson. To the first question —should there be a proclamation of neutrality?—Hamilton answered yes, Jefferson, no. Jefferson argued, first, that the question of neutrality (like that of war) was one for Congress to determine; second, that neutrality, a boon to Great Britain, should be used to bargain with, not freely given. Jefferson agreed, however, that the President should warn American citizens against giving aid to either party to the conflict.

To the second question—were the treaties binding?—Hamilton answered no, since, among other reasons, the government with which they were made had been destroyed. Even if the treaties were still in force, Hamilton added, the treaty of alliance was expressly a "defensive" one, and France, having declared war against England, was here the aggressor. Jefferson opposed Hamilton's reasoning, arguing that treaties were made by the government of Louis XVI acting as the agent of the French people, and that a mere change of agents did not invalidate the agreements. On this point, Jefferson's position was that now universally accepted in the conduct of international relations. A treaty is made with a nation and is not abrogated by a change in government. But while Jefferson would not repudiate the French treaties, neither would he so interpret them as to involve the United States in the war on the side of France. France, he said, had not yet asked the United States to fulfill its guarantee under the treaty of alliance. Should it do so, the United States could excuse itself on the ground that France, which had similarly undertaken to guarantee the sovereignty and territorial possessions of the United States, had given no aid in ending British occupation of the northwest posts. Thus Jefferson, though considered the head of the pro-French faction, was little less anxious than pro-British Hamilton to preserve American neutrality.

To the third question—should Genêt be received?—both Hamilton and Jefferson answered yes; but whereas Jefferson would receive him unconditionally, Hamilton would give him notice that the United States did not consider itself bound by the treaties of 1778.

Washington, thus finding his advisers divided on every question, was under the necessity of choosing between them. For the most part, he followed Jefferson. Genêt was received, upon his arrival at Philadelphia, without condition. His unconditional reception was a tacit acknowledgment that the treaties were still in effect. A proclamation of neutrality was issued (April 22, 1793), but out of regard for Jefferson's attitude, Washington avoided the use of the word "neutrality." He declared it to be the intention of the United States to "pursue a conduct friendly and impartial toward the belligerent Powers," called upon all citizens of the United States to avoid acts contrary to such a course, and warned them that, far from receiving the protection of the United States against the consequences of committing acts of hostility against any of the belligerents, they must expect prosecution for any violation of "the law of nations" committed "within the cognizance of the courts of the United States."

The arrival of Citizen Genêt and his impertinent attempts to exploit the United States for French purposes in defiance of the government in Philadelphia led before long to a request for his recall and to the passage by Congress of the first neutrality legislation in the history of the United States. Genêt obviously expected to find in the United States, if not an ally, at least a "nonbelligerent"—if we may borrow from the mid-twentieth century a term signifying a state that gives active assistance to one side without engaging in actual warfare. He made no demand for activation of the guarantees of the alliance, but he at once engaged in activities which were unwarranted by any provisions in the treaty of amity and commerce and which, if persisted in, would have compromised the neutrality of

the United States. Specifically, he fitted out and commissioned in American ports privateers to cruise under the French flag and to prey upon British commerce. He set up in American ports French prize courts to condemn prizes brought in by French privateers or cruisers.[4] He attempted to organize in the United States military expeditions to attack Florida and Louisiana, both at that time possessions of France's enemy, Spain. To enable him to finance these activities, he demanded that the United States pay before they were due installments of the debt owed to the French government for loans during and after the American Revolution—a demand that the American government refused. In all these ways, Genêt attempted to make the United States a base of French operations—by sea against Great Britain, by land against Spain. When Washington sought to interfere with these brash proceedings, Genêt appealed to the public over the President's head through letters to pro-French journals.

All this misbehavior, which even Jefferson could not condone, led after a few months to a request for Genêt's recall, which was complied with by the French government.[5] More important, the unfortunate experience with Genêt was largely responsible for the enactment by Congress of the neutrality law of June 5, 1794. A glance at this act will show that it forbade precisely those things that Genêt had been doing or trying to do—the arming or equipping of ships-of-war for a belligerent government in United States ports; the recruiting within American jurisdiction of persons to serve in the armed forces of a bellig-

---

4. It was Genêt's contention that the treaty of amity and commerce, in denying these privileges to the enemies of France, allowed them to France by implication.

5. Genêt did not return to France. The Girondist faction in the French National Convention, which had sent him to America, had fallen from power and its leaders were being sent to the guillotine. Not liking the prospects at home, Genêt asked and received permission to remain in the United States as a private citizen. He married the daughter of Governor George Clinton of New York and became the progenitor of an American family.

erent government; the setting on foot within the American jurisdiction of any armed expedition against a friendly power.

The law of 1794 is a landmark in the history of neutrality. Other nations had not been backward about laying claim to their neutral rights. The United States led the way in assuming responsibility for the carrying out of its neutral duties.

A Crisis with England

The termination of Genêt's mission temporarily eased relations with France but did little to help those with England, which was persistently violating what the United States held to be its neutral rights. Never having accepted the principles of the plan of 1776, the British government, in dealing with neutral commerce, was bound only by what it chose to recognize as the generally accepted law of nations; and this, as interpreted by the British, contravened the principles of 1776 in several respects. In violation of the dictum "free ships make free goods," British prize courts condemned enemy (French) property found in American ships. In partial disregard, at least, of the exclusion of provisions from the contraband categories of 1776, the British seized cargoes of American wheat, corn, and flour en route to France —not for confiscation, indeed, but for preemptive purchase, presumably to the injury of the shipper. Against the stipulation of 1776 that neutral ships should be free to trade to and between enemy ports, the British invoked their own so-called "Rule of the War of 1756," or simply the rule of 1756, which stated that trade illegal in peace was illegal in war. What this meant in practice was that France, which in peace confined trade between herself and her colonies to French ships, was not permitted in wartime to open that trade to neutral shipping, as she had done in the Seven Years' War and was again doing now. Neutral ships admitted to such trade, the British declared, would be considered as incorporated in the French merchant marine and hence subject to

confiscation like French property. Toward United States shipping, the British went even beyond the rule of 1756, seizing not only American ships trading between France and her colonies, but also those trading between the colonies and the United States—a trade that France had permitted in time of peace. The British also, in this period, began the practice of stopping American merchant vessels on the high seas and "impressing" members of their crews, presumed to be British subjects, for service in the Royal Navy.

These were the principal maritime grievances which, in conjunction with border troubles and nonfulfillment by both parties of the terms of the treaty of 1783, produced a crisis with Great Britain in 1794. On the frontier, British garrisons still held the border posts on American soil and British agents continued to encourage the Indians in their resistance to American land claims. Neither Congress nor the new government had attempted to oust the British by force from the posts. Viewing the Indian treaties of 1784 and later years as valid, Congress had provided for the government of the Northwest Territory in the Ordinance of 1787 and had sold large tracts of land north of the Ohio River to companies of prospective settlers and speculators, two of which planned settlements at Marietta and Cincinnati. When General Washington was inaugurated as first President of the United States in the spring of 1789, the settlement of the Northwest had begun, but it had become apparent that the Indians would not honor the land treaties until compelled by force to do so.

Two expeditions against the recalcitrant Indians in 1789 and 1791, led by General Joseph Harmar and Governor Arthur St. Clair, resulted respectively in an inconclusive campaign and a disastrous defeat for the Americans. Washington appointed "Mad" Anthony Wayne, an officer with a fine record in the Revolution, to command a third expedition. In the fall of 1793, with a thoroughly drilled army, Wayne advanced from Fort Washington at Cincinnati into the Indian country, went into winter quarters at Fort Greenville, and prepared for a decisive campaign during the following summer.

When Wayne moved into the Indian country in the fall of 1793, the United States and Great Britain were already engaged in a warm argument over the rights of neutrals. Congress had enacted a temporary embargo on American shipping and bills were introduced for the sequestration of British debts and other measures of retaliation. Lord Dorchester, Canadian governor general, at this point lost his head. Apparently assuming that war was inevitable and that Wayne, if successful against the Indians, would press on and attack Detroit, he sent orders to Governor John Graves Simcoe in Upper Canada to seize and fortify a strategic point at the Rapids of the Maumee River. As a result, the British flag flew at Fort Miami, many miles within the boundaries of the United States. In February 1794, Dorchester was visited at Quebec by a delegation of western Indians. In his "talk" to them he asserted that the United States had no desire for peace, that it had violated its treaty with Great Britain, and that war was certain within a year. Then, he said, the Indians could recover what was rightly theirs. This was little short of incitement to war.

Such was the ominous atmosphere in which Wayne began the second phase of his campaign in the spring of 1794. Slowly he advanced until on August 18 he was but two miles from the British fort on the Maumee. Here, in a mass of fallen timber—which gave a name to the battle—he came upon the assembled Indian warriors, reenforced, it must be added, by numerous Canadian volunteers. Scattering at a determined charge by Wayne's men, the Indians fell back under the guns of the British fort. "Inside the fort," writes Professor Bemis, "torches hovered above the breeches of loaded cannon trained on the American cavalry." [6] Would some rash British soldier discharge a cannon? Would Wayne attack? On these ques-

tions might hang peace or war, perhaps the fate of the American nation. Fortunately, "Mad" Anthony's actions belied his nickname. Campbell, the British commander, showed equal coolness, and the dangerous moment passed. Wayne left the vicinity of the fort. He had beaten the Indians soundly, and now turned to laying waste their villages and fields as the best means of bringing them to terms.

Jay's Treaty

While this crisis was passing on the frontier, another was passing in England. In April 1794, Washington had resolved to send to London John Jay, Chief Justice of the Supreme Court, in a final attempt to reach an agreement with England over the several matters in dispute. Jay was well chosen for such a mission of conciliation. A distinguished member of the Federalist party, he shared the desire of Hamilton, the party's head, for continued peace with Great Britain.[7] He was, furthermore, an experienced diplomat. He had represented the United States (albeit unrecognized) at the court of Spain (1779–1782), had been one of the American peace commissioners at Paris (1782–1783), and after his return to the United States had served as Secretary for Foreign Affairs for Congress under the Articles of Confederation. His policy in that office had

---

6. S. F. Bemis, *Jay's Treaty, a Study in Commerce and Diplomacy* (New Haven: Yale University Press, 1962), p. 247.

7. Alexander Hamilton, Secretary of the Treasury under Washington, was keenly interested in the success of the financial measures of which he was the father. He had funded the national debt, assumed the revolutionary debts of the states, and provided for the payment of interest and the gradual retirement of the principal of this debt. He had created the first Bank of the United States, the chief capital of which consisted of United States bonds. The success of his plans depended upon a steady flow of revenue into the Federal treasury, without which government credit would collapse. The principal source of this revenue was the duty collected upon imports. War with England would mean the ruin of this trade and would thus endanger Hamilton's whole financial structure. See C. A. Beard, *Economic Origins of Jeffersonian Democracy* (New York: The Macmillan Company, 1915), chap. 10.

rendered him acceptable to England; he had, in fact, condoned the British retention of the posts as justified by American infractions of the treaty. This fact, had it been generally known, together with his willingness at the same time to surrender the American demand upon Spain for the free navigation of the Mississippi,[8] might have led a westerner to fear that Jay would not be zealous in defense of western interests.

Jay was instructed, nevertheless, to secure fulfillment of the treaty of 1783, meaning among other things the surrender of the northwest posts. In the matter of neutral rights, he was to urge the British government to accept the principles of 1776 and was to seek compensation for seizures of American ships and cargoes in violation of those principles. His instructions, written by Randolph but shaped by Hamilton, were elastic, and it was probably not expected that Great Britain would yield much in principle. The dominant Federalist party, led by Hamilton, placed the maintenance of peace with Great Britain at the head of their list of desirables.

> In the last resort [writes Professor Samuel F. Bemis], to preserve peace and national credit, which depended for its revenues on commerce, they were willing, in the face of British sea power, to acquiesce in a complete reversion or suspension of the liberal principles incorporated in the American treaties with France, Sweden, Holland and Prussia.[9]

Negotiating in this spirit and faced by a Foreign Minister, Lord Grenville, who was secretly informed that the United States would not ally itself with the European neutrals for a joint defense of their interests,[10] Jay got nothing at all in the way of concessions in principle. On the contrary, in the treaty signed

on November 19, 1794, the United States agreed that enemy goods might be taken from neutral ships, that naval stores should be contraband, that provisions bound for an enemy might be taken from neutral ships if paid for. The rule of 1756 was left intact, and there was no definition of legal blockade—another point on which Jay had been told to seek clarification.

Under the treaty of amity and commerce of 1778 with France, French ships-of-war or privateers with prizes taken from the enemies of France were admitted freely to American ports, but enemy ships that had taken French prizes were excluded. The Jay treaty gave the same privilege to British ships-of-war and privateers and excluded those of Britain's enemies. This direct contradiction of the French treaty was partly nullified, however, by the inclusion of a clause declaring that nothing in the treaty should "operate contrary to former and existing public treaties with other sovereigns or States."

The West, which might have expected little from John Jay, fared rather better than other sections in the treaty. The document contained a promise, on the part of the British, that the posts would be evacuated not later than June 1, 1796. British traders at the posts might remain there if they chose, and the subjects or citizens of either country should be privileged "freely to pass and repass by land or inland navigation, into the respective territories and countries of the two parties, on the continent of America, . . . and to navigate all the lakes, rivers and waters thereof, and freely to carry on trade and commerce with each other,"— with the reservation that such privileges should not extend to the territories of the Hudson's Bay Company. The Mississippi River was, as under the treaty of peace, to be open to the use of both parties. A joint survey of the upper portion of that river was to be made, and if this survey should show that the river would not be intersected by a line drawn westward from the Lake of the Woods, the boundary in that quarter should be fixed by amicable negotiation. A joint commission should determine the identity of the St. Croix River, which

8. See p. 33.
9. Bemis, *Jay's Treaty,* p. 298.
10. Jay's bargaining position was weakened when George Hammond, British Minister to the United States, relayed to Grenville some indiscreet confidences of Alexander Hamilton, who had informed the minister that the United States would never ally itself with the European neutrals for the defense of its rights against Great Britain.

formed part of the northeastern boundary.[11]

From the point of view of the West, the great advantage of the treaty was the liberation of United States soil from British troops. For this gain, Jay deserves no great credit, since Grenville had resolved on this concession before the negotiations opened.[12] The accompanying provision for mutual freedom of travel and trade across the border enabled the British and Canadian traders to continue their profitable commerce and their Indian connections in United States territory, although it had little practical value for citizens of the United States. Jay had attempted unsuccessfully to secure disarmament on the lakes and an agreement that neither party would employ Indian allies in war against the other, supply the Indians with arms for war against the whites, or enter into political relations with Indian tribes upon the other's territory. These proposals Grenville had refused. On the other hand, Jay had resisted Grenville's attempt to secure for Great Britain a slice of territory reaching down the Mississippi River to navigable water in the vicinity of modern Minneapolis.

Jay's treaty also settled, after a fashion, a number of the other matters in controversy between the two countries. It provided for the adjudication and payment, on the one side, of pre-Revolutionary debts owed by Americans to British subjects and of British claims for damages resulting from Genêt's irregular proceedings; and, on the other, of claims arising from illegal seizures by British cruisers of American ships and cargoes. On these scores the United States paid $2,664,000 for debts and $143,428 for the Genêt claims and received $11,656,000 for injuries to its commerce. British claims for compensation of the Loyalists

were dropped, as were American claims for compensation for Negro slaves carried away by departing British troops in 1783. The commercial clauses of the treaty placed the United States on a most-favored-nation basis with reference to trade with the British Isles, opened the East Indian trade to Americans on fairly liberal terms, and also opened the more important West Indian trade, but on terms so unsatisfactory that the Senate struck out that article in approving the treaty. The treaty was approved by the Senate and ratified by the President and the necessary appropriations were made by Congress, but only after stormy sessions in both houses and widespread popular condemnation of John Jay.

Unsatisfactory though it was in some respects, the Jay treaty not only kept the peace at a critical time; it brought about the full execution by Great Britain of the peace treaty of 1783 and thus the acceptance by her of the United States as an equal and wholly sovereign state. This favorable result must be attributed in part to Great Britain's involvement in the European war and her reluctance to take on additional enemies. Freeing the northern frontier from British garrisons, the treaty was conducive to a settlement with the Indians. General Wayne followed up his victory at Fallen Timbers by a year of desultory campaigning in the Indian country. Deprived of the hope of British support, the tribes at length came to terms. At Fort Greenville on August 3, 1795, their deputies ceded to the United States all of the future state of Ohio except the northwest corner and a strip running thence along the shore of Lake Erie to the Cuyahoga River. With the signing of Jay's and Wayne's treaties, the control of the Northwest for the first time passed to the United States.

Pinckney's Treaty with Spain

Less than a year after the signing of the Jay treaty with Great Britain, Thomas Pinckney, at Madrid, signed a treaty with Spain that accomplished for the Southwest even greater things than Jay's treaty had achieved for the

---

11. A commission appointed under the terms of the treaty fixed upon the Schoodiac River as the eastern boundary of Maine—the St. Croix River of the Treaty of Paris. No survey of the upper Mississippi was made, however, and the line between that river and the Lake of the Woods remained undetermined.

12. Grenville disapproved strongly of Lord Dorchester's speech to the Indians and of his authorization of the occupation of Fort Miami, and rebuked that official so strongly that he resigned. Bemis, *Jay's Treaty*, p. 320.

Northwest. Spain, which had been an ally of Great Britain in the coalition against France, was drifting toward a peace with France that would eventually involve her in war against England, and the ministry regarded with apprehension the possibility of a joint Anglo-American attack upon the Spanish colonies. This fear was heightened when Godoy, the Prime Minister, learned (in July 1794) of Jay's mission to England. Friendly relations with the United States, even at the cost of large concessions, seemed the only safe policy for Spain.

At a hint from Madrid that the Spanish government was ready to form an alliance with the United States and to concede the American claims as to the boundary line and the navigation of the Mississippi, President Washington, in November 1794, appointed Thomas Pinckney as minister to Spain. Godoy was now really anxious for a settlement with the United States, and by the time that Pinckney reached Madrid, toward the end of June 1795, circumstances were most propitious for a successful negotiation. Peace negotiations between Spain and France were proceeding rapidly to a conclusion at Bâle, where a treaty was actually signed on July 22, 1795. The news that Jay had signed a treaty with Great Britain had also reached Madrid. Under these circumstances, the Council of State resolved, on August 14, 1795, to yield to the United States its principal demands without insisting upon a treaty of alliance in return. Haggling over details prolonged the negotiations, but on October 27, Pinckney and Godoy signed at the royal palace of San Lorenzo a treaty which for the time being settled the problem of the Southwest.

By the treaty of San Lorenzo, Spain accepted the 31st parallel of latitude from the Mississippi to the Chattahoochee as the southern boundary of the United States, agreed to the free navigation of the Mississippi from source to mouth by citizens of the United States, and consented that the latter might enjoy for three years the privilege of landing and storing their goods at New Orleans without other charge than a fair price for storage. This was the "right of deposit," which Pinck-

ney with considerable difficulty had wrung from Godoy. It was important for the westerners, who brought most of their cargoes down the river in flatboats and must have a place to store them while awaiting suitable ocean-going vessels. After three years, the privilege should be either renewed at New Orleans or provided at another suitable spot on the lower Mississippi. Each party to the treaty agreed to prevent its Indian inhabitants from molesting either whites or Indians in the territory of the other, and there were sections defining neutral rights and duties and providing for the establishment of consulates and the settlement of claims.

The Spanish displayed their usual procrastination in carrying out the terms of the treaty. Their frontier posts north of 31° were not evacuated until 1798. By the end of that year, however, all Spanish garrisons within the United States had been withdrawn, the long-disputed territory was in American hands, and the men of the western waters were freely navigating the great river and utilizing the storage facilities of New Orleans. In the Southwest as in the Northwest, the United States had at length made its sovereignty coextensive with the treaty boundaries of 1783.

Hostilities with France—and a New Treaty

A backward step in the promotion of neutral rights, Jay's treaty, with its gains in other matters, postponed a break with Great Britain to a period in which the United States was better able to endure it. In fact, it ushered in a decade of generally cordial relations with the British.[13] In American relations with France, however, it raised a storm that ended in undeclared hostilities.

When Jay was sent to England in 1794, James Monroe was sent to France to replace the Federalist minister, Gouverneur Morris, whose recall the French government had requested in return for Genêt's. Monroe, a fol-

13. Bradford Perkins, *The First Rapprochement: England and the United States, 1795–1805* (Philadelphia: University of Pennsylvania Press, 1955).

lower of Jefferson and a sympathizer with France, ingratiated himself with the National Convention, which then served as the French government, but when he learned of Jay's treaty, which was contrary to the spirit if not to the letter of American engagements with France, he joined the French in condemning it instead of defending it as became the representative of the United States government. Consequently, he was recalled and the South Carolina Federalist, C. C. Pinckney, was appointed to succeed him.

France was now (1796) under the rule of the unscrupulous group of politicians known as the Directory. Elated by a series of military victories in Europe, they were reducing the smaller neighbors of France to the role of satellites and tributaries. They proposed to do the same with the United States. Angered by Jay's treaty, they refused to receive Pinckney, suspended the functions of the French minister in Philadelphia, thereby severing diplomatic relations, ordered French cruisers and privateers to seize American ships (on the theory that what the British could do the French could do), and dabbled in American politics with a view to swinging the election of 1796 in favor of Jefferson and his Republicans and against the Federalist John Adams.[14] Adams (elected nevertheless) named a commission of three—John Marshall, Elbridge Gerry of Rhode Island (a Republican), and the rejected Pinckney—to seek a restoration of diplomatic

relations and a promise to respect American rights. Upon their arrival in Paris the commissioners were approached by intermediaries—designated by X, Y, and Z in the printed dispatches—who offered, on behalf of Foreign Minister Talleyrand, recognition by the Directory at the price of a loan to France, a substantial bribe to the Directors, and an apology for some unfriendly references to France in President Adams' recent message to Congress.

The commissioners spurned the proposal. Their report, submitted to Congress by President Adams, with the recommendation that the nation arm itself for defense, stimulated Congress to vigorous action. The lawmakers authorized the President to raise a "provisional army" of 10,000 men in addition to the Regular Army, and called George Washington back from retirement to command it. They created a Navy Department (the small Navy that the United States possessed had hitherto been administered by the Secretary of War) and authorized United States naval vessels and armed merchantmen to attack and capture armed French vessels in the western Atlantic and the Caribbean. And they declared the treaties of 1778 with France abrogated. The Army was not used, though Alexander Hamilton, as senior major general under Washington, would have liked to lead it against Florida and Louisiana, the possessions of Spain, formerly an enemy of France but now her ally. The little Navy, with considerable cooperation from the British,[15] gave a good account of itself, capturing between eighty and ninety armed French vessels.

This was the "quasi-war" with France of 1798 to 1800.[16] That it should become a full-

---

14. It was, in part, this French interference in American politics that inspired the warnings in Washington's Farewell Address of September 17, 1796. He cautioned his fellow countrymen against "inveterate antipathies against particular nations and passionate attachments for others." The current difficulties of relations with France also suggested the declaration that "it is our true policy to steer clear of permanent alliances with any portion of the foreign world." Often overlooked is the qualifying statement that "we may safely trust to temporary alliances for extraordinary emergencies." For a full discussion of the Farewell Address, see S. F. Bemis, "Washington's Farewell Address: A Foreign Policy of Independence," *American Historical Review*, 39 (1934), 250–68. On the partisan character of the "Farewell Address," see Alexander DeConde, *Entangling Alliance: Politics and Diplomacy under George Washington* (Durham, N.C.: Duke University Press, 1958), pp. 463–71, 503.

15. Bradford Perkins, *The First Rapprochement*, chap. 8.
16. In the first year of this undeclared war, a Pennsylvania Quaker, George Logan, went to France on his own responsibility to reassure French officials of the friendly attitude of the people of the United States. This adventure in private diplomacy led Congress to pass the "Logan Act," of January 30, 1799. The act prohibited any unauthorized negotiation by a citizen of the United States for the purpose of influencing the course of action of a foreign government in relation to any controversy with the United States.

scale war was not the desire of President Adams or of Talleyrand, or of General Napoleon Bonaparte, who in November 1799 overthrew the Directory and as First Consul, became the head of the French government. Adams, besides being a man of peace, had no wish to see military laurels gathered by his rival, Hamilton. Bonaparte and Talleyrand, now intent upon securing Louisiana, for that reason desired peace with both the United States and Great Britain. Adams, in one of his messages to Congress, had declared that he would never send another minister to France without assurance that he would be "received, respected, and honored as the representative of a great, free, powerful, and independent nation." Talleyrand sent word that a new minister would be thus received and treated. Adams, against the wishes of Secretary of State Timothy Pickering and other members of his cabinet, who wished the undeclared war to continue, named a new commission of three men, William Vans Murray, Oliver Ellsworth, and William R. Davie, to undertake a new negotiation with France.

The American negotiators were received in Paris with all proper respect. They found that Talleyrand, in his desire for a settlement, had already ordered an end to the seizure of American ships and was arranging for the release of captured American sailors. A commission headed by Joseph Bonaparte, the First Consul's brother, was appointed to negotiate with the Americans. Murray and his colleagues asked indemnity for French depredations upon American commerce and bilateral abrogation of the treaties of 1778—already abrogated insofar as an act of Congress could perform that function. The French commissioners pointed out that the claims for indemnity rested upon alleged French violations of the treaty of amity and commerce and said to the American commissioners in effect, "If you wish the indemnity, you must keep the treaties; if you insist upon cancelling the treaties, you must forgo the indemnity." No agreement proving pos-

sible on this choice of alternatives, the negotiators signed on September 30, 1800, a treaty of which the second article suspended the operation of the treaties of 1778 and left the question of indemnities undetermined, both to be the subjects of further negotiation "at a convenient time." As amended by the Senate and further qualified by Bonaparte before ratification, the treaty nullified the earlier treaties and cancelled the claims for indemnity. Thus the United States escaped from its "entangling alliance" with France—so indispensable during the Revolution, so inconsistent with American interest thereafter.

The treaty of 1800 restated almost intact the principles of 1776 with regard to neutral shipping and neutral trade. The ships-of-war and privateers of each nation, with their prizes, were to enjoy in the ports of the other the same treatment "as those of the nation the most favoured; and in general," the text continued, "the two parties shall enjoy in the ports of each other, in regard to commerce, and navigation, the privileges of the most favoured nation. . . ." Thus French privileges in American ports were placed on an equal footing, and no more, with those of England. As a measure toward liquidating the results of the hostilities terminated by the treaty, the document provided for the restoration to each party of all public ships taken by the other.

The chief importance of the treaty of 1800 with France lay in its termination of the treaty of alliance and of the special privileges enjoyed by France under the other treaty of 1778. Thus the United States was released from all obligations that compromised its neutral position in relation to the European belligerents. The restatement of the principles of 1776 was little more than a gesture. Napoleon Bonaparte's promises were kept only as long as they suited his convenience, and in any event a statement of neutral rights without the concurrence of Great Britain had small practical importance.

The treaties negotiated by John Jay and Thomas Pinckney in 1794 and 1795 validated the boundary provisions of the peace treaty of 1783. A vigorous young nation, however, was likely to overstep these boundaries wherever they proved weak and the land beyond them attractive. This was notably the case with the Spanish territories to the west and south. Settlers from the United States threatened to dominate Upper Louisiana and the eastern bank of the Mississippi in West Florida. At New Orleans, where the right of deposit was proving a boon to the growing settlements up river, American sailing ships far outnumbered all others. Eastward from New Orleans along the Gulf coast lay West and East Florida, sparsely inhabited but commanding the mouths of rivers that would become important to the United States as Georgia and Mississippi Territory filled with people and farms. The East Florida peninsula commanded the principal entrance to the Gulf of Mexico.

Clearly the United States would one day need New Orleans and the Floridas. But Thomas Jefferson, who took the oath of office as President on March 4, 1801, was content to let them remain for the present in the hands of Spain. With Spain, all serious controversies had been settled; Spanish rule in New Orleans and the Floridas had ceased to be a menace to the United States. "We consider [Spain's] possession of the adjacent country as most favorable to our interests," Jefferson wrote in July 1801, "and should see with an extreme pain any other nation substituted for them." Five months after writing this letter, Jefferson received evidence from the United States minister in London that such a substitution was in process of being made. By a secret treaty of October 1, 1800, Spain had retroceded Louisiana to the French Republic, then headed by Napoleon Bonaparte as First Consul.[1]

6

The Louisiana Purchase and Its Sequel

1. General Bonaparte became First Consul and, in reality, dictatorial head of the French government as a result of the *coup d'état* of November 9–10, 1799. On August 1, 1802, he had himself proclaimed Consul for Life, and thereafter chose to be known by his Christian name of Napoleon, after the fashion of other monarchs. In December 1804, he assumed the title, Emperor of the French.

Louisiana, originally a French colony, had been ceded by France to Spain in 1762, at the close of the French and Indian (or Seven Years') War. French interest in recovering it appeared on the eve of the French Revolution, and on several occasions during the 1790's French diplomats sounded the Spanish government on the possibility of a retrocession. Although Spain had found Louisiana unprofitable and impossible to defend against intrusions from the United States and Canada, the Spanish court resisted French approaches until the summer of 1800. Negotiations were then begun which culminated in the signing of the treaty of San Ildefonso, October 1, 1800.

The Retrocession of Louisiana

By the terms of the treaty, Spain agreed to "retrocede" to France the colony of Louisiana and to turn over six ships-of-war for the French navy. In return, Bonaparte promised to create for the Prince of Parma, nephew of the King of Spain, an Italian kingdom, to be known as Tuscany or Etruria, with at least a million subjects. Bonaparte's efforts to have the Floridas included with Louisiana in the cession were unavailing. Louisiana had formerly been French, but Florida was traditionally Spanish, and sentiment and pride forbade its surrender.

The treaty had been signed, but over two years elapsed before Spain was convinced that Bonaparte was carrying out his part of the bargain. The King of Etruria found his royalty a shadow, unrecognized by any major power save France. Spain, furthermore, insisted upon a promise that France would never alienate Louisiana to another power. The promise was solemnly given on July 22, 1802, and Bonaparte also undertook to induce Austria, Great Britain, and the dethroned Grand Duke of Tuscany to recognize the King of Etruria. Professing satisfaction with these assurances, the Spanish government on October 15, 1802, issued orders for the transfer of Louisiana to France. Still another year was to go by before the transfer actually took place.

It seems clear that Bonaparte, or Napoleon as he now called himself—using his first name after the style of other sovereigns—valued Louisiana as part of a balanced colonial empire, the heart of which would be the sugar island of Santo Domingo.[2] By the treaty of Bâle (1795) France had acquired title to the eastern or Spanish portion of the island and now nominally possessed the whole. But at the time of the retrocession of Louisiana, French authority in Santo Domingo had been reduced to a cipher by a violent slave revolt. Most of the whites had been killed or driven into exile, and control of the island had fallen into the hands of the Negro ex-slave Toussaint Louverture. Nominally acknowledging allegiance to France, Toussaint had actually established a military despotism and was making himself an independent sovereign.

The overthrow of Toussaint, the reestablishment of French authority in Santo Domingo, and the restoration of slavery were necessary preliminary steps in the building of the colonial empire of which Louisiana was to be a part. The opportunity for these measures came only upon the making of peace with England, for in the face of a hostile British navy, overseas ventures were not to be thought of. The preliminary peace terms of October 1, 1801, were followed by the Peace of Amiens, March 27, 1802. Without waiting for the latter, Bonaparte, in November 1801, dispatched his brother-in-law, General Leclerc, with an army of twenty thousand men, to restore French rule in Santo Domingo. This expedition was to be followed by another to take possession of Louisiana.

Though the Louisiana expedition never sailed, instructions were prepared for the two French officers who were designated to head the civil and military branches of administration in that colony. These instructions suggest the kind of neighbor France would have been in Louisiana. The French officials were in-

2. Custom has attached to the island the Spanish name of Santo Domingo. To the French, it was Saint Domingue. Embracing today the states of Haiti and the Dominican Republic, the entire island is known by its early Spanish name, Hispaniola.

structed to express "sentiments of great benevolence" for the United States. But these benevolent sentiments were not to prevent the French from doing everything in their power to supplant the American trade in the colonies, from maintaining "sources of information"—in other words, spies—in the western states, or from making alliances with the Indian nations of the American Southwest. In fact, the French agents were expressly instructed to do all of these things. The substitution of French energy for Spanish lethargy in Louisiana boded no good for the United States.

Jefferson and the Retrocession

The prospect of seeing a decadent Spain replaced in New Orleans by a vigorous and powerful France was alarming to Thomas Jefferson. In a letter to United States Minister Robert R. Livingston in Paris—the substance of which was to be made known to Bonaparte—Jefferson remarked that New Orleans, the outlet for the produce of three-eighths of the national territory, was the one spot on the globe "the possessor of which is our natural and habitual enemy." French possession of New Orleans, the President continued, would seal "the union of two countries who in conjunction can maintain exclusive possession of the ocean. From that moment we must marry ourselves to the British fleet and nation."

Friends in Paris, however, advised the President that Bonaparte could perhaps be more easily swayed by offers of money than by the threat of an Anglo-American alliance. Accordingly, through a letter from the Secretary of State, May 1, 1802, Livingston was instructed to ascertain the price for which France would sell New Orleans and the Floridas, if, as was commonly assumed in the United States, she had acquired the latter provinces in the same transaction with Louisiana.

In November ominous news reached Washington. It was learned that King Charles IV of Spain had actually issued orders for the transfer of Louisiana to France. At almost the same time came information that Morales, Spanish intendant at New Orleans, had on October 16 withdrawn the right of deposit guaranteed by Pinckney's treaty.

Though Morales acted on a secret order from the Spanish government, he maintained, in accordance with his instructions, that he was closing the deposit on his own responsibility. The reasons that he assigned were unimpressive. In reality, the change of policy resulted from the smuggling activities of certain Americans who had abused their privileges at New Orleans. It is difficult to explain, however, why Spain should have risked a breach with the United States over a situation in which her interest would cease within a few months by a transfer of Louisiana to France. The contemporary American belief that Spain was acting at the behest of France was reasonable but almost certainly unfounded.

To the American West, the closing of the deposit at New Orleans was an inconvenience rather than a disaster. The Mississippi remained open, and there was no obstacle to the transfer of cargoes directly from the river flatboats to oceangoing vessels, which at this season were present in adequate numbers. The Spanish action, nevertheless, was an undeniable violation of American treaty rights and, what was most alarming, seemed a foretaste of the policy of the new masters of Louisiana, whose advent was now imminent.

Westerners, for the most part, were willing to leave the solution of the Mississippi question to Jefferson's diplomacy, but eastern Federalists were bellicose. Their strategy was to force Jefferson to choose between war with France and surrender of western interests—either choice contrary to his principles and dangerous to his political supremacy. The strategy failed. Federalist resolutions calling for seizure of New Orleans were defeated in the Senate. From Paris came advice from Jefferson's friend, Pierre Samuel DuPont de Nemours, that New Orleans and the Floridas could probably be purchased for six million dollars. Jefferson resolved to send a special commissioner to Paris to follow up DuPont's suggestion. Successful or not, such a gesture would convince the West that its interests were not forgotten and might put a stop to Federalist talk.

On January 11, 1803, Jefferson sent to the Senate the nomination of James Monroe as minister extraordinary to France and Spain to assist the regular ministers there in "enlarging and more effectually securing our rights and interests in the river Mississippi and in the territories eastward thereof." Monroe was popular in the West, and his appointment was reassuring to that section. The Senate promptly confirmed Monroe's nomination, and Congress appropriated two million dollars for use in his negotiations. The committee of the House of Representatives that recommended this appropriation dwelt in its report upon the importance to the United States of the free navigation not only of the Mississippi but also of the Florida rivers to the eastward and concluded that

> the possession of New Orleans and the Floridas will not only be required for the convenience of the United States, but will be demanded by their most imperious necessities. . . . If we look forward to the free use of the Mississippi, the Mobile, the Apalachicola, and the other rivers of the West, by ourselves and our posterity, New Orleans and the Floridas must become a part of the United States, either by purchase or by conquest.

Monroe's instructions were not signed until March 2, nor were they drastic in tone. Should the French be willing to sell New Orleans and the Floridas, Monroe and Livingston were authorized to offer as much as $10,000,000 rather than lose the opportunity of obtaining them. Should France refuse to cede any territory, the commissioners were to do what they could to secure and improve the right of deposit guaranteed by the Spanish treaty of 1795. If France refused even the right of deposit, they were to refer the matter to Washington and await the decision of Congress. Only if they learned that France meditated hostilities against the United States or proposed to close the Mississippi entirely to American commerce, were the commissioners authorized to cross the channel and invite England to an alliance. Thus the marriage "to the British fleet and nation," of which Jefferson had warned DuPont, was to be resorted to only in a remote contingency.

The Purchase

Of the territories which Monroe and Livingston were directed to purchase if they could, France possessed only New Orleans, for Spain had refused to sell the Floridas. Before Monroe arrived in Paris, Napoleon had decided to offer not only New Orleans but all of Louisiana to the United States. On Easter Sunday, April 10, he called two of his ministers into conference and invited their advice on the proposal. On the next day he informed Barbé-Marbois, his Finance Minister, of his decision to sell and instructed him to open negotiations with Livingston.

The new proposal, however, came to Livingston not through Barbé-Marbois but through Talleyrand, who saw him on this same day (April 11) and inquired whether the United States would care to buy all Louisiana. As Monroe's arrival was expected within a day or two, Livingston properly deferred giving a definite answer until he could confer with his colleague.

The commissioners' instructions authorized them to purchase New Orleans and the Floridas. They were offered Louisiana, including the all-important town and island of New Orleans. In the mind of neither was there any serious doubt of the propriety of accepting the offer, and the twenty days that elapsed from Monroe's arrival (April 12) to the signature of the treaty (May 2) were spent in haggling over terms. Napoleon had told Barbé-Marbois to sell for fifty million livres; the thrifty minister asked one hundred million. Since this price considerably exceeded the outside figure in their instructions, Monroe and Livingston attempted to lower it. The negotiators finally agreed on eighty million livres ($15,000,000), of which three-fourths were to be paid to France, the remainder to Americans holding damage claims against the French government.

Virtual agreement was reached April 29, the treaty signed May 2, and it and the accompanying documents antedated as of April 30, 1803.

Quoting the language of the Franco-Spanish treaty of San Ildefonso, France by the new treaty ceded to the United States "the colony or province of Louisiana, with the same extent that it now has in the hands of Spain, and that it had when France possessed it; and such as it should be after the treaties subsequently entered into between Spain and other states." Other articles of the treaty promised the incorporation of the inhabitants of Louisiana in the Union of the United States with all the rights of citizens thereof, protected them in the meantime in the enjoyment of their liberty, property, and religion, and permitted French and Spanish ships laden with the produce of those countries or their colonies to enter and use the ports of Louisiana for twelve years upon the same terms as American ships.

Jefferson and his two ministers had achieved an impressive diplomatic success. It is apparent, however, that the only credit they deserve for it is the credit for being willing to accept a bargain when offered. Neither Jefferson nor Monroe nor Livingston—though the last had written a pamphlet to prove that France had nothing to gain from holding Louisiana—could justly claim to have persuaded Napoleon to sell the territory. The decision was Napoleon's own. Why, then, did he make it?

The sale of Louisiana was such a direct reversal of French policy, was so contrary to Napoleon's promises to Spain and even to the principles of the French constitution, was so unwelcome to many of Napoleon's supporters, including his brothers Joseph and Lucien,[3] that he and his Foreign Minister were hard put to find excuses and justifications for their action. The result was a rich crop of rationalizations, which historians have sometimes taken

too seriously. Thus, to the public and to his brother Lucien, Napoleon argued that he could not hold Louisiana during a war with England —an unimpressive argument, since he could have either peace or war with England as he chose. Talleyrand informed Decrès, the Minister for Colonies, that the purpose of the sale was to placate the United States, but the United States could have been placated merely by guaranteeing the navigation of the Mississippi and the right of deposit. Napoleon told Barbé-Marbois that the sale "affirms forever the power of the United States" and had "given England a maritime rival that sooner or later will lay low her pride"; but Talleyrand professed to foresee that the accession of western territory would in the end divide the United States into two separate nations. To accept both these views, as some historians have done, and to conclude that Napoleon planned first to strengthen the United States against England and then to divide it, seems obviously to dignify contradictory excuses as rational motives.

Yet other excuses were offered. Of all parties to the transaction, the one deeply wronged was Spain. The colony that Talleyrand had promised would be "a wall of brass" for her protection, Napoleon had brazenly sold to her chief rival for a pot of gold. One expedient for justifying his course was to blame Spain herself for it, and this Talleyrand did by charging that in first cancelling the right of deposit and later reviving it (as she had done in response to American protests), Spain had not only jeopardized French relations with the United States but also compromised French freedom of action with regard to the deposit. As Talleyrand, at an earlier date, had warmly congratulated the Spanish government on the closing of the deposit, this excuse rings no more true than the others.

More revealing than all the reasons offered after the event was an outburst of Napoleon's in January 1803. His guests at a small dinner were conversing of wines and other beverages, when Napoleon suddenly exclaimed, "Damn sugar, damn coffee, damn colonies!" It is not difficult to trace the source of this pent-up

3. Lucien Bonaparte had played an important part in securing Spanish consent to the retrocession, Joseph in negotiating the treaty of Amiens with England. Both were enraged at the sale of Louisiana and the accompanying rupture with England.

wrath. A few days previously Napoleon had learned of the death of General Leclerc in Santo Domingo and the virtual annihilation of his army there by a combination of yellow fever and renewed Negro insurrection. Santo Domingo had swallowed fifty thousand French troops and was no nearer subjection than at the opening of the campaign. This was a failure that had to be recognized. Santo Domingo must be abandoned. But without Santo Domingo, of what use was Louisiana? "The colonial system of France," writes Henry Adams, "centred in St. Domingo. Without that island the system had hands, feet, and even a head, but no body. Of what use was Louisiana, when France had clearly lost the main colony which Louisiana was meant to feed and fortify?" [4]

It is a safe inference that after January 1803 Napoleon was willing to dispose of Louisiana on the best terms he could get. His willingness may have been the greater because of the failure of his efforts to obtain Florida with its excellent harbors on the Gulf, and because of his fear of driving the United States into the arms of England. His actual offer may even have been timed by the receipt, April 8, 1803, of news of the introduction in the Senate of certain warlike resolutions.[5] But at the foundation of the structure was the failure in Santo Domingo. Anxious to divert popular attention from that failure, Napoleon jettisoned his American empire, toyed for a few weeks with projects of expansion in Egypt and India, and then turned to a renewal of the European war.

4. Henry Adams, *History of the United States During the Administrations of Jefferson and Madison,* 9 vols. (New York: Charles Scribner's Sons, 1889–1891), 2: 14. Cf. François, Marquis de Barbé-Marbois, *History of Louisiana,* in translation (Philadelphia: Carey & Lea, 1830), p. 200: ". . . Louisiana had been destined to supply the other colony with provisions, cattle, and wood; and as St. Domingo was lost to France, the importance of Louisiana was also diminished."
5. It has also been conjectured that the detention by ice in the port of Dunkirk of the fleet and army designated to take over Louisiana contributed to Napoleon's decision to sell. See Oscar Handlin, "The Louisiana Purchase: Chance or Destiny?" *Atlantic Monthly,* 175 (January 1955), pp. 44–49.

The Louisiana Purchase and the Constitution

The Louisiana treaty raised constitutional questions of great importance. Did the Constitution empower the President and Senate, through the instrument of a treaty, to acquire new territory, to promise its incorporation in the Union, and to confer special privileges upon foreign ships trading in its ports? All these things the treaty with France undertook to do, and to the last two, if not to all, students of the Constitution found serious objections.

Jefferson himself, as chief of the strict-constructionists, was the first to face the constitutional problem. A study of the Louisiana treaty persuaded him that its provisions went beyond the powers conferred upon the President and Senate. His proposed solution was a constitutional amendment expressly validating the purchase. Warned from Paris that the delay occasioned by seeking an amendment might mean the loss of Louisiana, Jefferson abandoned the plan for an amendment and agreed to participate in an act that he believed to be unconstitutional, "confiding," as he wrote, "that the good sense of our country will correct the evil of construction when it shall produce ill effects." He called Congress to meet six weeks before the usual date, and on October 17, 1803, submitted the treaty to the Senate.

Three days later the Senate gave its advice and consent to ratification, only the small Federalist minority opposing. The debate on the treaty was conducted in secret session, but in considering the legislation necessary for carrying out the treaty, both senators and representatives had an opportunity to state their views about the purchase. A bill empowering the President to take possession of the ceded territory and to govern it until Congress should establish a territorial government was passed with little opposition and became law on October 31. Most of the recorded debate concerned a second measure, which provided for the issuing of the $11,250,000 of United

States stock with which Napoleon was to be paid.

Division of opinion on the purchase was for the most part along party lines. Members of the Federalist party, now confined chiefly to New England, New York, and Delaware, foresaw certain doom for their party in the incorporation of new western and southern territory. They were opposed, therefore, to the acquisition of Louisiana, and especially to the article of the treaty promising the incorporation of the inhabitants into the Union. They did not deny the right of the federal government to acquire territory, either by purchase or by conquest. But incorporation was a different thing. The right of Congress to admit new states into the Union, they argued, applied only to states formed from the territory in the possession of the United States when the Constitution was adopted. Hence the treaty, with its promise of incorporation, was unconstitutional.

It was unconstitutional, in Federalist opinion, for another reason as well. To French and Spanish ships it promised, for twelve years, the use of the ports of Louisiana upon the same terms with ships of the United States. But this article conflicted, said the Federalists, with Article I, Section 9, of the Constitution, wherein it was declared that "no Preference shall be given by any Regulation of Commerce or Revenue to the Ports of one State over those of another."

Thus the Federalists, formerly the party of loose construction, adopted strict-constructionist views in order to defend their sectional interest. Conversely, the Republicans, in support of a policy that they believed beneficial, were ready to abandon their former strict-constructionist attitudes and to construe the Constitution liberally. One of them, John Taylor of Caroline, called attention to the wording of Article VI of the Constitution, where the requirement that laws must be made "in pursuance" of that instrument does not apply to treaties, and contended that the treaty-making power, possessed by the President and two-thirds of the Senate, was not restricted by the Constitution. As to the spe-

cial privileges accorded to French and Spanish ships in the ports of Louisiana, the Republicans pointed out that the constitutional restriction applied only to the ports of states. Louisiana was a territory, and as such was "in the nature of a colony whose commerce may be regulated without any reference to the Constitution."

Sure of their majority, the Republicans showed scant respect for the arguments of their opponents or for their own earlier opinions. The bill authorizing the creation of $11,250,000 United States stock (in modern terminology, bonds) passed the House by a vote of 90 to 25, the Senate by 26 to 5.[6] John Quincy Adams, newly elected as a Federalist senator from Massachusetts, voted with the Republican majority. Jefferson signed the bill on November 10.

There remained only the dual act of transfer, from Spain to France and from France to the United States. In a ceremony at New Orleans on November 30, 1803, the Spanish flag was lowered, to give place to the French tricolor, and the keys to the public buildings were presented by Governor Salcedo to Laussat, the French prefect. For twenty days France again ruled in New Orleans. At a second ceremony on December 20, Laussat surrendered the province to General James Wilkinson and Governor W. C. C. Claiborne of Mississippi Territory, the commissioners of the United States.

Thus Louisiana passed into the hands of the United States, and a precedent for the further acquisition of territory was established. The right to acquire territory and to govern it, the right to admit its inhabitants to the full status of American citizens, which Jefferson and Congress had assumed in this transaction, was set beyond dispute by Chief Justice

6. Napoleon needed to convert the United States bonds into cash to meet the costs of his war against England. Unable to arrange this transaction through the Bank of France, he sold the bonds to the British firm of Hope and Baring, who thus supplied the French dictator with funds for the war against their own country. E. W. Lyon, *Louisiana in French Diplomacy, 1759–1804* (Norman: The University of Oklahoma Press, 1934), p. 248.

John Marshall twenty-five years later. Speaking for the Supreme Court, Marshall declared:

> The Constitution confers absolutely on the government of the Union, the powers of making war, and of making treaties; consequently, that government possesses the power of acquiring territory, either by conquest or by treaty. [Until such territory becomes a state, it may be governed, without the participation of its inhabitants] by virtue of that clause in the Constitution, which empowers Congress "to make all needful rules and regulations, respecting the territory or other property belonging to the United States."

That such territory might be formed into states and admitted into full partnership in the Union was established by implication in the same decision.[7]

Making the Most of a Noble Bargain

But of what did Louisiana consist? To this question the treaty gave no answer. Instead of defining the boundaries of the territory, it described it, in language borrowed from the treaty of San Ildefonso, as having "the same extent that it now has in the hands of Spain, and that it had when France possessed it." To requests from the American commissioners for a more specific definition of limits, Talleyrand replied: "I can give you no direction. You have made a noble bargain for yourselves, and I suppose you will make the most of it."

Livingston was quick to discover that the two clauses describing the colony had different meanings: that Louisiana "when France possessed it" had a greater area than when "in the hands of Spain." French Louisiana (before 1762) had extended eastward along the Gulf coast to the Perdido River, thus including the town and bay of Mobile. Spain, on the other hand, had received from France only that portion of the colony bounded on the east by the Mississippi and a line from the Mississippi to

the Gulf by way of the Iberville River and Lakes Maurepas and Pontchartrain. The area between the Iberville and the Perdido, ceded to Great Britain in 1763, became part of West Florida and remained so when Spain recovered the Floridas 20 years later. Hence Spanish Louisiana was bounded on the east by the Mississippi-Iberville line.

Of the two conflicting descriptions, Livingston, with Monroe's backing, urged the President to adopt the one more favorable to the United States and to take possession of all Spanish territory between the Mississippi and the Perdido as included in the purchase. Jefferson and James Madison, his Secretary of State, accepted Livingston's interpretation (though not at this time his proposal to use force), and the claim that all of West Florida west of the Perdido was part of Louisiana henceforth became official American doctrine.

Spain, on the other hand, adhered consistently to the other interpretation of the treaty, insisting that Louisiana was bounded on the east by the Mississippi and the Iberville. This, indeed, was also the French interpretation. Napoleon had sought in vain to secure the Floridas from Spain and had finally accepted Louisiana with the Iberville as its eastern limit. France, therefore, supported Spain in her rejection of an American claim which had little basis in law or history.

Weak though the claim was, the disputed strip of Gulf coast was of such potential value to the United States that Jefferson made repeated efforts to secure it by devious methods that add up to one of the least creditable chapters in the history of American diplomacy. Jefferson tried first to bluff Spain into yielding possession of the territory. When Spain called his bluff, he tried the persuasions of diplomacy. When these proved unavailing, he offered Napoleon a large cash consideration if he would coerce his ally, Spain, into humoring the United States. Napoleon was not above such a deal, but after placing his brother Joseph on the throne of Spain in 1808, he quickly became a defender of Spanish interests.

It remained for Jefferson's successor, James Madison (1809–1817), to make good the

7. *American Insurance Co. v. Canter,* I Peters 542 (1828). The case concerned the annexation of Florida and the validity of the territorial government established therein.

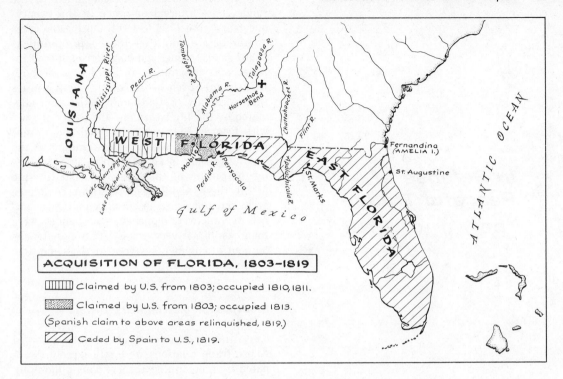

ACQUISITION OF FLORIDA, 1803–1819

[IIII] Claimed by U.S. from 1803; occupied 1810, 1811.

[...] Claimed by U.S. from 1803; occupied 1813.

(Spanish claim to above areas relinquished, 1819.)

[///] Ceded by Spain to U.S., 1819.

American claim to the disputed portion of West Florida. The imposition of a French king upon the Spanish people was the signal not only for revolt in Spain against French domination but also for rebellion in Spain's American colonies. The rebellion in West Florida was of a special character, for there the population was predominantly American in blood, speech, and loyalty. In the autumn of 1810, when revolts had begun in other Spanish colonies, the settlers along the Mississippi at the western extremity of West Florida seized the Spanish fort at Baton Rouge, proclaimed their independence, and invited the United States to annex them. President Madison acted promptly. In a proclamation of October 27, he stated anew the American claim to Florida west of the Perdido as a part of Louisiana and directed Governor W. C. C. Claiborne of Louisiana Territory to take possession of it in the name of the United States, so far as that could be done without employing force against Spanish troops. The United States took formal possession of Bation Rouge on December 10, 1810, and American authority was extended eastward to the Perdido with the exception of the bay and town of Mobile. A Spanish garrison at Mobile was the sole obstacle to the acquisition by the United States of Louisiana as it was "when France possessed it." The removal of that garrison in 1813 was to be an incident of a conflict with England over frontier rivalries and neutral rights.

7

In Defense of Peaceful Trade— The War of 1812

The Louisiana treaty was concluded in the single short interval of peace in the twenty-one years from 1793 to 1814. During the years of war before and after the Peace of Amiens (1801–1803) American commerce suffered injuries and indignities at the hands of both British and French—indignities and injuries that were only partially and temporarily alleviated by the Jay treaty and the treaty of 1800 with France. Even when England and France were at peace, American ships trading to the Mediterranean faced the hazards of capture by the pirates of the Barbary coast. In spite of all these handicaps, American commerce grew and flourished in these years. Old channels of trade were reopened, new channels were found, and the very wars that imposed risks on neutral commerce gave it at the same time a stimulus.

Breaches in Mercantilist Barriers

The United States was born into a world whose trade relations were still largely dominated by mercantilist theory. This philosophy taught, among other things, that a nation having colonies should monopolize their trade, that foreign ships should be excluded from their harbors, and that any exchanges between them and the outside world should be effected through, and for the benefit of, the mother country. No nation adhered one hundred percent to this policy; there were increasing departures from it, and in fact the whole system was soon to collapse under the attacks first launched by Adam Smith in his treatise, *The Wealth of Nations* (1776); but for nearly fifty years after winning its independence, the United States suffered from the mercantilist restrictions of other powers.

The United States was a nation without colonies, surrounded by the colonies of other nations. The most important of these colonial neighbors were British, and with the British colonies in the West Indies in particular, there had before the Revolution been a lively and profitable trade. Some five hundred vessels from New England and the continental colonies to the southward had been engaged in the West India trade. To the islands they carried lumber, livestock, fish, flour, and other provisions; they returned laden chiefly with sugar, molasses, rum, and coffee. The commodities exported to the islands from the continent regularly exceeded in value those imported in return. The balance was paid in specie, thus supplying the continental colonies (which produced no gold or silver) with an important medium of exchange and a means of settling their unfavorable trade balance with England.

This trade stopped with the Revolution and was not at once revived upon the return of peace. As previously noted, the British Parliament refused to follow William Pitt in his proposal to open the colonial trade to the Americans. The United States had thrown off British rule and was to be treated like any other foreign state. Certain essential commodities from the United States might be imported into the British West India islands, but only in British ships, and an even more drastic policy of mercantilist exclusion was applied to Canada and the other northern provinces, which were permitted no trade at all with the United States. Such, at least, was the general rule, but since it worked at least as much hardship on the colonies as on the United States, British provincial governors were given considerable latitude in relaxing the restrictions to meet emergencies. Such relaxations were especially common after the outbreak of war between France and Great Britain in 1793; and both before and after that event, the rigors of mercantilist policy were liberally tempered by smuggling. As a consequence of these breaches in the mercantilist wall and of trade with and by way of non-British islands, the West Indies trade of the United States as a whole rapidly revived and even by 1788 is estimated to have reached the level at which it had stood before the Revolution.[1]

The first significant retreat by Great Britain from her restrictive system was embodied in the Jay treaty of 1794, which permitted American ships to trade directly with British possessions in the East Indies and removed all restrictions, except the payment of normal tariff duties, from the overland trade between the United States and Canada. Article XII of this treaty, as originally signed, would also have allowed American ships of seventy tons burden or less to trade with the British West Indies, but subject to such limitations that the Senate expunged this article before approving the treaty.[2] The treaty, therefore, left the restrictions upon the West Indian trade as they had been before. American ships that visited the British islands did so either illegally or under emergency permits from the provincial governors. Such visits were allowed or winked at up to and even during the War of 1812.[3]

Fortunately for the United States, other powers with colonies in the West Indies were less bent than was England upon excluding the United States from the colonial trade. In the island colonies of Denmark (St. Thomas, St. John, St. Croix), Sweden (St. Bartholomew), and the Netherlands (St. Eustatia, Curaçao), American ships were free to enter, and American goods were received subject to trifling duties. The French islands (Martinique, Guadeloupe, and others) were permitted to import American foodstuffs (except salt pork), wood, and naval stores, and, as Thomas Jefferson reported in 1793, "our vessels are as free as their own to carry our commodities thither, and to bring away rum and

2. The United States would have agreed, had it accepted Article XII, to prohibit the exportation of molasses, sugar, coffee, cocoa, or cotton in American vessels "either from His Majesty's islands or from the *United States* to any part of the world except the United States, . . ." (Italics inserted.) The article was to continue in force during the existing war and for two years after its termination. The other commercial articles of the treaty were to expire at the end of twelve years. For other aspects of the Jay treaty, see Chapter 5.

3. F. L. Benns, *The American Struggle for the British West India Carrying-Trade, 1815–1830,* Indiana University Studies, Vol. X (Bloomington: University of Indiana Press, 1923), chap. 1.

1. Edward Channing, *A History of the United States,* 6 vols. (New York: The Macmillan Company, 1926), 3: 412. A. B. Keith, "Relaxations in the British Restrictions on the American Trade with the British West Indies, 1783–1802," *Journal of Modern History,* 20 (1948), 1–18.

molasses." Even Spain permitted some American trade with her colonies,[4] and the time was soon to come when the independence of continental Spanish America would open the ports of that area freely to the shipping and commerce of the United States.

Aiding the American Merchant Marine

The United States meanwhile was taking steps to build up its merchant marine by granting preferred status to American ships in American ports. The colonial merchant marine had never had to meet the competition of foreign ships, which had been excluded by the British navigation acts, but no sooner was independence won than merchantmen from a half-dozen European countries thronged American harbors, dealing a new blow to already depressed American shipping.[5]

For this foreign competition no effective remedy was found until the new government was set up under the Constitution. Then, by an act of July 4, 1789, fixing rates of duty on imported goods, Congress allowed a 10 percent discount in the rates on goods imported in ships of United States registry. A subsequent law (July 20, 1789) fixed tonnage dues at 6 cents per ton on ships built and owned in the United States and 50 cents per ton on foreign ships. American ships, furthermore, were subjected to the tonnage charge only once a year, while a foreign ship had to pay each time it entered an American port. This last provision had the effect of deterring foreign ships from engaging in the trade between American ports

—the coastwise trade. Possibly finding this multiplication of tonnage fees an insufficient deterrent, Congress in February 1793 expressly limited the coasting trade to "ships or vessels of the United States." From that time to the present, the coasting trade has continued to be monopolized by American ships.

For American ships trading with foreign ports, on the other hand, the discrimination in duties and tonnage charges proved necessary for only a limited period. In 1815 Congress authorized the President to remove these forms of discrimination for the shipping of nations which would abandon, or which did not practice, similar discrimination against ships of the United States. By mid-century practically all such discriminations had disappeared.[6]

Curbing the Barbary Corsairs

A problem that confronted the United States immediately upon independence and was not finally disposed of until more than thirty years later was the protection of American ships and sailors from harassment by the Barbary pirates. As British subjects, the colonists had been protected by the British government from the depredations of these marauders from the petty Moslem states of the North African coast. That protection ceased upon independence, and the United States was left to make its own terms with the Barbary governments. In 1786, it negotiated a satisfactory treaty with the Emperor of Morocco. Later treaties with Algiers, Tripoli, and Tunis were less favorable. Together they cost the United States over $800,000, chiefly in payment of ransom money for American prisoners held by the corsairs. The African signatories, furthermore, did not hesitate to violate the treaties and renew their attacks on American commerce whenever they thought they could get away with it.

In May 1801, the Pasha of Tripoli repudiated his treaty and declared war on the

4. Report by Jefferson on "Commercial Privileges and Restrictions," December 16, 1793. *American State Papers, Foreign Relations,* 1: 300–304. Jefferson stated that *"Spain* and *Portugal* refuse to those parts of America which they govern, all direct intercourse with any people but themselves." New Orleans, however, had since 1787 been open to American commerce, and apparently Spanish restrictions elsewhere were less rigid than Jefferson indicated. Cf. Channing, *History,* 3: 412.

5. S. E. Morison, *The Maritime History of Massachusetts, 1783–1860* (Boston: Houghton Mifflin Company, 1921), pp. 34–35.

6. See Chapter 10 for the later phases of the controversy with Great Britain over the West Indian trade.

United States. President Jefferson accepted the challenge and for four years the United States waged a desultory naval war against Tripoli in the Mediterranean. The war—which incidentally furnished excellent training for the officers and men of the young American navy—ended in a compromise settlement. The Pasha was made more amenable to reason by the threat of an overland expedition from Egypt, led by the eccentric American, William Eaton, which penetrated as far as Derna on Tripoli's eastern frontier. By the treaty, signed June 4, 1805, the United States agreed to pay $60,000 for the release of prisoners held by the Pasha and received assurances of future respect for its peaceful commerce.

During the War of 1812, several of the Barbary governments permitted British cruisers to take American prizes in their supposedly neutral coastal waters. To exact damages for these injuries and to chastise the offenders for other indignities to the American flag, the United States in 1815 sent two naval squadrons to the Mediterranean. The commander of one of these, Stephen Decatur (a distinguished veteran of the earlier Tripolitan war), was able to dictate terms to the despots of Algiers, Tunis, and Tripoli, and enjoyed the novel experience of taking money from predatory governments accustomed to exacting it. This was the beginning of the end for North African piracy.

The Anglo-French War Renewed

Great Britain and France had signed a preliminary treaty of peace on October 1, 1801, and the formal treaty of Amiens on March 27, 1802. The unstable peace was broken in May 1803. The war then renewed raged unabated between France and England, with other powers participating from time to time, until Napoleon's abdication in April 1814, and flared up again briefly the next year in the Hundred Days' fighting following the imperial exile's return from Elba. In the life-and-death struggle of these giants, the rights of small neutrals got short shrift.

The Peace of Amiens gave a brief respite to neutrals from the exactions of the belligerents. The renewal of the war revived their difficulties. For the United States it meant new controversies over neutral rights with both belligerents. Though both were equally ruthless in their disregard of neutral interests, the offenses of Great Britain, being more varied and brought closer to home by the ubiquity of the Royal Navy, proved in the end more offensive to the party in power in the United States—traditionally the pro-French party. The British, furthermore, also gave offense by their relations with the Indians of the Northwest. Defense of neutral rights, coupled with certain grievances and ambitions of the American frontier, led to the abandonment of neutrality and the declaration of war against England in 1812.

In the realm of neutral rights, the chief belligerent practices of which Americans complained were the impressment of seamen from American ships, of which England alone was guilty, and sweeping "paper blockades," which each belligerent sought to impose upon the ports and coasts of the other.

The Impressment Question

Impressment was a rough-and-ready species of "selective service," by which His Majesty's Navy was kept manned in times of stress. From time immemorial, British naval officers had exercised the right of recruiting their personnel by seizing British subjects (experienced seamen preferred), afloat or ashore, and pressing them into service, willy-nilly. The impressment of British subjects, on British shores or from British ships, was no concern of the United States, but when the practice was applied, on the high seas, to members of the crews of American merchant vessels, it roused American resentment. Such practice was, as the Americans saw it, in direct violation of the sovereignty of the United States; the American flag should protect the crews of American ships.

This the British were unwilling to admit.

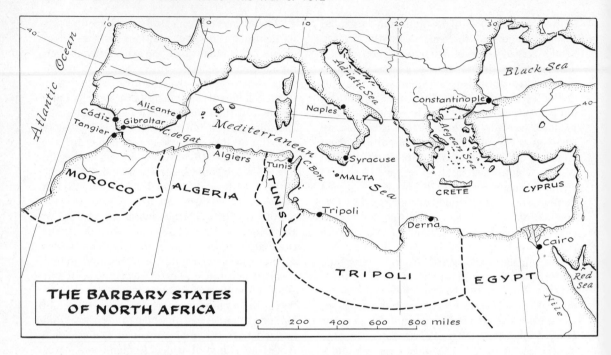

THE BARBARY STATES
OF NORTH AFRICA

In support of their position, they advanced the unquestioned facts that thousands of deserters from their Navy found employment in the American merchant marine, where the service was both pleasanter and safer, and that great numbers of these, through small bribes to American consuls or by other means, obtained false certificates of United States citizenship. To forgo the right of recovering such deserters forcibly from American ships would, as the British Admiralty viewed the matter, imperil the efficiency of the naval service in the struggle for existence against Napoleonic France.

If the British had exercised impressment with proper care to see that no injustice was done and that only deserters, or even only British subjects, were seized from American decks, perhaps the United States would have condoned the practice. But impressment was carried out, not by judicially-minded officials but by naval officers who needed seamen and were apt to resolve any doubt of a promising sailor's nationality in favor of themselves. From the arbitrary decisions of such naval

commanders, there was no appeal except through time-consuming diplomatic channels. When the British Foreign Office could be convinced that bona fide American citizens had been impressed, they were released—if still living—with regrets, but without indemnification for the injury.

The controversy was further complicated by a contradiction between British and American law on allegiance. The United States practiced naturalization on a large scale. Great Britain adhered to the principle of indelible allegiance—"Once an Englishman always an Englishman." The same man, therefore, might be at the same time an American citizen under American law and a British subject under British law. Hence even genuine evidence of American citizenship was not necessarily adequate protection against forced service in the British fleet.

All attempts to settle the controversy by diplomacy failed. The United States offered, in 1807, to take measures to exclude British deserters from American ships in wartime in return for British renunciation of the right of impressment, but the British Admiralty refused to forgo a valuable current practice for what it regarded as a dubious promise.

The impressment controversy reached a tragic climax in the *Chesapeake-Leopard* incident of June 1807. Ordinarily the British did not venture to interfere with American naval vessels, but in this instance the British frigate *Leopard* fired upon and boarded the American frigate *Chesapeake* and removed four members of the crew, alleged to be British deserters. The American vessel, unprepared for battle, put up only token resistance and suffered over twenty casualties in the melee. This time the British government realized that its naval agents had gone too far. It disavowed the action of the *Leopard's* captain and made tardy amends for the injuries inflicted. Meanwhile the impressment question, still unsettled, dropped somewhat into the background as new controversies held the stage. It was revived as a major issue on the eve of the War of 1812.

A Blow at American Commerce

In spite of impressments and in spite of restrictions placed upon neutral trade by both belligerents, American commerce flourished mightily, at least until 1807. The tonnage of American shipping employed in foreign trade grew from 363,100 in 1791 to 848,300 in 1807. Exports, with adjustments for changing price levels, increased nearly fourfold in the same years; imports grew by 75 percent.[7] This prosperity was in part a direct consequence of the war. American ships could trade with both belligerents. A form of activity that their owners found particularly profitable was the carrying of goods between France and Spain on the one hand and the French and Spanish Caribbean colonies on the other. French and Spanish ships, which in peacetime monopo-

7. W. A. Phillips and A. H. Reede, *The Napoleonic Period,* Vol. 2 of *Neutrality: Its History, Economics and Law,* 4 vols. (New York: Columbia University Press, 1935–1936), pp. 226–30, 234.

lized the colonial trade of their respective mother countries, were kept in port by the dominant British navy, and the two governments opened to neutrals a trade from which foreign ships were normally excluded. Of this, American shipping took the lion's share.

Such trade was, of course, contrary to the British rule of 1756, but for some years American shipowners had been able to circumvent that rule by the device of the "broken voyage." An American ship would take on a cargo of sugar, for example, at the French island of Martinique and would proceed to an American port, where the sugar would be entered as an import, probably without being removed from the ship, and either the import duty would be paid or the owner would give bond for its payment. The ship would then be supplied with new papers, showing the sugar as an export from the United States, most of the duty would be refunded as a drawback, and the ship would proceed on its way to a French port, where the cargo would be finally disposed of. Since neither segment of the voyage alone was forbidden by the rule of 1756 or otherwise, British admiralty courts at first declined to interfere with this species of transaction. But in the case of the ship *Essex* (1805) they held that the voyage—in this instance from Barcelona to Havana with an interruption at Salem, Massachusetts—was to be considered "continuous" and hence prohibited by the rule of 1756.

The *Essex* decision was a serious matter for the American carrying trade, a turning point for the worse in Anglo-American relations. Congress retaliated by an act (April 18, 1806) prohibiting the importation of certain English manufactures but suspended its operation pending the outcome of an attempt to reach agreement by diplomacy. For the latter purpose, Jefferson sent William Pinkney, a Maryland lawyer, to assist James Monroe, the regular minister in London. It was Jefferson's hope that the two envoys might secure satisfactory settlement of the whole complex of issues involving neutral rights—blockade, contraband, the rule of 1756, the continuous voyage interpretation, and impressment. Negotiating with friendly British commissioners, Monroe and Pinkney succeeded in getting a relaxation of the rule of 1756 and the doctrine of continuous voyage, but little else. On the right of impressment, particularly, the British would yield nothing more than a promise to remedy abuses in exercising it. The treaty that Monroe and Pinkney signed, nevertheless, on December 31, 1806, was not well received in Washington. Jefferson refused to send it to the Senate. He instructed the envoys to try again but to make no treaty without a provision against impressment. Monroe and Pinkney found the new British Foreign Secretary, George Canning, even less conciliatory than his predecessors. Their mission had failed.

A Competition in Paper Blockades

In the meantime, the two major belligerents had embarked upon a course of economic warfare which added immeasurably to the hardships of neutrals. Napoleon launched his "Continental System," designed to ruin England economically and thus destroy her power to make war. Embodied in his Berlin and Milan decrees (November 21, 1806, and December 17, 1807), it sought to bar continental Europe to British ships and British trade. Neutral ships which had called at British ports or submitted to search by British naval vessels were declared liable to confiscation. The British retaliated through a series of orders-in-council (especially those of January 7, 1807, and November 11, 1807), which forbade trade with France and her allies, in Europe and the colonies, and threatened with confiscation all neutral vessels attempting to trade with those areas. An important exception was made for neutral ships in the provision that they might trade with enemy ports if they first put in at British ports and paid certain duties on their merchandise. It is evident that the British blockade of France was not designed to cut off trade with the continent; its purpose was to compel such trade, carried in

neutral bottoms, to pay tribute to Great Britain.

The combination of decrees and orders-in-council—both of them, in American eyes, constituting illegal "paper blockades"—placed neutral shipping in a truly precarious situation. If an American sea captain obeyed the British orders, touching at an English port on the way to the continent, he exposed his vessel and cargo to confiscation by the French. If he sought to conform to the French decrees by avoiding contact with British ships or shores, he stood little chance of escaping confiscation by the British.

Jefferson's "Peaceable Coercion"

Jefferson was unwilling to submit to the "paper blockades" and other—in American eyes—illegal infringements upon American maritime rights; he was equally unwilling to go to war to defend those rights. He undertook instead to bring the belligerents to terms through economic weapons. It was his belief that trade with the United States was of such vital importance to both France and Britain that exclusion from it could be used to coerce them into respecting American rights. At his suggestion, Congress passed (December 22, 1807) an embargo act which closed American ports to all foreign shipping and forbade American ships to leave port except to engage in the coastwise trade. When the embargo, while subjecting the American economy to serious hardship, produced no change in French or British policy, it was replaced by a series of milder measures. The last of these—known as Macon's Bill No. 2 (May 1, 1810) [8] —opened American ports to the commercial vessels of all nations, but provided that if either England or France should revoke its orders-in-council or decrees so far as they infringed American neutral rights, and if the other belligerent failed to do likewise within

8. From Nathaniel Macon, a representative from North Carolina and speaker of the House of Representatives, 1801–1807.

three months, ships and trade of the latter should be barred from American ports.

By signing Macon's Bill No. 2, President James Madison put himself in the hands of a completely unscrupulous French government. Napoleon's Foreign Minister promptly informed the American minister in Paris that the Berlin and Milan decrees, in so far as they affected American ships, would cease to operate on November 1, 1810, upon the understanding that England would thereupon repeal its orders or else that the United States should "cause their rights to be respected by the English." In reality, Napoleon continued to enforce the decrees against American ships. Madison apparently accepted the repeal as genuine and reimposed nonimportation restrictions upon Great Britain (February 2, 1811).

The British government, seeing through Napoleon's subterfuge, refused to revoke or modify the orders-in-council. Though a new Secretary of State, James Monroe, made a genuine effort to reach agreement with a new British minister, A. J. Foster, it was evident by July 1811 that an impasse had been reached. Monroe insisted that the repeal of the French decrees was genuine and demanded that England revoke her orders-in-council. Foster denied that the French decrees were really repealed and demanded therefore that the United States give up its nonimportation policy against Great Britain. This Monroe refused until the orders-in-council were revoked. It was a vicious circle, from which, as it turned out, the only exit was war.

According to Madison's biographer, Irving Brant, Madison had believed from the beginning of his presidency that if England continued to violate American rights, America must fight. He now called Congress to meet in November, a month before the usual time. In his message, he complained of the unfriendly conduct of both belligerents, but he reserved his most wrathful comments for the British, whose practices, he said, "have the character as well as the effect of war on our lawful commerce." To resist their "hostile in-

flexibility in trampling on rights which no independent nation can relinquish," he asked Congress to put the United States "into an armor and an attitude demanded by the crisis."

Drifting into War

This Congress failed to do, even under the whiplash of the "war hawks," a group of newly elected representatives, most of them young men from western and southern states. Outstanding among them were Henry Clay of Kentucky—elected speaker in his first session in the House—John C. Calhoun of South Carolina, John A. Harper of New Hampshire, and Peter B. Porter of western New York. Such men were infuriated at seeing their country treated year after year as a second-class power. Insults and injuries, they felt, must be avenged by force of arms. Continued submission to humiliation and wrong, some believed, would endanger the very existence of the Republic.[9]

To most of the war hawks, in all probability, the principal grievance was the British interference with American seaborne trade. Such interference touched the pocketbook nerve as well as the sense of national honor. The British, at any rate, were widely blamed for a serious decline in the prices of western products which had recently been observed. Some of the war hawks had still another grievance. They blamed the British and their agents in Canada for an epidemic of Indian hostilities in the Northwest. Stimulated by the able Shawnee chieftain, Tecumseh, the Indians of the area from the Ohio to the Mississippi had undertaken to unite in resistance

9. Roger H. Brown, *The Republic in Peril: 1812* (New York: Columbia University Press, 1964). On the identity and motives of the war hawks (if their existence as a class was not "an historical myth"), see articles by Roger H. Brown and Reginald Horsman, with comments by Alexander DeConde and Norman K. Risjord, in *Indiana Magazine of History,* 60 (June 1964), 121 ff.

to the surrender of further Indian lands to agents of the United States government. Sporadic attacks on frontier settlers were followed by a dramatic clash between Indians and an army commanded by General William Henry Harrison near the shores of Tippecanoe Creek in Indiana, on November 7, 1811.

The British in Canada were well known to be friendly to Tecumseh and his plans, and when British arms were found among weapons left by the Indians at Tippecanoe, many westerners were confirmed in their belief that expulsion of the British from Canada was essential to peace with the Indians of the Northwest. The conquest of Canada became a secondary motive for war with England. If the annexation of Canada threatened to upset the sectional balance of the Union in favor of the North, there was the further possibility of enlarging the southern boundaries by the acquisition of that part of Florida still remaining in the hands of Spain. An attempt to acquire East Florida by subversion met with a well deserved failure in the spring of 1812. But Spain was now an ally of England, and not a few southerners foresaw in a war with England a justification of completing the conquest of the Floridas. It was, in fact, charged with some plausibility by Federalist opponents of the war that northern and southern expansionists had made a deal on the anticipated spoils of war: Canada for the North, Florida for the South.[10]

As one accomplished student of the period has remarked of the causes of the War of 1812, the British orders-in-council were "the central structure"; others—impressments, Indian troubles, expansionist ambitions—were mere "flying buttresses."[11] It was ironical, therefore, that the central structure was being dismantled at the very time that Congress was declaring war. Congress had dillydallied all winter and spring. It had provided neither men nor ships nor money adequate for a war

with England. It had at one point almost voted itself into a recess—a sure path to inaction. Urged on by the war hawks, by Monroe, and by Madison, who sent in a final war message on June 1, 1812, it finally declared war on June 18, with large minorities opposing in both houses (79 to 49 in the House, 19 to 13 in the Senate).

Two days earlier the British government had announced its intention of repealing the orders-in-council, and they were actually repealed on June 23. The repeal was—too late— a victory for Jefferson's policy of peaceable coercion. British merchants and manufacturers had been hard hit by the loss of the American market, and it was pressure from this source that achieved what neither American diplomacy nor the threat of an American war had availed to bring about.[12] Had the United States been competently represented in London, it could have foreseen the repeal of the orders, but Minister Pinkney had taken an "inamicable leave" in February 1811, leaving only a chargé d'affaires at the legation, and the latter failed to see or to report what was in the wind.[13]

The British expected this major concession to stop the war if it did not prevent it, but the news of repeal reached America weeks after war had begun and proved insufficient to halt it. Officially, the war went on because the British had not renounced the right of impressment. Other factors, presumably, were the West's aroused appetite for Canada and a feeling that a war begun in defense of the na-

10. J. W. Pratt, *Expansionists of 1812* (New York: The Macmillan Company, 1925).

11. Bradford Perkins, *Prologue to War: England and the United States, 1805–1812* (Berkeley: University of California Press, 1961), p. 431.

12. The British government had discounted the chances of the United States going to war. It had been assured by the Federalists and the British minister in Washington that Mr. Madison "couldn't be kicked into a war."

13. The British had sworn that they would not repeal the orders till they had evidence that Napoleon had revoked the decrees. They were enabled to save face when Joel Barlow, the United States minister in Paris, forwarded a spurious "decree of St. Cloud," antedated April 28, 1811, purportedly declaring the Berlin and Milan decrees revoked with respect to American vessels. This appears to have been produced on the spur of the moment by the French Foreign Minister in response to Barlow's plea for an "authentic act" giving evidence of the repeal of the decrees.

tional honor should not be adjourned without some bloodletting.

An Indecisive War

The War of 1812 began on June 18, 1812, and was ended by the Treaty of Ghent, signed on Christmas Eve, 1814. The failure of the United States to achieve any of the maritime concessions or territorial gains which the war hawks had contemplated was the result of inadequate preparation, incompetent administrative and military leadership, and internal dissensions.

Though Congress had authorized a Regular Army of 35,000 men, fewer than 10,000 had been raised; a large portion of these were raw recruits, and when the war began they were scattered about the country in small garrisons, unavailable for prompt or vigorous action. The state militia were poorly trained, poorly officered, and many of them were ready to take advantage of their supposed exemption from duty on foreign soil. The higher officers, who commanded the Regular Army at the beginning of the war, were without exception incompetent. Under these circumstances, it is not surprising that the early attempts to invade and conquer Canada resulted in dismal failures. By the summer of 1814, when able officers—notably Generals Jacob Brown and Winfield Scott—had risen to high command and had instilled discipline and courage into their little army, the chance of conquering Canada had vanished. Napoleon was at Elba, and Wellington's veterans were pouring into Canada. The problem was not how to conquer Canada, but how to defend the United States.

While military incompetence and unreadiness were frustrating northern hopes of winning Canada, southern designs on Florida were frustrated by northern opposition. Two attempts to empower the President to take possession of East Florida were defeated in the Senate by the votes of Federalists, who opposed the war *in toto*, and northern Republicans, who disliked the administration's Florida policy. The only gain on that front was the occupation of Mobile, to which the United States had long laid claim as part of Louisiana.

On the high seas, where the United States in 1812 had some seventeen naval vessels, none of the first class, to oppose the thousand ships of the British navy, American naval commanders put up a gallant but hopeless fight. A few brilliant victories in single-ship actions could not shake British control of the seas. Before the fighting ended, virtually all units of the American navy had been either captured or bottled up in port, and American commerce was excluded from the seas by a tight blockade. The only American naval victories that counted strategically were those on Lake Erie and Lake Champlain. The former (September 10, 1813) enabled the United States to recover Detroit, lost in the first weeks of the war, but did not prevent British occupation of most of Michigan and the Wisconsin-Minnesota area. The latter (September 11, 1814) turned back a formidable British army intent upon invading New York.

All things considered, the United States was fortunate in being able—except in the region of Lake Michigan and the upper Mississippi—to defend its own territory. The battle of Lake Champlain saved New York from serious trouble. Another British army—having taken Washington and burned the public buildings—was repulsed before Baltimore. At New Orleans, two weeks after the signing of the peace treaty, Andrew Jackson inflicted upon a third British force the most crushing defeat of the war.

The Treaty of Ghent

The defensive character which the war had assumed was evident in the final instructions to the American peace commissioners, who opened negotiations with the British at Ghent in August 1814.[14] Earlier drafts had proposed abandonment of impressments as an indis-

14. The American commissioners were John Quincy Adams, Albert Gallatin, Henry Clay, Jonathan Russell, and James A. Bayard (a Federalist senator from Delaware).

pensable condition of peace and had expressed a hope also for a definition of legal blockade and abandonment of the rule of 1756. But by the summer of 1814, military failure and the defeat of England's other antagonist, Napoleon, had so weakened the American bargaining position that all these proposals were dropped, and the commissioners were told to ask only a return to the *status quo ante bellum*.

The British commissioners had come to Ghent with more ambitious demands—cessions of territory in Maine, New York, and between Lake Superior and the Mississippi, and the creation of a permanent Indian territory embracing a great area in the American Northwest. The American commissioners rejected these demands at once. While the British hesitated, came news of the American victories at Lake Champlain and Baltimore. The Duke of Wellington, Napoleon's conqueror, advised the Cabinet to accept the American terms, unless it was prepared for an expensive prolongation of the war in America—a burden which the hard-pressed British taxpayer would be reluctant to carry. The British accepted the American terms. The treaty, signed December 24, 1814, provided for restoration of all territory that had been occupied by the forces of either party. Such of Britain's Indian allies as were still at war with the United States were to recover their land holdings of 1811. Finally, joint commissions were to settle certain boundary disputes between the United States and Canada. The United States had won not a single concession in the matter of maritime rights, not a foot of Canadian soil. Yet the treaty was joyously greeted by the American public and on February 16, 1815, was unanimously approved by the United States Senate.

The Treaty of Ghent did not register all the results of the war, and an awareness of some of the unregistered results may partly explain the general satisfaction with the treaty. In the Northwest, the Indian menace that had contributed to the war fever was removed or greatly reduced. Tecumseh died in battle in 1813; his confederacy dissolved; the Indians who had taken the British side made peace with the United States, the nearer tribes during the war, the others soon afterwards. British support of the Indians ceased. There was no further serious trouble about acquiring or settling Indian lands.

A somewhat similar development had marked the war in the South. There the powerful Creek confederacy, perhaps under British influence, had gone on the warpath in 1813. Its power was broken by Andrew Jackson's Tennessee troops at the battle of Horseshoe Bend, March 27, 1814, and the Creek chieftains were forced to cede a great area of some 23 million acres in southern Georgia and the future state of Alabama. The occupation of Mobile has been mentioned. These gains were direct consequences of the war. Indirectly, Indian troubles growing out of Jackson's treaty with the Creeks were to lead to the acquisition of the remainder of Florida in 1819.[15]

If the war brought gains to both northern and southern frontiers, it did nothing to establish the American position on neutral maritime rights. That the United States had for many years no further occasion to defend its rights as a neutral was the consequence not of its prowess in the War of 1812 but of the fact that for a century after Waterloo, there was no great war among the maritime states of Europe. An attempt by John Quincy Adams as Secretary of State in 1823 to secure international acceptance of a comprehensive code for the regulation of maritime war was abandoned when the British government refused even to discuss the impressment question. Not until the Declaration of Paris of 1856 was any progress made in the definition of neutral rights. That famous declaration embodied most of the principles for which the United States had long contended.[16]

15. See Chapter 8.
16. See Chapter 17. The British government never formally abandoned the right of impressment, but never again practiced it against American ships. By a convention of 1870, however, it abandoned the principle of indelible allegiance, thus recognizing the right of British subjects to change their allegiance under American naturalization laws.

The United States and Great Britain did not, after the War of 1812, obey the scriptural injunction to love one's enemies. Acrimonious disputes and occasional "crises" were still to mar the relations of the two English-speaking countries. But the more significant fact is that instead of going to war over such disputes, the two governments hereafter invariably settled them peaceably, either through negotiation or some form of arbitration. Much of the credit for this improvement in Anglo-American relations should go to Robert Stewart, Viscount Castlereagh, British Foreign Secretary, 1812–1822, and to two successive British ministers in Washington, Charles Bagot (1815–1820) and Stratford Canning (1820–1823). All three, while by no means lovers of the United States, avoided disputation and sought reasonable settlements of the controversies of the period.[1]

Beginnings of the Peace Movement

It may be more than coincidence that this long reign of Anglo-American peace began at the same time as the organized peace movement in the United States. The abolition of war was of course no new idea. The Quakers (Society of Friends) had been pacifists from their beginning. Benjamin Franklin, though no pacifist, had averred that there never was "any such thing as a *good* war or a *bad* peace." There had been serious proposals that the post of Secretary of War in the federal executive be balanced by another office for a Secretary of Peace. It was, however, reaction against the Napoleonic Wars and especially the War of 1812—a quite needless war as many believed —that supplied the impetus for the launching of an organized peace campaign. Federalist opponents of that particular war had organized themselves as "Friends of Peace" and under other names while the war lasted. In the year of its close, 1815, the Massachusetts and the New York Peace Societies were formed. These were speedily followed by other local societies —there were some fifty of these before 1861— and in 1828 the American Peace Society ap-

8

Friendly Settlements with Great Britain and Spain

1. Bradford Perkins, *Castlereagh and Adams: England and America, 1812–1823* (Berkeley: University of California Press, 1964).

peared, a body with wide ambitions that was destined for a long life.

The peace movement in the United States had its counterparts and affiliates abroad, in England and on the continent. At home, it was but one manifestation of the belief in the perfectibility of human society so characteristic of the early nineteenth century. The age was one of reform movements—antislavery, temperance, prison reform, educational reform, the quest for women's rights, and various others. But what evil worse than war beset suffering humanity? In an age when "the idea of progress" was generally accepted, it was not hard to believe in the evolution depicted in Tennyson's vision, which sped on

> Till the war-drum throbb'd no longer,
>   and the battle-flags were furl'd
> In the Parliament of man, the
>   Federation of the world.

American leaders in the movement—notably William Ladd, William Jay, and Elihu Burritt, the "learned blacksmith"—conducted propaganda at home and some of them participated in a series of international peace congresses held in Europe in the 1840's and 1850's. These congresses had a comprehensive program, which they sought to bring to the attention of the governments of Europe and America. It embraced such familiar concepts as reduction of armaments, a congress of nations, a court of arbitration, permanent and obligatory arbitration treaties, and prohibition of loans and sales of war materials to belligerents. None of these aims was achieved during the nineteenth century; yet the existence and influence of the peace societies should not be forgotten in any study of the growing resort to arbitration and other peaceful modes of settlement during that period.

The "Unguarded Frontier"

One of the earliest achievements of peace-minded Americans was the agreement with Great Britain in 1817 to dismantle existing naval forces on the Great Lakes and Lake Champlain and to maintain there only such trifling naval armament as would be needed to enforce the customs and revenue laws. When the War of 1812 ended, the two governments were engaged in a costly competition for naval supremacy on Lake Ontario; both recognized the dangers inherent in such a contest. Negotiations in London and Washington terminated in an exchange of notes (April 28 and 29, 1817) between Richard Rush, acting Secretary of State, and Charles Bagot, British minister in Washington. By the agreement (later approved by the Senate and thus given the authority of a treaty), the two governments consented to limit their naval armament on the lakes to vessels not exceeding 100 tons in burden nor carrying more than one 18-pound gun each. Of these each party should maintain not more than one on Lake Champlain, one on Lake Ontario, and two on the upper lakes. Either government might terminate the agreement by giving six months' notice.

The Rush-Bagot agreement, subject to some technical violations and to occasional modifications or interpretations,[2] continued in effect from 1817 to the present day. The common belief that the agreement inaugurated an era of an "unguarded frontier" is, however, without justification. Not for over half a century did Anglo-American peace seem sufficiently secure to warrant either party's disarming the frontier. The existing naval forces on the lakes were dismantled but not destroyed. Navy yards on the lakes were maintained for several

2. In 1838, for example, the British built and commissioned gunboats on the lakes to deal with filibustering in connection with the insurgent activities of 1837–38. In 1842–44 the United States built the iron gunboat *Michigan* on the upper lakes, a vessel of 582 tons, which was in service for many years thereafter. In November and December 1946, by an exchange of notes between the acting Secretary of State and the Canadian ambassador in Washington, the two governments agreed that the stationing of naval vessels on the Great Lakes for training purposes should be regarded as consistent with the spirit of the Rush-Bagot agreement, provided that full information in regard to such vessels was supplied by each government to the other. *Documents on American Foreign Relations,* 8: 788–90.

years. Land fortifications were maintained and were strengthened at times of crisis in Anglo-American relations. Not until 1871, with settlement of the *Alabama* claims assured, did the two governments by tacit consent gradually permit their land fortifications to fall into a state of decay. The "unguarded frontier" dates from 1871, not 1817.[3]

Arbitration Becomes a Habit

It was not an accident that both the Rush-Bagot agreement and the later demilitarization of the frontier followed agreements to submit troublesome Anglo-American controversies to arbitration.[4] No feature of Anglo-American relations in the nineteenth century is more striking than the growing realization that there were better methods than war for settling any disputes that were likely to arise between the two countries.

A good beginning had already been made under the terms of the Jay Treaty of 1794. That instrument had provided for arbitration of four controversies: (1) the identity of the St. Croix River, designated by the treaty of peace as the boundary between Maine and Nova Scotia; (2) the amount to be paid by the United States to British creditors in satisfaction of debts that they had been unable to collect by reason of "lawful impediments" imposed by the states in contravention of the treaty of peace; (3) the compensation to be paid by Great Britain to American claimants for illegal seizures of vessels and other prop-

erty in the current Anglo-French war; (4) the compensation to be paid by the United States to British claimants for losses resulting from violations of American neutrality by French armed vessels. Arbitration by mixed commissions adjudicated all of these controversies except the second, which in the end was settled by negotiation. The commission on the St. Croix River concluded that of several rivers which had been known by that name, the treaty-makers had meant to designate the Schoodiac, as claimed by Great Britain, not the Maguadavic, as claimed by the United States. Under the third and fourth headings, American and British claimants were awarded $11,656,000 and $143,428.14 respectively. Payment to British creditors under the second heading, as determined by a negotiated convention, was in the amount of $2,664,000.

The Treaty of Ghent provided for arbitration of four boundary controversies between the United States and British Canada, embracing certain islands off the coast of Maine and the overland boundary from the head of the St. Croix (Schoodiac) River to the Lake of the Woods. Possession of the islands and the fixing of the boundary line through the St. Lawrence River and other waters to the head of Lake Huron presented no great difficulty. On the segments of the boundary from the St. Croix to the St. Lawrence and from Lake Huron to the Lake of the Woods, agreement at this time proved impossible. On the line from Lake Huron to the Lake of the Woods, the arbitrators failed to make a report. The line from the St. Croix to the St. Lawrence was submitted to the King of the Netherlands as arbitrator. Instead of deciding in favor of one of the contestants, he recommended a compromise line, which the United States rejected. Both questions were settled in the Webster-Ashburton Treaty of 1842.[5]

The Northern Boundary and Oregon

The Treaty of Ghent made no provision for determining the boundary between the Lake

---

3. C. P. Stacey, "The Myth of the Unguarded Frontier, 1815–1871," *American Historical Review,* 56 (1950), 1–18.

4. International arbitration is the submission of a dispute to some supposedly impartial sovereign, government, individual, group, or judicial body, with power to settle it and with full obligation on the part of the disputants to accept the settlement so arrived at. Arbitration is not resorted to unless ordinary diplomatic negotiation has failed to produce a solution. Arbitration is superior to other forms of participation by third parties—"good offices," "mediation," "conciliation"—in that the disputants agree in advance to accept the decision. Thus, unless there is some slip, agreement to arbitrate insures a settlement.

5. See Chapter 10.

of the Woods and the Rocky Mountains or for adjusting conflicting British and American claims to the Pacific coast region that was coming to be known as Oregon.

The treaty of 1783 had described the boundary line as running from the northwestern-most point of the Lake of the Woods due west to the Mississippi—an impossible line since the Mississippi rose far to the south of the Lake of the Woods. No substitute line had been agreed upon when the United States acquired Louisiana with an undefined northern boundary. Monroe and Pinkney in 1806 tentatively agreed with their British fellow negotiators to fix the boundary at the 49th parallel from the Lake of the Woods to the Rocky Mountains, but the convention embodying the agreement was never signed. The American commissioners at Ghent proposed this same solution but dropped it when the British insisted upon coupling with it a stipulation giving them access to the upper Mississippi and free navigation of that river.

Agreement on a boundary line to the Rocky Mountains, if that were achieved, would still leave unsettled conflicting American and British (as well as Spanish and Russian) claims to the Oregon country. To such American claims as could be founded upon the discovery and naming of the Columbia River in 1792 by Captain Robert Gray of Boston and the explorations of Lewis and Clark (1804–1806), there was now added one based upon actual settlement. In May 1811, representatives of the fur merchant, John Jacob Astor, had established a fort and trading post, which they named Astoria, at the mouth of the Columbia on its southern shore. Their occupancy was brief, however. News of the outbreak of war, and the danger that their post and stores might be captured by the British induced them to sell out, in October 1813, to local representatives of the North West Company of Montreal. Two months later a British sloop of war, the *Raccoon,* arrived on the scene; her commander took formal possession of the fort and surrounding country in the name of the British King and renamed the fort Fort George.

The injection of military conquest into what had hitherto been a commercial transaction gave the United States ground for claiming that Astoria should be restored to the United States under the terms of the Treaty of Ghent. The British government did not contest the claim, and on October 6, 1818, the British flag was lowered and the stars and stripes raised over Fort George. The British Foreign Secretary, Lord Castlereagh, emphasized the point that he was not recognizing the American claim to sovereignty at the mouth of the Columbia; he was merely acknowledging that that claim had as much, or as little, force in 1818 as it had had in 1813. It soon became apparent, however, that the British were willing to concede priority of rights south of the Columbia to the United States.

The Boundary Treaty of 1818

Just two weeks after the "restoration" of Astoria, Richard Rush and Albert Gallatin, American commissioners in London, signed a treaty fixing the boundary line from the Lake of the Woods to the Rockies and establishing a temporary *modus vivendi* for the Oregon country. The British were now ready to accept the 49th parallel as the boundary from the Lake of the Woods [6] to the Rocky Mountains, without insisting upon the renewal of their right to navigate the Mississippi. When the Americans proposed extending the same line to the Pacific, the British intimated that they would accept instead the Columbia River from its mouth to its intersection with the 49th parallel, with the understanding that the river and the harbor at its mouth should be open to both British and American shipping. When neither party would accept the other's proposal, a compromise was agreed upon by which all territory on the northwest coast claimed by either Great Britain or the United States should be equally

6. More precisely, from a line drawn due north or south—south as it turned out to be—from the most northwestern point of the Lake of the Woods to its intersection with the 49th parallel.

open during a ten-year period to the vessels, citizens, and subjects of the two powers, without prejudice to the claims of other governments (Spain and Russia). This arrangement —the so-called "joint occupation"—was embodied, with the fixing of the boundary east of the Rocky Mountains, in the treaty signed on October 20, 1818.

The same treaty settled another question of considerable importance, especially to New England. The treaty of 1783 had granted to United States citizens the "liberty" of inshore fishing along the coasts of British North America. The British asserted that this "liberty" had been canceled by the War of 1812. Americans were anxious to see it restored. The British now offered a compromise which the American negotiators accepted. In return for the perpetual "liberty" to take fish inside the three-mile limit on the west coast and part of the south coast of Newfoundland, on the coast of Labrador, and in the waters about the Magdalen Islands, the United States renounced its claim to the inshore fisheries on all other parts of the coasts of British North America. American fishermen were also allowed to land and cure their fish in the unsettled bays and harbors of Labrador and that portion of the south coast of Newfoundland where inshore fishing was permitted.[7]

With the signing of the treaty of 1818 and the creation of the arbitration commissions provided for in the Treaty of Ghent, it was hoped that most of the troublesome issues between the United States and Great Britain had been disposed of, at least temporarily. Certainly there was an easing in Anglo-American tensions. But the West Indies trade problem had not been solved; the Oregon controversy had been merely postponed; and two questions that had been submitted to the arbitral process—the northeast boundary and the Lake Superior-Lake of the Woods boundary questions had proved incapable of being settled in that manner. Much work remained to be done before Anglo-American relations could be viewed with entire satisfaction.

7. For later developments and final settlement of the fisheries controversy, see p. 146 and Chapters 20, 25.

The Transcontinental Treaty with Spain

While Gallatin and Rush, in London, were fixing the northern boundary of Louisiana and holding the British to a draw in the diplomatic sparring over Oregon, Secretary of State John Quincy Adams, in Washington, was engaged in negotiations that eventually settled the longstanding controversies with Spain. Spain had never accepted the American claim to the Perdido River as the eastern boundary of Louisiana, and American occupation of the strip of land between the Perdido and the Iberville, before and during the War of 1812, had been without Spain's consent. The United States desired an acknowledgment of its title to this area; it desired also to acquire Florida east of the Perdido, to which it had no similar claim. The western boundary of Louisiana had never been defined. The United States, with little justification, claimed to the Rio Grande. Spain placed the boundary well to the eastward of the Sabine. Thus Texas and part of the state of Louisiana were in dispute.

Added to the boundary controversies were certain damage claims which each country held against the other. The United States claimed compensation for allegedly unneutral conduct on Spain's part during American hostilities with France in 1798–1800 and for damages suffered by American commerce from the withdrawal of the right of deposit at New Orleans in 1802. Spain claimed damages for American incursions into Florida before and during the War of 1812 and for hospitality accorded in United States ports to privateers sailing under the flags of Spain's revolting colonies. The United States paid little heed to Spain's damage claims. In satisfaction of its own, it was willing to accept all of Florida, East and West, of which Spain still held possession. Secretary Adams and Spanish Minister Don Luis de Onis were exchanging ideas about the boundary and damage claims in the spring of 1818, when they were interrupted by warlike noises from Spanish Florida.

Florida, after the War of 1812, was in a state of near anarchy, which Spanish governors at St. Augustine and Pensacola were powerless to remedy. Amelia Island, on the Atlantic coast just south of the United States border, became a haven of freebooters, who claimed to operate under letters of marque from one or another of Spain's revolting colonies. When one of them, Luis Aury, claimed East Florida as part of Mexico, President Monroe sent in United States troops to take possession.[8]

Farther west, Creek warriors, fugitives from Jackson's campaign of 1814, had taken refuge with their kinsmen, the Florida Seminoles. In their hostility to the United States, they were abetted by several British adventurers who had remained in Florida after the British defeat at New Orleans. When the Creeks undertook to interfere by force with the surveying and settling of their former lands in Georgia and Mississippi Territory, the United States resolved to punish and subdue them, even if that meant pursuing them across the border into Florida—a right which the United States claimed under the 1795 treaty with Spain. This task was handed to General Andrew Jackson, commanding a small army of regulars and militia.

Jackson acted upon the theory that he was expected not only to chastise the Indians but to take possession of Florida for the United States. For this assumption he later claimed to have had verbal authority from Monroe through an intermediary—a claim that Monroe firmly denied.[9] With or without

the President's secret assent, Jackson seized and occupied the Spanish town and fort of St. Marks and after burning a hostile Indian town from which the warriors escaped, turned his attention to Pensacola, seat of government of the Spanish remnant of West Florida. On the excuse that the Spanish were harboring hostile savages, Jackson took possession of the town and fortifications, deposed the governor, seized the archives, appointed one of his officers civil and military governor of West Florida, and directed him to enforce the revenue laws of the United States at the port of Pensacola. As if this affront to Spain were not enough, he had executed—after court-martial—two British subjects, Robert Ambrister and Alexander Arbuthnot, who had fallen into his hands at St. Marks, and whom he charged with being in conspiracy with the hostile Indians.

Well satisfied with his work, the happy warrior returned to Tennessee. In his report to the Secretary of War (John C. Calhoun), he justified his actions on the ground of "the immutable principles . . . of self defence" and urged that in the interest of security the United States hold the Gulf coast in preference to an indefensible "imaginary line"—the 31st parallel.

Reports of Jackson's aggressive course in Florida, accompanied by violent protests from Onis, the Spanish minister, created consternation in Monroe's cabinet. Fortunately for Jackson, he found a warm supporter in the Secretary of State. In opposition to Calhoun and others, Adams insisted that Jackson's acts must be sustained. Rejecting Spain's demands that Jackson be punished or disavowed, Adams took the offensive. He justified Jackson's actions as necessitated by self-defense. He denounced as unfriendly the conduct of the governor of West Florida and the commandant of St. Marks and demanded that those officials instead of Jackson be punished. Pensacola, he said, would be turned over to a proper Spanish official; St. Marks to a force competent to hold it against Indian attack. In a later note, Adams presented Spain with an ultimatum: let her either place in Florida

---

8. Monroe acted under authority of an act of Congress of January 15, 1811, which empowered the President to take possession of any part of Florida in the event of an attempt to occupy it by any third government.

9. Jackson had written Monroe that if the President desired possession of all Florida, this could be accomplished "without implicating the government." Let the President simply send him word to that effect through Congressman J. Rhea of Tennessee. Jackson asserted later that he had received the suggested go-ahead signal through Mr. Rhea. Monroe denied having sent such a message or even having read Jackson's letter in time to have acted on it. Most historians have credited Monroe's account rather than Jackson's. There is considerable literature on the "Rhea letter" controversy.

a force sufficient for the maintenance of order and the fulfillment of her obligations, or cede the province to the United States.[10]

Even before perusing this forceful argument, the Spanish government had resolved to make whatever concessions were necessary to reach an understanding with the United States. Fear of war with the United States, failure of efforts to get assurances of support from England, France, or Russia, and a desire to keep its hands free to put down rebellion in its American colonies induced Spain to give in.

In October 1818 the Spanish consented to reopen the boundary negotiations, which they had broken off upon news of Jackson's exploits. They were willing to cede the Floridas if the United States would agree to a satisfactory western boundary for Louisiana. This was achieved after months of negotiation in an agreement by which the United States surrendered whatever claim it had to Texas in exchange for Spanish claims on the Pacific coast north of California. The "transcontinental treaty," as it has been called, was signed on February 22, 1819. By its terms the King of Spain ceded to the United States "all the territories which belong to him, situated to the eastward of the Mississippi, known by the name of East and West Florida." This wording was so devised as to permit each party to adhere to its opinion as to whether Florida west of the Perdido had been included in the Louisiana purchase. Each government renounced its damage claims, and those of its citizens or subjects, against the other, and the United States agreed to satisfy the claims of its citizens against Spain to an amount not to exceed five million dollars.

On the west, the international boundary followed the western bank of the Sabine from the Gulf to the 32nd parallel; thence it ran due north to the southern bank of the Red, which it followed to the meridian of 100° west longitude, thence by that meridian to the

south bank of the Arkansas and along that bank to the source of the river; from the source of the Arkansas it ran north to the 42nd parallel, which it followed to the Pacific.

Despite some mutterings over the surrender of Texas, the United States Senate gave its prompt and unanimous approval to the treaty, and Monroe ratified it on February 25. The Spanish King, Ferdinand VII, however, delayed ratification not only beyond the period of six months specified in the treaty, but for a full year and a half. A dispute had arisen over the validity of certain Spanish land grants in Florida which, if recognized, would have absorbed all the vacant land in the ceded territory. This difficulty was settled to the satisfaction of the United States, but only over the resistance of influential individuals at the Spanish court. More serious was the attempt of Spain to exact from the United States, as a condition of ratification, a promise not to recognize the independence of Spain's revolting colonies. Such a pledge was firmly refused. A revolution in Spain early in 1820 compelled Ferdinand to accept a liberal constitution, which added a new hurdle to the treaty's course: approval by the legislative body, or Cortes. This was finally given, and in October 1820 the King ratified the treaty. The Senate again consented, and ratifications were exchanged in Washington on February 22, 1821, exactly two years from the date of signature.

John Quincy Adams and Manifest Destiny

In the mind of John Quincy Adams, the treaties of 1818 and 1819 with Great Britain and Spain, praiseworthy though they were, were but steps in the inevitable absorption of all North America by the United States. That such absorption should occur was, he remarked in a cabinet meeting in 1819, "as much a law of nature . . . as that the Mississippi should flow to the sea." It was "a physical, moral, and political absurdity" that European colonies "should exist permanently

---

10. In his second note to Spain, Adams also defended Jackson's execution of Ambrister and Arbuthnot. The British government had not made an issue of their case.

contiguous to a great, powerful, and rapidly growing nation." Thus Adams was an early expounder of the faith that was later called "manifest destiny." [11]

The elimination of Spain's claims to the Pacific coast north of 42° was soon followed by a similar limitation of the Russian claim. The Russian government, in 1821, put forward a claim to exclusive possession of the Pacific coast of North America north of 51° north latitude. Inasmuch as this claim was resisted by both Great Britain and the United States, Secretary Adams proposed that the two governments negotiate jointly with Russia a treaty fixing the southern boundary of Russian America. The British government, however, took exception to an accompanying statement in which Adams denied that "any European nation" had the right to practice "colonial principles of exclusion . . . upon any part of the Northwest Coast of America," and refused to join with the United States in the negotiations. By two separate treaties, therefore, with the United States in 1824 and Great Britain in 1825, Russia agreed to set up no establishment south of 54°40′ while the other powers promised to set up none north of that line.[12] Thus between 42° and 54°40′, all claimants to Oregon other than Great Britain and the United States had been eliminated.

The Florida peninsula, now safely in the possession of the United States, was like a finger of destiny pointing to the island of Cuba. John Quincy Adams, like Jefferson before him, was convinced that the island must one day be annexed. This was not a task for the immediate future. "But," said he, "there are laws of political as well as of physical gravitation; and if an apple severed by the tempest from its native tree cannot choose but fall to the ground, Cuba, forcibly disjoined from its own unnatural connection with Spain, and incapable of self-support, can gravitate only towards the North American Union, which by the same law of nature cannot cast her off from its bosom." [13]

Adams' metaphor was called forth by one of the rumors, continually current from 1817 to 1825, that Spain was about to dispose of Cuba, and perhaps Puerto Rico as well, to either Great Britain or France. While Adams did not wish the island immediately for the United States, he viewed with alarm the prospect that it might pass from Spain to a stronger power. The apple should remain on the tree until the day of its ripening. Consequently he instructed the American minister in Madrid that he should "not conceal from the Spanish government the repugnance of the United States to the transfer of the Island of Cuba by Spain to any other power." Two years later, when Adams was President and Henry Clay Secretary of State, the latter reiterated Adams' declaration with more vigor and finality. "We could not consent," wrote Clay, "to the occupation of those islands [Cuba and Puerto Rico] by any other European power than Spain under any contingency whatever."

The "non-transfer principle," thus stated by Adams and Clay with reference to Cuba and Puerto Rico,[14] was in the course of time to become a regular feature of American foreign policy. It was, in fact, to be associated with the Monroe Doctrine, which had been formulated two years earlier.[15]

---

11. See pp. 106–7.
12. The United States had first proposed 55° as the dividing line, this being the southern limit of a grant by the Czar to the Russian American Company in 1799; but when it was pointed out that this line would cut off the southern end of Prince of Wales Island, which was otherwise Russian, the American minister agreed to accept 54°40′.

13. *The Writings of John Quincy Adams,* W. C. Ford, ed., 7 vols. (New York: The Macmillan Company, 1913–1917), 7: 372–73.
14. Congress, by a resolution of January 15, 1811, had already stated the same principle with reference to the Floridas.
15. J. A. Logan, Jr., *No Transfer: An American Security Principle* (New Haven: Yale University Press, 1961).

Atlantic Ocean

Claimed by U.S. as
part of Louisiana;
occupied 1810-1813.

Gulf of Mexico

Lake of
the Woods

Mississippi River

Red R.

Missouri River

Platte R.

Arkansas River

Red River

Sabine R.

Trinity R.

Brazos R.

Colorado R.

Pecos R.

Rio Grande

100°

49°

CONTINENTAL DIVIDE

42°

Pacific Ocean

LOUISIANA
AND THE BOUNDARY TREATIES
OF 1818 AND 1819

Natural boundary of Louisiana.

Claimed by U.S. as part of Louisiana but relinquished
by Treaty 1819.

Claimed by U.S. on principle of "contiguity"; Spanish claims
acquired 1819; joint occupation with Great Britain,
1818-1846.

Louisiana with northern and western limits as defined in 1818 and 1819.

9

The Monroe Doctrine and Latin American Independence

Of all Presidents of the United States from 1789 to the 1960's, James Monroe alone was honored by having his name attached to a sacred national dogma—the Monroe Doctrine. There is no Washington, Jefferson, Jackson, Lincoln, or Wilson Doctrine, and the so-called Truman and Eisenhower Doctrines of 1947 and 1957 failed to capture the imagination or affection of the American people. The Monroe Doctrine, therefore, stands alone. Rarely, during the last one hundred years, has any American admitted doubt concerning this article of faith. It has been invoked by isolationists on the one hand and internationalists on the other. In the famous fight over American participation in the League of Nations,[1] opponents denounced such participation as contrary to the Monroe Doctrine, while Woodrow Wilson praised the League as providing a "Monroe Doctrine for the world." Neither side ventured to repudiate the Doctrine or to question its relevance to American policy decisions a century after its enunciation.

It seems safe to say that the Monroe Doctrine owes its long-continued popularity to the circumstance that it was the first official and public pronouncement of a deep-seated American belief—the belief that the Atlantic and Pacific Oceans divide the world so effectively into distinct hemispheres that the nations of the New World should be able to insulate themselves from the quarrels, the interferences, and the colonizing ambitions of the Old World powers. From this belief stem both the neutrality policy of the United States and the Monroe Doctrine. Insofar as the belief meant American abstention from European quarrels, it spelled neutrality. Insofar as it meant exclusion from the Americas of the political interference and the colonizing activity of Europe, it was set forth in President Monroe's message to Congress of December 2, 1823.

The "doctrine" expounded by Monroe on that occasion was not his spontaneous invention. In the formulation of one of its essential features, the noncolonization principle, Secretary of State John Quincy Adams had played a more important role than the President. On

1. See Chapter 29.

an earlier occasion, President Washington had declared in his Farewell Address (1796): "Europe has a set of primary interests, which to us have none or a very remote relation." Thomas Jefferson, writing in 1813 of the independence movement in the American colonies of Spain, observed:

> But in whatever government they end, they will be *American* governments, no longer to be involved in the never-ceasing broils of Europe. The European nations constitute a separate division of the globe; their localities make them a part of a distinct system; they have a set of interests of their own in which it is our business never to engage ourselves. America has a hemisphere to itself. It must have its separate system of interests; which must not be subordinated to those of Europe. . . .

President Monroe's ideas were similar to those of Washington and Jefferson. He was led to state them as he did by specific situations that confronted him in 1823. Perhaps it will be best to see first just what he said in his celebrated message, and then to look at the circumstances that called forth his pronouncements.

What Monroe Said

After describing recent negotiations with Russia concerning her claims to territory on the Pacific coast of North America, the President said:

> . . . In the discussions to which this interest has given rise . . . the occasion has been judged proper for asserting, as a principle in which the rights and interests of the United States are involved, that the American continents, by the free and independent condition which they have assumed and maintain, are henceforth not to be considered as subjects for future colonization by any European powers. . . .

This statement embodies what is generally called the "noncolonization" principle.

Later in the message, after alluding to the recent suppression of liberal movements in Spain and Italy, Monroe stated what has since been called the "noninterference" principle.

> . . . Of events in that quarter of the globe [he said], with which we have so much intercourse and from which we derive our origin, we have always been anxious and interested spectators. The citizens of the United States cherish sentiments the most friendly in favor of the liberty and happiness of their fellow-men on that side of the Atlantic. In the wars of the European powers in matters relating to themselves we have never taken any part, nor does it comport with our policy so to do. It is only when our rights are invaded or seriously menaced that we resent injuries or make preparation for our defense. With the movements in this hemisphere we are of necessity more immediately connected, and by causes which must be obvious to all enlightened and impartial observers. The political system of the allied powers is essentially different in this respect from that of America. This difference proceeds from that which exists in their respective Governments; and to the defense of our own, which has been achieved by the loss of so much blood and treasure, and matured by the wisdom of their most enlightened citizens, and under which we have enjoyed unexampled felicity, this whole nation is devoted. We owe it, therefore, to candor and to the amicable relations existing between the United States and those powers to declare that we should consider any attempt on their part to extend their system to any portion of this hemisphere as dangerous to our peace and safety. With the existing colonies or dependencies of any European power we have not interfered and shall not interfere. But with the Governments who have declared their independence and maintained it, and whose independence we have, on great consideration and on just principles, acknowledged, we could not view any interposition for the purpose of oppressing them, or controlling in any other manner their destiny, by any European power in any other light than as the manifestation of an unfriendly disposition toward the United States. In the war between those new Governments and Spain we declared our neutrality at the time of their recognition, and to this we have adhered, and shall continue to adhere, provided no change shall occur which, in the judgment of the competent authorities of this Government, shall make a

corresponding change on the part of the United States indispensable to their security.

The Origin of Noncolonization

The noncolonization principle was the brain-child of John Quincy Adams, Monroe's Secretary of State. Adams had a strong distaste for the presence of European colonial establishments in the neighborhood of the United States. He disliked the commercial exclusiveness with which colonizing powers still surrounded their dependencies, distrusted monarchical neighbors, and desired, in the words of a recent authority, to "keep North America open as a preserve for the republic of the United States to expand over at leisure." Thus noncolonization was "a principle of territorial containment." [2]

The ostensible occasion for putting forth the noncolonization principle at this time was an inclination on the part of Russia to enlarge her holdings upon the Pacific coast of North America. Russian traders had found lodgment on the northwest coast since the voyages of Vitus Bering between 1727 and 1741, but not until 1799 was the Russian American Company chartered, with exclusive trading rights and jurisdiction along the coast as far south as 55° north latitude. The company not only planted settlements north of that line, but in 1812 set up the trading post of Fort Ross on Bodega Bay only a few miles north of San Francisco Bay. The American government seems never to have been seriously concerned about Fort Ross. It was alarmed, however, by an imperial ukase of September 1821, by which the Russian government extended its exclusive claims down the coast to 51° and forbade all non-Russian ships to come within one hundred Italian miles of the American coast north of that latitude. Discussion of this new claim with Baron Tuyll, the Russian minister in Washington, gave Adams an opportunity to state the idea that he had been turning over in his mind for several years. The

United States, he told Tuyll in July 1823, would assert the principle "that the American continents are no longer subjects for *any* new European colonial establishments." A few days later he embodied the same idea in instructions to the United States ministers in both Russia and Great Britain, stating it even more emphatically to Richard Rush in London than to Henry Middleton in St. Petersburg.

Thus, though the Russian ukase provided the occasion for the launching of the noncolonization principle, the statement was perhaps aimed less directly at Russia than at Great Britain, whose rivalry in territorial expansion Adams feared more than he feared Russia's. It seems likely, furthermore, that Adams was here indulging in an early instance of the game of twisting the British lion's tail for political purposes. Adams was an active candidate for the succession to the presidency in the impending contest of 1824. Political enemies were charging him with having betrayed American, and especially western, interests to Great Britain and Spain in the treaties of 1818 and 1819. A forthright statement forbidding further European colonization not only in North America but in "the American continents" might be useful in silencing such criticism.[3]

That Adams, or the government that he represented, had any *right* to veto further colonial enterprises in the great areas of North America that still remained unoccupied and unexplored can hardly be maintained. Nor was Adams himself consistent in his position. Two years before, he had asserted to the British minister that Great Britain had no rights on the northwest coast; and only the arguments of his cabinet colleagues had restrained him from telling Tuyll that Russia had no right to *any* territory in North America. Yet in the treaty of 1818 he had in effect acknowledged the equality of British with American rights in the Oregon country; he was willing, in 1824 and later, to divide that region with the British at the 49th parallel; and in 1824 he accepted the Russian claim to exclusive

2. Frederick Merk, *Albert Gallatin and the Oregon Problem, A Study in Anglo-American Diplomacy* (Cambridge: Harvard University Press, 1950), p. 28.

3. Merk, *Gallatin and Oregon*, pp. 28–34. For the treaties of 1818 and 1819, see Chapter 8.

sovereignty north of 54°40′. Thus Adams himself did not attempt to enforce the noncolonization dogma. No European government ever recognized it. "There is room to doubt its wisdom as a diplomatic move," writes Dexter Perkins, "and a harsh critic might even go so far as to describe it as a barren gesture." [4]

A summary of the negotiations with Russia, supplied by Adams and using almost the exact language of his statement to Tuyll, was incorporated verbatim by Monroe in his message of December 2, 1823, and thus took its place as an integral part of the Monroe Doctrine.

The Origin of Noninterference

The second fundamental principle of the Doctrine—the announced opposition of the United States to European interference with the independent nations of the New World—has a more complicated origin. Immediately, it was the American answer to a British proposal for a joint Anglo-American declaration of such opposition. The situation that produced the British proposal was itself the product of two separate trains of events, one in Europe, the other in America.

The destinies of Europe, after the overthrow of Napoleon in 1815, were guided for some years by an alliance of the four powers that had made the chief contribution to his defeat—Russia, Prussia, Austria, and Great Britain. At Vienna in 1815, the four agreed to use their joint efforts to prevent France from again becoming the plaything of "revolutionary principles" and also to hold further meetings from time to time to consider measures that might prove "most salutary for the repose and prosperity of Nations and for the maintenance of the Peace of Europe." The members of the Quadruple Alliance thus formed met in a series of congresses for the purpose stated—at Aix-la-Chappelle (1818), Troppau (1820), Laibach (1821), and Verona (1822). At all except the first, they found serious work to do, for the liberal spirit, suppressed by the settlement at Vienna, was again raising its head. Liberal revolutions in the kingdoms of Naples, Piedmont, and Spain compelled the sovereigns of those states to accept constitutions that rigidly limited their prerogatives. It was this liberal spirit that the Quadruple Alliance, under the leadership of Prince Metternich, Austrian Foreign Minister and Chancellor, was resolved to crush. At the congresses of Troppau and Laibach the powers commissioned Austria to send troops into Italy to suppress the uprisings there; at Verona they sent French armies into Spain and thereby suppressed the liberal constitution of 1820 and restored Ferdinand VII to his former status as an absolute monarch.

During these proceedings, the composition of the Quadruple Alliance had suffered an unannounced change. France under the restored Bourbon sovereign, Louis XVIII, had shown such a strong disposition to reliable behavior that it had been virtually accepted into the alliance. England, on the other hand, though under a conservative Tory government, had protested repeatedly against the armed interventions practiced in Italy and Spain. She thus, in effect, drifted out of the alliance, and France took her place. When, having restored Ferdinand to power in Spain, the continental statesmen began to talk of restoring his authority also in Spain's former American colonies, England went completely into opposition and sought cooperation from the United States.[5]

4. Perkins, *History of the Monroe Doctrine,* p. 32.

5. The work of the Quadruple Alliance is often attributed to the Holy Alliance as if the two were synonymous. The Holy Alliance treaty, which originated in the brain of Czar Alexander I of Russia, was a harmless declaration to the general effect that the signatory sovereigns would be guided by Christian principles in their relations with one another and with their subjects. It was signed by all the sovereigns of Europe except the Pope, the Sultan of Turkey, and the British Prince Regent. The United States was invited to adhere but sent a polite declination. The original signers were the Czar, the Emperor of Austria, and the King of Prussia. Since these three sovereigns were also members of the Quadruple Alliance, it is not surprising that contemporary writers and later historians confused the two alliances. In reality the Holy Alliance was in the clouds, the Quadruple Alliance very much of this world.

The Spanish colonies that Ferdinand would have liked to recover had been in the process of establishing their independence since 1810. Napoleon's attempt (1808) to set a French king on the throne of Spain had, in their eyes, absolved them from any allegiance to that throne. The restoration of Ferdinand had done nothing to tempt them back, and by 1822 Spanish rule had been effectively overthrown in all the mainland colonies from Mexico to Argentina and Chile. The elimination of Spain's monopoly of the trade of her colonies had been economically beneficial to Great Britain and, to a minor extent, to the United States. For that reason, neither of them wished to see Spanish rule restored. Both had other reasons, however, for frowning upon any such intervention as rumor was forecasting. Great Britain feared that France might take advantage of Spain's necessity to appropriate some of the colonies for herself. Americans felt a natural sympathy for colonial populations who had won the fight for independence as they themselves had done a scant forty years earlier. They rejoiced at the success of the Spanish Americans and would have resented any attempt by the reactionary powers of Europe to restore the despotic rule of Spain.

The Problem of Recognizing Spain's Revolted Colonies

The United States, moreover, had just recognized the independence of Colombia, Mexico, the United Provinces of Rio de la Plata (Argentina), and Chile, and other recognitions would follow in due course. Recognition had come only after a suitable period of watchful waiting. The United States government had taken an interest from the beginning in the independence movement south of the border. Emissaries of the new governments were received cordially, though unofficially, in Washington, and "agents for seamen and commerce" (for a while, regular consuls) were sent to watch over American interests in the rebellious countries. When the European war ended and Spain undertook by force to recover control in America, the United States adopted a position of neutrality between the parties, thus allowing colonial vessels the privilege of frequenting United States ports and procuring war materials and other supplies. Henry Clay, speaker of the House of Representatives, called for immediate recognition of the new governments. Exclaiming, "Let us become real and true Americans, and place ourselves at the head of the American System," he attacked the President and Secretary of State, Monroe and Adams, for timidity and subservience to Europe in their postponement of recognition.

Monroe and Adams had good reason for hesitation. Heretofore the recognition by one power of the rebellious subjects of another had been but a prelude to war. The government of France had recognized the independence of the United States only when ready to go to war with England to support it. The British government had accepted the challenge and later had seized upon an unauthorized draft treaty with the United States subscribed to by a Dutch agent as an excuse for making war upon the Netherlands. The United States now had no intention of going to war with Spain in behalf of the revolted colonies, but there was a chance that Spain, following the British precedent, might regard recognition as an act of war and that, if so, she might be aided by the powers of the Quadruple Alliance. That was a chance that Henry Clay might be willing to take, but not Adams or Monroe.

Under what conditions could recognition be granted to a state that had established itself by revolution, without giving just offense to the parent state? International law had as yet no clear answer to that question, and the government in Washington had to make its rules as it went. For the recognition of revolutionary governments, Jefferson had stated the thesis, in 1792, during the French Revolution, that "It accords with our principles to acknolege [*sic*] any government to be rightful which is formed by the will of the nation substantially declared." "The only thing essential is the will of the nation," he said on another occasion. This assertion left open the question of how "the will of the nation" was to be ascertained. Henry Clay, in 1818, proclaimed that the essential test for recognition was and had been a more practical one. "We have constantly proceeded on the principle," he announced, "that the government *de facto* [in fact] is that we can alone notice. . . . As soon as stability and order are maintained, no matter by whom, we have always considered and ought to consider the actual as the true government."

Clay came very close to stating what was to become the standard American doctrine of recognition, but Adams added some important qualifications. The government of a state or a colony in rebellion might properly be recognized, he said, "when independence is established as a matter of fact so as to leave the chance of the opposite party to recover their dominion utterly desperate." But he also insisted upon certain standards of behavior in the government of the new state: it must carry out its responsibilities and duties as a member of the international community. Complaining of the lawless acts of privateers carrying letters of marque from the unrecognized Latin American governments, Adams wrote that those governments "cannot claim the rights & prerogatives of independent States, without conforming to the duties by which independent States are bound."

In these discussions, brought on by the Latin American wars of independence, can be found the principles of the permanent recognition policy of the United States. A government that has come to power by revolution (whether in an old or a new state) may properly be recognized when it (1) is effectively exercising the powers of government, (2) shows promise of stability, and (3) shows willingness and ability to carry out its international obligations.[6]

The problem of Monroe and Adams was to ascertain, first, whether these requirements were met by the new Latin American governments, and, second, whether Spain and her European friends would resent an act of recognition to the point of taking hostile action against the United States.

In 1817, when Clay began his campaign for recognition, victory for the revolutionists was still far from certain and the quality of the new governments was open to doubt. Commissioners sent by Monroe to Buenos Aires and elsewhere in South America disagreed among themselves as to whether the situation would justify recognition. Nevertheless, Adams, at Monroe's suggestion, inquired of Great Britain, France, and Russia whether they were disposed to join the United States in recognizing the new governments. When the responses were negative, the Washington statesmen thought it best to postpone action until the new governments could give better evidence of permanence and stability.[7]

By 1822 military victories over Spanish arms in South America had made it obvious that Spain, unaided, could never restore her rule on the mainland. The emancipated colonies were making encouraging progress toward orderly government, and some of them, at least, had put an end to privateering under their authority. It seemed unlikely that recog-

---

6. At various times, the United States has also insisted upon approval of a new government by popular or legislative suffrage as a prerequisite to recognition. Such was the implication of Jefferson's dictum that in order to deserve recognition a government must be "formed by the will of the nation substantially declared." For some twenty-five years after the Civil War it was customary to require that a revolutionary government (as in Latin America) be approved by either an election or an act of the legislature prior to recognition. See Julius Goebel, Jr., *The Recognition Policy of the United States* (New York: Columbia University Press, 1915), chap. 8. Woodrow Wilson inaugurated a similar policy in 1913. Today such a policy is generally condemned as intervention in the affairs of the other state, though the appearance of communist governments maneuvered into power by outside influence, has raised new questions.

7. It has been generally supposed that Adams postponed recognition in order to avoid offending Spain during the negotiation of the Florida treaty (see Chapter 8). The postponement seems to have been due rather to the persistence of an unsatisfactory situation in Latin America, and recognition did not come about till more than a year after the treaty had been ratified. See A. P. Whitaker, *The United States and the Independence of Latin America, 1800–1830* (Baltimore: The Johns Hopkins Press, 1941), pp. 270–74.

nition would lead to war with Spain or her European backers. The time had come, thought Monroe and Adams, to recognize the new governments to the southward without awaiting the concurrence of the powers of Europe. A special message of March 8, 1822, conveyed that opinion to Congress, which responded with an appropriation to cover the expenses of diplomatic missions to such of the American nations as the President might deem proper. By the end of January 1823, accordingly, the United States had entered into formal diplomatic relations with Colombia (comprising not only modern Colombia, but also Ecuador and Venezuela), Mexico, Chile, and the United Provinces of Rio de la Plata. Having officially recognized these states as independent sovereignties, the American government was even less sympathetic than formerly to any plan for the suppression of their independence by force.

Canning and Monroe Warn the European Allies

Such was the situation in the Americas in August 1823, when reports reached George Canning, British Foreign Secretary, that when France had completed her work of intervention in Spain, a new congress of the powers would probably be convoked to deal with the colonial question. Canning had already, in the preceding March, warned France that any attempt on her part to appropriate any of the Spanish colonies would be opposed by Great Britain. He now suggested to Richard Rush, the United States minister in London, that either by signing a convention or by an exchange of notes, the British and American governments signify their disapproval of any attempt by the European powers to restore the rule of Spain in her lost colonies. Great Britain, he said, subscribed to the following principles, which he believed to be also accepted by the United States:

1. We conceive the recovery of the Colonies by Spain to be hopeless.

2. We conceive the question of the recognition of them, as Independent States, to be one of time and circumstances.

3. We are, however, by no means disposed to throw any impediment in the way of an arrangement between them, and the mother country by amicable negotiations.

4. We aim not at the possession of any portion of them ourselves.

5. We could not see any portion of them transferred to any other Power, with indifference.

If any European power, Canning added, contemplated the forcible subjugation of the former colonies on behalf of Spain or in her name, or the acquisition of any of them for itself, a joint declaration by Great Britain and the United States of the principles indicated "would be at once the most effectual and the least offensive mode of intimating our joint disapprobation of such projects."

Since Great Britain alone, with her unchallenged control of the seas, would have been able to veto any attempt of the continental powers to restore Spanish rule in America, why should Canning have sought the cooperation of the United States? It seems obvious, in the first place, that such cooperation, even though the United States of 1823 was less than second-rate in naval and military power, would have bolstered England's diplomatic position. But scholars have suggested further reasons for Canning's proposal. Acceptance by the United States of Canning's fourth principle would be agreeable to Canning as a disclaimer of any American intent to acquire Cuba. It has been conjectured, furthermore, that Canning hoped, through courting American cooperation in the international field, to secure a continuance of a tariff-free American market for British textiles and ironware—a hope, however, which received a rebuff in protectionist proposals in Monroe's famous message.[8]

Rush had no instructions that would have empowered him to join with Canning in such a statement. He was, nevertheless, greatly at-

8. George Dangerfield, *The Era of Good Feelings* (New York: Harcourt, Brace & World, Inc., 1952), pp. 291–92, 319.

tracted by the proposal. Could he have secured from Canning an immediate recognition of the independence of the Spanish American states, he would have been ready to make a statement on behalf of his government that it would "not remain inactive under an attack upon the independence of those states by the Holy [Quadruple] Alliance," leaving it for his government to disavow his action if it saw fit. But Canning, whose policy, though backed by the Prime Minister, Lord Liverpool, was opposed by other cabinet colleagues and by the King, was not ready to risk recognition; [9] nor was Rush willing to accept a mere promise of future recognition, which Canning tentatively offered. Rush, therefore, could do no more than report the negotiations to his government and await instructions.

Adams was at home, in Quincy, Massachusetts, when Rush's account of the momentous conversation reached Washington. Monroe sought the advice of the two living Virginian ex-Presidents, Jefferson and Madison. Should the United States join with Great Britain in the proposed declaration? Both elder statesmen answered affirmatively. Madison even proposed that the "avowed disapprobation" be extended to cover the French intervention in Spain and that the two governments issue also a declaration in behalf of the Greeks, then engaged in their war for independence against Turkey.

John Quincy Adams was yet to be heard from. In November, when Monroe's cabinet discussed Canning's proposal, the Secretary of State frankly opposed joint action with Great Britain. "It would be more candid, as well as more dignified," he argued, "to avow our principles explicitly to Russia and France, than to come in as a cock-boat in the wake of the British man-of-war." Adams' ideas prevailed. Rush was instructed to decline Canning's proposal for a joint declaration, though at the same time assuring the Foreign Secretary that the United States accepted all of his stated principles except the second, which left the question of recognition to "time and circumstances." On this point, said Adams, "we considered that the people of these emancipated Colonies, were, *of right* independent of all other nations, and that it was our duty so to acknowledge them." Adams made no reservation on the fourth point, though he suspected its purpose in relation to Cuba. He added, on behalf of the United States,

> that we could not see with indifference, any attempt by one or more powers of Europe to restore those new states to the crown of Spain, or to deprive them, in any manner, whatever of the freedom and independence which they have acquired.

The note did not close the door entirely to the possibility of a joint declaration,[10] should an emergency make it expedient, but the decision upon such a declaration was reserved to the Washington authorities, who would, said Adams, "according to the principles of our Government, and in the forms prescribed by our Constitution, cheerfully join in any act by which we may contribute to support the cause of human freedom, and the Independence of the South American Nations."

It was President Monroe who proposed that the American position be announced to the whole world through a presidential message instead of being buried in diplomatic correspondence. The notes for his annual message, which he read to his cabinet, included a vigorous statement of the noninterference principle; they also expressed disapproval of the French intervention in Spain and sympathy with the Greek revolt. To these latter expressions Adams objected. "The ground I wish to take," he said, "is that of earnest remonstrance against the interference of European powers by force in South America, but to disclaim all interference on our part in Europe; to make an American cause, and adhere inflexibly to that." The President yielded. The message, while branding European intervention in the New World as "dangerous to

9. Bradford Perkins, *Castlereagh and Adams: England and America, 1812–1823* (Berkeley: University of California Press, 1964), pp. 321–23.

10. This point is well developed in G. W. McGee, "The Monroe Doctrine—A Stopgap Measure," *Mississippi Valley Historical Review,* 38 (1951), 233–50.

our peace and safety" and as "the manifestation of an unfriendly disposition toward the United States," likewise disclaimed on the part of the United States the taking of any part "in the wars of the European powers *in matters relating to themselves.*"

The last phrase is here italicized because it left a door wide open for American participation in the wars of Europe, if and when such wars should invade or seriously menace American rights or American security. When this passage was written, the Treaty of Ghent was less than eight years old. Monroe, who had been Secretary of State and for a short time Secretary of War during the War of 1812, had not forgotten that the wars of the European powers were not always concerned solely with "matters relating to themselves." They could endanger the rights, even the security, of the United States.

Effects of the Message in Europe

To James Monroe and the members of his cabinet, who concurred in the content and phraseology of his message to Congress of December 2, 1823, the threat of European intervention in America was real—to all, at least, except Adams, who was convinced that it would not be tried. The British warnings had been reinforced by a communication from the Russian Foreign Office exulting over the successes of the Quadruple Alliance in Europe and declaring it to be the Czar's policy to guarantee "the tranquillity of all the states of which the civilized world is composed"—an expression which, the Russian minister informed Adams, comprehended "the supremacy of Spain over the revolted colonies." The warning against intervention was therefore appropriate. For a young and weak nation thus to challenge the four principal powers of continental Europe appeared audacious, but Monroe was not bluffing; he had an "ace-in-the-hole"—the British navy. For while there was no agreement, not even an "understanding," with Great Britain, Canning had revealed enough to Rush to assure Monroe that

Great Britain would oppose armed intervention in the Americas.

What neither Monroe nor Adams knew was that Canning had already served an ultimatum on France and received a satisfactory response. Discouraged by Rush's insistence upon conditions that he was unwilling to meet, Canning had approached the Prince de Polignac, the French ambassador in London, and in a series of conferences in October had received from him assurances that France had no intention or desire to appropriate to herself any of the Spanish possessions in America, nor "any design of acting against the Colonies by force of arms." With the substance of these assurances embodied in a memorandum, Canning had lost interest in obtaining cooperation from the United States; he no longer needed it to secure British objectives, and he dropped the matter with an abruptness that shook American confidence in his good faith.

After the secret Canning-Polignac conversations, there was no danger that the Quadruple Alliance powers would intervene by force in Latin America, if, indeed, any such danger had ever existed. Modern scholarship, especially the work of Dexter Perkins, has shown that no one of the four governments involved—French, Russian, Austrian, and Prussian—had any matured plan for the use of force against Spain's former colonies, and that Prince Metternich, most influential of Quadruple Alliance statesmen, was realist enough to know that the restoration of Spain's rule in the New World was impossible.[11] Under these circumstances, it can hardly be supposed that a congress, had one been held, could have agreed upon a policy of force in America. Certainly after the Canning-Polignac conversations in October, such an outcome was unthinkable.

Unknown to Monroe and Adams, therefore, a practically nonexistent danger had been completely dissipated by Canning's warning to Polignac nearly two months before Monroe's message went to Congress. The message,

11. Dexter Perkins, *The Monroe Doctrine, 1823–1826* (Cambridge: Harvard University Press, 1927), chap. 4.

consequently, had little or no practical effect upon the course of events in Europe. Canning was probably exaggerating its effectiveness when he declared that the proposed congress on the "colonial question" "was broken in all its limbs before, but the President's speech [*sic*] gives it the *coup de grace*."

From the courts of the continental powers, the message elicited considerable unofficial abuse—it was described as "blustering," "monstrous," "arrogant," "haughty," and "peremptory," [12]—but no official protests. The United States was still a small power, and its attitude on international questions was of minor significance. Continental reaction to Monroe's message may be summarized as holding that his declaration was impertinent but unimportant.

George Canning, whose proposals to Rush had led to the inclusion of the noninterference principle in Monroe's message, was understandably annoyed at Monroe's independent pronouncement—a pronouncement that rested upon a knowledge of Canning's position but gave him no credit for it. Monroe, he felt, had stolen a march upon him and was courting the favor of the Latin American republics as the principal protector of their independence. To establish British priority in that role, Canning published the Polignac memorandum of October 1823, which showed that the British government had anticipated the United States in warning the continental powers against intervention. Later, after Great Britain had extended recognition to the new governments in December 1824, Canning boasted, "I called the New World into existence to redress the balance of the Old." By such claims, and in more direct ways, he sought to undermine the prestige of the United States with the Latin American governments and to establish England as their first and most powerful friend.

The other basic dogma of Monroe's message, the non-colonization principle, contributed further to Canning's pique at the United States. With vast portions of North America still unoccupied, Great Britain could not assent to the right of the United States to veto all further colonizing enterprises in that area. For this reason, Canning refused to join the United States in tripartite negotiations with Russia over claims on the northwest coast and took an unyielding stand toward the United States on the Oregon boundary question.[13] In the course of time, Great Britain and the United States would come to see eye to eye on the Monroe Doctrine, but the initial effect of Monroe's message upon Anglo-American relations was irritating rather than soothing.

As for Russia, against whose expanded territorial claims the noncolonization principle had been ostensibly directed, she readily consented, in separate treaties with the United States (1824) and Great Britain (1825), to limit her territorial claims in North America to the area north of latitude 54°40′. This she would have done, it seems safe to say, even had she never been confronted with the sweeping assertion put forth by John Quincy Adams.

The Reception of the Message in America

Monroe's message was received with some enthusiasm by the press of the United States. In Congress there were both praise and criticism. A resolution of endorsement, introduced by Henry Clay in the House of Representatives, never came to a vote. The principles of the message remained, therefore, a simple pronouncement of the President of the United States, without legal standing at home or in the international community.

In the Latin American states, supposedly the beneficiaries of the message, liberal and republican elements applauded the American President's declaration, but they soon discovered that the United States was little prepared to back up words with action. Five of the new

---

12. Perkins, *The Monroe Doctrine, 1823–1826,* pp. 161–84, 223–40, analyzes the reception of Monroe's message in Europe.

13. See pp. 73–74.

governments, Argentina, Brazil, Chile, Colombia, and Mexico, applied to the authorities in Washington for either treaties of alliance or promises of assistance against possible European intervention. All received negative replies. Of special interest was John Quincy Adams' reply (August 6, 1824) to the Colombian minister in Washington, since it plainly meant that without the support of Great Britain the United States could not undertake to defend the Americas against the Quadruple Alliance. Thus Latin American liberals learned what their conservative and monarchist rivals had known from the beginning, that the chief bulwark of their newly won independence was the British navy, not the pronouncement of an American President.

The United States Renounces New World Leadership: The Panama Congress

Both the caution of the United States and the influential position of Great Britain in Latin America were illustrated in the incident of the Panama Congress of 1826. Simon Bolivar, the "Liberator" of northern South America, invited the nations that had recently won their independence to send delegates to a meeting on the Isthmus of Panama, then a part of Colombia. There he proposed that they should form an organization to serve as a protector of their liberties against possible attack from Europe, as an interpreter of treaties and an umpire in disputes, and as a council for consultation in emergencies. In his invitations Bolivar included the empire of Brazil, which had declared its independence of Portugal, but not the United States. Bolivar was convinced that the democratic institutions of the northern republic would not serve the needs of the Latin American states, and he looked to Great Britain as the land that could provide both a model for their government and an alliance for their protection. The United States simply did not fit into his picture.

The invitation to the United States which

the Liberator had deliberately omitted was, however, supplied by the governments of Colombia, Central America, and Mexico, where liberal elements distrusted Bolivar's monarchical tendencies and saw the United States as embodying their ideals of democracy. These invitations reached Washington after John Quincy Adams had become President and Henry Clay, Secretary of State. Clay's enthusiasm was at once aroused. Here was an opportunity to take the lead in creating that "American System" of which he had spoken in glowing terms during his advocacy of the recognition of Latin American independence—a system which, he had said then, "would constitute the rallying point of human wisdom against all the despotism of the Old World." Adams, who had once scoffed at Clay's exuberance, was now a partial convert to the ideas of his brilliant Secretary of State. He nominated two delegates to attend the congress at Panama and in a special message to Congress, December 26, 1825, asked for an appropriation to cover their expenses. To extend the principles of commercial reciprocity with the neighbors to the south and to hand down to future generations "the most cordial feelings of fraternal friendship," was, said Adams, "congenial to the highest policy of the Union."

But in Congress the plan met unexpected opposition. The period was one of bitter factional strife. The partisans of Andrew Jackson, maintaining that their hero had been cheated of the presidency by a "corrupt bargain" between Adams and Clay, were attacking the administration at every opportunity. In opposing the plan to send delegates to Panama, they appealed to the warnings of Washington and Jefferson against foreign alliances. Southerners professed to see a peril to slavery in the proposal that the Panama meeting consider the status of Haiti, the unrecognized Negro republic; and while northern commercial cities hoped that the meeting would lead to improved trade with Latin America, the South saw more prospect of competition than of profitable markets in the nations south of the border. Eventually the

Senate confirmed the delegates, and Congress provided for their expenses, but so much time had been consumed in the debate that the delegates failed to reach Panama. One, the minister to Colombia, died en route from Bogotá; the other learned of the adjournment of the Panama meeting in time to avoid a useless journey.

Although the United States was unrepresented at Panama, Henry Clay's instructions to the prospective delegates are interesting as a revelation of administration policy, a policy toned down, no doubt, by the ardor of the congressional opposition. The instructions exhibit none of Clay's earlier enthusiasm for an "American system." The United States, he told the delegates, would not consent to any restriction upon its freedom of action by participating in either a confederacy or an alliance. The delegates were to oppose the recognition of Haiti and any plan for expelling Spain from Cuba or Puerto Rico—islands that the United States would not willingly see pass under any control other than Spain's. On the affirmative side, they were to devote their efforts to devising means of preserving peace in the Americas and promoting peace between Spain and her former colonies; to securing acceptance of the American conception of neutral rights; to the promotion of equality in trade and reciprocal freedom of navigation; to the forwarding of a plan for an isthmian canal; to a general endorsement of the noncolonization principle of the Monroe Doctrine; to the protection of religious freedom and the advancement of republican ideals.

Delegates from Colombia, Peru, Central America, and Mexico formally convened at Panama on June 22, 1826, and adjourned on July 15. Buenos Aires (Argentina), Brazil, Chile, Bolivia, and Paraguay were unrepresented. Observers attended from Great Britain and the Netherlands. The congress was a fiasco. The delegates agreed on a treaty "of perpetual union, league, and confederation," one article of which embodied the equivalent of the noncolonization principle. Other treaties provided for future meetings of the congress and for an international army and navy

to be made up of contingents from the various states. Not one of the treaties was ever ratified except by Colombia.

The Panama Congress was profitable to no one, unless perhaps to Great Britain. The British government had shown some concern lest the United States place itself at the head of a league of American republics in opposition to conservative, monarchical Europe. Of that, as has been shown, there was no danger. Foreign Secretary Canning had also feared that the Latin American states might adopt American ideas of neutral rights and a liberal system of navigation and trade, adverse to British interests. The United States delegates were not present to argue their case, but Edward J. Dawkins, the British agent, reported that only the Colombian delegates were disposed to accept those North American principles. The endorsement of the noncolonization dogma was innocuous. In the meantime, Dawkins was able to sow distrust of the United States by playing up its unwillingness to see Cuba taken by Colombia or Mexico. Although Canning discouraged Bolivar's overtures for an alliance, the Panama Congress marked a step of some significance in the program of building up British influence in the Americas at the expense of that of the United States. As a forerunner of the Pan-American movement of later days, it left a heritage of ideas and nothing more.

Europe and America Ignore the Monroe Doctrine

The specter of Quadruple Alliance intervention in the New World soon disappeared, and with its disappearance the principles of President Monroe entered upon a long slumber, from which they were not awakened until 1845, despite several minor disturbances that might well have aroused them earlier. The period was not one of abstention by Europe from interferences, or even from colonizing activities, in America, though none of these intrusions seemed seriously to endanger the security or the vital interests of the United

States. Great Britain and France were the chief offenders, if offense there was. Great Britain seized the Falkland Islands, off the tip of South America (1833), occupied the Caribbean island of Roatan, claimed by Honduras (1838–1839), arbitrarily extended the boundaries of her settlements at Belize (British Honduras) and elevated them to the status of a crown colony (1840), enlarged the area claimed for her protégés, the Mosquito Indians, on the east coast of Nicaragua, and finally (1841) occupied as part of their territory the port of San Juan, or Greytown, at the mouth of the San Juan River. France, meanwhile, attempted to enlarge her colony of French Guiana at the expense of Brazil (1835), occupied the port of Vera Cruz in an attempt to exact payment of claims from Mexico (1838), blockaded the coast of Argentina, and interfered in the internal politics of both Argentina and Uruguay (1838–1840).

Such activities as these would, at a later day, have excited public opinion in the United States and have called forth official protests in the name of the Monroe Doctrine. Nothing of the sort occurred. There was no official protest. Monroe's message was not once mentioned by the executive, was cited only once in Congress—in a House resolution calling for information about the French interventions at Vera Cruz and in the La Plata area—and was rarely mentioned outside of government circles. Partly, no doubt, because none of these actions constituted a serious threat to American interests, the United States let them proceed almost unnoticed.

As yet, no one spoke, or thought, of the "Monroe Doctrine." Not until nearly thirty years had passed did that phrase enter the national vocabulary, and during still another decade, it remained a principle of one political party, the Democratic, rather than a national heritage. Only when the United States had grown to such a stature that it could support its principles by effective force did the Monroe Doctrine win assent or command respect among the nations of the Old World.[14]

14. See pp. 122, 150 and Chapter 19, for the revival of the Monroe Doctrine by President Polk in 1845 and its development and application in the next few decades. The eclipse of the Doctrine between 1825 and 1845 is described in detail in Dexter Perkins, *The Monroe Doctrine, 1826–1867* (Baltimore: The Johns Hopkins Press, 1933), chap. 1.

Outstanding diplomatic problems in the two decades following the issuance of the Monroe Doctrine were the controversy with Great Britain over Oregon and the policy of the United States toward Texas, first as a province of Mexico, then as an independent state. The Texas question eventually led, with other things, to war with Mexico. The Oregon dispute brought the country to the brink of war with Great Britain. Each of these topics deserves a chapter to itself. Before taking them up, it will be well to dispose of a number of international problems which, although of less critical importance than Texas and Oregon, were nevertheless provocative of serious friction until their solutions were found. Among them were questions of boundaries, trade restrictions, claims, neutrality, and suppression of the slave trade.

Opening the West India Trade

By 1815, trade with all parts of the British Empire other than the West India islands was on a generally satisfactory footing. The British and American governments reciprocally abandoned discriminations in favor of their own ships in their home ports. The commercial treaty of 1815 put trade between the United States and the British Isles on a mutual most-favored-nation basis and admitted American ships to trade with the East Indies. In these respects, the new treaty resembled Jay's treaty of 1794. Also like Jay's treaty in its final form, it failed to admit American ships to the trade of the British West Indies. Furthermore, now that peace had returned, certain liberties that had been allowed in time of war were withdrawn, and the United States found its situation relative to the West India trade worse than ever. The British did make some minor concessions. American ships were allowed to carry certain specified articles to Bermuda, whence British ships could take them to the West Indies; and in 1818 an act of Parliament made St. John in New Brunswick and Halifax in Nova Scotia free ports for commodities needed in the West Indies. But the direct trade between the United

10

A Diplomatic Miscellany

States and the West Indies was still confined to British ships.

The United States now initiated a program of retaliation, which culminated in an act of Congress of May 15, 1820. This act closed United States ports after September 30, 1820, to British vessels coming from any British possession in the Americas and prohibited the importation from such possessions of any goods not wholly the product of the colony from which they entered the United States. The effect of this legislation was to put an end to all direct trade between the United States and the West Indies and to prevent the importation of West Indian products by way of Canada, New Brunswick, or Nova Scotia. The trade continued by way of the Danish, Dutch, and Swedish islands as intermediate points, but with the consequence that British West India planters, because of higher transportation costs, received less for their products and paid more for their supplies.

The planters petitioned for relief in the form of a reopening of the direct trade with the United States. Their applications were supported in England by a group of economic thinkers who had been converted to free trade doctrines and were pressing for a relaxation of the mercantilist restrictions.[1] Such innovations were opposed by the beneficiaries of the existing arrangements, especially the producers of food and lumber in British North America, but eventually the new ideas won the day. An act of Parliament of July 24, 1822, opened certain enumerated ports in Britain's American colonies to ships from independent countries in North and South America or from foreign islands in the West Indies. Such ships might import enumerated commodities from the countries or colonies to which the ships belonged and might export

1. R. L. Schuyler, *The Fall of the Old Colonial System: A Study in British Free Trade, 1770–1870* (New York: Oxford University Press, Inc., 1945), chap. 3. For the United States and the West India trade, see F. L. Benns, *The American Struggle for the British West India Carrying Trade, 1815–1830,* Indiana University Studies, Vol. 10 (Bloomington: University of Indiana Press, 1923).

from the British ports to their home countries any commodities except arms and naval stores. In the interest of the northern British provinces, fish and salt provisions were excluded from the list of enumerated commodities, and foreign livestock, provisions, and lumber were subject to a duty of about 10 percent not collected on similar items from British Empire sources. Duties on such articles were the same whether the latter were imported in British or foreign ships, and all ships paid the same harbor dues. All the privileges mentioned, however, could be denied to the ships of foreign countries that refused equality of treatment in their own ports to British vessels.

Promptly upon learning of the adoption of the new British policy, President Monroe proclaimed (as Congress had empowered him to do) that American ports were open to British ships bringing to the United States the produce of the British possessions in North America or the West Indies. That carrying trade was now open to both British and American vessels. With respect to ships coming from the British colonies, however, the United States did not remove the higher tonnage dues paid by foreign shipping or the higher tariff rates imposed on goods imported in foreign ships. It justified the continuance of these discriminations by the argument that they were a proper offset to the British discrimination in tariff rates in favor of the products of other British colonies. It demanded that Great Britain abandon this form of "imperial preference" as a condition to equalizing the fees paid in American ports by American ships and British ships coming from the West Indies or British North America.

The British retorted that "imperial preference" was as much a domestic matter as was the general tariff policy of the United States. Since they treated equally British and American ships trading between their colonies and the United States, they demanded that the United States do the same. When the United States refused, the British imposed higher harbor dues on American than on British ships in this branch of trade, and higher duties on their cargoes. The game of retaliation began again and reached a climax in 1826–1827, when the British government again closed its colonial ports in the Western Hemisphere to American ships and the United States again prohibited the importation of colonial products in British ships. The situation had reverted to the status before 1822, and once more, trade between the United States and the British West Indies was forced into roundabout and expensive channels.

The impasse was not broken until 1830 when the Jackson administration, with the support of Congress, dropped the demand that Great Britain abandon "imperial preference" as a price for removal by the United States of its discriminatory harbor dues and tariff rates assessed against British ships and their cargoes. Jackson's proclamation of October 5, 1830, admitting British ships from the colonies to American ports on the same terms as United States ships, was quickly followed by a British order-in-council of similar purport. A key pillar of the mercantile system had fallen.[2]

Collecting Damage Claims from France

Andrew Jackson also settled a long-standing claims controversy with France. There were monetary claims on both sides. By a general claims settlement of 1831, France agreed to pay the United States 25,000,000 francs, chiefly in compensation for seizures of American ships and cargoes during the war period, 1803–1815. The American government, in return, agreed to pay a much smaller sum (1,500,000 francs) in settlement of all French claims against the United States. Delay by the French Parliament in appropriating the funds necessary to carry out the agreement led to harsh words from President Jackson in his annual message of 1834, including a proposal that French property in the United States be sequestrated to satisfy the acknowledged but unpaid claims. The French government, resenting such forthright language, thereupon severed diplomatic relations. Through friendly British "good offices" amicable intercourse was resumed. President Jackson denied, in his next annual message, that he had intended "to menace or insult the Government of France." The French Parliament thereupon appropriated the necessary funds, and the claims were paid.[3]

2. Actually, Jackson's predecessor, John Quincy Adams, had offered to make the same concessions that Jackson made in 1830. The timing and the circumstances of the earlier offer had led the British to reject it.

3. Included among the French claims covered by the lump sum payment of 1,500,000 francs were claims of the heirs of Beaumarchais for aid furnished to the United States during the early years of the American Revolution. The United States had resisted these claims on the ground that the materials supplied through Beaumarchais' fictitious company, Hortalez et Cie., came out of French government arsenals without cost to Beaumarchais.

Besides the claims against France, numerous other monetary claims of American citizens against foreign governments were settled during the years between 1815 and 1861, some by arbitration, others by direct negotiation. Claims against Russia, Denmark, Spain, Portugal, the Two Sicilies, Sweden, and several Latin American states were settled, as were the French claims, by negotiation. There were arbitrations with Great Britain, France, Denmark, Spain, Portugal, Mexico, and other Latin American countries. Mexico's failure to pay the damages awarded by a mixed commission of 1839 (two commissioners from each country and an umpire named by the King of Prussia) was one of several causes leading to the war of 1846. See Chapter 13. Notable for its success was the arbitration under a convention of February 8, 1853, of all unsettled Anglo-American monetary claims that had arisen since 1815. The two commissioners, one American and one British, agreed without difficulty upon an umpire, one Joshua Bates, American born but at the time a member of the banking firm of Baring Brothers and Company of London. In sixteen months the commissioners and umpire adjudicated 115 claims, awarding $329,734.16 to American claimants, $297,102.88 to British. Of this arbitration Secretary of State Seward later remarked that it "had the prestige of complete and even felicitous success." A concise account of claims settlements between 1815 and 1861 is given in S. F. Bemis, *A Diplomatic History of the United States,* 3rd ed. (New York: Holt, Rinehart & Winston, Inc., 1950), pp. 284–91. For the arbitrations see J. B. Moore, *History and Digest of the International Arbitrations to Which the United States Has Been a Party . . .,* 6 vols. (Washington, D.C.: Government Printing Office, 1898), 2, *passim.*

The Northeastern Boundary Dispute

Failure of the joint commissions provided for by the Treaty of Ghent to agree on the northeastern boundary and on the line from the Neebish Rapids to the Lake of the Woods, and the subsequent rejection of the recommendation of the King of the Netherlands for settlement of the former controversy, threw these two problems again into the hands of the diplomats. It will be well here to examine the conflicting conceptions of the boundary between the state of Maine and the British provinces of New Brunswick (detached from Nova Scotia in 1784) and Quebec.

The dispute over this section of the boundary turned upon the meaning of the language of Article II of the treaty of peace with Great Britain of 1783, the relevant portion of which described the boundary as follows:

> . . . From the NorthWest Angle of Nova Scotia, viz. That Angle which is formed by a Line drawn due North from the Source of Saint Croix River to the Highlands along the said Highlands which divide those Rivers that empty themselves into the River St. Lawrence, from those which fall into the Atlantic Ocean, to the Northwestern-most Head of Connecticut River: Thence down along the middle of that River to the forty-fifth Degree of North Latitude; From thence by a Line due West on said Latitude until it strikes the River Iroquois or Cataraquy [St. Lawrence]; . . .

The identity of the St. Croix River having been established and its source located pursuant to the Jay treaty, the Americans proposed to draw a line from that point due north to the watershed between the St. Lawrence basin and the southward-flowing rivers, and to follow that watershed to the northwestern source of the Connecticut. That seemed, and still seems, the plain meaning of the treaty. The British, however, demurred. From their point of view, there were practical objections to a line so drawn. Such a line, as the map will show, would cut across the St. John River, leaving its source in Maine and its mouth in New Brunswick. It would also,

by pushing the boundaries of Maine far up toward the St. Lawrence, drive a wedge between the provinces of Quebec and New Brunswick and interfere with British plans for a vital military road to run from Fredericton, New Brunswick, to Riviere du Loup on the St. Lawrence.

The British, therefore, insisted that the line should be drawn south of the St. John River, leaving the river and the line of the proposed military road in British possession. They resisted the American interpretation of the treaty, in the first place, by arguing that the rivers flowing south from the highlands picked by the Americans drained not into the Atlantic Ocean but into the Bay of Fundy. Hence, they said, these could not be the highlands of the treaty. The Americans, on their side, contended that the Bay of Fundy was comprehended under the term Atlantic Ocean. The more persuasive British argument was based upon what they contended must have been the intent of the treaty-makers. These negotiators, they argued, would not knowingly have divided the source of an important river like the St. John from its outlet or have driven a wedge between two of His Majesty's provinces. Finally, they asserted, where the treaty spoke of "Highlands," it must have referred to some conspicuous elevation, not to the almost indistinguishable line that divided the tributaries of the St. Lawrence from the streams flowing southward. Such a conspicuous elevation was conveniently found in Mars Hill south of the St. John and a line of hills running thence westward, always south of that stream. There, said the British, must be the "Highlands" mentioned in the treaty.

The Americans, in addition to having what seems the fairest interpretation of the treaty in support of their case, had also, like the British, material reasons for insisting on their claims. North of Mars Hill and south of the St. John lay the valley of the Aroostook, a tributary of the St. John, a fertile valley constituting Maine's "last agricultural frontier." This area the people of Maine and their backers in Massachusetts (which still held title to lands in Maine) were determined not to give up.[4] When lumbermen from New Brunswick entered the Aroostook Valley and began cutting timber, they were expelled by Maine militia in what was locally dubbed the "Restook War" of 1838–1839. Serious trouble threatened. General Winfield Scott was sent to the Aroostook, where he arranged a *modus vivendi* between Maine and New Brunswick, each party to remain in possession of territory actually occupied without preujdice to its disposition in a final settlement.

The Webster-Ashburton Treaty

A final settlement was manifestly desirable, but until 1842 every attempt to negotiate a settlement or to submit the dispute a second time to arbitration encountered insuperable obstacles. For the United States, any compromise arrangement was rendered difficult by the contention of Maine and Massachusetts, both politically important, that no abatement of the American claim could be made without Maine's consent. In 1842 there arrived in Washington Alexander Baring, Lord Ashburton, commissioned as special envoy of the British government to seek a settlement of all existing difficulties between Great Britain and the United States. Among the chief of these was the northeastern boundary dispute. Daniel Webster, Secretary of State under President John Tyler, was, like Lord Ashburton, anxious to reach a settlement. Both men were prepared to make concessions.

The British had been willing, since 1831, to accept a compromise line similar to that proposed by the King of the Netherlands— a line that in its most vital portion would follow the west-east course of the St. John River, roughly halfway between Mars Hill on the south and the highlands claimed by the Americans to the north. Such a line would leave the Aroostook Valley to the people of Maine and the site for the military road to

the British. For such a line Lord Ashburton was ready to make concessions on other points. He was empowered to permit the Americans of the Aroostook the free navigation of the St. John to its mouth for the exportation of their farm and forest products. He was empowered to yield to the American claims on several other unsettled portions of the boundary. He might accept the American contention that the head of Hall's Stream was the northwesternmost source of the Connecticut River, thereby yielding to the United States some 150 square miles of forest land claimed by Great Britain. He might also accept, in lieu of the true 45th parallel from the Connecticut to the St. Lawrence, the line inaccurately surveyed as such in 1774, which lay about three-fourths of a mile north of the true line. This discrepancy was important chiefly because Fort Montgomery, a newly constructed American military work on Rouse's Point at the outlet of Lake Champlain, was situated just north of the true 45th parallel. Retention of the old line would leave the fort in United States territory. The importance attached to this fort and to the British plan for a military road throws interesting light on the myth of the "unguarded frontier" in this period.[5] Lord Ashburton was also authorized to make concessions to the United States on the boundary from the head of Lake Huron to the Lake of the Woods.

The chief obstacle to an agreement on the lines indicated was the opposition of the people and authorities of Maine to the relinquishment of their claims north of the St. John River. This opposition was quieted, partly by compensating Maine and Massachusetts, $150,000 to each, for the land titles surrendered; partly by skillful newspaper propaganda, some of it apparently paid for out of the secret service fund at Webster's disposal; [6] partly by bringing secretly to the attention of the Maine and Massachusetts authorities certain old maps that appeared to support the

4. Thomas LeDuc, "The Maine Frontier and the Northeastern Boundary Controversy," *American Historical Review,* 53 (1947), 30–41.

5. See Chapter 8.
6. R. N. Current, "Webster's Propaganda and the Ashburton Treaty," *Mississippi Valley Historical Review,* 34 (1947), 187–200.

British contention in regard to the identity of the "Highlands" of the treaty. Though subsequent discoveries have shown that Webster's maps were without authority and that authentic maps, which were not known to the negotiators, supported the American claim, Webster's strategy was effective, and the New Englanders agreed not to obstruct the compromise settlement.[7]

7. For a discussion of the famous episode of the "red line maps," see S. F. Bemis, *John Quincy Adams and the Foundations of American Foreign Policy* (New York: Alfred A. Knopf, Inc., 1949), chap. 23. Professor Bemis is scathing in his criticism of Webster, who,

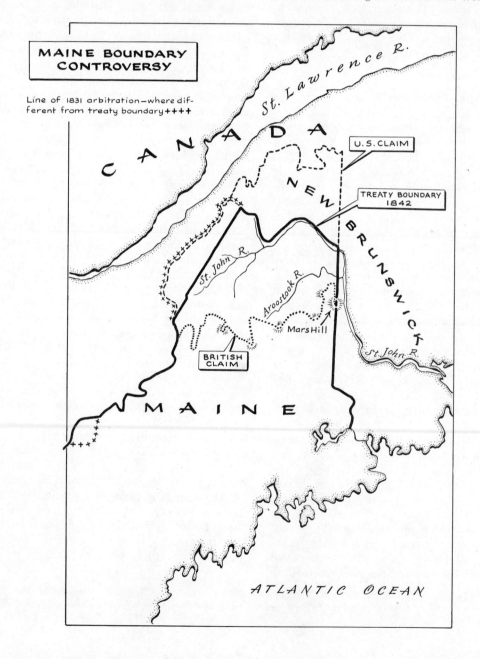

MAINE BOUNDARY CONTROVERSY

Line of 1831 arbitration—where different from treaty boundary ++++

By the Webster-Ashburton treaty, signed August 9, 1842, the United States secured slightly less of the disputed territory in Maine than it would have received by accepting the arbitral recommendation of the King of the Netherlands, as the following figures indicate:

	Arbitral Award 1831	Treaty 1842
To the United States	7,908 sq. mi.	7,015 sq. mi.
To Great Britain	4,119 sq. mi.	5,012 sq. mi.

as he says, "wilfully relinquish[ed] millions of acres of good American territory." He implies that Webster was motivated by selfish personal, even pecuniary, considerations in making his "surrender." It may be guessed that the final verdict of history will treat Webster more charitably. Lord Ashburton's British critics charged that it was he who had made the surrenders.

Granting that on the best interpretation of the treaty of 1783 the United States had a sound claim to the whole of the disputed territory, and granting that Webster could have exacted a better price from Lord Ashburton for what he yielded—the latter certainly could have been persuaded to foot the bill for compensation to Maine and Massachusetts and would probably have consented to grant the navigation of the St. Lawrence River—one may still feel considerable satisfaction at the termination of this long controversy. It is not clear that continued insistence upon all that the United States believed it was entitled to under the treaty would have exacted a peaceful surrender from Great Britain. It will hardly be contended that the five thousand square miles relinquished were worth a war.

The boundary settlements of the treaty, furthermore, cannot be assessed properly without weighing gains in the west against losses in the east. Webster and Ashburton inherited the unsettled boundary from the Neebish Rapids to the Lake of the Woods, a segment of the line that had baffled the Treaty of Ghent commissioners. The chief points in controversy in this area were the ownership of St. George's or Sugar Island in the St. Mary's River and the location of the line from Lake Superior to the Lake of the Woods. The treaty of 1783 described the boundary as leaving Lake Superior at "Long Lake" and running thence by the water communication to the Lake of the Woods. The commissioners found no "Long Lake" emptying into Lake Superior, but Mitchell's Map of North America of 1755, which they had every reason to suppose had been used by the peace commissioners, showed a Long Lake in the position of what had come to be called Pigeon River, which was not a lake at all. Both commissioners were at first disposed to run the line through Pigeon River, but Anthony Barclay, the British representative, later claimed that St. Louis River at the extreme western end of Lake Superior best answered the description of the treaty. Choice of this line would have added some 6,500 square miles of territory to the British possessions. Thereupon the American agent, Joseph Delafield, made out a case for the Kamanistegua or Dog River, some distance east of the Pigeon, as the proper boundary. He showed that its course included a stretch of water called Long Lake (though some distance from Lake Superior) and that a water route, with portages, led thence to the Lake of the Woods. It was the expectation of Delafield and of Peter B. Porter, the American commissioner, who adopted his claim, that the British would agree to accept Pigeon River as a compromise. The British stood firm for the St. Louis, however, and this portion of the boundary remained undetermined until the Webster-Ashburton negotiations. The diplomats then assigned St. George's Island to the United States and adopted Pigeon River as the "Long Lake" of the earlier treaty.[8]

8. Robert McElroy and Thomas Riggs, eds., *The*

By relinquishing the British claims between Lake Superior and the Lake of the Woods, Lord Ashburton yielded to the United States some 6,500 square miles of territory, which, though the negotiators were unaware of it, embraced a large proportion of the future iron ore fields of northern Minnesota, including the eastern portion of the famed Mesabi range. In any economic balance, the iron deposits of this section of Minnesota would certainly outweigh the forests surrendered to New Brunswick.[9]

The African Slave Trade and the Right of Search

Webster and Ashburton also included in their treaty an article providing for cooperative American and British action to further the suppression of the traffic in African slaves. Both governments had long since forbidden the slave trade to their own citizens or subjects (the United States as of January 1, 1808); and both had followed up the prohibitions by declaring the trade to be piracy, punishable by death. British and American action alone, however, could not give the slave trade the status of piracy under international law; and in the absence of special treaties providing for international action, each nation could enforce the law only against its own nationals.

By Article Ten of the Treaty of Ghent, the British and American governments had promised to "use their best endeavors to accomplish" the "entire abolition" of the slave trade. In 1824 British and American negotiators agreed on a convention that would have permitted reciprocal right of search of vessels suspected of engaging in the forbidden traffic; British cruisers could have searched ships fly-

Unfortified Boundary; A Diary of the First Survey of the Canadian Boundary Line from St. Regis to the Lake of the Woods, by Major Joseph Delafield (New York: Privately printed, 1943), pp. 63–123.
9. Thomas LeDuc, "The Webster-Ashburton Treaty and the Minnesota Iron Ranges," *Journal of American History,* 51 (December 1964), 476–81.

ing the American flag and vice versa. The proposal called up old and bitter memories of British cruisers hovering off American ports and searching American ships for alleged deserters from His Majesty's navy. The Senate, therefore, amended the convention to make it inapplicable to waters off the North American coast. The British government refused to accept this amendment, and the convention was never ratified.[10]

The division in the Senate over the convention of 1824 was not sectional, but within a few years thereafter, the American controversy over slavery grew bitter, while Great Britain, abolishing slavery in her colonies in 1833, became the international champion and promoter of the antislavery movement. This combination of circumstances aroused the slaveholding South to oppose any arrangement that would concede to British cruisers the right to search American ships for evidence that they were carrying slaves; and northern allies of the South, such men as Lewis Cass of Michigan, took the same view. When, in the late 1830's, British men-of-war off the African coast began stopping vessels flying the American flag, John Forsyth of Georgia was Secretary of State, and Andrew Stevenson of Virginia was minister to Great Britain. Forsyth and Stevenson took violent exception to this new British assertion of the right of search.

Lord Palmerston, British Foreign Secretary, was as vigorous in stating the British case as was Stevenson in setting forth that of the United States. He claimed for Great Britain, he said, not the right of search but merely a "right of visit"—the right to board a ship to ascertain whether she was really of the nationality that her flag indicated. He pointed out that, since England had treaties permitting reciprocal rights of search with numerous states of Europe and Latin America, it was becoming common practice for slave traders of various nationalities to seek protection by flying the United States flag. If British cruisers were

debarred from visiting such vessels to discover whether they were bona fide American or were sailing under false colors, said Palmerston, suppression of the slave traffic would be impossible.

Stevenson replied that the "right of visit" was merely the right of search under another name, and that the United States would never consent to having its ships searched by foreign cruisers except for contraband or evidence of other illegal trade in time of war. The controversy grew warm and, added to the disputes over the Maine boundary and others over the *Caroline* and Alexander McLeod, to be described below, produced something of a crisis in Anglo-American relations in 1841.

Chances for a friendly settlement improved when the conciliatory Lord Aberdeen replaced Palmerston in the Foreign Office and the conciliatory Webster succeeded Forsyth as Secretary of State. The questions of the slave trade and the right of search in connection with it were included in the agenda for the Webster-Ashburton conferences. To Lord Aberdeen, Ashburton pointed out that the American objection to the right of search arose largely from its association with the impressment controversy and asked permission to conciliate American opinion by assuring Webster that Great Britain no longer claimed the right to impress sailors from American ships. This proposal was firmly rejected by the Foreign Secretary, but Ashburton nevertheless assured Webster in writing that the practice of impressment had "wholly ceased" and could not be "under present circumstances renewed." [11]

This concession, unauthorized by the British government, did not alter the American attitude toward the right of search. Webster and Ashburton sought to terminate the controversy by eliminating the need for reciprocal rights of visit and search. Article Eight of the treaty stipulated that each government should maintain off the African coast an adequate cruising squadron carrying not fewer than eighty guns, "to enforce, separately and respectively, the laws, rights, and obligations, of

10. This whole subject is well covered in H. G. Soulsby, *The Right of Search and the Slave Trade in Anglo-American Relations, 1814–1862* (Baltimore: The Johns Hopkins Press, 1933).

11. Soulsby, *The Right of Search,* pp. 84–85.

each of the two countries, for the suppression of the Slave Trade, . . ." The two squadrons would be independent of each other, but it was agreed that the two governments would give such orders to their squadron commanders as would "enable them most effectually to act in concert and cooperation, upon mutual consultation, as exigencies may arise, . . ."

Thus the United States agreed to take measures adequate to enforce, against its own nationals or ships flying the American flag, its laws forbidding the African slave trade. This solution removed the issue from the field of controversy for fifteen years but did not settle it. The United States failed to implement the agreement effectually. It fulfilled its promise to keep eighty guns in African waters by using a few large and slow sailing ships when the situation called for numerous small but speedy craft. It was tardy in assigning steamers to the service. The base of the American squadron, in the Cape Verde Islands, was too far from the slave coast to permit effective operation. The slave trade, therefore, continued to flourish, a large share of it under the United States flag. Until 1857, nevertheless, the British refrained from visiting suspicious vessels flying the Stars and Stripes. In that year they renewed the practice and thereby revived the controversy. Lewis Cass, now Secretary of State,[12] combatted vigorously the British reassertion of the "right of visit." This time the British government gave ground, abandoning in 1858 its claim to rights of visit and search in time of peace, except where such rights were specially conceded by treaty.

The final chapter of the story was written in 1862, after the secession from the Union of the slaveholding South. A treaty with Great Britain, then signed and ratified, permitted the cruisers of each power not only to search ships of the other but also, if the search showed reasonable grounds for suspecting participation in the slave trade, to seize the suspect ship and send it for adjudication to one of several mixed British and American courts created for the purpose. The end of slavery in the South removed one important market of the illicit traffic. This event was soon followed by the abolition of slavery in the remaining civilized lands where it still had legal existence, in Brazil between 1871 and 1888, in Puerto Rico in 1873, and in Cuba in 1880. The closing of these last markets removed all incentive to the prohibited commerce.

The Caroline and Alexander McLeod

Another controversy that Webster and Ashburton inherited from their predecessors and succeeded in terminating amicably was the affair of the steamer *Caroline,* an outgrowth of a short-lived Canadian rebellion against British rule in 1837–1838. In this minor civil struggle, the United States, following the precedent that it had set in the Spanish-American wars of independence,[13] declared its neutrality. In a proclamation of January 5, 1838, President Van Buren warned citizens of the United States against committing any act that would "compromit the neutrality of this Government."

Despite official American efforts to prevent the giving of aid to the Canadian insurgents, the American lake steamer *Caroline* was used for the running of arms and recruits from Buffalo to an insurgent encampment on Navy Island in the Niagara River. On the night of December 29, 1837, a party of Canadian militia crossed the river to Schlosser on the American shore (now in Niagara Falls, New York), boarded the *Caroline,* routed her crew,

---

12. In 1841, as United States minister in Paris, Cass had worked against French ratification of a quintuple treaty (Great Britain, France, Austria, Prussia, Russia) declaring the slave trade piracy and allowing limited reciprocal rights of search. Such a treaty would have gone far to isolate the United States in regard to the slave trade. Whether or not because of Cass's exertions, France withheld ratification. Four years later she abrogated an earlier treaty with Great Britain permitting reciprocal rights of search. France, however, acted more vigorously than the United States in preventing slave-trading by its own nationals.

13. See Chapter 9.

killing at least one American, set her on fire, and towed her out into the river, where she sank.

This flagrant invasion of American territorial waters the British sought to justify on the ground that the rebellion was a criminal conspiracy and hence that the *Caroline* had the character of a pirate craft and might, as such, be destroyed wherever found. This whole argument was denied by the United States, which demanded apology for the attack on the *Caroline* and asserted that the rebellion must be regarded as a war, conferring belligerent status on the participants. This thesis was stated as follows in a note from Andrew Stevenson, American minister in London, to Lord Palmerston, British Foreign Secretary:

> The following principles are assumed as incontrovertible:
> That civil wars are not distinguishable from other wars, as to belligerent and neutral rights; that they stand upon the same ground, and are governed by the same principles; that whenever a portion of a State seek by force to overthrow the Government, and maintain independence, the contest becomes one *de facto* of war. That in such contests the principles of public law in relation to belligirants [*sic*] must govern, and all the rights which a state of war gives to public enemies are to be allowed to the respective parties engaged in them.[14]

This passage is quoted here because it contrasts radically with the position taken by the United States toward its own Civil War in 1861 and supports the attitude of Great Britain toward that later conflict.[15]

The *Caroline* affair remained unsettled for nearly five years. Meanwhile, in 1840, a Canadian named Alexander McLeod, a deputy sheriff whose efforts to prevent gunrunning had made him enemies on the American side of the line,[16] was arrested in New York and

indicted by a state grand jury on charges of having participated in the attack on the *Caroline* and hence of being guilty both of arson and of the "murder" of Amos Durfee, the one American known to have lost his life in the encounter. Lord Palmerston, for the British government, demanded McLeod's release on the ground that any share he might have had in the affair was performed under orders from the British authorities in Canada and hence that he was not personally responsible for his act. Should New York State hang McLeod for murder, Palmerston threatened, Great Britain would fight to avenge his death.

Webster, who became Secretary of State in the midst of this crisis, accepted the British contention that McLeod could not be held responsible for acts committed under orders. But McLeod was in the hands of the sovereign state of New York, which insisted that the trial must go on. The New York Supreme Court refused to order his release but did direct a change of venue from Lockport, where feeling against McLeod was strong, to Utica, distant from the scene of the "crime." At the trial, McLeod produced an alibi, and state witnesses who were reported to have seen him in the *Caroline* affray failed to appear. McLeod was acquitted, and the crisis passed.[17]

To prevent the recurrence of such collisions between state and national authority, Webster suggested and Congress passed (1842) an act providing that, in the future, cases against persons acting under the authority of a foreign government could be removed from state to federal jurisdiction.

With McLeod safely restored to his family and fireside, Webster and Ashburton could turn calmly to a settlement of the *Caroline* case. The British government had dropped its contention that the *Caroline* was in effect a pirate ship and excused the admitted invasion

14. *House Executive Document* 183, 25 Cong. 3 sess., p. 6.
15. See Chapter 17.
16. Alastair Watt, "The Case of Alexander McLeod," *Canadian Historical Review,* 12 (1931), 145–67, refutes the traditional story that McLeod's arrest followed his drunken boasting of his share in the *Caroline* raid.

17. Alastair Watt, who has made a detailed study of the case, "The Case of Alexander McLeod" states that McLeod was not in the *Caroline* party but that his brother, Angus McLeod, was a member of it. William H. Seward, governor of New York, refused to halt the prosecution but assured Webster privately that McLeod had an alibi but that if nevertheless he should be convicted, he would be pardoned.

of United States territory as an act of necessary self-defense. But although he claimed that "there were grounds of justification as strong as were ever presented in such cases," Lord Ashburton added that "no slight of the authority of the United States was intended" and expressed regret "that some explanation and apology for this occurrence was not immediately made." He hoped that "all feelings of resentment and ill will, resulting from these truly unfortunate events, may be buried in oblivion, and that they may be succeeded by those of harmony and friendship." This quasi-apology atoned for the violation of American sovereignty. Since the *Caroline* had confessedly been engaged in illegal activity, no reparation for her loss was demanded.

The Oregon country was, by the treaty of 1818, open to the use and occupation of both British subjects and American citizens. For many years this arrangement played into the hands of the British, for it was they who were on the ground, with the organization and experience needed to exploit the country. The North West Company, which had purchased Astor's post and trading goods in 1813, monopolized the trade of the Columbia River until the company itself was absorbed in 1821 by its rival, the Hudson's Bay Company. The Hudson's Bay Company tightened still further the monopoly of the Oregon trade, until there were few areas west of the Rockies in which traders from the United States dared compete with the great corporation. With the fur trade effectually closed to Americans, Oregon seemed for the moment to have little else to offer. Not only was it difficult of access, but Lewis and Clark and other early explorers had pictured it as mountainous, barren, and unattractive, and this remained the popular impression for many years.

The United States, nevertheless, maintained an interest in the Oregon country. A few men in Congress, notably Senator Thomas Hart Benton of Missouri, and Representative John Floyd of Virginia, repeatedly called attention to its future importance to the United States, Benton viewing it as part of a route to the commerce of the Orient. In diplomatic negotiations in the 1820's, the United States, while asserting the validity of its claim to the entire area, adhered to its offer of 1818, to accept the 49th parallel as the boundary. The British with equal consistency insisted upon the Columbia River, from its mouth to its intersection with the 49th parallel, as the dividing line. They were willing, however, to concede to the United States a detached fragment of territory, an enclave, on the Olympian peninsula, giving access to harbors on Puget Sound.[1] Since neither government was

1. The United States based its claim to Oregon upon (1) the principle of "contiguity," Oregon being regarded as a natural extension of Louisiana; (2) the explorations of Captain Gray and Lewis and Clark, and the settlement of Astoria; (3) the acquisition of Spanish rights under the treaty of 1819. The British denied the validity of (1) and (3). Any exclusive

11

Oregon

willing to back down, and since the ten-year period of joint occupation would terminate in 1828, the negotiators agreed simply to extend that arrangement indefinitely, with the proviso that either party might terminate it by giving twelve months' notice. A convention to that effect was signed on August 6, 1827.

Americans Colonize Oregon

The two decades that followed were to see a pronounced change in the situation, with the balance in *de facto* occupation of Oregon turning sharply in favor of the United States. Oregon suddenly became attractive to colonizers from the United States. The discovery (actually a rediscovery) of South Pass through the Rockies in 1824 greatly alleviated the physical difficulty of overland migration. This route was utilized in 1832 and again in 1834 by one Nathaniel J. Wyeth, a Massachusetts business man, who had visions of profitable enterprise on the lower Columbia. His business venture proved a failure, but he had established the route that came to be called the Oregon Trail. On his second journey, moreover, he had assisted a group of Methodist missionaries headed by Jason Lee. The Methodists settled in the Willamette Valley, south of the Hudson's Bay Company post at Fort Vancouver. They had little success in converting the Indians to Christianity, but they prospered as an agricultural colony, and their settlement proved a magnet to restless spirits in the East. They were followed two years later (1836) by the Presbyterian missionaries, Dr. Marcus Whitman and the Reverend H. H. Spalding. No more successful than the Methodists in proselytizing the natives, they too became effective advertisers of the attractions

of Oregon. The fact that their brides had accompanied them on the overland trek, handily surviving the hardships of the journey, opened to families what had hitherto been regarded as strictly a man's enterprise.

It was not until the early 1840's, however, that migration to Oregon reached significant proportions. The one hundred emigrants of 1842 swelled to nearly a thousand the following year. A census taken in 1845 showed 2,109 persons in Oregon, and the migration of that year brought nearly three thousand more. These settlers had need of some regular form of government and of some means of securing titles to the lands they occupied.[2]

These purposes could have been accomplished through the establishment of either British or American control, but since a great majority of the settlers had come from the United States, they hoped to see Oregon become American. Following the dispatch of several petitions to Congress asking that the United States assume control of the area, the settlers in July 1843 established an Oregon Provisional Government. In amending their organic act two years later, they stated in a preamble that its provisions were to apply only "until such time as the United States of America extend their jurisdiction over us." The next move was up to Congress and the diplomats.

The Oregon Question in Politics

Neither Congress nor the diplomats had been entirely idle. In Congress, Senator Lewis F. Linn of Missouri had assumed the role of protagonist of American rights in Oregon. Beginning in 1838, he introduced a series of resolutions which, though they never became law, furnished a sort of program for advocates

---

Spanish rights, they contended, had been canceled by the Anglo-Spanish Nootka Sound Convention of 1790. This also disposed of the claim derived from Louisiana, which in 1790 was a Spanish possession. They admitted that American explorations had some weight but asserted that their own explorations gave them claims as good as the American to the Columbia River and better to the north of it.

2. The Hudson's Bay Company exercised jurisdiction over its employees, and the British Parliament, in 1821, had extended the laws of Canada over British subjects in Oregon, but until ownership of the country was settled between Great Britain and the United States, there was no agency that could confer legal title to land.

OREGON BOUNDARY
CONTROVERSY, 1818-1846

Entire area 42° to 54°40' subject to joint occupation,
1818 - 1846

Claimed by Polk administration, 1845 - 1846.

Never seriously claimed by Great Britain.

Consistently claimed by U.S. and Great Britain, 1818 - 1846.

BRITISH

NORTH AMERICA

54°40'

NORTHERN LIMIT OF U.S. CLAIM

CONTINENTAL

VANCOUVER I.

BOUNDARY LINE
OF 1846

49°

BOUNDARY OF 1818

OLYMPIC PENINSULA
offered by Gt. Britain
to U.S., 1826, 1844.

DIVIDE

Columbia R.

Columbia River

Willamette R.

Snake River

42°

SPANISH-AMERICAN BOUNDARY, 1819

UNITED STATES

of American supremacy in Oregon. They asserted the American right to Oregon as beyond dispute, called for extension of American law over American citizens in Oregon and for military protection of the emigrant road, and proposed a grant of 640 acres of land to every white male inhabitant of Oregon who should cultivate and use the tract for five consecutive years. Explicitly or implicitly they called upon the President to give the necessary twelve-months' notice of the termination of joint occupation.

During the Webster-Ashburton negotiations of 1842, so successful in settling other matters in controversy,[3] informal discussion revealed that Great Britain was still, as in 1827, unwilling to concede to the United States the territory between the Columbia River and the 49th parallel. President Tyler suggested a possible compromise solution. If Great Britain would induce Mexico to recognize the independence of Texas and to cede Upper California to the United States, Tyler would be willing to accept the Columbia River as a northern boundary. Lord Ashburton stated that he had no authority to enter into any such arrangement. Acceptance of the Columbia River line would, in fact, have brought practically all the Oregon settlers under American jurisdiction, concentrated as they were in the Willamette Valley. The idea of surrendering the region north of the Columbia was discouraged, however, by reports from United States naval officers of the formidable bar at the mouth of the Columbia and excellent harbors on Puget Sound. The subject of Oregon, at any rate, never reached the stage of formal negotiation between Webster and Ashburton.

Rumors that Webster had offered to surrender northern Oregon in exchange for California created an uproar in the western states. It is evident that Senator Linn's Oregon proposals had struck a popular note among the people of the upper Mississippi Valley. Western newspapers and "Oregon conventions" in western towns expressed indignation at the suggestion of surrendering Oregon to Great Britain. The climax of this western agitation came in July 1843, when some 120 delegates from six states met in Cincinnati. Declaiming that the right of the United States to the whole of Oregon from 42° to 54° 40′ north latitude was "unquestionable," the delegates asserted it to be "the imperative duty of the General Government forthwith to extend the laws of the United States over said territory." The meeting directed that its declarations be sent to the President, to members of Congress, and to the governors of all the states.[4]

The United States was now on the eve of a presidential campaign in which the annexation of Texas was certain to figure as a major issue.[5] To strategists of the Democratic party, the party of expansion, it appeared expedient to link the two expansionist issues, Texas and Oregon, so that western votes for Texas might be obtained in return for southern votes for Oregon. After nominating James K. Polk, himself an advocate of taking possession of Oregon, the Democratic National Convention at Baltimore accordingly adopted the following platform declaration:

> *Resolved,* That our title to the whole of the territory of Oregon is clear and unquestionable; that no portion of the same ought to be ceded to England or any other power; and that the re-occupation of Oregon and the re-annexation of Texas at the earliest practicable period are great American measures, which this convention recommends to the cordial support of the Democracy of the Union.

The syllable "re," prefixed to "occupation" and "annexation," was designed to allay charges of aggression by suggesting that the nation was merely about to resume possession of what had once and rightfully been hers.

President Polk Looks John Bull in the Eye

Texas was more of an issue in the campaign than was Oregon. The phrase "Fifty-four

---

3. See Chapter 10.

4. M. C. Jacobs, *Winning Oregon: A Study of an Expansionist Movement* (Caldwell, Idaho: Caxton Printers, 1938), pp. 124–39, 169–76.
5. See Chapter 12.

forty or fight," traditionally supposed to have been a campaign slogan, was actually coined after the campaign, not during it.[6] But as there had been no serious Whig opposition to the Democratic pronouncement on Oregon, President Polk was within his rights in interpreting his electoral victory as a popular verdict in favor of a vigorous Oregon policy. Whether the verdict called for assertion of the claim to all of Oregon, even at the risk of war, or merely for a division at the 49th parallel, no one could be sure.

In his inaugural address Polk asserted, quoting the Democratic platform, that the American title to all of Oregon was "clear and unquestionable." But inasmuch as his predecessors had offered to settle for the 49th parallel, he instructed his Secretary of State, James Buchanan, to repeat the offer. When Richard Pakenham, the British minister, declined the proposal without even referring it to London, Polk directed Buchanan to withdraw it, intimating that the United States would stand upon its rights to the whole of Oregon. He was now determined to leave the next move to England and refused to permit Buchanan even to say that the United States would consider any proposal that the British government might care to make.

In his first annual message, December 2, 1845, Polk informed Congress of the course of the negotiations to that time. He was convinced, he said, "that the British pretensions of title could not be maintained to any portion of the Oregon territory upon any principle of public law recognized by nations." He had, nevertheless, made an offer of compromise. That offer, upon its being refused, had been withdrawn, "and our title to the whole Oregon territory asserted, and, as is believed, maintained by irrefragable facts and arguments." He recommended that Congress authorize him to give the required one year's notice of termination of joint occupation, that it extend the laws and jurisdiction of the United States over American citizens in Oregon, that it likewise extend to Oregon the laws

6. Edwin A. Miles, " 'Fifty-four Forty or Fight'—An American Political Legend," *Mississippi Valley Historical Review,* 44 (September 1957), 291–309.

regulating trade with the Indians, that it provide for a line of fortified posts from the Missouri to the Rockies and for the establishment of an overland mail route to the Columbia.

> At the end of the year's notice [said Polk], . . . we shall have reached a period when the national rights in Oregon must either be abandoned or firmly maintained. That they cannot be abandoned without a sacrifice of both national honor and interest, is too clear to admit of doubt.
>
> Oregon is a part of the North American continent, to which, it is confidently affirmed, the title of the United States is the best now in existence. . . . The British proposition of compromise . . . can never for a moment, be entertained by the United States without an abandonment of their just and clear territorial rights, their own self-respect, and the national honor.

Polk appeared to have closed the door to compromise, and the appearance was heightened some weeks later when Buchanan, under instructions from Polk, declined successively two British offers of arbitration, the first proposing to arbitrate an equitable division of the territory; the second, to arbitrate the whole question of title. To a timorous congressman, who expressed alarm lest Polk's bold stand lead to war with Great Britain, the President replied that "the only way to treat John Bull was to look him straight in the eye; . . . that if Congress faultered [*sic*] or hesitated in their course, John Bull would immediately become arrogant and more grasping in his demands."

John Bull Will Not Be Bluffed

President Polk has usually been given credit for adhering to this firm policy of looking John Bull straight in the eye, maintaining the American right to the 54°40' line, until the British government retreated, offering the traditional American solution of division at the 49th parallel. This impression, though doubtless the one that Polk wished to leave, credits him with more firmness and less discretion than he really exercised. Within a few days after his annual message, he permitted Buchanan to inform United States Minister Louis McLane, in London, that the President would feel inclined to submit to the Senate any reasonable proposal that the British government might make. Six weeks later, McLane was told that he might say to Lord Aberdeen, British Foreign Secretary, that although the President "would accept nothing less than the whole territory unless the Senate should otherwise determine," he might submit to the Senate for its advice a British proposal for a division at the 49th parallel.

Meanwhile, McLane was reporting two alarming interviews with Lord Aberdeen. Queried as to the purpose of extensive military preparations under way in England, the Foreign Secretary had expressed the conviction that "the President had determined to discourage any new proposition on the basis of compromise, and to concede nothing of the extreme demand." If this was true, said Aberdeen, he would not oppose measures for the defense of Canada and even for "offensive operations." McLane understood that such measures would include "the immediate equipment of thirty sail of the line, besides steamers and other vessels of war."[7]

McLane's dispatch conveying this information created distinct alarm in Polk's official circle, as well it might. Relations with Mexico had reached a state in which war was practically certain.[8] A war with Mexico and Great Britain at the same time could easily prove disastrous to the United States. Polk had carried his game of bluff too far and was sensible enough to realize it. Though publicly preserving a bold front, he permitted Buchanan to rush off by the next steamer a note to McLane in which the Secretary made a further bid for a compromise settlement. The President, he said, had always been ready "to receive and to treat with the utmost respect" any compromise proposal from the British government. McLane had expressed the opinion that he could secure from Lord Aberdeen an offer of settlement at the 49th parallel with one of several alternative modifications. Such an offer, Buchanan assured McLane, the President would send to the Senate; and he added in a private note that the Senate would certainly approve it.

Moderation Wins in Congress

Thus the President, through Buchanan's note to McLane (February 26, 1846), abandoned the claim to 54°40′ and secretly reverted to the 49th parallel boundary repeatedly proposed by his predecessors. There were still, however "Fifty-four forty" men in Congress. Early in February, the House of Representatives had passed a bill directing the President to give the year's notice of abrogation of the joint-occupation agreement, but only after prolonged wrangling did the Senate pass the measure. The Oregon debate in both houses was notable for two things: the popularization of the phrase "manifest destiny" and a dispute between spokesmen of the Northwest and the South over the proposed compromise on the boundary question.

The phrase "manifest destiny" had apparently been coined by one John L. O'Sullivan and first used in an editorial on the Texas question printed in the *Democratic Review* for July and August 1845. It appeared again in the New York *Morning News* (also edited by O'Sullivan) of December 27, 1845, in an editorial setting forth the writer's conception of "the true title" to Oregon. The "true title," according to this argument, was not to be found in rights of discovery, exploration, settlement, and contiguity—strong though the American case was on these grounds—but rather in

7. J. W. Pratt, "James K. Polk and John Bull," *Canadian Historical Review*, 24 (1943), 341–49. That Polk's retreat from his claim to the 54° 40′ boundary was hastened by McLane's report of February 3, 1846, is questioned by Frederick Merk, *The Oregon Question: Essays in Anglo-American Diplomacy and Politics* (Cambridge: Harvard University Press, 1967), pp. 337–47, but is borne out in Charles Sellers, *James K. Polk, Continentalist, 1843–1846* (Princeton: Princeton University Press, 1966), pp. 380–83. See also Pratt's review of the Merk volume in *Political Science Quarterly,* 83 (September 1968), 453–54.

8. See Chapter 13.

the right of our manifest destiny to overspread and to possess the whole of the continent which Providence has given us for the development of the great experiment of liberty and federated self-government entrusted to us. . . . The God of nature and of nations has marked it for our own; and with His blessing we will firmly maintain the incontestable rights He has given, and fearlessly perform the high duties He has imposed.

Within a few days the phrase "manifest destiny" was being quoted in Congress by opponents as well as advocates of terminating joint occupation; and though the opposition quoted it only to ridicule it, expressing mock surprise that so important a principle of international law was not mentioned by Grotius or Vattel and branding it as "the robber's title," the supporters of President Polk's policy were not ashamed now to cite "destiny" as an argument for expelling the British from Oregon.[9]

The sectional controversy arose from the fact that southern leaders like Calhoun, having secured Texas,[10] now favored compromise with Great Britain on Oregon. Northwestern expansionists, for whom Democratic Senators Hannegan of Indiana and Allen of Ohio were leading spokesmen, asserted that the Democrats had agreed at the Baltimore Convention that the South should get Texas and the Northwest the whole of Oregon, up to 54°40'. They took literally the slogan "Fifty-four forty or fight," though professing to believe that England would not fight if the United States stood firm. Hannegan not only charged the South with "Punic faith" in deserting the West after realizing its own objectives; speaking of rumors that Polk would compromise with Great Britain, he declared that, in that event: "I shall hold him recreant to the principles which he professed, recreant to the trust which he accepted, recreant to the generous

confidence which a majority of the people reposed in him."

Southern Democratic senators, on the other hand, joined with Whigs to pave the way for compromise. Whig senators shared the alarm of business and commercial groups at the possibility of a costly war with England. Calhoun's advocacy of compromise received warm praise in New York and New England. Daniel Webster, who set a low value upon Oregon and a high value upon peace with England, was working for compromise both in the Senate and out. The aged Albert Gallatin wrote a seventy-five page argument for postponement of the Oregon crises, including an estimate of "War Expenses" covering over twenty pages. An anonymous pamphlet published in Philadelphia declared that "monied men, for the most part, think very unfavorably of belligerent measures for the acquisition of Oregon" and declared that such men would not deem it prudent to invest money in government bonds "issued for the purpose of asserting a claim to worse than useless territory on the coast of the Pacific."[11]

Under such influences, the curt resolution passed by the House of Representatives was softened in the Senate. As amended and finally passed by both houses (April 23, 1846), it authorized the President to give the year's notice instead of directing him to do so. It made no mention of "clear and unquestionable" rights to all of Oregon but expressed a hope for "a speedy and amicable adjustment" of "the respective claims of the United States and Great Britain." Its adoption by the Senate by a vote of 40 to 14 gave assurance that the Senate would not reject a compromise settlement.

The Controversy Is Settled

Five days after passage of the resolution Buchanan forwarded the formal notice to

9. J. W. Pratt, "The Origin of 'Manifest Destiny'," *American Historical Review,* 32 (1927), 795–98; id., "John L. O'Sullivan and Manifest Destiny," *New York History,* 45 (1933), 213–34.
10. Texas was admitted to the Union December 29, 1845. A fine analysis of the Oregon debate in Congress is Merk, *The Oregon Question,* chap. 13.

11. Albert Gallatin, *The Oregon Question* (New York: Bartlett & Welford, 1846); *Oregon. The Cost and the Consequences,* by "a Disciple of the Washington School" (Philadelphia: J. C. Clark's Bookstore, 1846).

McLane for transmission to the British government. In doing so he reiterated the President's willingness to consider any suitable proposal made by Great Britain and his desire to preserve amicable relations.

Lord Aberdeen had awaited final congressional action upon the resolution before submitting the new British offer. Aberdeen, personally, had long been ready to accept the 49th parallel as a boundary. He attached little value to the disputed territory—to the whole of Oregon, in fact. He had, naturally, resented Polk's inaugural declaration that the American title to Oregon was "clear and unquestionable," and had replied, in a speech in the House of Lords, that England also possessed rights in Oregon which were "clear and unquestionable" and which, he added, "by the blessing of God, and with your support, . . . we are fully prepared to maintain." Undoubtedly the British government would have met with force any American attempt to occupy all of Oregon, but Aberdeen, at least, was ready to accept any compromise that could be reconciled with the national honor.

Aberdeen's real problem, in abandoning the British claim to the Columbia boundary and proposing the line that had been repeatedly offered by the United States and as often rejected by Great Britain, was to reconcile British opinion to the retreat. He must convince the British public that no vital British interests were being surrendered, and he must guard the cabinet, the Peel ministry, which had but a slender majority in Parliament, against a Liberal attack upon their conciliatory policy.

In the first undertaking, Aberdeen was assisted by events in Oregon itself. In past negotiations, the chief reason for insisting upon the Columbia River boundary had been the interest of the Hudson's Bay Company in that river and its watershed. In 1845, however, because of the decline of the fur trade on the Columbia and growing friction between the company's establishment at Fort Vancouver and the American settlers south of the river, the company had moved its headquar-

ters from Fort Vancouver to Vancouver Island, thus virtually abandoning the river. It was now possible, therefore, for Lord Aberdeen and his supporters to argue that the Columbia River boundary was not worth contending for.[12]

At home, Aberdeen and his associates were able to win over a large section of the British press to advocacy of compromise, and leaders of the Liberal party, now in opposition, prevailed upon the chauvinistic Viscount Palmerston, their spokesman in foreign affairs, to abstain from attack upon the proposed Oregon settlement. The prospect, furthermore, of an enlarged trade with the United States, founded upon the imminent repeal of the Corn Laws in Great Britain and the low-tariff policy of the Polk Administration, contributed to the desire for a friendly settlement of the Oregon question; and the work of the peace societies on both sides of the Atlantic, which were active in petitioning both governments and in promoting "friendly addresses" between English and American cities, should not be overlooked.[13] All in all, by the spring of 1846, Aberdeen was sure of his ground in England and could make a compromise proposal with assurance of its receiving British approval.

Aberdeen's offer, in the form of a treaty, was received in Washington on June 6. It proposed to draw the boundary line along the 49th parallel from the Rocky Mountains to the channel separating Vancouver Island from the mainland and thence through the channel around the south end of the island, leaving the entire island to the British. Other clauses

12. Merk, *The Oregon Question*, chap. 8. In promoting, through their obstreperous behavior, the company's abandonment of Fort Vancouver, the pioneers made a contribution of a sort to American acquisition of the territory between the Columbia River and the 49th parallel. Certainly they had not "occupied" the disputed territory, for not more than thirty-one Americans had settled north of the Columbia by 1846.
13. Merk, *The Oregon Question*, chaps. 9–11; T. P. Martin, "Free Trade and the Oregon Question," in *Facts and Factors in Economic History* (Cambridge: Harvard University Press, 1932), pp. 470–91; M. E. Curti, *The American Peace Crusade, 1815–1860* (Durham: Duke University Press, 1929), pp. 112–22.

recognized and safeguarded the lawfully acquired property rights, both north and south of the Columbia, of the Hudson's Bay Company and other British corporations and subjects. These provisions were acceptable to Polk. He objected, however, to a provision that navigation of the Columbia from the boundary line to its mouth should be "free and open to the Hudson's Bay Company, and to all British subjects trading with the same." In fact, he had said categorically that he would not accept such a provision. But the situation did not admit of delay. War with Mexico had begun, making a settlement with England imperative. In England, the Peel ministry, with Aberdeen as Foreign Secretary, retained power by a precarious hold, and Lord Aberdeen's successor was likely to be less compliant than he. On the advice of his cabinet, therefore, Polk resolved to send the treaty project to the Senate as it stood and to give or withhold his sanction depending upon the Senate's advice. Declaring, with dubious veracity, that the opinions expressed in his December message remained unchanged, Polk "passed the buck" to the Senate.

Two days later, on June 12th, the Senate voted, 38 to 12, to advise acceptance of the British proposal without change. The treaty was formally signed on June 15, and on June 18 the Senate gave its advice and consent for ratification by a vote of 41 to 14. The treaty was proclaimed on August 5, 1846. The long controversy was settled, apparently to the satisfaction of nearly everyone except the little group of "Fifty-four forty" men from the Old Northwest.[14]

14. A minor complication resulting from acceptance of the 49° boundary is the plight of Point Roberts, an area of 2,500 acres at the tip of a peninsula jutting southward from British Columbia into the Strait of Georgia. Point Roberts, part of the State of Washington, is cut off from the rest of that State by many miles of water and from British Columbia by the 49th parallel. Its 250 residents, American citizens, must travel 30 miles through Canadian territory to reach the nearest American town. School children are bused 60 miles daily. *New York Times,* March 23, 1969.

12

Texas

Some twenty years before the westward movement of population reached Oregon, it had begun to flow into Texas. Here there were no formidable physical barriers to migration, and the Spanish government, which had long prohibited the entry of Americans into Texas, modified that policy in 1821. In that year it granted to Connecticut-born Moses Austin, who had lived for a while under Spanish rule in upper Louisiana, permission to settle three hundred Louisiana families in Texas. The new policy was continued by the government of Mexico, which became independent soon thereafter. Moses Austin died before he could carry out his plan, and his son, Stephen F. Austin, assumed charge of the enterprise.

Under contracts with the Mexican authorities, Austin and other empresarios (contractors) received permission to settle specified numbers of families in the central portion of Texas. Mexican federal and state regulations made the acquisition of land easy and at a price far below that of public land in the United States. The population of Texas grew rapidly. Geographical location, soil, climate, the easy evasion of Mexican laws against slavery, all made Texas more attractive to the South than to other sections of the United States. By 1835 the population of Texas approximated thirty thousand, nearly all from the United States and the great majority from the slave states of the South.

In the meantime, the United States had sounded out the Mexican government as to its willingness to part with Texas. John Quincy Adams, in his negotiations with Spain, had surrendered the claim to Texas with reluctance, and the surrender had been criticized in the Southwest. As President, Adams permitted Joel R. Poinsett, first United States minister to Mexico, to suggest that Mexico celebrate her independence by making a new boundary treaty instead of accepting that made by Spain; but when the Mexican government showed no willingness to give up Texas or any part of it, Poinsett dropped the subject. A treaty signed in 1828, but not ratified till four years later, simply confirmed the boundary agreed upon between the United States and Spain in 1819. Andrew Jackson, when he became President, replaced Poinsett with Anthony Butler. "Vain, ignorant, ill-tempered, and corrupt," [1] Butler was a disgrace to the diplomatic service. His fruitless efforts to secure Texas by bribing Mexican officials led tardily to his recall in 1835.

Texans Win Their Independence

Alarmed by such attempts as Butler's and awake to the possibility that Texas might be lost through revolution by its American-born inhabitants (as West Florida had been lost by Spain in 1810–1811), the Mexican government tried too late to check the flow of immigrants or to subject them to military control. Such measures produced resentment without achieving their purpose. General Antonio Lopez de Santa Anna, elected President of Mexico in 1833, undertook a more drastic solution of the Texas problem. Abolishing the federal constitution, he transformed Mexico into a centralized state, in which the people of Texas stood to lose any vestige of local autonomy. The Texan response was rebellion, a declaration of independence (March 2, 1836), and the crushing defeat and capture of Santa Anna at the battle of San Jacinto (April 21, 1836). The remnant of Santa Anna's invading army retreated beyond the Rio Grande, and Texas had won *de facto* independence. Sam Houston, who had commanded the Texan army at San Jacinto, was rewarded for his victory by election to the presidency of the Republic of Texas.

The United States and the Texan Revolution

The Texans' fight for life against Santa Anna evoked widespread sympathy and material support from the United States. "Texas meetings" were held in cities ranging from New Orleans to Boston. Money and supplies were sent to Texas by sea, and hundreds of volunteers from the United States swelled the ranks of Houston's army. President Jackson, despite sympathy with the Texans and especially with Sam Houston, an old friend and comrade in arms, issued the appropriate orders for the enforcement of the neutrality laws. That these orders were not rigorously enforced was the result of strong pro-Texas feeling in the Southwest, which infected even federal district attorneys and United States army officers. The Mexican minister in Washington lodged protest after protest with the State Department against American activities in support of Texas and finally became so incensed that he withdrew from the capital.

Meanwhile both Congress and the President were weighing the question of recognition. Proposals for such action were heard in Congress as early as April 1836. The news of San Jacinto greatly strengthened the case for recognition. But aside from caution in recognizing a government that had not yet demonstrated a capacity to maintain itself, there was another obstacle in the rising antislavery sentiment in the North. Abolitionists opposed recognition as a step toward annexation. Once annexed, they feared, Texas might be subdivided into four or five new slave states. Despite such opposition—which found a powerful spokesman in ex-President John Quincy Adams, now a representative from Massachusetts—Congress and the President moved step by step toward recognition. On March 3, 1837, just before relinquishing the presidency, Jackson nominated a chargé d'affaires for Texas, and formal diplomatic relations were established in the following July.

But annexation was another matter. It was formally proposed by the Texan minister in August 1837 and was warmly favored by southern leaders. But Martin Van Buren's administration, already staggering under the burden of nationwide financial panic and economic depression, had no wish to take on a fight with the antislavery forces. The Texan offer of annexation was politely declined. Texas thereupon withdrew the proposal, and from 1838 to 1842, talk of annexation subsided in both countries.

---

1. G. L. Rives, *The United States and Mexico, 1821–1848,* 2 vols. (New York: Charles Scribner's Sons, 1913), 1: 235–36.

The Texas Question in Party Politics

By 1842 annexation was taking on new attractiveness on both sides of the border. Sam Houston, again elected to the presidency after three years out of office, found his government facing a heavy debt, an empty treasury, and renewed hostilities with Mexico. He saw two possible avenues of escape from these difficulties: annexation by the United States or continued independence under British protection. When he approached Washington on the possibility of annexation, he found the Virginian President, John Tyler, personally sympathetic but unable to act because of the opposition of his Secretary of State, Daniel Webster. But Webster resigned in May 1843, and his successor, Abel P. Upshur, like Tyler a Virginian, shared Tyler's desire to bring Texas into the Union.

The prospect that Texas might turn to Britain for protection, and the growth of British interest and influence in the "Lone Star Republic," had in fact aroused serious concern in all sections of the United States. It was the aim of Lord Aberdeen, British Foreign Secretary, to keep Texas independent, a market for British manufacturers, and a source of cotton for British mills. To remove the appeal of annexation by the United States, he sought to induce Mexico to recognize Texan independence. If at the same time Texas could be induced to follow Britain's example and abolish slavery, so much the better.

No part of this program was secret, and each part of it created alarm in the United States. To the South it meant danger to slavery as well as competition with the South's principal staple. To the commercial North it meant diversion of Texan trade from the United States into other hands—a diversion that was indeed already a reality. The surest cure for all these dangers was annexation. Annexation would also be profitable to an unknown number of speculators who held certificates of the Texas debt and scrip entitling them to Texas lands.

North as well as South, then, had begun to see advantages in the acquisition of Texas. When Secretary Upshur informed Houston in September 1843 that the administration had changed its policy and would be glad to conclude a treaty of annexation, he felt safe in assuring the Texan that such a treaty would certainly receive the Senate's approval.

Houston consented. Negotiations were interrupted by the death of Upshur, but were resumed under his successor, John C. Calhoun, and on April 12, 1844, an annexation treaty was signed. Texas was to be annexed to the United States as one of its territories, surrendering its public lands to the United States, which in turn would assume the Texan public debt to an amount not exceeding ten million dollars.

Had the treaty been acted upon promptly by the Senate, it would perhaps have received the better than two-thirds majority that had been indicated by a poll in January. The Senate, however, deferred action until after the party nominating conventions in May, and there events took a turn that sealed the treaty's fate. On the eve of the conventions the leading contenders for the nominations, Martin Van Buren, Democrat, and Henry Clay, Whig, published letters in which both opposed the immediate annexation of Texas, though leaving the door open to its future accomplishment. True to expectations, the Whig Convention nominated Clay and thereby committed the party against immediate annexation. The Democrats, on the other hand, unwilling to accept Van Buren's anti-Texas stand, set him aside and nominated the comparatively little known James K. Polk, a thorough-going expansionist. The Democrats also wrote into their platform a plank declaring for "the re-annexation of Texas and the re-occupation of Oregon." By both their candidate and their platform, the Democrats labeled themselves the party of expansion.

The effect of these party maneuvers was seen when the Senate, on June 8, 1844, voted on the Texas treaty. In view of Clay's stand against annexation, Whig senators could hardly support the treaty even if they so desired. The Van Buren Democrats, furthermore, were offended at the defeat of their hero and for the time being were unwilling to vote for a policy that he opposed. Thus party and factional politics had more weight than conviction in determining votes on the treaty. Of twenty-nine Whig senators, all but one (Henderson of Mississippi) voted No, and they were joined by seven of the twenty-four Democrats, while one Democratic senator did not vote. Thus, instead of the two-thirds vote for ratification predicted by Upshur in January, the vote stood thirty-five to sixteen against it.[2]

Whether defeat of the treaty disposed finally of Texan annexation, as some observers believed, or whether, as President Tyler suggested, there might be other means of accomplishing the same objective, was not immediately apparent. At any rate, nothing further could be done about it until the country had spoken in the presidential election.

Like most elections in the United States, that of 1844 could not rightly be considered a referendum on a single issue. The Texas question was prominent, but it could not be isolated from traditional party loyalties, divergence upon economic policies, nativism, and abolitionism. Nor was it clear that a vote for the Whig candidate was necessarily a vote against annexation. In his "Raleigh letter" in April, Clay had said that he was against annexation under the circumstances then existing. At the urging of southern supporters he now published an "Alabama letter," in

which he said that "far from having any personal objection to the annexation of Texas," he would "be glad to see it, without dishonor —without war, with the common consent of the Union, and upon just and fair terms." If elected, he said, and if called upon to make a decision on the Texas question, he would be guided by the conditions then prevailing.

Not all Clay votes, then, were against annexation, nor were all anti-annexation votes cast for Clay. Some thousands of these went to James G. Birney, candidate of the abolitionist Liberty party. An indeterminate number of others were cast for Polk, for in the North many Democratic opponents of annexation found it possible to support the party ticket on other grounds. With the exception of South Carolina, all the states in 1844 chose their presidential electors by popular vote. The returns, therefore, give a reasonably accurate idea of popular preferences as between the candidates. The figures were as follows:

	Popular Vote	*No. of States*	*Electoral Vote*
Polk	1,337,243	15	170
Clay	1,299,062	13	105
Birney	62,300	—	—

Thus (omitting South Carolina, from which there are no figures), Polk's plurality over Clay was 38,181 in a total vote of approximately 2,700,000. But if to Clay's vote is added that of Birney, the Liberty party candidate, the total exceeds Polk's by 23,819. If it could be assumed that every vote cast for Clay or Birney was a vote against the annexation of Texas, it would appear that a small popular majority was against annexation. But, for reasons already given, this cannot be assumed. Furthermore, there was no popular vote from South Carolina, where the electorate, had they had the opportunity, would certainly have supported Polk and annexation. It is obviously impossible to determine what was the popular will as to Texas.

On first examination the electoral vote appears much more decisive. Polk carried fifteen states with an electoral vote of 170; Clay,

2. Some northern votes for the treaty may also have been lost by publication of a note from Calhoun to the British minister in which he defended the treaty as necessitated by British encouragement of emancipation in Texas. He had added a long argument in defense of slavery and had cited facts and figures purporting to show the ill effects of freedom upon the health, morals, and general well-being of the Negro. This communication naturally antagonized northern opinion by stamping annexation as a proslavery measure. Not intended for publication, it had been leaked to the press by an antislavery senator. C. M. Wiltse, *John C. Calhoun, Sectionalist, 1844–1850* (Indianapolis: The Bobbs-Merrill Company, Inc., 1951), pp. 170–71.

thirteen states with an electoral vote of 105. Polk's majority, however, depended upon New York with its thirty-six electoral votes, and in New York the combined vote for Clay and Birney exceeded that for Polk by nearly nine thousand. Had only a portion of the Birney votes been cast for Clay, Clay would have carried New York and have had an electoral vote of 141 to Polk's 134. It has been contended, therefore, that Clay would have won the election if he had not, by his Alabama letter, driven antislavery voters into the Birney camp. But even of this no one can be sure. If the Alabama letter lost votes for Clay in the North, it presumably won votes in the South. Clay carried Tennessee, Polk's own state, by the almost invisible margin of 113 votes. Assuming that without the Alabama letter Clay would have lost Tennessee but have won New York and also Michigan (which Polk also carried by a mere plurality), we find that Polk would still have led with 142 electoral votes to Clay's 133.[3]

Whatever the history student may think of the meaning of the election, President Tyler admitted no doubt. To him, as he told Congress in his annual message, it appeared that both the people (through the popular vote) and the states (through the electoral vote) had decided. "A controlling majority of the people," he asserted, "and a large majority of the States, have declared in favor of immediate annexation." He recommended, therefore, that Congress should embody the terms of the late treaty in an act or joint resolution, "to be perfected and made binding on the two countries, when adopted in like manner by the government of Texas."

Invitation by Joint Resolution

The obvious advantage of action by joint resolution instead of treaty was that a resolution could be passed by a majority vote in

3. The figures on which this analysis is based are taken from Edward Stanwood, *A History of the Presidency from 1788 to 1897* (Boston: Houghton Mifflin Company, 1926), p. 223.

each house of Congress as compared with the two-thirds vote in the Senate required for a treaty. A joint resolution providing for admission of Texas to the Union as a state was passed by the House of Representatives on January 25, 1845. The change from the territorial status proposed by the treaty to that of statehood was designed to meet a constitutional point. For authority to acquire territory by joint resolution, the annexationists relied upon the constitutional provision that "new States may be admitted by the Congress into this Union."

In the Senate the Whig-dominated Committee on Foreign Relations reported against the resolution on the ground that foreign territory could be acquired only by treaty. While the Senate debated the committee's report, public opinion was expressing itself through the press, petitions to Congress, and resolutions of state legislatures. A preponderance of such sentiment, especially in the South and West, appears to have favored immediate annexation. Even in New England, the legislatures of Maine and New Hampshire passed annexationist resolutions. Goaded by instructions from the Missouri legislature, Senator Thomas H. Benton, who had opposed Tyler's treaty as likely to lead to war with Mexico, introduced a substitute for the House resolution, providing for admission of Texas upon terms to be agreed on by negotiation with Texas instead of terms defined unilaterally by the United States, as in the House measure.

In order to secure Benton's vote and the votes of other wavering senators, the Democratic managers attached Benton's bill to the House resolution as an alternative, giving the President the authority either to invite Texas into the Union on the House terms or to negotiate an agreement as Benton proposed. Upon assurances, as Benton later claimed, that Tyler would leave the choice of alternatives to Polk and that Polk would elect negotiation under Benton's plan, Benton and several other senators who had opposed the House resolution now voted for it in its amended form, and at a night session on February 27, 1845, the amended resolution passed the Senate by a vote of 27 to 25, the majority comprising all the Democratic senators and three southern Whigs. The House promptly passed the amended measure, and President Tyler signed it on March 1, 1845.

Tyler and Calhoun resolved to act in the short time remaining before the change in administration, and on March 3, Calhoun sent instructions to A. J. Donelson, the American chargé d'affaires for Texas, who was waiting in New Orleans, to invite Texas to enter the Union under the terms of the House resolution. Thus they discarded Benton's plan, much to the chagrin of that senator, and Polk, after a few days of apparent hesitation, decided to let Donelson proceed under Calhoun's instructions. It was now for Texas to decide.

Texas Accepts Annexation

Under the terms thus offered, Texas was invited to become a state in the Union, comprising "the territory properly included within, and rightfully belonging to the republic of Texas." All questions of the state's boundaries were to be left to negotiation between the government of the United States and "other governments." Texas was to cede to the United States its public buildings, ports, harbors, fortifications, and other means of defense, but it was to retain its public lands and to remain responsible for its debts; the latter should never become a charge upon the United States. A state constitution, republican in form, must be submitted to Congress on or before January 1, 1846. Additional states, not over four in number, might, with the consent of Texas, be formed out of her territory. In any such states lying north of 36°30′, the Missouri Compromise line, slavery was to be prohibited; states south of that line might be admitted with or without slavery, as the people thereof should determine.

Congress had acted. It was now for Texas to decide whether to accept annexation on the terms offered. There much depended upon

Sam Houston. His term as President ended in December 1844, when he was succeeded by Anson Jones, but his influence outlived his term in office. Houston had given his support to the treaty of annexation, but he had served notice that if Texas were again rejected by the United States, she would *"remain forever separate,"* and that the United States must expect that "she would seek some other friend." Texas had been again rejected, and Houston's attitude remained problematical.

Tyler and Calhoun, while they remained in office, did everything they could to conciliate Houston. In particular they sought to make use of Andrew Jackson's well known influence over the Texan. In August 1844, they had sent to Texas as chargé d'affaires Andrew Jackson Donelson, nephew and close friend of the old hero of the Hermitage. Through letters to both Houston and Donelson, Jackson sought to play upon whatever remained of Houston's loyalty to the United States in order to save him from falling under British influence. "How much more honorable," Jackson wrote, ". . . to be a senator representing a free and enlightened people, than the president of a people, a mere colony of England, and fighting against the United States that gave them birth, . . ." While Jackson thus hinted at a senatorship for this friend if Texas were annexed, other correspondents suggested that even the presidency of the United States might be within his reach.

Houston remained coy to such hints of preferment in the United States. In view of the uncertain temper of Congress, both he and Anson Jones would have been negligent of the true interests of Texas had they entirely closed the door upon a career of independence under British protection. At the same time, however, they left open the door to annexation. In his valedictory message to the Texan Congress (December 9, 1844), Houston pictured in glowing terms the future that might lie before an independent Texas, but at the same time spoke sympathetically of a possible union with "the beloved land from which we have sprung—the land of the broad stripes and bright stars"; and a few days later he wrote Jackson that if the United States should now make a proper offer of annexation, he would "not interpose any individual obstacle to its consummation."

Such was the situation in Texas when Congress passed the joint resolution and Donelson hastened back to Texas from New Orleans with the proposal made by Tyler and confirmed by Polk. Donelson found Houston at first seriously dissatisfied with the terms of the offer and disposed to insist upon negotiating under Benton's plan; but President Anson Jones, although agreeing with Houston that the United States should have offered better terms, assured Donelson that he would submit the proposal to the Congress and the people of Texas and that a special session of Congress for that purpose would be called to meet on June 16.[4] Weeks before that date,

Houston had been won over to support of annexation upon the terms offered.

The British government made a final effort to prevent annexation.[5] In the spring of 1845, Captain Charles Elliot, British chargé d'affaires in Texas, visited the Mexican capital, where he persuaded the Mexican government to agree to a treaty by which Mexico would recognize the independence of Texas in return for a promise by Texas never to annex herself to another power, the question of boundary being left for future adjustment. Elliot returned to Texas with this document shortly before the Texan Congress met in June, and Jones laid before Congress both the proposed treaty with Mexico and the proposal of annexation from the United States. Jones hoped, with the Mexican offer in hand, to be able to bargain for better terms from the United States, but Texan sentiment for annexation had become so overwhelming that the Texan Congress threw away the opportunity. By unanimous vote the Texan Senate rejected the treaty with Mexico, and both houses of Congress voted without dissent for annexation upon the terms offered. On July 4, a special convention confirmed this choice, and the convention's action, together with the state constitution that it had prepared, was ratified by popular vote in October. The final resolution admitting Texas as a state of the Union was passed by the American Congress and signed by President Polk on December 29, 1845.

---

4. Jones, in later years, claimed to have been "the architect" of annexation. He favored annexation, so he said, when Houston opposed it, and he took credit for the various measures that aroused and kept alive annexation sentiment in the United States. Anson Jones, *Memoranda and Official Correspondence Relating to the Republic of Texas, Its History and Annexation* (New York: Appleton-Century-Crofts, 1859), pp. 44, 58, 80–81. His statements, about both himself and Houston, need to be discounted. See Herbert Gambrell, *Anson Jones, The Last President of Texas* (Garden City: Doubleday & Company, Inc., 1948). Jones also asserted (pp. 46–51) that agents of President Polk tried to instigate him to renew hostilities with Mexico "so that, when Texas was finally brought into the Union, *she might bring a war with her.*" Some revisionist historians have seen in this incident evidence of a scheme by Polk to bring on a war with Mexico that would enable him to seize California (as actually happened a year later). See R. R. Stenberg, "The Failure of Polk's War Intrigue of 1845," *Pacific Historical Review,* 4 (March 1935), 39–69; G. W. Price, *Origins of the War with Mexico: The Polk-Stockton Intrigue* (Austin: University of Texas Press, 1967). There is no doubt that such agents, notably Commodore Robert F. Stockton of the Navy, tried to persuade Jones to permit the commander of the Texas militia to seek a confrontation with Mexican troops on the Rio Grande, but the contention that they were doing Polk's bidding in that respect lacks adequate proof and is contradicted by other known facts of Polk's policy at this time. See Charles Sellers, *James K. Polk, Continentalist, 1843–*

1846 (Princeton: Princeton University Press, 1966), pp. 222–26.

5. When the treaty of annexation was published in the spring of 1844, Lord Aberdeen had proposed an ambitious plan to preserve Texan independence. His scheme was what he called a "diplomatic act" by which Great Britain and France should join with Mexico and Texas in guaranteeing the independence of Texas and the boundaries of Mexico. France was interested, but the plan was dropped upon the advice of the British and French ministers in Washington. Any such European intervention, they warned, was certain to heighten the expansionist fever in Washington and to insure the election of Polk, the expansionist candidate.

The acquisition of Texas and of a clear title to Oregon south of the 49th parallel was quickly followed by the war with Mexico of 1846–1848 and the resulting addition of a still more notable slice of territory to the American domain. By the treaty that put an end to that two-year struggle, the United States secured the Rio Grande boundary, Upper California, and the vast intermediate region known as New Mexico. In three years, 1845–1848, the area of the United States had grown by over 1,200,000 square miles, an increase of more than 66 percent. It was no wonder that expansionist-minded Americans proclaimed their faith in Manifest Destiny.

Subjects of Contention with Mexico

The complicated factors that gave rise to the war with Mexico may be thus summarized: (1) Mexican resentment over the annexation of Texas by the United States, (2) a dispute as to what in reality constituted the southwestern boundary of Texas, (3) the failure of Mexico to pay certain damage claims of citizens of the United States, (4) President Polk's anxiety to acquire California for the United States. These factors interacted upon one another in a manner adverse to a maintenance of peaceful relations, Mexico's resentment over the annexation of Texas proved an insuperable obstacle to amicable negotiation over claims and boundary, and the glitter of California in the eyes of James K. Polk— for its shining harbors, not its still unknown golden treasure [1]—probably made him less forbearing toward Mexico on other points than he might otherwise have been.

From the time in Tyler's administration when the annexation of Texas was first seriously contemplated, Mexico had repeatedly served notice that it would regard such action on the part of the United States as a *casus belli*. Such warnings had been delivered in the summer of 1843 and the spring of 1844. Cal-

1. N. A. Graebner, *Empire on the Pacific: A Study in American Continental Expansion* (New York: The Ronald Press Company, 1955), emphasizes commercial interest in Pacific harbors as a major factor in the expansionism of the 1840's.

13

President Polk's Quarrel with Mexico

houn, after signing his abortive treaty of annexation in April 1844, had sent a special messenger to Mexico in a fruitless effort to mollify the Mexican government, which refused to negotiate on the subject but as yet maintained diplomatic relations with Washington. When, however, in March 1845, the joint resolution of annexation was passed by Congress and signed by President Tyler, the Mexican minister in Washington asked for his passports and shortly thereafter took his departure from the United States. As the Mexican government at the same time terminated relations with the United States minister, all formal diplomatic intercourse ceased. Mexico, however, fresh from one revolution and with another on the horizon,[2] was in no condition to inaugurate a war with the United States. It seems probable that Mexico would eventually have acquiesced in the accomplished fact of annexation had that been the sole subject of contention.

The dispute over annexation, however, was further embittered by a controversy over just what had been annexed. The United States, convinced of the propriety of its annexing Texas, had adopted the Texan claim that its boundary was the Rio Grande. Mexico, indignant that annexation had occurred at all, further insisted that Texas had never extended west or south of the River Nueces. The boundary question was of a kind that should have been susceptible of friendly adjustment had both sides been willing to await an examination and negotiation. An impartial examination would probably have sustained the Mexican contention. Texas, under Spanish and Mexican rule, it seems well established, had never extended beyond the Nueces. The

Texan claim to the Rio Grande boundary rested upon an early act of the Texan Congress, which could have no force against Mexico, and upon the fact that Santa Anna's armies, after San Jacinto, had retired beyond the Rio Grande. Thereafter, the land between the rivers had not been effectively occupied or controlled by either party to the dispute. The Texans had a settlement at Corpus Christi, south of the Nueces at its mouth; the Mexicans had a few scattered ranches and villages just north of the Rio Grande. Otherwise the strip was virtually no man's land. Texas had thus done little or nothing through *de facto* occupation to counter Mexico's historic claim. The claim of the United States was as strong as that of Texas, and no stronger. The joint resolution of annexation had merely provided that the boundaries of Texas should be subject to adjustment between the United States and other powers. American diplomats, indeed, now revived the claim that the Rio Grande had been the ancient boundary of Louisiana, but since the United States had definitely given up that claim by the treaty of 1819, it is difficult to see what bearing it had upon the question of the limits of Texas.

It seems regrettable, in retrospect, that the United States and Mexico did not agree to abstain from any attempt to occupy the disputed area until a settlement could be reached. On the Mexican side, however, such an agreement would have meant acquiescence in the annexation of Texas proper, and for this Mexico was not ready. President Polk, on the other hand, was determined to uphold the Texan claim to the Rio Grande boundary. He was willing to recognize merit in the Mexican contention to the extent of cancelling several millions of dollars of damage claims against Mexico in return for its surrender, but was not willing, in the meantime, to forgo occupation of the disputed territory.

In July 1845, as soon as the Texan legislature and convention had voted for annexation, Brigadier General Zachary Taylor, with some 3,900 United States troops, was ordered from the Sabine into Texas to defend it

2. Santa Anna, after his defeat and capture at San Jacinto had returned to Mexico in 1837. In the following year he had lost a leg but won additional military distinction in defending Vera Cruz against a French attack. From 1841 until November, 1844, he was again President of Mexico, but was then overthrown and banished. Herrera was then President for a brief period. In December 1845, he was overthrown by General Paredes, the same military chieftain who had engineered the revolution against Santa Anna thirteen months before.

against an anticipated Mexican invasion. He was instructed to take up a position south of the Nueces and as near the Rio Grande "as prudence will dictate," but not to disturb any posts occupied by Mexican troops, or Mexican settlements not under Texan jurisdiction. The obvious intent of these instructions was, while asserting title to the disputed territory, to avoid the initiative in any clash with Mexican forces. Exercising the discretion allowed him, Taylor in August stationed his army at Corpus Christi at the mouth of the Nueces, at a prudent distance from the Rio Grande. There he remained until March 1846.

A third subject of dispute with Mexico was the latter's failure to settle claims of American citizens to the amount of some millions of dollars. These claims had originated in supplies purchased on credit by the Mexican government and never paid for, and in damages to persons and property of United States citizens suffered during revolutionary disorders in Mexico. A treaty of 1839 had set up a mixed claims commission that had considered claims of over eight million dollars and made awards of slightly over two millions. Additional claims of over three millions had been submitted too late for adjudication by the commission. The two millions adjudicated, Mexico had agreed to pay in twenty installments over a five-year period; she had paid three installments, together with arrears of interest to April 30, 1843, and then had suspended payments. Since the Mexican treasury was chronically empty, there was little hope that payments in money would be resumed at any early date, if ever. But an alternative mode of settlement was possible. Following the precedents of the Louisiana and Florida transactions, Polk was willing to accept a boundary settlement in lieu of money. Specifically, if Mexico would recognize the annexation of Texas with the Rio Grande boundary, Polk would release Mexico from all monetary claims of American citizens, which would then be settled out of the treasury of the United States. But Polk wished to carry the settlement still further. If Mexico would yield additional territory, dearly coveted by Polk, the President stood ready to fill the bare Mexican treasury with good American dollars.

Polk's California Policy

In a conversation with George Bancroft, his Secretary of the Navy, soon after taking office, Polk remarked that two of the "great measures" of his administration would be "the settlement of the Oregon boundary question" and "the acquisition of California." [3] His success in settling the Oregon question was described in another chapter. In the acquisition of California he was likewise successful, but not without bloodshed.

California, the youngest of Spain's colonial enterprises in America, had received its first Spanish settlers at the time of the American Revolution. The area of effective Spanish, and later Mexican, control never extended farther north than the shores of San Francisco Bay or farther inland than the coastal area. The great inland valleys of the Sacramento and San Joaquin Rivers remained practically untouched until the coming of the Americans. Aside from the presidios and Franciscan missions, Spanish activities consisted principally of sheep and cattle ranching. The agricultural possibilities and mineral wealth of California were unexploited and almost undreamed of, and as late as 1846, the entire population of Spanish descent probably did not exceed seven thousand persons.

3. James Schouler, *History of the United States of America under the Constitution,* revised edition, 7 vols. (New York: Dodd, Mead & Co., 1894–1913), 4: 498. The paging differs slightly in different printings of this work. The source of the quotation is a letter from Bancroft to Schouler of February 1887. Schouler says the conversation between Polk and Bancroft is "still preserved." This may mean that Bancroft had preserved a contemporary memorandum of the conversation. If he relied upon his memory only, after forty-two years, we should of course question the accuracy of his statement. Polk mentioned "four great measures," of which the other two were "a reduction of the tariff" and "the independent treasury." Since all four were realized, Polk deserves to rank as one of our most successful presidents—if success is to be measured by having a definite program and carrying it out.

The first visitors to California from the United States came by sea, but in the 1820's, American fur traders were beginning to make their way overland, and soon there was a sparse population of drifting "mountain men" living among the Indians in the interior. The first party of bona fide homeseekers crossed the mountains in 1841, and thereafter there was a steady trickle of immigrants, who followed the Oregon Trail to Fort Hall in modern Idaho, and then turned southwest to cross the Great Basin and the Sierras.

Two reports of official explorations, both published in 1845, contributed to the growing interest in California. Lieutenant Charles Wilkes, commander of a naval exploring expedition, spent several months in Oregon and California in 1841. In his report, published four years later, he praised San Francisco harbor as "one of the finest, if not the very best harbour in the world." He found the country potentially rich but ill-governed under Mexico. He predicted that it would become independent and, probably joined with Oregon, would "perhaps form a state that is destined to control the destinies of the Pacific." John C. Frémont, a lieutenant in the Topographical Corps of the Army, after surveying the Oregon Trail, crossed the Sierras into California in the winter of 1843–1844 and returned to the United States by a southern route. His report painted an attractive picture of the California valleys.

Most important of the Americans living in California was Thomas O. Larkin of Monterey. Larkin, a New Englander, had come by sea in 1832 and had built up a prosperous trade. About 1840 he began writing articles about California for Boston and New York newspapers that became the foremost sources of information for readers in the eastern United States. In 1843 Larkin was appointed first United States consul in Monterey.

By 1846, according to the estimates of Consul Larkin, there were some nine hundred Americans in California, as well as three hundred non-Spanish whites of other nationalities, and the American contingent was rapidly growing; the newcomers of 1845 alone had

numbered between four and five hundred. This infusion of American blood into a Mexican province inevitably called to mind the histories of West Florida and Texas. Larkin's eastern correspondents began asking him whether there were not "enough wild Yankees in California to take the management of affairs in their own hands" and predicting that the American population would soon be "sufficiently numerous to play the Texas game."

The danger of another "Texas game" in California was quite apparent to the government in Mexico, but all orders from Mexico City for halting American immigration or expelling the Americans already there were disregarded by the local officials, who had neither the will nor the power to enforce them. In fact, the hold of Mexico upon California grew steadily weaker, and it was clear to visitors as well as to residents in the country that the sands of Mexican rule were running out. Lieutenant Wilkes foretold an independent California, perhaps joined with Oregon. With greater realism, Sir George Simpson of the Hudson's Bay Company, who visited California in 1842, warned his countrymen that only prior occupation by Great Britain could save it from falling into the hands of the United States. The hour was approaching when vigorous action by the United States might bring about a notable extension of American territory.

Presidents Jackson and Tyler had both displayed an interest in the possibility of acquiring California, and Tyler had received from Lord Ashburton an assurance that Great Britain would not object to such an accession to American territory.[4] Despite such assurances, there was a growing suspicion in the United States not only that Great Britain would oppose the acquisition of California by this country, but that she sought it for herself. Rumors emanating from Mexico City had it that Mexico had mortgaged or would mortgage California to Great Britain as security for the large Mexican debt held by British subjects. No such plan really existed, but Brit-

4. See p. 104.

ish subjects in Mexico and California persistently reminded the British government of the value of California, the danger of its falling to the United States, and the comparative ease with which Great Britain might take possession of it. Such suggestions were discouraged by Lord Aberdeen, who clearly had no desire for California. By the close of 1844, however, when he faced defeat in his efforts to save Texas from the United States, he had become distinctly averse to the thought of California's suffering a similar fate. He therefore directed that Californians who contemplated throwing off Mexican rule should be warned that Great Britain would be displeased by their accepting a protectorate from any foreign power; but neither British naval officers nor other British officials on the West Coast received orders to oppose actively the occupation of California by the United States. The British government was certainly not prepared to oppose American policy in California at the risk of war.

President Polk was not informed of the exact nature of British policy in California. He was well aware of Lord Aberdeen's attempt to thwart American policy in Texas, and the persistent rumors of British designs upon California must have seemed to him entirely credible. His anxiety for an early acquisition of that territory, therefore, was founded largely upon a genuine fear that if the United States failed to acquire it, Great Britain would do so.

Aside from war and conquest, Polk saw two possible methods of acquiring California. It might be purchased, if Mexico would listen to reason, and Polk was determined to try this if he received the slightest encouragement from Mexico City. But if Mexico refused to negotiate, the Californians might be induced to join the United States of their own free will. Polk's reliance here was not upon the recent immigrants from the United States, who might have evinced a willingness to "play the Texas game"; it was rather upon the bona fide Californians of Spanish descent. He was well informed, through Larkin and others, of the shaky hold of the distant Mexican government upon California, of the impatience of many of the native Californians with the ineptitude and inefficiency of Mexican rule. Was it unreasonable to suppose that these people might be persuaded to sever their ties with Mexico and to form with the United States a close connection that would eventually lead to statehood? At least it was worth the effort, if purchase failed. Indeed, both methods might be tried at once.

Thomas O. Larkin's informing reports had been so satisfactory that it was now resolved to make him the confidential agent of the government and to entrust to him the execution of one of the two branches of Polk's California policy. In instructions written by Secretary of State Buchanan and dated October 17, 1845, Larkin received his new appointment and was informed of his new duties. He was to seek to counteract foreign influence in California. He was to supply his government with full information in regard to conditions in the territory, the identity of its leading citizens and officials, its trade, and the amount and character of immigration from the United States. More significantly, however, Larkin was directed to do whatever he could to win the friendship of the Californians and to assure them that if California should declare her independence of Mexico, "we shall render her all the kind offices in our power as a sister republic." The United States, they were to be told, did not desire to extend its boundaries "unless by the free and spontaneous wish of all the independent people of adjoining territories." But, the instructions continued:

> Whilst the President will make no effort and use no influence to induce California to become one of the free and independent States of this Union, yet if the people should desire to unite their destiny with ours, they would be received as brethren, whenever this can be done without affording Mexico just cause of complaint.

But although expansion by compulsion was not its policy, the United States could not view with indifference the prospect of California passing under the control of Great Britain or any other European power. In the absence of any attempt at such a transfer, the true policy for the Californians should be to let events take their course—a course which, the writer evidently felt, would lead eventually to a voluntary union of California with the United States. These instructions, which could easily be interpreted as an invitation to the Californians to revolt from Mexico and join the United States, were entrusted to Lieutenant Archibald H. Gillespie of the Marine Corps and reached Larkin on April 17, 1846.

Polk Reasserts the Monroe Doctrine

While awaiting an expression from the Californians of their desire for union with the United States, Polk made use of his annual message (December 2, 1845) to notify Europe in general and Great Britain in particular that California was not open to European colonization and that a voluntary union of California and the United States would be the business of no one but the people directly concerned. In making the first point, he cited President Monroe's message of exactly twenty-two years earlier, thus becoming the first President since Monroe to refer to the Monroe Doctrine as a statement of official American policy. After quoting Monroe's noncolonization dictum,[5] Polk continued:

> This principle will apply with greatly increased force should any European power attempt to establish any new colony in North America. In the existing circumstances of the world the present is deemed a proper occasion to reiterate and reaffirm the principle avowed by Mr. Monroe and to state my cordial concurrence in its wisdom and sound policy. . . . it should be distinctly announced to the world as our settled policy that no future European colony or dominion shall with our consent be planted or established on any part of the North American continent. . . .[6]

Having thus warned England to keep hands

off California, Polk laid down another principle which has sometimes been called the "Polk corollary" to the Monroe Doctrine.

> We must ever maintain the principle [he wrote] that the people of this continent alone have the right to decide their own destiny. Should any portion of them, constituting an independent state, propose to unite themselves with our Confederacy, this will be a question for them and us to determine without any foreign interposition.

This declaration was a rebuke to the British government for its recent efforts to prevent the annexation of Texas. It was a rebuke to the French government for a recent speech in which Guizot, the Premier, had declared that there ought to be a "balance of power" in the Americas, in other words, a Latin counterweight to the United States. Most of all, perhaps, it was a warning that the United States would brook no European interference with its plan for the peaceful annexation of California. The reader, remembering that it was in this same message that President Polk asserted against Great Britain the American claim to all of Oregon, will hardly deny that this is one of the most nationally self-assertive documents in American history.

John Slidell's Mission

Thus Polk sought to pave the way for a voluntary union of California with the United States and to forestall foreign objection to such a union. At the same time, he was attempting to bring about a restoration of diplomatic relations with Mexico and at one stroke not only to purchase California but to effect a peaceful settlement of all questions in dispute with that country. Discreet inquiries as to whether the Mexican government would receive a minister and thus resume official intercourse were apparently well received in Mexico. When Polk sought more than verbal assurances, Consul Black obtained from Peña y Peña, Mexican Foreign Minister, a statement in writing (October 15, 1845) that President Herrera was "disposed to receive the commissioner [*comisionado*] of the United States, who may come

5. See Chapter 9.
6. It is to be noted that Polk referred repeatedly to *North* America, thus seeming, whether intentionally or not, to restrict the application of the noncolonization principle to that part of the western hemisphere. For comment, see Dexter Perkins, *The Monroe Doctrine, 1826–1867* (Baltimore: The Johns Hopkins Press, 1933), chap. 2.

to this capital with full powers from his government to settle the present dispute in a peaceable, reasonable, and honorable manner."

Thinking this invitation adequate, Polk at once despatched John Slidell of Louisiana to Mexico bearing a commission as envoy extraordinary and minister plenipotentiary of the United States. Polk and his cabinet had previously agreed to propose a boundary line following the Rio Grande from its mouth to El Paso in latitude 32° north or thereabouts, and thence directly westward to the Pacific—thus giving to the United States New Mexico and Upper California as well as the Rio Grande boundary. Polk believed such a line might be obtained by a payment of fifteen or twenty million dollars, but he was willing to pay as much as forty millions for it, if necessary.

Buchanan's instructions to Slidell (November 10, 1845) proposed a boundary settlement such as that described but showed a willingness to accept less as a minimum. Slidell was given four alternative propositions. If Mexico would accept the Rio Grande boundary and cede to the United States New Mexico and enough of California to include both Monterey and San Francisco, the United States would assume the American claims against Mexico and pay in addition twenty-five million dollars. If Mexico insisted upon holding Monterey but would accept these terms in other respects, the United States would assume the claims and pay twenty millions. For the Rio Grande boundary and New Mexico without California, the United States would assume the claims and pay five millions; for the Rio Grande boundary alone, it would assume the claims. This last proposal was practically an ultimatum. Slidell should make no settlement that did not secure the Rio Grande boundary in return for the assumption of the claims. But it is to be noted that Polk was willing to come to terms with Mexico without securing California or New Mexico—except that part of the latter east of the upper Rio Grande.[7] If

California could not be purchased, there was always the other alternative.

When Slidell arrived in Mexico, the government of President Herrera was facing imminent overthrow and dared not antagonize public opinion by an appearance of concessions to the Unitel States. By way of excuse, Peña y Peña complained that instead of a *comisionado*—a commissioner authorized merely to settle the Texas question as a preliminary to the restoration of friendly relations—the United States had sent an envoy extraordinary and minister plenipotentiary, implying a full restoration of diplomatic relations. In that capacity, said the Foreign Minister, Slidell could not be received. While Slidell waited, Herrera's government fell, and on January 2, 1846, General Paredes entered Mexico City and assumed the presidential authority. Slidell withdrew to Jalapa to await the decision of the new government. But Paredes, who had used Herrera's alleged friendliness to the United States as a weapon with which to overthrow him, was in no position to be conciliatory himself. On March 12, his Foreign Minister informed Slidell that he would not be received. "Be assured," wrote Slidell to Buchanan as he prepared to come home, "that nothing is to be done with these people, until they shall have been chastised." Polk was already of much the same opinion.

Polk Ponders War

Polk's attitude toward Mexico from first to last combined simultaneous gestures with the sword and the olive branch. Always willing to make what he considered a liberal settlement with Mexico, he was determined to have as a minimum the Rio Grande boundary as compensation for the American claims. He was, it seems safe to assume, sincerely hopeful that Slidell's mission would result in such a settlement, but if Mexico declined to accept that proffered olive branch, the sword was ready. A little saber rattling, he believed, might facilitate negotiations. Thus, on January 13,

7. Under the minimum proposal, the line would follow the Rio Grande from mouth to source, thus depriving Mexico of the eastern portion of New Mexico, including Santa Fe and Taos, and thence run due north to the 42nd parallel.

1846, upon learning of Herrera's refusal to negotiate, he ordered General Taylor to advance
from Corpus Christi and take up a position on
the Rio Grande.

A month later (February 13), Polk was
visited by one Colonel A. J. Atocha, a friend
of Santa Anna who was then in exile at Havana. Presumably speaking for the exiled dictator, Atocha assured Polk that if Santa Anna
were again in power, as he soon expected to
be, he would gladly, for a sufficient consideration, make such a territorial settlement as
Polk desired. Such a settlement might even be
made, he hinted, with the existing government,
but to reconcile Mexican public opinion to a
cession of territory, the United States would
have to take stronger measures. The army
should advance to the Rio Grande (as it already had orders to do), and Slidell, if he were
not received, should go on board a United
States man-of-war at Vera Cruz and deliver
an ultimatum supported by the guns of the
fleet.

Polk was favorably impressed by Atocha's
suggestions. Having already ordered General
Taylor to the Rio Grande, he now proposed to
his cabinet that Congress be requested to authorize the President, first, to present Mexico
with an ultimatum, and second, if Mexico still
rejected his terms, "to take redress into our
own hands by aggressive measures." This was
at a time, however, when the Oregon controversy was approaching a crisis, and Polk
accepted the advice of Secretary of State
Buchanan, who preferred not to precipitate
war with Mexico till he was sure of peace with
England. For the time being, the suggestion of
an ultimatum was dropped, and Slidell was
told not to hurry home even if Paredes refused
to receive him, since his return, before settlement of the Oregon dispute, "would produce
considerable alarm in the public mind and
might possibly exercise an injurious influence
on our relations with Great Britain."

Early in April Slidell's failure was known
in Washington. Polk, determined to take drastic measures against Mexico, delayed action
until Slidell could report to him in person.
Slidell reached Washington May 8, still of the

opinion that only "chastisement" could bring
Mexico to terms. Saturday, May 9, Polk informed his cabinet of his intention to send to
Congress the following Tuesday a message
recommending a declaration of war against
Mexico. All concurred except George Bancroft,
Secretary of the Navy, who, as recorded by
the President, "dissented but said if any act of
hostility should be committed by the Mexican
forces he was then in favour of immediate
war." On that very evening came tidings that
such an "act of hostility" had occurred.

The Clash of Arms

General Zachary Taylor, under his orders of
January 13, had set out with his army early in
March from Corpus Christi for the Rio
Grande. On the twenty-eighth he had reached
the river without meeting armed resistance and
had occupied and fortified the east bank some
miles from its mouth at the present site of
Brownsville, Texas, opposite the Mexican
town of Matamoros. Taylor's advance to the
farther edge of the disputed territory brought
to Matamoros the Mexican General Ampudia,
who on April 12 warned Taylor, upon pain of
hostilities, to withdraw his army beyond the
Nueces—thus, it would seem, giving a sort of
tacit assent to the annexation of Texas and
narrowing the quarrel to the controversial
area between the Nueces and the Rio Grande.
In reply, Taylor cited his orders from the
Secretary of War as authority for his movements. Furthermore, in retaliation for the
Mexican refusal to permit him to use the river
as a supply line, he instituted a blockade at its
mouth, thereby denying its use to the Mexicans at Matamoros. This measure Taylor characterized as "a simple defensive precaution."
It was, in reality, an act of war.

Upon receipt of the news of Taylor's blockade, President Paredes, April 23, proclaimed
the existence of a "defensive war" against the
United States. Next day (unaware as yet of
Paredes' proclamation) a Mexican force
crossed the river above Taylor's position. On
the twenty-fifth, a party of Mexican cavalry

attacked a company of sixty-three American dragoons commanded by a Captain Thornton, killed or wounded sixteen, and captured the remainder. So began the war with Mexico.

This was the news that reached President Polk on Saturday evening, May 9, 1846. Another cabinet meeting and a busy Sabbath produced a "war message" that went to Congress on Monday. The bulk of the message was as Polk had planned it prior to the coming of the news from the Rio Grande—a summary of Mexican offenses against the United States, with emphasis upon her "breach of faith" in refusing to receive Slidell after having agreed to do so. But the latest act in the drama enabled Polk to add a paragraph well calculated to fire the patriot heart.

> The cup of forbearance [he wrote] had been exhausted even before the recent information from the frontier of the Del Norte. But now, after reiterated menaces, Mexico has passed the boundary of the United States, has invaded our territory and shed American blood upon American soil. She has proclaimed that hostilities have commenced, and that the two nations are now at war.

Had Polk sent his contemplated message to Congress before the clash of arms on the Rio Grande was known, or had there been no such clash, there would almost certainly have been a long and bitter fight over the proposed declaration of war. But the shedding of American blood on "American soil," even though the soil in question was claimed with at least equal right by Mexico, supplied the necessary emotional element to give Polk the war he desired. Within two days Congress, by a vote of 173 to 14 in the House and 42 to 2 in the Senate, had declared that a state of war existed "by the act of the Republic of Mexico," had authorized the President to call out fifty thousand volunteers, and had appropriated ten million dollars for military and naval expenditures.[8]

Thus to the American public, unacquainted with the deliberations in Polk's cabinet, the ostensible cause of the war with Mexico was the Mexican attack upon Captain Thornton's dragoons. Thanks to James K. Polk's meticulous recording of his daily activities in his diary, it is now clear that he and his advisers, with a single dissenting vote, had chosen war before they knew of the attack—a war to punish the weak Mexican government for its refusal to receive Slidell and negotiate a settlement of the American claims and the disputed boundary. Back of these reasons lay Polk's determination to possess California—peaceably if he could, forcibly if he must.

8. The entire opposition vote was cast by northern Whigs: in the Senate, one vote from Massachusetts and one from Delaware; in the House, five votes each from Massachusetts and Ohio and one each from Maine, Rhode Island, New York, and Pennsylvania. Present but not voting in the Senate, however, in addition to a Whig Senator from Maine, were Berrien, a Whig from Georgia, and Calhoun of South Carolina, the sole Democrat to withhold a vote for war. There is an excellent analysis of the debate on the war resolutions in Charles Sellers, *James K. Polk, Continentalist, 1843–1846* (Princeton: Princeton University Press, 1966), pp. 416–21.

14

War and Peace
with Mexico

According to Senator Thomas H. Benton of Missouri, reluctant Democrats were assured by Polk or his advisers on the eve of the war with Mexico that there would in reality be no fighting and that all would be over in ninety or one hundred and twenty days. Polk may very well have believed this as a result of his conversations with Santa Anna's envoy, Colonel Atocha, in February 1846. Atocha had then reported that Santa Anna would be willing to make a treaty by which the Rio Grande would become the western boundary of Texas, "and the Colorado of the West down through the Bay of San Francisco to the Sea [sic] should be the Mexican line on the North," Mexico ceding to the United States all territory north and east of such a line for "a pecuniary consideration" of about thirty million dollars. Atocha added that Santa Anna would likely be able to return to Mexico by April or May.

Immediately after the declaration of war, steps were taken toward making peace through Santa Anna, and it was no doubt in the expectation that these efforts would succeed that members of Congress had been promised a short and easy war. The commander of the American naval squadron off Vera Cruz was instructed to let Santa Anna enter Mexico should he attempt to do so. A few weeks later Polk sent a personal representative, Commander Alexander Slidell Mackenzie of the Navy, to interview Santa Anna in Havana. To Mackenzie, Santa Anna expressed a desire to return to Mexico and "govern in the interest of the masses, instead of parties, and classes."

In expectation of Santa Anna's return to power, Secretary of State Buchanan on July 27 addressed a note to the Mexican Foreign Minister proposing negotiations for "a peace just and honorable for both parties." Before this note reached Mexico City, Santa Anna had actually returned to Mexico and assumed command of the "Liberating Army." While ostensibly keeping aloof from politics, he became in reality the directing force in the Mexican government. To Santa Anna's decision, therefore, is to be attributed the Foreign Minister's reply to Buchanan, postponing consideration of the peace offer until a new Mexican congress should meet in December. Justifiably angry at Santa Anna's double dealing, Buchanan rejoined that no choice remained for the United States "but to prosecute the war with vigor" until Mexico herself should exhibit a desire for peace.

Defining the Objects of the War

Long before this fading of the hope of an early peace, the objects of the war had come under discussion in Polk's cabinet. The first such discussion was precipitated by a proposal from Buchanan that a circular note be sent to the diplomatic corps disclaiming any intention of dismembering Mexico or acquiring New Mexico or California. Unless some such declaration were made, Buchanan feared intervention by foreign powers, especially England, with whom the Oregon settlement was not yet complete. Buchanan's fears were not shared by other members of the cabinet or by the President. Polk remarked that acquisition of territory was not the aim of the war, but that being in, the United States must not fail to take California as its sole means of indemnification. He would "meet war with either England or France or all the Powers of Christendom" rather than make such a pledge as Buchanan proposed. A further discussion some weeks later resulted in a general agreement that as a minimum the United States must secure the Rio Grande line, New Mexico, and Upper California—the maximum for which John Slidell had been directed to ask.

In order to make good these plans, it was proposed that General Taylor, already on the Rio Grande, should advance "toward the heart of the enemy's country" to bring Santa Anna to terms, while another expedition, setting out from Fort Leavenworth, should proceed to Santa Fe and thence to California, should occupy both California and New Mexico, and establish temporary governments therein.

The War in Northern Mexico

Taylor's army, already on the Rio Grande, was naturally the first in motion. During May,

Taylor drove the Mexican forces beyond the Rio Grande, crossed the river himself, and occupied Matamoros against but slight opposition. By the capture of Monterey in September, enemy resistance in northeastern Mexico was effectually broken, and Taylor was enabled to push on and take possession of Saltillo and Victoria. Thus before the close of 1846 the capitals of three Mexican states, Nuevo Leon, Coahuila, and Tamaulipas, were in American hands. Another American column, commanded by Colonel A. W. Doniphan, separating at Santa Fe from Brigadier General Stephen W. Kearny's California expedition, descended the Rio Grande to El Paso, pushed from there into the interior, and in March 1847 occupied Chihuahua.

The Occupation of California

Long before Doniphan reached Chihuahua, California had passed securely into American hands, but not through the peaceful agreement with the Spanish Californians for which Polk had hoped. Consul Larkin at Monterey received in April 1846 the secret instructions of the preceding October. He began conversations, as directed, with some of the leading Californians, but his efforts to win their loyalty were interrupted by the strange behavior of Captain John C. Frémont. This young Army officer, already a noted explorer, had set out for California in the spring of 1845 with a party of sixty-two soldiers. His ostensible purpose was to determine the most feasible route from Missouri to California. When Frémont undertook to winter in California, the presence of so many armed Americans alarmed the Mexican commandant at Monterey, who ordered the Americans to leave the province. This Frémont did after considerable bluster, leading his men up the Sacramento Valley and north into Oregon. Here, in May 1846, he was overtaken by Lieutenant Gillespie, who had brought instructions to Larkin and letters to Frémont. What the letters contained, or what verbal messages Gillespie may have brought, is not known. Obviously, they could not have conveyed tidings of war with Mexico, as Frémont later asserted. At any rate, Frémont returned to California and to the vicinity of San Francisco Bay, where he lent assistance to a group of American frontiersmen in an unprovoked rebellion against the Mexican authorities—the so-called Bear Flag revolt. This action brought him into direct conflict with the Spanish Californians whom Polk wished to conciliate, and worked at cross-purposes with Larkin's efforts to win their confidence.[1]

Having begun a private war of his own, out of harmony with the policy of his government, Frémont was rescued from serious embarrassment by receipt, early in July, of unofficial information that the United States and Mexico were at war. Frémont could now cooperate with Commodore John D. Sloat, and later with Captain Robert F. Stockton, both of the Navy, for the occupation of all California, but his erratic behavior had lessened the chances of effecting that occupation with the good will of the Californians.

Before the end of July, the United States flag was flying over all the settlements north of Monterey. Stockton and Frémont, accompanied by Larkin, then took their commands by sea to southern California, where in August

they took possession of San Diego, San Pedro, and Los Angeles, meeting no armed resistance from the Mexicans.

There now arrived from Washington the first official news of the declaration of war, and Stockton proclaimed the annexation of California by the United States.

So far, with the exception of the Bear Flag episode, the conquest had proceeded smoothly enough; but in September latent Mexican resentment flared into open revolt in Los Angeles, the small American garrison retreated to the coast, and for nearly four months the Americans were unable to reestablish their authority in the south. Not until after Brigadier General Stephen W. Kearny arrived in December with a hundred cavalrymen—he had sent the rest back to Santa Fe upon learning of Stockton's "conquest"—was it possible to repossess Los Angeles and reassert the authority of the United States. On January 10, 1847, the combined forces of Kearny and Stockton entered the city, and the conquest of California was complete.

A Blow at the Heart of Mexico

At every point American arms had triumphed, and all the territory that the administration desired to wrest from Mexico had been occupied. There remained the problem of terminating the war through a treaty by which Mexico would confirm such cessions as the United States wished to exact. Santa Anna, however, as yet showed no inclination to discuss peace terms. What, then, was to be done? One possible course, recommended by General Taylor, was simply to hold what had been taken and wait for Mexico to propose a settlement. This procedure at first appealed to Polk and most of his cabinet but, largely at the insistence of Senator Benton, was set aside for a more aggressive policy, and Polk resolved that an expedition should be despatched to seize Vera Cruz and thence, if circumstances seemed propitious, to advance against Mexico City. Since the existing military force was inadequate for such a campaign, ten regiments were to be added to the Regular Army and these

---

1. Larkin wrote Buchanan, July 20, that the Bear Flag revolt and the events that followed had created a hatred for the United States among the natives, who, with a little encouragement, would now favor British rule. Gillespie, on the other hand, claimed credit for having brought Frémont back from Oregon and thereby "frustrated British intrigue in California." *California Historical Society Quarterly*, 17 (1938), 279–80, 346. That no such "British intrigue" existed seems now well established. E. A. Wiltsee, "The British Vice-Consul in California and the Events of 1846," ibid., 10 (1931), 99–128, shows without question that Governor Pio Pico at Los Angeles and Commandant Castro at Monterey invited British protection against aggression from the United States. His further inferences—that British intervention was prevented only by Sloat's raising the United States flag at Monterey, that Sloat was persuaded to take this step by Frémont's activities, and that Frémont, acting under "secret instructions," had a clear plan from the time of his meeting with Gillespie— do not seem adequately supported by the evidence. See also R. W. Kelsey, *The United States Consulate in California,* Publications, Academy of Pacific Coast History, Vol. 1, No. 5 (Berkeley: University of California, 1910), pp. 77–82.

were to be supplemented by nine regiments of volunteers to serve for the duration of the war. In selecting a commander for the expedition, Polk, the politician, was embarrassed by the fact that Major General Winfield Scott, the highest ranking as well as the most capable general officer in the service, was a Whig in politics. After searching in vain for a competent Democratic general, Polk did the sensible thing by giving the command to Scott.[2]

Scott's army of some 10,000 men consisted partly of new regiments from the United States, partly of units detached from Taylor's command. The army was put ashore south of Vera Cruz early in March, 1847, and on March 29 received the surrender of the city. Not until Scott undertook to scale the mountain barrier back of Vera Cruz did he encounter the main Mexican force under General Santa Anna. The Mexican leader had seen an opportunity to overwhelm General Taylor's depleted army in the north, only to be himself soundly beaten in the hard-fought battle of Buena Vista (February 23–24, 1847). He was now routed again by Scott at the pass of Cerro Gordo, after Captain Robert E. Lee discovered a path through ravines and jungle to the Mexican rear. Scott pushed on to Puebla, Mexico's second city, which surrendered without opposition on May 15. The road to Mexico City lay open, but at Puebla, Scott found it necessary to await replacements for nearly four thousand of his one-year volunteers. Their terms of enlistment were near expiration, and only a handful proved willing to reenlist.

The Mission of Nicholas P. Trist

While Scott and his army rested at Puebla, a new attempt was made to bring the slippery Santa Anna to terms without further bloodshed. In violation of his promises, made through Colonel Atocha and Commander

Mackenzie, Santa Anna had hitherto refused to negotiate, demanding withdrawal of all American troops from Mexico as a condition precedent. News of the American victories at Buena Vista and Vera Cruz seemed to the administration in Washington to offer new opportunities for negotiation. On the chance that Santa Anna might now be ready to discuss peace, Polk resolved to send a commissioner to Scott's headquarters, empowered to negotiate a treaty whenever the Mexicans showed a willingness to talk.

The agent selected for this responsibility was Nicholas P. Trist, chief clerk of the State Department, who had formerly served as consul in Havana, who knew the Spanish language and was supposed to have some understanding of the Spanish character. Trist's instructions, drafted by Buchanan and signed April 15, 1847, directed him to insist upon the Rio Grande boundary and the cession of New Mexico and Upper California as a minimum. In compensation for such a boundary, the United States would assume the claims against Mexico and would pay, in addition, as much as $20,000,000, though Trist was to offer only $15,000,000 and was not to exceed the latter figure unless necessary to prevent a rupture of the negotiations. He was authorized, however, to pay an additional $5,000,000 for Lower California and a similar sum for the right of transit across the Isthmus of Tehuantepec— an outside figure of $30,000,000 for the maximum cessions suggested.

Trist arrived at Vera Cruz on May 6 and at once opened communications with Scott, to whom the visit of the commissioner was a complete surprise. Unfortunately General Scott, who already had reason to feel that he was not trusted by the President, received the impression that Trist, a civilian and a mere departmental clerk, had come to Mexico with authority superior to his own.[3] The general

---

2. Polk also considered creating a lieutenant generalship for Senator Benton, who was a good Democrat but of untried mettle as a general officer. Zachary Taylor, in addition to being a Whig, had disqualified himself by open criticism of the administration and by an exhibition of lack of military competence on the planning and strategic level.

3. William L. Marcy, Secretary of War, had written Scott: "Mr. Trist is clothed with such diplomatic powers as will authorize him to enter into arrangements with the government of Mexico for the suspension of hostilities." Trist made matters worse by requesting Scott to transmit Buchanan's sealed letter to the Foreign Minister without informing him of its contents, as he was authorized to do.

took offense and not only refused to transmit Trist's communications to the Mexican government but also sent Trist a lecture upon the latter's effrontery. Trist replied in kind, and the two men were presently engaged in an epistolary duel that did no credit to either. After some weeks of these unfortunate exchanges, the antagonists became reconciled, partly at least through the general's graciousness in sending a jar of guava jelly to his ailing opponent, and thenceforward the two worked in friendship and in perfect harmony.[4]

Before the reconciliation with Scott, which occurred at the beginning of July, Trist had made contact with Santa Anna through the good offices of Charles Bankhead, the British minister in Mexico City. Through this channel came an intimation that the use of money would facilitate the opening of negotiations; specifically, that Santa Anna would consent to treat for peace if he could have $10,000 at once and a promise of $1,000,000 upon ratification of a treaty by Mexico. Trist informed Scott of this proposal and the latter, after conferring with his officers, made the initial payment of $10,000 from his secret service fund. Once more Santa Anna double-crossed the Americans. After receiving the money, he pleaded the unwillingness of Congress as a bar to negotiations. Scott then had no alternative but to advance upon the Mexican capital.

On August 7, Scott broke camp at Puebla and, with less than eleven thousand ablebodied troops, began the march to Mexico City. In command at the capital was Santa Anna with an army several times the number of Scott's. But Santa Anna's force was poorly led, poorly disciplined, and poorly equipped; and to make matters worse, bitter feuds raged between Santa Anna and his generals and between Santa Anna, who had again assumed the presidential title, and rival politicians. The country was hopelessly divided in the face of the invader. Furthermore, Scott's fair and generous dealing with the Mexican people along

the route of his invasion had won their friendship and removed the menace of a hostile population to his long line of communications.[5] The American advance encountered no resistance until it had pentrated the mountain rim of the Valley of Mexico and reached the immediate approaches to the city. Here Scott cleverly avoided the strong defenses guarding the more direct and obvious route and by a turning movement to the south and two brilliant victories at Contreras and Churubusco (August 20, 1847) found himself at the southern gates of the Mexican capital.

Now, at last, Santa Anna sent to Scott through the British legation a proposal for a suspension of hostilities, and on August 23, commissioners from the two camps agreed upon an armistice to last until the end of peace negotiations or until forty-eight hours after either party should have given notice of its termination. It soon appeared that Santa Anna was but stalling for time. Upon his refusal to accept the terms offered by Trist, the negotiations were declared at an end, and with them the armistice. Hostilities were resumed, and on September 13 the Americans stormed the fortress of Chapultepec and on the following day occupied Mexico City. Santa Anna, with the remainder of his army, withdrew from the city and two days later resigned the presidency. A new government, headed provisionally by Peña y Peña, was set up at Querétaro, and early in October, Santa Anna was deprived of his military command.

Manifest Destiny

News of the breakdown of Trist's negotiations and the termination of the armistice reached Washington early in October. It was at once decided to recall Trist, to instruct Scott to occupy Mexico City and additional territory as rapidly as reinforcements made it practicable, and to await peace proposals from Mex-

4. The best defense of Trist is an article by L. M. Sears, "Nicholas P. Trist, a Diplomat with Ideals," *Mississippi Valley Historical Review,* 11 (1924), 85–98.

5. R. H. Gabriel, "American Experience with Military Government," *American Historical Review,* 49 (1944), 630–43, especially 630–37.

ico. Orders to this effect were sent to Trist and Scott on October 6.

Exasperated at Mexico's refusal to accept what they deemed generous terms of peace, Polk and his cabinet now talked of exacting from the defeated enemy much more than had at first been contemplated. They were agreed that the war should be prosecuted with increased energy, that the costs of occupation should be levied upon the Mexican people, that New Mexico and California should be regarded forthwith as permanent possessions of the United States and provided with territorial governments, and that, if necessary, the army in Mexico should assist in setting up and protecting temporarily a republican government willing and able to conclude an honorable peace.

There remained the question of what should be done if it proved impossible to make a satisfactory treaty even with a government set up under the protection of the United States. Two members of the cabinet, Buchanan and Secretary of the Treasury Robert J. Walker, were not averse to the possibility of conquering and absorbing all of Mexico, and both wished the President to intimate as much in his annual message, Buchanan suggesting a statement that "we must fulfill that destiny which Providence may have in store for both countries." Polk preferred to say that we should "take the measure of our indemnity into our own hands," and this was the wording of the message; but Walker and Buchanan were expressing the thought of a vocal group of politicians and journalists.

"Continental Democrats," as they were sometimes called, were urging the annexation of all of Mexico, or at least much more of it than had been contemplated at the beginning of the war. The long-prevalent view of this movement, like that of the war itself, ascribed the annexationist sentiment to southern cupidity for more slave territory and slave states. James Russell Lowell, in his antiwar and antisouthern *Biglow Papers,* announced:

> They just want this Californy
> So's to lug new slave-states in,

and derisively instructed the recruiting squad:

> Wal, go' long to help 'em stealin'
> Bigger pens to cram with slaves!

In reality, as even a casual examination of the evidence shows, there was nothing peculiarly southern about either the promotion of the war or the propaganda for larger annexations of Mexican territory. On the other hand, southern Whigs almost unanimously, and Calhoun and many southern Democrats, condemned the war and deplored the prospect of acquisitions of new territory. If they coveted more land for the slave economy, they saw little prospect of finding it in Mexico, where slavery had long since been abolished by Mexican law and where soil and climate were not propitious for the extension of the system. Even if physical conditions had been more favorable, the passage several times by the House of Representatives of the Wilmot Proviso, prohibiting slavery or involuntary servitude in any territory to be acquired from Mexico, had warned southerners that any attempt to extend slavery into new territory would meet with determined opposition from the North. So evident, in fact, did it become that any territory to be acquired from Mexico would be "free soil," that a few abolitionists abandoned their opposition to the war and to the absorption of territory and were ready to welcome new states from Mexico into the Union.[6]

The "all-Mexico" movement, however, was mainly neither proslavery nor antislavery. Sectionally, its greatest strength, or at least its most vocal support, was in New York and in the western states, from Ohio to Texas. Almost without exception its adherents were Democrats, and the arguments used in its behalf were those of Manifest Destiny. The *Democratic Review,* original propagator of that phrase, declared in October 1847: "This occupation of territory by the people, is the

6. An excellent analysis of the rise and decline of the movement for "all Mexico" is Frederick Merk, *Manifest Destiny and Mission in American History: A Reinterpretation* (New York: Alfred A. Knopf, Inc., 1963), chaps. 5–8.

great movement of the age, and until every acre of the North American continent is occupied by citizens of the United States, the foundations of the future empire will not have been laid." Similar ideas were expressed by the New York *Herald* and *Sun.* The New Orleans *Picayune* predicted that "the better order of Mexicans" would claim the protection of a power whose martial law they had found superior to the sort of native government they had experienced. "Nor is it," this journal added, "prophetic of the long dominion of a hybrid people, to have their flowers scented by any of Saxon origin." The incapacity for self-government of the Indian race, forming a large part of the Mexican population, was dwelt upon by the *Democratic Review* and the New York *Evening Post,* the latter remarking: "The aborigines of this country have not attempted and cannot attempt, to exist *independently* alongside of us. . . . The Mexicans are *aboriginal Indians,* and they must share the destiny of their race."

These are but a few samples of the type of expression that was becoming common in Congress and the press. *Niles' Register* printed a column of "'Manifest Destiny' Doctrines," and Calhoun, battling in the Senate against the proposed incorporation of Mexico with its hybrid race, declared: "I should be very glad indeed to think . . . that there is no person in the country who thinks of the extinction of the nationality of Mexico. Why, you can hardly read a newspaper without finding it filled with speculation upon the subject."

It was evident, then, that if the war should continue and American armies should occupy more and more of Mexico, there would be a numerous faction in the United States that would oppose surrendering any of the occupied territory. President Polk had not, as yet, aligned himself with this faction. Perhaps he would never have done so; yet the passage in his December message in which he said that if Mexico rejected peace offers, we "must continue to occupy her country with our troops, taking the full measure of indemnity into our own hands," was sufficiently elastic

to cover all eventualities. This was the state of affairs in the United States when, quite unexpectedly, there arrived in Washington a messenger bearing a peace treaty which Trist, despite his recall as commissioner, had negotiated with the provisional government of Mexico.

Mr. Trist Makes a Treaty

Not until November 16 did Trist receive Buchanan's letter of October 6 recalling him to Washington. In the same mail came a later note reiterating the order to return and rebuking him for alleged disregard of his instructions. In the meantime Trist had opened communications with the new Mexican government at Querétaro and had been informed that the government was anxious for peace and was about to appoint commissioners to treat with him. Trist's first act upon receiving his recall was to send to Querétaro an informal notice of the situation and to invite the Mexican government to give him peace proposals to take to Washington. The Mexican authorities, however, urged Trist to remain and negotiate despite his recall, and similar advice was given by General Scott and by Edward Thornton of the British legation, who played a useful role in bringing the parties together. For several weeks Trist hesitated, but on December 3 he informed the Mexican commissioners that he would withdraw his notice of recall and would proceed to negotiate if assured that Mexico would accept the minimum territorial demands of the United States.

The reasons for this unprecedented act of insubordination on Trist's part are clear and to his credit. He knew, much better than Polk or Buchanan, the political situation in Mexico and the nature of the people with whom he had to deal. He knew that neither the existing Mexican government nor any other could ever send a commission to Washington to sue for peace without committing political suicide. He knew also that the faction at that moment in power, the *Moderado* or Moderate party, was the only group in Mexico with which there was any hope of making a reasonable treaty. Experience had shown that Santa Anna and his following could never be dealt with. Certain other factions, such as the *Puros* (idealistic republicans) and the more substantial business elements, were attracted by the possible advantages of prolonged or permanent American rule. Knowing something too of the programs of the "all-Mexico" movement in the United States, and suspecting that Polk was in sympathy with it, Trist was convinced that the choice lay between a peace made at once with the Moderates on the basis of his original instructions, and a protracted military occupation of Mexico, complicated by guerrilla warfare and possibly ending in annexation of the whole country. The latter course he believed, as did Calhoun and many others, would be a major calamity for the United States; and he therefore resolved to disregard his recall and attempt to make a treaty, though he must have realized that a treaty made under these circumstances might be rejected in Washington and that in any case he was terminating his own official career.[7]

Despite good will on both sides, the negotiations moved slowly, and it was not until February 2, 1848, that the treaty was signed at Guadalupe Hidalgo, a suburb of Mexico City.

The treaty embodied the minimum territorial demands and the minimum monetary compensation proposed in Trist's instructions of April 15, 1847. The boundary line was to follow the middle of the Rio Grande from its mouth to the point where it crossed the southern boundary of New Mexico; was to follow that boundary to the southwest corner of New Mexico and proceed thence due north till it reached the nearest branch of the Gila

River, which it was to follow to its junction with the Colorado; and was to cross from the Colorado to the Pacific by way of the existing boundary line between Upper and Lower California. Thus the United States would secure the Rio Grande boundary and retain New Mexico and Upper California, both of which it had already occupied. The boundary rivers were to be open to the navigation of both parties, and the Colorado below the boundary line, as well as the Gulf of California, open to ships of the United States. The United States was to release Mexico from responsibility for all existing claims and to settle such claims itself to an amount not exceeding $3,250,000 and was to pay to Mexico $15,000,000.

The arrival of the treaty placed Polk in a serious dilemma. He was indignant at Trist, not only for his disregard of his letter of recall, but also because of the tone of his recent communications, which had been outspokenly critical of the President and had contained insinuations that Polk was really planning to extinguish Mexican nationality. Polk had come to regard Trist as "a very base man," and could not without pain accept his handiwork. On the other hand, Trist's treaty conformed to his official instructions and to Polk's public profession of his war aims, and if he rejected it merely because of the irregularity in its negotiation and chose to carry on the war, the President knew that he would be fiercely criticized and would meet with intensified opposition in Congress, where the Whigs, since the elections of 1846, held a majority in the House of Representatives.[8]

In view of all the facts, it seemed best to Polk not to reject the treaty. With suggestions for certain minor changes, but with a cautious statement of approval, he sent it to the Senate on February 22, 1848.

In the Senate the treaty was opposed by a strange alliance made up of those who wanted less territory than it secured, and those who wanted more. The former were Whigs; the

7. Upon his return to Washington after the ratification of the treaty, Trist found himself without a job. Polk even denied him his salary and expenses after November 16, 1847, the date on which he had received his letter of recall. Not until more than twenty years later did a more friendly administration award compensation for his services and expenses in the negotiation of the treaty.

8. On January 3, 1848, the House had voted, 85 to 81, that the war had been "unnecessarily and unconstitutionally begun by the President of the United States."

TERRITORY ACQUIRED FROM MEXICO
1845–1853

▦ Texas, annexed 1845; boundaries undefined and annexation not recognized by Mexico till 1848.

▨ Claimed by Texas (1836–1845) and by U.S. as part of Texas (1845–1848); ownership disputed by Mexico; title confirmed by Mexico, 1848.

▥ Acquired from Mexico 1848.

▨ Gadsden Purchase, 1853.

latter, expansionist Democrats. Daniel Webster, despite his well-known concern for Pacific commerce,[9] declared that New Mexico and California together were "not worth a dollar." He and fourteen other Whig senators joined in voting for an amendment that would have handed back to Mexico all territory west of the Rio Grande.[10] On the other side, eleven Democrats, one from New York and ten from the West and South, supported an amendment that would have added to the Mexican cession

all or large parts of the states of Chihuahua, Coahuila, Nuevo Leon, and Tamaulipas. Had the two groups of malcontents held together in opposition to the treaty, they would easily have defeated it. In the final vote, however, neither group held its lines intact, and the treaty was approved, March 10, by a majority of 38 to 14. Twenty-six Democrats and twelve Whigs made up the majority, while each party contributed seven votes to the minority.

The Senate had amended the treaty in a number of minor particulars, and it was therefore necessary to send commissioners to Mexico to explain the changes and secure the concurrence of the Mexican Congress. On May 19, 1848, that body approved the amended treaty, and on the thirtieth, ratifications were exchanged at Querétaro. The war

9. See pp. 138, 141.
10. This vote and Webster's remark suggest a need for some qualification of the thesis that expansion to the Pacific was motivated chiefly by commercial interests. See N. A. Graebner, *Empire on the Pacific: A Study in American Continental Expansion* (New York: The Ronald Press Company, 1955).

was over, and by July 30 the last soldiers of the invading army had embarked from Vera Cruz for home.

In his message to Congress on July 6, 1848, announcing the completion of the treaty, Polk expressed satisfaction that the annexed territories, which in Mexican possession had lain undeveloped and almost useless, would now be "productive of vast benefits to the United States, to the commercial world, and the general interests of mankind." Well might Polk feel gratification at the achievements of his three and a quarter years in the Presidency. A firm believer in the desirability of territorial expansion, he had completed the annexation of Texas, had acquired full title to the more valuable portion of Oregon, and by a short war, glorious to American arms and relatively inexpensive in lives and money, had secured the Rio Grande boundary, New Mexico, and the still unrealized wealth of California. Within less than two years the United States had become a Pacific power with a coastline stretching from San Diego to Puget Sound. Polk had taken serious chances, risking both a war with England and a prolonged and costly occupation of Mexico. If he owed his successes as much to good luck as to good management, the successes were nevertheless impressive, and it was but natural that he should claim for himself the chief credit.

15

Agents of Commerce
Open Doors
in the Far East

Long before the first American explorer reached the Pacific overland, ships from New York and New England were making the United States flag a familiar sight from the shores of California and Oregon to those of China and Southeast Asia. The search for new markets, so keenly pressed after the Revolution, led American merchants into distant seas where as colonials they had never ventured. As British subjects, they had been excluded from the trade of the Far East by the monopoly conferred upon the British East India Company. Now, as citizens of an independent state, Americans had no longer to respect that monopoly. The British themselves, by the Jay treaty, admitted American ships to the trade with the British East Indies. In other Far Eastern lands they needed only to secure the permission of the governments concerned. It was not long before Yankee skippers were trading with Oman, on the Indian Ocean, with Batavia in the Dutch East Indies, with Manila in the Spanish Philippines, with the kingdom of Siam, but above all, with the Chinese port of Canton.

The "Middle Kingdom" and Its Neighbors

The Chinese Empire of 180 years ago looked upon itself as the possessor of the world's only true civilization. It was the "Middle Kingdom," and those members of the human race outside its sacred circle were "barbarians" or "foreign devils," with whom the Chinese desired no intercourse. But as a favor, the foreigners were allowed very restricted privileges of trade. Foreign ships were admitted to the single port of Canton in south China, and at the same port foreign merchants were allowed to live in "factories" outside the city walls. Here they were shut off from all contact with the local population except the "co-hong" merchants, the small group of Chinese who had a monopoly of the foreign trade. China had no regular diplomatic relations with the outside world, no ambassadors or ministers abroad, no embassies, legations, or even recognized consulates in China. Foreign ambassadors were received at Peking only as tribute-bearers from governments of inferior states. The Emperor of the Middle Kingdom recognized no equals.

China's neighbors, Japan and Korea, were even more isolated from the outside world than was China. Korea acknowledged the overlordship of China, and her foreign trade was almost exclusively with that country. The Japanese had once been an active seafaring people; their ports had been open to foreign traders and even to Christian missionaries, who had made many native converts. But early in the seventeenth century, under Shoguns of the Tokugawa clan, Japan had closed her doors to the world, forbidden Japanese to go abroad, expelled the missionaries, and outlawed native Christianity. As one slight exception to this policy of exclusion, the Dutch were permitted to keep a trading post on Deshima island in the harbor of Nagasaki, to which they might bring one ship a year. Some trade with China was also allowed through Nagasaki, but otherwise the policy of Japan was to shield its people from all outside contacts and influences.

American Far Eastern Policy

Between the winning of American independence and the close of the nineteenth century, profound changes occurred in these nations of the Far East and in their relations with the Occident—changes to which the United States made important contributions. In China, the growth of trade led to the opening of regular diplomatic relations. In Japan (and in a much less significant way in Korea) the opening of diplomatic relations paved the way for the beginning of trade. In opening commercial and diplomatic relations with the Far East, the United States sometimes followed, sometimes preceded, the European powers. In its Chinese policy it at first followed England; in its Japanese policy, it led and Europe followed.

But American policy in the Far East developed in a somewhat different direction from the policy of Europe. American aims in this area were purely commercial; as yet the United States had no colonial ambitions. For its commerce it desired nothing better than most-favored-nation treatment, equality, or the "open door" as it came later to be called. When trade had once been opened, threats to the open door came not from China and Japan but from the colonizing powers of Europe, which were on the lookout for colonies, spheres of interest, and special favors in the Far East. A weak China or a weak Japan would be more likely to yield to such demands than a strong China or Japan. It was to the interest of the United States, therefore, to maintain or to build up the strength of both China and Japan. It was China's fate to be almost torn apart by internal strains and the encroachments of foreign powers. It was American policy to help China resist those disruptive forces—to maintain China's independence and "territorial integrity." Japan, on the other hand, after opening her door to western influences, began an amazing program of speedy westernization and modernization, building a strongly centralized government in place of a loose feudal organization. This course she followed in order to save herself from the helplessness against the West that she saw in China. In this policy of self-strengthening, which Europe at times sought to obstruct, Japan had the sympathy and moral support of the United States.

These American policies are usually associated with the period just before and after 1900, but they had their beginning much earlier. Their chief objectives were:

1. To secure and maintain an open door for American trade.
2. To keep China and Japan unified and strong as the surest means of keeping the door open.

Negatively, the United States had no wish for territorial acquisitions in the Far East; and it abstained from the use of force in pursuing its objectives. Other nations, the British and French, might use force. Whatever rights they gained, the United States gained too, through the operation of the most-favored-nation clauses in its first treaties with China and Japan. Thus its gains were made without bloodshed and without incurring the enmity of Chinese and Japanese. The development of these American policies will now be examined in some detail.

The "Old China Trade"

The first American ship to visit Canton was the *Empress of China,* which left New York in February 1784 and returned in May 1785. Her example was quickly followed by ships from New York, Boston, and other Atlantic ports, and before 1800 dozens of American vessels were engaged in the China trade. In the beginning these traders went primarily to bring back Chinese products—tea, spices, silk and cotton fabrics, chinaware—for which there was a market in the United States, and were hard put to it to find American commodities that could be disposed of in self-sufficing China. One such article was ginseng, a root found plentifully in the eastern United States, and esteemed in China for its supposed medicinal properties. Furs, from the sea otter of the northwest coast or the fur seals of the South Pacific, brought good prices in Canton. The value of such articles, however, was inadequate to pay for the return cargoes, and the balance was made up in Spanish silver dollars or in opium, for which China provided a growing but illicit market.

Beginning in the middle 1820's the United States exported to China growing amounts of coarse cotton cloth, and although imports from China remained far in excess of exports to it, Americans came to look upon China more and more as a future market for American manufactured goods. "After 1840," writes Tyler Dennett, "American policy in Asia was always directed with an eye to the future— to the day when Americans would supply the seemingly limitless markets of the East." [1]

1. Tyler Dennett, *Americans in Eastern Asia* (New York: The Macmillan Company, 1922), p. 74.

The First Treaties with China

The first effective blow against the Chinese policy of exclusion was struck by the British in the Opium War of 1839–1842. The Chinese authorities had long connived in the smuggling of opium. Most of this came from British India, where the tax on its production was the principal source of government revenue. Without warning, a new imperial official in 1839 suddenly cracked down on the practice, compelling British merchants to hand over 20,000 chests of opium valued at more than £2,000,000. This and other punitive measures against the British led to open hostilities, in which Chinese armies, fleets, and fortifications proved ineffectual against European armaments. The Chinese government was forced to capitulate. By the Treaty of Nanking, August 29, 1842, China ceded to Great Britain the island of Hong Kong, opened four new ports for trade, and agreed to pay an indemnity of $21,000,000 for the confiscated opium, the cost of the war, and debts owing to British merchants. The co-hong system was abolished; British traders might do business with any Chinese in the open ports. Aside from a boundary treaty with Russia of 1689, the Nanking treaty was the first made by China with any European power. It was the first step in a general opening up of China to western diplomacy, trade, and culture.

The United States was quick to follow the British lead. Caleb Cushing, a Whig politician from Massachusetts, was sent to China by President Tyler to make sure that American ships and trade should enjoy privileges at least equal to those granted to the British. Both Cushing and Secretary of State Daniel Webster, who wrote his instructions, represented that section of the country most interested in the China trade. On July 3, 1844, Cushing and a Chinese commissioner signed the Treaty of Wanghia (the name of a Chinese village near Canton). The treaty opened to American ships and trade the five ports of Canton, Amoy, Foochow, Ningpo, and Shang-

CHINA COAST AND JAPAN

hai and authorized the stationing of United States consular officers at these ports. It permitted American citizens to reside in the open ports with their families, to acquire sites for houses, places of business, hospitals, churches, and cemeteries, to purchase books, and to employ scholars to teach the Chinese language. It gave to Americans residing in China the right of extraterritoriality; that is, the right, when accused of crime or involved in civil cases, to be tried before an American official (normally the consul) and according to American law. It fixed at a low level the tariff to be paid by Americans on imports and exports and stipulated that the rates should not be changed without American consent. Finally, it contained a most-favored-nation article, assuring to the United States any additional rights or privileges that might be gained by any other power.

A few words of comment on some of these provisions are in order. The clauses permitting the building of churches, purchase of books, and employment of Chinese scholars were inserted at the instance of American missionaries who served Cushing as interpreters. The most notable of these was Dr. Peter Parker, a medical missionary who since 1834 had conducted a hospital at Canton.

The principle of extraterritoriality was supported by the arguments (1) that Chinese courts were unreliable, (2) that Chinese law, both civil and criminal, was so different from western law that the results of its application were often palpably unjust by western standards. The giving of criminal jurisdiction to American consuls was, however, attended with serious abuses. Consuls were rarely well trained for such duties or adequately paid, and there were no American jails for the confinement of convicted criminals.

For the fixing of tariff rates by treaty, instituted by the British in the Treaty of Nanking, it is difficult to find a valid excuse. Such a practice was wholly one-sided and subjected China to a surrender of sovereignty to which no western power would have submitted. It restricted the Chinese government's use of an important source of revenue and prevented the imposition of a duty on imports sufficient for the encouragement of domestic industry. There was much more justification for placing the collection of customs under the administration of foreigners, since native officialdom was both inefficient and corrupt. The Imperial Maritime Customs, staffed by foreigners of many nationalities but headed by Englishmen, originated in the 1850's during the disorders of the Taiping Rebellion [2] and continued to administer the customs until the

2. See below, p. 143.

eve of World War II. It won an enviable reputation for honesty and efficiency.

Because of the inclusion of extraterritoriality and tariff limitation in the Chinese treaties with Great Britain and the United States and in the later treaties with the other European powers, these documents came to be referred to as the "unequal treaties" and became a standing grievance of China against the West; but not until the western powers needed China as an ally in World War II were the last of these unequal provisions abrogated.

The United States Takes an Interest in Japan

In the opening of China it was Great Britain that played the leading role. In the opening of Japan the United States took the lead. Prior to 1853, British, Russians, and Americans had tried in vain to open diplomatic and trade relations with the island empire. American ships, government and private, which visited Japanese ports were received with varying degrees of courtesy but were always required to depart without doing business. Sailors from American whaling ships who, by mischance or design—as in the case of a group of deserters from the *Lagoda*—found themselves marooned on Japanese shores, were placed in confinement and transported to Deshima, whence they were repatriated via Dutch ships or, in one case, an American naval vessel. Those who complained of cruel treatment seem to have brought it upon themselves by unruly behavior,[3] but their complaints nevertheless helped to shape American policy.

In the meantime, the United States was

3. Shunzo Sakamaki, *Japan and the United States, 1790–1853* (*The Transactions of the Asiatic Society of Japan,* second series, Vol. 18, Tokyo, 1939). This study corrects the common impression that inhumane treatment of shipwrecked American sailors was standard Japanese practice. This myth is perpetuated in S. E. Morison, *"Old Bruin": Commodore Matthew C. Perry, 1794–1858* (Boston: Little, Brown and Company, 1966), p. 266.

rapidly becoming a Pacific power. The settling of the Oregon question in 1846 and the acquisition of California from Mexico in 1848 gave it a frontage of over 1,200 miles on the Pacific Ocean with magnificent harbors in San Francisco Bay and Puget Sound. Forward-looking Americans saw the dawn of a great commercial era on the Pacific. Japan's harbors lay close to the great circle route from San Francisco to the Chinese coast. Japan, furthermore, was reputed to have valuable deposits of coal, and coal was becoming a necessity of ocean commerce as the steamship nosed its way into the sea lanes. To open Japanese ports to trade, to gain access to Japanese coal, to insure humane treatment for American sailors shipwrecked on Japanese shores—these became objectives of American foreign policy in the 1850's. The efficient agents in attaining them were Matthew Calbraith Perry, the naval officer, and Townsend Harris, the diplomat.

Commodore Perry's original instructions, like those to Caleb Cushing, were written by Daniel Webster, serving now as Secretary of State under President Millard Fillmore (1850–1853), but Perry was permitted to rewrite the instructions to suit himself. He was, if possible, to deliver a letter from the President (Franklin Pierce replaced Fillmore in 1853), to the Emperor. He was to seek permission for American vessels to enter one or more of the ports of Japan for the purpose of selling their cargoes and obtaining supplies, including coal; permission to establish a coal depot on one of the islands was to be obtained if possible. But the objective most emphasized was assurance of protection of American seamen and property wrecked on the islands or driven into their ports by storm. Unless this was promised, the commodore was to warn the Japanese that any future acts of cruelty would "be severely chastised."

Perry paid two visits to Yedo (later Tokyo) Bay in July 1853 and February 1854. The Japanese were impressed by the haughty and determined demeanor assumed by the commodore, and by his formidable naval squadron. They were also aware of Oriental weakness vis-à-vis western naval armament, as shown in the recent Opium War, and they knew that both Britain and Russia were planning demonstrations for ends that might be more drastic than those sought by the United States. They considered it expedient, therefore, to give the American commodore most of what he asked for. Moderate concessions to the United States might shield them from immoderate demands of other powers. These factors help to account for Perry's success.

On his first visit Perry was able to deliver the President's letter to a representative not of the Emperor but of the Shogun, at this time the effective head of the Japanese government. When he returned seven months later, he found the Shogun's government ready to sign a treaty, and this ceremony took place at the village of Yokohama on March 31, 1854.

By Perry's treaty the United States merely got a toe, so to speak, inside the Japanese door; the door was not really opened. American ships, it was agreed, might enter two Japanese ports to procure supplies. The ports were isolated and unimportant—Shimoda, southwest from Yedo Bay, and Hakodate, in the northern island of Hokkaido—and all business must be transacted through Japanese officials; no trade with private individuals would be permitted. There was no mention of a coal depot, though coal was listed among the supplies that might be purchased. A United States consul would be permitted to reside at Shimoda. Japan agreed to give proper treatment to shipwrecked American sailors, and a most-favored-nation clause assured to the United States any rights that might subsequently be granted to any other power.

The United States Defines Its Policy in the Far East

As the treaties of Nanking and Wanghia had served as the models for other treaties with China, so Perry's treaty was accepted as the pattern for Japan. Within a few months after its signature, Japan had signed very similar treaties with Great Britain, Russia, and the Netherlands. Both China and Japan had made their first treaties under duress—China as a result of defeat in war, Japan under threat of unpleasant consequences if she refused. Neither nation intended to go further than it was compelled to go in carrying out the spirit or even the letter of its new obligations. The western powers, on the other hand, including the United States, were determined not only to enjoy the rights they had secured by the treaties but to gain additional rights as soon as possible. What methods were to be used in enforcing and enlarging treaty rights in China and Japan? Should reliance be placed upon force or persuasion?

Both Perry and Dr. Peter Parker, the medical missionary, who became United States commissioner to China in 1855, advocated an aggressive policy. As Britain had obtained a base at Hong Kong, they urged that the United States secure territorial bases in Far Eastern waters from which it might defend and promote its interests. Perry occupied the Bonin Islands, arranged for a supply depot on Okinawa in the Ryukyus, and suggested a protectorate over Formosa. Parker also had schemes for making Formosa a protectorate.

But as advocates of American territorial expansion in the Far East, both Perry and Parker were a half-century ahead of their time. The government in Washington turned a deaf ear to their proposals. Parker's successor as commissioner, appointed by President Buchanan in 1857, was told that the only interests of the United States in China were in "lawful commerce" and "the protection of the lives and property of its citizens." The United States had no motive "for territorial aggrandizement or the acquisition of political power in that distant region." Parker's suggestions for seizure of Formosa were ignored. Nothing was done to follow up Perry's occupation of the Bonins, and when Japan in 1861 reasserted an old claim to those islands, the American government made no objection.

The Tientsin Treaties

The United States in the 1850's had no wish for territorial conquest in the Far East, nor would it, like France and Great Britain, use armed force to advance its interests there.[4] It placed reliance upon the good faith of the Chinese and Japanese governments, upon the persuasiveness of its diplomats, and, in China especially, upon the operation of the most-favored-nation article in its treaty with that country.

In 1857 the French and British went to war with China in order to enforce respect for their rights under the earlier treaties and to gain further privileges. The United States and Russia remained neutral but sent their diplomatic representatives to cooperate with those of the allies in the negotiation of new treaties with China. Treaties with all four powers were signed at Tientsin in 1858. Through its own treaty or as a consequence of the treaties of the other powers, the United States gained for its citizens access to eleven additional ports on the coast and on the Yangtse River, the right to navigate the Yangtse as far as Hankow and to travel in the interior, and toleration for the Christian religion. Like the other governments concerned, the United States at last secured the right of diplomatic representation at Peking

4. American naval commanders in the Far East in a few instances used force on their own responsibility. In November 1856, while the Chinese were engaged in hostilities with the British at Canton, Chinese forts below the city fired on an American naval launch. Failing to receive a satisfactory explanation from the Chinese viceroy, U. S. Flag Officer James Armstrong silenced the forts by a naval bombardment and sent ashore a landing party which effectually demolished them. J. W. Pratt, ed., "Our First 'War' in China: The Diary of William Henry Powell, 1856," *American Historical Review*, 53 (1948), 776–86. In June 1859, U. S. Commodore Josiah Tattnall was present as an observer while British ships engaged the Chinese forts on the Pei-ho River below Tientsin. In the midst of the battle he went on board the British flagship to pay his respects to the wounded British admiral and with the celebrated remark, "Blood is thicker than water!" ordered the crew of his barge to assist the British seamen in serving the guns.

and the abandonment of the Chinese Emperor's pretensions to a status above that of other monarchs. Further fighting and the occupation of Peking by British and French forces proved necessary before the Emperor could be induced to ratify the treaties, but this final step was accomplished in 1860.

The chief gainer from the hostilities of 1857–1860 was neutral Russia. By the Treaty of Aigun (1858) China ceded to Russia the northern watershed of the Amur River. In the negotiations over ratification of the Tientsin treaties the Russian representative, General Ignatiev, acted as mediator between China and the allies and was rewarded by the further surrender of the area lying between the Amur and the Ussuri Rivers and the Sea of Japan. Thus the Czar's government came into possession of the Maritime Province and forthwith established the port of Vladivostok at its southern extremity.

The United States Opposes Partition of China

By its own Treaty of Tientsin and the inclusion in it of a new most-favored-nation article the United States was maintaining the principle of equality of treatment, or the open door. In the 1850's and 1860's also it was taking a stand against the disruption of the Chinese Empire, or in behalf of the preservation of China's territorial integrity. When the great Taiping Rebellion (1851–1865) in southern China threatened to split the empire asunder, the American commissioner at Canton, Humphrey Marshall, gave his sympathy to the imperial government in its struggle to hold China together. He suspected Great Britain and Russia of plans to take advantage of the rebellion by partitioning the country between them. Anson Burlingame, United States minister to China from 1861 to 1867, found the representatives of Great Britain, France, and Russia ostensibly willing to drop any claims for special privileges in China and any demands for further cessions of Chinese territory. His agreement with them, he reported to the Secretary of State, "is a guarantee of the territorial integrity of the Chinese Empire."

Townsend Harris and Japan

In China the United States had been content to leave leadership to the more aggressive British and French and to profit from their exploits. In Japan, on the other hand, it continued for some time to hold the leading position that it had assumed under Perry. The first American consul at Shimoda, appointed in accordance with the provisions of Perry's treaty, was Townsend Harris, a New York businessman who had had some years of experience in the Far East. It was his task to push open the door that Perry had merely unlocked.[5]

When Harris was deposited by an American warship at Shimoda in August 1856, he met with anything but a hospitable reception. In spite of the treaty, the Japanese had no wish to permit a foreign official to reside at Shimoda, and for months they made his stay as uncomfortable and as dreary as possible in the hope that he could be persuaded to leave. But Harris was a man of persistence, patience, and tact. Before many months he had won the respect if not the friendship of the officials. Within a year he had persuaded them to sign a convention (June 17, 1857) materially enlarging American privileges in Japan; and in the following year he was permitted to travel in state to Yedo, seat of the Shogun's government, where he secured (July 29, 1858) the first full-fledged commercial treaty that Japan signed with any western power. In obtaining Japan's signature to this treaty Harris was aided by contemporary events in China, where the British and French had soundly beaten the Chinese forces and compelled China to sign the treaties of Tientsin. Harris argued with effect that by accepting a reasonable treaty with the United States, Japan could divert the other powers from

5. A rather unflattering portrayal of Townsend Harris, based on Japanese as well as American sources, is Oliver Statler, *Shimoda Story* (New York: Random House, Inc., 1969).

making excessive demands. The American treaty did, in reality, become the model for those soon after made with the Netherlands, Russia, Great Britain, and France.

The convention of 1857 and the treaty of 1858 together opened four new ports to American ships, authorized the appointment of consuls for all the open ports, permitted trade with private parties in those ports, and gave to Americans the right to reside in the open ports, there to hold property, build churches, and practice their religion. After January 1, 1862, American citizens might also reside in Yedo, the Shogun's capital. The treaty permitted each government to appoint a diplomatic representative to reside at the capital of the other. Like the Chinese treaties, it gave extraterritorial status to Americans living in the Oriental country and fixed upper limits for duties on imports and exports. Perry had not included extraterritoriality in his treaty with Japan, and Harris did not approve the principle; but since the British, Dutch, and Russians had all inserted extraterritorial provisions in their treaties, Harris could not well forgo securing the same privilege for the United States. Thus Japan, like China, became a victim of "unequal treaties." The United States, however, was to be the leading advocate of a restoration to Japan of tariff autonomy and full jurisdiction over foreigners in her territory. Japan was relieved of the handicap of extraterritoriality before the end of the century and achieved tariff autonomy soon thereafter.

The End of Japanese Isolation

The treaties of 1858 were followed by a period of internal discord and strife in Japan. The Shogun's government had negotiated the treaties in the conviction that Japan must either make concessions to the western powers or, like China, suffer defeat and humiliation at their hands. The isolationist elements in society and those who were simply jealous of the Shogun, gathered around the Emperor, and for several years the imperial court at Kyoto was the center of opposition to the admission of the foreigners. An imperial decree ordered all foreigners out of the empire by June 25, 1863, and while no real effort was made to enforce this edict, foreigners were attacked and even murdered from time to time by irresponsible adherents of the isolationist party. In this difficult period the United States cooperated closely with the other powers in Japan, as it was doing in China under Minister Burlingame. United States naval forces joined in a punitive expedition against rebellious clans in southwestern Japan and the American minister was present (though on a British warship) at a joint naval demonstration at Osaka in 1865, which finally persuaded the Emperor to give his approval to the treaties signed seven years before.[6] The period ended with the overthrow of the Shogunate and the "restoration" of the Emperor to the actual possession of sovereign power. After this "Meiji Restoration" of 1868, the imperial court, its seat removed to Yedo, now rechristened Tokyo, was quickly converted to a belief in the necessity of throwing the door open to western ideas and western technology. Then began the marvelous transformation that was to bring Japan within a generation to a position among the leading world powers.

6. In July 1863 the United States steam sloop-of-war *Wyoming*, which had come to the Pacific in search of the Confederate raider *Alabama,* engaged single-handed with Japanese batteries and armed vessels in the straits of Shimonoseki, where American vessels had been fired upon by hostile Japanese.

If the 1840's are labeled the decade of Manifest Destiny Triumphant, the succeeding ten years may well be called the era of Manifest Destiny Frustrated. The faith in American democracy that had made acquisitions of new territory seem merely "extending the area of freedom" still persisted. So strong indeed was the democratic faith that not a few Americans were tempted to intervene in behalf of struggling democracy in Europe, in disregard of the warnings of earlier statesmen.

Such impulses were seen in the tumultuous enthusiasm that greeted the exiled Hungarian patriot, Louis Kossuth, when he visited the United States in 1851. In Washington, Kossuth was lavishly entertained at a banquet sponsored by members of Congress from both parties. He was cordially received by President Fillmore, but was clearly told by both the President and Secretary of State Webster that the United States would not depart from its policy of noninterference in the affairs of Europe. Kossuth was assured that Hungary's struggle for independence had American sympathy but could expect no American aid. Members of a group in the Democratic party calling themselves "Young America" were ready to go to almost any length in support of liberal or revolutionary movements in Europe, but their attempts were brought to nought by more conservative elements in the party.[1]

Faith in democracy, together with strategic and economic considerations, produced a profusion of new projects of territorial expansion, looking to the north, west, and south. But so deeply, in this decade, was the nation divided over the slavery question, that any proposal of expansion put forward by the pro-southern administration of either Franklin Pierce or James Buchanan was sure to be viewed with suspicion by the antislavery forces of the North. For this and for other reasons, few of the proposals for expansion were carried out. The only achievements of the decade in this respect were the narrow strip of territory purchased from Mexico by James Gadsden, certain rights of interoceanic transit across the

16

A Decade
of Frustration

1. M. E. Curti, "Young America," *American Historical Review,* 32 (1926), 34–55.

Isthmuses of Panama and Tehuantepec, and a few scattered and isolated "guano islands" in the Pacific and elsewhere.

Canada—Annexation or Reciprocity?

There seemed a possibility in the early 1850's that Canada, an objective of American arms and diplomacy in the Revolution and again in the War of 1812, might join the United States of its own accord. Dissatisfaction with a change in British commercial policy—repeal of the Corn Laws and the resulting loss of Canada's preferred status in British markets —combined with political discontents to produce a movement for peaceful separation from the British Empire and annexation to the United States. As was to be expected, the British government opposed any such solution for Canada's difficulties, and it undertook to meet these problems by liberalizing trade between Canada and her sister provinces [2] on the one hand and the United States on the other. This was accomplished by a reciprocity treaty, signed June 5, 1854, by Secretary of State William L. Marcy and the Earl of Elgin and Kincardine, Governor General of Britain's North American Provinces. The treaty provided free entry from Canada and the Maritime Provinces to the United States, and vice versa, of a long list of raw and semi-finished commodities, the products of farm, forest, mines, and the sea. It admitted American fishermen to the inshore fisheries of the British provinces from which they were excluded under the treaty of 1818, and gave similar privileges to Canadian fishermen on

2. Canada in 1849 comprised Quebec and Ontario (formerly Lower and Upper Canada), which had been united by the British Act of Union of 1840. Separate provinces or colonies were New Brunswick, Nova Scotia, Prince Edward Island, and Newfoundland. The Dominion of Canada, created by the North America Act of 1867, included at first Quebec, Ontario, New Brunswick, and Nova Scotia. Manitoba became a province of the Dominion in 1870, British Columbia in 1871, Prince Edward Island in 1873, Alberta and Saskatchewan in 1905, Newfoundland in 1950.

the eastern coast of the United States north of the 36th parallel of latitude. It also opened the St. Lawrence River and its canals to navigation by citizens of the United States, and in return admitted British subjects to the navigation of Lake Michigan.

The Marcy-Elgin Treaty was to remain in force for ten years, after which either party might terminate it by giving a year's notice. It proved beneficial to both countries, but was terminated by the United States in 1865. The principal reasons for this action were irritation at the allegedly pro-southern attitude of Canada during the Civil War, a belief that Canada profited more from the treaty than did the United States, and the protectionist philosophy of the then dominant Republican party.

The Pacific

The settlement of the Oregon boundary controversy and the acquisition of California made the United States a Pacific power. The opening of official relations with China and Japan in 1844 and 1854 respectively held out the prospect of a greatly increased commerce on the Pacific. Commodore Perry and Dr. Peter Parker, it will be recalled, urged the United States to follow the British example set at Hong Kong and acquire outposts of its own in the western Pacific, but the government in Washington repudiated such proposals.

The Hawaiian Islands were a different matter. Geographically an outpost of North America, they had come increasingly under United States influence. New England trading ships had begun frequenting them in the 1790's. New England whalers appeared some years later. New England missionaries, sent out in 1820 by the American Board of Commissioners for Foreign Missions, gained the ears of the royal family and within a few years had converted the entire Polynesian population to at least a nominal acceptance of Christianity. With Christianity in its American Calvinist form, the missionaries brought American ideas of education and of government. They set up printing presses, reduced the native language to writing, and provided a written constitution for the formerly despotic monarchy.

Culturally, Hawaii was becoming a colony of the United States. That it should not become politically a colony of any other power came to be a tenet of American foreign policy, first announced in 1842 by President Tyler and Secretary of State Webster. This was as far as they cared to go. Nine years later, in restating the principle, as in the earlier instance, against threatened interference by France, Webster declined an offer of a protectorate and disclaimed any thought of annexing the islands.

Franklin Pierce, Democratic President (1853–1857), was ready to adopt a more aggressive Hawaiian policy than his Whig predecessors. A treaty of annexation was actually negotiated in Honolulu in 1854, but the death of the reigning monarch produced a change in Hawaiian policy, and the treaty was never signed.

The only Pacific islands that came under American sovereignty in the 1850's were acquired as a result of the "Guano Law" of 1856. The law was the consequence of the discovery by American ship captains of deposits of guano, a valuable fertilizer, on certain uninhabited islands in the Pacific. It provided that such islands, if taken possession of and occupied by citizens of the United States, might "at the discretion of the President, be considered as appertaining to the United States." The first "appurtenances" acquired under this law were Baker and Jarvis Islands. Dozens of others were added in due course, most of them in the Pacific, a few in the Atlantic and Caribbean. Of no value then, save for the guano deposits, some of them were to assume unexpected importance in the air age.

One other possible Pacific acquisition, Russian America (or Alaska), received some attention at this time. Russia was not averse to selling, and President James Buchanan (1857–1861) let it be known that he stood ready to pay $5,000,000 for it. The project was

dropped when the Russian minister in Washington informed his government that under existing relations between President and Congress, no treaty sponsored by Buchanan was likely to get Senate approval.

Approaches to the Pacific: Railroad Schemes

Men who predicted a great future for the United States in the Pacific looked forward to speedier means of getting there than the prairie schooner plodding along the Oregon trail or the sailing ship beating laboriously around the Horn. There would be railroads across the continent or a canal through the isthmus; probably both. Asa Whitney, a New York merchant who had made a fortune in the China trade, labored vainly for years to persuade Congress to finance the building of a railroad from Lake Michigan to the mouth of the Columbia River. It proved easier to interest Democrats in Washington in a railroad by a southern route. The acquisition of such a route was warmly sponsored by Jefferson Davis, Secretary of War in Pierce's cabinet, and became an important object of James Gadsden's mission to Mexico in 1853.

The Gadsden Purchase

Gadsden was directed by William L. Marcy, Secretary of State, to secure a southward readjustment of the boundary with Mexico, between the Rio Grande and the Colorado, sufficient to permit the construction of a railroad within the limits of the United States. For this he could offer a maximum of $15,000,000. If Mexico would cede additional territory, Gadsden might offer more money, up to a top figure of $50,000,000 for a wide strip of northern Mexico, embracing portions of five states, and the peninsula of Lower California. In all, five alternative boundaries were suggested. Gadsden was also to secure the release of the United States from certain responsibilities of border policing that it had accepted in the Treaty of Guadalupe Hidalgo.

Events now began to take on a familiar pattern. The notorious Santa Anna was again in power in Mexico City and, as usual, was in need of money. Whether there was a duplicate of Colonel Atocha to carry hints to Gadsden the records do not reveal, but soon the minister was suggesting to Washington that an offer of a liberal down payment backed by threats of force might be expected to win valuable concessions. Accordingly, Gadsden was authorized to promise a large installment in cash for any one of the proposed cessions, and United States troops were moved ominously toward the Rio Grande.

Santa Anna this time proved compliant, but only to the extent of the minimum cession proposed by Gadsden. A treaty was signed on December 30, 1853. In the Senate it underwent considerable modification. As it emerged with Senate approval on April 25, 1854, it contained, in addition to the cession of territory between the Rio Grande and the Colorado, a guarantee to the government and the citizens of the United States of the use of any means of transit across the Isthmus of Tehuantepec, including the right of the government to protect the transit "when it may feel sanctioned and warranted by the public or international law." These rights, though never used, were not formally surrendered until 1937. The amended treaty also cancelled Article XI of the Treaty of Guadalupe Hidalgo, which had made the United States responsible for depredations that might be committed in Mexico by Indians from north of the border. The Senate reduced the monetary compensation from $20,000,000, of which $5,000,000 was to be paid to claimants in the United States, to $10,000,000, all to go to Mexico. All amendments were accepted by Santa Anna, and ratifications were exchanged in Washington June 30, 1854. Thus was acquired the route for a railroad subsequently utilized by the Southern Pacific.

Later attempts to secure rights-of-way on other possible railroad routes through Mexican territory were associated with chaotic political conditions in Mexico and the resulting danger of intervention from Europe. After Santa Anna's final elimination from Mexican politics in 1855, presidents followed one another in rapid succession, and soon there were rival governments at Mexico City and Vera Cruz. Americans and other foreigners lost lives and property in the disorders, and neither government would assume the obligation to settle damage claims. The situation was a standing invitation to foreign intervention, and President Buchanan feared that if the United States did not intervene, some European power or powers would do so, as eventually they did. He asked authority, therefore, to intervene by force in behalf of the "constitutional" government of Benito Juarez at Vera Cruz, to help in restoring order, and to establish, temporarily, a protectorate over certain of the northern states of Mexico. "As a good neighbor," he asked Congress, "shall we not extend to her a helping hand to save her?"

Northern men in Congress, suspecting that Buchanan's "good neighbor policy" cloaked designs for the extension of slave territory, saw to it that Congress refused or ignored all his requests. When his minister, R. M. McLane, signed a treaty with the Juarez government granting to the United States for $4,000,000 rights-of-way on two railroad routes—from the lower Rio Grande to Mazatlán and from Nogales to Guaymas—and the right to intervene for the protection of its citizens in Mexico, the Senate rejected it (May 31, 1860) by a vote of eighteen ayes to twenty-seven noes. Thus the way was left open for the Anglo-French-Spanish intervention of 1862 and the reign of Maximilian.[3]

The Search for a Canal Route: The Clayton-Bulwer Treaty

Keener than the interest in a transcontinental railroad route was that in the possibility of an interoceanic canal. Two sites for such a canal presented obvious advantages: Panama, where the inter-American isthmus was narrowest, and

3. See Chapter 19.

ATLANTIC
OCEAN

DANISH WEST INDIES

PUERTO RICO

SOUTH AMERICA

Môle St. Nicholas
(Samana Bay)
HAITI
SANTO DOMINGO

Caribbean Sea

CUBA

JAMAICA

NICARAGUA ROUTE–
TRANSIT TREATY, 1867

Greytown

NEW GRANADA
(COLOMBIA)

ISTHMUS OF PANAMA–
TRANSIT TREATY, 1846

UNITED STATES

Gulf of Mexico

YUCATAN PEN.

BELIZE (Br.)

HONDURAS

GUATEMALA

NICARAGUA

COSTA RICA

SALVADOR

Matamoros

Monterey

MEXICO

Mazatlan

ISTHMUS OF TEHUANTEPEC
– RIGHT OF WAY, 1853

PACIFIC
OCEAN

Nogales

Guaymas

U.S. INTERESTS IN MEXICO,
CENTRAL AMERICA, AND THE
CARIBBEAN, 1853–1871

••••••• Maximum proposed purchase line, 1853.

– – – Proposed purchase line, 1857.

ⅿⅿⅿⅿ Rights of way by McLane–Ocampo treaty (unratified).

Nicaragua, where a natural water communication by lake and river traversed all but a dozen miles of the distance between Pacific and Caribbean.

At Panama the United States had already, through no initiative of its own, acquired both rights and responsibilities. In 1846 Benjamin Bidlack, United States minister to New Granada (later known as Colombia), which embraced the isthmus, had been suddenly confronted with a surprising offer from the New Granadan government. If the United States would guarantee the neutrality of the isthmus and the sovereignty of New Granada therein, the government of New Granada would in return guarantee to the citizens of the United States the use of any means of transit that might be constructed across the isthmus upon the same terms as those enjoyed by the citizens of New Granada. Bidlack, though without instructions for such a contingency, signed the proposed treaty. Polk, after some hesitation because of the novel character of the plan, sent the treaty to the Senate, which eventually approved it.

Over control of the Nicaragua route an intense rivalry developed between local representatives of the United States and Great Britain. Fortunately, the governments in Washington and London were less ambitious and combative than the agents on the spot. A compromise settlement was achieved in a treaty signed by Secretary of State John M. Clayton and the British minister, Sir Henry Bulwer, April 19, 1850. Each party agreed never to obtain or maintain any exclusive control over the proposed Nicaraguan canal, never to erect fortifications in its vicinity, and never to colonize, or exercise dominion over, any part of Central America. Both agreed to lend support and encouragement to any company that should undertake the construction of a canal, to guarantee the neutrality of the canal when built, and to invite other friendly states to become parties to the treaty.

There were ambiguities in the Clayton-Bulwer Treaty, which resulted in misunderstanding and bickerings through much of the following decade. These concerned principally the question of whether the treaty required Great Britain to surrender certain holdings in the area, such as her protectorate over the Mosquito Indians of Nicaragua, or merely to refrain from acquiring new ones. In the diplomatic debates over these issues, the United States relied not only upon its interpretation of the treaty, but also upon President Monroe's message of December 2, 1823, which now for the first time came to be referred to as the Monroe Doctrine. Great Britain adhered to her own interpretation of the treaty and would admit no validity in the Monroe Doctrine. In practice, however, she eventually gave in, surrendering the footholds to which the United States had objected. In these British retreats, which were in keeping with the current loss of interest in colonial possessions in general, one may perhaps see the first real victory of the Monroe Doctrine.[4]

There was to be no isthmian canal for half a century, but both the Panama and Nicaragua routes were soon accommodating numerous travelers to and from the west coast of the United States. In Nicaragua, beginning in 1850, Cornelius Vanderbilt's Accessory Transit Company carried passengers by small steamer and coach between the Caribbean and the Pacific termini, to which steamers operated from New York and San Francisco. At Panama, by 1855, a railroad had replaced mule-back and other primitive modes of transportation across the isthmus.

Occasional disorders on both transit routes led to proposals for some sort of supervision by the United States. Riots in Panama disrupted transportation by that route. In Nicaragua, the incursion of the filibuster William Walker, the "grey-eyed man of destiny," kept things in turmoil for a year or two. To such interruptions of transportation over the isthmian routes President James Buchanan invited the attention of Congress in his first annual message in 1857 and in several subsequent messages. He proposed that Congress authorize the President to use the armed

4. Perkins, *History of the Monroe Doctrine,* pp. 101–2.

forces of the United States to keep the routes open.

One supporter of Buchanan's proposals was Sam Houston, now a senator from Texas. Houston questioned whether the United States had a right, under the Monroe Doctrine, to exclude European powers from intervention in the Americas "and yet do nothing ourselves by which these nations may be made useful to the community of nations, and advantageous to the cause of commerce, social organization and good government." Houston's position was close to that preached and practiced by Theodore Roosevelt half a century later. But Congress, where antislavery men suspected another scheme for extending slave territory, took no action. Buchanan was left to do what he could through normal diplomatic approaches to Nicaragua and New Granada.

Approaches to the Isthmus: The Cuban Question

The eastern approaches to the isthmus lie through the Caribbean, and the Caribbean is rimmed on the northwest and north by the peninsula of Yucatán and by Cuba, Hispaniola, and other islands to the eastward. Peninsula and islands command the sea lanes into the Caribbean, and Cuba in addition shares with Florida control of the eastern gateway of the Gulf of Mexico. In an era when the isthmian routes had become of such vital concern to the United States, it was inevitable that a similar concern should be felt for the territories dominating the entrances to the Caribbean. It is not surprising, therefore, that the expansionists of the period following the Mexican War sponsored projects for securing footholds for the United States in Yucatán, Hispaniola, and Cuba.

In Yucatán, which at the time considered itself independent of Mexico, the white inhabitants were endangered by a formidable Indian revolt. Through an agent in Washington, in April 1848, they offered the United States "dominion and sovereignty" over the peninsula in return for military aid against the Indians. Notification that similar offers had been made to Spain and Great Britain led President Polk to send the correspondence to Congress. There a debate on the desirability of forestalling Britain by taking possession of Yucatán was terminated by news that whites and Indians in the peninsula had patched up their differences.

Six years later, the expansionist administration of Franklin Pierce made an attempt to secure by cession or lease a site for a naval base at Samaná Bay in the Dominican Republic on the island of Hispaniola. The American agent, William L. Cazneau, seemed on the point of success when intervention by the British and French consuls dissuaded the Dominican government from executing the cession.

Far more important in American eyes than Yucatán or Samaná Bay was the island of Cuba. Thomas Jefferson and John Quincy Adams had viewed Cuba as inescapably linked by fate with the United States, and Adams and Henry Clay had warned Spain that the United States could never consent to its transfer to another European power. The new importance of Cuba in relation to the isthmian routes, renewed hints of British and French interest in the island and of projects for the emancipation of Cuban slaves, sympathy for an oppressed colonial people who made sporadic attempts to throw off Spanish rule—all linked themselves with the prevalent expansionist fever in the United States to promote a succession of schemes for the "liberation" of Cuba and its eventual annexation.

An informal offer from President Polk to purchase the island for $100,000,000 was emphatically rebuffed by the Spanish government. The Whig administrations of Taylor and Fillmore (1849–1853) showed no interest in the acquisition of Cuba and did what they could to prevent the filibustering adventures of the exiled Cuban patriot, Narciso Lopez. Lopez, whose ostensible object was an independent Cuba, nevertheless had the support of such American expansionists as John L. O'Sullivan of New York and Governor John A. Quitman of Mississippi. Twice he succeeded in slipping out of New Orleans and landing several hundred men on Cuban shores. Both attempts failed, and the second, in August 1851, ended in the capture and execution of Lopez and many of his followers.

Spain had appealed for British and French aid in resisting the filibusters. In the spring of 1852 the British and French ministers in Washington invited the United States to adhere to a tripartite convention by which the three governments would disclaim for all time any intention of acquiring the island of Cuba and would promise to discourage any such design on the part of other powers or individuals. This proposal was rejected by the Fillmore administration. Edward Everett, who had become Secretary of State upon Webster's death, informed the two ministers that although the United States did not seek the acquisition of Cuba, he considered its status "mainly an American question." The proposed agreement, he continued, was unequal, since the fate of Cuba was of much more vital importance to the United States than it could be to France or Great Britain. While Spain stood still, furthermore, the United States was an expanding power whose growth could not be arrested by any such paper agreement as that proposed. Such reasoning by the Whig Secretary of State was a close approximation to the Democratic dogma of Manifest Destiny.

The Pierce Administration and Cuba

Before Everett's note was written, the November elections had resulted in the defeat of the Whigs and the choice of the Democrat, Franklin Pierce, for the presidency. The new administration was avowedly expansionist. Pierce's inaugural declaration that his policy would "not be controlled by any timid forebodings of evil from expansion" probably alluded to a warning from outgoing President Fillmore that "serious peril" might result from the acquisition of Cuba. Pierce believed, on the contrary, that the acquisition of certain possessions—not named but certainly including Cuba—was "eminently important for our protection."

Spain's aversion to the idea of parting with Cuba was well known. Pierce and his Secretary of State, William L. Marcy, would perhaps have been willing to resort to other methods than negotiation had they been sure of support within their party. The *Black Warrior* incident seemed for a while to offer an opportunity. On February 28, 1854, Spanish authorities in Havana confiscated the cargo of the American steamer of that name for a purely technical violation of the customs regulations. This action drew from Washington a strong remonstrance and a demand for redress, refusal of which might conceivably be used as an excuse for war and the seizure of Cuba. At the same time, John A. Quitman, the former Mississippi governor who had supported Lopez, was organizing a filibustering plan of his own to save "white civilization" in Cuba and to bring the island into the Union as a slave state. Pending in the Senate was a proposal to suspend the neutrality laws, thus removing a barrier to Quitman's plan. England and France, now involved in the Crimean War, would hardly be in a position to interfere.

This seemingly fair prospect was dissipated by a rift within the Democratic party. Pierce's sponsorship of Senator Stephen A. Douglas' Kansas-Nebraska bill, opening Kansas and Nebraska territories to slavery, had incurred the displeasure of important sections of the northern Democracy. Virtual sponsorship of filibustering attacks on Cuba, demanded by proslavery southerners, might completely disrupt the party. In an attempt at compromise, Pierce repudiated the filibustering scheme and relaxed pressure on Spain for settlement of the *Black Warrior* claims, but promised more energetic measures for the acquisition of Cuba by diplomacy.

The American minister to Spain was Pierre Soulé, French-born radical and expansionist from Louisiana. He had been authorized by Marcy to attempt to purchase Cuba for as much as $130,000,000, and if purchase proved impossible, to seek other means "to detach that island from the Spanish dominion and from all dependence on any European power." Soulé's efforts had availed nothing. Marcy now proposed that Soulé, James Buchanan, minister to Great Britain, and John Y. Mason, minister to France, meet, consult together, "compare opinions as to what may be advisable, and . . . adopt measures for perfect concert of action in aid of [Soulé's] negotiations at Madrid." They were directed to report the result of their deliberations to Marcy by confidential messenger.

Out of the meetings of the three envoys at Ostend and Aix-la-Chappelle came their report, dated October 15, 1854, which was to become notorious as the "Ostend Manifesto." The term is a misnomer. The document was a confidential report to the Secretary of State and was published only at the insistence of the administration's enemies in the House of Representatives. It failed to give what Marcy presumably had desired—an objective appraisal of the attitudes of the principal European governments toward the Cuban question. It consisted principally of advice to the government of the United States as to why it needed Cuba and of advice to Spain on the advantages which that country could derive from selling the island. The sensational portion of the "manifesto" was a declaration that if Spain refused to sell Cuba and if conditions in Cuba should seriously endanger "our internal peace and the existence of our cherished Union," the United States would be justified in seizing the island upon the principle of self-defense.

The "Ostend Manifesto" failed completely in its purpose. Marcy repudiated the proposal for seizure, "the robber doctrine" he called it, whereupon Soulé resigned as minister. In December the Spanish Foreign Minister stated to an applauding Cortes: "To part with Cuba would be to part with the national honor." In the United States, the November elections went against the administration. Whatever chance Franklin Pierce may have had to acquire Cuba had been destroyed by the adverse northern reaction to the Kansas-Nebraska Act.

Pierce's successor, James Buchanan, fared no better than Pierce with respect to Cuba. The co-author of the Ostend Manifesto repeatedly called upon Congress for funds to facilitate negotiations with Spain for the acquisition of the island, but in the face of growing opposition his efforts were fruitless.

Could Buchanan have had his way, he would have purchased Cuba, stationed United States troops in Nicaragua and on the Isthmus of Panama, and used the army in Mexico to establish an orderly and solvent government. In proposing these policies, it seems safe to say, Buchanan was seeking to promote national rather than sectional interests—to guard the isthmian transit and the approaches to it and to forestall European intervention by removing the justification for it. He failed because of the supposed identification of his plans with the interests of slavery.[5]

5. For accounts of some private schemes of conquest in the Caribbean and Mexico, the plans of the "Knights of the Golden Circle" and of Sam Houston, see C. A. Bridges, "The Knights of the Golden Circle: A Filibustering Fantasy," *Southwestern Historical Quarterly,* 44 (1941), 287–302; Ollinger Crenshaw, "The Knights of the Golden Circle," *American Historical Review,* 47 (1941), 23–50; W. P. Webb, *The Texas Rangers: A Century of Frontier Defense* (Boston: Houghton Mifflin Company, 1935), chap. 10.

17

The Diplomacy
of the Civil War

The attack on Fort Sumter by the forces of the Southern Confederacy, April 12, 1861, opened the four-year struggle usually referred to as the American Civil War. Seven states of the lower South had seceded as a consequence of the election of Lincoln and at Montgomery, Alabama, had organized the Confederate States of America. Four additional states, Virginia, North Carolina, Tennessee, and Arkansas, joined them after the firing on Fort Sumter and Lincoln's call upon the states for troops to assist in suppressing the insurrection. The Atlantic and Gulf coasts from Chesapeake Bay to the Rio Grande lay within the Confederacy. This fact made it certain that the war would be fought by sea as well as by land and would involve many of the same troublesome questions between belligerents and neutrals that had been raised in the Napoleonic Wars.

The United States now found itself in an unaccustomed role—that of a belligerent in a war in which the great powers of Europe were neutral. It may be said in general that although the United States repudiated none of the principles for which it had previously contended, it adopted a new emphasis in their interpretation. It now insisted upon the *rights* of belligerents rather than their obligations, upon the *obligations* of neutrals rather than their rights. The consequence was an enlargement of belligerent rights and a more precise and exacting definition of neutral duties.

But the most momentous question that confronted the United States after the outbreak of hostilities was whether Europe, especially England and France, would remain neutral. It was the hope of Confederate leaders in 1861 that intervention by one or more of the European powers would insure the independence of the South, much as the intervention of France in 1778 had insured the independence of the United States. By the same token, avoidance of European intervention was vital to the triumph of the North.[1]

1. William H. Seward, Lincoln's Secretary of State, suggested to Lincoln (April 1, 1861) that provoking a foreign crisis, even war with Spain and France, might restore the Union. His suggestion was tactfully set aside by the President. Seward soon recovered from this "foreign war panacea" illusion and thereafter conducted the delicate diplomacy of wartime with exemplary discretion.

The Downfall of King Cotton

The first step toward intervention in behalf of the South would be formal recognition of the Confederacy as an independent state, and for this, Confederate agents in England and France worked unceasingly throughout the conflict. Napoleon III, the French Emperor, was frankly pro-southern in sympathy. He was ready to recognize the Confederacy and to intervene in its behalf at any time when the British government would cooperate. Without British support he dared not risk such action. All depended, therefore, upon the British attitude, and this in turn was determined by a number of factors.

The South had relied heavily upon the power of "King Cotton" to compel European intervention. This reliance proved illusory. Confidence that Europe, especially England, was so dependent upon the South's cotton that it must intervene to gain access to the white staple had failed to take account of the large surpluses of cotton and cotton goods in European warehouses in 1861. To the owners of these stocks, the cutting off of further supplies was a boon. By the time the surpluses were exhausted, substitutes were available. Neither the owners nor the employees of British cotton mills agitated for intervention.[2] Economic considerations, in fact, were more conducive to nonintervention than to intervention by Britain in the American war. Continuance of the war was profitable to British interests not only in the enhanced prices of textiles but also in the sale of war supplies to both sides and in the opportunity for destruction by Confederate cruisers of northern shipping, the chief competitor of England's merchant marine.[3] Intervention, furthermore, involving a break with the North, would entail serious risks for Great Britain. In Canada and the British merchant marine, the North held hostages for Britain's good behavior.

Apart from such material factors, British sympathies divided largely along class and ideological lines. The aristocracy, at that time still to a large degree the governing class, had much in common with the planter class of the South and were inclined to welcome the breakup of the Union as an object lesson in the failure of democracy. British liberals, like John Bright, likewise looked upon the war as a test of democracy and for that reason hoped for a northern victory and the preservation of the Union. British labor also favored the North, and though still unenfranchised, made its influence felt through numerous mass meetings and other forms of demonstration. Lincoln's emancipation policy, although deplored by the upper classes as a last desperate gamble and an invitation to a servile war, strengthened the support of the North on the part of liberal and labor groups.[4]

Viscount Palmerston and Earl Russell, Prime Minister and Foreign Secretary respectively, shared the sympathies of the British upper classes, but in so far as their official policy could be called pro-southern, it was the result of a widely held conviction that southern victory was inevitable and that hence the prolongation of the war meant useless bloodshed and destruction of property. In this conviction and under Russell's leadership, the cabinet was on the verge of intervention in October of 1862.

News of the southern repulse at Antietam, arriving at an opportune moment, made southern victory less certain and strengthened the

2. F. L. Owsley, *King Cotton Diplomacy: Foreign Relations of the Confederate States of America* (Chicago: University of Chicago Press, 1931), chap. 2; E. D. Adams, *Great Britain and the American Civil War,* 2 vols. (New York: Longmans, Green & Company, Inc., 1925), 2, chap. 10. The theory that accounts for British nonintervention by a supposed British dependence upon northern wheat is not tenable. Wheat was obtainable elsewhere. It came from the United States in large quantities chiefly because sale of war supplies to the North created a favorable exchange rate.

3. Owsley, *King Cotton Diplomacy,* chap. 19.
4. Adams, *Britain and Civil War,* 2, chap. 12; J. G. Randall, *Lincoln the President,* 3 vols. (New York: Dodd, Mead & Co., 1945–1953), 2: 176–80; 3, chaps. 13, 14. Public reaction in favor of emancipation and hence in favor of the North was apparently much more general in France and Spain than in England.

opponents of intervention. The cabinet drew back. In November the government rejected French proposals for joint intervention. Never again did Palmerston and Russell approach so close to recognition of the Confederacy.[5]

The War and Belligerent Rights

Although the Confederacy never secured the coveted recognition of its independence, the British government was prompt in according it belligerent rights. Such a course was not only in accord with American practice as seen in connection with the Canadian rebellion of 1837,[6] it was rendered unavoidable by the magnitude of the military preparations in America and by the Federal government's institution of a naval blockade of southern ports —clearly an act of one belligerent against another. British recognition of Confederate belligerency, accomplished through the issuance of a neutrality proclamation on May 13, 1861,

was promptly imitated by the other principal European governments. In practice it meant chiefly that Confederate naval vessels or privateers would be treated as legitimate ships of war, not as pirates. Though Lincoln and William H. Seward, his Secretary of State, resented the British proclamation as unfriendly, or at least as premature, nevertheless they found it necessary themselves to treat the Confederacy as a belligerent, not as a domestic insurrectionary movement, as Seward at first hoped.

The war, therefore, raised many of the old questions concerning the rights and duties of belligerents and neutrals.

To a considerable extent, these questions had been answered, for Europe at any rate, by the Declaration of Paris, adopted April 16, 1856, at the close of the Crimean War. The powers concerned (Austria, France, Great Britain, Prussia, Russia, Sardinia, and Turkey) had joined in declaring the following principles:

1. Privateering is, and remains, abolished;
2. The neutral flag covers enemy's goods, with the exception of contraband of war;
3. Neutral goods, with the exception of contraband of war, are not liable to capture under the enemy's flag;
4. Blockades, in order to be binding, must be effective; that is to say, maintained by a force sufficient really to prevent access to the coast of the enemy.

To this declaration the United States was invited to adhere. The second, third, and fourth articles stated principles for which the United States had long contended and which it rejoiced to see thus formally accepted by the great powers. But for the abolition of privateering it was not then ready. The United States had a large merchant marine but a navy far inferior to the navies of several European states. If it were unable, in a war with a European power such as England, to supplement its inadequate navy with privateers, it would be at a serious disadvantage. Its own merchant marine might be destroyed or driven from the seas by the British navy,

5. In rejecting Napoleon's proposal, Russell gave as one reason the unwillingness of the Russian government to join in the mediation. This was probably an excuse rather than a reason, since Russian support would have been of small value. Russian sympathy for the North during the war was part of the traditional Russian policy of building up the United States as a rival to England. The knowledge of Russia's friendly attitude, especially the supposed symbol of it in the visit of the Russian fleets in 1863 (see p. 165, n. 2), had a wholesome effect upon northern morale and may thus have made an intangible contribution to northern victory. See T. A. Bailey, *America Faces Russia: Russian-American Relations from Early Times to Our Day* (Ithaca, N.Y.: Cornell University Press, 1950), chap. 7. One obstacle to European recognition of the Confederacy was unquestionably the latter's commitment to the institution of slavery. Confederate propagandists tried to meet this objection by picturing American Negro slavery as a paternalistic and benevolent system, hardly slavery at all. In December 1864, when hopes of southern victory had become desperate, President Jefferson Davis offered emancipation of the South's slaves in return for British and French recognition of Confederate independence. In London the Confederate agents learned unofficially that the offer, which might possibly have been effectual a year and a half earlier, was now too late. Owsley, *King Cotton Diplomacy*, chap. 18; Adams, *Britain and Civil War*, 2:249–51.

6. See p. 99.

while the American navy could inflict only trifling losses on British commerce. Only on one condition would the United States consent to end privateering—if the other powers would agree to the immunity of all noncontraband belligerent property at sea. Secretary of State Marcy offered American adherence to the Declaration if it were amended to include this principle. There the negotiations had ended.

In the war now begun, privateering might well work to the advantage of the Confederacy and to the detriment of the United States. Lincoln and Seward, consequently, had reason to regret that their predecessors had not subscribed to the Declaration of Paris, which might now have been invoked to outlaw privateering under the Confederate flag. Seward, in fact, proposed to Great Britain and other signatories that they accept the adherence of the United States to the Declaration without the amendment upon which it had formerly insisted. Earl Russell in reply offered to accept the adherence of the United States, but only with the understanding that such acceptance should not "have any bearing . . . on the internal differences now prevailing in the United States." The qualification meant, of course, that Great Britain would not regard the ban upon privateering as applicable in the current conflict. Seward declined the offer thus qualified, but made it plain to the British Foreign Office that the United States proposed to adhere to the second, third, and fourth articles of the Declaration.[7]

In reality, all four principles of the Declaration of Paris came to be observed during the war. The Confederacy, after a few experiments with privateering, abandoned the practice as unprofitable. As for the North, although Congress in 1863 authorized President Lincoln to issue letters of marque, the President never made use of that authority.

Blockading the Confederacy

Observance of the fourth principle of the Declaration of Paris—that "blockades, in order to be binding, must be effective"—presented serious problems to the government in Washington. In a proclamation of April 19, 1861, Lincoln announced the intention of the government to institute a blockade of the ports of the seceded states. These ports, after Virginia and North Carolina joined the Confederacy, were scattered along 3,000 miles of coastline stretching from Chesapeake Bay to the Rio Grande. The Navy which would bear responsibility for closing some 185 ports or openings in this extensive coastline comprised initially about one hundred vessels, of which two-thirds were antiquated sailing vessels, while a number of the better steamers were in navy yards awaiting repairs. These were supplemented as rapidly as possible by the purchase of vessels of the most diverse types—steamers, tugs, ferryboats, even sailing vessels—since any craft that could carry a few guns and remain at sea could be utilized for blockade purposes. Over four hundred vessels were thus acquired during the war.[8]

Whether the blockade thus instituted was technically effective was at the time, and has been since, a matter of controversy.[9] There were a great many successful violations; just how many is not known. On the other hand, over 1,500 ships were captured or destroyed in attempted violations, and before the end of the

7. Department of State, *Policy of the United States toward Maritime Commerce in War,* prepared by Carlton Savage, 2 vols. (Washington, D.C.: Government Printing Office, 1934–1936), 1: 416–19, 432–35. Before answering Seward, the Foreign Office had sounded the Confederate government unofficially through the British consul at Charleston and had been informed that it would accept all articles of the Declaration of Paris except the first, which abolished privateering; Adams, *Britain and Civil War,* 1, chap. 5.

8. C. S. Alden and Allan Westcott, *The United States Navy: A History* (New York: J. B. Lippincott Co., 1943), p. 144.

9. Department of State, *Policy toward Maritime Commerce,* 1: 442. The leading modern critic of the blockade is Professor Owsley, who concludes, largely on the basis of estimates, that for the first two years of its duration the blockade of the South "made the old-fashioned English blockade look like a stone wall in comparison." Owsley, *King Cotton Diplomacy,* chap. 8.

war the principal Confederate ports were in Union hands. The British government, at any rate, accepted the blockade as effective and hence as binding under international law. Legality did not require, as Earl Russell wrote, that a blockade make access to a port impossible; it was sufficient if it created "an evident danger of entering or leaving it." There is good reason to suppose that the British government was not displeased at seeing the United States, hitherto the champion of neutral rights, now extending the rights of belligerents and setting precedents that might be useful to England in the future—as indeed they were.[10]

One of the precedents that were to prove of great value to Great Britain in years to come was the American application to blockade of that British invention, the doctrine of continuous voyage. This doctrine, it will be recalled, had first been announced by British courts in the case of the *Essex* (1805) in connection with the rule of 1756.[11] American courts adopted it in the enforcement of the Civil War blockade.

The actual running of the blockade was most successfully carried out by specially adapted steamers that brought cargoes from Bermuda, Nassau, or Havana into the ports of the Confederacy. Such steamers were hard to intercept, hard even to see. It was much easier to catch ships of more conventional type that brought the goods from Europe to the intermediate neutral ports. But could a voyage from Liverpool to Nassau be interfered with on the ground that the ultimate destination of the cargo was a blockaded port? The United States Supreme Court answered affirmatively. If the ship's papers or the character of the cargo showed conclusively that its real destination was a blockaded port, that the neutral destination was a subterfuge, then the voyage was *continuous* (even though in different ships) from origin to ultimate destination, and the cargo, whether contraband or not, was liable to confiscation for breach of blockade.

If the owners of the ship were aware of the ultimate destination of the cargo, the ship was also subject to confiscation.

Such was the opinion of the Supreme Court in the cases of the *Bermuda* and the *Springbok,* where the ultimate destination of the cargo was a blockaded port of the Confederacy. In the case of the *Peterhoff,* intercepted en route to Matamoros, Mexico, with a cargo destined for the Confederacy but not through a port actually blockaded, the court held that no breach of blockade was involved and that only the contraband goods in the cargo were seizable.[12]

It is significant that although continental jurists—French, German, and Dutch—vigorously attacked the doctrine of continuous voyage as applied by the Supreme Court in these cases, the British government said not a word in protest, although the property condemned was the property of British subjects. Apparently the British were content to see the United States adopt, adapt, and improve upon, a theory very useful to a belligerent controlling the sea lanes.

A Crisis with Great Britain: The Trent Affair

There were limits, however, to Britain's acquiescence in the stretching of law and precedent by the United States. An instance in which the British government firmly called a halt was the *Trent* affair in the first year of the war.

In November 1861, Captain Charles Wilkes, in the United States cruiser *San Jacinto,* took from the British mail steamer *Trent* the Confederate agents James M. Mason and John Slidell and their secretaries. Mason and Slidell, en route to represent the Confederacy in England and France respectively, had slipped through the blockade to Havana and there had taken passage on the

10. J. P. Baxter, III, "The British Government and Neutral Rights, 1861–1865," *American Historical Review,* 34 (1928), 9–29.
11. See p. 61.

12. *Bermuda,* 3 Wall. 514 (1865); *Springbok,* 5 Wall. 1 (1866); *Peterhoff,* 5 Wall. 28 (1866). J. W. Pratt, "The British Blockade and American Precedent," *U. S. Naval Institute Proceedings,* 46 (1920), 1789–1802.

Trent to St. Thomas, Danish West Indies, on their way to Europe. Wilkes, who had learned of their presence on the *Trent,* halted the ship and removed the four men over their protests and those of the British commander of the *Trent.* A week later (November 15) he landed them at Fortress Monroe, Virginia.

The news of Wilkes's bold action, which was taken wholly on his own responsibility, created great excitement in both the United States and England—in the former, exultation over the seizure of two important and dangerous Confederate personages with a slap at John Bull in the process; in the latter, resentment at an indignity to the British flag and insistence that the envoys be released and apologies made. In the United States, Wilkes was praised almost unanimously by the press and congratulated by the Secretary of the Navy. The House of Representatives passed a resolution thanking him for his "brave, adroit, and patriotic conduct." In England, Earl Russell penned instructions to Lord Lyons, British minister in Washington, directing him to demand the release of the envoys and an apology, and if these demands were not granted within seven days from their presentation, to close the legation and leave Washington. Few persons in England expected the United States to yield. Seward was suspected of a desire to provoke a war with Great Britain, and it was widely assumed that Wilkes had acted under his instructions. Since war seemed likely, British troops were ordered to Canada and the Navy was put in readiness for action.

Yet neither the British public nor the British government wished war. War with the United States would endanger Canada, bring disaster to the British merchant marine, and align Great Britain, leader in the crusade to end slavery, on the side of the slaveholding South. The instructions to Lyons had been softened, largely at the instance of Albert, the Prince Consort: the minister was not to "menace" the United States or to inform Seward of the seven-day time limit. Later he was told that an explanation would be accepted instead of an apology.

Seward was in a difficult dilemma. He knew that Wilkes's action had been irregular, that in defending him the United States would have a poor case, that European opinion solidly supported England, that to refuse the release of Mason and Slidell would mean war with England and the almost certain victory of the Confederacy. Seward, who had long since discarded his "foreign war panacea," wanted none of this. On the other hand, to surrender the Confederate agents would be flouting public opinion in the United States and might be politically disastrous to the administration.

Seward escaped from the trap with great skill. Having won Lincoln and the cabinet to his way of thinking in two long meetings, December 25 and 26, 1861, he promised the British minister that Mason and Slidell would be released, but gave the promise in a paper, at once made public, in which he made it appear that in releasing them he was vindicating a principle which the United States had long cherished and England had flouted. Reviewing Wilkes's conduct, he argued that the officer had been within his rights and had followed correct procedures in stopping and searching the *Trent* and that Mason and Slidell were properly liable to capture since— and here Seward advanced a novel doctrine— "persons, as well as property, may become contraband." [13] Wilkes's only error had been in removing the envoys on his own responsibility instead of bringing the *Trent* before a prize court where their status could be determined by proper judicial authority. But in committing this one error Wilkes had been guilty, said Seward, of the very practice of which the United States had complained so bitterly when it was followed by Great Britain

13. In instructions of the Secretary of the Treasury, May 23, 1862, only "military persons in the service of the enemy" were listed as contraband. This list was adopted by the Secretary of State in instructions to consular representatives, May 30, 1862. Mason and Slidell were of course not "military persons." A further difficulty about considering them as "contraband" was the fact that they were in transit between two neutral ports and that even their "ultimate destination" was not enemy territory.

—the arbitrary action of naval officers in assuming the right to remove persons from neutral ships. What was this but impressment? Seward continued:

> If I decide this case in favor of my own government, I must disavow its most cherished principles, and reverse and forever abandon its essential policy. The country cannot afford the sacrifice. If I maintain those principles, and adhere to that policy, I must surrender the case itself. . . . We are asked to do to the British nation just what we have always insisted all nations ought to do to us.

By the proposed adjustment of the present case, therefore, Seward declared, a question which had alienated the two countries for more than half a century would be "finally and rightly settled between them."

Seward could not resist the opportunity to take a dig at the two southern envoys, whose "comparative unimportance," he remarked, together with the "waning proportions of the existing insurrection," made it unnecessary for him to detain them on grounds of national security. Their self-esteem received a further blow when, upon reaching Europe, they not only met with a cool reception and no encouragement as to recognition, but were informed editorially by the London *Times* that "We should have done just as much to rescue two of their own Negroes."

Seward's surrender on these terms was well received in the United States and gladly accepted in England, though Earl Russell made it plain that he did not accept all of Seward's reasoning. Only southern agents and their sympathizers were disappointed. They found, in fact, that the crisis and its settlement had reacted against them and in favor of the North. Minister Adams reported to Seward that the *Trent* affair, "with just the issue that it had, was rather opportune than otherwise"; and Henry Hotze, the Confederate agent, complained that "the *Trent* affair has done us incalculable injury" and that Earl Russell was now "an avowed enemy of our nationality." [14]

14. Adams, *Britain and Civil War,* 1: 243.

The War and Neutral Obligations: The Confederate Cruisers

Except for the *Trent* affair and the close approach to British recognition of the Confederacy in the fall of 1862, the only misunderstanding with England that reached crisis level concerned the building of ships for the Confederate Navy in British shipyards and subsequent hospitality to such ships in British Empire ports. These activities were made possible, as Americans saw it, by the inadequacy of the British neutrality laws and their lax enforcement.

The British statute on neutral conduct, the foreign enlistment act of 1819, forbade the equipping, furnishing, fitting out, or arming within British jurisdiction of vessels for the purpose of attacking the commerce of friendly powers, or the augmentation of "the warlike force" of such vessels, but did not prohibit the building of such vessels. Taking advantage of this loophole in the law, Captain James D. Bulloch, the Confederate agent charged with such business, arranged with English shipbuilding firms for the construction of the ships, originally known as the *Oreto* and "No. 290," which became famous as the Confederate cruisers *Florida* and *Alabama*. In each case the ship was built but not "equipped, fitted out, or armed" in a British shipyard. Each put to sea without equipment and in a remote and unpoliced sanctuary—the *Florida* in the Bahamas, the *Alabama* in the Azores—met another steamer bringing her armament, officers, and crew. Each was then duly commissioned as a ship of the Confederate Navy and began her career as a commerce destroyer. The *Florida* made over forty prizes before she was herself captured by the U.S.S. *Wachusett* —by a violation of neutrality—in the port of Bahia, Brazil. The *Alabama* destroyed fifty-seven prizes and released many more on bond before she was sunk in a duel with the U.S.S. *Kearsarge* off the port of Cherbourg, France. Next after these two in destructiveness and notoriety was the *Shenandoah*, purchased for the Confederacy from her English owners and armed and manned at sea. Beginning her career late and cruising in the Pacific, she destroyed a large part of the New England whaling fleet at a time when, unknown to her officers or their victims, the Confederacy had ceased to exist.

In the cases of *Florida* and *Alabama,* Charles Francis Adams, the United States minister, had laid before the British government evidence that the ships were being prepared for the service of the Confederacy. The evidence against the *Alabama* was so strong that at the last moment Earl Russell ordered her held. The order came too late. The *Alabama* had steamed out of the Mersey River on a "trial trip" from which she never returned. The United States held Great Britain guilty of breaches of neutrality in permitting her escape and in the construction of the *Florida.*

The United States held also that Great Britain had violated the principles of neutrality in permitting Confederate cruisers to augment their strength in ports of the British Empire. The *Shenandoah,* for example, had put in at Melbourne, Australia, where, in spite of protests from the United States consul, she was allowed to make repairs, take on a supply of coal, and recruit additions to her crew. In addition to the actual destruction wrought by the *Alabama, Florida, Shenandoah,* and less celebrated raiders, their depredations had caused a skyrocketing of insurance rates, kept ships idle in port, and driven many northern shipowners to sell their vessels or transfer them to foreign registry. For all these losses, British negligence or partiality was held responsible.

The *Alabama* began her career in August 1862. Even before her escape, Captain Bulloch signed a contract with her builders, Laird Brothers, of Birkenhead, for the construction of two armored steamers, each to be equipped with four rifled guns mounted in turrets, and armed with a ram at the bow—ships more powerful than any in the United States Navy. It was reported that the "Laird rams," as the vessels were called, were being built for France or for the viceroy of Egypt,

but their real destination was common knowledge and their possession by the Confederacy would imperil the blockade and might well decide the outcome of the war. Adams bombarded Earl Russell with evidence of the true character and destination of the rams, most of it gathered by Thomas H. Dudley, the efficient United States consul at Liverpool. Adams' protests reached a climax with the warning, September 5, 1863, that should the rams be allowed to depart, "It would be superfluous in me to point out to your lordship that this is war."

Before receiving Adams' threat, Russell had ordered the rams detained; eventually they were purchased by the British government. There was, in reality, no danger that the rams would be allowed to escape. Russell was merely awaiting the most opportune time to halt them. Months earlier the British government had decided that it would not risk serious trouble with the United States by permitting repetitions of the *Alabama* episode. In April it had proceeded against the *Alexandra,* whose case resembled the *Alabama's,* and in September it detained the Laird rams. There were no more such incidents.

The suppression of Confederate transactions in English shipyards, together with England's continued refusal to recognize the Confederacy, made it clear to the Confederate government and its agents in Europe that British policy was actually beneficial to the North rather than the South. Mason withdrew from England under instructions in 1863, and in the same year British consuls in the South were expelled by the government at Richmond. Nonexistent diplomatic relations could not be broken, but these Confederate gestures were an equivalent manifestation of displeasure.

The Alabama Claims and the Geneva Arbitration

The British government's action against the *Alexandra* and the rams, although gratifying, did not atone for its earlier laxness, which had permitted the escape of the *Alabama* and *Florida* and had facilitated the destructive careers of those cruisers and the *Shenandoah*. The war's end, therefore, left the United States with a sense of grievance and a determination to insist upon compensation for damages resulting from Great Britain's too casual observance of neutral obligations.

An American proposal that the question of Great Britain's responsibility for the depredations of the Confederate cruisers be submitted to arbitration was at first rejected by the British government. By 1869, however, that government had concluded that the precedents set by the *Alabama* and her sisters might be injurious to British interests. In the event of an Anglo-Russian war, which seemed not unlikely, American shipyards might build cruisers for the Czar's navy, with disastrous consequences to the British merchant marine.[15]

Fear of such developments was at least one of the influences that led a new British ministry to agree, in 1869, to the Johnson-Clarendon convention, which provided for submission to arbitration of all claims on either side that had arisen since 1853, the year of the last general settlement. The *"Alabama* claims," as they were now called, were mentioned, but without special emphasis. There was no expression of regret or apology for British delinquencies, and the neutral member of the proposed court of arbitration was under certain circumstances to be chosen by lot, leaving much to chance.

All of these defects in the treaty, from the American point of view, help to explain its rejection by an unfriendly Senate with but a single vote in its favor, but Charles Sumner, chairman of the Foreign Relations Committee, in a celebrated speech, put forward additional reasons. The proposed arbitration, he complained, took account of but a small fraction of England's debt to the United States. England should pay, he argued, not only the

value of the ships and cargoes destroyed by the English-built cruisers, estimated at $15,000,000; she should pay also for the losses resulting from increased insurance rates and commerce driven from the sea or to the coverage of neutral flags. These items he put at $110,000,000. But that was not all. Only British encouragement, Sumner argued, had kept the Confederacy fighting after the battle of Gettysburg in July 1863. Britain ought, therefore, to pay half the cost of the war to the North, or two billion dollars. The total bill of $2,125,000,000, Sumner let it be known, could be paid only by ceding Canada and Britain's other American possessions to the United States.

Sumner's speech and the Senate's apparent endorsement of it in the 54 to 1 vote against the Johnson-Clarendon convention, placed an obstacle in the path of any settlement of the *Alabama* claims. No British government could agree to the "indirect claims," as Sumner's second and third categories were called. British spokesmen in Washington also pointed out that Canada could not be ceded contrary to its own wishes, and few Canadians wished for annexation by the United States.

Hamilton Fish, Secretary of State under President Grant, was anxious for a friendly settlement with Great Britain. He did not take Sumner's indirect claims seriously, but did believe that they should be put forward, if only to be set aside by an authoritative arbitral body. With the concurrence of Grant (who had at first been disposed to back Sumner's position), he brought this matter and others before a joint high commission (five Americans, four British, and one Canadian), which met at Washington in the spring of 1871. The resulting Treaty of Washington, signed May 8, 1871, provided, among other things, for the arbitration of the *Alabama* claims.[16]

The treaty featured an unqualified expression of

---

15. This danger was emphasized when the House of Representatives in July 1866 voted to repeal those clauses of the neutrality laws which forbade the sale of ships to belligerents.

16. In addition to providing for arbitration of the *Alabama* claims, the Treaty of Washington provided the following modes of settlement for other controversies: A mixed commission on British claims for

the regret felt by Her Majesty's Government for the escape, under whatever circumstances, of the Alabama and other vessels from British ports, and for the depredations committed by those vessels.

Although not exactly an apology or an admission of wrongdoing, this statement went far enough to satisfy most Americans. The treaty then provided for a tribunal of arbitration of five persons, one each to be named by the President of the United States, the Queen of Great Britain, the President of the Swiss Confederation, the King of Italy, and the Emperor of Brazil. To this body were to be submitted all claims growing out of the acts committed by the *Alabama* and other vessels, "generically known as the 'Alabama Claims.'" In reaching decisions the arbitrators were to be governed by three rules, in addition to such principles of international law as they might consider applicable. The three rules were crucial.

Of special importance was the first. It filled the principal gap in the foreign enlistment act by making it the duty of a neutral government to use due diligence to prevent the departure from its jurisdiction of any vessel intended to carry on war against a friendly power, "such vessels having been specially adapted, in whole or in part, within such jurisdiction, to warlike use." Since there could be little doubt that the *Alabama* and *Florida* had been so adapted within British jurisdiction, acceptance of these rules by the British government came close to being a surrender of its case.

property seized during the Civil War awarded $1,929,819 to British subjects. A mixed commission on the value of inshore fisheries (reciprocally agreed to for 12 years by the treaty) awarded to Great Britain (over U. S. protest) $5,500,000 for the estimated difference between the value of the privilege to Americans and that to British subjects. A dispute over the ownership of the San Juan Islands, lying in the straits between Vancouver Island and Washington Territory, was submitted for arbitration to the German Emperor, who in 1872 decided in favor of the American claim.

But when all seemed set for a happy ending to the controversy, a new crisis arose. When the court of arbitration convened in Geneva in December 1871, the case presented by the United States included the indirect claims, much as they had been drawn up by Charles Sumner. This course was adopted not with any expectation that the judges would accept them, but to satisfy the Senate and public opinion in the United States and, as Secretary Fish viewed the matter, to have the claims judicially disposed of, once and for all. The British, however, were under the impression that the United States had tacitly abandoned the indirect claims. They charged bad faith and refused to consent to any consideration of these claims by the court. It appeared that the court might have to adjourn with nothing accomplished, but a way was finally found around the obstacle. The court, in the absence of the British member, delivered an extrajudicial statement to the effect that the indirect claims were inadmissible. The opinion was promptly accepted by both British and American governments, and the tribunal proceeded to a consideration of the direct claims.

The decision of the tribunal was made public on September 14, 1872. On British responsibility for the depredations of the *Alabama* the judges were unanimous. That the British government was also responsible for the careers of the *Florida* and the *Shenandoah* the court held by votes of four to one and three to two respectively, the British member in each case voting in the negative. Claims based upon the careers of other cruisers were unanimously rejected. For the destruction wrought by the *Alabama, Florida,* and *Shenandoah* the court awarded damages of $15,500,000 to the United States. Sir Alexander Cockburn, the British member of the tribunal, declined to sign the award and in other ways showed himself a poor loser, but the British government promptly paid the bill. A troublesome controversy was settled, Anglo-American relations were restored to a cordial footing, and the obligations of neutrals were established with new precision.

18

Advance Agents of Empire

The secession of the southern states and the ensuing Civil War had put an end, for the time being, to plans for national expansion. The years immediately following the war, however, were almost as prolific in expansionist projects as the 1850's had been, though with different sponsorship and different motives. The Democratic party, formerly the party of Manifest Destiny, went into a long political eclipse. A few prominent individuals in the dominant Republican party—notably Secretary of State William H. Seward—became devotees of that doctrine but did not succeed in converting many of their colleagues. Several of the motives for expansion operative in the 1850's had disappeared in whole or in part. Slavery in the United States was ended. The need for an isthmian route to the Pacific became less urgent with the construction of the first transcontinental railroad —the Union Pacific-Central Pacific line— authorized in 1862 and completed in 1869. The menace of European intervention in the Caribbean region was removed; for Spain, which had reannexed her former colony of Santo Domingo in 1861, withdrew four years later, and France in 1867 abandoned her support of Maximilian's empire in Mexico.[1]

On the other hand, the experiences of the United States Navy during the Civil War had called attention to the need for insular naval bases in both the Caribbean and the Pacific. Seward, Secretary of State (1861–1869), sought to meet this need, as did President Grant after 1869. Seward in 1867 negotiated a treaty with Denmark for the purchase of the islands of St. Thomas and St. John in the Virgin Islands group, attractive to Seward and the Navy because of the fine harbor of Charlotte Amalie in St. Thomas. The price, $7,500,000, seemed excessive to many members of the American Congress; the more so since just at that time the islands were devastated by a series of natural disasters—an earthquake, a tidal wave, and a tropical hurricane. The House of Representatives warned that it would not feel bound to appropriate the money, and in the Senate, the treaty was never brought to a vote.

Seward then turned to dicker with the cur-

1. See Chapter 19.

rent dictator of the Dominican Republic, or Santo Domingo, for purchase or lease of Samaná Bay, a capacious harbor at the northeastern corner of the island. Buenaventura Báez, the dictator-president, was ready for a deal, as was President Andrew Johnson, but Congress showed itself averse to this proposal also, and soon thereafter Seward went out of office with the Johnson administration.

President Ulysses S. Grant (1869–1877) took up the Santo Domingo project where Seward had left it. Influenced by a pair of American speculators with axes to grind, and against the advice of his able Secretary of State, Hamilton Fish, he sponsored the negotiation of a treaty for the annexation of Santo Domingo by the United States, and tried to force it through the Senate. The Senate was inhospitable. It resented Grant's highhanded methods and an odor of corruption that sullied the entire transaction, and certain senators warned against the dangers inherent in an effort to extend American institutions into a climate, physical and human, where they could not flourish. Such a procedure, said one senator, would be to "embark the Government of the United States upon the vast and trackless sea of imperialism." The Senate rejected Grant's treaty by a vote of 28 to 28.

The Purchase of Alaska

But though Seward and Grant both met failure in their quest for Caribbean bases, Seward was more successful in another of his ambitions—his desire to make the United States a great Pacific power. By a treaty signed March 30, 1867, he acquired Russian America, thenceforth to be known as Alaska, an Indian name meaning "great land." Alaska had become a white elephant to the Czar's government, which for some years had been willing to dispose of it at a suitable price. This was intimated to Seward by the Russian minister, Baron Stoeckl, when he returned from a visit to St. Petersburg in the spring of 1867. Seward made an offer, and the two diplomats quickly agreed on a price of $7,200,000.

The treaty was promptly approved by the Senate, where it had the vigorous support of Charles Sumner, chairman of the Committee on Foreign Relations. Sumner made much of the importance of cultivating and perpetuating friendship with Russia, the only major power that had shown sympathy for the North in the recent war.[2] He also argued that the acquisition of Alaska was one more step in ousting the European monarchies from America. He and other legislators intimated that it was Britain's turn to go next—an idea that fitted in with several contemporary popular schemes for the annexation of Canada.[3] One member of the House of Representatives predicted that the British Empire would be shorn of its American possessions by the United States and its Asiatic possessions by Russia and that the day would come when "the two great Powers on earth will be Russia and the United States."[4]

2. The theory, long current, that the United States bought Alaska at an extravagant price as a means of compensating Russia for the friendly visits of her fleets was given reinforcement by an apocryphal story related in *The Letters of Franklin K. Lane* (Boston: Houghton Mifflin Company, 1922), pp. 260–61, and has been perpetuated in some American history textbooks despite its effective refutation by F. A. Golder in "The Russian Fleet and the Civil War," *American Historical Review,* 20 (1915), 801–12. Contemporary American opinion of the fleet visits is examined in W. E. Nagengast, "The Visit of the Russian Fleet to the United States: Were Americans Deceived?" *Russian Review,* 8 (1949), 46–55; E. S. Pomeroy, "The Myth after the Russian Fleet, 1863," *New York History,* 31 (1950), 169–76; T. A. Bailey, "The Russian Fleet Myth Re-Examined," *Mississippi Valley Historical Review,* 38 (1951), 81–90.

3. The net result of post-Civil War agitation for the annexation of Canada was to strengthen the Canadian sentiment of nationality and to expedite the movement for Canadian federation. This was achieved by the British North America Act of 1867, which created the Dominion of Canada.

4. Not for a year and a half after ratification of the treaty did Congress appropriate the money to carry out its terms. The delay occurred in the House of Representatives, where there was objection to being faced with a *fait accompli* by President and Senate and being expected to foot the bill. The delay was prolonged by efforts to divert part of the purchase price to pay certain questionable private American claims against the Russian government. Baron Stoeckl found it necessary to pay sizable sums of money to influential public men and newspapers in order to get the appropriation through Congress. W. A. Dunning,

By the purchase of Alaska the United States made its final acquisition of continental territory. It was a significant addition. Alaska contained mineral, forest, and animal resources that were to prove a mine of wealth. Although it was not, as many of its advocates predicted, a prelude to the absorption of Canada, it brought the United States, at Bering Strait, into sight of Asiatic shores, and in the Aleutian Islands to the south, carried the American flag into the western Pacific, in the longitude of the Marshall Islands and New Zealand. In that respect the purchase of Alaska was prophetic, as presumably Seward intended, of the destiny of the United States as a Pacific power.

In another respect the Alaska purchase was a turning point in the history of American expansion. In all earlier acquisitions of territory by treaty—Louisiana, Florida, the Mexican cession, the Gadsden purchase—the treaties of cession had stipulated not only that the inhabitants of the ceded territory should enjoy the rights and privileges of United States citizenship but also that they should be, in the language of the Louisiana treaty, "incorporated in the Union of the United States." The Alaska treaty provided that such civilized inhabitants as chose to remain in the territory should "be admitted to the enjoyment of all the rights, advantages and immunities of citizens of the United States"; but it made no promise of incorporation. Thus Alaska became the first bit of American soil not legally destined for statehood. Promising citizenship but not incorporation, the Alaska treaty was a transitional episode between the earlier treaties, which promised both, and the treaty of 1898 with Spain, which promised neither. It was the first step on the road to "imperialism." [5]

"Paying for Alaska," *Political Science Quarterly,* 27 (1912), 385–98; F. A. Golder, "The Purchase of Alaska," *American Historical Review,* 25 (1920), 411–25.

5. Although the Alaska treaty said nothing of incorporation, the Supreme Court later held that the treaty together with subsequent legislation extending the customs and other laws to Alaska had the effect of

Midway Island—and the End of an Era

Alaska and Midway Island were the only new possessions actually acquired in the immediate postwar period. Midway Island, about a thousand miles northwest of the Hawaiian group, was occupied by the Navy in the summer of 1867, at the suggestion of the China Mail Steamship Company. Under orders from the Navy Department, Captain William Reynolds, of the U.S.S. *Lackawanna,* took possession of the island in the name of the United States on August 28, 1867. Formerly known as Brooks Island from the name of its discoverer, it was rechristened in recognition of its situation approximately halfway from San Francisco to Yokohama. An attempt to dredge the entrance to the harbor was abandoned as too costly. In 1903 Midway became a station on the first transpacific cable. Otherwise it had no importance till the advent of transpacific air transportation some thirty years later.

The failure of Grant's attempt to annex Santo Domingo marked the end of the postwar revival of Manifest Destiny. The American public and the American Congress were, for the time being, simply not interested in schemes for the acquisition of insular possessions. But commercial expansion was another matter. The years after 1850 were the years of the industrial revolution in the United States. With the Civil War ended, American factories (like American farms) were soon turning out more products than the home market could absorb. The need for expanding foreign markets, therefore, impressed every administration from Grant's to McKinley's and became a constant, though generally undramatic, factor in the foreign policy of those decades. It played a part in President Cleveland's somewhat strained application of the Monroe Doctrine against Great Britain

---

making Alaska an incorporated territory. *Rassmussen v. U. S.,* 197 U. S. 516 (1905). Alaska became a state in 1959.

in Venezuela. Quite distinct in itself from the desire for further territorial acquisitions, it nevertheless on occasion provided a motive for such acquisitions, as at the time of the Spanish American War in 1898.[6] In the meantime, during Grant's years and later, it helped to account for a continuing American interest in the isthmian region, Hawaii, and the remote Samoan Islands.

The Isthmian Canal Question

The building of the transcontinental railroads diminished but did not eliminate the importance of the isthmian transit routes. Seward negotiated with Nicaragua a treaty which, like that of 1846 with New Granada (Colombia after 1863), insured to citizens of the United States equal rights with citizens of the sovereign state in the use of such transit facilities as might be constructed. President Grant was the first American statesman to proclaim publicly, in disregard of the Clayton-Bulwer Treaty with Great Britain, that any canal should be under the exclusive control of the United States. Grant in 1869 appointed an Interoceanic Canal Commission, which directed surveys of several proposed canal routes and in 1876 reported unanimously in favor of the route through Nicaragua.

While the United States deliberated, however, Europeans began to make the dirt fly. In 1881 a French corporation headed by Ferdinand de Lesseps, builder of the Suez Canal, operating under a concession from the government of Colombia, began the digging of a canal through the Isthmus of Panama. The prospect of a canal at Panama under European auspices was not relished in the United States. It was denounced as being in violation of the Monroe Doctrine. It brought

from President Rutherford B. Hayes (1877–1881) a declaration that "The policy of this country is a canal under American control." An isthmian canal, he continued, would be "virtually a part of the coast line of the United States," and it was "the right and duty of the United States to assert and maintain such supervision and authority over any interoceanic canal . . . as will protect our national interests." Hayes had voiced what was to become accepted American opinion—that sound national policy called for a canal controlled exclusively by the United States.

No attempt was made, however, to interfere with the operations of the French company. Instead, Congress chartered an American corporation, the Maritime Canal Company of Nicaragua, to exploit the rival Nicaraguan route, while Secretaries of State Blaine and Frelinghuysen strove in vain to induce Great Britain to abrogate or amend the Clayton-Bulwer Treaty and thus open the way for a canal nationally owned or controlled. Secretary Frederick T. Frelinghuysen, contending that the Clayton-Bulwer Treaty was no longer binding, negotiated in 1884 a treaty with Nicaragua, which gave the United States exclusive rights to the Nicaraguan route in return for a permanent alliance and a guarantee of Nicaragua's territorial integrity. This treaty was pending in the Senate when a change of administration in 1885 brought Grover Cleveland to the White House for his first term (1885–1889) and Thomas F. Bayard to the State Department. Upon Bayard's advice, Cleveland withdrew the treaty from the Senate. Its approval would certainly have brought on a controversy with Great Britain.

By the early 1890's the French company had gone bankrupt with only a minor portion of its work completed, and the Maritime Canal Company had failed to raise funds for its enterprise. It was evident that the United States government alone possessed the resources and the ability to do the work. The barrier to such a course was the Clayton-Bulwer Treaty, to which Great Britain as yet firmly adhered.

6. See Chapters 19, 22, for the Venezuela episode and the War with Spain. The urge for commercial expansion and its effect upon foreign policy in this period are stressed in Walter LaFeber, *The New Empire: An Interpretation of American Expansion, 1860–1898* (Ithaca, N.Y.: Cornell University Press, 1964).

International Rivalry in Samoa

President Grant's susceptibility to the pressures of businessmen and speculators, noted in connection with Santo Domingo, was also responsible for his interest in the Samoan Islands. In this case it was the head of a steamship company running steamers between San Francisco and Australia and New Zealand who drew the President's attention to the fine qualities of Pago Pago harbor in the Samoan isle of Tutuila. An American naval officer negotiated with the native chief of Tutuila a treaty giving the United States exclusive rights in Pago Pago harbor in return for assumption by the United States of a protectorate over the native government. Submitted to the Senate with Grant's qualified endorsement, the Samoan treaty was never brought to a vote.

In 1878 a native Samoan delegation visited Washington, seeking annexation or a protectorate. They were informed that this was impossible, but were given instead a treaty by which the United States agreed merely to use its "good offices" for the adjustment of differences that might arise between Samoa and any other government "in amity with the United States." In return the United States received the right to establish a coaling station in Pago Pago harbor. In the meantime, the Samoan economy had fallen under German domination, while the proximity of Samoa to Australia and New Zealand had led the British government to take a lively interest in the fate of the islands. The resulting three-power rivalry reached an intensity quite out of proportion to the weight of the issues involved. In the United States there was even reckless talk of war with Germany.[7] A three-power conference in Washington in 1887 failed to settle the controversy, but a second

7. On one occasion, in March 1889, American and German naval vessels were apparently on the verge of exchanging shots when a timely hurricane wrecked both squadrons on the reefs and beaches of Apia harbor.

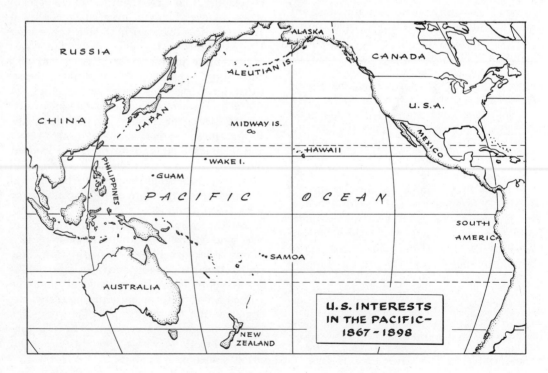

conference in Berlin two years later agreed on a compromise. The Treaty of Berlin, signed June 14, 1889, paid lip service to Samoan "independence" but in reality set up a three-power protectorate or condominium. Though the Samoan natives were given the right to choose their "king," real power thereafter resided in officials chosen by the three governments. The arrangement, though a clumsy one, was a victory for American policy. It prevented German political domination and preserved American rights in Pago Pago. Though it did not work without friction and left a residue of ill will against Germany, it did prevent serious international controversy during the ten years of its operation.

Toward Hawaiian Annexation

Unlike Samoa, Hawaii was a natural outpost of North America, and the interest of the United States in its destiny was almost as old as American independence.[8] The attempt to annex Hawaii made by the Pierce administration in 1854 was not renewed in the immediate postwar years. Seward, however, in negotiation over a proposed treaty of commercial reciprocity in 1867, informed the American minister in Honolulu that

> a lawful and peaceful annexation of the islands to the United States, with the consent of the people . . . is deemed desirable by this Government; and that if the policy of annexation should really conflict with the policy of reciprocity, annexation is in every case to be preferred.

Apparently some senators agreed with Seward in their preference for annexation rather than reciprocity, for some of the Senate votes that defeated the reciprocity treaty in 1867 were attributed to a fear that such an agreement might stand in the way of annexation.

In 1875, however, another attempt at reciprocity succeeded. A warning that Hawaiian sugar planters, if they failed to obtain a free market in the United States, might divert

both their trade and their political attachments to the British Empire, proved efficacious in securing American consent to the treaty. Its value to the United States was political and strategic, not economic. Exports from the United States to Hawaii expanded substantially under the stimulus of the free market, but the total value of such exports during the period of reciprocity was only some $82,000,000, while the loss of revenue to the United States treasury from the free admission of sugar and other Hawaiian products amounted to $91,000,000.[9] Obviously, the arrangement was not good business, considered in terms of dollars and cents. Its advantage to the United States lay in the fact that by holding Hawaii in the American economic sphere, it also held the little kingdom in the American political sphere. The treaty pledged the Hawaiian government not to alienate any port or territory in the islands to any other power, and not to grant to any other power the commercial privileges that the treaty conferred upon the United States.

The reciprocity treaty of 1875 was terminable by either party after seven years. A renewal treaty was negotiated in 1884, but the United States Senate, before approving it in 1887, attached an amendment by which the United States was to enjoy the exclusive right to the use of Pearl River Harbor in the island of Oahu as a coaling and repair station for its naval vessels. The reciprocity arrangement was thus extended to 1894 at least, and the United States was free during the same period to develop and use Pearl Harbor—a privilege of which it made no use.

The free American market provided by the reciprocity treaty gave a great stimulus to Hawaiian sugar production, which multiplied tenfold in the next twenty years. It also made Hawaiian prosperity so dependent upon the American market that a change in American tariff policy in 1890, admitting other foreign sugar on equal terms with Hawaiian and giving a bounty to American domestic producers,

8. See pp. 146–47.

9. U. S. Tariff Commission, *Reciprocity and Commercial Treaties* (Washington, D.C.: Government Printing Office, 1919), p. 136.

brought about an economic crisis, and contributed to a political crisis, in the Hawaiian kingdom.

The imperfect integration of two cultures in Hawaii had resulted in the existence side by side of a modern system of economy and a monarchical government that retained not a few primitive features. The dissolute and corrupt behavior of the last-but-one of the native monarchs, King Kalakaua, 1874–1891, invited revolution. In a bloodless coup in 1887, leaders of the white business community forced on Kalakaua a new constitution that effectually clipped his wings, making his ministers (without whose consent he could perform no official act) responsible to the legislature and so restricting the suffrage as to make the legislature appear securely under the control of the propertied classes.

Kalakaua was succeeded in 1891 by his sister, Liliuokalani. Educated in the local mission schools, active in local philanthropies, a composer of musical lyrics of some merit, "Queen Lil" was not endowed with political sagacity. She made no secret of her ambition to recover for herself and her native subjects the prerogatives and rights that her brother had signed away. In laying such plans, she underestimated the ability and determination of the white elite who had compelled Kalakaua to accept the reforms of 1887. Filled with apprehension at the course the Queen might follow, and suffering from the economic depression induced by the change in American tariff policy, many white businessmen and lawyers in the islands came to look upon annexation by the United States as a guarantee of both stable government and economic prosperity. They therefore planned to persuade or compel Liliuokalani to abdicate and then to offer the islands to the United States. One of their leaders, Lorrin A. Thurston, visited Washington in the spring of 1892 and received secret encouragement from members of the cabinet of President Benjamin Harrison (1889–1893) and from leaders in Congress.

Not until January 1893 did the revolutionists find a suitable occasion to carry out their plan. Their cue came in an announcement from the Queen that she proposed to proclaim a new constitution, an act that itself would have been unconstitutional and revolutionary. The annexationists immediately formed a committee of safety, set up a provisional government, and demanded the Queen's abdication. Their course had the sympathetic support of United States Minister John L. Stevens, who landed troops from the cruiser *Boston* and so disposed them as to give the impression that they would, if necessary, defend the provisional government, to which Stevens also granted precipitate *de facto* recognition. In this situation there was no course for the Queen but to yield her authority, as she said, "to the superior force of the United States of America," until such time as the United States government should "undo the action of its representative" and reinstate her "as the constitutional sovereign of the Hawaiian Islands."

The provisional government at once dispatched a commission to Washington to negotiate a treaty of annexation. In the negotiation they met with no serious difficulty, and on February 15, President Harrison sent to the Senate a treaty providing for the annexation of the Hawaiian Islands as "an integral part of the territory of the United States" and for the payment to the deposed Queen of a life annuity of $20,000. The treaty might well have received Senate approval had not the President-elect, Grover Cleveland, about to take office for his second term (1893–1897), let it be known that he preferred to have it left for him to deal with after the fourth of March. One of Cleveland's first acts as President was to withdraw the Hawaiian treaty from the Senate "for the purpose of reexamination." A few days later he appointed a former Democratic congressman, James H. Blount of Georgia, a special commissioner to the Hawaiian Islands to investigate the character of the annexation movement and especially to report to the President whether Minister Stevens had played an improper part in the revolution and whether annexation was desired by any large proportion of the natives or only by the ruling clique of whites.

Blount's investigation convinced both him and President Cleveland, first, that the revolution would not have been attempted and could not have been carried out without the encouragement and support of Minister Stevens; second, that the great majority of the native people were supporters of the Queen and opposed to annexation. Cleveland, therefore, not only declined to return the annexation treaty to the Senate, but concluded, somewhat quixotically, that he was under a moral obligation to undo "the great wrong done to a feeble but independent State" by restoring the Queen to her throne. But when Cleveland's minister, Albert S. Willis, sent to Honolulu for this purpose, had secured from Liliuokalani a reluctant promise of amnesty for the revolutionists, he received from the provisional government an unqualified refusal of his demand that they step down and make way for restoration of the ex-Queen. Only the superior armed force of the United States, said Hawaiian President Sanford B. Dole, could compel the provisional government (which the United States had formally recognized) to give up its authority.

Unprepared to make war on the provisional government, to right one wrong by committing another, Cleveland referred the whole matter to Congress, which resolved that nothing be done. In Hawaii a constitutional convention, held in 1894, provided the body politic with a regular republican constitution that perpetuated the power of the white minority who had overthrown the Queen. The new instrument worked smoothly; a small royalist uprising in 1895 was easily suppressed; a new United States tariff in 1894 restored Hawaiian sugar to its favored position in the American market. The Hawaiian republic enjoyed several years of peace and prosperity, but its leaders never lost sight of their chief desire, annexation by the United States. They could only wait patiently until a turn in the political wheel should bring into power in Washington an administration willing to reverse the policy of Grover Cleveland.[10]

10. See Chapters 21, 22, for the final phase in the acquisition of Hawaii.

19

The Monroe Doctrine and Pan Americanism

In the years in which the United States was uncertainly feeling its way toward a policy of overseas expansion, it was asserting the Monroe Doctrine with new emphasis and new assurance and winning for Monroe's pronouncement the explicit or the tacit assent of Europe's principal Atlantic powers. And while thus taking a more active role than formerly as a guardian of the Western Hemisphere, it was, by launching the Pan American movement, beginning to assume in that hemisphere the place of leadership that Henry Clay had urged in the early years of the century.[1]

Spain Defies the Monroe Doctrine

William H. Seward, Secretary of State (1861–1869) under Presidents Abraham Lincoln and Andrew Johnson, was eventually to win a signal victory for the Monroe Doctrine, but his first attempt to apply it earned him only a rebuff. Almost at once upon assuming office, Seward learned that Spain was about to reannex her former colony of Santo Domingo (now the Dominican Republic). The news led Seward to suggest to Lincoln that a war with Spain, and also with France, which was rumored to be involved in the transaction, might regain the loyalty of patriotic Southerners.[2] Lincoln put aside the Secretary's rash proposal, but did not prevent him from sending several strongly worded notes of protest to the Spanish government. In one of these Seward characterized Spain's action as "manifesting an unfriendly disposition toward the United States," and threatened forcible resistance. In another he expressly cited Monroe's message of 1823 as the basis for the American objection to Spain's reannexation of her former colony.

The Spanish Foreign Minister rejected Seward's protests. He acknowledged no legal force in the Monroe Doctrine and pointed out that Spain had agreed to reannex Santo Domingo at the behest of the representatives of the people of the island. By this time the United States was deeply involved in the Civil War. Unable to back his protests with

1. See above, p. 80.
2. See Chapter 17, n. 1.

force, Seward wisely dropped the subject. Spain withdrew from Santo Domingo in 1865, not as a result of protests from the United States but because of armed resistance to her rule by the island population.[3]

Napoleon III and Mexico

A far more serious challenge to the Monroe Doctrine than the short-lived Spanish regime in the Dominican Republic was the contemporary French intervention in Mexico and the establishment there of an empire under a European prince. The mastermind in this scheme to reestablish monarchy in the New World was the French Emperor Napoleon III, but he acted upon what he believed to be ample invitation from Mexico itself.

The monarchical ideal had never wholly disappeared in Mexico; in fact, there had always been a party there that saw in the establishment of a monarchy under a scion of some European royal house a solution for Mexico's internal disorders and a protection against further encroachments by the United States. Alarmed by the loss of Texas, California, New Mexico, and the Gadsden strip, and by the further acquisitive tendencies shown by the American government in the 1850's, monarchist elements in Mexico had repeatedly indicated their willingness to accept a European nominee for the Mexican throne. Many Europeans, too, wished to see a barrier erected which would halt the advance of the United States and preserve a balance of power in America. Europeans in Mexico, furthermore, had lost lives and property in the chronic state of disorder and civil war that beset the country. When, on top of all this, the government of President Juarez in 1861 was forced to suspend payments on its foreign obliga-

tions, even Great Britain was ready for a limited intervention in Mexican affairs.

Meeting in London in October 1861, representatives of France, Spain, and Great Britain signed a convention by which the three governments agreed to send a joint military expedition to Mexico. They declared its purpose to be the "more efficacious protection of persons and property of their subjects." They disclaimed any designs upon the territory or the independence of Mexico and any intention of interfering with the right of the Mexicans to decide for themselves upon the form of their government. At the insistence of Great Britain they invited the United States to participate.

This invitation to the United States Seward declined in a tactful note of December 4, 1861, on the grounds, first, of the American preference for abstaining from alliances with foreign nations, and second, of the friendship felt by the United States for Mexico as a neighboring republic. The President, said Seward, did not question the right of the three powers to make war upon Mexico for the redress of grievances, and he accepted their assurances that they aimed at no acquisition of territory and at no impairment of the Mexican people's right of self-government. Meanwhile, Seward was attempting to arrange a loan (with ample security) to the Mexican government, which might enable it to forestall intervention by meeting its foreign obligations, but this proposal found favor neither with the European governments nor with the United States Senate.

The allied forces landed in Mexico in December 1861 and January 1862. The British and Spanish soon withdrew, finding that France had plans which they were unwilling to support. The French Emperor, in fact, had in mind nothing less than the creation in Mexico of a monarchy, closely associated with France, which should keep alive the monarchical idea in the New World and serve as a barrier to the further southward expansion of the United States. Thus he would ensure that "balance of power" in America of which Guizot had spoken sixteen years earlier. France, he thought, would benefit commer-

---

3. In contrast with her attitude in the Santo Domingo affair, Spain in 1864 assured the United States of her intention to return to Peru certain Pacific islands seized in a current controversy. The Monroe Doctrine "would not be called in question," said the Spanish Foreign Office. Perkins, *History of the Monroe Doctrine,* pp. 138–47, covers these episodes.

cially, and he himself might recover the good will of French Catholics, which he had lost by espousing the cause of Italian unification at the expense of the temporal power of the Pope.

Napoleon's candidate for the Mexican throne was the Archduke Maximilian, brother of Emperor Francis Joseph of Austria, a young man of fine character and wholesome ambitions. To him the throne was offered by a handpicked Assembly of Notables, convoked by the French commander after French troops had occupied Mexico City. To satisfy Maximilian's democratic scruples, a "plebiscite" was held, though only the small fraction of Mexico under French control participated, and upon being informed of the favorable result of this dubious popular vote, Maximilian accepted. The new Emperor arrived in his capital in June 1864, only to find that his throne was supported by French bayonets. President Juarez, though driven from the capital, kept up a guerrilla war against the French occupation, and the authority of Maximilian was never secure far beyond the environs of Mexico City. The promised popular support was nonexistent.

Had an empire been erected in Mexico by purely Mexican forces, there is no reason to suppose that the United States would have interfered with it. The American government had made no objection to the long continuance of an imperial regime in Brazil (1822 to 1889). It was not monarchy in America in itself to which Monroe had objected, but monarchy imposed upon an American state by European powers. This, Napoleon III's adventure in Mexico certainly was, for though Napoleon may have been led to believe that monarchy would be popular in Mexico, a few months of experiment showed that the Mexican people desired none of it. Maximilian's empire was a thinly veiled French protectorate and, as such, was a manifest violation of the Monroe Doctrine.

The French intervention in Mexico, consequently, was distasteful to government and public in the United States from the time when its purposes first became apparent. The United States, however, involved in a desperate civil conflict, was in no position to offer resistance to the French. Seward had by this time seen the folly of his "foreign war panacea." From his experience with Spain in the affair of the Dominican Republic he had learned the futility of making threats that he could not back with force. From the same experience he had learned that European governments were unimpressed by citations of the Monroe Doctrine. With these lessons in mind, Seward acted with caution and prudence. Although warning that a monarchical regime, especially one headed by a non-Mexican, would be unlikely to endure in Mexico and would be unpopular in the United States, he made no threats that his government would interfere. He refused to receive a representative of Maximilian and continued to recognize Juarez as head of the legitimate Mexican government; but as long as the Civil War lasted in the United States, he did not entirely close the door upon a future recognition of Maximilian. In his correspondence with the French government he made no reference to President Monroe or to the Monroe Doctrine by name; but the principles of that doctrine were, in the words of Dexter Perkins, "implicit in all the more important of his dispatches; . . . they were on the lips of most American public men, and in the columns of many of the newspapers; and . . . they exercised a powerful influence upon the course of events at home and abroad." [4]

As the prospects for Union victory over the Confederacy improved, vocal opinion in the North and in Washington became bolder in its assertion of the principles of Monroe against the French experiment in Mexico. Both factions of the Republican party, regular and radical, denounced the intervention in their campaign platforms in 1864, and the House of Representatives passed unanimously a resolution referring to "the deplorable events now transpiring in the Republic of Mexico" and declaring that

it does not accord with the policy of the United

4. Dexter Perkins, *The Monroe Doctrine, 1826–1867* (Baltimore: The Johns Hopkins Press, 1933), p. 420.

States to acknowledge any monarchical government erected on the ruins of any republican government in America under the auspices of any European power.

That the fate of Maximilian's empire might hang upon the outcome of the Civil War in the United States was well enough realized both in Paris and in Mexico City, and both imperial courts watched the progress of the war with deep concern. Maximilian made repeated efforts to secure a hearing in Washington, where he hoped his efforts to give Mexico a stable and a liberal government would be appreciated. The death of Lincoln was little less of a blow to him than the surrender of Lee, for he had hoped for an understanding with the patient and forbearing man in the White House. Upon learning of these two momentous events, Maximilian dispatched a special envoy to the courts of Napoleon III and of his own father-in-law, Leopold I of Belgium, in the hope of securing a joint guarantee from the principal European powers against interference by the United States. This attempt to call into being a later version of the Quadruple Alliance failed completely. Even Napoleon III was heartily sick of an adventure which had proved costly and unpopular in France and which was not meeting with the anticipated success.[5]

The collapse of the Confederacy left the United States reunited and powerful, with a formidable army and navy. Military leaders, Grant, Sheridan, Schofield, would have relished the assignment of expelling Maximilian and his French backers from Mexico by force. Seward, confident that the same object could be accomplished peacefully, held the dogs of war in leash but raised the tone of his diplomacy. In November 1865 he informed Napoleon, through the United States minister in Paris, that the French intervention was "disallowable and impracticable" and that recognition by the United States of Maximilian's regime was out of the question. Dispatches

from Paris in the weeks that followed made it plain that France was preparing to retreat. By February 1866, Seward was convinced that he could present something approaching an ultimatum without risk of its being rejected. On February 12, accordingly, through the French minister in Washington, he requested the French Emperor to provide "definitive information of the time when French military operations may be expected to cease in Mexico." In the same note, to make the French retreat easier, Seward assured the Emperor that the United States would, after the French withdrawal, adhere to its usual policy of noninterference in the affairs of its neighbors: if Maximilian could sustain himself without French arms, the United States would not aid his foes. Seward made no reference to the Monroe Doctrine, but Monroe would have recognized his apprehensions in the following passage from the note:

> . . . the presence of European armies in Mexico, maintaining a European prince with imperial attributes, without her consent and against her will, is deemed a source of apprehension and danger, not alone to the United States, but also to all the independent and sovereign republican States founded on the American continent and its adjacent islands.

The result of the note was what Seward had expected. Early in April the government of Napoleon promised the withdrawal of French troops in three installments, in November 1866, March and November 1867. In reality, the last French soldiers embarked from Vera Cruz in the spring of 1867. Maximilian, rejecting the pleas of his wife and friends to seek safety in Europe, was captured and shot by the forces of Juarez. The persistent opposition to Maximilian in Mexico, the costliness of the adventure and its unpopularity in France, possibly the disturbed international situation in Europe—all or most of these factors had contributed to Napoleon's decision. But certainly decisive in timing if not in the final result had been the hostility of the United States. The Monroe Doctrine had won an impressive, indeed a tragic, success.

5. E. C. Corti, *Maximilian and Charlotte of Mexico,* trans. C. A. Phillips, 2 vols. (New York: Alfred A. Knopf, Inc., 1929), 2: 498–501.

The application of the Monroe Doctrine, even though unnamed, in the Mexican crisis had won for it respect in Europe, in practice if not in theory. That respect was due, rather obviously, to the great increase in the material and military power of the United States and the conviction that the United States would use that power, if necessary, to prevent political interference by Europe in the Americas. The Mexican episode had also had a profound effect upon the status of the Monroe Doctrine at home, converting it from a party dogma to a national principle. It was, significantly, a Republican Secretary of State, supported enthusiastically by a Republican Congress, who had invoked against Napoleon III the principles originally set forth by a Democratic President. Henceforth the nation was close to unanimity in its support of the doctrine.

The Beginning of the Pan American Movement

The Monroe Doctrine, in its origin and throughout the first century of its history, was a purely unilateral policy of the United States. The United States warned Europe against undertaking new colonization in the Americas, and against attempting to shape or control the governments of the independent American states. This it did in the interest of its own security. It gave no promises of protection to other American states (with the exception of such isolated cases as the Bidlack treaty with New Granada).[6] It assumed no obligation to them and asked no cooperation from them. The Monroe Doctrine was a policy of the United States, not a policy of the American republics.

The idea of cooperation of all the American republics for common ends and in support of common principles—an idea entirely absent from the Monroe Doctrine—is the heart of Pan Americanism. Henry Clay had envisaged an "American System" of republics, led by the United States. The Panama Congress of 1826

had been called with some such idea in mind. Though its promoter, Bolivar, would have limited the projected organization to the states of Spanish and Portuguese origin, the United States was eventually invited to send delegates. Its representatives, though appointed, failed to reach Panama.[7] During the next fifty years, no progress was made toward the Pan American ideal. Such congresses as were held by the Latin American states were sparsely attended and barren of achievement.[8] Not until 1881 did the United States attempt to lead its sister republics into a cooperative system.

James G. Blaine, Secretary of State in 1881 and from 1889 to 1892, was the chief agent in reviving the Pan American idea first voiced by Henry Clay. With the approval of President Chester A. Arthur, Blaine issued, November 29, 1881, an invitation to the other eighteen American states to send delegates to Washington in the following year "for the purpose of considering and discussing the methods of preventing war between the nations of America." Blaine's purpose, stated in his own words, was:

> First, to bring about peace and prevent future wars in North and South America; second, to cultivate such friendly, commercial relations with all American countries as would lead to a large increase in the export trade of the United States, by supplying fabrics in which we are abundantly able to compete with the manufacturing nations of Europe.

The maintenance of peace, as Blaine viewed the matter, was essential to a healthy growth of trade.[9]

6. See p. 150.

7. For the Panama Congress, see Chapter 9.
8. W. S. Robertson, *Hispanic-American Relations with the United States* (New York: Oxford University Press, 1923), pp. 384–89.
9. During his brief tenure as Secretary of State in 1881, Blaine attempted to promote the cause of peace in the Americas by offering the assistance of the United States in settling a boundary dispute between Mexico and Guatemala and in bringing to an end the "War of the Pacific" then being waged by Chile against Peru and Bolivia. In neither enterprise was Blaine successful. Preacher of peace though he was, Blaine had a reputation for chauvinism in his vigorous upholding of American rights and interests, as

Unfortunately for Blaine's plans, President Arthur, who had inherited Blaine as a member of the cabinet of the assassinated President Garfield, desired a Secretary of State politically more congenial to himself. Consequently, within three weeks of the issuance of the invitations to the conference, Blaine was replaced by Frederick T. Frelinghuysen. The new Secretary disapproved of Blaine's conference plans and, with the President's consent, withdrew the invitations. His official excuse for so doing was fear that friendly European states might regard the calling of an exclusively American conference as an affront to them.

The idea did not die, however. Congress, in 1888, requested the President to call a conference of American states for the purpose of promoting trade and preserving peace among the free nations of the hemisphere. For the promotion of trade, the resolution proposed the creation of an American customs union, the improvement of transportation and communications, and the adoption of uniform customs regulations, a common system of weights and measures, and a common silver coin. For the preservation of peace, it proposed an agreement to submit to arbitration all disputes that could not be settled by ordinary diplomacy. Thomas F. Bayard, Secretary of State under President Cleveland, sent out the invitations in July 1888. Before the conference met in October 1889, another turn of the political wheel had brought the Republican Benjamin Harrison to the White House and returned Blaine to the State Department. It was Blaine, therefore, who welcomed the American delegates to Washington and was chosen by them to preside over the conference. Thus Blaine, the proposer of the conference in 1881, became its presiding officer when it finally met eight years later.

Invitations had been sent to Mexico, to all the republics of Central and South America, and to Haiti and the Dominican Republic in the Caribbean—eighteen in all. All but the Dominican Republic accepted and sent delegates. Including the United States, therefore, eighteen governments were represented. The delegates, numbering thirty-seven, were organized in fifteen committees to study the proposals made to the conference and to recommend action upon them.

The results were disappointing. The proposal for a customs union was rejected; instead, the conference recommended separate reciprocity treaties. The proposal of a common silver coin (evidently a measure designed to check the falling price of silver) was reported adversely. No progress was made toward uniformity in weights and measures or in customs regulations. A railroad connecting North and South America was recommended, but nothing was done to make it a reality. A general arbitration treaty providing for settlement by arbitration of all questions except such as might compromise the independence of one party, was agreed upon (with the Chilean and Mexican delegations dissenting) but was never ratified. A resolution declaring against recognition of any future acquisition of territory by conquest suffered a similar fate.

The one tangible achievement of the conference was the setting up in Washington of the Bureau of American Republics, later renamed the Pan American Union, essentially an agency for the exchange of information, economic, scientific, and cultural. More significant, however, was the precedent set by the conference of 1889–1890 for the holding of inter-American meetings to discuss problems of common interest. It was the first of a long series of inter-American conferences, which gained in importance with the passage of time. The early conferences avoided all political commitments. Those held in the 1930's and

---

in relation to the isthmian canal question, the northeastern fisheries, and the fur seal controversy. See Chapter 20. He was equally vigorous in exacting from the government of Chile apology and reparation for an attack on members of the crew of the cruiser *Baltimore* by a Valparaiso mob in 1891. He attempted to acquire naval bases for the United States in the Caribbean, looked forward to the acquisition of Cuba and Puerto Rico, and gave tacit encouragement to the plan to overthrow the royal government in Hawaii in preparation for annexation to the United States. See J. W. Pratt, *Expansionists of 1898* (Baltimore: The Johns Hopkins Press, 1936), pp. 23–33 and chap. 2.

later, on the other hand, were successful in smoothing disagreements, particularly between the United States and its southern neighbors, and in unifying the American republics in resistance to totalitarian aggression from without. In this way, the Pan American movement, in its later phases, virtually adopted and "continentalized" the Monroe Doctrine.[10]

Great Britain and Venezuela

Aggressive assertion of the Monroe Doctrine as a unilateral policy of the United States, interpreted and maintained by the United States alone, reached a climax in 1895 in a diplomatic note penned by Secretary of State Richard Olney and a special message addressed to Congress by President Grover Cleveland.

This episode was the outgrowth of a boundary controversy between the republic of Venezuela and the adjoining colony of British Guiana. Venezuela had won its independence from Spain in the years after 1810 and had been recognized by the United States in 1822, being then a portion of Colombia. The neighboring western portion of Guiana had been ceded to Great Britain by the Netherlands in 1814. Spain and the Netherlands had never agreed upon a mutual boundary line. In 1840 the British explorer, Sir Robert Schomburgk, drew a line that the British accepted but the Venezuelans rejected. As time passed and gold deposits were discovered in the interior, the drawing of a boundary increased in importance, and both parties inflated their claims. Venezuela, the weaker party, repeatedly proposed arbitration. Great Britain offered to arbitrate her claims west of the Schomburgk line but not east of it, where British settlers had for years occupied areas now claimed by Vene-

zuela. Venezuela insisted upon arbitration without such limitations, and made appeal after appeal to the United States for support. Diplomatic relations were broken off, restored, and again severed. The United States recommended arbitration to Great Britain from time to time, but not until 1895 did its recommendations actually assume the nature of an ultimatum.

The new urgency that marked the diplomacy of 1895 must be attributed in part to the economic depression that followed the panic of 1893 in the United States. Every economic depression led to revived emphasis on the need for expanding foreign markets. This one, with its railroad strikes and armies of the unemployed marching on Washington, seemed to pose a threat to the nation's social fabric. Foreign markets seemed essential to the preservation of social stability, and American businessmen were eyeing with jealous interest the competition of Europe in the markets of South America. As a British publication remarked in the fall of 1895, there was "an unwritten Monroeism working like yeast in the commercial world of America."[11] There is little doubt that Cleveland and Olney were thinking in terms of this "unwritten [economic] Monroeism," though it must be read between the lines of the official documents.

Skillful propaganda also played a role in bringing on the confrontation. In the previous year, William L. Scruggs, a paid agent of the Venezuelan government, had published a pamphlet entitled *British Aggressions in Venezuela, or the Monroe Doctrine on Trial,* in which he unblushingly set forth the Venezuelan side of the case. To aid in arousing American concern, he advanced the theory that the upper waters of the Orinoco River

10. See Chapter 35. There is a good concise account of the Washington Conference of 1889–1890 in J. B. Lockey's sketch of James G. Blaine, in Samuel F. Bemis, ed., *The American Secretaries of State and Their Diplomacy,* 10 vols. (New York: Alfred A. Knopf, Inc., 1927–1929), 8: 164–81. See also T. F. McGann, *Argentina, the United States, and the Inter-American System, 1880–1914* (Cambridge: Harvard University Press, 1957), chaps. 10, 11.

11. *British Trade Journal,* quoted in Walter LaFeber, *The New Empire: An Interpretation of American Expansion, 1860–1898* (Ithaca, N.Y.: Cornell University Press, 1963), p. 195. Cleveland's Secretary of State Walter Q. Gresham had already taken vigorous action to sustain a government in Brazil friendly to American business interests and to end the last British pretensions to a protectorate over the Mosquito Indians of Nicaragua. Ibid., pp. 210–29.

interlocked with those of the Amazon and the La Plata; hence, if the British held, as they claimed, the southern shore of the Orinoco at its mouth, they would hold "the key to more than a quarter of the whole continent." [12] Scruggs not only secured wide circulation for his pamphlet; he lobbied directly with members of the House, the Senate, the Cleveland administration, and with the President himself. He deserved at least some of the credit when both houses of Congress early in 1895 passed unanimously a joint resolution calling upon the President to recommend "most urgently" to Great Britain and Venezuela that they settle their dispute by arbitration.

Walter Q. Gresham, Cleveland's Secretary of State (1893–1895), began the preparation of a note to Great Britain. Upon his death in May 1895, the task was taken over by his successor, the vigorous Boston lawyer Richard Olney. Olney resolved to rest his case against Great Britain on the Monroe Doctrine as he interpreted it. The "noninterference" principle of the Doctrine, he contended, would be violated if Great Britain should take by force any territory claimed by Venezuela without submitting the question of its ownership to impartial adjudication. Such a policy, he argued, "in effect deprives Venezuela of her free agency and puts her under virtual duress."

In an effort to show that the United States had a legitimate interest in such a controversy, Olney resorted to the argument that if Britain succeeded in appropriating Venezuelan territory, other European powers would follow her example; the powers of Europe would be "permanently encamped on American soil," and the United States would be deprived of the happy situation under which it "is practically sovereign on this continent, and its fiat is law upon the subjects to which it confines its interposition."

Olney closed his note by requesting a reply in time for the President to submit it to the session of Congress that would open early in December. The entire note savored of an ultimatum.

Lord Salisbury, British Foreign Secretary, took the American demand less seriously than it deserved. He took his time in replying; his answer—which the United States ambassador forwarded by mail instead of cable—did not reach Washington until after the opening of Congress. At the expenditure of considerable verbiage, it made two simple points: (1) the Monroe Doctrine was in no way binding upon Great Britain, which recognized no special rights of the United States in the Western Hemisphere; (2) even if the Monroe Doctrine were recognized as valid international law, it would have no bearing upon a mere boundary dispute between an American state and a British possession. The British government's position remained unchanged: it would arbitrate claims beyond the Schomburgk line, but not within it.

It is hard to refute the British logic, but the controversy had passed, in the United States, from the area of logic into that of emotion—and of politics. Public opinion, resentful of British procrastination and stubbornness in the Venezuelan affair, had found another grievance in the British occupation, in the spring of 1895, of the Nicaraguan port of Corinto as a means of enforcing payment of claims by Nicaragua. Some Democrats as well as most Republicans were denouncing Cleveland's foreign policy as weak, both in his failure to prevent the Corinto incident and in his shelving of the treaty for the annexation of Hawaii. Cleveland and Olney were being urged to bolster their own position and that of the Democratic party by making a strong stand in support of Venezuela.[13] Cleveland, a stubborn man in his own right, was in no mood to accept Salisbury's rebuff complacently.

In a special message to Congress, December 17, 1895, the President submitted the correspondence with the British government and with it, his recommendations. Since Great Britain had declined to submit her claims to

12. John A. S. Grenville and G. B. Young, *Politics, Strategy, and American Diplomacy: Studies in Foreign Policy, 1873–1917* (New Haven: Yale University Press, 1966), chap. 5.

13. N. M. Blake, "Background of Cleveland's Venezuelan Policy," *American Historical Review,* 47 (1942), 259–77.

arbitration, he proposed that Congress authorize him to appoint a commission to determine where the boundary ought to be, and that when the commission had reported, the United States assume responsibility for enforcing its decision. The President was aware, he said, of all the consequences that might follow his recommendation. It was, he observed, "a grievous thing to contemplate the two great English-speaking peoples . . . as being otherwise than friendly competitors in the onward march of civilization," but even war, he implied, would be preferable to "a supine submission to wrong and injustice and the consequent loss of national self respect and honor."

Thus Cleveland, like his predecessor, President James K. Polk, looked John Bull "straight in the eye." At home the message received enthusiastic support, and though many bankers and some businessmen, clergymen, and academic people deplored the risk of war over what seemed a trivial matter, Congress promptly gave the President the authority he had asked and provided for the expenses of the proposed commission.

Actually, despite the bold language, there was little risk of war. The message, composed by Olney, "was a most skillful piece of work; it satisfied even the wildest jingoes without, in fact, involving the United States in any real danger of conflict." [14] The work of the proposed boundary commission would take time; not until it was completed would there be a showdown, and in the interval pacific counsels were likely to prevail.

In fact, they prevailed without awaiting the report of the commission. If American opinion was chauvinistic, prevailing British opinion was quite the reverse. Newspapers and public men, including the Prince of Wales, hastened to express themselves in terms of friendship for the United States. The German Kaiser diverted British irritation from Washington to Berlin by a telegram congratulating President Paul Kruger of the Transvaal on the repulse of a filibustering expedition by Englishmen— the Jameson raid. Lord Salisbury wanted no war over the Venezuela boundary. He had underrated American determination and was ready for a retreat if a formula could be found that would accept arbitration and yet save British face.[15] Such a formula was devised in a rule that "adverse holding or prescription during a period of fifty years shall make a good title." Thus Great Britain was protected against loss of territory long settled or held by British subjects. A court of arbitration, provided for by treaty between Great Britain and Venezuela and composed of two justices of the United States Supreme Court, two Englishmen, and a Russian jurist selected by the four, rendered its decision in October 1899. The line agreed upon differed from the Schomburgk line chiefly in assigning to Venezuela possession of the south bank of the Orinoco River at its mouth and another bit of territory in the interior.[16]

The Monroe Doctrine had scored a second notable victory, for Lord Salisbury, although denying it in theory, had conformed to it in practice, even in the extreme and questionable interpretation given it by Richard Olney. Judged pragmatically, Cleveland and Olney

14. Grenville and Young, *Politics, Strategy, and American Diplomacy*, p. 167; cf. Bradford Perkins, *The Great Rapprochement: England and the United States, 1895–1914* (New York: Atheneum, 1968), p. 17.

15. The negotiations were cooled by a temporary shift from official to unofficial channels with the editor of the *Times* of London speaking for Salisbury and his American correspondent for Olney. See J. T. Mathews, "Informal Diplomacy in the Venezuela Crisis of 1896," *Mississippi Valley Historical Review*, 50 (September 1963), 195–212.

16. The Venezuela boundary question was reopened in the 1960's when publication of the papers of Mallet Prevost, a junior counsel at the arbitration, revealed evidence that the award had been the result of a political deal between the British members of the tribunal and its Russian president. Venezuela thereupon laid claim to 58,000 square miles of the territory of British Guiana, which became independent Guyana in 1966. A four-man mixed commission created in 1966 and charged with reaching a settlement within four years had not reached agreement in June 1970, but the two governments—Venezuela and Guyana—then announced a decision to shelve the dispute for at least twelve years. *New York Times*, December 19, 1966; June 21, 1970.

had been right. Whether they were justified in running the risk of war with England, minimal though it was, over a boundary dispute that in itself was of minor importance, was and remains debatable. It was their contention that by bringing the dispute to a head when they did, they foreclosed a greater risk of war that would have arisen later if Britain and Venezuela had drifted into hostilities.

Strangely enough, a controversy that for a few days had the United States and Great Britain seemingly on the verge of war, marked a definite turning point for the better in Anglo-American relations. A general arbitration treaty between the two, the Olney-Pauncefote Treaty negotiated in 1897, fell short of Senate approval by only three votes.[17] When the United States went to war with Spain over the Cuban question in 1898, it was warmly supported by British opinion. Within the next dozen years, all Anglo-American misunder-

standings of any significance were amicably adjusted, and the way was made easier for Anglo-American cooperation in World War I.[18]

Olney's aggressive assertion of the Monroe Doctrine was less resented in England, at which it was aimed, than on the continent of Europe. In France, Germany, Austria-Hungary, Italy, Spain, Holland, and Russia, official and newspaper opinion showed hostility to this new assumption by the United States of a predominant position in the Western Hemisphere. Nor was Latin America universally appreciative of Uncle Sam's taking upon himself the role of a protector whose "fiat is law" upon the continent. Venezuela, Colombia, Brazil (which had a boundary dispute with French Guiana), Peru, and the states of Central America showed varying degrees of enthusiasm or approval for the Cleveland-Olney policy. In Mexico, Argentina, and Chile, on the other hand, there was suspicion and hostility, and a thinly attended congress of American states, meeting in Mexico City in 1896, clearly betrayed distrust of the growing power and pretensions of the "Colossus of the North."[19] To have a powerful protector was all very well, but it was clear that some of Uncle Sam's neighbors were growing fearful that the protector might lay claim to certain rights of overlordship.

17. The Olney-Pauncefote Treaty bound the parties to submit to arbitration by mixed commissions any future differences between them not involving claims to territory and not susceptible of adjustment by diplomacy. A territorial dispute would be submitted to a tribunal of six judges, three chosen by each party. Its decision would not be binding unless concurred in by five of the six judges. Viewed with pride by Cleveland and Olney, praised by President McKinley in his inaugural address, and acclaimed by the press and public, the treaty failed to hurdle the Senate barrier. Senatorial jealousy of that body's prerogatives, dislike of advance commitments to arbitration, and hostility on the part of the large "free silver" bloc to England, home of the gold standard, accounted for the adverse vote. W. S. Holt, *Treaties Defeated by the Senate* (Baltimore: The Johns Hopkins Press, 1933), pp. 154–62.

18. This subject is brilliantly covered in B. Perkins, *The Great Rapprochement*.

19. The European and Latin American attitude to the Cleveland-Olney policy is conveniently summarized by D. Perkins, *History of the Monroe Doctrine,* pp. 186–90.

20

Fisheries, Fur Seals, and Far Eastern Interests

The Venezuela boundary controversy, although the most serious threat, was not the sole threat to Anglo-American amity in the last quarter of the nineteenth century. An ancient dispute over inshore fishing rights along the coasts of British North America flared up with new heat in the 1880's. At about the same time, a fresh misunderstanding arose over the American claim of an exclusive right to regulate the taking of fur seals in the waters of Bering Sea. Both controversies were eventually settled by arbitration; the fur seal dispute in 1893, the northeast fisheries question not until 1910. While the United States was defending its economic interests in these matters in protracted arguments with the British government, it was feeling new concern about a future market for its growing surplus of industrial products and was ready to take alarm when an apparently promising market in China seemed about to be preempted and monopolized by other powers. These topics are the principal subject matter of the present chapter.

The Northeastern Fisheries Controversy

Participation by New England fishermen in the fisheries along the coasts of British North America had been a perennial source of Anglo-American friction. The "liberty" to engage in inshore fishing granted to citizens of the United States in 1783 had been renounced in 1818, with the exception of the waters, bays, and harbors on the coast of Labrador north of Mount Joly, the western and part of the southern coasts of Newfoundland, and the Magdalen Islands. The privilege of fishing in these latter waters the Americans were to enjoy "forever." [1] The Marcy-Elgin reciprocity treaty of 1854 admitted American fishermen to the coastal waters of all British North America, as under the treaty of 1783, but when the reciprocity treaty was abrogated in 1866, the restrictions of 1818 again became operative.

The Treaty of Washington of 1871, whose chief title to fame was provision for arbitra-

1. See above, pp. 71, 146, for the earlier phases of this controversy. See also map, p. 249.

tion of the *Alabama* claims, reopened the prohibited waters to American fishermen. In return, Canadian fishermen were permitted to engage in inshore fishing along the coasts of the United States north of 39°, and Canadian fish and fish oil were admitted to the United States free of duty.[2] These provisions of the treaty were to run for ten years; at the end of that time either party might terminate them by giving two years' notice. The Canadians claimed that the privileges gained by the United States under this arrangement greatly exceeded in value those accruing to Canada. A commission of three, set up to adjust this discrepancy, fixed the difference over a twelve-year period at $5,500,000 and directed the United States to pay that amount to Great Britain. This award, made over the objection of the American member of the commission, was considered excessive in the United States and was the principal reason that led Congress, in 1883, to direct that the arrangement be abrogated at the end of the two-year interval specified in the treaty.[3]

Termination of the fisheries article in 1885 exposed American fishermen to a variety of petty annoyances by the local authorities of Canada and Newfoundland, where a growing population of fisher-folk resented the competition of the Yankees. By a narrow and legalistic interpretation of the treaty of 1818, American fishing vessels entering Canadian or Newfoundland harbors for the permitted purposes of shelter, repairs, or obtaining wood or water, were required to enter and clear at customs houses and pay pilotage fees, and were refused the privilege of buying bait and tackle. Ships were seized by Canadian patrol vessels for trifling violations of such requirements and prohibitions. American anger flared up at British "wrongs," and the friction was aggravated by the approach of the presidential campaign of 1888 and the need felt by both parties to court the Irish vote by speaking harsh words to John Bull.

The Republican Senate refused President Cleveland's request for authority to join with Great Britain in appointing a joint commission that might settle the controversy by treaty. The President proceeded, nevertheless, to invite Great Britain to negotiate, and named three commissioners, headed by the Secretary of State. The British government likewise named a three-man commission. A compromise treaty, signed February 15, 1888, was defeated in the Senate in the following August. A Republican senator explained to one of the British commissioners: "We cannot allow the Democrats to take credit for settling so important a dispute." [4]

Cleveland's counterstroke in the political game was to recommend a form of retaliation against Canada so drastic that the Republican Senate feared to pass it. Fortunately, no retaliation proved necessary. The negotiators, foreseeing that the treaty might meet with delay or rejection, had arranged a *modus vivendi* that met the principal American complaints. Fishing vessels were exempted from reporting to customs and from arrest for trifling causes and were permitted, in return for moderate fees, to purchase bait and other necessities of their calling in Canadian harbors. Though of only two years' duration, the *modus vivendi* was renewed from time to time and prevented further serious friction with Canada. It did not end difficulties with New-

2. Canada at this time made every effort to secure a renewal of the trade reciprocity inaugurated in 1854 and terminated in 1866. The United States was unwilling to go further than the free admission of fish and fish oil.

3. Over the twelve-year period during which the fisheries provisions were in force, payments by the United States were about eight times the value of the fish taken by American vessels in the waters opened to them by the treaty. Raymond McFarland, *A History of the New England Fisheries* (New York: Appleton-Century-Crofts for the University of Pennsylvania, 1911), pp. 329–30n.

4. Allan Nevins, *Grover Cleveland, A Study in Courage* (New York: Dodd, Mead & Co., 1932), p. 412. A detailed account of this phase of the fisheries negotiation is given in C. C. Tansill, *The Foreign Policy of Thomas F. Bayard, 1885–1897* (New York: Fordham University Press, 1940), chaps. 6–10. The later famous Joseph Chamberlain, one of the British negotiators, though he failed to get a completed treaty, negotiated a successful marriage with the daughter of Secretary of War Endicott.

THE BERING SEA
AND PRIBILOF ISLANDS

35° and 180°: Pelagic Sealing forbidden to British and Americans north and east of this line by arbitral award, 1893.

30°: Pelagic Sealing forbidden north of 30° by 1911 Convention between U.S., Great Britain, Russia, and Japan.

foundland, however, and not until the arbitration of 1910 were all the angles of this troublesome question disposed of.[5]

5. See Chapter 25. A sequel of the fisheries negotiation of 1887–1888 was the *faux pas* of the British minister, Sir Lionel Sackville-West (by the death of an elder brother, he became Lord Sackville just before leaving Washington), which resulted in his dismissal by Cleveland. Some Republicans laid a trap for this diplomat. A man signing himself Murchison and pretending to be a former British subject, now a naturalized American, asked the minister's opinion as to whether Cleveland, if reelected, would be friendly to British interests. His affirmative answer, published by the Republicans a few days before election, was useful

The Bering Sea Arbitration

The purchase of Alaska in 1867 brought under United States sovereignty the Pribilof Islands in the Bering Sea, the summer home and breeding ground of the principal Pacific herd

political ammunition, but its effect was at least partly nullified by Cleveland's prompt action—smart in domestic politics but unjustifiably drastic in international comity—in giving Lord Sackville his walking papers. See C. S. Campbell, Jr., "The Dismissal of Lord Sackville," *Mississippi Valley Historical Review*, 44 (March 1958), 635–48.

of fur seals. Here, during the summer months, the mature bulls, or "beach-masters," reign over their numerous harems, while the young bachelors live apart, awaiting their turn to become patresfamilias. Because of these biological habits and the tame and cooperative behavior of the species, it is an easy matter to despoil the male seals of their elegant skins to furnish adornment for human females. And because of the seals' polygamous family life, young males can be slaughtered in great numbers without endangering the perpetuation of the herd.

Soon after acquiring the islands the United States prohibited the taking, except under license, of fur-bearing animals in Alaska and "in the waters thereof." Subsequently it leased to a corporation, the Alaska Commercial Company, the exclusive right to take seals in the Pribilofs, limited the number to be taken annually, and forbade the killing of females and their young. All this it had an unquestioned right to do. Foreign sealers, especially Canadians, excluded from the island breeding-grounds of the seals, began resorting to so-called "pelagic" sealing—that is, shooting, harpooning, or otherwise killing the seals as they swam outside the territorial waters of the United States in search of food or in their annual migrations. By this method females were more likely to be killed than males, and the death of a female might easily mean also the death of one dependent pup and one unborn. Furthermore, since many of the animals killed were not recovered, there was a high percentage of waste. The growth of the practice, therefore, threatened the herd with extermination and a lucrative business with extinction.

To prevent such an unhappy result, American revenue cutters under instructions from the Treasury Department seized Canadian sealing ships in the waters of the Bering Sea on the theory that those waters were under American jurisdiction. Such seizures were upheld by the United States District Court at Sitka, Alaska, and Congress in 1889 directed the President to take steps to seize all vessels and arrest all persons violating the laws of the United States within "all the dominion of the United States in the waters of Behring Sea." In order to justify these proceedings, the United States had to assert some kind of exclusive jurisdiction over the waters of the Bering Sea outside the three-mile limit. Such a claim was embarrassing, since the United States, traditionally an upholder of "freedom of the seas," had objected strenuously to the Russian ukase of 1821, claiming jurisdiction one hundred miles from the shores of the Pacific, and had exacted from Russia in the treaty of 1824 a guarantee that "in any part of . . . the Pacific Ocean, . . . the respective citizens or subjects of the high contracting Powers shall be neither disturbed nor restricted, either in navigation or in fishing." [6] Since Russia had made a similar agreement with Great Britain in 1825, and since the United States was in the Bering Sea as heir to Russia, American Secretaries of State found it difficult to defend the American claim against British protests.

Secretary James G. Blaine, upon whom fell the brunt of the defense, was unable to impress the British government with the arguments (1) that pelagic sealing was *contra bonos mores*—"a pursuit which of necessity involves a serious and permanent injury to the rights of the Government and people of the United States"; and (2) that the United States was entitled by prescription—long British acquiescence in Russian and American authority over the seal herd even at sea—to exercise jurisdiction over the waters of the Bering Sea in this one respect only. Blaine did not assert, as the federal judge at Sitka had asserted, that the Bering Sea was in all respects *mare clausum*, a closed sea, as a part of the territorial waters of Alaska.

An attempt to prohibit pelagic sealing by international agreement was blocked by the objections of Canada. After a prolonged diplomatic wrangle, the British and American governments on February 29, 1892, agreed to submit the whole controversy to arbitration. The tribunal was composed of two representatives each of the United States and Great Britain and one member each named by the President

6. See p. 74.

of the French Republic, the King of Italy, and the King of Sweden and Norway.

The court convened in Paris in February 1893. John W. Foster, the American agent, argued his case somewhat differently from Blaine, who had resigned as Secretary of State some months before. The Bering Sea, he contended, was not a part of the Pacific Ocean and hence was not embraced in the concessions made by Russia in 1824 and 1825. Russia then, said Foster, had continued to exercise full jurisdiction not over the entire sea but over all of it within one hundred miles of shore until 1867, when she ceded Alaska to the United States. Thereafter the United States enjoyed all the rights that had been Russia's before the cession.

Unfortunately for this part of the American case, Foster made the discovery that he was relying upon falsified documents. A certain Ivan Petroff, employed as a translator, had hoped to ingratiate himself with the United States by interpolating in his translations of Russian documents passages asserting claims of jurisdiction that Russian officials had never made. The detection and withdrawal of these falsifications greatly weakened the American argument.[7]

Foster's other principal argument was the novel one that the fur seals of the herd frequenting the Pribilof Islands were domestic animals, the property of the United States; that when swimming abroad they were like cattle wandering on the range, still subject to the control of their owners and not to be taken or killed by others. Some portions of this interesting argument deserve quotation.

First. That the Alaskan fur seal, begotten, born and reared on the Pribilof Islands, within the territory of the United States, is essentially a land animal, which resorts to the water only for food and to avoid the rigor of winter, . . .

that it is domestic in its habits and readily controlled by man while on land; . . . that at all times, when in the water, the identity of each individual can be established with certainty, and that at all times, whether during its short excursions from the islands in search of food or its longer winter migration, it has a fixed intention, or instinct, which induces it to return thereto.[8]

Other sections of the American argument stressed the value of the herd as it had developed under Russian and American regulation, the danger of its extermination by pelagic sealing, which was described as "illegitimate, improper, and wasteful, . . . barbarous and inhuman," and the disproportion between the small profits and the great destructiveness of that method of sealing.

The court of arbitration, asked to decide upon the American claims to exclusive jurisdiction in the Bering Sea and to property rights in the seal herd when outside territorial waters, decided against the United States on all points. The Bering Sea, it held, was part of the Pacific Ocean; hence any exclusive rights that Russia might once have had in that area she had relinquished in 1824 and 1825. Russia, therefore, had no exclusive rights to pass on to the United States in 1867. The American claim to property rights in the seals as "domestic" animals, the court treated with scant respect. American rights in the seals ended when they passed the three-mile limit outward bound.[9]

A subsequent arbitration by a mixed commission assessed damages against the United States of $473,151.28 for the seizure of Canadian ships and cargoes in the enforcement of

---

7. J. B. Moore, *History and Digest of the International Arbitrations to Which the United States Has Been a Party . . .*, 6 vols. (Washington, D.C.: Government Printing Office, 1898), 1, 814–16; J. W. Foster, *Diplomatic Memoirs*, 2 vols. (Boston: Houghton Mifflin Company, 1909), 2: 40–41; R. A. Pierce, "New Light on Ivan Petroff, Historian of Alaska," *Pacific Northwest Quarterly*, 59 (January 1968), 1–10.

8. Moore, *History and Digest of Arbitrations*, 1: 812. Foster gives credit for this argument to Benjamin F. Tracy, Secretary of the Navy in Harrison's cabinet (Foster, *Memoirs*, 2:28). It has been facetiously commented that Foster stopped just short of claiming American citizenship for the fur seals.

9. Of the seven members of the court, the two Americans alone voted to uphold the American claim to property rights in the seal herd: only one of the Americans (Senator John T. Morgan of Alabama) voted to sustain the American claim to exclusive jurisdiction within one hundred miles of the shores of the Bering Sea.

the prohibitions that the court had held un-warranted. The court had, as provided by the treaty creating it, prescribed a set of regula-tions for the better preservation of the seal herd. These were put into effect by the two governments for their own citizens and sub-jects (including Canadians) but could not govern the practice of Japanese or Russians. Japanese sealers became especially active and aggressive. They sometimes failed to heed the three-mile limit and on one occasion actually landed and began slaughtering seals on the Pribilof Islands, where several of the poachers were killed and others captured by American officers. The United States claimed, further-more, that the regulations were not strictly enforced even against Canadian sealers. It threatened from time to time to exterminate the herd on the Pribilof Islands by "mercy killings" and so end once and for all what President Theodore Roosevelt denounced as "the hideous cruelty now incident to pelagic sealing." [10] Not until 1911 did a four-power treaty, signed by the United States, Great Britain, Russia, and Japan, forbid pelagic seal-ing in the North Pacific with provision for an equitable division among the four nations of the skins legitimately taken. Under these regu-lations the herd of fur seals thrived and multi-plied. In October 1940, however, Japan gave the required one year's notice of abrogation, and the treaty terminated October 23, 1941. Temporary agreements between the United States and Canada, later joined by Japan, were superseded in 1957 by a four-power con-vention—those powers and the Soviet Union —by which each signatory agreed to prohibit pelagic sealing by its nationals in the North Pacific north of the 30th parallel. This con-vention, originally for a minimum of six years, was extended to twelve by amendments signed in 1963.[11]

10. C. C. Tansill, *Canadian-American Relations, 1875–1911* (New Haven: Yale University Press, 1943), chap. 12.
11. T. A. Bailey, "The North Pacific Sealing Conven-tion of 1911," *Pacific Historical Review,* 4 (1935), 1–14; *United States Treaties and Other International Agreements,* 8: 2283–93; 15: 316–35.

Chinese Immigration Presents a Problem

American interest in the Far East in the thirty years after the Civil War was kept alive by a slow growth of trade and a continuing support by American churches of missionary activity in that area. Relations with Japan after the Meiji Restoration of 1868 were un-eventful and generally cordial. There were few causes of friction between the two govern-ments, and the United States sympathized with and encouraged Japan's attempts to throw off the shackles of the unequal treaties.

American relations with China in the same period suffered some deterioration. Anson Burlingame, after serving successfully for six years as United States minister to China, resigned in 1867 to become a member of a three-man commission to represent China in negotiations with the United States and the governments of Europe. His two colleagues were Chinese. In Washington, Burlingame signed with Secretary Seward (July 28, 1868) a treaty assuring most-favored-nation treat-ment to Chinese visiting or residing in the United States (and reciprocally to Americans in China). It withheld from such Chinese, however, the privilege of naturalization, which by an act of Congress of 1870 was limited to immigrants of European or African origin.

At the time when this treaty was made and approved, cheap labor was in much de-mand on the Pacific coast, and no objection was raised to the importation of Chinese of the working class. The completion of the Cen-tral Pacific railroad in 1869 threw thousands of laborers out of work and depressed wages. Soon thereafter came the panic of 1873, fol-lowed by a long economic depression. It was not surprising that white workers on the Pacific coast and their spokesmen in politics raised a storm against the Chinese, whose cus-tomary standard of living was so low that they were glad to work for a fraction of the wage considered adequate by native Ameri-cans or Europeans. From California came reports of anti-Chinese riots and insistent demands for prohibition or limitation of Chinese immigration.

When Congress in 1879 passed a limitation bill, however, President Hayes vetoed it as a violation of the Burlingame treaty. An American commission sent to China the next year (1880) returned with a new treaty by which China consented that the United States might "regulate, limit, or suspend, but not absolutely prohibit" immigration of Chinese laborers. Accordingly, an act of 1882 suspended for ten years the immigration of Chinese laborers, and in 1892 the suspension was renewed for an additional ten years. This suspension was later extended to 1904, with Chinese consent, and in 1904, without such consent, the exclusion of working-class Chinese was made permanent.

Such racial discriminatinn, whether justified or not, produced resentment in China. On the other hand, a grudging acceptance by the Chinese of American missionaries and the occasional mistreatment of such persons made for anti-Chinese feeling in the United States. Hence as China and Japan drifted toward war over their conflicting interests in Korea, American sentiment tended to favor Japan rather than China.

Japan and China Fight over Korea

Korea, the "hermit kingdom," had long paid tribute to China and, until 1832, to Japan also. Such submission, however, was ceremonial rather than political. In 1876 Japan, imitating the technique that Perry had used against the Shogun, made a naval demonstration in Korean waters and secured a treaty by which Korea declared itself to be a sovereign and independent state, thus repudiating any allegiance to China and opening the way for Japanese penetration.

The Chinese government had from time to time denied any responsibility for what befell foreigners in Korea, thus shielding itself from demands for satisfaction for the murder of missionaries or for other wrongs. But when the Chinese saw Japanese footprints leading to the Korean door, they began to reassert their claims to suzerainty. Thus when Commodore R. W. Shufeldt of the United States Navy was sent to the Far East with authority to make a treaty with Korea, he found Li Hung-chang, the Chinese viceroy at Tientsin, anxious to demonstrate that the proper approach to Korea was through China.[12] Commodore Shufeldt accepted the proffered good offices. A treaty was negotiated at Tientsin between Li and Shufeldt and signed in Korea on May 22, 1882. The treaty opened Korea to American trade, permitted residence of Americans in the open ports, fixed import and export duties, and provided temporary rights of extraterritoriality.

There now followed a period of intrigue for hegemony in Korea between China and Japan, with Russia, now a neighbor of Korea on the north, also taking a hand. The Russians withdrew for the time being, and after some years of see-saw between China and Japan, marred by assassinations, kidnappings, and deportations, an antiforeign uprising brought both Chinese and Japanese troops into the peninsula. Attempts of the western powers to persuade both to withdraw were unavailing, and on August 1, 1894, Japan declared war upon China. Characteristically, she had struck her first naval blow a week before. The United States was officially neutral and maintained friendly relations with both powers, but its attitude was on the whole more favorable to Japan than to China. It refused to join the other powers in making a one-sided protest to Tokyo against the opening of hostilities by Japan. It gave Japan a friendly warning that if she forced too drastic

12. This was not the first attempt of the United States to open relations with Korea. Secretary Seward was willing in 1868 to join with France in sending a naval expedition to avenge wrongs to missionaries and to effect a forcible opening, but the French government let the matter drop. In 1871 Mr. F. F. Low, the American minister to China, with a naval force, visited the Han River below Seoul, the capital. The squadron was fired upon by the shore batteries. In return it inflicted several hundred casualties on the Korean defenders but failed to open communications with the government.

surrender terms upon China, she might bring on intervention by the European powers—a warning that Japan failed to heed. To both belligerents the United States was useful in helping to initiate peace negotiations, the first steps to which were taken through the American legations in Tokyo and Peking.

Japan surprised the world by winning an easy victory on both land and sea over her gigantic but clumsy foe. In the treaty of Shimonoseki (April 17, 1895) she exacted hard terms from China—recognition of the independence of Korea (meaning, really, a free hand for Japan in that country), the cession of Formosa and the Pescadores Islands and of the Liaotung peninsula on the mainland of southern Manchuria, the grant of new commercial privileges, and payment of a large war indemnity. Now, however, came the outside intervention of which the United States had warned Japan. The ink on the treaty was hardly dry when Russia, backed by France and Germany, notified the Tokyo Foreign Office that the three powers, "in the interest of the peace of the Far East," could not consent to Japanese acquisition of territory on the mainland. Japan was forced to return to China the Liaotung peninsula, receiving instead an increased war indemnity. The part played by Russia in this diplomatic maneuver marked her as Japan's next rival.

The Open Door Is Threatened

Over the outcome of the Sino-Japanese war the United States showed no great concern, but it was deeply concerned over the events that quickly followed. The three powers that had vetoed Japan's acquisition of the Liaotung peninsula soon showed that their motive was not the preservation of China's territorial integrity but merely the prevention of its violation by Japan. They had no qualms about taking slices of Chinese territory for themselves.

Early in November 1897 two German missionaries were murdered by Chinese in Shantung province. Within two weeks of the event,

a German naval and military force expelled the Chinese garrison at Tsing-tau on Kiaochow Bay on the southern side of the Shantung peninsula and took possession of the port. The German government demanded from China an indemnity for the murders, punishment for the provincial governor, consent to the establishment of a German coaling and naval station in Kiaochow Bay, and exclusive mining and railroad rights in Shantung province. The Chinese government, having no means of resistance and no allies, bowed to the German demands and on March 6, 1898, signed a convention granting them in full.

The German action was the signal for similar demands by other powers. Russian naval vessels appeared at Port Arthur on the Liaotung peninsula, and Russia exacted from China a twenty-five year lease of Port Arthur as a naval base, of the neighboring commercial port of Dairen, and of additional portions of the peninsula. With these virtual cessions of territory Russia secured exclusive railway and other economic rights in Manchuria, with privileges of policing and administration that left little more than a shadow of Chinese authority in that area.

France had already (between 1862 and 1885) annexed Cochin China and established a protectorate over the remainder of the Indo-Chinese peninsula, at the expense of Chinese claims to suzerainty. Not to be outdone by Germany and Russia, she now demanded and got a lease of Kwangchow Bay on the south China coast and special mining and railroad rights for French citizens in China's three southern provinces, adjoining the French protectorate.

Great Britain's interests, like those of the United States, would have been best served by preserving China's territorial integrity against such encroachments as those of Germany, Russia, and France, but after trying in vain to dissuade those powers from the game of grab that they were playing, she joined in it herself. For the port of Weihaiwei, facing Port Arthur across the Strait of Pechili, she obtained a lease for as long as Russia should hold Port Arthur. She also secured an enlargement of her leased territory of Kowloon on the mainland adjoining Hong Kong and recognition of her peculiar economic interests in the Yangtse Valley.

The "break-up of China" had apparently begun. The Chinese government was unable to resist the aggressions of great powers armed with modern weapons. If the process now begun should continue, China would soon be carved up into colonies and spheres of influence of the competing states of Europe. For American interests in China, the future looked dark. American policy since 1844 had been to insist on equality of opportunity—the open door—for American trade with China; and as a means of keeping the door open, it had fostered the preservation of China's territorial integrity. Now China was faced with being torn apart piece by piece, and who could hope that the powers that appropriated the pieces would not favor their own nationals and discriminate against outsiders like the Americans?

The Chinese Market and the American Surplus

The prospect of being excluded from the Chinese trade was particularly alarming to American business interests in the 1890's, for China had come to hold a prominent place in their vision of future markets for American products. American industry was turning out an increasing surplus of manufactured goods. The agricultural South and West were afflicted with falling prices for their cotton, tobacco, and foodstuffs—the result, in part at least, of inadequate markets. Realizing that if the United States would sell its surpluses abroad, it must accept the complementary surpluses of foreign lands, James G. Blaine and other leaders advocated the reciprocal lowering of tariff barriers. The failure of Blaine's plan for an American customs union was mentioned in another chapter.[13] Blaine did suc-

ceed in securing an amendment to the McKinley tariff of 1890 which empowered the President to impose specified rates of duty upon certain commodities (otherwise duty-free) when imported from any country which should impose upon products of the United States duties which he deemed "reciprocally unequal and unreasonable."

Armed with this bargaining weapon, Secretary Blaine succeeded in negotiating executive agreements with ten countries by which they reduced or abolished import duties on various American agricultural and manufactured products.[14] The ten were Brazil, the Dominican Republic, Guatemala, Honduras, Nicaragua, Salvador, Spain (for Cuba and Puerto Rico), Great Britain (for her West India islands and British Guiana), Germany and Austria-Hungary (the last two as producers of beet sugar). There was also "an informal commercial arrangement with France," by which the French government agreed to apply minimum tariff rates to a small number of American products.[15]

By the Wilson-Gorman tariff of 1894, Congress abruptly terminated these agreements, arousing the resentment of the American and European nations that had participated in them. When the Dingley tariff of 1897 raised American duties to new high levels, European antagonism became more general. The products of American low-cost manufacture were penetrating European markets, competing successfully with European industry in its home area, while the United States on economic grounds found a mouth piece in the Austro-Hungarian Foreign Minister, Count Goluchowski. In an address in the late autumn of 1897, he complained of the "destructive competition with transoceanic countries" and warned that the peoples of

13. See p. 177.

14. The actual negotiation of these agreements was placed in the hands of John W. Foster. See D. S. Muzzey, *James G. Blaine, A Political Idol of Other Days* (New York: Dodd, Mead & Co., 1934), pp. 437–58, for a good account of this episode.
15. U. S. Tariff Commission, *Reciprocity and Commercial Treaties* (Washington, D.C.: Government Printing Office, 1919), pp. 153–55.

Europe "must fight shoulder to shoulder against the common danger" and "must close their ranks in order successfully to defend their existence." [16]

Anticipating such resentment abroad, and realizing that in the long run any nation must import in order to export, advocates of reciprocity had succeeded in incorporating certain mild reciprocity provisions in the Dingley tariff act of 1897. One of these, the so-called "argol provision," empowered the President to lower the American rates on argols, brandies, wines, paintings, and statuary imported from countries that would agree to make equivalent reductions in favor of products of the United States.[17] A second provision directed the President to impose specified duties on coffee, tea, tonka beans, and vanilla beans —articles otherwise on the free list—when imported from any country whose duties or other exactions upon products of the United States the President should deem to be "reciprocally unequal and unreasonable." A third provision empowered the President to negotiate reciprocal trade treaties with other governments, but with the "joker" that such treaties must not only be approved by the Senate in the usual way but must also secure approval of the House of Representatives.

The results of these cautious gestures toward reciprocity in a tariff act that erected new high barriers against international trade may be quickly stated. Under the treaty provision, treaties with seven countries were negotiated but never ratified. Threat of im-

position of a duty on coffee under the penalty provision made possible negotiation with Brazil of an agreement establishing favorable rates for American flour, condensed milk, watches and clocks, rubber articles, and other items. The "argol provision" of the act proved to have some bargaining value. Agreements made under this provision secured reductions of tariff rates on American imports into Great Britain, France, Germany, the Netherlands, Italy, Spain, Portugal, and Bulgaria. Most of the reductions in duty thus secured were small, however, and had little effect upon the course of American trade. The agreements were terminated by the next tariff act, adopted in 1909, but most of the reductions made in favor of the United States were permitted to continue.[18]

The "argol agreements" and the prospect (though unfulfilled) of reciprocity treaties to be made under the provisions of the act of 1897 alleviated somewhat the danger of European discrimination against American industry—the threat that Count Goluchowski had voiced so dramatically. The threat itself, however, had the effect of turning American eyes afresh to the Far East, especially to China. China had been to some extent a market for American goods for a century. If Europe should close her markets to American exports, there was still China, where the stirrings of a modernization movement seemed to promise "four hundred million customers" for the products of the West. It was for these reasons that threats to the open door in China were so alarming to some Americans in 1898.

16. *Literary Digest,* 15 (December 11, 1897), 964.
17. *Argol* is defined by Webster as "a grayish or reddish crust or sediment in wine casks; crude tartar."

18. U. S. Tariff Commission, *Reciprocity and Commercial Treaties,* pp. 213, 261.

21

The United States Looks Outward

The last three chapters have traced United States foreign policy along parallel paths from the close of the Civil War to the middle or late 1890's. Chapter 18 presented the story of schemes of territorial expansion and their fate, from Seward's fruitless quest for Caribbean bases to Cleveland's rejection of a treaty for the annexation of the Hawaiian Islands. Chapter 19 followed the development of the Monroe Doctrine from the rise and fall of Maximilian's Mexican Empire to Cleveland's and Olney's vigorous assertion of the doctrine in 1895, with some attention to the beginnings of the kindred Pan-American movement. Chapter 20, finding a unifying theme in certain economic interests—fisheries, fur sealing, foreign markets, and the China trade—arrived at a point where the future of China as a vast market for American exports appeared imperiled by the aggressions of the European powers against the Middle Kingdom at a time when the depression of the 1890's gave that market special significance. In all these matters, in its attitude toward Latin America, toward expansion, toward defense of the open door in China, the United States had reached a turning point in its history. Though few Americans were aware of the fact, the nation stood at the threshold of a career as a world power.

Thirty years before (in 1868), Secretary Seward had complained that "the public mind," preoccupied with the domestic questions resulting from the Civil War, refused "to entertain the higher but more remote questions of national extension and aggrandizement." That the attitude of "the public mind" had changed since Seward's day became apparent when Cleveland's rejection of the Hawaiian treaty was widely denounced in Congress and the press, by Republicans generally and even by some Democrats. The enthusiastic and bipartisan support given Cleveland when he threw down the gauntlet to Great Britain in the Venezuela dispute was evidence of the same change.

By the 1890's the United States was, as the naval historian Mahan expressed it, "looking outward." Expansion was again popular;

a new phase of Manifest Destiny had begun.[1] The Republicans revived that phrase in 1892, and four years later wrote into their platform an ambitious expansionist program. They called for a foreign policy "firm, vigorous, and dignified," for "a naval power commensurate with [the nation's] position and responsibility," for control of the Hawaiian Islands, for a Nicaraguan canal "built, owned and operated by the United States," and for "a proper and much-needed naval station in the West Indies." Republican victory in 1896 was followed by the War with Spain, the acquisition of a colonial empire in the Caribbean and the Pacific, and the assumption of leadership among the powers in the defense of the open door in China and of China's territorial integrity. The party that had launched this program won easily at the polls in 1900. The "public mind" evidently approved an aggressive foreign policy.

The New Manifest Destiny

The reasons for this change in popular psychology are not susceptible of precise definition or measurement. It is possible, however, to point to certain intellectual currents and material facts that help to account for the change.

One such intellectual current was the Darwinian theory of evolution, popularized in the United States by historian John Fiske and others. Darwin taught that in the biological world, higher life-forms evolved through natural selection—the "survival of the fittest" in the "struggle for existence." This hypothesis was easily adapted to sociological theorizing, even in the international sphere.[2] If a ruthless struggle for existence among biological species resulted in the survival of the "fittest," or biologically "best," a similar struggle among races or nations might be expected to produce similar results. Thus ruthless international competition could be justified in the name of "progress." With a frank racism, popular writers like Fiske and the Congregational clergyman Josiah Strong foretold the day when Anglo-Saxons, especially the American branch of the family, through their energy and the virtues of their institutions, should dominate the world. "And can anyone doubt," asked Strong, "that the result of this competition of races will be the 'survival of the fittest'?"[3]

Another racist approach was represented by a leading political scientist of the day, Professor John W. Burgess of Columbia University; but Burgess, after two years of advanced study in German universities, included Germans with Anglo-Saxons as constituting the world's elite in the arts of government. The Teutonic nations, which had perfected, in the national state, the best form of government yet devised on earth, were, he wrote, "called to carry the political civilization of the modern world into those parts of the world inhabited by unpolitical and barbaric races; i.e., they must have a colonial policy."[4]

This language would seem to mean that the expansion of the United States into backward and misgoverned areas, which Fiske and Strong had seen as destiny, in Burgess' teach-

1. Frederick Merk in *Manifest Destiny and Mission in American History: A Reinterpretation* (New York: Alfred A. Knopf, 1963), chap. 11, objects to the use of "manifest destiny" to characterize the expansionism of the 1890's. His contention that, in contrast to the "colonialism" of the later period, the earlier manifest destiny always assumed the consent of annexed populations, needs considerable qualification. At any rate, expansionists of the 1890's believed in destiny, as did their grandfathers, and used the same phrase.

2. See Richard Hofstadter, *Social Darwinism in American Thought, 1860–1915* (Philadelphia: University of Pennsylvania Press, 1944).
3. These writers are discussed in this context in J. W. Pratt, *Expansionists of 1898* (Baltimore: The Johns Hopkins Press, 1936), chap. 1, and from a dissenting viewpoint in Merk, *Manifest Destiny and Mission*, pp. 238–46.
4. J. W. Burgess, *Political Science and Comparative Constitutional Law*, 2 vols. (Boston: Ginn and Company, 1890), 1: 30–39.

ing took on the character of an obligation to civilization. It was apparently so understood by one of his students in Columbia Law School, young Theodore Roosevelt. Strangely enough, when as a result of the war with Spain, the United States set out to "have a colonial policy," Burgess bitterly dissented and even censured Roosevelt, his own pupil, for his part in promoting that policy.[5]

These men had wide circles of readers, and their expansionist language must have helped to shape the national mood, whether it was basic to their own thinking or only peripheral.

A fourth writer, about whose influence on public opinion and public men there can be no doubt, was Captain (later Rear Admiral) Alfred Thayer Mahan. In the year of Burgess' treatise (1890), Mahan published his own masterpiece, *The Influence of Sea Power upon History, 1660–1783.* The simple thesis of this work was that a wise cultivation of sea power had raised England in a century and a quarter from a second-rate power to the world's most powerful state, and from this he theorized that without sea power no nation could attain a position of first importance in the world. Being a patriotic American, he was naturally anxious to see his own nation profit by the British example. Not only in his original book, but in essays published in various magazines throughout the 1890's,[6] he urged his fellow countrymen to build up their sea power in order that the United States might be enduringly prosperous and influential. Widely read and respected at home and abroad, friend and confidant of Theodore Roosevelt and Senator Henry Cabot Lodge, Mahan exerted a potent influence upon the current of affairs.

What was the nature of the "sea power" whose possession Mahan thought indispensable to national greatness? He defined it broadly as "all that tends to make a people great upon the sea or by the sea." Thus it included commerce, merchant marine, navy,

naval bases at strategic points, and overseas colonies. All of these England had. The United States had a growing commerce—most of it carried in ships under other flags; it had, when Mahan first wrote, only the rudimentary beginnings of a modern navy. It possessed no colonies or outlying naval bases. Without these, the ships of war of the United States would

> be like land birds, unable to fly far from their own shores. To provide resting-places for them, where they can coal and repair, would be one of the first duties of a government proposing to itself the development of the power of the nation at sea.[7]

Specifically, in addition to the upbuilding of her navy, Mahan urged the United States to acquire bases in the Caribbean and the Pacific. Without American control of the Caribbean and the isthmian region, the piercing of the isthmus by a canal would be "nothing but a disaster to the United States." Bases in the Caribbean, then in the hands of other powers, the United States must not obtain "by means other than righteous; but," he declared with an obvious fling at the rejection of Seward's and Grant's annexation projects,

> a distinct advance will have been made when public opinion is convinced that we need them, and should not exert our utmost ingenuity to dodge them when flung at our head.[8]

Like Seward, Mahan foresaw a great commercial future in the Pacific. But he went further than Seward in his prophecy that that ocean would be the theater of a gigantic struggle between Western and Oriental civilizations—a struggle in which the United States would be in a front-line position. Hence the possession of outposts in the Pacific was of crucial importance. The issue of such a contest might well be determined by "a firm hold of the Sandwich [Hawaiian] Islands by a

5. Pratt, *Expansionists of 1898,* p. 11; Merk, *Manifest Destiny and Mission,* p. 245.

6. Collected in the volume, A. T. Mahan, *The Interest of America in Sea Power, Present and Future* (Boston: Little, Brown and Company, 1897).

7. A. T. Mahan, *The Influence of Sea Power upon History, 1660–1783* (Boston: Little, Brown and Company, 1890), p. 83.

8. Mahan, *The Interest of America in Sea Power,* pp. 102–3.

great, civilized, maritime power," and the United States was "naturally indicated as the proper guardian for this most important position."

Mahan's philosophy was basically economic. At the root of sea power was trade, the source of national wealth and power. Without trade, a nation might still need a navy for coast defense, but other elements of sea power —colonies, bases, merchant marine—would lose their significance. Thus Mahan was quite in accord with the current urge for trade expansion, for wider foreign markets.

The intensified quest for wider markets was one consequence of the economic depression of the 1890's. Another consequence, at least in the opinion of one historian, was a psychic crisis in the American collective mind. The depression, together with the revelation in 1893, in Frederick Jackson Turner's famous essay, "The Significance of the Frontier in American History," that the American frontier had ceased to be, led to widespread frustration. This feeling was expressed, in the words of Richard Hofstadter, in "an intensification of protest and humanitarian reform" on one hand and, on the other, in a mood "of national self-assertion, aggression, expansion." The war with Spain was to fit this mood exactly, serving "as an outlet for expressing aggressive impulses while presenting itself, quite truthfully, as an idealistic and humanitarian crusade." [9]

The intellectual atmosphere and the psychological mood suggested by these samplings help to explain why American public opinion was more receptive to proposals of overseas

expansion in the 1890's than it had been in Seward's day. There was also the contagion of European neo-imperialism. From the 1870's onward, the great powers of Europe were engaged in a new race for colonial possessions, in Asia, in Africa, and among the islands of the Pacific—a race brought home to the United States by the triangular quarrel over Samoa. If there was, indeed, any virtue in colonies, the United States would need to act quickly in order to get its share. "The great nations," wrote Henry Cabot Lodge in 1895, "are rapidly absorbing for their future expansion and their present defence all the waste places of the earth. It is a movement which makes for civilization and the advancement of the race. As one of the great nations of the world, the United States must not fall out of the line of march." [10]

The fact should, however, be emphasized that the influences responsible for the new expansionism were as yet chiefly intellectual and emotional, not economic. Despite the growing importance of foreign markets for the surplus of America's industrial production, most businessmen were still unconvinced of the need for colonies. Colonies, in the eyes of the average businessman, were not only difficult and expensive to administer; they meant foreign complications, perhaps war. Rather than engage in risky colonial ventures, he preferred to rely on the high quality and low prices of American products, backed by such assistance as the government could give through favorable treaties and the like, to insure their entry into the world's markets. Not until the spring and summer of 1898 did changes in the international picture convince the American businessman that colonial possessions might be economically advantageous; and even then the possessions that caught his eye—the Philippines, primarily—were valued less for themselves than for their supposed utility in affording entry to the markets of China.[11]

9. Richard Hofstadter, "Manifest Destiny and the Philippines," in Daniel Aaron, ed., *America in Crisis: Fourteen Crucial Episodes in American History* (New York: Alfred A. Knopf, Inc., 1952), pp. 173–200. Turner's essay is reprinted in F. J. Turner, *The Frontier in American History* (New York: Henry Holt and Company, 1920), pp. 1–38. Another writer credited with influencing expansionist policy was Brooks Adams, who believed that control of Asia might postpone for America the decline into "barbarism" that was the common fate of empires. See Walter LaFeber, *The New Empire: An Interpretation of American Expansion, 1860–1898* (Ithaca, N.Y.: Cornell University Press, 1963), pp. 80–85.

10. H. C. Lodge, "Our Blundering Foreign Policy," *The Forum*, 19 (1895), 8–17.

11. Pratt, *Expansionists of 1898,* pp. 252–59.

Expansion Becomes Republican Policy

The administration of Benjamin Harrison (1889–1893) was the first to show substantial evidence that it had been influenced by the ideas and tendencies just described. Harrison's Secretary of the Navy, Benjamin F. Tracy, had either read the manuscript of Mahan's *Influence of Sea Power upon History* or been otherwise indoctrinated with that author's sea power philosophy. He was the first Navy Secretary since the Civil War to propose the building of an up-to-date fighting fleet. His *Annual Report* of 1889 called for a fleet of twenty battleships, twelve for the Atlantic and eight for the Pacific, equal to the best in armor, armament, and speed. Congress in the next year authorized the building of three first-class battleships, the *Indiana, Massachusetts,* and *Oregon,* which, with the *Iowa,* were to form the backbone of the fleet in the war with Spain in 1898.[12]

Harrison's first Secretary of State, James G. Blaine, emulated Seward and Grant in attempts to secure naval bases in Santo Domingo and Haiti. He failed because of political complications in the two island republics. Harrison himself urged Congress repeatedly but unavailingly to assist in the building of a Nicaragua canal by guaranteeing the bond issues of the Maritime Canal Company and acquiring in return, for the United States, ownership of all or a majority of the company's stock. Harrison, Tracy, and John W. Foster, Blaine's successor in the State Department, were all sympathetic to the proposal for annexation of Hawaii. They would probably have succeeded in accomplishing it by treaty if the opportunity had occurred before

12. See Harold and Margaret Sprout, *The Rise of American Naval Power, 1776–1918* (Princeton: Princeton University Press, 1939), chaps. 12, 13; G. T. Davis, *A Navy Second to None* (New York: Harcourt, Brace & World, Inc., 1940), chaps. 3–6. The new navy had begun with the authorization in 1883 of three steel cruisers and a dispatch boat (the "White Squadron"). From 1883 to 1889 Congress had authorized some thirty additional vessels, including the second-class battleships *Maine* and *Texas.*

the Democratic victory of November 1892.

The second Cleveland administration (1893–1897), therefore, while alert to the need of foreign markets, was, in terms of territorial expansion, an interlude between two Republican regimes, of which the first attempted, and the second carried out, an aggressively expansionist foreign policy. It is true that in the 1896 presidential race the battles over "free silver" and the tariff absorbed popular attention almost to the exclusion of foreign policy issues. It is also true that William McKinley, the successful Republican candidate, had devoted his political career to such domestic problems as tariff and currency and was innocent, when he entered office, of any aggressive intentions in the international sphere. Taking office in the midst of the depression, he hoped, like his friend and political sponsor, Mark Hanna, that his administration could be signalized by a "policy of domestic economic amelioration." Foreign complications were the last thing that he desired. To the anti-expansionist Carl Schurz he gave verbal assurance that under his administration there would be "no jingo nonsense," no scheming for the annexation of Hawaii. The aging John Sherman, his first Secretary of State, was of like mind—"opposed to all acquisitions of territory not on the main land."

But McKinley was soon to yield to the expansionist forces within the Republican party, and before he had been in the White House eighteen months, the United States had annexed Hawaii and was involved in a war from which it emerged with a colonial empire in the Pacific and the Caribbean.

Hawaiian Annexation Revived

McKinley's first surrender to the expansionists was on the Hawaiian question. Forgetful, apparently, of his promise to Carl Schurz, the President gave his consent to the negotiation of a new treaty of annexation, and such a treaty, providing for the annexation of Hawaii as a territory, was signed on June 16,

1897, and sent to the Senate on the same day. The Senate took no action, however, prior to the adjournment of the special session of Congress.

Former opponents of annexation, Democrats and domestic sugar men, rallied to oppose the new treaty. An unexpected protest from Japan, which had a special interest in Hawaii because of the large number of Japanese that had recently settled in the islands, brought a vigorous response from Washington. Theodore Roosevelt declared to Mahan: "If I had my way we would annex those islands tomorrow . . . I would . . . hoist our flag over the island leaving all details for after action." While the State Department assured the Japanese minister that annexation would not jeopardize vested Japanese rights, secret instructions were sent to the commanding officer of the United States naval forces in Honolulu to raise the United States flag and declare a provisional protectorate over the islands at the first indication of a resort to force on the part of the Japanese, and preparations were made to dispatch the new battleship *Oregon* to Hawaii in case of need. Such precautions proved unnecessary. The Japanese government professed itself satisfied with the assurances given by the State Department, and in December 1897, its protest was withdrawn.

The "yellow peril" in Hawaii, although it stimulated the friends of annexation in the United States, failed to convert its opponents. By March 1898, it was evident that the treaty could never command a two-thirds majority in the Senate. The alternative of a joint resolution had already been considered, and on March 16 such a resolution was introduced in the Senate, only to languish there until the War with Spain and the victory at Manila Bay provided a new argument for the need of Pacific naval bases.

Civil War in Cuba

The War with Spain was itself not the product of an expansionist urge in the United States, but of a distressing situation in Cuba that became intolerable to American sentiment. Spain's misgovernment of its Cuban colony had been notorious for many decades, and Cubans had periodically risen in armed revolt to demand independence or at least autonomy. Reforms promised by the Spanish government at the close of the Ten Years' War (1868–1878) had ended slavery in Cuba but otherwise had brought little relief to the Cuban people. The cost of the war had been saddled upon the island population. Ninety percent of the revenues collected in Cuba went either into service on the debt or into the pockets of Spanish officialdom and military in the island. Cuba continued under the autocratic rule of a Spanish captain general, while a benighted commercial policy hampered Cuba's trade with its neighbors, like the United States, and even laid heavy taxes on exports to Spain itself.

An already bad situation was made worse by the worldwide economic depression that began in 1893 and by the United States tariff law of 1894, which reimposed a duty upon raw sugar from abroad. Economic distress now combined with political discontent to produce, in February 1895, an armed revolt against Spanish rule. A so-called republican government was set up in eastern Cuba, where large sections fell under insurgent control, and a Cuban *junta* in New York dispensed propaganda and tried desperately to secure money and arms from sympathetic Americans.

In Cuba the war was waged with ruthless ferocity on both sides. The insurgents made it their policy to destroy cane fields, sugar mills, and other property in the hope of thus rendering the island valueless to Spain. In February 1896, the newly appointed captain general, Valeriano Weyler, inaugurated a "reconcentration" policy, ordering the entire population of large districts of central and western Cuba into the cities and towns, which were surrounded with *trochas* or trenches, fortified with barbed wire and guarded by blockhouses at frequent intervals. Cubans who disobeyed the order were regarded as insurgents and were shot on sight. For the many thousands of women, children, and old men herded in the concentration camps, there was no provision of adequate shelter, food, or sanitation. Famine and disease were rife, and by the spring of 1898 it was estimated that at least 200,000 of the *reconcentrados* had died out of a total population of only 1,600,000.

The Cuban war affected intimately American economic interests and American humanitarian sentiment. American capital to the amount of forty to fifty million dollars was invested in Cuba—in sugar and tobacco plantations, sugar mills, manganese and iron mines, and other properties. Trade between Cuba and the United States, in good years, amounted to as much as $100,000,000. The effect of the war upon many of these enterprises was disastrous. The sugar crop dropped from 1,050,000 tons in 1894 to 200,000 in 1896; tobacco from 450,000 to 50,000 bales. Exports fell from $60,000,000 in 1895 to $15,000,000 in 1896. American businessmen who made their living from investments in Cuba or trade with Cuba had an obvious reason for desiring a termination of the war. Much more important, probably, was the reaction of humanitarian and religious sentiment in the United States to the barbarities attendant upon the Cuban conflict, especially to the suffering and death inflicted upon innocent noncombatants in the concentration camps.

Of these barbarities the American public was supplied with vivid and frequently exaggerated accounts by the "yellow press," led by William R. Hearst's New York *Journal* and Joseph Pulitzer's New York *World*. These and other papers sent talented reporters and artists to Cuba, and their descriptions of conditions in the island were widely published through the news services of the metropolitan papers that employed them. Spanish atrocities were played up to the virtual exclusion of insurgent ruthlessness, and a wave of sympathy for the *reconcentrados* swept the United States. Americans contributed with customary generosity for the relief of suffering, but as the war dragged on without prospect of victory for either side, there was a rising demand that the United States intervene to end the struggle and to secure independence for Cuba.

The demand for intervention, which would almost inevitably involve war with Spain, arose plainly from humanitarian rather than from economic considerations. While much of the Protestant religious press and numerous daily newspapers, both Democratic and Republican, clamored for intervention in behalf of the Cubans, mouthpieces of business—trade journals and resolutions of boards of trade and chambers of commerce—with few exceptions advocated a hands-off policy.[13] American business in general, which by the fall of 1897 was rapidly recovering from a prolonged economic depression, was fearful that a war with Spain would interrupt its upward march to prosperity. Fear of the losses that the Spanish navy might inflict upon American commerce was joined with fear that war expenditures might produce inflation. Practically the only business interests which agitated for intervention were seaboard firms that normally engaged in trade with Cuba, and such firms advocated neither Cuban independence nor armed intervention. They voiced a simple desire for the restoration of peace in order that trade might flourish. Nor is there any evidence that Americans with investments in Cuba worked for or desired intervention by the United States. There is proof, on the contrary, that a number of such persons or companies warned the State Department that they would suffer more heavily from a war between Spain and the United States than from the existing civil war.

Intervention on humanitarian grounds ought to be divorced from any motive of profit for the intervening power, and it is notable in this case that the advocates of intervention usually said nothing of annexing Cuba or, if they mentioned that possibility at all, did so only to disclaim it. Senator Lodge, who in 1895 had spoken of Cuba as a "necessity" to

13. The attitude of business and the churches toward intervention in Cuba is elaborated in Pratt, *Expansionists of 1898,* pp. 232–52, 279–89.

the United States, indicated a year later that he would be satisfied if it were "in friendly hands, in the hands of its own people." Other senators, speaking for intervention, either declared themselves opposed to annexation or professed a willingness to wait until the hand of destiny and the desire of the Cuban people should bring about union in some indefinite future. Most of the prominent newspapers also disclaimed all selfish designs on Cuba. Although the New York *Tribune* preferred to leave the question open, the *Journal, World, Sun, Herald, Times,* and *Journal of Commerce,* of the same city, denounced any suggestion of annexation. "No annexation talk so far as Cuba is concerned!" declared the *Sun. ".* . . For human lives and the liberty of human beings, for Cuba Libre; not for an extension of United States territory!" And the *World* concurred: "We are not going to filibuster under the guise of honor or philanthropy." As far as the American public was concerned, intervention, if it came, should be intervention for *Cuba libre*—for a Cuba free and independent, not a Cuba transformed from a colony of Spain to a colony of the United States.

The United States Intervenes

The situation in Cuba that made such a strong appeal to the humanitarian sentiment of the American public, was also one of which the United States government could not avoid taking official cognizance.[14] American citizens, usually naturalized Cubans, were frequently arrested by the Spanish authorities, and official interposition was necessary to secure their release, which was effected in every instance. It was also necessary to patrol the coasts of the United States, at considerable expense to prevent or break up attempts at "gunrun-

ning" by Cuban sympathizers. In the spring of 1896 both houses of Congress passed a concurrent resolution declaring that belligerent rights should be accorded the insurgents, but this declaration, being merely a statement of opinion on the part of Congress, was ignored by President Cleveland and Secretary of State Richard Olney.

Both Cleveland and President William McKinley, who succeeded him on March 4, 1897, desired to avoid intervention. Both, however, tendered their good offices to Spain for a settlement of the difficulty. Cleveland, furthermore, intimated in his last message to Congress, that the United States could not indefinitely stand aside and watch the cruel struggle continue, and McKinley made this position still clearer in instructions to the new minister to Spain in July 1897. Prospects for a settlement brightened in September when the assassination of the Spanish Prime Minister, Cánovas, brought in the Liberal Sagasta ministry, which was pledged to a more generous and humane colonial policy. The new ministry recalled General Weyler, gave assurance that the reconcentration policy would be abandoned, and promised a limited degree of autonomy to the Cuban people through the election of their own legislature or *cortes*.

President McKinley welcomed the reform program in his annual message of December 6, 1897, and bespoke for Spain an opportunity to carry it out, but warned again that if the new policy failed to pacify the island, "our obligations to ourselves, to civilization and humanity" might require intervention.

The grant of limited autonomy to Cuba was, as it turned out, doomed to failure. It was not acceptable to the insurgent leaders, who now declared they would accept nothing short of complete independence, nor was it acceptable to the many peninsular Spaniards in Cuba, who resented the prospect of being ruled by a native Cuban legislature. Any chance for success that it may have had was frustrated by a series of unfortunate incidents that suddenly inflamed relations between Spain and the United States.

On February 9, 1898, the New York

14. For elaboration of the diplomacy leading to the War with Spain, see J. W. Pratt, "The Coming War with Spain," in P. E. Coletta, ed., *Threshold to American Internationalism: Essays on the Foreign Policies of William McKinley* (New York: Exposition Press, 1970), pp. 35–76.

Journal printed, with a photographic facsimile, a private letter from Dupuy de Lôme, Spanish minister in Washington. The letter, which had been stolen from the minister's correspondent by an insurgent sympathizer in Havana, described President McKinley in unflattering terms as "weak and a popularity-hunter." The letter also raised doubts about Spain's good faith in carrying out the reform program and in current trade negotiations with the United States. De Lôme's immediate resignation and an apology from the Spanish government ended the episode but left an increment of ill will and distrust.

Six days later the United States battleship *Maine* was destroyed by an explosion at her anchorage in the harbor of Havana, whither she had been sent on a "courtesy call" following some rioting in that city early in January. Some 266 American seamen lost their lives. The cause of the catastrophe was never determined. The *Maine's* forward magazines had exploded, but a board of American naval officers, examining the wreck with divers, found unmistakable evidence that the initial explosion had been that of a submarine mine, which had in turn set off the magazines.[15]

The report of the navy board was not made public until March 28, when the President sent it to Congress, but in the meantime many of the American people, guided by the sensational newspapers, had adjudged Spain guilty of the act of destruction. "The readers of *The Journal*," boasted that New York paper in March, "knew immediately after the destruction of the *Maine* that she had been blown up by a Spanish mine."[16] "Remember the Maine!" became the popular watchword.

While Congress, for the most part, refrained from recrimination over the *Maine* tragedy until after the naval experts had reported, there was, after the middle of March, an intensified denunciation in the Senate of Spanish

atrocities in Cuba. On March 17, Senator Redfield Proctor of Vermont described to the Senate what he had seen and heard during a recent unofficial visit to Cuba, in the course of which he had toured the four central and western provinces. Outside of Havana, where conditions seemed almost normal, the situation, he said, "is not peace nor is it war. It is desolation and distress, misery and starvation." Of about 400,000 persons who had been driven into the concentration camps, "one-half have died and one-quarter of the living are so diseased that they can not be saved." Outside the camps there was only desolation—no crops, no domestic animals; everything of value was destroyed. He described Captain General Blanco, Weyler's successor, as an "amiable gentleman" with good intentions but without capacity to relieve the situation or put down the rebellion. Proctor made no recommendation beyond remarking that he was opposed to annexation. He merely reported his observations, in calm and unimpassioned language.

Senator Proctor's speech convinced many who had been skeptical of the revelations of the yellow press. Even the business interests that had hitherto opposed intervention now began to concede that something must be done and that business could stand the shock of war without disaster. The *Wall Street Journal* reported on March 19 that the speech had "converted a great many people in Wall Street." Senator Proctor's statements, "as many of them expressed it, . . . made the blood boil."[17]

By this time the President was under heavy

---

15. A second investigation made by the Navy thirteen years later, when the hull was raised, reached the same conclusion. A Spanish board of investigation, meeting just after the disaster, concluded that the only explosion had been an internal one.

16. *Literary Digest,* 16 (1898), 367.

17. LaFeber, *The New Empire,* p. 403, conjectures that of the forces pushing McKinley toward war in late March and early April 1898, "perhaps the most important was the transformation of the opinion of many spokesmen of the business community who had formerly opposed war." This idea runs through pp. 379–406. His thesis is repeatedly qualified by "perhaps," as in the sentence quoted. The period that he emphasizes in this chapter is one in which war had become almost inevitable, and businessmen were telling themselves that war might not hurt so much after all and would perhaps be preferable to continued uncertainty. He apparently assumes, furthermore, that businessmen always reached their decisions for business reasons, overlooking the fact that they were not

pressure from the public, the press, and from virtually all Democrats and many Republicans, in House and Senate, to take vigorous action against Spain. Some historians have pictured him as yielding to such pressure against his better judgment and his devotion to peace. A more likely analysis depicts him as simply following up the policy stated in his July instructions and repeated in his annual message—that is, unless Spain could, within a reasonable time, bring peace to Cuba, the United States would intervene. Spain thus far had not only failed to pacify Cuba; she was now held responsible for the loss of the *Maine* and the death of 266 American sailors. McKinley's patience was exhausted, but he would give the Spanish government one more chance. On March 27, he sent to Madrid his final proposal for a peaceful settlement of the Cuban question. Let Spain, he said, abandon at once the reconcentration policy, grant an armistice until October 1, and enter, through McKinley, into peace negotiations with the insurgents. A telegram on March 28 added that the President regarded Cuban independence as the only satisfactory outcome of the proposed peace negotiations.

In Madrid, the Sagasta ministry were caught on the horns of a dilemma. If they refused McKinley's demands, a disastrous war with the United States appeared certain. If they conceded those demands in full, popular indignation in Spain might overthrow the ministry and even the reigning dynasty. The only hope of salvation lay in securing support from the European powers against intervention by the United States. Such support the Spanish government had already sought from all the major courts and cabinets of Europe, and in every capital except London it had received expressions of willingness to participate in a joint demonstration against the United States—if someone else would take the lead.

The crowned heads of continental Europe, and the government of the French Republic as well, all desired the preservation of the shaky Spanish Empire and dynasty; none was willing to assume leadership in such a crusade. In England, Queen Victoria was sympathetic to the Spanish Queen Regent, as was her Foreign Secretary, Lord Salisbury; but British public opinion was overwhelmingly pro-United States, and neither Salisbury nor any other member of the ministry dreamed of opposing American policy in Cuba. The only result of the Spanish supplications, aside from a hazy suggestion for mediation by the Pope, was a visit to President McKinley by the ambassadors of six powers on April 6, in which they begged him, in the interest of humanity, to refrain from armed intervention in Cuba. McKinley replied politely that intervention, if it came, would be in the interest of humanity.[18]

Without hope of substantial support from Europe, the Spanish government went as far as it dared toward meeting McKinley's proposals. In its reply (cabled to Washington on March 31) it announced that reconcentration was being abandoned and that an armistice would be granted upon application by the insurgents. Instead of accepting McKinley's proposal of mediation, the note stated that the Cuban parliament, provided for by the autonomy arrangement, was to meet in May and should be the instrument of pacification—an evident rejection of the demand for independence. Spain was willing to submit to arbitration the question of responsibility for the destruction of the *Maine*.

A few days later, April 9, the Spanish government declared an armistice on its own initiative, and on the following day Minister Stewart L. Woodford cabled from Madrid that he believed a solution satisfactory to all parties was obtainable.

Paying slight heed to these last-minute concessions and assurances, which still fell short of his demands, McKinley sent to a warlike Congress on April 11 a message in

immune to humanitarian sympathy. One need not doubt that the last-minute conversion of many businessmen made it easier for McKinley to follow the course dictated by the logic of his earlier consistent statements, but that is quite different from implying that his decision for war was economically motivated.

18. Orestes Ferrara, *The Last Spanish War: Revelations in "Diplomacy"* (New York: Paisley Press, 1937).

which he described the outcome of the recent negotiations as unsatisfactory and declared that:

> In the name of humanity, in the name of civilization, in behalf of endangered American interests which give us the right and the duty to speak and to act, the war in Cuba must stop.

He asked authority to use the military and naval forces of the United States "to secure a full and final termination of hostilities between the Government of Spain and the people of Cuba."

Congress, which had been champing at the bit for weeks, seized upon the President's message with eagerness, but debated for a week whether the resolutions that it was about to pass should constitute merely a recognition of the independence of the Cuban people or should include also recognition of the existing but insubstantial republican government of Cuba. The administration, opposing recognition of the existing regime, which it did not believe could meet Cuba's needs, finally prevailed. Between one and three on the morning of April 20 (though officially on April 19), Congress adopted the resolutions, the final vote being 42 to 35 in the Senate, 311 to 6 in the House.[19]

The resolutions as adopted, and approved by the President on April 20, declared that "the people of Cuba are, and of right ought to be, free and independent," demanded that Spain "at once relinquish its authority and

government in the Island of Cuba and withdraw its land and naval forces from Cuba and Cuban waters," and empowered the President to use the armed forces of the United States to enforce this demand. Without a record vote or any expression of dissent, the Senate had adopted, and the House had accepted, a fourth resolution prepared by Senator Henry M. Teller of Colorado, declaring:

> That the United States hereby disclaims any disposition or intention to exercise sovereignty, jurisdiction, or control over said Island except for the pacification thereof, and asserts its determination, when that is accomplished, to leave the government and control of the Island to its people.

The Colorado senator had remarked that he wished to make it impossible for any European government to say, "when we go out to make battle for the liberty and freedom of Cuban patriots, that we are doing it for the purpose of aggrandizement for ourselves or the increasing of our territorial holdings." He wished this point made clear in regard to Cuba, "whatever," he added, "we may do as to some other islands."

Thus with a specific renunciation of annexationist designs in Cuba but with freedom of action with respect to Spain's other colonies —Puerto Rico, the Philippines, the Carolines and Marianas—the United States entered the conflict with Spain. Upon being informed of the approval of the Cuban resolutions, the Spanish government at once severed diplomatic relations and on April 24 declared war. Congress responded with a declaration of war the next day, making it retroactive to April 21. On the twenty-second the President had instituted a blockade of portions of the coast of Cuba.

---

19. The large minority vote in the Senate is not to be construed as opposition to intervention but as dislike of the form of the resolutions. The Senate had originally passed, by a vote of 67 to 21, its own resolutions including recognition of the republican government in Cuba.

The war, begun for motives that were primarily humanitarian and sentimental, was to have momentous consequences for both Spain and the United States. For Spain, it meant the loss of the last remnants of her once great colonial empire. To the United States, it brought the sudden assumption of unprecedented imperial responsibilities and elevation to the status of a "world power." And all this was accomplished in one of the shortest and least costly wars in history.

22

The War with Spain and Its Fruits

The Collapse of Spanish Power

The military and naval details of the war require only brief mention. The conflict was pathetically one-sided from the beginning. The Spanish navy, which on paper appeared something like the equivalent of the American fleet, had really nothing to match the four new United States battleships, the *Massachusetts, Indiana, Iowa,* and *Oregon,* the last of which had joined the Atlantic Fleet after a two-months' voyage around the Horn from San Francisco. Spanish ships and crews, moreover, were in a wretched state of inefficiency, and the officers were imbued with a defeatist spirit, while the United States Navy, thanks to the energetic efforts of Assistant Secretary Theodore Roosevelt, was well prepared and spoiling for a fight. The Spanish army in Cuba outnumbered the American expeditionary forces but was ill-equipped for war, and though Spanish soldiers fought bravely and stubbornly, the severance of their supply line from Spain made their case hopeless.

Though Cuba had furnished the sole cause of the war, the first important blow fell in the Far East. Months before the outbreak of war, the President had been briefed by Senator Orville H. Platt of Connecticut and by Assistant Secretary of the Navy Theodore Roosevelt on the importance of Manila as a commercial port, and Roosevelt had submitted a memorandum suggesting that in the event of war with Spain, the Asiatic squadron "should blockade, and if possible take Manila." [1]

1. T. J. McCormick, *China Market: America's Quest for Informal Empire, 1893–1901* (Chicago: Quadrangle Books, 1967), pp. 107–8.

Even earlier, in June 1896, a naval officer, Lieutenant William W. Kimball, had prepared a contingency plan for such an operation.[2] Contrary to long tradition, therefore, Roosevelt was not acting on a sudden inspiration on February 25, 1898, when he cabled Commodore George Dewey, in Hong Kong, to "begin offensive operations in the Philippines" as soon as he should be informed of a declaration of war. And although other drastic orders issued by the impatient Roosevelt on that day when Secretary Long had left him as acting Secretary were countermanded by his superiors, the orders to Dewey were allowed to stand. It may be assumed, therefore, that they represented administration policy.

Dewey, whom Roosevelt had personally picked for the command and had provided with the necessary ships and ammunition, received the news of war at Hong Kong. After putting his ships into war trim at neighboring Mirs Bay on the Chinese coast, he steamed south to the Philippines and in the early morning of May 1 led his squadron of light cruisers past the forts and through the rumored mine fields that guarded the entrance to Manila Bay. At dawn he spied the Spanish ships, equal in number to his own but hopelessly antiquated, anchored in line off the naval station of Cavite. Circling repeatedly past the enemy squadron, the American cruisers fired so effectively that before noon the entire Spanish naval force lay sunk or burning, at the cost, to the American squadron, of eight men slightly wounded. Dewey occupied Cavite and held control of Manila Bay, while the War Department prepared to send an army to take possession of the city of Manila, the Philippine capital. By the end of July, some eleven thousand United States troops under General Wesley Merritt had arrived in the Philippines, and on August 13 they entered Manila against little more than token resistance by the Spanish. As an incident of their expedition to the Orient, the American forces had occupied the

island of Guam in the Spanish Marianas. Unconnected with the outside world by cable, the Spanish officials in Guam knew nothing of the war until the cruiser Charleston entered Apra harbor and tossed a few shells into a deserted fort. Unable to return the fire, which they had at first mistaken for a salute, they surrendered without resistance.

Meanwhile, the main Spanish fleet, four armored cruisers and three destroyers, commanded by Admiral Cervera, had left the Azores for Cuban waters. Dodging American patrols, it slipped into Santiago harbor on the south coast of Cuba. Capture or destruction of this fleet now became the prime objective of the war in this theater, since without a fleet Spain could not possibly defend Cuba for any extended period. The Atlantic Fleet, under Commodores William T. Sampson and Winfield Scott Schley, closed in around the narrow entrance to Santiago Bay, while an army of sixteen thousand regulars and volunteers, commanded by Major General W. R. Shafter, landed on the Cuban coast a few miles east of Santiago and fought its way toward that city. On July 1, in the hard-fought engagements of El Caney and San Juan Hill, the Americans pierced the outer defenses of Santiago and reached high ground, whence they could look down on the city and harbor. Cervera was caught between the Army and Navy of the United States. On the morning of July 3, under orders from the captain general in Havana, he led his squadron out of the harbor in a dash for a safer haven farther west. In a running fight westward along the coast, all his ships were sunk or run ashore in a burning condition. American losses were one man killed and one wounded. On July 16 the city of Santiago was surrendered to the Americans.

The war was now virtually over, and on July 18 the Spanish government requested the good offices of France in arranging for a termination of hostilities. Before the fighting ended, however, another American expeditionary force, commanded by General Nelson A. Miles, landed in Puerto Rico and proceeded, against feeble Spanish resistance, to take possession of that island.

2. J. A. S. Grenville and G. B. Young, Politics, Strategy, and American Diplomacy (New Haven: Yale University Press, 1966), pp. 269–78.

McKinley and the Philippines

With the Spanish application for peace terms before them, President McKinley and his advisers had some difficult decisions to make. The independence of Cuba was a foregone conclusion; it must obviously be detached from Spain, and the Teller Amendment to the resolutions of intervention eliminated the possibility of annexation. But what of Spain's other islands—Puerto Rico, Guam, and above all the Philippines, an extensive and populous area where Spanish misrule had brought about native rebellion only less formidable than that in Cuba? The Teller Amendment said nothing of these, and its author had expressly excluded "some other islands" from his ban on the annexation of Cuba.

McKinley had approved the plan to attack the Philippines. On the day after Dewey's victory, and before its completeness was known in Washington, the President decided to send an army to occupy Manila, and on May 11 he approved a State Department proposal to insist on cession by Spain of a "coaling station" in the Philippines, presumably Manila. The intention at this stage was to allow Spain to retain the remainder of the archipelago.[3] That plan was abandoned in the course of the summer. The point to be emphasized here is that McKinley was well aware of the significance of the Philippines in the commercial strategy of the Far East and was determined to profit from Dewey's victory by acquiring a base within five hundred miles of the coast of China. Decisions to push the annexation of Hawaii and to occupy Guam as a stepping stone between Hawaii and the Philippines were part of the same pattern.

McKinley, then, seems to have needed little prodding from the group of Republicans in Washington who had been urging expansion ever since Hawaii had invited annexation five years earlier. Prominent in this group were Roosevelt, Senator Henry Cabot Lodge, and Captain Mahan, who had been recalled from

inactive duty to help guide the strategy of the war as a member of the Naval War Board. Roosevelt had resigned his office as Assistant Secretary of the Navy to go to Cuba as lieutenant colonel of the "Rough Riders" regiment, but he kept in touch by letter with his friend Lodge. Before going to Cuba, he seems to have felt some temporary qualms about taking the Philippines,[4] but he was soon writing Lodge of the importance of securing possession of those islands as well as Puerto Rico. Lodge had written to another friend, three days after Dewey's victory: "We hold the other side of the Pacific, and the value to this country is almost beyond recognition." On no account, he added, must we "let the islands go . . . they must be ours under the treaty of peace." Now he was able to assure Roosevelt: "Unless I am utterly and profoundly mistaken the Administration is now fully committed to the large policy that we both desire."[5]

A number of influential senators also favored the "large policy," as did the powerful New York *Tribune* and large sections of the press that spoke for business and religion.

American businessmen, who had generally opposed intervention in Cuba and had seen no need for colonies, underwent a sudden conversion on the latter point in the spring of 1898. It was at this time that American business was taking alarm at the aggressions of the powers in China, described in an earlier chapter.[6] In February and March, chambers of commerce and boards of trade in cities on both the east and west coasts of the United States were urging the State Department to take energetic measures for the protection of Ameri-

---

3. McCormick, *China Market,* pp. 107–8.

4. R. H. Miller, ed., *American Imperialism in 1898: The Quest for National Fulfillment* (New York: John Wiley and Sons, Inc., 1970), p. 10.
5. Except as otherwise indicated, the account of the settlement with Spain is based chiefly on J. W. Pratt, *Expansionists of 1898* (Baltimore: The Johns Hopkins Press, 1936), pp. 259–78, 289–316, and chap. 9. For a recent detailed account of the negotiations, see P. E. Coletta, "The Peace Negotiations and the Treaty of Paris," in P. E. Coletta, ed., *Threshold to American Internationalism* (New York: Exposition Press, 1970), chap. 4.
6. See Chapter 20.

can interests. An American Asiatic Association was formed in New York to agitate for the preservation of American rights and interests in the Orient. The New York *Journal of Commerce,* which had hitherto scoffed at colonies, isthmian canal schemes, and big-navy programs, now declared itself in favor of an isthmian canal, the annexation of Hawaii, and an increased navy—all for the purpose of strengthening the United States in the Pacific and safeguarding its rights in China.

Dewey's victory at Manila found the Chinese situation unimproved but seemed to many to offer an effective remedy. With a naval base in the Philippines, way-stations in Hawaii and perhaps in Guam, with a growing navy and the prospect of an isthmian canal through which the fleet could slip easily into the Pacific, might not the United States become at last a great Pacific power, quite capable of defending its interests in the Orient against aggressions from Europe? Many trade journals in all parts of the country agreed with the New York *Journal of Commerce,* which declared that to give up those islands now "would be an act of inconceivable folly in the face of our imperative future necessities for a basis of naval and military force on the Western shores of the Pacific."

Converted to a belief in colonialism by the special situation in the Far East, American businessmen found it easy to apply the same philosophy to the Caribbean. The erstwhile anti-imperialist *Journal of Commerce* insisted that Puerto Rico be retained and suggested that it might be necessary to keep control over Cuba in spite of the Teller Amendment. The former Spanish islands might furnish not only outlets for trade but also profitable fields for investment. It seemed that the war for humanity might be made to pay dividends in hard cash.

But the war might also pay dividends in the salvation of human souls. Of this the larger Protestant churches were as firmly convinced as were businessmen of its material advantages.[7] Religious groups that had favored the war as a humanitarian crusade regarded the quick and easy victory as a sure sign of divine approval and as a divine command to continue the good work in islands freed from Spanish tyranny. Although there were some dissenting voices, in general Methodists, Baptists, Presbyterians, Congregationalists, and Episcopalians, together with several of the minor sects, united in urging that the United States accept the civilizing and Christianizing mission that Providence had placed before it; and just as businessmen prepared to take advantage of the opportunities for trade and investment in the former possessions of Spain, so the churches began laying plans for new missionary enterprise. If the new career upon which the United States was about to enter was to be tinged with economic imperialism, it was also to be, as one religious writer remarked, "the imperialism of righteousness."

Businessmen were interested in the Philippines principally because of their proximity to China and would presumably have been satisfied with the retention of a secure naval base in the islands. To that, McKinley had been committed since the first week of the war. But the churches wanted something more—an opportunity to practice their benevolence among the seven million people of the Philippines. Their zeal may have helped to shape the President's decision to demand cession of the entire archipelago. On one occasion, at any rate, he attributed his decision to religious influence. Months after the decision had been reached, he told a Methodist delegation at the White House that in answer to his earnest prayers

---

7. Quakers and Unitarians, who had opposed the war, were skeptical of any benefit accruing from "imperialism." The Catholic Church was excusably dubious about Protestant enthusiasm for missionary work in islands that had for centuries been Catholic under Spanish rule. "The unfortunate people of Manila," said *Ave Maria,* "will remember Dewey's bombardment as a restful holiday compared with the times that will come if the preachers ever invade the Philippines, bringing divorce and sundry other things with them." Other Catholic publications, however, and several members of the Catholic clergy joined with Protestants in welcoming the opportunity for civilizing work in the islands. They expressed little fear of the results of Protestant competition.

for guidance the revelation had one night come to him that "there was nothing left for us to do but to take them all, and to educate the Filipinos, and uplift and civilize and Christianize them, and by God's grace do the very best we could by them as our fellow-men for whom Christ also died."

Spain Surrenders Her Colonial Empire

The decision to demand from Spain the cession of all the Philippines was not reached, however, until after months of uncertainty. The reply to the Spanish request for peace terms offered an immediate cessation of hostilities on condition that Spain relinquish all authority over Cuba, cede to the United States Puerto Rico and an island in the Ladrones (Marianas), and consent to American occupation of the city and harbor of Manila pending the conclusion of a definitive peace treaty that should determine the future of the Philippines. On this basis an armistice protocol was signed on August 12. American and Spanish peace commissioners were to meet in Paris not later than October 1. Thus several months would be allowed for discussion and the testing of public opinion before the final decision on the Philippines would need to be made.

As peace commissioners to represent the United States, the President selected William R. Day, who resigned as Secretary of State to become chairman of the commission, Senators Davis and Frye, Republicans, and George Gray, Democrat, and editor Whitelaw Reid of the New York *Tribune*. A majority of the commission—Davis, Frye, and Reid—were expansionists; all three favored retention of the entire Philippine archipelago. Gray, formerly a strong supporter of Cleveland's Hawaiian policy, was still an "anti," while Day occupied a middle ground.

Instructions to the peace commissioners were dated September 16. By this time the desires of American business and religion had had ample opportunity to be heard, and McKinley had also received from abroad significant hints that the United States would do well

to retain the Philippines. John Hay, formerly ambassador to Great Britain, who now succeeded Day as Secretary of State, had previously sent word that England would be glad to see the United States keep the islands. Japan expressed a similar preference, though adding that Japan herself would be willing to join with the United States and a third power in a joint administration. These friendly gestures were presumably designed to forestall the possibility that the Philippines might fall into the possession of a Germany still hungry for Pacific islands. The American ambassador in Berlin, Andrew D. White, had dropped an unauthorized hint, after Dewey's victory, that the United States did not wish the islands, and the Germans had sent a naval squadron to Manila, where its commander, Admiral von Diederichs, made things difficult for Dewey by his disregard of the latter's rules of blockade. Should the United States decide to abandon the Philippines, the Germans were on hand to promote their own interests.[8]

By the instructions of September 16, the American commissioners were told that the United States could not accept less than full sovereignty over the principal island of Luzon. In Paris the commissioners were advised by Americans who had been in the Philippines that division of the islands was undesirable. The archipelago formed an economic unit with Manila as its commercial center. Davis, Frye, and Reid, accordingly, cabled to the President a strongly worded argument for the retention of the entire group. McKinley, who had just sounded public opinion during a tour of the Midwest, had apparently reached a similar conclusion. On October 26 Secretary Hay cabled the commissioners that the United States must retain all the Philippines. Small heed was paid to the group of Filipino natives, led by Emilio Aguinaldo, who demanded inde-

8. The old idea that either von Diederichs or his government wished to provoke hostilities with the United States or to seize the Philippines by force has been discredited. See T. A. Bailey, "Dewey and the Germans at Manila Bay," *American Historical Review,* 45 (1939), 59–81; L. B. Shippee, "Germany and the Spanish-American War," ibid., 33 (1925), 754–77.

pendence and had set up a government of their own near Manila. It was generally agreed, by whites who knew the Philippines, that the natives were not prepared for self-government. Independence under these conditions might breed anarchy and anarchy would invite foreign—quite possibly German—intervention.

Spain, reluctant to surrender the last remnants of her once great colonial empire, held out as long as possible for retention of all or part of the Philippines, but in the end could do nothing but accept the American terms. The blow was softened somewhat by an agreement to pay her $20,000,000 for public works and improvements in the islands.[9]

By the treaty of peace signed in Paris on December 10, 1898, Spain relinquished "all claim of sovereignty over and title to Cuba," ceded to the United States the Philippine Islands, Guam in the Marianas or Ladrones, Puerto Rico, "and other islands now under Spanish sovereignty in the West Indies."[10] The inhabitants of the ceded territories were promised "the free exercise of their religion," but it was stipulated that their "civil rights and political status" should "be determined by the Congress." For the first time, in a treaty

9. The American commissioners were unsuccessful in an attempt to purchase the island of Kusaie in the Carolines, which was of considerable interest to American missionaries and was also desired as a cable station by capitalists planning to lay a cable from Hawaii to Manila. The German government, disappointed in the Philippines, had exacted from Spain a secret promise not to cede the Carolines to the United States. They were subsequently sold to Germany, and with them went also the Pelew Islands and the Marianas with the exception of Guam. Pratt, *Expansionists of 1898*, pp. 302–4, 340–44. Aside from the disposition of the Philippines and Carolines, the only serious disagreement between the American and Spanish commissioners at Paris was over the Cuban debt. Spain wished this assumed by either the Cubans or the United States. The United States insisted successfully that responsibility for it be retained by Spain.

10. The "other islands" of Spain in the West Indies were Culebra and other tiny islands off the east end of Puerto Rico and the Isle of Pines south of the west end of Cuba. Long in dispute between Cuba and the United States, the Isle of Pines was finally made over to Cuba in 1925.

acquiring territory for the United States, there was no promise of citizenship. As in the case of Alaska, there was no promise, actual or implied, of statehood. The United States thereby acquired not "territories" but possessions or "dependencies" and became, in that sense, a "colonial" power.

The Senate Debates Imperialism

The treaty, however, still had to run the gauntlet of the Senate, and there it encountered determined opposition. Few senators appear to have objected seriously to the annexation of tiny Guam or of Puerto Rico, which was near by and peopled chiefly by the white race, though of alien tongue. But annexation of the Philippines was a much greater break with American tradition. Their distance, six thousand miles from San Francisco, their population of seven million Malays, including a minority of pagans and Mohammedans, the existence of a vigorous independence movement whose leaders were as hostile to American as to Spanish sovereignty —all these factors made their acquisition seem to many, in and out of the Senate, a dangerous venture in imperialism and a violation of time-honored American principles. An Anti-Imperialist League was organized to combat annexation, while in the Senate many Democrats and a few Republicans made clear their purpose to vote against ratification of the treaty.

Debate on the treaty was in executive session, but beginning weeks before the treaty was sent to the Senate (January 4, 1899), senators found opportunity for public expression of their views in debating a number of resolutions dealing with the acquisition of colonial territory. The most important of these, introduced by Senator Vest of Missouri, declared:

That under the Constitution of the United States no power is given to the Federal Government to acquire territory to be held and governed permanently as colonies.

Democratic senators, ably supported by Republican George F. Hoar of Massachusetts, argued that under the Constitution there was no place for a colonial system like that of the European powers—a system based "upon the fundamental idea that the people of immense areas of territory can be held as subjects, never to become citizens." It was against that very system that Americans had rebelled in 1776. If the Philippine Islands were taken under American sovereignty, therefore, their inhabitants must become citizens with all the rights of citizens. They could not be governed as subjects, nor could they and their products be excluded from the United States by restrictions on immigration and importation. American agriculture and American labor would thus be subjected to unchecked competition from the Filipinos. It was foolish to suppose, furthermore, that American free institutions would operate successfully among a people so widely different in race, language, religion, and customs from the people of the United States. Both those who opposed and those who favored annexation regarded colored races and any bred in the tropics as unqualified to participate in democratic self-government.[11]

But even if it were granted that the United States might constitutionally annex the Philippines and govern them as a colony, was it expedient to do so? No, answered opponents of the treaty. Departure from the spirit of our republican institutions in the government of colonies would spell the destruction of those institutions at home. Possession of the Philippines, moreover, would embroil the United States in the international politics of the Far East and endanger the Monroe Doctrine. How could we forbid Europe to interfere in the Western Hemisphere when we were interfering in the Eastern? "The Monroe Doctrine is gone!" lamented Senator Hoar. Opposition senators also minimized the trade advantages to be expected from annexation

and ridiculed the religious argument. "In order to Christianize these savage people," said one senator, "we must put the yoke of despotism upon their necks; . . . Christianity can not be advanced by force."

All of these arguments were answered by the supporters of the treaty. Of special interest is the constitutional argument advanced by Senator Orville H. Platt of Connecticut, since it anticipated subsequent decisions of the Supreme Court.[12] The right to acquire and the right to govern territory, said Platt, were sovereign rights, which the United States enjoyed in common with other sovereign nations, and the right to govern implied the right to establish whatever form of government was suitable to the condition of the territory and the character of its inhabitants—be they savages, barbarians, or civilized folk. Platt denied that there would be any obligation to admit the Philippines as a state or to confer citizenship upon the Filipinos. He denied that either the people or the products of the islands could be admitted to the United States without the consent of Congress.

Senator Platt affirmed, in brief, precisely what his opponents denied—that the United States had all the powers necessary to establish and maintain a full-fledged colonial system.

The debate continued from early December until February 6, 1899, the date set for a vote on the treaty. Since Democratic votes were essential for ratification, it was important that Senator Gray of Delaware, a leading Democrat, had been a member of the peace commission, and though at first opposed to taking the Philippines, now defended the treaty in the Senate. William Jennings Bryan, titular head of the Democratic party, came to Washington to urge Democratic support of the treaty, arguing that peace should be made as soon as possible and that the question of freeing the Philippines could be disposed of later. It is possible that he won two votes that might

---

11. Christopher Lasch, "The Anti-Imperialists, the Philippines, and the Inequality of Man," *Journal of Southern History,* 24 (August 1958), 319–31.

12. *Downes* v. *Bidwell,* 182 U.S. 244 (1901); see also J. W. Pratt, *America's Colonial Experiment* (Englewood Cliffs, N.J.: Prentice-Hall, Inc., 1950), pp. 157–64.

otherwise have been cast against the treaty.[13] On February 6, 1899, the Senate approved the treaty by a vote of 57 to 27—a single vote above the necessary two-thirds majority. Fifteen Democratic, Populist, or Independent senators voted with the Republican majority, while two Republicans, Hoar of Massachusetts and Hale of Maine, voted in the negative.

Meanwhile, on February 4, two days before the Senate approved the treaty, hostilities had broken out between American troops at Manila and Filipino insurgents led by Aguinaldo, who were ready to fight for their independence against Americans as they had fought against Spaniards. In annexing an empire the United States had also annexed a war, which was to prove much longer and more troublesome than that with Spain. Not until July 1902 was armed resistance in the Philippines effectually subdued.

Hawaii, Wake, and Tutuila

The War with Spain, which gave the United States Puerto Rico, the Philippines, and Guam, also furnished the impetus necessary to effect the long-delayed annexation of Hawaii, and it was followed within a year by the partition of the Samoan group, in which the United States received the island of Tutuila, where since 1878 it had possessed rights for a coaling station in Pago Pago harbor.

In March 1898, as previously noted, the advocates of Hawaiian annexation abandoned hope of accomplishing their object by treaty and brought into the Senate a joint resolution of annexation. The resolution, however, made no headway until June.[14] Dewey's victory at Manila turned American eyes to the Pacific as never before. If the American flag was to remain in the Philippines—if the United States, from the Philippines as a base, was to

defend its rights in China—Hawaii, it was argued, was essential as a naval base and coaling station en route to the Far East.[15] The Hawaiian government, on advice from its minister in Washington, instead of proclaiming its neutrality in the war, placed all the facilities of Honolulu harbor at the disposal of the United States and even offered to make an alliance. The alliance offer was not accepted, but the friendly attitude of Hawaii and the fact that by aiding the United States it was subjecting itself to possible Spanish reprisals, enabled the annexationists to argue that Hawaii should be brought under the American flag as a reward for friendly aid and for its own protection. Thus the war situation greatly strengthened the case for annexation. Much was also said of the "yellow peril" in Hawaii—the rapid growth of its Japanese population and the danger that Hawaii might be absorbed in Japan's waxing empire.

These arguments proved adequate, in the end, to secure a victory for the annexationists. A new joint resolution was introduced in the House of Representatives on May 4, three days after Manila Bay, and passed the House by a large majority on June 15. Senate opponents brought out all the timeworn arguments. They could delay but could not defeat the measure, which passed the Senate on July 6, 1898, by a vote of 42 to 21, and received the President's signature on the seventh. On the following August 12—the date of the signature of the armistice protocol with Spain— Hawaii passed formally under the jurisdiction of the United States as a part of its territory.

The Hawaiian Islands, their outpost at Midway, acquired by the United States in 1867,[16] and Guam provided stepping stones to the Philippines and the Far East in general. The wide gap between Midway and Guam was soon filled in by the annexation

---

13. P. E. Coletta, *William Jennings Bryan,* 3 vols. (Lincoln: University of Nebraska Press, 1964–1970), 1: 233–36.

14. For details of the passage of the joint resolution annexing Hawaii, see Pratt, *Expansionists of 1898,* pp. 317–26.

15. Opponents of annexing Hawaii argued that the United States already had, at Kiska in the Aleutians, a fine harbor much nearer the great-circle route to the Orient than was Hawaii. The claim was correct as far as it went, but it took no account of climatic and supply difficulties in the Aleutians.

16. See Chapter 18.

of Wake Island, 2,130 miles west of Honolulu and 1,034 miles from Midway. The naval explorer, Commander Charles Wilkes, had asserted title to Wake for the United States in 1841, but for nearly sixty years no effort had been made to enforce the claim. On January 17, 1899, Commander E. D. Taussig, commanding the gunboat *Bennington,* landed at Wake and took formal possession in the name of the United States.

The year of the Spanish-American War witnessed a new outbreak of native trouble and international friction in Samoa, which was solved the following year by a partition of the islands, the United States receiving Tutuila, while Upolu and Savaii passed to Germany. Britain relinquished all claims to Samoa, receiving as compensation the surrender of German rights in the Tonga and part of the Solomon Islands and territorial concessions in Africa. A treaty of partition was signed in Washington on December 2, 1899. From the treaty the United States obtained no title to Tutuila (subsequently, with the small neighboring islands, known as American Samoa), but merely a renunciation in its favor of German and British claims. All three powers had hitherto maintained the fiction of Samoan sovereignty and independence. The native chiefs of Tutuila, however, formally ceded their island to the United States in 1900, and those of the nearby Manu'a group followed suit in 1904. These cessions were accepted by President Theodore Roosevelt without submission to the Senate or to Congress. The American title seems not to have been questioned, but to remove all doubt Congress, by a joint resolution of February 20, 1929, accepted, ratified, and confirmed the cessions of 1900 and 1904.

The People's Verdict

The expansionist policies growing out of the War with Spain had, in general, been sponsored by Republicans and opposed by Democrats, though with many exceptions in both parties. Under the circumstances it was perhaps inevitable that "imperialism" should become an issue in the presidential campaign of 1900 and that the Democrats should attack their opponents for holding the Philippines by armed force against the will and despite the resistance of the most vocal native faction. Accordingly, while the Republican platform of that year sought to justify the establishment of American sovereignty in the Philippines as a necessary consequence of the breakdown of Spanish rule and promised to confer upon the Filipinos "the largest measure of self-government consistent with their welfare and our duties," the Democrats officially denounced "the Philippine policy of the present Administration" and "the greedy commercialism" which had dictated it. "We are unalterably opposed," said the Democratic platform, "to the seizing or purchasing of distant islands to be governed outside the Constitution and whose people can never become citizens."

> . . . we favor [the platform continued] an immediate declaration of the Nation's purpose to give to the Filipinos, first, a stable form of government; second, independence; and third, protection from outside interference such as has been given for nearly a century to the republics of Central and South America . . .

the last reference obviously being to the Monroe Doctrine. "Imperialism," said the Democrats, "is the paramount issue" in the campaign.

Mr. Bryan, the Democratic candidate, fully endorsed—probably had dictated—the party's platform declarations with regard to the Philippines. The attack upon imperialism, however, was not confined to the Democrats. Many prominent men of both parties joined hands in the Anti-Imperialist League, which conducted a vigorous campaign of propaganda based upon the principle of "government by the consent of the governed."[17] Opposed, from the beginning, to annexation of the Philippines, the League joined the Democratic

17. F. H. Harrington, "The Anti-Imperialist Movement in the United States, 1898–1900," *Mississippi Valley Historical Review,* 22 (1935), 211–30; R. L. Beisner, *Twelve against Empire: The Anti-Imperialists, 1898–1900* (New York: McGraw-Hill Book Company, 1968).

party in denouncing the war of subjugation against the Filipino insurgents and in demanding that they be given independence. After some discussion of the formation of a third party, the League's leaders resolved instead to support Bryan for the Presidency.

Thus, on the surface, the political issue for 1900 seemed clear-cut, but as usual in presidential campaigns, the "paramount issue" did not stand alone.[18] Bryan had insisted upon incorporating, as in 1896, a "free-silver" plank in the Democratic platform. "Bryan would rather be wrong than President," quipped Thomas B. Reed, Republican speaker of the House. Many Republican anti-imperialists, like Senators Hoar and Hale, discovered that they preferred McKinley, with the gold standard and a little imperialism, to Bryan and free silver. Bryan himself, as the campaign progressed, found that his diatribes against imperialism excited little popular enthusiam and shifted his emphasis to an attack on the trusts, the plutocracy, and special privilege. But even if attention had been concentrated on the single issue, there was no black and white difference between the Democratic and Republican positions on the Philippines. Republicans promised "self-government" and had never expressed a determination to hold the Philippines as a permanent possession.

18. T. A. Bailey, "Was the Presidential Election of 1900 a Mandate on Imperialism?" *Mississippi Valley Historical Review,* 24 (1937), 43–52.

The Democrats made no proposal to surrender to Aguinaldo and his insurgents. They promised to "give" the Filipinos "a stable form of government" and independence, but under "protection from outside interference"—a "protectorate" of undefined duration. Who could say whether Filipino liberties would be safer under Republican or Democratic auspices, or under which the United States would run less risk of being involved in Far Eastern politics?

Thus when American voters went to the polls in November 1900, to cast their ballots for McKinley or Bryan, it is none too clear what their votes meant with respect to policy in the Philippines or colonial expansion in general. Certainly those who wished to vote for McKinley and the gold standard, or for McKinley and a continuation of the prosperity that had come in with his administration, could persuade themselves that they were voting for little more "imperialism" than was implicit in the Democratic proposals. But there must have been very many, influenced by the propaganda of business and the churches, who were anxious to vote for a profitable imperialism that was at the same time an "imperialism of righteousness."

At any rate, when McKinley and Roosevelt won the election by a handy popular plurality of nearly 900,000 votes, the Republicans could be pardoned for assuming that the nation had accepted and approved their "large policy" of territorial expansion.

The Spanish-American War, it has been often said, raised the United States to the status of a "world power." After 1898, certainly, the weight and influence of the United States were felt throughout the world as never before. Three phrases sum up the new role of the United States in international politics: (1) dominance in the Caribbean, (2) leadership in the Far East, (3) participation (in a modest way until 1917) in the affairs of Europe. The nation that had suddenly acquired Puerto Rico, Hawaii, and the Philippines had ceased to be land-bound and isolationist. These acquisitions did not cause Uncle Sam's assumption of new world responsibilities; rather, they were a result and a symbol of a new attitude toward the world. Had the United States not been ready to play a part as a world power, it would hardly have insisted upon keeping the Philippines.

The policies that the United States followed during the war and after it were precisely the policies that Admiral Mahan had been preaching throughout the 1890's.[1] Build up the Navy, he had urged; own and control fully whatever isthmian canal is dug; make sure of bases on the Caribbean approaches to the canal; secure Hawaii as an outpost of the Pacific coast. Part of this program was achieved by the events of the war and the resulting Treaty of Paris. The remainder of it was rapidly accomplished thereafter, particularly under the direction of Mahan's disciple, Theodore Roosevelt, who entered the White House in September 1901, after McKinley's assassination.

Roosevelt found a Navy that already comprised some seventeen battleships, built and building. Under his leadership it grew steadily. The United States, which in 1890 had been negligible as a naval power, stood in fifth place in naval strength in 1904, in second place in 1907. After 1912 the German fleet took a small lead, but when war began in 1914, the United States was easily one of the three foremost powers in battleship strength.[2] Outlying naval bases had been developed at Guantanamo Bay in Cuba and at Pearl Harbor in

23

Latin America and the Caribbean, 1899–1917

1. See pp. 194–95.
2. G. T. Davis, *A Navy Second to None* (New York: Harcourt, Brace & World, Inc., 1940), chaps. 8, 9.

the Hawaiian island of Oahu. In the meantime the United States had built its own isthmian canal at Panama and, as a means of safeguarding that vital defense link against European interference, had ringed the Caribbean Sea with protectorates whose governments were friendly and dependable.

The attainment of American supremacy in the Western Hemisphere was facilitated by British accommodation. British retreat in the Venezuela controversy and British friendliness during the Spanish-American War were early steps in what has been called "the great rapprochement," a process that removed all serious causes of Anglo-American friction before the outbreak of war in Europe in 1914. Alarmed by the threat of rising German commercial and naval rivalry, Britain closed or deactivated her naval bases at Halifax and on Puget Sound, concentrated her naval power in European waters, and conceded naval supremacy on both American coasts and in the Caribbean to the United States. In the same spirit she yielded to American desires with reference to isthmian canal policy and the boundary of Alaska, approved the institution of American protectorates in the Caribbean, settled by arbitration a long-standing dispute over fishing rights, and accepted an American policy for Mexico with which her statesmen strongly disagreed. The traditional enemy had become a cooperative friend.[3]

Acquiring the Panama Canal Zone [4]

The focal point of American interest in the Caribbean region was at the site, whether in Nicaragua or Panama, of the future isthmian canal. Here was the key to the naval strategy and national security of the future—a boon to

the United States if firmly held in American hands, a menace if controlled by potential enemies. An earlier chapter [5] has recounted the initial failure of French efforts at Panama, the attempt by American private capital to construct a canal through Nicaragua, and the growing belief in the United States that only a canal under American control was admissible. The events of the war with Spain—the voyage of the *Oregon,* the acquisition of new possessions and new interests in the Pacific—had hardened this belief into a national conviction that was well voiced by President McKinley when he remarked in his annual message of December 5, 1898, that "the construction of such a maritime highway is now more than ever indispensable" and that "our national policy now more imperatively than ever calls for its control by this Government."

For the successful pursuit of such a "national policy" the situation in 1898 seemed more favorable than ever before. Both the Panama and Nicaragua routes were available. At Panama, the new Panama Canal Company, successor to the original French company, had come to the end of its resources and was willing to dispose of its rights if the consent of Colombia could be obtained. In Nicaragua, the Maritime Canal Company had forfeited its concession because of failure to fulfill its contract. The governments of Nicaragua and Costa Rica were willing to dicker with the United States for the rights necessary for the construction of a canal by that route. Finally, Great Britain, which since 1850 had clung to the Clayton-Bulwer Treaty, barring national control of an isthmian canal, was at last in a mood to withdraw or modify that prohibition.

The obstruction of the Clayton-Bulwer Treaty was removed by a new treaty signed by Secretary of State John Hay and Lord Pauncefote, the British ambassador, on November 18, 1901.[6] The new treaty expressly

3. Bradford Perkins, *The Great Rapprochement: England and the United States, 1895–1914* (New York: Atheneum, 1968), pp. 157–59, 185, 230, *et passim.*
4. The account of the acquisition of the Panama Canal Zone and the institution of the Caribbean protectorates is condensed from J. W. Pratt, *America's Colonial Experiment* (Englewood Cliffs, N.J.: Prentice-Hall, Inc., 1950), chaps. 3 and 4. Source citations will be found in that work.

5. Chapter 18.
6. This was the second of two canal treaties signed by Hay and Lord Pauncefote. The first had been amended by the Senate in ways which the British government refused to accept, but the second treaty actually embodied the substance of the Senate's amendments.

abrogated the Clayton-Bulwer Treaty, thus freeing the United States to construct, manage, and police its own canal. The only obligation assumed by the United States was a guarantee that the canal should be open to the vessels of commerce and war of all nations "on terms of entire equality." The treaty was approved by the Senate on December 4, 1901.

The choice of a route was the next hurdle to be overcome. Nicaragua had for years been the favorite location, and it was powerfully supported in Congress by Senator John T. Morgan of Alabama. But Panama now had persuasive advocates, notably William Nelson Cromwell, of the New York law firm of Sullivan and Cromwell, and the Frenchman, Philippe Bunau-Varilla. Both represented the interests of the New Panama Canal Company, whose only hope of saving something from the

wreck of its enterprise lay in sale to the United States. They were fortunate in enlisting in their cause the influential Senator Mark Hanna of Ohio.

The battle of the routes makes a long story, of which only a few high spots will be related here. A commission of engineers reported first in favor of Nicaragua, then switched to Panama when the Company lowered its price for its rights from $109,000,000 to $40,000,000, the figure which the commission had suggested as reasonable. The House of Representatives passed a bill for a Nicaraguan canal. The Senate, after a long debate, amended it to favor Panama. The report of the commission and the persuasive argument of Mark Hanna largely accounted for the change, but they were aided by convulsions of nature. A major volcanic eruption in the island of Martinique and reports of a minor one and an earthquake in Nicaragua itself, pointed to danger to a canal in that volcanic country. Panama seemed exempt from such phenomena.[7] The Isthmian Canal Act, making the Panama route the first choice, was signed by President Theodore Roosevelt on June 28, 1902.

The next act in the drama is one of the most controversial episodes in the history of American foreign policy. The United States needed the consent of Colombia to the transfer of rights from the New Panama Canal Company to the United States, and its consent also to the exercise by the United States in the proposed Canal Zone of the authority necessary to operate and protect the canal. The consent was given in a treaty signed by Secretary of State John Hay and Colombian chargé d'affaires Dr. Tomás Herrán, January 22, 1903. The Colombian Senate, however, unanimously rejected the treaty, holding that the price ($10,000,000) was too low and the impairment of Colombian sovereignty too sweeping.[8] Thereupon the Department of Panama revolted, was promptly recognized as independent and shielded from Colombian vengeance by the United States. A few days later, November 18, 1903, its representative in Washington signed a treaty giving the United States even more privileges than it would have received under the treaty with Colombia. The

United States received in perpetuity the use of a zone across the isthmus, ten miles in width (five miles on each side of the canal), in which it might exercise all the rights and authority that it would possess if actually sovereign. It might take steps to ensure sanitation and to maintain public order in the cities of Colon and Panama, and it might fortify and defend the canal. The United States, in turn, would pay to Panama $10,000,000 at once and $250,000 annually beginning after nine years —the same compensation earlier offered Colombia. In addition, the United States guaranteed and promised to maintain "the independence of the Republic of Panama."

The treaty, it is interesting to observe, was signed for Panama by Philippe Bunau-Varilla. The Frenchman had promoted and helped to finance the revolution and in return had been named the first minister of Panama to the United States.

The circumstances of the Panama revolution—the appearance of American collusion, the veto by the United States of Colombian attempts to suppress the uprising, the unusual haste with which recognition was extended and an advantageous treaty made—created bitter resentment in Colombia and divided opinion in the United States. Mr. Roosevelt, supported by his Secretaries of State and War (Hay and Elihu Root), energetically defended his handling of the Panama crisis. "By far the most important action I took in foreign affairs," he said of it in his *Autobiography*. "I took the canal zone and let Congress debate," he boasted in a public address in 1911. Recent scholars have not shared Roosevelt's confident assurance that he followed the only right procedure, but are inclined to think his action unnecessarily precipitate and unjustified by treaty or precedent.

Colombia, naturally enough, believed that she had suffered a grievous wrong at the hands of the United States. For nearly twenty years all attempts to appease her failed. The United States consistently refused to submit the propriety of its conduct to arbitration. Finally, in 1921, the United States paid Colombia $25,-000,000, the amount that the Colombian

7. Bunau-Varilla took advantage of the Martinique disaster by placing on the desk of every Senator a Nicaraguan postage stamp featuring a smoking volcano in the middle of Lake Nicaragua. Though there was no love lost between Bunau-Varilla and Cromwell, and though each later spoke disparagingly of the other, the two appear to have worked cooperatively during the "battle of the routes" in 1902. See C. D. Ameringer, "The Panama Canal Lobby of Philippe Bunau-Varilla and William Nelson Cromwell," *American Historical Review,* 68 (January 1963), 346–63; but cf. A. H. Dean, *William Nelson Cromwell, 1854–1948* (New York: Privately printed, 1957), pp. 140, 147.

8. D. C. Miner in *The Fight for the Panama Route* (New York: Columbia University Press, 1940), has given the first adequate account in English of conditions in Colombia at the time of the canal negotiations.

Senate presumably would have settled for in 1903. The payment, though accompanied by no apology, was a tacit admission of wrong-doing on the part of the United States. It was reported that senatorial approval of the treaty was made easier by pressure from American capitalists who were to be rewarded with oil concessions in Colombia for bringing about a satisfactory settlement of the old quarrel over Panama.[9]

Transfer of the French property on the Isthmus to the United States took place on May 4, 1904. Construction of the canal, though attended with some bungling at the outset, went forward rapidly, and on August 15, 1914, the Panama Canal was opened to the traffic of the world.

Protectorates in the Caribbean

Control of the Caribbean did not rest solely upon outright annexations of territory, as in Puerto Rico, acquired from Spain in 1898, and the Virgin Islands, purchased from Denmark in 1916,[10] or upon perpetual leases, almost the equivalent of annexation, as in the Panama Canal Zone. Between 1901 and 1917 the United States instituted a system of "protectorates," by which it gained sufficient control of a number of small republics rimming

9. J. F. Rippy, *The Capitalists and Colombia* (New York: Vanguard Press, Inc., 1931), pp. 103–21.
10. The United States had several times negotiated for the purchase of the Danish West Indies, the islands of St. Thomas, St. John, and St. Croix. Seward's treaty of 1867 had died in the Senate. John Hay had signed a second treaty in 1902, only to see it defeated in the Danish Parliament. Fear that Germany might absorb Denmark and claim the islands led Secretary of State Lansing in 1916 to make a generous offer, coupled with a warning that the United States might find it necessary to seize them to prevent their falling into German hands. By a treaty signed on August 4, 1916, the United States purchased the three islands for $25,000,000. After the transfer of sovereignty, March 31, 1917, they were known as the Virgin Islands of the United States. The entire story of the efforts of the United States to acquire the islands is told in C. C. Tansill, *The Purchase of the Danish West Indies* (Baltimore: The Johns Hopkins Press, 1932).

the Caribbean to bind them securely into an American "sphere of influence." The term "protectorate," however, like the word "colony," had no place in the American official vocabulary.

The principal recipients of American "protection" were Cuba, Panama, the Dominican Republic, Nicaragua, and Haiti. The special relations of the United States to these republics were embodied in treaties, no two of which were exactly alike. To only one such state— the Republic of Panama—did the United States actually promise "protection," in the declaration that "the United States guarantees and will maintain the independence of the Republic of Panama." Other treaties, such as those with Cuba and Haiti, contained engagements on the part of the "protected" states not to impair their independence or cede any of their territory to a third party; and the same two treaties permitted intervention by the United States for the maintenance of independence or of orderly government. Since careless public finance was likely to lead to foreign intervention and possible loss of independence, a number of the treaties—those with Cuba, Haiti, and the Dominican Republic—contained restrictions upon, or gave the United States supervision over, financial policy. By the treaties with Cuba and Nicaragua, the United States gained the privilege of using naval bases within the territorial limits of the "protected" states, and by that with Nicaragua, it obtained exclusive canal rights through Nicaraguan territory.

In all the countries of this Caribbean semi-circle of protectorates American investments existed. These no doubt benefited from the increased stability and financial responsibility induced by governmental policy. In the Dominican Republic, Haiti, and Nicaragua that policy resulted in a transfer of the ownership of government obligations from European to American bankers. Yet in none of the five republics save Cuba were American financial interests large or important, and the charge that the Caribbean policy of the United States was primarily one of "financial imperialism" is not sustained by the facts. The dominant motive was clearly political and strategic rather than economic. The acquisition of the Canal Zone and the building of the Panama Canal made the isthmian area a vital spot in the American defense system. It became, then, a matter of the utmost importance that the United States itself should control the bases requisite for the defense of the canal and that no rival great power should obtain a foothold in the vicinity of the canal or on the approaches to it. Hence the securing of base rights in Cuba and Nicaragua, and hence the exaction of nonalienation agreements from Cuba and Haiti and the control of the public finance of these and other Caribbean republics. The establishment of protectorates thus became a species of "preventive intervention," which Theodore Roosevelt, in his celebrated "corollary" message of December 1904, sought to justify as merely an application of the Monroe Doctrine. Still another motive, which influenced different administrations in the United States to varying degrees, was a genuine desire to substitute orderly democratic processes for the chronic addiction to armed revolution that afflicted most of the Caribbean and Central American states.

Panama, whose special relations with the United States have just been described, was the second Caribbean republic to become a protectorate of the United States. Cuba had preceded it, and it was followed by the Dominican Republic, Nicaragua, and Haiti.

Cuba and the Platt Amendment

The end of the war with Spain had left Cuba occupied by the armed forces of the United States but with its future status not clearly defined. Spain had relinquished sovereignty over the island, and the United States had renounced any thought of annexing it. But that renunciation did not absolve the United States, in its own eyes, from responsibility for Cuba's future. President McKinley remarked in his annual message of December 5, 1899, that the United States had assumed "a grave responsibility for the future good government

of Cuba." The island, he continued, "must needs be bound to us by ties of singular intimacy and strength if its enduring welfare is to be assured."

What those ties were to be was defined by Elihu Root, McKinley's Secretary of War. General Leonard Wood, who had achieved many useful reforms as military governor of Cuba, convoked a Constitutional Convention, which sat in Havana from November 1900 to February 1901. It completed a constitution for independent Cuba but failed to carry out a directive of the governor to provide for the relations to exist between the Cuban government and the government of the United States. Secretary Root outlined his concept of what those relations should be in a set of proposals which were introduced in the Senate by Senator Orville H. Platt of Connecticut and were known henceforth as the Platt Amendment. Actually an amendment to the Army Appropriation Bill of March 2, 1901, the amendment authorized the President to terminate the military occupation of Cuba as soon as a Cuban government should have been established under a constitution which provided, among other things, that Cuba should never permit any "foreign power" to gain foothold on its territory, or contract any debt beyond the capacity of its ordinary revenues to pay; that Cuba should consent that the United States might intervene in its affairs for the preservation of Cuba's independence or "the maintenance of a government adequate for the protection of life, property, and individual liberty"; and that Cuba should lease or sell to the United States lands necessary for coaling or naval stations at points to be agreed upon.

The Cuban Convention at first rejected the terms of the Platt Amendment but later accepted them after receiving assurances from Secretary Root that the United States would exercise the right of intervention only in the event of foreign threat or serious domestic disturbance, not in a spirit of "intermeddling or interference with the affairs of the Cuban government."

The new Cuban government was inaugurated on May 20, 1902. The Platt Amendment took its place as an Annex to the Cuban Constitution and was embodied in the permanent treaty of 1903 between Cuba and the United States. It remained in force until 1934, when all of the treaty except the naval base article was abrogated. Under that article the United States enjoyed the use of Guantanamo Bay, on the south coast near Santiago, as a naval station. Under Article 3 the United States exercised the right of intervention from time to time, notably in 1906–1909, following a breakdown of the Cuban government, but so frequently in subsequent years as to violate, in the opinion of many, Root's promise that the article would not result in "intermeddling or interference."[11] Such intervention ceased after 1934, with the treaty basis for it. In the meantime the United States had not only its naval base at Guantanamo, which it kept after 1934, but also the assurance that no rival power would secure a foothold in Cuba.

The Roosevelt Corollary of the Monroe Doctrine

Secretary Root had spoken of the Platt Amendment as supplying a basis in international law for intervention by the United States under the Monroe Doctrine to protect the independence of Cuba. But with how much justice or logic could the United States enforce the Monroe Doctrine against European intervention in turbulent American republics if it took no responsibility for the behavior of such republics or for the fulfillment of their obligations to Europe? The Platt Amendment, by restricting the debt-contracting power of Cuba and by permitting the United States to intervene for the preservation of orderly government, had hinted that the Monroe Doctrine involved certain policing responsibilities for the United States. That idea, though previously suggested from time to time, was now

for the first time written into law. Need for such a principle was emphasized by events in Venezuela in 1902–1903.

In 1901, when the German and British governments were contemplating the use of force to collect debts from the Venezuelan dictator, Cipriano Castro, Roosevelt (as yet only Vice President) wrote to a German friend: "If any South American country misbehaves toward any European country, let the European country spank it"; and in his first annual message as President, a few months later, he declared that the Monroe Doctrine gave no guarantee to any American state against punishment for misconduct, provided that punishment did not take the form of acquisition of territory. When, however, in the winter of 1902–1903, Germans and British actually undertook to bring Castro to terms by a "pacific blockade," anti-German sentiment flared up in the United States, and Roosevelt became alarmed over the possibility that such a situation might produce a serious quarrel between the United States and some European power. The Venezuelan crisis was settled when Castro agreed to submit the question of his debts to arbitration, but no one knew when Venezuela or one of its neighbors might present a new invitation to coercion. It seemed to Roosevelt desirable to find a formula by which all excuse for European intervention in the New World might be removed.[12]

The formula was announced by Roosevelt in 1904, first in May in a letter to Secretary Root, later, in almost identical language, in his annual message of December 6, 1904. As

11. T. P. Wright, Jr., "United States Electoral Intervention in Cuba," *Inter-American Economic Affairs,* 13 (Winter 1959), 50–71.

12. Roosevelt's handling of the Venezuela crisis of 1902–1903 is still a subject of disagreement among historians. One recognized authority, Dexter Perkins, in *The Monroe Doctrine, 1867–1907* (Baltimore: The Johns Hopkins Press, 1937), chap. 5 and pp. 407–11, discounts completely Roosevelt's dramatic story of how he brought the Kaiser to accept arbitration. On the other hand, Howard K. Beale, in *Theodore Roosevelt and the Rise of America to World Power* (Baltimore: The Johns Hopkins Press, 1956), pp. 395–431, and J. W. Pratt in *Challenge and Rejection* (New York: The Macmillan Company, 1967), pp. 22–28, express the belief that the story had some factual basis. Many others have argued that question, pro and con.

stated in the annual message it read as follows:

> Any country whose people conduct themselves well can count upon our hearty friendship. If a nation shows that it knows how to act with reasonable efficiency and decency in social and political matters, if it keeps order and pays its obligations, it need fear no interference from the United States. Chronic wrongdoing, or an impotence which results in a general loosening of the ties of civilized society, may in America, as elsewhere, ultimately require intervention by some civilized nation, and in the Western Hemisphere, the adherence of the United States to the Monroe Doctrine may force the United States, however reluctantly, in flagrant cases of such wrongdoing or impotence, to the exercise of an international police power.

The Dominican Receivership

This "Roosevelt Corollary of the Monroe Doctrine"—so called because it was assumed to follow as a necessary consequence of the Monroe Doctrine—was to serve, whether expressly mentioned or not, as the theoretical basis for the subsequent establishment of protectorates in the Caribbean—in the Dominican Republic, Nicaragua and Haiti. Uncle Sam now assumed the role of international policeman—kindly to the law-abiding, but apt to lay a stern hand upon little nations that fell into disorder or defaulted on their obligations, since disorder or default, if allowed to continue, might invite intervention from outside the hemisphere. The first application of the new doctrine was in the Dominican Republic. In fact, it was a threatening situation in the Dominican Republic that had led to Roosevelt's pronouncement.

The government of the Dominican Republic, or Santo Domingo, since that state won its independence from Haiti in 1844, had been a dictatorship generously tempered by revolution.[13] Revolutions are costly, and by 1904

13. According to Carl Kelsey, "The American Intervention in Haiti and the Dominican Republic,"

the Dominican debt had grown to a figure—some $32,000,000—which the national revenues, as administered by native collectors of taxes and customs, were incapable of servicing. The foreign debt was widely distributed. Portions of it were held in France, Belgium, Italy, and Germany. The largest single creditor, representing both American and British capital, was the San Domingo Improvement Company of New York. From time to time the Dominican government had pledged the customs duties at various ports as security for its debts, and the pledges sometimes conflicted. Intervention by the United States in behalf of the Improvement Company resulted, in 1903 and 1904, in that company's being placed in charge of the collection of customs at Puerto Plata and Monte Cristi on the north coast, bringing protests from the European creditors, who claimed that those same revenues had previously been pledged to them. An international scramble for control of the Dominican customhouses threatened, with the possible development of a situation resembling that in Venezuela which had alarmed Roosevelt a scant two years earlier.

It was under these circumstances that Roosevelt formulated his famous "Corollary," which was without doubt intended as a forecast of coming events. With the encouragement of Thomas C. Dawson, United States minister to the Dominican Republic, President Morales invited the United States to take charge of the nation's custom-houses and administer the collection of import duties for the purpose of satisfying the creditors of the Republic and providing its government with revenue. An executive agreement to this effect was signed on January 20, 1905, but this attempt of Roosevelt to bypass the Senate excited so much criticism that Minister Dawson

Annals of the American Academy of Political and Social Science, 100 (1922), 109–202, 175, in the seventy years, 1844–1914, the Dominican Republic had nineteen constitutions and fifty-three presidents, of whom only three completed the terms of office for which they were elected. See above, pp. 172–73 for an account of the brief restoration of Spanish rule, 1861–1865.

was instructed to put the agreement into the form of a treaty, subject to ratification in the constitutional manner. The treaty was duly signed and its approval urged upon the Senate by President Roosevelt with reasoning based, like his Corollary message, upon the Monroe Doctrine.

Democratic opposition prevented action upon the treaty, but the President, with characteristic determination, put the essence of the arrangement into effect by a new executive agreement, referred to as a *modus vivendi,* signed April 1, 1905. The Dominican government agreed to appoint as receiver of customs a citizen of the United States who should have been nominated by the American President. As in the proposed treaty, 45 percent of the receipts were to be turned over to the Dominican government; the remainder, less costs of collection, was to be deposited in a New York bank, to be apportioned among the creditors of the Republic if the Senate approved the treaty, or returned to the Dominican government if the treaty was finally rejected.

The *modus videndi* remained operative for over two years. During that period the creditors of the Dominican government agreed to a downward adjustment of the debt from over $30,000,000 to $17,000,000. A new $20,000,000 bond issue was floated in the United States, and the proceeds were applied to the paying off of the adjusted debt and to the execution of needful public works in the island. In February 1907, a new treaty was signed, which the Senate promptly approved through the switch of a few Democratic votes to its support. The treaty, proclaimed July 25, 1907, perpetuated the arrangement under the *modus vivendi,* with minor modifications. A general receiver of Dominican customs, named by the President of the United States, was to have full control of the collection of customs duties until the $20,000,000 bond issue should have been liquidated.

The Dominican receivership, under the *modus vivendi* and the subsequent treaty, produced gratifying results. For some four years after the conclusion of the treaty the Republic experienced the unaccustomed blessings of

financial solvency and political stability. Then began a new series of revolutionary disturbances that led to a more drastic form of intervention by the United States.[14]

"Dollar Diplomacy" in Nicaragua

The next Caribbean country to receive the "protection" of the United States was Nicaragua. Intervention in Nicaragua, initiated under William H. Taft as President (1909–1913) and Philander C. Knox as Secretary of State, was a prominent example of the "dollar diplomacy" usually associated with that administration. Dollar diplomacy had a dual character. On one side, it was the use of diplomacy to advance and protect American business abroad; on the other side, it was the use of dollars abroad to promote the ends of American diplomacy. In the first sense it was practiced by many an administration before Taft and since. The employment of American dollars to advance the political and strategic aims of diplomacy was a less familiar technique. There was a hint of it in the Platt Amendment. It was plainly seen in the refunding of the debt and the instituting of the receivership in the Dominican Republic under Theodore Roosevelt. Invoking, as Roosevelt had done, the Monroe Doctrine as their justification, Taft and Knox made a similar arrangement with Nicaragua and sought unsuccessfully to do the same with Honduras and Guatemala.

The setting up of the Nicaraguan customs receivership came at the conclusion of some years of turmoil in Central America, largely the work of the Nicaraguan dictator, José Santos Zelaya. Having lent support to the ousting of Zelaya, Taft and Knox were anxious to bring peace and order to Central America by applying there the same remedy that had been applied with some success for the Dominican Republic. They found a cooperative leader in Nicaragua in the person of Adolfo Díaz, who had eventually succeeded

14. See Chapter 23.

Zelaya as President. A businessman who despised militarism and craved order and good government, Díaz was willing to compromise his country's independence by granting to the United States broad powers of intervention. When he was faced with insurrection, the United States, at his request, landed over two thousand marines in Nicaragua, suppressed the rebellion, deported its leader, and left at Managua, the capital, a "legation guard" of marines that for the next thirteen years (1912–1925) "stabilized" the Nicaraguan government under Díaz and his successors.

Secretary Knox's attempt, with the aid of Díaz, to set up a customs receivership in Nicaragua by treaty was blocked in the Senate, but a receivership was established nevertheless by agreement between Nicaragua, certain American banks, and the State Department. A mixed claims commission reduced claims against Nicaragua from $13,750,000 to a mere $1,750,000. Another mixed commission was given limited control over Nicaragua's spending policy. The policy of Taft and Knox was continued by their successors, President Woodrow Wilson and his first Secretary of State, William Jennings Bryan. To meet Nicaragua's urgent need for funds, and at the same time to provide for the future canal needs of the United States, a treaty signed August 5, 1914, and approved nearly two years later, the Bryan-Chamorro Treaty, provided for a payment of $3 million to Nicaragua in return for the grant of certain concessions to the United States. These included the perpetual and exclusive right to construct a canal through Nicaragua and the right for ninety-nine years to establish naval bases at either end of the route, in the Corn Islands in the Caribbean and on the Gulf of Fonseca on the Pacific.

Two of Nicaragua's neighbors, Costa Rica and El Salvador, contested Nicaragua's right to grant these concessions, which they claimed infringed on their sovereignty. The two governments submitted their case to the Central American Court of Justice, where they won a verdict against Nicaragua. Neither Nicaragua nor the United States accepted the decision.

The Court, created in 1907 with the blessing of the United States, went out of business in 1918 as a consequence of this defiance of its authority.

Thus by 1916 the United States had secured from Nicaragua at trifling cost a perpetual monopoly of the canal route through that country and the privilege of setting up naval bases, if they should be needed, at each end of the route. It had also succeeded, not by treaty but by informal agreement with Nicaragua and the bankers, in reducing and simplifying the Nicaraguan debt and in setting up a customs receivership which would see to it that a suitable portion of the national revenue was applied on the debt. Application of the Roosevelt Corollary, implemented by dollar diplomacy and the landing of a few marines, had made Nicaragua secure against any violation of the Monroe Doctrine.

Wilsonian Intervention

That the treaty which consummated the success of dollar diplomacy in Nicaragua bore the name of William Jennings Bryan was ironical, for Bryan, out of office, had been a severe critic of dollar diplomacy. Other inconsistencies were to follow. The anti-imperialist Wilson administration (1913–1921), with first Bryan and later Robert Lansing as Secretary of State, although promoting independence for the Philippines and self-government for Puerto Rico, was to impose upon Haiti a protectorate treaty of unprecedented severity, and to set up a regime of pure force in the Dominican Republic.

There is perhaps less of contradiction than at first appears between the new administration's policy in the Philippines and Puerto Rico and its policy toward the independent republics of the Caribbean. The Philippines and Puerto Rico, under American tutelage, had been learning the lessons of democracy and conducting orderly elections in which ballots, not bullets, determined the outcome. Perhaps a few years of American tutelage would suffice to complete the political education of the natives of Haiti and the Dominican Republic, who hitherto had found the bullet a more congenial instrument than the ballot. At the very beginning of his administration, Wilson made it clear that he would frown upon revolutions in the neighboring republics. "I am going to teach the South American republics to elect good men!" he remarked with optimism to a British visitor.

Such remarks foreshadowed a new turn in American interventionist policy, in which the promotion of democracy would take its place as an objective beside the preservation of the Monroe Doctrine and the protection of the economic and strategic interests of the United States. Unfortunately, although the new measures were effective in restoring order and preventing revolutions by force, they did little or nothing toward providing a substitute for revolutions in the form of free and fair elections. Whether because of the absorption of effort in World War I or for other reasons, the Washington schoolmaster quite neglected to "teach the . . . republics to elect good men," or to elect any men at all by democratic methods.

Haiti—the Fifth Protectorate

The Negro republic of Haiti, unlike the Dominican Republic, had maintained its independence continuously since the time of Toussaint Louverture. It had also been more successful than its neighbor in meeting the interest payments on its rather large foreign debt; but in the prevalence of corrupt tyranny complicated by frequent revolution it surpassed its rival on the island. In the early twentieth century, corruption grew more flagrant and revolution more frequent, and bankruptcy, default, and the menace of European intervention loomed on the horizon.

Under these circumstances the United States began urging upon Haitian Presidents measures designed to bring some order out of the chaos into which the country had fallen and to guard against European intervention. Mr. Bryan asked for the United States the

right to appoint a customs receiver, as in Santo Domingo, and a financial adviser. He asked the right to supervise Haitian elections, and he asked a nonalienation pledge as to Môle St. Nicolas, a potential naval base at the northwest corner of the island. Negotiations along these lines proceeded, but so kaleidoscopic were the changes in Haitian administrations that no results had been achieved by July 1915, when President Guillaume Sam, following the coldblooded massacre of 170 political prisoners in the government jail, was pulled by an angry mob from his sanctuary in the French legation, thrown into the street, and there assassinated. On the same afternoon (July 28), the U.S.S. *Washington*, flagship of Rear Admiral Caperton, dropped anchor in Port au Prince harbor, and before nightfall the marines had occupied the town.

Exasperated at the long reign of anarchy in Haiti and at the failure of treaty negotiations, Washington was resolved to use the new crisis to enforce its demands upon the Haitian government. By taking control of the customhouses and impounding the revenue, and by the threat of continued military government if its wishes were not obeyed, the United States was able to dictate the choice of a President as successor to Guillaume Sam and to prevail upon him and the National Assembly to accept a treaty embodying all the American demands.

The Treaty of 1915 with Haiti went further in establishing American control and supervision than the Platt Amendment treaty with Cuba or the Dominican treaty of 1907, or than both combined. It provided that the following officials should be appointed by the President of Haiti upon nomination by the President of the United States: a general receiver of customs, a financial adviser, an engineer, or engineers, to supervise measures of sanitation and public works, and officers of the newly organized native constabulary. All Haitian governmental debts were to be classified and arranged, and to be serviced from funds collected by the general receiver; Haiti was not to increase its debt without the consent of the United States. Haiti agreed to do nothing to alienate any of its territory or impair its independence. Finally, as in the case of Cuba, the United States might take any necessary measures to preserve Haitian independence or to maintain "a government adequate for the protection of life, property, and individual liberty." The treaty was to remain in force for ten years, but a clause permitting its extension for another ten-year period upon either party's showing sufficient cause was invoked by the United States in 1917, thus prolonging to 1936 the prospective life of the treaty.

Aside from the immediate restoration of order and the elimination of all excuse for European intervention, it was presumably hoped that the tying up of the revenues and the organization of an efficient constabulary would remove at once the chief motive for revolution and the chance of its succeeding. Unfortunately neither at this time nor in the new constitution, drafted with American aid in 1918, were any steps taken to complement these reforms with the introduction of democratic political processes. The result was a reasonably efficient dictatorship dominated by the United States treaty officials with the support of the Navy and Marine Corps.

The Navy Governs the Dominican Republic

Interest in the Caribbean area now shifted eastward to the Dominican Republic. Here, until 1911, the customs receivership of 1905 and 1907 had worked admirably. Under the Presidency of Ramón Cáceres (1906–1911) stable government and orderly finance had been the rule; constitutional reforms had been adopted, and surplus revenues had been applied to port improvements, highway and railroad construction, and education. Such a novel employment of the powers and resources of government was displeasing to many Dominican politicians, and on November 19, 1911, Cáceres fell victim to an assassin's bullet. At once the Republic reverted to its

seemingly normal condition of factional turmoil and civil war, and the necessities incident to the conducting and suppressing of revolutions resulted in the contraction of a large floating debt, contrary to the spirit, if not to the letter, of the 1907 treaty with the United States.

Thus the Wilson administration found in the Dominican Republic a situation as difficult as that in Haiti. Under a plan drafted by Wilson himself and accepted by the Dominican leaders, the United States supervised the 1914 elections. From the new President, Jiménez, the United States now demanded a treaty providing for the appointment of a financial adviser with control over disbursements, for the extension of the authority of the general receiver to cover internal revenue as well as customs, and for the organization of a constabulary. These demands were rejected as violative of Dominican sovereignty, and in the spring of 1916 the situation went from bad to worse when the Dominican Secretary of War, Desiderio Arias, launched a new revolution and seized Santo Domingo, the capital. On May 15 United States marines were landed in Santo Domingo, and their occupation was gradually extended to other ports and to the interior of the island. Jiménez resigned the presidency. His successor, chosen by the lesgislature, also refused to accept the proposed treaty. President Wilson thereupon directed that the Dominican Republic be placed under military government.

Accordingly, on November 29, 1916, Captain H. S. Knapp, the naval officer commanding at the capital, proclaimed the establishment of a military government by the forces of the United States in Santo Domingo. Cabinet posts were taken over by Marine Corps officers, the legislature was suspended, and for the next six years the government of the Dominican Republic was administered by the United States Navy Department. The situation differed from that in Haiti in that the Haitian government by consenting to the protectorate treaty demanded by the United States, had preserved some vestiges of its independence, whereas the Dominican government by refusing less drastic demands, had seen all its functions taken over by officers of a foreign power. Had Haiti similarly refused, there is little doubt that it likewise would have been subjected to alien military rule. In both republics, though in slightly different ways, the Wilson Administration had carried to its logical conclusion the "international police power" doctrine of Theodore Roosevelt.

Wilson and Mexico

The problems presented by the little states of the Caribbean were solved, after a fashion, by bringing their governments under varying degrees of control by the United States. No such simple solution sufficed for the most serious crisis in Latin American affairs that confronted Wilson during his early years in the White House. In Mexico the dictator-President, Porfirio Díaz, who had governed the country since 1877, had been overthrown in 1911. Leader of the revolution against Díaz, and his successor for a brief period of sixteen months, was Francisco I. Madero, a man of good will, who attempted to give Mexico a democratic government and to reform the Mexican economy in the interest of small farmers and landless workers, both rural and urban. Powerful interests, foreign as well as Mexican, opposed his program. Madero lacked the political adroitness that might have brought lasting success. In February 1913, his foes engineered a revolt of elements in the army at Mexico City. General Victoriano Huerta, to whom the President had entrusted the defense of the government, betrayed him, ordered his arrest, and, after compelling him to resign, had him shot. The official excuse asserted that the shooting occurred during an attempt by Madero's followers to rescue him, but the evidence pointed to a coldblooded assassination.

Huerta then arranged for his own elevation to the Mexican presidency. Foreign interests, including the American ambassador, Henry Lane Wilson, welcomed the accession of Huerta. They had had little patience with Ma-dero's attempted reforms and looked upon Huerta as a strong man, another Díaz, who would keep the Mexican peon in his place and continue Díaz' considerate treatment of foreign capital.[15] Huerta's government, though facing armed opposition from former followers of Madero, was recognized by Great Britain, by other European powers, and by Japan.

President Taft, in the few days that remained of his administration, took no step toward recognition of the Huerta government. The omission was the result not of any qualms about the means of Huerta's rise to power, but rather of the State Department's hope of securing settlement of certain disputes as the price of recognition. Wilson and Bryan viewed the question differently. Shocked by the assassination of Madero, Wilson looked upon the Huerta regime as "a government of butchers," unworthy of recognition.[16] On March 11, 1913, he announced in a press release that friendship and cooperation with the "sister republics" of Latin America would be possible

> only when supported at every turn by the orderly processes of just government based upon law, not upon arbitrary or irregular force. . . . We can have no sympathy with those who seek to seize the power of government to advance their own personal interests or ambition.

Although called forth by rumors of revolutionary plots in Nicaragua, this statement was obviously applicable also to Mexico. It hinted at what was to become an established feature of Wilson's foreign policy vis-à-vis Latin America: a refusal to recognize governments that had attained power only by force and violence. Thus he deviated from the practice, followed quite consistently since Jefferson's day, of recognizing, regardless of origin, any

15. For a competent account of the Madero regime and Huerta's *coup d'état* see C. C. Cumberland, *Mexican Revolution: Genesis under Madero* (Austin: University of Texas Press, 1952).

16. A. S. Link, *Woodrow Wilson and the Progressive Era, 1910–1917* (New York: Harper & Row, Publishers, 1954), p. 109. Chapter 5 of this work gives an excellent analysis of Wilson's Mexican policy. See also H. F. Cline, *The United States and Mexico* (Cambridge: Harvard University Press, 1953), chaps. 7–9.

U.S. POSSESSIONS AND PROTECTORATES IN THE CARIBBEAN

GULF OF MEXICO

ATLANTIC OCEAN

FLORIDA

Key West

BAHAMA ISLANDS

Nassau

M E X I C O

ISLE OF PINES

C U B A

Guantánamo

JAMAICA

HAITI

DOMINICAN REPUBLIC

PUERTO RICO

VIRGIN ISLANDS

LEEWARD ISLANDS

WINDWARD ISLANDS

C A R I B B E A N   S E A

BRITISH HONDURAS

GUATEMALA

HONDURAS

SALVADOR

FONSECA BAY

NICARAGUA

CORN IS.

COSTA RICA

PANAMA

Colón

Panamá

COLOMBIA

VENEZUELA

PACIFIC OCEAN

U.S. Possessions or equivalent.

U.S. Protectorates, c. 1917.

government that was firmly seated and capable of performing its duties, internally and externally.[17]

Refusing to be guided by the advice of Ambassador Henry Lane Wilson, the President sent his own investigators to Mexico to inform him of the character of Huerta's regime. Their unfavorable reports confirmed the conclusions he had reached through reading and reflection about Mexico. He had come, he said, to feel a "passion . . . for the submerged eighty-five percent of the people of that Republic who are now struggling toward liberty." [18] Huerta, he believed, besides owing his position to brute force, would not serve the interests of "the submerged eighty-five percent." He let it be known that he would recognize Huerta only if the latter would agree to hold a fair election in which he himself should not be a candidate. When Huerta not only refused these promises but also, on the eve of the election, arrested 110 opposition members of the Mexican Congress, Wilson made up his mind that the dictator must go.

In determining to oust Huerta from the Mexican presidency, Wilson was clearly intervening in the domestic politics of Mexico. This act of intervention he justified on the ground that it was in the interest of the Mexican people and that, as he later told a group of Mexican editors:

> . . . our sincere desire was nothing else than to assist you to get rid of a man who was making the settlement of your affairs for the time being impossible.[19]

Not until July 1914 did Wilson's campaign against Huerta achieve its result in the latter's resignation and flight to Europe. In attaining his end Wilson had withheld recognition; had lifted a previously instituted arms embargo, thus enabling Huerta's opponents to secure arms in the United States; had persuaded

the British government to remove from Mexico a minister, Sir Lionel Carden, antagonistic to American policy; and finally had occupied the city and port of Veracruz (April 21, 1914). The occupation of Veracruz, accomplished only after considerable fighting, was ostensibly designed to secure an apology for a minor indignity to the United States flag; in reality it was a means of ousting Huerta by depriving him of the revenues from an important port and cutting him off from European sources of arms and ammunition. It was, of course, an act of war; but Wilson insisted that he was not making war upon Mexico, only upon Huerta and his supporters.

When Huerta resigned, July 14, 1914, he left as his leading opponent and probable successor Venustiano Carranza, a former follower of Madero and governor of Coahuila, who had taken up arms against Huerta after Madero's death. Carranza and his forces, Constitutionalists as they called themselves, occupied Mexico City on August 20, 1914, but peace did not come to Mexico nor harmony to Mexican relations with the United States. Carranza's rule was contested by Emiliano Zapata in the south and by Francisco Villa, a former Carranza lieutenant, in the north. Civil war continued, and with it loss of lives and property of foreigners. Carranza, though he had risen to power as a result of Wilson's policy, was so unreceptive to suggestions from Washington that Wilson and Bryan for a while looked with favor upon Villa, the illiterate ex-bandit, as a probable successor to Carranza. This idea had to be abandoned when Carranza's forces, led by General Álvaro Obregón, soundly defeated Villa and drove him back into northern Mexico. Lansing, now Secretary of State, sought aid from other American republics. In the previous year (1914), in its dispute with Huerta, the United States had accepted an offer of mediation from Argentina, Brazil, and Chile. Lansing now called into conference the representatives of these "ABC" powers, together with those of Uruguay, Bolivia, and Guatemala. The conference recommended recognition of Carranza as head of a *de facto* government of Mexico,

17. See Chapter 9.
18. R. S. Baker, *Woodrow Wilson, Life and Letters,* 8 vols. (Garden City, N.Y.: Doubleday & Company, Inc., 1927–1939), 4: 245.
19. Baker, *Woodrow Wilson,* 8: 195.

and the United States took this step in October 1915.

Carranza's enemies continued their resistance. It became the object of Villa to embroil Carranza with the United States. To this end his guerrilla forces, in January 1916, held up a train carrying seventeen American mining engineers and shot all but one. On the following March 9, Villa's cavalry dashed across the international border and shot up the peaceful town of Columbus, New Mexico. A punitive expedition under Brigadier General John J. Pershing followed Villa into Mexico but failed to catch him. Although Carranza had given grudging consent to the pursuit of Villa, he resented the presence of United States troops in Mexico, and on June 21, 1916, in a clash with Mexican government forces at Carrizal, twelve United States soldiers were killed and twenty-three captured. Thereupon Wilson ordered the National Guard to the border, and the two nations were very close to war. The United States declined another Latin American offer of mediation but accepted a suggestion from Carranza (who wanted war no more than did Wilson) for the setting up of a joint commission to study the entire situation. The commission sat from September 1916 to January 1917. It found no solution acceptable to both governments, but the United States members finally advised withdrawal of troops from Mexico and the granting of full diplomatic recognition to the Carranza government.

In accordance with this advice, General Pershing and the last of his troops left Mexican soil on February 5, 1917, and on March 3, Mr. Henry P. Fletcher presented his credentials as ambassador of the United States. Within a few weeks thereafter the United States entered the war against Germany. Throughout the period of that conflict, relations with Mexico continued to be marked by bickering—now over border disturbances, now over threatened expropriations of American property under the new Mexican constitution [20] —but there was no further danger that the

United States might have to fight a war in its back yard as well as upon and across the Atlantic.

Woodrow Wilson's Mexican policy had been marred by errors, inconsistencies, and vacillations. These had resulted, in large part, from his own misjudging of the Mexican character and his lack of well qualified advisers. But when all is said, his policy had had three merits that outweighed its faults. First, he had avoided war with Mexico when to drift into war would have been easy and even popular. Second, he had shown a willingness to consult the other American republics in shaping his course toward Mexico. Third, he had contributed to the success of a regime committed to the social progress of the Mexican people rather than to the exploitation of Mexican riches by foreign capital.[21]

A Policy of Contradictions

Viewed as a whole, Woodrow Wilson's policy toward Latin America presented curious contradictions, which are confusing to the historian and must have been still more confusing to Wilson's Latin American contemporaries. Wilson was aware, when he took office, of a growing air of suspicion toward the United States on the part of its southern neighbors. Theodore Roosevelt's support of revolution in Panama; the Roosevelt Corollary; the interventions in Cuba, the Dominican Republic, and Nicaragua; the frank invoking of dollar diplomacy by Taft and Knox —all had contributed to distrust of "Yankee imperialism." Apprehensive of further interventions by the United States or "imperialist" powers of Europe, the Latin Americans had evolved formulas for the protection of bor-

20. See Chapter 35.

21. The revolution of Madero and Carranza was strongly anticlerical, that is, opposed to the power of the Roman Catholic Church in Mexico; it was sometimes marked by acts of violence against church property, priests, and nuns. By giving aid and comfort to such a regime Wilson incurred the enmity of much of the Catholic hierarchy in the United States. Link, *Wilson and the Progressive Era,* p. 135.

rowing countries against the exactions of their creditors. The "Calvo Doctrine," first announced by an Argentine jurist of the last century, attempted to bind the foreigner who invested in an American country not to go beyond the courts of the latter in seeking protection for his investment; to bind him, in other words, not to seek the intervention of his home government in support of his interests. Another Argentinian, Foreign Minister Luis M. Drago, later set forth the doctrine that bears his name. Suggested by the Anglo-German blockade of Venezuela in 1902–1903, it declared inadmissible armed intervention to enforce payment of the public debt of an American nation. A convention adopted at the Second Hague Conference in 1907 accepted the Drago Doctrine with the qualification that intervention was permissible if the debtor government refused arbitration or, having accepted arbitration, refused to carry out the award. This qualified acceptance of the principle failed to satisfy the Latin Americans. No South American country ratified the convention; distrust and suspicion lived on.

It was Wilson's desire to reassure the Latin Americans by convincing them that the United States had no aggressive purposes. In his public statement of March 11, 1913 (quoted above in connection with Mexico), he declared:

> One of the chief objects of my administration will be to cultivate the friendship and deserve the confidence of our sister republics of Central and South America. . . .

Later in the year, addressing a Southern Commercial Congress at Mobile (October 27, 1913), he denounced the "hard bargains" that had been driven with the Latin American states by foreign moneylenders and added: "I rejoice in nothing so much as in the prospect that they will now be emancipated from these conditions, and we ought to be the first to take part in assisting that emancipation." Later in the same address he declared: "I want to take this occasion to say that the United States will never again seek one additional foot of territory by conquest."

Such words as these must have sounded hopeful to Latin American ears; yet before many months had passed the Wilson administration twice sent armed forces into Mexico; acquired from Nicaragua exclusive rights to the canal route and to naval base sites on both coasts; flouted a decision of the Central American Court of Justice; landed marines in Haiti and forced both a treaty and a constitution upon that ill-governed little state; and handed to the Navy the task of governing the Dominican Republic. These actions, though almost certainly intended in the interest of the people concerned, were hard to reconcile with the anti-imperialist professions of both Wilson and his first Secretary of State, William Jennings Bryan.[22]

But against these interventionist actions, again, must be weighed other acts indicative of a very different attitude. Wilson sponsored the negotiation of a treaty (not then ratified) with Colombia, bestowing an apology and substantial compensation for the loss of Panama. Far from adopting a go-it-alone policy toward Mexico, he called other American republics into consultation and was largely guided by their advice. And he refrained, though sorely tempted, from making actual war upon Mexico. Finally, he proposed for adoption, first by the United States and the "ABC" powers, eventually by all the American republics, a Pan American treaty mutually guaranteeing the territorial integrity and political

22. Bryan, a severe critic of Taft's dollar diplomacy, would, had Wilson permitted, have carried dollar diplomacy a step further than Taft had done. Once Secretary of State, he became as sensitive as his predecessors to any threat to the security of the Canal Zone. To keep dangerous rivals at a distance, he proposed a new corollary to the Monroe Doctrine by which the United States government should itself become banker to the republics of the Caribbean, supplying on easy terms the funds needed to liquidate their European debts and to promote essential economic development and social services. Wilson never accepted this proposal. Selig Adler, "Bryan and Wilsonian Caribbean Penetration," *Hispanic American Historical Review,* 20 (1940), 198–226; P. E. Coletta, "Bryan, Anti-Imperialism, and Missionary Diplomacy," *Nebraska History,* 44 (September 1963), 167–87.

independence under republican forms of government of all the signatories. A precursor of the famous Article X of the League of Nations Covenant,[23] the proposed guarantee was also an anticipation of the "continentalizing" of the Monroe Doctrine, later accomplished by Franklin D. Roosevelt.

23. For Article X, see p. 287. Argentina and Brazil showed interest in the proposed inter-American guarantee; Chile was cool to it. Wilson dropped the plan in favor of the more inclusive Article X.

On the eve of the Spanish-American War, it will be recalled, Germany, Russia, France, and Great Britain had seized harbors suitable for naval bases on the coast of China and had exacted from the Chinese government long-time leases of these harbors and grants of economic concessions in the neighboring areas, which thereby became "spheres of interest" of the powers named. The United States had a small but at this time a rapidly growing trade with China. It was looking to China as a market for the surplus products of its industry, which European statesmen were threatening to exclude from their own shores. Since signing its first treaty with China in 1844 the United States had been assured of most-favored-nation treatment, or the "open door," in its trade with that country. That open door now appeared to be threatened by the creation of spheres of interest in the hands of governments which might be expected to discriminate in favor of the trade and other interests of their own nationals. It was largely the belief that a foothold in the Philippines would enable the United States better to defend its interests in China that had led to the decision to keep the islands.[1]

John Hay and the Open Door in China

Of all the powers concerned, Great Britain had interests most akin to those of the United States. An invitation from Great Britain to join with her in defending the open door in China was rejected by Secretary of State John Sherman in March 1898. But Sherman soon gave place to William R. Day and he in turn (August 1898) to John Hay, who came home from the London embassy to take the job. Admittedly an Anglophile, Hay would have welcomed close cooperation with Great Britain in the Far East. But public and senatorial opinion would have rejected anything like an alliance, and the most that Hay could do was to invite the powers chiefly concerned with China to agree to respect the open door principle, hoping, as Monroe and Adams had

24

The United States and the Far East, 1898–1914

1. See pp. 205–6.

hoped in 1823, that Great Britain would back the American position.

A suitable occasion for such a proposal was offered by the Russian government in an imperial ukase in mid-August 1899, giving assurance that Russia would not interfere with or control the collection of Chinese customs in her sphere of interest, or place any restrictions on "foreign commerce and trade" in that sphere. Sensing in the unexpected Russian move an excellent opportunity to get general assent to preservation of the open door principle, Hay instructed his chief adviser on Far Eastern matters, W. W. Rockhill, to prepare a memorandum for presentation to the governments concerned. Rockhill and an English friend, Alfred E. Hippisley (an employee, on leave, of the Inspectorate of Maritime Customs in China), had, as a matter of fact, been urging such a course upon the Secretary for weeks, and their memorandum was virtually ready.[2] In the form of similar diplomatic notes, it was presented to the governments of Great Britain, Germany, Russia, France, Italy, and Japan.[3] The note of September 6, 1899, to the United States ambassador in Berlin stated that

> . . . the Government of the United States would be pleased to see His German Majesty's Government give formal assurances, and lend its cooperation in securing like assurances from the other interested powers, that each, within its respective sphere of whatever influence—
> *First.* Will in no way interfere with any

treaty port or any vested interest within any so-called "sphere of interest" or leased territory it may have in China.

> *Second.* That the Chinese treaty tariff of the time being shall apply to all merchandise landed or shipped to all such ports as are within said "sphere of interest" (unless they be "free ports"), no matter to what nationality it may belong, and that duties so leviable shall be collected by the Chinese Government.

> *Third.* That it will levy no higher harbor dues on vessels of another nationality frequenting any port in such "sphere" than shall be levied on vessels of its own nationality, and no higher railroad charges over lines built, controlled, or operated within its "sphere" on merchandise belonging to citizens or subjects of other nationalities transported through such "sphere" than shall be levied on similar merchandise belonging to its own nationals transported over equal distances.

The notes, it will be observed, did not propose the abrogation of spheres of interest; these, Hay and his advisers assumed, would have to be recognized as facts. What they asked was assurance that within those spheres the regular Chinese tariff should continue to be collected and that the trade of all nations should be treated without discrimination as to tariffs, railroad rates, and harbor dues. They asked an opportunity for American trade to expand in China without the American government's being burdened with colonial responsibilities or the obligations of protectorates. "In short, a most interesting hybrid of anti-colonialism and economic imperialism." [4]

Five of the six governments addressed replied that they were willing, in their spheres of interest, to abide by the principles set forth by Secretary Hay if all the other governments concerned would agree to do the same. The Russian reply was less forthright. It dealt specifically only with the question of tariffs and was equivocal even on that point; it contained a declaration that "the Imperial Government has no intention whatever of claiming any privilege for its own subjects to the exclusion of other foreigners," but in a context

---

2. T. J. McCormick, *China Market: America's Quest for Informal Empire, 1893–1901* (Chicago: Quadrangle Books, 1967), pp. 128, 141–45. McCormick downgrades the importance of Hippisley and Rockhill as progenitors of the Open Door notes, as claimed, for example, in G. F. Kennan, *American Diplomacy, 1900–1950* (Chicago: University of Chicago Press, 1951). Hay, in McCormick's view, needed no prodding and was merely waiting for a sign that his policy might be well received by other governments. The Russian ukase was precisely such a sign.

3. The notes to Great Britain, Germany, and Russia were dated September 6, 1899; the others were not sent till November. They were addressed to the United States ambassadors or ministers in the respective countries.

4. McCormick, *China Market*, p. 128.

which suggested that the promise applied to Chinese territory outside, not inside, the Russian sphere of interest. The Russian Foreign Office, nevertheless, authorized Hay to treat the reply as favorable, and on March 20, 1900, he notified the six governments that the United States regarded acceptance by all as creating a binding agreement. Thus, as Hay's biographer writes, "What began as straightforward diplomacy . . . ended in diplomatic prestidigitation." [5]

John Hay and the Boxer Rebellion

John Hay had asked only that the powers observe the principles of the open door with respect to foreign trade within their spheres of interest; he had not proposed that they surrender those spheres or agree not to enlarge them. While the diplomats were still debating the significance of the notes and the replies to them, events occurred in China that threatened to provide an excuse for a further partitioning of the empire among the western powers—perhaps even for a final extinction of its independence.

Chinese leaders at the turn of the century were of two minds. A reform party, headed by the well-meaning but weak Emperor, Kuang Hsü, wished to westernize and modernize China in emulation of Japan. A reactionary party, which secured the support of the Dowager Empress, Tzu Hsi ("Old Buddha" as foreigners called her), advocated the expulsion of the "foreign devils" and the destruction of their influence. The spearhead of the reactionaries was the secret society known to the West as "Boxers," from the emblem of a clenched fist. When the Emperor attempted to institute a reform program, "Old Buddha" came out of retirement and seized the reins of government. With her secret connivance, the Boxers began a campaign of violence, at first directed against foreign missionaries and

their Chinese converts in Shantung province, but soon broadened to include the elimination from China of all foreign influence. From Shantung the Boxer hordes advanced against the imperial capital of Peking, took possession of the city, murdered the German minister in the streets, and laid siege to the legation quarter, where foreign diplomats and other foreign residents set up precarious defenses. For weeks in the summer of 1900 the foreigners in Peking were cut off from all communication with the outside world, where it was feared that all might have perished.

The Boxers had persuaded themselves and many others, including the Empress, that they had magic powers which made them invulnerable. Otherwise they could hardly have counted upon a successful defiance of the western nations. The long-run danger was not that western influence in China would be destroyed, but rather that the western powers would seize upon the Boxer outrages as an excuse for partitioning China among them. If China's independence and territorial integrity were thus violated, few would predict a long life for the open door principle. It became the policy of the United States, as voiced by John Hay, to liquidate the Boxer outbreak in a manner that would not involve further seizures of territory by foreign governments.

While, therefore, preparations were being made for the dispatch of an international army for the relief of the legations in Peking, Hay insisted that the powers were not at war with China but only with a rebellious faction within the empire. He kept in contact with friendly groups in China and through them succeeded in reopening communications with the American minister in Peking, thus obtaining the welcome news that the legations were still holding out. Most celebrated, if not most important, of Hay's measures was his circular note to the powers of July 3, 1900, setting forth the aims of American policy. The purpose of the President, he said, was to act concurrently with the other powers in rescuing those in danger in Peking, protecting American lives, property, and legitimate interests wherever they might be imperiled, and pre-

5. Tyler Dennett, *John Hay, from Poetry to Politics* (New York: Dodd, Mead & Co., 1933), p. 293.

venting the spread of disorders to other provinces of China. In regard to the means for obtaining these results, Hay continued,

> the policy of the Government of the United States is to seek a solution which may bring about permanent safety and peace to China, preserve Chinese territorial and administrative entity, protect all rights guaranteed to friendly powers by treaty and international law, and safeguard for the world the principle of equal and impartial trade with all parts of the Chinese Empire.

Thus Hay recognized the relationship between the preservation of China's territorial integrity (this term, rather than "entity," came to be generally used) and the maintenance of the open door in China.[6] It was, he said, the policy of the United States "to seek a solution" that would preserve both.

Orally or in writing, the governments of France, Great Britain, Germany, Russia, and Italy expressed concurrence with Hay's statement, and on October 29, 1900, Hay could state that the United States had had "the gratification of learning that all the powers held similar views." [7]

A month after the dispatch of the circular note of July 3, an international army of 19,000 men, chiefly Japanese and Russian but including 2,500 American troops from the Philippines, set out from the coast for Peking. The Empress fled from the city disguised as a peasant woman. Resistance collapsed and on August 14 the expeditionary force entered the Chinese capital, bringing succor to the besieged foreigners, among them a future President of the United States, Herbert Hoover. Gradually order was restored, the anti-foreign movement disintegrated, and the Chinese government agreed to the payment of an indemnity for foreign lives lost and property destroyed. Whether or not as a result of Hay's statement of American policy, the governments concerned did not ask additional cessions or leases of territory, and the United States exerted its influence to reduce the amount of money indemnity demanded. A figure of $333,000,000 was finally fixed upon, of which slightly less than $25,000,000 was assigned to the United States. When it was discovered that all American losses could be covered by little more than half of this sum, the United States voluntarily agreed to remit the balance. China thereupon put the remitted portion into a fund for the education of young Chinese in American universities.[8]

In addition to the payment of an indemnity, the Chinese government agreed to punish those persons chiefly responsible for the attacks on foreigners, and to permit the foreign powers to police the railroad line connecting Peking with the coast near Tientsin, a right that they continued to enjoy until World War II.

While befriending China with respect to the amount of indemnities to be paid, the United States never lost sight of its main objective, the China market. In tariff negotiations that accompanied those on indemnities, the United States was in accord with the European powers in withholding tariff autonomy from China, and the rates were so adjusted as to discourage China from developing "a more balanced, advanced, and sophisticated economy." China must still look to the West for all but the simplest products of the machine age.[9]

---

6. Rockhill's correspondence with Hippisley prior to the issuance of the open door notes of 1899 shows that Rockhill even then wished to speak out for the preservation of China's territorial and administrative integrity. Indirectly he did so in the proposal in those notes that the tariff duties levied at ports in the spheres of interest "shall be collected by the Chinese Government." P. A. Varg, *Open Door Diplomat: The Life of W. W. Rockhill,* Illinois Studies in the Social Sciences, Vol. 33, No. 4 (Urbana: The University of Illinois Press, 1952), pp. 31–32.

7. *Foreign Relations of the United States, 1900* (Washington, D.C.: Government Printing Office, 1902), pp. 304, 316, 317, 324, 328, 344, 345, 359.

8. As a consequence of this first remission and a later one in 1924, the United States retained only some $6,000,000 of the Boxer indemnity. Tsing Hua College, designed to prepare Chinese students for American universities, was instituted and supported largely from Boxer indemnity funds. W. W. Willoughby, *Foreign Rights and Interests in China,* 2 vols. (Baltimore: The Johns Hopkins Press, 1927), 2: 986–87, 1012–17.

9. McCormick, *China Market,* p. 179.

What Did Hay Accomplish?

John Hay's Chinese policy—his espousal of the open door and of China's territorial integrity—was hailed in his own day and for many years thereafter as a great achievement in American diplomacy. Later his policy was subjected to criticism not only as ineffectual but even as detrimental to the true interests of the United States—as embroiling that nation needlessly in the international strife in a distant continent.

The last criticism seems devoid of substantial foundation. Hay was under steady pressure from American business concerns to protect their current and future interests in China.[10] Certainly the United States had a legitimate interest in keeping the Chinese market open to American trade without adverse discrimination, even though contemporary notions of that market's importance were exaggerated. And certainly the preservation of China's independence and territorial integrity would be essential to keeping the market open. These objectives, though perhaps not worth fighting for, were nevertheless legitimate and proper objects of diplomacy.

There seems no good reason, therefore, to doubt that Hay's efforts were in the national interest. But we may well question whether they were successful and whether the United States consistently practiced the policy that it asked others to follow. If the United States really believed in an open door policy in the Orient, it could have set an example in its newly acquired possession, the Philippines. It did not do so. At the earliest moment permitted by the terms of the treaty of peace with Spain it established there a preferential system favoring the United States at the expense of other powers.[11]

But, consistency aside, was Hay's policy successful? Could diplomatic notes and ambiguous promises alone preserve China's territory intact and prop open the door? Could incantations subdue greedy imperialism? Such was not the belief of England and Japan, the two powers whose wishes were then most nearly in accord with those of the United States. Japan, anticipating correctly that Russia would seek to strengthen her economic and political hold on Manchuria, inquired what attitude the United States would take if Russia should violate her promises. Hay replied that the United States was not prepared to back up its policy with force, either alone or in concert with other powers. Whatever Hay's personal desires, he had to recognize that neither would the Senate accept a treaty of alliance, nor would public opinion support a war, in defense of the nation's Far Eastern policies. Consequently, when first Russia and later Japan strengthened their hold on Manchuria and violated the spirit of the open door, the United States could do no more than write ineffectual diplomatic protests. That there was no immediate extension of the boundaries of the spheres of interest in China is to be attributed to the balance of power among the governments interested rather than to the notes of the brilliant Secretary of State.

This is not to say that Hay's notes were without effect. They may perhaps have aided in restraining some imperialistic ambitions; they may have made Russia and Japan more cautious and moderate than they would otherwise have been in squeezing foreign trade out of their Manchurian spheres of interest. But that John Hay had struck "a tremendous blow . . . for the triumph of American principles in international society," is, as George

---

10. C. S. Campbell, Jr., *Special Business Interests and the Open Door Policy* (New Haven: Yale University Press, 1951).

11. Hay was not responsible for American economic policy in the Philippines, but in another matter he laid himself open to a charge of inconsistency, though the facts came to light only many years later. In December 1900, at the instance of American military and naval officers, he prepared to request from China

permission to establish a naval base in Samsah Bay on the Chinese coast opposite Formosa. He took the precaution, however, of sounding Tokyo first. Japan, which had a nonalienation agreement with China for Fukien province, where Samsah Bay is located, discouraged the project, and Hay dropped it. The correspondence in regard to Samsah Bay was published in *Foreign Relations, 1915* (1924), pp. 113–15, note.

F. Kennan has said, largely a "myth."[12] Later attempts to establish the Hay policies by international consent won a number of verbal triumphs, as will subsequently appear, and put some temporary restraints upon Japan; but the sequel was to show that Japan could not be restrained by words.

The Russo-Japanese War

While the United States relied upon words alone, England and Japan looked about for more substantial means of defending their interests in Asia. The British government turned first to Germany, and in October 1900 concluded an agreement by which both powers promised to respect the integrity of China and the open door, unless aggressions by a third power should compel them to reconsider their decision. This document was so phrased, however, as not to apply to Manchuria, where Germany desired to see Russia have a free hand. But since Russia was England's chief rival in Persia and Afghanistan and Japan's chief rival in the Far East, it was only natural that Great Britain and Japan should draw together in an alliance designed to check Russia. This they did in 1902. By the Anglo-Japanese alliance of that year the two governments, although declaring their devotion to the maintenance of the territorial integrity of both China and Korea, and the open door in both, recognized each other's special interests in China, while Great Britain also recognized the special interests, "politically as well as commercially and industrially," of Japan in Korea. In order to protect those interests in China and Korea from encroachment by a third power, each of the allies promised to remain neutral if the other became involved in war with a third power and to come to the support of the other should it be attacked by two or more enemies.[13]

Within two years the chief purpose of the

12. Kennan, *American Diplomacy*, p. 37.
13. The Anglo-Japanese alliance was renewed in stronger terms in 1905 and again renewed for a ten-year period in 1911. See Chapter 31.

treaty was revealed—the protection of Japan from attack by other powers while she expelled Russia from the latter's holdings in southern Manchuria. Since the Sino-Japanese war of 1894–1895, the clash of Russian and Japanese interests had been acute. Russia had posed as a friend of China, had taken the lead in forcing Japan to restore the Liaotung peninsula to China, and had been compensated by permission to extend the Trans-Siberian Railway across northern Manchuria to Vladivostok. With this portion of the line, known as the Chinese Eastern Railway, Russia acquired also extensive economic and policing rights. In 1898, as was noted earlier, Russia exacted from China a twenty-five-year lease of the same Liaotung peninsula which Japan had been required to disgorge. With the lease went also the right to build and police a railroad line (the South Manchuria Railway) from Harbin on the Chinese Eastern south to Port Arthur at the tip of the Liaotung peninsula. Economic and policing rights also accompanied the new concession; and at Port Arthur Russia proceeded to build a great naval base. The Boxer outbreak gave the Czar's government an excuse for moving large numbers of troops into Manchuria. Under pressure from other powers, Russia agreed in 1902 to withdraw these troops, but neglected to do so. Russia was obviously transforming Manchuria from a part of the Chinese empire into a Russian colony.

More alarming to Japan than Russia's encroachments in Manchuria were those in Korea, the nominally independent kingdom which since 1895 had come under strong Japanese influence. Korea was, in the words of an old saying, "a dagger pointed at the heart of Japan." Japan could not in safety permit Russia to grasp the hilt of the dagger, nor could she afford to see Korea's economic resources pass into any hands but her own.

In 1903 Japan and Russia opened negotiations in an effort to settle both the Manchurian and Korean questions. Japan demanded in effect a free hand in Korea, although conceding Russia's superior economic interests in Manchuria. Russia demanded a free hand in

Manchuria; in return she would recognize Japan's special interests in southern Korea but proposed that Korea north of the 39th parallel be treated as a neutral zone. Neither party would meet the demands of the other. In February 1904 Japan broke off the negotiations and without awaiting a formal declaration of war made a surprise attack on the Russian fleet, which imprudently lay at anchor outside the defenses of Port Arthur.

The Russo-Japanese war, thus begun, lasted for a year and a half and ended in a complete victory for Japan. Russia's Far Eastern fleet, divided between Port Arthur and Vladivostok, was destroyed piecemeal. Her Baltic fleet, after a long voyage from European waters, was annihilated in a one-sided battle in Tsushima straits, May 27, 1905. Meanwhile Port Arthur had surrendered (January 2, 1905) after a long siege, and the main Russian army had been defeated in the battle of Mukden, February–March 1905.

Roosevelt the Peacemaker

The United States, though sympathetic to Japan, adopted a correctly neutral attitude. It assisted in securing from the belligerents an agreement to respect the neutrality of China, with the important exception of the Manchurian provinces, where the land war was fought. Informally, the United States aligned itself with Great Britain in support of Japan, against France, Russia's ally, and Germany, which encouraged Russian adventuring in the Far East. President Roosevelt admired the Japanese and had little but contempt for Russian officialdom. He assured Japan at the beginning that American neutrality would be "benevolent" toward her. He warned Germany and France, so he reported later, that he would intervene if necessary to protect Japan from being robbed of the fruits of a successful war, as she had been in 1895 after defeating China.[14]

If Roosevelt's preferences were partly sentimental, they were also based upon his conception of American interest as affected by the balance of power in the Far East. In 1904, Russia presented the chief threat to that balance and hence to the territorial integrity of China and the open door. Therefore Roosevelt backed Japan against Russia. As the war developed into a series of brilliant Japanese victories, he became apprehensive lest the power pendulum swing too far in Japan's direction. The prospect that, if war continued, Japan might take and hold all of Eastern Siberia he viewed with some alarm.[15] It was perhaps partly for this reason that he welcomed the opportunity to assist in making peace.

Japan, though everywhere victorious, had strained her resources to the limit and was anxious to bring the war to a close. She so intimated confidentially to Mr. Roosevelt in the spring of 1905, asking that he, "on his own initiative," propose a peace conference. This he did, and in August 1905 Russian and Japanese delegates met at Portsmouth, New Hampshire.

The principal obstacle to the conclusion of a peace treaty was Japan's demand for a large money indemnity, six hundred million dollars or more, to cover the cost of the war. This Russia resolutely refused, and over this issue the conference was close to breaking up in failure. At this point, however, President Roosevelt persuaded Japan to drop the indemnity from her list of demands, and a treaty was signed, September 5, 1905. The signing took place in an atmosphere of amity and good will strangely in contrast with the relations of opposing diplomats in some later international

14. E. E. Morison, ed., *The Letters of Theodore Roosevelt*, 8 vols. (Cambridge: Harvard University Press, 1951–1954), 4: 1284.

15. Morison, *Letters*, 4: 1315. The suggestion here that Roosevelt promoted peace in order to prevent an undue predominance of Japan in the Far East is contradicted by his alleged statement to a friend that from the standpoint of pure national interest he would have preferred to see the war continue until both belligerents were completely exhausted; that in taking on the role of peacemaker he bowed to American public opinion against his better judgment. See H. L. Stoddard, *It Costs to Be President* (New York: Harper & Row, Publishers, 1938), pp. 148–52.

controversies. The negotiators clasped hands across the conference table. Baron Rosen, of Russia, then rose, as he said, to "fulfill a most agreeable duty in acknowledging that in negotiating with our hitherto adversaries we have been dealing with true and thorough gentlemen to whom we are happy to express our high esteem and personal regard." [16]

By the treaty of Portsmouth, Russia recognized the paramount interest of Japan in Korea and ceded to her the southern half of the island of Sakhalin, all Russian rights in the Liaotung peninsula, and the South Manchuria Railway extending from Port Arthur and Dairen to Changchun. Both powers agreed to withdraw from Manchuria all troops other than railway guards and to restore Manchuria to Chinese civil administration.

In July 1905, before the delegates met at Portsmouth, Mr. William H. Taft, then Secretary of War in Roosevelt's cabinet, visited Tokyo. In a confidential meeting with the Japanese Premier, Count Katsura, Taft received assurances that Japan would respect United States sovereignty in the Philippines and in return promised American approval if Japan should find it necessary to assume control of the international relations of Korea. President Roosevelt gave his emphatic endorsement to the attitude thus expressed by his emissary. Accordingly, in the following November, when Japan announced that she was taking full charge of Korea's foreign relations, the United States gave immediate approval and promptly closed its legation in Korea. Nor did the United States protest when, five years later, Japan transformed her protectorate over Korea into complete sovereignty.

At the close of the Russo-Japanese war, then, the governments of Japan and the United States enjoyed relations of mutual friendliness and cordiality. The American people, too, had shown overwhelming sympathy for Japan—little David in a struggle with giant Goliath. But the terms of peace

16. *New York Times,* August 20, 1950, Sec. 1, p. 7. For his share in ending the war, President Roosevelt was awarded the Nobel Peace Prize.

were bitterly disappointing to the Japanese public, who had been led to expect much more—a huge money indemnity and the cession of all of Sakhalin, perhaps even Vladivostok and Russia's maritime province. For what they considered the meagerness of the peace terms, the Japanese press and public blamed partly their own government, partly the United States and President Roosevelt. When the terms were announced, angry mobs rioted in Tokyo and other cities, attacking government buildings and the pro-government press, threatening foreigners, and burning Christian churches, most of them American. A regime of martial law put an end to the disorders, but the popular attitude boded ill for the future of Japanese-United States relations. Soon the governments, too, were engaged in controversy.

Japanese Immigration and the "Gentlemen's Agreement"

The United States soon had reason to doubt Japan's devotion to the open door principle, though she had warmly endorsed Secretary Hay's original proposal and had assured President Roosevelt that, if she were victorious in her war with Russia, she would maintain the open door in Manchuria. But once Japan was inside the door, her enthusiasm for keeping it open abated. As early as February 1906, the State Department had cause to complain of discrimination against American trade in Japan's Manchurian sphere of interest. Japan repeated her avowals of adherence to open door policy but continued in subtle ways to violate it. The United States, unwilling now as before to back up words with action, could only continue to deliver ineffectual notes of protest.

More dangerous to Japanese-American relations than Japan's light regard for her open door pledges were the manifestations of anti-Japanese sentiment in the United States, particularly in California. The immigration of Japanese, unlike that of Chinese, was not prohibited by American law. Since 1900, it is true, the Japanese government had itself refused passports to Japanese laborers to come to continental United States. Indirectly, however, via Hawaii, Canada, or Mexico, Japanese did enter in considerable numbers, as many as a thousand per month in 1906, and most of them settled in Pacific coast states. Japanese immigrants seem to have been well behaved and to have been objectionable only on grounds of race prejudice and of their willingness to work for a lower wage than their Caucasian competitors.

The most troublesome manifestation of anti-Japanese feeling occurred in October 1906, when the San Francisco school board barred Japanese children—there were only 93 of them and they were generally model pupils —from the city's regular public schools, requiring that they attend instead an Oriental school established long before for Chinese and Korean children. This action fixed upon the Japanese a stigma of inferiority which their nation, having just handily defeated one of the "great powers" of white Europe, regarded as an insult. The Japanese ambassador [17] protested, and the Japanese press, which like the American had its sensational and jingo elements, engaged in warlike talk.

The management of San Francisco schools was a matter outside of federal jurisdiction, unless, which was doubtful, the case was covered by a most-favored-nation clause in the treaty of 1894. Rather than have the matter tested in the courts, President Roosevelt tried persuasion on the San Francisco officials. The mayor, the superintendent of schools, and the school board were invited to Washington. By pointing to the danger of war (which would fall most heavily upon the Pacific coast) and by promising action to check Japanese immigration, the President secured from the San Francisco authorities a promise to rescind their order for school segregation. He then concluded with the Japanese ambassador a "gentlemen's agreement": Japan would continue to refuse passports to laborers coming to

mainland United States; it would make no objection if the United States barred Japanese from coming from intermediate points such as Hawaii, Canada, or Mexico. An executive order put the new immigration policy into effect.

The "gentlemen's agreement" continued in force till 1924, when it was superseded by prohibitive legislation.[18] It worked well except for one loophole. The Japanese government reserved the right to give passports to subjects who had already resided in the United States or to wives and children of residents. This proviso was so interpreted as to permit the entry of "picture brides"—young women married in Japan to bridegrooms *in absentia* residing in the United States. Even this abuse (if such it was) was terminated before 1924.

A Naval Demonstration and a Seeming Diplomatic Victory

The "gentlemen's agreement" of 1907 did not end Japanese-American friction. Later in the year there were anti-Japanese riots in San Francisco, despite the fact that Japan had donated generously to victims of the earthquake and fire of April 1906. Rumors of impending war circulated in the American press and were rife in the capitals of Europe, where bettors placed odds on Japan to win. Roosevelt was so far disturbed by these rumors that he expressed to Taft an inclination to give independence to the Philippines, which, in a possible conflict with Japan, would "form our heel of Achilles." In October 1907 he sent Taft again to Tokyo, whence the Secretary of War sent home a long cable reporting that Japan's intentions were altogether peaceful.

Roosevelt's handling of relations with Japan exemplified his dictum, "Speak softly, but carry a big stick." On the one hand, he treated all Japanese complaints with courtesy and consideration. On the other hand, he prepared an impressive demonstration of force— no less than sending the entire United States

17. In May 1906 the United States and Japanese legations in Tokyo and Washington respectively were raised to the rank of embassies.

18. See p. 329.

battleship fleet around the world. This, Roosevelt hoped, would convince the Japanese that the United States was no "push-over," like Russia. It would also be excellent advertising for the Navy and might aid Roosevelt in getting adequate naval appropriations from Congress.

The "Great White Fleet"—sixteen battleships attended by colliers and other auxiliary craft—visited Tokyo harbor by invitation of the Japanese government. There were those who, remembering Japan's surprise attacks on China and Russia, predicted that the American fleet would find a watery grave in the bay where Perry, fifty-four years earlier, had wrested a treaty from a reluctant Shogun.[19] The visit passed without untoward incident, however, and with impressive displays of courtesy on both sides. War talk died down, and a few weeks after the fleet had left Tokyo, Secretary of State Elihu Root and Kogoro Takahira, the Japanese ambassador in Washington, by an exchange of notes, agreed to a set of principles in tune with United States policy.

By the Root-Takahira agreement (November 30, 1908) the governments of Japan and the United States declared themselves "firmly resolved reciprocally to respect the territorial possessions belonging to each other" in the Pacific area, and announced their determination

> to preserve the common interest of all powers in China by supporting by all pacific means at their disposal the independence and integrity of China and the principle of equal opportunity for commerce and industry of all nations in that Empire.

Since the text of the Root-Takahira agree-

ment seemed entirely to favor the United States—even adding equality of treatment for industry to that previously asked for trade—historians have searched for some hidden price paid by the United States for these concessions. Some have found it in a clause of the agreement in which the two governments declared it to be their purpose to maintain "the existing status quo" in the region referred to, and have interpreted this language as a tacit recognition by the United States of Japan's special interests in Manchuria. There is no evidence of such an understanding in the records of the Root-Takahira conversations, and the circumstantial evidence is ambiguous. State Department records show that on the day the notes were signed, Root received from Tokyo a report of an official conversation in which Foreign Minister Komura had declared "that South Manchuria constituted Japan's outer line of defense and that Japan no longer considered the principle of China's integrity to include Manchuria." Whether Root had read this report before signing the note by which the United States promised to respect the status quo in the area is not known. If he had done so, his acceptance of the status quo could be construed as acceptance of the status of South Manchuria as defined by Komura.[20] This interpretation is supported by Roosevelt's action two years later, when he warned his successor, President Taft, against giving the Japanese in Manchuria any reason to feel that the United States was "a menace—in however slight a degree—to their interests."

The Root-Takahira agreement contained no provision to protect the interests of Japanese residing in the United States. Within a week after it was signed, Roosevelt was expressing alarm at the possible effect in Japan of legislation proposed in California that would have excluded Japanese residents from the ownership of land. He was "thankful that our squadron left Japanese waters before California and other Western States began this

---

19. The Japanese main fleet, with fewer battleships than the American, but with large contingents of cruisers, destroyers, and submarines, all in battle trim, was engaged in maneuvers between Japan and the Philippines during the U.S. visit. In a confrontation the U.S. would have been at a great disadvantage. See R. A. Hart, *The Great White Fleet: Its Voyage Around the World, 1907–1909* (Boston: Little, Brown and Company, 1965).

20. R. A. Esthus, *Theodore Roosevelt and Japan* (Seattle: University of Washington Press, 1966), chap. 16.

idiotic procedure, . . ." [21] Roosevelt, working through the Republican governor of California, was able at that time to dissuade the California legislature from enacting discriminatory land laws. Four years later, President Wilson was less successful. Despite his best efforts and those of Mr. Bryan, his Secretary of State, California in 1913 passed legislation forbidding ownership of land to "aliens ineligible for citizenship," that is, Japanese. Despite a protest from the Japanese ambassador so vigorous that the Joint Army-Navy Board incurred Wilson's anger by urging him to put the Navy on guard,[22] California refused to rescind or modify its alien land law, and other western states were soon enacting similar legislation.

"Dollar Diplomacy" in the Far East

In the four-year interval between Roosevelt and Wilson, President William H. Taft and his Secretary of State, Philander C. Knox, were giving a new turn to the open door policy. John Hay's notes had asked for equal treatment in matters of trade only. Few Americans in 1899 were interested in putting money into the development of Chinese industry or the exploitation of China's natural resources. Taft and Knox became interested in securing entry into China for American capital, particularly in the field of railroad building.

Taft and Knox owed their inspiration chiefly to Willard Straight, formerly United States consul general at Mukden in Manchuria, and for some months in 1908–1909 acting chief of the newly formed Division of Far Eastern Affairs in the State Department. Straight, in turn, was in close touch with the American railroad king, E. H. Harriman, who dreamed of extending his railroad empire to

Asia and in the fall of 1905 had received some encouragement from Japan in a plan to purchase the South Manchuria Railway. A Japanese change of heart, the financial panic of 1907, and Harriman's death in 1909 all contributed to the defeat of this particular scheme, but Straight did not abandon the general idea. Straight viewed the investment of American dollars in China, not primarily with the eyes of an investor seeking profits, but rather with those of a statesman pursuing high policy. He believed that only a substantial stake in the country would enable the United States to block Japan's plans for taking over southern Manchuria and perhaps additional slices of the tottering Chinese empire. It was his wish that dollars should be made to serve the ends of diplomacy.

But first diplomacy must open the door for dollars. Acting in this sense, President Taft, in July 1909, took the unusual course of addressing a letter to the Chinese Prince Regent, asking that American bankers be admitted with those of England, France, and Germany to a proposed banking pool to finance Chinese railroad construction. The request, though resisted by the other banking groups, was eventually granted. Still later, Russian and Japanese bankers were also included, thus forming the so-called Six-Power Consortium. Results in railway construction were not large.

Secretary Knox, in the meantime, proposed (November 1909) that American and European banking groups purchase and thus "neutralize" the railroads of Manchuria—the Chinese Eastern owned by Russia, and the South Manchuria owned by Japan. A novice in handling delicate international relations, Knox assumed that by thus taking ownership of the railroads out of the hands of Japan and Russia, China would be enabled to recover her complete sovereignty over Manchuria. He was apparently unaware that in 1907 Japan and Russia had formally recognized one another's spheres of interest in southern and northern Manchuria respectively and had secured approval of that arrangement from France and Great Britain and from China her-

21. L. F. Abbott, ed., *The Letters of Archie Butt* (Garden City, N.Y.: Doubleday & Company, Inc., 1924), pp. 220–21.
22. J. A. S. Grenville and G. B. Young, *Politics, Strategy, and American Diplomacy* (New Haven: Yale University Press, 1966), p. 322.

self. Japan and Russia not only regarded themselves as in Manchuria to stay; they had also delimited their spheres of interest in Mongolia: Outer Mongolia for Russia, Inner Mongolia for Japan. No wonder that they received Knox's proposals with cool disapproval; nor did Knox get encouragement from England, which he tried to use as an intermediary. England, allied with Japan, had now settled her differences with Russia. She needed the friendship of both in her growing rivalry with Germany, and could not afford to antagonize them by supporting Knox's plans for Manchuria. Thus Knox met complete defeat in his effort to rescue Manchuria from the imperialistic clutches of Russia and Japan.

An opportunity to use the resources of the Six-Power Consortium for a purpose other than railroad construction occurred after the Chinese revolution of 1911, which overthrew the Manchu Dynasty and resulted in the setting up of a republic with Yüan Shih-k'ai as President. In serious financial straits, the new government opened negotiations with the six-power banking group for a loan of $300,000,-000 to be used for the reorganization of the administration. The proposed terms involved some control over expenditure and over collection of the salt tax, or gabelle, which was pledged as security.

Arrangements for the loan were pending in March 1913, when Taft surrendered the presidency to Woodrow Wilson. It seems evident that the bankers of the American group did not find loans to China attractive on their merits and were willing to participate only if the United States government desired that they do so for political ends. Five days after Wilson took office, representatives of the American banking group (one of whom was Willard Straight, who had left government service some time previously) had an interview with Secretary of State Bryan. They in-

formed Mr. Bryan that the American bankers would seek their share of the proposed loan only if the new administration should so request.

After discussion in two cabinet meetings, but without consulting the experts in the State Department or the other governments concerned, Wilson issued a statement to the press. The administration, he said, would not request the American bankers to participate in the loan,

> because it did not approve the conditions of the loan or the implications of responsibility on its own part which it was plainly told would be involved in the request.
> The conditions of the loan seem to us to touch very nearly the administrative independence of China itself, and this Administration does not feel that it ought . . . to be a party to those conditions. The responsibility on its part which would be implied . . . might conceivably go the length in some unhappy contingency of forcible interference in the financial, and even the political, affairs of that great Oriental State, just now awakening to a consciousness of its power and of its obligations to its people. . . .

Thus Wilson frowned upon this form of dollar diplomacy and in so doing put an end to the participation of American bankers in the Consortium. Several years later, when he saw that Japan was enjoying a practical monopoly of loans to China and was thus strengthening its influence there, Wilson reversed his position and encouraged American bankers to take part in a new consortium. But before this new turn in American policy, the war in Europe had greatly altered the picture, diverting the attention of the West to problems nearer home and giving Japan a rare opportunity to rivet chains on China. How the United States met Japan's new aggressive moves will be told in a later chapter.

In the period from 1899 to 1914, between the Spanish-American War and the First World War, while the United States consolidated its hold on the Caribbean and played a prominent rôle in the politics of the Far East, it was also taking an increasing part in the affairs of Europe. In particular it was lending its support to efforts for the peaceful settlement of international disputes.

These fifteen years were the heyday of the peace movement. The peace societies became affluent and respectable; the Permanent Court of Arbitration was established at The Hague; arbitration and conciliation treaties were concluded in dozen lots; and the United States continued its tradition of settling amicably its controversies with other states. Some people who lived through those calm and peaceful years can recall arguing in all seriousness that the day of wars, at least of major wars, was past. It seemed clear that, given the costly and destructive potentialities of modern warfare, even the victors in such a struggle would lose more than they could possibly gain. Man, it was assumed, was a rational animal, and could see the folly of squandering his resources in a game of self-destruction.

Prosperity of the Peace Societies

The peace societies, whose early history was touched upon in a previous chapter,[1] had hitherto drawn their membership mainly from the clergy and from idealists who had little standing in the worlds of business and politics. After the turn of the century there was a noticeable increase in the number of prominent and "practical" men who took part in their affairs. The American Peace Society, before 1914, counted among its members the President and the Secretary of State of the United States—Woodrow Wilson and William Jennings Bryan. In 1906 the New York Peace Society chose as its president Andrew Carnegie, the steel king, who had already donated a magnificent "Peace Palace" at The Hague.[2] At a New York Peace Congress, sponsored in

25

The Paths of Peace

1. See Chapter 8.
2. See p. 244.

1907 by the society and its president, the participants included "ten mayors, nineteen members of Congress, four supreme court justices, two presidential candidates, thirty labor leaders, forty bishops, sixty newspaper editors, and twenty-seven millionaires."[3] In 1910, the Boston publisher, Edward Ginn, established the million dollar World Peace Foundation, which sponsored numerous publications in the fields of international law and international relations. In the same year, Carnegie, not to be outdone, set up the more wealthy and pretentious Carnegie Endowment for International Peace, which likewise sponsored publications but also granted subsidies to other organizations working for the same ends.[4]

Organizations of business men vied with the churches and with such religious groups as the Y.M.C.A. and the Christian Endeavor Society in their apparent zeal for the abolition of war. When President Taft, in 1910, proposed general arbitration treaties with Great Britain and France, almost three hundred chambers of commerce in as many cities supported him. There was, of course, little that the United States wanted that could be gained by war. Many businessmen, furthermore, had probably reached the same conclusion as the Englishman Norman Angell who in his book, *The Great Illusion*, published in 1910, argued convincingly that no one wins in modern war.

The Hague Peace Conferences

The private sponsors of the peace movement in these years were not only more respectable, better heeled, and more optimistic than their predecessors; they were far more influential in, or at any rate more in accord with, the actual policies of the government. The United States participated, with twenty-five other powers, in the conference on disarmament, generally referred to as the First Hague Peace Conference, called by the Russian Czar in 1899. In its attempt to put limits on military and naval expenditure (the principal object for which it had been called), the conference failed completely. Its efforts in this direction were not aided by Captain A. T. Mahan, one of the United States delegates, who remarked privately to a British representative that the new responsibilities of the United States in the Pacific would require that it have more navy, not less.[5] The conference adopted conventions on treatment of prisoners, including sick and wounded, the status of flags of truce, respect for the Red Cross, the outlawing of such allegedly "inhumane" implements of war as missiles dropped from balloons, poisonous gas, and expanding bullets—in general, agreements to alleviate the effects of war rather than to prevent it. In practice, even such modest agreements as these were soon to be violated.

The most celebrated achievement of the First Hague Conference was the creation of the Permanent Court of Arbitration—the international body for which, together with the Permanent International Bureau that served as its secretariat, Andrew Carnegie built the famous "Peace Palace." This was not really a court at all but a panel of jurists—four named by each of the twenty-six member nations—from which the parties to a dispute might select the judges if they agreed to arbitration. The signatory governments made no promises to take disagreements between them to the Court for arbitration. They agreed merely to use their best efforts to insure the peaceful settlement of international disputes. The Court, with its panel of jurists, was there for whoever cared to use it.

3. Merle Curti, *Peace or War: The American Struggle, 1636–1936* (New York: W. W. Norton & Company, Inc., 1936), p. 207. Chapter 7 of this work summarizes the nongovernmental aspects of the American peace movement, 1900–1914.

4. In the 1970's both the World Peace Foundation and the Carnegie Endowment continued to carry on their useful work. If they had not preserved the peace, they had at least, through their many publications, contributed to a more realistic understanding of international relations. Carnegie's optimism is illustrated by his directive to his trustees to the effect that when they had attained "the speedy abolition of international war between so-called civilized nations," they should turn their attention to the "next most degrading remaining evil."

5. G. P. Gooch and Harold Temperley, eds., *British Documents on the Origins of the War, 1898–1914,* 11 vols. (London: H. M. Stationery Office, 1926–1938), 1: 231.

The Second Hague Peace Conference met in 1907, again at the call of the Czar, who in the interval had engaged in the disastrous war with Japan. At the suggestion of the United States, invitations had been sent to all the republics of Central and South America, with the result that forty-four governments sent representatives. Again, no steps were taken for the limitation of armaments, nor did the Conference agree to the proposal of the United States that a genuine international court of justice be established. Aside from extending most of the conventions agreed to eight years previously, the Conference could point to only two promising achievements, and in neither of these was the promise fulfilled. First, it adopted a modified form of the Drago Doctrine,[6] which, because of the modifications, proved unacceptable to the Latin American states chiefly interested. Second, it provided for the creation of an International Prize Court of Appeals for maritime prize cases; and, since there were differences of opinion about points of international law that such a court would administer, it was agreed that a conference should meet in London to codify the international law of maritime war. The London Conference, meeting in 1908–1909, issued its findings in a Declaration of London, but when war began in 1914, neither the Declaration nor the convention creating the International Prize Court had received the necessary ratifications. Nor did they ever do so.[7]

The Root Arbitration Treaties

The existence of a court of arbitration, such as that at the Hague, had little importance if the nations of the world were under no obligation to use it. President Theodore Roosevelt and his two Secretaries of State (John Hay, 1898–1905; Elihu Root, 1905–1909) were willing to accept such obligation for the United States in certain categories of cases. Hay, accordingly, taking a recent Anglo-French treaty as a model, negotiated a number of bilateral arbitration treaties, under which the parties would agree to submit to the Hague Court questions of a legal nature or relating to the interpretation of treaties, not affecting "the vital interests, the independence, or the honor" of the two states, or the interests of third parties. The exceptions listed, which apparently excluded all important questions from the obligation to arbitrate, were broad enough; but the Senate weakened the agreements still further by adding the requirement that every arbitration under the treaties be preceded by a special agreement made with the advice and consent of the Senate, that is, requiring approval by a two-thirds vote.

In Hay's opinion, the Senate amendments made the treaties valueless, and upon his advice President Roosevelt let them die. Secretary Root, on the other hand, considered even such weak treaties better than none. In 1908–1909, accordingly, he negotiated twenty-five treaties similar to Hay's but containing the Senate amendment and having a duration of five years. Of the twenty-five, all but three were ratified by the other parties. Most of them were renewed at five-year intervals until replaced by the Kellogg treaties of 1928–1931.[8]

President Taft's Abortive Arbitration Treaties

Speaking at a peace meeting in New York, March 22, 1910, President Taft voiced his belief that the time had come when even questions affecting national honor could safely be submitted to arbitration. This pronouncement was generally so well received that Taft instructed Philander C. Knox, his Secretary of State, to negotiate general treaties of arbitration with France and Great Britain. The two

---

6. See p. 229.
7. See pp. 257–58. The British Parliament rejected the Declaration of London as restricting too far the naval activities of belligerents. The United States Senate had given its advice and consent to the ratification of both documents, conditional upon their acceptance by the other governments concerned.

8. See Chapter 30, n. 10. Argentina, Bolivia, and Chile neglected to ratify. Treaties were not signed with Germany or Russia.

treaties, signed August 3, 1911, provided for the submission to the Hague Court or other suitable tribunal of all "justiciable" questions, that is, questions "susceptible of decision by the application of the principles of law or equity," which could not be settled by ordinary diplomacy. The treaties provided machinery for determining whether or not questions were justiciable. The Senate, however, amended the treaties to reserve this determination for itself and appended a long list of subjects to which the agreements should not apply. The excluded subjects embraced the admission of aliens to the United States and to the educational institutions of the United States (clearly referring to the Japanese question in California and her neighbor states), the alleged monetary indebtedness of any state (a reference to the Reconstruction debts of the South), and questions involving the Monroe Doctrine. Unwilling to ask the French and British governments to accept the Senate amendments, President Taft pigeonholed the mutilated treaties.[9]

The Bryan Conciliation Treaties

A final phase of treaty-making in the interest of peace preceded the outbreak of the First World War. Secretary of State William Jennings Bryan, although not a pacifist in the extreme sense, was a staunch opponent of war and had electrified many an audience with his oration, "The Prince of Peace"—second in fame only to his "Cross of Gold" speech of 1896. Soon after taking over his official duties, he began the negotiation of a series of conciliation treaties, popularly known as "cooling-off" treaties because they would have the effect of at least postponing a resort to arms till the parties to a controversy had had time to think it over. Supplementary to the Root arbitration treaties, they provided a procedure in questions which the parties might be unwilling to arbitrate.

9. J. P. Campbell, "Taft, Roosevelt, and the Arbitration Treaties of 1911," *Journal of American History,* 53 (September 1966), 279–98.

Under the Bryan treaties—of which thirty were negotiated and twenty-one ratified and proclaimed—the parties agreed that any dispute which diplomacy should fail to adjust should be submitted for study to an international commission of five persons, two to be chosen by each government (one from among its own citizens and one from a third state) and a fifth to be agreed upon by the two governments. The commission should, within one year, make a recommendation for settlement. The parties were not obligated to accept the recommendation, but they agreed not to declare war or begin hostilities until the commission should have made its report.

Putting the Hague Court to Work

The United States, as was observed in an earlier chapter, had already made a good record in submitting troublesome disputes to arbitration. It soon took advantage of the creation of the Permanent Court of Arbitration at The Hague to lay a dispute before a panel of jurists from that tribunal. At the suggestion of a French visitor that the United States might set a good example by sending a case to the court, President Roosevelt in 1902 persuaded Mexico to agree to the arbitration of the "Pious Fund" controversy—the question of Mexico's obligations to Franciscan missions in California, which before the Mexican War had received their support from a fund in Mexico. The dispute was arbitrated in 1902, and Mexico was directed to pay over $1,400,000 for the support of the missions.[10]

The Alaska Boundary Controversy

A more serious controversy than that over the Pious Fund was the Alaska boundary dispute. President Roosevelt, convinced of the complete justice of the American case, and re-

10. Curti, *Peace or War,* pp. 190–91; F. J. Weber, "The Pious Fund of the Californias," *Hispanic American Historical Review,* 43 (February 1963), 78–94.

garding the Canadian pretensions as "dangerously near blackmail," refused to submit this dispute to the Hague Court or to any tribunal where a neutral might cast the deciding vote. In fact he denied that the mode of settlement adopted, a procedure by which the United States could not lose, was really arbitration.

The Alaska controversy, involving the boundary between British Columbia and southern Alaska, depended upon the interpretation of the Anglo-Russian boundary treaty of 1825. The rights to which Russia was entitled by that treaty were inherited by the United States when it purchased Alaska in

ALASKA
BOUNDARY DISPUTE

- - - - - U.S. claim.
• • • • • • British claim.
———— Boundary decision of 1903.

1867. The ownership of certain islands in the Portland Channel was in dispute, but the principal disagreement concerned the location of the boundary line from the head of that estuary to the meridian of 141° west longitude. The treaty prescribed that the line should parallel the coast at a distance of ten leagues (thirty miles) inland. Until the 1890's it was generally assumed that the thirty miles were to be measured from the head of tidewater; but when the gold rush to the Klondike gave sudden importance to the Lynn Canal and the boom towns of Dyea and Skagway at its head, the Canadians produced the theory that the thirty miles should be counted from the outer limits of the irregular coast, in which case Dyea and Skagway would be left on the Canadian side of the boundary.

British attempts to secure concessions by the United States in Alaska in return for British concessions in Panama failed. A *modus vivendi* agreed upon in 1899 left Dyea and Skagway for the time being under American jurisdiction. Not until 1903 did the British and American governments agree on a procedure for final settlement. The treaty of that year provided for submission of the question to the decision of a commission composed of six "impartial jurists," three American, two Canadian, and one British. Here was a possibility, obviously, of a tie vote and no settlement.

The British government named to the commission Lord Alverstone, Lord Chief Justice of England, and two Canadians who, if not wholly "impartial," were at any rate jurists of some repute. President Roosevelt followed the questionable course of appointing his Secretary of War, Elihu Root, and two senators—Lodge of Massachusetts and Turner of Washington. Root was a great lawyer but had presumably formed his opinion of the controversy; the other two could hardly be called either jurists or impartial. In justification of Roosevelt's choice, it may be said, first, that he had tried unsuccessfully to persuade two justices of the Supreme Court to accept appointments; second, that an advance and confidential assurance that "safe" men would

be named was perhaps necessary to secure Senate approval of the treaty.[11] Canadians considered Roosevelt's selections contrary to the spirit of the treaty, if not its letter; and though it cannot be said that the decision reached was unjust to Canada, the episode left a residue of ill will north of the border.

The commissioners met in London in September 1903. So determined was Roosevelt to have the decision his way that he engaged in what sounded definitely like saber-rattling, sending troops to southern Alaska (where they were perhaps needed for the preservation of order) and letting it be known informally to the British ministry that if the commission deadlocked, he proposed, as he put it, "to run the boundary on my own hook." It is to be hoped that Lord Alverstone was not swayed by these hints but rather by the documents in the case, which undoubtedly upheld the American contention. For whatever reason, he voted, on the most controversial issue, with the three Americans and against the two Canadian jurists. The disputed islands were divided between the contestants, but the mainland portion of the line was established eastward of the heads of the inlets, thus leaving Lynn Canal with Dyea and Skagway securely on the American side.

Arbitration of the Northeast Fisheries Dispute

A better example of genuine arbitration than the Alaska boundary settlement was the submission to the Hague Court of the northeast fisheries controversy. The *modus vivendi* of 1888,[12] extended from time to time, had prevented friction with Canada, but Newfoundland, upon whose ports and inshore waters New England fishermen largely depended for bait, had continued to harass the Americans

11. T. A. Bailey, "Theodore Roosevelt and the Alaska Boundary Settlement," *Canadian Historical Review*, 18 (1937), 123–30. See also P. C. Jessup, *Elihu Root*, 2 vols. (New York: Dodd, Mead & Co., 1938), 1: 389–401.
12. See p. 183.

with a variety of troublesome and unreasonable regulations, which the United States contended were contrary to the spirit if not the letter of the treaty of 1818. Newfoundland would have relaxed her impositions in return for the duty-free admission of her fish to the American market, but a proposal to this effect was rejected by the United States Senate.

After prolonged negotiation, the United States and British governments agreed in 1909 to submit the entire question of the fisheries to a panel of five judges selected from the membership of the Hague Court of Arbitration. The panel was composed of one American and one Canadian jurist and one each from Austria, The Netherlands, and Argentina. The panel decided all the principal questions in favor of the United States. The most important feature of the award was the ruling that all local regulations affecting visiting fishermen must be "reasonable" and that their reasonableness

should be subject to determination by a mixed commission representing both parties. Certain restrictions that Newfoundland had sought to impose upon American fishing vessels were definitely ruled out by the court.

An interesting question, but one that had long ceased to make serious trouble, was the definition of inshore waters on those coasts where American fishermen were excluded from inshore fishing. Was the three-mile line, beyond which Americans must not go, to follow all the sinuosities of the coast, as Americans claimed, or to be drawn from headland to headland across the mouth of every bay, as was the Canadian contention? Though practical understandings on this point had long since been reached, it was placed before the Hague panel for final determination. The panel adopted the arbitrary rule that when the entrance to a bay did not exceed ten miles in width, the waters of the bay should be

NORTHEAST FISHERIES CONTROVERSY

Inshore fishing rights ·······
Inshore fishing and curing rights – – –

counted as inshore waters; in wider bays the three-mile line should mark the limit of the prohibited area.[13] Thus another troublesome dispute, the longest in American diplomatic history, was finally and amicably disposed of.

The Panama Canal Tolls Question

Still another disagreement with Great Britain, one that might properly have been submitted to arbitration but was handled in a different way, was the controversy over tolls to be charged for use of the Panama Canal. The Hay-Pauncefote Treaty of 1901 had stipulated that the canal should be "open to the vessels of commerce and of war of all nations . . . , on terms of entire equality." When Congress, in 1912, legislated for the operation of the canal, which was nearing completion, it provided that United States ships engaged only in the coastwise trade, as from New York to San Francisco, should be exempt from the payment of tolls for the use of the canal. This provision was at once attacked by the British as inconsistent with the equality of treatment promised by the treaty. American supporters of the measure contended that, since foreign ships were excluded from the coastwise trade, exemption of American coastwise shipping from payment of tolls was not discrimination. Foreigners replied that the loss of tolls resulting from the exemption of American coastwise shipping would necessitate higher tolls on other shipping, which would therefore suffer discrimination.

The Democratic platform on which Woodrow Wilson won the presidency in 1912 supported the tolls exemption in the recently enacted law. Wilson soon became convinced,

however, that the British had good ground for their objections. He believed, as did leading Republicans like Roosevelt, Root, and Lodge, that the question was a suitable one for arbitration. But arbitration could be instituted only through a treaty, and there was little chance that such a treaty would be approved by two-thirds of the Senate. Wilson decided, therefore, to ask Congress for outright repeal of the tolls exemption.

Wilson's case for repeal was strengthened by the fact that Britain had accepted—though disliking—his anti-Huerta policy in Mexico and had removed her minister, who had befriended Huerta. It was America's turn to make a concession, especially in a matter in which Britain appeared to many to have right on her side.[14] Wilson used this argument by implication, without specific mention of Mexico, when on March 5, 1914, he asked Congress to repeal the tolls exemption, "in support of the foreign policy of the administration." Leading Republicans like Root, now a senator from New York, and Lodge gave Wilson their support. The repeal bill became law on June 15, 1914.

Europe Drifts Toward War

The same years that saw so much apparent progress toward the substitution of arbitration for war in the settlement of international controversies, saw also a steady intensification in the rivalries of the principal European powers. Europe, in fact, became divided into two mutually antagonistic armed camps.

At the turn of the century a Dual Alliance of France and Russia faced a Triple Alliance of Germany, Austria-Hungary, and Italy. Aside, however, from the French desire to recover Alsace-Lorraine, surrendered to Germany in 1871, the rift between the groups was not too deep. In fact, as appeared in the story of Far Eastern developments, Germany on some occasions cooperated with France and Russia. Great Britain as yet held aloof, not

13. A good analysis of the award and its background is in Robert Lansing, "The North Atlantic Coast Fisheries Arbitration," *American Journal of International Law,* 5 (1911), 1–31. Besides adopting the general rule described above, the panel recommended acceptance of specific lines as marking the entrances to certain of the bays involved.

14. See p. 227.

aligning herself with either group of powers. Her chief rivalries in the 1890's were with France in Africa and with Russia in Persia, Afghanistan, and China.

The rise of Germany as a great industrial, commercial, and naval power gave Great Britain a new rival, one more to be feared than France and Russia, her traditional enemies. As a consequence, Great Britain settled her differences first with France and then with Russia. In 1904 England and France composed their colonial rivalries in Africa and the Pacific, forming what was called the *Entente Cordiale*. In 1907 England and Russia came to terms over their conflicting interests in Asia; the *Entente Cordiale* became the Triple Entente of France, Russia and Great Britain —not an alliance (except between France and Russia) but an understanding that the three powers would work for common objectives. Japan, furthermore, was allied with Great Britain after 1902 and in 1907 reached agreement with Russia in regard to Manchuria. Italy, moreover, showed signs of drifting away from her Teutonic allies in the direction of better relations with France.

The chief scenes of rivalry after 1904 were in North Africa, where French and German ambitions clashed, and in the Balkans, where Austria-Hungary, backed by Germany, worked at cross-purposes with Russia.

In North Africa, by the agreement of 1904, France had given up, for the benefit of England, any claim to the Egyptian Sudan, receiving in return from Great Britain a free hand in Morocco. A subsequent agreement with Spain divided Morocco, though still nominally independent, into French and Spanish spheres of interest. Germany resented the partitioning of Africa without regard to German interests and, in particular, took exception to the French assumption of paramount interest in Morocco. Taking advantage of the weakening of the Dual Alliance by Russia's disastrous war with Japan, Germany in 1905 provoked a crisis with France over Morocco, forced the resignation of the ambitious French Foreign Minister, Théophile Delcassé, and brought about an international conference at Algeciras, Spain, in which the United States took part. At Algeciras, Germany secured recognition of her limited economic interests in Morocco and assurances that an open door policy would be followed there. On two later occasions, 1909 and 1911, Germany rattled the saber over the Moroccan question. Unable to break French political predominance in Morocco, Germany exacted, in compensation for her acquiescence, the cession of certain French territories in central Africa.

More perilous to peace than the question of Morocco was great-power rivalry in the Balkan peninsula. Here a German-Austro-Hungarian *Drang nach Osten*—an eastward thrust through the Balkans and Turkey, symbolized by the Berlin-to-Baghdad Railway— ran counter to Russia's traditional desire to control the Bosporus and Dardanelles and her more recent assumption, as leader of a Pan-Slavic movement, of a sort of guardianship over the Slavs of the Balkans, especially the Serbs and Bulgars. Russia, still debilitated by her defeat by Japan, was too weak to resist when Austria-Hungary, in 1908, annexed Bosnia and Herzegovina, Slavic provinces of the crumbling Turkish Empire. But she did nothing to restrain anti-Austrian activities on the part of Serbia. Serbia bitterly resented Austria's seizure of the Slavic peoples of Bosnia-Herzegovina. Among them and among other South Slavic groups living under the Dual Monarchy the Serbs launched a propaganda aimed at liberating their kinsmen from Austro-Hungarian rule as they themselves had been liberated from the tyranny of the Turk.

In the Balkan Wars of 1912–1913, Serbs, Bulgars, Greeks, and Rumanians expelled the Turks from most of the remnants of their European possessions outside the city of Constantinople, and then fought among themselves over the spoils. Most significant, however, was the intervention of Austria-Hungary to prevent Serbia from using her victory to secure a port on the Adriatic. This action added fuel to the fire of Serbian hatred for Austria, which was to have its tragic outcome in the assassination at Sarajevo of Archduke

Francis Ferdinand, heir to the thrones of Austria and Hungary.

The growing tension between Austria-Hungary and Serbia meant growing tension also between the Dual Monarchy and Russia, friend of Serbia. And since France and Germany were bound by alliances with Russia and Austria-Hungary respectively, while England had at least moral commitments to France and Russia, it was obvious that a spark in the Balkans might set off a general European conflagration. Recognizing the danger, and at the same time increasing it, all continental powers in 1913 enlarged their armies by extending the periods of military service. Great Britain increased her naval budget. Germany and Russia were building strategic railroad lines. The world talked of peace, but Europe prepared for war.

Theodore Roosevelt and the Moroccan Question

Americans in general, although they deplored the signs of increasing tension and growing militarism in Europe, felt little direct personal concern about them. Europeans might foolishly go to war; Americans would remain at peace. Theodore Roosevelt was more aware than most of his countrymen of the realities of European politics and of their implications for the United States. He had a wide circle of acquaintances among Englishmen, French, and Germans. He kept up, as President, a lively correspondence with the German Kaiser, whose vagaries he viewed with an amused condescension. The Kaiser aided Roosevelt in his efforts to make peace between Russia and Japan and in turn appealed to him for support in the Moroccan crisis with France in 1905. Roosevelt responded by urging France to agree to a conference on Morocco but in doing so assured the French government of American support in resistance to any unreasonable German demands. The United States was itself represented at the ensuing conference at Algeciras, January to April 1906. Roosevelt found an excuse for American par-

ticipation in the fact that a commercial treaty of 1880 with Morocco gave the United States a legitimate interest in keeping the Moroccan door open to American trade. Roosevelt's real purpose, however, was to maintain the balance of power in Europe, with the American weight thrown temporarily into the scale instead of Russia's; to prevent the humiliation of France, to improve Anglo-German relations, and to reduce the chances of a European war.

By the resulting treaty of Algeciras the powers, including the United States, avowed their devotion to the independence and territorial integrity of Morocco, the sovereignty of the native Sultan, and the preservation of the open door in the Sultan's dominions. They devised measures for administrative and financial reform, assured Germany of a substantial share in an International Bank set up at Tangier to handle Moroccan finance, but gave to France and Spain the authority to officer and instruct a native police force. On the whole, France had come out well, German ambitions had been restricted within small bounds, and Roosevelt had succeeded in his aims. The United States had been able, as Secretary of State Elihu Root phrased it, to "preserve world peace because of the power of our detachment." [15]

Last-Minute Efforts to Prevent War

In participating actively in the Algeciras Conference, Theodore Roosevelt ventured further than any other American President before 1917 into the intricacies of European politics.[16]

15. Jessup, *Elihu Root,* 2: 59.
16. The Senate, in approving the Algeciras treaty, sought to dispel the impression that American participation in conference and treaty was a departure from standard United States policy. It appended a reservation explaining that the United States had taken part because of its treaty of 1880 with Morocco and adding that participation was "without purpose to depart from the traditional American foreign policy which forbids participation by the United States in the settlement of political questions which are entirely European in their scope."

President Taft and Secretary Knox directed their international activities principally toward the Far East and the Caribbean. By the time Woodrow Wilson entered the White House, European tension had reached an alarming pitch. This fact did not escape the attention of Walter Hines Page, United States ambassador in London, or of Colonel Edward M. House, Wilson's confidential friend and adviser. Both Page and House had ideas for preventing the war that they correctly sensed to be just around the corner.

To Page it seemed that the only hope was to find some useful and constructive work in which the great European armies might be employed instead of fighting each other. He suggested a clean-up campaign in Mexico and unspecified tropical countries—"to clean out bandits, yellow fever, malaria, hookworm—all to make the country healthful, safe for life and investment, and for orderly self-government at last. . . . conquest for the sole benefit of the conquered, worked out by a sanitary reformation. . . . And the tropics cry out for sanitation, which is at first an essentially military task." [17]

House had something of the same idea. To the German ambassador in Washington he suggested "a sympathetic understanding between England, Germany, Japan, and the United States. . . . They could ensure peace and the proper development of the waste places." [18] In House's conception "the proper development of the waste places" appeared to be not "an essentially military task" but a problem of guaranteed investments at reasonable rates of interest. If Germany could find outlets in this way, if, for example, she could be encouraged to "exploit South America in a legitimate way," tensions might be reduced, and armies also. In the hope of working out such an arrangement—reduction of armaments based upon an internationally accepted program of overseas investments—House visited Berlin and other European capitals in May, June, and July 1914. He received some encouragement, but on June 28, while he was in London, Archduke Francis Ferdinand, heir to the thrones of the Dual Monarchy, was assassinated at Sarajevo, Bosnia, by a young Bosnian under secret Serbian sponsorship.[19] When the colonel sailed for home on July 21, Austria-Hungary was on the point of presenting to Serbia the fateful ultimatum that touched off the First World War.

17. B. J. Hendrick, ed., *The Life and Letters of Walter H. Page,* 3 vols. (Garden City, N.Y.: Doubleday & Company, Inc., 1923–1925), 1: 272–73. Reprinted by permission of The Odyssey Press.

18. Charles Seymour, ed., *The Intimate Papers of Colonel House,* 4 vols. (Boston: Houghton Mifflin Company, 1926–28), 1: 239–40. Quotations from *The Intimate Papers of Colonel House* reprinted by permission of the publisher. Walter Millis, *Road to War: America 1914–1917* (Boston: Houghton Mifflin Company, 1935), pp. 21–27.

19. Vladimir Dedijer, "Sarajevo Fifty Years After," *Foreign Affairs,* 42 (July 1964), 569–84.

26

The Road to War

Though informed Americans had been aware of the growing tensions in Europe, the actual outbreak of war took both the American public and government completely by surprise. The assassinations at Sarajevo (June 28) made newspaper headlines for a day and then were largely forgotten. For over three weeks there were few hints of serious trouble brewing. Then, on July 23, Austria-Hungary presented to Serbia a forty-eight-hour ultimatum whose terms, if accepted, would have gone far toward extinguishing Serbian sovereignty. Rejecting Serbia's partial acceptance as unsatisfactory, Austria-Hungary on July 28 declared war upon the Serb kingdom. Two days later, Russia mobilized, determined to defend her small protégé. On August 1, Germany declared war against Russia; on August 3, against Russia's ally, France, which had refused to give assurance of remaining neutral; on August 4, against Belgium, which had denied passage to German armies en route to France. On August 4, also, Great Britain declared war upon Germany—ostensibly as a joint guarantor of Belgian neutrality; more realistically, because of moral commitments to France and Russia and unwillingness to acquiesce in the domination of Western Europe by her most dangerous rival. Subsequently, Turkey and Bulgaria entered the war as allies of Germany and Austria-Hungary —the "Central Powers"; while Italy (repudiating her Triple Alliance ties) and Rumania eventually joined the side of the Triple Entente powers—the "Allies," as they were called in American parlance. Meanwhile, Japan had declared war upon Germany on August 23, 1914, and set out to seize for herself German holdings in China's Shantung peninsula and German islands in the North Pacific. Eventually no less than thirty-two nations—including the British Dominions and India—were involved in the war against Germany.

American Opinion and the War

To the average American the war in Europe seemed remote—a deplorable tragedy indeed, which might entail inconvenience to his trade or travel but was unlikely to involve him in any more serious way. But some Americans saw it in a different light, as a struggle that might have deep significance for the United States. Elihu Root wrote to an English friend:

> Underlying all the particular reasons and occasions for the war, the principle of Anglo-Saxon liberty seems to have met the irreconcilable conception of the German State, and the two ideas are battling for control of the world.[1]

Robert Lansing, who in July 1915 became Wilson's Secretary of State, took a view similar to Root's and drew from it a practical conclusion:

> . . . Germany must not be permitted to win this war or to break even, though to prevent it this country is forced to take an active part. . . . American public opinion must be prepared for the time, which may come, when we will have to cast aside our neutrality and become one of the champions of democracy.[2]

Still other Americans foresaw a danger to the United States in an upsetting by Germany of the European balance of power. Great Britain and France were "satisfied" powers; so long as they dominated the eastern Atlantic, the United States had nothing to fear. But should their place be taken by imperial Germany, "unsatisfied" and hungry for colonies and colonial markets, the United States might have to surrender the Monroe Doctrine or fight to defend it.[3]

But these were the opinions of a select few. To most Americans, though they might sympathize with one side or the other, the war was a European affair. It took the German

1. P. C. Jessup, *Elihu Root,* 2 vols. (New York: Dodd, Mead & Co., 1938), 2: 313. Quotations from *Elihu Root* reprinted by permission of the publisher.
2. *War Memoirs of Robert Lansing* (Indianapolis: The Bobbs-Merrill Company, Inc., 1935), p. 21. Quotations from *War Memoirs of Robert Lansing* reprinted by permission of the publisher.
3. Walter Lippmann, *U.S. Foreign Policy, Shield of the Republic* (Boston: Little, Brown and Company, 1943), pp. 33–39. The various motives for American intervention are discussed in detail in Part Two of R. E. Osgood, *Ideals and Self-Interest in American Foreign Relations* (Chicago: The University of Chicago Press, 1953).

submarine attacks on American lives and American ships—attacks which, in American eyes, were both inhumane and illegal—to bring the United States to the point of intervention.

President Wilson issued a formal proclamation of neutrality on August 4, 1914. Fifteen days later, in a message reminiscent of Washington's Farewell Address, Wilson appealed to his countrymen to avoid taking sides in the European struggle. Otherwise, he warned, Americans might "be divided in camps of hostile opinion, hot against each other, involved in the war itself in impulse and opinion if not in action."

> The United States [he continued] must be neutral in fact as well as in name. . . . We must be impartial in thought as well as in action, must put a curb upon our sentiments as well as upon every transaction that might be construed as a preference of one party to the struggle before another.

Wilson attempted, during the next two and one-half years, to keep the United States "neutral in fact as well as in name," though consciously or unconsciously American interpretations of international law were consistently favorable to the side of the Allies. But no one could compel or persuade the American people to be "impartial in thought," and this lack of impartiality was conspicuous in the President's own official family. Mr. Bryan, Secretary of State until July 1915, was, indeed, as impartial as one could well be, seeing little to commend the British case over the German. Lansing, second man in the State Department in 1914 and Bryan's successor the next year, believed that the United States must enter the war if necessary to prevent a German victory. Walter H. Page, ambassador to Great Britain, saw the war as a crusade in which England and her allies were to Germany as St. George to the dragon. Edward M. House, Wilson's unofficial ambassador to Europe on several occasions, was almost as pro-Ally as Page. Wilson himself, however impartial at first, had come by May 1915 to a belief that "England is fighting our fight." A year later, exasperation at certain British practices had driven him back to a relatively impartial attitude.

Public opinion from the beginning tended to be pro-Ally. Americans had ties of race, language, culture, and political ideals with England and bonds of ancient friendship with France, which had no substantial counterpart in their relations with Germany. Only in communities where the German or Irish heritage was strong was there likely to be much pro-German (or anti-British) sentiment. Both sides in the war made their propaganda appeals to American public opinion. The British had the advantage—in a day when wireless transmission of news was relatively unimportant—of controlling the cables and hence of shaping news from the war fronts to suit their purposes. German "atrocities" were magnified or even invented. Such exaggerated stories were often accepted as sober truth. German propaganda, on the other hand, was more often spotted as such and discounted accordingly.

British propaganda, however, was probably less influential in building anti-German sentiment than authentic words and deeds of German leaders and the German armed forces. Chancellor von Bethmann-Hollweg's injudicious reference, in his closing conversation with the British ambassador, to the treaty neutralizing Belgium as a "scrap of paper" sounded a false note to American ears, as did the actual invasion of neutralized Belgium and the destruction of the great library of the University of Louvain. The execution as a spy of the English nurse Edith Cavell by the German armies seemed to the American public an act of wanton cruelty. Later, the German U-boat campaign against merchant ships and cases of sabotage against American suppliers of war material for the Allies—whatever one thinks of them in retrospect—contributed to a popular conception of a Germany careless of neutral rights and of human life.

Such pro-Ally sentiment was stronger along the Atlantic coast than in the interior; stronger among the well-to-do classes than among the less affluent. Many American businessmen had banking and commercial ties with England; many had found a playground in France. Similar links with Germany were relatively few.

The American Economy and the War

The war itself bound the United States with new and powerful bands to France and Great Britain. The initial effect of the war on the American economy was disastrous. German markets were cut off by the British Navy. German merchant shipping was bottled up in port, and Allied ships were in many cases diverted from their customary routes and services. Luxury purchases virtually ceased. American business, already wallowing in the trough of a minor cyclical depression, was still further depressed by these disruptions of the foreign market. Soon, however, relief came in the form of large munitions orders from the Allies, and by the closing months of 1915, the United States was enjoying a war-born prosperity.

The sale of munitions of war to the Allies raised the question of neutral obligations. German sympathizers complained that such sales, being made exclusively to the Allied side, were unneutral. To such a critic Mr. Lansing replied:

> If one belligerent has by good fortune a superiority in the matter of geographical location or of military or naval power, the rules of neutral conduct cannot be varied so as to favor the less fortunate combatant.

Such a change in the rules would in itself be unneutral. There was no doubt that this position was correct in law and precedent. Sale of munitions of war to belligerents was no breach of neutrality. That only one set of belligerents could buy was the result of their control of the seas, not of United States policy. The sale of munitions continued, therefore, at a rapidly climbing rate. Exports of explosives, six million dollars in value in 1914, jumped to $467,000,000 in 1916.

In the first few days of the war, it became apparent that the Allies, if their munitions purchases were to continue over a long period of time, would need to finance them by borrowing in the American money market. In August 1914 the New York firm of J.P. Morgan and Company inquired of Secretary Bryan what would be the attitude of the government to such transactions. Bryan replied that loans by bankers to belligerent governments were "inconsistent with the true spirit of neutrality." Whatever the ethics of Bryan's position, it had no legal standing. Loans by neutral bankers to belligerent governments were common enough. Both North and South had borrowed in Europe to finance the American Civil War. Japan had borrowed extensively in England and the United States to pay for her recent war with Russia, and Russia had fought back with money borrowed in France.

Bryan was apparently convinced by the French ambassador, J. J. Jusserand, that his position was untenable. He disguised his retreat by distinguishing between loans and "credits." In October 1914, with State Department consent, Morgan granted a ten-million-dollar "credit" to the French government.[4] Other credits followed, but "loans" were still banned when Bryan resigned as Secretary of State. In September and October 1915, Secretary Lansing and Secretary of the Treasury William G. McAdoo persuaded Wilson to abandon Bryan's position completely, arguing that without large-scale loans, Allied purchasing would taper off and the country would face a depression. Thereupon the Morgan firm, which became purchasing agent in the United States for the Allied governments, assisted in floating an issue of a half-billion dollars in Allied war bonds. Before American entry into the war in 1917, the Allied governments had borrowed over two and one-quarter billion dollars in the United States, of which nearly one and one-half billion dollars went to Great Britain.

The loans, and the trade that they supported, made and kept the United States prosperous until its own entry into the war. That prosperity was dependent upon a continuance of Allied purchases in the United States. In 1915–1916, half of American foreign trade was with France and Great Britain. The German submarine campaign of 1917, besides violating the American interpretation of international law, threatened to destroy this trade altogether. There is no evidence that President Wilson was swayed by such economic considerations in his decision to accept the German challenge. The most that can be safely said is that the existence of these strong economic ties with the Allies, compared with almost no such ties with Germany, made it easy to break with Germany when occasion arose.

The British Navy Revives Old Issues

Observance of neutral obligations was a relatively simple matter for the United States in 1914–1917. Enforcement of its rights as a neutral raised more complicated and difficult problems. It embroiled the State Department in long arguments with the leading belligerents on both sides and eventually led to a declaration of war against Germany.

The rights in question were mainly those of trade and travel by sea. Each belligerent attempted, so far as it dared and with the instruments at its disposal, to shut off neutral trade with its antagonist, raising again the old questions of contraband and blockade and new questions of the immunity of commercial vessels, with their crews and passengers, from lethal attack by submarines. Each belligerent denounced the other's methods as illegal, and the United States, as the leading neutral, saw illegalities in both.

The London Naval Conference of 1908–1909, referred to in the preceding chapter, had attempted to reach agreement upon disputed points of maritime law and had issued its findings in the Declaration of London. On nearly all controversial points, the Declaration would have restricted belligerent activities and thereby would have enlarged the

---

4. See "A Communication" from Charles A. Beard, *New Republic,* 87 (June 17, 1936), 177.

rights of neutrals and also those of the inferior naval power—the belligerent that did not control the sea. For this very reason, the British Parliament had withheld its approval, and at the outbreak of war, the Declaration had no legal standing.

Secretary Bryan proposed, nevertheless, that the belligerents agree to abide by the rules laid down in the Declaration. Germany and Austria-Hungary expressed their willingness to accept the Declaration if their opponents would do so. The British government agreed only with qualifications and reservations that virtually nullified the Declaration. In particular, the British rejected the rigid categories of contraband, noncontraband, and conditional contraband [5] commodities set up by the Declaration; they made, from time to time, sweeping additions to the contraband lists and in the end wiped out the distinction between contraband and conditional contraband. The British also refused to be bound by the articles of the Declaration which provided that blockading forces "must not bar access to the ports or to the coasts of neutrals," and that the doctrine of continuous voyage,[6] although applicable to stoppage of contraband, could not be invoked for enforcement of blockade with respect to noncontraband goods.

It is a fact worth noting that the British government never formally declared a blockade of Germany. It accomplished the same end by other means. The lists of contraband were gradually enlarged until they included not only foodstuffs and cotton but nearly all articles of consequence that Germany was in the habit of importing. By a drastic order-in-council of March 11, 1915, Great Britain announced that thereafter goods "of enemy destination, ownership, or origin" would not be permitted to proceed to or from Germany, directly or indirectly. This was a blockade in all but name. It was a blockade, furthermore, that applied to trade via neutral ports, such as those of Holland and Denmark, as well as trade via German ports. By this order the British carried the doctrine of continuous voyage to its logical conclusion.[7] Neutral states with access to Germany which desired to import goods by sea were required to guarantee not only that such goods would not be re-exported to Germany, but also that like goods of domestic production, for which the imports might be substituted, would not be so exported.[8]

Against these interferences with its trade —trade with Germany and with Germany's neutral neighbors—the United States from time to time protested. It protested, too, against other and incidental British wartime practices—the taking of American ships into British ports for search, with consequent interminable delays; interference with the mails; the blacklisting of American firms alleged to have some German connections; the flying of the American flag on British ships for purposes of disguise. Although these protests were sometimes strongly worded [9] (to satisfy suffering American shippers and to balance contemporary protests to Germany), they never reached the ultimatum stage. Mr. Lansing never lost sight of the possibility that the United States might become an ally of Great Britain and might then even wish to engage in some of the very practices against

5. "Conditional contraband" comprised commodities susceptible of both military and nonmilitary uses, which became "contraband" (and so liable to confiscation) only when consigned to the armed forces or a government department of the enemy state.
6. See pp. 61, 158.

7. In the case of noncontraband neutral property stopped en route to Germany, the British did not assert the right of confiscation, as they could have done for breach of blockade. German property and neutral contraband property were subject to confiscation as such.
8. In their blockade policy, the British did not always "play fair" with neutrals. To a considerable extent, they allowed British exporters to ship to Scandinavian countries "the very products which they intercepted when bound to such destinations from America." Jessup, *Elihu Root*, 2: 320, and compare M. W. W. P. Consett and O. H. Daniel, *The Triumph of Unarmed Forces* (New York: Brentano's, 1923).
9. Ambassador Page, who had no patience with his government's objections to British practice, described one of Lansing's notes as "an uncourteous monster of 35 heads and 3 appendices."

which it was protesting. Consequently, as he wrote later:

> The notes that were sent [to England] were long and exhaustive treatises which opened up new subjects of discussion rather than closing those in controversy. Short and emphatic notes were dangerous. Everything was submerged in verbosity. It was done with deliberate purpose. It insured continuance of the controversies and left the questions unsettled, which was necessary in order to leave this country free to act and even to act illegally when it entered the war.[10]

The United States, as a matter of fact, came close to giving its case away as early as December 26, 1914, when it acknowledged that "imperative necessity to protect their national safety" might justify the Allies in committing acts that would otherwise be illegal. Subsequent protests against British blockade policy, Sir Edward Grey, British Foreign Secretary, was able to answer more or less effectively with the arguments that:

1. The British interference with trade to the European neutrals was based upon, and went little beyond, the practice followed by the United States in the Civil War.
2. New instrumentalities of trade necessitated modifications of international law. With modern steam transportation a blockade of German ports would be futile if trade to Danish and Dutch ports were unmolested.
3. Extension of the contraband lists to cover food and other commodities largely for civilian use was justified by the fact that in modern war the entire nation participates, the factory or railroad worker behind the lines no less than the soldier in the trenches.

Although the United States never accepted this reasoning as satisfactory, it took no steps, beyond making protests, to enforce its conception of maritime rights against Great Britain. In the controversy with Germany over the submarine, Colonel House and Wilson himself assured the German government that in return for German concessions to the American position, the United States would put pressure on England to make corresponding concessions. These promises were never effectively carried out.

The German Submarine Raises New Problems

The British practices against which the United States had occasion to protest violated property rights only; they exposed no neutral lives to danger. In this respect they differed radically from the German use of the submarine for warfare upon commerce, which became the chief grievance against Germany. President Wilson made clear the American attitude toward the two kinds of grievance in a speech of September 2, 1916. When American rights became involved, he said,

> this was our guiding principle: that property rights can be vindicated by claims for damages when the war is over, and no modern nation can decline to arbitrate such claims; but the fundamental rights of humanity cannot be. The loss of life is irreparable.[11]

"The fundamental rights of humanity," as Wilson saw them, were violated by the German submarine.

On February 4, 1915, the German government announced that the waters around the British Isles would thenceforth be considered a "war zone" in which enemy merchant vessels would be sunk at sight by German submarines. Furthermore, because the British had adopted the practice of disguising their ships with neutral flags, Germany could not guarantee the safety of neutral vessels that ventured into the war zone.[12]

---

10. *War Memoirs of Robert Lansing,* p. 128.

11. R. S. Baker and W. E. Dodd, eds., *The Public Papers of Woodrow Wilson: The New Democracy,* 2 vols. (New York: Harper & Row, Publishers, 1926), 2: 282.

12. The Germans had early begun laying mines in the North Sea. The British had asserted the right to retaliate, and on November 2, 1914, had proclaimed the entire North Sea to be a "war area," which merchant vessels would enter at their own risk. The United States had not seen fit to join the Scandinavian governments in protesting this action. C. C. Tansill, *America Goes to War* (Boston: Little, Brown and Company, 1938), pp. 176–77.

To this unprecedented innovation in maritime warfare the United States replied promptly on February 10. For any loss of American ships or lives as a result of the new policy, the German government would be held to "a strict accountability," and the United States would take any necessary steps "to safeguard American lives and property and to secure to American citizens the full enjoyment of their acknowledged rights on the high seas." So began the controversy that after two years was to involve the United States in the war.

To the use of the submarine as a weapon against enemy naval vessels there could be no objection. The objection to its use as a commerce destroyer arose from the fact that it could not easily conform to established rules for commerce destruction. Recognized practice called for visit and search of the commercial vessel by the enemy warship, inspection of its papers, and, if possible, the bringing of the suspected ship into port—a home port of the captor—for adjudication by a prize court. But when the latter part of this process was impossible—as it obviously was for a German submarine in the face of the British navy—international law permitted the destruction of the prize at sea, *but only if adequate provision was made for safety of crew and passengers.*

A submarine was a small and cramped vessel which could not possibly take on board and care for the noncombatants from a large freighter or passenger ship. The best it could do, if it destroyed the ship, was to give passengers and crew an opportunity to take to the lifeboats and in them to face precariously the perils of the deep. But a submarine was also a weak and vulnerable craft; and since the British armed their merchant ships and instructed them to fire upon or ram enemy submarines, the Germans contended that only by torpedoing such ships without warning could they use the submarine safely and effectively. The United States complained that this practice violated the principle that noncombatant lives must be protected. The Germans replied that armed merchant ships foreferited

their immunity from attack and, furthermore, that old concepts of international law must be adapted to new conditions and the employment of new weapons.

The United States Objects

Opinions differed within the State Department itself on how the United States should meet the new German policy. Bryan, who saw that a challenge to Germany on this issue might lead to war, favored submission: he would warn American citizens who chose to travel on belligerent ships that they did so at their own risk. Lansing, on the other hand, contended that American citizens had a right to travel on British ships, even though the latter were defensively armed, and that the United States government must defend its citizens in the enjoyment of such rights. Lansing was apparently wrong on two counts: (1) persons of whatever nationality traveling on a British ship could properly look only to the British government for protection; (2) an armed merchant vessel, even though the armament was defensive, forfeited its immunity from armed attack.[13] Wilson, nevertheless, accepted Lansing's position rather than Bryan's. From then on, the United States contended that its citizens had the right to travel in safety on British ships and to look to their own government for protection in that right. It mattered not that the British ships were armed or that they carried, as most of them did, cargoes of munitions for Allied armies.

Two attempts were made to solve the problem of submarine warfare by compromise. Soon after the original German announcement, the United States proposed that Germany restrict its use of submarines against merchant vessels to legal visit and search, in

13. E. M. Borchard and W. P. Lage, *Neutrality for the United States,* 2nd ed. (New Haven: Yale University Press, 1940), pp. 87–88, 136–37, 177–83. Tansill, *America Goes to War,* p. 649. There are indications that Lansing later realized he had been wrong but was unwilling to acknowledge it.

The Road to War   261

return for a relaxation of the British food blockade and a British promise to abandon the use of neutral flags. This attempt failed when Germany demanded free access to raw materials for her industry as well as food. The second attempt was made early in 1916. Lansing then proposed that the British give up arming their merchant ships in return for a German agreement that submarines would not attack unarmed ships without warning and without taking precautions for the safety of those aboard. This proposal failed to meet a favorable response in London and Paris. A move in Congress to support it by warning American citizens against travel in armed belligerent ships (the Gore and McLemore resolutions) was blocked at the request of President Wilson, who wrote to the chairman of the Senate Foreign Relations Committee that he could not "consent to any abridgment of the rights of American citizens in any respect."

The Lusitania Crisis

Long before this second attempt at compromise, German-American relations had passed through their first serious crisis, brought on by the torpedoing of the British Cunard liner *Lusitania* off the Irish coast on May 7, 1915. The vessel sank in eighteen minutes. Of the 1,198 persons who lost their lives, 128 were American citizens. Despite the fact that the German embassy had published warnings to Americans to avoid the *Lusitania*, there was apparently no deliberate German plot to "get" that particular ship. The commander of the offending submarine, the *U-20*, had actually begun his homeward voyage when the big liner hove in sight, steaming with culpable disregard of precautions prescribed by the British Admiralty.[14]

14. T. A. Bailey, "The Sinking of the *Lusitania*," *American Historical Review*, 41 (October 1935), 54–73. According to the best available evidence, the *Lusitania* was not armed and did not, as the Germans claimed, carry Canadian troops. She did, however, carry munitions, including 4,200 cases of rifle cartridges.

The phrase "strict accountability" was now put to the test. Lansing and some others in or close to the administration wished a declaration of war against Germany but realized that public opinion would not support that course. Over Bryan's protest and finally despite his resignation, President Wilson made and reiterated a demand upon the German government for disavowal of the sinking, reparation for the injury caused, and the taking of "immediate steps to prevent the recurrence" of such acts. The German government, unwilling to make a public surrender but not ready to risk a break with the United States, issued secret orders to submarine commanders not to attack passenger ships without warning. In Washington the German ambassador, Count von Bernstorff, hard pressed by the State Department, exceeded his authority and permitted publication of his assurance that: "Liners will not be sunk by our submarines without warning and without safety of the lives of non-combatants, provided that the liners do not try to escape or offer resistance." After months of further negotiation the German government conceded its "liability" for the sinking of the *Lusitania*.[15]

Germany Retreats

The continuance of German-American amity was again endangered in March 1916, when the French channel steamer *Sussex*, an unarmed passenger vessel, was torpedoed in the English Channel. The *Sussex* managed to make port, and no American lives were lost, though American passengers were injured. It seems well established that the submarine commander who attacked the *Sussex* mistook her for a type of British mine-layer which in

15. Tansill, *America Goes to War*, chaps. 13, 14. Bernstorff did not present his assurance that liners would not be sunk until September 1, 1915. In the meantime on August 19, the White Star liner *Arabic*, en route from Liverpool to New York, had been sunk without warning, with two American lives lost. For this sinking, which was apparently in violation of orders, the German ambassador expressed disavowal, regret, and offer of indemnity.

silhouette she closely resembled.[16] At the time, however, the incident appeared to be a deliberate violation of the assurance given after the *Lusitania* sinking. Lansing and House advised breaking off diplomatic relations with Germany. Wilson, not ready to go so far without another attempt at an understanding, presented a vigorous ultimatum to the German government.

> Unless the Imperial Government [Wilson wrote] should now immediately declare and effect an abandonment of its present methods of submarine warfare against passenger and freight-carrying vessels, the Government of the United States can have no choice but to sever diplomatic relations with the German Empire altogether.

Again the German government yielded, giving definite assurance (May 4, 1916) that merchant vessels would "not be sunk without warning and without saving human lives, unless these ships attempt to escape or offer resistance." The note concluded, however, by stating the expectation that, in return for German concessions, the United States would compel England to abandon her allegedly illegal practices, and by warning that unless England should alter her methods, "the German Government would then be facing a new situation, in which it must reserve [to] itself complete liberty of action."

The British Try Wilson's Patience

The eight months following settlement of the *Sussex* crisis were the most satisfactory period of the war in German-American relations. The Germans were on their good behavior. German submarines continued to prey upon Allied commerce but acted within the rules of law and humanity. At the same time the Allies, especially the British, were exasperatingly uncooperative.

During the early months of 1916, Wilson had permitted Colonel House to make an effort to end the war, coupled with a conditional

16. Tansill, *America Goes to War*, p. 491.

offer of American intervention on the side of the Allies if the effort should fail. The plan was as follows: At a secret signal from the Allies, Wilson was to invite both groups of belligerents to meet in a peace conference. The Allies would accept. If Germany declined, as was expected, or if, after accepting, she refused to make peace on "reasonable" terms (which were to have been agreed upon in advance between Wilson and the Allies), the United States would enter the war against Germany. A memorandum to this effect, agreed upon by House and Sir Edward Grey, was cabled to Wilson from London for his approval. The President, who under the Constitution could not promise a declaration of war, inserted the word "probably" in the clause predicting American action. Whether because of this element of uncertainty or because they hoped for victory without agreeing to terms that would satisfy Wilson's idealism, the Allied governments never signified their readiness for Wilson's invitation.

Apparently Wilson was, like House, chagrined at this cool treatment of a generous offer. It is clear that he was intensely annoyed at a blacklist of American business concerns issued by the British government in July 1916. The blacklist contained the names of nearly one hundred American firms or individuals with which, because of supposed German connections, British subjects and corporations were forbidden to have any business dealings; nor could firms in neutral countries do business with them except at the risk of being themselves blacklisted. Even Ambassador Page considered this British move "tactless and unjust," and the usually pro-Ally *New York Times* characterized it as "quite the most tactless, foolish, and unnecessary act of the British government during the war."

The blacklist, coupled with a contemporary British order-in-council setting aside all that remained of the Declaration of London, and with the British government's ruthless suppression of an Irish rebellion in April 1916, aroused a storm of anti-British feeling in the United States, in which Wilson shared. "I am . . . about at the end of my patience with

Great Britain and the Allies," he wrote House. "This blacklist is the last straw." And to Page, home on vacation from the London embassy, Wilson remarked that earlier public sympathy for England and the Allies "had greatly changed. He saw no one who was not vexed and irritated by the arbitrary English course.[17]

Not loving Germany more but Britain less, Wilson reverted at this time to an attitude close to the impartiality in thought that he had advised in August 1914. He allowed his supporters to campaign for his reelection with the slogan "He kept us out of war," carrying the implication that if reelected he would continue to do so. At the same time, he had permitted himself to be won over to a program of military preparedness for the United States—a program for strengthening and improving the Army and greatly increasing the Navy. The naval increases, for whatever reason, were not in the small, swift ships that would be effective in combating submarines, but in battleships which might be expected to contest control of the seas with the British Grand Fleet. To House, with whom in September the President was discussing British relations, he remarked: "Let us build a navy bigger than hers and do as we please."

A Peace by Compromise or a "Knockout Blow"?

Had the German government continued to act with wisdom and moderation, it might well have capitalized upon Wilson's growing irritation at Great Britain, have insured the continued neutrality of the United States, and have won the war on the European continent. For after the collapse of Russia, which began

in March 1917, only the entry of the United States could save the Allies from defeat. Chancellor von Bethmann-Hollweg and other civilian elements in the German government desired to hold to a policy of conciliating the United States, but they were under constant pressure from the military and naval leaders, who wished either to make peace at once on their terms, or else to use the full power of the enlarged fleet of submarines to starve Great Britain into surrender.

Victorious against Russia in the east and against Rumania, which had rashly entered the war, in the Balkans, and holding their own on the western front in France and Belgium, Germany and her allies wished to conclude a peace that would reflect their favorable military situation. Through the fall they urged Wilson, as head of the leading neutral state, to invite the belligerents to a peace conference. When he procrastinated (chiefly, perhaps, because Colonel House opposed his taking such a step without Allied approval), the German government itself announced, December 12, 1916, that it was ready to begin peace negotiations.

In England, where a few months earlier proposals for a compromise peace might have got a hearing, David Lloyd George had replaced Asquith as Prime Minister, and Lloyd George had declared that only the defeat of Germany by a "knockout blow" could ensure a lasting peace. The Allies, therefore, contemptuously rejected the German invitation. When Wilson, hoping still to find a compromise, asked both sides to state their peace terms, the Central Powers refused, explaining that the proper place for such a statement would be the peace conference that they had suggested. The Allies, on the other hand, named terms so extravagant that only complete victory could have justified them.[18]

17. Congress empowered the President to retaliate for the British blacklist by refusing clearance to the ships of nations that discriminated against American commerce or to ships that refused to carry the products of blacklisted firms. The authority was not used because of advice from the Department of Commerce that British countermeasures might be disastrous to American industry. Tansill, *America Goes to War*, pp. 535–47; A. S. Link, *Woodrow Wilson and the Progressive Era, 1910–1917* (New York: Harper & Row, Publishers, 1954), pp. 219–22.

18. Wilson's biographer, Arthur Link, found evidence that Lansing secretly advised the British and French to name impossible conditions in order to insure the renewal of unrestricted submarine warfare and American participation in the war. Arthur S. Link, *Wilson* [5]: *Campaigns for Progressivism and Peace* (Princeton: Princeton University Press, 1965), pp. 221–25.

Wilson was under no illusions in regard to the probable consequences of the failure of these attempts to end the war. He knew that their failure must lead to resumption by Germany of unrestricted submarine warfare; that in that event he would have no course but to break off diplomatic relations with Germany; that severance of diplomatic relations would almost certainly be but a prelude to war. In his desire to halt this chain of events, the President made one last effort at peace. For months there had been forming in his mind the conception of a league of nations which, when the current war should end, would guarantee the world's peace against future wars.[19] The United States, he believed, should be a participant in such a league, but only if the terms of peace, which the league must guarantee, should conform to American ideals. It now occurred to him, apparently, that an outline of the kind of peace that America would be willing to support might serve as a basis for negotiations.

Accordingly, in an address to the Senate, January 22, 1917, Wilson undertook to state the conditions under which, as he said, the government of the United States "would feel justified in asking our people to approve its formal and solemn adherence to a League for Peace." His conditions were these: The peace must be "a peace without victory," since a peace forced by the victor upon the vanquished sows the seed of future wars. It must be a peace based upon the equality of rights of all nations, upon the principle of government by the consent of the governed, upon access to the sea for "every great people," upon freedom of the seas, and upon a general reduction of armaments. Here was an unprecedented offer to exert the influence and power of the United States for the maintenance of a just peace if the warring governments would but agree to make one.

The Germans Abandon Moderation

Whatever effect Wilson's pronouncement might have had if made earlier, it came too late to be useful. Three days before it was delivered, Ambassador von Bernstorff had been informed of his government's decision to resume unrestricted submarine warfare beginning February 1. Von Bernstorff, knowing better than his masters in Berlin what American entry into the war would mean, labored during the time that remained to persuade them to reconsider their decision. He had Wilson's promise, he reported, that if Germany would adhere to the *Sussex* pledge and offer reasonable peace terms, Wilson would use whatever pressure was needed to bring the Allies into line. His pleas were unheeded, and on January 31 he carried out his orders by announcing to Lansing that, because Great Britain was continuing her illegal practices, Germany would resume the "freedom of action" reserved in the *Sussex* note and beginning the next day, would sink all vessels encountered in the seas adjacent to the British Isles and the coasts of France and Italy. Neutral ships that had set out prior to the notification would be spared, and one American steamer weekly, carrying no contraband and painted with red and white stripes to insure identification, might proceed unmolested from New York to Falmouth, England.

On February 3, 1917, von Bernstorff was given his passports, and Ambassador Gerard was recalled from Berlin. Wilson still hoped to avoid war. The mere breaking of diplomatic relations, he hoped, might deter Germany from actually carrying out her threat. Unlike Lansing, he would, at least at this juncture, have stood aside while Germany won the war, provided only that she refrained from destroying American ships and American lives on the high seas.[20]

But Germany had not been bluffing. Her

---

19. Wilson had spoken to this effect at a dinner of the League to Enforce Peace, held in Washington, May 27, 1916. Henry Cabot Lodge spoke on the same occasion and in much the same sense.

20. In the hearings on the treaty with Germany in 1919, Wilson was asked: "Do you think that if Germany had committed no act of war or no act of injustice against our citizens that we would have

military masters were confident of crushing England by submarine blockade before the United States could take a telling part in the war. Sinkings began at once. Recalling, perhaps, the "armed neutralities" of days gone by, Wilson asked Congress for authority to arm American merchantmen against submarine attack and to use "any other instrumentalities or methods" to protect American lives and commerce. In the Senate "a little group of willful men" (Wilson's words) filibustered the bill to death in the closing days of the Sixty-fourth Congress; [21] but upon Lansing's advice that the necessary authority existed anyway, Wilson announced on March 12 that merchant ships would be provided with guns and gun crews.

In the meantime, February 24, the State Department had received from British Naval Intelligence an intercepted note from Herr Arthur Zimmermann, German Foreign Minister, to the German minister in Mexico, proposing that if the United States went to war, Mexico should ally herself with Germany and seek to persuade Japan (Great Britain's ally!) to do the same. For her cooperation Mexico would be rewarded by restoration of her "lost provinces" of Texas, New Mexico, and Arizona. The Zimmermann proposal, absurd though it was, was no more immoral than the secret treaties by which the Allies had agreed to apportion conquered enemy possessions among themselves. Nevertheless, its publication on March 1 created great indignation in the United States, particularly in the Southwest, where anti-German feeling had so far been at a minimum. It also added to Wilson's distrust of Germany and brought him a step

nearer to asking a declaration of war.[22]

On the same day (February 26) on which Wilson had asked for authority to arm merchantmen, it had become known that two American women had died when a German submarine sank the Cunard liner *Laconia* on February 25.[23] When to this act was added the torpedoing on March 18 of three American merchant ships, it became fully apparent that the German submarine campaign was on in deadly earnest, and that neither American lives nor American ships would be spared. For Wilson the only choice was between humiliating retreat and war. He chose the latter. In an address, April 2, 1917, to a special session of Congress, he related the history of the submarine controversy with Germany, denounced the current submarine campaign as "a warfare against mankind" and "war against all nations," and advised Congress to "accept the status of belligerent which has thus been thrust upon it." Going beyond the immediate purpose of defeating Germany, he declared it to be the purpose of the United States "to vindicate the principles of peace and justice . . . and to set up amongst the really free and self-governed peoples of the world such a concert of purpose and of action as will henceforth insure the observance of those principles." And again, in his final paragraph, he declared:

---

gotten into this war?" He replied: "I do think so." *Peace Treaty Hearings* (*Senate Document* 106, 66 Congress 1 sess.), p. 536. This later opinion is contradicted by what is known of the attitude of Wilson and the country in general in 1917. See the discussion in Link, *Wilson: Campaigns*, pp. 277–81.

21. The objections were to the broader authority asked by Wilson rather than to the mere arming of merchant vessels. For earlier armed neutralities, see pp. 22, 42.

22. Wilson was particularly indignant at the way in which the note had been sent. Because of British control of the cables, von Bernstorff had been permitted, by a technical violation of neutrality, to communicate with his government in cipher through the State Department and the American embassy in Berlin. Zimmermann's proposal to dismember the United States had been sent through this privileged channel to von Bernstorff in Washington and relayed by him to Minister von Eckhardt in Mexico City. British Intelligence, having possession of the German code, caught the communication from the cable and also as sent by wireless. R. S. Baker, *Woodrow Wilson, Life and Letters,* 8 vols. (Garden City: Doubleday & Company, Inc., 1927–1939), 6: 470–79; B. J. Hendrick, ed., *The Life and Letters of Walter H. Page,* 3 vols. (Garden City: Doubleday & Company, Inc., 1923–1925), 3: chap. 12.

23. Samuel R. Spencer, Jr., *Decision for War, 1917* (Peterborough, N. H.: Richard R. Smith Co., Inc., 1953), chap. 2.

. . . we shall fight for the things which we have always carried nearest our hearts,—for democracy, for the right of those who submit to authority to have a voice in their own Government, for the rights and liberties of small nations, for a universal dominion of right by such a concert of free peoples as shall bring peace and safety to all nations and make the world itself at last free. . . .

Four days later, April 6, 1917, Congress resolved: "That the state of war between the United States and the Imperial German Government which has been thrust upon the United States is hereby formally declared." The vote was 373 to 50 in the House, 82 to 6 in the Senate. On the same date the President proclaimed the existence of war.

The United States had quarreled with Germany, not with Germany's allies. Following the declaration of war, however, Austria-Hungary and Turkey broke off diplomatic relations with the United States. Bulgaria did not do so, nor did the United States sever relations with Bulgaria or declare war against Turkey. On December 7, 1917, after the disaster to the Italian Army at Caporetto, Congress declared war against Austria-Hungary upon advice that such action would bolster Italian morale.

With the British and French and their allies and associates in the war, the United States made no treaty of alliance. Its relation to them was described as that of an "associated power." The distinction was not important—a mere gesture out of respect to the American tradition against "entangling alliances"—for no ally could have given more complete military cooperation than did the United States.

President Wilson, in his war message, had indicated the forms that American cooperation might take: "the most liberal financial credits"; "the organization and mobilization of all the material resources of the country"; "the immediate full equipment of the Navy in all respects but particularly in supplying it with the best means of dealing with the enemy's submarines"; "the immediate addition to the armed forces of . . . at least five hundred thousand men, . . . and also the authorization of subsequent additional increments of equal force so soon as they may be needed and can be handled in training." The increments to the armed forces, Wilson added, "should, in my opinion, be chosen upon the principle of universal liability to service."

The program thus outlined by Wilson was the program actually followed, with details taking shape as the war progressed. Credits advanced to the Allied powers, exclusive of reconstruction credits granted after the armistice, totaled over seven billion dollars. The industrial resources of the country were, as never before, channeled into the production of goods needed for winning the war. A War Industries Board, created for the purpose, attained the status of an economic dictatorship. Food, rail transportation, and shipping were similarly controlled for the purpose of meeting

27

Preparing for the Peace Conference

most effectively the war-connected needs of the United States and its friends in Europe. American shipyards were mobilized and enlarged to produce replacements for the hundreds of ships sunk by submarine attack. The Navy, shelving temporarily its ambitious big-ship program, devoted itself to the war against the submarine. Destroyers and smaller "submarine-chasers" received priority in construction. An effective convoy system was introduced in cooperation with the British; and in the last year of war a great mine-barrage was laid across the narrows of the North Sea as a barrier to the exit of enemy submarines. The Army grew, with selective service as the chief factor in its increase, from two hundred thousand to four million men, of whom half were in Europe before the fighting ended.

In military policy, the United States threw its influence in favor of a united command over all armies on the western front, which was finally agreed to in the spring of 1918, with the French General Foch as supreme commander. General John J. Pershing, commander of the A. E. F. (American Expeditionary Force), resisted, with government backing, the Allied demand that American troops be brigaded with British and French. He insisted, at the cost of some delay in getting them into the line, that they be employed as a distinct United States Army, and he had his way. His insistence, also, that the United States Army be trained for open fighting, not merely for trench warfare, paid off when the great German retreat began.

Meantime, American ideas, particularly President Wilson's statements of war aims, were helping to win the war. In the war's closing months, airplanes and balloons dropped 100,000 leaflets daily far behind the German lines. These carried translations of Wilson's Fourteen Points and other addresses,[1] which called for no "unconditional surrender" but stressed his concept of a peace that should be fair and just to all, and his insistence that America's quarrel was with the German gov-

ernment, not with the German people, toward whom, he had said in his war message, "we have no feeling . . . but one of sympathy and friendship." Such propaganda, in the opinion of German military leaders, was effective in shattering the war morale of the German people and in preparing the way for both the German surrender and the Kaiser's abdication.[2]

The military history of the war would be out of place in this narrative. Suffice it to say that the withdrawal of Russia from the war after the Bolshevik revolution of November 1917 [3] enabled Germany to shift large forces from the eastern to the western front and to launch a succession of formidable offensives in the spring of 1918. With France and England near exhaustion after almost four years of war, only the timely arrival of American reinforcements prevented a German victory in France. With American aid the German drives were halted, and the last one, launched in July, was turned into a retreat that ended only with the signing of the armistice in November. By mid-August the German high command knew that victory was impossible and awaited only some minor success as an occasion for proposing peace. No minor success occurred. While the German armies were pushed back, Germany's allies were succumbing one by one. Bulgaria surrendered September 29, Turkey a month later. An Austrian proposal for a peace conference (September 16) was rejected by

1. See pp. 269–71.

2. W. P. Slosson, *The Great Crusade and After, 1914–1928*, Vol. 12 of *A History of American Life* (New York: The Macmillan Company, 1931), p. 65.

3. The government of the Czar was overthrown in March 1917 and succeeded by a provisional government representative of middle-class elements and headed by Prince Lvov as Premier and Professor Miliukov as Foreign Minister. These leaders tried to continue the war against Germany, as did the socialist Alexander Kerensky, who in July 1917 replaced Lvov as Premier. War weariness among soldiers, workers, and peasants played into the hands of the Communist, or Bolshevik, leaders, Lenin and Trotsky, who on November 7, 1917, overthrew the provisional government and substituted a government of soviets (working-class committees) headed by themselves. On December 15, 1917, they signed a military armistice with Germany and on March 3, 1918, agreed to the treaty of Brest-Litovsk.

Wilson, speaking for the Allies. Finally, on October 6 and 7, Germany and Austria-Hungary offered, through the neutral Swiss and Swedish governments, to make peace upon the terms previously set forth by President Wilson. Those terms must now be examined.

Wilson's Peace Program: The Fourteen Points

A few weeks before the United States entered the war, President Wilson had described in brief and general terms the kind of peace which, in his opinion, the American people would support.[4] For many months thereafter, the mobilization of the war machine absorbed his attention, but before the end of the year he felt that a more explicit statement of war aims was desirable. Such a statement might please liberal opinion in the United States and England and commit the Allied governments to a peace of justice rather than a peace of vengeance. It might win support among liberals and socialists in Germany. Most important, perhaps, it might satisfy the Bolshevik leaders in Russia and possibly dissuade them from making a separate peace with Germany.

Immediately after seizing power on November 7, 1917, the Bolshevik leaders had issued an appeal to all the belligerents to make peace on a basis of universal self-determination, a peace without annexations or indemnities. Only Germany and her allies responded favorably to this proposal, offering the prospect of a separate Russian-German peace. Colonel House, in Europe, tried to persuade the Allied leaders to match the Soviets in an idealistic declaration of war aims, hoping thereby to induce the Russians to adhere to the alliance. When the French and Italian Premiers refused to disavow their nationalistic objectives, Wilson resolved to issue a unilateral statement of the war aims of the United States. This he did in the famous Fourteen Points address to Congress of January 8, 1918.

That the address was aimed particularly at

Russia was made clear in the introductory paragraphs. Here the President referred to the negotiations then in progress between the Soviet government and the Central Powers and contrasted the reasonable proposals of the former with the imperialistic demands of the latter. He assured the Russian people of the deep sympathy of the people of the United States. ". . . It is our heartfelt desire and hope," he declared, "that some way may be opened whereby we may be privileged to assist the people of Russia to attain their utmost hope of liberty and ordered peace."

The President then came to his statement of American war aims, the object of which, he said, was "that the world be made fit and safe to live in; and particularly that it be made safe for every peaceloving nation. . . ." The Fourteen Points, briefly summarized, comprised:[5] "open covenants of peace, openly arrived at," freedom of the seas, removal of economic barriers, limitation of armaments, recognition of the interests of native populations in the adjustment of colonial claims, evacuation and restoration of Allied territory invaded by the Central Powers, readjustment of the boundaries of Italy, the Balkan States, and Turkey on lines of nationality, an independent Poland, opportunity for autonomous development for the peoples of Austria-Hungary, and the creation of "a general association of nations."

Point 6 dealt with Russia. It called for the evacuation of all occupied Russian territory and a sincere welcome of Russia "into the society of free nations under institutions of her own choosing; . . . The treatment accorded Russia by her sister nations in the months to come," the President continued, "will be the acid test of their good will, of their comprehension of her needs as distinguished from their own interests, and of their intelligent and unselfish sympathy."

Wilson's address had no effect on the Soviet-German peace negotiations. Neither did a speech on February 11, in which he specifi-

---

4. See p. 264.

5. See the end of this chapter for the Fourteen Points in full.

cally endorsed the Russian peace formula of "no annexations, no contributions, no punitive indemnities," nor a special message of friendship to the Russian people a month later. An armistice had been signed in December, and negotiations proceeded, with several interruptions, until March 3, 1918, when the Russians, in the treaty of Brest-Litovsk, accepted the harsh German terms. In that document, which the Congress of Soviets ratified on March 15, Russia surrendered title to Finland, the Baltic provinces, Lithuania, Russian Poland, and the Ukraine. Russia withdrew from the war, and German armies were shifted westward for the spring offensive in France.

But though Wilson's Fourteen Points failed to achieve their purpose in Russia, they did offer an idealistic peace program and gained for it a worldwide hearing. Because the Allied governments did not at the time repudiate or take exception to them, the Fourteen Points were generally accepted as a statement of the war aims of the Allies. Together with principles stated in several later addresses, they became the basis on which Germany offered to make peace.[6]

6. Scholars have detected thirteen additional or supplementary points in Wilson's addresses of February 11, July 4, and September 27, 1918, but nearly all of these are restatements or generalizations of principles (like that of self-determination) already explicit or implicit in the original fourteen. The following may be considered additions: (1) the renunciation of annexations, contributions, and punitive indemnities, cited above; (2) a statement in the same address (February 11, 1918) that "each part of the final settlement must be based upon . . . such adjustments as are most likely to bring a peace that will be permanent"; (3) a designation as an aim of first importance of "the destruction of every arbitrary power anywhere that can separately, secretly, and of its single choice disturb the peace of the world; or, if it cannot be presently destroyed, at the least its reduction to virtual impotence." Since Germany asked for peace on the basis of the Fourteen Points *and subsequent addresses,* these last two broad statements could be cited to justify the imposition of terms that seemed in conflict with the Fourteen Points. See T. A. Bailey, *Woodrow Wilson and the Lost Peace* (New York: The Macmillan Company, 1944), pp. 297–98. The later addresses are found in R. S. Baker and W. E. Dodd, eds., *The Public Papers of Woodrow Wilson: War and Peace,* 2 vols. (New York: Harper & Row, Publishers, 1927), 1, *passim.*

The Armistice

President Wilson now took it upon himself (despite objections from overseas) to act as spokesman for "the principal Allied and Associated Powers" in answering the Austrian and German peace overtures. As far as Austria was concerned the President replied that the Fourteen Points were no longer wholly applicable. Point 10 had declared for the autonomous development of the peoples of Austria-Hungary, but subsequently the United States had recognized a Czechoslovak National Council as a *de facto* government and had also given encouragement to the South Slavs under Austrian rule in their aspirations for independence. Hence, said the President, it was for those nationalities, not for him, to say what concessions from the Austro-Hungarian government would satisfy them.

To Germany, Wilson specified the conditions upon which the Allies would be willing to enter into peace negotiations. He insisted upon four things: full acceptance of the Wilson terms; complete evacuation of Allied territory; abandonment of illegal practices (obviously referring in part to submarine warfare) on sea and land; assurance that the German government which was to conduct the negotiations should represent the people, not "the military masters and the monarchical autocrats," of Germany. The last stipulation was construed in Germany as requiring the abdication of the Kaiser. This occurred on November 9, 1918, and on the same day there was organized a provisional German People's Government, headed by the socialist deputy, Friedrich Ebert.

In the meantime, Germany had accepted Wilson's other conditions. Then, however, it became apparent that Wilson's idealism had outdistanced the more mundane thinking of his European associates. Not until after a protracted argument and even a threat that the United States might make a separate peace with Germany did Colonel House, representing Wilson in Europe, secure acceptance of the Fourteen Points by the governments of England, France, and Italy. Even then, the acceptance was qualified by two reservations. On Wilson's second point, "freedom of the seas," a phrase open to varied interpretations, they reserved complete freedom of decision. Wilson's statement that territory occupied by the enemy should be "restored" as well as freed, they construed as meaning that Germany must pay compensation "for all damage done to the civilian population of the Allies and their property by the aggression of Germany by land, by sea and from the air." With this second reservation, which was to serve as the basis of the large reparations bill presented to Germany, Wilson indicated his complete agreement. The reply of the Allies, including the reservations, was communicated to the Germans on November 5,[7] and they were informed that Marshal Foch would formulate the military terms of an armistice. These included evacuation of all Allied territory and of the German lands west of the Rhine, and surrender of the German fleet, of heavy military equipment, and of large numbers of locomotives and freight cars. Acceptance of these terms would render Germany incapable of renewing the struggle.

German armies were still intact and held an unbroken line on foreign soil. But morale in both the civilian population and the armed forces had so nearly collapsed—witness a mutiny in the High Seas Fleet at Kiel on November 3—that the high command feared to continue the war. To prevent a destructive invasion of the Fatherland, the German government accepted Marshal Foch's terms. In a railway car near Compiègne, which served Foch as headquarters, the German commissioners signed the armistice at 5 A.M., November 11, to become effective six hours later.[8] Austria and Italy had signed an armistice on

November 3. The Austrian surrender terms did not, strictly speaking, include the Fourteen Points. Morally, however, Austria was entitled to expect that her peace settlement would conform to Wilson's principles.

Wilson Goes to Paris

Before the signing of the armistice, President Wilson had decided to attend the peace negotiations in person. For this decision he has been much criticized. His critics argue, first, that if he had remained in Washington, at a distance from the angry debates in Paris and immune from the compelling persuasiveness of Lloyd George and Clemenceau, he could have held out for a settlement more in accord with his ideals than that actually reached. They argue, in the second place, that in Washington he would have kept in touch with American opinion and might have avoided the collision with the Senate that in the end undid his work at Paris. Neither point can be proved. There is something to be said for Wilson's evident conviction that only his presence would ensure the acceptance of the kind of treaty that he deemed essential. Lloyd George himself, less than two years previously, had urged: "The President's presence at the peace conference is necessary for the proper organization of the world which must follow peace." [9] But whether Wilson's resolve to attend the conference was wise or mistaken, there is no doubt that he showed poor judgment in selecting the other delegates. The men chosen— House, Lansing, General Tasker H. Bliss, and the diplomat Henry White—were all estimable people, but not one of them possessed the kind of political influence that would be useful in seeing the treaty through the Senate. President McKinley, a smaller man but a wiser politician than Wilson, had named three senators, two Republicans and a Democrat, as members of

7. Not communicated to Germany with the reply of the Allies was a point-by-point interpretation of the Fourteen Points, worked out by Walter Lippmann and Frank Cobb, under Colonel House's direction. This is printed in *Foreign Relations, 1918, Supplement 1,* 1: 405–13, and conveniently reprinted in H. S. Commager, ed., *Documents of American History,* 7th ed. (New York: Appleton-Century-Crofts, 1963), 2: 139–43. There is nothing in this interpretation that would have been any more disturbing to the Germans than the second Allied reservation.

8. In this same railway car at Compiègne, on June

22, 1940, Adolf Hitler dictated armistice terms to a defeated France. He then had the car and the nearby monument to the former French victory transported to Berlin.

9. *Foreign Relations, 1917, Supplement 1,* p. 44.

the commission to make peace with Spain. Thus he not only flattered the *amour propre* of the Senate but also ensured bipartisan support for the treaty in that body. Wilson took no senator to Paris, and the only Republican among the delegates was Henry White, a career diplomat who did not count in Republican politics.

Wilson's failure to make a bid for Republican support was particularly imprudent, for the Senate that would pass upon the treaty would be controlled by a Republican majority. Just before the congressional elections of 1918, Wilson had appealed to the electorate to return Democratic majorities in House and Senate in order that he might, as he said, "continue to be your unembarrassed spokesman in affairs at home and abroad." The appeal had failed. Not only did the voters elect Republican majorities in both houses of Congress; Wilson's appeal, at a time when Republicans had supported the war as loyally as Democrats (though they had begun to attack his peace program), offended the party leaders and made it certain that they would view critically any treaty that Wilson might lay before the Senate.[10]

Under these circumstances Wilson would have been well advised to include at least one prominent Republican on his peace commission. Henry Cabot Lodge would, after March 4, 1919, become chairman of the Senate Committee on Foreign Relations. He would have been, for this reason, the logical choice. But if Wilson found Lodge objectionable, Elihu Root, William H. Taft, and Charles Evans Hughes were all prominent Republicans who sympathized generally with Wilson's program for a peace settlement and a league of nations.

Politically, then, the American delegation was weak. The fact that its members lacked detailed knowledge of the intricate problems facing them was not a serious deficiency, for the commission was to have the advice of a group of experts—historians, economists, bankers, geographers, ethnologists—who had been brought together at the instance of Colonel House. Though Wilson made less use of their advice than he might have done, the members of "The Inquiry" (as the group was called) won the hearty respect of their British opposite numbers and, in collaboration with the experts of other nationalities, actually wrote the less controversial portions of the treaty with Germany.[11]

Could Wilson Put Over His Program?

Wilson's grand purposes at Paris were two: (1) a peace settlement of justice, based, with respect to territorial adjustments, upon the principle of self-determination—a settlement that would leave no sores to serve as centers of infection productive of future wars; (2) the creation of a league of nations to ensure preservation of peace, the covenant of the league to be an integral part of the peace treaties, so that no government could participate in the peace settlement without becoming a member of the league. Adherence to the principles of the Fourteen Points, Wilson believed, would accomplish these objectives.

Wilson had advantages on his side but serious obstacles in his path. His chief advantage was the extraordinary position of moral leadership to which he had risen. His eloquent statements of idealistic war aims had made him a hero to liberals everywhere and had led war-weary or oppressed populations throughout the world to hail him as their deliverer. This moral leadership was fated to decline as ideals were forced to compromise with practical considerations and as the aspirations of different national groups—such as Italians and Yugoslavs—proved to be mutually incompatible.

One obstacle to a Wilsonian peace was the group of secret treaties and agreements that the Allies had made among themselves before

10. A factor in the Democratic defeat in 1918 may have been Wilson's consent to parley with the Germans when there was a popular hue and cry for an "On to Berlin" policy. Bailey, *Wilson and the Lost Peace*, pp. 40–41. The defeat has generally been ascribed more to domestic issues. See Selig Adler, "The Congressional Election of 1918," *South Atlantic Quarterly,* 36 (1937), 447–65.

11. L. E. Gelfand, *The Inquiry: American Preparation for Peace, 1917–1919* (New Haven: Yale University Press, 1963).

the United States entered the war. Thus France had been promised by Russia, although not by Great Britain, not only the return of Alsace-Lorraine, but also possession of the Saar Valley and the conversion of German territory west of the Rhine into an independent "buffer state." Italy had been assured of large accessions of Austrian territory in the Trentino or southern Tyrol and about the head of the Adriatic; and Japan had been promised the German islands in the North Pacific and the inheritance of German rights in Shantung. Russia also had been promised Constantinople and other Turkish territory, and still other portions of the Ottoman Empire had been apportioned prospectively among France, Great Britain, Italy, and Greece. The Russian claims were renounced by the Bolshevik government. The other Allies pushed their claims with varying degrees of persistence. The French and Italian claims in Europe and Japan's claim to Shantung were destined to give Wilson more headaches than any other problem of the Conference. The claims derived from the secret treaties conflicted with the principle of self-determination and specifically with Wilson's declaration (February 11, 1918) that "peoples and provinces are not to be bartered about from sovereignty to sovereignty as if they were mere chattels and pawns in a game." [12]

Wilson (despite a later denial before the Senate Committee on Foreign Relations) had certainly known of the existence of these treaties, with the exception of that concerning Shantung, since shortly after the United States entered the war. He had made no effort to have them set aside, and he rejected a French proposal for a conference agenda which stated, among other things, that all secret treaties should be suspended. In the showdown the principle of self-determination was in part sacrificed to claims based on these treaties.

A second obstacle in Wilson's path was the vindictive spirit prevalent among the peoples of the Allied countries, not excluding the United States—a spirit which, for the very reason that these countries were democratic, had to be taken into account. Lloyd George, Clemenceau, and Orlando (the Italian Premier) had all made extravagant promises to their electorates—that Germany should be made to pay for the war, the Kaiser should be hanged, and so forth. Now, often against their better judgment, they were under compulsion to exact the pound of flesh from the prostrate foe. Thus the very democracy that Wilson and Lansing thought a safeguard against war proved to be a barrier to a statesmanlike peace.[13]

Still a third obstacle to Wilson's success was the awareness on the part of the other negotiators that he had been in a manner repudiated in the recent congressional elections. He himself, in his pre-election appeal to the voters, had warned: "The return of a Republican majority to either house of the Congress would . . . be interpreted on the other side of the water as a repudiation of my leadership." When the election had given majorities in both houses to the Republicans, Theodore Roosevelt exulted in a public statement: "Our allies and our enemies and Mr. Wilson himself should all understand that Mr. Wilson has no authority whatever to speak for the American people at this time." Under analogous circumstances, Lloyd George or Clemenceau or Orlando would have had to resign his premiership. In their eyes Wilson's loss of the election inevitably lessened his bargaining power.

The Fourteen Points

[From Address of President Wilson to the Congress of the United States, January 8, 1918]

. . . The programme of the world's peace, . . . is our programme; and that programme, the only possible programme, as we see it, is this:

12. The texts of most of the secret agreements are found in H. W. V. Temperley, ed., *A History of the Peace Conference of Paris,* 6 vols. (London: Henry Frowde and Hodder & Stoughton, Ltd., 1920–1924), *passim.* Most of them were first published by the Bolshevik government of Russia in December 1917, as illustrative of the crimes of imperialism.

13. T. W. Lamont, *Across World Frontiers* (New York: Harcourt, Brace & World, Inc., 1951), p. 111.

I. Open covenants of peace, openly arrived at, after which there shall be no private international understandings of any kind but diplomacy shall proceed always frankly and in the public view.

II. Absolute freedom of navigation upon the seas, outside territorial waters, alike in peace and in war, except as the seas may be closed in whole or in part by international action for the enforcement of international covenants.

III. The removal, so far as possible, of all economic barriers and the establishment of an equality of trade conditions among all the nations consenting to the peace and associating themselves for its maintenance.

IV. Adequate guarantees given and taken that national armaments will be reduced to the lowest point consistent with domestic safety.

V. A free, open-minded, and absolutely impartial adjustment of all colonial claims, based upon a strict observance of the principle that in determining all such questions of sovereignty the interests of the populations concerned must have equal weight with the equitable claims of the government whose title is to be determined.

VI. The evacuation of all Russian territory and such a settlement of all questions affecting Russia as will secure the best and freest co-operation of the other nations of the world in obtaining for her an unhampered and unembarrassed opportunity for the independent determination of her own political development and national policy and assure her of a sincere welcome into the society of free nations under institutions of her own choosing; and, more than a welcome, assistance also of every kind that she may need and may herself desire. The treatment accorded Russia by her sister nations in the months to come will be the acid test of their good will, of their comprehension of her needs as distinguished from their own interests, and of their intelligent and unselfish sympathy.

VII. Belgium, the whole world will agree, must be evacuated and restored, without any attempt to limit the sovereignty which she enjoys in common with all other free nations. No other single act will serve as this will serve to restore confidence among the nations in the laws which they have themselves set and determined for the government of their relations with one another. Without this healing act the whole structure and validity of international law is forever impaired.

VIII. All French territory should be freed and the invaded portions restored, and the wrong done to France by Prussia in 1871 in the matter of Alsace-Lorraine, which has unsettled the peace of the world for nearly fifty years, should be righted, in order that peace may once more be made secure in the interest of all.

IX. A readjustment of the frontiers of Italy should be effected along clearly recognizable lines of nationality.

X. The peoples of Austria-Hungary, whose place among the nations we wish to see safeguarded and assured, should be accorded the freest opportunity of autonomous development.

XI. Rumania, Serbia, and Montenegro should be evacuated; occupied territories restored; Serbia accorded free and secure access to the sea; and the relations of the several Balkan states to one another determined by friendly counsel along historically established lines of allegiance and nationality; and international guarantees of the political and economic independence and territorial integrity of the several Balkan states should be entered into.

XII. The Turkish portions of the present Ottoman Empire should be assured a secure sovereignty, but the other nationalities which are now under Turkish rule should be assured an undoubted security of life and an absolutely unmolested opportunity of autonomous development, and the Dardanelles should be permanently opened as a free passage to the ships and commerce of all nations under international guarantees.

XIII. An independent Polish state should be erected which should include the territories inhabited by indisputably Polish populations, which should be assured a free and secure access to the sea, and whose political and economic independence and territorial integrity should be guaranteed by international covenant.

XIV. A general association of nations must be formed under specific covenants for the purpose of affording mutual guarantees of political independence and territorial integrity to great and small states alike.

In regard to these essential rectifications of wrong and assertions of right we feel ourselves to be intimate partners of all the governments and peoples associated together against the Imperialists. We cannot be separated in interest or divided in purpose. We stand together until the end.

28

The Treaty
of Versailles

President Wilson arrived in Paris on December 13, 1918, but not until the following January 12 did the representatives of the great powers hold their first formal meeting. Since November 1917, the British, French, and Italian Prime Ministers, with the occasional attendance of Colonel House representing President Wilson, had exercised direction of the war as the Supreme War Council. Now the three Prime Ministers—Lloyd George, Clemenceau, and Orlando—President Wilson, and the ranking Japanese delegate, representing the "Big Five" powers, took full charge of the Conference and assumed authority to make all crucial decisions. They determined what states should be represented, the number of delegates allowed to each, and the makeup of the commissions that did the bulk of the work of the Conference.

The Problem of Russia

The Conference comprised the representatives of the thirty-two "allied and associated powers," including the four British dominions and India. Neither the enemy states nor the neutrals had been invited to send delegates, nor had the Bolshevik (or Soviet) government of Russia. None of the states represented at the Conference had recognized that government. France, in particular, held that in making a separate peace with Germany the Soviet leaders had betrayed their allies and had forfeited any right to be represented at the general peacemaking. Wilson's plea in the Fourteen Points for a generous treatment of Russia did not, apparently, comprehend Russia's current rulers. Both he and Lloyd George, however, believed that the Russian people should be represented at a conference that was to remake the map of Europe, but since Russia was still in the throes of civil war between "Reds" and "Whites," there was no government or party that could speak for the Russian people as a whole.

At Wilson's suggestion, the Conference leaders proposed that all contending Russian factions agree to a cease-fire and send representatives to the island of Prinkipo in the Sea of Marmora to confer with one another and with spokesmen for the Allies and the United States. There was a faint hope that in this way the civil war might be ended, extremist positions moderated, and a delegation representing all Russian factions might be sent to Paris. The plan collapsed, despite qualified Soviet acceptance, when the chief "White" leaders (with French encouragement) refused to cooperate. Later an American secret mission to Russia, approved by Lloyd George and headed by William C. Bullitt, brought back a conciliatory offer from Lenin. News of the mission, meanwhile, had leaked to the press and caused such a furor in conservative quarters that Lloyd George repudiated it and Wilson refused even to see Bullitt when he returned to Paris.[1]

Soviet Russia, therefore, remained without visible representation at the Peace Conference. The threat of Bolshevism, however, was always present, like Banquo's ghost at the feast, and influenced in various ways the decisions of the Allied statesmen.[2] So far as their very limited resources permitted, the British and French gave aid to anti-Bolshevik Russian generals—Denikin in the South, Kolchak in Siberia. They had persuaded President Wilson in July 1918, after months of resistance, to consent to the landing of American troops at Archangel on the White Sea, and, with Japanese contingents, at Vladivostok, in Eastern Siberia. The Allies clearly hoped to use these troops in the fight against Bolshevism but were blocked by Wilson's stipulation that the American forces were to take no part in the contest between Russian factions.[3]

All such attempts at military counterrevolution were destined to failure, as was an American plan to bribe the Soviets into virtual surrender by providing food for the Russian people, reduced as they were to near starvation. As hope for destruction or subversion of the Soviet regime faded, the conservative Allied statesmen in Paris fell back upon "containment" as a second choice. Reliable anti-Communist governments of old and new nations in Eastern Europe—Rumania, Poland, Czechoslovakia—were strengthened by material aid and accessions of territory in order to form a *cordon sanitaire* on Russia's western border.

The problems arising from the prevalence of Communism in Russia and threats of its raising its head elsewhere in Eastern Europe (e.g. the short-lived regime of the Communist Béla Kun in Hungary, March to August 1919) were distracting but did not prevent the Conference from getting on with its other work. The Conference held a number of plenary sessions—ten from January to June—but these meetings were mainly ceremonial and served to rubber-stamp decisions already reached by the delegates of the Big Five powers. These, at the beginning of the Conference, began holding sessions as the so-called Council of Ten, comprising the heads of government and foreign ministers of Britain, France, Italy, and the United States and two of the Japanese delegates. This group became the dominating committee of the Conference and so remained until the latter part of March, when it was replaced by a still smaller group, the Council of Four—Wilson and the three prime ministers, Lloyd George, Clemenceau, and Orlando. During several weeks in April and May, while Orlando was sulking in Italy,[4] the Council of Four became a Council of Three. All crucial questions affecting Europe were decided, up to the signing of the treaty with Germany, by these three or four states-

1. G. F. Kennan, *Russia and the West under Lenin and Stalin* (Boston: Little, Brown and Company, 1961), chap. 9.
2. This thesis is expounded in great detail in A. J. Mayer, *Politics and Diplomacy of Peacemaking: Containment and Counterrevolution at Versailles, 1918–1919* (New York: Alfred A. Knopf, Inc., 1967), and more briefly, with specific reference to American policy in N. G. Levin, Jr., *Woodrow Wilson and World Politics: American Response to War and Revolution* (New York: Oxford University Press, 1968). Levin depicts Wilson's policy as a conscious attempt to steer a middle course between revolution and reaction.
3. See p. 309. I cannot accept the contention of Levin, *Wilson and World Politics,* pp. 197 ff., that

Wilson, contrary to the plain meaning of his words, intended that American troops should be used against the Bolshevik government.
4. See p. 281.

men. The great bulk of the detailed and routine work of the Conference, however, was done by commissions, composed of delegates and expert advisers. Fifty-two such commissions were organized, and it was they who actually wrote most of the treaty with Germany, subject always to the final decision of the Ten or the Four.

Until sometime in the spring, it was quite generally assumed that the Conference then in session was preliminary; that it would be followed by one in which the defeated powers would be permitted to negotiate, as the French had done at Vienna after the downfall of Napoleon, and perhaps would be allowed to mitigate some of the harsh features of the treaty. Such plans were laid aside. There were no second conference and no negotiation. The victors wrote the treaty and summoned the vanquished to sign on the dotted line.

Wilson's Great Victory— The League of Nations

Wilson's most conspicuous success at the Conference was the adoption of the Covenant of the League of Nations and the decision that it should be made an integral part of each peace treaty. Wilson himself was chairman, and Colonel House a member, of the commission appointed to draft the Covenant. The commission held ten sessions, from the third to the thirteenth of February, and on the fourteenth presented to a plenary session of the Conference the document which, with a few changes, became the Covenant of the League.[5]

With this initial triumph in his pocket, Wilson boarded the steamer *George Washington* to return to the United States, where his presence was necessary at the end of the congressional session, March 4. Supporters and

opponents of the League of Nations idea were already busy in the United States. In the Senate, where any treaty must run the gauntlet, partisan opposition was developing, joining hands with opposition that was honestly isolationist. Wilson, having "sold" his plan in Paris, must now attempt to convince his own countrymen.

At Colonel House's suggestion, Wilson had invited the members of the Senate Foreign Relations and House Foreign Affairs Committees to meet with him for discussion of the League Covenant. They dined at the White House (Senators Borah and Fall declining) on February 26. Wilson defended his pet project but won no converts among the doubters. A few hours before Congress adjourned, Senator Lodge read in the Senate a statement signed by thirty-seven Republican senators or senators-elect, declaring that "the constitution of the league of nations in the form now proposed . . . should not be accepted by the United States"; that peace with Germany should be made as soon as possible "and that the proposal for a league of nations to insure the permanent peace of the world should be then taken up for careful and serious consideration."

This famous "Round Robin," signed by four more senators than were needed to block a treaty,[6] Wilson met first by defiance and later by an attempt at conciliation. In a speech at the Metropolitan Opera House, New York, just before heading back to Paris, he told his opponents that when his work was done the treaty of peace would be tied with so many threads to the League Covenant that it would be impossible to separate them. It did not occur to him, apparently, that such organic union might result, not in acceptance of the Covenant, but in rejection of the treaty.

On the advice, however, of both Democratic and Republican friends of the League—the latter group including ex-President Taft and President Lowell of Harvard—who warned that without some changes the Covenant

---

5. See Chapter 29 for an analysis of the Covenant. The Covenant was not adopted at this plenary session. It was "deposited with the Bureau of the Conference for examination and study by all the interested powers." Stephen Bonsal, *Unfinished Business* (Garden City, N.Y.: Doubleday & Company, Inc., 1944), p. 57.

6. Really six more, for two additional senators signed later.

would never receive Senate approval, Wilson reconvened the League of Nations Commission and asked that the Covenant be amended. The changes deemed essential to insure Senate approval were four: (1) recognition of the right of members to withdraw from the League; (2) exemption of domestic questions (such as tariff and immigration) from League jurisdiction; (3) a statement that no member would be required, against its will, to accept a mandate over a former enemy colony; (4) a declaration safeguarding the Monroe Doctrine.

On two of these proposed changes—the right of withdrawal and the Monroe Doctrine —Wilson met stiff opposition, particularly from the French delegates, who argued that these changes would weaken the protection which France expected from the League. France, Great Britain, Italy, and Japan all tried to exact *quids pro quo* for their consent to the American amendments. France asked for an international general staff to direct action against new aggressions. Great Britain (outside the League Commission) demanded that the United States give up its ambitious naval building program. Italy stepped up its insistence that its new boundaries include Fiume, a city and port on the Adriatic.[7] Japan revived a proposal, made and discarded earlier, for a recognition of racial equality in the Preamble of the Covenant. After many days of apparent deadlock, Wilson secured the desired amendments without accepting the changes in the Covenant proposed by others. There is no doubt, however, that he paid in concessions in other matters for acquiescence of his colleagues in his embarrassed effort to placate the United States Senate or that his insistence upon what appeared to be special privileges for the United States weakened his moral position at Paris.[8] The amended Cove-

nant was adopted at a plenary session of the Conference on April 28.

The Peace and the Fourteen Points

In Wilson's mind the making of the League of Nations was the most important item in the peace settlement. To get the Covenant adopted, incorporated in the treaties with Germany and the other enemy states, and accepted by the principal Allied governments was an achievement so precious that he was willing to pay for it with concessions in other matters—concessions that in many cases contravened the principles of the Fourteen Points. What did some injustices here and there in boundaries or other particulars matter if the world had, in the League, machinery to prevent war and to correct wrongs by peaceful process? So the Fourteen Points, though not forgotten, were sometimes stretched till they were hardly recognizable. It would be a great mistake, however, to conclude that Wilson yielded on everything except the League. The surprising fact is not that he compromised on some points but that he saved as much of his program as he did.[9]

Apart from the League Covenant, the fruits of Wilson's efforts at Paris may best be estimated by comparing the terms of the peace settlement with the ideals set forth in the Fourteen Points and later addresses.

Wilson was successful in gaining assurances that hereafter international engagements would be "open covenants," as provided by the first of the Fourteen Points. Article 18 of the League Covenant required that every treaty or international engagement thereafter

7. See p. 281.
8. Bonsal, *Unfinished Business,* pp. 144–217, gives an excellent firsthand picture of this phase of the negotiations. The American amendments appear in Articles 1, 15, 21, and 22 of the Covenant. The Monroe Doctrine statement (Article 21) read: "Nothing in this Covenant shall be deemed to affect the validity of international engagements, such as treaties of arbitration or regional understandings like the Monroe doc-

trine, for securing the maintenance of peace." In the recognition of "regional understandings like the Monroe doctrine," the Japanese, Bonsal believes, saw an opportunity to bolster their position in relation to Manchuria and China. Did they not have "regional understandings" with regard to that area?
9. T. A. Bailey, *Woodrow Wilson and the Lost Peace* (New York: The Macmillan Company, 1944), chap. 20; Paul Birdsall, *Versailles Twenty Years After* (New York: Reynal & Company, Inc., 1941), *passim.*

entered into by any member of the League be registered with the League Secretariat and published as soon as possible. No treaty should be binding unless so registered. By Article 20 all engagements inconsistent with the terms of the Covenant were declared abrogated.[10]

Of point 2, "freedom of the seas," upon which the Allies had reserved freedom of decision, nothing further was heard. Nor was any step taken to implement point 3, removal of economic barriers, beyond the innocuous promise in Article 23 of the Covenant that members of the League would make provision to secure and maintain "equitable treatment for the commerce of all Members of the League."

The Covenant, in Article 8, recognized the necessity for the reduction of armaments (point 4) in the interest of peace and charged the Council of the League with formulating plans for such reduction. But members of the League were not obliged to accept such plans, and in practice no armaments were limited except those of the enemy states.

Point 5 had called for "a free, open-minded, and absolutely impartial adjustment of all colonial claims," with a view to the interests of the colonial populations no less than to the rights of the claimants. How was this principle to be applied to the former German colonies in Africa and the Pacific, all of which had been conquered during the war, and to the non-Turkish parts of the Ottoman Empire, which had been occupied by the Allied armies?

Had the precedents of the past and the secret understandings of wartime been followed, these areas would simply have been annexed by the conquerors, and this was what at least some of the conquerors desired. Such a solution, however, would have violated the spirit of point 5 and would have made ridiculous the professions of high moral purpose by the Allies and the United States. The dilemma was solved by the system of mandates, devised chiefly by one of the American experts, Professor G. L. Beer, and persuasively sponsored by Prime Minister Jan Christiaan Smuts of South Africa. As embodied in Article 22 of the Covenant, it provided that colonies and territories which had been detached by the war from the states that formerly governed them, and which were not prepared for self-government, should be placed under the tutelage of advanced nations which were competent and willing to undertake the responsibility. The nations accepting such assignments, or "mandates," should exercise authority on behalf of the League and should report annually to an organ of the League, a permanent Mandates Commission.

Wilson had hoped to see the mandates assigned to small neutral countries like Switzerland and the states of Scandinavia. In practice they were all given to the victorious Allies—the United Kingdom, the British Dominions, France, Belgium, and Japan—a distribution closely following the provisions of the secret understandings. Different mandatory powers took their obligations with varying degrees of responsibility. That the system was something more than the old imperialism camouflaged is shown by the progress toward, and final attainment of, independence by such of the mandated areas as Iraq, Jordan, Palestine, Syria, and Lebanon, even before the insistent anticolonial urge of the 1960's.[11]

Japan received the mandate for the former German islands in the North Pacific—the Marshalls, Carolines, and Marianas—but her claim to former German rights in Shantung was not thus disposed of. In 1915, as a feature of the Twenty-One Demands,[12] Japan had forced China to agree in advance to any ces-

10. The phrase "openly arrived at" in point 1 of the Fourteen was thus explained away in the House interpretation referred to above (p. 281, note 10): The phrase "was not meant to exclude confidential diplomatic negotiations involving delicate matters. The intention is that nothing which occurs in the course of such confidential negotiations shall be binding unless it appears in the final covenant made public to the world."

11. Bailey, *Wilson and the Lost Peace,* chap. 11; H. D. Hall, *Mandates, Dependencies and Trusteeships* (Washington: Carnegie Endowment for International Peace, 1948). Iraq, Trans-Jordan, and Palestine were British mandates; Syria and Lebanon, French.
12. See p. 306.

sion of rights that Japan might exact from Germany at the close of the war. Later she secured British and French promises to support her claim. China, asserting that her promise had been made under duress, now demanded the return to her of all German rights, privileges, and property in Shantung. Wilson was eager to restore to China what German imperialism had wrested from her, but Lloyd George and Clemenceau backed the Japanese claim. Japan played her trump card in a threat that unless humored in Shantung she would not join the League of Nations. To this menace Wilson yielded. The treaty assigned to Japan the German rights in Shantung, but Wilson did receive from the Japanese a promise that they would "hand back the Shantung Peninsula in full sovereignty to China retaining only the economic privileges granted to Germany and the right to establish a settlement . . . at Tsingtao."[13] This compromise, though probably representing the greatest concession that Japan could have been induced to make, was rejected by the Chinese delegation, which refused on that account to sign the treaty. Its unpopularity in the United States became one obstacle to approval of the treaty by the Senate.[14]

Self-Determination—for Friends but Not Always for Foes

Wilson's points 6 to 13 were concerned principally with the "restoration" of territory occupied by the enemy and the redrawing of national boundaries along lines of nationality or self-determination. In this respect the peace settlement registered some significant achievements but also some unfortunate surrenders.

(Point 6, on Russia, had presumably been rendered invalid by Russia's defection from the alliance.) Alsace-Lorraine was restored to France. The new states of Poland, Czechoslovakia, and Yugoslavia emerged from the breakup of Austria-Hungary and also from the detaching of Polish territory from Germany and Russia. Germany ceded to Denmark, Belgium, and Czechoslovakia small areas inhabited chiefly by people of those nationalities. Austria and Hungary were separated, and Transylvania was taken from Hungary and added to racially kindred Rumania. These were but the more significant of the changes in the European map made in response to the demands of nationalism. In the Near East, the Arab portions of the Ottoman Empire became independent (like Saudi Arabia) or were put on the road to independence under the mandate system. All this was in accord with the Fourteen Points.

The same can be said of Wilson's unyielding resistance to Italian demands for Fiume and French demands for German territory west of the Rhine. The city of Fiume on the Adriatic had a population more than half Italian, but its hinterland was Slavic and it was the natural outlet to the sea for both Yugoslavia and Austria. Although the secret treaty of London had not assigned Fiume to Italy, Italy now demanded both Fiume and non-Italian portions of the Dalmatian coast to assure her naval control of the Adriatic. Wilson refused. He even issued an appeal to the Italian people over the heads of the Italian delegates. He continued to refuse when those delegates, Orlando and Sonnino, dramatically left Paris and returned after two weeks during which they were enthusiastically acclaimed by the Italian people and given a vote of confidence by the Italian parliament.[15]

13. R. H. Fifield, *Woodrow Wilson and the Far East: The Diplomacy of the Shantung Question* (New York: Thomas Y. Crowell Company, 1952), treats the subject in great detail. Japan actually returned Shantung to Chinese sovereignty and renounced preferential rights in the province after the Washington Conference of 1921–1922. See below, Chapter 31. Japan failed in her attempt to insert in the League Covenant a declaration against racial discrimination.
14. See Chapter 29. China became a member of the League of Nations by signing the treaty with Austria.

15. The question of Fiume was not solved in Paris but was left to Italy and Yugoslavia to settle. In September 1919 the city was seized and occupied for Italy by the Italian poet-adventurer, Gabriele D'Annunzio. Late the following year, Italy and Yugoslavia agreed to recognize it as a "free state," and Italian troops expelled D'Annunzio's filibusters. This arrangement proving unsatisfactory, the two governments in 1924 divided it between them, Fiume proper going to Italy and the adjacent Port Baros to Yugoslavia.

France, for her part, demanded that the Rhineland (German territory west of the Rhine) be separated from Germany to serve as a buffer state, and that the Saar basin, valuable for its coal mines, be annexed to France. These demands (which had been agreed to by Russia in a secret exchange of notes in February 1917) the French attempted to justify on grounds of security, reparation for French coal mines flooded by the German armies, and the fact that France had exercised temporary sovereignty over the Saar a century before. In Wilson's mind, the French proposals were plainly in violation of the principle of self-determination. In a compromise solution, the Rhineland, although remaining under German sovereignty, was demilitarized as was a strip of land fifty kilometers wide east of the Rhine, and as additional security, the Allies were given for a period not to exceed fifteen years bridgeheads east of the river. France received title to the Saar coal mines, and for a fifteen-year period the Saar territory was to be administered by a commission of the League of Nations. At the end of that time the inhabitants would determine by plebiscite whether they should rejoin Germany, be annexed to France, or continue under international control.[16]

As a means of inducing the French government to abandon its designs upon the Saar and Rhineland—designs motivated by an understandable French concern for military security—Wilson consented to a tripartite agreement by which the United States and Great Britain promised to come to the aid of France if she should again be attacked by Germany. The American treaty was duly sent to the Senate but never reported out of committee.

But if Wilson fought for self-determination on the questions of Fiume and the Rhineland, he surrendered without a struggle in some other cases where that principle was involved. At the opening of the Conference, he promised the Italians the strategic frontier of the Bren-

ner Pass (which they claimed under the secret treaty of London), although that involved surrender by Austria of the South Tyrol or Trentino, populated by over 200,000 Austrian Germans. Likewise, with his consent, Austria with its seven million Germans, a small and feeble country since the destruction of the great empire once ruled from Vienna, was forbidden to unite with Germany. Such a natural solution of its problems was ruled out by French fears of an enlarged Germany. It would be easy to mention numerous other violations of self-determination—always in the interest of the victorious powers. Yet, by and large, self-determination won at Paris. "Many more millions of minority groups were released from alien domination than were consigned to alien domination. The result was the closest approximation that modern Europe has ever had to an ethnographic map coinciding with a political map." [17] Whether or not such an order of things is necessarily good, it was what Wilson had aimed at.

Reparations

In the light of subsequent events, it may be that Wilson's most serious failure at Paris was his consent to the reparations clauses of the treaty; for, although these brought little benefit to the victor powers and were in the end largely nullified, they created in Germany a feeling of grave injustice, a sense of grievance that boded ill for the future.

In his speech of February 11, 1918, the President had declared that there should be "no contributions, no punitive damages." [18] This speech was one of the "subsequent addresses" which, with the Fourteen Points, had been accepted as the basis of Germany's surrender. This particular stipulation had been

16. In 1935, after a vigorous campaign of Nazi propaganda, the people of the Saar voted overwhelmingly for reannexation to Germany.

17. Bailey, *Wilson and the Lost Peace,* p. 316.
18. The account of the reparations settlement is adapted with slight changes from J. W. Pratt, *Challenge and Rejection: The United States and World Leadership, 1900–1921* (New York), pp. 189–91. Copyright 1967 by The Macmillan Company. Selections from *Challenge and Rejection* reprinted by permission of the publisher.

qualified by the Allied reservation that Germany's obligation to "restore" occupied territory was to embrace payment "for all damages done to the civilian population of the Allies and their property by the aggression of Germany by land, by sea and from the air." This phrasing seemed to preclude any attempt to levy the cost of the war upon Germany, but Allied statesmen, particularly the British in the parliamentary election campaign of December 1918, had promised to do just that.

When Wilson rejected "war costs" as contrary to the terms of the armistice, Lloyd George brought forward the specious contention that pensions and separation allowances paid to Allied soldiers and their dependents could properly be classified as "damages done to the civilian population." In British eyes this thesis had the merit not only of doubling the aggregate reparations bill but of substantially increasing Britain's share, since actual damage to British civilian property had been comparatively slight. Wilson allowed himself to be convinced by the British argument, apparently under the impression that inclusion of pensions would merely increase the British share of a fixed sum based on calculations of Germany's capacity to pay.

The claim based on pensions and separation allowances was in fact added to claims for other losses. It brought the total reparations bill to a sum far exceeding any reasonable estimate of Germany's capacity to pay, particularly when other features of the treaty deprived her of resources that could have facilitated payment. These included her colonies, most of her merchant marine, German-owned property in Allied countries, the coal of the Saar, the iron ore of Lorraine, and a substantial fraction of both her industrial and her agricultural capacity. Wilson and his American advisers would have preferred to fix the sum to be paid then and there. The Allies, unable to agree on a figure, left it to be determined after the Conference by a Reparations Commission. It was eventually set at $33,000,000,000—thirty-three times the indemnity that Germany had imposed on France in 1871. Though only a small part of

it was ever actually paid,[19] the enormous bill left Germany with a justified sense of having been double-crossed. This feeling was aggravated by the imposition of the "war guilt" clause (Article 231) of the treaty by which Germany was required to accept for herself and her allies responsibility "for causing all the loss and damage" which the Allies and their nationals had suffered "as a consequence of the war imposed upon them by the aggression of Germany and her allies." This thesis of the exclusive responsibility of the Central Powers for the war may have been generally believed by the men who wrote the treaty. Accepted by the Germans under duress, it was not believed by them and is not sustained by history.

There are two prudent ways, thought Machiavelli, of dealing with a defeated enemy: either destroy him altogether or treat him so generously that he will become your friend. Any middle course is perilous. At Paris, Wilson and the Allies had chosen a middle course.

Germany Accepts

When the delegates of the Allied and Associated Powers had finished their wrangling over the terms of peace, they summoned the Germans to Paris—not to discuss the treaty, but to receive and prepare to sign it. At a plenary session of the Conference on May 7, 1919, Premier Clemenceau, as president of the Conference, handed the lengthy document of 440 articles to the German delegation headed by Count Brockdorff-Rantzau. The Germans received the treaty with a display of sullenness and discourtesy and made their reply on May 29 in a similar spirit. Thereby they injured their own case. Had they shown themselves conciliatory, had they singled out only the worst features of the treaty for criticism, they might have found much sympathy and support among the Allies, for many in the Allied delegations, having at last seen

19. See Chapter 32.

the treaty as a whole, were appalled at its severity. It had been written in sections, with the authors of each section largely in ignorance about the proceedings of others. Some of the commissions, furthermore, had worked with the idea that they were preparing "asking terms," which would be whittled down in negotiation. When the sections were assembled and stamped as final, their combined weight surprised even the authors.

Dissatisfaction with the severity of the treaty was especially strong among members of the British delegation. Had the Germans been good diplomats, they might have divided their opponents and have won large concessions. By their resentful attitude and by making a violent attack on all major features of the treaty, they helped to consolidate the Allied delegations around Clemenceau, who opposed any substantial moderating of the terms. A few concessions were in fact granted —slight modifications of the boundaries between Germany and Poland and Denmark, agreement that the disposition of a part of Upper Silesia should be decided by plebiscite instead of by outright cession to Poland, better German representation on the commissions that were to control German rivers, and assurance that the limitation of armaments imposed on Germany was "also the first step towards that general reduction and limitation of armaments . . . which it will be one of the first duties of the League of Nations to promote." With such minor changes and assurances as these, the Germans had to be content—unless they preferred to renew the war and have the Allied armies march on Berlin.[20]

On June 23, 1919, an hour and a half before the deadline set for expiration of the armistice, the Germans accepted the treaty. Formal signature by the delegations of thirty-two governments took place on June 28 in the Hall of Mirrors at Versailles—the hall in which the victorious Prussians had in 1871 proclaimed the establishment of the German Empire.[21]

Just before leaving Paris, President Wilson was asked at a press conference: "Mr. President, do you feel that you achieved here the peace that you expected to make?"

"I think," replied Wilson, "that we have made a better peace than I should have expected when I came here to Paris." [22]

---

20. The German counter-proposals and the allied reply are printed in *Foreign Relations of the United States: The Paris Peace Conference,* 13 vols. (Washington, D.C.: Government Printing Office, 1942–

1947), 6: 800 ff. See also J. T. Shotwell, *At the Paris Peace Conference* (New York: The Macmillan Company, 1937), chap. 4; H. W. V. Temperley, *A History of the Peace Conference of Paris,* 6 vols. (London: Henry Frowde, Hodder & Stoughton, Ltd., 1920–1924), 2: 1–20.

21. The treaty with Germany took effect—but not for the United States—on January 10, 1920. Treaties with the other Central Powers were signed as follows: with Austria at St. Germain-en-Laye, September 10, 1919; with Bulgaria at Neuilly-sur-Seine, November 27, 1919; with Hungary at the Trianon, June 4, 1920. A treaty with Turkey was signed at Sèvres, August 10, 1920, but the Nationalist revolution in Turkey prevented its taking effect. A treaty with the new Turkish government was signed at Lausanne, July 24, 1923. The United States shared in the negotiation of the treaties with Austria, Bulgaria, and Hungary but they were not sent to the Senate. The United States was not represented at Sèvres. At Lausanne an American "observer" negotiated two separate treaties with Turkey—a general treaty and an extradition treaty. The Senate rejected the former and approved the latter only in 1934, but diplomatic and consular relations with Turkey were reestablished by executive agreement in 1927.

22. *The Autobiography of Lincoln Steffens* (New York: Harcourt, Brace & World, Inc., 1931), pp. 788–89.

The Treaty of Versailles, making peace with Germany and embodying the Covenant of the League of Nations, was submitted by the President to the United States Senate on July 10, 1919. To most of the terms of peace with Germany there was little objection in the United States; only the cession to Japan of German rights in Shantung met serious opposition. American criticism centered on the League Covenant—that novel departure from the tradition of non-participation by the United States in the politics and controversies of the other hemisphere. What was the nature of the proposed League, and what were the responsibilities that the United States would assume if it accepted membership?

In Time of War Prepare for Peace

The outbreak of World War I had illustrated tragically the futility of such well-intended peace machinery as that set up at The Hague. A court of arbitration that no one was required to use might suffice for the settlement of minor problems; it would not be invoked in disputes affecting "vital interests" and "national honor"—the very disputes likely to lead to war. If the events of 1914 showed the inadequacy of the existing arrangements for preventing war, the destructiveness of the conflict that ensued convinced many that either war must be abolished or civilization would perish. Hence many men in many countries set to work to devise an effective method by which the nations of the world might organize to preserve the peace.

In the United States the most important unofficial effort in this direction was organized in Independence Hall, Philadelphia, June 17, 1915. Meeting in that historic spot, some three hundred distinguished citizens formed the League to Enforce Peace, chose William H. Taft as president, and put out a program in harmony with the name of the organization. The program proposed that the United States join a league of nations binding the members: (1) to submit all justiciable disputes to judicial settlement by a genuine international court of justice; (2) to submit all other disputes to a council of conciliation for study and

29

The League of Nations and the Senate

recommendation; (3) to participate jointly in economic or military sanctions, or both, against any nation that went to war without resorting to one of these methods of peaceful settlement; (4) to hold periodic conferences for the codification and revision of international law. The League to Enforce Peace held an impressive meeting in Washington on May 27, 1916, and heard sympathetic addresses from President Wilson and Senator Henry Cabot Lodge. Chambers of commerce throughout the United States endorsed its program and voted overwhelmingly that the United States should take the initiative in forming an international organization to carry it out.

Parallel movements were in progress in other countries. A Central Organization for a Durable Peace, organized at The Hague in April 1915, represented both neutral and belligerent opinion. In the following month, a British League of Nations Society was founded. In September 1916 the British Cabinet set up a committee headed by the distinguished jurist, W. G. F. (later Lord) Phillimore, to study the same subject. Its proposals, known as the Phillimore Report, became one of the important sources of the League Covenant.[1]

President Wilson endorsed, at least in principle, the program of the League to Enforce Peace; he seems never to have sought the advice of its leaders or to have taken them into his confidence. In January 1917, as was recorded in an earlier chapter,[2] he assured the warring nations that the United States would cooperate in preserving a peace made upon terms consistent with American ideas of fairness and justice. A year later, in the Fourteen Points address, "a general association of nations" held the climactic position in the list. Not until the summer of 1918, however, did he attempt to work out the details of the proposed organization. Taking the Phillimore

1. D. F. Fleming, *The United States and World Organization, 1920–1933* (New York: Columbia University Press, 1938), pp. 11–15; R. J. Bartlett, *The League to Enforce Peace* (Chapel Hill: University of North Carolina Press, 1944), pp. 40–41.
2. See p. 264.

Report as a starting point, he and Colonel House then devised a draft of their own, in which were later incorporated suggestions from other sources, American and foreign. At Paris a final draft by Wilson was combined with another British draft, and the two were worked together by American and British legal experts into the draft that was laid before the League of Nations Commission and, variously amended by it, became the Covenant of the League of Nations. The Covenant was a product of many minds. Wilson, only in part its author, became its principal champion.

The League of Nations Covenant

Original membership in the League was to include the signatories to the treaty (with the exception of Germany) and thirteen additional states named in an annex, or as many of them as should accede to the Covenant without reservation. Any other "fully self-governing State, Dominion or Colony" might, upon giving certain guarantees, be admitted to membership by a two-thirds vote of the League Assembly. A member of the League might withdraw after two years' notice if it had fulfilled all its international engagements and its obligations to the League. A member could be expelled for violation of "any covenant of the League."

The Covenant named three organs of the League: an Assembly in which every member should be represented and have one vote; a Council comprising representatives of the "Big Five" powers (the United States, Great Britain, France, Italy, and Japan) and of four other powers to be selected from time to time by the Assembly; and a permanent Secretariat. In addition, Article 14 directed the Council to formulate and submit to the members for adoption plans for a Permanent Court of International Justice. Geneva, Switzerland, was designated as the seat of the League, subject to the right of the Council to fix it elsewhere.

The Covenant of the League, and hence

the League itself, were primarily political in character. The Covenant, it is true, showed some concern for the economic and social betterment of the peoples of the world. It pledged the members to "endeavour to secure and maintain fair and humane conditions of labour for men, women, and children" and to establish for that purpose "the necessary international organizations"; [3] to "undertake to secure just treatment of the native inhabitants of territories under their control"; to entrust the League with supervision of "the execution of agreements with regard to the traffic in women and children, and the traffic in opium"; to ensure freedom of communications and transit and equitable treatment of the commerce of League members; and to "endeavour to take steps in matters of international concern for the prevention and control of disease." The Covenant provided also that the League might take over, with the consent of the governments concerned, existing international bureaus, some of which might be concerned with economic and social matters, and that any such bureaus established in the future *should* be under League direction; and it promised encouragement for voluntary national Red Cross organizations for the purpose of improving health, preventing disease, and mitigating suffering throughout the world. But mention of these objectives occupies a very small space in a document in which the emphasis was overwhelmingly on the peaceful settlement of international disputes and the prevention of international aggression and war.

How the League Would Keep the Peace

The "heart of the Covenant," in Wilson's words, was Article 10, which read:

> The Members of the League undertake to respect and preserve as against external aggres-

3. Part XIII of the treaty with Germany provided for the creation of the International Labor Organization.

sion the territorial integrity and existing political independence of all Members of the League. In case of any such aggression or in case of any threat or danger of such aggression the Council shall advise upon the means by which this obligation shall be fulfilled.

The Preamble of the Covenant mentioned "the acceptance of obligations not to resort to war" as one of the means by which the signatory powers hoped "to achieve international peace and security." Articles 12, 13, and 15 embodied these obligations, although, as will be seen, the obligation not to resort to war was not quite complete. Member states agreed to submit either to arbitration or to study by the Council "any dispute likely to lead to a rupture" (unless it arose out of a matter wholly within the domestic jurisdiction of one of the parties), to abide by an arbitral award, and, if the Council should agree unanimously upon a recommendation (not counting the votes of parties to the dispute), not to go to war with any party to a dispute that complied with such recommendation.[4] Thus there could be no "legal" war between members of the League if a dispute was settled either by arbitration or by a unanimous vote of the Council (barring the votes of the parties to the dispute). But if the dispute was referred to the Council and that body failed to make a unanimous report or recommendation, the members of the League reserved to themselves "the right to take such action as they shall consider necessary for the maintenance of right and justice." Under these circumstances, in other words, members of the League might go to war with one another without violating their engagements under the Covenant.

In these ways and with the exception described, members of the League obligated

4. The Council might upon its own initiative, and must at the request of any party to a dispute, refer the dispute from itself to the Assembly. In the latter body, the equivalent of a unanimous recommendation of the Council would be a report "concurred in by the Representatives of those Members of the League represented on the Council and of a majority of other Members of the League exclusive in each case of the Representatives of the parties to the dispute."

themselves not to resort to war as a means of settling their disputes with one another. But what of the state that should violate these promises? What penalties would it suffer? What "sanctions" were its fellow members bound to impose? This important—potentially all-important—question was answered in Article 16. Any member that resorted to war in disregard of its "covenants" under Articles 12, 13, and 15 was declared to have committed, *ipso facto,* "an act of war against all other Members of the League." Against such a covenant-breaking state the members of the League undertook

> immediately to subject it to the severance of all trade or financial relations, the prohibition of all intercourse between their nationals and the nationals of the covenant-breaking State, and the prevention of all financial, commercial or personal intercourse between the nationals of the covenant-breaking State and the nationals of any other State, whether a Member of the League or not.

In other words, members of the League undertook to subject to complete blockade, in trade, finance, and communications, any one of their number that made war in disregard of its promises. They might even declare it to be no longer a member of the League. There was no explicit promise to use armed force, but the next paragraph made it

> the duty of the Council in such case to recommend to the several Governments concerned what effective military, naval or air force the Members of the League shall severally contribute to the armed forces to be used to protect the covenants of the League.

This statement carried the plain implication that it would be the duty of member governments to provide the armed forces recommended by the Council.

Such were the peacekeeping features of the League of Nations Covenant that Wilson brought back with him from Paris. They were not watertight, but they gave reasonable promise, if all the great powers joined and lived up to the letter and spirit of their com-

mitments, of preventing aggression and war for a long time to come. If the Covenant as a whole, and especially Article 10, looked too much like a "freezing" of the *status quo,* there was hope of alleviation, of peaceful change, in Article 19, which declared:

> The Assembly may from time to time advise the reconsideration by Members of the League of treaties which have become inapplicable and the consideration of international conditions whose continuance might endanger the peace of the world.[5]

The League of Nations might work successfully if the great powers gave their wholehearted cooperation. One great power, the United States, was already assured of a special status in the League. Article 21, inserted in the Covenant by Wilson on the advice of American friends of the League declared:

> Nothing in this Covenant shall be deemed to affect the validity of international engagements, such as treaties of arbitration or regional understandings like the Monroe doctrine for securing the maintenance of peace.

Would the Senate be satisfied with this concession to American tradition, and those others that Wilson had pushed through the Commission at Paris? Would the United States, having cooperated magnificently (if tardily) in winning the war, now cooperate in maintaining the peace?

---

5. *Other features of the Covenant.* Mentioned in the preceding chapter were the provision for the mandate system (Article 22), the directive to the Council to work out a scheme of arms limitation (Article 8), the requirement that all treaties be registered with the Secretariat and published (Article 18), and the agreement that acceptance of the Covenant abrogated all international obligations inconsistent with it. Article 11 empowered the League, on its own initiative, to take action for meeting any war or threat of war and declared it the right of each member to bring to the attention of Council or Assembly any situation which threatened to disturb the peace. Article 17 prescribed procedures in the event of disputes with or between states not members of the League. Article 26 made amendment of the Covenant comparatively simple.

The Opposition Organizes

Wilson officially laid the treaty before the Senate on July 10, 1919. To the senators the document was not new. Weeks earlier Senator William E. Borah of Idaho, a leading opponent of the League, had procured a copy with the assistance of a Chicago *Tribune* journalist and had read the long text verbatim into the *Congressional Record,* so that not only senators and members of the House, but any of the public who cared to, might peruse it. The general nature of Part I, the League of Nations Covenant, had been known since February, and had been debated by both friends and foes. The amendments subsequently added to the Covenant had also been published, and Senator Henry Cabot Lodge, who had rebuffed an inquiry from Delegate Henry White as to what changes would satisfy the Senate, had let it be known that Wilson's changes did not satisfy him. From the time that the Senate met in special session in May, Republican opponents of the treaty in its existing form had been planning strategy. Senator Knox (formerly Taft's Secretary of State) introduced a resolution to separate Covenant from treaty so that the latter could be approved without accepting the League. A more indirect method was adopted. Senator Lodge, who almost certainly desired to see the treaty defeated despite his protestations to the contrary,[6] believed that sentiment for the League was so strong both in the country and in the Senate that the treaty could not be defeated by direct attack. The course adopted was a dual one: first, to delay action by prolonged hearings and debate, giving pro-League enthusiasm time to cool; second, to load the treaty down with amend-

ments or reservations and then count upon Wilson and the Democrats to reject it. Such tactics would appear to shift the responsibility for killing the treaty from its opponents to its friends.[7]

Opposition to the treaty stemmed from varied motives. Sincere isolationists feared the League as a "super-state," which would destroy American independence and drag the United States into quarrels with which it had no concern. A resurgent nationalism saw treason in an attempt to subject the will of the American people to any form or degree of international control. "If the Savior of men," said Senator Borah, "would revisit the earth and declare for a League of Nations, I would be opposed to it." The League, he said, was "the first step in internationalism and the sterilization of nationalism." A western "progressive" in domestic politics, Borah charged that the League was designed as a tool of Wall Street bankers and big businessmen. His feeling was shared by many liberals, former supporters of Wilson, who now attacked him for surrendering his principles and selling out to British, French, and Japanese "imperialists." Socialists of nearly all varieties would have none of the League because, as they charged, it enthroned capitalism.[8] While liberals and radicals were damning the League as an invention of big business, isolationist Senators Knox and Brandegee were obtaining from millionaires Andrew W. Mellon and Henry Clay Frick funds with which to fight the treaty. The battle made strange bedfellows.

Racial groups in the United States stemming from "oppressed" nationalities to whom the Paris settlement had brought neither independence nor self-determination were bitter against the treaty and the League. Most

6. H. C. Lodge, *The Senate and the League of Nations* (New York: Charles Scribner's Sons, 1925), p. 209. For an opposite view, see especially Fleming, *The U.S. and World Organization,* pp. 19–25; also D. F. Fleming, *The United States and the League of Nations, 1918–1920* (New York: G. P. Putnam's Sons, 1932), pp. 475–87.

7. Lodge, *Senate and the League of Nations,* p. 164.
8. The liberals' break with Wilson is well described in Selig Adler, *The Isolationist Impulse: Its Twentieth Century Reaction* (New York: Abelard-Schuman Limited, 1957), chap. 3. Especially illuminating was the defection of the weekly periodicals *New Republic* and *Nation.* Chapter 5 of the same work describes the resurgence of nationalism.

numerous, best organized, and most influential were the Irish, who through their society, "Friends of Irish Freedom," missed no opportunity to damn Wilson and the League for failing to rescue Ireland from British tyranny. Egyptians and Indians, though not numerous in the United States, found many friends who added their voices to those of Erin. American committes were organized to promote freedom for Korea and for Armenia, other neglected nationalities. Italian-Americans resented Wilson's refusal to give Fiume to Italy. German-Americans, of course, deplored the harsh terms imposed on the Fatherland. All these groups gave their support to the senators opposing the treaty.[9]

Partisanship and personal feuds made their contributions to the opposition. Republicans, with an eye on the 1920 campaign, even suspecting that Wilson might run for a third term, were reluctant to place such an impressive achievement as the League in Democratic hands. Senatorial jealousy of the executive and personal dislike for Wilson on the part of some senators were certainly among the motives that stimulated the fight against the League Covenant and the treaty of which it it was a part.

Leader and organizer of the Senate opposition was Senator Henry Cabot Lodge, chairman of the Committee on Foreign Relations in the newly elected Senate, which the Republicans controlled by the slender majority of 49 to 47. Lodge found a complex picture in the Senate. Of forty-nine Republicans, fifteen were bitter-end opponents of the League—"irreconcilables" they came to be called. They would vote with Lodge for any reservations he cared to propose and at the end would vote against the treaty even with reservations. Thirty-four would vote for reservations of varying degrees of strictness and would vote for the treaty with reservations that suited them. Eight to ten of these were "mild reservationists," strongly pro-League. About eighteen stood with Lodge for strong reservations or amendments. The remainder were somewhere between these and the "mild

reservationists." Lodge's first problem was to unite the Republican majority behind a set of reservations strong enough to "make the League safe for the United States" if the treaty passed, or perhaps strong enough to ensure its defeat by the Democrats. The Senate Democrats, too, were divided. Reed of Missouri voted always with the Republican irreconcilables; Gore of Oklahoma and Shields of Tennessee would support the treaty only with strong reservations. Several others, pro-League but not 100 percent pro-Wilson's Covenant, would support Lodge at least part way. The remaining Democrats were divided about equally between those who insisted on the Covenant as it was and those who would take it either with or without reservations.

An Unsympathetic Committee

The first hurdle for the treaty was the Committee on Foreign Relations. Lodge, the chairman, had seen to it that the committee was "packed" with senators unfriendly to the League. Of the ten Republican members, six —a disproportionately large number—came from the irreconcilable group. They included such redoubtable foes of the League as Borah of Idaho, Knox of Pennsylvania, and Hiram Johnson of California. Two others, Harding of Ohio and New of Indiana, were reliable party men. Only McCumber of North Dakota, among the Republicans, could be described as genuinely pro-League. The seven Democrats on the committee were fairly representative of their party in the Senate; even one of them, Shields of Tennessee, agreed more with Lodge than with Wilson.[10]

Officially printed copies of the treaty were available to the committee on July 14. As a part of the strategy of delay, however, hearings were not begun until July 31. Wilson himself was heard—the committee meeting with him at the White House August 19—as was Secretary Lansing. Lansing, who did not share Wilson's enthusiasm for the League, did

9. Adler, *The Isolationist Impulse,* chap. 4.

10. Lodge, *Senate and the League of Nations,* p. 151.

not betray his skepticism to the committee; but another witness, William C. Bullitt, bared the rift in the American delegation. Bullitt, one of the "experts" attached to the delegation, had resigned in a huff in Paris. He now voluntarily revealed to the committee a confidential conversation with Lansing, in which the Secretary reportedly had described the League of Nations as "entirely useless" and had added that "if the Senate could only understand what this Treaty means, . . . it would unquestionably be defeated." Though Lansing asserted that his language had been distorted, Bullitt's testimony was damaging to the chances of the League. So also was much of the other testimony, for the committee heard, for the most part, unfriendly witnesses.

An Appeal to the People

Wilson, in his testimony before the committee, had stated that he would not object to interpretative or clarifying reservations, provided these were not incorporated in the resolution of ratification. If they were so incorporated, he explained (inaccurately), he would have to obtain the consent of the other parties to the treaty before ratification could be completed. It now appeared that the committee, and perhaps the Senate, would insist on much more than the interpretative reservations that Wilson was willing to accept.

Wilson, consequently, resolved to appeal to the country over the heads of the Senate, and, like President Andrew Johnson before him, set out on a "swing around the circle." His tour was routed through the Old Northwest, the Upper Mississippi Valley, and the Far West—the sections that furnished much of the opposition to the treaty. Despite the rather academic and "literary" style of his addresses, Wilson roused much popular enthusiasm with his appeal for a League that should make unnecessary a repetition of recent sacrifices, and his warning that failure to make the League work would surely open the way for new aggressions in Europe and new necessity for intervention by the United States. His

reception was particularly warm and enthusiastic on the Pacific coast and at his last appearance, in Pueblo, Colorado.

But although Wilson had captivated popular audiences, he had no success in winning the needed senatorial support. His references to his opponents were unconciliatory, tactless, and in some instances offensive. He offered no compromise; the Senate, he said, must take the treaty as it was or have no treaty at all. Senators who would withhold the support of the United States from the peace organization would be, he said, "absolute, contemptible quitters." Isolationist senators trailed his footsteps, giving their side of the argument to the same public he had addressed. Wilson won no votes in the Senate, and his opponents, if they were changed at all, were more bitterly defiant than before.

Practically speaking, the trip was a failure, and it ended in tragedy. The strain of the effort—the thirty-six formal addresses in addition to numerous "whistle-stop" back-platform speeches, the intense heat without benefit of air conditioning, the unrelenting personal interviews and press conferences—was too much for a constitution already weakened by the long struggle in Paris. After the speech at Pueblo, September 29, Wilson's health gave way. He was rushed back to Washington, a very ill man. A few days later came the paralytic stroke that made him for months an almost helpless invalid and from which he never fully recovered. Secluded from friends and shielded from sound advice by the solicitous Mrs. Wilson, the sick man in the White House clung to his insistence that the treaty must be approved as he had written it or not at all. It would have been far better had he stayed in Washington and continued the effort, begun in July and August, to reach agreement with the "mild reservationists" and the moderate Republicans.[11]

11. Kurt Wimer, "Woodrow Wilson Tries Conciliation: An Effort That Failed," *The Historian*, 25 (August 1963), 419–38. Wilson's speaking tour and its results are well described and appraised in T. A. Bailey, *Woodrow Wilson and the Great Betrayal* (New York: The Macmillan Company, 1945), chaps. 6, 7.

Senator Lodge's Fourteen Points

Meanwhile, the Foreign Relations Committee had completed hearings on the treaty, and on September 10 the majority made its first report, proposing forty-five amendments and four reservations. This action was too drastic even for many Republicans. About a dozen of them joined the Democrats in voting down the committee's amendments and others offered from the floor. The idea of amending was given up, and on November 6, Lodge proposed a resolution of advice and consent to ratification subject to fourteen reservations. Of these, twelve were accepted by the Senate and two more added, restoring the number to fourteen. In adopting the reservations, the Republicans held together almost solidly and had the aid of a number of Democratic votes, ranging from four to ten on different reservations.[12]

The substance of the reservations thus adopted may be described without taking them up point by point. The majority of them simply made explicit the retention of powers by the United States or by Congress that under the Covenant could hardly have been denied them. They declared, for example, that the United States should judge, in case it withdrew from the League, whether it had fulfilled its obligations. They reserved to the United States the right to decide what questions were (for it) domestic and hence outside the jurisdiction of the League, and they specified as domestic questions immigration, labor, coastwise traffic, the tariff, commerce, and the suppression of traffic in women and children and in opium and other dangerous drugs. They reserved to Congress the right to determine whether the United States should accept a mandate or should participate in the International Labor Organization proposed in Part XIII of the treaty; the right to provide by

law for the appointment of United States representatives to the League, to appropriate funds for the American share of League expense, and to give or withhold assent to interference by the Reparations Commission with trade between the United States and Germany. Such provisions as these were comparatively harmless. Much more controversial were those on Article 10 (the mutual guarantee of independence and territorial integrity), the Monroe Doctrine, the multiple votes of the British Empire, and the Shantung section of the treaty.

The second reservation stated:

> The United States assumes no obligation to preserve the territorial integrity or political independence of any other country or to interfere in controversies between nations—whether members of the league or not—under the provisions of article 10, or to employ the military or naval forces of the United States under any article of the treaty for any purpose, unless in any particular case the Congress, which, under the Constitution, has the sole power to declare war or authorize the employment of the military or naval forces of the United States, shall by act or joint resolution so provide.

The fifth reservation declared that the United States would not submit to arbitration or to inquiry by the Assembly or Council of the League any question that in its judgment depended upon or related to "its long-established policy, commonly known as the Monroe doctrine," and announced further, that that doctrine was "to be interpreted by the United States alone" and was "wholly outside the jurisdiction" of the League.

Reservation 6 withheld the assent of the United States from the Shantung settlement.

Reservation 14, alluding to the fact that the four British dominions and India were to be members of the League, announced that the United States assumed no obligation to be bound by any decision of the Council or Assembly in which "any member of the league and its self-governing dominions, colonies, or parts of empire, in the aggregate have cast more than one vote"; and furthermore that

---

12. On the third reservation, declaring that the United States should accept no mandate without consent of Congress, there was no objection and no record vote. Lodge, *Senate and the League of Nations,* p. 185.

it assumed no obligation to be bound by a decision "arising out of any dispute between the United States and any member of the league if such member, or any self-governing dominion . . . [etc.] united with it politically has voted."

These four were the reservations likely to cause trouble. The introductory resolution stated that ratification would not take effect until the reservations had been accepted by an exchange of notes by three of the four "principal allied and associated powers"— Great Britain, France, Italy, and Japan. Would Great Britain accept reservation 14 limiting the voting power of the dominions? Would France, already worried about security, accept the qualification to the guarantees of Article 10? Would Japan ratify the treaty in the face of American refusal to recognize her rights in Shantung? Would any three of them agree to the sweeping reservation on the Monroe Doctrine? But these questions were as yet academic. The immediate problem was whether Wilson and his friends in the Senate would accept the Lodge program. Would the invalid in the White House, despite his defiant utterances on the stump, consent to take half a loaf rather than no bread? Would Democratic senators vote to approve the treaty with the Lodge reservations?

The First Defeat

Wilson was not opposed to all compromise. Before setting out on his speaking tour he had handed to Senator Gilbert M. Hitchcock, minority leader in the Senate, four reservations that he would be willing to accept if such a course were necessary to get the treaty approved. These dealt with withdrawal from the League, Article 10, the Monroe Doctrine, and domestic questions, and differed from the Lodge reservations on the same points more in wording than in substance. They were so similar to proposals made by the Republican mild reservationists as to suggest that the latter and the Democrats could readily have

reached a compromise had Wilson encouraged such an effort. But when, in November, Hitchcock introduced the substance of the Wilson reservations, adding a fifth on the British Empire's six votes,[13] the moderate Republicans had committed themselves to the Lodge program and complained with reason that Hitchcock came late with his appeal for compromise.

This far Wilson was willing to go, but no farther. The Lodge reservation on Article 10 he had denounced as "a rejection of the covenant." As the day approached for the vote on the treaty with the fourteen reservations, he wrote from his sickbed to Senator Hitchcock that affirmative action would mean not ratification but "nullification of the treaty." "I trust," he added, "that all true friends of the treaty will refuse to support the Lodge resolution."

Hitchcock and the Democrats heeded the word of their stricken leader. Some of them, perhaps, hoped as he did that defeat of the treaty with the Lodge encumbrances would clear the way for a favorable vote on the treaty without, or with only mild, reservations—a vote in which enough moderate Republicans would join the Democrats to provide the needed two-thirds. And so, on November 19, 1919, all but four of the Democrats joined the Republican irreconcilables to defeat the treaty with the reservations by a vote of 39 to 55. A second vote showed a slight shift, 41 to 50. The Senate refused to reconsider the treaty with Hitchcock's reservations and then voted down, 38 to 53, a resolution to approve it with no reservations. Here all breeds of Republicans (with the sole exception of Senator McCumber) joined against most of the Democrats. Neither with the Lodge reservations nor without any could the treaty command a bare majority of the Senate, not to mention the required two-thirds. The Senate adjourned *sine die*.

13. Wilson's and Hitchcock's reservations are printed in parallel columns in Bailey, *Wilson and the Great Betrayal*, pp. 393–94. Hitchcock did not reveal the source of the reservations.

The Last Chance

By no means all "true friends of the treaty" favored Wilson's uncompromising course. House (no longer in the President's good graces) had urged compromise. Herbert Hoover, a professed friend of the League, had urged acceptance of the Lodge reservations, as had also the League to Enforce Peace and its president, William H. Taft. When the next session of Congress convened in December, new hopes for compromise arose. At the Jackson Day dinner in Washington, January 8, 1920, William Jennings Bryan told his fellow Democrats that democracy required that the President bow to a majority of the Senate. From across the water came word that Great Britain would welcome American ratification with or without the Lodge reservations, although Viscount (formerly Sir Edward) Grey registered a caveat at the reservation on British Empire voting,[14] and Lloyd George hoped that the other governments might be allowed to consent by silence rather than by affirmation.

But Wilson stood firm. To the same Jackson Day dinner that Bryan addressed, he sent a letter saying that the United States must take the treaty "without changes that alter its meaning, or leave it"; that, if there was any doubt as to what the people of the country thought on this vital matter, the next presidential election should be made "a great and solemn referendum" in which the people's will could be ascertained.[15] He himself was convinced "that the overwhelming majority

of the people of this country desire the ratification of the treaty." Long written pleas from Joseph P. Tumulty, his private secretary, urging that he yield gracefully to majority opinion in the Senate, either did not reach him —for Mrs. Wilson excluded even the faithful Tumulty from his presence—or, if he saw them, failed to budge him from his position.[16]

Nevertheless, attempts at compromise went on. During the latter half of January 1920, Republican and Democratic senators, including Lodge and Hitchcock, in a series of informal meetings sought to find common ground in a modified set of reservations. Reports from the secret conferences were so optimistic that the irreconcilable senators took alarm. A delegation of them, meeting with Lodge and New were assured, in Lodge's words, "that there was not the slightest danger of our conceding anything that was essential or that was anything more than a change in wording." [17] The conferences reached agreement on some minor points but not on the crucial questions of Article 10 and the Monroe Doctrine. Lodge was a prisoner, more or less willingly, of the irreconcilables; the Democrats, or a goodly number of them, were bound hand and foot by Wilson.

On February 10, 1920, Lodge again reported the treaty to the Senate, with a few changes in the November reservations in conformity with tentative agreements reached in the recent conferences. From then until the middle of March, the Senate went over the old ground, readopting the Lodge reservations with changes that were hardly material. One exception should be made to that statement. The resolution of ratification provided, as Lloyd George had suggested, that failure of the allied and associated powers to object to

14. Canada had threatened not to join if her voting rights were in any way restricted.
15. Prior to writing the Jackson Day letter, Wilson had contemplated challenging the opposition senators to resign and stand for reelection on the League issue, promising that, if a majority of them won, he and Vice President Marshall would resign after making way for one of the opposition (through appointment as Secretary of State) to succeed to the Presidency. Kurt Wimer, "Woodrow Wilson's Plan for a Vote of Confidence," *Pennsylvania History, Quarterly Journal of the Pennsylvania Historical Association*, 28, No. 3 (July 1961), 2–16.

16. J. M. Blum, *Joe Tumulty and the Wilson Era* (Boston: Houghton Mifflin Company, 1951), pp. 230–39.
17. Lodge, *Senate and the League of Nations*, p. 194. According to Senator Borah's biographer, Borah and his fellow irreconcilables threatened Lodge with deposition from his post of Republican leader if he compromised with the Democrats. C. O. Johnson, *Borah of Idaho* (New York: Longmans, Green & Company, Inc., 1936), pp. 246–48.

the reservations should be counted as acceptance. But even this apparent gain was balanced by giving the right of objection to all or any of the allied and associated powers, rather than only to the Big Four, as in the original reservation. In the reservations themselves, it is hard to see any change that could have made them more palatable to Wilson; nor were they made more acceptable by the assertion in reservation fourteen that if the British Empire had six votes, the United States should have the same, or by the addition of number fifteen, introduced by Senator Gerry of Rhode Island and adopted by a close vote. This final reservation, more relevant to domestic politics than to ratification of the treaty, affirmed the Senate's interest in the cause of Irish independence and its hope that, once this independence was achieved, Ireland would be promptly admitted to the League of Nations.

Wilson wrote again on March 8, urging his supporters to defeat ratification on Lodge's terms. On the day of the voting, March 19, 1920, members of his cabinet, according to Lodge, were on the floor of the Senate to hold wavering Democrats in line. Such efforts were successful in defeating the treaty but not, this time, in maintaining an unbroken Democratic front. The vote stood:

	Ayes	*Nays*
Republicans	28	12
Democrats	21	23
	49	35

Thus the treaty, with the revamped Lodge reservations, received the votes of a majority of the senators but of fewer than two-thirds of those present. Twenty-one Democrats broke away from administration dictation and voted for ratification. Had only seven of the remaining 23 done likewise, the treaty would have been approved, 56 to 28. Such a result, however, would hardly have changed history,[18] for the ill and stubborn President

would almost certainly have refused to ratify the treaty with the reservations that he had repeatedly denounced as nullification. In any event, the treaty was dead. On Lodge's motion it was returned to the President.

Who Was Responsible?

Defeat of the treaty with the Lodge reservations can unquestionably be laid at the door of President Wilson. But what would have been the situation if Wilson and his supporters had consented to take the treaty in that form? Would the other "allied and associated powers" have accepted the reservations? Would the reservations, if accepted, have impaired the strength of the League?

Considering the second question first, the crucial fact was that the Senate had reserved to the United States Congress the right to decide in each case whether, and how, the United States would assist in carrying out the guarantees under Article 10 and other provisions of the Covenant. Such a reservation certainly raised an element of doubt as to the effective operation of the League's enforcement machinery. But in practice, the right of every member of the League to determine what enforcement action it would take came to be recognized very soon anyway.[19] Thus any weakening of the League that would have resulted from the Senate's reservation on Article 10 came about by other means. It seems fair to say, therefore, that the League would have gained much more from having the United States as a member than it would have lost by accepting the Senate's reservations.

But would the other members of the League have accepted the Senate's reservations? To this question there can be no cer-

---

18. If the Senate had approved the treaty and Wilson had pigeonholed it, the Republican party would have stood committed to ratification with the Lodge reservations. That this would have meant resubmission, reapproval, and ratification by President Harding is possible but hardly seems probable.

19. F. P. Walters, *A History of the League of Nations,* 2 vols. (London: Oxford University Press, 1952), 1: 259.

tain answer. Some of the reservations would certainly have presented difficulties, especially when we bear in mind that the March resolution of advice and consent, unlike that of November, gave a potential veto to each of the other thirty-one signatories of the treaty. It would have been difficult for Japan to accept the reservation on Shantung; for the Latin American republics to accept that on the Monroe Doctrine; for the British Dominions to agree to the restriction on their voting rights. On the other hand, such was the power, the wealth, and the prestige of the United States that any member of the League that hoped to see the world organization function effectively would perhaps have consented to some sacrifice of pride or "face" in order to insure American participation. In the opinion of T. A. Bailey, a recognized authority on the question, the other governments would have ended by reconciling themselves to the American reservations, perhaps with some adjustments.[20] If not, the responsibility for America's failure to join the League would have rested clearly with them and with the Senate. Wilson would have done his utmost.

It seems in retrospect that the ill and stubborn President made a tragic mistake in holding out for the impossible instead of accepting an available second-best.

20. Bailey, *Wilson and the Great Betrayal,* pp. 281–84.

The Senate's rejection of the Treaty of Versailles left the United States still technically at war with Germany. When Congress attempted, by a joint resolution of May 21, 1920, to declare the war with Germany and Austria-Hungary at an end, Wilson vetoed the measure as "an action which would place ineffaceable stain upon the gallantry and honor of the United States." It may be well at this point to round out this phase of the story by recording how the United States finally made peace with its former enemies. An act of Congress of March 3, 1921 made that day the date of expiration of all emergency war legislation. Under the new Republican administration, the joint resolution to terminate the state of war was revived, passed, and signed by President Harding on July 2, 1921. Treaties of peace with Germany, Austria, and Hungary, negotiated by the new administration, were approved by the Senate on October 18, 1921. All were ratified and proclaimed before the end of the year. The treaties reserved to the United States, in accordance with the terms of the joint resolution of July 2, all the rights to which it would have been entitled under the treaties of Versailles, St. Germain, and Trianon, while relieving it of all the responsibilities it would have assumed as a party to those treaties. So the United States brought to an inglorious close its crusade in behalf of democracy, international law, and world peace.[1]

30

The United States Renounces War but Spurns Peace Machinery

1. Secretary of State Hughes would have preferred ratification of the treaties of Versailles, St. Germain, and Trianon without the League Covenant, but was warned by the Senate irreconcilables that they would fight any effort to resurrect the Treaty of Versailles in any shape or form. To settle American claims against Germany, a mixed commission was set up by executive agreement. Secretary Hughes assured the German government in advance that the United States would make no claim for pensions or separation allowances, as it might have done under the reparations section of the Versailles Treaty. Germany reciprocated this gesture of good will by proposing that the umpire of the claims commission be an American. M. J. Pusey, *Charles Evans Hughes,* 2 vols. (New York: The Macmillan Company, 1951), 2: chap. 42.

The Senate having rejected a general treaty made with Turkey at Lausanne in 1923, diplomatic and consular relations were restored by executive agreement in 1927.

The League of Nations in the Campaign of 1920

The events last described took place after the fateful presidential campaign and election of 1920, which must now be considered. Wilson, it will be recalled, had proposed that the approaching election be made "a great and solemn referendum," in which the voters of the country might declare themselves for or against the League—Wilson's League without paralyzing reservations. It was not possible, of course, to isolate the League issue in the campaign; other questions competed for the voters' attention. Furthermore, the Republican position toward the League was so ambiguous that a vote for the Republican candidate could be counted as a vote either for or against the League.

The Democratic convention took a forthright stand in favor of "immediate ratification of the treaty without reservations that would impair its essential integrity" but disregarded a rather plain hint from the ailing President that he would welcome a renomination and an opportunity to run for a third term with the League as an issue.[2] The nominee, Governor James M. Cox of Ohio, campaigned valiantly for American entry into the League, though suggesting that he would go further than Wilson in the direction of compromise.

The Republican platform declared that the party stood "for agreement among the nations to preserve the peace of the world . . . without the compromise of national independence." It denounced the Covenant signed at Paris as failing "signally to accomplish this great purpose" and commended the senators who had prevented its approval. Threatened with a possible bolt by the irreconcilable minority,

2. J. M. Blum, *Joe Tumulty and the Wilson Era* (Boston: Houghton Mifflin Company, 1951), pp. 239–47; C. W. Stein, *The Third Term Tradition: Its Rise and Collapse in American Politics* (New York: Columbia University Press, 1943), chap. 9; W. M. Bagby, *The Road to Normalcy: The Presidential Campaign and Election of 1920* (Baltimore: The Johns Hopkins Press, 1962).

the Convention refrained from committing the party to ratification of the treaty with the Lodge reservations. Senator Warren G. Harding, the Republican candidate, had stood with Lodge and had voted for ratification with the Lodge reservations. Early in the campaign he announced that he would support an "association of nations" and added that he would keep the good and reject the bad in Wilson's Covenant. As the campaign progressed, his speeches became more and more anti-League and in a speech at Des Moines, Iowa, October 7, 1920, he said the issue was clear: "In simple words it is that he [Cox] favors going into the Paris League and I favor staying out." It was noticeable that isolationist senators like Borah and Johnson, cool to Harding at first, later came out strongly in his support.

In view of the candidate's anti-League statements, there was cause for surprise when thirty-one prominent pro-League Republicans published, three weeks before election, a statement in support of Harding *and the League*. The thirty-one, including Elihu Root, Henry L. Stimson, Herbert Hoover, Abbott Lawrence Lowell, and Charles Evans Hughes (soon to be Secretary of State), argued thus: With Harding in the White House, the United States might persuade the other powers to eliminate from the Covenant Article 10, a provision "very objectionable to great numbers of the American people." A Covenant thus modified, the United States could accept. On the other hand, if Cox were elected and if he held, like Wilson, that Article 10 was "the heart of the Covenant," the deadlock of the previous winter would be repeated.

The perplexed voter who wished to support Harding, therefore, could tell himself either that he was voting with Root and Lowell for American entry into a League without Article 10, or that, with Borah and Johnson, he was voting against American participation in a league of any kind. Under these circumstances there was no justification for interpreting the Republican landslide of November 1920 (16,000,000 for Harding to 9,000,000 for Cox) as a popular mandate against any connection with the League.[3] It was thus interpreted, nevertheless, by the irreconcilables in the Senate and by all opponents of the League in or out of Congress. Charles Evans Hughes, who became Secretary of State under Harding, hoped at first to carry out the program of the "Thirty-One"— entry into the League without Article 10. But Borah, Johnson, and other isolationist senators threatened, if this were attempted, to retaliate by blocking other parts of the administration's program, and pro-League senators could give no assurance that the Senate would approve a modified Covenant. President Harding decided against making a fight either for the League or for a different "association of nations." He informed Congress, April 12, 1921, that "there will be no betrayal of the deliberate expression of the American people in the recent election . . . the League Covenant can have no sanction by us." Hughes accepted the President's decision. No subsequent administration, Republican or Democratic, attempted to revive the League issue.[4]

Relations of the United States and the League of Nations

The League of Nations became a living organism on January 10, 1920, following the deposit in Paris of the requisite number of ratifications. The United States at this time was represented on the Reparations Commission and was participating in other Allied agencies that would now fall under the aegis of the League. After the Senate's final rejection of the Covenant (March 19, 1920), the Wilson administration withdrew from all association with the League. The American representative on the Reparations Commission

was recalled, and the State Department became negligent in replying to communications from the Secretariat or other League organs. This practice continued, apparently unknown to Hughes, for several months after he took office. He then gave orders that League correspondence be treated with ordinary courtesy.

Secretary Hughes did not share, though he did not openly repudiate, the attitude toward the League expressed by George Harvey, the new United States ambassador to Great Britain. Harvey assured a London audience that the United States would not "have anything whatsoever to do with the League or with any commission or committee appointed by or responsible to it, directly or indirectly, openly or furtively." Hughes, on the contrary, attempted to resume official participation in the Reparations Commission and other agencies of the League, but he was blocked by objection from the Senate. That body, now apparently hypnotized by the irreconcilables, approved the separate peace treaty with Germany (October 18, 1921) subject to a reservation declaring that the United States should "not be represented or participate in any body, agency or commission . . . unless and until an Act of the Congress of the United States shall provide for such representation."

Although thus prevented from participating officially in the business of the League, Hughes made increasing use of "unofficial observers," who attended meetings of League commissions and conferences to report their proceedings to Washington. As years passed, the United States, through such "observers" and through conventions signed in common with members of the League, cooperated more and more actively in the social and humanitarian work of the League. It thus took part in the regulation of the traffic in opium and other drugs, the suppression of the international white slave traffic, and even in such political matters as the discussion of limitation of armaments. Such cooperation, however, was always with the understanding that the United States assumed no responsibility whatever for the collective security features

3. There is evidence that many thousands, if not millions, of voters cast their ballots for Harding in the belief that he would steer the United States into a modified League of Nations, as predicted by the "Thirty-One." D. F. Fleming, *The United States and World Organization, 1920–1933* (New York: Columbia University Press, 1938), p. 37.

4. Pusey, *Chas. Evans Hughes*, 2: chap. 41.

of the League or for its attempts to settle international disputes. Furthermore, American representatives sat *with,* not *in,* League commissions like those dealing with the opium traffic; they could suggest but, not being members, could not vote. Not until 1934 did the United States officially join the International Labor Organization, which had been set up in pursuance of Part XIII of the Treaty of Versailles. In 1934, also, it finally agreed to submit its treaties to the League Secretariat for registration and publication.[5] The cooperation of the United States with the League in the Manchurian crisis of 1931–1932 will be treated in another place.

The World Court Fulfills an American Dream

No international organization could have been more American in conception or purpose than the Permanent Court of International Justice, or the World Court, as it was usually called. Such a court—a court of law as distinct from a court of arbitration—had been proposed, under instructions from Secretary Hay, by the American delegation at the First Hague Conference in 1899. Secretary Root had repeated the proposal when the Second Hague Conference met in 1907, and that Conference would probably have established such a court if it had been able to find a method of selecting judges that was agreeable to both great and small powers. An international court of justice had been a keystone of the program of the League to Enforce Peace, and Charles Evans Hughes, as the Republican presidential candidate in 1916, had warmly endorsed the idea. Nowhere had the substitution of law for force in international relations had more hopeful advocacy than in the United States.

5. Pusey, *Chas. Evans Hughes,* 2: chap. 41; F. P. Walters, *A History of the League of Nations,* 2 vols. (London: Oxford University Press, 1952), 1: 348–51; Fleming, *The U.S. and World Organization,* chaps. 4, 9. Pusey tries, not altogether successfully, to refute the charge that Hughes was so far intimidated by the irreconcilables as to be guilty for a time of a rather petty attitude toward the League.

Of this aspiration the League of Nations Covenant took account in Article 14, which directed the Council to "formulate and submit to the Members of the League for adoption plans for the establishment of a Permanent Court of International Justice." The Council, promptly after its organization, appointed an Advisory Committee of Jurists to formulate plans for the Court and, quite appropriately, named Elihu Root as a member of the Committee. During June and July 1920, the Advisory Committee, meeting at The Hague, drew up a statute for the Court. The statute, amended by the League Assembly, was ratified by the requisite number of members of the League and became effective in September 1921. Judges were elected, rules of procedure were adopted, and on May 12, 1922, the Council declared the Court open to all nations.

Unlike the so-called Hague Court of Arbitration, which was merely a panel of jurists willing to be drawn as arbitrators, the Permanent Court of International Justice was as much a true court as is the Supreme Court of the United States. It was composed of eleven judges and four deputy judges (later, of fifteen judges of equal status) chosen for nine-year terms from a list of nominees presented by the national groups of judges constituting the Hague Court of Arbitration. The problem of election, which had baffled the architects of 1907, was neatly solved through use of the organs of the League of Nations. Election was by majority vote in the Council and Assembly sitting separately. Thus the interests of both great and small powers were safeguarded. No two judges might be of the same nationality.

The jurisdiction of the Court extended to all cases that the parties thereto might refer to it either by special agreement or under general treaties or conventions. By the so-called "optional clause," members *might* agree in advance to refer to the Court any disputes between them which they were unable to settle by diplomacy and which should fall within any of the following categories: (1) interpretation of a treaty; (2) any question of international law; (3) the existence of a fact which, if established, would constitute a breach of an international obligation; (4) the nature and extent of reparations to be made for a breach of such an obligation. The Court was also empowered to give "an advisory opinion upon any dispute or question referred to it by the Council or by the Assembly."

The law to be applied by the Court in making its decisions was to comprise international conventions and custom, general principles of law recognized by civilized nations, judicial decisions, and the opinions of the best authorities on international law. Hearings and arguments before the Court were to be public (unless otherwise by special decision or upon demand of one of the parties). The Court would hold its deliberations in secret. Decisions would be by majority vote, and the basis of the Court's conclusions must be announced. English and French were the official languages of the Court.

Isolationists Block American Participation in the World Court

Although created pursuant to an article of the League Covenant and tied through the process of election to the League organs, the Court owed its legal existence to ratification of the statute by the member states acting individually, and membership in it was open to states not members of the League. In rejecting the League, therefore, the United States had not debarred itself from participation in the Court, of which it had been the original promoter. Under urging from Secretary Hughes, President Harding on February 24, 1923, sent to the Senate a proposal that the United States adhere to the statute of the Court with four reservations proposed by Hughes. The reservations stipulated (1) that in joining the Court the United States contracted no legal relationship with the League of Nations; (2) that the United States should participate equally with members of the League in the election of judges; (3) that the United States should pay a fair share of the expenses of the

Court, to be determined and appropriated by Congress; (4) that the statute of the Court should not be amended without the consent of the United States.[6]

Unfortunately for the plans of Harding and Hughes, the Senate Foreign Relations Committee, through which any such proposal must pass, was still dominated by the irreconcilables who had defeated the Treaty of Versailles; for many years they and their equally isolationist successors were able to control it. Lodge, who had practically moved over into the isolationist camp, died in 1924, but his place as chairman was taken by Borah, a man of great integrity but one of the extreme isolationists in the Senate. Such men professed belief in *an* international court of justice but held that the only such court in existence was contaminated by its connection with the League. It was a "League Court" and hence one to be avoided by the United States.

Tactics of delay, which had helped to defeat the League, were again resorted to. Hearings were postponed from time to time. Impractical schemes for divorcing the Court from the League were advanced. Thus action was delayed for nearly three years, and this in spite of evidence of overwhelming popular approval of membership in the Court.

When at last public pressure became too strong to be further withstood, the Foreign Relations Committee reported, and the Senate passed (January 27, 1926), a resolution of adherence to the protocol of the Court, embodying not only the four Hughes reservations but three in addition. One required the consent of the Senate for the submission of any case to the Court. A second reaffirmed the "traditional attitude" of the United States

6. Hughes made a bad beginning, in the opinion of enthusiastic friends of the Court, by dissuading the four American Hague Court judges from making nominations for the new judgeships when requested by the League Secretariat to do so in June 1921. His reason, as stated to Elihu Root, was fear that the proposed action would raise a storm among the Senate irreconcilables and imperil the success of the conference on naval limitation for which Hughes was then preparing. Pusey, *Chas. Evans Hughes,* 2: 595–97, and see below, Chapter 31.

"toward purely American questions." A third, expressing a newly aroused isolationist alarm at one of the functions of the Court, stipulated that the Court should not, without the consent of the United States, "entertain any request for an advisory opinion touching any dispute or question in which the United States has or claims an interest." [7]

The Senate resolution required that this last reservation, as well as the four Hughes reservations, be agreed to individually by all other members of the Court, now forty-eight in number, before the completion of United States ratification. This requirement led to objections, compromise proposals, and more delay, for which the Coolidge and Hoover administrations must share responsibility with isolationist senators. Finally, under a compromise formula devised by Elihu Root and acceptable to other members of the Court, the protocol of adherence came to a vote in the Senate on January 29, 1935. This was in the dawn of the neo-isolationism of the 1930's.[8] A veritable storm of adverse propaganda assailed the Senate before the vote, and despite an urgent appeal in behalf of the Court from President Roosevelt, the protocol went down to defeat with 52 votes for to 36 against—a majority but, like the final vote on the Treaty of Versailles, seven votes short of the necessary two-thirds.[9]

7. An advisory opinion may be defined as an opinion of the legality or constitutionality of an action that has not yet been taken, as contrasted with a judgment in regard to a completed action. Advisory opinions are not given by the U.S. Supreme Court but are given by the highest courts of a number of the States. The United States could not be bound but might be embarrassed by an advisory opinion of the World Court.

8. See Chapter 34.

9. The story of the long fight over the Court is told in D. F. Fleming, *The United States and the World Court* (Garden City, N.Y.: Doubleday & Company, Inc., 1945). Failure of the United States to join the Court did not prevent American jurists from serving as judges. John Bassett Moore, Charles Evans Hughes, Frank B. Kellogg, and Manley O. Hudson were in turn elected to the bench. For U.S. adherence to the post-World War II World Court, see below, pp. 418, 418n.

The Kellogg-Briand Pact

In the decade following its participation in World War I, the United States rejected membership in the League of Nations—the organization through which it might have taken an active part in the promotion of international justice and the preservation of peace. It held for years at arm's length and finally rejected, chiefly because of its connection with the League, the Permanent Court of International Justice, a tribunal embodying an old American ideal and built almost to American specifications. While it rejected these opportunities to work with other nations in the interest of peace, it revived the old habit—possibly to ease a guilty conscience—of signing arbitration treaties qualified by conditions that made them worthless, and concluded a new series of "cooling-off" treaties of the kind dear to Mr. Bryan.[10] It also took a leading, though at first a reluctant, part in promoting the most grandiose project of the period, the Kellogg-Briand Pact, or Pact of Paris, by which it joined the other nations of the world in renouncing war as an instrument of national policy.

10. For the earlier Root and Bryan treaties, see Chapter 25. Secretaries of State Frank B. Kellogg (1925–1929) and Henry L. Stimson (1929–1933) negotiated sixteen new conciliation treaties on the Bryan pattern. Kellogg replaced Root's arbitration treaties with "Kellogg treaties" and concluded a number of treaties of the latter type with states with which the United States had previously had no arbitration treaties, including new states that had emerged from the war. The Kellogg treaties differed from the Root treaties chiefly in dropping the "vital interests and honor" escape clause and substituting domestic questions and questions involving the Monroe Doctrine. Of these treaties, 27 were in effect by 1936. With the American republics, the United States negotiated multilateral treaties of conciliation (1923 and 1929) and arbitration (1929). The conciliation treaty was similar to the Bryan bilateral treaties. The arbitration treaty obligated the parties to arbitrate disputes arising from justiciable questions with the exception of (a) domestic questions, (b) questions affecting a state not a party to the treaty. By 1942 the conciliation treaty had been ratified by 18 and the arbitration treaty by 16, of the American republics, including the United States in each case.

In spite of multitudes of such arbitration and conciliation treaties as the United States had sponsored; in spite of the obligation assumed by members of the League to submit disputes between themselves to arbitration or judicial settlement [11] or to study by the Council or the Assembly, the possibility of "legal" war—war not in violation of the Covenant [12] —still remained. The more earnest and idealistic advocates of peace sought means to make all war illegal, to "outlaw war," in the hope that no nation would risk being branded by the rest of mankind as a criminal. Salmon O. Levinson, a Chicago lawyer, became the leading propagandist for the "outlawry of war." [13] He found a convert, surprisingly, in Senator Borah. A foe of all positive collective security measures, Borah was not averse to the plan to call all war, except war in self-defense, illegal. Even less objectionable from Borah's point of view would be a general renunciation of war— a promise not to resort to it. Levinson, Borah, and others had prepared a partly sympathetic climate in the United States for the proposal that came from Aristide Briand, French Foreign Minister, in the spring of 1927.

Briand's message to the American people, communicated through the Associated Press on April 6, 1927, was inspired by—was in fact written by—Professor James T. Shotwell of Columbia University. A disappointed proponent of American entry into the League of Nations, a believer that civilization and modern war are incompatible, Shotwell took advantage of an interview with Briand to suggest that the latter take a first step toward a general renunciation of war by proposing a treaty renouncing it between France and the United States.

Briand apparently saw in the suggestion a chance to tie the United States in a negative way to the system of alliances that France was building as protection against a feared renewal of German aggression—treaties with Belgium, Poland, Czechoslovakia, Rumania, and Yugoslavia. A treaty with the United States mutually renouncing war would at least insure the benevolent neutrality of the United States in a future conflict between France and Germany.[14] Whether that was his purpose or not, Briand chose April 6, the tenth anniversary of the American declaration of war against Germany, to publish an open letter to the people of the United States. France, he said, "would be ready publicly to subscribe, with the United States, to any mutual engagement tending, as between those two countries, to 'outlaw war,' to use an American phrase." The signatories to the Covenant of the League of Nations, he continued, were already familiar with the concept of

> the renunciation of war as an instrument of national policy. . . . Any engagement subscribed to in the same spirit by the United States with another nation such as France would greatly contribute in the eyes of the world to broaden and strengthen the foundation upon which the international policy of peace is being raised.

Both Secretary Kellogg and President Coolidge were somewhat annoyed at Briand's disregard of diplomatic niceties in making his appeal to the American people instead of the State Department. They were annoyed also because France at this time was acting uncooperatively in regard to war debts and naval arms limitation. Kellogg, furthermore, was cool to the proposed treaty with a single European state as looking too much like an alliance. He at first ignored Briand's proposal,

11. The phrase "judicial settlement" was introduced into Articles 12, 13, and 15 of the League Covenant after the World Court had been established.

12. See p. 287.

13. J. E. Stoner, *S. O. Levinson and the Pact of Paris* (Chicago: University of Chicago Press, 1943). The latest and most authoritative account of the origin of the Pact of Paris is R. H. Ferrell, *Peace in Their Time; The Origins of the Kellogg-Briand Pact* (New Haven: Yale University Press, 1952). See also D. H. Miller, *The Peace Pact of Paris* (New York: G. P. Putnam's Sons, 1928); J. T. Shotwell, *War as an Instrument of National Policy* (New York: Harcourt, Brace & World, Inc., 1929).

14. That such was Briand's purpose is the well reasoned conclusion of R. H. Ferrell in his previously cited *Peace in Their Time,* especially pp. 73–74. Professor Shotwell, on the other hand, insists that Briand had no such hidden motive.

but under prodding from President Butler of Columbia University,[15] *The New York Times,* and other sources, he finally indicated a willingness to discuss the proposal. Thereupon Briand, June 20, 1927, handed the United States ambassador in Paris a draft treaty, which supplied the wording for the multilateral pact finally adopted.

For over six months, however, Briand's proposal remained unanswered. Kellogg did not like it, but public opinion, stirred by Briand's friendly appeal and cultivated by Levinson and his circle, demanded that something should be done. Meeting with the Senate Foreign Relations Committee, December 22, 1927, Kellogg learned that the committee would not support the proposed treaty if made with France alone but would support it if it were converted into a general multilateral treaty for the renunciation of war.[16] Accordingly, on December 28, he dispatched the latter proposal to France.

Briand was reluctant to accept an arrangement so different from the intimate bilateral treaty that he had proposed, but Kellogg, now grown quite enthusiastic over the plan, pushed it with vigor. Having secured from Briand a tentative acceptance, he invited the governments of Great Britain, Italy, Japan, and Germany to join in the discussions. Agreement was reached in July, and on August 27, 1928, the treaty was ceremoniously signed in Paris by representatives of the six governments already named and of nine others—fifteen in all.[17] The Kellogg-Briand Pact, or Pact of

Paris, was thrown open to general signature and was eventually signed and ratified by nearly all the nations of the world. Its signers included Germany, Italy, Japan, and the Soviet Union. It was approved by the Senate with but one dissenting vote and was proclaimed in effect by President Hoover on July 24, 1929.

The essential portions of the Pact are the following:

Article I. The High Contracting Parties solemnly declare in the names of their respective peoples that they condemn recourse to war for the solution of international controversies, and renounce it as an instrument of national policy in their relations with one another.

Article II. The High Contracting Parties agree that the settlement or solution of all disputes or conflicts of whatever nature or of whatever origin they may be, which may arise among them, shall never be sought except by pacific means.

The Senate approved the Pact without reservation. Secretary Kellogg had said, in fact, that he would have no "reservations," although he did not object to "qualifications" or "interpretations." Of these there had been a number. The French had made it plain, with Kellogg's consent, that the Pact did not prohibit wars of self-defense or wars in pursuance of France's obligations under the League Covenant, the Locarno treaties, or her postwar treaties of alliance, and that breach of the Pact by one party would release others from its obligations. Kellogg had not objected when Sir Austen Chamberlain, speaking for the British government, pointed out that

there are certain regions of the world the welfare and integrity of which constitute the special and vital interest for our peace and safety. His Majesty's Government have been at pains to make it clear in the past that interference with these regions cannot be suffered. Their protection against attack is to the British Empire a measure of self-defense. It must be clearly understood that His Majesty's Government in Great Britain accept the new treaty upon the distinct understanding that it does not prejudice their freedom of action in this respect.

---

15. N. M. Butler, *Across the Busy Years,* 2 vols. (New York: Charles Scribner's Sons, 1939–1940), 2: 202–12. Butler had hitherto ridiculed the "outlawry" idea. Charles A. Lindbergh's dramatic solo flight from New York to Paris, May 20–21, 1927, stimulated popular interest in closer United States-French relations.

16. There is disagreement as to whether the idea of a multilateral treaty originated in Kellogg's mind or was suggested by Senator Borah in the committee hearing or had still other sources. Apparently the same idea occurred to several people. See Ferrell, *Peace in Their Time,* pp. 138–41, and sources there cited.

17. The other original signatories were Belgium, Poland, Czechoslovakia, Ireland, India, Canada, Australia, New Zealand, and South Africa.

Now the Senate Committee on Foreign Relations in reporting the treaty favorably to the Senate, stated its understanding that (1) the treaty did not impair the right of self-defense, of the necessity of which each nation is the sole judge; (2) since the Monroe Doctrine was an element in American self-defense, the treaty did not rule out armed support of the Monroe Doctrine; (3) the United States assumed no obligation to enforce the treaty against signatories that might violate it—"the treaty does not provide sanctions, express or implied."

Though none of these interpretations was attached to the treaty in the form of a reservation, there is no doubt that they determined the meaning of the Pact of Paris,[18] or perhaps, indeed, rendered it meaningless. The latter was the opinion of Senator Carter Glass

18. Ferrell, *Peace in Their Time,* chap. 13.

of Virginia. Though he proposed to vote for its ratification, he said,

> I am not willing that anybody in Virginia shall think that I am simple enough to suppose that it is worth a postage stamp in the direction of accomplishing permanent international peace. . . . it is going [he added] to confuse the minds of many good and pious people who think that peace may be secured by polite professions of neighborly and brotherly love.

The minds of senators were not so confused. Having approved with one dissenting vote (that of Senator John J. Blaine of Wisconsin) the treaty renouncing war, the Senate turned to the next item of business—the appropriation of $270,000,000 for fifteen 10,000-ton cruisers for the United States Navy. The bill was duly passed and was signed by President Coolidge within less than a month from the day when he had ratified the Pact of Paris.

31

The Washington Conference and Its Sequel

One notable success in international understanding stands out amid the diplomatic futilities of the 1920's. A nine-power conference in Washington in 1921–1922 disposed for the time being of a number of troublesome controversies in the Pacific and the Far East and halted a costly and dangerous competition in armaments between the world's three leading naval powers.

Japanese and American Policies Clash in China

Though the United States and Japan had fought on the same side in the recent war, the partnership had been productive of discord rather than concord between them. Japan took early advantage of the war in Europe to press demands upon China that she would have hesitated to make under normal circumstances. In January 1915 she presented secretly her Twenty-one Demands to President Yüan Shih-k'ai. These were arranged in five groups, of which the first four were mainly economic, while the fifth was political and military. Most important in the first category were demands that China agree to Japan's acquisition of German rights in Shantung and grant to Japan new rights of exploitation in Manchuria and adjoining eastern Inner Mongolia. The proposals in Group V would require China to employ Japanese advisers in financial, political, and military matters, to accept joint administration of the police in the principal Chinese cities, to procure munitions in Japan, and to establish a joint Chinese-Japanese arsenal under the direction of Japanese technical experts. Group V, if accepted, would have gone far toward making China a protectorate of Japan.

The Chinese government shrewdly permitted the secret demands to "leak." The European powers were in no position to offer support to China, but from Washington came a warning (May 11, 1915) drafted by Lansing and signed by Secretary of State Bryan, that the United States

cannot recognize any agreement or undertaking . . . between the Governments of Japan and China, impairing the treaty rights of the United

States and its citizens in China, the political or territorial integrity of the Republic of China, or the international policy relative to China commonly known as the open door policy.

As a result of such pressure from the United States and resistance from China, Japan shelved, temporarily at least, the demands in Group V, while China agreed to most of the others. Japan fortified her position by a secret treaty with Russia in 1916, by which the two powers delimited their spheres of interest in Manchuria and Inner and Outer Mongolia, and by understandings of the next year with Great Britain and France, who agreed to support Japan's claims in Shantung and in the Pacific islands that she had seized from Germany.

The Lansing-Ishii Agreement

After the United States entered the war, Japan sent a special envoy, Viscount Ishii, to Washington to seek an understanding with regard to China. By an exchange of notes (November 2, 1917), known as the Lansing-Ishii agreement, the two governments declared their continued adherence to the policy of respecting the independence and territorial integrity of China and the preservation there of the open door for commerce and industry. These phrases embodied the traditional policy of the United States, but they were preceded by a statement scarcely in harmony with them and giving Japan a reasonably free hand in China.

> The Governments of the United States and Japan [the statement read] recognize that territorial propinquity creates special relations between countries, and consequently the Government of the United States recognizes that Japan has special interests in China, particularly in the part to which her possessions are contiguous.

Even though this declaration was qualified by a secret protocol (not published until 1938) in which the two governments promised that they would "not take advantage of the present conditions to seek special rights or privileges in China which would abridge the rights of the subjects or citizens of other friendly states," the recognition of Japan's "special interests" in China represented a retreat for the United States. It is partly to be explained, as are the earlier agreements with Japan on the part of Great Britain, France, and Russia, by discreet hints that Japan, unless treated generously, might desert the allied and associated powers and cast her lot with Germany.[1] China, quite aware of the fact that Japan was being paid in Chinese coin, informed the United States that "the Chinese Government will not allow herself to be bound by any agreement entered into by other nations."

At the Paris Peace Conference, as related in a previous chapter, Wilson reluctantly agreed to the transfer to Japan of German rights in Shantung, accompanied by a Japanese promise to restore sovereignty of the province to China. But since China refused to sign the treaty and the United States did not ratify it, the Shantung settlement had the consent of neither government. The Shantung question remained, therefore, as a sore spot in the relations of Japan with both China and the United States.

The Japanese Mandate and Yap

By its failure to ratify the Versailles Treaty the United States had also withheld its assent from the transfer of the former German islands, the Marshalls, Carolines, and Marianas, to Japan as a mandate. These island groups formed a perfect screen between the Hawaiian and Philippine islands and quite surrounded the little American outpost of Guam in the Marianas. That Japan's seizure of them early in the war did not alarm the United States is to be explained, first, by confidence in Japanese assurances that occupation was temporary; second, by Wilson's belief that the Philippines were ready for indepen-

1. F. W. Iklé, "Japanese-German Peace Negotiations During World War I," *American Historical Review,* 71 (October 1965), 62–76.

dence and hence that the United States need no longer concern itself over defending them. Before the Peace Conference met, it was evi-

dent that Japan intended to keep the islands. Wilson insisted that they should not pass under Japanese sovereignty but acquiesced in

Japan's receiving the mandate to administer them.

Wilson did not, however, acquiesce in the inclusion under the mandate of the little island of Yap in the Carolines. Yap was a cable station of importance, the meeting-point of cables from Guam, Shanghai, and Menado in the Dutch East Indies. For the United States it commanded the only cable connection with the Dutch East Indies and the best connection with China.[2]

At Paris Wilson insisted emphatically that Yap must be internationalized. He claimed subsequently that such had been the understanding when the Council of Four gave the mandate for the Carolines to Japan. The Japanese, on the other hand, maintained that Yap was embraced in the mandate, and in this claim they were backed by the British. A heated controversy over the disposition of Yap arose in the closing months of the Wilson administration.

When Secretary Hughes inherited the controversy in March 1921, he broadened it to include the whole question of the islands mandated to Japan. Without the consent of the United States as one of the conquerors of Germany, he argued, German possessions could not be legally disposed of, and that consent could only be given in a treaty properly ratified. Thus Hughes called in question the right of Japan to the control not only of Yap but of all the mandated islands. The position was a good one for bargaining purposes.[3]

Japanese Imperialism in Siberia

Still another source of friction with Japan was the Japanese occupation of Eastern Siberia and northern Sakhalin. Japanese and American troops had entered Siberia through Vladivostok in 1918, after the Soviets' surrender to Germany. Their ostensible purpose was to guard military supplies (which it was feared

might fall into German hands) and to assist in the escape across Siberia of the Czechoslovak legion, a body of troops formerly prisoners of Russia but now liberated and moving along the Trans-Siberian railroad toward Vladivostok. The American troops, in reality, had been sent partly to keep an eye on the Japanese, who were rightly suspected of having imperialistic designs on the mainland. When the ostensible aims had been accomplished, however, the United States troops, commanded by General William S. Graves, were withdrawn (April 1920), but the Japanese, who had far outnumbered the Americans, stayed on. Japanese newspapers began to speak of the Sea of Japan as "the new Inland Sea," and it was evident that Japanese imperialists were intent upon permanent occupation of Eastern Siberia.

Although the United States had not recognized the Russian Soviet government, Secretary Hughes opposed Japanese expansion at the expense of Russia no less than at the expense of China. He warned Japan that the United States would not recognize "any claim or title arising out of the present occupation" nor acquiesce in any action that "might impair existing treaty rights or the political or territorial integrity of Russia."[4]

Three-Cornered Naval Rivalry

Thus in Shantung, in Siberia, in Yap, in the mandated islands, American and Japanese policies were in conflict. Furthermore, despite the promises of the Lansing-Ishii agreement, the menace of Japanese domination still hung over China as a whole; the fifth group of the Twenty-one Demands had been shelved for the time being but not renounced, and Japanese promises to observe the open door principle in her sphere of interest had been found not wholly dependable. War clouds darkened the relations of the two countries. In 1919 the United States moved the major part of its battle fleet to the Pacific and announced that

2. R. L. Buell, *The Washington Conference* (New York: Appleton-Century-Crofts, 1922), pp. 52–53.
3. M. J. Pusey, *Chas. Evans Hughes,* 2 vols. (New York: The Macmillan Company, 1951), 2: chap. 43.

4. Pusey, *Chas. Evans Hughes,* 2: 524.

it would remain there. This move and the American program of naval expansion, initiated in 1916 and resumed at the end of the war, were countered by a new Japanese program calling for a fighting fleet of eight battleships and eight battle cruisers with annual replacements of one ship of each type. Here was naval rivalry that involved not only the United States and Japan but Great Britain also, for Great Britain would not willingly surrender her traditional mastery of the sea, and this mastery was threatened by the naval program of the United States.

The naval expansion bill passed by Congress in 1916 called for an unprecedented amount of naval construction—ten battleships, six battle cruisers, and over one hundred smaller types, to be built over a five-year period. The war with Germany diverted American shipyards from battleship construction to the turning out of destroyers and "subchasers" for use against the U-boat, but in July 1918 Congress ordered the resumption of the program of 1916, and later in the year the Navy Department proposed a second five-year plan similar to the first, which would have given the United States a fighting fleet equal to the existing strength of all other navies combined.[5] This prospect naturally alarmed the British, and at the Paris Conference Lloyd George, in return for support of Wilson's amendments to the League Covenant, received assurances that the President would not push the Navy's second five-year plan. But even at that, England's traditional naval supremacy was threatened and could be maintained, if at all, only by an expensive building program that the British pocketbook could ill afford.

The Anglo-Japanese Alliance

That Americans should feel it necessary to compete not only with Japan but also with England in naval building was due to several

causes. With Germany removed from the scene, the United States would be England's chief commercial rival, and such rivalry might breed hostility. British attempts to monopolize the petroleum resources of the Middle East were particularly alarming to Navy men. More serious, however, was the continued existence of the Anglo-Japanese alliance. The alliance had been renewed in 1911 for a ten-year period. To placate the United States the British had then inserted a clause to the effect that neither party to the alliance should be obligated to go to war with a third power with which it had "a treaty of general arbitration." This phrase alluded to the "Taft treaty" of arbitration then under negotiation between Great Britain and the United States.[6] Taft's refusal to ratify the amended treaty nullified the escape clause in the alliance, for it was doubtful whether either a "Root treaty" or a "Bryan treaty" could be described as a "treaty of general arbitration."

A possibility existed, therefore, that if friction between the United States and Japan should lead to war, Great Britain might have to side with Japan. This possibility was highly distasteful not only in the United States but in Canada as well. At a British Imperial Conference in London in June 1921, Canadian Prime Minister Arthur Meighen opposed renewal of the Anglo-Japanese alliance, which was due to expire that year, and won the Conference to acceptance of his position over the initial opposition of Australia and New Zealand. This move placed Lloyd George in a difficult position. If he was to remain on good terms with Japan, he must find something to offer her as a substitute for the alliance she was asked to give up. Such a substitute could be found, if at all, only through an understanding with the United States in regard to the Far East and the Pacific. A conference for that purpose seemed called for.

Limiting the World's Navies

Already moves were on foot for a conference to end the naval armaments race. In Washing-

5. This program was inspired, at least in part, by the surrender of the German High Seas Fleet to the British and uncertainty as to its future disposition. This particular problem was solved when the German crews scuttled the ships at Scapa Flow in June 1919.

6. See Chapter 25.

ton, Congress adjourned in March 1921 without appropriating funds for naval expansion, and the new Congress passed, almost unanimously, a resolution introduced by Senator Borah calling upon the President to invite Great Britain and Japan to a conference on the subject. In England, a spokesman for the Admiralty expressed a willingness to accept naval parity with the United States instead of the "two-power standard" that Britain had long maintained. An exchange of communications between Washington and London, in which the United States, for obvious reasons, proposed including Far Eastern questions in the agenda, enabled President Harding to announce, July 11, 1921, that the powers concerned (Soviet Russia excepted) were being invited to a conference on naval armaments and the Far East, to meet in Washington on the following November 11, Armistice Day. Included, in addition to the United States, the British Empire, and Japan, were France and Italy (naval powers of lesser rank), Portugal, The Netherlands, Belgium, and China, all with interests in the Far East. Sponsors of the Conference hoped to end the threat of a three-power race in naval armaments and, as a means to that end, to compose the disputes in the Far East which stimulated the naval competition. They were, in the short run, highly successful.

Three major treaties and a number of minor treaties and agreements emerged from the Washington Conference, which met from November 11, 1921, to February 6, 1922. Most dramatic was the Five-Power Treaty on naval limitation (signed February 6, 1922), which Secretary of State Hughes and the delegation that he headed steered through the Conference with great skill. Taking as a basis the tonnage of capital ships (battleships and battle cruisers) built and under construction,[7] the American delegation proposed a ratio of 5-5-3

for the United States, Britain, and Japan respectively. All construction of such types was to be stopped for ten years; all such ships under construction (and numerous obsolescent craft) were to be scrapped. At the end of ten years, the parties might begin building replacements for their older ships, but the new battleships were to be limited to 35,000 tons displacement and to mount no guns of more than 16-inch bore. When all older ships had been replaced by the new type prescribed, the United States and Great Britain would each have fifteen battleships of an aggregate 525,000 tons and Japan, nine of 315,000 tons. The much smaller French and Italian navies would each be limited to five battleships totaling 175,000 tons.

Japan was reluctant to accept a figure less than that of the United States or Britain and consented only when those powers agreed not to build new fortifications or to strengthen those existing in the Western Pacific—west of Hawaii for the United States, north of Singapore for Britain.[8] Japan also agreed not to fortify her outlying possessions, but the ban on American or British bases within thousands of miles of Japan presumably made her militarily the equal of either of the others in the area of her principal concern.

Outside the category of capital ships, only aircraft carriers were limited: 135,000 tons each for the United States and Britain, 81,000 tons for Japan, 60,000 tons each for France and Italy. Carriers were normally not to exceed 27,000 tons displacement, but as an

---

7. This basis was chosen as most favorable to the United States. On the basis of completed ships Great Britain would have had a much larger quota than the United States. On the basis of ships built, building, and projected, Japan would have been only slightly below the United States. G. T. Davis, *A Navy Second to None* (New York: Harcourt, Brace & World, Inc., 1940), pp. 277–78. Other excellent ac-

counts of the Washington Conference are found in Pusey, *Chas. Evans Hughes;* Harold and Margaret Sprout, *Toward a New Order of Sea Power* (Princeton: Princeton University Press, 1940); Buell, *The Wahsington Conference;* Merze Tate, *The United States and Armaments* (Cambridge: Harvard University Press, 1948), chap. 9. The Davis and Tate volumes are also useful for the later conferences described in this chapter.

8. U.S. Military Intelligence had broken the Japanese diplomatic codes and supplied the State Department with translations of confidential messages between Tokyo and the Japanese delgation. Hughes knew, therefore, just how far the Japanese would retreat. H. O. Yardley, *The American Black Chamber* (Indianapolis: The Bobbs-Merrill Company, Inc., 1931), chap. 16.

exception to this rule, the United States was permitted to convert into carriers two vessels that had been begun as battle cruisers and that as carriers would displace 33,000 tons each. These ships became the *Lexington* and *Saratoga,* famous flattops of World War II.

Hughes had hoped to limit also the building of smaller types of ships—cruisers, destroyers, and submarines—but met with refusal from France and achieved nothing more than a "qualitative" limitation, stipulating that no cruiser should exceed 10,000 tons in displacement or carry larger than 8-inch guns.

The Five-Power Treaty was to remain in force until December 31, 1936 and thereafter was subject to termination by two years' notice by any one of the signatories.

The Nine-Power Treaty on Policy in China

Signed by all the participating delegations, also on February 6, 1922, the Nine-Power Treaty was something of an achievement for the United States. It gave solemn treaty form for the first time to the traditional policies of the United States with relation to China. The signatories other than China herself agreed "to respect the sovereignty, the independence, and the territorial integrity of China," to allow China the fullest opportunity "to develop and maintain for herself an effective and stable government," and to use their influence for establishing and maintaining the open door for commerce and industry throughout China. Borrowing the language of the secret protocol attached to the Lansing-Ishii agreement, Hughes planted it in the new treaty in the pledge of the signatories:

> To refrain from taking advantage of conditions in China in order to seek special rights or privileges which would abridge the rights of subjects or citizens of friendly States, and from countenancing action inimical to the security of such States.

The signatories, other than China, agreed not to do anything, nor to support their subjects or citizens in doing anything, that would infringe the principles here stated, or that would tend to create spheres of influence or exclusive opportunities in any part of China. China, on her part, agreed not to discriminate in any way between nationals of different countries. Other governments having treaty relations with China and recognized by the signatory powers would be invited to adhere to the treaty.

Ending the Anglo-Japanese Alliance: The Four-Power Treaty

One purpose of the Washington Conference, as previously noted, was to terminate the Anglo-Japanese alliance by finding some substitute that would be acceptable to Japan. Hughes had made his dislike of the alliance clear to the British Ambassador before the Conference met. Now that Germany and Russia had ceased to be obstacles in Japan's path, he remarked, Americans regarded the alliance as aimed at the United States. The Secretary feared, too, that the alliance with Great Britain tended to encourage Japan to undertake imperialist adventures in Asia that she would otherwise avoid. Discussions with Arthur James Balfour, head of the British delegation, led to agreement on a formula proposed by Hughes that was then accepted by Japan, and, at Hughes's suggestion, by France. In a Four-Power Treaty, signed on December 13, 1921, the signatories agreed to respect one another's rights in their Pacific insular possessions, to consult with one another if any controversy should arise between any two of them with respect to such rights, or if such rights should be "threatened by the aggressive action of any other Power." The Anglo-Japanese alliance would terminate upon ratification of the new treaty, which would remain in effect for ten years and thereafter until terminated by any one of the parties giving one year's notice.

For the United States the Four-Power Treaty had a double value: it abrogated the Anglo-Japanese alliance, and it reaffirmed, in treaty form and with British and French endorsement, Japan's promise to respect United States sovereignty in the Philippines.

Of all the Washington treaties, however, it alone met serious opposition in the Senate, where isolationist senators suspected that a commitment to consult implied further obligations. The Senate approved it by a vote of 67 to 27 but only after attaching a reservation asserting that the treaty involved "no commitment to use armed force, no alliance, no obligation to join any defense."

Other Treaties and Understandings

In addition to the Four-Power, Five-Power, and Nine-Power Treaties, the Washington Conference made other contributions to the settlement of Pacific and Far Eastern problems. A treaty between China and Japan (February 4, 1922), negotiated with the assistance of Hughes and Balfour, provided for the restoration of Chinese sovereignty in Shantung, the withdrawal of Japanese troops, and the purchase by China from Japan of the principal railroad in the province. Thus Japan carried out her promise made to President Wilson in Paris in 1919. In a statement to the Conference, the Japanese delegation announced the surrender of special privileges in China obtained under the Twenty-one Demands and abandoned Group Five of those demands, which in 1915 had been "postponed for future negotiations."

A treaty between the United States and Japan (February 11, 1922) assured the United States of free access to the island of Yap for purposes connected with cable and radio communications, rights of residence and property-holding for American citizens, and freedom of cable and radio communications from censorship and taxes. By the same treaty, the United States gave its consent to the exercise by Japan of its mandate over the Caroline, Marshall, and Mariana islands, while Japan promised the United States freedom for missionary enterprise and respect for property rights in the islands and application there of the provisions of existing Japanese-American commercial treaties. Among the stipulations of the mandate, which thus became part of the agreement between Japan and the United States, was Japan's promise that "no military or naval bases shall be established or fortifications erected in the territory." Japan also agreed to submit to the United States a duplicate of each annual report to the League of Nations on the administration of its mandate.

One other subject of friction, the Japanese occupation of Russian territory in Siberia and northern Sakhalin, was not disposed of by treaty, but Baron Shidehara, one of the Japanese delegates, gave assurance, in a speech before the Far Eastern Committee of the Conference, that the Japanese troops would soon be withdrawn. The process was not a rapid one, but the Japanese did in fact evacuate Siberia later in 1922 and northern Sakhalin in 1925.[9]

Work of the Conference Appraised

The Washington Conference was hailed in its own day as a brilliant achievement in American diplomacy. In the short run that acclaim was justified. From the point of view of the national interest alone, the United States gained acceptance by the powers concerned,[10] and for the first time in treaty form, of its traditional policy toward China. It secured the withdrawal of Japan from Shantung and a promise to withdraw from Siberia. It gained assurances of use, on satisfactory terms, of cable and radio facilities on the island of Yap and of freedom of missionary enterprise and most-favored-nation commercial treatment in the remainder of the mandated islands. It acquired naval parity with England, five-to-three naval superiority over Japan, and relief

9. Under pressure from Hughes, but not until more than a year after the Conference, Japan agreed to set aside the Lansing-Ishii agreement of 1917 in which the United States had recognized the "special interest" of Japan in China. J. C. Vinson, "The Annulment of the Lansing-Ishii Agreement," *Pacific Historical Review*, 27 (February 1958), 57–69.

10. The one exception was Russia, whose Soviet government was not recognized by the participating powers and not invited to send representatives to Washington. The Soviet government resented its exclusion and served notice that it would not be bound by any decision made in its absence.

for ten years from the burdens of an expensive competition in capital ships. It effected an easing of tensions with Japan and termination of the objectionable Anglo-Japanese alliance.

These were substantial gains. They were not secured without a price, but the price, measured in realistic terms, appears trifling. The United States agreed to scrap a large number (twenty-eight to be exact) of battleships and battle cruisers, of which the majority were obsolete and the remainder under construction with little prospect that Congress would provide money for their completion. It surrendered the right to improve its position in bases and fortifications in the Philippines and other islands west of Hawaii. But here again, although the right existed on paper, Congress had shown no disposition to exercise it. If the United States erred in limiting its Navy and forgoing the building of bases, if by the two measures combined it conceded supremacy to Japan in the waters bordering Asia, the fault was that of Congress and public opinion, not of the diplomats in Washington. The price paid by the United States for termination of the Anglo-Japanese alliance was adherence to a consultative pact that entailed no obligation to follow consultation with material action of any kind. All things considered, the contemporary impression that Secretary Hughes had served his country well seems quite justified. In the words of one authority writing in the 1930's, "the treaties went as far as pen and ink could go to preserve a peace founded on such antithetical elements as those inherent in the *status quo* in the Far East." [11] Time was to show that pen and ink could not restrain those antithetical elements for more than a decade.

The Sequel to Washington

The failure of the Washington Conference to limit the building of auxiliary naval vessels— cruisers, destroyers, and submarines—was not

11. A. W. Griswold, *The Far Eastern Policy of the United States* (New York: Harcourt, Brace & World, Inc., 1938), p. 331.

regarded too seriously at the time. The American expectation was that, without express agreement, strength in these categories would be limited in approximately the same ratio as that set for capital ships. But although the United States, where both Congress and President Coolidge were economy-minded, refrained for several years from building new cruisers, both Great Britain and Japan embarked upon building programs in the unrestricted categories. The United States, therefore, found actual parity with Great Britain slipping from its grasp and its superiority over Japan being whittled down. In the hope of correcting this situation by fixing limits for auxiliary craft, President Coolidge invited the other four naval powers to meet in Geneva in the summer of 1927.

The Geneva Conference of 1927 was as conspicuous for its failure as that at Washington had been for its success. France and Italy refused to attend. The American and British delegations were at odds over large versus small cruisers. The United States, which had few naval bases outside home waters, had a preference for 10,000-ton cruisers (armed with 8-inch guns), which had a long cruising radius, and wished to be free to include in its total tonnage as many of this type as it saw fit. The British, on the other hand, with their great network of commercial lanes and strategically placed naval stations in the seven seas, had little need of large cruisers. What they needed was a large number of smaller vessels with guns no larger than 6-inch. They did not wish the United States left free to build a large fleet of big cruisers, whose fighting power, ton for ton, exceeded that of the small ships. They proposed that the number of such ships be limited to fifteen for each navy, the remainder of a suggested total of 600,000 tons to be made up of 6-inch-gun cruisers of not over 7,500 tons displacement. Of the latter, they wanted a larger number than the Americans thought reasonable. What the British really wanted was parity in battle fleets and their essential auxiliaries, and *in addition* enough light cruisers to guard their commerce, whereas the United States insisted on mathematical parity. The Conference adjourned on August 4, 1927 after six weeks of futile argument.

Failure at Geneva and subsequent revelations brought out the fact that elements in the British government, including Winston Churchill, then Chancellor of the Exchequer, were not really willing to concede full naval parity to the United States. The United States, on the other hand, had a growing commerce and no guarantee of neutral rights in future wars. Its naval strategists were intent upon having a navy capable of defending its sea-borne trade against potential belligerent interference from Great Britain. A new acrimony entered British-American relations. President Coolidge, in his 1928 Armistice Day address, complained, alluding to a tentative Anglo-French understanding, that "foreign governments made agreements limiting that class of combat vessels in which we were superior, but refused limitation in the class in which they were superior." He urged the passage of a bill authorizing the building of fifteen 10,000-ton cruisers, which in the last session of Congress the House had passed but the Senate had rejected. The bill was passed and signed in February 1929, a few weeks after the United States, by ratifying the Kellogg-Briand Pact, had "renounced war as an instrument of national policy." [12]

The London Conference of 1930

The inauguration, March 4, 1929, of President Herbert Hoover, who had both a keen desire for peace and an understanding of British problems, was followed within three months by the ousting of the British Conservatives and the installation of a Labour government headed by Ramsay MacDonald. Statesmen on both sides of the water deplored the naval rivalry and asked why British and Americans should build against each other, now especially, when both had subscribed to the Kellogg-Briand Pact. This new spirit quickly

12. See Chapter 30.

dissolved the differences that at Geneva had seemed insoluble. In the fall, MacDonald visited Hoover in the White House and at the President's rural retreat in Virginia. "On a log by the Rapidan," the two statesmen came to a full understanding on the naval problem, and a new conference was called for the following year in London.

At the London Naval Conference of 1930, the American delegation was headed by Secretary of State Henry L. Stimson, who fully shared Hoover's desire for Anglo-American understanding. Anglo-American harmony was restored. France and Italy were again represented. Japan brought an insistent demand for improved ratios in auxiliary vessels.

The dispute that had broken up the Geneva Conference was easily disposed of. The United States dropped its demand for twenty-one 10,000-ton cruisers. Great Britain agreed that it might have either eighteen of these and an overall cruiser tonnage some 15,000 tons below Great Britain's, or fifteen of the big cruisers and parity (339,000 tons) with Great Britain in all cruiser categories. A rather complicated formula gave Japan a cruiser strength approximately seventy percent of that of the United States and Great Britain. Destroyer and submarine tonnage was also limited— Japan receiving a 7 to 10 ratio in the former and parity with England and the United States in the latter. Replacement of capital ships, which by the Washington treaty was to begin in 1931, was deferred until 1936, thus saving many millions of dollars for all participants. Of the capital ships then in commission it was agreed that Great Britain should destroy five, the United States three, and Japan one, leaving capital ship strength at fifteen, fifteen, and nine respectively. France and Italy, being unable to agree on cruiser ratios, accepted only parts of the treaty. An "escalator clause" reserved to the three principal signatories the right to exceed the quotas agreed upon if their security should be threatened by new naval construction by a power not a party to their agreement. The five participants, and later all other important naval powers, agreed that the submarine should in future be used against commerce only in accordance with the rules of international law and humanity. This provision was to be of indefinite duration; other portions of the treaty would expire December 31, 1936.

The End of Naval Limitation

The London Conference of 1930 was the last successful attempt to limit the size of navies by international agreement. The period of peace and comparative harmony following World War I was ended in 1931 by Japanese aggression in Manchuria, described in a later chapter. Japanese militarists, who had always resented the inferior naval ratios accepted by Japan at Washington and London, gained control of the government. In 1934, Japan served notice that for her the limitations of the Washington and London treaties would terminate December 31, 1936. An attempt to reach agreement was made at another conference in London in 1935–1936, but the Japanese delegation withdrew when British and Americans refused their demand for parity in all categories. The only agreement reached on that occasion was a treaty for "qualitative" limitation between Great Britain, France, and the United States. It placed no limit upon the number of ships in any category but limited the size of battleships to 35,000 tons and the bore of guns to 14 inches instead of the 16 inches allowed by the Washington treaty. It limited the size of other vessels also, declared a six-year holiday in the building of heavy cruisers, and provided for exchange of information regarding any new naval construction. Another "escalator clause" released the signatories from these restrictions upon receipt of evidence that any other power was exceeding the dimensions named.

The Washington Five-Power Treaty, consequently, came to an end on the last day of 1936. Thereafter there was no treaty limit on the number of naval vessels to be built by any government. Rumors that Japan was building 45,000-ton battleships, and the Japanese government's refusal to confirm or deny such reports, led the United States, Great Britain, and France in 1938 to invoke the "escalator clause" of the treaty of 1936. Thereafter, "the sky was the limit" in number, size, and armament of the world's navies.

A consequence of the First World War whose significance was little realized was the sudden transformation of the United States from a debtor to a creditor nation. Like other new countries, the United States had hitherto been consistently a borrower. Its canals, railroads, and industry had been built, in large measure, with capital borrowed in Europe, which it had been enabled to service by an excess of exports over imports. By the end of the century, the United States was also lending or investing money abroad (e.g., some $50,000,000 invested in Cuba before 1898), but in 1914 it was still on balance a debtor, owing Europe from 4½ to 5 billion dollars against 2½ billion American dollars invested abroad, chiefly in Canada, Mexico, and Cuba.[1]

Early in the war large quantities of American securities held abroad were sold in New York in order to finance purchases of American war materials by the Allied governments. By the fall of 1915, those governments found it necessary to float a bond issue of $500,-000,000 in the United States through the agency of J. P. Morgan and Company, and such borrowings continued until the United States entered the war. The role of lender was then assumed by the United States government, which advanced to friendly governments over 7 billion dollars before the armistice of November 11, 1918, and 3¼ billions in subsequent months. Without counting interest, therefore, the United States government at the close of the war was a creditor of its wartime associates to the extent of $10,350,000,000. The war also, although it impoverished Europe, brought sudden wealth to the United States and thereby created a large fund of surplus capital ready to seek investment abroad. By 1928 private investments in foreign lands totaled between 11½ and 13½ billions of dollars. Deducting the still-existing American indebtedness to foreign investors, we find the United States, ten years after the armistice, a net creditor, on both public and private account, to the extent of well over 20 billion dollars.

Acceptance of the new creditor role should

1. B. H. Williams, *The Economic Foreign Policy of the United States* (New York: McGraw-Hill Book Company, 1929), p. 17.

32

Economic Foreign Policy between Two World Wars

have entailed changes in policy, especially tariff policy, which American statesmenship proved incapable of making. But before considering this problem of adjustment, it will be well to glance at the American attitude toward the war debts and toward investment in and trade with foreign countries.

Settling the War Debts

The 10⅓ billion dollars advanced by the United States to friendly governments during and immediately after the war had unquestionably been regarded as loans by both lender and receivers. In the United States Congress, it is true, a few voices were raised in support of the thesis that the advances should be viewed simply as part of America's contribution to the war, as a means of enabling others to do what, for the moment, the United States could not do with its own Army and Navy. There were warnings, too, of the ill will that might result from an American effort to collect the debts from governments which the war would leave close to bankruptcy.[2] But such pleas and warnings went almost unnoticed, and President Wilson and his advisers rebuffed all proposals for cancellation of the debts or for discussing them at the Paris Peace Conference.[3]

In June 1921 President Harding proposed that Congress empower the Secretary of the Treasury to negotiate with the debtor governments adjustments of the war debts as to

2. Williams, *U.S. Economic Foreign Policy,* pp. 219–20.

3. Great Britain, which had loaned to its allies more than it had borrowed from the United States, and which had cancelled debts owed to it at the close of the Napoleonic wars, suggested twice in 1920 a general cancellation of inter-Allied debts in the interest of European recovery. The British were advised that neither Congress nor public opinion in the United States would sanction cancellation in whole or in part. The United States, it was pointed out, had gained no territory or other advantages from the war, and the American taxpayer would not willingly shoulder the burden of paying off the Allied indebedness. H. G. Moulton and Leo Pasvolsky, *War Debts and World Prosperity* (Washington: Brookings Institution, 1932), pp. 52–70.

terms, interest rates, and dates of maturity. Congress responded by an act (February 9, 1922) creating the World War Foreign Debt Commission with the Secretary of the Treasury as chairman, and authorizing it to negotiate settlements upon terms defined by the act. No portion of any debt might be cancelled; the interest rate must be not less than 4¼ percent; nor the date of maturity later than 1947. The commission found no debtor government willing to settle on these difficult terms. The procedure it adopted, therefore, was to make with each debtor the best terms possible (taking into account in the later settlements "capacity to pay") and then to ask Congress in each case to approve the departure from the formula originally prescribed.

In this way, between May 1923 and May 1926, the World War Foreign Debt Commission negotiated settlements with thirteen governments. Settlements with Austria and Greece were later made by the Treasury Department. With the exception of Austria, which received special treatment, all the settlements provided for annual payments over sixty-two years. In theory, no part of the principal (which included accrued interest to the date of settlement) was cancelled; in practice, the rates of interest were so adjusted downward that varying portions of the debts were actually forgiven. Comparing the total amounts to be paid under the settlements with the amounts that would have been paid at the interest rate of 4¼ percent originally prescribed by Congress, we find effective cancellations ranging from 19.3 percent for Finland and 19.7 percent for Great Britain to 52.8 percent for France and 75.4 percent for Italy. The amounts of the principal funded, the rates of interest to be paid, and the portions of the debts that were in effect cancelled, are shown in the following table: [4]

4. Moulton and Pasvolsky, *War Debts,* pp. 91, 101. Minor variations between percentages of cancellation for countries with same interest rates result from slight adjustments in amounts of principal and accrued interest to reduce total to round figures. The United States had not recognized the Soviet government of Russia, and there was no settlement of the Russian debt.

Country	Principal	Rate of Interest	Percentage of Cancellation
Austria	$ 24,614,885	—	70.5
Belgium	417,780,000	1.8	53.5
Czechoslovakia	115,000,000	3.3	25.7
Esthonia	13,830,000	3.3	19.5
Finland	9,000,000	3.3	19.3
France	4,025,000,000	1.6	52.8
Great Britain	4,600,000,000	3.3	19.7
Greece	32,467,000	0.3	67.3
Hungary	1,939,000	3.3	19.6
Italy	2,042,000,000	0.4	75.4
Latvia	5,775,000	3.3	19.3
Lithuania	6,030,000	3.3	20.1
Poland	178,560,000	3.3	19.5
Rumania	44,590,000	3.3	25.1
Yugoslavia	62,850,000	1.0	69.7
Total	$11,579,435,885		

The Reparations Problem

Throughout the debt settlement negotiations the European debtor governments argued that payments on the debts should be dependent upon the collection of reparations from Germany. The United States refused consistently to recognize any relation between the two transactions. In American eyes, the Allied governments that had borrowed from the United States—had "hired the money," as President Coolidge put it—were under obligation to repay their borrowings without regard to what they might be able to collect from Germany. In actual fact, however, it was obvious that the ability of the Allied governments to pay their debts would be affected by their success or failure in collecting reparations, and the United States took a sympathetic attitude toward efforts to solve the reparations problem.

The Peace Conference, it will be recalled, had left to the Reparations Commission the determination of the amount to be paid by Germany. In May 1921 the Commission set the figure at 132 billion marks, or approximately 33 billion dollars. Germany accepted the figure under threat of occupation of additional German territory. Annual payments of a minimum of 2 billion marks were to begin at once, later payments to be adjusted in the light of estimates of capacity to pay and evaluation of payments in kind already made.

Within fifteen months of the settlement, Germany was in default on the required payments, whether willfully or through inability to meet the schedules. Over British objection (backed by that of the American observer) the Reparations Commission authorized occupation of the great German industrial area of the Ruhr. French and Belgian armies carried out the mandate in January 1923 and held the Ruhr till September 1924. Germany met the occupation with passive resistance. The German economy suffered a prolonged and disastrous inflation. Reparations payments stopped entirely.

In the meantime, Secretary of State Hughes (in an address to the American Historical Association in New Haven, December 29, 1922) had proposed that a committee of experts study Germany's capacity to pay and devise a plan to facilitate payments. Late in 1923 all the governments concerned agreed to the suggestion, and the Reparations Commission appointed two committees to study different aspects of the problem. One of the committees was headed by the Chicago banker, Charles G. Dawes, and the arrangement adopted is known on that account as the Dawes Plan.

The Dawes Plan, in effect September 1, 1924, was admittedly a temporary expedient, providing for a rising scale of reparations payments over a period in which it was hoped the German economic and monetary system could be restored to a healthy condition. Germany received an international loan of $200,000,000. She agreed to make reparations payments beginning at 1 billion gold marks the first year and rising to $2\frac{1}{2}$ billions the fifth year and thereafter. Payments would be made in German currency to an Agent General for Reparations. Thereupon Germany's responsibility would cease. The problem of converting the marks into foreign currencies would be the responsibility of an inter-Allied Transfer Committee. No attempt was made to reassess the total or to set a date for the termination of payments.

During the prosperous years 1924 to 1928, the Dawes Plan worked satisfactorily, and by the latter date, the time appeared ripe for an attempt at a final settlement. A new committee headed by another American, the New York financier Owen D. Young, proposed the Young Plan, which was agreed to by Germany and her creditors in January 1930. By the new arrangement, which was intended to make a final disposition of the reparations problem, Germany agreed to make thirty-seven annual payments averaging a little over $500,000,000 followed by twenty-two annual payments averaging slightly under $400,000,000. By the end of the fifty-nine years, Germany would have paid altogether about 9 billion dollars of principal and 17 billions of interest—a drastic reduction from the 33 billions of principal at first demanded by the Reparations Commission. Furthermore, the Young Plan clearly recognized the relationship between reparations and war debts through a concurrent agreement (not participated in by the United States) that any scaling down of the debts would bring about a corresponding reduction in reparations. The

annuities to be distributed under the plan were so proportioned as to cover the war debt payments to be made by the recipients. So long as Germany continued to pay the Young Plan annuities, the debtor governments would have the wherewithal to satisfy their creditors, of whom the chief was Uncle Sam. If general prosperity continued, the plan would be workable.

Emigrant Dollars

No one foresaw, apparently, that Uncle Sam himself would supply a large share of the funds which would be used by Germany to pay reparations and then by the recipients of reparations to pay war debts to the United States. But such was the case. The schedules of both the Dawes and the Young Plans were in theory adjusted to Germany's estimated capacity to pay. But Germany, with her credit established, found it easier to pay by borrowing abroad than out of her own resources. The German government, governments of states and municipalities, and German industry all engaged in borrowing. By purchasing the securities of the German government, German municipalities, business enterprises, and the like, American investors supplied the dollars that the Germans could then use for reparation payments. In the period 1924–1931, while the German government was paying some $2\frac{3}{4}$ billion dollars in reparations, the same government, local German governments, and industry were borrowing abroad about $4\frac{1}{2}$ billion dollars, of which approximately half came from the United States. In the same years, the United States received some 2 billion dollars in payment on the war debts. Thus the United States government (and in the last analysis, the taxpayer) was receiving indirectly [5] from Germany 2 billion dollars while American investors were supplying Ger-

5. The United States received directly from Germany a small amount of reparations—3.2% of the Young Plan payments. The figures here given, translated from marks to dollars, are from Moulton and Pasvolsky, *War Debts,* p. 300.

many with 2¼ billions. Since, after the world economic depression began in 1929, the German securities acquired shrank in value to near zero, the American taxpayer was really paid by the American investor.[6]

The American private funds invested in German securities were but a part of the flood of dollars that went abroad in the 1920's. American dollars were plentiful, and rates of interest obtainable abroad were generally higher than those at home—by 1 or 2 percent, sometimes more.[7] The United States government encouraged such foreign investments or, more accurately, did not discourage them so long as they were not in conflict with some national policy.[8] The State Department, through expressions of disapproval, in effect vetoed loans to governments unrecognized by

6. Some such investors were destined to recover their money, or a part of it. Large quantities of German bonds were repurchased by the issuers during the 1930's at greatly depreciated figures. For the original purchasers of these there was no recourse. On the other hand, investors who held their German bonds until after the war could hope to profit from an agreement on German external debts reached in London in 1952, by which the Federal Republic of Germany undertook to see that service should be resumed upon such bonds. Since many of the bonds that had been repurchased for cancellation had been stolen or disappeared during or after the war, a validation procedure was necessary to identify bonds still genuinely outstanding. *Department of State Bulletin,* XXIV, 444–47; XXVII, 252–60, 608–9 (March 19, 1951; August 18, October 20, 1952); *New York Times,* August 30, 1953, Sec. III, pp. 1–4.

7. Williams, *U.S. Economic Foreign Policy,* p. 23n.

8. Five classes of loans that were considered "objectional" and hence frowned upon by the State Department were the following:
   "1) Loans to governments for balancing of budgets as a result of insufficient taxation;
   "2) Loans for military purposes;
   "3) Loans for assistance to foreign monopolies where their conduct is such as to maintain prices against the American consumer;
   "4) Loans to governments not recognized by the United States;
   "5) Loans to governments or citizens in countries who have failed to maintain their obligations to the United States."

From a State Department statement of July 1929, quoted in Herbert Feis, *The Diplomacy of the Dollar: First Era, 1919–1932* (Baltimore: The Johns Hopkins Press, 1950), pp. 18–19.

the United States, such as that of Soviet Russia. It similarly discouraged loans to France until the French government had agreed to settle its war debt. Although it frowned upon loans for military purposes, it did not obstruct loans designed to enlarge and modernize heavy industry in Germany, Italy, and Japan. Thus, as one writer has phrased it, "our financial mechanism was busily creating future targets for our bombers."[9] But in general the American administrations of the 1920's—those of Presidents Harding, Coolidge, and Hoover—regarded foreign lending and investment by the American public as a healthy activity. With such encouragement, American private investments abroad grew mightily, from a mere 2½ billion dollars in 1914 to an estimated 11½ to 13½ billion dollars in 1928. Such investments and loans, like the war debts, were economically sound only if foreign governments and other foreign borrowers could find means to pay the interest on them and over the years to repay the principal. In the long run, they could pay only by exporting their products, or selling their services, to the United States.

Adjusting the Tariff— in the Wrong Direction

It becomes relevant, therefore, to inquire into the attitude of the United States toward the acceptance of foreign goods and services as payment of interest and principal on the war debts and the private investments abroad and in exchange for the goods and services that the United States itself desired to dispose of abroad. In particular, was the United States tariff policy appropriate to a nation that had become a large-scale international creditor?

At this point it may be useful to glance at the course of United States tariff policy since the turn of the century. Traditionally, the Republican party was committed to a high-tariff policy, and the Republicans were in full control of the presidency and Congress from

9. Feis, *Dollar Diplomacy,* p. 43.

1897 to 1911. Throughout those years they adhered, with minor exceptions, to their traditional policy. The Dingley tariff of 1897 raised again the protective rates that the Democrats had lowered in 1894. By 1908 popular discontent with rising prices—the "high-cost-of-living"—induced the Republicans in the presidential campaign of that year to promise tariff revision, presumably downward revision. But the Payne-Aldrich tariff, passed in 1909, failed to make significant changes, leaving import duties on the average close to what they had been before. The Republicans, in consequence, were charged with repudiating their campaign promises and in the elections of 1910 lost their majority in the House of Representatives. During their years of control the Republicans had made one small breach in the tariff wall through a reciprocity agreement of 1903 with Cuba. Designed primarily to aid the struggling economy of the liberated island, the agreement admitted Cuban products (notably sugar) to the United States at rates of duty 20 percent below the prevailing rates, while American products exported to Cuba received reductions of 20 to 40 percent. Republican Congresses had also instituted free trade with the new territories of Hawaii and Puerto Rico, both of which were brought within the United States tariff wall, and had provided a preferential arrangement, which eventually became full free trade, with the Philippines. Thus the United States failed to practice, in its new possessions, the open-door principle that it asked other powers to observe in China.

After the passage of the unpopular Payne-Aldrich tariff, President Taft and Canadian Premier Sir Wilfrid Laurier, both in search of means to improve their popularity with their respective electorates, hit upon the old idea of a reciprocal trade agreement between the two countries. The idea was popular in the farm country of the Canadian west, in manufacturing areas in the United States, with American newspapers that wished free importation of wood pulp and pulpwood from Canada, and generally with Democrats, who by tradition and interest looked with favor

upon low tariffs. It proved unpopular in the western farm belt of the United States and in the Canadian east. An agreement was signed in January 1911, to be put in effect not by treaty but by concurrent legislation. It provided generally for free trade in raw materials and reduction of duties on a substantial list of manufactured products. President Taft, after many months of effort, and with the support of Democrats and eastern Republicans, got the measure through Congress. In Canada the proposal was attacked less on economic than on nationalistic grounds. Some unfortunate remarks in the United States, especially by Speaker Champ Clark of the House of Representatives and by the Hearst press, had pictured reciprocity as a step toward annexation. Canadian opponents of reciprocity made the most of these slips, warning their countrymen that their status in the British Empire was at stake. From England the imperialist poet Rudyard Kipling warned: "It is her own soul that Canada risks today." Reciprocity became a party issue between Laurier's Liberals and the opposing Conservatives. Sir Wilfrid was forced to dissolve Parliament and appeal to the electorate. In the ensuing election the Conservatives swept the country, and reciprocity was dead.[10]

The Democrats, who in 1912 won the presidency and majorities in both houses of Congress, signalized their victory by passing in 1913 the Underwood tariff, the lowest since the Civil War. Wartime conditions, which followed soon after, made it impossible to estimate the normal results of a low tariff on the national economy. A postwar economic slump and the sweeping Republican victory in the 1920 elections produced an outcry for restoration of high protective duties. An emergency tariff bill was passed in the closing days of the expiring Congress and vetoed by President Wilson in one of his last state papers, March 3, 1921. Calling attention to the necessity of accepting the products of Europe if

10. The story of this ill-fated proposal is exhaustively treated in L. E. Ellis, *Reciprocity 1911: A Study in Canadian-American Relations* (New Haven: Yale University Press, 1939).

Europe was to settle her debts and to buy from the United States, the President remarked: "Clearly, this is no time for the erection here of high trade barriers."

Wilson's influence was at an end, however, and a few weeks after his veto message a special session of Congress passed, and President Harding signed (May 27, 1921), an emergency tariff imposing high duties on a number of staple farm products. A year later (September 19, 1922) the President approved the Fordney-McCumber tariff "with rates higher than any in the long series of protective measures of the whole period." [11]

Completely fantastic as the policy of a nation that was seeking to collect its huge debts and to increase its exports, the high rates of the tariff of 1922 were immediately less injurious than might have been expected. Their consequence was postponed as long as the United States remained able and willing to loan to foreigners the money that they needed to pay their debts and to purchase American exports. So, during the boom years of the 1920's, the United States continued to insist upon payment of the war debts, to invest in what were assumed to be profitable ventures in foreign countries, to exert every effort for expanding its exports, to enlarge its merchant marine. All these activities logically implied a hospitality to imports from abroad. That such hospitality was belied by contemporary tariff policy was concealed by the piling of foreign loan upon foreign loan. [12]

This process could not go on indefinitely, and a halt came with the stock market crash of October 1929. Easy American money disappeared practically overnight, and with it vanished the ability of the foreign world to pay its debts to the United States and to buy American products. A lowering of the tariff wall would have been at least a partial remedy. Instead, Congress raised it still higher. Called in special session to pass a tariff for the hard-pressed farmer, Congress got out of hand and in the Hawley-Smoot tariff of 1930 raised rates all across the board. President Hoover approved the bill (June 17, 1930) despite a protest signed by 1028 American economists, pointing out that an increase in rates would impede the export trade, place obstacles in the way of debt collection, incur retaliation in kind from other countries, and create worldwide ill will toward the United States.

All these gloomy predictions were realized. Thirty-four foreign governments lodged official protests against the increase in rates, and many of them followed the American example, raising their own tariff rates or fixing quotas on imports. [13] International trade declined dis-

---

11. F. W. Taussig, *The Tariff History of the United States,* 8th ed. (New York: G. P. Putnam's Sons, 1931), chap. 10. Taussig ascribes the postwar revival of protectionism to two causes: (1) a war-induced craving for economic self-sufficiency; (2) a sharp fall in agricultural prices and a belief, especially in the western states, that higher duties would ensure higher prices. Asking protection for themselves, the western agrarians could not well refuse it to eastern industry.

12. Herbert Hoover, in his *Memoirs,* boasts of how, as Secretary of Commerce and President, he promoted the export trade, developed domestic substitutes for high-priced foreign products, and enlarged the merchant marine. There is no suggestion that these policies and the insistence on debt collections were in conflict with tariff policy. *The Memoirs of*

Herbert Hoover: [2] *The Cabinet and the Presidency, 1920–1933* (New York: The Macmillan Company, 1952), pp. 79–80, 83–84, 248. Dexter Perkins, "The State Department and Public Opinion," in G. A. Craig and Felix Gilbert, eds., *The Diplomats, 1919–1939* (Princeton: Princeton University Press, 1953), p. 307, comments sharply on the apparent blindness to economic realities of otherwise able Secretaries of State like Hughes and Stimson. Two explanations may be offered for the seeming "economic illiteracy" of American trade and financial policy in the 1920's: (1) The agricultural depression that existed throughout that otherwise prosperous period and the illusion that higher tariff rates could cure the farmer's ills built up intense political pressure for higher rates; (2) preoccupation with the "boom" in industry, real estate, and the stock market diverted the better minds of the business community from serious consideration of economic foreign policy. 13. Switzerland, for example, in retaliation for increased American rates on Swiss watches, raised its duties on American automobiles, gasoline, electrical and household equipment, office appliances, and meat products to practically prohibitive levels. Swiss imports from the United States fell by 29.6 percent astrously. There seems no reason to doubt that the American tariff deepened the depression. It helped to raise anew the thorny questions of reparations and war debts.

President Hoover's Moratorium

An already unsound and dangerous economic and financial situation in Europe was aggravated in March 1931 by an announcement that Germany and Austria had agreed to form a customs union. This move was denounced in France as a first step toward *Anschluss*—union of Germany and Austria—which was forbidden by the peace treaties. Eventually the proposed customs union was ruled out by the World Court as contrary to treaty obligations, but in the meantime French banks had brought pressure upon both Germany and Austria by demanding of banks in those countries payment of short-term loans to an estimated amount of three hundred million dollars. "It was the last push against an already tottering economic structure in Europe." [14] The strain was too much for the banks involved. In June the *Creditanstalt,* largest of Austria's private banks, was saved from collapse only by the intervention of the Austrian government. The panic spread to Germany, which seemed again, as in the early 1920's, on the brink of national bankruptcy.

To President Hoover in Washington it appeared that a temporary suspension of the payment of reparations and war debts might alleviate sufficiently the strain on Germany and her neighbors to permit recovery and stave off worldwide financial disaster. After consulting congressional leaders of both parties (Congress not being in session), he announced on June 20, 1931, that (subject to

---

compared with a drop of only 5.4 percent in imports from all countries. Hull, *Memoirs,* 1: 355. Cf. J. M. Jones, Jr., *Tariff Retaliation: Repercussions of the Hawley-Smoot Bill* (Philadelphia: University of Pennsylvania Press, 1934), chap. 4.

14. *The Memoirs of Herbert Hoover:* [3] *The Great Depression, 1929–1941* (New York: The Macmillan Company, 1952), p. 62.

confirmation by Congress) the United States would waive all intergovernmental payments during the year beginning July 1 if other governments would do the same. The American people, he said, should "be wise creditors in their own interest and be good neighbors."

Other governments were prompt to accept the proposed moratorium (an agreed-upon period of delay in meeting an obligation). France alone held out for three weeks before consenting, thereby contributing to the closing of practically all banks in Germany and Austria. To Congress, when it met in December 1931, the President recommended approval of the moratorium and also the recreation of the World War Foreign Debt Commission with authority to reexamine the debt situation and report on it to Congress. Congress gave its consent to the one-year moratorium but refused to call the commission back to life. In fact, it declared it to be "against the policy of Congress that any of the indebtedness of foreign countries to the United States should be in any manner canceled or reduced." Congress expected, in other words, that the regular schedule of payments would be resumed on December 15, 1932, the first payment date after the expiration of the moratorium.

The End of Reparations—
and of War Debts

Such optimism proved unfounded. An appeal from Germany for more substantial relief than that afforded by the one-year postponement led to a meeting with her European creditors at Lausanne, Switzerland, in June and July 1932. It was there agreed that Germany might liquidate her reparations obligation by depositing with the Bank for International Settlements bonds to the amount of three billion gold marks (approximately $715,000,000). The bonds would not bear interest for the first three years, nor thereafter until sold by the bank. At the end of three years the bank should offer them for sale to the public, and such bonds as proved unsalable on reasonable terms at the end of 15 years would be cancelled.

In thus forgiving nine-tenths or more of Germany's remaining reparations bill, the European governments expected to get corresponding relief from their own creditors. Ratification of the Lausanne agreement was in fact made contingent upon the securing of such relief. This meant, of course, that the United States, as the end creditor, was invited to bear the principal cost of the cancellation of reparations. But Congress had already shown that it was in no mood to consent to even partial cancellation. President Hoover was more aware than Congress of the realities of the situation. He feared that by insisting on all the United States might lose all. He sought in vain the support of President-elect Roosevelt, victor in the November 1932 election, in a second effort to persuade Congress to reconstitute the War Debt Commission. Congress would do nothing, and the President had no choice but to send to the debtor governments notices of the payments due December 15. Most of the debtors paid on this occasion, but thereafter, with the exception of Finland (which had a small debt and an export surplus which provided her with dollar exchange), none of them made more than token payments. Even these ceased after the Attorney General of the United States ruled that token payments did not save the debtor governments from being held in default.

For all practical purposes, therefore, payments both on reparations and on war debts (Finland's excepted) came to an end with the Hoover moratorium. Payments that had not been too burdensome in prosperous times and with the aid of American loans became too much for human nature to bear in the depths of the great depression. The United States, by its tariff policy, had contributed to the difficulty, but Congress, unconscious of any responsibility in the matter, proceeded to "punish" the recalcitrant debtors. By the Johnson Act of April 13, 1934 (sponsored by isolationist Senator Hiram Johnson of California) it forbade within the jurisdiction of the United States the making of loans, by sale

of securities or in any other way, to any government which was in default upon its debts to the United States. The Johnson Act stimulated no resumption of debt payments but added appreciably to the stock of international ill will. It seems safe to say that both the United States and the world at large would have been better off if the former had consented in the beginning to consider its loans in the light of contributions to the common war effort.

President Roosevelt Torpedoes the World Economic Conference

Before the end of the Hoover administration the United States had joined in plans for a World Economic Conference, to meet in London for a concerted attack on the worldwide depression. A commission of experts appointed to prepare the agenda of the conference found that barriers to trade, the failure to reach agreement on the war debts, the cessation of foreign loans, and the departure of some governments—notably the British—from the gold standard, all contributed to the prolongation of the depression, and that each of these factors aggravated the others. The best hope for recovery, the commission believed, lay in a concerted international attempt to remove or alleviate these malign influences, not singly but all together.[15]

The date for the conference was finally set for June 1933. During the spring, representatives of eleven governments visited Washington to discuss conference plans with President Roosevelt. All seem to have agreed, and Roosevelt with them, that stabilization of currency exchanges should have high priority at the conference. As late as May 16, 1933, Roosevelt announced that the conference "must establish order in place of the present chaos by a stablization of currencies."

In the meantime, however, the United States had itself gone off the gold standard,

15. W. O. Scroggs, *The United States in World Affairs, 1933* (New York: Harper & Row, Publishers, 1934), pp. 7–8.

and as the dollar had declined in relation to gold, commodity prices had risen. To Roosevelt, the restoration of prices to pre-depression levels, in the interest of hard-pressed debtor groups, was an objective of the utmost importance. If this could be achieved domestically by currency manipulation, then the right to manipulate the currency was not to be surrendered, and hence the United States should not for the present enter into any international agreement to stabilize currencies. Unfortunately, Roosevelt seems to have come to this conclusion only after the American delegation, headed by Secretary of State Cordell Hull, had departed for the London Economic Conference, and the members of the delegation were not adequately informed of the change in policy. The "gold bloc" at the conference—the gold standard countries led by France, Italy, Switzerland, Belgium, and The Netherlands—insisted that stabilization of currencies and a return to the gold standard by those who had left it were measures essential to recovery. To meet them halfway, the United States and British delegations agreed to an innocuous declaration. Espousing eventual return to gold and agreeing to discourage speculative fluctuations in currencies, the statement left the United States and Great Britain free to determine when and at what level the dollar and pound should be stabilized.

This declaration was cabled to President Roosevelt for approval. His rejection of it, July 2, 1933, had been referred to both as a "bombshell" and as the "torpedo" that sank the conference. He would regard it as a great catastrophe, said the President,

> if the great conference of nations, called to bring about a more real and permanent financial stability and a greater prosperity to the masses of all nations, should . . . allow itself to be diverted by the proposal of a purely artificial and temporary expedient affecting the monetary exchange of a few nations only. . . .

The President's complete repudiation of an effort to achieve one of the principal objectives for which the conference had been called ended whatever slim chances for achievement the meeting may have had. The delegations of Great Britain and the gold bloc favored immediate adjournment, putting the blame for failure at the President's door. The urging of Hull and his colleagues, backed by the delegates from the British dominions, kept the conference in session for three weeks longer, but it could do nothing beyond passing resolutions on some minor subjects and acknowledging disagreement on others more important. The American delegates had been forbidden to discuss the intergovernmental debts. Secretary Hull, whose chief enthusiasm was for the lowering of trade barriers, had hoped to negotiate reciprocal trade agreements, but Congress had adjourned without passing the necessary legislation. The conference adjourned, July 27, with nothing substantial to show for six weeks of labor. On the part of the United States it was a sad example of poor preparation, lack of understanding between President and delegates and among the delegates themselves, and changing of the target after the arrow left the bow.[16]

The Hull Reciprocal Trade Agreements Program

The authority to negotiate reciprocal tariff agreements that Secretary Hull had failed to get at the time of the London Conference was given him a year later. Hull, imbued with the traditional low-tariff views of a southern Democrat, also had a fervent belief that the lowering of economic barriers was a cornerstone of international peace.

> . . . To me [he wrote] it seemed virtually impossible to develop friendly relations with

16. See Scroggs, *U. S. in World Affairs, 1933,* chaps. 7, 8; E. K. Lindley, *The Roosevelt Revolution* (New York: The Viking Press, Inc., 1933), chap. 6; Hull, *Memoirs,* 1: chaps. 18, 19; *The Memoirs of Herbert Hoover:* [3] *The Great Depression, 1929–1941,* pp. 363–68; Raymond Moley, *After Seven Years* (New York: Harper & Row, Publishers, 1939), chap. 7; A. J. Toynbee, *Survey of International Affairs, 1933* (Oxford: Oxford University Press, 1934), pp. 35–81; Pratt, *Cordell Hull,* 1: chap. 3.

other nations in the political sphere so long as we provoked their animosity in the economic sphere. How could we promote peace with them while waging war on them commercially? [17]

For many years, as a representative and senator from Tennessee, he had fought consistently for lower tariffs. As Franklin Roosevelt's Secretary of State, and with a Congress overwhelmingly Democratic, he saw an opportunity to realize a lifelong objective.

The first year of the New Deal, however, was not propitious for a lowering of tariff rates. President Roosevelt, intent upon raising domestic prices through the NRA and AAA, foresaw the possibility that higher rates on imports might be necessary to offset higher prices of home products. Nevertheless, at the Inter-American Conference at Montevideo in December 1933, Hull won great acclaim by his proposal for the reciprocal lowering of rates. This success, in part, won the President to his program, and with presidential support, Congress passed the Reciprocal Trade Agreements Act of June 12, 1934.

The purpose of the law, as stated officially in the preamble, was that "of expanding foreign markets for the products of the United States (as a means of assisting in the present emergency . . .)"; essentially, it was an anti-depression measure. Technically an amendment to the Hawley-Smoot tariff of 1930, it empowered the executive to negotiate with other governments agreements lowering (or raising) by as much as 50 percent the existing rates on imports from those countries, or "freezing" existing rates or import restrictions, in return for reciprocal concessions on American products imported into the foreign countries. Due notice must be given and hearings must be held before the opening of negotiations for lower rates on any commodity, so that domestic interests might have their say;

and the President must seek (though he need not follow) the advice of the Tariff Commission and the Departments of State, Agriculture, and Commerce. But once made, the agreement required no action either by the Senate or by Congress as a whole to put it into effect. Thus agreements under the new act escaped the pitfalls that had been fatal to most attempts at such agreements in the past.[18]

Another novel feature of the act of 1934 was its directive that the trade agreements embody the most-favored-nation principle in its unconditional form. The United States had, as a matter of fact, made the shift from the conditional to the unconditional form of treaty in 1923, but it now appeared for the first time in reciprocal trade agreements. It meant that when an agreement with Brazil, for example, lowered the duties on certain imports from Brazil, the same reduction took effect on similar goods imported from other countries, provided only that the countries in question did not discriminate against the trade of the United States. Thus each agreement had the effect of lowering duties on a wide front, not only between the two parties to the pact. In practice, agreements would normally be negotiated for commodities of which each of the negotiators was principal supplier to the other.

Every agreement under the act was to be effective for three years and thereafter until one party terminated it by giving six months' notice. The power to conclude agreements conferred upon the President was of three years' duration, but its term was extended from time to time for periods of three years or less. The three-year renewal of July 5, 1945, was particularly significant in that it permitted a 50 percent reduction in the rates of January 1, 1945, instead of those of the 1930 tariff. Thus rates that had already been reduced by 50 percent could now be lowered by an additional 50 percent, making a total reduction of 75 percent from the 1930 rates.

From 1934 to 1947 the executive nego-

17. *The Memoirs of Cordell Hull,* 2 vols. (New York), 1: 355. Copyright 1948 by The Macmillan Company. Quotations from *The Memoirs of Cordell Hull* reprinted by permission of the publisher. Hull's account of the beginning of the reciprocal trade program is in ibid., 1: chaps. 26, 27. See also Pratt, *Cordell Hull,* 1: chap. 5.

18. See pp. 190–91.

tiated bilateral reciprocal trade agreements with twenty-nine countries, resulting in the reduction or binding of duties on commodities constituting about 70 percent of all dutiable imports. In 1947, at Geneva, Switzerland, the United States negotiated with twenty-two other countries the General Agreement on Tariffs and Trade (GATT), by which numerous bilateral agreements were combined into a multilateral program. By 1963, membership in GATT had expanded to forty-four countries, while some thirty others enjoyed some form of affiliation with it. Together they accounted for well over four-fifths of the world's international trade.[19]

As a consequence of tariff reductions under the Reciprocal Trade Agreements Act, the average rate on dutiable goods imported into the United States had dropped from 46.7 percent in 1934 to 12.5 in 1951; while the average rate on all imports, dutiable and free, had fallen from 18.4 percent to 5.6 percent. These figures, based upon the value of all imports and the duties collected thereon, are misleading, since rates so high as to be prohibitive do not enter into the calculations at all. Part of the reduction, furthermore, is accounted for by increases in the prices of articles on which the duties are specific, that is at rates of so much per pound or per yard, instead of *ad valorem*. Thus a rate on sugar of two cents a pound will be 40 percent when sugar sells for five cents a pound, but only 20 percent if the price advances to ten cents. But when allowance is made for these elements in the picture and for other barriers to trade, such as quotas, which the United States Congress often resorted to, the reciprocal trade program had done much to facilitate the flow of international commerce and the payment of in-

ternational debts.[20] As Secretary of State Acheson stated to the House Ways and Means Committee in 1951, "Tariffs have been reduced over a wider area of world trade than ever before."

Though more popular with big business than with agriculture, and with Democrats than with Republicans, the reciprocal trade program in the end received a measure of the bipartisan support for which Secretary Hull had labored. It was repeatedly extended, though in some instances with weakening amendments, by both Democratic and Republican Congresses, with the support of President Eisenhower as well as with that of the Democratic Presidents who preceded and followed him. In order to enable the President to bargain effectively with the European Common Market, Congress, in the Trade Expansion Act of 1962, gave the Executive tariff-cutting powers much more comprehensive than those bestowed by the Act of 1934 or its various extensions.[21]

19. *U. S. in World Affairs, 1962,* p. 382; Isaiah Frank, "Issues before the U.N. Conference," *Foreign Affairs,* 42 (January 1964), 210–26.

20. *Trade Agreements Extension Act of 1953.* Hearings before the Committee on Ways and Means, House of Representatives, Eighty-third Congress, First Session, on H.R. 4294 (Washington: Government Printing Office, 1953), pp. 1728–31. U. S. Tariff Commission, *Effect of Trade Agreement Concessions on United States Tariff Levels Based on Imports in 1952* (Washington: U. S. Tariff Commission, 1953), Table 7, shows the rates which the imports for consumption in 1952 would have paid if imported before any reciprocal trade agreements were concluded, compared with the rates applicable January 1, 1953, as follows:

Rates of Duty	Percent of Total before Any Agreement	Percent of Total Jan. 1, 1953
10% or less	32.2	52.3
10.1 to 20.0	19.6	30.2
20.1 to 30.0	23.2	11.5
30.1 to 40.0	10.0	4.1
40.1 to 50.0	4.1	1.0
50.1 or more	10.9	.9
	100.0	100.0

21. See Chapter 43, n. 18.

The peace system set up by the Treaty of Versailles in 1919, reinforced by the Washington treaties of 1921–1922 and the Pact of Paris of 1928, suffered its first serious breach in 1931.[1] The peace-breaker then was Japan, and the scene was Manchuria.

For almost a decade after the successful Washington Conference of 1921–1922,[2] Japan was on her good behavior and Japanese-American relations were generally cordial. Such friction as existed was the result of American rather than Japanese action. Americans, it is true, contributed generously to relief of the victims of the destructive Japanese earthquake of September 1, 1923. But the good will thus won was largely dissipated by the Johnson Immigration Act of 1924. By this measure Congress prohibited the immigration of Japanese and other Orientals—aliens ineligible for citizenship—instead of admitting them on a quota basis as in the case of Europeans. To the Japanese, who had in good faith carried out the Gentlemen's Agreement of 1907, this discrimination was a needless affront—needless, because Japan's quota of immigrants, had she been given one, would have been so small as to be negligible.[3] President Coolidge and Secretary of State Hughes both disapproved of the ban on Japanese immigration. Their efforts to dissuade Congress from imposing it were hindered rather than helped by a protest from Japanese Ambassador Hanihara. The ambassador warned Secretary Hughes that such discriminatory treatment would bring "grave consequences . . .

1. The period 1919–1931 was not one of unbroken peace. There were armed conflicts between Poland and Russia, Poland and Lithuania, Greece and Turkey, as well as armed intervention by the western powers and Japan in the Soviet Union. But all these were of short duration and were settled without endangering the peace of the great powers.
2. See Chapter 31.
3. For Gentlemen's Agreement see Chapter 24. The Immigration Act of 1924 fixed, after July 1, 1927, a maximum annual immigration of 150,000 (exclusive of immigrants from Western Hemisphere countries and certain other non-quota immigrants) and assigned to each European nationality a fraction of the 150,000 equal to the percentage of persons derived from that nationality in the total population of the United States in 1920. If Japan had been placed on this basis, her quota would not have exceeded 185 in any year.

33

The Manchurian Crisis and Its Aftermath, 1931–1936

upon the otherwise happy and mutually advantageous relations between our two countries." The implied threat angered Congress and hastened passage of the bill containing the offensive provision.

Passage of the Johnson Act produced a new flurry of anti-American pronouncements in the Japanese press, but the excitement soon subsided. On the American side there was a growing appreciation of Japan's point of view, and by 1931 there was good reason to hope that Congress would repeal the exclusion provision of the Johnson Act and permit Japanese immigration under the quota system.[4] This possibility was destroyed when the Japanese army launched its campaign for the conquest of Manchuria.

Sino-Japanese Rivalry in Manchuria

The motives of the army in its Manchurian adventure are clear enough. Since 1922 and especially since 1924 the Japanese armed services had been losing ground to the civilian elements in government. This was a period of rising democracy at home and conciliatory behavior abroad. Baron Kijuro Shidehara, Foreign Minister 1924–1927 and 1929–1931, followed a policy of treaty observance, friendliness with the West, and moderation toward China, where the rising tide of nationalism endangered both Japanese and western interests and treaty rights. Shidehara and Premier Hamaguchi, leaders of the Minseito, the more moderate Japanese party, were responsible for Japan's signing the London naval treaty of 1930, by which Japan continued to accept naval limits inferior to those of the United States and Great Britain.[5] Their success in persuading the Emperor to ratify the treaty despite the opposition of his military and naval advisers seemed to the armed services to imperil their privileged position in the Japanese government. Their resentment was

shown in the assassination of Premier Hamaguchi in November 1930, but Shidehara continued as Foreign Minister, and the new Premier, Wakatsuki, had been one of the negotiators of the London treaty. Only some drastic action, it seemed, could save the armed services from being subjected to civilian control.

They found an occasion for drastic action in Manchuria. Still nominally the "Three Eastern Provinces" of China, Manchuria had long since been divided into Japanese and Russian spheres of interests.[6] Russia's hold upon the northern portion had weakened as a result of the Soviet Revolution. Japan, holding the Liaotung Peninsula (embracing Port Arthur and Dairen) and the zone of the South Manchurian Railway, had come to regard all of Manchuria as her economic "lifeline," to be controlled by her in the future. The Japanese, therefore, were understandably disturbed when the new Nationalist government of China began to reassert Chinese authority in Manchuria. China, since the revolution of 1911, had been divided and almost powerless. Its reunification under Chiang Kai-shek and the Kuomintang (Nationalist People's Party) began in 1926 when Chiang's armies swept north from Canton to the Yangtze Valley, where a new seat of government was established at Nanking. In 1928 the drive was extended northward and Peking, the old imperial capital, now rechristened Peiping ("Northern Peace" instead of "Northern Capital"), was brought under the Nationalist government. In the same year Marshal Chang Tso-lin, the autonomous war lord of Manchuria, was killed when his train was blown up (supposedly by Japanese agents). His son, Chang Hsüeh-liang, the "Young Marshal," inheriting his father's position, declared his allegiance to the Nationalist government, which was thus put in a position to reassert Chinese authority over Manchuria. Japan, therefore, faced the prospect of a China reunified and strong, extending its control over Japan's Manchurian "lifeline."

4. A. W. Griswold, *The Far Eastern Policy of the United States* (New York: Harcourt, Brace & World, Inc., 1938), pp. 378–79.
5. See Chapter 31.

6. See p. 241.

China, moreover, was disposed to regard lightly (as accepted under duress) certain treaties of 1915 and earlier,[7] by which she had recognized Japan's special interest in Manchuria and had agreed, among other things, not to build railroads to compete with the Japanese-owned South Manchurian line.

Out of this situation, friction inevitably developed between Japan and China. In the summer of 1931 the Japanese press published sensational accounts of an attack by Chinese upon a group of Korean farmers (Japanese subjects) engaged in peaceful pursuits in Manchuria. A more serious incident was the killing by Chinese troops of Captain Nakamura, a Japanese army officer in disguise, who was pursuing a mysterious mission in central Manchuria. The Japanese government under Wakatsuki and Shidehara sought a peaceful settlement of such incidents. The Army hoped to make them an excuse for seizing control of Manchuria and reasserting its authority in the government. It is significant that on September 17, 1931, the Nakamura case was reported to be on the verge of amicable adjustment.[8] With this incident about to slip out of its grasp, the Army seized—more probably created—another.

The September Eighteenth Incident

Japan was entitled to keep troops in the Liaotung leased territory and as railway guards along the line of the South Manchurian Railway. On the night of September 18, 1931, a Japanese patrol north of Mukden, according to report, heard an explosion on the railway and, upon investigation, discovered that a section of rail had been broken off by a

mine. The damage was so slight that an express train passed over the spot without injury a few minutes later, and it seems probable that the occurrence was a synthetic one. At any rate, Chinese soldiers were charged with an attempt to blow up the track, and with a speed and efficiency that bespoke careful planning, Japanese troops surrounded the Chinese barracks at Mukden, captured the garrison and military stores, and within a few hours seized other key points on or near the railway line. All this was done by the Army on its own initiative without the consent of the Premier or the Foreign Office.[9]

The Chinese government at Nanking appealed at once both to the United States and to the League of Nations for protection against Japan. Japan's action, as interpreted by all parties concerned except the Japanese themselves, appeared to be in violation of Japan's obligations as a member of the League, in violation of the Nine-Power Treaty of 1922 (by which she had promised to respect the independence and territorial and administrative integrity of China), and in violation of the Kellogg-Briand Pact or Pact of Paris. The United States, not a member of the League, was a party to the two treaties mentioned. If, through invoking any or all of these international engagements, Japan could be stopped, the cause of peace would have won a notable victory. If Japan got away with her act of aggression, her success would be an example to other ambitious and unscrupulous governments. Civilization had reached a turning point.

The United States Joins Hands with the League

The Council of the League, meeting in Geneva, promptly took up China's appeal. A proposal to send a commission of inquiry to the scene of the dispute was dropped upon the objection of Japan, backed by disapprov-

7. See account of the "Twenty-one Demands," pp. 306–7.

8. S. R. Smith, *The Manchurian Crisis, 1931–1932: A Tragedy in International Relations* (New York: Columbia University Press, 1948), p. 127. See also Armin Rappaport, *Henry L. Stimson and Japan, 1931–1933* (Chicago: University of Chicago Press, 1963); R. N. Current, *Secretary Stimson: A Study in Statecraft* (New Brunswick: Rutgers University Press, 1954).

9. R. H. Ferrell, "The Mukden Incident: September 18–19, 1931," *Journal of Modern History,* 27 (March 1955), 66–72.

ing comment from the United States. In a resolution adopted September 30, the Council took note of a Japanese promise to withdraw all troops to the railway zone as soon as safety should permit, and called upon both parties to do nothing that would tend to aggravate the dispute. It then adjourned until October 14.

In Washington, Henry L. Stimson, Secretary of State, was perplexed by conflicting opinions in his own department, where there were pro-Japanese as well as pro-Chinese experts. Stimson wished, within limits, to cooperate with the League. He was, however, inclined at first to be sympathetic to Japan and was anxious not to appear more anti-Japanese than the members of the League Council. For reasons of domestic politics, too, he wished to make it plain that the United States was making up its own mind and not merely following the League's lead. These considerations induced a caution that made Stimson's protests to Japan in conjunction with the League appear dilatory and half-hearted.[10]

Stimson, furthermore, fell at the beginning into the natural error of believing that if he treated the Japanese government, that is, Wakatsuki and Shidehara, gently, he would strengthen their hands in putting restraints on the Army, whereas "tough talk" addressed to them would unify popular sentiment behind the militarists. For this reason, during the early stages of the controversy, he "pulled his punches," and even when he did speak firmly, he withheld his notes from publication. Thus both the Japanese and the American

public got the impression that Stimson was more inclined to condone Japanese action than actually was the case.

To both the United States and the League Council, Shidehara replied in a conciliatory spirit, promising that the unruly soldiers would be called back within the limits of the railway zone. Probably these promises were made in good faith, but they were not kept. Such was the nature of the Japanese government that neither the Premier nor the Foreign Office had any effective control over the Army. Disillusion first came on October 8, 1931, when Japanese planes bombed Chinchow in southwestern Manchuria. It was here that Chang Hsüeh-liang, the "Young Marshal," had set up his government after being expelled from Mukden. General Honjo, commanding the Japanese forces in Manchuria, had resolved to drive Chang and his government from that area without regard to promises given by the Foreign Minister.

The bombing of Chinchow led Stimson, with President Hoover's approval, to instruct an American representative, Consul Prentiss Gilbert in Geneva, to sit with the League Council when next it discussed the Manchurian question. Gilbert, however, was directed to participate in the proceedings only when the bearing of the Kellogg-Briand Pact was under discussion. His joining the circle at the Council table was hailed with enthusiasm in Geneva (except by the Japanese representative, who had opposed inviting him). It was viewed with misgivings by isolationists in the United States. His presence, though symbolizing the unity of purpose of the League and the United States, had little practical effect.

The Council, meeting from October 14 to October 24, finally passed a resolution calling upon Japan to withdraw her troops into their legitimate zone by November 16. Stimson, nearly two weeks later, sent a note with a similar request but setting no deadline date. The Japanese Army showed its contempt for the polite notes from Geneva and Washington by launching a campaign for control of northern Manchuria. On November 18, two days after the date set by the Council for with-

10. Smith, *Manchurian Crisis,* emphasizes the ineffectual character of Stimson's cooperation with the League. Much the same view is taken in D. F. Fleming, *The United States and World Organization, 1920–1933* (New York: Columbia University Press, 1938), chap. 13, and in F. P. Walters, *A History of the League of Nations,* 2 volumes (New York: Oxford University Press, 1952), 2: chap. 40. For Stimson's own view, see H. L. Stimson, *The Far Eastern Crisis: Recollections and Observations* (New York: Harper & Row, Publishers, 1936), and H. L. Stimson and McGeorge Bundy, *On Active Service in Peace and War* (New York: Harper & Row, Publishers, 1948), chap. 9.

drawal, Japanese forces occupied Tsitsihar, north of the Chinese Eastern Railway.

The Council of the League met again on November 16, this time in Paris. Charles G. Dawes, United States ambassador to Great Britain and formerly Vice President under Coolidge, was directed to go to Paris to cooperate with the Council; whether he should sit with it, as Gilbert had done at Geneva, was left to his discretion. He chose not to attend the Council meetings either as a participant or as an observer. Setting up his quarters at the Hotel Ritz, he held sessions with the Japanese and Chinese representatives and tried to contribute to a settlement. But what the Council could not do, neither could Dawes.

It was apparent by this time that Japan would not yield to persuasion or to diplomatic pressure. That she should be forced to yield seemed to Secretary Stimson a matter of great importance to the United States. To permit Japan to have her way in Manchuria, he believed, would impair American prestige in China, would injure American trade and endanger its Pacific possessions, and, most serious, would be a blow to the cause of world peace. Stimson had by now lost hope that conciliatory treatment would enable the Japanese moderates to bring the military to heel and, in contrast to his early posture of foot-dragging, he now took the lead in seeking collective measures to halt Japan. Yet what could he do? Economic sanctions were discussed, though not publicly, both in Washington and in the League Council in Paris. But in Washington President Hoover was unalterably opposed to American participation in such measures, which he believed to be a step toward war. Hence, while Stimson could cheer for economic sanctions by the League, he could promise none by the United States, saying only that this country would not interfere with any that the League might impose. And as for the League, while delegates of the small powers could talk of sanctions, the British and French governments felt more than a little sympathy for Japan and would not go beyond words in criticism of her policy.

The Council, therefore, could do little but repeat its hope that Japan would remove her troops. It did, however, resolve—this time at Japan's suggestion—to appoint a commission of inquiry to visit the Far East, examine the issues between China and Japan, and recommend a solution which would reconcile the interests of both parties. From this resolution came the Lytton Commission, so called from the English Earl of Lytton who became its chairman.

The Hoover-Stimson Doctrine

With economic sanctions ruled out on both sides of the Atlantic, President Hoover and his Secretary of State discussed means of subjecting Japan to purely moral pressure. It was apparently Hoover who suggested reviving the device first used by Secretary Bryan in 1915;[11] namely, a declaration that the United States would not recognize any situation brought about by action in violation of its treaty rights. The idea was held in reserve so long as there was any faint hope that Japan would draw back from her career of aggression in Manchuria. Such hope did not long persist. On December 11, 1931 (the day after the adjournment of the League Council in Paris), the Wakatsuki cabinet resigned. It was replaced two days later by a cabinet of the Seiyukai party, a party more amenable than the Minseito to Army influence. On January 3, 1932, the Japanese army occupied Chinchow at the southwestern extremity of Manchuria. Four days later, Secretary Stimson addressed to Japan and China identical notes setting forth what came to be known as the Stimson Doctrine (more accurately the Hoover-Stimson Doctrine). In these notes the Secretary informed the governments of China and Japan that the government of the United States

---

11. Current, *Secretary Stimson,* pp. 79–80; *The Memoirs of Herbert Hoover:* [2] *The Cabinet and the Presidency, 1920–1933* (New York: The Macmillan Company, 1952), pp. 362–78. On Bryan, see pp. 306–7.

can not admit the legality of any situation de facto nor does it intend to recognize any treaty or agreement entered into between those governments, or agents thereof, which may impair the treaty rights of the United States or its citizens in China, including those which relate to the sovereignty, the independence, or the territorial and administrative integrity of the Republic of China, or to the international policy relative to China, commonly known as the open-door policy; and that it does not intend to recognize any situation, treaty, or agreement which may be brought about by means contrary to the covenants and obligations of the pact of Paris of August 27, 1928, to which treaty both China and Japan, as well as the United States, are parties.

Nonrecognition, if practiced by the United States alone, would clearly have little value as a weapon. Before publishing his notes, Stimson had informed Great Britain and France of his plan and invited them to adhere to his declaration; he had hoped that other governments would follow suit. France made no response. The British government, in a communiqué released to the press, announced that it relied on Japan's promises to keep the door open to trade in Manchuria and saw no need for adopting the American position.

The British attitude changed somewhat when, late in January, 1932, the Japanese attacked the Chinese section of Shanghai. The purpose of this maneuver was to compel the Chinese to drop their boycott of Japanese goods, the peaceful yet potent weapon with which they had retaliated for aggression in Manchuria. The attack on Shanghai endangered the populous and important International Settlement (which, with the French concession, constituted the foreign area of the city); it was also a blow at the heart of the British sphere of interest in the Yangtse Valley. Now the British joined the Americans in protesting the Japanese aggression and in promoting direct negotiations between Chinese and Japanese. These negotiations, also sponsored by the League of Nations, resulted in March in a suspension of hostilities in the Shanghai area and on May 5 in the signing of

an armistice. Between March and May, Japanese troops at Shanghai were reduced to the small number normally kept in the International Settlement.[12]

Manchuria Becomes "Manchukuo"

But while at Shanghai Japan yielded to stubborn Chinese resistance and to international pressure, she was consolidating her gains in Manchuria. As each portion of Manchuria was occupied by Japanese troops the civil administration was reorganized with Japanese in key positions. Japanese civil and military officials, in close touch with aggressive militarists in Tokyo, "made use," in the words of the Lytton Report, "of the names and actions of certain Chinese individuals, and took advantage of certain minorities among the inhabitants, who had grievances against the former administration," to organize an independence movement. Such a movement, said the Report "had never been heard of in Manchuria before September 1931."[13] On February 18, 1932, the independence of Manchuria was proclaimed, the country henceforth to be known as "Manchukuo," the Country of the Manchus.

This was a plain challenge to the American doctrine of nonrecognition. Stimson responded in a letter of February 23, to Senator Borah, chairman of the Senate Foreign Relations Committee. He invited other governments to adhere to the nonrecognition policy and added, by way of warning to Japan, that, since the

12. Secretary Stimson attributed the Japanese surrender to international pressure at Shanghai in part to the presence of the United States battleship fleet in the Pacific, whither it had come for previously scheduled maneuvers centered at Hawaii. Current, *Secretary Stimson*, p. 103. As a further warning to Japan, he persuaded Hoover to keep the battle fleet at Hawaii and with it the scouting force, which otherwise would have returned to the Atlantic. Rappaport, *Stimson and Japan*, pp. 161–62.

13. League of Nations, *Appeal by the Chinese Government: Report of the Commission of Enquiry*, September 4, 1932 (Series of League Publications: VII. Political 1932. VII. 12), p. 97. (Cited hereafter as *Lytton Report*.)

Washington treaties of 1922 were all inter-related, a violation of one of them by one signatory released other signatories from their obligations under other treaties in the group. In other words, if Japan violated the territorial or administrative integrity of China, protected by the Nine-Power Treaty, the United States was no longer bound by the limitations on her naval strength and her fortifications in the Pacific imposed by the Five-Power Treaty. This warning made no more impression upon Japan than the earlier nonrecognition note. Nor did the United States carry out the implied threat.

But if Stimson was unable to deflect Japan from her course, he did have the satisfaction of seeing his (or Hoover's) doctrine officially adopted by the League of Nations. On February 12, 1932, China had requested the transfer of her appeal from the Council of the League to the Assembly. The latter body, on March 11, 1932, adopted a resolution in effect endorsing the nonrecognition doctrine and declaring it incumbent upon members of the League not to recognize any situation "brought about by means contrary to the Covenant of the League of Nations or to the Pact of Paris."

The League and the Lytton Report

The five-man Commission of Enquiry, or Lytton Commission, with the British Earl of Lytton as chairman and General Frank R. McCoy as the American member, arrived in Tokyo on February 29, 1932, and spent six months in Japan, China, Manchuria, and Korea. Its report, dated September 4, 1932, although recognizing that Japan had legitimate rights in Manchuria that had been endangered by Chinese policy, concluded, nevertheless, that Japan's military action, initiated on September 18, 1931, had not been justified, as Japan claimed, as legitimate self-defense. It concluded that the establishment of independent Manchukuo did not represent the wishes of the population of Manchuria but had been engineered by Japan as a part of her

program of expansion. The government of Manchukuo, it found, was dominated by Japanese, of whom there were nearly two hundred in the central government alone.

The Commission did not, however, recommend a return to the status quo before September 1931, a status that had not adequately protected Japanese interests. It proposed, instead, a special administration for the Three Eastern Provinces (Manchuria), under Chinese sovereignty, but with a large degree of autonomy in local affairs. Both Chinese and Japanese troops would be withdrawn, and a special gendarmerie would be entrusted with the maintenance of order. Japanese interests would be safeguarded in a treaty to be negotiated between Japan and China. The Commission recommended also that Japan and China negotiate a commercial treaty and a treaty of arbitration and conciliation, nonaggression and mutual assistance. The essence of the proposal was reconciliation of Chinese sovereignty in Manchuria with protection of legitimate Japanese economic interests.[14]

The Lytton Report, conscientious and reasonable as it appears to an unprejudiced eye, was spurned by Japan. In fact, without even awaiting its publication, Japan on September 15, 1932, officially recognized her puppet state of Manchukuo. The League Assembly, on the other hand, approved the Commission's recommendations and at the same time (February 24, 1933) advised all League members not to recognize Manchukuo "either *de jure* or *de facto*." Japan's response was to give the required two-year notice of withdrawal from the League.

Neither the Stimson doctrine nor the letter to Borah, the retention of the Pacific fleet in Hawaiian waters nor an address by Stimson declaring that the United States could not remain neutral in a war between aggressor and victim [15] had the slightest effect upon Japanese policy—partly, perhaps, because the Japanese knew that Stimson's threats were a

---

14. *Lytton Report, passim.*
15. Rappaport, *Stimson and Japan,* p. 169.

bluff. Stimson had taken a high moral position, but the chief practical effect had been to incur Japanese ill will by making the United States appear the chief opponent of Japanese expansion in Asia.[16]

A More Cautious Policy

A few days after the League Assembly rendered its verdict against Japan and the puppet state of Manchukuo, Franklin D. Roosevelt entered the White House in Washington, and Cordell Hull replaced Stimson in the State Department. Stimson had conferred at length with Roosevelt during the winter and had been assured that in the Far East the new administration would continue the policy of the old.[17] The United States, accordingly, persisted in refusing recognition to Manchukuo and accepted a nonvoting membership in an Advisory Committee on the Far East set up by the League of Nations. Roosevelt also kept the battleship fleet in the Pacific, where it had been since 1932, and announced that the Navy would be built up to treaty limits.

Yet the diplomacy of the new administration toward Japan was in a much lower key than Stimson's. There had, in fact, been a change in priorities. "In particular," writes Dorothy Borg, "the emphasis which had been placed upon the necessity of supporting the peace system began to be shifted to another objective: the avoidance of a conflict between the United States and Japan."[18] Having announced that it would not recognize the new situation in Manchuria, the United States gave up protesting against it. The change was noted by the Japanese and called forth appreciative comments.[19]

Actually, Japanese military aggression came to a pause soon after Roosevelt and Hull

16. Rappaport, *Stimson and Japan*, pp. 176–77, 202–3.
17. Current, *Secretary Stimson*, chap. 6.
18. Dorothy Borg, *The United States and the Far Eastern Crisis of 1933–1938* (Cambridge: Harvard University Press, 1964), p. 522.
19. Hull, *Memoirs*, 1: 270, 274.

took office. In February and March 1933 the province of Jehol (pronounced ray-hō), adjoining Manchuria and formerly a part of Inner Mongolia, was annexed to Manchukuo. Japanese troops engaged in this operation penetrated south of the Great Wall into the Chinese province of Hopei. Here they met firm resistance, and here, on May 31, 1933, they signed the Tangku truce, which established a demilitarized zone south of the Great Wall in Hopei. Chinese troops were to withdraw to a line just north and east of the cities of Peiping and Tientsin; Japanese were to retire beyond the Great Wall. The truce ended active hostilities between Japanese and Chinese forces for four years and reduced United States-Japanese tension.

Closing the Open Door

Tension was kept alive, however, by other Japanese actions. Japan was quietly promoting disregard of the open door principle by the puppet government of Manchukuo. Intermittently during 1934, Hull was protesting to Tokyo over discriminations against American trade in that area. Japan had initially given assurances that the open door principle would be respected in Manchukuo, but in April 1935 the British and American ambassadors were told by Foreign Minister Hirota that these assurances

> had been given on the understanding that "Manchukuo" would be recognized by other nations and that until the existence of "Manchukuo" were recognized "no dispute whatever could be entertained with regard to that country."

On another occasion Ambassador Grew was informed that since Manchukuo was an independent country, protests should be addressed to Hsinking, the Manchukuo capital,

> but that if foreign countries claim that Manchuria is still a part of China they should protest to Nanking, . . .

The Foreign Office spokesman added that

"Japan does not consider that the Nine Power Treaty applies to 'Manchukuo.' " [20]

Thus Japan evaded all responsibility for discrimination against non-Japanese trade in Manchukuo. The United States rejected the Japanese evasions but for the time being limited its opposition to rather mild protests and to moralizing upon the virtue of keeping promises.

In other ways Japan was making clear its determination to establish its supremacy in the Far East, free from American or European interference. In April 1934, Eiji Amau, spokesman for the Foreign Office, told a press conference that because of Japan's "position and mission," she alone had the duty "to keep peace and order in East Asia." Japan objected, he said, to "any joint operations, even in the name of technical or financial assistance," such as the League of Nations had proposed for China. Japan would also object to aid or advice of a military or political nature furnished to China by foreign nations acting individually.[21] Secretary Hull protested mildly. Nevertheless, the United States canceled current plans for aid to China.[22]

A few weeks after the Amau statement, Hiroshi Saito, the new Japanese ambassador, proposed to Hull an eight-point agreement between Japan and the United States. The heart of the agreement was to be recognition of American and Japanese spheres in the Pacific and an undertaking on the part of the two governments, "so far as lies within their proper and legitimate power to establish a reign of law and order in the regions geographically adjacent to their respective countries." This proposal for what the Japanese sometimes referred to as a "Japanese Monroe Doctrine"—a proposal that would have given Japan a free hand in China with no compensating gain to the United States—was politely rejected by Secretary Hull. It turned up from time to time in the Japanese press as a rumor of an accord about to be reached.[23]

By 1935 the Japanese had become dissatisfied with their gains. Economically, Manchukuo had been disappointing, and Japan coveted the markets and raw materials of northern China. Seeking a less expensive and less offensive method than conquest, Japanese agents undertook to stimulate native autonomy movements in five provinces, three in China proper and two in adjoining Inner Mongolia. These attempts had little success, and though the Japanese Army was disposed to insist on "independence" for those five provinces, the Foreign Office preferred another path. During 1935 and 1936, it pressured the Nanking government for a diplomatic settlement on the basis of three principles: (1) cessation of anti-Japanese activity in China, (2) tacit *de facto* recognition by China of Manchukuo, (3) cooperation between China and Japan for the suppression of Communism in the Far East. Such a settlement, in the opinion of American diplomats in Tokyo and Peiping, would eventually mean domination of China by Japan without the need of military conquest, and apparently Washington was prepared, however reluctantly, to acquiesce in such an outcome.[24]

20. Joseph C. Grew, *Turbulent Era: A Diplomatic Record of Forty Years, 1904–1945*, ed. Walter Johnson, 2 vols. (Boston: Houghton Mifflin Company, 1952), 2: 970, 979–80. Quotations from *Turbulent Era* reprinted by permission of the publisher.
21. *Foreign Relations, Japan, 1931–1941*, 1: 224–25. League of Nations experts had been at work on plans for the economic reconstruction of China. The United States, Germany, and Italy were assisting in different ways in the building of a Chinese air force. H. M. Vinacke, *A History of the Far East in Modern Times*, 5th ed. (New York: Appleton-Century-Crofts, 1950), p. 548.
22. Borg, *The U. S. and the Far Eastern Crisis*, p. 523.

23. Hull, *Memoirs*, 1: 281–84; Grew, *Turbulent Era*, 2: 997. One report expanded the accord to include Great Britain, which was to keep peace in a European sphere.
24. Borg, *The U. S. and the Far Eastern Crisis*, chaps. 5, 6, and p. 528. Cordell Hull stated in his *Memoirs* (1, 290–91) that after Japan's refusal to renew the Washington and London naval treaties and their expiration at the end of 1936, he and the President reached a decision "to continue to insist on the maintenance of law, on our legitimate rights and interests in the Far East, and on observance of the treaties and declarations that guaranteed an independent China." It appears from Borg's study that no such fateful decision was made at this time. Even

The negotiations were complicated by sporadic Sino-Japanese "incidents," usually attacks by Chinese on Japanese subjects, and by an invasion of the province of Suiyuan by Manchukuoan and Japanese forces. The repulse of this invasion stiffened Chinese resistance, and in December 1936 the Japanese moderated their demands. The Nanking government was being advised by the British to make reasonable concessions,[25] but any chance of agreement was lost when, following the "Sian incident," [26] Chiang Kai-shek came to an understanding with the Chinese Communists for a common front against Japan. Negotiations with Japan ceased. The following July was to witness the opening of full scale hostilities between Japan and China. These events will be treated in a later chapter.[27]

---

after the outbreak of Sino-Japanese hostilities in 1937, the United States avoided a course that might lead to a military showdown. Only after Japan aligned itself with the Axis and proclaimed its Greater East Asia program did the U.S. government resolve that Japan must be stopped whatever the cost. See below, Chapters 36, 38.

25. The various stages in these negotiations are reflected in Grew, *Turbulent Era,* 2: 1003–14, *passim.*

26. In December 1936 Chiang Kai-shek was kidnapped at Sian by the forces of Marshal Chang Hsüeh-liang, who instead of fighting the Chinese Communists were fraternizing with them. No agreement was put in writing, but before his release Chiang evidently reached an understanding with the Communists for cessation of the civil war and a united front against Japan.

27. See Chapter 36.

While the Japanese militarists and nationalists were seizing control of their government and launching Japan upon an aggressive career of expansion in the Far East, similar developments were taking place in the politics of two of Europe's leading states. Fascism rose to power in Italy and nazism in Germany. Both movements were anti-communist but also anti-democratic and totalitarian. German nazism was, in addition, violently anti-Semitic. Both set up one-party states, in which all opposition was suppressed. Freedom of speech, of the press, of teaching, of association were abolished. Control of the national economy was assumed by the government. Both fascism and nazism were nationalistic to the point of chauvinism. Benito Mussolini, the founder of fascism, aspired to reestablish for Italy something of the grandeur of imperial Rome, at least to make Italy supreme in the Mediterranean. Adolf Hitler, who built his National Socialist Party (Nazis for short), upon the Italian model, sought not only to make Germany supreme in Europe, bringing into the Reich all German populations living under other sovereignties, but also to conquer for Germany *Lebensraum* (living space) at the expense of her eastern neighbors, to recover the German colonies lost in World War I, and to elevate Germany to a position of world leadership superior to that which she had held under Kaiser Wilhelm II. Such purposes, which Hitler set down in writing in his book *Mein Kampf (My Struggle),* published in 1924, could be attained only by tearing up the peace settlement of 1919.

Mussolini came to power in Italy, following the Fascist "march on Rome" in October 1922. Most Americans were not greatly concerned with the anti-democratic features of his domestic regime, the strong-arm measures of his "Black Shirts," the elimination, even by assassination, of parliamentary opponents. That he had suppressed communism and socialism (though himself formerly a socialist), put an end to strikes, and "made the trains run on time," seemed, to the average American visitor, to justify his unconventional methods. Not until the middle 1930's, when he set out to conquer an empire, did Mussolini's activities seriously affect American thought or American policy.

34

European Dictators and American Neutralism

Hitler followed Mussolini by a decade. His first bid for power, the Munich beer hall *Putsch* of 1923, failed completely. Not until 1930 (when the German Republic was hard hit by depression and unemployment) did his National Socialist followers make a respectable showing at the polls, and not until January 30, 1933 (five weeks before the accession of Franklin Roosevelt) was Hitler named Chancellor of the Reich by President von Hindenburg. In March, following new elections, the Reichstag gave Hitler dictatorial powers for four years. When President von Hindenburg died in 1934, Hitler united in himself the powers of President and Chancellor, though preferring his Nazi title, *der Führer* (the Leader), to that of President.

Although acting promptly to suppress opposition parties, deprive Jews of citizenship, and substitute a centralized for the federal state—in other words to set up his totalitarian, anti-Semitic system within Germany—Hitler moved more cautiously in foreign policy. In fact, his early moves in the international field were more conciliatory than had been expected. The tragic significance for the whole world of his rise to power was not at once realized; certainly not in the United States.

The General Disarmament Conference Fails

One of the first international problems to confront both Hitler and Roosevelt as they took up their new duties was the question of disarmament by international agreement. The General Disarmament Conference, which had first convened a year earlier, was sitting at Geneva in the spring of 1933.

The history of this attempt at a general limitation of armaments goes back to the Treaty of Versailles and the League of Nations Covenant. Article 8 of the latter had made it a responsibility of the Council of the League to "formulate plans for . . . reduction [of armaments] for the consideration and action of the several Governments." The treaty had strictly limited Germany's armed forces, but placed no restriction upon those of the victors. In 1926 the Council appointed a Preparatory Commission for the Disarmament Conference. Included were representatives of Germany and the United States, and ultimately of the Soviet Union, as well as representatives of the League powers. The Commission sat intermittently from 1926 to 1930 and at length drew up an outline for a treaty on disarmament, details of which the Conference itself would have to fill in.

The General Disarmament Conference first met at Geneva, February 2, 1932, with representatives from sixty nations, including Germany (now a member of the League), the United States, and the Soviet Union. The most serious obstacle to agreement lay in the relations between France and Germany. Germany was now insisting upon her right to "equality" in armaments instead of the Versailles limitations. France, with bitter memories of 1870 and 1914, insisted upon some new guarantees of security before she would consent to German rearmament. Attempts of President Hoover to break the deadlock failed to satisfy France.

Upon Hitler's accession to power, Germany's insistence upon equality in armament grew more urgent. In May 1933, President Roosevelt made a new attempt to bring about agreement. Urging the Conference to adopt a compromise plan for progressive disarmament offered by the British, he proposed a solemn nonaggression pact by which the signers would promise, during the implementation of the disarmament program, not to send their armed forces outside their own territory. A few days later (May 22, 1933), through an address by Delegate Norman H. Davis at the Conference, Roosevelt offered an agreement to consult with other governments in the event of a threat to the peace, and to refrain from interfering with League sanctions against an aggressor if the judgment of the United States as to the aggressor coincided with that of the League. These promises of cooperation with the League, which went beyond any previously offered by the United States and which were given in the hope of satisfying the French craving for security, were conditional upon the adoption of a general plan for disarmament—a plan that should include abolition of offensive weapons and reduction of others.[1]

Meanwhile, on May 17 (the day after Roosevelt's proposal of a nonaggression pact), Hitler addressed the Reichstag, which he had convoked in special session. Germany was willing, he said, to go as far as her neighbors in disarmament. She was even willing to defer for five years the attainment of equality. But she would not be bound by majority votes in the Conference and would sign no document perpetuating her inferiority in armaments.

In spite of these good omens of success, the Conference recessed in June without agreement. Before the date set for reconvening in October, Hitler's fleeting interest in cooperation had dissolved. On October 14, 1933, Germany announced her withdrawal from both the Disarmament Conference and the League of Nations. The German secession ended any hope for an agreement on disarmament. The meeting of the Conference planned for October was postponed until May 1934. After two weeks of futility, it adjourned June 11, never to meet again.

Hitler Repudiates Versailles

Hitler's withdrawal from the Disarmament Conference and the League of Nations was a prelude to the rearmament of Germany in disregard of the Versailles Treaty. On March 16, 1935, the Führer announced that Germany was resuming compulsory military service (forbidden by the treaty) and increasing her army to 500,000 men (five times the treaty limit). The treaty limitations on Germany's armament, he argued, were nullified by the failure of the powers to carry out the plan for general disarmament; but he assured an anxious world that Germany would continue

to observe all other articles of the Versailles Treaty, including those on boundaries and the demilitarization of the Rhineland.

Great Britain joined with France and Italy, both in the League Council and outside, in condemning Hitler's violation of treaty engagements; but in June 1935, the British government condoned Hitler's action by formally consenting to the building of a German navy 35 percent the size of Britain's—far beyond the limit set by the Versailles Treaty.

In March 1936, when Mussolini's invasion of Ethiopia had driven a wedge between Italy and her former allies, England and France,[2] Hitler seized the occasion to proclaim his repudiation of the entire Treaty of Versailles and also of the Locarno Pact of 1925, by which Germany had joined in guaranteeing the frontiers of her western neighbors. Simultaneously he announced the remilitarization of the Rhineland and occupied it with thousands of German troops. The League Council and the signers of the Locarno Pact condemned the German action as in violation of treaty obligations. The possibility of sanctions was discussed but failed to receive adequate support in the Council. Hitler "got away with" his breach of the peace system as Japan and Italy had been permitted to do with theirs.

The United States Is Warned of Hitler's Purposes

What was known in the United States about Hitler's aggressive plans, and what, if anything, did Americans propose to do about them? American representatives in Europe were fully aware of the trend in German policy, and from 1934 on, they were sending alarming reports to the State Department. As early as April 1934, the acting American commercial attaché in Berlin, Douglas Miller, thus described German purposes:

The fundamental purpose is to secure a greater share of the world's future for the Germans, the expansion of German territory and

1. The President's proposal and Davis's address are printed in U. S. Department of State, *Peace and War: United States Foreign Policy, 1931–1941* (Washington: Government Printing Office, 1943), pp. 179–82, 186–91.

2. See pp. 344–45.

growth of the German race until it constitutes the largest and most powerful nation in the world, and ultimately, according to some Nazi leaders, until it dominates the entire globe.

Elsewhere in the same report, Miller predicted: "Germany is to engage in a gigantic struggle with the rest of the world to grow at the expense of its neighbors." And, eleven months before Hitler announced his plans for rearmament, Miller reported that the Nazis were "building a tremendous military machine" and were "determined to secure more power and more territory in Europe. If this is voluntarily given to them by peaceful means," he continued, "well and good, but if not, they will certainly use force. That is the only meaning behind the manifold activities of the movement in Germany today."[3]

Similar warnings were passed along from time to time during the next two years by Ambassador William E. Dodd in Berlin. In April 1935, he reported German opinion as holding that American intervention had prevented Germany from dominating Europe in 1918, and as now believing: "Since American intervention will not be repeated the Third Reich will at strategic moment seize the [Polish] corridor or Austria and if war follows win what was lost in 1918 . . ."[4] Chancellor Hitler, Dodd reported a few months later, had "repeatedly said that he could make no arrangement with any Powers which might deny German advances into Lithuania, Latvia and Esthonia—'barbaric peoples,' he said to Sir John Simon." Hitler looked to those states as part of a plan to encircle Russia.[5] Dodd assured the State Department, furthermore, that Hitler could count on the support of "an overwhelming majority of the German people in

any venture he might undertake," even if it were "one of outright conquest."[6]

The United States Chooses Neutrality

By 1935 it was apparent that the postwar system of peace and collective security, already ruptured by Japan in Asia, was further imperiled by the aggressive designs of Germany and Italy in Europe. New wars in Europe seemed certain, unless the "peace-loving" states in the League could act more energetically to preserve the peace than they had done to suppress Japanese aggression or to prevent Germany from tearing up the Versailles Treaty. This they were not likely to do; certainly they would not do it without the active support of the United States. The United States faced a choice between active support of collective security to prevent war on the one hand, and, on the other hand, an attempt to insulate itself from whatever war might come. The United States chose the latter course. Assuming that new wars were inevitable, it set up safeguards against being drawn into them as it had been drawn in in 1917.

Whether this decision was right or wrong, the reasons for it are clear. The basic one was disillusionment with the results of World War I. Woodrow Wilson had justified that war to the American people, and to himself, with idealistic arguments. The war was to "make the world safe for democracy," to end secret diplomacy, to ensure the self-determination of peoples, to set up a League of Nations that should suppress aggression and prevent wars in the future. Having been led to expect too much, the American people were doomed to be disappointed with the practical realities of the postwar world. Idealists had been shocked by some of the compromises of the Paris peace settlement, and their opposition had helped to prevent ratification of the treaty. At Paris and in the subsequent years, much had been accomplished for democracy, for self-deter-

3. U. S. Department of State, *Peace and War,* pp. 211–14.
4. *Foreign Relations, 1935,* 2: 320–21. At almost the same time that Dodd was reporting thus, the German ambassador in Washington was declaring to Secretary Hull that Germany had no designs on the Polish corridor, Austria, or portions of Czechoslovakia; in fact, no aggressive designs whatever. Ibid., p. 318.
5. *Foreign Relations, 1935,* p. 337.

6. *Foreign Relations, 1936,* 2: 152.

mination, and for open diplomacy. Even the League of Nations had been successful in settling many minor disputes, besides making useful contributions in the economic and social fields. But Americans were prone to emphasize its weaknesses rather than its successes, and their skepticism about the League was reinforced by its failure to take vigorous action against Japan and Germany. Few of them paused to reflect that American membership in the League might have closed the gap between failure and success.

After 1931, furthermore, Americans were impatient with the refusal of their former associates to settle their war debts.[7] Not always appreciative of Europe's problems, such as the French passion for security, they resented the expenditure on new European armaments of money which might have been used to pay back to Uncle Sam the generous loans that had saved Europe from conquest by Germany.

All in all, as the average American saw it, the United States had participated in World War I for altruistic reasons and at great cost. Then its former associates had used the war and the peace settlement for their own selfish advantage, had repudiated the ideals for which America had fought, and had shown neither gratitude for American aid nor a disposition to pay their just debts. This was a partial and a distorted view of history. It took no account, for example, of the perils that German victory would have held for the United States, and of the idea that hence, in aiding to defeat Germany, the United States had been effectively safeguarding its own future.[8] But it was a widespread and a popular view, in Congress no less than with the general public. It pointed unmistakably to the conclusion: Our entry into World War I was a grave mistake; we must never repeat it.

If the interest of the United States was in keeping out of future wars in other continents, the investigation of a Senate committee beginning in the fall of 1934 suggested how that end might be attained. The committee, headed by Senator Gerald P. Nye, of North Dakota, was organized for the purpose of investigating the operations of manufacturers of, and dealers in, arms and munitions of war. In months of sensational public hearings, the committee convinced itself and a large share of the public that a hidden reason for American entry into the war in 1917 had been to protect its trade in munitions with the Allies and the loans made to those same Allies by American bankers. It was no news that the presence in the war zones of American citizens traveling on ships of the belligerents had also contributed in an important way to drawing the United States into the war. The conclusion was obvious: If the activities of bankers, munitions-makers, and citizens traveling in war zones dragged the country into war in 1917 against its own best interests, such activities should be prohibited in connection with future foreign wars.[9]

Congress Legislates Neutrality

By the summer of 1935 a foreign war was clearly imminent. In the preceding December, Italian and Ethiopian troops had clashed at a place called Wal Wal near the boundary of Ethiopia and Italian Somaliland. When Italy, although professing to desire a peaceful settlement, obstructed all attempts at arbitration and conciliation and began mobilizing her war machine, it was evident that Mussolini was bent upon conquering an African empire. Now, thought some senators and congressmen, was the time for legislation that might protect the United States against a repetition of the mistake of 1917.

7. See Chapter 32.
8. Cf. Walter Lippmann, *U. S. Foreign Policy: Shield of the Republic* (Boston: Little, Brown and Company, 1943), pp. 33–39; R. E. Osgood, *Ideals and Self-Interest in America's Foreign Relations* (Chicago: University of Chicago Press, 1953), pp. 397–400.

9. Osgood, *Ideals and Self-Interest,* pp. 365–66. Secretary Hull believed the Nye Committee unrivaled in its unfortunate effects on American foreign policy, except by the committee that prepared the way for rejection of the League of Nations. Hull, *Memoirs,* 1: 398.

Here the aims of Congress and the administration diverged. President Roosevelt and Secretary Hull, wished legislation flexible enough to empower the President to forbid the exportation of arms and munitions to an aggressor government while permitting their sale to the victim of aggression. A bill to this effect had been prepared by the State Department. Such discretionary power would have enabled the President to cooperate with the League of Nations in withholding arms from a nation adjudged the aggressor. Such action, however, would have meant taking sides in a conflict and possible involvement in war. This Congress did not wish to risk. The Senate set aside the administration bill and passed a substitute requiring the President, in the event of a foreign war, to forbid arms shipments to both belligerents without distinction. A joint resolution in this form, usually referred to as the First Neutrality Act, was passed by both houses of Congress and became law on August 31, 1935. President Roosevelt signed it reluctantly because of its failure to permit any discrimination between attacker and attacked in cutting off war material.[10]

The new law directed the President, upon the outbreak of war between two foreign countries, to proclaim the existence of such war, and prohibited thenceforth the exportation from the United States of arms, ammunition, and implements of war to or for either belligerent. It also forbade American ships to carry such articles from any point to or for a belligerent; and it empowered the President, at his discretion, to warn American citizens that they would travel on belligerent ships only at their own risk. Another section of the Act created a National Munitions Control Board, with the Secretary of State as chairman. Every person engaged in manufacturing, exporting, or importing arms, ammunition, or implements of war was required to register with the Secretary of State and to obtain a license for every transaction by which such commodities were exported from, or imported into, the United States.

10. Hull, *Memoirs,* 1: chap. 29.

The Italo-Ethiopian War and American Neutrality

This was the legislation governing President Roosevelt's action when Italy, without formally declaring war (she had renounced war by signing the Pact of Paris), invaded Ethiopia early in October 1935. The President acted promptly. In a proclamation of October 5, he announced that actual war existed between Italy and Ethiopia, even though there had been no declaration. He therefore prohibited the exportation of arms, ammunition, or implements of war to or for either country. In this instance, the necessity of including both belligerents in the embargo did not displease the President. Ethiopia, a completely landlocked country with poor overland communications, could not have imported significant amounts of material from America in any case; the practical effect of the embargo was, therefore, felt less in Ethiopia than in Italy, the aggressor power.

But what Italy needed most was oil, and since oil was not classified as ammunition or an implement of war, the President had no authority to forbid its export. He and Secretary Hull did, however, resort to a "moral embargo" on oil and other commodities, appealing to American exporters to hold their shipments to Italy to normal prewar levels.[11]

In the meantime, the Council of the League of Nations, acting with more vigor than it had yet shown, declared Italy an aggressor and imposed sanctions. It forbade the shipment to Italy, by members of the League, of arms, ammunitions, or implements of war; forbade loans to Italy, either to the government or to private parties; prohibited acceptance of imports from Italy; and embargoed shipments to Italy of various commodities produced chiefly by League powers.[12] Omitted from this list

11. Hull, *Memoirs,* 1: chap. 31.
12. F. P. Walters, *A History of the League of Nations,* 2 vols. (New York: Oxford University Press, 1952), 2: chap. 53, gives a good account of League policy in the Italian crisis. See also Herbert Feis, *Seen from E.A.* (New York: Alfred A. Knopf, Inc., 1947), pp. 193–283.

were oil, iron and steel, coal and coke, which were obtainable in non-League countries.

Great Britain also made an impressive showing of force, moving her Mediterranean fleet to the vicinity of the Suez Canal and her home fleet to Gibraltar.

These, and similar French gestures, however, turned out to be principally bluff. Great Britain and France were now deeply concerned over the plans of Hitler's Germany. Anxious to divide Mussolini from Hitler and retain the friendship of the former, they agreed between themselves not to push sanctions to a point that might provoke Italy to war. In December, the British and French Foreign Secretaries, Sir Samuel Hoare and Pierre Laval, proposed a settlement that would have given Italy most of what she desired at the expense of Ethiopia. This proposal for appeasement was so strongly condemned in England that Hoare resigned, and Anthony Eden became Foreign Secretary.

A proposal for an embargo on oil—really the key commodity in the Italian campaign—was then seriously made and discussed; but before a decision could be reached, Hitler proclaimed the end of the Treaty of Versailles and marched his legions into the Rhineland. These events stole the spotlight from Italy and added to France's reluctance to take drastic action against a power that she might need as a friend. They ended talk of an oil embargo and virtually assured an Italian victory, since Great Britain declined to take the one other step that might have been effective—closing the Suez Canal. On May 5, 1936, an Italian motorized column entered Addis Ababa, the Ethiopian capital. Four days later, Mussolini decreed the annexation of all Ethiopia to the Italian empire. Resistance to the invaders collapsed, and in July the League Assembly voted to put an end to the sanctions against Italy. For the third time, collective security had failed to restrain the aggression of a major power. Italy, angered by the League's attempt to curb her and by the Assembly's refusal to unseat the Ethiopian delegation, withdrew from membership, as had Japan and Germany before her. The Assembly failed to take a stand against recognition of the conquest, as it

had done in Manchuria, and one by one, members of the League recognized Italy's sovereignty in Ethiopia.

The attitude of the United States toward the League in its battle with Mussolini was sympathetic but not very helpful. The "moral embargo" on oil and other commodities not on the prohibited list was, says Hull, "reasonably successful." An attempt to give the President discretionary authority to impose a legal embargo on such commodities was defeated in Congress before passage of the Second Neutrality Act of February 29, 1936 (the date on which most provisions of the original act were due to expire). The League powers knew, therefore, that if they should impose an embargo on oil, the President of the United States would have no authority to join in it, except insofar as he could persuade American exporters to restrict voluntarily their oil shipments. This situation was certainly a deterrent to an oil embargo by the League.

The Second Neutrality Act, furthermore, contained a new feature that was hardly encouraging to those who might consider using stronger sanctions against Italy. The act of 1935 *authorized* the President, when a new belligerent entered an existing war, to extend the embargo to cover dealings with the new entrant. The act of 1936 *directed* him to do the same. This meant, for example, that if imposition of sanctions upon Italy should lead her to attack Great Britain, the latter, as a belligerent, would be cut off from "arms, ammunition, and implements of war" produced in the United States. It cannot be said that such misgivings about the attitude of the United States to possible sanctions were *the* reason for the halfheartedness of League action; they may well have been *one* of the reasons.[13]

The Second Neutrality Act contained two other provisions not found in its predecessor. It forbade loans to belligerent governments, through purchase of their securities or other-

---

13. Feis, *Seen from E.A.,* pp. 280–81. As a matter of fact, the League had no positive assurance that the U.S. would submit to a complete or partial blockade of Italy should the League impose one.

wise, by "any person within the United States." This was clearly an application of the Nye Committee's thesis that loans to the Allies by American bankers had been a factor in seducing the United States into war in 1917. The other new provision, which might be regarded as a corollary of the Monroe Doctrine, exempted from the bans on munitions, loans, and the like, an American republic engaged in war with a non-American state, "provided the American republic is not cooperating with a non-American state or states in such war."

Except for these modifications, the Second Neutrality Act extended the provisions of the First to May 1, 1937.

The Spanish Civil War and American Neutrality

The neutrality regulations were applicable to wars between foreign states; they made no mention of civil wars. A new problem was raised, therefore, when, in July 1936, General Francisco Franco launched his insurrection against the Republican government of Spain. The Spanish Civil War, thus begun, was fought bitterly for nearly three years, finally ending in victory for Franco and his so-called Nationalists. What was to be the American policy with regard to the sale of arms to the opposing Spanish groups? If the United States had followed the practice that had been customary in dealing with civil wars in Latin America, the legitimate government of the Spanish Republic would have been permitted to purchase freely in the American market, while that privilege would have been denied to the insurgents. But Europe adopted a different course, and the United States conformed to it. The Spanish Civil War contained the germ of a possible international conflict. It was known that Germany and Italy sympathized with Franco, while Russia, France, and to a less degree Great Britain were friendly to the Republican or Loyalist side. Intervention by these powers in behalf of the opposing parties in Spain might bring them into armed collision with one another and set off a new world war.

In August 1936, therefore, upon French initiative, the European governments agreed upon a policy of nonintervention in Spain and set up a committee in London to supervise its operation and to prevent assistance to either side from the cooperating powers.

That Germany and Italy would violate their nonintervention agreement on a large scale, and so ensure Franco's victory, could not be foreseen.[14] It seemed best to Messrs. Roosevelt and Hull in Washington to adopt a policy parallel to that of Europe. In August 1936, accordingly, the Secretary of State announced that though the President had no authority to institute an arms embargo in a civil war, he hoped nevertheless that American exporters would refrain from shipping war material to either side in Spain. Thus they would be conforming to the spirit of the Neutrality Acts.

This "moral embargo" was not observed in all instances, and early in January 1937, the President asked Congress to make it legal. Accordingly, in a joint resolution signed on January 8, 1937, Congress prohibited the export of any arms, ammunition, or implements of war to either of the opposing forces in Spain. The wisdom of thus shutting off war materials from the Loyalist government in Spain has been much debated pro and con.[15] In retro-

---

14. Russia, too, violated the agreement, sending what aid she could to the Loyalists, who included an influential Communist contingent, but for geographical reasons Russia was not able to match the aid given by the Fascist powers.

15. Hull, *Memoirs,* 2: chap. 34, vigorously defends the policy. Congress recognized, he says, that American aid to the Spanish government might lead to a spread of the war "and that our peace and security required our keeping aloof from the struggle" (p. 491). On the other hand, Sumner Welles, Assistant Secretary of State at the time, believed that the Roosevelt administration committed "no more cardinal error [in foreign policy] than the policy adopted during the civil war in Spain." *The Time for Decision* (New York: Harper & Row, Publishers, 1944), pp. 60–61. Welles wrote under the erroneous impression that Roosevelt reluctantly signed the law, whereas in reality he strongly urged it. Basil Rauch, *Roosevelt from Munich to Pearl Harbor* (New York: Creative Age Press, 1950), pp. 34–41, also believes the Spanish policy was a mistake, a reversal of

spect, it appears certain that American policy, like British and French nonintervention policy, played into the hands of Hitler and Mussolini, enabling them to assist in establishing a friendly Fascist government in Spain. There is, on the other hand, a strong probability that a Loyalist victory would have meant eventually a Spain under Communist domination.

Making Neutrality "Permanent"

The new neutrality had now become established American policy. The new neutrality, in essence, was a waiving of rights that had been claimed under the old neutrality—rights of doing business with belligerents, especially on the high seas,—because insistence upon those rights meant a risk of war. The laws of 1935 and 1936 had been experimental; their provisions would expire May 1, 1937. Before that date Congress undertook to put them in permanent form, with various modifications and improvements. The result was the Third Neutrality Act, signed May 1, 1937. The new act (technically, like the others, a joint resolution) extended indefinitely the main features of the acts of 1935 and 1936. Its provisions were to be applied whenever the President should find that war existed between two or more foreign states. They might also be applied in a foreign civil war if the President should find that export of arms and munitions "would threaten or endanger the peace of the United States." American citizens were now forbidden to travel on belligerent ships instead of being merely warned that such travel was at their own risk. A temporary "cash and carry" provision (to expire May 1, 1939) empowered the President, at his discretion, to prohibit the export to or for a belligerent of commodities not included in the lists of arms, ammunition, and implements of war, (a) in any American vessel, and (b) until ownership had been transferred to the foreign purchaser. The obvious intent was to prevent "incidents" that might arise from destruction of American property by one of the belligerents; but since this portion of the act expired before there was any occasion to use it, it was of no practical importance.

The United States was now fortified, or so it seemed, against being drawn into any "foreign war" through such violations of "freedom of the seas" as had involved it in 1812 and 1917. Freedom of the seas, as earlier understood, had been surrendered, or at least waived for the time being. The legislation had the merit of reserving to the United States itself the decision whether it should enter a "foreign war." Such entry was no longer to be dependent on the decision of a foreign government, as war or peace in 1917 had hung upon whether Germany did or did not resort to unrestricted submarine warfare. The United States could now make its own decision, based upon national interests more vital than the right of American ships or citizens to sail the oceans unmolested, or the right of American munitions-makers to sell their products to belligerent governments.

But if the new neutrality had this merit from the point of view of the United States alone, from a broader view it did a disservice to the cause of peace. It was notice to well-armed dictators like Hitler and Mussolini, that if they chose to attack their democratic neighbors, the latter could get no aid from the United States, either in direct war material or in loans of money or credit. Had such laws been on the books in 1914, the Kaiser's Germany would have won the First World War. Should these laws remain on the books, Hitler's Germany might expect to win the next war, for the American "arsenal of democracy" would be closed to the democracies of Europe. To President Roosevelt and Secretary Hull, who had accepted this policy reluctantly, it was evident that it encouraged aggression. But the American Congress was so intent upon keeping America out of the next war that it deliberately passed legislation which, by encouraging aggression, made that war more probable.

Roosevelt's policy toward Italy. He attributes it in part to the influence of the Catholic Church, which was incensed at the anticlerical policy of the Spanish Republicans.

35

A Good Neighbor Policy for the New World

While the United States was setting up safeguards against involvement in the wars of Europe and Asia, it was acting to reduce friction and to improve friendly relations with its neighbors of the New World. Relations with the other American republics had suffered as a consequence of the policy of intervention in the Caribbean and Central America practiced under Presidents Theodore Roosevelt, Taft, and Wilson.[1] The role of international policeman assumed by Uncle Sam had not endeared him to his neighbors, and the neighbors could not forget that in the Panama episode of 1903 the policeman had participated in what many of them thought an act of larceny. Woodrow Wilson, as was noted before, tried to allay the fear of "Yankee imperialism" that flourished south of the border, but his reassuring words were contradicted by his vigorous acts of intervention in Haiti and the Dominican Republic. Wilson's Republican successors, Harding, Coolidge, and Hoover, made varying contributions to an improvement of relations with Latin America, but it remained for Franklin D. Roosevelt to go the whole way in surrendering the policy of intervention that his Republican cousin had instituted.

First Withdrawals from the Caribbean [2]

Warren G. Harding, while campaigning for the presidency in 1920, had criticized President Wilson's policy of intervention in the Caribbean. As President (1921–1923) he took steps to liquidate the most objectionable of the protectorate regimes—that in the Dominican Republic. In 1922 a native provisional government was installed as successor to the United States Navy's military regime. Two years later regular elections were held, and as the elected government began to function, the last United States marines left the island. A new treaty provided for continuance of the

1. See Chapter 23.
2. The account of the withdrawal from the protectorates in the Caribbean and Central America is adapted from chapter 8 of J. W. Pratt, *America's Colonial Experiment* (Englewood Cliffs, N.J.: Prentice-Hall, Inc., 1950). Source citations are given in that chapter.

348

customs receivership instituted in 1907 until bond issues authorized by the new agreement should have been retired.

President Calvin Coolidge (1923–1929) under whose administration the restoration of self-government in the Dominican Republic was completed, also called home the legation guard of marines from Managua, the capital of Nicaragua. Since 1912 this small force had effectively deterred the Nicaraguan opposition from resorting to arms to overthrow the pro-United States government of Adolfo Díaz and his successors. Peaceful habits seemed so well established that in 1925 Coolidge deemed it safe to remove this symbol of American power. Within a few months, civil war broke out between rival claimants to the presidency. Díaz, the Conservative and a friend of the United States, again held the office. Sacasa, a Liberal, had some basis of claim to it and had the backing of the government of Mexico. Díaz appealed to the United States for aid. Early in 1927 the marines were sent back, not to fight for Díaz but to neutralize certain areas and to protect American and other foreign lives and property.

The renewed intervention in Nicaragua provoked widespread criticism in both the United States and Latin America. President Coolidge defended the intervention as warranted by "the proprietary rights of the United States in the Nicaraguan canal route" and "the obligations flowing from the investments of all classes of our citizens in Nicaragua." The United States, he said, could not

> fail to view with deep concern any serious threat to stability and constitutional government in Nicaragua tending toward anarchy and jeopardizing American interests, especially if such a state of affairs is contributed to or brought about by outside influences or by any foreign power.

But when it appeared that President Díaz, even with the advantage of arms supplied by the United States, was unable to suppress his Liberal opponents, and that Nicaragua faced the probability of a prolonged civil war, the United States undertook to bring about a compromise settlement. For this purpose Coolidge requested Colonel Henry L. Stimson, who had served as Secretary of War under President Taft, to go to Nicaragua as a special representative of the United States and to confer with the leaders of both factions.

Stimson's mission was successful. Díaz was, as usual, willing to accept United States intervention on almost any terms. He readily agreed to Stimson's proposal that both sides be disarmed by the United States forces. So did General Moncada, the Liberal commander, when informed that the United States proposed to disarm forcibly those who would not disarm voluntarily. An agreement, known as the "peace of Tipitapa," was signed after a month of negotiation. The national army was to be replaced by a National Guard, to be trained and temporarily officered by United States marines. Díaz was to continue in office, with Liberals admitted to his cabinet, until the 1928 elections, which were to be supervised, and then fairness guaranteed, by the United States.

The arrangement committed the United States to further intervention in Nicaragua. The occupation forces, it turned out, supervised not only the elections of 1928 but those of 1930 and 1932 as well. The fairness of those elections is sufficiently attested by the fact that all three were won by the Liberals—traditionally the anti-American party—Moncada being elected to the presidency in 1928 and Sacasa in 1932. One Liberal leader, Sandino, had refused to abide by the terms of the peace and carried on for three years a guerrilla warfare against the marines, thus keeping the bloody aspects of intervention steadily before the American public. By February 1931, peace was so far restored that Mr. Stimson, now Secretary of State under Herbert Hoover, announced that the marines would be gradually withdrawn, leaving the further suppression of guerrillas to the National Guard, and that the intervention would be terminated after the elections of 1932. This decision was not altered when a new outbreak of guerrilla warfare occurred in the interior in April 1931. In January 1933, the last of the marines were withdrawn, leaving as the only element of American control the customs receivership agreed upon in 1911 and modified in 1917.[3]

The End of the Roosevelt Corollary

The withdrawal of the marines from Nicaragua, and especially the refusal to augment the existing force during the disturbances of 1931, typified the new Hoover-Stimson policy toward Latin America. This "new policy toward Latin American countries" was described in the *New York Times* on "high authority" as representing "a determination on the part of the United States not to intervene in the internal affairs of any of those countries." [4] The policy was exhibited in the prompt abandonment of the Wilsonian practice of refusing recognition to revolutionary governments—a form of intervention—and a return to the traditional American policy of recognizing any government that was *de facto* in control and able and willing to observe its international obligations.[5] It was supported by the publication in 1930 of a *Memorandum on the Monroe Doctrine,* prepared in 1928 by Under Secretary of State J. Reuben Clark. Though never actually made official doctrine, it amounted to a repudiation of the Roosevelt Corollary.

> The [Monroe] doctrine [it declared] states a case of United States *vs.* Europe, not of United States *vs.* Latin-America.
> Such arrangements as the United States has made, for example, with Cuba, Santo Domingo,

Haiti, and Nicaragua, are not within the Doctrine as it was announced by Monroe.[6]

It is to be noted that the Clark *Memorandum* did not repudiate the right of the United States to intervene in the affairs of neighboring states when its interests were endangered. It merely denied that such right found any basis in the Monroe Doctrine. Arrangements such as those with Cuba and the other states mentioned, it stated, "may be accounted for as the expression of a national policy which . . . originates in the necessities of security or self-preservation." Here was no admission that the United States had done wrong in intervening in the states of Central America and the Caribbean, no promise that it would not intervene again in the interest of "security or self-preservation." But since virtually all the interventions after 1904 had been given a basis in the Roosevelt Corollary of the Monroe Doctrine, and since that basis was now discarded, the issuance of the *Memorandum* was an important step in the direction of complete nonintervention. Taken with other features of the Hoover-Stimson Latin American policy, it warrants the assertion that those two statesmen laid the basis of the "good neighbor policy" of the 1930's.[7]

3. See p. 222.
4. *New York Times,* April 16, 1931.
5. Early occasion for the application of the new policy was afforded by an epidemic of revolutions occurring in 1929–1930 in Argentina, Bolivia, Brazil, Dominican Republic, Panama, Peru. Until 1934, when the five Central American republics terminated the treaty binding them mutually not to recognize revolutionary governments, the United States made for those republics an exception to its general policy of recognizing *de facto* governments. For Secretary Stimson's defense of this feature of his foreign policy, see H. L. Stimson, "The United States and the Other American Republics," *Foreign Affairs,* 9 (1931), No. 3, Special Supplement.

6. U. S. Department of State, *Memorandum on the Monroe Doctrine,* prepared by J. Reuben Clark (Washington: Government Printing Office, 1930), p. xix. Secretary of State Hughes had anticipated the Clark interpretation in 1923, declaring that the Monroe Doctrine afforded no support for any idea of superintendence or overlordship in the Western Hemisphere on the part of the United States. Perkins, *History of the Monroe Doctrine,* pp. 333–36.
7. In fact, Hoover repeatedly used the term "good neighbor" in the "good will tour" of Latin America that he made between his election and his inauguration. Alexander De Conde, *Herbert Hoover's Latin American Policy* (Stanford: Stanford University Press, 1951), chap. 2. Cf. Bemis, *Latin American Policy,* pp. 218–23. On the other hand, Latin Americans blamed Hoover for the Hawley-Smoot tariff (above, p. 323), which had disastrous effects on their economy. Sumner Welles, *The Time for Decision* (New York: Harper & Row, Publishers, 1944), pp. 190–91. It is one of the ironies of this period of history that a chief motive of Hoover's new Latin American policy was to build up trade by removing political antagonism, whereas the tariff bill that he signed had just the opposite effect.

Changing American Opinion

Franklin Roosevelt, as Assistant Secretary of the Navy, under Woodrow Wilson, had played a small part in the American interventions in Haiti and the Dominican Republic; he boasted, in fact, during the campaign of 1920, that he not only had "had something to do with running" those two republics, but had himself written Haiti's constitution of 1918. Before reaching the presidency, however, he had come to repent of these actions and to feel that the United States should renounce "for all time" its practice of "single-handed intervention . . . in the internal affairs of other nations." If intervention should be necessary to put an end to disorder in some American state, it should be carried out as a joint enterprise by the American republics, not by the United States alone.[8]

This attitude, which Roosevelt shared with Secretary of State Cordell Hull and Assistant Secretary Sumner Welles, prepared the way for acceptance by the United States of a doctrine of nonintervention which for some years Latin American governments and jurists had been advocating as a principle of American international law, but which the United States hitherto had declined to accept. One of the chief reasons for the exercise by the United States of the right of intervention had now vanished, however, with the elimination of German naval power in World War I. American naval supremacy in the Western Hemisphere was now unchallenged. There was no longer the fear that a rival power might seize a foothold near the Panama Canal if disorder or nonpayment of debts furnished an excuse. To be a "good neighbor" was easier and safer for the United States than it had been before 1914. The trend toward nonintervention, which had begun under Harding and accelerated under Hoover, reached its high point under the second Roosevelt.

8. F. D. Roosevelt, "Our Foreign Policy: A Democratic View," *Foreign Affairs*, 6 (July 1928), 573–86.

A Policy "Opposed to Armed Intervention"

President Franklin D. Roosevelt's original "good neighbor" declaration had no special reference to Latin America and was quite innocuous in any event.

> In the field of world policy [he announced in his first Inaugural Address, March 4, 1933] I would dedicate this Nation to the policy of the good neighbor—the neighbor who resolutely respects himself and, because he does so, respects the rights of others.

More significant was his declaration at a Woodrow Wilson Foundation dinner, December 28, 1933, that "the definite policy of the United States from now on is one opposed to armed intervention." This statement, while it went much further than the Clark *Memorandum,* was, like it, unilateral. It was a statement of policy that could be altered or revoked at will; it was in no sense a contract with other governments.

Two days before Roosevelt's speech, however, the United States delegation at the Seventh International Conference of American States at Montevideo had signed a Convention on the Rights and Duties of States that declared, in Article 8: "No state has the right to intervene in the internal or external affairs of another." Thus the United States acquiesced in a renunciation of the right of intervention that was more sweeping than that which it had rejected five years before at Havana.

The Montevideo Conference was one of the high points in the diplomatic career of Secretary Cordell Hull, who headed the United States delegation. By accepting the Latin American position on intervention and by his tactful and self-effacing behavior, Hull not only removed a large share of the distrust that Latin Americans felt for the United States; he even won the friendly cooperation of the Argentine Foreign Minister, Carlos Saavedra Lamas, the leading opponent of the United States among Latin American statesmen. Saavedra Lamas had attempted to blanket the achievements of the Conference by proposing his own antiwar treaty, containing a declaration against intervention, whether by arms or diplomacy, and by getting it signed, a few weeks before the Conference opened, by five South American states and Mexico. Hull, instead of treating Saavedra Lamas as a rival, offered to sign his treaty on behalf of the United States and persuaded him to introduce a resolution (which Hull seconded) calling upon all the American republics that had not done so to ratify not only the Argentine peace treaty but the inter-American conciliation treaties of 1923 and 1929, the inter-American arbitration treaty of 1929, and the Kellogg-Briand Pact of 1928.[9] Saavedra Lamas, in turn, agreed to support a resolution calling for the lowering of trade barriers, which Hull introduced and which was a prelude to adoption of the reciprocal trade agreement program mentioned in a previous chapter.[10]

Unlike the earlier Fifth and Sixth Inter-American Conferences (Santiago, 1923; Havana, 1928), which had been featured by ill-natured attacks on the United States, the Montevideo meeting resembled a love feast. The nonintervention article had been the goal for some years of the Latin American governments. Its acceptance by the United States caused surprise and gratification. None of the delegations, apparently, realized the full significance of proscribing intervention in "the external affairs" of any American state. If in the future some American state should develop affinity for a Fascist or Communist regime in the Old World, would Article 8 of the Montevideo convention bar its neighbors from acting against it in their own defense? The question

was not even asked at Montevideo. Unvoiced there, it was to become crucial twenty years later.[11]

At any rate, the United States Senate approved the convention without a record vote, appending only a mild reservation that Hull had injected at the Conference. The gist of this was a statement that the United States reserved its rights under "the law of nations as generally understood." Even this was omitted when nonintervention was reaffirmed at Buenos Aires three years later. The protocol then signed by Hull and approved without reservation by the Senate proclaimed:

> The High Contracting Parties declare inadmissible the intervention of any one of them, directly or indirectly, and for whatever reason, in the internal or external affairs of any other of the Parties.

Nonintervention in Practice

Meanwhile Roosevelt and Hull were giving evidence of their sincerity by liquidating those protectorates where the right of intervention had formerly been exercised—in Haiti, the Dominican Republic, Nicaragua, Cuba, and Panama.

In Haiti, where Hoover had already gone far in returning control of government and services to the Haitian people, Roosevelt accomplished by executive agreement (August 7, 1933) the last step which had eluded Hoover through Haitian rejection of a treaty. The native *Garde d'Haiti* was completely Haitianized, the United States marines were withdrawn, and responsibility for payment of Haiti's bonded indebtedness was conferred first upon a "fiscal representative" nominated by the President of the United States, and after 1941, upon the National Bank of Haiti, with representatives of both the Haitian government and the bondholders on its board of directors. Thus the United States government

9. See Chapter 30 for the treaties mentioned. Argentina had ratified none of them, and other states were delinquent in different degrees. Despite passage of the resolution, Argentina ratified only the treaty that she had originated. The United States ratified the Argentine treaty; it had previously ratified the others. The story of the Montevideo Conference is told in Hull, *Memoirs,* 1: chaps. 23–25; Bemis, *Latin American Policy,* chap. 15; E. O. Guerrant, *Roosevelt's Good Neighbor Policy* (Albuquerque: University of New Mexico Press, 1950), pp. 6–9.
10. See Chapter 32.

11. Bemis, *Latin American Policy,* pp. 272–73. It was not clear from the wording of Article 8 whether or not collective intervention was admissible in the event of such danger as is suggested.

withdrew from the picture altogether. By a somewhat similar arrangement, the United States relinquished the right to name the general receiver of customs in the Dominican Republic. In Nicaragua the last of the American loans secured by the customs revenue were paid off in 1944, and the collector general was thereafter responsible only to the government of Nicaragua.[12]

In the case of Cuba, the right of intervention embodied in the Platt Amendment of 1901 and the treaty of 1903 was surrendered through a new treaty signed in May 1934. This abandonment of the right of intervention, however, was preceded by an act of diplomatic, not military, intervention, by which Sumner Welles, serving temporarily as United States Ambassador, secured the resignation of the harsh and oppressive Cuban dictator-president, Gerardo Machado, and the election of a successor acceptable to the United States, with whom the new treaty was negotiated. The treaty abrogated the Platt Amendment, reserving to the United States only the right to use the naval base at Guantanamo Bay until that right should be set aside by mutual consent. Thus the United States surrendered all claim to financial control of Cuba and all right to intervene in its affairs.[13]

By a treaty with Panama, signed March 2, 1936, replacing that of 1903, the United States dropped its guarantee of Panama's independence and renounced its right to intervene in Panamanian affairs and to acquire, by eminent domain, additional lands in Panama needed for operation of the canal. The Senate approved the treaty after a three-year delay,

upon being assured that in an emergency the United States might utilize positions on the soil of Panama for defense of the canal, with consultation between the two governments to follow instead of preceding such action.[14]

Thus in the 1930's the United States divested itself of all the protectorates in the Caribbean area which it had assumed under the administrations of Theodore Roosevelt, Taft, and Wilson. It thereby accepted, in theory, the principle of the sovereign equality of all independent states. The American control or supervision had provided a degree of stability previously unknown in the states affected. Unfortunately, it had not induced habits of democratic behavior, as evidenced by the flock of dictators that followed withdrawal of American control: Trujillo in the Dominican Republic, the Somozas in Nicaragua, "Papa Doc" Duvalier in Haiti, Batista and Castro in Cuba.

"Continentalizing" the Monroe Doctrine

When the Montevideo Conference met in December 1933, there was no apparent threat from without to the security of the Western Hemisphere. Hitler had been in power less than a year and had not yet fully revealed his aggressive proclivities. Mussolini's conquest of Ethiopia was still in the future. Japan was quietly digesting her first big bite of Chinese territory. The chief problems confronting the American republics were the elimination of the distrust that the Latin members felt for "the Colossus of the North"; the freeing of trade, and the halting of such quarrels as pre-

---

12. Under the Bryan-Chamorro treaty of 1916, the United States still retained its exclusive rights to the Nicaraguan canal route and to bases near the termini. These concessions were resented by Nicaraguan nationalists, but not until March 1970 did the United States offer to reexamine the treaty. *Department of State Bulletin,* 62 (April 27, 1970), 560–61.

13. Signed May 29, 1934, the treaty was approved by the Senate two days later without a dissenting vote. Opponents of Machado had charged that the Platt Amendment, with its threat of American intervention to preserve "order" in Cuba, was a barrier to his removal by revolution.

14. In keeping with the abandonment of the protectorate over Panama, was the conclusion in 1937 of a new treaty with Mexico abrogating Article 8 of the Gadsden Treaty of 1853. This never-used article had guaranteed to the United States the use of a proposed plank-and-rail road across the Isthmus of Tehuantepec for its citizens, its mails, its property, and its troops, and had authorized the United States to extend its protection to the route whenever it should feel such protection "sanctioned and warranted by the public or international law."

vailed among the Latin sister republics themselves—notably the destructive war between
Bolivia and Paraguay over possession of the
Gran Chaco. Something was achieved in all
these directions.[15]

Normally, the next Inter-American Conference would have met in 1938, but alarming
developments in Europe—the increasing aggressiveness of Nazi Germany and Fascist
Italy, the penetration of German and Italian
influence and trade into Latin America, and
later, the Italo-Ethiopian War—seemed to
menace the peace of the New World as well
as the Old. They led President Roosevelt to
suggest the calling of a special conference to
consider how best to safeguard the peace of
the American republics. Feelers put out in
1935 brought favorable responses, Argentina
stipulating that her acceptance was conditional upon the choice of Buenos Aires as the
site of the Conference. Consequently, the Inter-American Conference for the Maintenance
of Peace convened in the Argentine capital on
December 1, 1936. Again Secretary Hull
headed the United States delegation, and to
emphasize the importance of the occasion,
President Roosevelt made the long voyage to
Buenos Aires and addressed the opening session of the Conference.

Apart from the adoption of a strengthened
declaration of nonintervention, the most important achievements of the Buenos Aires
Conference were a consultative agreement,
officially labeled the Convention for the
Maintenance, Preservation and Reestablishment of Peace; and a Declaration of Principles of Inter-American Solidarity and Cooperation. The Convention provided that the

governments of the American republics should
consult together upon methods of peaceful
cooperation, (a) "in the event that the peace
of the American Republics is menaced,"
(b) "in the event of war, or a virtual state of
war between American States," or (c) "in the
event of an international war outside America
which might menace the peace of the American Republics." In the last named contingency, which under the circumstances was the
most important, the consultation should "determine the proper time and manner in which
the signatory States, if they so desire, may
eventually cooperate in some action tending
to preserve the peace of the American Continent." [16]

The other principal document emanating
from the Buenos Aires Conference, referred
to in brief as the Declaration of Solidarity,
proclaimed four principles as "accepted by the
international American community." These
were: (1) nonrecognition of territorial acquisitions by conquest, (2) nonintervention,
(3) illegality of the collection of debts by
force, and (4) peaceful settlement of all disputes among American states. In subscribing
to the Declaration, the United States once
more endorsed the nonintervention dogma and
also accepted, in point 3, the Drago Doctrine
without qualification. The heart of the Declaration, however, was the assertion

> That every act susceptible of disturbing the
> peace of America affects each and every one of
> them [the American nations], and justifies the
> initiation of the procedure of consultation pro-
> vided for in the Convention . . . executed at
> this Conference.

It is this paragraph of the Declaration,
coupled with the Convention's provision for
consultation, that has given rise to the statement that the Buenos Aires Conference "continentalized" the Monroe Doctrine. That doctrine was not mentioned in the documents, it
is true, but henceforth any threat from Europe

---

15. Rivalry between Argentina and the United States
extended even to attempts to end the Chaco War by
mediation. For a time two neutral commissions, led
by the two rivals, were engaged in the effort. At
Montevideo a degree of cooperation was achieved,
and produced an armistice that lasted for only
eighteen days. Eventually another neutral commission, including both Argentina and the United States
and operating under League of Nations auspices,
brought the war to an end by an armistice of June
14, 1935. Bemis, *Latin American Policy*, p. 285.

16. Of the expression "if they so desire," Hull remarks that the Argentines "were able to emasculate
this resolution by inserting four words." Hull,
Memoirs, 1: 500.

(or Asia) to the peace or independence of any part of America—any threat that would have led the United States to invoke the Monroe Doctrine—was now declared to affect "each and every one" of the American nations and to justify their consulting together. Consultation, of course, did not guarantee action, but neither did the Monroe Doctrine.

A weak spot in the Buenos Aires program was the failure to define how and through whom consultation should take place. The cog thus omitted from the machinery at Buenos Aires was inserted at the Eighth International Conference of American States at Lima, Peru, in December 1938. The Conference convened shortly after the Munich settlement in Europe, but few of the delegates shared Neville Chamberlain's faith that Munich assured "peace in our time." The likelihood of war in Europe spurred the American statesmen to action. The Declaration of Lima proclaimed any threat to "the peace, security, or territorial integrity of any American Republic" to be the concern of all and provided that to consult upon methods of meeting any such threat, the Foreign Ministers should meet together upon the call of any one of them.

Thus before the war began in Europe, the twenty-one American republics were prepared, to a degree without precedent, to present a common front to danger from abroad. The outbreak of war led to a series of conferences of Foreign Ministers, under the Lima plan, at Panama (September–October 1939), at Havana (July 1940), and after the United States was attacked by Japan, at Rio de Janeiro (January 1942).[17] Eventually all the American republics followed the United States into the war, though Argentina, which harbored an ill-disguised sympathy for the Axis powers, hung back to the last possible moment. Argentina was the weakest spot in the Pan American united front. A state which cooperated in that front, but which in the 1920's and 1930's had sorely tried the patience of the United States, was Mexico.

17. See pp. 396–97.

Mexico Tests the Good Neighbor Policy

In considering United States relations with Mexico in the interwar period, it is necessary to remember that in those years Mexico was passing through the tremendous social revolution that had been launched by Carranza with the issuance of the Constitution of 1917. This was Mexico's "New Deal," a reform movement much more radical than the "Roosevelt Revolution" in the United States. Its theoretical aims were the betterment of the lot of peasant and worker in Mexico and, as a necessary preliminary of such betterment, recovery by Mexico of control of important elements in its resources that had passed into the possession of foreigners. Thus the Revolution took on a "Mexico for the Mexicans" coloration.

This attitude toward foreigners was a reversal of the policy that had prevailed under Porfirio Díaz (1877–1911). Díaz had welcomed foreign capital to Mexico. Foreigners, chiefly Americans and British, had invested in Mexican agricultural, grazing, and timber lands, in Mexican mines, and, especially after 1900, in Mexican oil fields. Without accepting the Mexican thesis that such investments had amounted to "exploitation" of the Mexicans, it can readily be admitted that foreign ownership stood in the way of parts of the new Mexican reform program.

The two aspects of that program that chiefly collided with American property rights were land reform and the nationalization of subsoil properties, especially petroleum.[18] The common lands or *ejidos,* that had once been appurtenances of Mexican villages had to a large extent been absorbed in private landed estates, some owned by Mexican, some by

18. A third aspect of the program that aroused much antagonism in the United States, though not on economic grounds, was anticlericalism. The campaign against the Roman Catholic Church, especially against its control of education, was deplored by Catholics in the United States.

foreign landlords. It became a major object of the Revolution to restore the *ejidos* to the peasantry. In the earlier and more conservative phase of the Revolution (1920–1934), dominated by the "Northern Dynasty"[19] of Álvaro Obregón and Plutarco Elías Calles, the lands were distributed in individual holdings; under the more leftist Lázaro Cárdenas (1934–1940), the favored system was communal ownership. In obtaining the lands for distribution, the Mexican government resorted to expropriation (the taking of property with compensation) rather than confiscation (uncompensated seizure). Trouble with foreign owners and their governments arose when compensation was long delayed or inadequate.

The *ejidos* made less international trouble than the petroleum properties. Article 27 of the Mexican Constitution of 1917 nationalized subsoil resources. Petroleum or gold or silver, that is, was the property of the nation, not of the person or corporation who owned the surface above it. This was the common rule in Spanish countries and had been the rule in Mexico until 1878.[20] During the Díaz period, however, purchasers of Mexican lands had acquired subsoil as well as surface rights, and in this way large petroleum properties had come into the possession of United States and British corporations.

No one denied the right of Mexico to nationalize petroleum deposits not already in private hands. The crucial question was: is Article 27 retroactive? Will oil men who acquired their properties from Díaz now be required to obtain permits and pay fees for the privilege of removing the oil that they

claim is theirs? Carranza had promised privately that Article 27 would not be applied retroactively to American-owned properties, and then had broken his promise. Obregón, who in 1920 overthrew Carranza and was then duly elected to the presidency of Mexico, repeated the promise, but refused the request of Secretary of State Hughes to put it in a treaty. Hughes, therefore, withheld recognition from Obregón.

The Mexican Supreme Court, in a series of oil cases, enunciated the "positive acts" principle: if the owner of an oil property had before 1917 performed some "positive act," such as drilling a well, his full ownership could not be questioned. If he had performed no such act, he forfeited subsoil rights. This was a compromise acceptable to the State Department if its permanency could be guaranteed. Obregón, fearful of domestic repercussions if he yielded too much to Washington pressure, still refused to make a treaty. He did, however, subscribe to an "extra-official pact," known as the Bucareli agreement, which embodied the "positive acts" principle and made other concessions to the United States. On this basis the United States accorded Obregón *de jure* recognition, August 31, 1923. In the following year, when he faced a formidable rebellion, arms and airplanes supplied by the United States helped him to rout his enemies.

Under Obregón's successor, Calles (1924–1928), the Mexican Congress evidently regarded the Bucareli agreement as no longer binding. It passed legislation limiting to fifty years the ownership of petroleum rights acquired before 1917. This apparent breach of faith, aggravated by attacks on the Catholic Church in Mexico and by open Mexican support of the Sacasa insurrection in Nicaragua,[21] produced a crisis in United States-Mexican relations. The Hearst press, the oil companies, other interested parties, agitated for intervention. President Coolidge sent to Congress on January 10, 1927, a special message on Nicaragua, in which he complained that Mexico

---

19. The phrase "Northern Dynasty" is applied to this phase of the Revolution by H. F. Cline in his study, *The United States and Mexico* (Cambridge: Harvard University Press, 1953). Obregón (1920–1924), Calles (1924–1928), and the "puppet presidents" (1928–1934) who took orders from Calles all came from northern Mexico and were less socialistic in outlook than many of the southern leaders.

20. The United States Congress in 1910 and 1914 reserved to the government ownership of subsoil rights in public lands granted for agricultural purposes. *U. S. Statutes at Large,* 36: 583; 38: 509.

21. See p. 349.

alone had recognized Sacasa's insurrectionary government, and that Sacasa had been supplied with arms belonging to the Mexican government through the active agency of Mexican officials. A few days later Secretary of State Kellogg released to the press a statement attempting to link the Mexican government and its interference in Nicaragua with the Communist party in the United States and hence with Russian Bolshevism. Communist Russia, he charged, was seeking footholds in Latin America.[22]

These alarmist pronouncements were received coolly in Congress and in the country at large. On January 18, Senator Joseph T. Robinson of Arkansas introduced a resolution urging arbitration of the controversies with Mexico. The Senate passed it a week later by a vote of 79 to 0. President Coolidge took his cue from the Senate. In an April 25 address to the United Press, he reported friendly assurances from the Mexican ambassador and avowed his conviction that "it will surely be possible to reach an amicable adjustment." [23] Soon thereafter he sent to Mexico a new ambassador, Dwight W. Morrow, with instructions to do whatever was necessary to prevent war. Morrow, though a Wall Street banker, a member of the Morgan firm, showed great sympathy for Mexico and an aptitude for cultivating Mexican good will. From the first he got on well with Calles. Under the latter's influence, the Mexican Supreme Court again entered the picture, reaffirming the principle that "positive acts" before 1917 conferred full ownership. In December 1927, the Mexican Congress adopted a new Petroleum Code, following the court decision and embodying the terms of the Bucareli agreement. The State Department expressed itself as satisfied that American interests could thenceforth rely for protection upon the Mexican courts.

So matters rested, as far as petroleum was concerned, until 1938. Lázaro Cárdenas, who came to the Mexican presidency in 1934, was

the first non-northern President since the overthrow of Díaz. Though he owed his rise to Calles, he was more socialistic in his thinking than the "Northern Dynasty" and soon showed that he was no one's puppet. Somewhat like the contemporary Roosevelt, he catered to the small farmer and the working man and placed new emphasis upon the slogan "Mexico for the Mexicans." In his attitude to American interests he may have drawn courage from Roosevelt's acceptance of the nonintervention principle at Montevideo and Buenos Aires.[24] In any event, he stepped up the expropriation of agricultural lands to a new tempo and brought about the effective organization in one union of the scattered employees of the foreign oil companies. Extravagant demands of this union, for increased wages and "fringe benefits," some of which would have amounted almost to management of the businesses, were rejected by the companies. The demands were found "reasonable" by a not wholly impartial commission and ordered into effect by a Federal Board of Arbitration. When the companies again refused, Cárdenas, in a decree of March 18, 1938, ordered their properties expropriated.[25]

The Mexican Settlement of 1941

The expropriation of the American and British oil properties involved Mexico in new arguments with both governments concerned. British protests were so strong that Mexico responded by breaking off diplomatic relations. In Washington, Cárdenas' highhanded action

22. *Congressional Record,* 68 Cong. 2 sess., pp. 1649–51.

23. *Foreign Relations, 1927,* 3: 217.

24. S. F. Bemis emphasizes the effect of nonintervention on Cárdenas' policy in *Latin American Policy,* pp. 345–50. See also the same author's long chapter on Mexico in *A Diplomatic History of the United States,* 4th ed. (New York: Holt, Rinehart & Winston, Inc., 1955), chap. 30.

25. Cline, *The U. S. and Mexico,* pp. 229–38, believes that Cárdenas did not premeditate the act of expropriation, that he was on the point of accepting a compromise proposal by the companies when their request that he put his promises in writing seemed to him a reflection upon his own and the nation's honor and touched off the decree of March 18.

and his refusal to submit the American claims for expropriated property to international arbitration exhausted the patience of Secretary Hull. He would have taken as strong a position as the British, and presumably with similar results, had he not been dissuaded by Josephus Daniels, the sympathetic American ambassador in Mexico, and by President Roosevelt. Roosevelt, no great friend of corporations, announced that he felt more concern for expropriated American farmers in Mexico than for the oil companies. The latter, he said, could rightly expect payment for the amount of their invested capital but not for the value of oil still in the ground, which formed a large part of their claim. The United States acknowledged the right of the Mexican government to expropriate private property, and ultimately consented to leave the amount and method of compensation to negotiation rather than arbitration.[26]

The American companies negotiated directly with the Mexican government. Their claims totaled $260,000,000. Compromises were suggested, but no agreement was reached. Subsequently, one of the companies, Sinclair Oil, negotiated apart from the others and accepted $8,500,000 in settlement of its claims.

By this time the clouds of World War II were drifting over the New World. In Mexico, friction with the United States and Great Britain was assisting Nazi infiltration, which was not welcomed either by Cárdenas or by his successor, Manuel Avila Camacho (1940–1946). The United States was anxious both to eliminate the Nazi influence and to close the rift in the Inter-American front before the war actually reached American shores. The

situation was favorable for compromise, and a compromise was arranged.

An agreement signed November 19, 1941, settled all outstanding controversies between the United States and Mexico and assured Mexico of all the benefits of good neighborliness. The United States promised a reciprocal trade treaty, credits through the Export-Import Bank, continued purchases of Mexican silver at the world price, and help toward modernization of Mexico's obsolete military establishment. In return Mexico agreed to pay a total of $40,000,000 for agrarian and other American claims, exclusive of those derived from oil properties. Of this total, six millions had already been paid; the remainder was to be paid in annual installments of $2,500,000. The task of evaluating the expropriated oil properties and recommending a method of compensation for them was assigned to two commissioners, one from each country, who were to report within five months. Mexico made a down payment of $9,000,000 on the debt that was thus to be adjudicated. The commissioners valued the expropriated properties, exclusive of Sinclair's, at just under $24,000,000. They recommended that one-third of the sum in excess of the $9,000,000 already advanced be paid July 1, 1942; the remainder in five equal annual installments. The companies protested but were told the State Department would not support them in asking more. They accepted, and payments were made on schedule. By 1949 the American oil claims had been liquidated.

In all, including principal and interest, the payments to Sinclair, and the purchase price of a few small companies that were not expropriated but were bought out, Mexico paid about $42,000,000 for oil properties owned in the United States. The British, who waited until after the war for a settlement, secured somewhat better terms. By an agreement of 1947, Mexico agreed to pay to the expropriated British companies a principal of $81,-250,000, with interest, in annual installments to end in 1962.[27]

26. Bryce Wood, *The Making of the Good Neighbor Policy* (New York: Columbia University Press, 1961), chaps, 8, 9. Hull argued that under the inter-American arbitration treaty of 1929, Mexico was obligated to accept arbitration of such claims as those of the oil companies. The position of Mexico and other Latin American governments was that compensation for expropriated property was a domestic matter not subject to arbitration. The United States accepted this position rather than jeopardize the fruits of the Good Neighbor Policy.

27. Cline, *The U. S. and Mexico*, pp. 239–51.

There is no doubt that in accepting this settlement with Mexico the government of the United States sacrificed the interests of some of its citizens. How far the claims that were surrendered or abated were ethically justifiable is a problem too complicated to be attacked here. How those claims could have been collected in full without armed intervention and conquest is not easy to see. Of American policy toward Mexico, as of the voluntary grant of independence to the Philippines, history will perhaps record that the United States was first among western powers to recognize that the sun had gone down upon old-fashioned imperialism, whether political or economic. At any rate, in applying the Good Neighbor Policy to Mexico under trying circumstances, the United States made good the pledges given at Montevideo and Buenos Aires and assured itself of cordial Latin American support in the impending war. Three weeks after the signing of the Mexican agreement, Japanese bombs fell upon Pearl Harbor.

36

The Rising Tide
of Aggression

The three powers whose initial acts of aggression were described in two earlier chapters [1] operated until 1936 quite independently of one another. It was natural, however, that Germany, Italy, and Japan should be drawn together. All three were "dissatisfied" powers, not content with the territorial heritage left them by the last war and the peace settlement. They could realize their ambitions only by destruction of the status quo established in 1919 and sanctified by the treaties of Washington and Locarno and the Pact of Paris. All three, furthermore, were ideologically compatible. In all, the governing cliques held democracy in contempt and paid little respect to treaty obligations. An alliance or understanding between them should have surprised no one.

Up to 1936 there had been one point of serious rivalry between Germany and Italy. Hitler was anxious to annex Austria, his native land, to Nazi Germany. Mussolini had no wish to face a powerful Germany at the Brenner Pass. In 1934, when Austrian Nazis murdered Chancellor Dollfuss and tried, unsuccessfully, to take over the government, with *Anschluss* (union with Germany) as an objective, Mussolini mobilized Italian troops on the Austrian frontier and in effect served notice that he would defend Austria's independence. But by 1936, the situation had changed. Hitler had maintained a sympathetic attitude to Italy during the war in Ethiopia, when the League powers were trying to halt Italy with sanctions. The outbreak of the Spanish Civil War found the two dictators benevolently disposed to Franco. In July, Hitler promised to respect Austria's independence and to abstain from interfering in her internal politics. On October 25, 1936, Hitler and Mussolini signed an accord pledging collaboration in their policy toward Spain and in the defense of Europe against Communism, and arranging for economic cooperation in southern Europe. Hitler recognized Mussolini's Ethiopian empire and was rewarded with economic privileges there and in other Italian colonies. The "Rome-Berlin Axis" had come into being.

Just a month after the Rome-Berlin accord,

1. See Chapters 33, 34.

Germany and Japan signed (November 25, 1936) an Anti-Comintern pact. Ostensibly aimed at the Communist International, or Comintern, and pledging the signatories to consultation and cooperation in measures to combat Communism, the pact contained a secret addendum providing for political, or even military, cooperation against the Soviet Union. When Italy signed the document a year later, the combination was referred to as the Rome-Berlin-Tokyo Axis. Henceforth each of the three could expect the sympathetic understanding of the others in its efforts to break down the status quo.

Beginning of the "China Incident"

When Mussolini adhered to the Anti-Comintern pact (November 6, 1937), Japanese troops were already engaged in large-scale operations against China. What the Japanese called the "China Incident" or "China Affair" (but never the China war!) began with a seemingly unpremeditated clash between Chinese and Japanese troops at Lukouchiao, or the Marco Polo bridge, near a village just outside Peiping, on the night of July 7, 1937. The Japanese troops involved were in Hopei province by virtue of the Boxer protocol of 1900, which permitted guards along the Peiping-Tientsin railway. The Japanese had made excessive use of that privilege, but there is no convincing evidence that the collision of armed forces was planned, and there seems to have been a real effort to settle the resulting controversy through negotiations between the local commanders.[2] New fighting broke out, however, both in the Peiping area and at Shanghai. A Chinese proposal made through the British embassy in Tokyo, that hostilities cease and that all troops withdraw to the lines held before the clash, was not answered by the Japanese government.[3] After three weeks of futile negotiations, during which Japanese civilians were warned to leave China and Japanese reinforcements were sent to the mainland, the Nipponese opened a full-scale offensive.

Whatever were the intentions of the Japanese Premier (Prince Konoye) and Foreign Office, it is hard to escape the conclusion that the Army found in the incident of July 7 an excuse to secure by force its main objective in China, the control of the five northern provinces. Since 1933 the objective had been sought in vain by negotiation and by the encouragement of autonomy movements in the northern provinces. Time was strengthening China's hands. Chiang Kai-shek had put down a rebellion in the south and as a result of the "Sian incident," [4] had agreed to join with the Chinese Communists in a united front against Japan. Japanese expansionists must have felt, as they had felt in 1931, that it was now or never for their plans in China.

The United States and the China Incident

The United States took at first an impartial attitude toward the two belligerents. This was in accord with the ideas of Ambassador Joseph C. Grew, who advised a threefold policy: (1) noninvolvement in the conflict, (2) protection of American lives, property, and rights in China, (3) maintenance of friendship with both parties. In the protection of American citizens and their properties and rights in China, the United States adopted what was described as a "middle-of-the-road" policy, neither abandoning its nationals and their rights nor resorting to intervention for their protection. Additional American marines were sent to Shanghai for the protection of the International Settlement, but Americans in China who could leave were advised to do so. The governments of both Japan and China were notified that the United States reserved all its treaty rights in China and the right to compensation for damages inflicted.

2. F. C. Jones, *Japan's New Order in East Asia: Its Rise and Fall, 1937–1945* (New York: Oxford University Press, 1954), pp. 30–49.
3. J. C. Grew, *Turbulent Era: A Diplomatic Record of Forty Years, 1904–1945*, 2 vols. (Boston: Houghton Mifflin Company, 1952), 2: 1049–50, 1052.

4. See p. 338 and note.

Since there had been no declaration of war, the President refrained from invoking the Neutrality Act, though advised to invoke it by Ambassador Grew and by numerous peace societies in the United States. The President thus reversed the policy that he had followed in the similarly undeclared war between Italy and Ethiopia. His reason was, presumably, that application of the act would be more injurious to China than to Japan; it would cut off arms and the use of American ships, both of which China needed and Japan did not. The President did, however, forbid the use of government-owned ships to carry arms, ammunition, or implements of war to either party, and he warned private shipowners that they would engage in such trade at their own risk.[5]

Early in October 1937, the United States departed from its policy of impartiality to join with the League of Nations in labeling Japan a treaty-violator. On October 5, in a speech in Chicago, President Roosevelt deplored the fact "that the epidemic of world lawlessness is spreading" and suggested a "quarantine" for those nations infected with it. Although the President mentioned no nation by name, he was clearly alluding to Japan. What he meant by a "quarantine" he did not spell out, but there is good evidence that he had in mind complete severance of relations with a nation adjudged to be an aggressor.[6]

The "quarantine" speech met with a mixed reaction in the United States. There was much favorable comment, but the President, apparently more impressed by the very vocal isolationist criticism, did not pursue the idea. On the day after the speech, however, the League of Nations Assembly, sitting in Geneva,

adopted a report holding that Japan's invasion of China violated both the Nine-Power Treaty and the Pact of Paris. The State Department announced its concurrence on the same day (October 6, 1937). Thus the United States stood committed in behalf of China and against Japan. This series of events came as a shock to Ambassador Grew in Tokyo. For five years Grew had striven to build a firm structure of Japanese-American friendship; he was convinced of the "hopelessness of deterring aggression by moral judgments." The United States had, he feared, "chosen the road which might lead directly to involvement . . . in the Far Eastern mess."[7]

The Brussels Conference

The League Assembly, at the same time that it charged Japan with treaty violation, suggested that the signers of the Nine-Power Treaty undertake a settlement of the dispute. Accordingly, the Belgian government issued invitations to a conference to be held at Brussels. Invitations went to the original and subsequent signers of the treaty, and also to Germany and the Soviet Union.[8] Japan declined the invitation, on the grounds that the League had already condemned Japan without hearing its side of the case and furthermore, that the quarrel was one purely between Japan and China and in no way concerned the other Nine-Power Treaty powers. Germany also declined to attend. Italy sent a representative, who, as it turned out, supported the views of Italy's axis partner.

The Brussels Conference, attended by delegates from nineteen nations, met from November 3 to November 24, 1937. In Japan's absence and in the face of her refusal to con-

---

5. On September 16 the S.S. *Wichita,* operated by the U. S. Maritime Commission, was required to unload at San Diego, California, a cargo of airplanes that it was transporting from Baltimore to China.

6. W. L. Langer and S. E. Gleason, *The Challenge to Isolation, 1937–1940* (New York: Harper & Row, Publishers, 1952), p. 19; Dorothy Borg, "Notes on Roosevelt's Quarantine Speech," *Political Science Quarterly,* 72 (September 1957), 405–33; T. B. Jacobs, "Roosevelt's Quarantine Speech," *Historian,* 24 (August 1962), 483–502.

7. Grew, *Turbulent Era,* 2: 1167–68n.

8. Bolivia, Denmark, Mexico, Norway and Sweden had signed the Nine-Power Treaty subsequently to its negotiation. To the Brussels Conference, Canada, Australia, New Zealand, South Africa, and India, which had been represented in the British Empire delegation at Washington in 1922, sent independent delegations. In all, nineteen nations were represented.

sult with representatives of any of the partici- pating powers, no attempt at composing the conflict was feasible. President Roosevelt, seemingly made cautious by the reaction to his "quarantine" speech, had ruled out any mention of sanctions. The Conference, there- fore, could do little more than reaffirm (Italy dissenting) that the principles of the Nine- Power Treaty were applicable to the con- troversy, and serve notice that any settlement of the conflict must be consistent with those principles.[9]

On Japanese policy this notice had no effect whatever. In justification of her course in China, Japan kept insisting: (1) that she was acting in self-defense against Chinese vio- lence and Chinese infringement of Japanese rights; (2) that the Nine-Power Treaty was obsolete and the Pact of Paris inapplicable to the Far East; (3) that the dispute con- cerned only Japan and China and that inter- vention of third parties was inadmissible.

The Panay Bombing

A few weeks after the Brussels Conference, Japanese-American relations were imperiled when young Japanese aviators, on December 12, bombed and sank the American gunboat *Panay*, escorting American tankers in the Yangtze River. Two American crew members were killed and many injured. The attack occurred under conditions of excellent visi- bility and could not be explained as a mistake. The Japanese government was deeply per- turbed. The Foreign Minister came in person to the American embassy in Tokyo to offer abject apologies and a promise of reparations for the injured and the families of the killed, and Japanese civilians contributed generously to a fund for the same purpose. American public opinion took the matter calmly—in contrast to the "Remember the *Maine*" furor

of 1898. Within two weeks the Japanese apology was accepted and the crisis passed.[10]

The "New Order" in East Asia

In the meantime Japan was pushing the war in an effort to destroy Chinese resistance and compel the government of Chiang Kai-shek to make peace on Japan's terms. In so doing, the Japanese did not hesitate to bomb Chinese cities from the air—a practice to which they had resorted at Chinchow in 1931, which had been followed by Italian and German aviators serving Franco in the Spanish Civil War, but which was still regarded with abhorrence by the democracies. The bombing of Nanking in September 1937, and of Canton and other cities later, led the United States, in July 1938, to place a "moral embargo" on sales of airplanes to Japan. This took the form of a letter from Secretary Hull to American air- plane manufacturers stating that the govern- ment was "strongly opposed" to the sale of such equipment to nations guilty of bombing civilian populations. This request was, for the most part, adhered to by the companies con- cerned.[11]

The bombings were in part preparatory to land campaigns against the Chinese cities. Nanking was taken December 15, 1937. The Chinese government had withdrawn to Han- kow. In October 1938, Hankow and Canton were occupied, and the government retreated to Chungking on the upper Yangtze. All prin- cipal ports, the coast cities, and the main rail- way lines were now in Japanese hands and, by the ordinary rules of the game, China should have acknowledged defeat and have made peace on Japan's terms. But the Chinese armies, though beaten, had not been de-

9. *The Conference of Brussels, November 3–24, 1937, Convened in Virtue of Article 7 of the Nine-Power Treaty of Washington of 1922*, Department of State Conference Series 37 (Washington: Government Printing Office, 1938).

10. The United States government preferred not to pass on the private donations to the American sufferers. Arrangements were therefore made to have the fund devoted to "some constructive purpose in the interests of Japanese-American friendship." Grew, *Turbulent Era*, 2: 1205. See also M. T. Koginos, *The Panay Incident: Prelude to War* (Lafayette, Ind.: Purdue University Studies, 1967).

11. *New York Times,* January 10, 1939, pp. 1, 8.

stroyed, and the government of Chiang Kai-shek fought stubbornly on.

Since Chiang would not negotiate, the Japanese conquerors set up puppet governments in the occupied area. A Peking Provisional Government was established in the north in December 1937; a Reformed Government of the Chinese Republic at Nanking in March 1938. Two years later a once prominent Kuomintang politician, Wang Ching-wei, was persuaded to head the latter, which Japan recognized as the government of China.

While extending her military control over eastern China, Japan was consolidating her economic hold upon the country, and following a policy of restricting the activities of foreign business firms, if not forcing them out altogether. At the same time, American and other foreign missions in China found that Japanese bombs had a more than chance affinity for their churches, schools and hospitals. The Open Door was being closed to both the business and the culture of the West.

The opposing Japanese and American positions were clearly stated late in 1938. A Japanese Foreign Office statement, issued on November 3, 1938, proclaimed that Japan was inaugurating a "new order" that would "insure the permanent stability of East Asia," a new order having "for its foundation a tripartite relationship of mutual aid and co-ordination between Japan, Manchukuo and China in political, economic, cultural and other fields." [12] American complaints that the "new order" might infringe treaty rights met with the declaration that no useful purpose would be served by "an attempt to apply to present and future conditions without any changes, concepts and principles which were applicable to conditions prevailing before the present incident." [13]

To this statement Ambassador Grew, speaking for Secretary Hull, replied that the United States was aware that conditions changed and was willing to adapt existing treaties to new conditions through orderly "processes of negotiation and agreement," but could not assent to "the abrogation of any of this country's rights or obligations by the arbitrary action of agents or authorities of any other country." As for the "new order," the United States could not admit the right of any one power to "prescribe . . . the terms and conditions of a 'new order' in areas not under its sovereignty and to constitute itself the repository of authority and the agent of destiny in regard thereto." [14]

Thus by the end of 1938 the United States and Japan seemed to have reached a complete impasse in regard to China. During the course of that year, however, the center of international tension had shifted from the Far East to Europe.

Hitler Opens His Drang nach Osten

During 1938 Hitler took the first two steps in his *Drang nach Osten* or drive to the east. He annexed Austria and the predominantly German sections of Czechoslovakia. In order to win Italian support, Hitler had, as noted above, promised to respect Austrian independence and to refrain from interfering in the small republic's internal politics. At heart, he had never abandoned his hope of uniting the land of his birth with his adopted fatherland, and by the spring of 1938 he felt strong enough to cast his promises to the winds.

In February he summoned Schuschnigg, the Austrian Chancellor, to a conference at Berchtesgaden, the Führer's mountain retreat in Bavaria, and demanded the admission of prominent Austrian Nazis to the cabinet. Schuschnigg complied, but called for an immediate plebiscite, which he felt sure would demonstrate popular opposition to union with Germany. The Nazis were apparently of the same opinion, for they at once demanded the resignation of Schuschnigg and a postponement of the plebiscite, threatening invasion by German troops as the alternative. Schuschnigg

12. *Foreign Relations, Japan, 1931–1941,* 1: 478.
13. *Foreign Relations, Japan, 1931–1941,* 1: 800.

14. U. S. Department of State, *Peace and War: United States Foreign Policy, 1931–1941* (Washington: Government Printing Office, 1943), pp. 445–47.

resigned on March 11. His successor as Chancellor, the Nazi Seyss-Inquart, immediately called in German troops, allegedly to suppress disorders in Austria. On March 12 the German government proclaimed Austria to be a state of the German Reich, and two days later Hitler entered Vienna amid a great show of rejoicing. *Anschluss* was complete. France and Great Britain protested, but no one raised a hand in resistance, least of all Mussolini, who had blocked the way in 1934.

Chamberlain Goes to Berchtesgaden

Hitler next turned to "rescue" what he termed the "tortured and oppressed" Germans of Czechoslovakia, the most democratic state of Central Europe. Of Czechoslovakia's 14,500,000 people, about 3,500,000 were Germans. These lived for the most part in the Sudeten area that fringed the western end of the republic, facing German territory to the north, west, and south. The Sudeten Germans, comprising one of numerous racial minorities in Czechoslovakia, had shown little dissatisfaction with their government until 1932, when the Nazi movement first gained some strength among them. From then on to 1938, the Sudeten Nazis, led by one Konrad Henlein, kept up a growing agitation, first for complete cultural and political autonomy within Czechoslovakia, finally for union with Nazi Germany.

The Czechoslovak government made a succession of compromise offers, but these were one by one rejected by Henlein, who consulted Hitler at each step. By September 1938 it was evident that nothing less than cession of Sudentenland to Germany would satisfy the Führer. The Czechoslovak government did not propose to yield to dismemberment without putting up a fight. It had a good army and a defensible frontier. It also had defensive alliances with France and Russia. If it were attacked by Germany, and if its allies fulfilled their obligations, a general European war was certain. This would, in all probability, involve England also.

In an effort to find a peaceful settlement for the Sudeten problem, Prime Minister Neville Chamberlain of Great Britain paid two visits to Hitler, at Berchtesgaden and at Godesberg. In the first (September 15, 1938) Chamberlain ascertained that the Führer would take nothing less than surrender of the Sudetenland to Germany. In the second, a week later, he submitted to Hitler a plan for the prompt and peaceful transfer to Germany of the areas of Czechoslovakia with population more than 50 percent German, the fixing of the new frontier by an international commission, and an international guarantee of the independence of a Czechoslovakia shorn of these important segments of her territory and population. These terms the Czech government had agreed to under combined British and French pressure.

To Chamberlain's consternation, Hitler rejected this proposal as too slow. Instead, he demanded the immediate withdrawal of all Czech military and official civilian personnel from areas that he specified, with plebiscites to follow in other areas where the percentage of German population was doubtful. German troops, he said, would occupy the specified areas October 1, whether or not Czechoslovakia accepted his ultimatum.

Czechoslovakia at once rejected this proposal and mobilized its army of 1,500,000 men. France followed with partial mobilization, as did Belgium. France and Britain made it clear that they would assist Czechoslovakia if it were attacked, while Mussolini announced his intention of standing by his Axis partner. The threat of war was very real.

The United States Has a Finger in Appeasement

At this point (September 27, 1938) President Roosevelt entered the picture. Urging Hitler to lay the controversy before an international conference, he added:

> Should you agree to a solution in this peaceful manner I am convinced that hundreds of millions throughout the world would recognize

your action as an outstanding historic service to all humanity.

Roosevelt also joined with Chamberlain and French Premier Daladier in a plea to Mussolini to persuade Hitler to accept a peaceful settlement that would give him substantially all he asked for. Hitler yielded to the extent of agreeing to meet with Mussolini and the French and British Premiers at Munich. There, on September 29, Hitler and Mussolini, Chamberlain and Daladier agreed on a plan that the Czech government perforce accepted. It differed little from Hitler's ultimatum of a week before, merely allowing slightly more time for Czech withdrawal from the surrendered area. Thus, it was assumed, war had been averted.[15] Prime Minister Chamberlain told the people of England that he had brought back "peace with honour. I believe," he added, "it is peace in our time."

The Munich settlement proved to be but the prelude to the complete extinction of Czechoslovakia as an independent nation. Hungary and Poland at once demanded and received slices of territory where Magyars and Poles were numerous. Internal dissension between Czechs and Slovaks afforded Hitler an excuse for taking control of the destinies of those two ethnical divisions of the former republic. In March 1939, Bohemia-Moravia and Slovakia became German protectorates.

While Hitler was helping himself to terri-tory in Central Europe, Mussolini seized the occasion to strengthen Italy's position in the Mediterranean. On April 7, 1939, Italian troops occupied the independent state of Albania, which was, a few days later, added to the realms ruled over by Mussolini in the name of King Victor Emmanuel III.

The Threat to Poland

Hitler had declared at Munich: "This [Sudetenland] is the last territorial claim which I have to make in Europe."[16] His absorption of Czechoslovakia had given the lie to that declaration, and by April 1939 he was pressing Poland for consent to annexation of the free city of Danzig and a sort of German corridor across the Polish Corridor to give Germany freer access to East Prussia. By this time Mr. Chamberlain had lost faith in Hitler's promises. He abruptly abandoned appeasement and, with France, gave guarantees of aid against aggression to Poland and later to Rumania and to Greece, the latter threatened by Italy's April occupation of Albania. Geography would make it difficult to implement these guarantees effectively, but they at least served notice on the Axis powers that further aggression against their small neighbors would mean war with the great western democracies.

The United States Tries to Shake Off Its Fetters

In Washington, the sympathies of the administration were unequivocally on the side of the European democracies and against the Fascist and Nazi dictatorships. In his annual message to Congress, January 4, 1939, Mr. Roosevelt remarked that although the United States had no intention of using other than peaceful methods to discourage aggressors, there were "many methods short of war, but stronger and more effective than mere words, of bringing

---

15. There is some reason to believe that Hitler was bluffing at Godesberg and Munich. His Chief of Staff, Marshal Keitel, was asked after the war whether Germany would have attacked a Czechoslovakia backed by France and Great Britain. He replied: "Certainly not. We were not strong enough militarily." The object of the Munich settlement, he said, "was to get Russia out of Europe, to gain time, and to complete the German armaments." Quoted by Winston S. Churchill, *The Gathering Storm*, Vol. 1 of *The Second World War* (Boston: Houghton Mifflin Company, 1948), p. 319. Quotations from *The Second World War* are reprinted by permission of Houghton Mifflin Company and Cassell & Co. Ltd., London. That American policy in the Munich crisis weakened the French spirit of resistance to Hitler is the conclusion of John McV. Haight, Jr., "France, the United States, and the Munich Crisis," *Journal of Modern History*, 32 (December 1960), 340–58.

16. Churchill, *The Gathering Storm*, p. 345.

home to aggressor governments the aggregate sentiments of our own people." But "methods short of war," if that phrase meant material aid, were barred by the neutrality law which, as the President complained in the same message, "may actually give aid to an aggressor and deny it to the victim." Thus began a long campaign to have the neutrality law repealed or revised.[17]

On April 15, a week after the Italian invasion of Albania, Roosevelt addressed a surprise message to Hitler and Mussolini. Referring to the fear of war that hung over the world, he suggested that the two dictators could dispel it by giving a ten-year non-aggression guarantee to their neighbors in Europe and the Near East—the President named thirty-one. He believed that he could, in return, secure similar promises from the governments named. Could this be accomplished, he promised, the United States would gladly participate in discussions aimed at easing the burden of armaments and freeing the channels of international trade.

To this communication Mussolini made no reply. Hitler answered it two weeks later, in a speech to the Reichstag. He had, he said, inquired of all the thirty-one governments named by Mr. Roosevelt as to whether they feared aggression by Germany and therefore felt the need of such promises as the President had proposed. In each case, he said, the answer had been negative. Any fear of German aggression, he implied, must exist only in President Roosevelt's imagination.[18]

As spring turned to summer and as European tension built up over the Polish question, President Roosevelt and Secretary Hull became more and more convinced that the neutrality law, especially the arms embargo, served as an encouragement to aggression. It assured Hitler that in a general European war, Great Britain and France could purchase no arms, ammunition, or implements of war in the United States. Repeal of the arms em-

bargo, the administration reasoned, would make Hitler think twice before inviting war with the democracies. During June and July, therefore, administration leaders in Congress made an attempt to secure repeal of that provision, while leaving the remainder of the law intact or slightly modified. The House passed a bill so mutilated as to be worthless. In a final effort, the President and Secretary Hull met with leading senators and sought to impress upon them the danger of war in Europe, and the perils that would confront the United States if the Axis won, as it might well do. The surest road to security for America, they argued, lay in taking action that would assure Great Britain and France of access to American materials and so deter Hitler from starting a war. Senator Borah, always the isolationist, replied that he had sources of information in Europe more reliable than those of the State Department, and that his sources assured him that there would be no war. Isolationist sentiment was strong in the Senate, and the administration's friends were forced to admit that they did not have the votes to pass the repeal bill. Congress adjourned without taking action.[19]

Hitler Precipitates War

While Roosevelt asked in vain for legislation to strengthen the hands of the democracies, the British and French were seeking the only available means of making effective their guarantees to Poland and Rumania; namely, the support of the Soviet Union. Though Russia had been ignored at Munich, Stalin in April 1939 offered to make with France and Great Britain a defensive alliance against further German aggression. Negotiations began in April and dragged on into August. The stumbling block was the refusal of Poland, Rumania, and the Baltic States to accept a Russian guarantee of their territory, which would

17. Langer and Gleason, *Challenge to Isolation,* pp. 46–48.
18. Langer and Gleason, *Challenge to Isolation,* pp. 83–90.

19. Langer and Gleason, *Challenge to Isolation,* pp. 136–47. It is the opinion of these authors that repeal of the arms embargo at this time would probably not have altered Hitler's course.

imply a right to occupy it for protection against German aggression. To the Russians this right seemed an essential element in their plans for defense. To the small states lying between Germany and Russia, the eastern giant was at least as great a peril as the western. When the British and French balked at forcing Russia's attentions upon its neighbors against their will, the Kremlin secretly opened parallel negotiations with Germany. On May 3, Maxim Litvinov, a friend of the West and of the League of Nations, was replaced as Foreign Commissar by that diplomat of ill omen, Vyacheslav M. Molotov. For three months Molotov shrewdly kept two paths open, one to Berlin, one to Paris and London. The first clue to the outcome was the announcement on August 20 that Russia and Germany had signed a trade agreement. Immediately thereafter Nazi Foreign Minister Joachim von Ribbentrop flew to Moscow and on August 23 signed with Molotov a non-aggression pact that assured Hitler of Russian neutrality if he invaded Poland. Accompanying it was a secret agreement for the partition of Poland between Germany and Russia and for delimitation of their spheres of influence in the Baltic States.[20]

Hitler now pressed peremptorily his territorial demands on Poland, hoping to avoid war with England and France but willing to face it rather than retreat. Last minute efforts at settlement by negotiation broke down. On September 1, 1939, German armies crossed the Polish frontier, and German airplanes rained bombs on Polish cities. Two days later (September 3), Great Britain and France declared war against Nazi Germany. It was the beginning of World War II.

20. Germany claimed only Lithuania, conceding paramount Russian interest in Finland, Estonia, and Latvia.

In Washington, the President issued on September 5, 1939, the customary proclamation of American neutrality. In this instance, with war having been formally declared by all the principal belligerents, he had no choice but to invoke the provisions of the neutrality law whose amendment he had earlier sought from Congress. The arms embargo and other features of the act were applied against both belligerent camps. There was, however, no repetition of Wilson's appeal for impartiality in thought, nor was there any pretense of impartiality on the part of the administration.

An analysis of President Roosevelt's position is appropriate at this point. His first priority was to prevent an Axis victory, which in his mind would present a deadly peril to the United States. This he felt from the first, but even more keenly after the German victories of 1940 revealed the frightful power of the Nazi war machine. An Axis victory, he believed, would mean eventual encirclement of the United States by the Berlin-Rome-Tokyo combination, followed by economic strangulation if not by military disaster.[1]

Secondly, there seems no good reason to doubt that he sincerely desired to keep the United States out of the war, unless American participation should become necessary to prevent an Axis victory. In that event, as he saw it, better war now with dependable allies than war later when those allies should have been crushed by the Axis. At some point along the

---

1. The fears felt by President Roosevelt were probably the same as those that were voiced by the American chargé d'affaires in Berlin, Alexander Kirk, in a memorandum of June 17, 1940. Hitler, he wrote, would, if successful in Europe, "exercise his power with a view to eliminating it [the United States] as a great power as soon as possible. He will not attack the Americans by force, as he can attain his aims by other methods, once he has established his domination over the countries of Europe. He will strangle the United States economically and financially and . . . he will confront the United States within a brief measure of time with the impossible tasks of adjusting its system to an economy in which it will be excluded from access to all foreign markets. . . ." Quoted in H. L. Trefousse, *Germany and American Neutrality, 1939–1941* (New York: Bookman Associates, 1951), p. 56. Reprinted by permission of the publisher. See chap. 1 of this monograph for an analysis of the totalitarian threat to the United States.

37

The United States as a Nonbelligerent

way, probably in the summer of 1941, he became convinced that only American entry into the war could insure Allied victory. It should be added that, although believing participation in the war might be necessary to American security, Mr. Roosevelt never took the American people fully into his confidence.

Thirdly, unless or until America should enter the war, the President believed that it should give all possible material and moral aid to the opponents of the Axis. Only thus was there hope of an Allied victory without American participation. This program meant scrapping the neutrality legislation so laboriously written in the 1930's. It meant also complete disregard of the old rules of neutrality, which prescribed impartial treatment of the belligerents and forbade a neutral government to give aid to a belligerent. Justification for this departure from old-fashioned neutrality was found in (a) the argument that the Pact of Paris had made neutrality obsolete, (b) Germany's complete disregard of international law and treaty promises, (c) the imperative needs of national security. Thus the United States moved from a status of neutrality to a newly recognized status known as nonbelligerency—the status of a nation not at war but giving active aid to one belligerent.

In President Roosevelt's open stand for all-out aid for the Allies short of war, and in his unpublicized belief that war itself would be a lesser evil than an Axis victory, he had important segments of public opinion both with him and against him. The isolationist sentiment that had promoted the neutrality laws was still strong. It opposed aid to the Allies as a step toward war, and it felt that America's sharing in "Europe's wars" was the greatest of evils. It was organized most effectively in the America First Committee, with General Robert E. Wood of Chicago as president and Colonel Charles A. Lindbergh as leading orator. It received the support of, among other journals, the *Chicago Tribune* and the Hearst newspapers. The America First Committee was "going strong" up to the afternoon of the Pearl Harbor attack.

On the other side, the most important organized vehicle for the expression of public opinion was the Committee to Defend America by Aiding the Allies, headed for some time by the well known Kansas editor, William Allen White, and often referred to as the White Committee. Organized in the spring of 1940, it stood for all material aid to the Allies short of war; part of its membership favored outright participation in the war. Some persons sharing this latter view, from both within and without the White Committee, formed the Fight for Freedom Committee in April 1941. They held that, in asking others to do all the fighting, America was playing an ignoble role, and urged that America take its place as a full-scale belligerent in the "fight for freedom." [2]

From Neutrality to "Shooting War"

We may now trace the principal steps by which the United States moved away from neutrality and nearer to war with the Axis powers.

Repeal of the arms embargo. The first step was a modification of the neutrality law along the lines earlier proposed by the administration. Roosevelt called Congress to meet in special session on September 21 and asked legislation to permit the sale of arms to the Allies. After six weeks of debate and by safe majorities, Congress passed a Fourth Neutrality Act, which became law on November 4, 1939. It repealed the embargo on arms, ammunition, and implements of war and placed sales to belligerents of goods of all kinds on a cash and carry basis. It empowered the President to designate "combat areas," which American ships and American citizens would be prohibited from entering. Other restrictions of the earlier legislation were generally retained. The great importance of the new law was in opening the American market in war goods to the French and British, since they

2. The story of the two opposing committees is told in two useful monographs: W. S. Cole, *America First: The Battle against Intervention* (Madison: University of Wisconsin Press, 1953); Walter Johnson, *The Battle against Isolation* (Chicago: University of Chicago Press, 1944).

alone, of the European belligerents, could buy and carry away.

The promise of aid to "the opponents of force." In Europe, a lightning German campaign against Poland was followed by months of comparative inactivity—the *Sitzkrieg* (sitting war) or "phony war." But in April, 1940 the *Sitzkrieg* suddenly became a *Blitzkrieg* (lightning war). Denmark, Norway, the Netherlands, and Belgium were quickly overrun by German airborne troops and motorized columns. The French armies were crushed, the Maginot Line taken in the rear. The British Expeditionary Force escaped, as by a miracle, from Dunkirk, but left on the beaches all its heavy equipment and most of its small arms. On June 10, Mussolini, who hitherto had preserved a nonbelligerent status in his partner's war, declared war upon stricken France. On June 22 France surrendered. All of northern and western France became occupied territory. The south and east Hitler left to a government established by Marshal Pétain at Vichy.

President Roosevelt's response to these events was prompt and emphatic. Speaking at Charlottesville, Virginia, June 10, he remarked, with reference to Mussolini's attack on France: "The hand that held the dagger has struck it into the back of its neighbor." More important was his declaration:

> In our American unity, we will pursue two obvious and simultaneous courses: we will extend to the opponents of force the material resources of this nation, and at the same time we will harness and speed up the use of those resources in order that we ourselves in the Americas may have equipment and training equal to the task of any emergency and every defense.

The beginning of rearmament. During the summer of 1940, Congress, at Roosevelt's request, took important steps toward strengthening the armed forces of the United States and stepping up production of war material for the use of the "opponents of force." The Army was to be enlarged from an authorized strength of 280,000 men to 1,200,000 as soon as the men could be raised and trained, with other increments to follow. Army and Navy air

strength was to be augmented by over 18,000 planes, and a production goal of 50,000 planes annually was set. Authorization of an unprecedented naval increase of 1,325,000 tons laid the basis for a "two-ocean Navy." The total defense appropriation of over 5 billion dollars, more than the President had asked, broke all peacetime records while authorizations for future construction contracts brought the grand total to some 16 billions. In September, Congress passed the first peacetime selective service act in American experience. Fear of Hitler had stimulated a tardy but impressive drive for rearmament.

The destroyer-bases deal. The surrender of France soon after the President's Charlottesville speech left only two active "opponents of force" in the world, Great Britain in the west, China in the east. Roosevelt's most immediate concern was with Great Britain, now assailed from the sea and air by victorious Germany. If Britain should fall, if her fleet should be destroyed or pass into hostile hands, the future for America would look dark indeed. Britain's most pressing need at the moment was for swift naval vessels for antisubmarine patrol and convoy duty. The United States had fifty overage destroyers, which in the President's mind would serve the United States better if put to active use by the British than laid up "in moth balls" in American harbors. Attorney General Robert Jackson found ingenious paths for the President through both domestic and international law, and on September 2 Mr. Roosevelt agreed to turn over the destroyers to the British Navy in return for the right, over a 99-year period, to set up and maintain American military bases in eight British possessions stretching from Newfoundland to British Guiana.[3] The bases made possible a naval and air screen covering the approaches to the Atlantic coast of the United States and to the Caribbean. In announcing the deal to Congress (he had not asked their consent), the President claimed: "This is the most important action in the reinforcement of our national defense that has been taken since the

3. The other base sites were Bermuda, the Bahamas, Jamaica, Antigua, St. Lucia, and Trinidad.

Louisiana Purchase." Congress and public opinion for the most part acquiesced in the President's startling *fait accompli*. The transfer of the destroyers to Great Britain was, as Winston Churchill later wrote, "a decidedly unneutral act by the United States." But though it would, in Churchill's words, "according to all the standards of history, have justified the German Government in declaring war," [4] Hitler did not waste time in making official protests.

President Roosevelt's reelection, 1940. In July the Democratic party had broken precedent by nominating Mr. Roosevelt for a third term as President. The President's prior move of inviting into his cabinet two prominent Republicans, Henry L. Stimson as Secretary of War and Frank Knox as Secretary of the Navy, did nothing to appease the Republican party. But the Republican candidate, Wendell L. Willkie, shared the President's belief in the importance of aid to Britain. Isolation, therefore, was not an issue in the campaign. Neither was its antithesis of joining in the war, for both platforms and both candidates declared emphatically against participation in "any foreign war," though the Democratic platform added the qualification "except in case of attack." The Republicans, however, painted Roosevelt as the war candidate, and the President found it expedient, as the campaign climaxed, to reiterate, "again and again and again," the assurance: "Your boys are not going to be sent into any foreign wars." Roosevelt won the election easily, though with a majority much reduced from that of 1936.

"The arsenal of democracy": lend-lease. After reelection the President received from Prime Minister Churchill a long letter setting forth Great Britain's financial straits. That nation was scraping the bottom of the barrel to pay for goods already ordered and would need "ten times as much" for the extension of the war. Churchill hoped that Roosevelt would regard his letter "not as an appeal for aid, but as a statement of the minimum action

necessary to achieve our common purpose." [5] The problem, as Roosevelt saw it, was how to aid England in the common cause without incurring such a breeder of ill will as the war debt problem after World War I. After brooding over the matter for days during a Caribbean cruise on the cruiser *Tuscaloosa*, he came up with the ingenious idea of lending goods instead of money. He wanted, as he told a press conference, to get away from that "silly, foolish old dollar sign," and he compared what he proposed to do to lending a garden hose to a neighbor to put out a fire that might otherwise spread to one's own house. [6]

In a "fireside chat" on December 29, 1940, he pictured the United States as the "arsenal of democracy," and in his message to Congress a few days later he made officially the proposal that resulted in the Lend-Lease Act of March 11, 1941.

The Lend-Lease Act was the complete negation of old-fashioned neutrality. It empowered the President to make available to "the government of any country whose defense the President deems vital to the defense of the United States" any "defense article," any service, or any "defense information." "Defense articles" might be manufactured expressly for the government that was to receive them, or they might (after consultation with top military and naval advisers) be taken from existing stocks in the possession of the United States. Launched on a modest scale, the lend-lease program eventually conveyed goods and services valued at over $50,000,000,000 to the friends and allies of the United States in World War II; and it left in its wake no such exasperating war debt problem as that of the 1920's. [7]

Planning for joint military action. From

4. Winston S. Churchill, *Their Finest Hour,* Vol. 2 of *The Second World War* (Boston: Houghton Mifflin Company, 1949), p. 404.

5. The letter and comment are printed in Churchill, *Their Finest Hour,* pp. 555–67.
6. Basil Rauch, *Roosevelt from Munich to Pearl Harbor* (New York: Creative Age Press, 1950), p. 296.
7. Against the 50 billions of lend-lease aid furnished by the United States, it received approximately 10 billions in so-called reverse lend-lease from its allies. After the war the United States negotiated settlement agreements with most of the recipients. These were

January to March, 1941, while Congress was debating the lend-lease proposal, British and American military and naval officers were holding secret staff conferences in Washington. Their purpose was to plan coordination of the American and British effort, (a) on the basis of lend-lease while the United States remained nonbelligerent; (b) in joint military and naval operations if and when the United States entered the war. The conferences reached the fundamental decision that if Japan entered the war, Germany was still to be regarded as Enemy Number One, and her defeat to be given priority over that of Japan. One reason for this decision was fear that the German scientists, if given time, might perfect new super-weapons. There was no such apprehension as to Japanese achievement.[8] After conclusion of the conferences, American officers went to England to select sites for future naval and air force bases.

Coordinating the defense program with Canada's. Akin to this tie-up with belligerent Britain were contemporary arrangements with belligerent Canada. In August 1938, a year before the outbreak of war, President Roosevelt and Prime Minister Mackenzie King had

exchanged assurances of mutual assistance in case of need; the President declaring that the United States would not "stand idly by if domination of Canadian soil is threatened by any other empire."[9] Meeting at Ogdensburg, N.Y., August 17, 1940, while the battle of Britain still hung in the balance, the two statesmen agreed to set up a Permanent Joint Board of Defense for the protection of their two countries. After the passage of the Lend-Lease Act they met again at Roosevelt's home at Hyde Park, April 20, 1941, and took steps to gear together the production facilities of the United States and Canada for their own defense and that of Britain. A Joint Defense Production Committee was established on November 5, 1941. Thus months before the United States became a belligerent, it was working closely with Canada for a common objective: defeat of the Axis powers.

The Atlantic Charter. In August 1941, the Prime Minister of belligerent Great Britain and the President of the nonbelligerent United States met secretly for their first conference at Argentia, Newfoundland. In explaining his desire for such a meeting, Mr. Churchill wrote afterwards that "a conference between us would proclaim the ever closer association of Britain and the United States, would cause our enemies concern, make Japan ponder, and cheer our friends."[10] The two statesmen discussed a variety of topics connected with the war, including means of deterring Japan from attacking the British or Dutch possessions in the Far East.[11] But the most famous if not the most important achievement of the conference was the production of the document known as the Atlantic Charter.[12] This pronouncement, which came chiefly from Churchill's pen, may

in general on the theory that lend-lease materials not used in the war should be returned or paid for, but the settlements were also shaped by the proviso written into the original lend-lease agreements, that final settlement terms should "be such as not to burden commerce but to promote mutually advantageous economic relations . . . and the betterment of world-wide economic relations." As of December 31, 1953, settlement agreements totaling over $1,577,-000,000 had been negotiated, on which $477,000,000 had been paid. The U.S.S.R., which had received over $11,000,000,000, was the only large debtor that had failed to agree to a settlement. *Thirty-fifth Report to Congress on Lend-Lease Operations* (Washington: Government Printing Office, 1954).

8. S. E. Morison, *The Battle of the Atlantic, History of United States Naval Operations in World War II*, Vol. 1 (Boston: Little, Brown, & Company, 1947), pp. 46, 47; Winston S. Churchill, *The Grand Alliance*, Vol. 3 of *The Second World War* (Boston: Houghton Mifflin Company, 1950), pp. 137–38; Maurice Matloff and E. M. Snell, *Strategic Planning for Coalition Warfare, 1941–1942* in *United States Army in World War II: The War Department* (Washington: Department of the Army, 1953), chap. 3.

9. E. W. McInnis, *The Unguarded Frontier: A History of American-Canadian Relations* (Garden City, N.Y.: Doubleday & Company, Inc., 1942), pp. 355–56.

10. Churchill, *The Grand Alliance*, p. 427.

11. See pp. 381–82.

12. The text of the Atlantic Charter is as follows:
    The President of the United States of America and the Prime Minister, Mr. Churchill, representing His Majesty's Government in the United Kingdom, being met together, deem it right to make known certain

be compared roughly to Wilson's Fourteen Points in World War I. Like Wilson's formulation, it set up idealistic objectives that might be expected to appeal to liberals everywhere. That it brought the United States a step nearer to war was clearly seen and appreciated by Churchill, who wrote:

> . . . The fact alone of the United States, still technically neutral, joining with a belligerent Power in making such a declaration was astonishing. The inclusion in it of a reference to "final destruction of the Nazi tyranny" . . . amounted to a challenge which in ordinary times would have implied warlike action. . . .[13]

common principles in the national policies of their respective countries on which they base their hopes for a better future for the world.

First, their countries seek no aggrandizement, territorial or other;

Second, they desire to see no territorial changes that do not accord with the freely expressed wishes of the peoples concerned;

Third, they respect the right of all peoples to choose the form of government under which they will live; and they wish to see sovereign rights and self-government restored to those who have been forcibly deprived of them;

Fourth, they will endeavor, with due respect for their existing obligations, to further the enjoyment by all States, great or small, victor or vanquished, of access, on equal terms, to the trade and to the raw materials of the world which are needed for their economic prosperity;

Fifth, they desire to bring about the fullest collaboration between all nations in the economic field with the object of securing, for all, improved labor standards, economic advancement and social security;

Sixth, after the final destruction of the Nazi tyranny, they hope to see established a peace which will afford to all nations the means of dwelling in safety within their own boundaries, and which will afford assurance that all the men in all the lands may live out their lives in freedom from fear and want;

Seventh, such a peace should enable all men to traverse the high seas and oceans without hindrance;

Eighth, they believe that all of the nations of the world, for realistic as well as spiritual reasons must come to the abandonment of the use of force. Since no future peace can be maintained if land, sea or air armaments continue to be employed by nations which threaten, or may threaten, aggression outside of their frontiers, they believe, pending the establishment of a wider and permanent system of general security, that the disarmament of such nations is essential. They will likewise aid and encourage all other practicable measures which will lighten for peace-loving peoples the crushing burden of armaments.

Patrolling the Atlantic sea lanes. The lend-leasing of "defense articles" to Great Britain was worse than useless unless the articles could be delivered. The protection against German submarines of convoys from North American to British ports strained the resources of the British and Canadian Navies. The problem was further complicated when Hitler attacked the Soviet Union, June 22, 1941, and the United States determined to make the U.S.S.R. a beneficiary of lend-lease. The northern sea route to Russia stretched around the northern tip of Norway to its terminus at Murmansk. The British navy could not protect the Murmansk convoys unless it got relief elsewhere.

For the United States to convoy British shipping carrying lend-lease "defense articles" would have been stretching nonbelligerency to a point that even Roosevelt thought inexpedient. But a substitute method was found. A Conference of American Foreign Ministers at Panama in September–October 1939 had proclaimed the neutrality of a wide belt of the western Atlantic and had warned the belligerents against acts of war in these waters.[14] Though neither England nor Germany had paid any heed to this declaration, Roosevelt decided, in the spring of 1941, to have the navy "patrol" not only the waters so defined, but the entire North Atlantic west of 26° west longitude and to "publish the position of possible aggressor ships or planes when located in the American patrol area."[15] Thus British convoys would be warned of the positions of Nazi submarines located by the United States navy.

Patrolling was facilitated by the American occupation of Greenland under an agreement made with the Danish minister in Washington, April 9, 1941.[16] German aerial activity had been observed over Greenland's east coast and German weather stations had been set up on

13. Churchill, *The Grand Alliance,* p. 444.
14. See p. 396.
15. Churchill, *The Grand Alliance,* p. 140.
16. The minister, Henrik de Kauffmann, was at once repudiated by the government of Denmark, but since that government was a prisoner of Germany, the United States paid no attention to its action.

the island. To these activities the United States now put a stop. Three months later, July 7, 1941, United States forces occupied Iceland, by agreement with the local government and with the British authorities, who had previously landed troops there as a precautionary measure. The United States now had a legitimate reason for convoying its own supply ships to Iceland. On July 19, 1941, Admiral E. J. King, Commander-in-Chief, Atlantic Fleet, directed a naval task force to "escort convoys of United States and Iceland flag shipping, *including shipping of any nationality which may join such . . . convoys, between United States ports and bases, and Iceland.*" [17] Thus the United States navy, in company with that of Canada, began actually escorting British lend-lease convoys as far as Iceland, where the British navy picked them up.

A "shooting war" begins. Such "nonbelligerent" activity could not continue for long without bringing on clashes with German U-boats. On September 4, 1941 the destroyer *Greer,* while trailing a submarine and signaling its position to a British plane, was made a target for two torpedoes from the U-boat, both of which missed their mark. A week later President Roosevelt, without describing the circumstances of the incident, denounced the German attack as "piracy" and warned "German or Italian vessels of war" that they entered American waters at their own peril; he had, he said, issued orders to "shoot on sight" at such craft.

Other torpedoings followed. On October 17, the destroyer *Kearny,* doing convoy duty on the Iceland run, was hit by a torpedo with the loss of eleven men killed. On October 31 the *Reuben James* lost 96 men in a similar attack. Speaking October 27, after the attack on the *Kearny,* the President told the country: "We have wished to avoid shooting. But the shooting has started. And history has recorded who fired the first shot. . . ."

Reclaiming "freedom of the seas." While the country was still excited over the "attack"

17. E. J. King and W. M. Whitehill, *Fleet Admiral King: A Naval Record* (New York: W. W. Norton & Company, 1952), p. 343 (italics inserted).

on the *Greer,* the President thought the time had come to get rid of as many as possible of the troublesome remaining restrictions of the neutrality law. On October 9, 1941, he asked Congress for repeal of the section forbidding the arming of merchant vessels. "We intend," he said, "to maintain the policy of protecting the freedom of the seas against domination by any foreign power which has become crazed with a desire to control the world." In spite of large anti-interventionist blocs in both houses of Congress, in spite of warnings that repeal meant war, Congress passed and the President signed on November 17, 1941, a law that went further than he had asked. It not only permitted the arming of American merchantmen, but also repealed the cash-and-carry and combat area provisions of the law of 1939. American merchant ships were now free to arm themselves and to sail anywhere on the globe, carrying, if their owners wished, arms, ammunition, and implements of war for the British, the Russians, or the Chinese.[18] American destroyers and German submarines were already trading depth charges for torpedoes in the North Atlantic. With all restrictions removed from American merchant ships, it is any one's guess how long the country would have waited before an accumulation of "incidents" would have drawn a declaration of war from a reluctant Congress—or a reluctant Führer. The Japanese eliminated any such period of waiting.

Hitler Declines a Challenge

There can be little doubt that by the fall of 1941 Roosevelt wished war with Germany, that he had concluded that only through active participation by the United States could Germany and Italy be defeated. He never said so publicly nor, so far as the records have revealed, privately. He exasperated the more

18. The bill passed Congress by votes of 50 to 37 in the Senate, 212 to 194 in the House. Its passage left intact the National Munitions Control Board, the section forbidding Americans to travel on belligerent ships, and the ban on loans to belligerent governments. The last-named provision had been rendered academic by the lend-lease policy.

war-minded of his advisers, like Secretary Stimson, by his failure to share frankly with the American people his apparent conviction that the road to national security lay through war. He feared, we may assume, to call for a declaration of war as long as the response of Congress and the public was in doubt. As late as November 5, 1941, a poll conducted by the American Institute of Public Opinion showed 63 percent noes to 26 percent yeses in answer to the question: Should Congress pass a resolution declaring that a state of war exists between the United States and Germany? [19] In Congress, the bill for arming merchant ships had carried by a vote, in the two houses, of 262 in favor, 231 against. To a declaration of war a still more formidable opposition might be expected. A defeat on this crucial issue would, from the President's point of view, have been disastrous. A victory by such a slender margin would have been an inauspicious beginning of a war for survival.

So, it would appear, the President tried to provoke Hitler into declaring war or into committing an overt act that would silence American opposition to war. The President's words and actions toward Germany, from August to November 1941, were not the words or actions of a man who wished peace. He committed himself, in the Atlantic Charter, to "the final destruction of the Nazi tyranny," he sent the navy out to "shoot on sight" at German U-boats, and declared "The shooting has started." In reverting to a defense of "freedom of the seas," in sweeping away virtually all the safeguards against war in the neutrality legislation, he was inviting collisions with Germany that must surely lead to war.

Why, in the face of American unneutrality, did Hitler shun war with the United States? From the time of the destroyer deal in September 1940, the United States had committed one unfriendly act after another. It was overtly aiding Hitler's foes in ways that a belligerent would hardly have stood for in any prior war. Yet Hitler issued no ultimatum, threatened no reprisals. He said merely, after Roosevelt's shoot-on-sight order, that German submarines would defend themselves.[20] The reasons for Hitler's forbearance are clear enough. However irrationally he may have acted in other matters, in this one he was realistic and rational. He well knew the result of American participation in the war of 1914. Germany had lost that war by inviting attack from the United States. The Führer was determined to avoid repeating that mistake if possible, until he had won his war in Europe. When he had crushed Russia and defeated or cowed Britain, there would be time enough to reckon with America.

19. Hadly Cantril, ed., *Public Opinion, 1935–1946* (Princeton: Princeton University Press, 1951), p. 1172. It is interesting to compare this result with that of another poll taken after the Japanese attack on Pearl Harbor but before the German declaration of war. To the question: Should President Roosevelt have asked Congress to declare war against Germany as well as Japan? 90 percent answered yes, 7 percent no. Ibid., p. 1173.

20. This whole subject is well presented in Trefousse, *Germany and American Neutrality.*

While the United States was drifting into an undeclared naval war with Germany in the Atlantic, it was approaching a crisis in its relations with Japan in the Pacific. Japan followed up its announcement of the "New Order for East Asia" by seizing, in February 1939, the large island of Hainan off the south China coast, and, a month later, the Spratly Islands in the South China Sea. Hainan, a Chinese island, was in the French sphere of influence; it also lay in close proximity to the British shipping lane between Singapore and Hong Kong. The Spratly Islands, claimed by France, were uncomfortably close to French Indochina and the American Philippines. Japan, in other words, while ostensibly fighting only China, was moving southward into an area where her forces constituted a potential threat to the possessions of France, the United States, and Great Britain, and even to those of the Netherlands. At the same time she continued her policy of gradually closing the door of China to western trade and western culture.

Ambassador Joseph C. Grew, at home in the United States during the summer of 1939, found, as he wrote, "an unmistakable hardening of the Administration's attitude toward Japan and a marked disinclination to allow American interests to be crowded out of China." [1] This hardening attitude took tangible form when, on July 26, 1939, the United States gave the required six months notice of the abrogation of its 1911 commercial treaty with Japan; thus it would be free, early in 1940, to restrict Japan's trade with the United States in any way it might deem expedient. "Methods short of war" were in the making.

Upon returning to his post in Tokyo, Grew publicly warned the people of Japan that the policy of their government was alienating the friendship of the United States. In a speech (October 19, 1939) to the America-Japan Society of Tokyo, which he described as coming "straight from the horse's mouth," the ambassador pointed out that the American people

38

Pearl Harbor

1. J. C. Grew, *Turbulent Era: A Diplomatic Record of Forty Years, 1904–1945,* 2 vols. (Boston: Houghton Mifflin Company, 1952), 2: 1211–12.

have good reason to believe that an effort is being made to establish control, in Japan's own interest, of large areas on the continent of Asia and to impose upon those areas a system of closed economy. It is this thought, added to the effect of the bombings, the indignities, the manifold interference with American rights, that accounts for the attitude of the American people to Japan today. . . .[2]

When this speech was delivered, Europe had been at war for seven weeks. The "phony war" of the following months had little effect on the Far Eastern situation, but the spring and summer of 1940 seemed to open magnificent opportunities to the ambitious Japanese. First the Netherlands and then France succumbed to German might; only the English Channel and the Royal Air Force and Navy barred Hitler from the conquest of Great Britain, and how long those barriers would hold no one could foretell. French Indochina, the Netherlands East Indies, and British Malaya appeared as tempting prizes to Hitler's Asiatic partner. A new Japanese ministry, headed, like that of 1938, by Prince Konoye, proclaimed on August 1 a "New Order for Greater East Asia." This enlargement of Japan's prospective empire, also called the "Greater East Asia Co-prosperity Sphere," was chiefly the plan of the new Foreign Minister, Yosuke Matsuoka. Aggressive, boastful and garrulous, pro-Axis and anti-United States, Matsuoka was described by Secretary Hull as being "as crooked as a basket of fishhooks." The Greater East Asia Co-prosperity Sphere was defined, under his inspiration, by a Liaison Conference (cabinet and Army and Navy leaders) in Tokyo, September 19, 1940, as comprising the former German islands under mandate to Japan since 1920 (the Carolines, Marianas, and Marshalls), French Indochina and French islands in the Pacific, Thailand, British Malaya and Borneo, the Dutch East Indies, Burma, Australia, New Zealand, and India, "with Japan, Manchuria, and China as the backbone." An item conspicuously missing from this list, no doubt out of temporary def-

erence to the United States, was the Philippines. To take care of such omissions, Matsuoka had added an "etc." at the end of his enumeration and in addition had commented that "this sphere could be automatically broadened in the course of time."[3]

In April, after the fall of Holland, Secretary Hull had put up a no-trespassing sign on the Netherlands East Indies, warning that any alteration of their status by other than peaceful means "would be prejudicial to the cause of stability, peace, and security . . . in the entire Pacific area." The Japanese heeded the caution for the time being, but in August submitted to the local officials in Indochina a demand for access to the ports, cities, and airfields of the northern part of the French possession. These were important to the Japanese because they commanded a principal supply route to the Chinese at Chungking. Pressure by Hitler on the Vichy regime forced the French to give way. Representatives of Vichy continued in office in the colony, but on September 22 key centers in the Tonkin area were occupied by Japanese forces. They could now halt supplies to China via the railroad from Hanoi, and their planes could threaten traffic over the Burma Road.

The Tripartite Pact

Matsuoka, in the meantime, had opened negotiations for an outright alliance with Germany and Italy.[4] On September 27, 1940, representatives of the three powers signed in Berlin a Tripartite Pact, comprising mutual recognition by the three partners of the "new orders" instituted by them in Europe and Greater East Asia respectively, and also a defensive alliance. By the latter (Article Three) Germany, Italy, and Japan agreed:

---

2. Grew, *Turbulent Era*, 2: 1219–20.

3. Herbert Feis, *The Road to Pearl Harbor: The Coming of the War Between the United States and Japan* (Princeton: Princeton University Press, 1950), pp. 114, 120.
4. The Anti-Comintern Pact had become a dead letter upon Hitler's entering his partnership with Stalin in August 1939.

to assist one another with all political, economic and military means when one of the three contracting powers is attacked by a power at present not involved in the European war or in the Chinese-Japanese conflict.

This article was obviously aimed at the United States, since another article excluded Russia from its application. Its purpose was to deter the United States from entering the war against either Germany or Japan by the warning that by so doing it would have to fight all three Axis powers. With American interference thus fended off, Matsuoka believed, Japan could readily take possession of French, Dutch, and British colonies in Greater East Asia. He hoped, too, that the pact would enable Japan to improve her relations with the Soviet Union and, by isolating China, to compel Chiang Kai-shek to make a peace satisfactory to Japan.[5] This was the bright mirage that dazzled Yosuke Matsuoka and led Japan along the road to disaster.

The United States Applies Pressure

Far from intimidating the United States, the Tripartite Pact still further stiffened the American attitude toward the Axis. The threat of encirclement made the two wars one in American eyes, and, in the mind of President Roosevelt at any rate, strengthened the determination to aid Britain. Roosevelt followed up his reelection in November by proposing the lend-lease policy, which became law in March 1941. In a letter to Ambassador Grew he explained the "global strategy" that he thought imperative in the interest of American

security. The President wrote, January 21, 1941:

> Our strategy of giving them [the British] assistance toward ensuring our own security must envisage both sending supplies to England and helping to prevent a closing of channels of communication to and from various parts of the world, so that other important sources of supply will not be denied to the British and be added to the assets of the other side.[6]

The President referred specifically in this connection to the Dutch East Indies and British Malaya, sources of rubber, petroleum, and tin. A few weeks later (February 14, 1941), Mr. Dooman, of the American embassy in Tokyo, passed on this idea to the Japanese Vice Minister for Foreign Affairs. He added that the United States had a direct as well as an indirect interest in the products of Malaya and the N.E.I. and that "a Japanese threat to occupy areas from which the United States procured essential primary commodities would not be tolerated."[7]

As the fateful year 1941 dawned, friction between the United States and Japan was increasing. Resentful of Japan's assaults upon China's independence and of violations of the open door, the United States was now seriously concerned about Japan's affiliation with the European Axis and her threatened appropriation of the rich raw materials of Southeast Asia. During 1940, the United States had begun to exert economic pressure upon Japan. The launching of the rearmament program in the spring and summer furnished a pretext for cutting off supplies from Japan on the ground that they were needed at home. On July 25, 1940, the President prohibited the export without license of petroleum, petroleum products, and scrap metal. Six days later he placed an embargo upon the export of aviation gasoline to all countries outside the Western Hemisphere, except for the use of American planes in the service of foreign countries. As an answer, presumably, to the Japanese landings in Indochina and the advance news of

5. F. C. Jones, *Japan's New Order in East Asia, 1937–1945* (New York: Oxford University Press, 1954), pp. 195–202; Feis, *Road to Pearl Harbor,* pp. 111–17. By a secret exchange of notes at the time of signing the pact, the parties agreed that any question of whether one of the powers had been attacked within the meaning of Article Three would be decided by consultation between them. The Soviet Union had signed a non-aggression treaty with Nationalist China in August 1937 and from that time until attacked by Germany in 1941, sent to China large quantities of military supplies, including several hundred airplanes.

6. Grew, *Turbulent Era,* 2: 1259–66.
7. Grew, *Turbulent Era,* 2: 1307.

the signing of the Tripartite Pact, the President on September 26, placed a similar embargo on exports of scrap iron and steel, making shipments to Great Britain the only exception.[8] Other gestures designed as warnings to Japan were a $25,000,000 loan to China through the Export-Import Bank, and a notice to all American citizens in the Far East urging that they return to America.

Deadlocked Negotiations

Such measures as these, and the possibility of still more drastic ones, without doubt gave Japan serious concern, for her industry and her ability to make war were heavily dependent upon her trade with the United States. Japanese policy in the winter and spring of 1941 apparently had a three-fold purpose: (1) to reach agreement with the United States if this was possible at not too great a cost; (2) to bring the Netherlands East Indies into the Co-prosperity Sphere, peaceably if possible, forcibly if necessary; (3) to remove the danger of an attack from the Soviet Union if Japan's southward expansion should involve her in war with the United States or Great Britain.

Serious negotiations with the United States began in April, following the arrival in Washington of a new Japanese ambassador, Admiral Kichisaburo Nomura. Nomura's negotiations with Hull were complicated by the presence in Washington of two Roman Catholic clerics, Bishop James E. Walsh and Father James M. Drought of the Maryknoll Society, who had returned from a visit to Japan bringing what they thought to be an offer from the Japanese

government. Japan, they reported, was ready to recall Japanese troops from China and to nullify the Tripartite Pact insofar as it was a threat to the United States. The source of this supposed offer is unknown.[9] Hull soon discovered that it misrepresented Japanese intentions.

Actually, as the conversations with Nomura revealed, Japan was asking the United States to press Chiang Kai-shek to accept Japan's terms (including merger of his government with the puppet government in Nanking, and retention of some Japanese troops in North China and Inner Mongolia). Should he refuse, the United States should deprive him of any further aid. The United States was also to restore normal trade with Japan (insofar as articles needed by Japan were available) and to assist Japan in obtaining raw materials from Southeast Asia to meet her needs. In return, Japan would promise to use only peaceful means in seeking her ends in Southeast Asia and would reserve to herself the right to interpret her obligations under the Tripartite Pact; in other words, if the United States went to war with Germany, Japan would decide independently whether she was bound to assist her Axis partner.

The United States, for its part, asked Japan's acceptance of four general principles set forth by Secretary Hull: (1) respect for the sovereignty and territorial integrity of all nations; (2) noninterference in the internal affairs of other countries; (3) the open door, or equality of commercial opportunity; (4) no disturbance of the status quo in the Pacific except by peaceful means. Specifically the United States asked that Japan withdraw her armed forces from China and Indochina, accept the government of Chiang Kai-shek as the only legitimate government of China, and disavow the Tripartite Pact as aimed at the

8. The use of such measures was encouraged by Ambassador Grew, who reversed his former disapproval of economic sanctions. In what he described as a "green light telegram," September 12, 1940, he advised the State Department: "Until such time as there is a complete regeneration of thought in this country [Japan], a show of force, together with a determination to employ it if need be, can alone contribute effectively to the achievement of [an equitable adjustment of the Pacific problem] and to our own future security." Grew, *Turbulent Era,* 2: 1229.

9. John H. Boyle, "The Drought-Walsh Mission to Japan," *Pacific Historical Review,* 34 (May 1965), 141–61. See also R. J. C. Butow, "The Hull-Nomura Conversations: A Fundamental Misconception," *American Historical Review,* 65 (July 1960), 822–36, and W. L. Langer and S. E. Gleason, *The Undeclared War, 1940–1941* (New York: Harper & Row, Publishers, 1953), pp. 314–15, 321, *et passim.*

United States. Each government adhered inflexibly to its set of demands, and by June 1941, an impasse had been reached.

By June, also, Japan had been rebuffed in her attempt by negotiation to take over practical control of the Netherlands East Indies. The Netherlands government, in exile in London, proved more intractable than had the Vichy government of France, and a Japanese mission, which had gone to Batavia in September 1940 in quest of special concessions, returned home empty-handed in June 1941.[10]

With Russia the Japanese government was more successful, though the success there was illusory. On April 13, 1941, in Moscow, Matsuoka signed with Molotov a five-year treaty of neutrality, pledging each party to remain neutral if the other should become involved in war. Russia agreed to respect the territorial integrity of Manchukuo, and Japan gave a similar promise with respect to Outer Mongolia, which had fallen under Soviet influence. Matsuoka, believing that Japan's southward drive might bring conflict with Great Britain or the United States or both, thought the promise of Russia's neutrality worth a price. He promised surrender of Japanese economic concessions in North Sakhalin (a promise that was not carried out). He did not know, though he had just come from Berlin, that Hitler was preparing to attack the Soviet Union. When that event took place, on June 22, 1941, the neutrality pact was of more value to the U.S.S.R. than to Japan.[11]

Japan Moves South and Is Rebuked

Matsuoka, as a matter of fact, wished to violate the pact that he had just made and to join Germany in war against the Soviets, but he was overruled. His cabinet colleagues and the top military men preferred a southward drive combined with neutrality in the Russo-German war. An Imperial Conference on July 2 decided upon an advance into southern Indo-

china and Thailand, even at the risk of war with the United States and Britain. Indochina would serve as a takeoff point for attacks on Singapore and the Netherlands Indies. A cabinet reorganization eliminated Matsuoka from the Foreign Office. On July 24, with the reluctant consent of the Vichy government, Japanese troops landed in southern Indochina. An accord with Vichy, signed a few days later, permitted the Japanese to establish air and naval bases in the colony, while Japan promised to respect French political and territorial rights there.

This renewal of aggressive action by Japan, clearly designed as a prelude to armed attack upon Malaya and the Netherlands Indies,[12] brought quick response from the United States, Great Britain and the Netherlands. The Japanese excuse—that the occupation was a defensive measure against alleged British designs—was answered by President Roosevelt with a proposal that Indochina be neutralized. This suggestion was refused by Japan. In the meantime, the United States had broken off the discussions with Nomura that had been proceeding since April, and had announced, July 25, the freezing of all Japanese funds in the United States. Within a few days Great Britain and the Netherlands took similar action. This was the final stroke in cutting Japan off from her most important markets and sources of raw material. Would Japan submit or fight, or was some compromise still possible?

There were those in both England and the United States who believed that Japan would retreat before a united front of the democracies. With this idea in mind, Winston Churchill, at the Atlantic Conference in August,[13] urged President Roosevelt to warn

---

10. Jones, *Japan's New Order,* pp. 242–46.
11. Jones, *Japan's New Order,* pp. 210–20.

12. U. S. Naval Intelligence had broken one of the principal Japanese codes and in the operation known as "Magic" was regularly intercepting and translating Japanese broadcasts to diplomatic representatives abroad. Thus the United States and, through it, the British government, knew in advance not only of the plan against Indochina but also of the proposed further moves against British and Dutch possessions. Jones, *Japan's New Order,* p. 263.
13. See p. 373.

Japan that an attack on British or Dutch possessions in the Far East would compel the United States "to take counter-measures, even though these might lead to war between the United States and Japan." These fighting words, which Roosevelt had apparently agreed to, were toned down at the insistence of the State Department, and the warning that the President read to the Japanese ambassador on August 17 was as follows:

> This Government now finds it necessary to say to the Government of Japan that if the Japanese Government takes any further steps in pursuance of a policy or program of military domination by force or threat of force of neighboring countries, the Government of the United States will be compelled to take immediately any and all steps which it may deem necessary toward safeguarding the legitimate rights and interest of the United States and American nationals and toward insuring the safety and security of the United States.

The warning was accompanied by an offer to reopen the interrupted conversations and to institute a helpful economic program for the Pacific area if Japan were willing "to suspend its expansionist activities . . . and to embark upon a peaceful program for the Pacific . . ." [14]

Konoye Seeks a Meeting with Roosevelt

Upon Roosevelt's return from the Atlantic Conference with Churchill, he had found awaiting him a proposal for a Pacific Conference with Prince Konoye, the Japanese Premier. Konoye had suggested that a personal meeting of the two statesmen might settle controversies that seemed otherwise insoluble. The proposal was heartily endorsed by Ambassador Grew. Grew believed that Japan was ready to make important concessions. As he saw it, the inconclusive and costly war in China, economic pressure from the democ-

racies, and growing distrust of Germany had combined to convince the cabinet, the Emperor, and many top military men that Japan was following a ruinous course. Retreat would be difficult and would meet strenuous opposition, but Grew believed, and the entire embassy staff shared his view, that a dramatic meeting of Premier and President, productive of a promising economic program, even though at the cost of important concessions, would catch the popular imagination and overwhelm the opposition. Confidence in this outcome was strengthened by the assurance that such a program would have the full support of the Emperor. Specifically, Grew believed that Konoye was ready to satisfy the United States in regard to the Tripartite Pact and to withdraw Japanese troops both from Indochina and from China, "with the face-saving expedient of being permitted to retain a limited number of troops in North China and Inner Mongolia temporarily." [15]

President Roosevelt was at first quite taken with the suggestion of a Pacific Conference. Secretary Hull, however, threw cold water on the idea. He doubted the ability of the Premier, whatever his intentions, to gain the consent of the militarists to a program acceptable to the United States; and he insisted that the general lines of an acceptable agreement be sketched out before the meeting. Otherwise, he feared the meeting would result in a fiasco, which Japanese propaganda would then turn against the United States. On the necessity of a preliminary agreement, the President accepted Hull's position, and Konoye was asked to state Japan's terms.

In a talk with Grew on September 6, Konoye stated that he accepted "conclusively and wholeheartedly" (the Foreign Office later added the weasel words "in principle") the four principles of international behavior previously set forth by Secretary Hull.[16] But on

---

14. Langer and Gleason, *The Undeclared War*, pp. 670–77, 694–95; Winston S. Churchill, *The Grand Alliance,* Vol. 3 of *The Second World War* (Boston: Houghton Mifflin Company, 1950), pp. 440, 446.

15. Grew, *Turbulent Era,* 2: 1355. This whole question is treated in much detail in ibid., pp. 1262–1375, with valuable footnotes by the editor, Walter Johnson. Grew continued to believe after the war, as he believed in 1941, that a Roosevelt-Konoye meeting might well have succeeded in averting war.

16. Grew, *Turbulent Era,* 2: 1326, 1331.

specific confessions that they were willing to make, the Japanese refused to commit themselves, possibly, as Grew believed, because they feared that leaks in the Foreign Office would reveal such proposals prematurely to Matsuoka and other extremists. In the absence of specific advance commitments by Japan, President Roosevelt was unwilling to meet the Premier. On October 16 the Konoye ministry resigned, and whatever chance there was for an agreement at the top level was lost.

Was Grew right in thinking there was a chance for agreement? Konoye's memoirs, published after his postwar suicide, reveal at least part of what was in his mind. In seeking the consent of the Army and Navy to his plan, Konoye assured the War and Navy Ministers that Japan would "insist, of course, on the firm establishment of the Greater East Asia Co-prosperity Sphere," while American claims would be based on the Nine-Power Treaty. The two were incompatible; but, Konoye pointed out, the United States had stated its readiness to discuss revision of the treaty "through legal means," while Japan could not expect immediate fulfillment of her "ideal" of the Co-prosperity Sphere. There was, in other words, enough flexibility in each program to enable Konoye to say: "I do not believe that Japanese-American talks are an impossibility if they are carried out with broad-mindedness. . . ."

But Konoye was ready with an alternative plan if the meeting did not result in an agreement. If the President did not "understand," Konoye would

> be fully prepared to break off the talks and return home. It is, therefore [he added] an undertaking which must be carried out while being fully prepared for war against America. [If the talks should fail] the people will know that a Japanese-American war could not be avoided. This would aid in consolidating their determination. The world in general, also, would . . . know that great efforts were made [by Japan] in behalf of maintaining peace in the Pacific. . . .[17]

17. Quoted in Grew, *Turbulent Era,* 2: 1303n.

It seems a fair supposition that Konoye had real hopes of coming to an agreement with Roosevelt but at the same time had in mind the propaganda value of a meeting that failed—blame for the failure, of course, to be saddled upon the United States. In view of the reluctance, certainly of the Navy, possibly of the Army, to face a war with the United States (to be mentioned below), it seems at least possible that a Roosevelt-Konoye meeting might have produced an agreement. One may question whether such a meeting would have involved any risks for the United States serious enough to justify the American refusal.

Final Negotiations

The discussions of a possible Roosevelt-Konoye meeting were carried on simultaneously with Japanese planning for war if no agreement with America were reached. An Imperial Conference on September 6 had decided upon war with the United States, Great Britain, and the Netherlands if by the beginning of October the negotiations did not show promise of a satisfactory outcome. The Emperor had accepted this decision unwillingly, and, though the Supreme Command ("top brass" of the Army and Navy) had proposed it, levelheaded men in both services had misgivings. Early in October, General Tojo, Minister of War, intimated to Konoye that if the Navy would state explicitly its opposition to war with America, "the Army would have to reconsider its position." When the Navy refused to take the odium by advertising its reluctance, Tojo advised that the cabinet resign and proposed that Prince Higashikuni, a member of the royal family, become Premier and take the responsibility of reversing the decision of September 6.[18] This solution proved unfeasible, and on October 18 General Tojo himself became Premier. Halfhearted

18. This is the course of events described by Toshikazu Kase, a Foreign Office official, in *Journey to the Missouri* (New Haven: Yale University Press, 1950), pp. 46–64. On the attitude of the Navy see also Jones, *Japan's New Order,* pp. 290–91.

attempts were made, by the Emperor and others, to avoid a war that few responsible people wanted, but Japan had got herself "out on a limb" and could not crawl back without serious loss of face, as well as possible assassination of officials responsible for a retreat.

Upon Tojo's taking office it was announced that the change in cabinets meant no change in policy and that negotiations with the United States would continue. An Imperial Conference of November 5 resolved to continue the negotiations still further. A few concessions were agreed to, and another ambassador, Saburo Kurusu, was sent to assist Nomura in Washington. The Emperor requested that efforts at a peaceful agreement with America be redoubled. At the same time, the Conference resolved that preparations for war should be completed by early December. Time was now really running out.

During the next two weeks, operation "Magic"—the decoding and translation by Naval Intelligence of intercepted Japanese messages—picked up a steady stream of messages passing back and forth between Tokyo and the Japanese embassy in Washington. It was thus known that the Japanese envoys had been given two sets of proposals to lay before the American government, Plan A and Plan B, the latter to be presented if the former were rejected. Plan B represented the greatest concessions that Japan was willing to make. It was known, too, that Japan had set a deadline, first November 25, later November 29, by which time the negotiations must be completed. "After that," ran one intercepted message, "things are automatically going to happen." Pleas from the ambassadors (Kurusu arrived in Washington November 15) for more time and further concessions met with blunt refusals in Tokyo. Washington knew, therefore, that unless by November 29 the United States accepted Japanese Plan B, or persuaded Japan to take something less, "things" were "going to happen." Washington did not know what or where, but Japanese concentrations of troops and transports pointed to attacks on British Malaya, Thailand, the Dutch East Indies, or possibly the Philippines.

It was assumed in Washington that an attack on the British or Dutch possessions would, or at least ought to, bring the United States into the war. President Roosevelt had, in fact, given secret assurances to this effect to the British. Such a course was in line with Roosevelt's "global strategy" and had been made plain to Japan. But neither the Army nor the Navy was prepared for war in the Pacific; both desperately needed time. Secretary of War Stimson, in particular, believed that in three months he could build up a force of B-17's (Flying Fortresses) in the Philippines that could block Japan's southward expansion.[19] So the Army and Navy pleaded for a postponement of the showdown, for three months at least, and there was talk of a possible temporary *modus vivendi* if no permanent agreement could be reached.

Japanese Plan A having been presented piecemeal and rejected by Secretary Hull, the envoys brought in on November 20 their Plan B, which they described as a *modus vivendi*, or way of getting along, presumably only temporarily. The proposals were as follows: (1) neither government to send armed forces into the Southeast Asia or South Pacific area, except Indochina; (2) the two governments to cooperate to secure needed commodities from the Netherlands Indies; (3) commercial relations to be restored to their status before the freezing of funds, the United States to supply Japan with "the required quantity of oil"; (4) the United States "not to resort to measures and actions prejudicial to the endeavors for the restoration of general peace between Japan and China"; (5) Japan to move its troops in southern Indochina into the northern portion upon the conclusion of this agreement, and to withdraw all troops from Indochina upon the making of peace with China "or the establishment of an equitable peace in the Pacific area."

In regard to Japan's relations with Ger-

---

19. This belief of Stimson's betrayed a naive faith in the capacity of unsupported air power, particularly since no adequate force of fighter planes would be available for protection of the bombers. Feis, *Road to Pearl Harbor*, p. 300.

many, not mentioned in the document, Kurusu had said to President Roosevelt on November 17 that Japan could not openly abandon the Tripartite Pact but "had no intention of becoming a tool of Germany nor did she mean to wait until the United States became deeply involved in the battle of the Atlantic and then stab her in the back." [20]

These proposals the United States rejected. Acceptance of them, as Cordell Hull wrote later, "would have placed her [Japan] in a commanding position later to acquire control of the entire western Pacific area. . . . It would have meant abject surrender of our position under intimidation. . . ." But since the Army and Navy were pressing for time, Hull prepared a *modus vivendi* of his own. This he thought of proposing to the Japanese as a basis for a three months' truce, during which either a permanent agreement might be reached or, if not, the armed forces would have had that much more time to prepare for war. The new proposals comprised mutual pledges of peaceful policy; promises that neither would advance further in the Pacific area by means of force or threat of force; withdrawal of Japanese forces from southern to northern Indochina and limitation of those in that area to 25,000; resumption of trade with Japan on a limited scale; sale of petroleum to Japan for civilian use only; any settlement between Japan and China to be "based upon the principles of peace, law, order, and justice."

The difference between these proposals and Japan's Plan B was not so wide as to rule out possible agreement. On the other hand, they provided so little for China (nothing but a "pious hope," in fact), that China, which, with the United Kingdom, the Netherlands, and Australia, was consulted about them, protested bitterly. Since neither the British nor the Dutch greeted them with enthusiasm, and since their publication at home was sure to bring charges of "appeasement," Hull decided reluctantly and after consulting with Roosevelt, to discard the *modus vivendi* en-

20. Jones, *Japan's New Order,* p. 304.

tirely and to submit instead a ten-point program for a permanent settlement along strictly American lines. Since this program called for withdrawal of all Japanese troops from China and Indochina and for a virtual disavowal of the Axis Pact, Hull must have known when he presented it on November 26 that Japan would spurn it and that "things" would begin to happen. He made this clear next day by telling Stimson: "I have washed my hands of it, and it [the situation] is now in the hands of you and Knox, the Army and Navy."

Would the United States Fight if Not Attacked?

The note of November 26, sometimes referred to as an ultimatum, was, more accurately, a rejection of Japan's ultimatum of November 20. As far as the United States was concerned, it left the door open for further negotiation. In fact, the Army and Navy still hoped for at least a postponement of hostilities. Intercepted messages, however, directing Japanese envoys in the democracies to burn their codes and destroy their code machines and referring to war as imminent, made it plain that Japan was bent on war. The movement of a large Japanese convoy down the China coast in the direction of Indochina pointed surely to a southern campaign. Its objective might be Thailand, British Malaya, the Netherlands Indies, or the Philippines—any or all of these. Prevailing opinion in Washington in these last days of peace held that Japan would not deliberately attack United States territory, and the problem that most exercised the minds of the President and his advisers was whether American opinion, in Congress and out, would support the administration in making war if the Japanese attack should fall only upon British or Dutch or Thai territory.

To meet this contingency the President set his advisers to work drafting a message to Congress for the purpose of demonstrating to the legislators that any further Japanese advance in Southeast Asia would threaten the vital interests of the United States and thus justify armed resistance.[21] But this message to Congress was to be preceded by a last ditch attempt to dissuade Japan from aggression— a direct appeal from the President to the Emperor. The idea of an appeal to the Emperor was threshed over for at least a week before the message was sent. One draft revived the idea of a *modus vivendi,* with a ninety-day truce between Japan and China as well as between Japan and the western powers.[22] The message actually sent, on the evening of December 6, too late to have any effect, contained no such proposal. It reviewed the long friendship between Japan and the United States and the current threats to it and described the occupation of Indochina as a threat hanging over the peoples of Malaya, the Netherlands Indies, Thailand, and the Philippines. It offered guarantees that no other power would occupy Indochina if Japan withdrew, and promised: "Thus a withdrawal of the Japanese forces from Indo-China would result in the

assurance of peace throughout the whole of the South Pacific area." It is notable that this last appeal to Japan placed all the emphasis upon Southeast Asia, none upon China. This final attempt to stave off hostilities reached Ambassador Grew in Tokyo too late for delivery to the Emperor until almost the moment of the fateful Pearl Harbor attack.

The Japanese reply to the American note of November 26—a long complaint against American policy in the Far East ending with notice of the breaking off of the negotiations —was presented by the ambassadors to the Secretary of State at 2:20, Washington time, on Sunday afternoon, December 7, 1941. The hour set for its delivery had been one o'clock, a few minutes before the first bombs were to fall on Pearl Harbor. Delay in decoding postponed the envoys' call upon Secretary Hull. When they reached his office, he knew, as they did not, of the Japanese surprise attack. After glancing at the note (of whose content he was already apprised through "Magic"), Mr. Hull castigated it as "crowded with infamous falsehoods and distortions," and showed the ambassadors the door. Later in the day came word that Japan had formally declared war, some two hours after the Pearl Harbor attack. Congress responded the next day (December 8) with a declaration of war against Japan. The British government had done the same a few hours earlier. On November 29 Japan had received assurance that Germany would join her if she went to war with the United States. On December 11 Germany and Italy declared war. The United States was in the war "up to its neck," in Europe and in the Pacific.

21. The so-called "War Cabinet," comprising the President, Secretaries of State, War, and Navy, the Army Chief of Staff and the Chief of Naval Operations, discussed this problem in meetings on November 25 and 28. Secretary Stimson recorded in his diary of the earlier meeting that the President remarked on the probability of a surprise attack by the Japanese, "and the question was how we should maneuver them into the position of firing the first shot without allowing too much danger to ourselves." This passage has been cited in support of the thesis that Roosevelt "maneuvered" the Japanese into making the attack on Pearl Harbor. The most plausible explanation of the quoted passage is probably that advanced by Richard N. Current, namely, that, taken in context, the passage referred to the problem of convincing Congress and the public that an attack on friendly British, Dutch, or Thai territory would be equivalent to an attack on the United States, that is, "firing the first shot." Stimson himself had advocated striking the Japanese convoy from the air as it passed the Philippines. Other members of the "War Cabinet" preferred to wait until it committed a hostile act, such as an unmistakable approach to friendly territory. See R. N. Current, "How Stimson Meant to 'Maneuver' the Japanese," *Mississippi Valley Historical Review,* 40 (June 1953), 67–74; also id., *Secretary Stimson: A Study in Statecraft* (New Brunswick: Rutgers University Press, 1954), chap. 7.
22. The appeal to the Emperor and the proposed message to Congress, as well as the dilemma of what to do if Japan attacked others but not the United States, are discussed in detail in Langer and Gleason, *The Undeclared War,* pp. 911–35.

Post-Mortem on Pearl Harbor

The naval task force under Admiral Nagumo that launched the surprise attack on Pearl Harbor had been assembled behind a perfect screen of secrecy at Hitokappu Bay on Etorofu Island in the Kuriles. It had set out for the vicinity of Hawaii on November 25 with orders to launch the attack at dawn December 7 (December 8, Tokyo time), but with the understanding that it would be recalled if a settlement were reached in the meantime. Its assignment was performed with complete success but with results disastrous for Japan. Nothing could have so unified sentiment in the United States as the "sneak attack" at Pearl Harbor.

The phrase "sneak attack," however, was a convenient rationalization which helped to divert attention from the culpable negligence that made the surprise possible. There were several reasons why the attack should have been anticipated. In the "war games" of 1932, American carriers had launched a successful Sunday morning attack on the defending force at Pearl Harbor. This exploit gave the Japanese a perfect pattern but had apparently been forgotten by responsible Americans. As early as January 1941, Ambassador Grew reported to the State Department, Tokyo rumors that Japan would open hostilities with an air attack on Pearl Harbor. From September 1941 to the eve of the attack, intercepted Japanese instructions to the Japanese consul general in Honolulu showed a suspicious curiosity about the exact location of ships at Pearl Harbor. In November, when negotiations were approaching a climax, Ambassador Grew warned that hostile Japanese action might come "with dangerous and dramatic suddenness"; and Secretary Hull remarked to a meeting of the "War Cabinet" at the White House that the Japanese "might make the element of surprise a central point in their strategy," that "they might attack at various points simultaneously. . . ." The Japanese habit of striking first and declaring war later was well known. Why was Pearl Harbor asleep?

In answering that question, we may discard at once the discredited theory that President Roosevelt deliberately enticed the Japanese to attack Pearl Harbor in order to get the United States into the European War by the "back door." [23] That Roosevelt would voluntarily

have invited destruction of a major weapon, the Pacific Fleet, as a means toward involvement in a two-front war which he did not want, stands the test neither of reason nor of the evidence. The explanation for the disaster lies not in a conspiracy of FDR and a few close advisers, but in complacency and negligence, both in the administration in Washington and in the high command in Hawaii.

Certainly Washington was remiss in its failure to alert the Hawaiian commanders more emphatically to the possibility of surprise attack. "War warnings" were sent to the Army and Navy commanders there and in the Philippines on November 27, the day after the final note was handed to Japan. The warnings were not followed up as it seems clear they should have been when intercepted messages revealed that the zero hour was approaching. For reasons of security, knowledge of the "Magic" intercepts was limited to a very few persons in Washington. Their content was not communicated to the commanders in Hawaii or the Philippines. Even if it had been, there is no certainty that Admiral Husband E. Kimmel and General Walter C. Short in Hawaii would have acted with more foresight than they actually exhibited. The intercepts showed unmistakably that war was coming—somewhere. The only item that pointed specifically to an attack on the fleet at Pearl Harbor was the display of Japanese interest in the precise location of the ships there; and, as Roberta Wohlstetter has shown in her impressive study of the shortcomings of American intelligence operations in 1941, the Japanese were showing similar curiosity about ship locations in Panama, San Diego, San Francisco, Portland, Vancouver, and elsewhere.[24] Washington intelligence failed to see any special threat to Pearl Harbor (even though Pearl Harbor sheltered the prime target for Japanese attack). With the same

23. The most formidable presentation of this conspiracy theory is C. C. Tansill, *Back Door to War: The Roosevelt Foreign Policy* (Chicago: Henry Regnery Co., 1952). Others are listed in the Bibliographical Essay at the end of the book.

24. Roberta Wohlstetter, *Pearl Harbor: Warning and Decision* (Stanford: Stanford University Press, 1962), p. 390. A judicious brief summary of the mistakes and mischances that contributed to the Pearl Harbor disaster is M. S. Watson, *Chief of Staff: Pre-War Plans and Preparations* (Washington: Department of the Army, Historical Division, 1950), especially pp. 518–19.

information, Kimmel and Short might well have similarly failed in its interpretation. In the absence of more specific warnings from Washington, Admiral Kimmel and General Short took measures for protection against submarine attack and sabotage respectively. These measures apparently satisfied their superiors in Washington. They were not told to, nor did they, take special precautions against attack from the air.

Neither in Washington nor in Hawaii, it seems in retrospect, was there the alert imagination that imminent war with a tricky enemy called for. For Washington, the rather obvious explanation (certainly not a justification) of the blind spot is the fact that all eyes were fixed so intently on the Far East that earlier warnings of danger to Hawaii were forgotten. Japanese concentrations in Formosa (threatening the Philippines), large Japanese convoys heading for Malaya, other concentrations in the Carolines pointing toward the Netherlands Indies—all these were known, were real, were watched with anxiety. No one had spotted Admiral Nagumo's task force, plowing through the North Pacific toward Hawaii. No one dreamed, apparently, that Japan could be aiming another major blow in addition to the several for which preparations were visible.

There are other intriguing questions. Why did Roosevelt keep the Pacific Fleet at Pearl Harbor when its former commander, Admiral James O. Richardson, had advised that it would be both safer and more effective if operated from Pacific Coast bases? The probable answer is that Roosevelt, though realizing the military soundness of Richardson's advice, took a calculated military risk rather than withdraw the fleet in a move which both the Japanese and their Chinese victims would have viewed as a retreat by the United States.

Why did the Japanese, aware of the greatly superior material and human resources of the United States, initiate a war in which the long-range odds were so heavily against them? The answer lies partly, of course, in their reliance upon the prowess of their German ally, but also in their drawing a false lesson from history. Records of prewar military discussions suggest that Japanese optimists expected to repeat the achievements of their fathers against Russia in 1904–1905. In that conflict, a succession of early and impressive victories had worn down the determination of a stronger foe and led to a favorable peace. Would not the same strategy work against America? [25]

Finally, why did the United States think it necessary to oppose Japan's program of expansion up to the point where Japan had either to abandon it or to fight for it? American policy may have been right or wrong, but it had historical roots and a logical pattern. The United States had objected from the beginning to Japan's step-by-step domination of China. It began to talk of forcible resistance only after Japan allied herself with Germany and threatened to absorb in her Greater East Asia Co-prosperity Sphere areas considered vital to the free world. There may have been errors of judgment and missed opportunities for compromise, as Ambassador Grew believed; but the fact remains that Japan was bent upon expanding its empire in ways incompatible with Roosevelt's "global strategy," with his commitments to Great Britain, and with his moral commitments, at least, to Chiang Kai-shek. The United States did not choose to fight; it blocked Japan's path and left the choice to her.

25. Nobutaka Ike, ed., *Japan's Decision for War: Records of the 1941 Policy Conferences* (Stanford: Stanford University Press, 1967), p. xxv.

Upon entering World War II, the United States did not, as in 1917, hold itself aloof from its associates. In 1917–1918 the United States had described itself as an "associated power," not one of the Allies. In the later war, although it made no formal treaty of alliance, it took the lead in drawing up and signing, January 1, 1942, the Declaration by United Nations, which for practical purposes amounted to the same thing. Other signatories were the United Kingdom, the Soviet Union, and China; the five nations of the British Commonwealth, the governments in exile of eight European countries overrun by the Axis powers; and nine states of Latin America that had followed the United States into the war. The original signers numbered twenty-six; before the war's end the number had grown to forty-seven.[1]

The signatory governments, endorsing the "program of purposes and principles embodied in the . . . Atlantic Charter," and avowing their conviction "that complete victory over their enemies is essential to defend life, liberty, independence, and religious freedom, and to preserve human rights and justice," declared:

1. Each Government pledges itself to employ its full resources, military or economic, against those members of the Tripartite Pact and its adherents with which such government is at war.

2. Each Government pledges itself to cooperate with the Governments signatory hereto and not to make a separate armistice or peace with the enemies.

1. The original signers, in order of signing, were the United States, the United Kingdom, the U.S.S.R., China, Australia, Belgium, Canada, Costa Rica, Cuba, Czechoslovakia, Dominican Republic, El Salvador, Greece, Guatemala, Haiti, Honduras, India, Luxembourg, Netherlands, New Zealand, Nicaragua, Norway, Panama, Poland, Union of South Africa, Yugoslavia. Subsequent signers were Bolivia, Brazil, Chile, Colombia, Ecuador, Egypt, Ethiopia, France, Iran, Iraq, Lebanon, Liberia, Mexico, Paraguay, Peru, Philippines, Saudi Arabia, Syria, Turkey, Uruguay, Venezuela. All of these governments declared war against one or more of the Axis powers. Argentina declared war on March 27, 1945, but did not sign the Declaration by United Nations. *Documents on American Foreign Relations,* 7; July 1944–June 1945, pp. 301, 344–45. The text of the Declaration is in ibid., 4: 203, 208.

39

The Grand Alliance

In signing this declaration, with its pledge to employ the nation's full resources for war and its promise not to make a separate peace, President Roosevelt, as one authority has remarked, "virtually contracted an alliance, and this without the consent of any legislative body, and indeed almost without a voice raised in criticism." [2]

The members of this "grand alliance" contributed to the common cause in proportion to their ability combined with their enthusiasm, the contributions of many being purely nominal. The brunt of the fighting was borne by the "Big Three," the United States, the United Kingdom, and the Soviet Union, with China a poor fourth. The British Dominions, the Yugoslav guerrillas, and the Free French under General Charles de Gaulle did their full share. All the allies that contributed to the war, and some that did not, received the benefits of the lend-lease program of the United States.[3]

The United States and Great Britain

The most intimate cooperation was that between the United States and the United Kingdom. This cooperation originated at the highest level. Within a few hours after receiving the news from Pearl Harbor, Winston Churchill was planning a visit to Washington. He spent several weeks at the White House in December and January (with excursions to Ottawa and to Palm Beach). This conference (which was given the code name of "Arcadia") was the first of a notable series of meetings in which President and the Prime Minister and their advisers made decisions on matters of high strategy, both political and military.[4]

Not always did they see eye to eye, but they always resolved their differences amicably. The President, commanding the greater resources in men and matériel, had his way more often than did the Prime Minister.

On one basic matter there was never any difference of opinion between the two men: Hitler's Germany was Enemy Number One. This decision had been reached, it will be recalled, in staff conferences nearly a year before the United States entered the war.[5] Germany was a more dangerous foe than Japan, and her defeat must have priority. From the British point of view this was an obvious truth. To an American, after Pearl Harbor, it was less obvious, particularly to American commanders like General MacArthur and Admiral King, who had the task of fighting Japan. Even General Marshall, the Chief of Staff, sometimes wavered. Yet Roosevelt adhered consistently to the Germany-first policy and would have had the satisfaction, had he lived, of seeing Japan surrender three months after the defeat of Germany.

On some other important aspects of the war there were differences. Roosevelt rated much more highly than Churchill the importance of China and of assisting Chiang Kai-shek, perhaps because he expected that China would follow the American lead in international policy. This difference was not of too great practical importance, since available aid for Chiang was severely limited. The war against Japan was won not on the Chinese mainland but by sea and air attacks upon the Japanese homeland and its communications.

In the strategy of the war in Europe, such differences as arose were between the two men's military advisers rather than between Roosevelt and Churchill themselves. The Americans, anxious to deliver a knockout blow at Germany at the earliest possible moment, urged a crossing of the English Channel by Anglo-American forces in the spring

---

2. Dexter Perkins, *The American Approach to Foreign Policy* (Cambridge: Harvard University Press, 1952), pp. 138–39. For text of the Atlantic Charter see above, pp. 373–74n.
3. See p. 372.
4. In addition to the Atlantic Conference of August 1941 and the "Arcadia" Conference, meetings of the President and the Prime Minister occurred as follows: Washington, June 1942; Casablanca, January 1943; Washington, May 1943 ("Trident"); Quebec, August

1943 ("Quadrant"); Cairo, November 1943 (with Chiang Kai-shek); Teheran, November–December 1943 (with Stalin); Cairo, December 1943; Quebec, September 1944; Yalta, February 1945 (with Stalin).
5. See p. 373.

of 1943, with a possible preliminary crossing still earlier. The British, with tragic memories of the trench warfare of World War I, would not agree to such a crossing until assured of possession of overwhelming force and adequate landing equipment, and until Germany had been further worn down by blockade, bombing, and attrition on the Russian front. Nineteen forty-three, they insisted, was too early. In the face of this refusal, General Marshall proposed shifting the main American effort to the Pacific. Roosevelt at once vetoed this suggestion. A compromise was found in TORCH, the North African landing, in November 1942, followed by the advance into Sicily and Italy in 1943, and OVERLORD, the Normandy landing, in June 1944. The dispute had been over timing, not over the final objective. A proposal of Churchill's in 1944 that troops in Italy, earmarked for southern France, be sent instead across the Adriatic into Yugoslavia and perhaps as far as Vienna and Hungary (where they might have anticipated the Russian armies) was vetoed by Roosevelt. Churchill, disturbed by the advance of the Red armies,[6] was more concerned for the political future of Central Europe than were Roosevelt and his advisers, who tended to think in strictly military terms.[7]

One real difference in outlook between the two men is deserving of a paragraph. Roosevelt, an anti-imperialist, had no enthusiasm for preserving or restoring the colonial holdings of the French or the British, and occasionally urged upon Churchill the claims to independence of India or other British possessions. Churchill took a dim view of such ideas. Proud as Rudyard Kipling of his nation's imperial achievements, he proclaimed in the House of Commons, soon after the Anglo-American landing in North Africa: "I have not become the King's First Minister in order to preside over the liquidation of the British Empire."[8]

The anticolonialism of Roosevelt and Cordell Hull was traceable in principle to Woodrow Wilson's preaching of self-determination, to carry it no further back, but it had, too, an important economic significance. Colonial empires, even the liberal British Commonwealth, were associated with "imperial preference," with partially closed economic systems. These were contrary to the nondiscriminatory, or "open door," principle which Hull had tried to promote through the reciprocal trade treaties and the terms of the lend-lease agreements; but the best assurance of the end of "imperial preference" would be the end of empires. Here, as in some other matters, American principles were in harmony with American economic interests.[9]

Between conferences Roosevelt and Churchill kept in touch through frequent letters, telegrams, and telephone conversations. Roosevelt's friend, Harry Hopkins, was frequently in England and was in Churchill's confidence. In these various ways, regular diplomatic channels were largely bypassed.

---

6. Churchill's skepticism about Russia had interfered not at all with his welcome to Russia as an ally in June 1941. Cf. his classic remark apropos of Hitler's attack upon Russia: "If Hitler invaded Hell I would make at least a favourable reference to the Devil in the House of Commons." Winston S. Churchill, *The Grand Alliance*, Vol. 3 of *The Second World War* (Boston: Houghton Mifflin Company, 1950), p. 370.
7. K. R. Greenfield, *American Strategy in World War II: A Reconsideration* (Baltimore: The Johns Hopkins Press, 1963), pp. 16–48; R. M. Leighton, "Overlord Revisited: An Interpretation of American Strategy in the European War, 1942–1944," *American Historical Review*, 68 (July 1963), 919–37. An American suspicion that Churchill wished to substitute a thrust from the Mediterranean at the "soft underbelly" of Hitler's Europe for the cross-Channel invasion seems to have been unfounded. See, however, Chester Wilmot, *The Struggle for Europe* (New York: Harper & Row, Publishers, 1952), chap. 23; H. W. Baldwin, *Great Mistakes of the War* (New York: Harper & Row, Publishers, 1950), pp. 25–45.

8. R. E. Sherwood, *Roosevelt and Hopkins: An Intimate History* (New York: Harper & Row, Publishers, 1948), p. 656.
9. American economic objectives in the war are stressed in Gabriel Kolko, *The Politics of War: The World and United States Foreign Policy, 1943–1945* (New York: Random House, Inc., 1968). Kolko contends that the United States aimed to supplant Britain in the world's economy and to maintain or restore the capitalist status quo, even where its basis had been destroyed by war, as in Eastern Europe. See also below, Chapter 40, note 1.

As one consequence of the Arcadia Conference there was set up in Washington in January 1942 a body known as the Combined Chiefs of Staff. This was made up of the Joint Chiefs of Staff of the United States (the Army, Navy, and Air Force Chiefs, together with, later on, the Chief of Staff to the President) and deputies of the corresponding British Chiefs, the deputies being quartered in the Pentagon in offices adjacent to those of the American Chiefs. This body was charged with making and executing plans for the strategic conduct of the war, for meeting war requirements in matériel, for allocating munitions and transportation facilities, all, of course, under the general direction of the President and the Prime Minister.

Further machinery for Anglo-American collaboration took the form of a number of Combined Boards, of which the most important were those for Raw Materials, Munitions Assignments, Shipping Adjustment, Production and Resources, and Food. These were all created in 1942, with American and British members. On the last two, Canada also was represented. The purpose was to direct all materials and services available to the United Nations into channels where they would contribute most to winning the war.

There was, of course, friction between Americans and British at various levels, but on the whole, the branches of the English-speaking world cooperated with gratifying smoothness and success.

Wartime Relations with Russia: The Background

With the third member of the Big Three, the Soviet Union, such close and mutually trustful relations proved impossible, despite an undoubted wish on Roosevelt's part to create them. It would, indeed, have been miraculous if the sudden partnership in the war against Hitler had produced friendship and confidence where incompatible ideologies had long bred hatred and suspicion.

It will be well at this point to summarize briefly the story of prewar relations between the United States and the Soviet Union. The United States had hailed with enthusiasm the overthrow of the Czar in March 1917 and the establishment of a liberal provisional government in Russia, but enthusiasm had turned to dislike and suspicion when the Bolshevists, led by Lenin and Trotsky, seized power in November, made a separate peace with Germany, and adopted a program of world revolution. Communist Russia was excluded from the Paris Peace Conference and was long refused recognition by the United States. The reasons for withholding recognition (after an initial period when the permanence of the new regime was in doubt) were: (1) refusal of the U.S.S.R. to recognize the financial obligations of its predecessors; (2) its refusal to recognize claims of American citizens for damages sustained as a result of the revolution; (3) its denial of the validity of international agreements; (4) the subversive activities of the Communist International, the propaganda agency of the Moscow government, operating through Communist parties in the United States and other capitalist countries.

For a brief period in 1918–1919 American troops joined British and French forces in Archangel in futile cooperation with Russian anti-Bolshevik elements. The Siberian expedition of 1918–1920, on the other hand, was designed partly to safeguard Russian territory against Japanese expansionism.[10] At the Washington Conference of 1921–1922, though Russia was not invited to participate, the United States took the position that no action injurious to Russia must be taken, and was successful in persuading Japan to evacuate Siberia and return northern Sakhalin to Russia. The United States again took Russia's part in 1929, when Nationalist China undertook to oust Russia from the Russian-built and Russian-owned Chinese Eastern Railway. In other words, the United States, although

10. See p. 309.

withholding recognition from the Soviet government, took action repeatedly to protect the interests of the Russian people.

By 1933, some of the arguments against recognition had lost a part of their force. In Russia, Leon Trotsky, chief apostle of world revolution, had been expelled from the Communist party and from the country, and Stalin had adopted the slogan "Socialism in one country." To a considerable extent, the Soviet government had settled the claims of American individuals and corporations, as the price of doing new business with them. The economic depression of the early thirties aroused a hope that official recognition of Russia would expand the Russian market for American products. The Manchurian crisis had reemphasized the common interest of Russia and the United States in opposing Japanese expansion on the Asiatic mainland. Finally, the Roosevelt administration was not, like its predecessor, committed to a policy of nonrecognition. Consequently, at Roosevelt's invitation, the Soviet government sent Maxim Litvinov to Washington, and on November 16, 1933, the United States established regular diplomatic relations with Moscow.

By an exchange of notes prior to recognition, the Soviet government agreed not to sponsor, nor to permit within its jurisdiction, propaganda or other activity aimed at the overthrow of the government of the United States; to allow religious freedom and protection in the courts of American nationals residing in Russia; and to negotiate for a settlement of debts and claims. The results were disappointing. No agreement on claims was reached. Moscow-sponsored Communist activity in the United States continued. Trade figures were far below expectation; and there was no cooperation in opposing Japan.

If a lack of cordiality characterized Russian-American relations until 1939, the events of that year and of 1940 turned American sentiment violently against the Soviets. Stalin's pact with Hitler was quickly followed by Russia's occupation of eastern Poland. The Baltic states of Lithuania, Latvia, and Estonia were first required to admit Russian troops for their "protection" and then quietly incorporated in the Soviet Union.[11] When Finland refused to grant in full the Kremlin's demand for bases on Finnish territory and was attacked and invaded in consequence, it put up a brave but hopeless fight, which won the sympathy of the democracies and led to the expulsion of Russia from the League of Nations—the League's last, futile gesture against aggression. All of these Russian acts alienated whatever sympathy American non-Communists may have felt for the U.S.S.R. and were poor preparation for partnership.

Wartime Relations with Russia: Strains and Stresses

When Hitler turned his arms against his former partner on June 22, 1941, the United States joined Great Britain in welcoming Russia into the fellowship of the nations engaged in combating totalitarianism. Secretary Hull, ill at home, phoned the President: "We must give Russia all aid to the hilt. We have repeatedly said we will give all the help we can to any nation resisting the Axis." [12] Roosevelt stated at once that the United States was prepared to give all possible assistance to the Soviet Union.

Convinced through on-the-spot investigations by Harry Hopkins, Averell Harriman, and others that Russia would hold out if adequately supplied, he informed Stalin on October 30 that military equipment and munitions to the value of one billion dollars would be supplied under lend-lease. A week later he instructed the Lend-Lease Administrator that he had "today found that the defense of the Union of Soviet Socialist Republics is vital to

11. The Molotov-Ribbentrop pact of 1939 had assigned Lithuania to the German sphere of influence. Lithuania was later shifted by agreement to the Russian sphere, but friction arising from Russia's absorption of it was a contributing cause of Germany's break with Russia in June 1941.
12. Hull, *Memoirs,* 2: 967.

the defense of the United States," and that defense supplies were therefore to be transferred to the Soviets under lend-lease. This was the first installment of lend-lease goods to the amount of $11 billion to be supplied to the Soviet Union during the war. Shipments went via Murmansk, via Vladivostok (under the noses of the Japanese), and via the Persian Gulf and Iran.

In return, the Russian armies and people, through their heroic resistance, played an indispensable role in defeating Nazi Germany. Apart from this, the Soviet government made certain gestures of good will. Speaking through the Soviet ambassador in London, it endorsed the liberal principles of the Atlantic Charter, though with a qualification that provided a loophole; namely, "Considering that the practical application of these principles will necessarily adapt itself to the circumstances, needs, and historic peculiarities of particular countries." [13] The Soviet Union was one of the original signers of the Declaration by United Nations, January 1, 1942. In May 1943, furthermore, the Communist International, or Comintern, was dissolved by the action of its own governing body, and all former supporters of the Comintern were called upon "to concentrate their energies on the whole-hearted support of and active participation in the war of liberation of the peoples and the states of the anti-Hitlerite coalition . . ." [14] Thus was soft-pedaled, for the time being, the basic antagonism of Soviet Communism for the capitalist world.

On the American side there was much wishful thinking, to the effect that the cooperation of wartime would survive the destruction of Hitler. Neither Roosevelt nor his advisers, whether civil or military, seemed aware of the danger of a too powerful postwar Russia; or, if the danger occurred to them, their remedy was to conciliate the monster rather than clip its claws. If faith in Russia's good intentions wavered, there was another reason for "being

nice to Russia"—fear: fear that Russia might turn again to Hitler and make a separate peace, or fear that Russia would not aid in defeating Japan after Germany had been crushed. The idea prevailed in Washington that the United States needed Russia more than Russia needed the United States. Therefore Stalin could name his price, and sometimes even got more than he asked. Lend-lease aid, for example, was sometimes pressed upon indifferent Russian recipients.

The Soviet Union, for its part, showed no such naive trust in its Western allies. It was not without grounds for suspicion, for a common British hope had been to see Germany and Russia tear each other to pieces while the West stood by. So now, almost from the time the United States entered the war, Stalin demanded the opening without delay of a second front in Europe, to relieve the pressure on the Russian armies. Misleading assurances about a second front in 1942 were given Molotov on a visit to Washington in May and June of that year, and Churchill later had difficulty in persuading Stalin that the landing in North Africa (November 1942) was the only offensive possible to the Western Allies at that stage. Up to the Normandy landing in June 1944, there were periodic complaints from Moscow that the Anglo-American forces were dragging their feet. And as late as March 1945, Anglo-American negotiations looking to the surrender of German troops in northern Italy brought from Stalin angry accusations that his allies were planning a separate peace.

In the meantime there was endless friction in negotiation over comparatively minor matters—over the use of bases in Soviet territory, over liberated prisoners of war, even over the details of lend-lease, where the Russians were given to haggling over prices of goods for which they would never be called upon to pay. One difficulty arose from the almost invisible amount of discretion allowed to Soviet negotiators at all but the top levels; virtually all decisions had to be referred to higher authority. And when Soviet authorities made concessions on paper, they too often failed to

---

13. *Documents on American Foreign Relations,* 4: 216. All quotations from *Documents . . .* reprinted by permission of Council on Foreign Relations.
14. Ibid., 5: 527–30.

implement them in practice.[15] When the President and the Secretary of State met with their Russian opposite numbers, as they did on several occasions, superficial harmony was generally achieved; but in these meetings the Russians generally had their way, and such concessions as they made to the American or British point of view were too often forgotten when the time came to apply them. Since the conferences with Stalin and Molotov dealt largely with postwar matters, an account of them is deferred until later.[16]

China as an Ally

In its character of nonbelligerent (rather than neutral), the United States had been assisting China against Japan for some time before December 1941. China, that is, the government of Chiang Kai-shek, had received, since 1937, loans or credits to the amount of $120 million from the Export-Import Bank in Washington. It had been made eligible for lend-lease assistance. Its principal air force, the American Volunteer Group (A.V.G.) or Flying Tigers, was commanded by a retired United States Air Force officer, Claire L. Chennault; the planes were American planes and they were flown and fought by American Air Force pilots, who had been permitted to resign or take leave with the object of serving in China. An American military mission was in China for the purpose of instructing and training Chinese

personnel in the use of American equipment.[17] Since all Chinese seaports were in Japanese hands, material aid from the United States was sent by way of Rangoon and the Burma Road into southwest China.

The Japanese attack at Pearl Harbor made China and the United States full-fledged allies. American policy toward China, as defined by Secretary Hull, now assumed two purposes: (1) to ensure Chinese cooperation in waging effective war against Japan; (2) to raise China to the status of a great power, not only for the better prosecution of the war, but also that she might serve as a stabilizing factor in the postwar Far East.[18]

In pursuance of the policy of elevating China to great-power status, the United States granted to the Chinese government and people an equality that had been denied them since the first entry of the West into Chinese affairs. By a treaty with China signed January 11, 1943, the United States surrendered the extraterritorial rights that it had enjoyed since 1844, as well as the policing rights accorded at the time of the Boxer Rebellion, and its political and jurisdictional rights in the Diplomatic Quarter at Peiping and in the International Settlements at Shanghai and Amoy. The British signed a similar treaty on the same day. Thus, in theory, China recovered jurisdiction over her territory and over foreigners residing in China. The last of the "unequal treaties" were abrogated by the voluntary action of the United States and Great Britain.[19] Later in the same year Congress repealed the Chinese exclusion laws which, in some form or other,

15. A case in point concerned treatment of American prisoners of war liberated by the Russian armies. After long delay the Russians finally signed an agreement providing for repatriation of such prisoners with American supervision in the process. The agreement was satisfactory but it was not carried out. One American mission was allowed to visit Poland, the location of many of the prisoners, but its movements were so restricted that it could accomplish little. American prisoners were either left to shift for themselves or were kept in filthy camps and shipped in box cars to Odessa. J. R. Deane in Raymond Dennett and J. E. Johnson, eds. *Negotiating with the Russians* (Boston: World Peace Foundation, 1951), chap. 1. See also J. R. Deane, *The Strange Alliance: The Story of American Efforts at Wartime Cooperation with Russia* (New York: The Viking Press, Inc., 1947).

16. See Chapter 40.

17. Herbert Feis, *The China Tangle: The American Effort in China from Pearl Harbor to the Marshall Mission* (Princeton: Princeton University Press, 1953), p. 4; C. L. Chennault, *Way of a Fighter: The Memoirs of Claire Lee Chennault,* edited by Robert Hotz (New York: G. P. Putnam's Sons, 1949).

18. Hull, *Memoirs,* 2: 1583–87.

19. The treaty and related documents are printed in *Documents on American Foreign Relations,* 5: 485–501. By an exchange of notes at the time of signing the treaty the United States also surrendered special rights formerly enjoyed by United States shipping in the coastal trade of China and special rights that had been accorded to United States naval vessels in Chinese waters.

had been on the statute books since 1882. By the same act it placed Chinese immigration on the same quota basis as immigration from Europe and made Chinese immigrants eligible for naturalization.[20]

By these measures the United States removed the taint of inequality that had always marked its relations with China. It went further in bringing about the association of China with itself, Great Britain, and the Soviet Union, as one of the "Big Four" powers. With the other three, China signed the Moscow Declaration on General Security, of October 30, 1943, sponsored the call for the United Nations Conference on International Organization at San Francisco in 1945, and became one of the five permanent members of the United Nations Security Council.[21]

These important reforms, accomplished by the approving and signing of certain documents, were relatively easy to achieve. Giving effective military support to Chiang Kai-shek was a more difficult matter and was never accomplished to the Generalissimo's satisfaction.

The early decision to give the European war priority over that in Asia limited the amount of aid available for China. The amount was further limited when the Japanese, early in 1942, overran Burma and closed the Burma Road. Until the Ledo (or Stilwell) Road from India to Yunnan was opened in the fall of 1944, all material for China had to be flown in "over the hump" from bases in northeast India. What could be done was done, however. The "Flying Tigers" evolved into the Fourteenth Air Force, which fought the enemy effectively in southern China. General Joseph W. Stilwell, who had had previous experience in China, was sent in to command United States ground forces, to serve as Chief of Staff to Chiang Kai-shek, and to act in part under the direction of the British commander of the China-Burma-India theater. He was effective as a trainer and commander of Chinese troops. He succeeded in recovering northern Burma

from the Japanese and in opening the road from Ledo, that was named in his honor. Unfortunately, he disagreed with General Chennault, commander of the Fourteenth Air Force, about the relative importance of air and ground action; and he developed a strong dislike for Chiang Kai-shek, to whom he referred contemptuously as "the Peanut." His demand that he be entrusted with full command of all Chiang's armies and be permitted to amalgamate with them the Communist armies in north China, led to his recall at Chiang's peremptory request in the fall of 1944. By that time the approach to Japan by way of the Philippines and the Marianas was deemphasizing the importance of the war in China, and there was a consequent tapering off in the effort to build up Chiang's military power. This change in policy had its bearing on Chiang's later defeat by the Communists.[22]

Good Neighborliness Is Reciprocated

By its Good Neighbor Policy of the 1930's, the United States had laid the basis for New World solidarity in confronting Axis aggression. Axis sympathizers were influential in Argentina and to a lesser degree in Chile. The rest of Latin America cordially supported the United States during both its nonbelligerency and its participation in the war.

Following the outbreak of war in Europe, the Foreign Ministers of the American Republics met in conference at Panama in September and October 1939. There they approved a General Declaration of Neutrality of the American Republics and announced rules of neutral conduct which, like the United States Neutrality Act of 1939, favored the European democracies. In the Declaration of Panama they undertook to prohibit any belligerent act in the waters adjacent to the American continents (south of the Canadian boundary) and delimited those waters as extending on the average three hundred miles to sea. It was in this Declaration that President Roosevelt found justification for patrolling North Atlan-

---

20. *Documents on American Foreign Relations,* 6: 607–17. The President fixed the annual quota of Chinese immigrants at 105.

21. See p. 413. France was the fifth permanent member.

22. Feis, *The China Tangle,* p. 196.

tic waters for the detection of Axis submarines.[23]

The German victories over the Netherlands and France in the spring of 1940 raised the question of the fate of the French and Dutch possessions in the Caribbean. The possibility that they might be claimed or seized by Germany called forth reassertions by the Secretary of State and by Congress of the non-transfer principle long associated with the Monroe Doctrine. It led also to another conference of American Foreign Ministers at Havana, in July 1940. There, by the Act of Havana, the Foreign Ministers provided that an "emergency committee," one member from each republic, might set up a "provisional administration" for any European colony in the American area that might be threatened with a change of sovereignty. In urgent cases, a single American republic might act without waiting for a meeting of the committee. Upon the ending of the danger, the colony in question should either become independent or return to its former status. A convention, giving permanent form to the provisions of the act, also signed at Havana, was ratified and proclaimed early in 1942.

Such drastic action as that contemplated in the Act and the Treaty of Havana proved unnecessary. The landing of American troops in Greenland and Iceland was done with the consent of the Danish minister in the first case and the Iceland government in the second. By arrangement with the Netherlands government, United States and Brazilian troops aided in the protection of the bauxite mines in Surinam, whence came 60 percent of the ore for the American aluminum industry. In the spirit of Havana, however, the United States informed the American republics of its action in Surinam, and declared open to the use of any of them the bases acquired from Great Britain in the destroyer deal and any that it might establish in Greenland.[24]

The attack on the United States at Pearl Harbor and the declarations of war by the Axis powers brought the real test of inter-American solidarity. The results were in the main gratifying. All of the Central American and Caribbean republics (many of them former objects of intervention by the United States) promptly declared war against the Axis powers and were on hand to sign the United Nations Declaration, January 1, 1942. Mexico, Colombia, and Venezuela severed diplomatic relations with the Axis. The other republics without exception sent friendly messages to the United States. Not one subjected it to the restrictions that normally would have been imposed upon a belligerent.

For a third time the Foreign Ministers or their deputies met in January 1942, this time at Rio de Janeiro. Here they declared that an act of aggression against one is aggression against all, and recommended that all member states that had not yet severed relations with the Axis powers do so without further delay. This recommendation met with prompt compliance, except by Chile, which delayed until January 1943, and Argentina, which continued to harbor Axis diplomats until January 1944.

Eventually all the American republics declared war against Germany or Japan or both —Argentina not until March 27, 1945. All except Argentina and Panama received lend-lease assistance.[25] Brazil sent an expeditionary force to Europe. Brazil, Cuba, Ecuador, and Panama permitted the United States to establish military bases within their territory. Otherwise, except in the furnishing of raw materials at good prices, their positive contributions to the war effort were not great. But the assurance that enemy agents would not find harborage in neighboring territory was an advantage of no small consequence to the United States.

23. See Chapter 37. The Panama meeting also set up several Inter-American committees to deal with different problems of the war and neutrality and took steps for cooperation in suppressing unlawful activities in favor of any belligerent. Bemis, *Latin American Policy,* chaps. 21, 22, gives a good account of developments through the Rio de Janeiro Conference of 1942.

24. *U. S. Department of State Bulletin,* 5 (November 29, 1941), 425. See above, Chapter 37, for the Greenland, Iceland, and destroyer incidents.
25. *Documents on American Foreign Relations,* 7: 344–45.

The European Neutrals and the War

A number of European countries remained neutral or nonbelligerent throughout the war or until near the end. Eire, Sweden, and Switzerland kept out of it entirely, as did Turkey until February 1945, when it joined the United Nations. Portugal, too, did not enter the war, but in October 1943 made an air base in the Azores available to Great Britain and the United States. The government of Spain, headed by General Franco, made no effort to disguise its pro-Axis sympathy, though the practical expressions of that sympathy faded and disappeared at the same rate as the prospects for Axis victory. France, after June 1940, had two governmental entities, each professing to speak for the French people. The government of Marshal Pétain at Vichy was a prisoner of Hitler, and of such pro-Hitler Frenchmen as Pierre Laval. General Charles de Gaulle, head of the Free French movement and claiming to be the spokesman of the true France, carried on the war against the Axis from foreign shores. Of these countries, the wartime relations of the United States with France and Spain were important.

Marshal Pétain's government broke off relations with Great Britain in July 1940, when the British navy attacked a portion of the French fleet at Oran in Algeria, to end all possibility of its falling into German or Italian hands. The break with England made it the more important for the United States to maintain relations with Vichy. Such contact, it was hoped, could reduce Hitler's influence to a minimum, prevent the surrender to the Axis of the French fleet or French bases in Africa, and serve as a channel of information in regard to Axis plans and activities. For American ambassador to Vichy, Roosevelt picked a distinguished naval officer, Admiral William D. Leahy, who held the office from January 1941 to May 1942.[26] His presence there was a reminder of both the friendliness and the power of the United States. It made possible the negotiation of the Murphy-Weygand agreement, by which the United States undertook to provide French North Africa with essential food supplies and other commodities, and was authorized to supervise their distribution. The presence of American agents in Algiers and French Morocco, ostensibly for that purpose, was of importance in preparing the way for the Anglo-American landings of November 1942. At the news of those landings, Marshal Pétain broke off relations with the United States, though reportedly sending secret directions to Admiral Darlan, in Algiers, to stop resistance to the invaders.[27]

While maintaining relations with Vichy, the United States had recognized the Free French National Committee of General Charles de Gaulle, to the extent of granting lend-lease aid to forces operating under its direction and dealing with colonial regimes that accepted its authority, such as the government of New Caledonia. At a conference at Casablanca, Morocco,[28] soon after the landings in North Africa, Roosevelt and Churchill brought about a meeting of de Gaulle and General Henri H. Giraud, who had been their choice to command French forces in North Africa. Some months later de Gaulle and Giraud joined in setting up a Committee of National Liberation, which from then on served as a sort of French government in exile. Giraud was soon eased out,

---

26. Leahy's story of his ambassadorship and other wartime activities is told in W. D. Leahy, *I Was There* (New York: Whittlesey House, 1950). See also W. L. Langer, *Our Vichy Gamble* (New York: Alfred A. Knopf, Inc., 1947); D. C. McKay, *The United States and France* (Cambridge: Harvard University Press, 1951), chap. 6.

27. Admiral Jean François Darlan, French Minister of Marine and powerful Vichy politician, had been sympathetic to the Axis cause, but before the North African landings had sent secret intimation of his readiness to cooperate with the Anglo-Americans. His offer was not accepted, and his presence in Algiers at the time of the landings was accidental. It was also fortunate, since French commanders in North Africa obeyed his cease-fire order; they refused to recognize the authority of General Giraud, who had landed with the Americans and British. American embarrassment at having to deal with a man of Darlan's reputation was ended when, on December 24, 1942, Darlan was assassinated by a young French fantatic. Langer, *Our Vichy Gamble,* 321–23, 345, 352–54, 379.

28. See p. 401.

and de Gaulle became the unquestioned head of the Committee. Unfortunately, General de Gaulle had antagonized Secretary Hull [29] and had failed to ingratiate himself with President Roosevelt. The United States, therefore, held back when Churchill proposed to recognize de Gaulle's Committee of National Liberation as the provisional government of France. Only after the Allies had taken Paris in the summer of 1944 was such recognition finally granted.

With the Spain of General Franco, the leading problem of both American and British diplomacy was to prevent nonbelligerency from slipping into belligerency. The pro-Axis sympathies of Franco were well known. Serrano Suñer, his brother-in-law and, from October 1940 to September 1942, his Foreign Minister, was even more of a Germanophile than Franco himself. Spain, though a poor and weak nation, held a vitally important strategic position. Should she, with or without German aid, capture Gibraltar, she would be able to forbid access to the Mediterranean from the west. Thus she might have prevented the North African offensive; or, had she intervened after that campaign was launched, she might have frustrated it by severing its communications with the Atlantic.[30]

The means of preventing this course, first devised by the British, was to take advantage of Spain's economic weakness, supplying just enough essential raw materials, especially petroleum, to meet her day-to-day needs but none for stockpiling. The United States, where Franco was much detested and where emotion often interfered with the expedient course, was slow in adopting this policy, but eventually did so. Thus Spain was made to feel keenly her dependence upon British and American good will.[31]

How far Franco's decision not to enter the war was influenced by British and American pressure is not easy to determine. He was nearest to intervention in the fall of 1940, when he had a personal meeting with Hitler at Hendaye, France. An agreement that Spain should join the Axis seems then and there to have been reached, but the time for the move was not set. Thereafter Franco, aware of Spain's weakness and more and more convinced that the war would be a long one, postponed the date of entry and raised his price. Hitler abandoned his plan for a campaign through Spain and turned east to strike Russia. Franco cooperated by sending the "Blue Division" to fight Communism on the eastern front, by conniving at the supplying of German U-boats from Spanish ports, and by facilitating the purchase of wolfram (tungsten ore) from Spanish mines by German agents. The tungsten purchases went on, despite Anglo-American protests and preclusive buying, until April 1944.

But Franco did nothing whatever to interfere with the Allied landings in North Africa or to hamper the ensuing campaign; and as the prospects of an Axis victory faded, he became more and more cooperative with the Allies. Instead of moving from nonbelligerency into war (as Mussolini had done, to his sorrow), Franco moved from nonbelligerency to neutrality—a neutrality that became increasingly benevolent to the Allies as their prospects of victory brightened. In the words of an American poet on a different occasion,

> But consistency still wuz a part of his plan,—
> He's ben true to one party,—an' thet is himself.[32]

29. Especially by his unheralded seizure of the islands of St. Pierre and Miquelon in December 1941, when Hull had reached an understanding with the Vichy authorities about French New World possessions. Pratt, *Hull*, 2: 533–42.

30. A principal reason for the landing at Casablanca on the Atlantic coast of Morocco in November 1942 was to make sure of an overland communication with the Mediterranean if Spain should close the straits. Herbert Feis, *The Spanish Story: Franco and the Nations at War* (New York: Alfred A. Knopf, Inc., 1948), pp. 180–81.

31. W. L. Langer and S. E. Gleason, *The Undeclared War, 1940–1941* (New York: Harper & Row, Publishers, 1953), pp. 761–67. See also Feis, *The Spanish Story;* C. J. H. Hayes, *Wartime Mission in Spain, 1942–1945* (New York: The Macmillan Company, 1945); Sir Samuel Hoare, Viscount Templewood, *Ambassador on Special Mission* (London: Collins, 1946).

32. James Russell Lowell, *The Biglow Papers,* First Series, No. 3.

40

Ending the War

Plans for ending the war and arranging for the peace to follow it began many months before the United States became a belligerent. The chief planners were the United States and the Soviet Union. American plans were highly publicized in the pronouncements of Franklin Roosevelt, idealistic in the main but not neglectful of American material interests. Stalin talked little but moved quietly to safeguard the Russian future. Winston Churchill, a poor third in the possession of power, accepted the American program with skepticism and watched the Russian strategy with misgiving.

Roosevelt, in proposing the lend-lease program to Congress, January 6, 1941, described the kind of world that the program was designed to make secure—"a world founded upon four essential human freedoms." These were freedom of speech and expression, freedom of religion, freedom from want, and freedom from fear, the last to be achieved by a worldwide reduction of armaments to such a point that no nation would be able to commit an act of aggression against a neighbor. Seven months later, in the Atlantic Charter, Roosevelt and Churchill joined in a declaration of their objectives, Churchill as head of a government at war, Roosevelt as head of a nonbelligerent government committed to all aid short of war. Notable among those objectives were the "desire to see no territorial changes that do not accord with the freely expressed wishes of the people concerned"; respect for "the right of all peoples to choose the form of government under which they will live"; and the "wish to see sovereign rights and self-government restored to those who have been forcibly deprived of them." The Charter contemplated also "the establishment of a wider and permanent system of general security."

The fourth point of the Charter, proposing for all states "access, on equal terms, to the trade and to the raw materials of the world which are needed for their economic prosperity," committed the signers to the principle of elimination of economic barriers, or the "open door," which Secretary of State Cordell Hull had considered vital to the preservation of world peace. While nominally idealistic, this principle was also undoubtedly conducive to the economic prosperity and growth of the

United States. It was rarely lost from sight in American planning for the postwar world.[1]

The principles of the Atlantic Charter were, as recorded above, endorsed by the Soviet Union with an interpretative qualification,[2] and were accepted by the governments signing the Declaration by United Nations of January 1, 1942. Thus they became, at least in theory, a part of the program of the nations allied against the Axis powers.

Stalin, in the meantime, was working toward ends that directly contradicted the principle of self-determination so prominent in the Atlantic Charter. Anthony Eden, British Foreign Secretary, visiting Moscow in December 1941, was confronted with a demand that Great Britain recognize Russia's annexation of the Baltic States and a slice of Finland. Eden agreed to pass on the Russian proposal to Great Britain and the United States. The United States rejected this demand as in conflict with the Atlantic Charter, despite Churchill's argument in favor of expedient concessions to the Kremlin.[3] Both powers, furthermore, refused to accede to Molotov's demand, a few months later, that they recognize Russia's claims to eastern Poland and a part of Rumania. Molotov settled for a twenty-year treaty of alliance with Great Britain, in which both governments agreed to "act in accordance with the two principles of not seeking territorial aggrandizement for themselves and of non-interference in the internal affairs of other

States."[4] This phraseology accorded well with the Atlantic Charter, but at the Teheran Conference (November–December 1943) Stalin informed Roosevelt that the status of the former Baltic States was not open to discussion, since they had voted to join the Soviet Union. At the same conference the Western powers agreed to the Russian proposals for the boundaries of Poland.[5] Here as elsewhere, the principles of the Atlantic Charter yielded, first, to the urgent need of holding Russia as an ally, and later, to the persuasive presence of victorious Russian armies.

"Unconditional Surrender"

The frequent meetings of Roosevelt and Churchill, mentioned in the preceding chapter, were concerned very largely with the conduct of the war. As military prospects improved, however, their meetings and those that they held with Stalin and Chiang Kai-shek dealt increasingly with the shape of the peace and with postwar problems.

In January 1943, two months after the successful landings in North Africa, the President and the Prime Minister met at Casablanca, on the Atlantic coast of Morocco. Premier Stalin was invited to attend the meeting but, in the words of the official communiqué, "was unable to leave Russia at this time on account of the great offensive which he himself, as Commander-in-Chief, is directing." The principal business of the conference was the planning of campaigns to come, in the Mediterranean theater and elsewhere, but in his remarks to the press correspondents at the close of the conference (January 26, 1943) the President used a momentous expression. Recalling the phrase, "unconditional surrender," used by General Grant in the American Civil War, Roosevelt informed the reporters: "The democracies' war plans were to compel the 'unconditional surrender' of the Axis." The use of

1. The text of the Atlantic Charter is printed above, pp. 373–74n. On Hull, see Chapter 32. To one school of historians, "open door" has become a dirty word, signifying an alleged American drive for worldwide economic predominance which, in their opinion, blocks a wholesome economic development of the backward areas and is largely responsible for the cold war and other ills. See William A. Williams, *The Tragedy of American Diplomacy,* rev. ed. (New York: Dell Publishing Co., Inc., 1962); Gabriel Kolko, *The Politics of War: The World and United States Foreign Policy, 1943–1945* (New York: Random House, Inc., 1968). Such analyses in this writer's opinion, exaggerate the role of economic motivation in wartime and postwar policy.
2. See p. 394.
3. Winston S. Churchill, *The Hinge of Fate,* Vol. 4 of *The Second World War* (Boston: Houghton Mifflin Company, 1950), p. 327.

4. *Documents on American Foreign Relations,* 4: 254–57.
5. See pp. 404–5.

this phrase, which had been approved in advance by Churchill and the British War Cabinet, was apparently designed to convince the Russians that America and England were determined to fight the war to a finish. In the opinion of most analysts, it had the unintended and unfortunate effect of stiffening enemy resistance and postponing the day of surrender, certainly of Germany and Japan, perhaps of Italy. Conducing to the complete destruction of German and Japanese military potential, it helped to ensure the collapse of the balance of power and the military ascendancy of the Soviet Union in Europe and Asia.[6]

Similarly unfortunate in its hardening effect on German resistance was the endorsement by Roosevelt and Churchill, in September 1944, of the so-called "Morgenthau Plan" for the postwar treatment of Germany. In the words of the memorandum signed by the two heads of government at Quebec, September 16, 1944:

> This programme for eliminating the war-making industries in the Ruhr and in the Saar is looking forward to converting Germany into a country primarily agricultural and pastoral in its character.

The program was the work of Henry Morgenthau, Jr., Secretary of the Treasury. It was vigorously opposed by Secretaries Hull and Stimson in Washington, but Roosevelt invited Morgenthau to Quebec, where he had an opportunity to present it to the President and the Prime Minister. Roosevelt later explained lamely to Stimson that he must have signed the document "without much thought," but that "England was broke" and that under the Morgenthau Plan she "might inherit Ger-many's Ruhr business." Churchill recalled that he had "at first . . . violently opposed the idea,"

> but the President, with Mr. Morgenthau—from whom we had much to ask—were so insistent that in the end we agreed to consider it.

The suggestion here is that British acceptance of the plan was looked upon as a price to be paid for postwar loans from the United States. In any event, both Roosevelt and Churchill soon had their eyes opened to the preposterous nature of a program that would have eliminated the most productive industrial workshop in Europe, leaving a void in the European economy and starving millions in western Germany. The plan was quietly shelved, but not before it had "leaked." To Joseph Goebbels, Minister of Information in Berlin, it had obvious propaganda value.[7]

The Foreign Ministers' Conference at Moscow

Roosevelt was to meet Stalin for the first time in November 1943. But a month before that, Secretary Hull, despite his seventy-two years and frail health, had flown to Moscow to confer with Molotov and Anthony Eden. Italy had surrendered to Anglo-American forces in September, and the German divisions that still held much of the peninsula were being steadily pushed back. The Russian armies, too, had taken the offensive. The tide of war had turned, and it was none too soon to consider postwar arrangements.

At the close of a twelve-day conference (October 19–30, 1943) the Foreign Ministers of the Big Three issued a communiqué and a

6. Roosevelt's remarks, as reported to the *Christian Science Monitor,* are printed in *Documents on American Foreign Relations,* 5: 254–55. For discussion of the phrase and its effects see Churchill, *The Hinge of Fate,* pp. 683–91; H. W. Baldwin, *Great Mistakes of the War* (New York: Harper & Row, Publishers, 1950), pp. 14–25; W. H. Chamberlin, *America's Second Crusade* (Chicago: Henry Regnery Company, 1950), pp. 285–93; Anne Armstrong, *Unconditional Surrender: The Impact of the Casablanca Policy on World War II* (New Brunswick: Rutgers University Press, 1961).

7. H. L. Stimson and McGeorge Bundy, *On Active Service in Peace and War* (New York: Harper & Row, Publishers, 1948), pp. 568–83 (the memorandum is on pp. 576–77); Winston S. Churchill, *Triumph and Tragedy,* Vol. 6 of *The Second World War* (Boston: Houghton Mifflin Company, 1953), pp. 156–57; Chamberlin, *America's Second Crusade,* pp. 301–10, Hull, *Memoirs,* 2: chap. 115; Henry Morgenthau, Jr., *Germany Is Our Problem* (New York: Harper & Row, Publishers, 1945).

number of declarations. They had agreed upon setting up in London a European Advisory Commission (EAC) to study and make recommendations upon questions that might arise as the war developed. An Advisory Council for Italy, to include a representative of the French Committee of National Liberation, and eventually representatives of Greece and Yugoslavia, was to make recommendations for coordinating Allied policy in Italy. A Declaration regarding Italy promised a government "made more democratic by the introduction of representatives of those sections of the Italian people who have always opposed Fascism." It also promised to the Italian people restoration of freedom of speech, the press, political belief, public meeting, and religious worship. A Declaration on Austria promised liberation from German domination and recorded the wish of the three governments "to see reestablished a free and independent Austria."

At the urging of Secretary Hull, China was invited to join in what thus became a Declaration of Four Nations on General Security. In this the four governments pledged that the united action of wartime would be "continued for the organization and maintenance of peace and security," and recognized "the necessity of establishing at the earliest practicable date a general international organization" for that purpose. Here was the first definite international commitment to the idea of a postwar substitute for the League of Nations. In Secretary Hull's mind, the fact of having secured a Russian pledge to cooperate with the Western powers in a postwar security organization was an important achievement. In reporting on the work of the conference to a joint session of Senate and House of Representatives, he prophesied:

> As the provisions of the Four-Nation Declaration are carried into effect, there will no longer be need for spheres of influence, for alliances, for balance of power, or any other of the special arrangements through which, in the unhappy past, the nations strove to safeguard their security or to promote their interests.[8]

8. Hull, *Memoirs*, 2: 1314–15 (chaps. 92–94 for full account of conference); Winston S. Churchill, *Closing*

"While Six Million Died"

The Foreign Ministers at Moscow also issued a declaration on German atrocities over the signatures of Roosevelt, Churchill, and Stalin. This promised punishment for crimes committed against nationals of the countries occupied by German armed forces but said nothing about Nazi atrocities against their own Jewish nationals. Merciless persecution of German Jews had begun immediately upon Hitler's accession to power in 1933. It had grown more cruel with the years and had been promptly extended into the countries annexed or occupied by the Third Reich.

While such racial persecution was deplored in the United States, the American people, with some millions unemployed, showed no disposition to make places for refugees from the Nazi terror, and the State Department, partly out of fear that spies might slip in as refugees, displayed a surprising indifference to the sufferings and death of millions of European Jews and to the plight of thousands of Protestant and Catholic Christians who were also victims of Nazi persecution. Contrary to precedent, the Department, with Roosevelt's approval, took the position that the United States had no right to interfere with the German government's policy toward its own nationals. Even after receipt in August 1942 of conclusive evidence that Hitler's "final solution" of the Jewish question was the extermination of all European Jews, the State Department declined to protest.[9]

Omission of all mention of the plight of the Jews from the Moscow Declaration aroused deep indignation among Jews in the United States and Britain. In the ensuing month, how-

the Ring, Vol. 5 of *The Second World War* (Boston: Houghton Mifflin Company, 1951), Book 1, chap. 16. Communiqué and declarations are in *Documents on American Foreign Relations,* 6: 226–31.
9. Arthur D. Morse, *While Six Million Died: A Chronicle of American Apathy* (New York: Random House, Inc., 1968); David S. Wyman, *Paper Walls: America and the Refugee Crisis, 1938–1941* (Amherst: University of Massachusetts Press, 1968).

ever, Secretary of the Treasury Henry Morgenthau, Jr., and members of his staff were able to convince Roosevelt that some effort should be made to save those European Jews who had not yet been sent to the gas chambers. On January 20, 1944, the President set up the War Refugee Board, which acted vigorously and with some success to save many thousands of Jews remaining in satellite countries. In a strong statement two months later, Roosevelt described Nazi treatment of the Jews as "one of the blackest crimes of all history" and gave assurance of American "determination that none who participate in these acts of savagery shall go unpunished." [10]

The new policy bore some fruit. It should have been tried years earlier, although the threats of punishment owed their efficacy to the growing conviction that Hitler was doomed to defeat.

Cairo and Teheran

During the Moscow Conference, arrangements had been perfected for a meeting of Roosevelt, Churchill, and Stalin at Teheran, the capital of Iran or Persia. This was as far as the Russian dictator could be induced to journey from his own borders. Chiang Kai-shek, on the contrary, did not hesitate to fly to Cairo to confer with Roosevelt and Churchill as they stopped there en route to Teheran. From Cairo the three statesmen issued a declaration (released December 1, 1943) of importance for the postwar Far East.

> . . . It is their purpose [said the declaration] that Japan shall be stripped of all the islands in the Pacific which she has seized or occupied since the beginning of the first World War in 1914, and that all the territory Japan has stolen from the Chinese, such as Manchuria, Formosa

and the Pescadores, shall be restored to the Republic of China. Japan will also be expelled from all other territories which she has taken by violence and greed. The aforesaid three great powers, mindful of the enslavement of the people of Korea, are determined that in due course Korea shall become free and independent.[11]

At Teheran, where the Big Three leaders and their advisers conferred from November 28 to December 1, 1943, Roosevelt, as he reported to Congress, " 'got along fine' with Marshal Stalin," and on the basis of this experience predicted "that we are going to get along well with him and the Russian people—very well indeed." The meeting was, in fact, quite harmonious. Important military decisions were reached; notably that the cross-Channel invasion, known as OVERLORD, should be launched in May or June 1944, with a supporting landing on the south coast of France and a simultaneous Russian offensive in the east. Stalin repeated the promise, made to Hull at Moscow, that as soon as Germany was defeated, Russia would enter the war against Japan. He mentioned no price for such intervention, but Churchill expressed sympathy with the Russian desire for an ice-free port, and Roosevelt suggested that access to Dairen in South Manchuria would meet that need. It was agreed that in Yugoslavia all aid should be given to Tito and his partisans—a decision that insured Communist, though not necessarily Russian, domination of that country.

On the political side, the most important questions debated were the boundaries of Poland and the future of Germany. The three leaders were in general agreement that Poland's eastern boundary should be the Curzon Line, a supposedly ethnographical de-

---

10. Morse, *While Six Million Died,* p. 337. President Roosevelt had voiced at least one earlier public denunciation of Nazi anti-Semitism. After the massacre of the "Night of Broken Glass" in November 1938, he recalled the U.S. ambassador from Berlin and remarked at a press conference: "I myself could scarcely believe that such things could occur in a twentieth century civilization." *Ibid.,* p. 231.

11. With the reluctant assent of Churchill, Roosevelt promised Chiang that a large-scale amphibious operation would be launched from India against southern Burma, to be synchronized with a land campaign from China in the north. This plan, designated Operation ANAKIM, was abandoned after the Teheran Conference because of the need for all available landing craft for OVERLORD, the cross-Channel invasion.

marcation proposed in 1919. Poland would thus lose some White Russian and Ukrainian areas that she had held from 1921 to 1939. For these losses in the east she was to be compensated in the west by accessions of German territory up to the Oder River. Neither Churchill nor Roosevelt betrayed any moral scruple about these territorial changes, to be made, contrary to the promise of the Atlantic Charter, without "the freely expressed wishes of the peoples concerned," though Churchill did insist upon Polish boundaries that he could defend to the Polish government in exile in London.[12]

Nor did either Roosevelt or Churchill reveal any uneasiness over the proposed elimination of Germany as a military factor and the consequent destruction of the balance of power in Europe. Both agreed with Stalin that the revival of German military might must be made impossible. Roosevelt proposed that Germany be partitioned into five independent states, excluding the Ruhr-Saar and Kiel areas, which should be internationally controlled. Churchill preferred to isolate Prussia on the one hand, and, on the other, to construct a Danubian Confederation along lines resembling those of the former Austro-Hungarian Empire. Stalin preferred Roosevelt's solution to Churchill's. No decision was reached, but the debate showed to what an extent the Nazi peril had blinded Roosevelt, and even Churchill, to the menace of a strong Communist Russia.[13]

Churchill at Moscow

Roosevelt and Stalin did not meet again until the celebrated Yalta Conference in February 1945. In the interval, Churchill paid a visit to Moscow, in October 1944, with the principal object of seeking an understanding on the affairs of Poland and the Balkan States. The latter problem proved the easier to solve, temporarily and superficially. It existed because of the advance of the Russian armies into Rumania and Bulgaria and a threatened conflict between Russian and British interests, especially in Greece and Yugoslavia. A temporary arrangement of the previous June, giving to Russia predominance for three months in Rumania and to Britain the same in Greece, had been acceded to by President Roosevelt over the objections of the State Department. Now Churchill proposed and Stalin accepted (at least he made a blue check mark on Churchill's memorandum) an extension of this arrangement on a mathematical formula. According to Churchill's notation, as amended overnight by Molotov, Russia should have 90 percent predominance in Rumania and Great Britain (presumably in accord with the United States), 90 percent in Greece. Russian influence should predominate 80 to 20 percent in Bulgaria, 75 to 25 percent in Hungary, while in Yugoslavia the proportion was to be 50–50.[14] It seems clear that this exercise in arithmetic had no binding force, particularly since Roosevelt had cautioned Stalin that he would not be bound by any tête-à-tête agreement made in his absence, but it is useful in indicating the thinking of Stalin and Churchill at the time.

At Churchill's urging, Stanislaw Mikolajczyk, head of the Polish government in exile in London, came to Moscow during the conference. There he and several of his colleagues met with representatives of a Russian-sponsored Polish government set up at Lublin. The

12. Churchill had claimed for the "unconditional surrender" formula the merit that it would deprive Germany of any claim to be treated in accordance with the Atlantic Charter as a matter of right. Churchill, *The Hinge of Fate,* p. 689.
13. The conference also issued a Declaration regarding Iran, promising postwar economic assistance in return for Iran's wartime cooperation, and expressing the desire of the three governments "for the maintenance of the indepedence, sovereignty and territorial integrity of Iran." *Documents on American Foreign Relations,* 6: 235–36. For accounts of the Cairo and Teheran Conferences see Churchill, *Closing the Ring,* Book 2, chaps. 1–6; R. E. Sherwood, *Roosevelt and Hopkins: An Intimate History* (New York: Harper & Row, Publishers, 1948), pp. 771–802; W. D. Leahy, *I Was There* (New York: Whittlesey House, 1950), chap. 14.

14. Churchill, *Triumph and Tragedy,* pp. 227, 232; John A. Lukacs, "The Night Stalin and Churchill Divided Europe," *New York Times Magazine,* October 5, 1969; Kolko, *Politics of War,* pp. 144–47.

two groups failed to agree as to their respective shares in a new government for Poland. Mikolajczyk finally consented to urge his London colleagues to accept the Curzon Line, but the outcome was in doubt. Because of the exigencies of American politics, the unsatisfactory status of the Polish negotiations was kept quiet until after the presidential election of November 7.[15]

Europe at the Yalta Conference

Reelected for a fourth term, Roosevelt proceeded with preparations for another meeting with Churchill and Stalin, this time at Yalta in the Russian Crimea, recently liberated from the German invader. Here the three statesmen, with their diplomatic and military staffs— seven hundred British and Americans were flown in a night from Malta to Yalta—met from February 4 to 11, 1945. Four principal subjects occupied the time of the Conference: (1) details of the proposed United Nations Organization; (2) the treatment of defeated Germany; (3) restoration of self-government in the countries of eastern Europe, now occupied in whole or in part by Russian armies; (4) the terms of Russia's entry into the war against Japan. The first of these subjects is deferred to the next chapter; the others are considered here.

Treatment of defeated Germany. The future of Germany was left undecided. The governments of the United Kingdom, the United States, and the Soviet Union were declared to possess "supreme authority" to "take such steps, including the complete disarmament, demilitarization and dismemberment of Germany as they deem requisite for future peace and security." Study of the procedure of dismemberment was referred to a committee consisting of the British Foreign Secretary and the American and Russian ambassadors in London, who might at their discretion bring in a French member. In the meantime, Germany was to be divided into four zones of

15. Churchill, *Triumph and Tragedy,* pp. 235–43.

military occupation, a French zone to be formed out of previously agreed upon American and British zones.

Germany was to pay reparations in kind, in the first instance to the nations that had borne the main burden of the war, suffered most heavily, and "organized victory over the enemy." Reparations were to be of three categories: (1) removal, over a two-year period, of capital goods located either within or without German territory, "chiefly for the purpose of destroying the war potential of Germany"; (2) "annual deliveries of goods from current production for a period to be fixed"; (3) "use of German labor." A reparations commission representing the three governments was to be set up in Moscow. The American and Soviet delegations agreed in recommending that the commission should take, "as a basis for discussion," a total reparations figure of twenty billion dollars, one-half to go to the Soviet Union. The British delegation was opposed to naming any figure, pending consideration by the commission.

The question of punishment of major war criminals was left for inquiry and later report by the three Foreign Secretaries.

Poland and liberated Europe. The Conference agreed that a new Polish Provisional Government of National Unity should be established, constituted by including with the existing (Communist) Provisional Government at Lublin "democratic leaders from Poland itself and from Poles abroad." The new government should be "pledged to the holding of free and unfettered elections as soon as possible on the basis of universal suffrage and secret ballot." The "three heads of Government" considered that Poland's eastern boundary should be the Curzon Line, with some deviations in favor of Poland, and that Poland should receive "substantial accessions of territory in the north and west." These accessions were not defined.

For other portions of liberated Europe and for former Axis satellites (such as Hungary, Rumania, and Bulgaria) the three statesmen promised assistance in the establishment of internal peace, in relief of suffering, in the setting up of interim governments "broadly representative of all democratic elements," and in "the establishment through free elections of Governments responsive to the will of the people."

The Far East at the Yalta Conference

Both the American and British governments had for some time considered Russian aid indispensable against Japan if the war in the Far East was to be brought to an early conclusion. Stalin had promised such aid to Hull in Moscow, to Roosevelt at Teheran, and to Churchill during his visit to Moscow in October 1944. Beyond specifying that he would need to stockpile over a million tons of lend-lease goods for the campaign in the Far East, Stalin had hinted in October 1944 that there were political questions that should be "clarified" before Russia entered the war. In an interview between Stalin and Ambassador Averell Harriman in December 1944, the questions became demands. These demands Harriman telegraphed to Roosevelt on December 15. The President knew of them, therefore, six weeks before setting out for Yalta and had ample time to consider them.[16] They were embodied almost word for word in the Yalta agreement.

By that agreement Stalin promised that the Soviet Union would enter the war against Japan "in two or three months" after the German surrender, upon the following conditions:

1. Preservation of the status quo in Outer Mongolia; that is, continuance of the Soviet-sponsored Mongolian People's Republic in an area long claimed by China.
2. Restoration of "the former rights of Russia violated by the treacherous attack of Japan in 1904"; namely: (a) return to the Soviet Union of southern Sakhalin; (b) internationalizing of the port of Dairen, with safeguards for the "preeminent interests of the Soviet Union," and restoration to Russia of the lease of Port

Arthur for a naval base; (c) the Chinese Eastern and South Manchurian Railroads to be operated by a joint Soviet-Chinese company, with safeguards for "the preeminent interests of the Soviet Union" and retention of Chinese sovereignty in Manchuria.

3. Cession of the Kurile Islands to the Soviet Union.

President Roosevelt undertook to obtain the concurrence of Chiang Kai-shek in the provisions in regard to Outer Mongolia and the Manchurian ports and railroads, but all three heads of government agreed that the conditions should be "unquestionably fulfilled" after the defeat of Japan. Stalin, for his part, expressed a readiness to conclude a treaty with Chiang's government for the purpose of aiding in "liberating China from the Japanese yoke." [17]

Criticism of the Yalta Agreements

No single act of President Roosevelt's career has been more harshly criticized than his group of agreements with Stalin at Yalta. One of his principal critics, William Henry Chamberlin, states this point of view in the following:

> These agreements grossly violated the Atlantic Charter by assigning Polish territory to the Soviet Union and German territory to Poland without plebiscites. They violated the most elementary rules of humanity and civilized warfare by sanctioning slave labor as 'reparations.' And the whole historic basis of American foreign policy in the Far East was upset by the virtual invitation to Stalin to take over Japan's former exclusive and dominant role in Manchuria.[18]

16. Herbert Feis, *The China Tangle: The American Effort in China from Pearl Harbor to the Marshall Mission* (Princeton: Princeton University Press, 1953), pp. 232–33.

17. The Yalta agreements are printed in *Documents on American Foreign Relations,* 8: 919–24. The best appraisal of the conference is J. L. Snell, ed., *The Meaning of Yalta* (Baton Rouge: University of Louisiana Press, 1956). See also E. R. Stettinius, Jr., *Roosevelt and the Russians: The Yalta Conference* (Garden City, N.Y.: Doubleday & Company, Inc., 1949); Leahy, *I Was There,* chap. 18; Sherwood, *Roosevelt and Hopkins,* pp. 850–69; Feis, *The China Tangle,* chaps. 22, 23.

18. W. H. Chamberlin, *America's Second Crusade* (Chicago: Henry Regnery Company, 1950), p. 220. Reprinted by permission of the publisher.

In weighing these criticisms, several basic facts must be borne in mind: (1) Russian armies had overrun all or nearly all of Poland, Rumania, Bulgaria, Hungary, and Yugoslavia. The Western Allies, in consequence, had little bargaining power with regard to eastern Europe. They could ask but not demand. (2) Both Roosevelt and Churchill, especially the former, still relied on the good will and trusted the promises of the Soviet Union, and they were sure that they required its cooperation for the peace no less than for the war. (3) No one, at that stage, was disposed to be very tender toward the Germans. "Unconditional surrender," as Churchill had remarked, excluded the enemy from any claim to the benefits of the Atlantic Charter. (4) The opinion prevailed in influential quarters that Japan was capable of prolonged resistance, that she had a powerful army in Manchuria, and that Russian participation might greatly shorten the war and reduce the cost of victory to the United States by perhaps a million casualties. Therefore Russia's price must be paid. No doubt, also, a tortured sense of justice made it seem right to restore to the Soviets what Japan had once taken from the Czar.

The student who wishes to understand the Yalta agreements must try to put himself into the mood and the state of knowledge of the men who made them. He will then perhaps regard both the men and the agreements with more indulgence than has been shown by some critics equipped with 20–20 hindsight. The Polish boundaries had been previously agreed upon at Teheran. For the Curzon Line (with deviations in favor of Poland) there were sound ethnographical arguments, and Mikolajczyk had reluctantly agreed to recommend it to his London colleagues. This cannot be called a decision in "accord with the freely expressed wishes of the people concerned," but it was the best that the Soviets were willing to concede. The compensation of the Poles with German territory, and likewise the inclusion of German labor as a form of reparations, cannot be justified; they can be understood only as manifestations of the hate-engendered thesis that

Germans had forfeited all claim to humane treatment. The promises of free elections open to all democratic elements in Poland and liberated Europe sounded fair and generous. No one as yet realized that the Russians would equate democracy with acceptance of Communism and would enforce this view ruthlessly in areas that they held vital to their security.

The least excusable of the agreements made at Yalta was that concerning the Far East. The pretense that it restored to Russia rights of which Japan had robbed her was hollow. Russia had been the most active aggressor in the Far East between 1895 and 1904,[19] and her moral claim to Dairen, Port Arthur, and the Manchurian railroads was no better than Japan's. All had been exacted from China by the threat of force. To restore to Russia these rights and properties, with recognition of her "preeminent interest" in Manchuria, was a contradiction of American policy since John Hay's time. It was paying Russia for her assistance with Chinese coin. Yet on the assumption that Russian assistance might save the lives of a million American soldiers, would another President in Roosevelt's place have refused it?

The tragic irony of this part of the story is that Russian aid was not needed. The postwar U.S. Strategic Bombing Survey concluded that without Russian entry into the war, without invasion of the homeland, and without use of the atomic bomb, Japan would have surrendered before December 31 and probably before November 30, a month after the date set for the first Anglo-American invasion of the home islands. This estimate, of course, was not known to Roosevelt or his advisers at Yalta, but it is to be noted that both the Navy and the commander of the Strategic Air Force were skeptical about the need for invasion or Russian assistance. It was the Army that misjudged the situation and was chiefly

19. See pp. 189, 236. There was no historical justification for Russia's demand for the Kuriles. She had relinquished all claim to them in 1875 in return for Japan's relinquishment of claims to Sakhalin.

responsible for Roosevelt's decision to pay Stalin's price.[20]

To say that the agreement on the Far East was both unnecessary and morally hard to justify is not to endorse all that has been written of its evil results. Critics have charged that it betrayed Chiang Kai-shek, made the Soviet Union a Pacific power, and paved the way for the triumph of Communism in China, Indochina, and northern Korea. This reasoning seems to betray a naive view of the power of paper agreements, particularly as they affect the Soviet Union. It is difficult to believe that, had there been no agreement, the Soviet Union would have abstained from attacking Japan or from taking what it wished in the Manchurian area. The only way to prevent it would have been to follow a course more Machiavellian than President Roosevelt was willing to follow or the American public to endorse—such as making an easy peace with Japan that would have left her, though shorn of her conquests, still a formidable military power. Shrewd American statesmanship would have aimed at preserving a balance of power in both Asia and Europe, but both Roosevelt and Hull had repudiated the balance of power concept as one of the techniques of an evil and war-ridden past.

The German Collapse

Events moved swiftly after the Yalta Conference. Russia was soon displaying a callous disregard of her Yalta pledges, in both Poland and Rumania. She did, however, give warning of her intention to join in the war against Japan by serving notice, on April 5, 1945, that she would not renew the neutrality treaty of 1941 upon its expiration. Russia would thus be freed to attack Japan but only—if she kept faith—after April 13, 1946. On April 12, President Roosevelt died of a cerebral hemorrhage at Warm Springs, Georgia. Meanwhile,

Allied armies were pouring into Germany from east and west, and the German front in Italy was collapsing. On May 1 it was reported that Russian forces had entered Berlin and that Hitler had died in the Reichchancellery. Admiral Karl Doenitz headed a short-lived provisional government. On May 7, representatives of the German Army signed surrender terms at Reims, and on the following day President Truman and Prime Minister Churchill proclaimed V-E (Victory in Europe) Day. On May 9 the formalities of surrender were completed in Berlin, and Stalin announced the end of the war to the Russian people. Early in June an Allied Control Committee for Germany began functioning in Berlin. It consisted of General Eisenhower and Marshals Montgomery and Zhukov.

Japan Surrenders

The war in Europe was ended; that in the Pacific went on, but Japanese surrender was nearer than most responsible Allied statesmen supposed. From the time of the first Japanese naval reverses in the Coral Sea and at Midway, in May and June 1942, there had been a peace party in Japan, headed by certain ex-Premiers, and this group had gained in strength with every Japanese defeat. It was not, however, until the appointment of a cabinet headed by the octogenarian Admiral Suzuki, in April 1945, that the peace group felt strong enough to oppose the Army, which favored resistance to the bitter end. But even the peace-minded men of the Suzuki cabinet found an obstacle in the "unconditional surrender" formula. Loyalty to the Emperor and the dynasty prescribed that as a minimum the Emperor system must be preserved.[21] Begin-

20. Herbert Feis, *The Atomic Bomb and the End of World War II* (Princeton: Princeton University Press, 1966), pp. 190–93.

21. The best account of the events leading to the Japanese surrender is R.J.C. Butow, *Japan's Decision to Surrender* (Stanford: Stanford University Press, 1954). See also F. C. Jones, *Japan's New Order in East Asia: Its Rise and Fall, 1937–1945* (New York: Oxford University Press, 1954), pp. 420–49; Toshikazu Kase, *Journey to the Missouri* (New Haven: Yale University Press, 1950), chaps. 6–11;

ning in June, Japan made a series of attempts to secure Russian mediation in getting a peace with at least this face-saving condition. The Soviet government, for understandable reasons, turned aside these proposals.

In Washington, meanwhile, the War Department was planning an invasion of Japan's home islands, to begin November 1. At the same time, those who believed that there was a responsible peace party in Japan were seeking ways to make surrender easy and avoid the frightful costs of invasion. A beginning was made by President Truman on V-E Day, in his proclamation announcing the German surrender. Calling upon the "Japanese military and naval forces"—not the Japanese government—to "lay down their arms in *unconditional surrender*," he added the assurance: "Unconditional surrender does not mean the extermination or enslavement of the Japanese people." On the same day, Captain Ellis M. Zacharias, the Navy's leading expert on Japan, began a series of Japanese-language broadcasts designed to show the Japanese that they could surrender without loss of honor, sovereignty, or "national structure." [22] Former Ambassador Joseph C. Grew, now Under Secretary of State, wished to tell the Japanese in plain language that the United States would not object to their retaining a constitutional monarchy, and he was supported by Secretary of War Stimson. A Proclamation to the People of Japan, containing such an assurance, was prepared under their joint direction; but before it was issued from Potsdam, July 26, 1945, over the signatures of Truman, Attlee (who had succeeded Churchill), and Chiang Kai-shek, that particular assurance was deleted. [23]

This document, often referred to as the Potsdam Declaration, called, as had Truman earlier, for the unconditional surrender of the Japanese armed forces, for the complete elimination of militarism and militarists, the setting up of "a new order of peace, security and justice," the removal of obstacles to democratic tendencies, the punishment of war criminals, and the carrying out of the terms of the Cairo Declaration. The Japanese, it promised, would not be "enslaved as a race or destroyed as a nation." Allied forces would occupy designated points in Japanese territory until the objectives were accomplished and until there should have been "established in accordance with the freely expressed will of the Japanese people a peacefully inclined and responsible government." [24]

This declaration held out enough hope to encourage the peace party in Japan, but since the government had not yet despaired of securing Russian mediation, the Foreign Minister advised that no response be made until a reply was received from Moscow. Premier Suzuki gave the Cabinet the impression that he accepted this advice, but under pressure from the military he told the press that Japan would "ignore" the declaration. [25] This unfortunate note of defiance led to the decision in Washington to drop atomic bombs on Hiroshima and Nagasaki (August 6 and 9). [26] It also allowed time for Russia to enter the war, as she did on August 8, sending armies into Manchuria and Korea. From Tokyo on August 10 there came by way of Switzerland an ac-

J. C. Grew, *Turbulent Era: A Diplomatic Record of Forty Years 1904–1945*, 2 vols. (Boston: Houghton Mifflin Company, 1952), 2: chap. 36; Stimson and Bundy, *On Active Service in Peace and War*, chap. 23; R. N. Current, *Secretary Stimson: A Study in Statecraft* (New Brunswick: Rutgers University Press, 1954), pp. 220–37.
22. E. M. Zacharias, *Secret Missions: The Story of an Intelligence Officer* (New York: G. P. Putnam's Sons, 1946), chap. 31.
23. For the Potsdam Conference, which dealt for the most part with European matters, see Chapter 42.

24. *Documents on American Foreign Relations*, 8: 105–6.
25. Butow, *Japan's Decision to Surrender*, pp. 143–49; Feis, *The Atomic Bomb and the End of World War II*, pp. 107–10.
26. What seems unnecessary haste in using the atomic bomb at Hiroshima has suggested to some analysts that its principal purpose was to warn the Soviet Union that the U. S. had exclusive possession of a potent new weapon which would give it a great advantage in negotiations over the fate of Eastern Europe and other pending controversies between the wartime allies. This is the thesis of Gar Alperovitz, *Atomic Diplomacy: Hiroshima and Potsdam. The Use of the Atomic Bomb and the American Confrontation with Soviet Power* (New York: Simon and Schuster, 1965). See also Feis, *The Atomic Bomb and the End of World War II*, pp. 196–201.

ceptance of the Potsdam terms, but with the understanding that the declaration "does not comprise any demand which prejudices the prerogatives of His Majesty as a Sovereign Ruler." To the request for an "explicit indication" that this understanding was warranted, James Byrnes, now Secretary of State, replied that during the occupation the authority of the Emperor would be subject to the Supreme Commander of the Allied Powers, and that the ultimate form of Japan's government should be determined "by the freely expressed will of the Japanese people."

On the question of whether to surrender on the basis of the Potsdam Declaration thus interpreted, the Supreme War Direction Council divided three to three—the Premier, Foreign Minister, and Navy Minister for, the Army Minister and the two Chiefs of Staff against. In the face of this deadlock, the Premier appealed to the Emperor to make the decision (as he had already done in a similar situation in the preliminaries). The Emperor chose peace. Japan's surrender was proclaimed by President Truman on August 14. The formal signing of surrender terms took place on the battleship *Missouri,* in Tokyo Bay, September 2, 1945.

41

The United States
and
the United Nations

The Japanese attack at Pearl Harbor, and the German and Italian declarations of war that followed, silenced, if they did not kill, isolationism in the United States. The elaborate neutrality legislation of the 1930's had failed to insulate the United States from war in Europe and Asia. To many Americans it appeared that in future the United States could hope to avoid war only by joining in a system of collective security capable of preventing war. To such people American membership in an improved and strengthened League of Nations seemed the only hope of peace.

Almost from the outbreak of war in Europe, Secretary Hull and his State Department subordinates began planning for a new world organization, of which the United States should be a member. In January 1940 Hull announced the appointment of an Advisory Committee on Problems of Foreign Relations, with subcommittees to study political, economic, and security questions. In addition to State Department personnel, members of the House and Senate, both Democrats and Republicans, were brought in, as were experts from private life. Notable among these were Isaiah Bowman, well known geographer and president of Johns Hopkins University, and Hamilton Fish Armstrong, editor of the influential quarterly, *Foreign Affairs*. As time went on, a number of nongovernmental organizations were brought into consultation with the State Department, among them the Federal Council of Churches of Christ in America and the Council on Foreign Relations. The latter, aided by a grant from the Rockefeller Foundation, conducted several series of studies by experts in close liaison with the Department, to which it sent 682 memoranda in the period 1939–1945.[1]

Hull, a former follower of Woodrow Wilson and advocate of the League of Nations, was acutely aware of Wilson's mistakes and determined to avoid them. In particular, he was careful to take Republicans as well as Demo-

1. Hull, *Memoirs,* 2: 1625–1713; Pratt, *Cordell Hull,* 2: chap. 22; U. S. Department of State, *Postwar Foreign Policy Preparation, 1939–1945* (Washington: Government Printing Office, 1950), *passim; The War and Peace Studies of the Council on Foreign Relations* (New York: Council on Foreign Relations, 1946).

crats into his confidence. No one would be able to charge this time that the administration's plans for the postwar world were tinged with partisanship.

Franklin Roosevelt, though he may have shared the belief of his Secretary of State that the United States must lead in the preparation for a new League of Nations, at first feared the political reaction to public announcement of such a view. At the Atlantic Conference in August 1941,[2] he rejected a declaration, proposed by Churchill, for a peace that would, "by effective international organization . . . afford to all States and peoples the means of dwelling in security." Such an expression, he feared, would rouse the suspicion of the isolationists, in Congress and out. But he let himself be persuaded by Churchill and Harry Hopkins into accepting a statement of the same idea in different words. Paragraph 8 of the Atlantic Charter proposed the disarmament of aggressor nations, "pending the establishment of a wider and permanent system of general security." [3]

By the fall of 1943, the political hazards of advocating American participation in a collective security organization had been eliminated. By large majorities, the Senate and the House of Representatives, respectively, had passed the Connally and Fulbright Resolutions, declaring that the United States, acting "through its constitutional processes," should participate in international machinery to prevent aggression and preserve the peace of the world. A Republican Post-War Advisory Council, meeting at Mackinac Island in September, adopted a resolution of similar purport.[4]

In the spring of 1944, speeches by the Secretary of State, by Assistant Secretary Breckinridge Long, and by the President himself informed the public that the State Department was making plans for a postwar international organization to keep the peace.

2. See Chapter 37.
3. R. E. Sherwood, *Roosevelt and Hopkins: An Intimate History* (New York: Harper & Row, Publishers, 1948), pp. 359–60.
4. *Documents on American Foreign Relations,* 6: 315–18.

They even sketched out its general lines: an assembly representing all members of the organization, a smaller body with power to act against aggression, an international court of justice. The structural similarity to the League of Nations is obvious. The planners hoped to avoid the weaknesses of the League, first, by including all the great powers in the membership; secondly, by vesting in the enforcement agency power of vigorous action.

The Dumbarton Oaks Conference

Hull relates that in State Department discussions he emphasized the belief that

> there was no hope of turning victory into enduring peace unless the United States, the British Commonwealth, the Soviet Union, and China agreed to act together.[5]

The Four Nations' Declaration, issued at Moscow, October 30, 1943, was a good omen for such agreement. In order to make sure of a plan that would be acceptable to the governments of these four powers, the United States invited the other three to send delegations to Washington in August 1944 to cooperate in producing a tentative charter for a permanent United Nations Organization. The conference was held at Dumbarton Oaks (a Washington estate owned by Harvard University), from August 21 to October 7. The Soviet Union, still at peace with Japan, refused for that reason to confer with belligerent China. Hence the conference had two phases: the United States, Great Britain, and Russia, August 21 to September 28; the United States, Great Britain, and China, September 29 to October 7. For the most part, the Chinese delegation accepted the work already done by the other three.

The Dumbarton Oaks Proposals, published October 9, 1944, contained most of the provisions that took lasting form in the United Nations Charter. They proposed the creation of a permanent organization to be known as the United Nations, open to "all peace-loving

5. Hull, *Memoirs,* 2: 1651.

states" and based on the "sovereign equality" of such states. Its purposes should be (1) to maintain peace and security through collective measures; (2) to develop friendly relations between states; (3) to effect cooperation in the solution of international economic, social, and humanitarian problems; (4) to afford a center for harmonizing the action of nations for their common ends. The principal organs would be a General Assembly, a Security Council of eleven members (four permanent, the others chosen for two-year terms), a Secretariat, an Economic and Social Council (subsidiary to the General Assembly), and an International Court of Justice. It was the hope of the architects of the plan that the General Assembly and the Economic and Social Council would remove or alleviate causes of friction, the International Court would settle peaceably any disputes susceptible of judicial determination, and the Security Council would assist in the peaceful settlement of disputes and suppress any acts of aggression or breaches of the peace that might unfortunately occur.

On several questions the delegations at Dumbarton Oaks had failed to reach agreement. When and where should a general meeting be held to write the Charter with the Proposals as a starting-point? What nations should be invited to that meeting and thus become original members of the United Nations? What should be done with the former Japanese mandated islands, most of them certain to be in United States possession at the end of the war? Should the constituent republics of the U.S.S.R., or any of them, have separate membership in the United Nations? Most crucial of all, should each of the great powers, permanent members of the Security Council, have the right to veto its decisions? These questions were taken up by Roosevelt, Churchill, and Stalin, when they met at Yalta in February 1945.

The Yalta Decisions

The three heads of government reached agreement on these pending problems without great difficulty. The date for the conference on world organization was set at April 25, 1945, and the place at San Francisco. The governments invited to participate would be those already cooperating as the United Nations and such others as might declare war "on the common enemy" by March 1, 1945. Stalin had once intimated that all sixteen republics of the U.S.S.R. should be separately represented—bringing from Roosevelt the rejoinder that in that case he would ask separate membership for all forty-eight states of the U.S.A. The Russian dictator now moderated his demands, asking separate membership in the San Francisco Conference and in the proposed world organization only for the Ukraine and White Russia. Roosevelt and Churchill agreed to support this request at the Conference. Stalin, in return, offered to support the United States if it should ask for three votes in the General Assembly to balance Russia's three. In theory, at least, these proposed multiple votes were intended to offset the six votes of the British Commonwealth of Nations. (It may be noted here that when the time came, the United States did not ask for or receive extra votes.)

It was tentatively agreed to replace the Mandate System of the League of Nations with a system of territorial trusteeships—much the same thing under a different name. It was to apply to (a) existing mandates of the League of Nations, (b) territories taken from the enemy in the current war, (c) any other territory that a sovereign power might voluntarily place under trusteeship.

On the question of voting in the Security Council—in other words, the right of veto—the State Department had prepared a formula. Some members of the Department, notably former Under Secretary Sumner Welles, had opposed granting any power the right, in Welles's words, "to veto action against itself if it undertook to pursue policies of aggression." [6] To Secretary Hull, however, it was clear that neither the Soviet Union nor the Senate of the United States would accept a

6. Sumner Welles, *Where Are We Heading?* (New York: Harper & Row, Publishers, 1946), pp. 24–25.

charter that failed to vest the right of veto in the permanent members. The great-power veto was a practical necessity. The hope was that it would not be abused.

The formula devised by the State Department, approved at Yalta, and eventually adopted at San Francisco, permitted decision in procedural matters by the votes of any seven of the eleven members of the Security Council. In all substantive matters, however, the seven affirmative votes must include the votes of all five [7] permanent members, with the unimportant qualification that a member which was a party to a dispute should not vote if the question were one merely of investigation or of recommending peaceful methods of settlement. Thus a permanent member could veto the use of sanctions against itself or even a motion finding it guilty of an act of aggression. If a dispute concerned not itself but one of its satellites, it could even veto a proposal for an investigation.

The price of securing the adherence of the Soviet Union, and of ensuring a favorable vote by the United States Senate, was thus a veto provision that would paralyze the Security Council in any controversy between two or more of the Big Five powers. It was frankly recognized at the time, and became tragically apparent later, that only through friendly cooperation of the Big Five could the United Nations operate successfully as a security organization.

President Roosevelt, however, returned from Yalta in a mood of confidence. Reporting to Congress on March 1, 1945, he said:

> The Crimean Conference was a successful effort by the three leading nations to find a common ground for peace. It spells the end of the system of unilateral action and exclusive alliances and spheres of influence and balances of power and all the other expedients which have been tried for centuries—and have failed.
>
> We propose to substitute for all these a universal organization in which all peace-loving nations will finally have a chance to join.[8]

7. It was agreed at Yalta to include France as one of the permanent members of the Council. See p. 427 for enlargement of the Security Council in 1965.
8. *Documents on American Foreign Relations,* 7: 28.

The San Francisco Conference

The members of the American delegation to the San Francisco Conference (officially the United Nations Conference on International Organization, or UNCIO) were named by President Roosevelt before his death. In choosing the delegates, as in other aspects of preparation for the U.N., Roosevelt profited from Woodrow Wilson's errors.[9] Headed by the Secretary of State, Edward R. Stettinius, Jr., the delegation was bipartisan and contained distinguished members of both Senate and House: the chairmen and ranking minority members of the Senate Committe on Foreign Relations and the House Committee on Foreign Affairs.[10] No one could make the charge that Roosevelt had slighted either the Senate or the Republican party, as Wilson had been accused of doing. Of special importance was the selection of Senator Vandenberg. A trusted Republican leader and long an outspoken critic of Roosevelt, he did effective work at San Francisco and conjured away Republican opposition when the Charter came before the Senate.[11]

9. See Chapter 29.
10. Besides Stettinius and Cordell Hull, who was prevented by ill health from attending the Conference, the delegation had the following members: Senators Tom Connally (Dem.) and Arthur H. Vandenberg (Rep.), Representatives Sol Bloom (Dem.) and Charles A. Eaton (Rep.), Dean Virginia C. Gildersleeve of Barnard College, and Commander Harold E. Stassen, U.S.N.R., a former Republican governor of Minnesota. John Foster Dulles, chairman of the Commission on a Just and Durable Peace of the Federal Council of the Churches of Christ in America, was one of several official advisers to the delegation.
11. A prewar isolationist, Vandenberg had declared himself strongly in favor of international organization in a Senate speech of January 10, 1945. For his part before and during the San Francisco Conference, see A. H. Vandenberg, Jr., ed., *The Private Papers of Senator Vandenberg* (Boston: Houghton Mifflin Company, 1952), chaps. 8–11. John Foster Dulles has given a first hand, though brief, account of the San Francisco Conference in his *War or Peace* (New York: The Macmillan Company, 1950), chap. 5. The documents pertaining to Dumbarton Oaks and San Francisco are collected in L. M. Goodrich and Edvard Hambro, *Charter of the United Nations: Commentary and Documents* (Boston: World Peace Foundation, 1946).

The nations originally invited to send delegations to San Francisco were forty-six—the forty-seven that had signed the United Nations Declaration by March 1, 1945, minus Poland, whose government had not yet been reconstituted according to the Yalta formula. In fulfillment of Roosevelt's promise at Yalta, the United States delegation helped to secure from the Conference the admission of delegates from the Ukraine and White Russia. The Latin American republics consented reluctantly to this action and in return asked for and obtained the admission of Argentina, which had been a laggard in breaking with the Axis. Denmark, now liberated from Axis occupation, was also admitted, raising to fifty the number of nations participating. These became "charter members" of the United Nations. It was agreed that Poland, though not admitted to the Conference, should also be considered an original member. In future, membership in the organization was to be open to "all other peace-loving states" that should accept the obligations contained in the Charter and should be judged able and willing to carry these out.

The United Nations Charter

The Conference labored for two months, from April 25 to June 26. The Charter, signed by the delegates on the latter date, followed closely the Dumbarton Oaks Proposals in general structure. To the four "principal organs" originally proposed—General Assembly, Security Council, Secretariat, and International Court of Justice—the Conference added two: the Economic and Social Council (raised from subsidiary level) and a Trusteeship Council.

It will be useful here to comment briefly upon some of the ways in which the Charter of the United Nations altered, added to, or elaborated upon the plan sketched out at Dumbarton Oaks.

Idealistic phraseology. In the Preamble, the statement of Purposes and Principles, and elsewhere, the Charter is profuse in such expressions as "fundamental human rights," "the equal rights of men and women," "social progress and better standards of life," and the like. Senator Vandenberg considered it an achievement to have obtained the insertion of the word "justice" as expressing one of the objectives of the organization.

A more important role for the General Assembly. The original proposals had lodged almost all power in the Security Council, which would be dominated by the Fig Five and was expected to function partly through the use of force, economic or military. Senator Vandenberg, believing that in the long run moral force—mobilized world opinion—might count more than material force, led a movement to make the General Assembly "a town meeting of the world" by giving it practically unrestricted freedom to debate, and to make recommendations upon any matter of international concern. This was finally accomplished over strenuous opposition from the Russian delegation.

Restriction of the veto in the Security Council. The right of the permanent members to veto *action* by the Security Council had been generally accepted as inescapable, whether desirable or not. At San Francisco, however, it became apparent that the Russians conceived of the veto power as extending also to discussion. No subject, they claimed, could be brought before the Security Council for consideration without the consent of all five permanent members. To the Americans, and apparently to all other delegations not under Soviet influence, this seemed an intolerable infringement of free speech. This issue very nearly broke up the Conference. An appeal to Stalin, through Harry Hopkins and Ambassador Averell Harriman in Moscow, finally brought about a Russian retreat.

Action through regional organizations. A conference of the American States in Mexico City in February and March 1945, had adopted the Act of Chapultepec,[12] which declared an act of aggression against one American state to be aggression against all and obligated the several states to consult, in such

12. *Documents on American Foreign Relations,* 7: 717–20.

a case, "upon the measures it may be desirable to take." A provision (Article 53), however, had been incorporated in the United Nations Charter forbidding enforcement action by regional agencies without the authorization of the Security Council. It was plain to the Latin American delegations, and to Nelson Rockefeller, United States Assistant Secretary of State for Latin American Affairs, that a Council veto, by Russia, for example, could, under this article, prevent the American republics from taking any action under the Act of Chapultepec; could, in fact, make impossible action to uphold the Monroe Doctrine. To meet this situation the American delegation made a proposal that eventually took the form of Article 51 of the Charter. This reserved to member nations "the inherent right of individual or collective self-defense" in case of attack, until the Security Council should have taken "measures necessary to maintain international peace and security." It would be difficult to exaggerate the importance of this article, which like the guarantees of free discussion in the Assembly and Council, was accepted only after prolonged Russian opposition. Its recognition of the right of "collective self-defense" served to reconcile with the Charter not only the inter-American security arrangements but the later North Atlantic Treaty Organization and mutual defense treaties beween the United States and Australia, New Zealand, the Philippines, Japan, Nationalist China, and the Republic of Korea, and the later Southeast Asia pact.[13]

The International Court of Justice. This was a new tribunal, not a revised form of the World Court established in 1922. The reason for making it so was the practical one that revision of the statute of the old World Court would have required the consent of all its members, several of which were in the enemy camp. It was simpler to let it die (as the League of Nations died) and set up a new body.[14] The new Court was in most respects similar to the old one. The chief difference was that it was an organic part of the United Nations, not separate, as the World Court had been from the League. The Statute of the Court was an annex of the U.N. Charter, and all members of the U.N. were *ipso facto* members of the "I.C.J."

The Economic and Social Council. This wholly new body was given considerable powers of initiative in sponsoring studies, making recommendations, and preparing draft conventions in relation to international economic, social, cultural, educational, and medical matters. It might "make recommendations for the purpose of promoting respect for, and observance of, human rights and fundamental freedoms for all." In addition, it was made the coordinating body for various "specialized agencies," some old, some new, such as the International Labor Organization, the International Bank and Monetary Fund, the World Health Organization, the Food and Agricultural Organization, the United Nations Educational, Scientific and Cultural Organization (UNESCO), and others.

Trusteeship arrangements. Aims and principles for the administration of non-self-governing territories were set forth in some detail, and a Trusteeship System was made the successor to the Mandate System of the League, with a Trusteeship Council as the supervising body. In the United States, the Army and Navy had objected strongly to placing under trusteeship the former mandated islands taken from Japan at great cost. The armed services would have preferred outright annexation. But the United States had forsworn territorial aggrandizement as an object of the war and had sponsored the trusteeship system. It could not consistently annex the islands. The American delegation at San Francisco worked out a compromise, which was embodied in Articles 82 and 83 of the Charter. These specified that any area in a trust territory might be declared a "strategic area" and that all United Nations functions relating to such an area should be exercised under direction of the Security Council. The United States, having a veto in that body, could block any attempt that it

13. See Chapters 42, 45, 46.
14. F. P. Walters, *A History of the League of Nations,* 2 vols. (New York: Oxford University Press, 1922), 2: chap. 67.

might make to interfere with American administration of any "strategic area" under its charge. Eventually the former Japanese mandated islands—the Marshalls, Carolines, and Marianas—were assigned to the United States as a trust territory and were designated a "strategic area." [15]

The United States Accepts the U.N.

The action of the Senate and the Congress on the United Nations Charter contrasts strikingly with the Senate's mutilation and final rejection of the Covenant of the League. The Second World War had changed the senatorial attitude, but, as has been remarked before, Roosevelt, Hull, and their successors had learned much from Wilson's mistakes.

The Senate gave its approval of the Charter on July 28, 1945, by a vote of 89 to 2, the two nays being cast by Senators Langer of North Dakota and Shipstead of Minnesota.[16] Congress later provided that after contingents of American armed forces had been designated for use at the call of the Security Council, the President might use them at the Council's call without awaiting special permission by Congress. The Senate, which had rejected membership in the original World Court, now, by a vote of 60 to 2, accepted compulsory jurisdiction of the International Court of Justice in certain types of cases by approving the "optional clause" in the Statute of the Court.[17]

One may well wonder how the history of the world might have been changed if the United States had entered the League of Nations in a spirit of international cooperation such as that which it initially showed toward the United Nations.

Beginnings of a Rift

The fundamental purpose of the United Nations was, of course, the prevention of acts of aggression, whether these were accomplished by force or the threat of force. Its chief function was a policing function. For this purpose the Security Council was empowered, if efforts at peaceful settlement of a controversy failed, to call upon members of the U.N. to sever diplomatic relations with an offender and to apply economic sanctions. If such measures proved inadequate, the Security Council was to have at its disposal armed force contingents made available to it in advance by the members, and might use these as it saw fit against the offender. Immediate direction of such forces would be in the hands of a Military Staff Committee, made up of the chiefs of staff of the permanent members of the Council, or representatives of those chiefs of staff. But all action by the Security Council, it must be remembered, must have the concurrence of the five permanent members; it was subject to veto by any one of them.

In reality, this enforcement machinery, so impressive on paper, was paralyzed from the beginning by the rift between the Soviet Union and the West. No contingents of armed forces were made available to the Security Council, because the Military Staff Committee could not agree on their composition. The British and Americans wished specialized forces: they

15. J. W. Pratt, *America's Colonial Experiment* (Englewood Cliffs, N.J.: Prentice-Hall, Inc., 1950), pp. 362–67. For nonstrategic territories the Trusteeship Council was responsible to the General Assembly, where there was no veto.

16. Senator Hiram Johnson, whose "unchangeable isolationism" would presumably have led him to cast a third negative vote, was in the hospital. Vandenberg, *Private Papers*, pp. 128, 218.

17. *Documents on American Foreign Relations*, 8: 509–17. The "optional clause" was similar to that in the Statute of the earlier Court. See above, pp. 300–301. The Senate attached to its approval of the "optional clause" a reservation sponsored by Senator Tom Connally, excepting "disputes with regard to matters which are essentially within the domestic

jurisdiction of the United States of America as determined by the United States of America." The Connally reservation appreciably weakened the effectiveness of American adherence to the Court and in the opinion of some jurists actually nullified U.S. acceptance of the optional clause, but through the year 1970, all efforts to have it repealed had failed.

would furnish the principal naval and air contingents and expect the U.S.S.R., with its huge army, to provide most of the land forces. The Russians insisted upon equal and similar contributions from all five of the major powers. This disagreement was never composed.

A similar fate befell attempts at disarmament, notably the effort at international control of atomic energy and prevention of its use for warlike purposes. After August 1945, the specter of atomic war hung over the world. The United States, having for the time being an advantage in atomic knowhow and the possession of atomic weapons, took the lead, in company with Great Britain and Canada, in proposing international control. In January 1946, the U.N. Assembly established a United Nations Atomic Energy Commission. To this Commission, on June 14, 1946, the American member, Bernard Baruch, submitted a proposal thereafter generally referred to as the Baruch Plan. It called for the creation of an International Atomic Development Authority, to have complete control over the primary production of fissionable materials and over all dangerous forms of atomic energy development, as well as licensing and inspection authority over nondangerous forms. It should have unrestricted rights of inspection, aerial and otherwise. As soon as the proposed system of control and inspection was set up and functioning, the United States would dispose of its stockpile of atomic weapons, and the production of such weapons would thereafter be strictly prohibited. Any violation of this or other prohibitions would be subject to prompt and severe punishment; and here the Baruch Plan emphasized the point that no veto must stand in the way of punishment for this one type of offense.

The Baruch Plan was rejected by the Soviet Union, which would neither surrender national control of atomic activities, submit to effective inspection, nor waive the veto. It insisted, on the other hand, that existing atomic bombs be at once destroyed and the manufacture and use of others be strictly prohibited. The impasse, which developed in

1946, had not been resolved in September 1949, when it was revealed that the Soviet Union had perfected the technique of constructing atomic weapons, nor in August 1953, when both the United States and the U.S.S.R. had succeeded in producing the still more potent and frightful hydrogen bomb.

Attempts to limit conventional armaments had been equally futile. In 1952 a new United Nations Disarmament Commission, representing twelve nations, replaced both the U.N. Atomic Energy Commission and a separate Commission for Conventional Armaments.[18] The new Commission underwent repeated changes in size, eventually (in 1958) comprising representatives of all members of the U.N. Regardless of numbers, its deliberations were consistently unproductive, and further negotiations on disarmament between East and West were held for the most part outside the United Nations.[19]

18. A proposal made by President Eisenhower, December 8, 1953, for the creation of an International Atomic Energy Agency to promote peaceful uses of atomic energy, was adopted by the General Assembly a year later. The Soviet Union, initially cool to the proposal, eventually joined with the United States and other nations to establish the Agency, which was set up at Vienna in July 1957. The Agency found much useful work to do, but Eisenhower's hope that a modest beginning in cooperation for the peaceful uses of atomic energy might lead to agreement upon international control of its warlike uses was still unfulfilled after seventeen years.

19. In 1960 the U.S., Britain, France, and the U.S.S.R. set up a ten-nation disarmament committee in Geneva. Enlarged in 1962 by the addition of the representatives of eight nonaligned states to the original five Communist and five Western-bloc members, it came to be known as the Eighteen-Nation Disarmament Committee (E.N.D.C.)—a misnomer, since France's refusal to participate reduced its number in practice to seventeen. In 1969 its nominal membership was increased to twenty-six. (*New York Times,* July 30, 1969.) Its principal achievements to the end of 1970 were the negotiation of a nuclear non-proliferation treaty and a treaty prohibiting the placing of nuclear weapons on the ocean floor. The test-ban treaty of 1963 was negotiated directly between the United States, the U.S.S.R., and Britain. The treaty on the peaceful uses of outer space, on the other hand, was negotiated in a special U.N. committee and approved by the General Assembly. See below, p. 456.

Paralysis of the Security Council

On political questions, no less than on those of military forces and atomic energy, the hoped-for unanimity of the Big Five powers gave place to chronic deadlock between the Soviet Union and the democracies. From the first meeting of the Security Council, in January 1946, nearly every question submitted to it was one on which Soviet Russia and the United States took opposite sides. And from the beginning, Soviet Russia, which usually was in the minority, used its veto power freely to block action contrary to its wishes. By 1969 the U.S.S.R. had cast 105 vetoes.

The Security Council was able nevertheless, in its early meetings, to accomplish something merely by publicity. Thus, Soviet troops which had remained in Iran contrary to treaty engagements, withdrew following the raising of the issue in the Security Council, though Andrei Gromyko, the Russian member, boycotted a discussion that he could not veto. Complaints from Syria and Lebanon against the continued presence of British and French troops in those newly independent lands were answered by a majority vote in the Council favoring withdrawal of the troops. Though this resolution received a Soviet veto as being too weak, the British and French acted upon it as though it had official force.

The Security Council succeeded also, without a rift, in bringing about a cease-fire between Dutch and native forces in Indonesia, followed by a political agreement between Netherlands and Indonesian leaders; and it voted unanimously to send a commission to investigate disturbances on Greece's frontier with her Communist neighbors, Albania, Yugoslavia, and Bulgaria; it sent to Palestine a mediator who helped put a stop to hostilities between Jews and Arabs in 1949.

But with these achievements, and with one other, to be mentioned later, the record of the first five years ends. The commission to investigate the Greek frontier divided on ideological lines, the Russian and Polish members holding Greece responsible, the others blaming the Communist states. The Security Council divided similarly. It was the same in a dispute between Great Britain and Albania over damage to British destroyers by mines in the strait of Corfu; the same in an attempt to choose a neutral governor for Trieste, pending settlement of the boundary dispute between Italy and Yugoslavia. Even in the recommendation of new members to be elected by the General Assembly, the Security Council was long deadlocked. The West "blackballed" the satellites of the U.S.S.R.: Albania, Bulgaria, Hungary, the Mongolian People's Republic, Rumania, North Korea, and North Vietnam. The Soviet Union, while ready to engage in "horse-trading," vetoed recommendation of the following states desired by the western powers: Austria, Cambodia, Ceylon, Eire, Finland, Italy, Japan, Jordan, Laos, Libya, Nepal, Portugal, South Korea, South Vietnam.[20]

The only action by the Security Council that at all conformed to the vigorous role that had been planned for it was its decision, in June 1950, to resist by force the Communist invasion of South Korea.[21] This action, stimulated by the energetic leadership of the United States, was possible only because the Soviet Union was at the time boycotting the Council. If the Soviet delegate had been present, a veto would certainly have prevented a decision.

Some Accomplishments of the General Assembly

The General Assembly was not handicapped, as was the Security Council, by a right of veto. It made decisions by a two-thirds majority, in which the votes of all nations had equal weight. But the General Assembly could

20. The following new members were admitted: Afghanistan, Iceland, Sweden, Thailand (1946); Pakistan, Yemen (1947); Burma (1948); Israel (1949); Indonesia (1950). Total membership at end of 1954 was sixty. New members are elected by the General Assembly upon recommendation of the Security Council.
21. See Chapter 44.

only make recommendations to the members of the U.N., which were under no obligation to carry them out, whereas they were pledged to abide by decisions of the Security Council.

In spite of its lack of power, the General Assembly in its early years had to its credit some important achievements in the political field. It recommended the organization of a government for a United Korea and sent to Korea a commission to supervise the process. Excluded from North Korea by the Soviet occupation, the commission supervised the holding of elections in South Korea, and the General Assembly recognized the resulting government of the Republic of Korea. Later, when Chinese armies took the part of North Korea against the Republic of Korea and the United Nations, the General Assembly labeled Communist China an aggressor and recommended an embargo on shipment of war materials to China or North Korea.[22]

The General Assembly recommended the partition of Palestine into independent Jewish and Arab states, supplying the initiative to a movement that was actually carried out by Jewish arms and brought to a close by mediators acting under the direction of the Security Council.

The General Assembly achieved a settlement of the problem of disposition of the former Italian colonies. This problem was placed on the Assembly's doorstep by the Big Four Council of Foreign Ministers, who were unable to settle it themselves,[23] and who agreed in advance to accept the recommendation of the Assembly. The decision promised independence to Libya from January 1, 1952; to Italian Somaliland after a ten-year period under a trusteeship administered by Italy (1960); and directed that Eritrea be federated with Ethiopia.

Proposals for Strengthening the U.N.

Various proposals for strengthening the United Nations in its collective security func-

22. See Chapter 44.
23. See p. 437.

tion were made from time to time. These usually took the direction either of limiting the use of the veto in the Security Council, or of giving more authority to the General Assembly, where there was no veto. Proposals to amend the Charter were generally recognized as futile, since any amendment must have the approval of all the permanent members of the Security Council. The veto was self-protecting. Any limitation in its use, therefore, would have to be by voluntary agreement. The British proposed that the Big Five agree on a code of conduct in the use of the veto. The United States proposed that certain types of questions—thirty-one in all—be declared procedural and thus protected from the veto when they arose in the Security Council. Neither these nor other suggestions for restricting the veto were ever adopted.

More successful, at least in getting adopted, was an American proposal for empowering the General Assembly to act against aggression when the Security Council, because of lack of unanimity, failed to do so. This plan, labeled "United Action for Peace," was introduced into the General Assembly by Secretary of State Dean Acheson, September 20, 1950. The war in Korea was in full swing. The Security Council, in the absence of the Russian delegate, had taken vigorous action to repel aggression, but had been quickly reduced to the customary paralysis when that delegate returned. The need for finding a way around the veto had never been more evident.

The "United Action for Peace" plan proposed that the General Assembly undertake four types of action:

1. That it recommend appropriate collective measures by the members in cases of aggression or breach of the peace, when the Council fails to exercise its responsibility; the General Assembly to meet on twenty-four hours' notice.

2. That it establish a Peace Observation Commission, or peace patrol, to observe and report upon any area in which international conflict threatens.

3. That it recommend maintenance by each member of the United Nations of contingents of armed forces that could be made promptly

available for service to the United Nations upon recommendation of either the Security Council or the General Assembly.

4. That it establish a Collective Measures Committee to report to the Security Council and the General Assembly on methods for maintaining and strengthening international peace and security.[24]

Here was a set of reforms which, if adopted and if acted upon cooperatively by members of the U.N., might enable the veto-free General Assembly to do the work of the Security Council when that body was deadlocked. The proposals were adopted, November 3, 1950, by a vote of 55 to 2. It was after the adoption of these proposals that the General Assembly found Red China guilty of aggression and recommended a partial embargo on shipments to her. But the General Assembly took no further action under the authorization, unless one includes some of the peace-keeping operations between small states or rival factions as described below.

Finding neither the Security Council nor the General Assembly dependable as agencies for resisting Communist aggression in what had come to be called the cold war, the United States turned more and more to regional collective security organizations, for which Article 51 of the United Nations Charter had left the door open.

The U.N. Shows New Vigor

Beginning in 1956, however, the United Nations began to show new vigor. On a number of occasions the Security Council was able to act, but for the most part the new energy displayed by the world organization stemmed from the General Assembly (greatly enlarged in membership after 1954) and from the election in 1953 of a new Secretary-General, Dag Hammarskjöld, who brought outstanding courage, initiative, and imagination to the office.[25]

24. *Documents on American Foreign Relations,* 12: 179–86.
25. Hammarskjöld, a Swede, was the U.N.'s second

The new spirit of the United Nations was exhibited most strikingly in its handling of the Suez crisis of 1956 and the Congo crisis of 1960–1963, and in its dedication to the campaign against the remnants of "colonialism," especially from 1960 onward. The story of the Suez crisis is told elsewhere.[26] It is sufficient here to point out its significance in the evolution of United Nations policy.

In the Suez crisis, brought on by Israeli and Anglo-French attacks on Egypt following Nasser's seizure of the Suez Canal, and in the contemporary Soviet aggression against Hungary, the Security Council was, as usual, paralyzed. Anglo-French vetoes in the first instance, a Russian veto in the second, prevented action. The General Assembly, however, promptly passed resolutions calling for the withdrawal of the invading forces. The British, French, and Israelis, under pressure from the United Nations and the United States and threatened by the Soviet Union, obeyed the resolutions and withdrew their forces from Egypt. The Russians paid no heed to the demand that they leave Hungary. Here were one victory and one defeat for the United Nations. The novel feature of the episode was not in the withdrawal resolutions and the divergent responses to them but in the subsequent creation, pursuant to another resolution of the Assembly, of the U.N. Emergency Force (UNEF), whose role it was to maintain peace on crucial segments of the border between Israel and Egypt. Supplied initially by ten governments, numbering 5,500 men, and maintained at a cost of about $2 million a month, the UNEF remained as a peacekeeping force until Egypt demanded its withdrawal on the eve of the Six-Day War of June 1967.[27]

Secretary-General. His predecessor, the Norwegian Trygve Lie, had made an excellent record, though he had shown less initiative than his successor. He resigned because of a boycott instituted against him by the Soviet bloc in consequence of his stand against Communist aggression in Korea.
26. See Chapter 47.
27. See Chapter 47. In the minor Middle Eastern crisis of 1958, the Security Council sent observers to Lebanon to check reports of aggression from without. Later, under a resolution of the General Assembly,

Operation Congo

The United Nations also found work to do in the Congo, the former Belgian colony,[28] which attained its independence on June 30, 1960. Premature independence was followed by mutiny of the native army, a general condition of anarchy, and the return of Belgian troops for the protection of Europeans. The native government requested the U.N. to send in a military force to restore order and replace the Belgians. In this instance the United States and the U.S.S.R. concurred in a vote by which the Security Council authorized the Secretary-General to comply with the Congo's appeal for military assistance. The military force thus provided for and designated United Nations Operation in the Congo (ONUC) eventually attained a peak strength of some 20,000, drawn largely from other African states, and from Ireland, Sweden, India, Indonesia, and Malaya. The United States gave warm support to the United Nations Operation in the Congo. That operation seemed the best safeguard against unilateral Soviet intervention, which would have been welcomed by local left-wing elements, and which might in turn have necessitated direct counter-intervention by

the United States, with incalculable consequences. The United States made a major contribution in airlifting men and equipment into the troubled area. It also helped to provide emergency food supplies for a population that the breakdown of the internal economy threatened with starvation, "and supported a wide variety of supplementary United Nations measures undertaken on the authority of the Secretary-General with the aim of averting a complete breakdown in civilian services and public health condition." [29]

The harmony that had enabled the Security Council to act in this case was of short duration. The Soviet Union was soon finding fault with the Secretary-General for failing to suppress the secessionist Moïse Tshombé of Katanga province and to expel his European mercenaries. After the overthrow and death of the pro-Soviet premier, Patrice Lumumba, the U.S.S.R. launched a virulent attack against Dag Hammarskjöld. Joined by the other members of the Communist bloc, it withdrew recognition from him as Secretary-General and demanded that he be replaced by a "troika," a three-man committee with one member each from the West, the Communist bloc, and the non-committed nations, whose decisions must be by unanimity. This was obviously an attempt to reduce the office of

---

the Secretary-General stationed a U.N. "presence" in Lebanon and Jordan to observe and report upon the withdrawal of American and British troops, which had been sent in for the protection of these small states. In the Six-Day Arab-Israel War of June 1967, the Security Council, in addition to issuing a series of cease-fire orders, agreed unanimously to a resolution (November 22, 1967) proposing terms of settlement. After three years, however, the resolution had not been acted upon by the parties to the dispute.

28. The two adjacent Congo Republics, one formerly a Belgian dependency, the other formerly French, are often distinguished from each other by printing the names of their seats of government in parentheses after the names of the nations. Thus the one-time Belgian and French colonies are referred to respectively as Democratic Republic of the Congo (Kinshasa) and Republic of the Congo (Brazzaville). By 1965 native names had replaced the European names of many of the principal towns. Thus Léopoldville, Elisabethville, and Stanleyville became respectively Kinshasa, Lubumbashi, and Kisangani.

29. *U. S. in World Affairs, 1960*, p. 180. In addition to UNEF and ONUC, the U.N. had in 1963 maintained an observation force in Kashmir, in dispute between India and Pakistan; a Temporary Executive Authority in West Irian (New Guinea) during the transition from Netherlands to Indonesian rule; and an observation mission in Yemen, where the United Arab Republic and Saudi Arabia were backing opposing sides in a civil war. The Secretary-General had also, in 1963, sent a group of U.N. officials to Sarawak and North Borneo to determine whether the population of those British colonies desired to federate with Malaya and Singapore to form Malaysia. Introduction to Annual Report of the Secretary-General, in the *New York Times*, August 26, 1963. For U.N. operation in Cyprus see below, p. 426. In November 1964 U.S. planes landed Belgian paratroops at Stanleyville in the Congo to rescue several hundred Europeans and Americans whose lives were threatened by rebel forces. What the U.S. and Belgians regarded as a humanitarian act was denounced as "imperialism" in many African states and the Communist world.

Secretary-General to the same impotence that afflicted the Security Council. Since the Soviet Union and its supporters were at the same time refusing to pay their assessments for either ONUC or UNEF, the United Nations faced both a constitutional and a financial crisis.

The constitutional crisis was solved, in part at least, by the death of Dag Hammarskjöld, September 18, 1961. After the failure of a variety of efforts to bring Katanga peacefully back into the Congo, fighting broke out in Elisabethville, the Katanga capital, between U.N. troops and Tshombé's forces. Hammarskjöld was on his way to a conference with Tshombé when his plane crashed and he was killed. The Russians, after some hesitation, abandoned their insistence on a "troika" and consented to the election, November 3, 1961, of the chief Burmese delegate, U Thant, as Acting Secretary-General for the remainder of Hammarskjöld's term. A year later U Thant was elected for a full five-year term, with nothing said about the "troika." He was re-elected for another term in 1966.

Who Pays for Peacekeeping?

The financial crisis admitted of no such simple solution. The operations of ONUC and UNEF were costing about $10 million per month, far more than the normal budget of the U.N. In theory, UNEF and ONUC were supported by special assessments to be paid by members in the same ratios as their normal contributions, meaning that nearly one-third of the cost would be borne by the United States.[30] But not only the Soviet bloc, but also France, the Latin American nations, and some others were refusing to pay their special assessments.[31]

The U.N. treasury faced a deficit of over $100 million by the end of 1961 and double that by the end of the next year. Voluntary contributions over and above their assessments by the United States and some other advanced nations alleviated but did not cure the deficit. As a temporary expedient, the General Assembly voted in December 1961 to issue bonds up to the amount of $200 million, of which the United States Congress agreed to purchase an amount equal to the purchases of all other governments, to a maximum of $100 million. Before the end of 1962 over two-thirds of the authorized bonds had been subscribed. The U.N. was enabled to continue its operations in the troubled Congo. By January 1963, Katanga's resistance to the central government had collapsed. A native army was undergoing training, chiefly at the hands of Europeans, but not before the middle of 1964 was it expected to be ready for the responsibility of maintaining order in the Congo. Until that time (June 30, 1964) the General Assembly had provided for the continued presence of a U.N. force of 5,350 men.[32]

Meanwhile the World Court had been appealed to and in an advisory opinion on July 20, 1962, had ruled that assessments for the U.N.'s peacekeeping operations had the same obligatory character as the regular annual contributions. In theory, this ruling opened the way for a species of sanctions against nonpaying members. Article 19 of the U.N. Charter provides that any member delinquent to the extent of two years' dues shall lose its vote in the General Assembly. The Soviet Union reached that degree of delinquency early in 1964.

The United States was determined to apply Article 19 against the Soviet Union when the General Assembly met in its nineteenth regular session in 1964. The U.S.S.R., for its part, threatened to withdraw from the General Assembly if denied its vote, possibly as a

---

30. Until 1961, the United States was assessed 32.2 percent of the normal budget, the Soviet Union, 13.5 percent. In 1961, the U.S. share was reduced to 32.02 percent, the Soviet share raised to 14.97 percent. *U.S. in World Affairs, 1961,* pp. 364–66. By 1967 the U.S. share had fallen to 31.57 percent.
31. The U.S.S.R. and France denied the legality of the UNEF and all but the initial Congo operations on the ground that they had been ordered by the

General Assembly instead of the Security Council. Other delinquent members pleaded inability to pay the assessments.
32. *New York Times,* October 6, 1963, Sec. 4, p. 2.

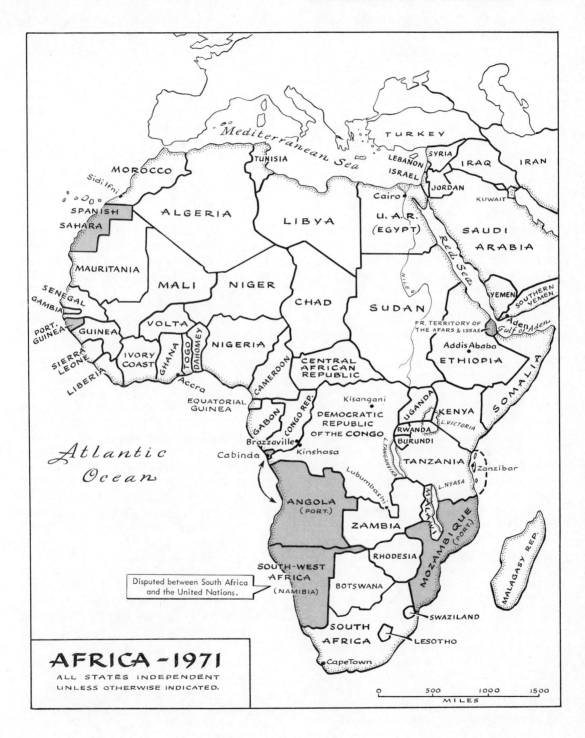

Disputed between South Africa and the United Nations.

AFRICA — 1971
ALL STATES INDEPENDENT
UNLESS OTHERWISE INDICATED.

prelude to leaving the U.N. altogether. The U.N. faced a serious crisis. To avoid such a showdown the meeting of the General Assembly was postponed from September to December in the hope that the contending powers might reach an accommodation. When they failed to do so and the Assembly met, December 1, its business was limited by common consent to noncontroversial matters in which no state-by-state vote was required, and hence the United States had no occasion to challenge the vote of its adversary. Finally, at the very end of the session, February 18, 1965, Communist Albania challenged a ruling of the president. Only a vote would decide the issue, and the United States surrendered, agreeing not, on this technical point, to invoke Article 19 against the Soviet Union. Before the next regular session of the General Assembly it had abandoned its position rather than risk a rupture of the United Nations. The Soviet Union and France had given some reason to think that, if not pressed as to their supposed legal obligation, they would make voluntary contributions to the costs of peacekeeping. They did not do so, and a committee of thirty-three, appointed to find a solution for the financial problem, had no success. By 1970, contributions were so far in arrears that the U.N. had to resort to borrowing to meet its payroll.

Meanwhile, a conflict which had arisen between the indigenous Greek and Turkish populations of newly independent Cyprus threatened to drag Greece and Turkey into war. The U.N. peacekeeping force which was sent to the island in 1964 and was still there in 1970, had to be paid for by voluntary contributions. These were furnished in part by the United States and Britain, in part by the small nations providing the troops. While the U.N. forces helped to keep the hostile factions from each other's throats, mediators from the U.N., NATO, and the United States sought means of settling the prolonged quarrel. Particularly successful was an American mediator, Cyrus R. Vance, sent to the area by President Johnson during an especially dangerous phase of the dispute in 1967. His efforts brought about a provisional understanding between the governments of Greece, Turkey, and Cyprus but did not eliminate the need for peacekeeping forces.

But while the attitude of the Soviet Union and France prevented any systematic financing of the U.N.'s peacekeeping activities, there was more dependable provision for the armed forces needed for such operations. The practice had been to draw such forces from the small nations (and from India, which was small in terms of military power). The Scandinavian countries had been particularly cooperative in this respect, and early in 1968 they —Denmark, Sweden, Norway, and Finland— as well as Austria, informed Secretary-General U Thant that they had taken practical steps "to provide peacekeeping forces to the United Nations on short notice." Canada had also "earmarked contingents for peacekeeping use." [33] This was a far cry from the armed forces contingents which the framers of the Charter had envisaged as supplied primarily by the great powers. The difference between expectation and reality on this point was characteristic of the U.N. in general.

New Members, New Purposes

By 1970 the original membership of the United Nations had risen from 51 to 127. The deadlock of 1954 had been broken the next year with the admission of sixteen new members, and nearly every year thereafter saw further additions.[34] The number of new Asian nations, former colonies or dependencies of Europe, was noteworthy, but they were now outnumbered by the new African states, formerly colonies of Britain, France, and Belgium. Ghana, the former British Gold Coast,

33. *New York Times,* March 21, 1968.
34. See above, p. 420. The only independent states remaining outside the U.N. in 1970 were Switzerland (by its own choice), Communist China, East and West Germany, North and South Korea, North and South Vietnam, Western Samoa, and the tiny European states of Monaco, Andorra, San Marino, and Liechtenstein.

was admitted in 1957—the first member (other than Liberia) from Black Africa south of the Sahara. President de Gaulle's invitation to France's African colonies to become independent within a French Community produced a swarm of new states, beginning with Guinea in 1958. By the end of 1969, all of Africa, with a population approaching 330 million, held thirty-nine seats and cast thirty-nine votes in the General Assembly; the United States, with its population of 200 million, enjoyed one seat and one vote in that body.

The multiplication of the United Nations members aggravated the problem of so-called "microstates" or "ministates." Many of the new states, like a few of the original members, were insignificant in area and population. Gabon, for example, had a population of 452,000, the Maldive Islands, 97,000. Yet each ministate in the General Assembly had the same voting power as the United States or the Soviet Union. This created a situation where in theory, as observed by Secretary of State Rusk, a two-thirds majority of General Assembly votes could be cast by states representing only 10 percent of the world's population or by states responsible for only 5 percent of the United Nations budget.[35]

This unhealthy disparity between voting strength and the capacity for action in realistic terms drew comment from Secretary General U Thant in his Annual Report for 1967. His suggestion that a form of associate membership be established for nations below some specified level of population or resources was not acted upon at the time, but two years later, under prodding by the United States, the Security Council named a committee to study the possibility of such associate membership as U Thant had proposed. The United States, as a member of that committee, received little support in its efforts to find a remedy. The other great powers—Britain and the Soviet Union—were reluctant to take action that might offend the existing small states. It appeared possible that the United States might be forced to use its veto in the Security Council to prevent the further dilution of the General Assembly by the admission of some sixty to seventy-five additional infant "countries," the remnants of dissolving colonial empires.[36]

The General Assembly in its early years had been dominated by the United States and its partners in Europe and Latin America. Now Asia and Africa together held a majority of the seats; with the Soviet bloc they held a safe majority. When the twenty Latin American states joined them, as they often did on such issues as colonialism, the combination easily commanded the two-thirds majority required for important decisions.

The African-Asian group, commanding a majority in the General Assembly, with an Asian Secretary-General and with Asians and Africans filling many positions in the Secretariat, understandably desired a more influential role in other U.N. bodies than had originally been assigned them. To meet their wishes an amendment to the Charter, adopted in 1965, enlarged the Security Council from eleven to fifteen members, the Economic and Social Council from eighteen to twenty-seven. It gave the Africans and Asians five of the ten elective seats on the Security Council and required a majority of nine instead of seven votes for decisions on important matters, the five permanent members retaining their right of veto.[37]

Two attitudes characterized virtually all of the new U.N. members. They were neutralist, or at least uncommitted, in the cold war, and they were bitterly hostile to what remained of colonialism and its accompaniment, racial discrimination. These attitudes the United States could accept, with reservations as to the sec-

35. *U.S. in World Affairs, 1964,* p. 315. Fiji (population 520,000) became the 127th member in October 1970. *New York Times,* October 14, 1970.

36. *New York Times,* September 30, 1967, August 28, 1969; William R. Frye in *Buffalo Evening News,* April 2, 1970. Cf. F. T. P. Plimpton, "The U.N. Needs Family Planning," *New York Times Magazine,* September 18, 1966.

37. This "inflation" of the Security Council membership, in the opinion of an experienced public man, "altered its character and impaired the chances of its effective operation." G. W. Ball, "Slogans and Realities," *Foreign Affairs,* 47 (July 1969), 623–41.

ond. Washington had come far since the days when Secretary Dulles had branded neutralism as immoral. It now accepted as natural the desire of the new states to avoid involvement in the struggle between East and West, asking only that they maintain genuine independence. As for colonialism, the United States had always felt sympathy for peoples struggling for independence, though in these days it would have preferred to see independence attained more gradually and with better preparation. It was also embarrassed when caught between the urgent desire of colonial populations for immediate independence and the preference of its European allies for a more leisurely pace or, in the case of Portugal, for preservation of the *status quo*.

The Anticolonial Urge

The principal targets of the Asian-African states' anticolonial displeasure after 1958 were Portugal and the Union of South Africa, with the addition, in 1965, of Rhodesia. Portugal refused even to consider independence for her African possessions of Angola, Mozambique, and Portuguese Guinea. Portugal maintained that these possessions were not colonies but provinces of Portugal, but this quibble could not disguise the fact that some millions of black Africans were ruled by Portuguese governors. The South African government, wholly controlled by whites, practiced a policy of extreme racial discrimination, known as *apartheid* (apartness), against blacks, "coloreds" (persons of mixed blood), and Asiatics, who outnumbered the "master race" more than four to one. South Africa also applied her racial policy in Southwest Africa, a pre-World War I German colony which South Africa had administered as a mandate. She had refused, after 1945, to place it under the Trusteeship System. Rhodesia, formerly the British colony of Southern Rhodesia, issued a unilateral declaration of independence on November 11, 1965 (the first British colony to secede without British consent since 1776). The purpose of the secession was to preserve the rule of the white minority of 220,000 over the majority of 4 million blacks, against a British policy of gradual conversion to majority rule. Rhodesia thereby joined South Africa and the Portuguese colonies as a third exemplar of racial oppression in southern Africa.

The vigor of anticolonialism in the United Nations, as measured by votes, was displayed when the General Assembly, December 14, 1960, resolved 89 to 0, that "immediate steps" should be taken to transfer all governmental powers in the remaining colonies to the native people. Unimpressed by the recent exhibition of anarchy in the Congo, the eighty-nine delegates declared: "Inadequacy of political, economic, social or educational preparedness should never serve as a pretext for delaying independence." The United States was one of nine members that abstained from voting on the resolution.[38] In the following year, however, it parted company with Britain, France, Spain, and South Africa, in voting for the creation of a Committee of Seventeen (later twenty-four) to oversee the implementation of the resolution.

The United States, the U.N., and Africa

The shift to a more uncompromising stand on the anticolonial issue, indicated by the two votes just mentioned, coincided with a change of administration in the United States from Eisenhower to John F. Kennedy. It was during the Eisenhower administration (1953–1961) that Africa had first loomed large in the perspective of American foreign policy. In earlier years, when most of Africa consisted of colonies of European states, such African matters as came to the attention of the State Department were normally handled through the diplomatic channels to Europe. In 1937 responsibility for much of the African area was

38. *Documents on American Foreign Relations, 1960,* pp. 575–77; *U.S. in World Affairs, 1960,* pp. 352–56. The resolution was an Asian-African substitute for an even more drastic one proposed by Premier Khrushchev, calling for the complete elimination of colonialism immediately.

transferred to the Bureau of Near Eastern Affairs, which later became the Bureau of Near Eastern, South Asian, and African Affairs. In 1958, after several former African colonies or protectorates had attained their independence, Congress provided for a separate Bureau of African Affairs, headed by an assistant secretary of state.[39] Kennedy's choice for this office, G. Mennen ("Soapy") Williams, former governor of Michigan, brought to his task a fresh enthusiasm for African self-determination.[40]

Before the new administration had been in office two months, its representative in the Security Council, Adlai Stevenson, joined the Russian and Afro-Asian delegates in voting for a resolution admonishing Portugal to conform to U.N. policy toward colonialism. The new administration seemed thus to have gone nearly all the way in opposition to the chief remnants of colonialism in Africa. Though it abstained from voting on a later resolution calling on all states to refrain from supplying Portugal with arms,[41] it supported a similar resolution a few days later, calling for denial of arms to South Africa. On this occasion, Ambassador Stevenson declared it to be within the prerogatives of the U.N. to seek to induce South Africa to abandon *apartheid,* primarily a "domestic question" though that might be. He announced that after January 1, 1964, the United States would stop the sale of all arms to that country.[42]

The United States made it plain, however, that it would not support punitive measures against Portugal or South Africa and that it would oppose their expulsion from the United Nations—a measure of which there was talk among African and Asian delegations.

American policy remained much the same during the Johnson administration. When Rhodesia declared its independence in defiance of British refusal, the British government imposed financial and commercial sanctions, and the U.N. Security Council, at British prompting, did the same. Rhodesia was expelled from the sterling bloc, subjected to an oil embargo (which was evaded through imports via South Africa), and denied a market for her tobacco, chrome, and other products. Britain's Prime Minister Harold Wilson made it plain, however, that he would not use military force to suppress the independent Rhodesian government of Ian D. Smith and stuck to this policy despite the angry demands of the spokesmen of Black Africa that Britain use force to do

39. Vernon McKay, *Africa in World Politics* (New York: Harper and Row, Publishers, 1963), pp. 290, 292.

40. Williams' alleged remark in Nairobi, Kenya, in February 1961, that America believed in "Africa for the Africans," was so disturbing to the British that an American paper headlined a story, "BRITISH IN LATHER OVER SOAPY." Williams may have been misquoted. At any rate, he explained that by "Africans" he understood all who made their homes in Africa, including Europeans and Asiatics. McKay, *Africa in World Politics,* pp. 351–52.

41. *New York Times,* August 4, 1963, Sec. 4, p. 2. Assistant Secretary Williams explained the abstention on the ground that the language of the resolution would not encourage Portugal to join in the necessary "dialogue." The United States, in other words, still hoped to win its end by persuasion. *Department of State Bulletin,* 49 (September 16, 1963), 434–36.

42. *New York Times,* August 11, 1963, Sec. 4, p. 2. The United States had already stopped the sale of "offensive" weapons to South Africa. The white population of that country, already heavily armed, obtained most of their military supplies from Britain, which did not join the embargo. The South African matter was brought before the Security Council by spokesmen for 32 African governments, all but South Africa itself. In the preceding May, the heads of state of 28 of these nations had assembled at Addis Ababa in Ethiopia. They had unanimously adopted an African Charter, one provision of which demanded the elimination from the continent of all forms of colonialism (of which apartheid was one). There was talk then and later about a resort to military action against Portugal and South Africa if milder measures failed. Ibid., May 26, 1963, Sec. 4, p. 2. In November 1963, members of the Afro-Asian group were pressing for further action against South Africa; e.g. an embargo on petroleum and petroleum products, in order to compel her to recognize the right of the people of Southwest Africa to independence. The petroleum embargo failed of adoption, but on December 4 the Security Council adopted, this time unanimously, a resolution urging a worldwide embargo on the shipment to South Africa of equipment for manufacturing and maintaining arms and ammunition. Ibid., November 6, December 5, 1963.

what economic sanctions were failing to accomplish. The United States backed its British ally one hundred percent, refusing recognition to the Rhodesian government, cooperating in the economic sanctions, and supporting Britain in her refusal to use force against the rebellious colony.[43]

In the case of South West Africa, the World Court, in July, 1966, evaded the responsibility of passing upon the legality of South Africa's rule, based as it was on a mandate from the long defunct League of Nations. The U.N. General Assembly thereupon (October 27, 1966) declared that South Africa's mandate over the territory was terminated and that South West Africa therefore came "under the direct responsibility of the United Nations." The United States voted in favor of this resolution and accepted membership on a fourteen-nation committee charged with recommending means by which South West Africa should be administered. But when this committee (its American member was William P. Rogers, future Secretary of State) failed to agree on a recommendation, the United States parted company with the Asian-African majority. Under domination of the latter group, supported by the Communist bloc, the General Assembly (May 19, 1967) set up a Council to take over and administer South West Africa—later rechristened Namibia—and to speed it on its way to independence. The Council, however, was given no means by which to oust a defiant South Africa from the territory, other than a *pro forma* request to the Security Council to "take all appropriate measures"—a request that had no chance of being complied with. The United States was one of thirty

members that abstained from voting on this futile measure, which nevertheless was adopted by a vote of 85 to 2.[44]

The American position on these African issues, in 1967 and to the end of the decade, was, on the one hand, to make plain its sympathy with Black Africa's drive against racial inequality and the remnants of colonialism; but, on the other hand, to oppose the use of force in seeking these objectives and to discourage irresponsible and utopian legislation by the anticolonial majority in the General Assembly. Thus the United States opposed the use of force to bring Rhodesia to terms or to expel South Africa from its "mandated territory"; it opposed a suggested blockade of South Africa to halt shipments of oil to Rhodesia; and it opposed General Assembly resolutions calling for support of guerrilla warfare against the white racist regimes in Rhodesia and South Africa. As Arthur Goldberg, United States ambassador to the U.N., remarked in a 1967 address on African affairs, "the best way to solve difficult problems is not by dramatic confrontations but by patient dialog." [45] This was a sound position for the United States to take in the light of its own interests. Needless to say, it did not satisfy the Asian-African majority in the United Nations, though Secretary of State William P. Rogers, in an unprecedented fifteen-day tour of ten African states in February 1970, was apparently quite successful in allaying African criticism of the American attitude.

The United States and the U.N.: Economic Development and Human Rights

In the economic and social activities of the United Nations, the United States had played a major role from the beginning. It had taken a leading part in the creation of a dozen or more "specialized agencies" of the U.N., such as the World Bank and the World Health Or-

43. It was in support of British policy in Rhodesia that the United States cast its first veto in the Security Council. On March 1, 1970, Rhodesia severed its last tie with the British Crown and declared itself a racially segregated Republic. On March 17 the U.S. joined Britain in vetoing a Security Council resolution which not only condemned Britain for refusal to use force, but called upon all states to sever not only diplomatic and economic relations but all forms of communication with the Rhodesian regime. The U.S. had already emphasized its nonrecognition of the Rhodesian government by announcing that it would close its consulate in Salisbury. *New York Times,* March 2, 10, 18, 1970.

44. *Documents on American Foreign Relations, 1966,* pp. 309–11; ibid., *1967,* pp. 300–303.
45. *Department of State Bulletin,* 56 (February 20, 1967), 292; *New York Times,* October 13, November 21, 1969; *Buffalo Evening News,* November 13, 1968.

ganization, and was the largest single contributor to their upkeep. It had initiated the founding of the International Atomic Energy Agency and contributed generously in cash and commodities to a World Food Program. It had led in the creation of a billion dollar International Development Association and had inspired the General Assembly, in December 1961, to declare the 1960's to be the United Nations Development Decade. Unfortunately, the purpose of the last-named enterprise—narrowing the gap between the backward, or "developing," nations and the industrialized nations (North America, Europe, and Japan) —was not realized. The gap was wider at the end of the decade than at the beginning. The period would be known to history, it was suggested, as the Decade of Discouragement.[46]

For this failure the United States must bear a considerable share of the responsibility. It had, it is true, after long resistance, accepted the proposal that the industrialized nations should grant generalized tariff preferences to the developing countries, and had joined in endorsing the proposal in principle at the Second U.N. Conference on Trade and Development (UNCTAD II) at New Delhi in February and March 1968. But the details of this program remained to be worked out, and its usefulness had still to be tested.[47] Meanwhile, the costs of the war in Vietnam, an adverse balance of payments, and a growing aversion to "give-away" programs on the part of Congress had resulted in drastic curtailment in the amounts of foreign aid granted by the United States to developing countries.[48]

In its response to one field of U.N. activity —international legislation on human rights— the United States had been distinctly laggard; its record in this area approximated those of Spain and South Africa. From 1945 to 1948 the United States, in the U.N. Commission on Human Rights, led the movement for a Universal Declaration of Human Rights, which was adopted by the General Assembly in December 1948. Since 1948 different U.N. agencies have completed twenty or more conventions or treaties on different aspects of human rights. Of these, the United States, up to December 1970, had ratified exactly two. One of the first to be completed was a convention of December 1948 outlawing genocide. This was sent to the Senate by President Truman but never acted upon. Secretary Dulles at the beginning of the Eisenhower administration (1953–1961) announced that the United States would not become a party to any human rights convention, on the ground that under the American federal system a treaty cannot be used to effect domestic reform. The United States, said Dulles, would promote human rights, but by means of "persuasion, education, example."

President Kennedy took a different attitude. In July 1963, he sent to the Senate three treaties on the subjects of slavery, forced labor, and women's rights. Of these the Senate —four years later—approved one, an innocuous treaty forbidding slavery. It later approved one on refugees. Though President Johnson had signed a Convention on the Elimination of All Forms of Racial Discrimination, adopted by the General Assembly in 1965, he had not sent it to the Senate, and the year 1968, declared by the General Assembly to be the International Year for Human Rights, found the United States with but two human rights treaties on its books.[49] The same record held two years later, when President Nixon, February 20, 1970, urged the Senate to approve the Genocide Convention of 1948.[50]

46. Secretary General U Thant as cited in *Manchester Guardian Weekly,* January 3, 1970; *U.S. in World Affairs,* 1967, p. 352.

47. *U. N. Monthly Chronicle,* April 1968, pp. 74–82; *New York Times,* March 22, 27, April 15 (editorial), 1968; W. M. Blumenthal, "A World of Preferences," *Foreign Affairs,* 48 (April 1970), 549–60.

48. W. L. Thorp, "Foreign Aid: A Report on the Reports," *Foreign Affairs,* 48 (April 1970), 561–73.

49. William Korey, "Human Rights Treaties: Why Is the U.S. Stalling?" *Foreign Affairs,* 45 (April 1967), 414–24.

50. Nixon's message on genocide treaty with report by Secretary Rogers, *Department of State Bulletin,* 62 (March 16, 1970), 350–53. As of June 18, 1970, six treaties on different aspects of human rights awaited action by the Senate. Letter from Human Rights Division, Department of State, to author, June 18, 1970. To the end of the year there was no report of further action.

42

Europe and
the Cold War

The rift in the United Nations between the Soviet Union, backed by its satellites, and the United States, generally supported by the other democracies, reflected a mounting antagonism between the two groups. The origin of this antagonism and of the resulting contest, dubbed the "cold war," has itself been a subject of controversy. One interpretation, until recently generally accepted in the United States, finds the origin of the strife in the supposed determination of the Soviet leaders to make the whole world Communist, by force if necessary. They had, according to this theory, used the alliance with the West for the destruction of Nazism. That accomplished, the alliance had lost its value to them, and they quickly abandoned it to pursue their goal of world revolution. In violation of the promises subscribed to at Yalta, they set up Communist regimes in "liberated Europe" and only awaited a favorable occasion to impose such regimes on the nations of Western Europe, allies of the United States. The cold war began when the United States resisted such Communist expansion through the "containment" policy described below.

Alternative Theories

One school of historians, commonly referred to as the New Left, offers a directly opposite interpretation, placing the chief blame for the cold war upon the United States. Viewing economic motives as all-important, historians of this group interpret American foreign policy since 1945, like that of the preceding half-century, as "imperialistic" and counterrevolutionary. The cold war, they say, began when President Harry Truman, apprised of the prospect of American possession of a potent secret weapon, the atomic bomb, resolved to require Stalin to relax his grasp of the nations of Eastern Europe and permit them to enjoy an "open door" (to American capitalism). In this plan he had the hearty support of James F. Byrnes, who became his Secretary of State in July 1945. In this general framework, these scholars cite specific actions by the United States which at best were less than gracious toward a wartime ally: the abrupt termination of lend-lease to Russia after the German surrender; denial of a reconstruction loan to Russia on terms acceptable to the Kremlin, while making a postwar loan of 3¾ billion dollars to Britain; the withholding from Russia of the secret of the atomic bomb, etc.[1] Thus, in their view, Stalin was driven into an antagonistic position by the aggressive policies of "American imperialism."

The New Left's explanation of the cold war has had a wholesome effect in correcting some of the excessively nationalistic and moralistic views popular in the United States, but like other mono-causational interpretations of history, it goes much too far. As a Hegelian antithesis, it will some day contribute to a new and more acceptable synthesis.

A third interpretation takes account of American materialistic motives and ungracious actions toward the Soviet Union as contributing factors in producing the cold war but finds the main cause elsewhere. It acknowledges that American fears of Soviet expansionism were genuine but believes that they were largely ill-founded. This theory, accepted today by many students of Soviet policy, holds that the Soviet leaders were less interested in spreading Communism than in safeguarding Russia against further attacks from the West, such as those delivered by Germany in 1914 and 1941, to say nothing of Napoleon in 1812. Thus, in discussing the fate of Poland at Yalta, when Churchill remarked that for Britain the question of Poland was one of honor, Stalin replied that for Russia the question was "one of life and death. . . . Throughout history," he added, "Poland has been the corridor for attack on Russia." The Soviet leaders, in other words, put national security ahead of world revolution, and sought security much as the Czars had done, by establishing firm control over the small states on their western frontier.

1. Inspirer and teacher of many of the young historians of the New Left is William Appleman Williams, whose *The Tragedy of American Diplomacy,* rev. ed. (New York: Dell Publishing Co., Inc., 1962), applies this thesis to the whole period since 1898. See Charles S. Maier, "Revisionism and the Interpretation of Cold War Origins," *Perspectives on American History,* 14 (1970), 313–47.

In accord with this theory was Stalin's agreement with Churchill in October 1944[2] conceding British or British-American predominant influence in Greece in return for predominant Soviet influence in Rumania, Bulgaria, and Hungary, with a fifty-fifty split in Yugoslavia. Why Stalin seemingly abandoned this position at Yalta,[3] accepting Roosevelt's proposal for an assurance of democracy and self-determination in Poland and "liberated Europe," is not clear. At any rate, he secured a loophole in unofficial assurances at Yalta that those neighbor states should have "friendly" governments, which the Russians later interpreted to mean Communist governments.

Put in different words, the Soviets were insisting on a sphere of influence in Eastern Europe while conceding a similar sphere to the Western Allies in Greece, Italy, and Western Europe in general, and also, a little later, reluctantly, in occupied Japan. Unfortunately for the future of East-West harmony, Stalin made promises at Yalta which, if taken literally, could not be reconciled with his sphere-of-influence agreement with Churchill. Churchill, in fact, was the first Allied statesman to object to the Soviets' riveting their control on Rumania and Bulgaria. As for the United States, it could not cheerfully accept Soviet domination of those states, which violated the American dogma of self-determination and the American economic principle of the Open Door. Its adherence to principle was no doubt reinforced by the presence in the electorate of several million persons of Polish and other East European ancestry.

Eventually the United States did recognize the Russian-imposed Communist governments in Eastern Europe, thus in effect accepting Russia's sphere of influence in that area, but it did so with such ill grace and with such persistent demands for fulfillment of the Yalta promises, that the Kremlin suspected its former ally of planning to "liberate" Eastern Europe once more, this time from its Russian

2. See Chapter 40.
3. See Chapter 40.

"liberators." Meanwhile, the Western powers were equally suspicious of Soviet purposes, which they assumed to embrace the subjection of all Western Europe to Communism, if need be by the use of the huge Russian armies.

Soviet suspicion of Western intentions (as distinct from wishes) had no basis in fact; and it seems probable today that Western suspicions of Soviet purposes were almost equally unfounded. But suspicion bred suspicion, and each defensive measure taken by one party was viewed by the other as aggressive and so calling for more defense. Hence the spiral of escalation in fears and in armaments. In this theory, the "cold war" was a product of exaggerated mutual suspicion, which in turn derived partly from a failure of communication, perhaps inevitable between parties harboring such antipathetic ideologies.

If this interpretation is correct, Stalin's decision to abandon cooperation with the West did not come at once as a consequence of the German surrender. There is good reason to believe that for some time after May 1945 he expected that cooperation to continue. This can be inferred from the advice that he was giving to Communist leaders in the Far East and in Europe: Mao Tse-tung should accept the supremacy of Chiang Kai-shek; Tito should welcome King Peter back to Yugoslavia; the French and Italian Communists should avoid "adventurism." Not, apparently, until some time in 1946 or early 1947 did he take a wholly uncompromising position on the chief issues that divided the former Grand Alliance.[4]

The Future of Germany

The rift that began over the fate of Eastern Europe was widened when the Allied governments undertook to determine the fate of Germany—a matter of the first importance for the future peace of Europe. The statesmen at Yalta had reached no decision on what its ultimate fate should be. Germany was, it is true, to be de-Nazified and demilitarized and to pay a large (but as yet undetermined) amount of reparations. Whether it was to remain one nation or to be dismembered, and if so, how, had not been decided, but arrangements had been made for temporary military occupation by the victor powers. A European Advisory Commission established by the Big Three in London, drew the boundaries of the German zones that were to be occupied, after the German surrender, by Russian, British, American, and later, French armies. The zone assigned to Russia, including Mecklenburg-Pomerania, Brandenburg, Saxony-Anhalt, Thuringia, and all to the eastward, contained 40 percent of the territory, 36 percent of the population, and 33 percent of the productive resources of pre-1937 Germany.[5] This no doubt seemed a fair division at the time, but it had, as was learned later, two great disadvantages: it brought the advanced posts of the Russian occupation within less than one hundred miles of the Rhine, and it placed Berlin far within the Soviet zone, distant a hundred miles or more from the nearest point in the British zone. State Department representatives saw the danger in the latter arrangement and proposed reserving a corridor into Berlin from the western zones, but were told by the War Department that this was a question for the military only. The consequence was that, except by air, American and British access to Berlin was at the mercy of the Russian occupiers.[6]

4. Joseph R. Starobin, "Origins of the Cold War: The Communist Dimension," *Foreign Affairs,* 47 (July 1969), 681–96. James McGregor Burns, in *Roosevelt: The Soldier of Freedom* (New York: Harcourt Brace Jovanovich, Inc., 1970), pp. 373–74, finds the origin of the cold war in Russian resentment at the postponement of the Anglo-American second front in Europe until 1944.

5. P. E. Mosely, "The Occupation of Germany: New Light on How the Zones Were Drawn," *Foreign Affairs,* 28 (July 1950), 580–604.

6. Mosely, "The Occupation of Germany." Admiral Leahy recalled later that the details of the agreement for free access to Berlin "did not seem too important at the time. I do not believe any of us, in the late spring of 1945, thought that three years later a state of virtual armed truce would exist in Berlin with the Russians enforcing a land blockade . . ." W. D. Leahy, *I Was There* (New York: Whittlesey House, 1950), p. 382.

The zones were not designed to limit the areas of initial military operations but those alone of subsequent occupation. The unexpectedly rapid advance of the Anglo-American armies brought them into the Soviet zones of Germany and Austria and also into western Czechoslovakia, which the Russians viewed as within their sphere. Prime Minister Churchill, convinced, as he wrote later, "that Soviet Russia had become a mortal danger to the free world," [7] wished to take advantage of Western military success by seizing Berlin and holding all the territory occupied until Stalin could be induced to live up to the promises made at Yalta. Otherwise, Churchill warned, the "iron curtain" which the Russians had already "drawn down upon their front," would descend over a much wider area, and "a broad band of many hundreds of miles of Russian-occupied territory will isolate us from Poland." [8] But Eisenhower, supported by Roosevelt and then by Truman, declined to pay the cost of what he thought a useless advance to Berlin, and Truman refused to postpone the withdrawal of American troops from the Russian zone beyond July 1. The Russians took Berlin, Prague, and Vienna—the three great capitals of Central Europe.[9]

The Potsdam Conference

The Big Three heads of government held their last wartime meeting at Potsdam, just outside the ruins of Berlin, July 17 to August 2, 1945. Truman replaced Roosevelt, and midway through the Conference the victory of the Labour party in the British elections removed Churchill and Eden and substituted Clement Attlee and Ernest Bevin as Prime Minister and Foreign Secretary respectively.

The atmosphere was friendly and the discussions were generally good-tempered, but many controversial issues were passed over with no agreement. Such issues were Western complaints of one-party domination in Bulgaria and Rumania, and the Russian request for British and American recognition of the governments of these countries; [10] Soviet desire for control of the Dardanelles and a trusteeship over former Italian possessions in the Mediterranean; an American interest in the internationalizing of such waterways as the Dardanelles and the Danube.

On a number of important matters there was agreement, superficial though it was. The task of drawing up treaties with Italy and with the Axis satellites, Hungary, Bulgaria, Rumania and Finland,[11] was assigned to a Council of Foreign Ministers of the American, British, French, and Russian governments, which was to meet in London. China would also be represented but would not participate in European settlements.

The three leaders agreed that supreme authority in Germany should rest in the hands of the commanders of the four occupying armies, each in his own zone, and acting together in Berlin as a Control Council in matters affecting Germany as a whole. Germany was to be demilitarized, de-Nazified, and democratized. War criminals were to be punished. Local German governments were to be established. Though for the time being there was to be no central German government, certain central administrative departments were to be set up

7. Winston S. Churchill, *Triumph and Tragedy,* Vol. 6 of *The Second World War* (Boston: Houghton Mifflin Company, 1953), p. 456.
8. Churchill, *Triumph and Tragedy,* p. 573.
9. Churchill, *Triumph and Tragedy,* pp. 603–5; Chester Wilmot, *The Struggle for Europe* (New York: Harper & Row, Publishers, 1952), p. 696. It is worth noting that the Saxony-Thuringia area, occupied and then abandoned by American troops, contained rich uranium deposits. It was estimated in 1954 that enough uranium had been produced here to make forty-four atomic bombs. *New York Times,* August 27, 1954.

10. The government of Poland was for the time being removed from the field of controversy. At the end of May, Truman had sent Harry Hopkins to Moscow to seek agreement on Poland. Stalin had then consented to the admission of Mikolajczyk and other non-Communist Poles to the Provisional Government of National Unity, which had been recognized by the United States and the United Kingdom.
11. Finland, having been defeated and despoiled of part of her territory by Russia in 1939–1940, had joined Germany in the war against the Soviets after June 1941.

in such fields as finance, transport, communications, foreign trade, and industry. As this last provision suggests, Germany was to be administered as an economic unit, with establishment of common policies in all major fields of economic activity. Production policies were to be adjusted to meet the needs of the occupying forces and displaced persons, and to maintain for the German population a standard of living no higher than the average for other European countries, exclusive of the United Kingdom and the Soviet Union.

As *faits accomplis* the President and Prime Minister accepted the Polish occupation of German territory up to the Oder-Neisse line (except the Königsberg area of East Prussia, which was claimed by the Soviets) and the expulsion from that area of the German population, though nominally the fixing of Germany's eastern boundary was reserved for the future treaty of peace.

For reparations, the Potsdam agreement authorized each occupying power to remove property from its own zone and to seize Ger-

ALLIED OCCUPATION IN GERMANY AND AUSTRIA

International occupation.

Area occupied by U.S. and British forces and released to the Russians.

Adapted from a map in Winston S. Churchill, *Triumph and Tragedy*, with the permission of Cassell and Company, Ltd., London, and Houghton Mifflin Company, Boston.

man assets abroad. In order to balance the predominance of industry in the Western zones against that of agriculture in the East, Russia was entitled to 10 percent of industrial equipment taken from the Western zones, plus another 15 percent which was to be exchanged for products of the East, chiefly coal, raw materials, and foodstuffs. What remained of the German merchant marine and the German navy were to be divided equally among the United States, the United Kingdom, and the Soviet Union.[12]

The Satellite Treaties

The Council of Foreign Ministers met in London (September 1945), Moscow (December 1945), Paris (April–May and June–July 1946), and New York (November–December 1946), in prolonged and finally successful efforts to make treaties with the former so-called "Axis satellites."

The first meeting of the Council, to which Secretary Byrnes went "with the atomic bomb in his pocket," produced nothing but an unseemly wrangle. Though the agenda was limited to Europe, Molotov complained repeatedly of the exclusion of the Soviets from a share in the control of Japan.[13] At Moscow, three months later, a better spirit prevailed. Concessions were made on both sides. The Soviet Union consented to the holding of a conference of the Big Five with the sixteen other nations that had made more than nominal contributions to the war in Europe.[14] This

Conference sat in Paris from July 29 to October 15, 1946. It could only recommend. All final decisions were made by unanimous vote of the Council of Foreign Ministers. Agreement was reached in New York in December 1946, and the treaties were signed in Paris on February 10, 1947.

The treaties imposed monetary indemnities upon all the former Axis satellites, Finland, Hungary, Rumania, and Bulgaria, as well as upon Italy. They required Finland and Rumania to cede territory to the Soviet Union, and Italy to surrender her African conquests; and they imposed strict limits upon the armed forces of all. Unable to agree upon the disposition of Italy's former African possessions— although the Soviet Union dropped its demand for a trusteeship over Libya—the Foreign Ministers turned over the problem to the U.N. General Assembly, which put Libya and Italian Somaliland on the road to independence and federated Eritrea with Ethiopia.[15]

The most difficult problem faced by the Foreign Ministers in connection with the satellite treaties was the conflict over Trieste between Yugoslavia and Italy. The Yugoslav

---

12. The Soviet Union was to take care of Poland's claims for reparations; the United States, the United Kingdom, and France were to share with other claimant governments. The protocol of the Potsdam Conference is printed in *Documents on American Foreign Relations,* 8: 925–38. Accounts by participants are Churchill, *Triumph and Tragedy,* pp. 630–67; Leahy, *I Was There,* chap. 22; J. F. Byrnes, *Speaking Frankly* (New York: Harper & Row, Publishers, 1947), chap. 4; H. S. Truman, *Memoirs:* Vol. 1, *Year of Decisions* (Garden City, N.Y.: Doubleday & Company, Inc., 1955), pp. 332–412.

13. On Japan see Chapter 44. On Byrnes and the bomb, see p. 432.

14. The sixteen were White Russia and the Ukraine,

the four British Dominions and India, Belgium, the Netherlands, Czechoslovakia, Poland, Yugoslavia, Greece, Norway, Brazil, and Ethiopia. The function of the sixteen was advisory only. It had been agreed at Potsdam that the great powers should make the treaties, with the exceptions that France should participate only in drawing the treaty with Italy and that the United States, which had not been at war with Finland, should not be a party to the Finnish treaty. For texts of treaties and an account of the negotiations see A. C. Leiss and Raymond Dennett, eds., *European Peace Treaties after World War II,* supplementary to *Documents on American Foreign Relations,* 8 and 9. (Boston World Peace Foundation, 1954.)

15. The Soviet Foreign Minister, at the New York meeting, consented to the holding of a conference on the free naviation of the Danube River, to be participated in by the United States, the United Kingdom, France, and Russia, and by the riparian states, or states fronting on the river, Austria excluded. When this conference met in 1948, the riparian states voted to exclude the nonriparian states from all voice in control of the river. Russia had become a riparian state by annexing Bessarabia, once a Russian possession, but from 1919 to 1940 a part of Rumania.

claim was backed by Russia, the Italian claim by the Western powers. The compromise solution was to place the territory of Trieste temporarily under the Security Council of the United Nations. In practice, the Security Council could never agree on the appointment of a governor for Trieste, and until 1954 the territory remained under military occupation, the city and northern portion (Zone A) by Anglo-American forces, the remainder (Zone B) by the Yugoslav Army. Efforts of the United States and Great Britain to bring about a settlement were at long last rewarded. By an agreement signed on October 5, 1954, Italy received Zone A, with slight adjustments in the boundary; Zone B was retained by Yugoslavia. The Soviet Union, more flexible since Stalin's death (1953), created general surprise by announcing that it approved the settlement.

The United States was a party to, and in due time ratified, all these treaties except that with Finland. By signing the treaty with Bulgaria, the United States recognized the Communist-dominated government of that country, as it had already done in the case of Rumania. At Moscow, in December 1945, Stalin had promised a relaxing of one-party control in Rumania and Bulgaria. The United States had recognized Rumania without waiting for the promise to be fulfilled, and Bulgaria, after waiting a year in vain. In so doing it tacitly acquiesced in Soviet domination of these two countries, in plain disregard of the promises of Yalta.

Austria Regains its Independence

Austria presented problems more complicated than those of the satellite states. At Moscow in 1943, the Big Three Foreign Ministers had promised that Austria, as "the first free country to fall a victim to Hitlerite aggression," should be "liberated from German domination" and reestablished as "free and independent"; and that the way should be opened for the Austrian people to find "political and economic security." The statesmen at Potsdam

had declared Austria exempt from the payment of reparations. Yet this little country, with the area of South Carolina and the population of Michigan, was subjected, like Germany, to a four-power occupation, with the Russians holding Vienna and the most productive agricultural and industrial districts.

In November 1945, the Austrians were permitted to elect their own Parliament, which was, and remained thereafter, overwhelmingly anti-Communist and pro-Western. Negotiations for a treaty, which should liberate the country from military occupation, were begun in 1946, but were endlessly prolonged by the Russians. Not until the spring of 1955, two years after Stalin's death, did the Russians cease their obstruction. On May 15, 1955, a treaty was signed which ended the occupation and reestablished Austria as a free and independent state. Separate agreements with the Soviet Union and the Western powers guaranteed its neutralization.

Deadlock in Germany

But relations between East and West in Austria appeared harmonious when compared with their relations in Germany. There, the Four-Power Control Council, established in Berlin, soon reached a condition of chronic deadlock, resulting from the requirement that all decisions be by unanimous vote. The French, miffed at their exclusion from Yalta and Potsdam, were guilty of some obstructionist tactics in the early months of the occupation; but in the end it was the Russians who sabotaged attempts at a common policy for the four zones by repudiating in practice the Potsdam agreement that Germany should be treated as an economic unit.

The consequence was that each of the four powers applied its own ideas in its own zone. The Americans undertook to build democracy, starting from the grass roots, combined with a system of free enterprise. The Russians, finding German Communists too few to rule their zone, forced a union of Communists and Social Democrats to form the Socialist Unity

Party, which became their instrument of government. Large landed estates were broken up and large industries were nationalized. The French and British were less zealous for democracy than the Americans, and the British, under a Labour government, talked little of free enterprise and much of nationalizing the giant Ruhr industries, located in their zone. But policies in the three Western zones were sufficiently alike to make their economic and political union an easy matter.

The Russians' independent course on reparations—taking from their zone whatever they wished in capital goods and current production without giving an accounting to their allies—and their refusal to send food and raw materials to the Western zones, led to an abandonment of the reparations policy in the latter in the spring of 1946 and, a few months later, to the economic union of the American and British zones. The Russians refused an invitation to merge their zone with the "Bizonia" thus formed, denouncing it as a step toward a permanent division of Germany. France, unwilling to offend the Soviets, also held aloof.

The trend of events was clearly in the direction of a Germany divided by the iron curtain. In order to prevent such division, and to put an end to the necessity of economic support that weighed heavily upon the Western powers, Secretary of State James F. Byrnes, in a speech at Stuttgart, September 6, 1946, proposed that Germany be reunited not only economically but politically, with a central government on a federal pattern. To quiet French or Russian fears of a revived and rearmed Germany, Byrnes repeated an earlier offer on the part of the United States, to sign a twenty-five- or even forty-year four-power treaty to keep Germany disarmed, and to leave American troops in Germany as long as any armed occupation should be necessary.[16]

This offer of American participation in a

treaty to guarantee German disarmament was rejected by the Soviet government. It was rejected again in March 1947, when George Marshall, then Secretary of State, went to Moscow for another meeting of the Council of Foreign Ministers. The West made another bid for German unification, economic and political—a bid the failure of which was to lead to the organization of West Germany as a separate entity. The Soviets would agree to economic union on two conditions: a share in control of the industry of the Ruhr, and recognition by the West of Russia's claim to 10 billion dollars in reparations, a claim that had been waived at Potsdam and revived later. On neither point would the Western powers yield. The two camps were equally far apart on political organization, the Western allies proposing a rather loose federal system, the Russians insisting on a strongly centralized government. The former, it was felt would be a barrier against Communism; the latter might facilitate the communizing of the entire German state. The Moscow Conference adjourned without agreement on any significant point. "Moscow really marked the end of the road which began at Teheran and Yalta."[17]

The Policy of Containment: The Truman Doctrine

The antagonism that disrupted the Moscow Council of Foreign Ministers in March 1947 had been building up through the preceding year. Two speeches early in 1946 sounded like unofficial declarations of war. Stalin, on February 9, restated the Marxist-Leninist dogma of inevitable war between Communism and capitalism and called for three five-year plans to prepare the Soviet Union for the struggle. A month later Winston Churchill— not then a member of the British cabinet, be it noted—delivered at Fulton, Missouri, his famous denunciation of the "iron curtain" and urged "a fraternal association of English-speaking peoples" to defend the free world.

---

16. *Documents on American Foreign Relations,* 8: 210–18. This was a startling offer in the light of President Roosevelt's statement to Stalin that American troops would remain in Europe no longer than two years.

17. *U.S. in World Affairs, 1947–1948,* p. 78.

Stalin followed this speech with a tightening of the Kremlin's hold upon the governments of Eastern Europe, an intensified suppression of human liberties in the Soviet Union, and a campaign of propaganda directed against the West, especially the United States.[18] Actions on both sides contributed to the growing tension: final breakdown of negotiations for an American loan to Russia; Soviet rejection of Secretary Byrnes' Stuttgart offer; disruption of the reparations program; pressures of Russia or Russian satellites upon Greece and Turkey; replacement of negotiations by propagandist oratory in the meetings of the Council of Foreign Ministers (opened to the press and public in April).

Yet to the end of 1946, hope of accommodation was not wholly ended. The satellite treaties were made and ratified. Soviet troops, whose presence in Iran contravened wartime promises, were finally withdrawn, and Stalin sometimes talked affably with visitors from the West of peaceful coexistence between opposing systems. Not until the spring of 1947, with the failure of the Moscow Conference and the simultaneous announcement by the United States of the policy of "containment," did the break become clearly irreparable and the cold war begin in earnest.

The new American policy was based upon the thesis that the Soviet Union had a persistent tendency to expand the boundaries of its empire wherever possible but would not undertake to do so at the risk of major war. The United States, therefore, by exerting counterpressure, should "contain" the U.S.S.R. and its Communist satellites within their existing bounds, hoping that time and internal strains would eventually sap the strength of the Red Empire.[19]

The first notice of the new policy came on March 12, 1947. While the Foreign Ministers were wrangling in Moscow, President Truman went before Congress to ask for $400 million in military and economic aid for Greece and Turkey. Since 1945 the royal government of Greece had been struggling against Communist forces within aided by heavy infiltrations from Greece's three northern neighbors, all satellites of the Soviet Union. Turkey was reported to have been pressed by Moscow to yield control of the Dardanelles and to surrender the districts of Kars and Ardahan at the eastern end of the Black Sea, which Russia had surrendered at the end of World War I. Great Britain, which had been aiding both Turkey and Greece, informed the United States in February 1947 that she would no longer be able to do so. Mr. Truman promptly accepted the responsibility for the United States. In asking authority and funds to assist Greece and Turkey, he propounded a general principle that came to be referred to as the "Truman Doctrine."

> I believe [said the President] that it must be the policy of the United States to support free peoples who are resisting attempted subjugation by armed minorities or by outside pressures . . .

President Truman's proposal met a generally favorable response in the United States, though some critics thought its scope too broad. Congress acted after two months of debate. An act of May 22, 1947, authorized the expenditure of $100 million in military aid to Turkey and, for Greece, $300 million equally divided between military and economic assistance. The act also empowered the

---

18. Starobin, "Origins of the Cold War."
19. Authorship of the "containment" policy is often attributed to George F. Kennan, a Foreign Service officer who, after spending some years in Russia, became head of the new Policy Planning Staff in the State Department in the Spring of 1947. Kennan expounded the general philosophy of "containment" in an anonymous article (signed "X"), "The Sources of Soviet Conduct," in *Foreign Affairs*, 25 (July 1947), 566–82; republished in G. F. Kennan, *American Diplomacy, 1900–1950* (Chicago: University of Chicago Press, 1951), pp. 107–28. He was, however,

critical of Truman's message of March 12. He disapproved military aid to Greece and Turkey and the later military emphasis on containment. He and his staff, on the other hand, played an important part in formulating the Marshall Plan, as did also Under Secretaries of State Dean Acheson and William L. Clayton. See G. F. Kennan, *Memoirs, 1925–1950* (Boston: Altantic Monthly Press, 1967), chaps. 14, 15; Joseph M. Jones, *The Fifteen Weeks (February 21–June 5, 1947)* (New York: Viking Press, 1955), pp. 154–55, 255; Dean Acheson, *Present at the Creation: My Years in the State Department* (New York: W. W. Norton & Co., Inc., 1969), chaps. 24–26.

President to send military and civilian experts as advisers to the Greek and Turkish governments. American aid, thus begun and continued from year to year, proved effective as a means of "containment" in that quarter. But the Truman administration moved quickly on to assume broader responsibilities.

The Marshall Plan

Greece and Turkey might thus be strengthened against armed aggression or the threat of it. But to Europe as a whole the danger from Communism lay principally in the economic stagnation that had followed the war. Western Europe in the spring of 1947 was facing catastrophe after an exceptionally severe winter. Food and fuel were in short supply, and foreign exchange, notwithstanding the large dollar loan to England, would be exhausted by the end of the year. Large Communist parties in France and Italy stood ready to profit from the impending economic collapse and human suffering.

The best protection against the spread of Communism to Western Europe would be economic recovery. So, at least, it appeared in Washington, and on this theory Secretary of State George Marshall, speaking at the Harvard Commencement, June 5, 1947, offered American aid to such European nations as would agree to coordinate their efforts for recovery and present the United States with a program and specifications of their needs. Marshall drew no distinction between Communist and non-Communist Europe, but the Soviet Union spurned the proposal as a new venture in "American imperialism," a threat to the sovereignty of small nations that might accept it. The satellite governments obeyed the dictum from Moscow, as did Finland and Czechoslovakia, which dared not offend the Soviet giant. They had been tempted, as had Poland, by Marshall's proposal, and all three declined it with regret. Rejection of the offer by the Soviet bloc no doubt contributed greatly to its endorsement by Congress.

The other sixteen nations of Europe (excluding Spain, which was not invited, and Germany, which as yet had no government) formed a Committee of European Economic Cooperation, which, in September 1947, presented to the United States a report proposing the achievement by 1951 of a self-sufficient European economy, at an estimated cost to the United States of $19.3 billion. In December, President Truman laid the proposal before Congress, with a request for $6.8 billion for the first fifteen months of the program and $10.2 billion for the succeeding three years—a total of $17 billion. In explaining the motive for his request, the President said:

> I am proposing that this Nation contribute to world peace and to its own security by assisting in the recovery of sixteen countries which, like the United States, are devoted to the preservation of free institutions and enduring peace among nations.

Congress slashed the figure somewhat, but on April 3, 1948, established the Economic Cooperation Administration to handle the program and at the end of June appropriated an initial $4 billion for the purpose, which might be spread over either twelve or fifteen months at the discretion of the administrator of the program. So was launched the Marshall Plan, or European Recovery Program, which was to continue for three years, to cost the United States $10¼ billion, to contribute to an impressive economic recovery in Europe, and to be broadened to serve many non-European countries.[20] Unlike later programs of military assistance, the Marshall Plan has had few critics from the American New Left.

Point Four

The Marshall Plan was designed to aid in the recovery of nations with advanced economies that had been dislocated by the war. By increasing production and trade, by alleviating unemployment and poverty, its authors ex-

---

20. Nominally, the program lasted four years and cost approximately $13,350,000,000, but virtually all the aid in the fourth year went for defense or defense support under the Mutual Security Agency, which in 1951 supplanted the E.C.A.

pected it to halt the growth of Communism among the working classes of Europe. But Communism was also a threat among the poverty-stricken masses in countries of Asia, Africa, and Latin America, where the modern economy had made little or no impress. The "containment" of Communism called for measures to raise the standard of living in countries such as these.

It was with this purpose in mind that President Truman, in his second-term Inaugural Address, January 20, 1949, proposed his "Point Four," or Technical Assistance program.

> . . . we must [he said] embark on a bold new program for making the benefits of our scientific advances and industrial progress available for the improvement and growth of underdeveloped areas.[21]

The Point Four program got under way in 1950, with a modest appropriation of $35 million. Authorized expenditures for the three years 1951–1954 totaled nearly $400 million. In 1953 the program was placed, with other forms of foreign aid, under the Foreign Operations Administration (FOA).

The West German Republic

In the meantime there had been important developments in Germany. Failure of the Foreign Ministers to reach agreement at Moscow in March 1947, and at London in November and December of the same year, led to moves by the Western powers toward the creation from their three zones of a unified and self-governing West Germany. The British and Americans had already taken one step in that direction in the economic merging of their zones. Consultations in London in the

spring of 1948 by representatives of France, Great Britain, the United States, and the three Benelux countries (Belgium, the Netherlands, and Luxembourg) resulted in agreements, announced June 7, proposing the creation of a West German government and, as a safeguard against a too strong Germany, control of the Ruhr industries by an international authority representing the six states and West Germany. The Germans of the Western zones would elect members of a constituent assembly. This body would then draw up a constitution for a federal state, which might eventually include the Eastern zone. The new government would exercise sovereignty over its domestic affairs and limited control over foreign relations; but the ban on rearmament would remain, and the military occupation would continue "until the peace of Europe is secured." [22]

The West German Constituent Assembly met in Bonn, September 1, 1948, and proceeded with its work of preparing a constitution. A German Federal Republic, comprising the three Western zones, was inaugurated at Bonn in September 1949. Military government terminated, although occupation forces remained. Allied authority was exercised through a High Commission, to which the United States, France, and the United Kingdom each appointed one member. The Federal Republic was soon made eligible for Marshall Plan aid and was given a voice in the international control of the Ruhr. Under its first Chancellor, Konrad Adenauer (1949–1963), it showed a spirit of willing cooperation with the West.

Divided Germany

The Russians had not viewed these developments without protest and countermoves. The Marshall Plan they interpreted as an aggressive scheme of the United States, aimed eventually at "liberating" the satellite states of Eastern Europe. Their response was the hold-

21. *Documents on American Foreign Relations,* 11: 10. This was the fourth point in the foreign policy program outlined by the President. The first three were support of the United Nations, continuation of the European Recovery Program, and the strengthening of "freedom-loving nations against the dangers of aggression." The last referred especially to the North Atlantic Treaty then under negotiation.

22. *Documents on American Foreign Relations,* 10: 106–27.

ing of a conference of nine East European states in Warsaw (September 1947), which resolved to do everything possible to defeat the program of "American imperialism." Communist-inspired strikes in France and Italy sought in vain to deter these countries from accepting Marshall Plan aid. The Communist Information Bureau, (Cominform), a successor of the Comintern, dissolved in 1943, was set up at Belgrade. Treaties of defensive alliance linking the Soviet Union with Bulgaria, Finland, Hungary, and Rumania were added to treaties previously negotiated with Czechoslovakia, Poland, and Yugoslavia.

More violent reaction accompanied the early steps toward the unification of West Germany. In February 1948 a Communist coup overthrew the democratic government of Czechoslovakia and installed one firmly attached to Moscow. This blow to the West was partly compensated for later in the year, when Yugoslavia, under Tito's leadership, broke with the Cominform and with Moscow. The government remained firmly Communist but ceased to take orders from the Kremlin and took a basically neutralist position. With the opening of the six-power talks on Germany in London, the Soviets complained that the Western powers were destroying the four-power control of Germany agreed to three years before, and hence that they had no further business in Berlin. The Western Allies, on the other hand, maintained that they were in Berlin by virtue of their part in the defeat of Germany.

At any rate, the Russians now began an attempt to squeeze the Western Allies out of Berlin, which, it will be recalled, lay wholly within the Soviet zone with no guaranteed surface corridor communicating with the West. Restrictions upon movement to and from the city were first imposed in April 1948. In June all surface transportation between Berlin and the Western zones was halted. The Western powers must now either withdraw their garrisons from Berlin in admitted defeat or find means of supplying not only them but the two million people of West Berlin. Rejecting advice that he "call the Russian bluff"—open

the roads by military force—President Truman (and the British) resorted to air transport, the only means for which they had signed agreements with the Russians. The "air lift" started at once, and by September 1, American and British planes were flying in four thousand tons of supplies daily. Russian planes occasionally threatened the air lift but never ventured to attack. Allied persistence and patience eventually paid off. In May 1949, the Soviet Union agreed to end the blockade and to participate in another meeting of the Big Four Foreign Ministers. The meeting achieved no agreement, but the blockade was ended.

In October 1949, after the inauguration of the German Federal Republic at Bonn, a so-called People's Council in Berlin proclaimed a new government for the Soviet zone of Germany. Styled the German Democratic Republic, it rested upon a constitution designed, like that at Bonn, to unite all of Germany. Two Germanys had come into being, one totalitarian, the other democratic; one under the domination of the Soviet Union, the other closely tied to Western Europe and America.

Collective Self-Defense

The Communist coup in Czechoslovakia and the Berlin blockade alarmed the Western powers. Though the blockade had been beaten, there was no guarantee that the Russians might not make a new attempt to oust the Western Allies from Berlin or to prevent the formation of the German Federal Republic. It was true that the Soviets, since 1945, had reduced their armed forces from eleven and a half million men to fewer than three million,[23] but they still far outnumbered those available in the West. Their numerical superiority, it was feared, might tempt the Russians to commit some aggressive act against a weak spot in the fragile Western armor. "Containment" of Russia, till now dependent chiefly upon

23. Adam B. Ulam, *Expansion and Coexistence: The History of Soviet Foreign Policy, 1917–1967* (New York: Praeger Publishers, 1968), p. 404.

economic and political means, appeared to need military backing. If the Soviet Union could be warned that an act of aggression against any one of the free nations of Western Europe would mean a conflict with the others and also with the United States, it might be deterred from such acts. The United Nations, because of the Soviet veto, could not supply such a deterrent, but Article 51 of the U.N. Charter legalized "collective self-defense" by groups within the U.N.,[24] and to agreements under Article 51 the free world now turned.

In the Americas, the Rio Pact of September 2, 1947 [25] had already invoked Article 51 in a hemispheric collective security agreement. In Europe a beginning was made in March 1948, when Great Britain, France, and the Benelux countries signed at Brussels a fifty-year treaty of economic, social, and cultural collaboration and collective self-defense. But in order to constitute an impressive warning, such a treaty needed the backing of the United States. Such backing was promptly proposed by President Truman in an address to Congress on March 17, 1948. In the same address, the President spoke frankly of the danger from Russia; in order to enable the United States to meet it, he called for adoption of a universal military training program and temporary reenactment of selective service legislation.[26] The United States had allowed its military might to disintegrate since 1945. It must grow strong again and must show its willingness to pool its strength with that of like-minded nations.

The build-up of American armed strength began with the enactment by Congress of a new selective service, or draft, law in June 1948. With the aid of this and under the stimulus of war in Korea, which began in June 1950, the strength of the Army, Navy, and Air Force grew from 1,350,000 in 1948 to 3,630,000 in June 1952.

The way for collective action was cleared when the Senate, in the Vandenberg Resolu-

tion of June 11, 1948, voiced the opinion that the United States should, among other measures for promoting peace, associate itself, "by constitutional process, with such regional and other collective arrangements as are based on continuous and effective self-help and mutual aid, and as affect its national security." The United States ought also, the resolution declared, to make clear "its determination to exercise the right of individual or collective self-defense under article 51 should any armed attack occur affecting its national security." [27]

The North Atlantic Treaty Organization

The Vandenberg Resolution was the prelude to the North Atlantic Treaty, an important and ambitious venture in search of collective security. The treaty—a pronounced break with the principle of "no permanent alliances" —was signed April 4, 1949, by twelve nations of the North Atlantic and Western European areas. This number was increased to fifteen by the accession of Greece and Turkey in 1952 and West Germany in 1955.[28] The parties agreed to settle peacefully all disputes between themselves and to develop their capacity to resist armed attack "by means of continuous and effective self-help and mutual aid." But the heart of the treaty was Article 5, which declared that an armed attack upon any one of the members in Europe or North America would be considered an attack upon all, and pledge each member in case of such an attack to assist the party attacked "by such action as it deems necessary, including the use of armed force." Thus began the North Atlantic Treaty Organization, or NATO. Its directing body was a North Atlantic Council,

24. See p. 417.
25. See p. 532.
26. *Documents on American Foreign Relations,* 10: 5–9.

27. *Documents on American Foreign Relations,* 10: 302; A. H. Vandenberg, Jr., ed., *The Private Papers of Senator Vandenberg* (Boston: Houghton Mifflin Company, 1952), pp. 403–11.
28. The twelve original signers were the United States, Canada, Iceland, the United Kingdom, France, Belgium, the Netherlands, Luxembourg, Denmark, Norway, Portugal, and Italy.

made up of the Foreign, Defense, and Finance Ministers of the member states.

The United States now took the lead in providing and organizing the military deterrent envisaged by the framers of the North Atlantic Treaty. The American position was stated in a secret document labeled NSC-68, prepared at President Truman's request by the State and Defense Departments in the spring of 1950. The document is still (1970) classified, but its substance has been revealed by, among others, Dean Acheson, who, as Secretary of State, played an important part in its composition.

NSC-68 started from an assumption as to Soviet intentions which, as Acheson admits, was opposed by the Soviet experts in the State Department though accepted by the Planning Staff. In this analysis the Russian threat, in Acheson's words, "combined the ideology of communist doctrine and the power of the Russian state into an aggressive expansionist drive, which found its chief opponent, and, therefore, target in the antithetical ideas and power of our own country." The threat to Western Europe, he thought, seemed "singularly like that which Islam had posed centuries before, with its combination of ideological zeal and fighting power." [29]

Such being the supposed threat to Western Europe and ultimately to the United States, NSC-68 recommended that the United States "strike out on a bold and massive program of rebuilding the West's defensive potential to surpass that of the Soviet world, and of meeting each fresh challenge promptly and unequivocally." With the security of the free world at stake, costs of such a program were immaterial. The country could afford to spend, if necessary, 20 percent of its gross national product on defense. President Truman approved NSC-68 in April 1950, and it thereby became official government policy.

The assumption of NSC-68 as to Moscow's aggressive purposes seemed to Acheson and others to be borne out by events in the Far East, as well as by the revelation in September 1949 that the U.S.S.R. had exploded its first atomic bomb. The Communist conquest of all mainland China was completed in the summer of 1949, and the government of the People's Republic of China was proclaimed at Peking on October 1. The Chinese Communists were then regarded as puppets of Moscow and their victory, as a major triumph in the Kremlin's program of world revolution. Then on June 25, 1950, two months after the approval of NSC-68, Communist North Korea invaded the South.[30] What part the Kremlin played in launching the Korean aggression we do not know, but in official circles in Washington in 1950 it was generally assumed that this was another Soviet blow for world conquest. Here was a "fresh challenge" of the kind which NSC-68 had said should be met "promptly and unequivocally."

While that challenge was being met,[31] the United States, working now through NATO, was building defenses in Western Europe against supposed Soviet plans for a Communist conquest of that incomparably important area. Early in 1951 the North Atlantic Council set up military headquarters near Paris, known as SHAPE (Supreme Headquarters, Allied Powers in Europe), with General Eisenhower as Supreme Commander. Its purpose was to build a defense force in Western Europe, not equal to the huge army maintained by the Soviet Union (175 Russian divisions and 60 or more divisions from the satellite states), but strong enough to make the Russians think twice before going to war, and, if war should come anyway, strong enough to hold the Russian armies in check until (it was hoped) the strategic air power of the United

29. Dean Acheson, *Present at the Creation: My Years in the State Department* (New York: W. W. Norton & Co., Inc., 1969), pp. 375–77, 752–53. Reprinted by permission of W. W. Norton and Hamish Hamilton, Ltd., London. NSC-68 is also discussed in Walter La Feber, *America, Russia, and the Cold War, 1945–1966* (New York: John Wiley & Sons, Inc., 1967), pp. 90–91, and summarized in Cabell Phillips, *The Truman Presidency* (New York: The Macmillan Company, 1966), pp. 306–8. The initials "NSC" stood for National Security Council, the body to which the document was submitted.

30. See Chapter 44 for events in China and Korea.
31. See Chapter 44.

States could destroy the centers of Soviet strength.

American aid to Europe now began to shift from economic to military. The Mutual Security Agency in 1951 replaced the Economic Cooperation Administration, and was in turn, in 1953, succeeded by the Foreign Operations Administration. From October 1949 to the end of 1953, the United States supplied nearly $6 billion worth of arms and military equipment to its European allies, as well as $1.7 billion worth to other countries. The United States also increased its divisions stationed in Germany and Austria from two to six, following a "great debate" in which the Senate approved this increase but advised against sending additional troops abroad without the consent of Congress. The European allies in the same period spent over $35 billion in building up their military forces and installations.[32] The result was an encouraging increase in the troops, planes, and airfields available for NATO service.

Throughout this period, the United States was pressing strongly for the inclusion of West German units in the defense forces. The prospect of a rearmed and nationalistic Germany was almost as alarming to France and the Benelux countries as the Russian danger. A French proposal for a European Defense Community (E.D.C.), which would make it possible to use and yet control German troops by integrating them with those of France, Italy, and the Benelux states,[33] was finally rejected by the French Assembly in August 1954, in spite of urgent pleas by U.S. Secretary of State John Foster Dulles.[34] A substitute was found in a set of treaties constituting Western European Union (W.E.U.), an alliance rather than an organic union as E.D.C. would have been. The treaties became effective on May 6, 1955.[35] Under this arrangement, Italy and the Federal Republic of (West) Germany were admitted to the Brussels Pact alliance of 1948 with Britain, France, and the three Benelux countries. West Germany recovered its sovereignty and was permitted to rearm, though pledging itself to manufacture no atomic, chemical, or bacteriological weapons. United States, British, and French troops were to remain in West Germany for its defense and that of the North Atlantic area until the Bonn government could provide its own defense forces. West Germany became a member of NATO, and the armed forces of the Western European Union, with certain exceptions, became subject to the NATO supreme command, referred to as SACEUR (Supreme Allied Commander, Europe). To quiet French fears of a rearmed Germany, Great Britain and the United States agreed to maintain substantial military forces on the continent, four ground divisions and a tactical air force for Britain, six divisions or the equivalent for the United States. To the British, American, and French forces and the smaller contingents to be furnished by Belgium and the Netherlands, were to be added, it was hoped by 1960 but actually not until 1963, twelve divisions from the German Federal Republic. Such an army, centrally commanded from SHAPE, should be able to

32. Outside NATO, the United States, on September 26, 1953, secured from the government of General Franco the right to establish naval and air bases in Spain in return for economic and military aid for the modernization of Spain's armed forces. A year later it further strengthened its position in the Mediterranean by an agreement for use of air bases in Libya. *New York Times,* September 27, 1953; September 10, 1954.

33. The six governments named had already, under the Schuman Plan, formed a Coal and Steel Community, a step toward integrating the economies of Western Europe. Plans for political federation were also being actively discussed. The United States government looked with favor upon all these plans. Great Britain, too, was sympathetic, but at this time held that participation in these organizations would conflict with her Commonwealth ties.

34. Dulles succeeded Acheson as Secretary of State when Eisenhower became President in January 1953. He attached such importance to E.D.C. that he warned that the U.S. might be driven to an "agonizing reappraisal" of its European policy if the plan was rejected.

35. The treaties and agreements are printed in U.S. Department of State, *London and Paris Agreements, September–October 1954.* Department of State Publication 5659. (Washington: Government Printing Office, 1954). See also F. S. C. Northrop, *European Union and United States Foreign Policy* (New York: The Macmillan Company, 1954).

put up a strong first line defense against aggression from the east.

Beginnings of an Arms Race

The Russians had watched with misgivings the formation of NATO and Western European Union, and especially the plans for rearming West Germany, and had tried to halt the process by threats, persuasion, and offers of compromise, but none that the Western leaders felt safe in accepting.[36] What the Russians feared most was the rearming of West Germany, especially the possibility that German troops, as NATO forces, might acquire atomic weapons. Having failed in their attempts to block these measures of the West, they turned to countermeasures. At Warsaw on May 14, 1955, the Soviets negotiated an alliance of eight Communist states—a sort of Eastern European Union—professedly for defense against the allegedly aggressive intentions of NATO.[37]

We may well ask today: was this inauguration of rival alliances and rival military build-ups necessary? Did the Soviet leaders of a country slowly recovering from a frightfully devastating war, actually plan armed aggression against Western Europe? There is no doubt that Truman and Acheson and their fellow planners in England and France believed the threat to be real. On the basis of what they believed, their precautions were

justified. But it is to be remembered that the Soviet experts in the State Department in 1950 were skeptical of Russia's aggressive intentions, and some careful students of Soviet policy twenty years later were convinced that Russia was too weak, and knew she was too weak, to attempt a takeover in Western Europe and a resulting confrontation with the United States. For their part, the Russians seem to have believed, partly as a result of such rhetoric as that of the Republican platform of 1952, that this country was determined to "liberate" the states of Eastern Europe from Soviet control. Thus, in the words of historian Adam Ulam:

> The Russians knew that they would not and could not move against the West. What, then, was the purpose of NATO, if not to push them from the positions they had secured in Eastern Europe between 1944 and 1947? Contrariwise, the Western statesmen, at least in 1949 and 1950, knew that they would not and could not reverse the *faits accomplis* in Poland, Rumania, etc. Why, then, did the Russians try to sabotage NATO unless they wanted a disarmed and weak Western Europe as their prey?[38]

The inevitable result of this atmosphere of mutual suspicion and fear was, in the words of Hans. J. Morgenthau, "a drastic militarisation of the Cold War in the form of a conventional and nuclear armaments race, the frantic search for alliances, and the establishment of military bases."[39]

Admitting, however, that neither alliance had any ambitious designs upon the territory or the sovereignty of the other, there remained the possibility that war might begin by accident or miscalculation. Berlin was the chief danger spot. Should the Russians or their puppets, the East Germans, try to seize the Western sector or to resume the blockade, the West would have to choose between surrender and

36. Russian offers to compromise on arms and the like always had gimmicks that the West could not accept. They would pull back their troops beyond the Polish boundary if the U.S. would remove its beyond the Atlantic. Any agency set up to police limitation agreements must be on the "troika" pattern, affording a veto to the Communists. If there was an agreement on mutual destruction of weapons, the West might see what the Soviets destroyed, not what they retained. Their super-secretive attitude always barred any effective arrangement for reciprocal inspection.
37. The signers of the Warsaw Alliance were the Soviet Union, Poland, Czechoslovakia, East Germany, Hungary, Rumania, Bulgaria, and Albania. A Communist Chinese observer promised the support of his government in the event of war.
38. Adam B. Ulam, *Expansion and Coexistence: The History of Soviet Foreign Policy, 1917–1967* (New York: Praeger Publishers, 1968), p. 511. Reprinted by permission of Praeger Publishers and The Pall Mall Press, Ltd., London.
39. Hans J. Morgenthau, "Arguing about the Cold War," *Encounter,* May 1967, p. 39.

conflict. Faced with this possibility and the Russian superiority in number of troops available, the West could hardly do otherwise than arm for defense. To a large degree, therefore, it might be said that the escalation of the cold war stemmed from the mistake of 1945 which left the West so vulnerable in Berlin.

The hopes of 1955 for a NATO army were never completely realized. The gain in strength from the addition of the West German army to NATO forces was largely offset by losses elsewhere. The nationalist rebellion against the French in Algeria, which had begun in 1954, drew off the greater part of the French forces that had been committed to NATO. Pressure for economy, doubt as to the efficacy of conventional forces in an age of nuclear weapons and long-range ballistic missiles, and occasional relaxation in East-West tensions, led to reductions in other national contingents. The goal of ninety-six divisions, set at the Lisbon meeting of the North Atlantic Council in 1952, was abandoned, and the "irreducible minimum" of thirty divisions, announced year after year by American Supreme Commanders at SHAPE was never attained.[40] Shortages of manpower, indeed, were compensated for by increases in firepower, as NATO troops in Europe were gradually equipped with tactical (low yield) atomic weapons. These were supplied by the United States, and their atomic warheads were kept under American custody, as required by the Atomic Energy Act. Any satisfaction afforded by this modernization of weaponry was qualified, however, by the reflection that the Russians were undoubtedly effecting similar improvements.

The weapons picture, in fact, had changed radically since the NATO treaty was signed in April 1949. Then the West held a monopoly of atomic weapons, and the United States, with the long-range bombers of the Strategic Air Command (S.A.C.), presumably possessed the capability of destroying Russian centers of population and industry without suffering comparable injury. Later in the same year, however, the U.S.S.R. exploded its first atomic bomb. Four years later it followed the United States by only a few months in setting off its first hydrogen, or thermonuclear, device, thus closing the gap between nuclear-weapon capabilities of the two major powers. The Russian success in launching the rocket-propelled satellites, Sputnik I and Sputnik II (October 4, November 3, 1957), ushered in the age of the intercontinental ballistic missile (ICBM) and its less potent relative, the intermediate-range ballistic missile (IRBM), which soon largely supplanted the slower and more vulnerable airplane as prospective carriers of nuclear destruction. By the early 1960's the Russians had developed, in the ICBM, means of delivery at least equal to those of the United States and also (as demonstrated in their tests in the fall of 1961) nuclear weapons of many megatons in potency.[41]

Something like a stalemate in nuclear weapons between the United States and the U.S.S.R. had been reached. Since each had the unquestioned power to destroy the other, nuclear war between them had become "unthinkable." The terms "balance of terror" or "mutual deterrence" described the relationship. Each government, however, was in constant search of more powerful and reliable weapons, and the search often took the form of exploding nuclear devices in the atmosphere with the resulting fallout of radioactive particles that created worldwide hazards to health. An unofficial moratorium on such tests was instituted in 1958, but in 1961 the Soviet Union resumed testing, and Britain and America felt it necessary to follow suit. Finally, on August 5, 1963, the three powers signed the Test Ban Treaty, by which they agreed to abstain from exploding nuclear de-

40. The ninety-six divisions proposed at Lisbon would have included the Greek and Turkish forces. The figure of thirty divisions referred to those on the main front from Denmark to Switzerland. General Eisenhower was succeeded as Supreme Commander by General Matthew B. Ridgway (May 1952), General A. M. Gruenther (July 1953), General Lauris Norstad (November 1956), General Lyman L. Lemnitzer (January 1963), and General Andrew T. Goodpaster (March 1969).

41. One megaton represents the equivalent of one million tons of TNT; a kiloton equals one thousand tons of the same. The "little" bomb that destroyed Hiroshima had a power of twenty kilotons.

vices in the atmosphere, in outer space, and under water. Underground tests were not banned. The treaty, which could be terminated by any signatory at three months' notice, was promptly ratified by the signers and adhered to by most of the governments of the world, excluding France, Communist China, and Cuba.[42]

42. Text of treaty in *Documents on American Foreign Relations, 1963*, pp. 130–32. On June 20, 1963, six weeks prior to the signing of the test-ban treaty, American and Russian representatives had signed at Geneva an agreement for a "hot line" emergency communications link between Washington and Moscow. Its purpose was to reduce the risk of war by making possible instant communication between the White House and the Kremlin in the event of a sudden crisis. It could, as the *New York Times* commented, "help to halt the war machines in an emergency until the real intentions of the potential antagonists could be clarified." Ibid., pp. 115–16. *New York Times,* June 15, 1963.

43

Peaceful Coexistence

Long before the major antagonists in the cold war had reached agreement on the test-ban treaty, important changes in personnel and in techniques had taken place in the Soviet Union. The death in March 1953 of Marshal Josef Stalin, the Russian dictator, was the prelude to the rise to power in Moscow of a leader whose aims were the same as Stalin's but whose methods were more flexible, more seductive, and more dangerous. Stalin's first successor as Premier, Georgi M. Malenkov, was quickly thrust aside to make way for Nikolai A. Bulganin, while Communist Party Secretary, Nikita S. Khrushchev, emerged as the man who really held the reins. In March 1958 Khrushchev took over the Premiership from Bulganin.

The new regime was more tolerant at home than its predecessor. With few exceptions its defeated opponents were relegated to obscure posts rather than liquidated in Stalinesque fashion, and the terrorism of the secret police largely disappeared. In foreign policy, the new rulers undertook to entice the uncommitted nations instead of frightening them. With a great show of affability, Bulganin and Khrushchev—popularly referred to as "B. and K."—paid friendly visits to India, Burma, and Afghanistan in 1955. There followed, for those countries and others, substantial grants or loans of economic and technical aid, to which, the Russians boasted, no political strings were attached.

When the Twentieth Congress of the Communist Party of the Soviet Union convened in Moscow in February 1956, Khrushchev, in a secret speech, roundly denounced Stalin's bloodthirsty methods and inaugurated a process of de-Stalinization calculated to degrade the dictator's name from its hitherto honorable place in Soviet history. It was at this time, too, that Khrushchev enunciated his policy of "peaceful coexistence," repudiating the Leninist doctrine of inevitable war between the Communist and capitalist societies, and declaring that Communism could achieve its victory by peacefully demonstrating its superiority. "We will bury you," he informed the capitalist world on a later occasion, but he meant that he would bury the system, not the people who lived under it. The Soviet government, meanwhile, having negotiated the Warsaw Pact in response to Western European Union, showed a spirit of conciliation by signing (May 15, 1955) the treaty ending the occupation of Austria and accepting on the same day an invitation from the United States, Great Britain, and France for a summit meeting of the Big Four heads of government at Geneva in July.

At Geneva, July 18 to 23, 1955, President Eisenhower, Prime Minister Anthony Eden (who had recently succeeded Winston Churchill), French Premier Edgar Faure, Russian Premier Bulganin, their Foreign Ministers, and other dignitaries (including, of course, Party Secretary Khrushchev), met face to face in an effort to resolve critical East-West difficulties. The meeting had been heralded from Moscow and Washington as promising agreement, and its sessions were conducted in a tone of cordiality which gave rise to the phrase, "spirit of Geneva." On substantive matters, however, no agreement was achieved. On the reunification of Germany, the Western proposal that it be effected by free elections won temporary assent from the Russians, but this assent was repudiated when the Foreign Ministers met later to work out details. This was not surprising, since it was well understood that a Germany unified by free elections would be anti-Communist and pro-West.

On disarmament, the West considered effective inspection essential; the Soviets held it inadmissible. President Eisenhower's generous proposal that East and West exchange "blueprints" of their armed forces and permit mutual "open skies" aerial inspection of their territory found no favor with the Russians. On European security, Russian insistence that NATO be disbanded and American troops withdrawn from Europe was equally unacceptable to the West. Only on such matters as freer cultural exchanges was there any real meeting of minds. The questions unresolved "at the summit" were referred to the four Foreign Ministers, who met late in October,

also in Geneva. Their failure to agree on anything significant left no doubt that East and West had reached a new impasse.

Tragedy in Hungary

From 1955 to 1963 relations of the United States and its NATO Allies with the Soviet bloc, so far as Europe was concerned, involved a series of alternating crises and détentes, with the status of West Berlin eventually taking a prominent place as a factor in the crises. The first serious crisis after the Geneva summit meeting of 1955, however, did not concern Berlin. The crisis of 1956 was a dual one produced by Russian suppression of an attempted anti-Communist revolution in Hungary and an attack on Egypt by Israel, France, and Great Britain. The Egyptian crisis is dealt with in the chapter on the Middle East. The Hungarian tragedy is considered here.

An important characteristic of Soviet policy after Stalin was a degree of relaxation in Moscow's control of Communist parties and governments in neighboring states. The dissident Marshal Tito of Yugoslavia, after playing host to Khrushchev, was welcomed on a visit to Moscow and assured that the Kremlin accepted the principle of "national Communism" which he espoused. Encouraged by this display of conciliation toward Yugoslavia, the Polish Communists installed a pronounced anti-Stalinist, Wladyslaw Gomulka, as Party Secretary and dissuaded Khrushchev from interfering. Still Communist and continuing to adhere to the Warsaw Alliance, the Polish regime had successfully defied the dictatorship of the Kremlin.

In Hungary, dissatisfaction took a more radical turn. Anti-Soviet and antigovernment riots in Budapest led to the installation, October 24, 1956, of a new government headed by Imre Nagy. A few days later, Nagy, though a Communist, admitted non-Communists to his government. On November 1 the government repudiated the Warsaw Alliance, declared Hungary a neutral state, and appealed to the United Nations for assistance.

This was more than the Soviet Union could let pass. Success in Hungary's secession from the Communist bloc could well lead to a complete breakup of Moscow's circle of satellites. Moscow reacted violently. After temporarily withdrawing its tanks and troops from Budapest, it sent them back in force, suppressed the popular uprising in the city, and connived at the installation of a new Communist government headed by János Kádar, which invited Russian assistance. Imre Nagy took refuge in the Yugoslav embassay. Enticed out by hints of office in the new government, he was seized, abducted to Rumania, and later executed. Weeks of fighting followed, but a virtually unarmed populace was no match for Russian tanks. No aid came from the West, and collapse of an heroic struggle for independence was inevitable.

In Washington President Dwight D. Eisenhower had been elected in 1952 after a campaign in which the Republican Party had condemned the "containment" policy of the Democrats as "negative, futile, and immoral," and promised to "again make liberty into a beacon light of hope that will penetrate the dark places." "Liberation" of peoples under the Communist yoke was to replace "containment" of Communism. How far the Hungarians and other captive peoples had been encouraged to hope for aid by these campaign declarations and by broadcasts from the official Voice of America and its unofficial American counterpart, Radio Free Europe, it is impossible to say. It is certain that neither President Eisenhower nor Secretary of State John Foster Dulles intended to encourage a popular rebellion against impossible odds or to assist such a rebellion at the risk of war with the Soviet Union. Even if the United States, or NATO, had wished to intervene in Hungary, it would have been seriously hampered by contemporary events in the Middle East.[1] But it seems clear that no such desire existed. Action by the United States was limited to the expression of sympathy for the Hungarian people, the sponsoring of resolutions by which the U.N. General Assembly futilely called upon the Soviet Union to withdraw its troops, and the offering of asylum in the United States to Hungarian refugees.

It should be added that the United States welcomed such varying degrees of independence from Moscow as were represented by Yugoslavia since 1948 and Poland under Gomulka's government.[2] America had for several years been supplying economic and even military aid to Yugoslavia and now began providing aid to Poland, chiefly in surplus food products. Such aid was based upon the theory that any measure which lessened the dependence of these regimes upon Moscow served the interests of the West.

Berlin and Camp David

The next serious crisis in NATO-Warsaw Pact relations concerned Berlin. In a speech of November 10, 1958, and in notes to the United States, Great Britain, and France on the 27th, Khrushchev demanded an end to the occupation of West Berlin by the three Western powers. In the notes, he insisted upon a solution within six months, threatening otherwise to make a peace treaty with East Germany and leave the Allies to negotiate their rights in Berlin and their access thereto with the East German government which they did not recognize. Any attempt to maintain their position against East Germany by force, Khrushchev warned, would be met by all the power of the Warsaw Alliance.

The Soviet ultimatum—for that is what it appeared to be—received a unified response from the Western powers. In Paris, December 14, the Foreign Ministers of the United States, Great Britain, France, and West Germany joined in an unqualified rejection of the Soviet ultimatum, and their position was endorsed two days later by the NATO Council. The reply of the United States to the Russian note

1. See Chapter 47.

2. Gomulka subsequently became a firm adherent of Kremlin policy.

of November 27 was dispatched on December 31. Briefly stated, the Western argument was that the Soviet Union had no right by unilateral action to cancel the rights of the Western Allies in West Berlin, which were theirs by virtue of the common victory over Germany. The Allies also emphasized their obligation to maintain the freedom of the more than two million people of West Berlin. They expressed their desire to see the Berlin question settled as a part of the German question as a whole, and repeated their proposal that Germany be unified through the holding of free elections in both parts of the divided country.[3]

Faced by determined and united Western opposition, Mr. Khrushchev softened the ultimative tone of his demand by letting it be known that the six months time limit need not be taken literally. It was then agreed that the Big Four Foreign Ministers should meet in Geneva in May to discuss Berlin, Germany, European security, and disarmament. It was further understood that if they should make progress toward an accord, their sessions would be followed by another summit meeting, which might perhaps end the cold war. From May 11 to June 30 and again from July 13 to August 5, the Foreign Ministers met at Geneva. They considered possible compromise solutions for the Berlin question but reached no agreement on this or on any of the other major issues before them. President Eisenhower, who had at first made some preliminary agreement a prerequisite of another summit meeting, now waived that requirement. He invited Nikita Khrushchev—now Chairman of the Council of Ministers of the U.S.S.R., or Premier—to visit him at Camp David, his mountain retreat in Maryland.

The meeting at Camp David, September 25 to 27, 1959, climaxed ten days in which Khrushchev's touring of the United States and his sensational proposal in the United Nations General Assembly of general and complete disarmament had enjoyed continuous spotlight. His conversations with Eisenhower were marked by cordiality on both sides, giving rise to talk of a "spirit of Camp David." The joint communiqué issued at the close of the meeting stated that while the talks were not undertaken to negotiate issues, they had been useful in mutually clarifying the positions of the two leaders and should thus contribute "to the achievement of a just and lasting peace." The two had agreed that the question of general disarmament was "the most important one facing the world today." On the Berlin question they had agreed that, subject to the approval of the other parties concerned, negotiations should be reopened in the hope of reaching a satisfactory solution. It was also agreed, Eisenhower told a news conference and Khrushchev concurred, "that these negotiations should not be prolonged indefinitely but there could be no fixed time limit on them." The leaders rejected the use of force in settling "outstanding international questions," and finally they agreed that President Eisenhower should visit the Soviet Union in the following spring, at a date to be arranged through diplomatic channels.[4]

Explosion at the Summit

In December, after the Camp David meeting, Great Britain and France joined the United States in proposing a summit meeting of the Big Four for the following spring. The Russians accepted, and the date was fixed at May 16, 1960, the place in Paris. Eisenhower's visit to the Soviet Union was to follow in June.

In the months prior to the Paris meeting, the "spirit of Camp David" was clearly deteriorating. There were renewed threats from Khrushchev of drastic action if the Berlin

3. The essential portions of the lengthy arguments are printed in *Documents on American Foreign Relations, 1958*, pp. 217–38; ibid., *1959*, pp. 219–96. The Russians argued that the Western Allies had violated the Potsdam Agreement by establishing West Germany and had thus forfeited their rights in Berlin, which, as the Russians told it, they had derived from the Potsdam Agreement.

4. *Documents on American Foreign Relations, 1959*, pp. 193–94, 199. A peace treaty with Germany and trade between the U.S. and the U.S.S.R. were among other subjects that had been discussed.

question were not soon settled, and assurances from Washington that the United States would never desert the people of West Berlin. Prospects of agreement, growing dim already, were completely destroyed by the Russian reaction to the U-2 incident early in May.

On May 1 a high-flying U.S. reconnaissance plane of the U-2 type was shot down while on a flight across Russia from Pakistan to Norway. The pilot, Francis Gary Powers, was captured unharmed, along with his photographic and other equipment. Khrushchev adroitly held back details while the State Department tried to explain the presence of the U-2 over Russia as the result of a navigational error. But when it became apparent that the Russians "had the goods" on Powers and his flight, Secretary of State Christian A. Herter admitted that the flight of the U-2 was but one of a number of such flights, conducted for the purpose of photographing installations in the Soviet Union. The President confirmed Herter's admission, and both men defended this type of espionage as a means of guarding against surprise attack, necessitated by Russian secretiveness, and as in no way more culpable than other forms of espionage notoriously practiced by the Soviet Union.

It seems evident that Khrushchev and his associates in the Kremlin seized upon the U-2 incident as an excuse for wrecking a summit conference in which they realized the West would never accept their terms for Berlin or Germany. Khrushchev came to Paris and in brutal and boorish language refused to negotiate unless President Eisenhower would, among other things, apologize for the U-2 flight and agree to punish those responsible for it. He also withdrew the invitation to Eisenhower to visit the Soviet Union. He was not mollified by the President's assurance that there would be no more U-2 flights during his term of office, or by the conciliatory efforts of President de Gaulle and Prime Minister Macmillan. The summit conference ended abruptly on May 17, one day after its opening.[5]

5. Powers tells the story of his flight and imprison-

Khrushchev and Kennedy

In spite of his violent diatribes in Paris, Chairman Khrushchev did not follow up his threat to conclude a peace treaty with the East German regime. On the contrary, he told an audience in East Berlin that the existing situation would have to be preserved for a while until there could be another summit conference, perhaps after six or eight months. It was plain that he hoped to find Eisenhower's successor more yielding.

It was not, however, until June 1961 that Mr. Khrushchev and President John F. Kennedy met for a two-day conference in Vienna. Although this meeting was on the surface friendly and courteous, the *aide-mémoire* which Khrushchev handed to the President resurrected the Berlin crisis in much the same terms as before, and again with a six-months time limit. Unless within that time the four governments could agree on a peace treaty or treaties with Germany, united or divided, the Soviets would conclude a separate treaty with what they called the German Democratic Republic, and occupation rights in West Berlin would terminate. West Berlin might continue as a "free city," and either neutral U.N. troops or "token forces" of the three Western powers and the Soviet Union might be stationed there, but it seemed clear that the city's contacts with the West would be at the mercy of the G.D.R.[6]

The United States replied to the *aide-mémoire* in a note of July 17. The United States had, it averred, together with its British and French Allies, "a fundamental political

ment in Francis Gary Powers and Curt Gentry, *Operation Overflight: The Story of U-2 Sky Pilot, Francis Gary Powers* (New York: Holt, Rinehart and Winston, 1970). For documents on the U-2 flight and the summit conference, see *Documents on American Foreign Relations, 1960,* pp. 106–67. Herter had succeeded John Foster Dulles as Secretary of State upon the latter's resignation in April 1959. Dulles had died of cancer a month later. Macmillan had succeeded Eden after the Suez crisis.
6. *Documents on American Foreign Relations, 1961,* pp. 137–41.

and moral obligation" to "maintain the freedom of over two million people in West
Berlin." Any attempt to hinder the fulfillment
of that obligation "would have the gravest
effects upon international peace and security
and endanger the lives and well-being of millions of people." In a nationwide broadcast,
July 25, the President told the country: "We
cannot and will not permit the Communists
to drive us out of Berlin, either gradually or
by force." Remarking that "we do not want
to fight, but we have fought before." Mr.
Kennedy announced that he was asking Congress for a $3.25 billion increase in the defense
budget, for increases in Army, Navy, and Air
Force manpower, and for authority to call
various reserve units to active duty. By increasing the conventional forces at home and
in Europe, the President intended "to have a
wider choice than humiliation or all-out nuclear action." [7]

Congress gave the President what he asked
for, and an additional force of 45,000 men
was moved to Europe. France and West Germany also strengthened their NATO forces.
All in all, General Norstad, NATO Supreme
Commander, now had twenty-five divisions or
the equivalent, most of them in markedly improved fighting condition. Whether or not
because of these warlike gestures, Mr. Khrushchev again removed the time limit from his
demand for a Berlin settlement. For a time in
the early months of 1962, there was Russian
harassment of Western planes in the air corri-
dors from West Germany to Berlin, accompanied by other forms of pressure, but after
March, the Berlin front was relatively quiet.

But if such concessions relaxed tension at
one point, other moves by Khrushchev or his
henchmen had the reverse effect. On August
13, 1961, the East German regime began construction of the wall separating East from
West Berlin, thus effectively putting an end
to West Berlin's important role as an "escape
hatch" from Communist East Germany. The
United States responded by protest only. At

the end of August, Khrushchev announced the
early beginning of a new series of nuclear tests
in the atmosphere, ending an informal moratorium begun in 1958, and necessitating further tests by the United States and Great
Britain. In December the Soviet government
announced a 10 percent increase in its defense
budget for 1962, acknowledging at the same
time that the original estimates for 1961 had
already been increased by nearly one-third.
The following year, 1962, was marked by the
most dangerous confrontation since 1945—
Khrushchev's audacious planting of nuclear
missiles in Cuba and his retreat when faced
by American firmness. For a few days the
world seemed indeed on the brink of nuclear
war. This story is told in another chapter.[8]

The Quest for a Détente with the Soviet Union

After the settlement of the Cuban missile
crisis, there seemed some hope for a real improvement of relations between the United
States and the U.S.S.R. Both had, apparently,
accepted the nuclear stalemate as a reality.
The questions of Germany and Berlin were
by no means settled; but the successors of
Chancellor Adenauer, who retired in October
1963, were less insistent than he upon German
reunification as an immediate goal, while on
the other hand, the Soviets refrained from
creating further crises over Berlin. There were,
it is true, sporadic threats and some harassing
of transportation into and out of West Berlin
on occasions when the West German Bun-
destag (Parliament) or its committees chose
to meet there—illegally from the East German
and Russian point of view; but these interferences were short-lived and did not threaten
the life of the city or the security of its Western garrisons.

Under these circumstances Presidents Lyndon B. Johnson (1963–1969) and Richard
Nixon (1969–   ) sought to improve relations with the Soviet Union and, as Johnson

7. The note of July 17 and the broadcast of July 25
are printed in *Documents on American Foreign Relations, 1961*, pp. 141–49 and 95–105, respectively.

8. See Chapter 48.

phrased it, to "build bridges" of trade and understanding with the smaller nations of Eastern Europe.

Johnson's efforts to improve trade relations with the Communist bloc were hampered by a reluctant Congress, while the war in Vietnam and Soviet backing of the Arabs against Israel in the Six-Day War of 1967 and thereafter [9] kept tensions alive between the United States and the U.S.S.R. Moscow viewed the war in Vietnam as a "war of national liberation" on one side and a war of American "aggression" and "imperialism" on the other. The Soviets, therefore, provided war equipment on a generous scale to the armies of Ho Chi Minh, and Premier Kosygin [10] told the editors of *Life* (February 2, 1968) that "we [the Soviets], for our part will do all we can so that the U.S. does not defeat Vietnam. American aggression," he added, "will be met with growing rebuff." Attempts by both Johnson and Nixon to persuade Moscow to assist in bringing Hanoi to accept the United States peace terms were fruitless.

In the Arab-Israeli Six-Day War of June 1967 the Soviet Union, if it did not instigate hostile moves by the Arabs, certainly did little to restrain them. It furnished no military aid to the Arabs during their disastrous war, but was quick, after the cease-fire, to replace the immense stores of military equipment destroyed or captured by the Israelis.

The war gave the Soviets an excuse to move a large naval force into the Mediterranean, where it monitored the movements of the American Sixth Fleet. This naval presence, plus the now unquestioned friendship of most of the Arab states, gave the Soviets a foothold in the Middle East which the most powerful of the Czars would have envied. By the same token, American influence in the area declined.

Eventually the U.S.S.R. and the United States agreed on the Security Council resolution of November 22, 1967,[11] recommending terms of settlement of the Arab-Israeli war, but differed as to its interpretation and implementation.[12] Meanwhile, a meeting of President Johnson and Premier Kosygin at Glassboro, New Jersey (June 23, 25, 1967), produced amicable discussion but no agreement on either the Middle East or Vietnam.

President Nixon entered office, January 20, 1969, with high hopes for, as he put it, substituting "negotiations" for "confrontation" in relations with the Soviet Union and for securing Soviet aid in bringing peace to both the Middle East and Vietnam. By the close of 1970 no apparent progress toward peace had been made in either area. It could safely be assumed that Moscow did not wish to see hostilities in either area escalate into major war, but that in neither was it willing to sacrifice its own interests for a settlement that would be acceptable to the United States.

Some progress had been made, nevertheless, in the negotiation of desirable treaties, both bilateral, between the United States and the U.S.S.R., and multilateral, including both as signatories. The nuclear test-ban treaty of 1963 was described in the preceding chapter. A U.S.-Soviet consular convention was signed in 1964 and ratified four years later. In July 1969 reciprocal arrangements were made for the opening of consulates in San Francisco and Leningrad. A multilateral treaty on the peaceful uses of outer space, signed in January 1967, went into effect later in the year. A treaty to prohibit the placing of nuclear weapons on the seabed beyond any nation's twelve-mile limit, sponsored jointly by the United States and the Soviet Union, was approved by the U.N. General Assembly's Political Committee on November 17, 1970. It would become effective when ratified by 22 governments. A treaty to halt the spread of nuclear weapons (the nuclear nonproliferation treaty), prepared by the United States and the Soviet Union and overwhelmingly approved by the

9. See Chapters 46, 47.

10. In October 1964 Nikita S. Khrushchev was removed from his two high offices and replaced by Aleksei N. Kosygin as Premier and Leonid I. Brezhnev as first Secretary of the Communist party.

11. See p. 526.

12. See pp. 526–27 for four-power attempts to find a peace plan for the Middle East.

U.N. General Assembly, was signed on July 1, 1968, by the United States, the U.S.S.R., and Britain, and approved by the United States Senate on March 13, 1969. It received the necessary ratifications and went into effect on March 5, 1970. Its importance was limited by the nonparticipation of the two minor but ambitious nuclear powers, France and Communist China.

There was hope, too, at the close of 1969, that the long-sought treaty halting competition in nuclear strategic weapons between the superpowers might at last be in sight. The banning of nuclear tests in the atmosphere [13] had not halted the race in nuclear weapons. During 1966 the United States learned that the Soviet Union was pushing the development of both offensive missiles and defensive antiballistic missiles (ABMs) in an effort to overcome assumed American superiority or even in a quest for "first strike" capability—the ability to destroy the retaliatory power of an enemy by a surprise attack. In the United States, the Nixon administration, after a long debate in the Senate, resolved to begin laying down a "light" ABM system, known as "Safeguard," theoretically for defense of missile sites. Both governments, also, were experimenting with the latest offensive device, the MIRV (multiple independently targetable reentry vehicle), an ICBM armed with not one but a number of nuclear warheads, which could be aimed at as many separate targets, cities, or missile sites, in the enemy country.[14] Since these weapons systems were almost unimaginably costly as well as destructive, common sense and common interests obviously called for an agreement between the United States and the U.S.S.R. to stop the race.

The prospect of the deployment of MIRVs by both parties made the need for a halt in the race particularly urgent. The number and location of ICBMs could be checked by photography from satellites, which each party was now assumed to employ as a matter of course. Each party to a limitation agreement would therefore be able to check on the performance of its rival as to the number of missiles deployed. But once the deployment of the hydraheaded MIRVs began, there would be no way of determining the number of warheads per missile and hence the total of the rival's nuclear armaments. If the arms race could not be halted before the deployment of MIRVs had proceeded very far, there was slim chance of halting it at all.

In June 1968 the Kremlin, reacting to a four-year old American proposal, had offered to begin talks on the subject in Geneva in September. The United States promptly agreed, but backed off when Russian armies invaded Czechoslovakia in August, and the question of arms talks was left for the Nixon administration to handle.

Richard Nixon, who in his campaign for the presidency in 1968 had talked of negotiating "from a position of superiority," spoke after his inauguration of "sufficiency" in nuclear arms as an acceptable basis for talks. The change was encouraging, since each of the nuclear giants already had weapons "sufficient" to destroy the other. Nixon showed no haste to begin the talks, however, and delayed action until he was assured that Congress would approve deployment of the ABM "Safeguard," which he felt would improve his negotiating position.

After the Senate's hairbreadth approval of "Safeguard" on August 6, 1969, the administration informed the Russians of its readiness to talk, with the result that the Strategic Arms Limitation Talks (SALT) opened at Helsinki, Finland, on November 17, 1969, in a mood of unusual cordiality and guarded optimism. On December 22 the negotiators adjourned after completing the preliminary phase of their talks. Further sessions were held in Vienna, April 16 to August 14, and in Helsinki, November 2 to December 18, 1970, with a fourth meeting scheduled for March 15, 1971, in Vienna. The cordial relations continued, but

---

13. See pp. 448–49.

14. Before the development of MIRV, the chief strategic nuclear weapons in the American arsenal were the land-based solid-fuel ICBM Minuteman and the Navy's IRBM Polaris, designed to be mounted on and fired from an atomic-powered submarine. The Soviet Union was armed with comparable weapons.

the negotiators were still far from any agreement. The United States, meanwhile, had begun equipping some hundreds of its Minuteman ICBMs with triplet MIRV warheads.[15]

NATO in Trouble

The relations of the United States with the Soviet Union were not separable from those of NATO with the Warsaw Alliance. NATO in its second decade had lost much of its cohesiveness and at least some of its importance. As the apparent danger of Soviet aggression declined, so did the bond that held the diverse members of the alliance together, and rifts appeared in the structure. Many of these were minor. Europeans resented an American habit of making unilateral decisions on defense and other matters. Americans felt that the NATO nations of a newly prosperous Europe were carrying less than their fair share of the burden of common defense. Some Americans deplored the failure of most of the NATO allies to sympathize with and support American policy in Vietnam and the insistence of some of them upon trading with North Vietnam as well as with Communist China and Cuba, which the United States sought to isolate. The United States found its usually faithful northern ally, Canada, uncooperative in continental defense policy during the prime ministership of John Diefenbaker (1957–1963). Portugal, for its part, resented its allies' faultfinding with its colonial policy in Africa [16] and threatened to deny them the use of bases in the Azores. Greece and Turkey, constituting the right flank of NATO's line of defense, were prevented from going to war over Cyprus only by the joint efforts of NATO, the U.N., and the United States.[17] Greece, in April 1967, was the scene of a military coup and a resulting dictatorship, which weakened its ties with its democratic allies in Europe and America.

15. *New York Times*, November 18, December 23, 1969; April 17, August 15, December 19, 20, 1970.
16. See pp. 428–29.
17. See p. 426.

De Gaulle Sabotages NATO

These misunderstandings and quarrels were of minor importance compared with the partial defection of France under President Charles de Gaulle (1958–1969). Called to power in France in June 1958 as the successor to a series of weak governments, de Gaulle quickly restored stability to French political life and ended the exhausting colonial war in Algeria, in all of which the United States rejoiced. But de Gaulle, the wartime leader of the Free French, was dissatisfied with France's minor role in world politics compared with that of the "Anglo-Saxons," as he was fond of saying. When President Eisenhower rejected his proposal for a three-power directorate—France, Britain, and the United States—to guide the policies of NATO, de Gaulle took position after position antagonistic to the United States—recognizing Communist China, condemning American policy in Vietnam, catering to anti-Americanism in Latin America, encouraging French separatism in Quebec, siding with the Arabs against Israel in the Six-Day War of 1967, rebuffing the United States as well as England in barring the United Kingdom from the Common Market.[18]

18. England, formerly aloof from the Common Market because of Commonwealth ties, had changed its position and applied for membership in 1961. The European Economic Community (E.E.C. or Common Market) was formed by France, West Germany, Italy, and the three Benelux countries by a treaty signed in Rome on March 25, 1957. The same governments at the same time established the European Atomic Energy Community (Euratom). They were already linked in the European Coal and Steel Community. The three interlocking organizations promised a high degree of integration in the economies of this important area of Western Europe and a consequent enhancement of both its economic prosperity and its defense capabilities. This development, which might be considered a culmination of the Marshall Plan, had received consistent encouragement from the United States, despite the prospect that such an integrated Europe would offer intensified competition to American industry and agriculture. A wide power to reduce U.S. tariff rates granted to the President in the Trade Expansion Act of October 11, 1962 was to take effect in full only if Britain became a member of the Common Market.

Most serious, however, was de Gaulle's policy toward NATO, a policy characterized by his fervent nationalism. In opposition to American policy, he insisted that France must have, at great expense, her independent nuclear force, or *force de frappe*. In justification of this costly policy, he warned the French people and their European allies that the United States would not defend Western Europe at the cost of a nuclear war with the Soviet Union.[19] He gave assurances that France would fulfill her obligations as an ally under the North Atlantic Treaty, but rejected, so far as France was concerned, the concept of a unified command—a fundamental concept of NATO. Measures of partial withdrawal from the command structure—detachment of the French Mediterranean fleet, denial of base and air rights to nuclear-armed American planes, etc.—climaxed in March 1966, when the French President served notice that all NATO military installations, including headquarters at SHAPE, must leave French soil by April 1, 1967.[20] Even before that date French officers were withdrawn from all SHAPE's planning committee.

NATO headquarters, civil as well as military, were moved to Belgium within the time allowed. France continued as an ally and made no move to withdraw when NATO's first twenty years ended in 1969. But the armed forces of France, the geographical and military keystone to the defense of Western Europe, could no longer be counted upon to take orders from SHAPE, and the problems of the Supreme Commander in the event of an attack from the East were greatly complicated.[21]

Other NATO members followed France, not in detaching their forces from SHAPE command but in reducing the number of forces immediately available. The United States, where the maintenance of 330,000 troops in Europe contributed (with the war in Vietnam) to a chronic foreign exchange deficit, transferred 35,000 troops from Europe to America in 1967, though these units were still committed to NATO and could be returned to Europe on short notice. Britain took similar action with 6,500 of her 51,000 troops on the continent. Canada, two years later, announced that it would cut its ground troops and air force in Europe by almost 50 percent. West Germany reduced her projected contribution to NATO forces from 508,000 to 400,000 men.[22]

Further reduction of NATO conventional forces seemed probable. In the United States, Democratic Senate Leader Mike Mansfield called year after year for a "substantial reduction" of American troops in Europe, and his proposal had wide support in Congress. It was, however, opposed by the Executive under both Presidents Johnson and Nixon, and shelved by the latter for at least a year and a half in December 1970. December 1970, indeed, saw not only President Nixon's reassurance that U.S. troops would remain in Europe, but also a pledge by ten European members to spend a billion dollars over the next five years on military installations, communications, and additional Nato forces.[23]

From Defense to Détente?

Weakening and revival of commitments to NATO were the result, actually, of fluctuating skepticism as to the reality of the danger of Russian aggression. Such skepticism grew as tension over Berlin relaxed and the Soviet Union became more deeply involved in a

19. It was partly to counteract de Gaulle's influence and to assure the German people that they could count upon American protection that President Kennedy visited Bonn and West Berlin in June 1963, declaring in the latter city: "Today, in the world of freedom the proudest boast is *'Ich bin ein Berliner.'*"

20. *Documents on American Foreign Relations, 1966,* pp. 107–8, 120–22.

21. President de Gaulle resigned in April 1969, after defeat of his proposed constitutional changes in a national plebiscite. His successor, Georges Pompidou, relaxed opposition to Britain's admission to the Common Market but in other respects remained faithful

to Gaullist foreign policies. De Gaulle died suddenly on November 9, 1970.

22. *U.S. in World Affairs, 1967,* pp. 201–4; *New York Times,* September 20, 1969.

23. *New York Times,* December 4, 1970.

quarrel with Communist China.[24] Western fears were reawakened in August 1968, when Russian armies invaded Czechoslovakia to suppress a liberalizing program in that Communist state. In justification of this action, Communist Party Chairman Leonid I. Brezhnev proclaimed, in what came to be known as the Brezhnev Doctrine, the right of the Soviet Union to intervene in any state of the Communist bloc to preserve the integrity of the socialist system.[25]

More alarming than the Brezhnev Doctrine were the arrival on the Czechoslovak-West German frontier of five Russian divisions and a statement from Moscow that Articles 53 and 107 of the U.N. Charter gave the Soviet Union the right to intervene in West Germany, a former enemy state. The threat brought about a more cooperative attitude on the part of France and led the governments of France, Britain, and the United States to warn Moscow to keep hands off the German Federal Republic.[26] The Moscow threat was probably bluff; it was not followed up, and the relaxation of tensions was resumed.

In March 1969, at Budapest, the Warsaw Pact powers proposed a conference on security by the nations of East and West Europe, bringing from the *New York Times* the editorial query, "From Defense to Détente?" [27] Nothing came from this proposal (as had happened repeatedly in the past), but in October 1969 the Warsaw Pact powers tried again, this time proposing Helsinki as a meeting place and—a novel feature in such proposals—leaving open the possibility that the United States and Canada might be included.

NATO's response came from Brussels at the end of a three-day meeting of the Council. The communiqué, issued December 5, 1969, declared that the NATO governments were "receptive" to suggestions of talks on "measures to reduce tension and promote cooperation in Europe," but stipulated that "prospects of concrete results" would be essential to their consent to the proposed conference. Listed as such "concrete results" were free access to West Berlin, a working agreement between East and West Germany, and an agreement on reduction of armed forces in Europe. It was reported that these preconditions for a conference were insisted upon by the United States over the objection of a number of the European allies. They led an American commentator to deplore the American attitude "that we can't enter a conference unless we know in advance what its outcome will be." [28]

But while NATO as a whole hesitated, Chancellor Willy Brandt of West Germany was making promising moves toward a détente with the Communist bloc. As Foreign Minister in the coalition cabinet of Chancellor Kurt Georg Kiesinger (1966–1969), he had refrained from pushing for reunification of Germany as an immediate goal and had dropped the demand of the previous regime of Ludwig Erhard (1963–1966) for access to nuclear weapons.[29] He had also violated an unofficial West German taboo by proposing to recognize the Oder-Neisse line as Germany's eastern boundary, thus surrendering claims to the formerly German territory occupied since 1945 by Poland and the U.S.S.R.[30]

As Chancellor after the victory of the Social Democrats in the German elections of September 28, 1969, Brandt offered to negotiate agreements renouncing the use or threat of force with the nations of Eastern Europe, agreements that would also guarantee mutual

24. See Chapter 45.
25. Cynics remarked that there was no great difference between the Brezhnev Doctrine and the Monroe Doctrine as applied in Guatemala and the Dominican Republic, where the U.S. had intervened to preserve the integrity of the free enterprise system. See Chapters 48, 49.
26. *New York Times*, September 18, 1968; Don Cook, "NATO." *Atlantic*, January 1970, p. 16.
27. *New York Times*, March 19, April 10, 1969.

28. *New York Times*, December 6, 1969; Zbigniew Brzezinski, "Détente in the '70s," *The New Republic*, January 3, 1970.
29. In an effort to satisfy the German desire for equality of status with respect to nuclear weapons, the United States had espoused a plan for a multilateral naval force (MLF), to be armed with Polaris missiles and officered and manned by personnel of mixed NATO nationalities. The proposal had evoked little enthusiasm except from Germany and had been strongly opposed by President de Gaulle as well as by the Soviet Union. It had been quietly allowed to die after 1966.
30. *New York Times*, March 19, 24, 1968.

respect for the territorial integrity of the signers, thus in effect insuring Poland and Czechoslovakia against any German irredentist claims. While unwilling to recognize East Germany as a sovereign state and insisting that all Germany was really one, the Chancellor stated his government's willingness to work for "contractually agreed cooperation" with East Germany and to abandon attempts to interfere with East Germany's economic and cultural relations with other nations.[31]

Meetings between Chancellor Brandt and East German Premier Willi Stoph, March 19 and May 21, 1970, met an obstacle in Stoph's insistence that Bonn accord full diplomatic recognition to East Germany as an independent sovereign state.[32] The meetings were not resumed until December, but meanwhile talks by Bonn with Warsaw and Moscow were more productive. The Moscow talks reached a culmination on August 7, when the Soviet and West German Foreign Ministers initialed a treaty by which both governments renounced the use of force in their mutual relations and agreed to respect existing national boundaries. In accompanying notes, the Bonn government reserved the right to seek the unification of Germany by peaceful means and assured the Western Allies that the treaty in no way infringed their rights in Berlin.[33]

Three months later, in a treaty with Poland, the West German government accepted the Oder-Neisse line as Poland's border with Germany. Treaties with Czechoslovakia and Hungary were expected to follow. Chancellor Brandt made it plain, however, that the Soviet treaty, and probably the others, would not be submitted to the Reichstag for ratification until East Germany agreed to relax tensions in Berlin and to ease restrictions on intercourse between Berlin and West Germany.[34]

Additional hope for relief of these tensions was found in the resumption, in Berlin, after twenty-two years, of amicable discussions of the Berlin problem between delegates of the four occupying powers.[35] A NATO offer in May to discuss "mutual and balanced force reductions" with the Warsaw Pact powers received an encouraging response, and prospects for a NATO-Warsaw Pact security conference some time in 1971 seemed good.[36] C. L. Sulzberger of the *New York Times* was led to remark: "Thus, suddenly, the diplomatic ice jam gives signs of breaking." [37]

Unfortunately, the hopeful signs were confined to Europe, and even here they were soon clouded. By December the four-power talks appeared stalled; indeed, there were new harassments of traffic between West Germany and Berlin when West German Social Democrats held a party meeting in the city. In Southeast Asia and the Middle East, East-West tensions showed no indications of abating. In the Middle East, alleged Soviet and Egyptian violations of a cease-fire agreement brought angry recriminations between Washington and Moscow, while Moscow denounced President Nixon's peace offer to Hanoi as "a great fraud," and Washington sternly warned Moscow against carrying out suspected plans for a nuclear submarine base in Cuba.[38] An easing of Sino-Soviet tensions—the signing of a trade agreement and an exchange of ambassadors after a four-year lapse [39]—relieved Moscow of one compulsion to placate the West. James Reston of the *New York Times,* visiting Moscow in December 1970, found Soviet officials "openly and uniformly critical" of American foreign policy under President Nixon. Their attitude had undergone "a marked change for the worse since the first of the year." [40] Thus a year that had begun in optimism seemed fated to end in gloom.

31. *New York Times,* October 29, 1969.
32. *New York Times,* March 20, May 22, 1970.
33. *New York Times,* August 7, 8, 12, 13 (editorial), 1970.
34. *New York Times,* November 21, 23 (editorial), 1970.

35. *New York Times,* March 29, June 10, 1970.
36. *New York Times,* May 28, June 27, August 19, 1970.
37. *New York Times,* July 5, 1970.
38. *New York Times,* September 26, 1970.
39. *New York Times,* November 24, 1970.
40. *New York Times,* December 20, 1970, sec. 4, p. 11.

44

The Postwar
Far East, I:
Beginnings—
The Korean War

For the postwar Far East the United States had, if not a program, at least a rather clear ideal. This ideal may be defined as anticolonialism or, more affirmatively, nationalism. Japan, in the first place, was to disgorge all the territories that she had taken at the expense of other nationalities. She was, furthermore, to be so thoroughly demilitarized and democratized that she would have neither the power nor the will to begin a new career of conquest. China, freed from the inequalities that she had endured for a century, was to be recognized as one of the great powers and to be assisted in becoming strong, united, and democratic. Korea, as had been promised at Cairo, was to become, "in due course," free and independent. In Southern and Southeast Asia, where Japanese conquest had weakened the fabric of European colonialism and given an impetus to nationalistic movements, progress toward independence was to be encouraged. Determined to carry out its prewar promise of independence for the Philippines in 1946, the United States was anxious to push other colonial powers—Great Britain, France, the Netherlands—along the path it had chosen for itself. Anticolonialism was, in fact, an old American ideal, which the nation had repudiated only partially and temporarily at the turn of the century.

If the general purpose was fairly clear, the performance was inconsistent and faltering, and the result more failure than success. The aim for China had been compromised in the agreement at Yalta, by which the Soviet Union was to be restored to the privileged position in Manchuria which Russia of the Czars had enjoyed before 1904. The Soviets, it is true, later surrendered most of these special privileges, but only after, in a major defeat for American policy, China had become a Communist state. The victory of home-grown Communism in China and China's subsequent alliance with the Soviet Union increased the danger that the Asiatic colonies of European powers might be added to the Communist empire instead of becoming free nations on the Western pattern, for Communism was skillful in allying itself with Asiatic nationalism against the remnants of Western imperialism. The break between Peking and Moscow, which began in the late 50's and reached the brink of war in 1969, destroyed the image of a monolithic world Communism, widely accepted in the United States, but the fact that Russia and China were now rivals instead of partners in spreading their gospel to the former colonial lands did not end the threat. There was danger, therefore, that in southern Asia, as in China, the victory of nationalism would be accompanied by subversion to Communism. The American conviction that here, as in Europe, Communism must be "contained" produced an Asiatic phase of the cold war, which, unlike that in Europe, became sporadically a hot war, as in Korea and later in Vietnam.

Twenty-five years after Japan's surrender, Western imperialism in Asia was dead, but Communism had made impressive gains. China and parts of Korea and Indochina had slipped behind the Iron Curtain, or the "Bamboo Curtain," as it was sometimes called in this area. Great Britain had granted independence to India, Pakistan, Ceylon, Burma, Malaya, Singapore, and other minor colonies. All except Burma had elected to remain within the British Commonwealth. In 1963, Singapore, North Borneo, and Sarawak were federated with Malaya to form Malaysia, but Singapore resumed its independence two years later. India, Ceylon, and Burma preferred neutralism to alignment with the West in the cold war. The states of former French Indochina had won their independence, but North Vietnam was Communist, and the U.S.-South Vietnamese war to save South Vietnam from Communism had spilled over into nominally neutral Cambodia and Laos and had involved independent Thailand. Indonesia, with U.S. encouragement, had won its independence from the Netherlands. Its demagogic leader, Sukarno, was on the verge of forming an alliance with Communist China when the Army (following an abortive premature attempt at a Communist coup, September 30, 1965) seized power and steered the nation back onto a neutral course, though friendly to the West. In Indonesia, in the former British colonies, in the Philippines, and in Japan, the United States could see some realization of its hopes of 1945.

Toward a Democratic and Peaceful Japan

Japan escaped the divided control that frustrated reconstruction in Germany and Austria. General Douglas MacArthur, bearing the title Supreme Commander for the Allied Powers (SCAP), received his orders from Washington. A Russian request to share in the occupation was refused. This refusal and the assumption by the United States of unilateral control over Japan offended the Russians and may have contributed to their uncooperative attitude in Europe and China. At the Foreign Ministers' Conference in Moscow (December 1945), the United States made concessions in form rather than substance. Thereafter, a four-power Allied Council for Japan, representing the United States, the Soviet Union, the British Commonwealth, and China, sat in Tokyo; it could advise the Supreme Commander but not compel him. A Far Eastern Commission in Washington, speaking for the eleven powers that had fought against Japan,[1] in theory made policy for the Occupation; in reality it acquiesced in SCAP's decisions.

General MacArthur's regal bearing and magisterial language appealed to the same Japanese traits that accounted for Emperor-worship. The people of the islands submitted to his rule with surprising docility and accepted, at least superficially, reforms that revolutionized their way of life. Japan's once great empire was cut down to the four islands that had formed her domain at the time of Commodore Perry's visit in 1853. Her armed forces were abolished, her war industries liquidated. In the new constitution, prepared by SCAP and put into effect May 3, 1947, the Japanese people "forever renounce war as a

1. The U.S., the U.S.S.R., the United Kingdom, China, France, the Netherlands, Canada, Australia, New Zealand, India, the Philippines. The Commission was enlarged to thirteen, November 17, 1949, by the addition of Burma and Pakistan.

sovereign right of the nation" and agree that "land, sea, and air forces, as well as other war potential, will never be maintained. The right of belligerency of the state will not be recognized." War criminals were punished; some, such as the war Premier, General Tojo, with the death penalty. Political life was purged of those individuals who could be held responsible for Japan's war policy. On the theory that democracies are pacific, the new constitution, although retaining the monarchy, placed all power in the representatives of the people. These were to be chosen by extremely democratic procedures, including the novelty of woman suffrage. The Emperor conformed to the new spirit. In his New Year's Rescript, January 1, 1946, he repudiated "the false conception that the Emperor is divine and that the Japanese people are superior to other races and fated to rule the world." By dissolving the great industrial and commercial combines, the Zaibatsu, and by consigning all but the smallest landed estates to peasant proprietorship, the Occupation attempted to democratize economic life. Educational reform accompanied these political and economic transformations. The dissolution of the Zaibatsu did not long outlast the military occupation; the other reforms promised to be more permanent.

The complete demilitarization of Japan, like that of Germany, was undertaken in the naive faith that the Soviet Union would continue friendly and cooperative with the West. Discovery that that faith was false suggested an entirely different approach to the Japanese problem. The change became imperative when China was drawn into the Soviet orbit.[2]

First Postwar Steps in China

At the Yalta Conference, Stalin, in return for concessions given him at China's expense, had offered to make a treaty of alliance with the Nationalist government of China and to assist in liberating China from the Japanese invaders. To United States Ambassador Hurley, who stopped in Moscow on his way to Chungking, and to Messrs. Hopkins and Harriman later, Stalin gave assurances that he wished to see China unified under Chiang Kai-shek, that he would not support the Chinese Communists, that he would respect Chinese sovereignty in Manchuria and the open door principle.[3] When the secret of the Yalta agreement was revealed to Chiang Kai-shek, qualified with these assurances, he expressed disappointment but did not seem greatly perturbed. He sent T. V. Soong to Moscow to negotiate an agreement with the Soviet Union. The treaty and agreements which Soong signed August 14, 1945 were generally in accord with the Yalta promises.

The treaty was one of friendship and alliance against Japan. Both parties promised cooperation to bring about Japan's defeat and to prevent a repetition of her aggression. They promised respect for each other's sovereignty and territorial integrity and noninterference in each other's internal affairs. Notes and agreements signed at the same time as the treaty provided for independence of Outer Mongolia if a plebiscite showed this to be the desire of the people; status of Dairen as a free port; joint use of Port Arthur as a naval base by the Soviet Union and China; the establishment of Chinese civil administration in Manchuria *pari passu* with the completion of Soviet military operations; joint ownership and management of the Chinese Changchun Railway, comprising the former Chinese Eastern and South Manchurian Railways. Reassuring to the Chinese were a reaffirmation by the Soviet Union of respect for "China's full sovereignty" over Manchuria and, especially, a promise that support and assistance would "be entirely given to the National Government as the central government of China." The last promise, if observed, would eliminate the danger of

2. For later phases of policy toward Japan, see pp. 475–80.

3. Herbert Feis, *The China Tangle: The American Effort in China from Pearl Harbor to the Marshall Mission* (Princeton: Princeton University Press, 1953), pp. 284–89, 309–12.

Soviet support for the Chinese Communists.[4]

Publication of this group of agreements was well received in the United States, the *New York Times* hailing it as a "victory for peace as great as any scored on the battlefield." With Sino-Soviet relations apparently harmonized, the United States could proceed with the development of its policy for the creation of a "strong, united, and democratic China." American postwar policy toward China was based on the fallacious belief, common at the time, that Communists and Kuomintang men could work together in a democratic government, like Republicans and Democrats in the United States. General Stilwell had sought during the war to bring the two groups together for united opposition to the Japanese invaders. With the war over, the peaceful unification of China became an immediate aim of United States policy. In the fall of 1945, United States Ambassador Patrick J. Hurley brought the Communist leader, Mao Tse-tung, to Chungking, where he spent six weeks in negotiations with Chiang Kai-shek. The two parted on apparently friendly terms, announcing that they had reached agreement on the majority of points in dispute and were not too far apart on the remainder.

In the meantime, while Chiang's Nationalist forces, with American aid, were reoccupying the coastal area of China and most of its large cities, Communist armies continued to hold large areas of the interior in the Northwest and North and were filtering into Manchuria. Here they took over arms and supplies from the surrendering Japanese and were soon receiving, *sub rosa*, assistance and cooperation from the Russians in direct contravention of recent Russian promises.[5] Armed clashes between Nationalists and Communists occurred with increasing frequency. It was evident that only energetic action by the United States could save China from disastrous civil war.

The Marshall Mission

To carry out this delicate mission, and to replace Ambassador Hurley who resigned in November 1945, President Truman picked General George C. Marshall, who had just retired as Army Chief of Staff. Marshall was directed to seek, first, a truce in the fighting; second, political unification through a conference of Nationalists, Communists, and other groups. He was given considerable discretion in the use of persuasion and pressure, but it was made plain that the existing Nationalist government, "the only legal government in China," was to form the foundation of the new political structure. That government, President Truman stated publicly, "is the proper instrument to achieve the objective of a unified China."[6]

Marshall's China mission lasted throughout the year 1946. After a promising beginning, during which the Communists apparently agreed to accept a minority position in a unified government and a subordinate position in a unified army, the two factions fell to fighting again, and nothing that Marshall could do could halt the drift into full-scale civil war. Marshall came home in December. His report, dated January 7, 1947, blamed the failure of his mission on "extremist elements on both sides." Between the Communists, who "frankly state that they are Marxists," and the conservative leaders of the Kuomintang, Marshall saw no hope of a compromise settlement.[7]

---

4. The texts of all these agreements are printed in *United States Relations with China,* Department of State Publication 3573. (Washington: Department of State, 1949), pp. 585–96.
5. There is reason to believe that Stalin at first intended to keep his promise not to aid the Communists. He is reported to have told the Yugoslav Vice Premier later that he had directed the Chinese Communists to drop their opposition to Chiang Kai-shek and take part in his government, but that they disobeyed his directive. Vladimir Dedijer, *Tito* (New York: Simon & Schuster, Inc., 1953), pp. 331–32.
6. Feis, *The China Tangle,* chap. 37; *U.S. Relations with China,* pp. 607–9.
7. *U.S. Relations with China,* pp. 686–89. Marshall was immediately appointed Secretary of State.

The Downfall of Chiang Kai-shek

The end of Marshall's mission meant also the end of the American effort at mediation in China's internal politics. The United States continued to recognize the government of Chiang Kai-shek as the legitimate government of China but was unwilling to give Chiang the massive military aid and cooperation that alone might have enabled him to win his war against the Communists.[8] The United States government had lost faith in Chiang's ability to solve China's problems. It was now, furthermore, committed to fostering European recovery under the Marshall Plan and to succoring Greece and Turkey with both economic and military aid. As during the war, Europe came first and China was relegated to a secondary position.

There followed a rapid deterioration in the position of the Nationalist government and a series of victories by the Communists that gave them control of all mainland China by the end of 1949. In December Chiang withdrew to Formosa (Taiwan), where he set up his new capital at Taipei. Incompetent military leadership and a collapse in morale rather than lack of military supplies accounted for the débacle. In fact, great quantities of American-made military matériel were surrendered to the Communists.[9]

The People's Republic of China

In September 1949, a Chinese People's Consultative Conference met at Peiping (to which the Communists now restored its ancient name of Peking) and produced a constitution for the People's Republic of China. The constitution followed closely the Soviet pattern. There was window dressing indicative of democratic character, but all real power was lodged in the Communist party or its leaders. The new government was inaugurated October 1, with Mao Tse-tung holding the office equivalent to the presidency and Chou En-lai as Premier and Foreign Minister. The Soviet Union and its satellites promptly recognized the new government as that of China, and a new treaty, signed in Moscow February 14, 1950, sealed an alliance between the Soviet Union and Communist China—a defensive alliance against aggression "by Japan or states allied with it." [10]

The People's Republic of China was recognized not only by the Soviet Union, its satellites, and Yugoslavia, but (after Chiang's flight from the mainland) by Great Britain and a number of other non-Communist governments in both Europe and Asia.[11] The United States was one of numerous governments that withheld recognition from Peking and continued to regard the Nationalist government on Formosa as the government of China. Certainly by the arrest and barbarous treatment of American consular officers, businessmen, and missionaries, and by its denunciation of "American imperialism," the People's Republic of China did nothing to invite recognition by the United States.

But although withholding recognition and opposing admission of "Red China" to the United Nations, the United States had apparently reconciled itself, at the beginning of

8. General Albert C. Wedemeyer, sent to China on a tour of investigation in the summer of 1947, advised that the United States give "moral, advisory and material support to China" on a large scale. He believed an advisory group of 10,000 officers and other qualified persons would be needed to effect the necessary reforms in Chiang's military establishment. *U.S. Relations with China*, p. 814. The text of Wedemeyer's report, not made public till 1949, is in ibid., pp. 764–814.

9. *U.S. Relations with China*, pp. 299–300.

10. After signing the treaty of alliance with the Peking government, the Soviet Union agreed to withdraw Russian troops from the Port Arthur area and to surrender to China its share in the Chinese Changchun Railway. It later agreed to assist in building two new railroads connecting China with Siberia and with Soviet Central Asia.

11. During 1949 and 1950, the following non-Communist governments recognized the new Chinese regime: United Kingdom, Norway, Denmark, Sweden, Switzerland, the Netherlands, Burma, India, Ceylon, Pakistan, and Israel. *Documents on American Foreign Relations*, 12: 506; *U.S. in World Affairs*, 1950, p. 35.

1950, to the prospect of Red China's taking over Formosa as well as the mainland. To congressional proposals that the United States should occupy, or at least defend, Formosa, President Truman responded in a statement of January 5, 1950, that the United States had no intention of establishing bases on Formosa or of providing "military aid or advice" to the Chinese forces there. A week later, in a speech defining the "defensive perimeter" of the United States in the Far East, Secretary of State Dean Acheson omitted Formosa (as well as Korea) from the areas that the United States considered it necessary to defend. Then, within a few months, the picture was changed by the war in Korea.

The Two Koreas

Primarily for the purpose of receiving the surrender of Japanese troops, Korea was divided at the 38th parallel into a Russian and an American zone. There was no thought, on the part of the United States, of a permanent division. The two parts of the country were complementary: the north supplied the electric power and most of the industry; the south was agricultural. The Russians, however, lowered the Iron Curtain at the 38th parallel. North of the line, local government was organized on a Communist basis; south of it provisional organs of government had a rightist tinge. The American and Soviet Foreign Ministers, at Moscow in December 1945 and again in March 1947, agreed to direct the military commanders in Korea to confer upon setting up a government for a united Korea. The conferences failed because of disagreement as to the Korean groups that were to be represented in the proposed government.[12] Finally, the

12. The Foreign Ministers' Conference of December 1945 proposed a four-power trusteeship for Korea, to last not over five years. All Korean elements except the Communists (who were told what to do) protested. Thereafter, the Soviet commander insisted that only groups that willingly accepted the Moscow decision be included in the proposed government. For obvious reasons the United States rejected the proposal.

United States placed the issue before the General Assembly of the United Nations. That body, in November 1947, appointed a Temporary Commission on Korea and directed it to hold elections for a constituent assembly. Excluded from the Russian zone, the Commission held elections in southern Korea. The assembly thus chosen drew up a constitution for the Republic of Korea, which was inaugurated at the old capital of Seoul in August 1948. Dr. Syngman Rhee, who had been educated and had long resided in the United States, became President.

North of the 38th parallel the Russians organized a Democratic People's Republic of Korea, with seat of government at Pyongyang and with Kim Il Sung as President. Thus there were two Korean governments, one recognized by the U.S.S.R. and its satellites, the other by the United States and the U.N. Assembly, though a Russian veto in the Security Council blocked its admission as a U.N. member. Each government aspired to extend its rule over the entire peninsula. Each had its army, that in the north trained and supplied by the Russians, that in the south by the Americans. But the Russians had equipped the northern army with tanks and heavy artillery; the Americans —largely because of Syngman Rhee's unconcealed ambition to conquer the north—had provided defensive weapons only, mostly small arms and light artillery. When the occupying armies withdrew, therefore—the Russians in 1948, the Americans by June 1949—the People's Republic in North Korea had a decided military advantage over its southern rival.

Hot War in Korea

The withdrawal from Korea of United States armed forces (with the exception of a military advisory group of about 400) perhaps created the impression that the United States would not defend the Republic of Korea against attack from the north. Such an impression would have been strengthened by certain pronouncements from Washington. In particular, Secretary of State Acheson, in an address to the

National Press Club, January 12, 1950, described the "defensive perimeter" of the United States in the Pacific (as had General MacArthur) as running through the Aleutians, Japan, the Ryukyus, and the Philippines. Areas beyond that line, he said, could not be guaranteed against military attack. Should an attack occur in such an area (e.g., Korea),

> the initial reliance must be on the people attacked to resist it and then upon the commitments of the entire civilized world under the Charter of the United Nations which so far has not proved a weak reed to lean on by any people who are determined to protect their independence against outside aggression.[13]

The Acheson statement, though certainly not a "green light" for aggression, did hold out the rather vague prospect of United Nations action instead of a warning that the United States would regard an attack on South Korea as a threat to its own security.

Whatever the reasoning behind the Iron Curtain, the North Koreans, on the morning of June 25, 1950 (Korean time), launched a well organized attack along the entire length of the 38th parallel. Within a few hours of receiving the news, President Truman requested a meeting of the U.N. Security Council, and on the afternoon of June 25 (New York time) that body adopted a resolution, introduced by the United States, declaring the North Korean action a "breach of the peace," demanding that the aggressors withdraw beyond the 38th parallel, and calling upon all members of the U.N. "to render every assistance to the United Nations in the execution of this resolution and to refrain from giving assistance to the North Korean authorities." [14]

The resolution passed the Security Council by a vote of 9 to 0, Yugoslavia not voting.

13. *Documents on American Foreign Relations,* 12: 431–32. A similar remark was made in May by Tom Connally, chairman of the Senate Committee on Foreign Relations.
14. This and numerous other documents illustrative of the Korean policy of the United States are printed in U.S. Congress, Senate, *The United States and the Korean Problem: Documents, 1943–1953,* Senate Document 74, 83 Cong. 1 sess. (Washington: Government Printing Office, 1953).

This temporary relief from the Council's chronic paralysis was due to the absence of the Russian delegate. Since January the Soviet Union had boycotted the Council and other U.N. agencies because of their refusal to seat the representatives of Communist China in place of those of the Formosa regime. Until Soviet delegate Yakov A. Malik returned on August 1 to take his turn as chairman, the Security Council was able to act with vigor. It followed the resolution of June 25 with another on the twenty-seventh, recommending that U.N. members "furnish such assistance to the Republic of Korea as may be necessary to repel the armed attack and to restore international peace and security in the area." On July 7 the Council requested the United States to name a commander for all U.N. forces serving in Korea. The President named General MacArthur.

President Truman had acted promptly in throwing the weight of the United States into the struggle. On June 27 he announced that he had ordered American air and sea forces "to give the Korean Government troops cover and support." Three days later, on the advice of General MacArthur in Tokyo, he authorized the use of United States ground troops in Korea, ordered a naval blockade of the Korean coast, and directed the air force to attack targets in North Korea "wherever militarily necessary."

In his announcement of June 27, President Truman revealed other action that constituted a distinct change of policy by the United States. It was now evident, he said, that "communism has passed beyond the use of subversion to conquer independent nations and will now use armed invasion and war." Under these circumstances, the occupation of Formosa by Communist forces would be a threat to the security of the Pacific area and to United States forces performing their duties there. He had, therefore, "ordered the Seventh Fleet to prevent any attack on Formosa." To obviate excuse for such an attack, he had called upon the Chinese on Formosa to cease all attacks on the mainland and had instructed the Seventh Fleet to "see that this is done." He was also accelerating military assistance to the Philippines and Indochina, the scenes of other armed conflicts with Communist forces. The stretching of the "defensive perimeter" to include Formosa very naturally antagonized Communist China, which claimed the island as part of its domain. It also resulted in friction with other U.N. members, many of whom had recognized the Peking government and endorsed its claim to Formosa.

Response to the Security Council's call for support was spotty. In all, fifteen nations, other than the United States and South Korea, sent armed forces to participate in the fighting.[15] As of February 1951, the others were supplying only 9 percent of the manpower, as compared with 48 percent by the United States and 43 percent by the Republic of Korea. Overall troop contributions for the period of the war were: Republic of Korea, 500,000; United States, 300,000; others, 40,000. Of 411,000 casualties (killed, wounded, captured, missing), the Republic of Korea suffered 63 percent, the United States 33 percent, others 4 percent.[16] It should be said in this connection, however, that Great Britain and France were actively fighting Communism on other fronts, Malaya and Indochina respectively, and that their exertions in those theaters must be counted as part of their contribution to the global struggle.

Such was the superiority of the North Korean troops in equipment and preparation that they were able to push back the South Koreans and the few U.N. troops at first available into the extreme southeast corner of Korea, an area that fortunately included the important port of Pusan. The tide turned suddenly on September 15, when General MacArthur in a risky maneuver landed U.N. forces at Inchon, far behind the North Korean lines. Large elements of the North Korean army

were destroyed or captured, and the remainder driven beyond the 38th parallel. Backed by the authority of a General Assembly resolution reiterating the objective of "a unified, independent and democratic Korea," U.N. forces crossed the 38th parallel on October 9 and pushed on toward the Yalu River, Korea's northern boundary.

Too little heed had been given to warnings, over the Peking radio and through the Indian delegate in the U.N. Assembly, that Red China might feel called upon to prevent the extinction of the Korean People's Republic. After a skillful build-up whose portentous significance eluded the American command, Chinese armies, late in November, launched a massive attack which in a few weeks threw the Allied armies back below the 38th parallel and recaptured Seoul, the South Korean capital.[17] By mid-January 1951, however, the line had been stabilized and the U.N. forces were ready for a counterattack, which eventually pushed Chinese and North Koreans again beyond the 38th parallel.

In the meantime, efforts by a U.N. committee to arrange a cease-fire agreement brought from the Chinese the declaration that they would make peace only on three conditions: withdrawal of all "foreign troops" from Korea, abandonment of Formosa by the United States, and admission of Red China to United Nations membership instead of the Nationalist government on Formosa. Such terms were unacceptable to the United States as the principal U.N. participant in the war.

In November the General Assembly of the U.N. had adopted the "United Action for Peace" plan, proposed by Secretary Acheson.[18] At the urging of the United States, the Assembly now (February 1, 1951) adopted a resolution declaring Red China an aggressor and appointing two committees: one to consider additional measures to be used against

15. The fifteen as listed in U.S. Congress, *The U.S. and the Korean Problem,* pp. 149–51, were: Australia, Belgium, Canada, Colombia, Ethiopia, France, Greece, Luxembourg, Netherlands, New Zealand, Philippines, Thailand, Turkey, United Kingdom, Union of South Africa.

16. *New York Times,* July 5, 1953.

17. A vivid account of the Chinese surprise attack is given in S. L. A. Marshall, *The River and the Gauntlet: The Defeat of the Eighth Army by the Chinese Communist Forces* (New York: William Morrow & Company, Inc., 1953).

18. See pp. 421–22.

the aggressors, the other to continue efforts for a peaceful settlement. On the advice of the former, the Assembly on May 18, 1951, recommended that member states prohibit the shipment to Communist China and North Korea of "arms, ammunition, and implements of war, atomic energy materials, petroleum, transportation materials of strategic value, and items useful in the production of arms, ammunition, and implements of war." These actions by the Assembly were taken, over the opposition of the Soviet bloc and with abstentions that showed considerable dislike of American policy, particularly on the part of the Asian and Arab members.

General MacArthur Comes Home

On April 11, 1951, President Truman relieved General Douglas MacArthur of his dual position as commander of U.N. forces in Korea and of the occupation forces of the United States in Japan. Growing friction between the general and the administration had resulted from MacArthur's impatience at the restraints placed upon his military activities and his habit of publicly voicing his disagreements with administration and U.N. policy. In particular, MacArthur had complained at the prohibition upon bombing enemy sources of supply and communications in what he termed the "privileged sanctuary" of Manchuria. His recall set off a violent debate in the United States, which continued in muted tones till well after the Korean War had been halted by an armistice. The issue was whether to limit the war to Korea or to go all out for victory against Red China at the risk of bringing in the Soviet Union. The arguments were epitomized in General MacArthur's assertion, "There is no substitute for victory," and the warning of General Omar N. Bradley, chairman of the Joint Chiefs of Staff, that a full-scale war against Red China would be "the wrong war at the wrong place, at the wrong time and with the wrong enemy." The administration's policy gave Europe first place and deferred to the opinion of Allies in the

U.N.; MacArthur believed Asia to be the decisive theater in the struggle with Communism and would have the United States "go it alone if necessary." A long investigation by two Senate committees ended inconclusively, and the administration adhered to its policy of limited war.[19]

The Korean Armistice

On June 23, 1951, in New York Mr. Yakov A. Malik, head of the Soviet delegation in the United Nations, responded to a secret feeler from the United States by stating publicly that the Korean conflict could be settled if both parties so desired. His statement led to the opening of armistice negotiations on July 10, 1951, at Kaesong, just north of the 38th parallel. There, and later at Panmunjom, the negotiations proceeded with a number of interruptions till July 27, 1953. The Chinese dropped their earlier demands in regard to Formosa, admission to the U.N., and withdrawal of foreign troops as indispensable conditions. The questions that proved most troublesome were the location of the cease-fire line, machinery for enforcing the armistice terms, and repatriation of prisoners. By the spring of 1952 agreement had been reached on all points but the last. The Communists demanded that all prisoners of war be repatriated, willy nilly. The U.N. spokesmen would not agree to compulsory repatriation of thousands of Chinese and North Korean prisoners who were unwilling to return to Communism.

On this issue the negotiations stuck until

19. *Military Situation in the Far East* (Hearings before the Committee on Armed Services and the Committee on Foreign Relations, United States Senate, 82 Cong. 1 sess. In five parts. Washington: Government Printing Office, 1951). The case for Truman is stated in lively fashion in R. H. Rovere and A. M. Schlesinger, Jr., *The General and the President* (New York: Farrar, Straus and Young, 1951). The same questions, with particular reference to later phases of the war, were revived by General James A. Van Fleet in an article entitled "Catastrophe in Asia," *U. S. News and World Report,* September 17, 1954.

after the 1952 presidential elections in the United States. The successful Republican candidate, General Eisenhower, after a visit to the Korean front in December, let it be known that he supported the U.N. stand on prisoners of war. He was determined to bring the war to an end and after his inauguration permitted the word to leak to the enemy that if an armistice were not soon agreed to, the United States might find it necessary to use atomic weapons against China. To this covert threat, and to his removal of President Truman's ban on operations from Taiwan (Formosa) against the mainland, the new President later attributed the decision of the Communists to accept U.N. terms.[20] In April 1953, armistice negotiations were resumed after a suspension of six months. The Communists were ready to make concessions on the prisoners of war issue, and in spite of the violent opposition of President Syngman Rhee, an armistice agreement was signed at Panmunjom on July 27, 1953.

The agreement provided for a cease-fire and withdrawal of the armies two kilometers from the existing battle-line. This ran northeasterly from a point just below the 38th parallel on the west coast to a point some thirty miles above it on the east. A neutral commission (Sweden, Switzerland, Czechoslovakia, Poland) would supervise enforcement of the armistice terms. Willing prisoners were to be exchanged and repatriated within sixty days. Disposition of others who still remained unwilling after a period of persuasion was to be settled by a political conference, but when plans for this fell through, the U.N. on January 24, 1954, began releasing the 22,000 Chinese and North Korean prisoners who had refused repatriation. Most of the Chinese were transported to Formosa. Three hundred fifty U.N. prisoners, including twenty-one Americans, refused repatriation and took their chances behind the Iron Curtain.

The Big Four Foreign Ministers, meeting in Berlin in January and February 1954,

20. Dwight D. Eisenhower, *The White House Years: Mandate for Change, 1953–1956* (New York: Doubleday & Company, Inc., 1963), pp. 178–91.

agreed that a conference on the Korean question should be held in Geneva in April. There the Republic of Korea and fifteen of the United Nations that had participated in the war confronted North Korea, Communist China, and the Soviet Union. A U.N. proposal for the unification of Korea after supervised free elections throughout the country was rejected by the Communists, and no agreement was reached. The United Nations had no stomach for Syngman Rhee's demand that Korea be unified by force, and armistice conditions—neither peace nor war—continued to prevail. A treaty of mutual defense, similar to others being negotiated by the United States in the Pacific area, was signed by representatives of the United States and the Republic of Korea on October 1, 1953. Korea consented to the stationing of United States armed forces "in and about" its territory. Two American army divisions remained in Korea, nominally as part of a U.N. force, and the United States continued to provide the Republic of Korea with economic aid of some $200 million annually and to help arm and sustain the Korean army at unspecified cost.

No War, No Peace, in Korea

President Syngman Rhee, the 85-year old patriot, was forced to resign in April 1960 as a consequence of unsavory methods employed in his reelection to a fourth term. His constitutionally elected successor, John M. Chang, was overthrown by a group of young army officers in May 1961. The United States recognized the junta as the *de facto* government. Its head, General Chung Hee Park, later laid aside his uniform and as a civilian candidate for the presidency was elected in a close and apparently fair election on October 16, 1963. He was reelected in May 1967, and in a popular referendum on October 18, 1969, won approval of a constitutional amendment that would permit him to seek a fourth four-year term as President. To the credit of the Park administration were a substantial upturn in the national economy and a treaty with Japan,

CONFLICT IN
KOREA

M A N C H U R I A

U.S.S.R.

Tyumen R.

Chongjin

Yalu River

Manpo

Hyesanjin

November 1950
Line of greatest U. N. advance

Sinuiju

NORTH

Hamhung

Hungnam

Sea of
Japan

Gulf of
Korea

Sinanju

KOREA

Wonsan

Pyongyang

WONSAN

TRUCE LINE
Agreed upon by both sides
July 26, 1953

Panmunjom

38°   38°

Kangnung

Seoul

Inchon

Wonju

Suwon

SOUTH

September 1950
Line of greatest
Communist penetration

KOREA

Yellow

Taejon

Sea

Pohang

Kunsan

Taegu

Pusan

Korea Strait

0   50   100   150   200
miles

signed June 22, 1965, which established normal relations between the two governments for the first time since 1945 and in addition provided for $800 million in grants and credits from Japan for Korea's further economic development—a kind of reparations for past injuries.

Relations between the Republic of (South) Korea and the U.S.–U.N. military command on the one hand and the People's Democratic Republic of (North) Korea on the other remained on the unsatisfactory armistice basis of 1953, with both parties guarding their respective sides of the demilitarized zone (DMZ) that straddled the cease-fire line. The neutral commission charged with supervising enforcement of the armistice terms was unable to function. It found its mission was obstructed in North Korea, whereupon its Communist members (Polish and Czech) were expelled from South Korea. Military build-up and modernization of equipment, contrary to armistice terms, proceeded on both sides. Spokesmen of the two military commands, U.S.–U.N. and North Korean, constituting the Military Armistice Commission, met from time to time [21] in Panmunjom on the armistice line. They met, ordinarily, to make and to hear complaints of violation of armistice terms, but actually in most instances to berate and insult each other, not to negotiate.

Each Korean government aspired to unite the country on its own terms. South Korea's endeavors to that end were limited, by U.N. resolution and by its dependence on the United States, to peaceful means. North Korea was not so restricted. When the United States became deeply involved in the Vietnam war, Premier Kim Il Sung apparently saw an opportunity to move toward his goal by force, perhaps in part by stirring up in South Korea the kind of guerrilla warfare that gave the United States so much trouble in South Vietnam. Beginning late in 1966, at any rate, there was a sharp stepping up of infiltrations through the DMZ and around it by water,

culminating in a series of dramatic incidents in 1968–1969, which could easily have brought renewal of the war.

On January 21, 1968, a suicide squad of thirty-one North Korean terrorists penetrated the DMZ and reached Seoul with the acknowledged mission of assassinating President Park. Their leaders were captured less than a mile from the presidential palace. Two days later the U.S. naval intelligence ship *Pueblo* was attacked and captured with its officers and crew while in international waters in the Sea of Japan. The North Korean claim that the *Pueblo* had entered national waters (within the twelve-mile limit) was denied by the United States. After eleven months of negotiations of the Panmunjom type, the eighty-two officers and men of the *Pueblo* (and the body of one killed at the time of the capture) were released to the United States. As a *quid pro quo* the U.S. commander had agreed to sign a confession and apology prepared by the North Koreans, but with the consent of the North Koreans that he should repudiate the document before signing it! [22]

Before President Richard Nixon (inaugurated January 20, 1969) had been three months in office there was another crisis. On April 14, 1969 (Washington time) an unarmed United States naval intelligence plane with a crew of thirty-one was shot down by North Korean planes over the Sea of Japan at an estimated distance of ninety miles from the Korean coast. President Nixon's first impulse was reported to have been to retaliate with air strikes upon North Korean targets. If so, he thought better of it and confined his response to a strong protest to the commission at Panmunjom and the dispatch of a large naval task force into the Sea of Japan, where, however, it remained only briefly.[23] The

21. The *New York Times,* September 22, 1968, reported that 278 meetings had taken place as of that date.

22. *New York Times,* December 23, 1968. The commander of the *Pueblo* describes the incident in Commander Lloyd M. Bucher, U.S.N., *Bucher: My Story* (Garden City, N.Y.: Doubleday and Company, 1970).

23. The Russians, who had cooperated with the United States in searching for debris and survivors from the destroyed plane, expressed concern over the proximity of the task force (officially of twenty-

President stated that such aerial reconnaissance as the lost plane had been conducting, which he described as essential to the safety of United States troops in South Korea, would be continued and that the planes engaged in it would in the future be protected.

There were no more such incidents during 1969 or 1970.[24] There was, furthermore, a distinct tapering off of Communist infiltrations and other incidents along the DMZ. Though talk of imminent war was heard from both sides of the line,[25] there were indications that Premier Kim Il Sung was adopting a new approach. A memorandum issued by the Pyongyang Foreign Office in October and communicated to U.N. Secretary-General U Thant renounced any design to reunify Korea by force of arms. Unification should come, it said, through general elections without outside interference. All foreign troops should be removed from Korea, presumably before the elections.[26]

Such a proposal had no chance of acceptance in South Korea, where it and the softening of aggressive tactics were interpreted as propaganda designed to persuade the United States that its 60,000 troops were no longer needed in South Korea. As a matter of fact, President Nixon's Guam (or Nixon) doctrine—that Asians should protect themselves against internal rebellion and subversion [27]— while of doubtful applicability to the Korean situation, appears to have been emphasized when Nixon and Park met in San Francisco in August 1969.[28] Contingency plans for the reduction of American troops in Korea had in fact been under consideration for some time, and Secretary of Defense Melvin Laird revealed on July 9, 1970, that the United States planned to withdraw a substantial proportion of its 60,000 troops from Korea, beginning after July 1, 1971. The Pentagon denied unofficial South Korean claims that a secret agreement linked the presence of U.S. troops in Korea with the participation of 50,000 South Korean troops in the war in Vietnam.[29]

---

nine ships, actually said to be nearer forty) to the Soviet base at Vladivostok. The task force was withdrawn presumably in deference to Russian objections. See *New York Times,* April 19 (President's press conference), April 23, 27, 28, May 4, 6, 1969.

24. In August an American helicopter on a training flight strayed into North Korean air space and was shot down and its three-man crew captured. The men were released in December, reportedly after an American apology, at Panmunjom. *New York Times,* August 18, December 3, 1969.

25. *New York Times,* January 9, August 19, 1969.

26. *New York Times,* November 11, 1969.

27. See p. 561.

28. *New York Times,* August 22, 23, 1969.

29. *New York Times,* October 15, 1969; July 10, 1970.

The outbreak of war in Korea in June 1950 led to a stiffening of American resistance to the spread of Communism in the Far East. President Truman's announcement of his intention to defend Formosa and to speed up assistance to anti-Communist forces in the Philippines and Indochina was noted above. The protection of the Nationalist regime of Chiang Kai-shek on Formosa, and refusal to recognize Communist China or to consent to her admission to the United Nations, became settled policies of the United States, emphasized even more under the Eisenhower administration (from January 1953) than under its predecessor. President Eisenhower, indeed, went one step beyond President Truman. He withdrew the ban upon Nationalist attacks against mainland China, while continuing to offer protection to the Nationalists against invasion from the mainland.

Japan as an Ally

The Korean War, too, accelerated a movement already begun to negotiate a peace treaty with Japan and to build up that former enemy country as a bulwark against Communism in Asia, as Germany was to be built up as a bulwark against Communism in Europe. John Foster Dulles, as a consultant to the Secretary of State, began in 1950 the delicate task of finding treaty terms acceptable to Japan and to as many as possible of the nations of the U.N. The Soviet Union was invited to share in the proceedings but took no part in making the treaty. After reaching agreement with Japan, the United Kingdom, France, and other states, the United States invited fifty-four nations to a conference in San Francisco, opening on September 4, 1951, not to negotiate but to sign a treaty already agreed upon. India, Burma, and Yugoslavia declined the invitation. Russia, Poland, and Czechoslovakia attended. When blocked in their efforts to amend the treaty, they refused to sign. The representatives of the other forty-nine governments signed the treaty.[1]

1. The text of the treaty and background material are printed in *Documents on American Foreign Relations*, 13: 458–79. For intimate details of treaty-mak-

45

The Postwar Far East, II: Japan and Communist China

Described as a "Peace of Reconciliation," the Japanese treaty (signed September 8, 1951) well deserved the name. Other than loss of her outlying territories, which was a foregone conclusion, it imposed no penalties and no disabilities on Japan. The question of reparations was left to negotiation between Japan and neighbors like the Philippines, Burma, and Indonesia, which had suffered heavily from Japanese invasion. By recognizing that Japan, as a sovereign state, possessed the right of self-defense, the Allies implicitly consented to her rearming. Some troublesome disputes were avoided by having Japan relinquish her colonial possessions (Formosa, Sakhalin, the Kuriles) without designating the recipients. Japan agreed that the United States should continue to occupy the Ryukyu and Bonin Islands, with the understanding that they might be placed under trusteeship with the United States as administrator. China not being represented at the Conference, Japan was left nominally free to make a treaty with whichever Chinese government she should choose to recognize. Japan acted in accordance with American policy in negotiating a treaty, April 28, 1952, with the Chinese Nationalist government on Formosa. It established no official relations with the Communist government in Peking.

A Security Treaty, signed at the same time as the other, permitted United States armed forces to remain in Japan "to contribute to the maintenance of international peace and security in the Far East and to the security of Japan." The right was to continue as long as it was needed to assure those objectives.[2] Upon the entering into force of the two treaties with Japan, April 28, 1952, the war in the Pacific came officially to an end,[3] and Japan regained her sovereignty. As a sequel to the Security Treaty, the United States and Japan on March 8, 1954, signed a mutual defense assistance agreement providing for progressive Japanese rearmament with American military and economic aid.

Some Pacific states were less pleased than the United States by the "Peace of Reconciliation" with Japan. The Philippines, which had been so recently a victim of Japanese aggression; Australia and New Zealand, which had narrowly escaped a similar tragedy—these three governments especially wished guarantees against possible dangers from a rearming Japan. To alleviate their fears, the United States signed, a few days before the Japanese treaties, a security treaty with the Philippines and another jointly with Australia and New Zealand. These treaties, less definite in their commitments than the NATO treaty, promised consultation in the event of any threat to the independence, territorial integrity, or security of any of the parties. Each party recognized that an armed attack on either of them "would be dangerous to its own peace and safety" and declared that "it would act to meet the common dangers in accordance with its constitutional processes."[4]

Refusal of the Soviet Union to sign the peace treaty with Japan left those two powers nominally in a state of war. So long as that situation obtained, the Soviet Union continued to block Japan's admission to the U.N. In 1956, however, an agreement was signed terminating the state of war and providing for the resumption of diplomatic relations. Upon its ratification in December, the Russians withdrew their objection to Japan's admission. Japan became a member of the U.N. on De-

---

ing and the conference, see Dean Acheson, *Present at the Creation: My Years in the State Department* (New York: W. W. Norton & Company, Inc., 1969), chaps. 46, 56.

2. *Documents on American Foreign Relations,* 13: 266–67.

3. President Truman had proclaimed an end of hostilities December 31, 1946, thereby ending the life of many kinds of wartime legislation. On October 19,

1951, he signed a joint resolution formally ending the state of war with Germany. *New York Times,* January 1, 1947; October 20, 1951.

4. *Documents on American Foreign Relations,* 13: 256–65. There was doubt whether the Senate would approve commitments as strong and automatic as those in the NATO and Rio de Janeiro treaties (pp. 444, 532). Hence the phrase "in accordance with its constitutional processes." *U.S. in World Affairs, 1951,* pp. 200–201.

cember 18, 1956. In the following October it was elected to one of the nonpermanent seats in the Security Council.[5]

The aim of American policy toward Japan after 1951 was to treat Japan increasingly as an equal and to promote its prosperity through facilitating its international trade. Above all, the United States was determined to attach Japan, the one industrially advanced nation of Asia, securely to the West and to circumvent the contrary designs of Japan's neighbors, Communist China and the Soviet Union. In the last-named undertaking the United States had the full support of a succession of Japanese cabinets and of the Liberal-Democratic majority in the Japanese Parliament. The Socialist Party, on the other hand, which with other opposition groups controlled over one third of the seats in Parliament, preached a policy of neutralism, recognition of the Peking government, and the cultivation of trade relations with China and the Soviet bloc.[6]

Liberal-Democratic premiers, however, while conforming to United States policy in refusing recognition to the Peking government, were unwilling to join in the American boycott of trade with mainland China, a natural and traditional Japanese market. Unofficial delegations of Japanese businessmen visited China from time to time, with so much success that by 1966 Japan's annual trade with China was over $600 million, exceeding that with Formosa by more than 50 percent.[7]

Japan had also developed a considerable trade with the Soviet Union, in which, however, Japan's imports far exceeded her exports. Japan was also being urged by Moscow to invest heavily in the economic development of Eastern Siberia, but on terms which so far had attracted little Japanese capital.[8]

The bulk of Japan's growing foreign trade was with the "free world." In 1955 the United States was instrumental in securing Japan's admission to the General Agreement on Tariffs and Trade (GATT). Its efforts to open markets for Japanese exports were hampered by discriminations practiced by some other governments and by demands in the United States for protection against certain exports from Japan, especially cotton textiles. The latter problem was met in part by persuading Japan to limit "voluntarily" her textile exports to the United States. Trade restrictions on both sides, as well as Japanese barriers to foreign investments, remained chronic irritants. In order to alleviate them, the two governments agreed in 1961 to establish at cabinet level a Joint U.S.–Japan Committee on Trade and Economic Affairs (patterned on a similar U.S.–Canadian committee), whose function was to seek solutions for economic problems through periodic discussions. Such discussions, however, reached an impasse in the summer of 1970, when Japan's refusal to restrict further her exports of textiles provoked Congress into a move to impose import quotas.

The United States, at any rate, remained Japan's best customer, and Japan was surpassed only by Canada as a market for American exports. Japan attained unprecedented prosperity in the two decades after the Peace Treaty. Her gross national product, minimal at the close of the war, reached $37.8 billion

5. The agreement of 1956 was not actually a peace treaty. Russia agreed that when a peace treaty should have been concluded she would return to Japan the small islands (Shikotan and the Habomai group) occupied by the Russians but not included in the cession of the Kuriles. As of December 1970 no peace treaty had been concluded. The Soviets, furthermore, had served notice that they considered the promise no longer binding after Japan's conclusion of the Security Treaty of 1960 with the United States. They continued to hold the islands and to harass Japanese fishing in neighboring waters.

6. The Socialists were strongly Marxist. The Communists cast only a few votes in elections, but were strong in the labor unions and in the universities. By the late 1960's the Socialists were losing ground to a new party, the Komeito (Clean Government Party), the political arm of a growing Buddhist sect, which won 47 seats in the House of Representatives in the election of December 27, 1969 (*New York Times,* January 4, 1970, Sec. 4). For a description of Komeito and its background, see Ivan Morris, "Soka Gakkai Brings 'Absolute Happiness,'" *New York Times Magazine,* July 18, 1965.

7. Jerrold L. Schecter, "Japan's New Bid for Leadership," *The Reporter,* May 18, 1967. Cf. *New York Times,* February 16, 1968.

8. *New York Times,* January 19, 1968; July 14, 1969.

in 1960 and $140 billion in 1969. Japan's economy thereby replaced West Germany's as third strongest in the world.[9] Japan's foreign trade in 1968 reached a total value of almost $26 billion, of which over one fourth was with the United States.

United States Troops and Bases in Japan

More serious sources of friction between the two countries were the continued presence of American troops in Japan and the American occupation, for strategic purposes, of the Bonin and Ryukyu Islands. In accordance with the Security Treaty of 1951, American troops remained in Japan in order to maintain the security of Japan and to preserve international peace and security in the Far East. Their presence and their requirements of more and more land for improved air bases incurred popular resentment. Their presence was needed, however, since Japan's capacity for self-defense was limited by the pacifist provisions of the "MacArthur Constitution," which could be amended only by an as yet unattainable two-thirds majority in each House of Parliament. Under a liberal interpretation of the Constitution, the Japanese government did organize "Defense Forces," but these, as of 1969, numbered not over 250,000, a force inadequate to protect Japan in the event of attack from China or the Soviet Union.

In a visit to Washington in June 1957, Premier Nobusuke Kishi secured an agreement that responsibility for Japan's defense should be transferred as rapidly as possible from the United States to Japan, and a promise that American ground combat troops should be promptly withdrawn. Navy and Air Force contingents remained.

Premier Kishi also initiated negotiations that resulted in a new Security Treaty, signed January 19, 1960. The new treaty, terminable by either party after ten years, replaced that

of 1951. It was designed to raise Japan from a position subordinate to the United States to that of an equal partner. The key provision, not in the treaty itself but in an accompanying exchange of notes, specified that consultation with Japan should precede any new deployment of American forces into Japan, any major changes in equipment (such as the introduction of nuclear weapons), or any use by American forces of bases in Japan for combat operations for any purpose other than the defense of Japan itself. The wording did not specifically give Japan a veto on such American activities, but President Eisenhower assured Kishi that the United States had no intention of acting contrary to Japan's wishes in the matters specified. Subject to these restrictions, American forces were to retain their base facilities in Japan.[10]

The treaty was approved by both Houses of the Japanese Parliament, in spite of riotous demonstrations against it in June, led by students and workers and motivated, in part at least, by fear that the alliance with the United States might drag Japan into nuclear war.[11] It went into effect on June 23, 1960. Premier Kishi, whose highhanded tactics in pushing the treaty through Parliament had aroused much opposition, resigned in July. In the November elections his Liberal-Democratic successor, Hayato Ikeda, easily won a safe majority in the House of Representatives.

9. Takashi Oka in the *New York Times*, January 5, 1970.

10. *Documents on American Foreign Relations, 1960,* pp. 416–31. In 1968, in response to growing popular and minority-party agitation for removal of American bases, the United States reached an agreement with the Japanese government for the surrender, joint use, or relocation of 50 of the 148 military base facilities still occupied in Japan. These would constitute about one-half of the area still held, much of it on choice land near urban areas. These changes, it was reported, could be made without detriment to the military capability of the United States. *New York Times,* December 24, 27, 1968; June 23, 1969.

11. *U.S. in World Affairs, 1960,* p. 267; E. O. Reischauer, "The Broken Dialogue with Japan," *Foreign Affairs,* 39 (October 1960), 11–26. The demonstrations, which were strongly anti-American, led to the abandonment by President Eisenhower of a proposed visit to Japan "to celebrate the emergence of postwar Japan into a position of full and equal partnership with the United States."

Return of the Bonins and Ryukyus

Removal of the other principal source of friction—American occupation of the Bonin and Ryukyu Islands—was reserved for Premier Eisaku Sato, who succeeded Ikeda in November 1964. Premier Sato and his first Foreign Minister, Takeo Miki, struck a new note in Japan's postwar foreign policy by calling for Japan's leadership, in collaboration with the United States, in what Miki described as "the grand task of developing Asia." [12] This proposed role for Japan, reminding some critics of Japan's aggressive prewar program of a "Greater East Asia Co-prosperity Sphere," [13] was in accord with an American wish to see cooperation among the non-Communist nations of East and Southeast Asia for both economic development and security. Japan was contributing to the economic development of the region through payment of reparations to the victims of her prewar aggression, through her participation as a large investor in the Asian Development Bank established in Manila in 1966, and through her membership in a series of regional economic conferences, initiated in South Korea in June 1966. Her participation in any security arrangements, however, was prevented by the provisions of the "MacArthur Constitution" as well as by pacifist and neutralist popular sentiment.

Premier Sato's policy was gratifying to the United States not only in his determination to have Japan share in the economic development of East Asia, but also in his personal endorsement—in the face of strong adverse public opinion—of United States policy in South Vietnam. This cooperative attitude strengthened his hand when he asked the United States for the return to Japan of the Bonin and Ryukyu Islands. The Bonins (with the nearby Volcano Islands, including Iwo Jima) presented no serious problem. Though conquered in 1945 at great sacrifice, they were not important in American postwar strategy. Their chief significance was sentimental. During a visit to Washington in November 1967, Premier Sato secured President Johnson's promise that they should be returned. In subsequent negotiations the Japanese agreed that the American flag on the summit of Mount Suribachi on Iwo Jima should be replaced by a permanent copper reproduction at the top of a stone monument, and below it a bronze replica of the famous photograph of the flag-raising by six dust-covered marines should commemorate the victory of February 23, 1945. On these terms the American flag on Iwo Jima was lowered at 12:15 P.M. on June 26, 1968, and replaced five minutes later by the Rising Sun flag of Japan. The Bonin and Volcano Islands were thereby returned to Japanese administration.[14]

The Ryukyus presented an altogether different problem, for there, on Okinawa, scene of one of the toughest campaigns of the Pacific War, the United States had built its chief military base—sometimes referred to as "the Gibraltar"—of the Western Pacific. Okinawa was, in effect, "an unsinkable aircraft carrier," from which American B-52 bombers could range as far as Korea on the north and Vietnam and Thailand on the south, to say nothing of Taiwan and the nearby Chinese mainland. Okinawa was also, it was well understood, stocked with nuclear weapons, which were barred by agreement from United States bases in Japan. The island was, in the words of Tom Wicker of the *New York Times*, "a general's dream," but at the same time it was a "politician's nightmare"—"a political time bomb ticking away at the heart of the Japanese-American security arrangement, which in turn is the central pillar of the United States position in the Pacific and East Asia." [15]

The time-bomb element was a dual one,

12. *New York Times,* August 13, 1967. Miki, a rival of Sato for the leadership of the Liberal-Democratic Party, was replaced as Foreign Minister in 1968 by Kiichi Aichi.
13. See p. 378.

14. *New York Times,* November 16, 1967; March 18, June 27, 1968.
15. *New York Times,* May 27, 1969. Cf. Takashi Oka, "Okinawa Mon Amour," *New York Times Magazine,* April 16, 1969.

comprising the Japanese Okinawans (slightly under a million in number), who had grown increasingly restive under American administration, and, more serious, a rising popular demand in Japan itself for the restoration of Japanese rule in the Ryukyus. So strong had this sentiment become that Premier Sato, after his party's success in elections to the Upper House of Parliament in July 1968, felt it necessary to stake his political future on the return of Okinawa by 1972, though at the same time acknowledging that continuance of the American bases on the island was vital to Japan's security.[16]

The United States faced a difficult dilemma. It had to choose between surrendering political and administrative control of the island harboring its most vital military base in the Western Pacific as well as presumably, the right to arm it with nuclear weapons, and, on the other hand, risking the loss of the friendship and cooperation of the one industrially advanced and politically stable nation of non-Communist Asia, a nation still weak militarily but possessing great military potential. Specifically, the continuation of the 1960 Security Treaty beyond 1970 might depend upon Washington's decision as to Okinawa.

A visit to Washington by Foreign Minister Kiichi Aichi in June 1969 prepared the way for a three-day visit by Sato in November. An agreement reached by Sato and President Nixon was published in a complicated and somewhat ambiguous communiqué of November 21. The President and the Prime Minister agreed that the two governments should at once enter into consultations with a view to the reversion of Okinawa to Japan during 1972, "without detriment to the security of the Far East, including Japan," and "with the necessary legislative support." Japan would "assume gradually the responsibility for the immediate defense of Okinawa" as part of her own territories, but in the meantime the United States would retain "such military

facilities and areas in Okinawa as required in the mutual security of both countries." The Security Treaty of 1960 should remain in force and should be applicable to Okinawa. Nuclear weapons would be removed from Okinawa. Whether they might, in emergency, be returned there under the treaty's provision for "prior consultation," was not clear. American officials maintained that they might, whereas Sato upon his return to Japan assured a news conference that Okinawa would remain free of nuclear weapons after its reversion to Japan. Elsewhere in the communiqué Sato stated that it was the intention of the Japanese government "to accelerate rapidly the reduction of Japan's trade and capital restrictions." [17]

Both statesmen expressed the hope that the war in Vietnam would end before the reversion of Okinawa, but declared that if that should not be the case the two governments would consult with each other "so that reversion would be accomplished without affecting the United States efforts" in behalf of the people of South Vietnam.

There would no doubt be difficulties in working out the details of the reversion of Okinawa, but at least the most serious issue between the United States and Japan had been placed on the road to final settlement. That the agreement was approved in Japan was demonstrated by the elections of December 27, 1969, which gave the Liberal-Democratic Party an increased majority (but still short of two-thirds) in the House of Representatives. Premier Sato interpreted the victory as "a mandate for continual close ties with the United States." [18] Indicative of his cooperative attitude was Japan's signing, February 3, 1970, of the nuclear nonproliferation treaty, sponsored by the United States, Great Britain, and the Soviet Union.[19]

16. *New York Times,* July 14, 1968.

17. Text of communiqué and analysis by Richard Halloran in the *New York Times,* November 22, 1969; summary of Sato's news conference by Takashi Oka in ibid., November 27, 1969.
18. *New York Times,* December 28, 29, 1969.
19. See p. 456, for the nuclear nonproliferation treaty.

Cold War with Peking

While Japan, the wartime deadly foe of the United States, was becoming her postwar friend and ally, mainland China, her wartime ally, had become her cold war foe. American policy, during the war and just after it, had aimed at the emergence of "a strong, united and democratic China," which could be counted on to help keep the peace of the Far East. Mainland China had indeed emerged strong and united (if not in spirit, at least under despotic central control). It was also "democratic" according to the Communist lexicon. But instead of the friendly and cooperative China that Roosevelt, Hull, and Truman had envisaged, it was a China which aspired to make all East Asia Communist and which never tired of proclaiming its undying enmity to "American imperialists." The United States was seen as Enemy Number One (at least until, strangely enough, Russia entered the competition), generally as the stronghold of world capitalism and "imperialism," more especially as the power which, by shielding the Nationalist government on Taiwan,[20] prevented the unification of China under Communism. This, as the Peking government viewed it, was aggression, interference in China's domestic affairs.

As the central purpose of American postwar policy in Europe was to prevent the expansion of Russian Communism, so the containment of Chinese Communism became after 1950 the central purpose of American policy in Asia. Theoretically, the Communist camp was indivisible. Actually, rifts soon appeared between Peking and Moscow, and even before that, the chief pressure in each area was exerted by the nearer of the two Communist giants.

The containment policy in Asia had been implemented in a costly war in Korea, in the treaties with Japan, the Republic of Korea,

20. The island long known to the West as Formosa was coming to be spoken of more and more by its Chinese name, Taiwan.

Reprinted from *The United States in World Affairs 1958*, Council on Foreign Relations, by permission of the publisher.

and the Philippines, and in other treaties yet to be described. Giving substance to the treaties were American armed forces stationed in Japan, Korea, Okinawa, Taiwan, the Philippines, and South Vietnam, the presence of the Seventh Fleet in Asiatic waters, and great quantities of economic and military aid around the perimeter from Japan and Korea to Thailand and Pakistan. Aspects of the same policy were the American refusal to recognize the government of Communist China and opposition to the seating of that government in the United Nations.

The assurances given Chiang Kai-shek by Presidents Truman and Eisenhower that his regime on Taiwan would be protected against attack from the mainland were put in binding form in a treaty signed in Washington, December 2, 1954. The treaty resembled closely the treaties with the Philippines and Japan. Each party agreed to regard an attack on the territories of the other in the West Pacific area as dangerous to its own peace and safety and to "act to meet the common danger in accordance with its constitutional processes." The territory of "the Republic of China" (the name still claimed by the Nationalists) was defined as meaning Taiwan and the Pescadores Islands. Other territories might be included by mutual agreement. This definition left in doubt the question whether the United States would help to defend certain small islands near the mainland—notably the Quemoy, Matsu, and Tachen groups—still occupied by Nationalist troops. The United States was given the right to station its armed forces "in and about Taiwan and the Pescadores as may be required for their defense." By an exchange of notes following the signing of the treaty, the parties agreed that military operations should be conducted from territory of the Republic of China only by joint agreement (except in cases of emergency self-defense). This agreement evidently debarred President Chiang Kai-shek from undertaking an invasion of the mainland without the consent of the United States. In other words, if Chiang had been "unleashed" by President Eisenhower in 1953, he was now leashed again.[21]

For the immediate future, however, the Chinese Communists seemed more likely than the Nationalists to initiate invasion. Communist Premier Chou En-lai had declared in August 1954 that it was "imperative that the People's Republic of China liberate Taiwan and liquidate the traitorous Chiang Kai-shek group," which, he charged, had turned Taiwan into a United States colony and military base. But since the U.S. Seventh Fleet barred the way to Taiwan, the Communists began their offensive, September 3, with an artillery bombardment of the islands of Quemoy and Little Quemoy, situated near the entrance to the

port of Amoy. These islands and the Matsus and Tachens farther north, though geographically appertaining to the mainland, had been held by the Nationalists when they withdrew to Taiwan. Some of them had been fortified, with American encouragement, and Quemoy at least was strongly garrisoned with some of Chiang's best troops. The usefulness of the islands for the defense of Taiwan was doubtful; they appeared better suited as stepping stones for a Nationalist invasion of the mainland—an enterprise which Chiang Kai-shek never ceased to cherish.

The bombardment of Quemoy and the resulting death of two American officers stationed there as advisers confronted President Eisenhower with a difficult decision. Should the United States regard itself as obligated to defend Quemoy against Communist attack? Overruling the majority of the Joint Chiefs of Staff, the President decided that the United States would aid in defending Quemoy only if the attack on that island was clearly preparatory to an attack on Taiwan.[22] The treaty of the following December left the question open. Congress, upon Eisenhower's recommendation, passed a joint resolution, signed January 29, 1955, authorizing the President to defend Taiwan and the Pescadores and such other positions as he might judge to be necessary for the defense of those islands. This left any future decision as to defending the offshore islands entirely in the President's hands.[23]

The British government and important segments of opinion in the United States held that the Nationalist stand on the off-shore islands was weak both politically and militarily, and that Chiang Kai-shek should be persuaded to evacuate them and fall back to a more defensible line. Chiang did, under American pressure, consent to withdraw from

21. *Documents on American Foreign Relations, 1954,* pp. 360–64.

22. *U. S. in World Affairs, 1954,* pp. 264–66; Dwight D. Eisenhower, *The White House Years: Mandate for Change, 1953–1956* (Garden City, N.Y.: Doubleday & Company, Inc., 1963), pp. 459–83. Stewart Alsop, "The Story behind Quemoy: How We Drifted Close to War," *Saturday Evening Post,* December 13, 1958.
23. *Documents on American Foreign Relations, 1955,* pp. 295–99.

the Tachens but refused to give up either Quemoy or Matsu. Communist pressure on Quemoy slackened and was not revived until August 1958, when a new bombardment was opened. On this occasion Secretary of State Dulles made it plain that the United States was not in sympathy with the retention of a large Nationalist garrison on Quemoy, but he refrained from pressuring Chiang to remove it, and the Seventh Fleet aided the garrison to the extent of escorting supply convoys to the vicinity of the island, though the escort vessels halted at the three-mile limit.

The incident ended in a curious kind of truce. Chiang Kai-shek, after a visit from Dulles, announced that the Nationalists' "sacred mission" of restoring freedom to mainland China would be carried out not primarily by force but through propagation of the Three Principles of Dr. Sun Yat Sen—"nationalism, democracy, and livelihood." Thereupon the Communist army command made known that henceforth Quemoy would be bombarded only on odd days of the month. On even days, island activities and even the arrival of convoys would not be disturbed, provided the latter were not under American protection.[24] Later the shells were sometimes filled with propaganda leaflets instead of shrapnel or high explosives.

The United States had repeatedly proposed to Communist China a mutual renunciation of the use of force with special reference to the Taiwan Strait between Taiwan and the mainland. These proposals had been made through diplomatic contacts that the United States had intermittently maintained with the Peking government since 1954, in spite of American adherence to a policy of nonrecognition of Peking. First on the consular, then on the ambassadorial level, at Geneva and later at Warsaw, these contacts had been ini-

tiated for the purpose of securing the release of some scores of Americans, military and civilian, held in Communist China. By the end of 1961 all but four of the detained Americans had been released; in return, 129 Chinese who had been denied exit visas from the United States because of nuclear or other technological skills gained here, were allowed to depart if they so desired. When the American negotiators turned from this subject to the suggestion of a formal cease-fire in the Taiwan Strait, they were met with demands that the United States in return abandon Taiwan, withdraw the Seventh Fleet, and lift its embargo on trade with China. On some occasions the Chinese spokesman also demanded a meeting of the two Foreign Ministers—a step toward recognition. Since the majority of these demands were unacceptable to the United States, there was no cease-fire agreement, and the intermittent bombardment of Quemoy continued. Tension in this area was relaxed but could be revived whenever Peking might wish.[25]

The Two Chinas

In consenting to the diplomatic contacts just mentioned the State Department had made it plain that it was by no means departing from its settled policy of refusal to extend diplomatic recognition to the Peking government. There were, after 1949, two governments, one in Peking, one in Taipei on Taiwan, each claiming to be the government of China. The Nationalist government in Taipei governed an area about equal to that of New Jersey and Connecticut, with a population of some thirteen million people, but claimed to be the legitimate government of all China, which it designated as the "Republic of China." The

24. *U. S. in World Affairs, 1958,* pp. 313–32. The question of defending Quemoy and Matsu was briefly an issue in the radio debate between Vice President Nixon and Senator Kennedy in the presidential campaign of 1960. Both candidates concluded, however, by supporting the stand of President Eisenhower. *Documents on American Foreign Relations, 1960,* p. 83.

25. In June 1962, reports of large movements of Chinese Communist forces to the mainland facing Quemoy led President Kennedy to reaffirm the position taken by President Eisenhower as to the defense of the offshore islands. *New York Times,* June 28, 1962.

Communist government at Peking, ruling over the "People's Republic of China," controlled an area larger than the United States with a population thought to exceed seven hundred million. It claimed Taiwan as a province of China and would in all probability have taken it had not the Korean War brought American intervention in support of the Nationalist government at Taipei.

The reason first given by the United States for nonrecognition of the Peking government was its refusal to observe generally accepted standards of international behavior, exemplified in its brutal mistreatment of American nationals in China when it came to power. Such mistreatment of both civilian and military personnel continued during and after the Korean War. Another reason, cited in 1951 by Dean Rusk, then Assistant Secretary of State for Far Eastern Affairs, was the conviction that the Nationalist government more authentically represented "the views of the great body of the people of China." [26] Secretary Dulles, some years later, asserted his belief that Communist rule in China, as elsewhere, was "a passing and not a perpetual phase," and that nonrecognition would contribute to its passing. Recognition on the other hand, Dulles believed, "would be a well-nigh mortal blow to the survival of the non-Communist governments in the Far East." Recognition, followed by admission to the U.N., would so increase the prestige and influence of the Chinese Communists in the Far East, "and so dishearten our allies there, that the Communist subversive efforts would almost surely succeed." [27]

The arguments against the seating of the Peking government in the U.N. were much the same as those against recognition. Here there was the further consideration that that government had been branded an aggressor by the U.N. General Assembly and had never purged itself of the charge. "You can't shoot your way into the U.N." was a common way of stating it; or as Secretary Dulles liked to

put it: "The U.N. is not a reform school for delinquent governments." This line of reasoning was reinforced by Communist China's ruthless suppression of dissent in Tibet in 1959 and its undeclared war against India over a border dispute in 1962.

The situation was further complicated by American responsibility to the Nationalist regime on Taiwan. The question was not one of admitting a new member to the U.N. but of choosing between rival governments of a nation which under the Charter was entitled not only to membership but also to one of the five permanent seats on the Security Council. If the Peking regime was seated, what would become of Chiang Kai-shek and his government? For the United States, which had fully committed itself to Chiang's support and had won his cooperation in carrying out impressive economic and social reforms in Taiwan, this was a vital question. While Chiang lived, at least, the United States could not withdraw its support.

Since admission of a new member was not involved, recommendation by the Security Council was not needed. In the General Assembly, year after year, the proposal was made to seat representatives of the People's Republic of China in place of those of the Nationalist government. Sponsored at first by the Soviet Union and by India (even in 1962, in the midst of the Chinese invasion of the latter country), the motion always had the support of the Communist bloc, a majority of the Asian and varying proportions of the African delegations, and the Scandinavian countries, which had earlier recognized the Peking regime. Year after year until 1961 the United States tactic was to move for a postponement of the issue, and each year it won by a majority of those voting, though the majorities steadily diminished. In 1961, however, the United States delegation resolved to let the question come up for debate and a vote. Having first resolved that the proposal was an important one, requiring a two-thirds vote for passage, the General Assembly rejected it by a comfortable margin in 1961 and repeated the performance in the next two years.

26. *U. S. in World Affairs, 1951,* p. 115.
27. *Documents on American Foreign Relations, 1957,* p. 343; *U. S. in World Affairs, 1958,* p. 339.

The votes on the proposal to seat Communist China were as follows: [28]

	Yes	No	Abstaining
1961	37	48	19
1962	42	56	12
1963	41	57	12

There was no vote in 1964, but in 1965, 47 states voted to seat the Peking government, 47 voted not to, while 20 abstained. Though the yes vote was far short of the necessary two-thirds, there were many predictions that the next Assembly would override American opposition and admit Communist China. But this did not occur. In 1966 the pro-Peking vote declined to 46 whereas the opposition rose to 57, with 17 absentions, and the ratio varied only slightly from these figures in the next three years, standing at 48–56–21 in 1969. Peking's support in the U.N. had peaked in 1965.

The explanation for the decline in the following years is to be found primarily in developments within China. The year 1965 had marked the beginning of the "Great Proletarian Cultural Revolution," an intense and nationwide struggle between the radical followers of Mao Tse-tung and more moderate elements in the Communist Party, in which the Maoists sought to stamp out alleged bourgeois tendencies in the Chinese populace and in the Party itself. At the height of this convulsive movement, hundreds of thousands of teen-age Red Guards roamed the country, invading homes, offices, and factories, assaulting suspected reactionaries, destroying books, and disrupting industry. Schools and universities were closed while their students participated in the Revolution, finding answers to all problems in the little Red Book containing *The Thoughts of Mao Tse-tung*.

If such near-anarchy detracted from the prestige of the Peking government, policies of the government itself tended to make enemies rather than friends among the uncommitted nations. Premier Chou En-lai, on visits to Africa in 1963–1964 and again in 1965, had proclaimed that continent, along with Latin America and parts of Asia, to be "ripe for revolution"—a proclamation that antagonized some independent African governments which wanted no revolution imported from China. Chou's excursion, against the background of the Cultural Revolution, presumably accounted for many of the sixteen African votes cast against Red China's admission in 1966.[29]

Then, in 1970, Peking staged an impressive recovery. The Cultural Revolution had ended and China was approaching stabilization under Mao Tse-tung and the army. Universities reopened. The government reestablished its diplomatic ties abroad, deliberately neglected during months of anarchy at home.[30] Reward came in new recognitions of the Peking regime, by Canada in October and Italy in November 1970, and in a markedly improved showing when the new test came on seating Red China in the U.N. The vote on November 20, 1970, was 51 in favor, 49 opposed, with 25 abstentions. For the first time a majority of the votes cast favored Peking. Though the pro-Peking vote was far below the required two-thirds, there was widespread opinion that it portended the early defeat of the American policy of denying China's seat in the U.N. to the Peking government.[31]

28. *U.S. in World Affairs, 1961*, pp. 363–64; *New York Times*, October 31, 1962; October 22, 1963.

29. *U.S. in World Affairs, 1965*, pp. 200–201; ibid., *1966*, pp. 366–69. A theoretical embodiment of Chou En-lai's revolutionary preaching was an article published in September 1965 by Marshall Lin Piao, who was emerging as Mao Tse-tung's second in command and probable successor. Entitled "Long Live the Victory of People's War!," the article predicted that as the Communist revolution in rural China had overwhelmed the capitalist cities, so the Communist revolution in the underdeveloped continents would overwhelm capitalist Europe and America. Ibid., *1965*, pp. 252–53; Donald S. Zagoria, "China's Crisis of Foreign Policy," *New York Times Magazine*, May 1, 1966.

30. Tilman Durdin in *New York Times*, November 17, 1970.

31. *New York Times*, November 21, 1970. The United States, while standing fast on its opposition to the seating of Communist China, softened its attitude by deploring the proposed expulsion of Taiwan from the U.N. rather than expressing antagonism to Peking.

The Sino-Soviet Quarrel

Associated with the Cultural Revolution was Communist China's bitter quarrel with the Soviet Union, with which it had once sworn "eternal friendship." Begun in the late 1950's, when Moscow had refused aid in producing nuclear weapons and begun withdrawing Russian technicians from China, it had developed into a dispute over ideology and conflicting territorial claims. Ideologically, the Chinese professed to be the true upholders of the doctrines of Marx and Lenin and charged the Russians with "revisionism" and even with conspiring with the United States against Peking. Peking and Moscow thus became rivals for the leadership of world Communism.

Territorially, China laid claim to enormous areas in Eastern Siberia and Central Asia which Czarist Russia had acquired by questionable means in the nineteenth century. Local disputes in two of those areas—an island in the Ussuri River and a spot on the Sinkiang-Kazakhstan border—led to armed clashes in March and August 1969 and to talk of war, even nuclear war, between the two formerly fraternal nations. A visit of Premier Kosygin to Peking in September paved the way for negotiation of the territorial dispute, which had not, nevertheless, been settled by April 1971.[32]

Under such circumstances the Soviet Union had ceased to be an active sponsor of Red China for membership in the U.N. and gave its candidacy only perfunctory support. Moscow was even suspected of encumbering the proposal for seating Peking with conditions certain to ensure its defeat.[33]

The United States Has Second Thoughts

It is interesting to note that in this period when Communist China was losing friends both within and without the Communist bloc, the United States was feeling gingerly for a chance to improve relations. Cut off from its alliance with Russia, China posed less of a threat than in the days of the "Communist monolith." Furthermore, both the Kennedy and Johnson administrations recognized the fallacy of the Dulles assumption that Communist rule in China was but a passing phase, soon to disappear. Mainland China was evidently to remain Communist for some time to come. Its 700 million people constituted one-fifth of the human race. To ignore their existence, or to boycott all trade and cultural relations with them, as the United States had done since 1951, was coming to be recognized as an unrealistic policy that neither weakened the Peking government nor produced any benefit for the United States. Informed American opinion was urging an opening of commercial and cultural channels with mainland China, if not formal recognition of the Peking government. Senate hearings in 1966 gave currency to the popular formula, "containment but not isolation." [34]

Another stimulus to American rethinking of its China policy was Communist China's unexpectedly rapid progress in nuclear and missile technology. The Atomic Energy Commission reported that China's first atomic explosion took place, probably in the desert area of Sinkiang Province, on October 16, 1964. This was followed by others on May 14, 1965, and May 8, 1966. The last of these was estimated to have been of 300 kilotons potency, fifteen times the strength of the bomb that destroyed Hiroshima. On October 27, 1966, according to the same authority, China fired a 20-kiloton bomb an estimated distance of 400 miles on a rocket missile, thus entering the IRBM class.[35] Her first thermonuclear (hydrogen) bomb, estimated at three megatons was exploded on June 17, 1967. By the end of September 1969, China had exploded at

32. *New York Times,* March 3, August 14, September 12, 1969; January 14, 1970.
33. Hermane Tavares de Sá, *The Play Within the Play: The Inside Story of the U.N.* (New York: Alfred A. Knopf, Inc., 1966), pp. 62–68.

34. *U. S. in World Affairs, 1966,* pp. 276–82.
35. China's success in missile propulsion was attributed to scientist Tsien Hsue-shen, "trained, nurtured, encouraged, lionized, paid and trusted" in the United States, and reluctantly permitted to return to China in 1955. *New York Times,* October 28, 1966.

least ten atomic or thermonuclear devices and was presumably well on the way to ICBM capability.[36]

If China, as a nuclear power, was to be governed by the restraints that other nuclear powers except France had accepted—the test-ban treaty and the nuclear nonproliferation treaty—she must obviously be brought onto speaking terms with the others; yet she was excluded from the U.N. and quarreling with Russia, while with the United States she had only the vestigial diplomatic contacts of the meetings at Warsaw—and even these the Peking government discontinued after January 8, 1968. Genuine diplomatic relations between Peking and Washington were precluded as long as the United States recognized and supported the Nationalist government on Taiwan, and the United States could not morally abandon Chiang Kai-shek or permit Taiwan to be seized by the Communists without the free consent of its people.

A Two-Chinas Policy?

A much-talked-of solution to the U.N.-membership problem was a "two Chinas" policy. What this phrase inaccurately denoted was recognition of the Peking government as the government of China (with China's rights in the U.N.) and a downgrading of the Nationalist government to the government of an independent Republic of Taiwan. The latter would abandon its pretensions to being the government of China and any hopes of returning to the mainland. Taiwan would become a member of the U.N. on a par with other small nations.[37] The fatal weakness of the plan, for the time being at any rate, was its unacceptability to both Peking and Taipei. The Communists would not surrender their claim to Taiwan, nor the Nationalists their pretension to being the legitimate government of China.

36. *New York Times,* October 5, 1969.
37. A. Doak Barnett, *Communist China and Asia: Challenge to American Policy* (New York: Harper & Row, Publishers, 1960), chaps. 14, 15.

"Ping Pong Diplomacy"

Under these circumstances there was little that the United States could do toward bettering relations, other than offering in minor matters to open channels of communication on its side of the "bamboo curtain," and this it did despite Peking's dedicated support of Hanoi against the United States in the war in Vietnam.[38] In late 1965 and the spring and summer of 1966, the United States relaxed the ban on travel to China by doctors and medical scientists, congressmen, businessmen, athletes, and some tourists, and offered permission for Chinese newspapermen, and for Chinese scientists and other scholars invited by American universities, to visit the United States. All of these gestures, obviously, depended for results upon cooperative action by the Peking government, and none was forthcoming. The American feelers were rebuffed. After January 1968, also, as stated earlier, Peking repeatedly postponed further meetings at Warsaw.[39]

Then, toward the end of 1968, came signs that Peking desired a lessening of tensions. As some China-watchers guessed, the Chinese may have been alarmed by the Czechoslovak incident and the Brezhnev Doctrine (which might have been thought applicable to

38. See Chapter 46.
39. *U. S. in World Affairs, 1966,* pp. 276–82. The United States had made a more restricted effort at breaking down barriers nine years earlier. In 1957 the State Department issued passports for travel in Communist China to a limited number of American journalists, but when the Department refused visas to a similar Chinese group, the Peking government canceled its invitation to the Americans. Barnett, *Communist China and Asia,* pp. 456–57. One American journalist who succeeded in entering mainland China in 1960 with the permission of both Washington and Peking was Edgar Snow, author of the famous *Red Star over China,* published in 1938. His book, *The Other Side of the River: Red China Today* (New York: Random House, Inc., 1962), painted Red China in brighter colors than those used by most Western writers, and argued strongly for American recognition. See Michael Lindsay's critical review of Snow's book in *New York Times Book Review,* December 9, 1962.

China),[40] and may have hoped for a change in American policy under President Nixon. Whatever the reason, the Peking government, on November 26, 1968, proposed that American and Chinese diplomats meet in Warsaw on February 20, 1969, to seek an agreement "on the five principles of peaceful coexistence." [41] The proposal for renewed talks was welcomed by the new administration in Washington, but two days before the meeting was to take place, the Chinese suddenly canceled it,[42] and Chinese officialdom resumed its customary diatribes against both the United States and the Soviet Union.

The United States, on the other hand, where President Nixon and his advisers genuinely desired a normalization of relations with China, made this attitude clear in statements from the White House and by the Secretary of State and through announcing significant relaxation in the restrictions on travel to China.[43] These American gestures of good will apparently bore fruit when a chance social meeting of American and Chinese diplomats in Warsaw in December 1969, led to agreement on resumption of the suspended diplomatic meetings. Such meetings were held, in an atmosphere of apparent cordiality, on January 20 and February 20, 1970, but a further meeting scheduled for May 20 was called off by the Chinese, presumably because of the American invasion of Cambodia on April 30.

After the vote in the U.N. General Assembly in November 1970 showed a majority in favor of seating the Peking government, President Nixon ordered a review of American policy toward China. The President himself, in his second "state of the world" message, February 24, 1971, broke precedent by referring to the Peking government by its official title, the "People's Republic of China." Almost equally novel was his declaration that an important challenge to the United States in the 1970's would be the drawing of China "into a constructive relationship with the world community." [44]

These and other conciliatory moves from Washington, including a further relaxation of the ban on American travel to China, were reciprocated in an unexpected manner when an American table tennis team, participating in an international meet in Tokyo, was suddenly, early in April 1971, invited to visit China. Three American newsmen were invited to accompany the team, and a few days later *New York Times* correspondent Tilman Durdin, a knowledgeable pre-1949 "China hand," was given a 30-day visa by the Chinese government. Speculation on the significance of "ping pong diplomacy" was heightened when Premier Chou En-lai greeted the visting team affably in person and observed that their visit had "opened a new page in the relations of the Chinese and American people." [45]

President Nixon responded to this unexpected show of friendliness from Peking by announcing at once an easing of the embargo on trade with China and informing a news conference some days later that he himself fully expected to visit mainland China, but at what time and in what capacity he declined to say.[46]

Authorities on Sino-American relations pointed out that in spite of all this euphoria, nothing had been said or done that touched the main obstacle to the improvement of those relations—American support of the Chinese Nationalist regime on Taiwan. Even on this difficult problem, however, there were signs of a new flexibility in Washington. On April 26, 1971, a presidential commission, appointed

40. See p. 460.
41. *New York Times,* November 27, December 8, 1968. The "five principles of peaceful coexistence," the formula of an earlier agreement between Communist China and India, comprised respect for territory and sovereignty, nonaggression, noninterference in one another's internal affairs, equality and mutual benefit, and (illogically) peaceful coexistence.
42. *New York Times,* February 19, 1969.
43. See *New York Times,* August 4, 8, September 6, 1969, for State Department and White House statements; July 22, December 20, 1969, for relaxation in travel restrictions.

44. *New York Times,* February 25, 1971. See also first-page story by Terence Smith, ibid., March 10, 1971.
45. *New York Times,* April 15, 1971.
46. *New York Times,* April 15, 30, 1971.

months before to review American policy in the United Nations, submitted a recommendation that the United States seek, "as soon as practicable," the admission to the United Nations of the People's Republic of China. The appended qualification that the United States should continue to oppose expulsion from the U.N. of the Nationalist government on Taiwan would almost certainly make the proposal in that form unacceptable to Peking, but it was clear that neither the commission (chaired by former Ambassador Henry Cabot Lodge) nor the President accepted the outworn fiction that the Taipei government was the legitimate government of mainland China. This at least was a step in the direction of realism.[47]

If world opinion was startled by President Nixon's hint in April that he hoped to visit the People's Republic of China, it was electrified, or in some capitals stunned, by his announcement on July 15, 1971, that he had received and accepted an invitation to visit Peking at some time before May 1972. The announcement, made simultaneously in Peking and in a special broadcast from the Western White House in California, followed a perfectly screened mission to Peking by the President's Assistant for National Security Affairs, Dr. Henry Kissinger, who had spent twenty hours in conference with Chou En-lai.

In the United States, the surprising news got a generally favorable reception, except in strongly conservative circles. It was recognized as a major step toward Nixon's well-known goal of normalization of relations with mainland China, an achievement which, it was supposed, might strengthen the position of the United States internationally and of President Nixon politically.

Abroad, the announcement had a mixed reception. It was generally hailed as realistic by allies like England and France, which had long since recognized the Peking regime themselves. But the President's reassurance that the search for a new relationship with Peking would "not be at the expense of our friends" and was "not directed against any other nation" was received in some quarters with skepticism. The ambassador of the Chinese Nationalist government delivered a strong protest at the State Department. Japanese Premier Eisaku Sato, who, like his predecessors, had consistently followed the American lead in his China policy, expressed resentment at not having been consulted, or even informed, before the announcement of this radical reversal of policy. The Soviet government, which could hardly be happy over a prospective rapprochement of its two chief rivals, withheld official comment for ten days. Then, in an article in *Pravda,* July 25, it took what may be described as a cool and "watchful waiting" rather than a hostile attitude.[48]

All details of the proposed agreement remained to be worked out, or at least to be made public. No one could predict with certainty what its effect would be on the war in Vietnam, on the fate of Taiwan, on U.S.-Japanese relations, or on pending negotiations with the Soviet Union on arms limitation or the status of Berlin. The one result that seemed almost certain was the early admission of the Peking government to the United Nations. Otherwise, it was anyone's guess whether the Nixon visit to Peking would be more productive of healing elixirs or of monkey wrenches.

47. *New York Times,* April 27, 1971. The Lodge commission also suggested possible U.N. membership for the two Germanys, the two Koreas, and the two Vietnams.

48. *New York Times,* July 16, July 18 (sec. 4), July 25 (sec. 4), July 26, 1971.

46

The Postwar
Far East, III:
Southeast Asia—
The War in Indochina

The war in Vietnam, into which the United States was gradually drawn during the 1960's, was, like the Korean War, a part of the program for containing Asiatic Communism. It differed from the Korean War in that it began not as invasion from the Communist North but as subversion in the non-Communist South. The Viet Cong (Vietnamese Communists) were actually participants in a civil war in South Vietnam. They were supported and eventually backed militarily by the Communist government of North Vietnam in Hanoi. How far they were initially instigated by Hanoi is in some doubt.

Also in doubt is the weight of the role played by Vietnamese nationalism as distinct from Communism in the resistance to France and later to the United States. Ho Chi Minh, who led the war against France and, until his death in 1969, against the United States, was a convinced Communist, but nationalism—his insistence upon independence for Vietnam—seems to have been his major motivation at least in the struggle with France, and the dedication of his followers must certainly be ascribed in part to hatred of foreign domination, whether by Japan, France, or the United States.

These are but a few of the questions that make the war in Vietnam extraordinarily hard to understand for the American public and for many of those called to serve in it.

The French in Indochina

Present-day North and South Vietnam, Laos, and Cambodia were known before World War II as French Indochina.[1] They had come under French rule by stages from the 1860's to the 1880's. The entire area was occupied by the Japanese, with the reluctant consent of the Vichy authorities, on the eve of World War II.[2] The Japanese permitted the French

1. Vietnam under French rule was divided into, from north to south, Tonkin, Annam, and Cochin China. The people of all were predominantly Vietnamese. Cochin China, comprising the Mekong Delta and Saigon, was a colony. Annam, Tonkin, Laos, and Cambodia were protectorates with native rulers guided by French advisers.
2. See Chapter 38.

officials to function until March 9, 1945. By a coup of that date they arrested the French officials and interned French troops, except for a few who escaped to the mountains or to China. The Japanese took direct control of southern Vietnam (Cochin China) but returned Cambodia, Laos, and northern and central Vietnam (called by the French Tonkin and Annam) to their native rulers—in Vietnam, to Bao Dai, Emperor of Annam. Thus things remained until the Japanese surrender, August 14, 1945.

Should Indochina be restored to French rule? To this question President Roosevelt, a foe of colonialism in general, had replied with an emphatic No. The French, he charged, had "milked" the country for nearly a hundred years, and the native people were worse off than at the beginning of the period. He proposed that Indochina be put under trusteeship in preparation for independence. After Roosevelt's death, however, such intentions were disavowed by the State Department; the Allied High Command designated Britain and China to receive the surrender of Japanese troops in southern and northern Indochina, respectively, and the Britain and Chinese, in turn, withdrew in favor of the French.

The French, however, met formidable resistance from the Viet Minh (Vietnam Independence League), a native nationalist organization headed by Ho Chi Minh. Ho was a Communist, but the Viet Minh at this stage was a united front of Communists and other nationalist elements, whose common objective was an independent Vietnam. The Viet Minh leaders persuaded Emperor Bao Dai to abdicate and on September 2, 1945, at Hanoi, Ho Chi Minh proclaimed the independence of the Democratic Republic of Vietnam, comprising, it was claimed, Tonkin, Annam, and Cochin China.

An independent Vietnam was not in accord with French plans. For reasons of both economics and prestige, France was determined to keep her prewar colonial empire, though modified to bear a distant resemblance to the British Commonwealth. Negotiations between French authorities and Ho Chi Minh led to

an agreement (March 6, 1946) by which France recognized Vietnam as a "free state" within the French Union, on condition (1) that Vietnam would be a member of an Indochinese federation, with Laos and Cambodia, which had again accepted the status of French protectorates, and (2) that a plebiscite in Cochin China should determine whether the latter would be included in Vietnam or constitute a separate "free state" in the Union.

The agreement broke down primarily over Cochin China, the most highly developed and productive section of Indochina. So intent were the French upon keeping it in their hands that they ignored the provision for a plebiscite (as did Ngo Dinh Diem ten years later) and set up a puppet "Cochin Chinese Republic." This and other disputes led to an outbreak of hostilities between the French and the Viet Minh under Ho Chi Minh in November 1946—a war which, with a brief interruption and a change in participants, was still raging in 1971. A principal stake at the end as at the beginning of those twenty-four years was whether the Communist Democratic Republic of Vietnam should dominate former Cochin China, today constituting the vital part of South Vietnam.

The French Fight a Losing War

The French, having broken with Ho Chi Minh, set up a rival Vietnamese government and induced the former Emperor, Bao Dai, to head it as chief of state. To this subservient government they gave the privilege, denied to Ho Chi Minh, of extending its rule over Cochin China. The Bao Dai government gained recognition from Britain and the United States, but since France still refused to grant full rights of self-government, the Bao Dai regime made little appeal to Vietnamese nationalism.

The Viet Minh, meanwhile, was abandoning Ho's united front policy, purging its non-Communist elements, and aligning itself with world Communism. The "Democratic Republic of Vietnam" thereby gained recognition and some material support from China and Russia but, in the words of one authority, "blundered across the no-man's land of the cold war into a position where it found itself confronted by the Communist-containment policy newly formulated by the United States."[3] France and the government of Bao Dai, as opponents of world Communism, could now count upon large-scale aid from the United States. Such aid was stepped up after the Korean War began,[4] until by 1954 the United States was bearing some 70 percent of the cost of the French military effort in Vietnam.

In spite of such massive material aid, the war went badly for the French. It reached a crisis in the spring of 1954 when a French and Vietnamese army of 20,000 men was surrounded and cut off by a superior force of Viet Minh troops in the frontier fortress of Dienbienphu. The French government, in appeals to Washington, warned that without direct military aid from the United States, Dienbienphu was doomed and that its fall might pave the way for Communist conquest of all Indochina, perhaps all of Southeast Asia.

To President Eisenhower, who likened the situation to the falling of a row of dominoes, and even more to Secretary of State John Foster Dulles, such a challenge to the containment policy must be met at almost any cost. When consultation with congressional leaders revealed strong opposition to American unilateral intervention, Dulles tried unsuccessfully to persuade the British government to join with the United States, France, and minor states in an alliance to save the French in Vietnam and to contain Communism in Southeast Asia. An international conference was about to meet in Geneva to deal with the problem of Korea[5] and also with that of Indochina, and the British were unwilling to take action that might prevent the success of the conference. Consequently nothing was done to save Dienbienphu, which fell on May 7.

3. Ellen J. Hammer, *The Struggle for Indochina* (Stanford: Stanford University Press, 1954), p. 247.
4. See pp. 468–69.
5. See Chapter 44.

The Geneva Conference of 1954

The Geneva Conference (April 26 to July 21, 1954), having failed to reach agreement on Korea, turned to Indochina, where it was more successful.[6] The United States, however, played little more than an observer's role in this phase of the Conference. Dulles, reluctant to meet the Chinese delegate Chou En-lai (whose government the United States did not recognize) and to subscribe to the inevitable cession of territory to the Communist Viet Minh, took little part in the Conference personally, and his deputy, Under Secretary Walter Bedell Smith, attended only intermittently. The United States signed no Conference documents.

The armistice terms agreed upon, July 20, ended the fighting in Cambodia and Laos (which had also been invaded by the Viet Minh) and in Vietnam, and divided Vietnam at the 17th parallel of north latitude. The Viet Minh, officially the Democratic Republic of Vietnam, was to take the north, including the cities of Hanoi and Haiphong. The State of Vietnam, soon to be known as South Vietnam, still nominally under Bao Dai, was to take all south of the line. The division, however, was to be temporary. The country was to be united on the basis of free general elections in July 1956. An international commission, composed of representatives of Canada, India, and Poland, was to supervise the carrying out of the armistice terms.

The United States acquiesced in the terms of settlement without being a party to them, and gave assurance that it would "refrain from the threat or use of force to disturb them" and would view any attempt by others to do so "as seriously threatening international peace and security." The State of (South) Vietnam also withheld approval from the settlement and protested against many of its terms, including the provision for elections.

6. Participants in this phase of the Geneva Conference were the United States, the U.S.S.R., Britain, France, Communist China, Cambodia, Laos, the Democratic Republic of (North) Vietnam, and the State of (South) Vietnam.

Under a new premier, Ngo Dinh Diem, the South Vietnamese government was acting independently of the French. Before the end of the year, in fact, France had agreed to the complete independence of all three states of Indochina.[7]

The SEATO Alliance

Since it appeared that only international action could prevent the further advance of Communism in the area, Secretary Dulles took the initiative in the creation of a Southeast Asia Treaty Organization (SEATO) to serve as a "container" of Communism in Southeast Asia, as NATO served in Europe. Unfortunately, several of the most important nations of Southeast Asia—India, Burma, Ceylon, and Indonesia—were so thoroughly committed to neutrality in the struggle between Russia and the West that they would have no part in such an organization. The states of Indochina—Vietnam, Cambodia, and Laos—were prevented from participation by the terms of the Geneva armistice. The Nationalist Chinese government on Taiwan, unrecognized by Great Britain, could not be included for that reason. Japan had no contribution to make to a defense organization. The Philippines, Thailand, and Pakistan were the only Asiatic nations that could be counted upon. Delegates of these three met in Manila on September 6, 1954, with representatives of the United States, Great Britain, France, Australia, and New Zealand. Thus five of the eight participating governments were of the West (in culture if not in geography); four were of the English-speaking world.

Such a gathering was certain to be denounced as "imperialist" by Communist spokesmen. Partly, at least, to head off this charge, the delegates adopted a proposal of President Ramón Magsaysay of the Philippines for a "Pacific Charter." The signatories of this document affirmed their faith in "the principle of equal rights and self-determination of peoples" and promised to

strive by every peaceful means to promote self-government and to secure independence of all countries whose peoples desire it and are able to undertake its responsibilities.

Having thus answered the charge of "imperialism," the eight delegations proceeded to their principal task, agreement upon a treaty, which was officially titled the "South-east Asia Collective Defense Treaty" and signed at Manila on September 8, 1954. The treaty followed the pattern of the Australia, New Zealand, and Philippines treaties rather than the NATO model. That is to say, instead of declaring an attack upon one to be an attack upon all, it stated that an attack upon one would be recognized as dangerous to the peace and safety of the others. Each member agreed, in such an event, to "act to meet the common danger in accordance with its constitutional processes." The treaty also provided for consultation and collective action if threats to any member developed in the form of subversion rather than armed attack from without. It provided for economic cooperation, including technical assistance, "to promote economic progress and social well-being"; and it declared, through an attached protocol, that Laos, Cambodia, and "the free territory under the jurisdiction of the state of Vietnam" should be eligible for both the protective features and the economic benefits that the treaty provided. To consider matters concerning the implementation of the treaty and to provide for military or other necessary planning in connection with it, the treaty called for the establishment of a council on which all parties should be represented, so organized as to be able to meet at any time.[8]

SEATO, with its annual Council meetings and its occasional joint military maneuvers, may have exercised some deterrent influence upon potential Communist aggression in Southeast Asia, but any such influence was

7. *Documents on American Foreign Relations, 1954,* pp. 283–318.

8. *Documents on American Foreign Relations, 1954,* pp. 318–23. The United States delegation incorporated in the treaty a statement that the obligations assumed by the United States to act against aggression applied to Communist aggression only, but that the United States agreed to consult with other signers "in the event of other aggression or armed attack."

U. S. TREATY COMMITMENTS
EAST ASIA

Parties with U.S.A., Great Britain, and France in Southeast Asia Collective Defense Treaty.

Protected by Southeast Asia Collective Defense Treaty but not parties to it.

Parties to separate mutual defense treaties with the United States.

plainly dependent upon the power and the determination of the United States. It was in Laos and South Vietnam that those factors were to be tested.

Upon French acknowledgment of the independence of Cambodia, Laos, and divided Vietnam, the United States promptly accredited ambassadors to the first two and to the State of (South) Vietnam and initiated programs of economic and military aid with a view to enabling them to maintain their independence. American influence soon overshadowed French. It was, in fact, deliberate American policy to supplant the French as supplier of aid and advice to the three states. America, Dulles believed, would not be subject to the suspicion that the native people would feel for their former "imperialist" masters. By thus replacing French influence in the area, the United States also took over from France, morally at least, responsibility for seeing that the Geneva terms were observed by the former protégés of France. Of the three states, Cambodia took an outspokenly neutralist position, seeming at times more suspicious of the West than of the Communist powers. The government of South Vietnam was uncompromisingly anti-Communist and pro-Western. Laos was in danger of being torn apart between leftist, neutralist, and rightist elements. On the morrow of the Geneva Conference, however, the most critical situation was that in South Vietnam.

The long struggle in Vietnam had called forth one interesting personality in the anti-Communist ranks. Ngo Dinh Diem, hitherto little known, had become Premier in June 1954, nominally under the absentee Emperor, Bao Dai. A Catholic Christian, a celibate, an ascetic, a nationalist patriot, he was uncompromising in his opposition to Communism and also to a continuance of French rule. It was he who, along with the United States, had refused to sign the Geneva agreement. Faced with apparently insuperable obstacles—remnants of the Viet Minh and other hostile armed factions at home, antagonism of the Riviera Emperor, hostility of the French, the problem of resettling nearly a million refugees from north of the 17th parallel—the Premier overcame them all, thanks partly to American aid but primarily to his own shrewdness and determination. When the Emperor sought to remove him, he refused to relinquish his post. In October 1955 he held a plebiscite in which the people of South Vietnam were asked to choose between him and Bao Dai. Victor by an enormous majority in an election allegedly "rigged" by his unscrupulous brother, Ngo Dinh Nhu, Diem declared the state a republic —henceforth the Republic of Vietnam—and himself President. By the end of the year he seemed to have the situation well under control. Already in evidence was the reliance on his family which, with the autocratic quality

that he displayed later, was to be his undoing.

Compromise in Laos

In the kingdom of Laos the history of the period from 1954 to 1963 is too complicated to permit of more than summary treatment in this narrative. The Geneva settlement had left the Communist Pathet Lao ("Lao nation") forces in occupation of two northeastern provinces adjoining North Vietnam and Communist China. Attempts of the neutralist Premier, Prince Souvanna Phouma, to integrate these forces and their political leaders into the Laotian army and government aroused rightist opposition and replacement of Souvanna Phouma (repeatedly, though never for long) with Premiers representing the right. Successive attempts of such rightist governments to suppress the Pathet Lao led to armed resistance, supported, so the Laos government claimed, by Communist troops from North Vietnam. An appeal by Laos to the United Nations for action against such aggression in 1959 led the Security Council, over Russian objection,[9] to send a subcommittee to investigate, whereupon the rebellion subsided. In 1960, on the other hand, Souvanna Phouma's renewed effort to come to terms with the Pathet Lao led to rebellion on the right, the flight of the Premier to Cambodia, the choice of still another rightist Premier by the Assembly, and civil war between right and left. Since the United States (which had assumed the task of training and supplying the Royal Laotian Army) was aiding the right and the U.S.S.R. was flying in military equipment for the Communists, there was danger that the civil war might escalate into a major conflict.

As the Royal Army proved unable to stay the Communist offensive, it became apparent in Washington that only some kind of intervention from outside could preserve even a neutral Laos. The SEATO Council, meeting

9. The Italian President of the Council ruled that the proposal for the subcommittee was a procedural matter and hence not subject to the veto.

in Bangkok, March 27–29, 1961, failed to take decisive action in spite of the urging of its three Asiatic members and presumably of the United States.[10] President Kennedy now accepted a British proposal that the co-chairmen (Britain and Russia) of the 1954 Geneva Conference call upon it to reconvene to consider an attempt to settle the Laotian muddle.

Accordingly, a fourteen-nation Conference met at Geneva in May 1961.[11] Its efforts were stimulated by the joint statement of President Kennedy and Premier Khrushchev from Vienna, June 4, reaffirming "their support of a neutral and independent Laos." It became apparent that the only neutralist solution for Laos would be found in a coalition government headed by neutralist Prince Souvanna Phouma and his rivals of the right and left, Princes Boun Oum and Souphanouvong respectively. The Conference, therefore, could not conclude its work until the three Princes had reached agreement. This required a year of hard bargaining, during which a new Communist offensive threatened to overflow into Thailand, a SEATO ally of the United States. The landing in Thailand of 1,800 marines from the Seventh Fleet, followed by token forces from Great Britain, Australia, and New Zealand, headed off any such danger and perhaps expedited agreement on Laos.[12]

At any rate, on June 11, 1962, the three Princes reached agreement. Souvanna Phouma became Premier, Prince Souphanouvong and General Phoumi Nosavan (for whom Prince Boun Oum had stepped aside), Deputy Premiers. On questions of foreign policy, defense, and police, decisions were to be concurred in by the three. In a statement of July 9 the new government guaranteed its neutrality and renounced the protection of "any alliance or

military coalition" (i.e. SEATO). The transaction was completed at Geneva on July 21, 1962, when the fourteen nations of the Conference signed documents undertaking to respect the independence, sovereignty, neutrality, and territorial integrity of the Kingdom of Laos and setting forth rules for the International Commission that was to supervise the settlement.[13] Since the Commission (Canada, India, Poland), like the Laotian government, operated on the "troika" principle except on procedural questions, its efficacy as a bulwark against further Communist encroachment was dubious. During the next year, in fact, intermittent pressure of Communist forces upon neutralist and rightist elements made it plain that the Laotian settlement was no more than a shaky armistice.

Diem Faces Guerrilla War

Many months before the Laotian settlement was reached, the United States found itself confronted by a crisis in South Vietnam (the usual appellation for the Republic of Vietnam, with capital at Saigon). The Communist government of North Vietnam (the Democratic Republic of Vietnam) at Hanoi had never abandoned its intention to "liberate" the South and thus unify the country under Communist rule. Ho Chi Minh had expected to accomplish this through the elections to be held in July 1956, and such was Ho's prestige as a nationalist patriot that there is good reason to believe that he could have won in a fair election in Vietnam as a whole. President Ngo Dinh Diem of South Vietnam, however, maintained, with reason, that no election in the Communist North could be fair, and since neither he nor the United States, which backed him in this argument, had signed the Geneva agreement, Diem was within his rights in refusing to hold the elections. In refusing to carry out this part of the Geneva settlement, however, it has been argued that he forfeited any right to be protected by the armistice, an-

10. *U. S. in World Affairs, 1961,* pp. 197–98; *Documents on American Foreign Relations, 1961,* pp. 296–99.
11. The governments taking part in the Conference were those of Burma, Cambodia, Canada, Communist China, France, India, Laos, Poland, Thailand, the U.S.S.R., the United Kingdom, the United States, North Vietnam, South Vietnam.
12. *U. S. in World Affairs, 1962,* p. 197.
13. *New York Times,* June 12, 13, July 10, 22, 1962.

other part of the same complex agreement.[14]

At any rate, Diem's refusal meant that no elections were held in 1956, and Ho Chi Minh's hope for unification of Vietnam by that process was frustrated. Here we reach a very controversial point in the narrative. Was the campaign of terrorism that began in the South in 1957—chiefly in the form of assassination of village officers, killing or kidnapping of schoolteachers, etc.—instigated by Hanoi, or did it spring from local grievances in South Vietnam—abolition of village elections, collection of back rent for absentee landlords, persecution of former Viet Minh and other opponents of the regime? The U.S. State Department has maintained consistently that the campaign of subversion was from the beginning engineered from Hanoi with the object of taking over the country. Some reputable scholars, both French and American, have concluded, on the contrary, that the rebellion against the Saigon government of Ngo Dinh Diem was indigenous to the South and that the Hanoi government came to its support only in 1960 when implored to do so by southern veterans of the former Viet Minh. The answer to this question, if it could be given with certainty, would have an obvious bearing on the character of the war. Was it a war of aggression of the North against the South? Or was it a civil war in the South with the North coming to the aid of one faction? American policy has of course been based on the former hypothesis.[15]

By 1958, at any rate, Diem's government had a guerrilla war on its hands, with the Viet Cong establishing control in many rural areas.

Both Diem and his American military advisers, however, were slow in facing the facts. With guerrilla war "breaking out all over," American military advisers provided the native army with training only for conventional war, on the Korean pattern, while political advisers were unable to persuade Diem to adopt economic and social reforms that might have held the loyalty of the peasantry.[16] In December 1960 the formation of the National Liberation Front (NLF) of South Vietnam was announced. This body, which seems clearly to have owed its inspiration to Hanoi,[17] was designated as the political arm of the movement in which the Viet Cong were the military. By 1961, Southerners who had withdrawn to the North at the time of the partition were returning to the South on a large scale and joining in the resistance. By the end of that year the Viet Cong had extended their influence to perhaps 80 percent of the South Vietnamese countryside.[18]

The United States to the Rescue

President John F. Kennedy had been in office only a short time when he received from President Diem an appeal for increased military aid. In May 1961 Kennedy sent Vice President Lyndon B. Johnson on a fact-finding mission to Vietnam and elsewhere in Asia. Johnson who as Senate Leader had opposed intervention to save Dienbienphu in 1954, found the Communist threat in Vietnam serious, and his report echoed the "domino theory" of President Eisenhower. Unless Communism was successfully fought in Southeast Asia, he told the President, "the United States, inevitably, must surrender the Pacific and take up our defenses on our own shores."

14. George McT. Kahin and John W. Lewis, *The United States in Vietnam* (New York: The Dial Press, Inc., 1967), p. 82. It is stated by these authors that the British and French, at a SEATO meeting in February 1955 served notice that if South Vietnam refused the elections, they would feel under no obligation to defend it against attack from the North.

15. The official interpretation is set forth in the State Department White Paper *Aggression from the North,* Department of State Publication 7839 (Washington: Government Printing Office, 1965). Kahin and Lewis, *The U.S. in Vietnam,* chap. 5, is an emphatic statement on the other side.

16. Bernard B. Fall, *The Two Viet-Nams: A Political and Military Analysis* (New York: Frederick A. Praeger, Inc., 1963), pp. 322–23.

17. Douglas Pike, *Viet Cong: The Organization and Techniques of the National Liberation Front of South Vietnam* (Cambridge, Mass.: MIT Press, 1966), chap. 4.

18. Pike, *Viet Cong,* p. 359.

The United States must decide whether "to attempt to meet the challenge of Communist expansion now in Southeast Asia by a major effort in support of the forces of freedom in the area, or throw in the towel." An affirmative decision would involve heavy costs "in terms of money, of effort, and of United States prestige" and might lead to the necessity of making "the further decision of whether we commit major United States forces to the area or cut our losses and withdraw should our efforts fail. . . . I recommend," Johnson added, "we proceed with a clear-cut and strong program of action." [19]

President Diem did not at this time ask for U.S. troops. General Maxwell D. Taylor, whom Kennedy sent on a similar mission a few months later, found that Diem, while not asking for combat troops, would welcome American military personnel to assist in logistics and communications.

President Kennedy responded to Diem's request and Taylor's report in a letter of December 14, 1961. He was convinced, he assured Diem, "that the campaign of force and terror now being waged against your people and your Government is supported and directed from the outside by the authorities at Hanoi." Since these activities on the part of Hanoi violated the provisions of the Geneva settlement, and since the United States viewed such violations "with grave concern," the United States, said the President, would "promptly increase our assistance to your defense effort." [20]

Now began a new phase of American aid to South Vietnam, which for the period 1955–1962 exceeded $2 billion in cost and by 1963 was at the rate of nearly $500 million annually. A dramatic indicator of the new policy was the arrival at Saigon, December 12, 1961, of an American escort carrier bearing over thirty helicopters, four single-engine training planes, and operating and maintenance crews to the number of about four hundred men. [21] This event was a prelude to the "helicopter war," in which United States personnel were to participate throughout the next three years, flying Vietnamese troops over jungles and rice fields in attempts, sometimes successful, sometimes not, to detect, intercept, and destroy units of the Viet Cong, or Communist guerrillas. In addition to the new mode of transport, the United States had undertaken to train the Vietnamese army in guerrilla tactics and had persuaded President Diem's government to launch a program of isolating the peasantry from the guerrillas by resettling them in fortified villages—a procedure which the British had found successful in fighting Communist guerillas in Malaya. The number of American troops in South Vietnam increased steadily, reaching some 16,500 before the end of 1963. Technically they were engaged only in transportation, training, and advice, but these activities inevitably exposed them to combat conditions. At first ordered to retaliate if fired upon, they were later authorized to shoot first if obviously about to be attacked. By the end of May 1964 more than two hundred Americans had been killed, about half of them in battle, since the beginning of the new program. A number of American planes had been shot down. [22]

The Fall of Diem

The American task in South Vietnam was rendered more difficult by a growing rift between President Ngo Dinh Diem and non-Communist elements in the population. His rule had become increasingly authoritarian. Members of his family, it was charged, exercised too much influence. This criticism ap-

19. Rowland Evans and Robert Novak, *Lyndon B. Johnson: The Exercise of Power* (New York: The New American Library, Inc., 1966, © 1966 by Rowland Evans and Robert Novak), pp. 321–23.
20. *Documents on American Foreign Relations, 1961,* pp. 323–24.
21. *New York Times,* December 13, 1961.
22. *Viet Nam and Southeast Asia.* Report of Senator Mike Mansfield et al. to the Committee on Foreign Relations, United States Senate. Printed for the use of the Committee on Foreign Relations (Washington: Government Printing Office, 1963), pp. 3–9; *New York Times,* November 3, 1962, Sec. 4, p. 1; November 15, 1963.

SCENE OF CONFLICT
IN
SOUTHEAST ASIA

plied especially to his younger brother, Ngo Dinh Nhu, who had become his principal adviser, and the latter's attractive and too outspoken wife. The President grew intolerant of criticism, whether voiced by his own people or by foreigners.[23] He resented, as outside interference, American suggestions for alleviating popular discontent or improving his administrative structure and techniques.

The war against the Viet Cong dragged along with no end in sight. A Senate subcommittee, visiting Southeast Asia late in 1962, found little ground for optimism. It warned, on the one hand, that any sudden termination of the aid programs in the area "would open the region to upheaval and chaos" and probable Chinese domination. On the other hand, it pointed to the danger that the war in Vietnam might be converted "primarily into an

23. See for example Stanley Millet, "Terror in Vietnam: An American's Ordeal at the Hands of Our 'Friends,'" *Harper's Magazine,* September 1962, pp. 31–39; Denis Warner, "Agony in Saigon: The Lady & the Cadaver," *The Reporter,* October 10, 1963.

American war, to be fought primarily with American lives." *"In present circumstances,"* the report observed, no interest of the United States in Vietnam would justify such a war. Primary responsibility for the survival of the Republic of Vietnam should rest with the Vietnamese government and people, and any further effort necessary to assure it should come from that source.[24]

Dissatisfaction, both native and American, with the rule of the Ngo Dinh family reached boiling point in the summer and fall of 1963. A basic cause of trouble was antagonism between the Catholic ruling family and the Buddhist majority (commonly stated at 70 percent) of the population. A bloody suppression, in May 1963, of a Buddhist procession in Hué (where a brother of Diem was the archbishop) led to Buddhist demonstrations, including a series of spectacular suicides by fire, in the capital, and in turn to government raids on Buddhist pagodas and the imprisonment of scores of Buddhist monks, or bonzes. Native resentment of the oligarchy became so intense that President Kennedy and his advisers were convinced that without a change in policies, if not in personnel, the war against the Viet Cong would hopelessly bog down. A new ambassador, Henry Cabot Lodge (grandson and namesake of Woodrow Wilson's antagonist) was sent to Saigon, and Diem was subjected to pressure by cuts in American aid. Lodge was unsuccessful in persuading Diem to part with his brother or to reform his administration. On November 1, a group of army officers, headed by General Duong Van Minh, carried out a carefully planned revolution, seized the royal palace, and captured the brothers Diem and Nhu, who had taken refuge in a church. Both were killed—for Diem a needless and tragic end to the life of a patriot who had served well his country and the anti-Communist cause, but whose later mistakes had impaired his usefulness.[25]

24. *Viet Nam and Southeast Asia,* op. cit., pp. 2, 8–9. The italics are the subcommittee's. What different circumstances might justify a primarily American war in the area it did not explain.
25. A detailed account of the *coup d'état* by correspondent David Halberstam was published in *New York Times,* November 6, 1963.

The military junta set up a civilian figurehead as Premier, promised free elections, released political prisoners, declared the press free, and began making dispositions for the more effective conduct of the war. The United States promptly recognized the new provisional government, hoping that it might save Washington from the dilemma suggested by Senator Mansfield's subcommittee: make the war in Vietnam "primarily American" or let the Viet Cong take the country.

Escalating the War

The overthrow and death of President Diem was followed in less than three weeks by the assassination of President Kennedy. Lyndon B. Johnson, the new President, was explicit in assuring the Saigon government of continued American support. In a letter of December 31, 1963 to General Duong Van Minh, chairman of the Military Revolutionary Council in Saigon, Johnson wrote: "The United States will continue to furnish you and your people with the fullest measure of support in this bitter fight."

The stability and efficiency that had been hoped for from the new government did not materialize, however. General Minh was overthrown in January 1964 by another general, and military coups followed one another at frequent intervals until June 1965, when General Nguyen Van Thieu became Chief of State with Air Vice-Marshal Nguyen Cao Ky as Premier. This pair continued to head the government for the remainder of the 1960's and into the next decade. Under a new constitution prepared by a popularly elected convention in 1966 and effective the next year, Thieu was elected President and Ky, Vice President, both for four-year terms. A Senate and House of Representatives were also elected by popular vote under the new constitution, and the government of South Vietnam took on the appearance of a democracy, though opponents of the regime who showed any inclination to compromise with Hanoi or the NLF were denied political rights and often their liberty.

In their relations with the United States,

Thieu and Ky were more cooperative and more amenable to suggestion than some of their predecessors had been. Some real progress was made in pacifying the villages and hamlets of the rural areas—winning their allegiance to the government and providing protection from further incursions of the Viet Cong. By September 1967, when elections were held, over 60 percent of the population of voting age were in areas where registration was possible without interference from the Viet Cong.[26]

During the year and a half after Diem's fall, however, the war had gone badly for the government, and President Johnson eventually found it necessary to make the decision that he had foreseen in 1961—"whether we commit major United States forces to the area or cut our losses and withdraw." He chose the former course, though the decision was made known in stages, each stage usually triggered by an allegedly provocative act by the enemy.

The first such episode was an attack by North Vietnamese PT-boats on American destroyers cruising in international waters in the Gulf of Tonkin (August 2, 1964, and again, so it was claimed, on August 4). The government retaliated by bombing North Vietnamese naval stations, and Congress, at the President's request, passed a joint resolution authorizing the President "to take all necessary measures to repel any armed attack against the forces of the United States," or "to assist any member or protocol state" (e.g., South Vietnam) of the SEATO treaty "requesting assistance in defense of its freedom."[27] This Tonkin Gulf Resolution, as it came to be called, passed the House of Representatives unanimously, the Senate by a vote of 82 to 2. Described by the State Department as "a functional equivalent of a declaration of war," it gave President Johnson congressional backing for such escalation of the war as he might choose to carry out. Its passage was later bitterly regretted by some of its sponsors, notably Senator Fulbright, chairman of the Committee on Foreign Relations, who

came to believe that the provocative incidents had been distorted or magnified and used by the President to secure a wide grant of power.[28]

The Gulf of Tonkin incident, as it happened, came in the thick of a presidential campaign in which the Republican candidate, Senator Barry Goldwater, was urging a more vigorous participation in the war by the United States. In defending his more restrained course, Lyndon Johnson gave repeated assurances that American boys would not be sent "nine or ten thousand miles away from home to do what Asian boys ought to be doing for themselves."[29] His sweeping victory in the election was presumably due in part to such assurances.

By January 1965 there were some 23,000 United States troops in South Vietnam, but these were still "advisers," only incidentally exposed to risks of combat. On February 7, however, at Pleiku, and three days later at Quinhon, attacks by Viet Cong on American barracks caused heavy casualties. In each instance the United States retaliated by bombing military targets in North Vietnam. Beginning as retaliation for specific hostile acts,

26. New York Times, September 3, 1967.
27. Documents on American Foreign Relations, 1964, pp. 216–17.

28. Joseph C. Goulden, Truth Is the First Casualty: The Gulf of Tonkin Affair—Illusion and Reality (Chicago: Rand McNally & Co., 1969); The Gulf of Tonkin, The 1964 Incidents. Hearing before the Committee on Foreign Relations, United States Senate, 90th Congress, 2d session, February 20, 1968 (Washington: Government Printing Office, 1968). There was no question about the attack on August 2. Evidence for that reported on August 4 was less conclusive. Some senators questioned whether the attacks had really been unprovoked and thought that, in any event, the U.S. response (64 air sorties) was excessive. On June 24, 1970, the Senate voted, 81 to 10, to repeal the Tonkin Gulf Resolution. The House of Representatives later concurred in their action, and President Nixon signed on January 12, 1971, an arms sale bill to which the repeal was attached. Buffalo Evening News, January 13, 1971. The President had not opposed the repeal, arguing that his actions in Vietnam and Cambodia "are validated by the President's constitutional power to protect the lives of American troops." New York Times, June 25, 26 (editorial), 1970.
29. Quoted, with other similar expressions, in A. M. Schlesinger, Jr., The Bitter Heritage: Vietnam and American Democracy, 1941–1966 (Boston: Houghton Mifflin Company, 1967), p. 29.

bombing from American carriers or land bases became more and more frequent until by the summer of 1965 it had become a regular campaign against North Vietnamese military targets. It continued to escalate and to broaden the range of targets, including oil installations at Hanoi and Haiphong, port facilities at Haiphong, iron works and railroad yards, and the railroad from Hanoi to China to within ten miles of the Chinese border.

Such a campaign took risks. Two Russian cargo ships were hit. Bombing so near the Chinese border might have resulted in hostile encounters with the Chinese. The danger of widening the war was evident. Bombing close to or within cities inevitably killed civilians, bringing charges of "war crimes" upon the United States abroad and among critics at home. U.N. Secretary General U Thant repeatedly called upon the United States to stop the bombing. President Charles de Gaulle of France declared it "destestable" for "a great nation to ravage a small one." [30] The bombing went on, nevertheless, until 1968, except for occasional pauses, of which it was hoped (in vain) that Hanoi would take advantage by indicating a desire for peace negotiations.

In the meantime, "American boys" were taking over an increasingly heavy share of the war on the ground. To counter the deterioration of the South Vietnamese military position in the interregnum after Diem's fall, the United States put ashore two Marine battalions at Danang (the former Tourane) on May 6, 1965 the first American troops to be actually deployed for combat in Vietnam. Thereafter the number grew rapidly: 180,000 by the end of 1965, 380,000 a year later, 542,000 in February 1969. Combat deaths at the end of 1970 exceeded 44,000.

Hawks versus Doves

The conflict had become a major American war, and yet there had been no declaration of war by Congress. How did the President justify carrying on a war of this scale without that supposedly essential formality? There was, of course, the Tonkin Gulf Resolution, but that resolution, apart from its assertion of the right to defend U.S. forces, found its basis in the SEATO treaty. Each party to that treaty had agreed that an armed attack in the area against any other party or against any state which they had unanimously designated (e.g. South Vietnam), "would endanger its own peace and safety" and that it would "act to meet the common danger in accordance with its constitutional processes." The State Department contended that South Vietnam had become an independent state and that infiltration from North Vietnam across the cease-fire line constituted armed aggression, which called for action under the SEATO treaty and also justified it as "collective self-defense" under Article 51 of the U.N. Charter. "Constitutional processes," according to the State Department, had been taken care of by the Tonkin Gulf Resolution.[31]

On grounds of national interest, furthermore, the President and the State Department viewed the defense of South Vietnam as essential to the containment of Chinese Communism, as a test of Lin Piao's theory of the inevitable success of Communist guerrilla war. A Communist victory in South Vietnam would be but a prelude to the conquest of Laos and Cambodia. Then would come the threat to Thailand, Malaysia, Indonesia, the Philippines, Taiwan, and Japan. If Communism were not stopped in this small country, only a much greater war could stop it later. There must not, then, be another Munich in Southeast Asia.

The United States, it was argued further, had promised protection to the government and people of South Vietnam. To ignore that promise would not only expose thousands of its friends and supporters in South Vietnam to bloody reprisals; it would also impair the prestige of the United States and destroy its credibility in the eyes of all its allies.

---

30. *U.S. in World Affairs, 1966,* p. 94.

31. *Aggression from the North* (see above, note 15); *U.S. in World Affairs, 1967,* p. 375.

Americans who thus argued for continuing the war or, as some of them did, for waging it more relentlessly, were called "hawks." Those who opposed it were "doves," and among them, to name but a few, were such notable figures as Senators J. W. Fulbright, Mike Mansfield, and Wayne Morse, former diplomat George Kennan, journalist Walter Lippmann, and political scientist Hans Morgenthau. In agreement with them were many public men of both political parties, such newspapers as the *New York Times* and *Washington Post,* and an overwhelming majority of the vocal youth of America, especially college youth.

Many doves saw the war in Vietnam not as an international war of aggression but as a civil war in which Vietnamese revolutionary nationalism fought a reactionary and corrupt government supported by a foreign power, yesterday France, today the United States. On this kind of war the SEATO treaty had no bearing. The United States had no obligation to intervene under that treaty.[32] It was intervening, furthermore, on behalf of an unpopular government and against a popular revolutionary movement. Furthermore, said some doves, the United States could not win, but in the effort to do so it was destroying the society which it professed to be saving. The war had outraged world opinion. It had divided the American people. It was wasting American resources, starving vital reform programs at home, and cutting down on salutary aid to the developing countries abroad.

A victory of North Vietnam, the doves conceded, might make all Vietnam Communist. But a Communist Vietnam would not be a puppet of China. The Vietnamese people had for centuries hated and feared China. A Communist Vietnam might well be a Yugoslavia of the Far East, Communist but unaligned. In any event, the Communist world was no longer a monolith. Rent by the deep fissure between Peking and Moscow, it was no longer the awesome giant of Stalin's day. Let the United States stop fighting a frightfully costly and destructive war, which it could not win, against a danger of greatly shrunken proportions.

The debate went on, in Congress and out, and the longer the war dragged on with no end in sight, the stronger grew the appeal of the doves to the badly disillusioned public.

The War a Stalemate

Despite the enormous American effort, supplemented by the operations of some 700,000 South Vietnamese troops and the smaller contingents from other allies, the war by 1968 had reached a condition of stalemate. The Viet Cong and North Vietnamese troops (of the latter, some 45,000 were estimated to be committed) obviously could not force the Americans out or destroy the Saigon government. The Americans and their allies, on the other hand, could not destroy the Viet Cong or, despite heavy bombing, prevent North Vietnamese supplies and reinforcements from reaching the battle area via the Ho Chi Minh Trail through Laos or through Cambodia. Nor could they prevent attacks on South Vietnamese cities by rocket-borne bombs or by occasional infiltration or invasion.

A tragic illustration of the vulnerability of the government-held area of South Vietnam was the Tet (Lunar New Year) offensive of January–February 1968. In November 1967 Ambassador Ellsworth Bunker and General William C. Westmoreland, commander of U.S. troops in Vietnam, were brought from Saigon to report in Washington. Both were optimistic on the pacification program as well as on the war. The general was quoted as saying, "We are winning a war of attrition" and as predicting that within two years the United States would be able to begin a slow

32. Was the United States more obligated to defend South Vietnam than other SEATO signatories? England, France, and Pakistan denied any such obligation. Australia, New Zealand, and Thailand sent small military contingents, and Thailand supplied air bases for American planes. The Philippines sent a 2,000-man construction battalion (paid for by the United States). The only nation that sent significant military support (some 50,000 troops) was South Korea, not a member of SEATO.

withdrawal of its forces, turning over a progressively larger share of the responsibility to the Vietnamese.[33]

Yet barely two months later, in the early morning of January 31, 1968, the Viet Cong made simultaneous surprise attacks on twenty-six or more provincial capitals and, as the New York Times reported, "uncounted numbers of district towns and American and Vietnamese air fields and bases." The most dramatic episodes were the seizure and six-hour occupation by twenty suicidal Viet Cong of the American Embassy compound in Saigon, and the capture of the old Annamese capital of Hué, including the ancient citadel, from which the intruders were driven only after weeks of fighting.[34] The Viet Cong took advantage of their occupation of Hué to murder an estimated 3,000 or more Vietnamese citizens, presumably supporters of the Saigon regime.

The Viet Cong were eventually expelled with heavy casualties from all the towns and cities that they had seized, and President Johnson proclaimed the Tet offensive "a complete failure." Yet it had quite destroyed the optimism produced by the reports of Bunker and Westmoreland, set back the pacification program many months, and shown the war to be truly a stalemate. From this point on, talk of "victory" in the war largely ceased. "Peace," a compromise peace, by negotiation, became the declared objective.

The Search for Peace

In fact, the offer of peace negotiations was as old as active American participation in the war. In a speech at Johns Hopkins University, April 7, 1965, President Johnson had stated the essence of the American peace terms in a few words: "an independent South Viet-Nam —securely guaranteed and able to shape its own relationships to all others—free from outside interference—tied to no alliance—a mili-

tary base for no other country." If peace were assured, he added, the United States would be ready to invest a billion dollars in development of the Mekong River area—a development in which he hoped North Vietnam would share.[35]

The Hanoi government responded next day with a four-point peace program comprising: (1) complete withdrawal of all U.S. troops from South Vietnam and cancellation of the alleged U.S.-South Vietnam "military alliance"; (2) observation of the 1954 Geneva agreement pending the unification of Vietnam; (3) settlement of the internal affairs of South Vietnam by the people of South Vietnam in accordance with the program of the NLF; (4) peaceful unification of Vietnam "to be settled by the Vietnamese people in both zones, without any foreign interference." [36] Later Hanoi imposed a fifth requirement or precondition: all bombing of North Vietnam must stop before negotiations could begin.

President Johnson was now under pressure from peace-minded persons and organizations at home and abroad to pave the way for negotiations by stopping the bombing of North Vietnam. Secretary-General U Thant, in particular, gave repeated assurances that Hanoi would negotiate if only the bombing were called off. Official and unofficial feelers were tried in efforts to learn Hanoi's real intentions. Responses to some of these seemed promising, and the administration was accused in some quarters of being unreceptive to pacific suggestions from Hanoi. To one such criticism a State Department spokesman replied that Secretary of State Rusk's "sensitive antenna" had perceived no willingness for "meaningful

33. New York Times, November 26, 1967, Sec. 4, p. 2.
34. New York Times, February 4, 1968, Sec. 4, p. 1.

35. Department of State Bulletin, 52 (April 26, 1965), 606–10.
36. M. G. Raskin and B. B. Fall, eds., The Viet-Nam Reader: Articles and Documents of American Foreign Policy and the Viet-Nam Crises (New York: Vintage Books, 1965), pp. 342–43. Matters included in the NLF program and not mentioned in that of Hanoi were removal of the Saigon government, agrarian and educational reform, improved living conditions, equal treatment of the minorities in Vietnam. Text in ibid., pp. 216–21.

talks" on the part of Hanoi.[37] In the light of the impasse that promptly developed when negotiations did begin in 1968–1969, Rusk's antenna was probably right. Those who hopefully urged negotiations overlooked the incompatibility of the opposing positions.

At any rate, Johnson was willing to experiment with the possible results of a bombing halt. A five-day cessation in May 1965 was criticized as being too short to give Hanoi a chance to respond. This criticism did not apply to a respite from Christmas Eve, 1965, to January 31, 1966. During these thirty-seven days of nonbombing, Johnson made a spectacular peace gesture by sending Vice President Hubert Humphrey, U.N. Ambassador Arthur Goldberg, Ambassador-at-Large Averell Harriman, and other less exalted personages on special missions to forty foreign capitals, to convince those governments of Washington's desire for peace and to enlist their aid in bringing Hanoi to the conference table. When this appeal failed and the bombing was resumed, the President, through Ambassador Goldberg, submitted the problem of finding a road to peace to the U.N. Security Council, which took no action.[38]

The bombing continued through 1966 and 1967, hitting targets in North Vietnam and along the Ho Chi Minh Trail in Laos. The Joint Chiefs of Staff considered the bombing essential in both areas to inhibit the movement of supplies and men from North Vietnam to the scene of fighting, though Secretary of Defense Robert S. McNamara was skeptical about its efficacy for that purpose. Johnson now took the position that he could not halt the bombing without some corresponding

de-escalation by the other party. In a speech in San Antonio, Texas, September 29, 1967, he set forth what came to be known as the San Antonio formula:

> The United States is willing to stop all aerial and naval bombing of North Vietnam when this will lead promptly to productive discussions. We, of course, assume that while discussions proceed, North Vietnam would not take advantage of the bombing cessation or limitation.[39]

The San Antonio formula was an offer to stop the bombing and begin negotiations on the basis of an assumption, rather than a promise, that the enemy would not utilize the respite to strengthen his position. Another concession was offered on November 2, 1967. Hitherto the United States had made it plain that it would not be willing, in any peace negotiations, to meet representatives of the National Liberation Front as a separate entity, though it would talk with them as a part of a North Vietnamese delegation. This position had been an obstacle to agreement with Hanoi. On November 2, however, Ambassador Goldberg stated—and the State Department concurred—that the United States would not resist participation of the NLF as a party in a peace conference.[40]

The response of Hanoi and the NLF to these invitations was the Tet offensive, described above. Despite President Johnson's description of that enemy effort as "a complete failure," it produced deep disillusion-

37. David Kraslow and Stuart Loory, *The Secret Search for Peace in Vietnam* (New York: Vintage Books, 1968), p. 105. The efforts, from 1965 to 1967, to bring Hanoi to the negotiating table are described by a participant in a chapter entitled "Tragedy of Errors" in Chester L. Cooper, *The Lost Crusade: America in Vietnam* (New York: Dodd, Mead & Company, 1970), pp. 325–68.

38. Neither North Vietnam nor its backer, Communist China, was a member of the U.N. They denied its right to interfere in the matter. This was but one of a number of attempts to get U.N. aid in the quest for peace.

39. *New York Times,* September 30, 1967. An appeal to Hanoi of another sort had been made eleven months before, at the close of a conference of the United States with its Vietnam allies in Manila. The joint communiqué of October 25, 1966, promised that Allied forces in Vietnam would be withdrawn within six months after enemy forces should have been withdrawn, infiltration from the North should have ceased, "and the level of violence thus subsides." *Documents on American Foreign Relations, 1966,* p. 250. Some Americans, such as Richard Nixon, thought this was a dangerous promise and feared that North Vietnam might make peace on that basis, get U.S. forces out of the country, and then renew its aggression. *United States in World Affairs, 1966,* p. 84.

40. *U.S. in World Affairs, 1967,* p. 71.

ment with the war in the United States.[41] Opposition to Johnson's war policy became formidable within the Democratic Party. On March 12, Senator Eugene McCarthy, running on an antiwar platform, won 42 percent of the vote in the New Hampshire Democratic presidential primary. Four days later, Senator Robert F. Kennedy, a more formidable critic of the war policy, entered the presidential race. Meanwhile, a ferment was working within the administration, apparently set off by an estimate of General Westmoreland that he needed an increase of 206,000 men in Vietnam and by the reaction of a new Secretary of Defense, Clark M. Clifford, who succeeded McNamara on March 1, 1968. Formerly known as a "hawk," Clifford now became convinced that it was useless to press for military victory in Vietnam and that the bombing should be halted as a step toward a negotiated peace. His arguments ultimately prevailed with Johnson. In a television address on the night of March 31, 1968, the President announced that the bombing would be ended on the following day over all of North Vietnam except the sparsely populated southern portion which contained the access routes to South Vietnam. In the same address the President announced that he would not seek or accept renomination for the Presidency.[42]

41. Of four articles on Vietnam in the April 1968 number of the influential quarterly *Foreign Affairs,* three were deeply pessimistic, as was the *Wall Street Journal* in an editorial of February 23, quoted by Richard Hofstadter, "Uncle Sam Has Cried 'Uncle' Before," *New York Times Magazine,* May 19, 1968.
42. *New York Times,* April 1, 1968; "The Vietnam Policy Reversal of 1968," a two-part article by Hedrick Smith and other *Times* reporters, ibid., March 6, 7, 1969; Clark M. Clifford, "A Viet Nam Reappraisal," *Foreign Affairs,* 47 (July 1969), 601–22; Townsend Hoopes, *The Limits of Intervention* (New York: David McKay Co., Inc., 1969), chaps. 8–10. Ex-President Johnson in a CBS televised interview with Walter Cronkite, broadcast February 6, 1970, gave chief credit for the reversal to Secretary Rusk. For discussion of Johnson's statement, see Townsend Hoopes, "LBJ's Account of March, 1968," *The New Republic,* March 14, 1970, and John P. Roche, "The Jigsaw Puzzle of History," *New York Times Magazine,* January 24, 1971.

Negotiations Begin

To the surprise of many, the Hanoi government responded to Johnson's announcement by agreeing to negotiate. After weeks of wrangling about a place for the talks, both sides accepted Paris, and there on May 10, 1968, delegations headed by veteran diplomat W. Averell Harriman for the United States and Xuan Thuy (pronounced "Swan Twee") for North Vietnam met at last. The results were disappointing, though not surprising, for now the North Vietnamese refused to discuss terms of settlement until the United States stopped all bombing of the North. The United States refused, on the ground that to stop bombing the access routes would increase the peril to U.S. troops south of the line. Not until October 31, five days before the presidential election, did Johnson yield, announcing the end of all bombing of North Vietnam.

Now it was the turn of the Saigon government to stall, this time over the status of the NLF delegation at the talks, symbolized by the shape of the table. Finally, on January 16, 1969, the delegations agreed that the table should be a round one, signifying equality of all participants. Four days later the new Nixon administration took office. Henry Cabot Lodge, twice U.S. Ambassador in Saigon, replaced Averell Harriman as chief negotiator.

When the four delegations met, January 25, 1969, for an actual beginning of negotiations, Lodge proposed as an eventual goal the withdrawal of all foreign (including North Vietnamese) troops from South Vietnam, but as an immediate objective the restoration of the neutralized character of the Demilitarized Zone (DMZ), which had been virtually taken over by the Communists for artillery and other installations. Five days later the North Vietnamese and NLF delegations rejected Lodge's proposal as an attempt to camouflage "American aggressive designs." The rejection was announced in a seven-hour session in which, as described by a *New York Times* reporter, "most of the proceedings were devoted to propaganda, recriminations and occasionally rough language." [43] The parties drew no nearer together in the weekly sessions that followed.

It seemed evident that confrontations in this spirit could hardly produce meaningful negotiation, and it was for this reason, presumably, that Nixon observed in March that only through secret talks with Hanoi could progress toward peace be expected. At the same time President Thieu revealed that he was ready to begin private talks with spokesmen of the NLF or Viet Cong.[44] Such secret talks were said soon thereafter to have begun but, if so, they were no more productive than the open sessions, and there were no signs of progress until early May, when both the NLF and President Nixon set forth their peace objectives.

On May 8 the NLF made public a ten-point peace proposal. Six days later President Nixon, in a television address to the nation, stated the American objectives.[45] A comparison of these two sets of proposals reveals the points of incompatibility which, in spite of some optimism at the time, were for many months to stand in the way of any agreement. First, Nixon called for the phased withdrawal of all non-South Vietnamese troops, the evacuation of the forces of the United States and its allies and of those of Hanoi to be completed at the same time. The NLF demanded the unconditional withdrawal of the forces of the United States and its allies but left the question of North Vietnamese forces in South Vietnam to be settled "by the Vietnamese parties among themselves."

Second, Nixon called for elections under the supervision of an international body to replace the existing governmental personnel, who would continue to function until the elections were held. The NLF proposed, on the other hand, that between the restoration of peace and the holding of elections a provisional government should be set up to include all parties in South Vietnam "that stand for peace, independence and neutrality." This provisional government, from which by definition the Thieu-Ky party was excluded, would supervise the American withdrawal and hold the general elections.

In fewer words, President Nixon was demanding, as the Johnson administration had demanded, that Hanoi withdraw its troops from South Vietnam and leave the South Vietnamese people to settle their own affairs in peace. Hanoi refused. Hanoi and the NLE were demanding the unilateral withdrawal of Allied troops and the creation of a South Vietnamese coalition government from which Thieu and Ky and their faction would be excluded. President Nixon was standing by Thieu and Ky until their successors should be chosen in general elections. If these positions were not clear in May 1969, they became so in succeeding months. They were not changed when the NLF transformed itself in June into the Provisional Revolutionary Government of South Vietnam or when the veteran leader Ho Chi Minh died on September 3, 1969.[46] Negotiations dragged along without result. Ambassador Lodge resigned in frustration on November 20, 1969. President Nixon neglected to replace him with another equally high-ranking spokesman, whereupon the head of Hanoi's delegation ceased to attend meetings, and Hanoi and the NLF all but boycotted the conference.[47] Formal meetings continued to be held but to no purpose.

Finally, July 1, 1970, after the completion of the military campaign in Cambodia,[48] the President announced that he was appointing David K. E. Bruce, a distinguished diplomat and a Democrat, to head the American negotiating team in Paris. Bruce, he said, would

43. *New York Times,* January 26, 31, 1969.
44. *New York Times,* March 26, 1969. These proposals were in accord with an earlier suggestion of parallel negotiations offered by Mr. Nixon's national security adviser. See Henry A. Kissinger, "The Viet Nam Negotiations," *Foreign Affairs,* January 1969, pp. 211–34.
45. *New York Times,* May 9, 15, 1969.

46. *New York Times,* June 11, September 4, 1969.
47. *New York Times,* November 21, December 12, 19, 1969.
48. See pp. 509–10.

take charge on August 1. The President re-stated the American peace terms. There was nothing new in the formula offered here, but the President promised that Ambassador Bruce would have "great flexibility." He hoped that this move would be reciprocated by the North Vietnamese.[49]

Actually, the chief Viet Cong negotiator, Mme. Nguyen Thi Binh, returned to the peace table on September 17, 1970, bringing with her an eight-point formula for settlement. The new proposal, like those before it, called for the unilateral withdrawal of all American and allied troops. There were some apparent con-cessions. Only the three top men in the Saigon government—Thieu, Ky, and Premier Tran Thien Khiem—were named as unacceptable in a proposed coalition government. The docu-ment spoke of a possible cease-fire and of willingness to discuss exchange of prisoners prior to a general settlement. There was a sufficient degree of "give" here, thought the *New York Times,* to warrant exploration through submission of new proposals by the United States.[50]

The new American proposals came in a tele-vision broadcast by President Nixon on the night of Wednesday, October 7. The novel features in the President's five-point plan were proposals for a "standstill" cease-fire, imme-diate exchange of prisoners, a widened peace conference to include Cambodia and Laos (tacit admission that the war had become an "Indochina war"), and a promise to with-draw *all* American troops upon a timetable to be agreed upon as part of an overall settle-ment. Mr. Nixon rejected emphatically the demand for elimination of Thieu and Ky before elections, and although the actual pro-posal did not repeat the insistence that with-drawal of troops be mutual, the accompanying briefing made it plain that this demand still stood.[51]

The new formula impressed many of

Nixon's former critics at home and abroad (including even Senator Fulbright) as fair and reasonable.[52] The response in the enemy camp, however, was disappointing. Moscow was prompt in describing the offer as "a great fraud," and it was totally rejected by the Hanoi and Viet Cong negotiators in Paris. Hope of an early peace settlement could be found only in the contention of the State De-partment that the enemy delegations did not mean what they said in public and would prove more conciliatory in secret negotia-tions.[53]

"Vietnamizing" the War

While still hoping to end the war through negotiations in Paris, President Nixon at-tempted to quiet criticism of the war at home by a process of "Vietnamization," that is, a gradual withdrawal of U.S. forces and their replacement by South Vietnamese troops with improved training and equipment. An an-nouncement on June 8, 1969, that 25,000 U.S. troops would be withdrawn during July, to be replaced by South Vietnamese, was fol-lowed a few days later by an expression of hope that more than 100,000 could be with-drawn before the end of 1970, and a further announcement on September 16 that an addi-tional 35,000 would be brought home by the end of 1969.[54]

The President's first comprehensive exposi-tion of the new policy came in a television address on November 3, 1969. All U.S. combat ground forces, said Mr. Nixon, would be with-drawn from Vietnam and replaced by Viet-namese forces "on an orderly scheduled time-table." He did not announce the timetable, since the rate of withdrawal would depend upon three variables: (1) progress of the peace negotiations, (2) "the level of enemy activity," and (3) progress in training the South Vietnamese forces. The peace negotia-tions seemed to be at a standstill, but the

49. *New York Times,* July 2, 1970; cf. John Osborne, "Why Cambodia?" *The New Republic,* July 11, 1970.
50. *New York Times,* September 18, 27, 1970.
51. *New York Times,* October 8, 1970; *The New Re-public,* October 17, 1970.

52. *New York Times,* October 9, 1970.
53. *New York Times,* October 11, 16, 1970.
54. *New York Times,* June 9, 21, September 17, 1969.

President spoke hopefully of the other two factors. He warned Hanoi that any increase in violence by North Vietnam would be met with "strong and effective measures," presumably exemplified by a partial renewing of the bombing of North Vietnam in November 1970. He suggested, with logic that seemed not to impress Hanoi, that the latter could make better terms with the United States than with Saigon after U.S. troops departed.[55]

The Vietnamization plan contained a number of ambiguities. It called specifically for the withdrawal of ground combat forces. Other elements—air, logistics, artillery—would presumably remain as long as needed to support Vietnamese ground forces. Furthermore, since the United States was still committed to the preservation of a free South Vietnam, even American ground forces could be expected to remain—in the absence of a peace settlement—until their South Vietnamese counterparts were able to cope with the threat from the North. On the basis of past experience that might take some time—"many years," predicted President Thieu in January 1970.[56]

Nixon's program of Vietnamization, as set forth in the announcements in June and September and in the November address, was further spelled out in a statement of December 15, 1969, that 50,000 additional U.S. troops would be withdrawn by April 15, 1970, and in a television address of April 20, 1970, forecasting that 150,000 more would be brought home by the spring of 1971. This, said

Mr. Nixon, would add up to a total reduction of 265,000 (sic) men by the latter period.

In spite of doubts and ambiguities, the President's plan seemed, for the time being, quite effective in quieting the antiwar clamor in the United States. A Gallup poll on the day after his November address showed 77 percent of those questioned supporting the President, 6 percent opposed, and 17 percent undecided. On December 2, the Democratic-controlled House of Representatives adopted by a vote of 333 to 55 a resolution expressing its support of the President "in his efforts to negotiate a just peace in Vietnam." Although there were further antiwar demonstrations in mid-November, Nixon's promise to withdraw even a part of the American troops in Vietnam seemed to have taken the steam out of the antiwar movement, an effect noted even on the nation's uneasy campuses. Such comparative harmony came to a sudden end with the President's announcement on April 30 that American and South Vietnamese forces were carrying the war into Cambodia.

The Cambodian Adventure

The declared purpose of the intrusion into Cambodia was to destroy Communist bases in areas adjoining South Vietnam which for years had been used as sanctuaries by Viet Cong and North Vietnamese forces with the tacit consent of nominally neutralist Prince Norodom Sihanouk, Cambodian Chief of State. The United States had long tolerated this breach of neutrality rather than take action which might drive Sihanouk into the enemy camp. But a new situation had arisen. Sihanouk had been overthrown in a coup d'état of March 18, led by pro-West Premier General Lon Nol, who now found his rule threatened by thousands of North Vietnamese troops from the sanctuaries. Should they succeed, the President explained, "Cambodia would become a vast enemy staging area and springboard for attacks on South Vietnam along 600 miles of frontier." Faced with these attacks, the government of General Lon Nol

55. *New York Times,* November 4, 1969. The President's address on Vietnamization came nineteen days after a nationwide peaceful demonstration or "moratorium," in which hundreds of thousands of people called generally for an "immediate" pullout of all U.S. forces in Vietnam. The President had rather ostentatiously ignored the demonstration—letting it be known that he preferred to watch a football game on TV—but there can be no doubt that the Vietnamization plan was a response to popular opposition to the war.

56. *New York Times,* January 11, 1970, Sec. 4, p. 5. Defense Secretary Melvin Laird raised new doubt about the withdrawal of American troops in making it dependent upon the release of U.S. prisoners by North Vietnam. Ibid., December 27, 1970, Sec. 4, p. 1.

had "sent out a call to the United States and a number of other nations for assistance."

Not only was the enemy threatening to take over Cambodia, he was, said Nixon, "concentrating his main forces in the sanctuaries where they are building up to launch massive attacks on our forces and those of South Vietnam." In view of this dual threat to the American program, the President's decision had been

> to go to the heart of the trouble. That means cleaning out major North Vietnamese and Viet Cong-occupied sanctuaries which serve as bases for attacks on both Cambodia and American and South Vietnamese forces in South Vietnam.

Tonight, the President continued, allied units would "attack the headquarters for the entire Communist military operation in South Vietnam"—the "key control center" that had operated for years "in blatant violation of Cambodia's neutrality."

The President insisted that the operation was "not an invasion of Cambodia" but was confined to areas "completely occupied and controlled by North Vietnamese forces, . . . Once enemy forces are driven out of these sanctuaries and their military supplies destroyed, we will withdraw." Success of the operation, the President intimated, would facilitate the previously announced withdrawal from Vietnam of 150,000 men over the next year.[57]

The move into Cambodia, invasion or not, looked to many in America like widening the war. Though the Gallop poll (May 4) showed a small majority favoring the President, the action produced a new round of demonstrations on university campuses, and in the Senate the introduction of several resolutions designed to prevent the President from expanding the area of war without consent of Congress. To conciliate his critics, Mr. Nixon gave assurance that American ground forces would penetrate no farther than 21.7 miles (35 kilometers) into Cambodia and that they and any advisers with South Vietnam forces would be withdrawn no later than June 30. United States aid to Cambodia would be limited to equipment and air support; whether this would be tactical as well as strategic (the bombing of enemy supply routes) was not clear. The Saigon government announced, however, that South Vietnamese troops would not be bound by the United States time-table but might remain to support the Lon Nol government and to assist in training its inexperienced troops.[58]

Upon completion of the sweep through the sanctuaries on June 30, the President issued a long report claiming outstanding success for the operation, even though the "key control center" of the Communist command had not been found. Enemy killed were estimated at over 11,000; enemy captured and detainees at 2,328. But the greatest gain had been in the vast amounts of enemy equipment—weapons, ammunition, vehicles, food (14 million pounds of rice)—and installations captured or destroyed. Enemy operations had been set back many months at least. The concept of sanctuaries in Cambodia had been demolished. The South Vietnamese troops had made an excellent showing, demonstrating the success of Vietnamization. In summary, the President predicted that the operation

> Will save American and allied lives in the future.
>
> Will assure that the withdrawal of American troops from South Vietnam will proceed on schedule.
>
> Will enable our program of Vietnamization to continue on its current time-table.
>
> Should enhance the prospects for a just peace.[59]

57. *New York Times*, May 1, 1970. In addition to the threats from the sanctuaries mentioned in his statement, the President had, in the opinion of some analysts, another motive for the invasion: to demonstrate to Communist nations that "had long been trifling with him in Indochina, Korea and the Middle East . . . that he could meet force with force." Ibid., June 30, 1970.

58. *New York Times*, May 31, 1970, Sec. 4, p. 3.
59. *New York Times*, July 1, 1970. It was in connection with the last point that the President announced a day later the appointment of David Bruce to head the negotiating team in Paris.

A New Indochina War?

There were other estimates of the probable consequences of Nixon's Cambodia gamble. In the opinion of one French expert on Southeast Asia, the war in Vietnam was in process of becoming the Second Indochina War, in which the United States and its allies would face a united front of North Vietnam, the NLF, the Pathet Lao of Laos, and the *Khmers Rouges*, or Cambodian Communists, with whom would now be numbered their former enemy, prestigious Prince Sihanouk.[60]

Sihanouk, who had been in Moscow when deposed in March, had gone thence to Peking, where he announced (March 23) that he would form a "national government" and a "national liberation army." On April 24 and 25 he met "at a certain spot in South China" with Communist leaders from North and South Vietnam and Laos to form an Indochinese revolutionary front. The conference issued a declaration denouncing the United States as an "imperialist aggressor" and calling upon the peoples of Vietnam, Laos, and Cambodia to "step up the fight against the common enemy—American imperialism and its lackeys in the three countries—until total victory." [61]

Hanoi radio applauded the conference, and in Peking Mao Tse-tung, in a violently anti-United States outburst, pledged the support of the Chinese people to "the people of the three Indochinese countries . . . in their revolutionary struggles against United States imperialism and its lackeys." [62]

How much substance there was behind this bluster remained to be seen; but the map issued with the President's report of June 30 showed over one-third of Cambodia under Communist domination, and other estimates were gloomier. When asked, in his television conversation of July 1, what his policy would be if Cambodia seemed on the point of becoming "the springboard for attacks on South Vietnam" of which he had warned, he replied that the South Vietnamese should be able to handle that problem. He refused at this time to say categorically that no American ground troops would be sent back into Cambodia, but months later, in a press conference of December 10, 1970, he stated that he could foresee no circumstances whatever under which American ground forces would be so used.[63]

---

60. Jean Lacouture, "From the Vietnam War to an Indochina War," *Foreign Affairs,* 48 (July 1970), 617–28.

61. *New York Times,* April 28, 1970. In Laos, the Geneva tripartite accord of 1962 had soon broken down. The Communist Pathet Lao, headed by Prince Souphanouvong, withdrew from the coalition and renewed sporadic warfare, while the neutralist and right-wing groups coalesced under Premier Prince Souvanna Phouma, whose royal government received military supplies and logistical aid from the United States, while the Central Intelligence Agency (CIA) sent advisers to the anti-Communist Meo tribesmen of the mountain areas. After a long stalemate, the Pathet Lao, with their North Vietnamese allies, went on the offensive in the winter and spring of 1970 and were reported to be stocking a region in southern Laos "as an expanded supply base for the war in Vietnam." Ibid., June 20, 1970.

62. *New York Times,* May 21, 1970.

63. *New York Times,* December 11, 1970. The renunciation of the use of U.S. ground forces in Cambodia did not apply to the Air Force. The Defense Department was evasive, but during August news despatches made it clear that U.S. Air Force planes were giving often close support to Cambodian troops. Ibid., August 5, 7, 31, 1970. Another possible source of military assistance to the Lon Nol government was Thailand. Thailand, the former Siam, was the most concerned (after the United States) of all the SEATO allies, for the obvious reason that it stood next to the states of Indochina in the "row of dominoes." It was itself the target of Communist subversion in four separate areas. A convinced advocate of collective action to halt Communism, the Thai government had allowed the United States to construct six major air bases on Thai territory, from which B-52 planes bombed the Ho Chi Minh trail and enemy areas in Vietnam. Thailand had also sent 12,000 troops to fight in Vietnam. Revelation that the United States had paid Thailand $50 million a year for the services of these troops and had entered into certain secret diplomatic and military agreements with the Thai government aroused serious criticism in the United States Senate. Senatorial criticism in turn roused the ire of Thai Foreign Minister Thanat Khoman, who vowed that no Thai troops would be sent into Cambodia "without a firm United States guarantee to underwrite financially the cost of their operations." *New*

The Senate preferred not to take chances. When the President, in November, added $145 million to an earlier request for $40 million for military aid to Cambodia,[64] the Senate attached to the authorization bill an amendment sponsored by Senators Church of Idaho and Cooper of Kentucky, which, as finally agreed to by the House of Representatives and signed by the President, forbade the sending of U.S. troops or advisers into Cambodia unless such action were specifically authorized by Congress.[65] It also stipulated that the

granting of aid should not be interpreted as a commitment by the United States to defend the Cambodian government. Its passage was an effort to reassert the constitutional authority of Congress over the war-making process.

Whether the war in Cambodia was to be fought by Americans or by South Vietnamese, by both, or by Cambodians alone, the expansion of the war area, as pointed out by French authority Jean Lacouture, was a "gift" to Hanoi's commander-in-chief, General Vo Nguyen Giap, who had repeatedly asserted "that every extension of the field of battle serves the revolutionary interests." And Lacouture added for good measure: "The evolution of the Indochina war is the fulfillment of Peking's hopes." [66]

Whether Nixon or Lacouture was the better prophet only time would tell.

York Times, June 28, July 2, 1970. For earlier phases, see the *New York Times,* May 21, August 16, 17, 1969, and June 8, 1970, and Robert Shaplen, *Time Out of Hand: Revolution and Reaction in Southeast Asia* (New York: Harper & Row, Publishers, 1969), pp. 275–97.

64. *New York Times,* November 19, 1970. The request for a total of $285 million included $100 million in economic aid and agricultural commodities.

65. *New York Times,* December 15, 23, 1970. The Cooper-Church amendment, in somewhat different form, had originally been passed by the Senate as an amendment to another bill on June 30, 1970, the day on which the President announced the departure of

the last U.S. ground troops from Cambodia. *New York Times,* July 1, 1970.

66. Lacouture, "From the Vietnam War to an Indochina War."

While the United States, under President Nixon, was endeavoring to disengage itself from the war in Southeast Asia, it was seeking to prevent renewal of a conflict that might involve it in hostilities in another corner of that vast continent—Southwest Asia, otherwise known as the Middle East. Here the new state of Israel was engaged in a war, alternately hot and cold, with its Arab neighbors, especially Egypt (now officially the United Arab Republic, or U.A.R.),[1] Syria, and Jordan. It was a war in which American and Soviet sympathies were engaged on opposite sides and which therefore presented frightening possibilities of major escalation.

47

American Policy in the Middle East

The Israeli Story

The story of this conflict begins in 1917. In the Balfour Declaration of that year (actually a bid for Jewish backing in World War I), the British government promised "the establishment in Palestine of a National Home for the Jewish people." To Britain's later embarrassment, her government had made conflicting promises to the Arabs of the area. The prospect of a Jewish state in a Palestine which had long been predominantly Arab aroused bitter resentment in the Arab world but was embraced with enthusiasm by the influential World Zionist Organization. As holder of a League of Nations mandate for Palestine, Britain found herself trapped by her conflicting promises to these rival forces. Until World War II she blew first hot and then cold upon Jewish aspirations for the National Home, first encouraging, and then attempting to check, Jewish immigration and acquisition of land in Palestine.

By 1947 an exhausted Britain found her position between those angry rivals more than she could bear and announced that she would surrender her mandate on May 15, 1948,

1. From 1958 to 1961 Egypt and Syria were united as the United Arab Republic; Egypt retained the name after their separation. Other Arab states that gave sympathy but little else to the three named were Iraq, Lebanon, Saudi Arabia, Yemen, the Sudan, Libya, Algeria, and Morocco. Tunisia tried to remain neutral. Neighboring Turkey and Iran, Moslem but not Arab, were not involved in the struggle.

yielding responsibility for Palestine to the United Nations. On November 29, 1947, the U.N. General Assembly recommended that Palestine be partitioned between an Arab and a Jewish state, with Jerusalem, containing the holy places of three great religions, to be placed under international administration. Immediately after the vote, the Arab delegates marched out of the Assembly, declaring that they would not be bound by the decision. The Palestine Arabs, with the support of their kinsmen in neighboring states, launched a civil war against the Palestine Jews. The Jews, meanwhile, were not only meeting Arab attacks successfully but were perfecting organs of government for Palestine. On the evening of May 14, 1948 (Washington time), they proclaimed the birth of the independent state of Israel. Within a few minutes thereafter, President Truman announced United States recognition, *de facto,* of the government of Israel.

Full-scale war now ensued between Israel and its Arab neighbors. The fighting was temporarily halted several times by cease-fire orders issued by the U.N. Security Council and finally ended by a series of armistice agreements negotiated by a United Nations mediator, Dr. Ralph Bunche. The armistice lines, fixed on the basis of territory occupied and held by the antagonists, gave Israel much more territory than the original partition proposal.

The armistice, however, proved to be that and nothing more. Armed clashes occurred from time to time along the border, despite the efforts of a U.N. Truce Supervision Organization. The United Nations resolution calling for an international regime in Jerusalem was unimplemented, and that city was cut in two by the armistice line between Israel and Jordan. The Arab states refused to negotiate peace treaties with Israel or to trade with it. Iraq refused to permit oil to flow through a pipe line to a refinery at Haifa. Egypt refused passage through the Suez Canal to Israeli ships or to ships with Israeli cargoes. Israel was blockaded on all its land frontiers.

A serious obstacle to any Israeli-Arab set-tlement was the plight of the Palestinian refugees, Arabs who had fled from their homes in Palestine during the war and were quartered in camps just outside the borders of Israel, in Syria, Lebanon, Jordan, and Egypt. Numbering some 800,000 to begin with, they were reported by the U.N. to have increased to 1,500,000 by 1967. Their places in Palestine were filled by the great influx of Jews—thousands of them driven from Arab lands—that followed independence. The Arab states would take no steps toward settling the refugees in permanent homes, since to do so would amount to surrendering their claim of right to return to their homes in Israel. The Arab governments would not make peace until Israel repatriated the refugees. Israel, for security reasons and later also because of lack of space, was unwilling to take back more than a token number. Meanwhile, the refugees were fed, clothed, and sheltered in their camps, chiefly through the exertions of the U.N. Relief and Works Agency for Palestine Refugees (UNRWA), established in 1948 and still functioning in 1970. The great majority of the refugees accepted their fate passively, but activists among them organized terrorist bands which waged guerrilla war against Israel from the neighboring states. Their activities and their opposition to any political settlement became a major obstacle to peace.[2]

Aims of the United States

Prior to World War I American interest in the Middle East—the land of the Bible and of the origins of the Christian religion—had been chiefly religious and archeological. American traders, too, had early found their way to the eastern Mediterranean and the ports of the Persian Gulf, but such trade had never been large.

In the years just before and during World War I, Americans first became conscious of the importance of the oil of the Middle East. British and French interests were on the

2. See pp. 522, 527, 528.

Nicosia ★
CYPRUS

Mediterranean Sea

Hama
Homs
SYRIA
Tripoli
Beirut ★ LEBANON
★ Damascus
Haifa
GOLAN HEIGHTS
Sea of Galilee
Tel Aviv
Jerusalem
Gaza
ISRAEL
★ Amman
Dead Sea
Beersheba
JORDAN
Kaf
IRAQ

Alexandria
Damietta
PortSaid
Suez Canal
El Arish
Tanta
El Giza ★ Cairo
Suez
(E G Y P T)
Elath Aqaba
Gulf of Suez
MT. SINAI
Gulf of Aqaba
Sharm el Sheikh
U.A.R.

SAUDI ARABIA

Red Sea

Nile

ISRAEL AND ADJACENT ARAB STATES

▨ Territory occupied by Israel, June 1967.

0   50   100   150   200
MILES

Note: In 1950 the Israel Parliament proclaimed Jerusalem the capital of Israel. The United States, however, does not recognize Jerusalem as the capital and maintains its embassy at Tel Aviv, the former capital.

ground first. In southern Iran the British, through the Anglo-Iranian Oil Company, attained and held a monopoly; but in Iraq and in the little sheikdom of Kuwait (500,000 people and one-seventh of the world's proved oil reserves!), American companies won a part interest, and in Saudi Arabia and the Bahrain Island field, they secured complete control.[3] World War II, with its terrific drain on the petroleum resources of the United States and Caribbean fields, emphasized the dependence of Western Europe (and even perhaps the future dependence of the United States), on the Middle East, under whose inhospitable surface lies more than half of all the proved oil reserves of the world.

It was the proximity of this vital region to the Soviet Union and the possibility of its subjection to Soviet influence or domination that made it a prime object of American attention in the years of the cold war. Russian desire to penetrate the region was undisguised. It was evident in the prolonged Soviet occupation of northern Iran, in Soviet pressure on Turkey for control of the Dardanelles, in the Russian desire for a trusteeship over former Italian conquests in North Africa.[4] Soviet ambitions had been frustrated at all these points, but no one could suppose that they had been abandoned. Hence exclusion of the Soviet Union from a dominant or influential role in the Middle East became an integral part of the American policy of containment.

The United States pursued its containment policy in the Middle East by three methods: (1) by attempting to compose disputes within the area which might tempt Soviet interference, especially the quarrel between Israel and its neighbors and controversies between Egypt and Iran on the one hand and Great Britain on the other; (2) by raising living standards through assistance in developing the region's

neglected natural resources; (3) by strengthening the area's military potential and its willingness to resist aggression or subversion originating in the Kremlin. In none of these approaches was the United States notably successful.

The United States did play a part, though a minor one, in bringing about two agreements between Britain and Egypt in 1954. By one of these England surrendered her share in the administration of the Anglo-Egyptian Sudan, which thereupon became the independent Republic of the Sudan. By the second agreement Britain agreed to withdraw her armed forces from her base on the Suez Canal over a period of twenty months. The United States also in the same year had a hand in settling a quarrel between Britain and Iran over the terms of Iran's nationalization of the Anglo-Iranian Oil Company.

But in its efforts to settle the Israeli-Arab dispute, the United States fared no better acting alone than through its participation in the U.N.'s Palestine Conciliation Commission. It did join with Britain and France in an attempt to guarantee each party to the controversy against aggression by the other. In a statement of May 25, 1950, the three governments declared that,

> should they find that any of these states was preparing to violate frontiers or armistice lines [they] would, consistently with their obligations as members of the United Nations, immediately take action, both within and outside the United Nations to prevent such violation.[5]

Ironically, on the only occasion when the United States acted under the terms of this guarantee, in the Israeli-Egyptian war of 1956, it was acting in opposition to the other signatories to the statement, which thus became a dead letter.[6]

In its efforts to raise the standard of living of the peoples of the Middle East (thereby, in theory immunizing them against Communism), the United States achieved little. It

3. The American companies chiefly involved are Standard of New Jersey and Socony-Vacuum in Iraq (and also in Qatar in the Persian Gulf); Gulf Oil Company in Kuwait; Standard of California, Standard of New Jersey, Socony-Vacuum, and Texas Company in Saudi Arabia and Bahrain.
4. See p. 435.

5. *Documents on American Foreign Relations,* 12: 658–59.
6. See p. 520.

signed Technical Assistance agreements with most of the states of the area. It promoted land development and resettlement programs in Egypt and Iraq and assisted the government of Saudi Arabia in modernizing its tariff and customs systems. The most ambitious proposal—development of the water resources of the Jordan River Valley for the benefit of all the people of the area—met an insuperable obstacle in the hostility of Jordan, Lebanon, and Syria to Israel. Any gain in influence that the United States, or the West, might have achieved by such measures was canceled out as the Soviet Union, though ostensibly friendly to Israel in 1948, quickly made itself, from 1956 on, the champion of the Arab states.

The Baghdad Pact

The third American line of approach, the building of military barriers against Soviet aggression in the area, received its principal impetus from Secretary of State John Foster Dulles, whose general policy it was to encircle the Soviet Union with military alliances. NATO (a pre-Dulles creation) reached into the eastern Mediterranean with the inclusion of Greece and Turkey. SEATO guarded Southeast Asia from anticipated Sino-Soviet aggression and, through the membership of Pakistan, came within a few miles of the Soviets' southern boundary. Dulles undertook to fill the gap between Pakistan and Turkey by an alliance of the "northern tier" of states —Turkey and Pakistan (already in NATO and SEATO respectively), linked by Iran and Iraq. The last-named was lured by the prospect of American military aid to draw apart, for the time being, from other Arab states and to sign a "Pact of Mutual Assistance" with Turkey, on February 24, 1955. Later in the year the pact was signed by Iran and Pakistan and also by the United Kingdom. Headquarters were established at Baghdad, the Iraqi capital, and the alliance was known as the Baghdad Pact.

The United States had promoted the alliance but did not become a member. It sent

observers to meetings, participated in certain committees, and gave military aid to the members individually, but what seemed to many its overly cautious abstention from full participation perplexed the British and the friends of the West in the other member states. It also emboldened the Russians and the anti-Western elements in the other Arab countries.[7]

The Baghdad Pact was based on a mistaken conception of the nature of the Russian threat in the Middle East, which lay not in military aggression but in infiltration and subversion. The fruits of these Soviet tactics were quickly apparent. Before the last signatures were appended to the Baghdad Pact, the government of Egypt announced a barter deal, arranged in Moscow, by which Egyptian cotton would be exchanged for arms from Czechoslovakia. Then followed quickly news of an alliance and a joint command agreement between Egypt, Syria, and Saudi Arabia; a Soviet-Syrian trade agreement; and a new treaty of friendship between Yemen and the Soviet Union. The Czech arms began arriving in October, and the next month a group of Egyptian fliers returned from a course of jet training in Czechoslovakia. The Baghdad Pact appeared to have given a sharp stimulus to Arab nationalism. This, in turn, was cultivated and abetted in Moscow, which felt no qualms about exploiting Arab hatred of Israel. The year of the Baghdad Pact saw impressive Soviet gains in the Middle East and a corresponding deterioration in British, French, and American influence.[8]

7. *U. S. in World Affairs, 1954,* p. 319; ibid., *1955,* pp. 154–57; John C. Campbell, *Defense of the Middle East* (New York: Harper & Row, Publishers for Council on Foreign Relations, 1958), pp. 61–62; Anthony Eden, *The Memoirs of Anthony Eden: Full Circle* (Boston: Houghton Mifflin Company, 1960), pp. 71, 374–75.

8. *U. S. in World Affairs, 1955,* pp. 159–67. France was confronted with rebellion in Algeria and knew that the Egyptian government was giving aid to the rebels. Britain's attempt to include Jordan in the Baghdad Pact touched off anti-Western rioting in Amman, the Jordanian capital, and led soon after to dismissal of the British commander of Jordan's army. Yemen supported anti-British tribesmen in the British protectorate of Aden.

The Suez Canal Crisis

The Americans and British attempted to recover their forfeited good will in Egypt by proposing to aid President Gamal Abdel Nasser [9] in financing a new high dam at Aswan on the Nile, a project that would provide hydroelectric power as well as irrigation for thousands of new farms. While Nasser was deliberating whether to accept the offer, British and American officials had second thoughts. Nasser had committed a large slice of Egypt's resources to pay for Czech arms. He seemed a poor risk for a loan such as that proposed. To Secretary of State Dulles, Nasser had not endeared himself by his further dickering with the Russians or his recent recognition of Communist China. Consequently, when Nasser's ambassador made a special trip to Washington in July 1956 to accept the loan, he was told abruptly that the offer was withdrawn. The British, who would have preferred a less spectacular refusal, had not been consulted, though the offer had been a joint one. They were annoyed, but Nasser was infuriated.[10]

Nasser's dramatic response, delivered July 26, was to nationalize the Suez Canal, owned chiefly by British and French stockholders and the vital link between Western Europe and the Middle Eastern oil fields. The Egyptian government, he indicated, would collect the tolls and apply a part of the proceeds to the building of the Aswan Dam. To the British and French this was an intolerable situation; to the United States it was objectionable but less crucial than to Europe. Secretary Dulles flew to London to confer with his British and French colleagues. A confer-

ence of twenty-four nations, principal users of the canal, was called to meet in London. A majority, the delegations of eighteen powers, recommended creation of a Suez Canal Board to take over management of the canal. When Nasser promptly rejected this solution, Dulles proposed the formation of a Suez Canal Users Association (SCUA), which might collect the tolls for use of the canal and assure that a proper share of the proceeds was used for maintenance of the canal and compensation to the stockholders of the canal company.

It was clear that Nasser would not accept the new proposal unless compelled to it by the use of force or some form of economic sanctions, such as a boycott of the canal. The British and French were willing to go to any necessary length for this purpose and assumed that Dulles, who had made the proposal, would be ready to back it up. They were chagrined, therefore, when he stated publicly that SCUA had no teeth. They turned for help to the United Nations and obtained from the Security Council, October 13, 1956, approval of a set of six principles for the management of the canal. These included a declaration of respect for the sovereignty of Egypt but also assertions that "the operation of the Canal should be insulated from the politics of any country," and that "there should be free and open transit through the Canal without discrimination, overt or covert." [11] Egypt accepted these principles. An attempt by Britain and France to attach an endorsement of the earlier eighteen-power plan and a request that Egypt cooperate with the Users Association was defeated by a Soviet veto. Observance of the six principles was left entirely to the good faith of the Egyptian government.

The British and French had no confidence

9. The corrupt and incompetent Egyptian King, Farouk, was overthrown in 1952 by a group of young army officers. The new government was at first headed by General Mohammed Naguib, but in 1954 he was replaced by strong man Col. Gamal Abdel Nasser, who became both Premier and Head of State (later President).

10. Eden, *Memoirs*, p. 470; Richard Goold-Adams, *John Foster Dulles: A Reappraisal* (New York: Appleton-Century-Crofts, 1962), p. 202.

11. *Documents on American Foreign Relations, 1956*, pp. 342–43. Other documents on the Suez crisis of 1956–57 are printed in ibid., pp. 289–373, and ibid., *1957*, pp. 195–290. Useful accounts are found in *U.S. in World Affairs, 1956*, pp. 251–74, 326–42; ibid., *1957*, pp. 157–74; Campbell, *Defense*, chap. 8; Eden, *Memoirs*, pp. 467–654; Goold-Adams, *Dulles*, pp. 208–33; Herman Finer, *Dulles over Suez: The Theory and Practice of His Diplomacy* (Chicago: Quadrangle Books, Inc., 1964).

in Nasser, whose pan-Arab nationalism was abetting rebellion against France in Algeria and denouncing British influence in Iraq and Arabia. They wished to humiliate and if possible to overthrow him. They felt with some reason that they had been led on and then let down by Secretary Dulles. It had become clear that neither he nor President Eisenhower would sanction the use of force or economic pressure against Nasser. Prime Minister Anthony Eden and French Premier Guy Mollet, therefore, planned their next move without taking the United States into their confidence.

The first nation to act, however, was Israel. Israel had been greatly alarmed at Egypt's acquisition of a great variety and profusion of military hardware from behind the Iron Curtain. An announcement in October of the formation by Egypt, Syria, and Jordan of

a joint military command, quite encircling the Jewish state, intensified the alarm. Israel's very existence seemed to be at stake. As Israelis saw it, only a preventive war could avert disaster.[12]

On October 29, 1956, therefore, Israeli forces struck without warning at Egyptian positions in the Gaza Strip and the Sinai Peninsula. The Egyptian armies, taken completely by surprise, were overwhelmed. Great stores of arms were captured, the Gaza Strip was overrun, and the invaders pushed on across the Sinai area toward the Suez Canal.

How much collusion there had been between the Israelis and the French and British is unknown. It seems well established that the

12. Nadav Safran, *The United States and Israel* (Cambridge: Harvard University Press, 1963), pp. 231–42.

THE MIDDLE EAST

French, at least, knew something of the Israeli plans; France, in fact, supplied a certain amount of air cover for the operation. Officially, the two Western governments on October 30 requested Israel and Egypt to accept a cease-fire, and when Egypt refused, announced that they would occupy positions along the canal to separate the belligerents and keep the canal open. This was the pretext for their intervention. Their real purpose, it would seem, was to restore the canal to international control and clip Colonel Nasser's wings, or, still better, bring him to ground altogether. At any rate, they began, through air attacks, to prepare the way for airborne landings at Ports Said and Fuad.

The United States reacted angrily to these resorts to force in violation of the U.N. Charter by one friendly state and two allies. In the U.N. Security Council on October 30 both the United States and the U.S.S.R. introduced resolutions calling for a cease-fire in the Israeli-Egyptian war. Both were vetoed by the British and French representatives. The General Assembly, meeting on the night of November 1–2, adopted an American resolution calling for an immediate cease-fire, suspension of military movements into the area, and withdrawal of armed forces behind armistice lines. Significant was the fact that the United States and the Soviet Union stood together against the former's two leading allies. The somewhat moralistic or legalistic position taken by the United States was typified by President Eisenhower in a broadcast of October 31. "There can be no peace without law," the President declared. "And there can be no law if we were to invoke one code of international conduct for those who oppose us and another for our friends." Mr. Eisenhower made plain his awareness of the provocations under which the three offending powers were acting; but he believed their actions had been "taken in error. For we do not accept the use of force as a wise or proper instrument for the settlement of international disputes." The President promised that the United States would not become involved in the existing hostilities and that the government would "do all in its power

to localize the fighting and to end the conflict." [13]

On November 5 the General Assembly recommended the creation of the Emergency Force for Palestine, described elsewhere.[14] With this as a face-saving device, under triple pressure from the United States, the U.N., and the U.S.S.R., and subjected to Russia's threats of "volunteers" at the seat of conflict and rockets on their home premises, the British, French, and Israelis agreed next day to a cease-fire. The Israeli campaign had been notably successful, winning virtually all its objectives. The British and French, inadequately prepared for the adventure, had destroyed much of the Egyptian air force but had landed only a few troops near the canal. Far from keeping the canal open, their avowed purpose, they had been unable to prevent Nasser from blocking it so completely with sunken ships that it was not open to normal use for six months.

The French and British had gained nothing whatever from their intervention. A humiliating retreat had impaired their prestige. The Israelis had destroyed a vast quantity of Egyptian war equipment and at least postponed the day of a new Arab offensive. From the stationing of the Emergency Force in the Gaza Strip and at the outlet of the Gulf of Aqaba, they gained protection from Egyptian border raids and access to the high seas from their port of Elath (Eilat). They were still debarred by Egypt from use of the canal. The complete success of their arms had raised their military prestige as it had lowered that of Egypt. Nasser, in spite of a humiliating military defeat, had been saved from complete disaster by the intervention of the U.N. backed by the U.S. and the U.S.S.R. He had

13. *Documents on American Foreign Relations, 1956*, pp. 49–55. Secretary Dulles was hospitalized for an emergency operation on November 3, and was immobilized for several weeks. When the Soviet Union, November 5, proposed joint action by the U.S. and U.S.S.R. against the three "aggressors," Eisenhower remarked that such action on the part of the United States would be "unthinkable."
14. See p. 422.

had to forgo for a while his attack on Israel, but he had his canal virtually on his own terms. His political prestige in the Arab world was enhanced. Aid for the Aswan Dam, denied him by the West, was provided instead by the Soviet Union.

The United States had made its point, that resort to force should not be allowed to pay. It had failed to show by what alternative means justice could be done. By equating the Anglo-French action at Suez with "colonialism," as both Dulles and Vice President Nixon had done, and by taking a leading part in opposing it, the United States had probably improved its standing in the Asian-African world. But by the same actions and by the equivocal character of Dulles' early support, it had impaired its relations with its two most reliable allies and opened a rift in NATO which required many months to heal.

The Eisenhower Doctrine

Though the Soviet Union had shown that military conquest was not its method of operation in the Middle East, the United States feared that states under Soviet influence might still resort to armed force to extend the boundaries of Communism. The chief objects of this fear were Egypt and Syria, both of which had developed strong economic ties with the Soviet Union and had been supplied with arms by the U.S.S.R. or its satellites. Egypt's losses in equipment in the war of 1956 were promptly restored with Soviet aid, and there was fear that President Nasser, perhaps with Syrian backing, might move to make himself the leader of a united Arab nation which would be, though not Communist, at least under strong Soviet influence.

To guard against such a possibility President Eisenhower secured from Congress (March 9, 1957) a joint resolution setting forth what came to be known as the Eisenhower Doctrine. The resolution empowered the President to use the armed forces of the United States, at the request of any nation of the Middle East, to protect it against overt armed aggression from any nation controlled by international Communism.[15]

Though no nation of the area made the type of request described in the resolution, President Eisenhower found two occasions to act at least in the spirit of it. A few weeks after the passage of the resolution, pro-Western King Hussein of Jordan was threatened by leftist agitators, who, with Egyptian and Syrian backing, called for his overthrow and the alignment of Jordan with Egypt and Syria. This situation brought from Eisenhower an announcement that he considered the independence of Jordan vital to the security of the United States, an order moving the American Sixth Fleet to the Eastern Mediterranean, and the grant to Jordan of $30 million in economic and military aid. These gestures, coupled with assurances of support to Jordan from Iraq and Saudi Arabia, put an end for the time being to the plot against Hussein's rule.

The year 1958 brought a more serious crisis. Early in the year Egypt and Syria merged to form the United Arab Republic (U.A.R.) under Nasser's presidency. This victory of Arab nationalism was a threat to the existing pro-Western regimes in Jordan and Iraq, as well as to Israel. As a countermeasure the kingdoms of Iraq and Jordan federated to form the Arab Union. This course was evidently unpopular in Iraq, where on July 14 a violent revolution overthrew the government. The King, the Crown Prince, and the Premier, all friends of the West, were assassinated. A new government, not Communist but friendly to the Soviet Union, took control. Iraq soon withdrew from the Baghdad Pact. Alliance headquarters were moved to Ankara in Turkey and the name was changed to Central Treaty Organization (CENTO).

15. *Documents on American Foreign Relations, 1957,* 195–204. In April 1970 the Senate Foreign Relations Committee voted to recommend repeal of the "Eisenhower Doctrine" resolution as well as the Tonkin Gulf Resolution. *New York Times,* April 11, 1970, and see above, p. 501. But the Eisenhower Doctrine was untouched by the rider that repealed the Tonkin Gulf Resolution in Public Law 91–672, January 12, 1971.

The immediate Western reaction to the Iraqi revolution, however, was an assumption (plausible but incorrect) that it had been engineered by Nasser and portended similar moves in Jordan and Lebanon. In Lebanon, in fact, there was already an armed rebellion in progress, with opponents of the regime receiving encouragement and support from the U.A.R., especially its contiguous Syrian branch. The governments of Lebanon and Jordan, on receiving news of the Iraqi revolution, appealed for military protection to the United States and Britain respectively, basing their pleas upon the right of collective self-defense guaranteed by Article 51 of the United Nations Charter.

The appeals met prompt response. The United States landed 14,000 marines and airborne troops in Lebanon, while the British dispatched 3,000 paratroopers to Jordan. While the Soviet Union denounced the intervention as a demonstration of "Western imperialism" and demanded immediate withdrawal of the foreign troops, and the U.N. Security Council was deadlocked, the quarreling Arab states excited general surprise by combining in the General Assembly to sponsor a resolution that broke the impasse. The resolution pledged the Arab states to respect one another's systems of government and to abstain from any action calculated to disturb those systems. It called upon the U.N. Secretary General to take steps toward seeing that this principle was observed with relation to Lebanon and Jordan and thus to prepare the way for an early withdrawal of foreign troops.[16] The danger of outside interference in Jordan and Lebanon was for the time being removed; the civil strife in Lebanon was terminated through the mediation of American diplomat Robert Murphy; and the foreign troops were withdrawn, the Americans in October, the British in November. Not for nine years did the Middle East see another crisis so serious.

16. *Documents on American Foreign Relations, 1958,* pp. 360–61.

Rifts in the Arab World

Those nine years, however, were by no means quiet or peaceful. They were marked, on the Arab side, by agreements made and broken, mutual denunciations, plots, counterplots, coups, and civil wars. The one constant was hatred of Israel, refusal to recognize its existence as a state, and a determination that as a state it must be destroyed. Of all the Arab leaders, only one, Habib Bourguiba of Tunisia, had the realism and courage to urge that the Arabs should accept Israel as a fact and make peace with it on the terms proposed by the U.N. in 1947. For this effrontery Bourguiba's government narrowly missed being expelled from the Arab League; nor did he get much credit from Israel, to which the terms of 1947 were no longer acceptable.

But practical Arab leaders, like Nasser, knew that as yet the Arabs were unprepared to fight another conventional war with Israel with any hope of success. There was, however, the possibility of guerrilla war, and for this purpose a Palestine Liberation Organization was formed among the refugees, spearheaded by a so-called Palestine Liberation Army with a fiery refugee, Ahmad Shukairy, as its leader. By 1966, this and other refugee groups were leading guerrilla raids into Israel from the neighboring states, most often from Syria, though such raiding parties frequently entered Israel from Jordan.

Israel retaliated, sometimes by air, sometimes by ground attack, against the states from which the attacks had come, often inflicting death or injury upon innocent parties, as when the Jordanian village of Es Samu was virtually destroyed by a tank-led Israeli force in November 1966. Such a reprisal was particularly unfortunate because, of all Israel's immediate neighbors, King Hussein of Jordan was most receptive to suggestions for a peaceful settlement, despite serious domestic opposition.

But although the Arab states, with the exception of Tunisia, were in agreement in their uncompromising hostility to Israel, they agreed about little else. They were divided ideologically into two groups. The "progressive" states, led by Egypt, Syria, Iraq, and Algeria (which won its independence from France in 1962), were in theory republican and socialistic and were sympathetic to the Soviet Union, though unwilling to be dominated by it. Saudi Arabia and Jordan, on the other hand, were conservative monarchies and preferred the friendship of the West to that of Moscow. President Gamal Abdel Nasser of the U.A.R., most dynamic of the Arab leaders, not only found his ambition to unite and dominate the Arab world blocked by the monarchies, but met with opposition even in Syria and Iraq, where pro-Nasser and anti-Nasser regimes alternated in consequence of a succession of coups. Syria withdrew from the U.A.R. in 1961 (though Nasser retained the name for Egypt alone), and attempts to reconstitute that union with the inclusion of both Syria and Iraq were frustrated by mutual jealousies.

The rift in the Arab world was deepened by a civil war in Yemen. In 1962 the Imam, the paternalistic sovereign of that backward little state, was ousted at the instigation of Nasser, and a nominally republican regime set up with Egyptian backing. The Imam, however, refused to bow to the revolution and was aided in his resistance by Saudi Arabia and Jordan. Nasser poured an estimated peak of 70,000 Egyptian troops (accompanied by Russian technicians) into Yemen, but royalist forces, with Saudi Arabian support, continued to resist, and the war dragged on until 1970, in spite of efforts of the U.N. and the U.S. to end it.[17]

Nasser at the same time, looking beyond Yemen, was denouncing British imperialism as exemplified in Aden and the neighboring British-protected South Arabian Federation.

In the face of acts of terrorism in this area and armed raids across the border from Yemen, Britain announced that she would withdraw from the entire area by 1968. Actually, Aden and the South Arabian Federation became independent as the People's Republic of Southern Yemen on November 30, 1967. Rightly or wrongly, Nasser was suspected of scheming to win control of all Arabia, including its petroleum resources and those of the Persian Gulf.[18]

American Preferences

United States policy during these years aimed primarily at keeping the peace in the area— peace for its own sake, and peace as the best means of preventing the growth of Soviet influence. In accord with this policy was President Kennedy's offer of assistance—specifically in resolving "the tragic Palestine refugee problem"—to all the states of the area that were determined to live in peace, maintain their independence, and improve the living standards of their people. Equally a part of this peace policy was the President's warning that, if necessary, the United States would act both through the U.N. and "on our own" to prevent or stop aggression by any state in the area.[19] The United States desired to maintain friendly relations with all states in the area. At the same time, it was fully committed to the right of Israel to exist as a nation, and hence necessarily opposed to the ultimate Arab goal—destruction of Israel; and

17. Egyptian troops were withdrawn during the Six-Day War of 1967, but the civil war continued until April 1970, when the royalist forces abandoned the contest at the instance of Saudi Arabia. *New York Times,* April 15, 1970.

18. Nasser also put pressure on Libya to terminate British and U.S. base rights in that country, due to expire in 1973 and 1971 respectively. Both agreed in 1964 to review their plans. Evacuation of British bases and American Wheelus Field was speeded up after a pro-Nasser military coup overthrew the King on September 1, 1969. The British were out by April 1, 1970; the Americans surrendered their $100 million air base at Wheelus Field in June 1970. *U.S. in World Affairs, 1964,* p. 256; *New York Times,* December 24, 1969; June 21, 1970.

19. *Documents on American Foreign Relations, 1961,* pp. 281–84; *New York Times,* May 12, 1963, Sec. 4, p. 2.

while it might, in theory, prefer the domestic policies of the "progressive" states to the paternalism of the monarchies, the affinity of the former group for the Soviet Union automatically aligned the United States with Jordan and Saudi Arabia in any contest between them and the U.A.R.

The peculiar consequence followed that whereas the United States had emphasized its desire to decelerate the arms race in the area, it found itself in 1966 contributing to that race on both sides of the Israeli-Arab contest. To balance Soviet (or satellite) arming of the U.A.R., the United States sold tanks and fighter-bombers to Jordan. To balance this increment to Jordan's tank forces, the United States then provided Israel with Patton tanks; and to balance Egypt's and Jordan's new aircraft (Soviet and American), the United States then found it necessary to sell small Skyhawk jet bombers to Israel. Israel and Saudi Arabia, meanwhile, had both been supplied by the United States with ground-to-air missiles.[20] Such business must have been profitable to American arms manufacturers.

The Six-Day War

The guerrilla attacks on Israel and Israeli counterattacks, which had become flagrant in 1966, intensified in the spring of 1967. Attacks from Syria, May 5 and 6, led the Israeli government to serve notice on the United Nations (which had repeatedly condemned Israeli reprisals with inadequate rebuke for the provocation) that Israel would defend itself. Abdel Nasser, who hitherto had shown a prudent caution, now committed a series of rash and provocative acts, stimulated in part by unfounded Soviet reports that Israel was mobilizing against Syria.[21] On May 18 he demanded

that the U.N. Emergency Force, which had policed the U.A.R.-Israeli border since 1956, be at once withdrawn. Secretary General U Thant complied; he contended that he had no choice, since the UNEF troops were stationed on Egyptian soil with Egypt's permission. Nasser then moved his armed forces into the Sinai Peninsula, apparently ready to cross the border into Israel. Then, on May 22, Nasser seized Sharm el-Sheikh, guarding the Strait of Tiran (occupied since 1956 by the UNEF), and declared the strait and the Gulf of Aqaba closed to Israeli shipping.

Closing the strait was virtually an act of war, but before resorting to force the Israeli government sought a diplomatic solution. Foreign Minister Abba Eban visited London, Paris, and Washington in a quest for support. From President de Gaulle he got only a warning not to fire the first shot—a warning that was to be invoked as the basis for France's later reversal of her hitherto sympathetic policy to Israel. In London, Prime Minister Wilson encouraged Eban to hope that Britain might act with other powers to keep the strait open. From President Johnson he got a promise to seek international pressure upon Nasser to open the strait, in accord with guarantees given to Israel by the United States in 1957 after the Suez crisis; but Johnson asked for two weeks' time and asked Israel meanwhile not to start the shooting. Thus Israel was left with only vague promises of future support and facing an enemy whose purpose seemed to be its immediate destruction.

The picture darkened on May 30, when King Hussein of Jordan flew to Cairo and signed a mutual defense pact with his former enemy, Nasser. Popular and military pressure for action now led Israeli Premier Levi Eshkol to name aggressive General Moshe Dayan, hero of the Suez War, as Minister of Defense. Early on June 5—claiming that radar screens

---

20. *U.S. in World Affairs, 1966,* pp. 204–5; *New York Times,* February 5, May 20, 1966.

21. The Soviet reports were apparently directly responsible for Nasser's determination to mobilize in the Sinai Peninsula, but Moscow was not consulted on his closing of the Strait of Tiran and at the last moment warned him against initiating military action. The Soviets did promise, however, that if Nas-

ser's acts led to war, they would match for him any aid that the U.S. might give to Israel. See Theodore Draper, *Israel and World Politics; The Roots of the Third Arab-Israeli War* (New York: The Viking Press, Inc., 1968). There is a good brief account in *U.S. in World Affairs, 1967,* chap. 3.

showed U.A.R. planes approaching to attack—Dayan launched a devastating offensive which in a few hours destroyed the air forces of the U.A.R., Jordan, and Syria, and left the way open for an equally invincible land campaign, which carried Israeli troops and tanks to the Suez Canal and Sharm el-Sheikh, to the west bank of the Jordan in Jordanian territory (including complete occupation of the Jordanian section of Jerusalem), and in the north to the summit of the Golan Heights, from which Syrian artillery had harassed Israeli settlements on the shores of the Sea of Galilee. No victory could have been more complete. By June 11, all belligerents had yielded to a series of cease-fire orders issued by the U.N. Security Council, and the Six-Day War was over.

The war had wide international repercussions. It destroyed for the time being any hope of better relations between the "progressive" Arab states and the West (except France). On the false charge that American and British planes had participated in the Israeli campaign, Nasser, who had already severed diplomatic relations with Britain, broke off those with the United States. His example was followed by Syria, Iraq, Algeria, and Yemen, while the oil-producing Arab states agreed to suspend oil shipments to the offending powers. This suspension, however, was short-lived, since it injured the suppliers of oil more than the purchasers. During the fighting Nasser had blocked the Suez Canal with sunken ships. It remained closed. The Israelis, occupying the east bank, would not consent to clearing operations without guarantees of nondiscrimination in its use. For the loss of this principal source of revenue, the U.A.R. was compensated by subsidies from the oil-rich Arab states, Saudi Arabia, Kuwait, and Libya.

On the other side of the board, the Soviet Union and its satellites broke off diplomatic relations with Israel, which they branded as the aggressor. Though President Johnson and Premier Kosygin assured each other on the "hot line," June 5, of their common determination not to become involved in the hostilities, Moscow's uncompromising espousal of the Arab cause—including immediate steps to re-place the estimated $1 billion worth of military equipment lost or destroyed—tended to widen the East-West rift. The meeting of the two statesmen at Glassboro, New Jersey, failed to narrow it.[22]

The Search for a Settlement

The cease-fire agreement of June 11, like its predecessors of 1949 and 1956, and like that of 1953 in Korea, ended hostilities for the time being but in no sense restored peaceful relations; in fact, between Israelis and Arabs there had been no peaceful relations to restore. Was there a chance now for a real settlement? The immediate question, since Israel held important areas of formerly Arab territory, was whether she should surrender these, and if so, upon what conditions? Both the Security Council and the General Assembly of the U.N. had struggled with this question in June and July but had failed to reach agreement. The great powers agreed, in general, that territory seized by force should be handed back. But whereas the U.S.S.R. contended that Israel, the aggressor, should restore the conquered territory at once and unconditionally, the United States and Britain recognized Israel's grievances and held that in return for surrendering her conquests she should receive recognition of her national existence and guarantees of security from attack and of nondiscriminatory treatment in international waterways, specifically in the Suez Canal and the Strait of Tiran.

President Johnson stated the American position in a few words in an address of June 19, 1967:

> Certainly troops must be withdrawn, but there must also be recognized rights of national life, progress in solving the refugee problem, freedom of innocent maritime passage, limitation of the arms race, and respect for political independence and territorial integrity.[23]

22. See p. 456.
23. *Department of State Bulletin,* 57 (July 10, 1967), 31–34.

Neither the United States nor the U.S.S.R. was able, during the summer, to secure the necessary votes for the approval of its position in either the Security Council or the General Assembly.

In August there was one hopeful indicator. At an Arab summit meeting in Khartoum, both Nasser and King Hussein of Jordan acknowledged the need for a diplomatic, as distinct from a military, solution of the problem; but such expression meant little in view of the continued insistence by the Arabs that they would not negotiate with the Israelis. Israel, for its part, was, as formerly, quite willing to negotiate, which would mean recognition, but as to the surrender of the Old City of Jerusalem, which had great sentimental value, and such strategically critical spots as Sharm el-Sheikh and the Golan Heights, Israel seemed unlikely to yield.

After months of tension during which the Security Council had several times to rebuke the U.A.R. and Israel for violations of the cease-fire agreement, that body on November 22, 1967, adopted unanimously a resolution, proposed by Great Britain, which held some promise as a basis for a compromise solution. The resolution called for the "withdrawal of Israeli armed forces from the territories occupied in the recent conflict"; termination of states of belligerency; "acknowledgement of the sovereignty, territorial integrity and political independence of every State in the area and their right to live in peace within secure and recognized boundaries free from threats or acts of force," and the guarantee of these rights "through measures including the establishment of demilitarized zones"; guarantee of "freedom of navigation through international waterways in the area"; and "a just settlement of the refugee problem."

Finally, the Secretary General was directed to name a special representative to act as mediator and to try to bring about a peaceful settlement based on the principles stated in the resolution.[24]

U Thant designated a Swedish diplomat, Gunnar Jarring, to undertake the delicate task of finding common ground between Arabs and Israelis. Jarring first attempted to bring representatives of the parties secretly to neutral territory in Cyprus, where they could exchange ideas through him as mediator (a technique used in negotiating the truce of 1949). This plan was abandoned when rumors of it leaked out, causing an uproar in Arab lands. The parties then agreed to work through Jarring at U.N. headquarters in New York, where the governments concerned were represented. When no results were achieved there, both U Thant and the French government proposed that the Big Four powers undertake to find a settlement. The proposal was endorsed by the Soviets and finally accepted by Britain and by the new Nixon administration in Washington. To warnings from Israeli Premier Golda Meir (Premier Levi Eshkol died in February 1969) that Israel would not accept an imposed settlement, Secretary of State Rogers responded that the Big Four would rely upon "the force of world opinion" to bring acceptance of a formula on which they might agree.[25]

The Big Four, however, became as deeply divided as the antagonists and along the same lines. Russia, seconded by France, supported the Arabs; the United States and Britain, though somewhat more flexible, backed Israel. The chief issues in dispute were clear. The Arabs would accept the U.N. terms of November 1967 but interpreted them to mean that Israel must surrender as a preliminary to negotiation all territory seized in the Six-Day War. The Israelis, on the other hand, would not surrender occupied territory until assured through negotiated treaties of their security against further hostilities and of their right to navigation of the Suez Canal and the Strait of Tiran. It became more and more clear, also, that the Israelis were determined to hold all of Jerusalem and were most unlikely to surrender the Golan Heights and Sharm el-Sheikh. These conflicting views were sufficient to block the road to understanding

24. *New York Times,* November 23, 1967.

25. *New York Times,* April 8, 1969.

without facing the complication of what constituted "a just settlement of the refugee problem." By January 1970 the Soviet Union and the United States were accusing each other of supporting demands that made settlement impossible.[26]

In the meantime the cease-fire had largely broken down. Nasser declared it void in April 1969, and U Thant observed in July that a virtual state of war prevailed in the Suez area. Israeli-Egyptian artillery duels roared across the canal. Guerrilla or commando bands—*fedayeen*—had been organized on an enlarged basis among the Palestinian refugees. They staged raids into Israel from Jordan and Syria, and resorted to acts of terrorism far from the borders of Israel, attacking or bombing Israeli planes or planes carrying Israeli passengers. Most important, through their politico-military organizations—of which Al Fatah was the most important—they denounced any plan for making peace with Israel and on occasion threatened with assassination any Arab ruler who should venture to negotiate for such a peace.[27] Thus they presented a new obstacle to a negotiated peace.

Israel responded to the commando activities by attacks, generally from the air, on the states that harbored them—Egypt, Jordan, Syria, even Lebanon when Palestinian commandos forced their activities on that would-be nonbelligerent little state. Egypt, however—or the U.A.R.—bore the brunt of the Israeli retaliation. Israeli planes dropped bombs as far within Egypt as the suburbs of Cairo, until Russia came to Egypt's support by deploying SAM-3 (surface-to-air) missiles, manned by Soviet crews, for the defense of the capital. In an even more ominous gesture, the U.S.S.R. sent in Russian pilots to fly Russian-built MIGs of the Egyptian air force, presumably for defense of the missile sites. More alarming than the obvious chance of clashes between Soviet and Israeli personnel was the danger that Russian participation might deprive Israel of its supremacy in the air and doom

it to a long war of attrition (3,000,000 Israelis against perhaps 90,000,000 Arabs) or actual destruction by Arab armies.

To offset Russian aid to its enemies, Israel looked to the United States, since France, its chief supplier prior to the Six-Day War, had cut off all planes to Israel and had, in fact, promised one hundred jets to Arab Libya. The United States, anxious not to exacerbate the arms race, delayed action on the Israeli request for 125 jet aircraft (Phantoms and Skyhawks), but in his TV "conversation" of July 1, 1970, President Nixon stated flatly: "We will do what is necessary to maintain Israel's strength vis-à-vis its neighbors. Not because we want Israel to be in a position to wage war —that isn't it—but because that is what will deter its neighbors from attacking it." [28]

Several days before the President's interview, Secretary of State Rogers had submitted to Israel and her neighbors a proposal for a ninety-day cease-fire and a resumption of peace negotiations under U.N. auspices. President Nasser, after a visit to Moscow, accepted the proposal (July 23); King Hussein of Jordan followed suit. The Israeli government also agreed, though with misgivings, after receiving assurances from the United States that the cease-fire would not be used to Israeli's military disadvantage. Syria and Iraq had rejected the proposal, and the Palestinian commando leader, Yasir Arafat, had served notice that his group would accept no cease-fire and no compromise settlement.[29]

The cease-fire became effective on the night of August 7–8, and on August 25 Gunnar Jarring began separate talks with the ambassadors of the three governments at the United Nations. Days earlier, however, Israel had charged that the U.A.R., with Russian assistance, had violated the cease-fire agreement by moving batteries of SAM-2 and SAM-3 missiles into the cease-fire zone west of the Suez Canal. Such reinforcement, the Israelis

26. *New York Times,* January 13, 23, 24, 1970.
27. *New York Times,* April 19, 1970 (editorial), Sec. 4, p. 16.

28. *New York Times,* July 5, 1970, Sec. 4, p. 10; *Buffalo Evening News,* July 2, 1970. Cf. G. W. Ball, "Suez Is the Front to Watch," *New York Times Magazine,* June 28, 1970.
29. *New York Times,* June 26–August 5, 1970, *passim.*

claimed, endangered Israel's command of the air over the canal and her ability to hold the east bank as her first line of defense.[30] The United States, at first skeptical, became convinced by September 1 that the U.A.R. had broken the truce agreement, and two days later called upon Cairo and Moscow to avoid further violations, but urged that the peace talks continue. Dissatisfied with this rather bland American posture, the Israeli government, which had already called home its ambassador at the U.N., announced on September 6 that it would not resume negotiations until the newly installed missiles in the cease-fire zone were removed.[31]

On that same day, with the evident purpose of putting a final end to the peace talks, Palestinian commandos hijacked three commercial jet airplanes in flight over Europe. One, a Pan American 747 jumbo jet, was flown to Cairo, where it was blown up after crew and passengers had made a hurried exit. The other two, an American TWA and a Swissair, were landed in the desert near Amman, Jordan, where they were joined three days later by a British BOAC plane, hijacked en route from Bahrain to London. By Friday, September 11, the passengers and crew members, numbering 414, had been removed from the planes. The planes were then blown up, and most of the passengers had been moved to hotels in or near Amman, whence they were flown to Cyprus; but some fifty-four (Israelis, Swiss, British, West Germans, and Americans) were separated from the others and held as hostages. The price of their release was to be the freeing of Arab terrorists imprisoned in Switzerland, West Germany, England, and Israel. American Jews, some of whom were reported to have dual U.S.-Israeli citizenship, were to be treated as Israelis.

Negotiations for the return of hostages were under way through the International Red Cross when King Hussein of Jordan installed a military government and on September 17 ordered his Bedouin army to have it out with the Palestinian guerrillas, with whom for weeks there had been intermittent fighting. Ten days of bloody and destructive warfare followed, ending in an apparent victory for Hussein's army and a truce arranged in Cairo September 25, between Hussein and Yasir Arafat under the supervision of the heads of other Arab states. By September 29 all of the hijacked hostages had been released. Thereupon, by agreement, the British, West German, and Swiss governments released their Arab terrorist captives.[32]

The Jordanian civil war had raised new threats of major international involvement. President Nixon had told a private gathering of news editors that the United States might have to intervene if King Hussein's regime should be threatened by interference from Syria or Iraq in behalf of the guerrillas. When Syrian tanks crossed the border on September 18, the President apparently considered direct intervention by the United States. He had already reinforced the Sixth Fleet, which was cruising between Crete and the coast of Israel, and alerted airborne troops in the United States and West Germany. What he had in mind was apparently a bold stroke which would at the same time sustain Hussein's throne and rescue the hostages.

Cautioned by the British ambassador against direct intervention, Mr. Nixon and his advisers concerted with Israel on a contingency plan by which, if it became necessary, Israeli forces would attack the invading Syrians, while the United States would protect the Israeli flanks and rear against possible attack from the U.A.R. or elsewhere. Fortunately,

---

30. The SAM-2 missile was effective only against planes flying at over 3,500 feet altitude. The more sophisticated SAM-3 could shoot down low-flying planes.

31. *New York Times*, August 8–September 7, 1970, *passim*.

32. *New York Times*, September 8–October 1, 1970, *passim*. Despite the perils of the hijacking operation and exposure to the civil war, there had not been a single death among the hostages—their number had, in fact, been increased by one birth—and many of those released, including some Jews, testified to the humane treatment they had received during captivity.

execution of the plan was not necessary. The Syrian tanks withdrew, probably impelled by advice from Moscow as well as by the threat from Israel and vigorous attacks by Hussein's air force and armor.[33]

The challenge to the Soviet Union over control of the Middle East and the Mediterranean, implicit in these events and in promises of increased military aid to both Israel and Jordan,[34] was made more explicit when the President, during a brief trip to Europe (September 27 to October 5, 1970), paid a ceremonial visit to the Sixth Fleet and declared in an address in Rome: "The Mediterranean is the cradle of many great civilizations of the past, and we are determined that it shall not be the starting place of great wars in the future." [35]

There were indications of a Soviet counter-challenge in the Caribbean. On September 25, the White House revealed information (which it had had for some time) of Russian naval activity at Cienfuegos on the south coast of Cuba. The information suggested the possibility that the Russians were preparing to construct a base for nuclear submarines in the Cuban harbor—a development which, the White House warned, the United States would view "with the utmost seriousness." [36] Mr. Nixon's ambition to substitute negotiation with Moscow for confrontation seemed, as James Reston observed, to have been at least temporarily thwarted.[37]

The suspension of fighting in Jordan brought some relief of tension. Then, on September 28, three days after presiding over the signing of the cease-fire agreement, President Gamal Abdel Nasser succumbed to a heart attack. Nasser had so dominated the Middle Eastern scene for the preceding eighteen years

that his passing made the future of the area more than ever unpredictable. His immediate successor as President, Anwar el-Sadat, vowed to continue Nasser's policies. His emphatic refusal, supported by Moscow, to remove a single SAM missile from the cease-fire zone made resumption of the peace talks seem at first unlikely. Israel, however, after strengthening her position on the east bank of the canal and receiving assurance of $500 million in military aid from the United States,[38] dropped her insistence upon the removal of the missiles. Urged by the United States to resume negotiations with the Arab states through Gunnar Jarring at the U.N., and given assurances of American support against extreme Arab demands, Israel finally agreed to resume the talks. The U.A.R. had already done so. Though neither side had indicated any yielding on its fundamental demands, the negotiations were expected to resume in January 1971.[39] The cease-fire had meanwhile been extended to February 5, 1971.

As matters stood in December 1970, the only real gainer from the Six-Day War and its sequel was the Soviet Union. Despite the humiliation of seeing her Arab protégés abjectly crushed and their Russian or Czech armaments destroyed or captured, Russia had gained immensely in the esteem of the Arab world. The most important of the Arab states looked to her as their prime friend among the great powers. France had salvaged something of her standing, but Britain and the United States, friends of Israel, were counted enemies of the Arabs. The Soviet Navy had the freedom of the Mediterranean, where it was now as much at home as the American Sixth Fleet. And not only the Mediterranean. Though the Suez Canal remained closed, Russian naval and commercial vessels were common sights in the Red Sea, the Gulf of Aden, the Indian Ocean, the Straits of Malacca, and so on to the Sea of Japan and home waters at Vladivostok. With Communist propaganda and sub-

33. The U.S.-Israeli plan was described by Benjamin Welles in the *New York Times,* October 8, 1970.
34. *New York Times,* September 13, 26, 1970.
35. *New York Times,* September 28, 1970.
36. *New York Times,* September 26, 1970. The charge was vigorously denied by the Soviet Union. Ibid., October 1, 14, 1970.
37. *New York Times,* September 27, 1970, Sec. 4, p. 15.

38. *New York Times,* October 24, 1970.
39. *New York Times,* December 7, 22, 29, 1970; January 1, 1971.

version played down, if not abandoned, Russia was behaving in Southern Asia like a "mercantile imperialist" power. In that capacity the U.S.S.R. seemed a formidable rival of the United States for successor to Britain's role in the area.[40]

40. Irving R. Levine, "The Mediterranean: The Sixth Fleet and the Russians," *The Atlantic,* February 1970; Welles Hangen, "The Russians in Asia," ibid., May 1970; T. B. Millar, "Soviet Policies South and East of Suez," *Foreign Affairs,* 49 (October 1970), 70–80. A desire to see the Suez Canal reopened may be one explanation for the Soviets' bolstering Egypt's defenses against the Israeli Air Force in the summer of 1970.

There was one portion of the world where the threat of Communism seemed insignificant in the early postwar period. The Western Hemisphere appeared dedicated to the ideals of human freedom and free enterprise. The governments of Latin America, too often undemocratic in practice, were still democratic in theory, and the trend, it was hoped, was toward an ever truer democracy. In the United Nations, Latin America habitually voted as a bloc with the United States. Hemispheric relations were still, presumably, governed by the Good Neighbor Policy, and the first three postwar years were marked by an elaboration of cooperative machinery to serve the inter-American system. In reality, however, that elaboration was accompanied by a deterioration in the cooperative spirit and in the degree of cordiality shown to the United States by its southern neighbors. Old-fashioned outcries against "Yankee imperialism" and "dollar diplomacy" were mingled with new complaints that Uncle Sam sent floods of dollars in every direction except southward. Governmental and financial instability, a low standard of living, and an unhealthy distribution of property and income combined to make parts of the region, within fifteen years after the war, a tempting field for exploitation by Communist agitators.

Formalizing the Inter-American System

Franklin Roosevelt's Good Neighbor Policy—essentially a negative policy of nonintervention in Latin American affairs—had exorcised for the time being much of the anti-Yankee prejudice in Latin America and had assured hemisphere support for the United States in World War II, with the exception of Argentina and, to a lesser degree, Chile. Its effect carried over for several years after the war, contributing to the acceptance of an inter-American collective security treaty, sponsored by the United States, and to the formalization of the hitherto loose inter-American system of treaties and understandings in the Charter of the Organization of American States (OAS).

48

The Western Hemisphere, I: Truman to Kennedy

The Inter-American Treaty of Mutual Assistance, signed at a conference at Rio de Janeiro on September 2, 1947, replaced a temporary agreement, the Act of Chapultepec, adopted at a wartime conference in Mexico City, February 15 to March 8, 1945. The delay of two and a half years in converting the act into a treaty was the consequence of an unfortunate quarrel between the United States and Argentina, going back to Argentina's pro-Axis sympathies during the war and culminating in an ill-conceived attempt by the United States to influence a postwar Argentine presidential election. The election was won by Juan D. Perón, the candidate whose alleged pro-Axis activities the State Department had exposed in a "Blue Book." Until the State Department changed hands from James F. Byrnes to George C. Marshall as Secretary, early in 1947, feeling between the two governments stood in the way of the proposed inter-American conference.[1]

The Rio Treaty was the first of a number of regional collective security agreements concluded by the United States in conformity with Article 51 of the Charter of the United Nations. It made it the duty of every American state to assist in meeting an armed attack upon another American state until the U.N. Security Council should have taken effective measures to repel the aggression. The nature of the action to be taken by the American states to meet such an armed attack was to be determined by a two-thirds vote of a meeting of Foreign Ministers called for the occasion (parties to the dispute not voting), with the proviso that no state should be required to use armed force without its consent. The treaty, following ratification by two-thirds of the signatories, went into force on December 3, 1948.[2]

The conference at Rio in 1947 was a special one. The next in the regular series, the Ninth International Conference of American States, met at Bogotá, Colombia, March 30 to May 2, 1948. Its principal achievement was to provide the Organization of American States for the first time with a charter or constitution. The Charter restated the "fundamental rights and duties of states" (including nonintervention), formulated and approved at conferences in the 1930's.[3] It named the organs of the organization and defined their powers and duties. As "supreme organ," the Inter-American Conference, meeting theoretically at five-year intervals, was replaced in 1970 by a General Assembly, meeting annually. Meetings of Foreign Ministers occur as needed. It is these meetings that determine, by a two-thirds vote, the action to be taken to repel aggression against an American state. The Council, consisting of one representative of each state, functions in Washington as an executive body; it may serve as a provisional "organ of consultation" pending a meeting of the Foreign Ministers. Operating under the direction of the Council are an Inter-American Council of Jurists, a Cultural Council, and an Economic and Social Council. The old Pan American Union became the Secretariat of the new Organization.[4]

Rifts Between Good Neighbors

The drafting and adoption of this elaborate Charter, which was ratified and went into effect in 1951, satisfied an American fondness for committing international agreements to paper, after the manner of the numerous arbitration and conciliation treaties and the Kellogg-Briand Pact, of earlier decades. It was

1. The real author of the intervention in Argentine politics was Spruille Braden, first as Ambassador to Argentina, then as Under Secretary of State. He resigned in June 1947. For Argentina's attitude during the war, see pp. 396, 397.

2. Text of treaty in *Documents on American Foreign Relations,* 9: 534–40.

3. See Chapter 35.

4. The Charter and a number of other agreements adopted at Bogotá are printed in *Documents on American Foreign Relations,* 10: 484–532. For the 1970 amendment to the Charter providing for General Assembly, see *Department of State Bulletin,* 62 (April 20, 1970), 529–30.

ironical that this paper work peak in inter-American relations came at a time when the spirit of those relations was deteriorating. Symptomatic of this trend was the temporary disruption of the Bogotá Conference in its second week by a violent outbreak of rioting in the Colombian capital. Whether or not Communist-inspired, as was charged, the riots were indicative of the widespread breakdown of orderly democratic processes in Latin America.

The Bogotá riots were symptomatic, too, of the revival of anti-Yankeeism which was making its appearance in many areas in Latin America. Never wholly extinguished, this resentment of the "Colossus of the North" had been overshadowed by the cordiality evoked by the Good Neighbor Policy. To Latin Americans, that policy had been identified with President Franklin Roosevelt. But Roosevelt was dead, and the policies followed by his successors, Presidents Truman and Eisenhower, brought many Latin Americans to the conclusion that the Good Neighbor Policy had died with him.

The truth was, not that the Good Neighbor Policy was dead, but that, in its strictly negative character, it no longer sufficed. The Latin Americans, like the peoples of other underdeveloped continents, were experiencing a postwar "revolution of rising expectations." They aspired to narrow the gap between their poverty (collectively speaking) and the affluence of the industrialized areas—Western Europe, North America, and now Japan. But the gap, instead of narrowing, was widening. Wartime prices of Latin America's raw materials—copper, tin, lead, petroleum, coffee—declined, while prices of their imported manufactures rose. Closing by the United States of wartime installations in such countries as Ecuador and Brazil worked economic disruption. Meanwhile, Latin Americans beheld their rich Uncle Sam dispatching billions of dollars in economic and military aid to Europe and the Far East, while they received little or nothing. They were not comforted by being told that the billions in aid were needed to combat the threat of Communism in Europe and Asia—a threat that supposedly did not exist in Latin America.[5]

What Latin Americans now demanded as the substance of good neighborliness was not simply the negative policy of nonintervention, important though that still was, but positive assistance in developing their economies and raising the standard of living of their rapidly growing population. This would involve such items as industrialization, improved transportation and agricultural techniques, and great advances in education in an area where illiteracy on the average was close to 50 percent. All of these things would require money in sums simply not available within the region. The Latin Americans, therefore, demanded two things of their good neighbor to the north: large-scale grants or loans on easy terms, preferably public, not private; and assistance in stabilizing at profitable levels the prices of their chief exports, especially coffee, metals, and petroleum.

To these proposed supplements to the Good Neighbor Policy, the United States reacted at first very negatively. While wholly in sympathy with the desire for industrialization, Washington spokesmen insisted that it should be accomplished chiefly through private investment and that the Latin American governments must attract private capital by offering it improved security—against nationalization, for example. This insistence on the paramount role of private investments as an agent of industrialization ran counter to a widespread Latin American antagonism to foreign private capital as exploitative and "imperialistic"—a prejudice which had some basis in past experience and was now itself exploited by the Communist apparatus, both native and imported. As to stabilization, the United States, itself involved in costly price guarantees to

5. Donald M. Dozer, *Are We Good Neighbors? Three Decades of Inter-American Relations* (Gainesville, Fla.: University of Florida Press, 1959), chaps. 6–10, gives a detailed analysis of the deterioration in the relations of the United States with its neighbors to the south.

American farmers, was unwilling to extend the operation into the international arena.

Beginning early in the Eisenhower administration (1953–1961), the United States gradually modified its position on both issues and eventually, under Kennedy in 1961, embarked upon an ambitious program of economic development and social reform for Latin America as a whole—the Alliance for Progress. This change in attitude owed something to altruistic humanitarian sentiment but most to a realization that an unhappy and resentful Latin America brought the threat of Communism to the doorstep of the United States.

The Communist Threat Comes Nearer

In its concern over the threat of Communism in Europe and Asia, the United States government had largely ignored conditions in Latin America which offered a favorable climate for Communist agitators. In a society which comprised a small but powerful upper class, or elite, a middle class insignificant in numbers and influence, and "a horde of uneducated 'have-nots,' a melancholy sea of misery," the need for economic and social reform was imperative. Unless this need could be met within the existing governmental framework, Communism would have a well-nigh irresistible appeal.

In his first year of office (1953), President Eisenhower, aware of the deteriorating relations between the United States and Latin America, sent his brother, Dr. Milton Eisenhower, as head of a mission to the ten republics of South America. The mission recommended certain modest measures for stabilization of prices, expansion of technical assistance (Point IV), encouragement of private investment, and carefully restricted public loans,[6] but more dramatic happenings were

needed to alert this conservative administration to the urgency of the situation.

The first such incident was the adoption of a Communist line, in both domestic policy and in alignment with the Soviet Union in the United Nations, by the administration of President Jacobo Arbenz Guzmán (1951–1954) in Guatemala. Any Communist beachhead in the Americas, no matter how small, seemed to Secretary of State John Foster Dulles not only a violation of the principles of the Monroe Doctrine but an actual threat to the security of the United States and its sister republics. At the Tenth International Conference of American States, meeting in Caracas, Venezuela in March 1954, Dulles secured the adoption of a declaration which, without naming Guatemala, condemned "the domination or control of the political institutions of any American state by the international Communist movement," and declared that such a situation would be ground for a meeting of consultation of Foreign Ministers "to consider the adoption of appropriate action in accordance with existing treaties."[7]

Whether Dulles could have persuaded two-thirds of the American Foreign Ministers to vote for intervention in Guatemala can only be conjectured. Such an effort was made unnecessary when Arbenz was overthrown in June 1954 by a fellow Guatemalan, Colonel Carlos Castillo Armas, assisted with American

---

6. *United States-Latin American Relations: Report to the President,* by M. S. Eisenhower, Special Ambassador, November 18, 1953, Department of State Publication 5290 (Washington: Government Printing Office, 1953). The current economic importance of Latin America to the United States is suggested by figures given in a *New York Times* editorial of November 22, 1954. Latin America furnished in 1953 one-third ($3,400,000,000) of United States imports and took over one-fifth ($2,900,000,000) of United States exports. Many of the imported commodities, such as tin, copper, lead, zinc, vanadium, petroleum, and sugar are vital to the United States economy. Latin America also surpassed any other single area in the amount of United States investments—about $6 billion.

7. *Documents on American Foreign Relations, 1954,* pp. 412–14. Many delegations at the Conference were reluctant to adopt a declaration that suggested a policy of intervention in the affairs of a sister republic. The vote was 17 to 1, Guatemala voting no, Mexico and Argentina abstaining. Costa Rica, not represented at the Conference, later indicated its concurrence in the declaration.

arms and planes, allegedly by the Central Intelligence Agency.[8]

If the brief apparition of Communist power in Guatemala shocked the Eisenhower administration, a perhaps ruder shock was the series of violent demonstrations that assailed Vice President Richard M. Nixon during his tour of South America in the spring of 1958. Nixon departed for South America on April 27, 1958, announcing that the purpose of his trip was to demonstrate "that these countries are not only our neighbors but our best friends." His reception varied from country to country, but in Lima, Peru, and Caracas, Venezuela, he was assailed by angry mobs. In Caracas, his life and that of Mrs. Nixon were in serious danger.[9] Upon his return to Washington, Nixon attributed his hostile reception in part to Communist agitation but in part also to a widespread popular impression that the United States government had shown itself too friendly to dictatorial regimes in Latin America. A relevant instance was the fact that Marcos Pérez Jiménez, the recently ousted dictator of Venezuela, was at that very moment enjoying a safe and comfortable asylum in the United States. As one aspect of its policy

of nonintervention, indeed, the United States had customarily made no distinction between dictatorial and democratic governments in its official relations with them. Nixon proposed no abandonment of the nonintervention policy, but he suggested that at least the United States might "have an 'abrazo' [embrace] for democratic leaders, and a formal handshake for dictators." This suggestion was endorsed by Dr. Milton Eisenhower, who in July 1958 made a good will and fact-finding tour of Central America.[10]

Fidel Castro's Revolution

One of the dictators with whom the United States was thought to have been too friendly was Fulgencio Batista, the one-time army sergeant who had seized power in Cuba in 1933 and had exercised it ever since, whether in or out of the presidential palace. In later years his regime had become "a cruel and corrupt dictatorship" and had grown increasingly unpopular. Consequently, when Fidel Castro, hitherto unknown in politics, launched his armed rebellion against Batista, the so-called 26th of July Movement, he quickly gathered popular support. Whatever may have been Castro's secret purposes, his movement in its days of struggle was neither Communist nor Communist-supported, and it elicited considerable friendly unofficial attention in the United States.[11]

The Washington government had maintained friendly relations with Batista and had supplied him, like certain other Latin American governments, with military equipment and advisers under the Mutual Security program. It now adhered to its policy of nonintervention with respect to Cuba. But inasmuch as it was making exertions to prevent clandestine aid from going to Castro, it termi-

8. *U.S. in World Affairs, 1954,* pp. 380–90; Dwight D. Eisenhower, *The White House Years: Mandate for Change, 1953–1956* (Garden City, N.Y.: Doubleday & Company, Inc., 1963), pp. 420–27; Philip B. Taylor, Jr., "The Guatemalan Affair: A Critique of United States Foreign Policy," *American Political Science Review,* 50 (September 1956), 787–806. Arbenz had appealed to the U.N. Security Council, charging aggression by Honduras and Nicaragua. The Soviet Union vetoed a proposal to refer the matter to the OAS. The Inter-American Peace Committee of the OAS, however, was preparing to investigate Arbenz' complaint when his government fell.

The Soviet Union and its European satellites were at this time expanding their trade with Latin America, which grew by 34 percent in 1955 alone. The U.S.S.R. was also advertising its desire for closer economic and cultural ties with the area and its willingness to provide technical assistance and advice—a Soviet counterpart of Point IV. *U.S. in World Affairs, 1956,* pp. 223–24.

9. Earl Mazo, *Richard Nixon: A Political and Personal Portrait* (New York: Harper & Row, Publishers, 1959), chaps. 13, 14; Richard M. Nixon, *Six Crises* (Garden City, N.Y.: Doubleday & Company, Inc., 1962), pp. 183–234.

10. *U.S. in World Affairs, 1958,* p. 371; *Documents on American Foreign Relations, 1958,* p. 510.

11. H. L. Matthews, *The Cuban Story* (New York: George Braziller, Inc., 1961); Theodore Draper, *Castro's Revolution: Myths and Realities* (New York: Praeger Publishers, Inc., 1962).

nated, in March 1958, the shipment of arms to the Cuban government, but did not withdraw a military training mission stationed in Cuba. Castro's rebellion gathered momentum throughout 1958, and on New Year's Day, 1959, Batista boarded a plane for the Dominican Republic, leaving the field to the bearded revolutionist.

Space does not permit a detailed catalogue of the steps by which Castro transformed his revolutionary regime into one frankly Communist and affiliated with the Communist bloc in Europe and Asia. It is enough to say here that early promises of free elections and a free press were repudiated; that foreign property (including United States property approximating $1 billion in value) was nationalized without provision for compensation; that Communists, notably Fidel's brother, Raúl Castro, and Ernesto (Ché) Guevara, gradually replaced moderates in Castro's entourage; and that large-scale economic aid and military equipment and promises of armed support were forthcoming from the Soviet Union and its satellites. Cuba, furthermore, became a center for Communist propaganda directed at the remainder of Latin America and a training school for Latin American revolutionists. Castro, who had based his 26th of July Movement in the Sierra Maestra Mountains of eastern Cuba, boasted that he would cast the Andes in a similar revolutionary role for South America.[12]

In view of the anti-Communist declaration adopted by the OAS at Caracas in 1954, the Eisenhower administration might have expected OAS support in combating Communism in Cuba. But two meetings of American Foreign Ministers, in Santiago, Chile, in August 1959, and in San José, Costa Rica, a year later, produced only inconclusive results. Though the Foreign Ministers at San José did not hesitate to call for a break in relations with the rightist dictatorship of Rafael Trujillo in the Dominican Republic, they refused to mention Castro or Cuba by name, merely condemning intervention in the Americas by

an outside power and rejecting any Sino-Soviet attempt to exploit a troubled situation in any American state.[13] In general, at this time and later, the states bordering on the Caribbean were ready for strong action against Castro, while Mexico and the larger South American republics avoided action that would antagonize his regime or offend pro-Castro minorities within their borders.

The United States, therefore, could take only unilateral action against Castro in retaliation for the latter's wholesale confiscation of American property and his continued abuse of the United States in his interminable speeches in Cuba and in his complaints in the United Nations. On July 6, 1960, President Eisenhower canceled about 95 percent of Cuba's remaining quota of sugar imports for the year. Some months later the United States canceled entirely the Cuban sugar quota for the first quarter of 1961; it also placed an embargo on all shipments to Cuba except foodstuffs, medicines, and medical supplies. On January 3, 1961, the President terminated all diplomatic and consular relations with the Cuban government. This was the American reply to a sudden Cuban order limiting the United States embassy staff in Havana to eleven persons and requiring all others to leave the island within forty-eight hours. The Swiss embassy in Havana assumed responsibility for American interests. A few days later, January 20, Eisenhower handed the Cuban problem over to John F. Kennedy.[14]

A "New Deal" for Latin America

Before bowing out, however, the Eisenhower administration had begun to yield to several long-cherished desires of the Latin Americans, hoping thereby to restore the atmosphere of

12. *U.S. in World Affairs, 1960,* p. 331.

13. *U.S. in World Affairs, 1960,* pp. 308–15; *Documents on American Foreign Relations, 1960,* pp. 516–18.
14. It became known later that the Eisenhower administration had sponsored the training of Cuban exiles for an attempt to overthrow Castro. This was the origin of the Bay of Pigs invasion, described below.

good neighborliness and thus to counteract the appeal of *Fidelismo* outside of Cuba. In 1958, following Nixon's ill-fated good will tour, the United States had shown an increased willingness to consider measures for combating fluctuations in the prices of raw materials; it had at long last accepted the proposal for an inter-American lending institution, or bank, to which it would be the principal contributor. It had, indeed, given the impression that it was ready to sponsor a "new deal" for Latin America as a whole; and it had sought to correct the supposition that it showed special consideration to dictators.[15]

The charter for the new Inter-American Development Bank was drawn up and approved during 1959, and the Bank began operations in Washington in October 1960. It would have an eventual lending capacity of $1 billion, of which $450 million would be subscribed by the United States. The United States, meanwhile, was supporting the efforts of the coffee-producing states to stabilize prices by limiting exports; it was looking with favor upon a plan for a free trade area embracing Mexico and several South American states and was lending assistance to a common market already functioning in Central America.

On July 11, 1960, President Eisenhower (who earlier in the year had paid a good will visit to several South American countries) announced a new program of aid for Latin America, which, unlike earlier programs, would emphasize meeting the human needs of the "bulk of the population." A month later he asked Congress to authorize the expenditure for this purpose of $600 million. One hundred million of this sum was intended for Chile, which had suffered a devastating earthquake. The remainder, as Secretary of State Herter explained, would be expended for "projects designed to contribute to opportunities for a better way of life for the individual citizens of the countries of Latin

America."[16] Congress promptly (though without enthusiasm) passed the authorization, and this measure gave a sense of reality to a program adopted at Bogotá in September by a Committee of Twenty-one, representing all the American republics. The "Act of Bogotá" envisaged a variety of social reforms, to be undertaken in the respective countries, with United States backing, in such fields as land-tenure and utilization, housing, taxation, education, and public health.[17] The program was termed "Operation Pan America" after a proposal along similar lines recently put forward by President Juscelino Kubitschek of Brazil.

The Alliance for Progress

"Operation Pan America," thus launched in the closing months of the Eisenhower administration, was taken over by President Kennedy and incorporated in his Alliance for Progress (*Alianza para el Progreso*). First suggested in his Inaugural Address, the plan was elaborated in an address to the Latin American diplomatic corps in Washington at a White House reception, March 13, 1961. Referring to the revolutions that had gained independence for the United States and its southern neighbors, the President declared:

> Our hemisphere's mission is not yet completed. *For one unfulfilled task is to demonstrate to the entire world that man's unsatisfied aspiration for economic progress and social justice can best be achieved by free men working within a framework of democratic institutions.*[18]

15. *U.S. in World Affairs, 1958,* pp. 350–71; good summary in ibid., *1959,* pp. 351–52.

16. *U.S. in World Affairs, 1960,* pp. 318–19; *Documents on American Foreign Relations, 1960,* pp. 50–51, 528–31.

17. *U.S. in World Affairs, 1960,* pp. 319–20; *Documents on American Foreign Relations, 1960,* pp. 539–46.

18. *Documents on American Foreign Relations, 1961,* p. 396. Italics in original. The entire address and the President's message to Congress on March 14 are in ibid., pp. 395–408. See also Milton S. Eisenhower, *The Wine is Bitter: The United States and Latin America* (Garden City, N.Y.: Doubleday & Company, Inc., 1963), pp. 302–9.

What the President was proposing was a ten-year plan of economic development and social progress and reform. "Only the most determined efforts of the American nations themselves can bring success to this effort," he commented; but if the Latin American countries would do their part, the United States "should help provide resources of a scope and magnitude sufficient to make this bold development plan a success," as it had done for Europe under the Marshall Plan. He mentioned no figures, but Treasury Secretary Douglas Dillon, speaking at an Inter-American Economic and Social Conference at Punta del Este, Uruguay, in August, estimated that at least $20 billion would be available from outside sources—North America, Europe, Japan—during the next decade, most of it from public agencies. The annual rate of economic growth required to meet the objectives of the Alliance was estimated by Dillon at 2.5 percent per capita, which meant, allowing for Latin America's "population explosion," a gross annual increase of 5 percent.[19]

The delegations at Punta del Este adopted a Charter defining the aims and procedures of the Alliance for Progress and a "Declaration to the Peoples of America," both signed August 17, 1961. The Declaration described the Alliance for Progress as "a vast effort to bring a better life to all the peoples of the Continent." The United States pledged itself to provide "a major part of the twenty billion dollars, principally in public funds," which Latin America would require from external sources over the next decade to supplement its own efforts.[20] Cuba was represented at Punta del Este by its leading Communist theoretician, Ernesto (Ché) Guevara. He did not sign the Charter, however, and Secretary Dillon made it clear that Cuba would receive no share of aid from the United States so long as it remained under Communist rule.

After being introduced with much fanfare,

the Alliance for Progress got off to a disappointingly slow start. Two years after its inauguration at Punta del Este, the United States had committed a total of $2,180,000,000 to the program and had disbursed over $1,500,000,000. These sums had been expended largely for such items as residential housing, hospitals, water systems, schools, textbooks, agricultural loans, and the like. This was all right as far as it went, but it made small contribution to the self-sustaining economic growth on which the long-run success of the program would depend. Private capital, essential to the success of the program, was being frightened away rather than attracted by threats of nationalization and cancellation of contracts. Reforms in landholding and taxation had been endorsed by a number of governments but their implementation was encountering powerful opposition.

As a means of promoting political democracy in the Western Hemisphere, the Alliance for Progress had been even more disappointing than in its economic and social role. Between the inauguration of the Alliance and the fall of 1963, six elected governments in Latin America had been overthrown or set aside by military juntas. In two of these countries—Argentina and Peru—the military juntas had permitted fair elections, which had resulted in the choice of reform-minded governments. The crushing defeat of the *Perónistas* in the Argentine election of July 7, 1963, was especially gratifying. But in the Dominican Republic and Honduras the revolutions of September 25 and October 3, 1963, respectively, were very discouraging to the United States. In both, the ousted presidents had been dedicated to the ideals of the Alliance for Progress; and in the Dominican Republic, President Juan Bosch, who had been chosen after the assassination of the long-time dictator, Rafael Trujillo, had become in American eyes a symbol of democratic progress. The United States responded to the revolutions in the Dominican Republic and Honduras by recalling its ambassadors and suspending all foreign aid.

19. *Documents on American Foreign Relations, 1961,* pp. 408–16; *U.S. in World Affairs, 1961,* pp. 326–32.
20. *Documents on American Foreign Relations, 1961,* pp. 416–35.

Within less than two months after these events, President Kennedy was dead and direction of the American participation in the Alliance for Progress passed to other hands.[21]

The Bay of Pigs

Between President Kennedy's announcement of the Alliance for Progress and the Conference at Punta del Este, Cuban exiles had made a disastrous attempt to land on the island and spearhead an armed rebellion against Castro's government. Unwilling itself to make war upon Castro, the United States government hoped to see him eliminated by the people of Cuba. Since March 1960 it had supplied training and equipment to several hundred Cuban refugees, some in the United States, more in Guatemala or elsewhere in Central America. Rumors of impending invasion gained credibility when the State Department, April 3, released a pamphlet entitled "Cuba." This document told the story of Castro's betrayal of his own revolution and his conversion of Cuba into a beachhead for Communism, "a fateful challenge to the inter-American system." Questioned at his press conference, April 12, President Kennedy denied categorically that there would be "an intervention in Cuba by United States armed forces." [22]

In the early hours of April 17, 1961, Cuban refugees numbering probably between 1,500 and 2,000 landed at Bahía de Cochinos (Bay of Pigs) on Cuba's southern coast. Here, in the absence of United States air support (which some of the exiles thought they had been promised), they were quickly overwhelmed by Castro's regular troops and militia, and were made prisoners to the number of 1,241. The expected popular uprising on the island had not occurred. The invasion was a fiasco and one very embarrassing to the United States, which had secretly sponsored it.[23]

To a message from Premier Khrushchev, threatening all-out war if the United States should invade Cuba, President Kennedy replied that the United States intended no military invasion of Cuba, but added: "In the event of any military intervention by outside force we will immediately honor our obligations under the inter-American system to protect this hemisphere against external aggression." Speaking a few days later to the American Society of Newspaper Editors, the President declared that the United States did not intend to abandon Cuba to the Communists. He again disclaimed, however, any intention of unilateral action by the United States. But, alluding to the nonintervention principle accepted by the American republics, he remarked that American restraint was not inexhaustible.

> Should it ever appear [he continued] that the inter-American doctrine of noninterference merely conceals or excuses a policy of nonaction—if the nations of this hemisphere should fail to meet their commitments against outside Communist penetration—then I want it clearly understood that this Government will not hesitate in meeting its primary obligations, which are to the security of our Nation.[24]

As for Fidel Castro, he was strengthened and emboldened by his success in crushing the invasion and by the resulting wholesale arrests of Cubans suspected of disloyalty to his regime. He quickly dispelled any doubt that may have remained about his commitment to Communism. On May 1 he proclaimed that Cuba was now a "socialist" state. Some months later he boasted that he was and would always remain a devotee of Marxism-Leninism.

---

21. See Chapter 49 for later developments in the Alliance for Progress.
22. The pamphlet, "Cuba," and Kennedy's statement of April 12 are reprinted in *Documents on American Foreign Relations, 1961*, pp. 438–55.

23. *U.S. in World Affairs, 1961*, pp. 308–20; Stuart Novins, "The Invasion That Could Not Succeed," *The Reporter*, May 11, 1961; Charles J. V. Murphy, "Cuba: The Record Set Straight," *Fortune*, September 1961.
24. *Documents on American Foreign Relations, 1961*, pp. 456–58, 67.

In the meantime, he announced that there would be no need of elections in Cuba, merged his 26th of July Movement with the Popular Socialist (Communist) Party, thereby making Cuba a one-party state, brought education under full state control, and took steps to curb the activities of the Catholic Church. In the following February (1962) he called for a continental civil war to enthrone Communism in all Latin America.[25]

The earlier of these activities aroused new apprehensions among Cuba's Latin neighbors and led to proposals from Peru and Colombia for a new meeting of American Foreign Ministers. With the reluctant acquiescence of Mexico and the larger South American republics, such a meeting was called, to take place at Punta del Este, January 22, 1962. The decisions of this conference were more cheering for the United States than had been those at Santiago and San José. Though the larger Latin states, with their vocal pro-Castro minorities, still resisted drastic action against Cuba, they all joined in unanimous votes (except Cuba's) declaring that the principles of Communism were incompatible with the principles of the inter-American system, and excluding the Communist government of Cuba from membership in the Inter-American Defense Board. By a vote of 16 to 1, with 4 abstentions (Mexico, Ecuador, Brazil, Chile), the conference ordered immediate suspension of trade with Cuba in arms and implements of war. By a vote of 14 to 1, with 6 abstentions (the 4 above plus Argentina and Bolivia), it excluded the Cuban government from participation in any of the organs of the OAS.[26] A beginning had been made toward collective OAS action against Communism in Cuba, but still opposed to any drastic measures were governments representing two-thirds of the

area and seven-tenths of the population of Latin America.[27]

Russian Missiles in Cuba

On the evening of Monday, October 22, 1962, President Kennedy made a startling and dramatic disclosure to the American people and to the world. Within the past week, he reported, unmistakable evidence had established the fact that a series of Soviet missile sites was in preparation on the island of Cuba. Their purpose, he explained, could be "none other than to provide a nuclear strike capability against the Western Hemisphere." Some of the sites were designed for medium-range ballistic missiles with a range of over a thousand miles—capable of reaching Washington, D.C., Cape Canaveral, the Panama Canal, or Mexico City. Other sites, not yet completed, appeared to be designed for intermediate-range missiles with a capability of reaching as far as Hudson's Bay to the north or Lima, Peru, to the south.[28]

Since the previous July, American reconnaissance had noted a heavy flow of traffic into Cuba in Russian ships. Cuban refugee sources and American secret agents in Cuba had reported construction of missile sites and John A. McCone, Director of the CIA, was convinced that these were designed for missiles of at least medium range. He urged as early as August 10 that this opinion be reported to the President, but during his prolonged absence in Europe his deputy clung to the theory that the sites were designed only for defensive surface-to-air (SAM) missiles, and administration officials repeatedly assured anxious inquirers that such was the case. Lower-level CIA officers became so alarmed at the complacency in the administration that they leaked their telltale information to a trusted reporter, Nat S. Finney of the *Buffalo Eve-*

25. *U.S. in World Affairs, 1961,* pp. 319–20, 341; *New York Times,* December 3, 1961; Adolf A. Berle, *Latin America: Diplomacy and Reality* (New York: Harper & Row, Publishers, for Council on Foreign Relations, 1962), pp. 102–3, 118; Draper, *Castro's Revolution,* esp. pp. 120–56.
26. Berle, *Latin America,* pp. 99–104; *New York Times,* February 1, 1962.

27. *New York Times,* February 4, 1962, Sec. 4, p. 1.
28. *Documents on American Foreign Relations, 1962,* pp. 374–80. A blow-by-blow account of the crisis was published in the *New York Times,* November 3, 1962.

ning News, who published a story on the subject on August 29.[29] Yet not until early October were orders given for high-level aerial photographic inspection of western Cuba, and not until Sunday, October 14, did American cameras obtain clear shots of missile sites near Cristobal in western Cuba; and not until the following Tuesday morning was the processing and analysis of the photographs completed. Then their evidence was convincing.

There followed a week of intense and almost continuous consultations among the President's top-level advisers, with the President himself sitting in from time to time. In order to avoid the appearance of a crisis, the President kept his regular appointments, including several speaking engagements in other cities. He canceled the last of these and returned to Washington on Saturday, October 20, with the fictitious explanation that he was suffering from a respiratory infection and a fever. His advisers—in effect an executive committee of the National Security Council—had meantime discarded proposals for an invasion of Cuba or an air strike against the missile installations, at least until less drastic measures had been tried. They recommended instead a selective blockade of the island, to prevent the importation of further weapons. This recommendation was accepted by the President and by Monday had been determined upon as the policy to be followed. But

since it might lead to outright hostilities, air and ground forces as well as naval vessels were mobilized and moved into appropriate strategic locations.

The President had resolved that the United States should act unilaterally, since time was precious and an appeal for collective action by the U.N. or the OAS was certain to lead to prolonged debate. Great care was taken, however, to brief all the allies of the United States, and the unaligned nations as well, upon the proposed action in the last hours before the President's address on Monday night. The response from both European and American allies was gratifying.

In his address, after describing the presence of the missiles as "an explicit threat to the peace and security of the Americas" and denouncing the "cloak of secrecy and deception" under which they had been spirited into Cuba, the President voiced a grave warning to Chairman Khrushchev. The United States, he said, would "regard any nuclear missile launched from Cuba against any nation in the Western Hemisphere as an attack by the Soviet Union on the United States requiring a full retaliatory response upon the Soviet Union." Let Chairman Khrushchev, he urged, "halt and eliminate this clandestine, reckless and provocative threat to world peace and to stable relations between our two nations." Meanwhile, said the President, he would initiate "a strict quarantine on all offensive military equipment under shipment to Cuba"; he would continue and increase "surveillance of Cuba and its military build-up"; he had already reinforced the United States naval base at Guantanamo and evacuated dependents of personnel stationed there. Finally, both the OAS and the U.N. would be asked to take or support action against this Soviet threat to the peace.

The blockade, or "quarantine," was to go into effect on Wednesday morning. On Tuesday Secretary of State Rusk convened the Council of the OAS and, surprisingly in view of past attitudes, secured a vote of 19 to 0 (the Uruguayan ambassador having no in-

29. Arthur Krock, *Memoirs: Sixty Years on the Firing Line* (New York, Funk & Wagnalls, 1968), pp. 377–80. Nat S. Finney in the *Buffalo Evening News,* August 29, 1962; November 23, 1968. Senator Kenneth F. Keating of New York, with information gained through a tip from Finney, raised the alarm in the Senate weeks before Kennedy's revelation. Yet the administration continued to give assurances that the weapons were defensive only. See also R. F. Kennedy, *Thirteen Days: A Memoir of the Cuban Missile Crisis* (New York: W. W. Norton and Company, Inc., 1969); A. M. Schlesinger, Jr., *A Thousand Days: John F. Kennedy in the White House* (Boston: Houghton Mifflin Co., 1965), pp. 795–830; Roger Hilsman, *To Move a Nation: The Politics of Foreign Policy in the Administration of John F. Kennedy* (Garden City, N.Y.: Doubleday & Company, Inc., 1967), pp. 159–229.

structions) in support of the American position. The resolution adopted called for "the immediate dismantling and withdrawal from Cuba of all missiles and other weapons with any offensive capability," and recommended that the member states, individually and collectively, take all necessary measures, including use of armed force, to prevent the further arming of Cuba by the Sino-Soviet powers, "and to prevent the missiles in Cuba with offensive capability from ever becoming an active threat to the peace and security of the continent." This unanimous endorsement by the OAS of the blockade of Cuba was given under authority of the Rio Treaty of Reciprocal Assistance of 1947. The State Department's experts on international law maintained that it provided sufficient legal basis for the blockade.[30]

The world now seemed to stand at the brink of nuclear war. The United States, backed by the OAS and its major European allies, had reacted with great firmness to an unexpected threat to its security and that of the hemisphere. It was the Russians who retreated, with some assistance from Secretary General U Thant of the United Nations. They did not challenge the blockade. Some Russian ships en route to Cuba voluntarily turned back. Others, ascertained to carry inoffensive cargoes, were allowed to proceed. In a series of exchanges with the President, lasting until Sunday, October 28, Chairman Khrushchev agreed to withdraw the missiles and also some thirty Russian long-range bombing planes that had been detected in Cuba, and to see to the dismantling of the missile sites. In return for these concessions, whose implementation was to be subject to international inspection, Kennedy promised that the United States would

not invade Cuba. But since Castro vetoed any international inspection, it could hardly be argued that Kennedy's promise was binding.[31]

The United States government, however, believed it had satisfactory evidence that the missiles and bombers were removed and the sites dismantled according to promise. It disclaimed, on its part, any intention of invading Cuba and took effective steps to discourage hit-and-run raids from American territory by Cuban refugees.

In any event, Russian troops and technicians remained in Cuba after missiles and bombers had been removed. Their number at the end of March 1963 was estimated at from 13,000 to 40,000. By the end of the year some estimates placed the number as low as 5,000 to 8,000. Cuba remained a Communist state under Soviet protection, and a training center and base for Communists operating elsewhere in the hemisphere. The situation was precisely of the kind that James Monroe had described in 1823 when he wrote that we should consider any attempt of the European powers "to extend their system to any portion of this hemisphere as dangerous to our peace and safety." Though Khrushchev had backed away from the most provocative aspects of his intervention in Cuba, it was hard to deny that he had successfully defied the Monroe Doctrine.[32]

30. *Documents on American Foreign Relations, 1962,* pp. 380–83.

31. *Documents on American Foreign Relations, 1962,* pp. 390–403. At one stage in the correspondence, Khrushchev proposed that the United States remove its missiles from Turkey in return for the removal of Russian missiles from Cuba, but did not press the point. The United States did, as a matter of fact, later abandon its missile bases in both Turkey and Italy, substituting Polaris submarines in the Mediterranean, but Kennedy had ordered them abandoned before the crisis.

32. In 1960 Khrushchev had declared that the Monroe Doctrine had "outlived its time" and "should best be buried as every dead body is." *New York Times,* July 13, 1960.

A year and a month after President Kennedy's dramatic announcement of the missile peril in Cuba, Kennedy died from an assassin's bullet, and Lyndon B. Johnson became President. Johnson promptly made clear his intention to follow the Kennedy policies, toward Latin America as elsewhere. Speaking on November 26, 1963, to the Latin American delegates in Washington for the Kennedy funeral, Johnson listed four principles constituting the essence of the Alliance for Progress. They were, in abbreviated form: nonintervention, human freedom (including participation in democratic government), social justice, and economic progress. The United States, Johnson assured his audience, would carry out its commitments under the Alliance.[1] In the Alliance for Progress and in relations with Castro's Cuba, Johnson's problems and policies were, with important variations, extensions of Kennedy's. In Panama and the Dominican Republic he faced new crises.

A New Crisis in Panama

Johnson had been in office only six weeks when he was confronted with a crisis in relations with the Republic of Panama. Panamanians had long resented the presence of Americans in the Canal Zone, with their high rates of pay, their continental standard of living, and the exercise by the United States of the substance of sovereign rights,[2] as a form of "colonialism." Nasser's nationalization of the Suez Canal had undoubtedly suggested a similar possibility here (though the situations were quite different), but the immediate cause of the trouble was a student quarrel over rival flags at a high school just inside the Zone. Presidents Eisenhower and Kennedy had consented to the flying of the flag of Panama beside that of the United States in the Zone as a symbol of the "residual sovereignty" of Panama. A lowering and alleged defilement of the Panama flag by angry American students

49

The Western Hemisphere, II: Johnson and Nixon

1. *Documents on American Foreign Relations, 1963*, p. 422.
2. See p. 216.

(January 9, 1964) led to an attempted invasion of the Zone by a Panamanian mob, their repulse by the American troops, and the death of three Americans and an unknown number of Panamanians in the melée.

It was difficult to place the blame for the brawl and the resulting deaths, but President Roberto Chiari of Panama broke off diplomatic relations with Washington, denounced the United States as an aggressor, and appealed for redress to both the U.N. Security Council and the OAS. A committee of the OAS undertook to mediate the dispute. After a period of semantic difficulty—Johnson would agree to *discuss* all matters in controversy but would not promise to *renegotiate* the existing treaty, as Chiari demanded, under pressure—a formula acceptable to both parties was found, and diplomatic relations were restored on April 4, 1964.[3]

In the following December, President Johnson revealed a plan for a new, sea level canal which might be constructed at any one of four sites, two in Panama, one in Nicaragua, and one in Colombia. The United States, said the President, was ready to negotiate a new treaty with Panama, which would (a) recognize the sovereignty of Panama in the Canal Zone, (b) provide for its own termination upon the opening of the new canal, and (c) provide for the effective discharge by the two states of their common responsibilities for hemisphere defense. Pending the conclusion of such a treaty, the existing treaties would continue in effect.[4]

Negotiations with the government of Panama under the new President, Marco A. Robles, proceeded slowly, but in June 1967, it was reported that three new treaties had been concluded. Though the texts were not made public, for fear of repercussions in a highly charged political atmosphere in Panama, it was understood that the treaties, though recognizing Panama's sovereignty in the Zone and giving her a voice in running the canal, would retain essential control for the United States; also that they provided for retention of United States bases in Panama.[5] Since some of these provisions seemed sure to provoke opposition in Panama (and others, in the U.S. Senate), President Robles apparently thought best not to submit them to the Panama National Assembly until after the next election, scheduled for May 12, 1968. Before that event, Panamanian politics became chaotic. The coalition of parties that had supported Robles broke apart; the National Assembly impeached Robles and declared him removed from office, but Robles held on, backed by the National Guard. Finally, the opposition candidate, Arnulfo Arias, a critic of the treaties, won the election on May 12, 1968. Inagurated on October 1, he was overthrown by officers of the National Guard after eleven days in office.[6]

Two National Guard officers formed a junta to serve as the government of Panama. One of them, Brigadier General Omar Torrijos, emerged as the "strong man" after an attempt by his aides to overthrow him in December 1969. He announced that he would name a civilian group to take over the presidential functions.[7]

An earlier intimation from the junta that they would welcome a renegotiation of the new canal treaties had been ignored by Washington, and on September 1, 1970, it was reported that the Panamanian government had notified the United States that the draft treaties were not acceptable even as a basis for renewing negotiation. An apparent impasse had been reached. Meanwhile, the treaty of 1903, as modified in 1936, remained in force, objectionable to Panama though it was.[8]

3. *U.S. in World Affairs, 1964,* pp. 226–34. The fact that presidential elections were pending in both the United States and Panama made concessions politically difficult for both presidents.

4. *Documents on American Foreign Relations, 1964,* pp. 312–14.

5. *New York Times,* June 27, 1967.

6. *New York Times,* December 2, 1967; March 25, May 31, October 13, 1968.

7. *New York Times,* December 16, 17, 19, 1969.

8. *New York Times,* September 2, 1969; September 3, 1970. See above, pp. 216, 353.

Intervention in the Dominican Republic

Johnson's handling of the Panama crisis had been, on the whole, considerate and tactful and had been well received in Latin America. Quite different was the reception of his intervention in the Dominican Republic in the spring of 1965. Here, it seems certain, he overreacted to a danger that was at least partly imaginary. In doing so, he violated the most basic principle of the Good Neighbor Policy, now solemnly incorporated in the OAS Charter, and although he extracted perfunctory support from a majority of the Latin American governments, his action produced, in the words of the *New York Times* (July 22, 1965) "a division of opinion between the United States and most of Latin America such as has rarely if ever existed in the last thirty years."

The Kennedy administration, it will be recalled, had deplored the overthrow, in September 1963, of Juan Bosch, the democratically elected President of the Dominican Republic, and had withheld recognition from the military-backed junta that replaced him. Kennedy's successor restored relations with the junta, headed by Donald Reid Cabral, and attempted to strengthen it with liberal grants of economic aid. The Reid Cabral government, nevertheless, soon found itself in economic difficulties. Its austerity measures, especially a cutting of military expenses, provoked a revolt, on April 24, 1965, by a group of young officers. They were promptly joined by the leaders of Bosch's Dominican Revolutionary Party. Designating themselves "constitutionalists," they organized a provisional government and proclaimed that their object was to restore Bosch to the presidency.

President Reid resigned, but a group of older officers, headed by Brigadier General Elias Wessin y Wessin, a strong anti-Communist, deployed their tanks and planes in opposition to the revolution. They were encouraged to do so, it seems clear, by local U.S. representatives—the chargé d'affaires and military attachés—the U.S. Ambassador being temporarily away from his post. The Embassy also had a hand in organizing a three-man military junta, headed by a Colonel Benoit, which undertook to function as a counterrevolutionary government. When the junta, facing probable defeat, requested U.S. intervention, they were told that the United States would intervene only for the purpose of protecting the lives of American citizens. Thereupon the Benoit junta made a new request, affirming that it was unable to guarantee protection to American citizens, of whom there were a thousand or more in the country, as well as other foreign nationals.

Upon receiving this revised request, endorsed by Ambassador W. Tapley Bennett, who had returned to Santo Domingo, President Johnson announced April 28 (with lurid details of the dangers threatening foreigners), that he was landing U.S. marines in the Dominican Republic "to give protection to hundreds of Americans . . . and to escort them safely back to this country."

The 556 marines landed at Santo Domingo at the time of this announcement were quickly reinforced by more marines and by airborne troops to a total of 21,000. In explanation of the sending of this large force, the President explained on April 30 that the revolutionary movement, originally democratic in purpose, had fallen under control of Communists, trained in Cuba and elsewhere, and that intervention alone could prevent the Dominican Republic from becoming another Cuba.

But American intervention was in direct violation of the OAS Charter, which declared: "No State or group of States has the right to intervene, directly or indirectly, for any reason whatever, in the internal or external affairs of any other State." It was Johnson's hope from the beginning to persuade the Latin American states, in spite of this plain language, to participate in an operation which they could regard as essential for hemisphere security. The American Foreign Ministers (actually represented by their deputies) met in formal session in Washington on May 1, but only after five days of persuasion by the United States did they provide the necessary two-thirds vote (14 to 5, with Chile, Ecuador, Mexico, Peru, and Uruguay voting no and Venezuela abstaining) to authorize the creation of an Inter-American Peace Force, including the U.S. troops already there, to assist in restoring normal conditions in the Dominican Republic.

Perhaps more disappointing to Johnson than the barely adequate majority for the resolution was the minimal participation of the Latin Americans in the Peace Force. Compared to the 21,000 U.S. troops on station, Honduras sent 250, Nicaragua 180, Costa Rica 20 policemen. None of the large states participated at all, except Brazil (at the time under military rule), which after some delay sent 1,250 soldiers under a high-ranking general, who was thereupon (May 24) made commander of the entire force, with the American commander as his deputy.

The American invading force, in the meantime, while nominally neutral, appears to have consistently favored the junta, thereby, in the opinion of qualified observers, insuring the defeat of the "constitutionalists." Early in May, United States officials took part in creating a new military-civilian junta, replacing that of Colonel Benoit. Headed by General Antonio Imbert Barreras (one of the assassins of Dictator Trujillo), the new group dubbed itself the Government of National Reconstruction. Fighting between the junta and the "constitutionalists," who had named Colonel Francisco Caamaño Deñó Provisional President, continued sporadically in spite of repeated cease-fire agreements negotiated by OAS representatives and others.

Finally a three-man OAS team, with members from Brazil, El Salvador, and the United States, secured acceptance by both factions of Héctor García Godoy, a businessman and former Foreign Minister, as Provisional President. He was sworn in on September 3, 1965. The Peace Force was to remain until its withdrawal was agreed upon by the provisional government and the OAS.

Such are the bare bones of the story of the intervention in the Dominican Republic by the United States, reluctantly assisted by the OAS. Whether it was justified will long remain in dispute. Was there, as the United States officially contended, a real danger that a "constitutionalist" victory and the restoration of Juan Bosch to the presidency would mean a Communist takeover? No one contended that Bosch was a Communist. Though the Kennedy administration had deplored his downfall, he had not been a strong President and had been more lenient with Communists than his critics thought wise. The American Ambassador at Santo Domingo and his staff, military and civilian, were apparently convinced that the return of Bosch to the presidency would be a victory for Communism and must be prevented at all hazards. They impressed Washington with their apprehensions, encouraged resistance by the Wessin group, and guided them in their plea for intervention. They, or the C.I.A., compiled a list of over fifty Communists said to be in the "constitutionalist" camp, thus providing President Johnson with his chief justification for the expanded intervention.

Subsequent investigation has thrown great doubt upon the seriousness of the Communist threat. It has also shown that, although street fighting and chaotic conditions existed in the city of Santo Domingo at the end of April, American and other foreign citizens were in no more danger than peaceful Dominicans. Justification for even the landing of the first contingent of marines is doubtful.[9]

9. A temperate but generally critical account of the episode is that by Richard P. Stebbins in *U.S. in World Affairs, 1965,* chap. 3. Unsparingly critical is Theodore Draper, *The Dominican Revolt: A Case Study in American Policy* (New York: Commentary, 1968). Another severe critic of American policy is Richard J. Barnet in *Intervention and Revolution: The United States in the Third World* (New York: The World Publishing Co., 1968), chap. 8. Intervention is defended by John Bartlow Martin, a one-time U.S. Ambassador to the Dominican Republic and special investigator for President Johnson in 1965, in *Overtaken by Events: The Dominican Crisis from the Fall of Trujillo to the Civil War* (Garden City, N.Y.: Doubleday & Company, Inc., 1966), and by Latin American expert Adolf A. Berle in John Carey, ed., *The Dominican Republic Crisis, 1965* (Dobbs Ferry, N.Y.: Oceana Publications, Inc., 1967), which also includes critical remarks by Wolfgang Friedmann.

Right or wrong, the Dominican intervention of 1965 had a happier sequel than might have been expected. Tension did not end, but comparative peace returned under García Godoy, backed by the Peace Force, whose numbers were gradually reduced. In the election of June 1, 1966, generally conceded to have been fair, Joaquín Balaguer defeated Juan Bosch as presidential candidate and was inaugurated on July 1. The last of the Peace Force departed in September. Balaguer included Bosch supporters in his cabinet. Restless military men of both factions were assigned to posts abroad. The United States provided substantial amounts of economic aid, and the country was for the most part peaceful, at least to the end of 1970. Balaguer's insistence upon being a candidate for reelection, with support of the military, led Bosch's Dominican Revolutionary Party to boycott the election of May 16, 1970. Bosch himself, who had gone into voluntary exile in Spain in 1967, returned in April, declaring that representative democracy could not solve the problems of the Dominican people. What was needed, he said, was "dictatorship with popular support." He approved his party's boycott of the election but opposed violence. With the chief opposition party holding aloof, Balaguer easily won reelection to another four-year term, but Bosch's repudiation of democratic procedures augured ill for a peaceful Dominican future.[10]

What Policy for the Future?

The question of what policy the United States should follow if the situation of 1965 should be repeated, in the Dominican Republic or elsewhere in Latin America, still remained.

Some critics of the policy of 1965, like Senator Fulbright, pointed out the contradiction between that policy and the aims of the Alliance for Progress.

> The direction of the Alliance for Progress is toward social revolution in Latin America [said the Senator in a speech of September 15, 1965]; the direction of our Dominican intervention is toward the suppression of revolutionary movements which are supported by Communists or suspected of being supported by Communists. . . .
>
> We simply cannot have it both ways; we must choose between the Alliance for Progress and a foredoomed effort to sustain the status quo in Latin America. . . .

A few days later, however, the House of Representatives adopted, by a vote in the ratio of 6 to 1, a resolution declaring that any one of the American republics might take any steps necessary "to forestall or combat intervention, domination, control, and colonization in whatever form by the subversive forces known as international communism and its agencies in the Western Hemisphere." [11]

The Johnson administration wished assurance that future threats of Communist takeover in the Hemisphere would be dealt with but without the necessity of unilateral action by the United States. At a Special Inter-American Conference at Rio de Janeiro in November 1965, Secretary of State Rusk tried to promote a plan for a permanent inter-American peace force which could deal with future crises on a multilateral basis. He received some encouragement from Brazil and Argentina, but the more democratic states, especially Mexico, Chile, and Uruguay, were so antagonistic to the concept of intervention, unilateral or multilateral, that Rusk's proposal had to be abandoned. Neither this plan nor any alternative had found favor with a majority of the OAS as late as December 1970. A proposal by Governor Nelson Rockefeller in 1969 for creation of a Western Hemisphere Security Council received no encouragement even in Washington.[12]

10. *New York Times,* April 20, May 18, 1970; letter from Theodore Draper, ibid., February 22, 1970. A hint of the dubious stability of conditions in the Dominican Republic was the decision of the OAS Council that the first meeting of the new General Assembly (created by the amended Charter) should meet in Washington in June 1970 instead of in Santo Domingo as originally planned. Ibid., June 9, 1970. For amendment of the Charter see above, Chapter 48, note 4.

11. *Congressional Record,* 89 Cong., 1 sess., 1965 (September 15, 20, 1965), 3: 23856, 24347.
12. See p. 552.

The proposals of Rockefeller and Rusk, and the House resolution quoted, all contemplated safeguards against Communist regimes imposed by outside intervention or internal subversion. But suppose the people of a Latin American state should choose a Communist government in a free election? This problem was raised in Chile in the fall of 1970. In an election on September 4, Dr. Salvador Allende Gossens, a Marxist Socialist, the candidate of a coalition which included the Communist party, won a plurality (36.3 percent) of the popular vote against two rivals. If precedent were followed, the Chilean Congress would choose Allende as the candidate with the highest popular vote.[13]

The prospect of a new Communist-backed government in an important American state created a stir in Washington. Though the State Department remained outwardly calm, "a very high official of the White House," in a briefing of September 16, expressed "dismay" at the prospect, and fear that Chile's neighbors, Argentina, Peru, and Bolivia, might follow her down the primrose path. At the same time, however, Washington was said to feel that the United States lacked leverage to change the course of events in Chile even if it desired to do so, while the American corporations with the largest investments in Chile were pictured as believing that their wisest course was to avoid antagonizing the new regime and hope for fair payment if their properties were nationalized.[14]

Dr. Allende made a course of nonintervention easier by agreeing, before his election by Congress (October 24) to support constitutional amendments which, if observed, would safeguard Chile against a totalitarian regime. Although President Nixon omitted the usual courtesy of congratulating President Allende on his election, he made amends by sending the Assistant Secretary of State for Inter-American Affairs to attend the inaugural ceremonies on November 3.

Once in office, President Allende promptly reestablished diplomatic relations with Communist Cuba, breaking with United States and OAS policy on that point. On the other hand, he launched his program for nationalizing the billion-dollar American-owned copper mines through the deliberate and strictly legal process of constitutional amendment and with the promise of compensation for the owners.[15] If Allende seemed unlikely to be another Castro, the fact remained that Communism had another bridgehead in the Americas.

Cuba after the Missile Crisis

After the dramatic events of October and November 1962, Castro's Cuba was destined to grow, or at least to seem, less formidable as an exporter of Communism to the Western Hemisphere. A year after the missile crisis, in fact, there were undercover negotiations between Havana and Washington, looking to a possible renewal of diplomatic and economic relations.[16] These negotiations were ended by Kennedy's assassination. Castro continued his efforts to subvert other Latin American governments, but without success. His almost frantic attempt to disrupt by terrorism the elections of 1963 in Venezuela failed completely. Four years later his chief lieutenant, "Ché" Guevara, met his death in an utterly futile attempt to carry Communism to the peasants and tin-miners of Bolivia. Although guerrilla activities with at least Communist coloration continued troublesome in Guatemala, Colombia, and Venezuela, it was evident that the Andes were not ready to become the Sierra Maestra of the Revolution.

Meanwhile Castro had exchanged unpleasant words with both his major patrons, Peking and Moscow. Early in 1966 the Cuban dictator accused the Chinese government of "a display of absolute contempt toward our country" in reducing by 115,000 tons the rice that it had allegedly agreed to exchange for

13. *New York Times,* September 6, 1970.
14. *New York Times,* September 21, 23, 1970; *The New Republic,* November 7, 1970.

15. *New York Times,* October 10, November 13, December 23, 1970.
16. William Attwood, *The Reds and the Blacks* (New York: Harper & Row, Publishers, 1967), pp. 142–46.

Cuban sugar.[17] Peking replied in kind. The loss in Chinese trade increased Cuba's dependence on Russia, yet in the following year (1967) Castro bitterly denounced the Soviet Union for cultivating diplomatic and cultural relations with the "oligarchic" governments of Latin America—a policy of "peaceful coexistence"—and for opposing Castro's policy of subversion and armed guerrilla tactics in that area.[18]

In 1966 and 1967, Cuba played host to two leftist international gatherings. The first, a "tricontinental conference," attended by delegates from 86 nations of Asia, Africa, and Latin America, met in Havana in January 1966. In speeches and resolutions it stressed the "duty" of giving aid to "national liberation movements," with special emphasis on those said to be operating in Latin American countries.[19]

A follow-up of the "tricontinental conference" was the "First Conference of the Organization of Latin American Solidarity" (OLAS), which met in Havana on July 31, 1967, with delegates from 27 countries or territories. Its declared purpose was "to unite, coordinate and step up the struggle against United States imperialism on the part of all the exploited peoples of Latin America." A novel feature was the presence of Black Power leader Stokely Carmichael from the United States and an effort to equate the contemporary urban riots in the United States with guerrilla activities in Guatemala and Colombia and the Viet Cong struggle in Vietnam. As noted by James Reston of the *New York Times*, however, one thing that the Solidarity Conference lacked was solidarity. The Moscow-oriented Communist parties of Argentina, Brazil, and Venezuela did not attend, and delegations from other Communist parties actually represented splinter groups or factions. The trumpet call for stepping up guerrilla wars in Latin America was in direct contradiction to Soviet policy, and as a matter of fact the Conference was followed by a decline

rather than an increase in guerrilla activity.[20]

The Organization of American States condemned the program of the OLAS Conference, as it had done that of the conference of the preceding year, and repeated earlier calls for a tightened quarantine of Cuba. By 1967, all members of the OAS except Mexico had severed diplomatic and commercial relations with Cuba. Mexico kept diplomatic channels open as well as air transport. The United States, which originally had exempted food and medicines from its embargo on exports to Cuba, had in 1964, made these subject to license.

An interesting exception to the ban on United States-Cuban communications was the airlift, arranged in 1965, by means of which Cubans (excepting men of military age) were permitted to emigrate to the United States to the number of from 2,000 to 3,000 per month.[21]

Rumors in 1968–1969 of an impending rapprochement between Cuba and the United States were vehemently denied by a spokesman for Cuba at a U.N. agency conference in Lima. Cuba, he insisted, would remain "an ideological base for violent revolution throughout Latin America." [22]

Progress (?) of the Alliance

Nine years after President Kennedy's launching of the Alliance for Progress, many of its goals seemed no nearer than they had been in 1961. The decade of the 1960's, observed a Latin American statesman and scholar in January 1970,

17. *New York Times,* February 7, 1966.
18. *New York Times,* March 15, 1967.
19. *U.S. in World Affairs, 1966,* pp. 306–9.

20. *U.S. in World Affairs, 1967,* pp. 323–26; *New York Times,* August 1, 2, 9, 1967.
21. *U.S. in World Affairs, 1965,* pp. 349–50. A crack in the OAS commercial boycott of Cuba appeared in 1970 when Chile signed an $11 million trade agreement with Castro's government. Several other Latin American governments were suggesting reconsideration of the Hemisphere boycott of the island. *Buffalo Evening News,* July 9, 1970. On the other hand, in September 1970, Mexico served notice of cancellation of her sixteen-year-old air transport agreement with Cuba, cancellation to take effect within one year. Ibid., September 15, 1970.
22. *New York Times,* April 27, 1969.

has been characterized by the frustrating contrast between the great hopes and promises with which it began, and the meager results with which it ended. It began with great possibilities of international aid, in a euphoria of development prospects, stimulated by the perspective of the Alliance for Progress and the desire to strengthen representative democracy.

It ended with the virtual breaking up of the alliance, with an overall standstill in development, with a worsening of economic and social problems, and return to military governments, of the traditional kind or in a new style.[23]

This was perhaps a too pessimistic estimate, yet it was largely supported by facts. The Alliance in its beginning was so much a personal conception of President Kennedy that his death, November 22, 1963, gave rise to doubts about its future under so different a personality as Lyndon Johnson. Kennedy, in fact, had given the Alliance a *mystique* which none of his successors could provide.

Kennedy's emphasis on the importance of democracy (whether or not he could have persisted in it had he lived) was an early casualty. Johnson's appointee as Assistant Secretary of State for Inter-American Affairs, Thomas C. Mann, was reported to have said in a quasi-official statement that the United States would make no distinction in its attitude toward democratic and military regimes. Prompt renewal of diplomatic relations with the military-backed governments in Honduras and the Dominican Republic seemed to confirm this apparent return to America's traditional recognition policy. Though Johnson, in a speech of May 11, 1964, reaffirmed the dedication of the United States to political democracy and "a peaceful, democratic social revolution across the hemisphere,"[24] the United States did no more than express mild disapproval by a brief withholding of recognition—and not always that—when the military seized power in Brazil (1964), Bolivia (1964, 1969), Argentina (1966), Panama (1968),

and Peru (1968). The military ruled more states of the OAS in 1970 than in 1960. Even if, as was claimed,[25] the generation of officers now asserting themselves were more reform-minded than their elders, military rule, however benevolent, was the antithesis of democracy.

For purposes of economic development, the United States had fulfilled the promise made at Punta del Este (1961) by making available to its Latin allies approximately a billion dollars annually in one form or another; but of the public funds supplied, the greater part was in loans, not grants, thus contributing to an increasingly heavy burden of debt. Loans were encumbered with provisions designed to benefit U.S. business, which sharply reduced their value and created resentment in the recipient countries.[26] As the decade progressed, furthermore, a reaction in Congress against foreign aid in general reduced year by year the public funds available for Latin America. As for private investments, which were counted as part of the contribution to development, Latin American economists complained that the profits on such investments taken out of their countries in every year since 1962 had exceeded the new capital put in.[27]

In trade, also, Latin America complained that U.S. and European barriers to the importation of its products kept their prices low and reduced Latin America's share of world trade

23. Arturo Uslar Pietri of Venezuela in the *New York Times,* January 26, 1970. © 1970 by The New York Times Company. Reprinted by permission.
24. *Documents on American Foreign Relations, 1964,* p. 257.

25. *U.S. in World Affairs, 1966,* p. 324.
26. Senator Frank Church, "Toward a New Policy for Latin America," *Christianity and Crisis,* March 2, 1970; A. F. Lowenthal, "Alliance Rhetoric Versus Latin American Reality," *Foreign Affairs,* 48 (April 1970), 494–508. Such provisions included "tying" stipulations, requiring that all purchases with aid funds be made in the United States (broadened by President Nixon to Western Hemisphere) and that one-half of goods purchased in the United States be transported in U.S. ships; that such goods must be in addition to items that would have been purchased had the loans not been made (relaxed by President Nixon). Other restrictions, e.g., the Hickenlooper amendment, required suspension of aid to a country which expropriated American property without making prompt provision for compensation, or to a country that purchased military equipment elsewhere than in the United States.
27. *New York Times,* June 12, 1969.

in the 1960's to little more than half what it had been in 1950.[28] This handicap (which many Latin Americans attributed to a conspiracy of the developed nations, led by the United States, to depress the prices of their primary products), combined with their growing burden of debt, limited the increase in economic growth. In the first seven years of the Alliance, the combined gross national product of member countries showed an average annual increase of 4.5 percent, but because of the high birth rate in the area, the per capita increase amounted to only 1.5 percent instead of the 2.5 percent proposed in the Charter of Punta del Este.[29] In some countries the figure was much lower. Though U.S. aid had produced important progress in public health and education, the rate of economic growth was not sufficient to support much self-generated social progress.

President Johnson, at a summit meeting at Punta del Este, Uruguay, in 1967, tried to meet Latin American complaints by promising to seek a general preferential lowering of trade barriers by the industrialized countries on behalf of all the developing nations, including Latin America. The United Nations Conference on Trade and Development (UNCTAD II) at New Delhi in 1968 approved such a policy in principle but left the details to be worked out.[30]

Johnson also, at Punta del Este, promised the assistance of the United States on plans for a Latin American Common Market, which might emulate the success of the Common Market in Europe. A Central American Common Market, formed in 1960, had already had a stimulating effect on the economies of the five member states. A Latin American Free Trade Association (LAFTA), embracing the nations of South America and Mexico, also formed in 1960, had scheduled a mutual aban-

donment of tariffs to begin by 1973. Negotiations for the first phase of LAFTA were disappointingly slow, and in May 1969 one group of states less inhibited than the others formed the Andean Group Association, comprising Colombia, Peru, Ecuador, Bolivia, and Chile. Their treaty provided for ending tariff barriers among themselves over an eleven-year period, but eventually they expected to join, with LAFTA, the Central American group, and a fourth grouping, the Caribbean Free Trade Association, to form the Latin American Common Market.[31]

President Nixon and Latin America

Actually, little had been accomplished by 1969, and the two-week war in July of that year between Honduras and El Salvador was a serious setback for the Central American Common Market. There was little prospect of improvement in the Latin American economy when Richard Nixon entered the White House. Nixon, in an address of April 14, 1969, assured the representatives of the OAS member states that their area had first priority in his thinking and that the times called for "new policies, new programs and new appointments." He was asking Governor Nelson Rockefeller of New York, a former adviser on Latin American affairs under Presidents Roosevelt and Truman, to make a tour of investigation and report to him on what the United States could do to meet Latin American needs.[32]

The Latin Americans, however, while not rejecting an investigation by Rockefeller, wished to present their own bill of particulars. Meeting at Viña del Mar, Chile, in May 1969, delegates from twenty-one Latin American countries [33] prepared an 18,000 word docu-

28. Wm. D. Rogers, *The Twilight Struggle: The Alliance for Progress and the Politics of Development in Latin America* (New York: Random House, Inc., 1967), pp. 148–50.

29. Report of Agency for International Development, cited by Felix Belair, Jr., *New York Times,* March 6, 1969.

30. See p. 431.

31. Galo Plaza, "A Common Market," *New York Times,* January 20, 1969; "Andean Trade Bloc Jelling," ibid., January 26, 1970.

32. *New York Times,* April 15, 1969.

33. Trinidad-Tobago and Barbados, after becoming independent from Britain in 1962 and 1966 respectively, joined the OAS. Jamaica became the twenty-fourth member of OAS on August 20, 1969. *New York Times,* August 21, 1969. Cuba did not participate in the Viña del Mar meeting.

ment, the "consensus of Viña del Mar," which was presented to President Nixon on June 11 by Foreign Minister Gabriel Valdés of Chile in the presence of the envoys of the twenty-one participating governments. It urged the elimination of barriers to the exports from Latin America to the United States and of political and military conditions for United States aid; asked alleviation of the burden of debt; and urged more effective assistance to hemispheric development in a wide variety of fields.[34]

Governor Rockefeller, in the meantime, was meeting with hostile demonstrations in many of the countries that he visited in the course of his four tours of Latin America, which began with Mexico on May 11 and ended with Barbados, July 6. The hostility may have been in part personal, because of the association of the Rockefeller name with the unpopular petroleum industry, but for the most part it seems to have been anti-United States rather than anti-Rockefeller. It was heightened by memories of U.S. intervention in the Dominican Republic and by current controversies with Peru and Bolivia over expropriation of American properties and with Peru and Ecuador over their claims to exclusive fishing rights in the Pacific up to 200 miles from their shores. So strong was the feeling in some quarters that Rockefeller was asked to cancel his proposed visits to Peru, Chile, and Venezuela.[35]

Governor Rockefeller's report, entitled "Quality of Life in the Americas," was submitted to the President on September 3, 1969, but not made public until early November. In regard to trade and aid its proposals were generally similar to those of the Viña del Mar consensus, but with the added suggestion that the entire U.S. sugar import quota be reserved for Latin America. The Governor had found an alarming growth of nationalism and anti-Americanism and a potential threat of "more Castros," which called urgently for a revival of U.S. interest and effort in behalf of Latin American economic development, but on a basis of real partnership and not paternalism.

He recommended the creation of a cabinet-level office of Secretary for Western Hemisphere Affairs (which Nixon qualified by proposing to upgrade the Assistant Secretary of State for Inter-American Affairs to Under Secretary). Rockefeller also proposed, rather unrealistically, creation of a Western Hemisphere Security Council to deal with subversion—a proposal that Nixon disregarded in making his own recommendations.[36]

Drawing ideas from the Rockefeller report, the Viña del Mar consensus, and other sources, President Nixon set forth his Latin American policy on October 31, 1969, in an address to the Inter-American Press Association.[37] Like Rockefeller, he insisted that the direction of Latin American policy must be determined by the Latin Americans, not by the United States.

> Our partnership [he said] should be one in which the United States lectures less and listens more, and in which clear, consistent procedures are established to insure that the shaping of Latin America's future reflects the will of the Latin American nations.

While avowing the dedication of the United States "to improving the quality of life in the Western Hemisphere," the President remarked that "the most pressing concerns center on economic development," and the greater part of his address dealt with those concerns. In line with his espousal of the partnership relation, he proposed that a multilateral inter-American agency—perhaps the already existing Inter-American Committee for the Alliance of Progress (C.I.A.P.)—"be given an increasing share of responsibility for development

34. *New York Times,* May 18, June 11, 1969.
35. *New York Times,* July 7, 1969.

36. *New York Times,* November 10, 1969 (excerpts and analysis), November 13, 1969 (editorial). The full text of the Rockefeller report was published as *The Rockefeller Report on the Americas, New York Times Edition,* with an introduction by Tad Szulc (Chicago: Quadrangle Books, 1969).
37. *New York Times,* November 1, 1969. Much of this was repeated in the President's comprehensive statement on foreign policy of February 18, 1970, *U.S. Foreign Policy for the 1970's: A New Strategy for Peace.* A Report to the Congress by Richard Nixon, President of the United States, February 18, 1970 (Washington: Government Printing Office, 1970), pp. 41–53.

assistance decisions." He promised to make an effort to lower non-tariff trade barriers maintained by most of the industrialized countries against Latin American products and—like Johnson in 1967—"to press for a liberal system of generalized tariff preferences for all developing countries." He announced that he was removing certain minor restrictions on the spending of the proceeds of loans made under U.S. aid programs and was asking that Congress consider modifying or eliminating others. He suggested that ways might be found for easing the debt load which hampered the development of some countries in the area. He made it clear that he maintained his faith in the good effect of foreign private investment in the developing countries and warned against policies that might frighten it away, but promised increased emphasis "on assistance to locally owned private enterprise." He promised, in response to the consensus of Viña del Mar, "an unprecedented effort to share our scientific and technological capabilities."

There was no lecturing of the Latin Americans on the need for reform in landholding, taxation, or other social policy, and although the President made clear the preference of the United States for democratic procedures, he observed: "On the diplomatic level, we must deal realistically with governments in the inter-American system as they are."

Mr. Nixon promised that the Latin neighbors of the United States would be treated with "respect for [their] national identity and national dignity." Whether this meant that there would be no more interventions like that in the Dominican Republic, no one could say.

In response to a feeling in some Latin American quarters that the United States "no longer cares," the President said emphatically, "We do care," and he assured his hearers of the firm commitment of the United States to the inter-American system and "to continued United States assistance for hemisphere development." He asserted, near the opening of his speech: "I offer no grandiose promises and panaceas. I do offer action." It was noted, however, that most of the action offered remained to come and would depend upon the uncertain attitudes of Congress, foreign governments, and international lending agencies to the President's proposals.

The Canadian Partner

More intimate than its relationship with its sister republics to the south was the association of the United States with its northern neighbor, Canada. Canada had not been a party to the inter-American conferences, organizations, or treaties. Though a "twenty-second chair" had been reserved for her at the Pan-American Union, it had never been filled, presumably because Canada was not a republic but a constitutional monarchy and a member of the British Commonwealth of Nations. The Mexico City Conference of 1945 expressed a hope for closer collaboration with Canada, and the Bogotá Charter of 1948 set up an Organization of American *States*, rather than *republics*, in order to include Canada if she so desired.

Many Canadians, after World War II, urged that Canada accept the invitation, but at least until 1970 the opposition arguments prevailed. Prominent among these was the realization that, as a member of the OAS, Canada would often have to take sides in controversies between the United States and Latin America, perhaps incurring the ill will of one or both. This argument gained force with growing Canadian disapproval of United States policy in Cuba and the Dominican Republic. American foreign policy, Canadians felt, tended to use the OAS when it could and to ignore it when it could not. Membership in such an organization would at times be frustrating. Canadian divergence from United States policy elsewhere, notably in China and Vietnam, lessened still further the attractions of OAS membership.[38]

But though Canada held aloof from the OAS and was unsympathetic to certain fea-

38. Gerald M. Craig, *The United States and Canada* (Cambridge: Harvard University Press, 1968), pp. 326–32.

tures of American foreign policy, similarity in race, language, culture, economic and political principles, and the need for a common defense system bound the two nations in a close, if not always comfortable, partnership. Before World War II, President Roosevelt and Prime Minister King had exchanged pledges of cooperation for mutual defense against the Axis powers. In 1940, the two nations had established a Joint Board on Defense and meshed together their production and defense mechanisms in the war that followed. The cold war found them again facing a common potential enemy. The prospect that hostilities might see long-range bombers, armed with nuclear weapons, striking across the north polar regions, heightened the military dependence of Canada and the United States on one another.

It was in the interest of both nations, therefore, to maintain the Joint Board on Defense as a permanent body, and this was supplemented in 1958 by the establishment at cabinet level of a Canada-United States Committee on Joint Defense.

Another important step had been taken in the preceding year (1957) with the creation of the North American Air Defense Command (NORAD), combining elements of both Air Forces. NORAD headquarters were established at Colorado Springs with an American commander-in-chief and a Canadian deputy commander. The purpose was the integrated use of the facilities of the two nations for the defense of the United States, including Alaska, and Canada against possible air attack from the Soviet Union. Another measure for the same purpose, the construction of a triple screen of radar warning stations drawn across Canada from ocean to ocean, was also complete and in operation by 1957.

It was ironical that the year of the completion of this screen and the creation of NORAD, both designed to safeguard the continent against attack by long-range bombing planes, was also the year of Sputnik; for Sputnik introduced the missile age, which would soon make bombers and defenses against them obsolete.

The transition from the bomber to the

ICBM, in fact, signalled a decline in U.S.-Canadian cooperation for defense. Canadian disapproval of the use of nuclear weapons asserted itself. Though the two governments had reached a tentative agreement for the arming of Canadian interceptor planes and short-range missiles with nuclear warheads, Conservative Prime Minister John Diefenbaker (1957–1963) refused to permit the stockpiling of the warheads in Canada, on the ground that they would be useless against ICBMs and would only expose Canada to nuclear attack. He also, during the Cuban missile crisis in 1962, refused to authorize what the United States command considered an adequate number of precautionary flights over Canada by nuclear-armed American planes.

Diefenbaker's uncooperative defense policy met criticism in both the United States and Canada and contributed to the fall of his government in February 1963 and the return to power of the Liberals. Lester Pearson, the Liberal Prime Minister, was less critical of the United States than was Diefenbaker, but, like Diefenbaker, was unhappy over the agreement which committed Canada to arming with nuclear weapons.

After 1963, the two nations diverged somewhat in their defense policies, though the official structure of alliance remained. "Canadians," writes Gerald Craig, "are increasingly doubtful that their country plays, or can play, any real role in making the decisions at NORAD headquarters," and many feel that Canada's limited military resources should be used for other purposes than continental (or NATO) defense; such, for example, as the U.N. peacekeeping activities in which Canada has played an active role. The United States, on its part, thought it unnecessary to consult Canada in advance about installation of the Safeguard ABM stations in North Dakota and Montana, though the interception missiles fired from those stations would presumably explode in Canadian airspace.[39]

39. Craig, *The U.S. and Canada,* p. 316; *New York Times,* March 20, 1969. For Safeguard, see above, p. 457.

Canada's sense of inequality with its giant neighbor in matters of defense was symptomatic of Canadian-U.S. relations in general. Canada, with its 21,000,000 inhabitants, vast territory, and rich resources, was an important "middle power," jealous of its independence and proud of its distinctive character and traditions. It was sensitive to what at times seemed a patronizing attitude on the part of the United States and resentful at having its goodwill and cooperation taken for granted, as they sometimes were. Economically, Canadians were unhappy at the steadily unfavorable balance—around $1 billion annually—in their trade with the United States and at the imposition of quotas or other restrictions upon imports to the United States of Canadian lead, zinc, and petroleum. They regarded as unfair the disposal abroad of American surplus wheat at less than world prices, undercutting the market for Canadian wheat. They were disturbed by the growing extent to which their industry and business were owned and controlled in the United States. Sixty percent of Canada's principal manufacturing industries, complained the Canadian Prime Minister in 1957, and a larger proportion of its mine and oil production, were owned and controlled by United States corporations or their Canadian subsidiaries, and few of these offered their stock to Canadian investors. Policies of the Canadian subsidiaries were apt to be determined on the basis of United States rather than Canadian interests and national policies. Canadians feared an impairment of their independence, both economic and political. They were further disturbed by the dominant position in the Canadian market of books, magazines, radio and television programs from south of the border. They did not admire all manifestations of the "American way of life" or wish to make it theirs.[40]

The United States, with a population almost ten times that of Canada and with a growing drain upon its natural resources, was coming, in the late 1960's, to the view that Canada's minerals, petroleum, natural gas, and abundant fresh water should be treated as "continental resources," to be disposed of, in other words, by joint agreement between the two governments. Not surprisingly, this view was not welcomed in Canada. As applied particularly to fuels, it brought from J. J. Greene, Canadian Minister of Energy, Mines, and Resources, in May 1970, the declaration that any bargaining with the United States on the subject of continental resources "must lead to Canadian solutions in a Canadian interest."[41]

Another Canadian worry arose from the discovery of oil on the Arctic slope of Alaska and the voyage, in the summer of 1969, of the giant icebreaking tanker *Manhattan* through the legendary Northwest Passage, in the effort to demonstrate that the oil could be transported by sea to East Coast ports. A natural fear of pollution from such traffic led Canadian Prime Minister Pierre Elliott Trudeau (1968–) to introduce in Parliament legislation to extend Canadian control of shipping over an area up to 100 nautical miles from Canada's shore line. Thus the Canadian government would be able to regulate oil transport and oil drilling in the waters of the Northwest Passage and to preserve what the Prime Minister called "the world's last big natural reserve." The United States took prompt exception to Canada's unilateral action and called for international talks to pass upon the Canadian claim to jurisdiction over what had hitherto been considered international waters.[42]

Such complaints as the United States had against Canada were chiefly, like this one, in the field of foreign policy. Canada's anti-Communist position was in general less rigid than that of the United States. Canada refused to accept Washington's view of Castro's Cuba. Canada maintained normal diplomatic and commercial relations with Cuba after the United States had broken them off, and, as said before, gave the United States less than

40. Joseph Barber, *Good Fences Make Good Neighbors: Why the U.S. Provokes Canadians* (Indianapolis: The Bobbs-Merrill Company, Inc., 1958), is a comprehensive treatment.

41. *New York Times,* May 31, 1970.
42. *New York Times,* April 10, 16, 20 (editorial), 1970.

complete cooperation in the Cuban missile crisis of 1962. Like the United States but unlike Great Britain, Canada until 1970 withheld recognition from Communist China. Canada refused, however, over a twenty-year period, to join the United States in a complete embargo on trade with China. In 1961, indeed, it granted a credit of $300 million to that famine-stricken country for the purchase of Canadian wheat, other grains, and flour. At last, Pierre Trudeau, the "swinging" young Liberal who became Prime Minister upon Pearson's retirement in 1968, announced that he would seek to establish normal relations with Peking as a step toward ending China's isolation from the non-Communist world. The establishment of diplomatic relations was announced in Ottawa and Peking on October 13, 1970, and at the same time Canada severed relations with the Chinese Nationalist government at Taipei. Canada made it plain, however, that she was not taking sides in Communist China's claim to sovereignty over Taiwan. In Washington the State Department took no issue with the Canadian decision, merely expressing concern for the adverse effect it might have on the international position of Nationalist China. The action would not, it was said, affect United States opposition to Red China's admission to the United Nations.[43]

Whatever the bickerings between the two neighbors, each was vitally essential to the other in economics and defense. They shared, moreover, the same world view. Both were democratic and freedom loving; both had stable governments that derived along different channels from British origins; both, as allies in NATO and the U.N., were dedicated to the preservation of order and peace in the world and against the spread of Communism. Responsible statesmen on both sides knew that cooperation was imperative.

These facts were recognized in a White Paper on foreign policy issued by the Trudeau government in June 1970. "The United States," declared this important document, "is Canada's closest friend and ally and will remain so." Recognizing at the same time the "constant danger that sovereignty, independence and cultural identity may be impaired" by this close relationship, the White Paper observed that "active pursuit of trade diversification and technological cooperation with European and other developed countries will be needed to provide countervailing factors." This broadening of Canada's external relations should be extended to Latin America, without, for the present, its becoming a member of the OAS—though this was suggested for some future time—and to the Far East, where Canada might assist in "bringing Communist China into a more constructive relationship with the world community." Canada would continue an active member of the United Nations and of NATO, though with reservations as to the extent of its military contribution to the latter. In contrast to the contemporary trend in the United States, Canada should "steadily increase its foreign aid contributions." In all this program, as the *New York Times* remarked editorially, there was "nothing to which Americans can legitimately object."[44]

Where interests differed, as they often would, "the need is clear," in the words of a joint study published in 1965, "for our two governments to confirm the practice of intimate, timely and continuing consultation on all matters of common concern, at the appropriate level, . . . "; and the author-diplomats added the sound advice: "It is in the interest of both countries that, wherever possible, divergent views between the two governments should be expressed and if possible resolved in private, through diplomatic channels."[45]

43. *New York Times,* October 14, 1970.

44. *New York Times,* June 26, July 4, 1970.
45. A. D. P. Heeney and Livingston T. Merchant, "Canada and the United States—Principles for Partnership," *Department of State Bulletin,* 53 (August 2, 1965), 193–208.

The first chapter of this volume enumerated what seem to have been the principal objectives of American foreign policy. It will be useful now, at the end of the narrative, to attempt to measure the successes and failures of American policy, during nearly two centuries, in the pursuit of these objectives. Has the government of the United States, using the tools of diplomacy and of force, done well or ill in striving toward its goals?

It is evident at a glance that the United States long since achieved the first and second of its objectives: independence with satisfactory boundaries, and the extension of those boundaries in the interest of security and other legitimate aims. From 1916 to the end of World War II in 1945, the United States neither acquired nor coveted foreign territory, and in the Atlantic Charter, issued a few months before entering that war, President Roosevelt renounced for the United States any "aggrandizement, territorial or other." But the postwar fear of the expansion of Russian Communism created new security problems, which called for a variety of American overseas bases, and although the United States actually acquired no new territory, it secured, by leases, by treaty, and under the trusteeship system, the right to occupy and use military, naval, and air bases in many parts of the world.

The third objective, the promotion and protection of the interests of American citizens abroad, is not one that can be achieved once and for all and safely stored away, like independence or a slice of territory. It requires more or less constant watching over. To protect commerce against organized piracy, the United States fought two wars with the Barbary States. To vindicate its conception of neutral rights in wartime, it engaged in undeclared hostilities with France in 1798 and in formal war with England in 1812 and with Germany in 1917. By none of these wars did it establish beyond dispute the principles for which it fought. Nor has it achieved conclusive results by numerous diplomatic negotiations over the security of American investments abroad. In so-called "backward" countries, renunciation by the United States of the right of intervention has removed a deter-

50

American Foreign Policy: Past and Future

rent to encroachments upon American interests, with the consequence that such investments have become increasingly liable to interference, sometimes to expropriation, by nationalistic governments. Much of what the United States had earlier gained in Asia, in economic privileges and political and social influence, it lost when Communism won in China. American postwar pressure for a worldwide "open door" to commerce and industry brought charges of "economic imperialism" from the New Left at home as well as from foreigners who resented a Yankee economic invasion. Where the pressure was resisted, as in Eastern Europe, it contributed to the onset of the cold war.

In its quest for the fourth objective, the preservation of neutrality and peace, the United States has clearly failed. It has been drawn into every major European struggle since winning independence; and this because, in the view of the statesmen in command on those occasions, neutrality was not compatible with the preservation of American security and vital interests. The United States has made frequent use of arbitration for the settlement of disputes and, during the early part of the present century, was very active in negotiating treaties of arbitration and conciliation and in constructing peace machinery in other and more elaborate forms. Yet it has engaged in seven foreign wars, one of which, that in Vietnam, was in its seventh year of direct American involvement in the autumn of 1970. Cold war, furthermore, had prevailed for years with the Soviet Union and Communist China. The "balance of terror" deterred the nuclear powers from risking war with each other, but both claimed the right to support their respective protégés in local "wars of liberation," and there was no guarantee that such wars might not escalate.

In the pursuit of the fifth objective, the protection of the Western Hemisphere against further colonization and against interference by non-American states, the United States had long been successful. In this it had been aided by circumstances, by the balance of power in Europe and the similarity in aims

between the United States and Great Britain. In the years since 1932 it had enlisted the other American republics in support of this principle, transforming the Monroe Doctrine from a unilateral to a multilateral policy, supported by the Organization of American States. Economic hardship and discontent, however, had undermined the new structure, creating weak spots where Communism might penetrate and find lodgment. The United States had sought to combat this tendency. A quasi-Communist regime was ousted in Guatemala. A revolution alleged to be Communist-infiltrated was thwarted by massive military intervention in the Dominican Republic. But in Cuba, Fidel Castro, using "salami tactics," had established a full-blown Communist regime, enjoying support and protection from the Soviet Union. This relationship, as Nikita Khrushchev had boasted, was undoubtedly a violation of the Monroe Doctrine.

It was remarked in the introductory chapter that after 1940 "the effort to protect the Americas from the spread of totalitarianism in its Nazi and Communist forms involved a struggle to protect all Western civilizations from the same peril." This was particularly true in the first postwar decade when world Communism seemed a monolithic structure propelled by Moscow; or, put in another way, when world Communism seemed the spearhead of Russian expansionism. It was in this decade that "containment"—prevention of the further spread of Communism, wherever it might threaten—became the dominant theme of American foreign policy; and because Moscow was believed to contemplate expansion by force, the United States made military alliances with over forty friendly states and stationed its armed forces on the periphery of the Communist empire in Europe, North Africa, and the Far East.

Containment necessitated not only the possession of force and the readiness to use it to resist aggression, but also the employment of measures to deprive Communism of its appeal by combating poverty, hunger, ignorance, and disease. Hence in the containment struggle, the humanitarian purpose mentioned as a sixth objective of foreign policy became linked with the more familiar means of promoting security. From the initiation of aid to Greece and Turkey in 1947 to the end of 1970, the United States had poured out vast sums in foreign aid.

It is of course apparent from this brief mention of containment that the United States faced a completely new situation in 1945. Through no choice or foresight of its own, it had become one of two mutually antagonistic great powers, surrounded by only second- and third-class nations in terms of economic and military potential. How this had come about needs no elaboration for readers of the earlier chapters of this narrative. For reasons of its own security, as seen by President Franklin Roosevelt and his advisers, the United States had cast its lot with those nations fighting to prevent world domination by the Axis—Germany, Italy, and Japan. So great was the military strength of the Axis that the Western democracies could not hope to defeat it without the aid of the other totalitarian power, the Soviet Union.[1] The Allied victory, by destroying or disarming the military forces of Germany and Japan, left the Soviet Union the dominant power on the Eurasian landmass. The democracies of Western Europe were impoverished and weakened by two world wars. The only nation capable of challenging Soviet power was the United States.

The Soviet Union under Stalin left no doubt of its determination to control Eastern Europe. How far beyond that its ambitions and plans actually extended is not known, but Western statesmen in both Europe and America assumed that Russian armies and local fifth columns, if unchecked, would carry Communism to the English Channel. True or false, this was then probably the only safe assumption.

The United States, breaking with long tradition, picked up the challenge. The Truman Doctrine, the Marshall Plan, and NATO were all initiated within a two-year period, 1947–1949. Their success in Europe was immediate. Economic recovery countered the threat of Communist subversion, and the United States commitment to the NATO alliance quashed any plans for conquest that Moscow may have nurtured. Unfortunately, the aggressive tone adopted by some NATO sponsors gave rise to apprehensions in Moscow and helped to accelerate the arms race.

So successful did NATO initially appear in Europe that a later administration undertook to copy it elsewhere. If the Communist empire could be contained by a military alliance on its western front, why not also on the south and southeast? Hence CENTO and SEATO were conjured up, but in areas where the threat was not primarily military and where the new allies differed widely in capacity, character, interests, and purposes. CENTO and SEATO did not share the success of NATO.

NATO itself, moreover, reached its twentieth year in a state of partial disarray. There were several reasons for the decline in its cohesiveness. First, the very success of the Marshall Plan in restoring the prosperity of the nations of Western Europe lessened their dependence upon the United States and revised their latent nationalism. Second, the loss by the United States of its virtual monopoly of nuclear weapons and the achievement of comparable nuclear capability by the Soviet Union impaired the credibility of the American deterrent. It fed de Gaulle's nationalism, strengthened his insistence that France have her *force de frappe,* and was presumably a factor in his decision to withdraw France from NATO's integrated defense structure.

Third, fission in the Communist world— the rise of hostility between Russia and China and the growing independence of the smaller Communist states—greatly mitigated the fear of Russian aggression in Western Europe. It

---

1. George F. Kennan, *American Diplomacy, 1900– 1950* (Chicago: University of Chicago Press, 1951), p. 75. Col. Charles A. Lindbergh, the famous aviator, who opposed American entry into the war at the time, believed thirty years later that the United States had made a mistake in joining the fray; that postwar Russia posed a greater threat to U.S. security than a victorious Axis would have done. *The Wartime Journals of Charles A. Lindbergh* (New York: Harcourt Brace Jovanovich, Inc., 1970).

also destroyed the postwar image of a monolithic world Communism, which had made a leftist revolution anywhere in the world appear as a dreaded expansion of an empire ruled from Moscow.

The United States's deep and persistent involvement in the war in Vietnam was a fourth factor in weakening the NATO alliance. Not one of its European allies shared Washington's belief in the importance of that struggle. France repudiated it completely, seeing as its only outcome either a settlement on Hanoi's terms or a perpetual involvement of the United States in the war. The British government gave only verbal support to American policy, while large segments of public opinion were hostile. West Germany, under Chancellor Willy Brandt, finding American attention and energy diverted from Europe to Indochina, acted independently in seeking a détente with the East. The fracturing of national unity, as well as the vast expenditures in resources and human lives, impaired the credibility of the United States as a NATO partner.[2] American persistence in the war documented the complaint of Europeans like former President de Gaulle, that the United States went its own way in world policy regardless of the opinions of its NATO allies.

An end to the war in Vietnam, and the giving of more weight in the future to the opinions of its allies seemed essential steps for the United States if NATO was to be restored to healthy life. NATO could not safely be allowed to die, for even if Russian Communism no longer seemed a menace to Western Europe, Russian imperialism threatened to take over the Middle East, the chief source of Western Europe's petroleum and hence a key to its prosperity and power.

If the mutual dependence of Western Europe and the United States gave a revivified NATO alliance a high priority among the objectives of American foreign policy in the 1970's,[3] what other desirable ends and means of that policy should be listed?

First, national survival depends upon avoidance of nuclear war with the Soviet Union. It can be assumed that neither party will begin such a war unless convinced that it has a "first strike" capability, that is, that by a surprise attack it can destroy the retaliatory capacity of the other. The aim of the United States should be to prevent the attainment of a "first strike" capability by the Soviet Union and in return to refrain from seeking such a capability on its own part. This means an urgent effort, through the SALT negotiations, to halt the extragavant race in MIRVs and ABMs, which threatens to bankrupt both nations without benefiting either. Halting of the arms race should be sought as a part of a détente not only between the United States and the Soviet Union, but between the NATO and Warsaw Pact powers in general.

Second, since the Soviet Union as an imperialistic power, regardless of ideology, threatens the vital interests of the United States and the other NATO nations in the Middle East, the United States should continue its efforts to establish or maintain peace among the nations of that area and to support their independence. This calls for skillful diplomacy and also for the maintenance of a balance in conventional weapons. Today the Soviets are rapidly overtaking the United States and Britain combined in naval power.[4] The Soviet fleet is new; much of the United States fleet is obsolescent. The supremacy of the American Sixth Fleet in the Mediterranean can no longer be taken for granted. There is a danger here that needs a remedy.

The danger today from the Soviet Union is a danger from a rival great power rather than from the chief exponent of Communism. Communism is still a weapon of Russian expansion, but its edge has been blunted. The developing nations—in Africa, for example—where its influence was greatly feared in the early 1960's, have proved largely immune to it. Such nations may incline to socialism, but they want their own brand, not that of either Russia or China.

It follows, third, that the United States

---

2. Stanley Hoffmann, "Vietnam and Western Europe," *The New Republic,* January 30, 1971.
3. Zbigniew Brzezinski, "America and Europe," *Foreign Affairs,* 49 (October 1970), 11–30.

4. *Jane's Fighting Ships, 1970–71,* cited in the *New York Times,* August 28, 1970.

should subdue its apprehension over threat- ened leftist revolutions in small states the world over. Such revolutions are bound to come. Where they are, or appear to be, in the hands of Communists, the United States should ask two questions: (1) Would a Com- munist regime in state X be a threat to the security or a vital interest of the United States? (2) If it would be, can the United States prevent its accession at a cost that would not exceed that of the apprehended danger? If the answer to either questions is no, the United States should keep hands off. In Vietnam, in the minds of a great many knowledgeable people, the answer would have been no to both questions.

Once the United States withdraws from Vietnam, the Nixon Doctrine offers a plausi- ble formula for a policy in East and Southeast Asia: provision of a shield against threats by a nuclear power to the freedom of a nation allied with the United States or vital to its security; arms and economic assistance but no U.S. troops to such nations facing other types of aggression.[5]

Fourth, the trend toward a more realistic China policy, accelerated in the spring of 1971, should continue. The United States should remove all discriminatory obstacles to travel to and from China, should encourage social and intellectual contacts, and should end the ban on trade with China, which dur- ing its twenty-year existence has served no discernible useful purpose. The United States should also abandon its opposition to the seat- ing of the Peking delegate as the representa- tive of China in the United Nations. If this can be accomplished while permitting the Na- tionalist government to retain its seat in the General Assembly as the government of Tai- wan, well and good. If such a "two Chinas" solution is rejected by one or both the govern- ments directly concerned, the United States may find it necessary to acquiesce in the de-

nial to the Nationalist government of U.N. membership. The United States would still be morally bound by its treaty commitments to the Chiang Kai-shek regime, and these may present, for some time, an obstacle to the establishment of normal diplomatic relations with the People's Republic of China.

Fifth, disillusionment with the experience in Vietnam should not lead to a revival of extreme isolationism, as some students of the subject have predicted.[6] The importance to the United States of the NATO alliance and of the preservation of a balance of power in the Middle East has been mentioned. The United States should not be indifferent to real threats to its security that may arise in other areas. National interest as well as humani- tarian sentiment prescribes assistance to the developing nations wherever such assistance can be effective in narrowing the gap between the poor and the affluent. In Latin America, where the Alliance for Progress has fallen far short of its goal, the United States should increase its efforts to promote economic pros- perity and social progress. A 50 percent de- cline in foreign aid appropriations from 1961 to 1971 and a revival of economic protec- tionism in the 91st Congress (1969–1971) represented tendencies that were contrary to the true interests of the United States and of international society as a whole.

Sixth, though many students of interna- tional relations have despaired of any great good coming out of the United Nations, that organization deserves to be respected for what it has achieved through its peacekeeping func- tion, through its economic and social subsidi- aries, and as a forum where the dissatisfied nations of the world may air their grievances. It should be not only preserved but strength- ened wherever possible. It is not inconceivable that an East–West détente might alleviate the chronic paralysis of the Security Council, that the dilution of the General Assembly by mini-states might be checked, or that the existing majority of small states might see the value of less cumbersome procedures and

5. *U.S. Foreign Policy for the 1970's: A New Strategy for Peace* (See above Chapter 49, n. 37), pp. 55–56. For discussion of ambiguities and possible booby-traps in the Nixon Doctrine, see Earl G. Ravenal, "The Nixon Doctrine and Our Asian Commitments," *For- eign Affairs,* 49 (January 1971), 201–17.

6. Cf. Selig Adler, "The Ghost of Isolationism," *For- eign Service Journal,* November 1969.

pay greater heed to the interests of the major powers. The United States, as the original leading sponsor of the United Nations, should not desist from working for its improvement, and its expanded use.

Finally, if the United States hopes to command respect and influence in the world through other means than sheer force, it should seek to improve its image in the eyes of other nations. Once viewed as the land of freedom and hope, today America appears to some Europeans (in the words of historian Arnold J. Toynbee) "the most dangerous country in the world," while another historian finds it "unfortunate that the role of leadership should have been thrust . . . on a nation unprepared for the role." [7] What many foreign observers see is a nation beset by crime, vio-lence, racial discrimination and strife, intoler-ance, and national disunity at home, and addicted to bloody intervention abroad. Such critics would certainly not depreciate the statesmanlike generosity of the Marshall Plan or the Foreign Aid program in general in its more flourishing years, or the American desire to see freedom prevail in the world; but of the America of 1971 there was all too much truth in their caricature. A change in national priorities is proposed by Hans Morgenthau. Instead of embarking upon costly interven-tions to impose its political and economic pro-cedures upon alien peoples, "the United States," he wrote, "ought to concentrate its efforts upon creating a society at home which can again serve as a model for other nations to emulate." [8]

7. Toynbee in *New York Times,* May 10, 1970, Sec. 4, p. 2; Walter Laqueur in the *New York Times Magazine,* August 16, 1970, p. 34.

8. Hans J. Morgenthau, *A New Foreign Policy for the United States* (New York: Praeger Publishers, Inc., 1969. Copyright by Council on Foreign Rela-tions).

A bibliography for a textbook covering nearly two centuries of American diplomatic history is necessarily highly selective; otherwise there would be no space for the narrative. I have tried to adapt the following essay to the immediate needs of teachers and students in undergraduate courses in the field, naming what seem to me the most useful books, together with a few key articles and suggestions for further bibliographical explorations. My rule has been to include older standard works that are still dependable for basic information and more recent books and articles presenting significant new interpretations and representing opposing points of view on controversial topics. The selective process becomes more exacting when applied to the flood of literature on the events of the last fifty years. My decisions on what to include necessarily reflect my personal judgments. I trust that others will accept most of these as sound.

The essay is divided into sections bearing Roman numerals. These do not correspond to chapters in the text, but each section gives indication of the chapter or chapters to which it is applicable. Bibliographical data and full titles, where long, are given only with the first citation of each book. Thereafter short titles are used with indications in each instance of the section of the original citation. Some items are cited so often, however, that repeated reference to the initial citation is superfluous.

A Selective Bibliographical Essay

I. Bibliographies, Sources, and Textbooks

Unique among *bibliographies* of the history of United States foreign relations is the *Guide to the Diplomatic History of the United States, 1775–1921*, compiled by Samuel Flagg Bemis and Grace Gardner Griffin (Washington, D.C.: Government Printing Office, 1935), an extraordinarily meticulous and intensive catalogue of the primary and secondary literature of the subject for the period covered. It is still indispensable as a starting point for the period to 1921, but its usefulness is obviously limited by its date of publication. For the period from 1919 to 1962, one may begin with the four volumes of *Foreign Affairs Bibliography*, published for the Council on Foreign Relations, the first three by Harper & Row, Publishers (New York, 1933–1955), the fourth by R. R. Bowker Co. (New York, 1964). These listings are compiled at ten-year intervals from the quarterly journal *Foreign Affairs*, in which they are continued to the present. Scholars investigating United States relations with Latin America will want to consult *A Bibliography of United States-Latin*

American Relations since 1810: A Selected List of Eleven Thousand Published References, compiled by David F. Trask, Michael C. Meyer, and Roger R. Trask (Lincoln: University of Nebraska Press, 1968). Useful also are such bibliographies of general American history as the *Harvard Guide to American History,* by Oscar Handlin and others (Cambridge: Harvard University Press, 1954); *The American Historical Association's Guide to Historical Literature,* edited by George F. Howe and others (New York: The Macmillan Company, 1962); and the annual volumes of the series, *Writings on American History,* the latest issue being that for the year *1959.* Useful bibliographies are also found in many textbooks.

The principal *official sources* of the history of American foreign relations are diplomatic correspondence and treaties and other international agreements. For an introduction to the published diplomatic correspondence, the student should consult Bemis and Griffin, *Guide to the Diplomatic History of the United States, 1775–1921* (cited above), items numbered 5339, 5340, 5341, 5344, and 5345–349. Several of these merit description here. *American State Papers. Class I, Foreign Relations,* 6 vols. (Washington, D.C.: Gales and Seaton, 1832–1859) [5341] contain the published diplomatic correspondence from 1789 to 1828. There is no similar collection for the years 1828–1861, but such correspondence as was published may be located through A. H. Hasse, ed., *Index to United States Documents Relating to Foreign Affairs, 1828–1861,* 3 vols. (Washington: Carnegie Institution of Washington, 1914–1921) [5344]. Beginning with 1861, the Department of State has published annual collections under the title *Papers Relating to the Foreign Relations of the United States* (title changed with the 1934 volume to *Foreign Relations of the United States: Diplomatic Papers*) [5345], usually cited simply as *Foreign Relations.* Publication in 1970 had reached the year 1946. A number of supplementary volumes dealing with specific topics have been published under the general title. The standard earlier collections of treaties (Bemis and Griffin, items 5371 and 5368 respectively) are *Treaties and Other International Acts of the United States of America,* 8 vols., edited by Hunter Miller (Washington, D.C.: Government Printing Office, 1931–1948), covering the period 1778–1863, much the best collection as far as it goes; and *Treaties, Conventions, International Acts, Protocols and Agreements between the United States of America and Other Powers, 1776–1937,* 4 vols., edited by W. M. Malloy and others (Washington, D.C.: Government Printing Office, 1910–1938). This was continued to 1950 in U.S. Department of State, *Treaties Series* and *Executive Agreement Series.* A new series, *Treaties and Other International Agreements of the United States of America,* 1950–1969 and continuing, was initiated in 1951. Other volumes under the same title will eventually cover the period from 1776 to 1950.

A new type of official document publication was initiated with the issuance in 1950 of *A Decade of American Foreign Policy: Basic Documents, 1941–1949* (*Senate Document* 123, 81st Cong., 1st sess.). This was followed in 1957 by *American Foreign Policy, 1950–1955: Basic Documents,* 2 vols. (Department of State Publication 6446), and, beginning with 1956, by annual volumes entitled *American Foreign Policy: Current Documents.* The volumes of this series contain important messages, addresses, statements, reports, diplomatic notes, and treaties, most, but not all, of these previously published. Classified documents are reserved for the *Foreign Relations* volumes. There are numerous unofficial anthologies of diplomatic documents. Two of the most convenient are R. J. Bartlett, ed., *The Record of American Diplomacy,* 4th ed. (New York: Alfred A. Knopf, Inc., 1964), and Dorothy B. Goebel, ed., *American Foreign Policy: A Documentary Survey* (New York: Holt, Rinehart & Winston, Inc., 1961). Others which combine documents with readings representing varying interpretations are: Robert A. Divine, ed., *American Foreign Policy* (New York: World Publishing Co., Meridian Books, 1960); Daniel M. Smith, ed., *Major Problems in American Diplomatic History: Documents and Readings* (Lexington, Mass.: D. C. Heath & Company, 1964); Norman A. Graebner, ed., *Ideas and Diplomacy: Readings in the Intellectual Tradition of American Foreign Policy* (New York: Oxford University Press, Inc., 1964); William A. Williams, *The Shaping of American Diplomacy: Readings and Documents in American Foreign Relations, 1750–1955,* 2 vols. (Skokie, Ill.: Rand McNally & Co., 1956). For the period from 1938 onward a useful collection is *Documents on American Foreign Relations,* published annually, 29 vols. to 1970 (Vols. 1–6, Boston: World Peace Foundation, 1939–1945; Vols. 7–13, Princeton: Princeton University Press, for World Peace Foundation, 1947–1953; Vols.

for 1952 to 1966, Harper & Row, Publishers, for Council on Foreign Relations, New York, 1953–1967; Vol. for 1967, Simon & Schuster, Inc., for Council on Foreign Relations, New York, 1968). Editors of these volumes are as follows: Vols. 1–3, S. S. Jones and Denys Myers; Vol. 4, L. M. Goodrich with the collaboration of S. S. Jones and D. P. Myers; Vols. 5–7, L. M. Goodrich and M. J. Carroll; Vols. 8–12, Raymond Dennett and R. K. Turner; Vol. 13, Raymond Dennett and K. D. Durant; Vols. for 1952, C. W. Baier and R. P. Stebbins; 1953–1954, P. V. Curl; 1955–1959, P. E. Zinner; 1960–1963, 1965–1967, R. P. Stebbins with the assistance of Elaine P. Adam; 1964, Jules David with the assistance of Elaine P. Adam.

Of *textbooks* in American diplomatic history, there has been a proliferation in recent years. Samuel F. Bemis, *A Diplomatic History of the United States,* 5th ed. (New York: Holt, Rinehart & Winston, Inc., 1965), and Thomas A. Bailey, *A Diplomatic History of the American People,* 8th ed. (New York: Appleton-Century-Crofts, 1969), retain the merits that have made them popular over many years. R. W. Leopold, *The Growth of American Foreign Policy: A History* (New York: Alfred A. Knopf, Inc., 1962), is an able analytical treatment, seven-eighths of it dealing with the period since 1889. A recent text of high quality is Robert H. Ferrell, *American Diplomacy: A History,* revised and enlarged edition (New York: W. W. Norton & Company, Inc., 1969). Among others worthy of mention are books by Wayne S. Cole, Alexander DeConde, L. Ethan Ellis, and Richard W. Van Alstyne.

II. Instruments and Procedures of Foreign Policy (Chapter 2)

An excellent general introduction to diplomatic practice is *Diplomacy* by Sir Harold Nicolson, 3rd edition (New York: Oxford University Press, Inc., 1963). *Diplomat,* by Charles W. Thayer (New York: Harper & Row, Publishers, 1959), performs a similar service from an American vantage point. James L. McCamy, *The Administration of American Foreign Affairs* (New York: Alfred A. Knopf, Inc., 1950), deals primarily with the Washington end of the American diplomatic machine. The same author, in *Conduct of the New Diplomacy* (New York: Harper & Row, Publishers, 1964), points to the ill effects of the

absence of coordination in the numerous agencies in the executive branch dealing with foreign policy. Elmer Plischke, *Conduct of American Diplomacy* (New York: Van Nostrand Reinhold Company, 1950), emphasizes "the principles, procedures, and governmental machinery involved in the conduct of our foreign relations," as do also W. Y. Elliott and others in *United States Foreign Policy: Its Organization and Control* (New York: Columbia University Press, 1952). The Department of State is treated historically and analytically by Graham H. Stuart in *The Department of State: A History of Its Organization, Procedure and Personnel* (New York: The Macmillan Company, 1949). The Foreign Service is treated comprehensively in William Barnes and J. H. Morgan, *The Foreign Service of the United States: Origins, Development, and Functions* (Washington, D.C.: Department of State [1951]), and more recently and more critically by W. Wendell Blancké in *The Foreign Service of the United States* (New York: Praeger Publishers, Inc., 1969). *The Secretary of State and the Ambassador,* edited by Senator Henry M. Jackson (New York: Praeger Publishers, Inc., 1964), comprises a study by a subcommittee of the Senate Committee on Foreign Relations and essays by six members of the State Department and the Foreign Service, including former Secretary Dean Rusk. Graham H. Stuart, *American Diplomatic and Consular Practice,* 2nd ed. (New York: Appleton-Century-Crofts, 1952), is a standard and still useful analysis. Eleanor Lansing Dulles, *American Foreign Policy in the Making* (New York: Harper & Row, Publishers, 1968), analyzes the machinery of decision-making from the President through the ambassador and gives case histories of "six critical decisions" in post-World War II foreign policy. Thomas A. Bailey, *The Art of Diplomacy: The American Experience* (New York: Appleton-Century-Crofts, 1968), sets forth "267 basic guidelines or maxims" for the conduct of diplomacy and supplies illustrative instances of both adherence and violation, with sometimes humorous comment. The same author has approached a basic problem in any democracy in *The Man in the Street: The Impact of American Public Opinion on Foreign Policy* (New York: The Macmillan Company, 1948). R. A. Dahl, *Congress and Foreign Policy* (New York: Harcourt Brace Jovanovich, Inc., 1950), is adequately characterized by the title. Two recent studies discuss the nature and purposes of the U.S. Information

Agency (including Voice of America): John W. Henderson, *The United States Information Agency* (New York: Praeger Publishers, Inc., 1969), and Ronald I. Rubin, *The Objectives of the U.S. Information Agency: Controversies and Analysis* (New York: Praeger Publishers, Inc., 1968). Harry H. Ransom, *The Intelligence Establishment* (Cambridge: Harvard University Press, 1970), is the best study of the Central Intelligence Agency and other United States secret agencies. David Wise and Thomas B. Ross, *The Invisible Government* (New York: Random House, Inc., 1964), is a journalistic portrayal of the role of the C.I.A. in foreign policy. Merle J. Pusey, *The Way We Go to War* (Boston: Houghton Mifflin Company, 1969), is a critique of the alleged usurpation of the war-making power by recent Presidents.

The role of the Secretary of State in the conduct of foreign policy is examined historically in *The American Secretaries of State and Their Diplomacy,* in seventeen volumes, as of 1970, and continuing. The first ten volumes, edited by Samuel F. Bemis, were published by Alfred A. Knopf, Inc. (New York: 1927–1929); the later volumes, edited by Robert H. Ferrell and Samuel F. Bemis, were published by Cooper Square Publishers, Inc. (New York, 1963–   ). Briefer treatments of the same theme are Alexander DeConde, *The American Secretary of State: An Interpretation* (New York: Praeger Publishers, Inc., 1962), and N. A. Graebner, ed., *An Uncertain Tradition: The American Secretaries of State in the Twentieth Century* (New York: McGraw-Hill Book Company, 1961).

Some Secretaries of State have left important personal records of their stewardship. Most voluminous of these are the *Memoirs of John Quincy Adams,* 12 vols. (Philadelphia: J. B. Lippincott Co., 1874–1877). In more recent times, John W. Foster, Robert Lansing, Henry L. Stimson, Cordell Hull, James F. Byrnes, and Dean Acheson have supplemented the official record with their personal recollections. These will be cited in due course.

Many American diplomats have published records of their experiences, often with observations, critical and otherwise, about American diplomatic machinery and procedures. Only a few can be mentioned here. Robert Murphy, *Diplomat Among Warriors* (Garden City, N.Y.: Doubleday & Company, Inc., 1964), and W. Averell Harriman, *America and Russia in a Changing World: A Half Century of Personal Observation* (Garden City, N.Y.: Doubleday & Company, Inc., 1971), have much to tell of the diplomacy of World War II and after. Joseph C. Grew, *Turbulent Era: A Diplomatic Record of Forty Years, 1904–1945,* 2 vols. (Boston: Houghton Mifflin Company, 1952), records a wide range of experience in the service, culminating in ten crucial years in Japan. Roger Hilsman, *To Move a Nation* (Garden City, N.Y.: Doubleday & Company, Inc., 1967), and John Kenneth Galbraith, *Ambassador's Journal* (Boston: Houghton Mifflin Company, 1969), recounted their diplomatic adventures during the administration of John F. Kennedy. Willard Beaulac, *Career Diplomat: A Career in the Foreign Service of the United States* (New York: The Macmillan Company, 1964), analyzes life and work in the Foreign Service for those considering it as a career. Ellis Briggs, *Farewell to Foggy Bottom: The Recollections of a Career Diplomat* (New York: David McKay Co., Inc., 1964), is partly appraisal, partly an anecdotal narrative. The same author's humorous and ironical approach characterizes his *Anatomy of Diplomacy: The Origins and Evolution of American Foreign Policy* (New York: David McKay Co., Inc., 1968). Henry S. Villard, *Affairs at State* (New York: Thomas Y. Crowell Company, 1965), explains some of the difficulties of conducting diplomacy in a situation where "the United States has changed its role in the world before it has had time to change its habits of mind." A critique of the conduct of American foreign policy by John P. Leacacos, a newsman with long experience both in Washington and abroad, is *Fires in the In-Basket: The ABC's of the State Department* (New York: World Publishing Company, 1968).

III. Diplomacy of the Revolution (Chapter 3)

The nearly three hundred years of diplomatic and military maneuvering for control of North America which preceded the American Revolution are comprehensively described in Max Savelle, with Margaret Anne Fisher, *The Origins of American Diplomacy: The International History of Anglo-America, 1492–1763* (New York: The Macmillan Company, 1967), a volume in the *American Diplomatic History Series,* edited by Armin Rappaport. The best concise account of the diplomacy of the Revolution is Samuel F. Bemis, *The Diplomacy of the American Revolution* (New York: Appleton-Century-Crofts, 1935). Essays on several phases of the struggle are included in the same author's *American Foreign Policy and the Blessings of Liberty and Other Essays* (New Haven: Yale University Press, 1962). Edwin S. Corwin, *French Policy and the American Alliance of 1778* (Princeton: Princeton University Press, 1916), long standard, is supplemented by William C. Stinchcombe, *The American Revolution and the French Alliance* (Syracuse, N.Y.: Syracuse University Press, 1969), which pays new attention to American opinion as expressed by the press and the clergy. Richard W. Van Alstyne, *Empire and Independence: The International History of the American Revolution* (New York: John Wiley & Sons, Inc., 1965), throws some new light on the role of France. All earlier accounts of the peace negotiations and their preliminaries have been superseded by Richard B. Morris, *The Peacemakers: The Great Powers and American Independence* (New York: Harper & Row, Publishers, 1965). The parts played individually by the principal American diplomats are related in Gerald Stourzh, *Benjamin Franklin and American Foreign Policy* (Chicago: University of Chicago Press, 1954) and in other biographies, among them, *Benjamin Franklin,* by Carl C. Van Doren (New York: The Viking Press, Inc., 1938); *John Jay,* by Frank Monaghan (Indianapolis: The Bobbs-Merrill Company, Inc., 1935); and *John Adams,* by Page Smith, 2 vols. (Garden City, N.Y.: Doubleday & Company, Inc., 1962).

IV. The Confederation and the Presidencies of Washington and John Adams (1783–1801) (Chapters 4, 5)

The foreign relations of this period concerned chiefly Great Britain, France, and Spain and have been generally so treated by historians. Not to be overlooked, however, are the general accounts in Edward Channing, *A History of the United States,* 6 vols. (New York: The Macmillan Company, 1926), Vol. 3, and A. B. Darling, *Our Rising Empire, 1763–1803* (New Haven: Yale University Press, 1940). A volume covering a long period of U.S.-British relations is A. L. Burt, *The United States, Great Britain, and British North America from the Revolution to the Establishment of Peace after the War of 1812* (New Haven: Yale University Press, 1940). The period from 1783 to 1795 is explored in the classic *Jay's Treaty: A Study in Commerce and Diplomacy,* by Samuel F. Bemis, rev. ed. (New Haven: Yale University Press, 1962). Some of Bemis's interpretations are now challenged by Jerald A. Combs in *The Jay Treaty: Political Battleground of the Founding Fathers* (Berkeley: University of California Press, 1970), in the field of domestic politics and by Charles R. Ritcheson in *Aftermath of Revolution: British Policy Toward the United States, 1783–1795* (Dallas: Southern Methodist University Press, 1969), as to British motivation. Relations with Britain after 1795 are perspicaciously covered by Bradford Perkins, *The First Rapprochement: England and the United States, 1795–1805* (Philadelphia: The University of Pennsylvania Press, 1955). For United States-Spanish relations the best accounts are Samuel F. Bemis, *Pinckney's Treaty,* rev. ed. (New Haven: Yale University Press, 1960), a companion volume to his *Jay's Treaty,* and two books by A. P. Whitaker, *The Spanish-American Frontier, 1783–1795* (Boston: Houghton Mifflin Company, 1927), and *The Mississippi Question, 1795–1803: A Study in Trade, Politics, and Diplomacy* (New York: Appleton-Century-Crofts, 1934). The French side of the picture has recently been explored by Alexander DeConde in two books: *Entangling Alliance: Politics and Diplomacy under George Washington* (Durham, N.C.: Duke University Press, 1958), and *The Quasi-War: The Politics and Diplomacy of the Undeclared War with France, 1797–1801* (New York: Charles Scribner's Sons, 1966). Specific problems of the period receive treatment in Felix Gilbert, *To the Farewell Address: Ideas of Early American Foreign Policy* (Princeton: Princeton University Press, 1961); Julian P. Boyd, *NUMBER 7: Alexander Hamilton's Secret Attempt to Control American Foreign Policy* (Princeton: Princeton University Press, 1964); B. H. Williams, *Economic Foreign Policy of the United States* (New York: McGraw-Hill Book Company, 1929); Marshall Smelser, *The Congress Founds the Navy* (Notre Dame, Ind.: University of Notre Dame Press, 1959). See also sketches in Bemis, *American Secretaries of State* (cited under II), Vols. 1 and 2, and "Washington's Farewell Address" and other essays in Bemis, *American Foreign Policy and the Blessings of Liberty* (cited under III).

V. Expansion, Neutral Rights, and War, (1801–1815) (Chapters 6, 7)

The classic general account of this period is Henry Adams, *History of the United States During the Administrations of Jefferson and Madison,* 9 vols.

(New York: Charles Scribner's Sons, 1889–1891). Though marked by a strong anti-Jefferson bias, it is still valuable. That bias is corrected by Marshall Smelser in *The Democratic Republic, 1801–1815* (New York: Harper & Row, Publishers, 1968), a well balanced volume based largely on fresh research. Volume 4 of Channing, *History of the United States* (cited under IV), and Volumes 3 and 4 of Bemis, *American Secretaries of State* (cited under II) are useful here also, as are Volumes 4, 5, and 6 of Irving Brant, *James Madison*, 6 vols. (Indianapolis: The Bobbs-Merrill Company, Inc., 1941–1961). Satisfactory accounts of relations with the pirates of North Africa are found in R. W. Irwin, *The Diplomatic Relations of the United States with the Barbary Powers, 1776–1816* (Chapel Hill: University of North Carolina Press, 1931), and in L. B. Wright and J. H. McLeod, *The First Americans in North Africa: William Eaton's Struggle for a Vigorous Policy Against the Barbary Pirates, 1799–1805* (Princeton: Princeton University Press, 1945). On the purchase of Louisiana, one of the best accounts is that by Henry Adams, *op. cit.*, but see also E. W. Lyon, *Louisiana in French Diplomacy, 1759–1804* (Norman: The University of Oklahoma Press, 1934), Darling, *Our Rising Empire*, and Whitaker, *The Mississippi Question*, both cited under IV.

Special aspects of trouble with Great Britain are treated by R. G. Albion and J. B. Pope in *Sea Lanes in Wartime* (New York: W. W. Norton & Company, Inc., 1942), by J. F. Zimmerman in *Impressment of American Seamen* (New York: Columbia University Press, 1925), and by J. W. Pratt in *Expansionists of 1812* (New York: The Macmillan Company, 1925), who emphasizes frontier problems and the desire for Canada and Florida. That whole subject is covered by A. L. Burt in *The United States, Great Britain* [etc.], (cited under IV), but by far the best survey of the events leading to the War of 1812 is Bradford Perkins, *Prologue to War: England and the United States, 1805–1812* (Berkeley: University of California Press, 1961). A convenient approach to the various theories of the causes of the War of 1812 is offered by either of two paperbacks: Bradford Perkins, ed., *The Causes of the War of 1812: National Honor or National Interest?* (New York: Holt, Rinehart & Winston, Inc., 1962), or G. R. Taylor, ed., *The War of 1812: Past Justifications and Present Interpretations* (Lexington, Mass.: D. C. Heath & Company, 1963); or by an earlier study, "The Origins of the War of 1812:

A Survey of Changing Interpretations," by W. H. Goodman, in *Mississippi Valley Historical Review,* 28 (1941), 171–86. Published too late to be included in these compilations are *The Republic in Peril: 1812* (New York: Columbia University Press, 1964), by Roger H. Brown, who surmises that war was thought necessary to save the Republic from disgrace and perhaps from collapse; and *The Causes of the War of 1812,* by Reginald Horsman (Philadelphia: University of Pennsylvania Press, 1962), a scholarly survey of the entire field.

The peace negotiations at Ghent, described in the general narratives listed above, get special attention from F. L. Engelmann in *The Peace of Christmas Eve* (New York: Harcourt Brace Jovanovich, Inc., 1962), in the third volume of Bradford Perkins's outstanding trilogy, *Castlereagh and Adams: England and the United States, 1812–1823* (Berkeley: University of California Press, 1965), and in Samuel F. Bemis's magisterial volume, *John Quincy Adams and the Foundations of American Foreign Policy* (New York: Alfred A. Knopf, Inc., 1949).

VI. Postwar Settlements and the Monroe Doctrine (1815–1826) (Chapters 8, 9)

The volumes just cited, by Bemis and Bradford Perkins, are of first importance for this period also, Perkins for relations with England, Bemis more generally. Bemis, *American Secretaries of State*, Vol. 4, and George Dangerfield, *The Awakening of American Nationalism, 1815–1828* (New York: Harper & Row, Publishers, 1965), are also useful. That special phase of Anglo-American relations which produced the Monroe Doctrine is included in Bradford Perkins' *Castlereagh and Adams* (cited in V) and is the subject of Dexter Perkins, *The Monroe Doctrine, 1823–1826* (Cambridge: Harvard University Press, 1927), the first of that historian's four authoritative volumes on the Monroe Doctrine. The fourth of these, *A History of the Monroe Doctrine* (Boston: Little, Brown and Company, 1955)—a revision of the earlier *Hands Off: A History of the Monroe Doctrine*, covers the period from 1823 to 1954. A principle that antedated the Monroe Doctrine but later became associated with it is the subject of J. A. Logan, Jr., *No Transfer: An American Security Principle* (New Haven: Yale University Press, 1961). Relations with Canada, still a British colony, are treated in E. W. Mc-

Innis, *The Unguarded Frontier: A History of American-Canadian Relations* (Garden City, N.Y.: Doubleday & Company, Inc., 1942). C. P. Stacey, "The Myth of the Unguarded Frontier, 1815–1871," *American Historical Review*, 56 (1950), 1–18, corrects a common but erroneous supposition.

The relation of the United States to the winning of independence by Spain's American colonies (the source of the Monroe Doctrine) is covered in Samuel F. Bemis, *The Latin American Policy of the United States: An Historical Interpretation* (New York: Harcourt Brace Jovanovich, Inc., 1943) and has also been the subject of a number of monographs, written from somewhat different angles: J. F. Rippy, *Rivalry of the United States and Great Britain over Latin America, 1808–1830* (Baltimore: The Johns Hopkins Press, 1929); A. P. Whitaker, *The United States and the Independence of Latin America, 1800–1830* (Baltimore: The Johns Hopkins Press, 1941); and C. C. Griffin, *The United States and the Disruption of the Spanish Empire* (New York: Columbia University Press, 1937). How America profited from Spain's difficulties is explained in P. C. Brooks, *Diplomacy and the Borderlands: The Adams-Onis Treaty of 1819* (Berkeley: University of California Press, 1939). The important and dramatic role played by Andrew Jackson in bringing about the settlement with Spain is related by two of his biographers: J. S. Bassett, *Life of Andrew Jackson,* 2 vols., 2nd ed. (New York: The Macmillan Company, 1916), and Marquis James, *Andrew Jackson, The Border Captain* (Indianapolis: The Bobbs-Merrill Company, Inc., 1933). The story of the ill-fated Panama Congress is told by J. B. Lockey in *Pan-Americanism: Its Beginnings* (New York: The Macmillan Company, 1920), and in Bemis, *John Quincy Adams and the Foundations of American Foreign Policy* (cited under V).

The beginning of the peace movement in the United States after the War of 1812 is described in M. E. Curti, *The American Peace Crusade, 1815–1860* (Durham, N.C.: Duke University Press, 1929).

VII. Minor International Controversies (Chapter 10)

Between the issuance of the Monroe Doctrine and the crises that arose with Mexico and with England over Oregon in 1846, several controver-sies of less moment were either settled or cooled for settlement later. The settlement of long-standing American claims against France is described in R. A. McLemore, *Franco-American Diplomatic Relations, 1816–1836* (Baton Rouge: Louisiana State University Press, 1941). F. L. Benns, *The American Struggle for the British West India Carrying Trade, 1815–1830, Indiana University Studies,* Vol. 10 (Bloomington: Indiana University Press, 1923), describes the course and happy ending of a sometimes acrimonious dispute. Another long controversy with England, put on a back burner in the 1840's but not settled until the Civil War, is the subject of H. G. Soulsby, *The Right of Search and the Slave Trade in Anglo-American Relations, 1814–1862* (Baltimore: The Johns Hopkins Press, 1933). Disputes over the boundary with Canada and its alleged violation are treated in A. B. Corey, *The Crisis of 1830–1842 in Canadian American Relations* (New Haven: Yale University Press, 1941). Relevant biographies are Bassett, *Life of Andrew Jackson,* and Bemis, *John Quincy Adams,* cited under VI; Marquis James, *Andrew Jackson, Portrait of a President* (Indianapolis: The Bobbs-Merrill Company, Inc., 1937); C. M. Fuess, *Daniel Webster,* 2 vols. (Boston: Little, Brown and Company, 1930). Alastair Watt, "The Case of Alexander McLeod," *Canadian Historical Review,* 12 (1931), 145–67, puts a persistent myth to rest.

VIII. Expansion to the Pacific (Chapters 11–14)

Under this head fall the settlement of the Oregon boundary question, the annexation of Texas, and the war with Mexico. Since President Polk played a leading role in all these events, biographies of him are important. E. I. McCormac, *James K. Polk, A Political Biography* (Berkeley: University of California Press, 1922), is now superseded by the work of Charles Sellers, of which two volumes have appeared: *James K. Polk: Jacksonian, 1795–1843,* and *James K. Polk: Continentalist, 1843–1845* (Princeton: Princeton University Press, 1957, 1966). Two long standard studies, J. S. Reeves, *American Diplomacy under Tyler and Polk* (Baltimore: The Johns Hopkins Press, 1907), and G. L. Rives, *The United States and Mexico, 1821–1848,* 2 vols. (New York: Charles Scribner's Sons, 1913), are still useful for the topic as a whole, as are the sketches in Volume 5 of Bemis, *American Secretaries of State.* A more recent study emphasizing the economic attraction of the Pacific Coast is N. A. Graebner, *Empire on the Pacific: A Study in American Continental Expansion* (New York: The Ronald Press Company, 1955). Dexter Perkins, *The Monroe Doctrine, 1826–1867* (Baltimore: The Johns Hopkins Press, 1933), finds in this period the reemergence of the Monroe Doctrine after a long quiescence. Frederick Merk, *The Monroe Doctrine and American Expansionism, 1843–1849* (New York: Alfred A. Knopf, Inc., 1966), shows how the principles of President Monroe were used (generally misused) to rationalize the expansionist schemes of the decade. J. W. Pratt, "John L. O'Sullivan and Manifest Destiny," *New York History,* 14 (1933), 213–34, identifies the origin of the phrase "Manifest Destiny." Frederick Merk, *Manifest Destiny and Mission in American History: A Reinterpretation* (New York: Alfred A. Knopf, Inc., 1963), philosophizes upon the meaning of the phrase and the ideas that underlay it, and follows their application in practice.

On Oregon in particular, another volume by Frederick Merk, *The Oregon Question: Essays in Anglo-American Diplomacy and Politics* (Cambridge: Harvard University Press, 1967), brings together over a dozen indispensable essays covering the whole history of the Oregon controversy. M. C. Jacobs, *Winning Oregon: A Study of the Expansionist Movement* (Caldwell, Idaho: The Caxton Printers, Ltd., 1938), treats more fully than Merk the American political aspects of the movement. F. N. Howay, W. N. Sage, and H. F. Angus, *British Columbia and the United States* (New Haven: Yale University Press, 1942), has chapters on the Oregon boundary question and later controversies. E. A. Miles, " 'Fifty-four Forty or Fight'—An American Political Legend," *Mississippi Valley Historical Review,* 44 (1957), 291–309, finds that the quoted phrase did not appear until after the campaign of 1844.

On the annexation of Texas and its preliminaries, the most detailed study is Justin H. Smith, *The Annexation of Texas* (New York: Baker and Taylor, 1911). O. P. Chitwood, *John Tyler: Champion of the Old South* (New York: Appleton-Century-Crofts, 1931), describes President Tyler's efforts for annexation. J. W. Schmitz, *Texan Statecraft, 1836–1845* (San Antonio, Tex.: Naylor Company, 1941) analyzes the Texas side of the story, as does, in a popular way, Marquis James, *The Raven: A Biography of Sam Houston* (Indianapolis: The Bobbs-Merrill Company, Inc., 1929). Anson Jones, *Memoranda and Official Correspondence Relating to the Republic of Texas, Its History and Annexation* (New York: Appleton-Century-Crofts, 1859), is a controversial account by an important participant, to be read in connection with Herbert Gambrell, *Anson Jones, The Last President of Texas* (Garden City, N.Y.: Doubleday & Company, Inc., 1948). E. D. Adams, *British Interests and Activities in Texas, 1838–1846* (Baltimore: The Johns Hopkins Press, 1910), is an excellent study of the British involvement in the Texas story, supplemented now by Clagette Blake, *Charles Elliot, R. N., 1801–1875* (London: Charter House Press, 1960), a biography of the energetic British chargé d'affaires in Texas.

On the war with Mexico, Justin H. Smith, *The War with Mexico,* 2 vols. (New York: The Macmillan Company, 1919), is still the most intensive account, but on the diplomatic side is marked by a nationalistic, almost chauvinistic tone. This defect is corrected in the works by Reeves and Rives, listed earlier in this section, and by G. W. Price, *Origins of the War with Mexico: The Polk-Stockton Intrigue* (Austin: University of Texas Press, 1967). Price properly takes Smith to task but is too ready to accept unproved charges against Polk. Allan Nevins, *Frémont, The West's Greatest Adventurer,* 2 vols. (New York: Harper & Row, Publishers, 1928), is good on a controversial phase of the conquest of California. One who played an important part in Frémont's California operations is the subject of a recent biography, *Messenger of Destiny: The California Adventure, 1846–1847, of Archibald H. Gillespie, U. S. Marine Corps,* by Werner H. Marti (San Francisco, Cal.: John Howell, 1960). R. L. Underhill, *From Cowhides to Golden Fleece: A Narrative of California, 1832–1858* (Stanford: Stanford University Press, 1939), tells the story of Thomas O. Larkin, first American consul at Monterey and confidential agent on the eve of the war. Nicholas P. Trist, who negotiated the peace treaty with Mexico and lost his job in consequence, has been the subject of two interesting essays: "Nicholas P. Trist, A Diplomat with Ideals," by Louis M. Sears, in *Mississippi Valley Historical Review,* 11 (1924), 85–98, and "The Thankless Task of Nicholas Trist," by R. M. Ketchum, in *American Heritage,* 21, No. 5 (August 1970).

IX. Opening China and Japan (Chapter 15)

On nineteenth-century United States relations with the Far East in general, Tyler Dennett, *Americans in Eastern Asia* (New York: The Macmillan Company, 1922), has long been standard, as has H. B. Morse and H. F. MacNair, *Far Eastern International Relations* (Boston: Houghton Mifflin Company, 1931). Akira Iriye, *Across the Pacific: An Inner History of American-Far Eastern Relations* (New York: Harcourt Brace Jovanovich, Inc., 1967), emphasizes the "images" of Japan and China held in the United States for over a century, and vice versa, and their effect on diplomatic relations. Richard O'Connor, *Pacific Destiny: An Informal History of the United States in the Far East, 1776–1968* (Boston: Little, Brown and Company, 1969), describes how the United States evolved as a Pacific rather than an Atlantic power.

Earliest relations of the United States with China are set forth authoritatively in K. S. Latourette, *The History of the Early Relations between the United States and China, 1784–1844* (New Haven: Yale University Press, 1917), and popularly by F. R. Dulles in *The Old China Trade* (Boston: Houghton Mifflin Company, 1930). Maurice Collis, *Foreign Mud* (New York: Alfred A. Knopf, Inc., 1947), describes the opium trade and the war brought on by China's efforts to suppress it. J. K. Fairbank, *Trade and Diplomacy on the China Coast: The Treaty Ports, 1842–1854*, 2 vols. (Cambridge: Harvard University Press, 1953), is supplemented by Te-kong Tong, *United States Diplomacy in China, 1844–1860* (Seattle: University of Washington Press, 1964), a study making extensive use of both American and Chinese sources. F. R. Dulles, *China and America* (Princeton: Princeton University Press, 1946), is a popular history.

The first forty years of American-Japanese relations are described in detail by P. J. Treat in *Diplomatic Relations between the United States and Japan, 1853–1895*, 2 vols. (Stanford: Stanford University Press, 1932). Interesting personal accounts of Commodore Perry's epoch-making mission are available in Roger Pineau, ed., *The Japan Expedition, 1852–1854: The Personal Journal of Commodore Matthew C. Perry* (New York: Random House, Inc., 1969), and A. B. Cole, ed., *With Perry in Japan* (Princeton: Princeton University Press, 1942). The same episode is well described in S. E. Morison, *"Old Bruin," Commodore Matthew C. Perry, 1794–1858* (Boston: The Atlantic Monthly Press, 1967), in A. C. Walworth, *Black Ships off Japan: The Story of Commodore Perry's Expedition* (New York: Alfred A. Knopf, Inc., 1946), and, through Japanese eyes, in Oliver Statler, *The Black Ship Scroll: An Account of the Perry Expedition at Shimoda in*

1854 (Rutland, Vt.: Charles E. Tuttle Co., Inc., 1963). How Townsend Harris built upon Perry's beginning is told with acclaim by Carl Crow in *He Opened the Door of Japan* (New York: Harper & Row, Publishers, 1939), and less flatteringly from Japanese sources, by Oliver Statler in *Shimoda Story* (New York: Random House, Inc., 1969).

X. The Pre-Civil War Decade (Chapter 16)

The lively but generally futile diplomacy of this period has called forth quite a body of literature. Bemis, *Latin American Policy*, deals with it briefly, as do the following works cited under VIII: Dexter Perkins, *The Monroe Doctrine, 1826–1867*; Frederick Merk, *Manifest Destiny and Mission in American History*, and *The Monroe Doctrine and American Expansionism, 1843–1849*. R. F. Nichols, *Advance Agents of American Destiny* (Philadelphia: University of Pennsylvania Press, 1956), relates the adventures of a number of diplomats and filibusters of the period. The same author's *Franklin Pierce, Young Hickory of the Granite Hills* (Philadelphia: University of Pennsylvania Press, 1931), and I. D. Spencer's *The Victor and the Spoils: A Life of William L. Marcy* (Providence, R.I.: Brown University Press, 1959), are biographies of a President and a Secretary of State who were responsible for some of the expansionist ventures of the decade. An illuminating essay is M. E. Curti, "Young America," *American Historical Review*, 32 (1926), 34–55.

American designs for new acquisitions from, or a protectorate over, a faction-torn Mexico are traced in detail in J. M. Callahan, *American Foreign Policy in Mexican Relations* (New York: The Macmillan Company, 1932), and in J. F. Rippy, *The United States and Mexico* (New York: Alfred A. Knopf, Inc., 1926), while P. N. Garber, *The Gadsden Treaty* (Philadelphia: The University of Pennsylvania Press, 1924), describes the one such venture that succeeded.

American Interest in Cuba, 1848–1855 (New York: Columbia University Press, 1955), by Basil Rauch, covers the crucial years of this angle of Manifest Destiny. A. A. Ettinger, *The Mission to Spain of Pierre Soulé, 1853–1855* (New Haven: Yale University Press, 1932), relates the career of an amazingly brash diplomat, while R. G. Caldwell, in *The Lopez Expeditions to Cuba, 1848–1851* (Princeton: Princeton University Press, 1915), writes of a series of filibustering expeditions backed by American "private enterprise." Another filibuster, William Walker, who briefly ruled Nicaragua, is the principal subject of W. O. Scroggs, *Filibusters and Financiers: The Story of William Walker and His Associates* (New York: The Macmillan Company, 1916). One of the financiers associated with Walker was Charles Morgan, of whom J. P. Baughman writes in *Charles Morgan and the Development of Southern Transportation* (Nashville, Tenn.: Vanderbilt University Press, 1968). Competition for control of the canal routes is described in Mary W. Williams, *Anglo-American Isthmian Diplomacy, 1815–1915* (Baltimore: Lord Baltimore Press, 1916).

American relations with the Hawaiian kingdom in this period are covered briefly in S. K. Stevens, *American Expansion in Hawaii, 1842–1898* (Harrisburg, Pa.: Archives Publishing Company, 1945), and in more detail in R. S. Kuykendall, *The Hawaiian Kingdom, 1778–1854* (Honolulu: The University of Hawaii, 1938).

For relations with Canada, one may consult L. B. Shippee, *Canadian-American Relations, 1849–1874* (New Haven: Yale University Press, 1939), or the more detailed study by C. C. Tansill, *The Canadian Reciprocity Treaty of 1854* (Baltimore: The Johns Hopkins Press, 1922).

XI. The Civil War and Foreign Relations (Chapter 17)

From the vast literature dealing with the Civil War, there is space here to list only a few items that should be most helpful to an understanding of the war's international aspects. Two brief but reliable narratives of the war in general are Volume 6 of Channing, *History of the United States* (cited under IV), and J. G. Randall, *The Civil War and Reconstruction* (Lexington, Mass.: D. C. Heath & Company, 1937). Bemis, *American Secretaries of State,* Volume 7, contains sketches of Seward and Fish, who receive extended treatment in two excellent biographies: G. G. Van Deusen, *William H. Seward* (New York: Oxford University Press, Inc., 1967), and Allan Nevins, *Hamilton Fish: The Inner History of the Grant Administration* (New York: Dodd, Mead & Co., 1936). (Fish is included here because he was Secretary of State at the time of the settlement of the *Alabama* claims, an outgrowth of the war.) President Lincoln's participation is interestingly told by Jay Monaghan in *Diplomat in Carpet Slippers: Abraham Lincoln Deals with Foreign Affairs* (Indianapolis: The Bobbs-Merrill Company, Inc., 1945).

Relations of the Washington government with particular countries or areas are dealt with in E. D. Adams, *Great Britain and the American Civil War,* 2 vols. (New York: Longmans, Green & Company, 1925), an outstanding work; Lynn M. Case and W. F. Spencer, *The United States and France: Civil War Diplomacy* (Philadelphia: University of Pennsylvania Press, 1970), as definitive for France as Adams is for England; Donaldson Jordan and E. J. Pratt, *Europe and the American Civil War* (London: Oxford University Press, 1931); Henry Blumenthal, *A Reappraisal of Franco-American Relations, 1830–1871* (Chapel Hill: University of North Carolina Press, 1959); R. W. Winks, *Canada and the United States: The Civil War Years* (Baltimore: The Johns Hopkins Press, 1960). Relations with Russia, minor though friendly, have been the source of some historical illusion. See the following articles: F. A. Golder, "The Russian Fleet and the Civil War," *American Historical Review,* 20 (1915), 801–12; W. E. Nagengast, "The Visit of the Russian Fleet to the United States: Were Americans Deceived?" *Russian Review,* 8 (1949), 46–55; T. A. Bailey, "The Russian Fleet Myth Re-Examined," *Mississippi Valley Historical Review,* 38 (1951), 81–90. See also T. A. Bailey, *America Faces Russia: Russian-American Relations from Early Times to Our Day* (Ithaca, N.Y.: Cornell University Press, 1950), and F. R. Dulles, *The Road to Teheran* (Princeton: Princeton University Press, 1944).

The foreign relations of the Confederacy are described in much detail in F. L. Owsley, *King Cotton Diplomacy: Foreign Relations of the Confederate States of America* (Chicago: University of Chicago Press, 1931), and briefly in chapters in Clement Eaton, *A History of the Southern Confederacy* (New York: The Macmillan Company, 1954), and David H. Donald, ed., *Why the North Won the Civil War* (New York: The Macmillan Company, Collier Books, 1967), the latter also containing a chapter on Northern diplomacy.

Questions of neutral and belligerent rights and obligations in relation to warfare at sea occurred throughout the war. These receive excellent treatment in the work by E. D. Adams, cited above, and in R. G. Albion and J. B. Pope, *Sea Lanes in Wartime* (cited under V), and in Stuart L. Bernath, *Squall Across the Atlantic: American Civil War Prize Cases and Diplomacy* (Berkeley: University of California Press, 1970). The American official position is explained in U.S. Department of State, *Policy of the United States Toward Maritime Commerce in War,* prepared by Carlton Savage, 2 vols. (Washington: Government Printing Office, 1934–1936). British policy is explained by J. P. Baxter, III, "The British Government and Neutral Rights, 1861–1865," *American Historical Review,* 34 (1928), 9–29. One dramatic episode is the subject of C. F. Adams, "The *Trent* Affair," *American Historical Review,* 17 (1912), 540–62. The best account of the Geneva arbitration is in Nevins, *Hamilton Fish,* cited above.

XII. From the Civil War to the Spanish American War (Chapters 18–20)

American foreign policy from 1865 to the eve of the war with Spain lacked such dramatic episodes as those of the 1840's or at the turn of the century. It was not, however, a period of isolation. This is clearly shown by Milton Plesur in *America's Outward Thrust: Approaches to Foreign Affairs, 1865–1890* (DeKalb: Northern Illinois University Press, 1971), and by Walter LaFeber, who demonstrates, in *The New Empire: An Interpretation of American Expansion, 1860–1898* (Ithaca, N.Y.: Cornell University Press, 1964), that American businessmen and diplomats were constantly in search of better foreign markets. Several previously cited works are applicable to this period: Bemis, *American Secretaries of State,* Volumes 7 and 8, and his *Latin American Policy;* the biographies of Secretaries of State Seward and Fish by Van Deusen and Nevins respectively (cited under XI); Dexter Perkins, *The Monroe Doctrine, 1826–1867;* also Perkins' third volume, *The Monroe Doctrine, 1867–1907* (Baltimore: The Johns Hopkins Press, 1937), and chapters from the one-volume condensed version of the work: Dexter Perkins, *A History of the Monroe Doctrine* (cited under VI). Important studies of other Secretaries of State are Alice F. Tyler, *The Foreign Policy of James G. Blaine* (Minneapolis: University of Minnesota Press, 1927); C. C. Tansill, *The Foreign Policy of Thomas F. Bayard, 1885–1897* (New York: Fordham University Press, 1940); Henry James, *Richard Olney and His Public Service* (Boston: Houghton Mifflin Company, 1923). F. R. Dulles, *Prelude to World Power: American Diplomatic History, 1860–1900* (New York: The Macmillan Company, 1965), is a useful survey of the entire period; and D. M. Pletcher, *The Awkward Years: American Foreign Relations under Garfield and Arthur* (Columbia: University of Missouri Press, 1962), is a more detailed study.

The postwar flurry of expansionism is described by T. C. Smith in "Expansion after the Civil War, 1865–1871," *Political Science Quarterly,* 16 (1901), 412–36, and on its negative side by D. M. Dozer, in "Anti-Expansionism During the Johnson Administration," *Pacific Historical Review,* 12 (1943), 253–75. C. C. Tansill analyzes two abortive projects of this period in two separate volumes: *The Purchase of the Danish West Indies* (Baltimore: The Johns Hopkins Press, 1932), and *The United States and Santo Domingo, 1798–1873* (same publisher, 1938). The one successful expansionist enterprise of the time is the subject of V. J. Farrar, *The Annexation of Russian America to the United States* (Washington, D.C.: W. F. Roberts Company, Inc., 1937). On this subject see also the items cited under relations with Russia in the preceding section, and F. A. Golder, "The Purchase of Alaska," *American Historical Review,* 25 (1920), 411–25. M. W. Williams, *Anglo-American Isthmian Diplomacy, 1815–1915* (cited under X) covers the growing interest in canal routes. Growing concern with the Pacific area is the subject of F. R. Dulles, *America in the Pacific* (Boston: Houghton Mifflin Company, 1932), and of L. H. Battistini, *The Rise of American Influence in Asia and the Pacific* (East Lansing: Michigan State University Press, 1960). American relations with Hawaii, culminating in annexation, are treated definitively in two studies by Merze Tate, *The United States and the Hawaiian Kingdom: A Political History* (New Haven: Yale University Press, 1965), and *Hawaii: Reciprocity or Annexation* (East Lansing: Michigan State University Press, 1968); and more briefly in S. K. Stevens, *American Expansion in Hawaii, 1842–1898* (cited under X); in J. W. Pratt, *Expansionists of 1898* (Chicago: Quadrangle Books, Inc., 1964); and in two volumes by W. A. Russ, Jr., *The Hawaiian Revolution (1893–1894)* and *The Hawaiian Republic (1894–1898) and Its Struggle to Win Annexation* (both published at Selinsgrove, Pa.: Susquehanna University Press, 1959, 1961). G. H. Ryden, *The Foreign Policy of the United States in Relation to Samoa* (New Haven: Yale University Press, 1933) covers that subject in detail.

For the Monroe Doctrine in relation to Maximilian's empire in Mexico, Dexter Perkins' volume on the 1826–1867 period, cited above, may be supplemented by E. C. Corti, *Maximilian and Charlotte of Mexico,* 2 vols. (New York: Alfred A. Knopf, Inc., 1929). The Venezuela affair of 1895–1896 is covered in Dexter Perkins' 1867–1907 volume, in LaFeber, *The New Empire,* and James, *Richard Olney* (all cited above), and also in Allan Nevins, *Grover Cleveland: A Study in Courage* (New York: Dodd, Mead & Company, 1932); in A. E. Campbell, *Great Britain and the United States, 1895–1903* (London: Longmans, Green & Co. Ltd., 1960); in two essays in J. A. S. Grenville and G. B. Young, *Politics, Strategy, and American Diplomacy: Studies in Foreign Policy, 1873–1917* (New Haven: Yale University Press, 1966); and in Bradford Perkins, *The Great Rapprochement: England and the United States, 1895–1914* (New York: Atheneum Publishers, 1968). The last two studies minimize the risks of war in Cleveland's policy.

Developments in Pan Americanism, largely revolving around Secretary of State James G. Blaine, are described in the studies by Bemis and Tyler, cited at the beginning of this section, and in T. F. McGann, *Argentina, the United States, and the Inter-American System, 1880–1914* (Cambridge: Harvard University Press, 1957).

XIII. The War with Spain and American "Imperialism" (Chapters 21, 22)

Good general accounts are found in Margaret Leech, *In the Days of McKinley* (New York: Harper & Row, Publishers, 1959), and in two books by H. Wayne Morgan, *William McKinley and His America* (Syracuse, N.Y.: Syracuse University Press, 1963), and *America's Road to Empire: The War with Spain and Overseas Expansion* (New York: John Wiley & Sons, Inc., 1965). Old but still useful accounts of United States Spanish prewar diplomacy and peace negotiations are F. E. Chadwick, *The Relations of the United States and Spain: Diplomacy* (New York: Charles Scribner's Sons, 1909), and the sketches in Bemis, *American Secretaries of State,* Vol. 9. P. E. Coletta, ed., *Threshold to American Internationalism: Essays on the Foreign Policies of William McKinley* (New York: Exposition Press, 1970), has essays by J. W. Pratt and P. E. Coletta, respectively, on the coming of the war and the peace negotiations. E. R. May, *Imperial Democracy: The Emergence of America as a Great Power* (New York: Harcourt Brace Jovanovich, Inc., 1961), is good on the reactions in European foreign offices to America's new aggressiveness in the 1890's, but less than convincing on the rationale of McKinley's policy. Orestes Ferrara, *The Last Spanish War: Revelations in "Diplomacy"* (New York: Paisley Press, Inc., 1937), describes Spain's desperate efforts for European support against American pressure. Grenville and Young, *Politics, Strategy, and American Diplomacy* (cited under XII) have several well-researched essays on the Cuban question and pre- and postwar diplomacy. P. E. Coletta, *William Jennings Bryan. I. Politician and Evangelist, 1860–1908* (Lincoln: University of Nebraska Press, 1964), tells of Bryan's relation to the war and to Senate approval of the treaty. H. Wayne Morgan, ed., *Making Peace with Spain: The Diary of Whitelaw Reid, Sept.–Dec., 1898* (Austin: University of Texas Press, 1965), gives a first-hand record of the peace negotiations.

Walter LaFeber, *The New Empire,* and J. W. Pratt, *Expansionists of 1898* (both cited under XII), assess the motives of the war. LaFeber stresses economics; Pratt, intellectual currents and humanitarian and religious sentiment, though they agree on the economic motives shaping the peace settlement. T. J. McCormick, *China Market: America's Quest for Informal Empire, 1893–1901* (Chicago: Quadrangle Books, Inc., 1967), explains McKinley's decision to keep the Philippines. P. A. Varg, *The Making of a Myth: The United States and China, 1897–1912* (East Lansing: Michigan State University Press, 1968), deflates the China market balloon. Much the same ground is well covered in Marilyn B. Young, *The Rhetoric of Empire: American China Policy, 1895–1901* (Cambridge: Harvard University Press, 1968). C. H. Brown, *The Correspondents' War: Journalists in the Spanish-American War* (New York: Charles Scribner's Sons, 1967), describes the role of newsmen in Cuba before and during the war. E. R. May, *American Imperialism: A Speculative Essay* (New York: Atheneum Publishers, 1968), seeks explanation for the brief foray into imperialism by a minority of the American "establishment," 1898–1900. R. L. Beisner, *Twelve Against Empire: The Anti-Imperialists, 1898–1900* (New York: McGraw-Hill Book Company, 1968), analyzes the attitudes of a dozen leaders in the anti-imperialist movement. Other accounts of the anti-imperialists are F. H. Harrington, "The Anti-Imperialist Movement in the United States, 1898–1900," *Mississippi Valley Historical Review,* 22 (1935), 211–30, and Christopher Lasch, "The Anti-Imperialists, the Philippines, and the Inequality of Man," *Journal of Southern History,* 24 (1958), 319–31.

Relations with England during the war are described in A. E. Campbell, *Great Britain and the United States, 1895–1903,* and Bradford Perkins, *The Great Rapprochement* (both cited under XII) as well as in C. S. Campbell, Jr., *Anglo-American Understanding, 1898–1903* (Baltimore: The Johns Hopkins Press, 1957), and in L. M. Gelber, *The Rise of Anglo-American Friendship: A Study in World Politics, 1898–1906* (New York: Oxford University Press, Inc., 1938). For narratives of the final stage in the annexation of Hawaii, see the items cited in the preceding section.

The expansion of the United States Navy and its employment in the Pacific are portrayed in Harold and Margaret Sprout, *The Rise of American Naval Power, 1776–1918* (Princeton: Princeton University Press, 1939); G. T. Davis, *A Navy Second to None* (New York: Harcourt Brace Jovanovich, Inc., 1940); and W. R. Braisted, *The United States Navy in the Pacific, 1897–1909* (Austin: University of Texas Press, 1958).

XIV. From the War with Spain to World War I (1900–1914) (Chapters 23–25)

There are important biographies of the Presidents and Secretaries of State of this period, supplemented, for Roosevelt, and soon to be for Wilson, by multivolume editions of their correspondence: *The Letters of Theodore Roosevelt,* edited by Elting E. Morison, 8 vols. (Cambridge: Harvard University Press, 1951–1954), and *The Papers of Woodrow Wilson,* edited by Arthur S. Link, Vol. 1 (Princeton: Princeton University Press, 1966), and in progress. Meanwhile, we have *The Public Papers of Woodrow Wilson,* edited by R. S. Baker and William E. Dodd, 6 vols. (New York: Harper & Row, Publishers, 1925–1927), of which the last four volumes contain material on foreign relations. Of the many biographies of Theodore Roosevelt, probably the best is W. H. Harbaugh, *Power and Responsibility: The Life and Times of Theodore Roosevelt* (New York: Farrar, Straus & Giroux, Inc., 1961). Also to be mentioned are the entertaining *Theodore Roosevelt: A Biography,* by H. F. Pringle (New York: Harcourt Brace Jovanovich, Inc., 1931), and *The Republican Roosevelt,* by John M. Blum (Cambridge: Harvard University Press, 1954), a brilliant interpretative essay. Howard K. Beale's *Theodore Roosevelt and the Rise of America to World Power* (Baltimore: The Johns Hopkins Press, 1956), though not a biography, is the product of intensive research and throws new light on Roosevelt's policy in Europe, the Far East, and the Caribbean. *Theodore Roosevelt: An Autobiography* (New York: The Macmillan Company, 1916), is a better clue to "T.R.'s" personality than to the precise historical record. H. F. Pringle, *Life and Times of William Howard Taft,* 2 vols. (New York: Farrar, Straus & Giroux, Inc., 1939), is good on Roosevelt's successor.

Until recently the most authoritative biography of Woodrow Wilson was R. S. Baker, *Woodrow Wilson, Life and Letters,* 8 vols. (Garden City, N.Y.: Doubleday & Company, Inc., 1927–1939), continued in the same author's earlier *Woodrow Wilson and World Settlement,* 3 vols. (Garden City, N.Y.: Doubleday & Company, Inc., 1922). Of the definitive biography by Arthur S. Link, *Wilson* (with a different subtitle for each volume), five volumes have so far been published (Princeton: Princeton University Press, 1947–1965), bringing the story up to 1917.

Link has published several other volumes on Wilson and his period, among them *Woodrow Wilson: A Brief Biography* (Cleveland: The World Publishing Company, 1963) and *Wilson the Diplomatist: A Look at His Major Foreign Policies* (Baltimore: The Johns Hopkins Press, 1957). Other useful biographies are H. F. C. Bell, *Woodrow Wilson and the People* (Garden City, N.Y.: Doubleday & Company, Inc., 1945); Arthur Walworth, *Woodrow Wilson,* 2nd ed., two volumes in one (Boston: Houghton Mifflin Company, 1965); and a sympathetic interpretative essay by John M. Blum, *Woodrow Wilson and the Politics of Morality* (Boston: Little, Brown and Company, 1956). A man very close to Wilson who conducted a number of important missions to Europe for him was Colonel Edward M. House. *The Intimate Papers of Colonel House,* edited by Charles Seymour, 4 vols. (Boston: Houghton Mifflin Company, 1926–1928), are an important source for the prewar and the war years. The relations of House and Wilson have been studied from a psychological angle by A. L. and J. L. George in *Woodrow Wilson and Colonel House: A Personality Study* (New York: The John Day Company, Inc., 1956).

Sketches of the Secretaries of State of the period are found in Bemis, *American Secretaries of State,* Vols. 9 and 10, and in N. A. Graebner, ed., *An Uncertain Tradition: American Secretaries of State in the Twentieth Century* (cited under II). Important biographies of Secretaries are Tyler Dennett, *John Hay: From Poetry to Politics* (New York: Dodd, Mead & Co., 1933); P. C. Jessup, *Elihu Root,* 2 vols. (New York: Dodd, Mead & Co., 1938); P. E. Coletta, *William Jennings Bryan,* 3 vols. (Lincoln: University of Nebraska Press, 1964–1970), especially Vol. 2. Useful general accounts of the diplomacy of the period are F. R. Dulles, *America's Rise to World Power, 1898–1954* (New York: Harper & Row, Publishers, 1955), and J. W. Pratt, *Challenge and Rejection: The United States and World Leadership, 1900–1921* (New York: The Macmillan Company, 1967). This book is also published in paperback as *America and World Leadership, 1900–1921* (New York: The Macmillan Company, Collier Books, 1970). It also covers the period of war and peacemaking. George F. Kennan, in a small book, *American Diplomacy, 1900–1950* (Chicago: The University of Chicago Press, 1951), analyzes what he considers some crucial errors in American foreign policy from the War with Spain to World War II and its sequel.

For American policy in Latin America and the Caribbean in general, there are Bemis, *The Latin American Policy of the United States,* Dexter Perkins, *The Monroe Doctrine, 1867–1907,* and *A History of the Monroe Doctrine* (both cited under XII); another brief book by Dexter Perkins, *The United States and the Caribbean* (Cambridge: Harvard University Press, 1947); W. H. Callcott, *The Caribbean Policy of the United States, 1890–1920* (Baltimore: The Johns Hopkins Press, 1942); D. G. Munro, *Intervention and Dollar Diplomacy in the Caribbean, 1900–1921* (Princeton: Princeton University Press, 1964); and J. F. Rippy, *Caribbean Danger Zone* (New York: G. P. Putnam's Sons, 1940). J. W. Pratt, *America's Colonial Experiment* (Gloucester, Mass.: Peter Smith, 1964), has a chapter on Caribbean interventions, with citation of books on individual countries in that area. An excellent recent study of a crucial episode in relations with Cuba is Allan R. Millett, *The Politics of Intervention: The Military Occupation of Cuba, 1906–1909* (Columbus: Ohio State University Press, 1968). Of the many books treating of the acquisition of the Panama Canal Zone, probably the most useful are Gerstle Mack, *The Land Divided: A History of the Panama Canal and Other Isthmian Canal Projects* (New York: Alfred A. Knopf, Inc., 1944), and D. C. Miner, *The Fight for the Panama Route* (New York: Columbia University Press, 1940). Miner is particularly good on the Colombian politics of the episode. On relations with Mexico under Wilson, there is important new material in Volumes 2, 3, and 4 of Link, *Wilson* (cited above). The standard account is H. F. Cline, *The United States and Mexico,* rev. ed. (Cambridge: Harvard University Press, 1963). This should be supplemented with C. C. Cumberland, *The Mexican Revolution: Genesis under Madero* (Austin: University of Texas Press, 1952); S. R. Ross, *Francisco I. Madero* (New York: Columbia University Press, 1955); R. E. Quirk, *An Affair of Honor: Woodrow Wilson and the Occupation of Veracruz* ([Lexington, Ky.]: University of Kentucky Press, 1962); John Womack, Jr., *Zapata and the Mexican Revolution* (New York: Alfred A. Knopf, Inc., 1969); and K. J. Grieb, *The United States and Huerta* (Lincoln: University of Nebraska Press, 1969). Womack writes of an agrarian revolutionary leader little understood in the United States. Grieb gives American readers for the first time a clear view of Huerta and his problems. A clear view of British policy in Mexico is given, also for the first time, in Peter Calvert, *The Mexican Revolution, 1910–1914: The Diplomacy of Anglo-American Conflict* (Cambridge: At the University Press, 1968).

On American policy in the Far East, Dennett, *Americans in Eastern Asia* (cited under VIII), ends with the Boxer rebellion of 1900. A. W. Griswold, *The Far Eastern Policy of the United States* (New York: Harcourt Brace Jovanovich, Inc., 1938), is highly critical of United States policy. F. R. Dulles has provided popular accounts of United States relations with the two principal powers of the Far East: *China and America: The Story of Their Relations Since 1784* (Princeton: Princeton University Press, 1946), and *Forty Years of American-Japanese Relations* (New York: Appleton-Century-Crofts, 1937). American economic interest in China and the Open Door has been the subject of several monographs. T. J. McCormick, *China Market,* and P. A. Varg, *The Making of a Myth,* were cited under XIII. Another contribution by P. A. Varg is *Open Door Diplomat: The Life of W. W. Rockhill,* Illinois Studies in the Social Sciences, Vol. 33, No. 4 (Urbana: University of Illinois Press, 1952). C. S. Campbell, Jr., *Special Business Interests and the Open Door Policy* (New Haven: Yale University Press, 1951) covers part of the same ground. Charles Vevier, *The United States and China,*

1906–1913 (New Brunswick, N.J.: Rutgers University Press, 1955), carries the story to Wilson's repudiation of "dollar diplomacy."

The ambivalent relations with Japan during the period have been the subject of a number of studies. Two recent volumes, both drawing upon Japanese as well as American sources, are R. A. Esthus, *Theodore Roosevelt and Japan* (Seattle: University of Washington Press, 1966), which covers the period of Roosevelt's presidency (1901–1909), and C. E. Neu, *An Uncertain Friendship: Theodore Roosevelt and Japan, 1906–1909* (Cambridge: Harvard University Press, 1967), limited as the title indicates. Older studies still useful are Tyler Dennett, *Roosevelt and the Russo-Japanese War* (Garden City, N.Y.: Doubleday & Company, Inc., 1925), and T. A. Bailey, *Theodore Roosevelt and the Japanese-American Crises* (Stanford: Stanford University Press, 1934). E. P. Trani, *The Treaty of Portsmouth: An Adventure in American Diplomacy* (Lexington: University of Kentucky Press, 1969), supplies some new details of that episode. R. A. Hart, *The Great White Fleet: Its Voyage Around the World, 1907–1909* (Boston: Little, Brown and Company, 1965), raises doubts about traditional views of that exploit. For a general account of the Navy in the Pacific in this period, see W. R. Braisted, *The United States Navy in the Pacific, 1897–1909*, cited under **XIII**.

The history of the peace movement in the United States is related by Merle Curti in *Peace or War: The American Struggle, 1636–1936* (New York: W. W. Norton & Company, Inc., 1936). The two peace conferences at the Hague are described in C. D. Davis, *The United States and the First Hague Peace Conference* (Ithaca, N.Y.: Cornell University Press, 1962), and J. H. Choate, *The Two Hague Conferences* (Princeton: Princeton University Press, 1913). Merze Tate, *The Disarmament Illusion: The Movement for a Limitation of Armaments to 1907* (New York: The Macmillan Company, 1942), carries the story through the Second Hague Conference. W. F. Kuehl, *Seeking World Order: The United States and International Organization to 1920* (Nashville, Tenn.: Vanderbilt University Press, 1969), is a detailed account of the development of American opinion on world organization from about 1903 to the Senate's rejection of the League of Nations, suggesting that Wilson had been deaf to the currents of American thinking on the subject. Sandra R. Herman, *Eleven Against War: Studies in American International Thought,*

1898–1921 (Stanford, Cal.: Hoover Institution Press, 1969), is an in-depth treatment of a few leading thinkers on the subject. The arbitration movement and the settlement of important controversies with Great Britain are covered in Bradford Perkins, *The Great Rapprochement*, and other works cited in the same connection under **XIII**; in H. C. Allen, *Great Britain and the United States: A History of Anglo-American Relations (1783–1952)* (New York: St. Martin's Press, Inc., 1955); and in C. C. Tansill, *Canadian-American Relations, 1875–1911* (New Haven: Yale University Press, 1943).

XV. The Diplomacy of Neutrality and Wartime (Chapters 26, 27)

The biographies of Wilson cited in the preceding section are relevant here, especially the fourth and fifth volumes of A. S. Link, *Wilson*, which bring the story down to the entry of the United States into the war. Other items from section **XIV**, relevant here, are Coletta, *William Jennings Bryan*, Vol. 2, *The Intimate Papers of Colonel House* (Seymour ed.), Kennan, *American Diplomacy, 1900–1950*, and Pratt, *Challenge and Rejection* (paperback, *America and World Leadership, 1900–1921*). The last-named has a serviceable bibliography. To be added to the writings of participants are Robert Lansing, Secretary of State, 1915–1920, *The War Memoirs of Robert Lansing* (Indianapolis: The Bobbs-Merrill Company, Inc., 1935), and B. J. Hendrick, ed., *The Life and Letters of Walter H. Page*, 3 vols. (Garden City, N.Y.: Doubleday & Company, Inc., 1923–1925).

An important revisionist interpretation of World War I by a German historian, stressing the aggressive expansionist aims of the German government, civilian as well as military, is Fritz Fischer, *Germany's Aims in the First World War*, translation (New York: W. W. Norton & Company, Inc., 1967). Of the numerous books on America's neutrality and final involvement in the war, perhaps the best is E. R. May, *The World War and American Isolation, 1914–1917* (Cambridge: Harvard University Press, 1959), which pays more attention than most accounts to British and German wartime politics. D. M. Smith, *The Great Departure: The United States and World War I, 1914–1920* (New York: John Wiley & Sons, Inc., 1965), is a briefer but judicious account, which covers also United States participation in the war and the Peace Conference.

The same author in an essay, "National Interest and American Intervention, 1917," *Journal of American History,* 52 (1965), 5–24, summarizes changing interpretations of the reasons for American entry into the war. C. C. Tansill, *America Goes to War* (Boston: Little, Brown and Company, 1938), emphasizes the offenses of the British while not denying those of the Germans. Walter Millis, *Road to War: America 1914–1917* (Boston: Houghton Mifflin Company, 1935), is a popular narrative reflecting the isolationist spirit of the 1930's. E. H. Buehrig, *Woodrow Wilson and the Balance of Power* (Bloomington: Indiana University Press, 1955), attempts to assess the importance of that concept in shaping Wilson's decision for war. Barbara W. Tuchman, *The Zimmermann Telegram* (New York: The Viking Press, Inc., 1958), analyzes a *faux pas* of the German Foreign Office. H. C. Peterson, *Propaganda for War* (Norman: University of Oklahoma Press, 1939), and H. C. Peterson and G. C. Fite, *Opponents of War, 1917–1918* (Madison: University of Wisconsin Press, 1957), illustrate the efforts to sway public opinion both against and for intervention. J. M. Cooper, Jr., *The Vanity of Power: American Isolationism and the First World War, 1914–1917* (Westport, Conn.: Greenwood Publishing Corp., 1969), describes "the birth of American self-conscious isolationism."

For the period of American participation in the war, the necessary volumes of Link's *Wilson* are not yet available, but the other Wilson biographies mentioned earlier in this section can be used. Much has been written on the relations of the United States with the European Allies ("Associates" of the United States). Arthur Willert, *The Road to Safety: A Study in Anglo-American Relations* (New York: Praeger Publishers, Inc., 1953), should be supplemented by W. B. Fowler, *British American Relations 1917–1918; The Role of Sir William Wiseman* (Princeton: Princeton University Press, 1969), the story of informal diplomacy between Colonel House and a British intelligence officer. L. A. R. Yates, *The United States and French Security, 1917–1921* (New York: Twayne Publishers, Inc., 1957), examines the American attitude to a major French problem during the war and the peacemaking. D. F. Trask, *The United States and the Supreme War Council: American War Aims and Inter-Allied Strategy, 1917–1918* (Middletown, Conn.: Wesleyan University Press, 1961), describes the sometimes strained cooperation of the United States with its chief European associates. L. E.

Gelfand, in *The Inquiry: American Preparation for Peace, 1917–1919* (New Haven: Yale University Press, 1963), writes of the body of experts organized under Colonel House to define American war aims in Europe. The development of those aims for Eastern Europe is described in V. S. Mamatey, *The United States and East Central Europe, 1914–1918* (Princeton: Princeton University Press, 1957), and L. L. Gerson, *Woodrow Wilson and the Rebirth of Poland, 1914–1920* (New Haven: Yale University Press, 1953).

On United States relations with Soviet Russia, the leading authority is G. F. Kennan. In addition to his two volumes (of a projected three-volume work, *Soviet-American Relations, 1917–1920*), *Russia Leaves the War* and *The Decision to Intervene* (Princeton: Princeton University Press, 1956, 1958), he has also published a less detailed work, covering the same period and much more: *Russia and the West Under Lenin and Stalin* (Boston: Little, Brown and Company, 1960). Robert D. Warth, *The Allies and the Russian Revolution* (Durham, N.C.: Duke University Press, 1954), also embraces American policy. Of several accounts of the American intervention in Siberia, perhaps the best is Betty M. Unterberger, *America's Siberian Expedition, 1918–1920* (Durham, N.C.: Duke University Press, 1946). The commander of that expedition, General William S. Graves, described the experience in his book, *America's Siberian Adventure, 1918–1920* (New York: Peter Smith, 1931). American wartime relations with the Far East in general are included in R. W. Curry, *Woodrow Wilson and Far Eastern Policy, 1913–1921* (New York: Twayne Publishers, Inc., Bookman Associates, Inc., 1957). Percy A. Martin, *Latin America and the War* (Baltimore: The Johns Hopkins Press, 1925), necessarily deals with Latin American relations with the United States.

XVI. The Making of the Treaty of Versailles and Its Rejection by the Senate (Chapters 28, 29)

The literature on the Paris Peace Conference is enormous. Only some suggestions can be given here. Probably the best concise history of the Conference in English is T. A. Bailey, *Woodrow Wilson and the Lost Peace* (New York: The Macmillan Company, 1944). The most comprehensive history of the Conference is H. W. V. Temperley, *A History of the Peace Conference at Paris,* 6 vols. (London: H. Frowde, Hodder & Stoughton, 1920–1924). R. S. Baker, *Woodrow Wilson and World Settlement* (cited under XIV), is the nearest approach to an American official history. Thirteen documentary volumes, *The Paris Peace Conference* (Washington, D.C.: Government Printing Office, 1942–1947), are included in the series, *Papers Relating to the Foreign Relations of the United States*. The biographies of Wilson by Bell, Walworth, and the Georges, and *The Intimate Papers of Colonel House,* edited by Seymour (all cited under XIV), are relevant here, as are the studies by Gelfand, Mamatey, Gerson, Trask, Yates, Warth, and Kennan, cited under XV. Robert Lansing, *The Peace Negotiations* (Boston: Houghton Mifflin Company, 1921), D. H. Miller, *The Drafting of the Covenant, 2 vols.* (New York: G. P. Putnam's Sons, 1928), and Charles Seymour, *Letters from the Paris Peace Conference,* edited by H. B. Whiteman, Jr. (New Haven: Yale University Press, 1965), are important among the many records by participants. Shorter first-hand accounts make up *What Really Happened at Paris,* edited by E. M. House and C. Seymour (New York: Charles Scribner's Sons, 1931). (See Pratt, *Challenge and Rejection,* cited under XIV, for additional items of this nature.) Some special problems of the Conference are discussed in Seth P. Tillman, *Anglo-American Relations at the Paris Peace Conference* (Princeton: Princeton University Press, 1961); Harold L. Nelson, *Land and Power: British and Allied Policy on Germany's Frontiers, 1916–1919* (London: Routledge & Kegan Paul, Ltd., 1963); Russell H. Fifield, *Woodrow Wilson and the Far East: The Diplomacy of the Shantung Question* (New York: Thomas Y. Crowell Company, 1952). Two recent studies which emphasize the influence of the Soviet Union and the fear of Bolshevism at the Conference are Arno J. Mayer, *Politics and Diplomacy of Peace-Making: Containment and Counterrevolution at Versailles, 1918–1919* (New York: Alfred A. Knopf, Inc., 1968), and N. Gordon Levin, Jr., *Woodrow Wilson and World Politics: America's Response to War and Revolution* (New York: Oxford University Press, Inc., 1968). On the other hand, John M. Thompson, in *Russia, Bolshevism, and the Versailles Peace* (Princeton: Princeton University Press, 1966), contends that fear of Bolshevism was a relatively minor influence at the Conference. See also the items on Russia cited in the preceding section.

On the defeat of the treaty in the Senate, the best single volume is T. A. Bailey, *Woodrow Wilson and the Great Betrayal* (New York: The Macmillan Company, 1945). Denna F. Fleming has also told the story in *The United States and the League of Nations* (New York: G. P. Putnam's Sons, 1932), and more briefly in *The United States and World Organization, 1920–1933* (New York: Columbia University Press, 1938). Ruhl J. Bartlett, *The League to Enforce Peace* (Chapel Hill: The University of North Carolina Press, 1944), is an account of a wartime American effort to promote the idea of a league of nations. F. P. Walters, *A History of the League of Nations,* 2 vols. (London: Oxford University Press, 1952), is the authoritative history of the League. Selig Adler, *The Isolationist Impulse: Its Twentieth Century Reaction* (New York: Abelard-Schuman Limited, 1957; paperback ed., New York: The Macmillan Company, Collier Books, 1961), analyzes the different currents of opposition to the League. W. Stull Holt, *Treaties Defeated by the Senate* (Baltimore: The Johns Hopkins Press, 1933), has an important chapter on this episode. Senator Henry Cabot Lodge, the principal architect of defeat, gives his version in *The Senate and the League of Nations* (New York: Charles Scribner's Sons, 1925). J. A. Garraty, *Henry Cabot Lodge, A Biography* (New York: Alfred A. Knopf, Inc., 1953), takes a more critical view. C. O. Johnson, *Borah of Idaho* (New York: Longmans, Green & Company, 1936), is a biography of a leading isolationist senator. The biographies of Wilson cited earlier in this section are still applicable. To these should be added J. M. Blum, *Joe Tumulty and the Wilson Era* (Boston: Houghton Mifflin Company, 1951). Kurt Wimer has published several articles on Wilson's fight for the League: among them, "Woodrow Wilson Tries Conciliation: An Effort That Failed," *The Historian,* 25 (1963), 419–28, and "Woodrow Wilson's Plan for a Vote of Confidence," *Pennsylvania History,* 28, No. 3 (1961), pp. 2–16.

Readings on the presidential campaign and election of 1920 will be found in the following section.

XVII. Republican Foreign Policy (1921–1933) (Chapters 30–32)

The campaign and election of 1920, including Wilson's unvoiced bid for a third nomination, are covered in a number of the biographies and special works cited under XVI. Charles W. Stein, *The Third-Term Tradition: Its Rise and Collapse in*

American Politics (New York: Columbia University Press, 1943), has a good chapter on 1920. Specialized accounts are those in Wesley M. Bagby, *The Road to Normalcy: The Presidential Campaign and Election of 1920* (Baltimore: The Johns Hopkins Press, 1962), and J. C. Vinson, *Referendum for Isolation: Defeat of Article Ten of the League of Nations Covenant* (Athens: University of Georgia Press, 1961). Selig Adler, *The Isolationist Impulse* (cited under XVI), has a brief account of the election in the course of his survey of the isolationist attitude from its beginnings to the years after World War II. Important biographical treatments are found in *The Available Man: The Life Behind the Masks of Warren Gamaliel Harding,* by Andrew Sinclair (New York: The Macmillan Company, 1965), and *Charles Evans Hughes,* by M. J. Pusey, 2nd. ed., 2 vols. (New York: The Macmillan Company, 1963). Wilson's widow, Edith Bolling Wilson, in *My Memoir* (Indianapolis: The Bobbs-Merrill Company, Inc., 1939), gives a personal view of Wilson's reaction to illness and failure, the subject also of the sympathetic but sometimes unreliable *When The Cheering Stopped: The Last Years of Woodrow Wilson,* by Gene Smith (New York: William Morrow & Co., Inc., 1964).

A reliable factual account of the Harding-Coolidge-Hoover foreign policy is L. Ethan Ellis, *Republican Foreign Policy, 1921–1933* (New Brunswick, N.J.: Rutgers University Press, 1968).

American opinion of the League, the World Court, and collective security in general, in the two decades after 1921, is dealt with by Selig Adler in *The Isolationist Impulse.* The same author, in his *The Uncertain Giant: American Foreign Policy Between The Wars, 1921–1941* (New York: The Macmillan Company, 1965; paperback edition, New York: The Macmillan Company, Collier Books, 1969), gives an excellent survey of two decades of American foreign policy, with comprehensive and illuminating bibliographical notes. D. F. Fleming, in *The United States and World Organization, 1920–1933* (cited under XVI) and *The United States and the World Court* (Garden City: N.Y.: Doubleday & Company, Inc., 1945), writes from a strongly internationalist point of view. On the Kellogg-Briand Pact, or Pact of Paris, the best account is R. H. Ferrell, *Peace in Their Time: The Origins of the Kellogg-Briand Pact* (New Haven: Yale University Press, 1952). See also D. H. Miller, *The Peace Pact of Paris* (New York: G. P. Putnam's Sons, 1928), J. C. Vinson, *William E. Borah and the Outlawry*

of War (Athens: University of Georgia Press, 1957), and L. Ethan Ellis, *Frank B. Kellogg and American Foreign Relations* (New Brunswick, N.J.: Rutgers University Press, 1961). J. T. Shotwell, *War as an Instrument of National Policy* (New York: Harcourt Brace Jovanovich, Inc., 1929), is written by one who played a role of some importance in bringing the pact to fruition.

R. H. Ferrell, cited above, is also the author of the sketches of Secretaries Kellogg and Stimson in Volume 11 of *The American Secretaries of State.* The tenth volume of that series contains a sketch of Secretary Hughes, who is also treated in the previously cited biography by Pusey, and in Dexter Perkins, *Charles Evans Hughes and American Democratic Statesmanship* (Boston: Little, Brown and Company, 1956). The labors of Elihu Root in his effort to bring the United States into the World Court are described in P. C. Jessup's *Elihu Root* (cited under XIV), and more briefly in R. W. Leopold, *Elihu Root and the Conservative Tradition* (Boston: Little, Brown and Company, 1954). Short but useful sketches of the Secretaries of State of the period are found in N. A. Graebner, ed., *An Uncertain Tradition* (cited under II).

On the Washington Conference of 1921–1922 and its accomplishments in naval limitation and Far Eastern adjustments, the biographies of Hughes and Root, just cited, are useful. A study of Hughes by Betty Glad, *Charles Evans Hughes and the Illusions of Innocence: A Study in American Diplomacy* (Urbana: University of Illinois Press, 1966), is less than convincing in the contention that Hughes' early life and training had not equipped him for the problems of the 1920's. An early scholarly account is R. L. Buell, *The Washington Conference* (New York: Appleton-Century-Crofts, 1922). More analytical is J. C. Vinson, *The Parchment Peace: The United States Senate and the Washington Conference, 1921–1922* (Athens: The University of Georgia Press, 1955), which pays special attention to the role of the Senate in the preliminaries of the Conference and in the handling of the Four-Power treaty. The agreements on naval limitation and their implementation are described in G. T. Davis, *A Navy Second to None* (cited under XIII), in Harold and Margaret Sprout, *Toward a New Order of Sea Power* (Princeton: Princeton University Press, 1940), and in Merze Tate, *The United States and Armaments* (Cambridge: Harvard University Press, 1948). On the Far Eastern angle, A. W. Griswold, *The Far Eastern Policy of the United States* (cited under XIV), gives a favorable verdict, on the whole, to the American negotiators. An early Japanese account of the Conference is Yamato Ichihashi, *The Washington Conference and After* (Stanford: Stanford University Press, 1928). A later Japanese appraisal is included in Chitoshi Yanaga, *Japan Since Perry* (New York: McGraw-Hill Book Company, 1949). The breaking of the Japanese diplomatic codes and the use of the resulting information by the American delegation is described in H. O. Yardley, *The American Black Chamber* (Indianapolis: The Bobbs-Merrill Company, Inc., 1931).

On economic policy under Republican Presidents Harding and Coolidge, there is a good summary in B. H. Williams, *The Economic Foreign Policy of the United States* (cited under IV). Herbert Feis, *The Diplomacy of the Dollar: First Era, 1919–1932* (Baltimore: The Johns Hopkins Press, 1950), deals especially with governmental policy toward foreign investments. *The Memoirs of Herbert Hoover,* Vol. 2, *The Cabinet and the Presidency, 1920–1933,* and Vol. 3, *The Great Depression, 1929–1941* (New York: The Macmillan Company, 1952), present Hoover's justification of his policy, economic and political, as Secretary of Commerce and as President. *Herbert Hoover and Economic Diplomacy: Department of Commerce Policy, 1921–1928* (Pittsburgh: University of Pittsburgh Press, 1962), by Joseph Brandes, is highly critical of Hoover's policy of encouraging investments abroad while failing to smooth the way for the return of their earnings. H. G. Moulton and Leo Pasvolsky, *War Debts and World Prosperity* (Washington: The Brookings Institution, 1932), is a contemporary analysis of a perplexing economic problem. J. M. Jones, Jr., *Tariff Retaliation: Repercussions of the Hawley-Smoot Bill* (Philadelphia: University of Pennsylvania Press, 1934), describes the disastrous consequences of a policy decision in which Hoover went along with a short-sighted Congress.

R. H. Ferrell, *American Diplomacy in the Great Depression: Hoover-Stimson Foreign Policy, 1929–1933* (New Haven: Yale University Press, 1957), treats the whole range of foreign policy in those troubled years, including the Hoover Moratorium, the preparations for world economic and disarmament conferences, and Japanese aggression in Manchuria. Ferrell's sketch of Secretary Stimson in *The American Secretaries of State,* Volume 11, was mentioned above, as were Volumes 2 and 3 of Hoover's *Memoirs,* also applicable here. Stimson left two accounts of his

part in handling the Manchurian crisis; H. L. Stimson, *The Far Eastern Crisis: Recollections and Observations* (New York: Harper & Row, Publishers, 1936); H. L. Stimson and McGeorge Bundy, *On Active Service in Peace and War* (New York: Harper & Row, Publishers, 1948), the latter volume covering his entire public career. Of Stimson biographers, Elting E. Morison, in *Turmoil and Tradition: A Study of the Life and Times of Henry L. Stimson* (Boston: Houghton Mifflin Company, 1960), is sympathetic and laudatory; while R. N. Current, in *Secretary Stimson: A Study in Statecraft* (New Brunswick: Rutgers University Press, 1954), finds Stimson's diplomacy both risky and ineffectual. Other useful accounts of the Manchurian crisis are Armin Rappaport, *Henry L. Stimson and Japan* (Chicago: University of Chicago Press, 1963), and Sarah R. Smith, *The Manchurian Crisis, 1931–1932: A Tragedy in International Relations* (New York: Columbia University Press, 1948). Griswold, *The Far Eastern Policy of the United States* (cited above) also covers this episode. Accounts of this crisis in F. P. Walters, *A History of the League of Nations* (cited under XVI), and D. F. Fleming, *The United States and World Organization* (cited above), emphasize the ineffectualness of American cooperation with the League.

Further readings on foreign economic policy and the sequel to the Manchurian crisis will be found in the next section.

XVIII. The Foreign Policy of the New Deal (1933–1941) (Chapters 33–38)

For the period in general, including foreign policy, a concise volume is William E. Leuchtenburg, *Franklin D. Roosevelt and the New Deal, 1932–1940* (New York: Harper & Row, Publishers, 1963), a volume in the *New American Nation Series.* Selig Adler, *The Uncertain Giant* (cited under XVII) is excellent for the period. Julius W. Pratt, *Cordell Hull,* Volumes 12 and 13 of *The American Secretaries of State* (1964), covers the entire period of Hull's incumbency, 1933–1944. *The Memoirs of Cordell Hull,* 2 vols. (New York: The Macmillan Company, 1948), are drawn largely from the Secretary's letters, memoranda, etc., and constitute an important source for the period of his service. Also important are the published papers of cabinet colleagues of Hull who often expressed vigorous ideas about foreign policy. One of these was Secretary of the Treasury Henry Morgenthau, Jr., from whose diaries and other papers generous selections have been edited by John M. Blum in three volumes under the title *From the Morgenthau Diaries* (Boston: Houghton Mifflin Company, 1959–1967). Much of the substance of the three volumes is reduced to one in John M. Blum, ed., *Roosevelt and Morgenthau: A Revision and Condensation* (Boston: Houghton Mifflin Company, 1970). Another colleague given to interfering in foreign policy was Secretary of the Interior Harold L. Ickes, the "Old Curmudgeon," whose outspoken ideas from 1933 to 1941 are recorded in *The Secret Diary of Harold L. Ickes*, 3 vols. (New York: Simon & Schuster, Inc., 1953–1954). Presidential papers dealing with foreign relations during the early years of the New Deal have been edited by Edgar B. Nixon as *Franklin D. Roosevelt and Foreign Affairs* (1933–1937), 3 vols. (Cambridge: Harvard University Press, Belknap Press, 1969). Another valuable source for some aspects of New Deal diplomacy is *The Moffat Papers: Selections from the Diplomatic Journals of Jay Pierrepont Moffat*, edited by Nancy H. Hooker (Cambridge: Harvard University Press, 1956). Moffat's diary gives many a glimpse of the inside workings of the Department of State.

Sumner Welles, who served as Assistant Secretary and later as Under Secretary of State from 1933 to 1944 (except for a brief interval as ambassador to Cuba), published three volumes after his retirement: *The Time for Decision, Where Are We Heading?*, and *Seven Decisions That Shaped History* (all New York: Harper & Row, Publishers, 1944, 1946, and 1951, respectively). The first and the third give first-hand (though frequently biased) insight into prewar and wartime policy-making. The second discusses problems of the immediate postwar period. Robert E. Sherwood, *Roosevelt and Hopkins: An Intimate History* (New York: Harper & Row, Publishers, 1948), is a valuable source, embodying extensive selections from the papers of Harry Hopkins, Roosevelt's confidential agent in foreign affairs from about 1940 to Roosevelt's death.

The economic features of New Deal foreign policy are discussed critically and from a somewhat "new leftist" angle by Lloyd C. Gardner in *Economic Aspects of New Deal Diplomacy* (Madison: University of Wisconsin Press, 1964). The World Economic Conference in London in 1933 is described in chapters in Pratt, *Cordell Hull;* in Raymond Moley, *The First New Deal* (New York: Harcourt Brace Jovanovich, Inc.,

1966); in *1933: Characters in Crisis*, by Herbert Feis (New York: Little, Brown and Company, 1966), and in A. M. Schlesinger, Jr., *The Age of Roosevelt*, Vol. 2, *The Coming of the New Deal* (Boston: Houghton Mifflin Company, 1959). The Reciprocal Trade Agreements program is described in a chapter in Pratt, *Cordell Hull*, Vol. 1; more fully in W. S. Culbertson, *Reciprocity: A National Policy for Foreign Trade* (New York: McGraw-Hill Book Company, Whittlesey House, 1937), and specifically in relation to Britain and Canada in R. N. Kottman, *Reciprocity and the North Atlantic Triangle, 1932–1938* (Ithaca, N.Y.: Cornell University Press, 1968).

The Good Neighbor Policy and its background in the 1920's are dealt with in an excellent chapter in Adler, *The Uncertain Giant*, with extensive bibliographical notes. Bemis, *Latin American Policy*, has several perceptive chapters on the subject. The abandonment by the United States of the earlier practice of intervention in the Caribbean area is described in Julius W. Pratt, *America's Colonial Experiment* (cited under XIV), chapter 8. Alexander DeConde, in *Herbert Hoover's Latin American Policy* (Stanford: Stanford University Press, 1951), shows how Hoover and Stimson paved the way for Roosevelt's Good Neighbor Policy. R. H. Ferrell also fills in the background in the studies cited under XVII, and in an amusing essay, "Repudiation of a Repudiation" in *The Journal of American History*, 51 (1965), 669–73, shows how a State Department "Memorandum on the Monroe Doctrine" became official policy in spite of being disowned by two successive administrations. The changing interpretation of the Monroe Doctrine is chronicled by Dexter Perkins in *A History of the Monroe Doctrine* (cited under VI). E. O. Guerrant, *Roosevelt's Good Neighbor Policy* (Albuquerque: University of New Mexico Press, 1950), is a sympathetic account, while Donald M. Dozer, *Are We Good Neighbors? Three Decades of Inter-American Relations, 1930–1960* (Gainesville: University of Florida Press, 1960), raises serious questions about the beneficence of the American policy, especially in its later stages. Bryce Wood, *The Making of the Good Neighbor Policy* (New York: Columbia University Press, 1961), shows how the United States, under stress of dangers in the other hemisphere, adapted its policy to Latin American concepts, especially of the rights of foreign investors. The most important locale of this adaptation was Mexico. Developments there are also described in H. F. Cline, *The United*

States and Mexico (cited under XIV), and the important part played by Ambassador Josephus Daniels in keeping U.S.-Mexican relations on an even keel is set forth by E. David Cronon in *Josephus Daniels in Mexico* (Madison: University of Wisconsin Press, 1960).

On the development of the American policy of neutrality in response to the dawning threat of new wars in Europe, a concise but indispensable guide is *Adler, The Uncertain Giant,* chapters 7 and 8, and the excellent bibliographical notes. Allan Nevins, *The New Deal and World Affairs: A Chronicle of International Affairs, 1933–1945* (New Haven: Yale University Press, 1950), and Dexter Perkins, *The New Age of Franklin D. Roosevelt, 1932–1945* (Chicago: University of Chicago Press, 1957), are lucid and generally sympathetic accounts of prewar and wartime diplomacy. The failure of the last efforts at arms limitation is recorded in Merze Tate, *The United States and Armaments* (cited under XVII), and in Hugh R. Wilson, Jr., *Disarmament and the Cold War in the Thirties* (New York: Vantage Press, Inc., 1963).

The American neutrality legislation of 1935–1937 is described in detail by R. A. Divine in *The Illusion of Neutrality* (Chicago: University of Chicago Press, 1962). The contribution of Senator Nye to the neutrality legislation is differently assessed in Wayne C. Cole, *Senator Gerald P. Nye and American Foreign Relations* (Minneapolis: University of Minnesota Press, 1962), and in John E. Wiltz, *In Search of Peace: The Senate Munitions Inquiry, 1934* (Baton Rouge: University of Louisiana Press, 1963). The initial testing of the neutrality legislation is described in Brice Harris, Jr., *The United States and the Italo-Ethiopian Crisis* (Stanford: Stanford University Press, 1964). A more severe testing came with the outbreak of the Spanish Civil War in 1936, which led some American isolationists to waver. That conflict itself is competently analyzed in Hugh Thomas, *The Spanish Civil War* (New York: Harper & Row, Publishers, 1961). Of several accounts of American policy toward the combatants, the most recent is the well researched and fair-minded *American Diplomacy and the Spanish Civil War,* by Richard P. Traina (Bloomington: Indiana University Press, 1968). Also useful for their analyses of conflicting currents in American opinion are F. J. Taylor, *The United States and the Spanish Civil War* (New York: Twayne Publishers, Inc., Bookman Associates, Inc., 1956), and Allen Guttman, *The Wound in the Heart: America and the Spanish Civil War* (New York: The Free Press, 1962).

The consequences to Europe of the American isolationist or neutrality policy are devastatingly set forth by Arnold A. Offner in *American Appeasement: United States Foreign Policy and Germany, 1933–1938* (Cambridge: Harvard University Press, Belknap Press, 1969). In Offner's opinion, the American policy weakened the will of Britain and France and whetted Hitler's appetite for aggression. American diplomats who perceptively assessed the Nazi threat were Ambassador William E. Dodd and commercial attaché Douglas P. Miller, both in Berlin. Dodd's impressions are recorded in *Ambassador Dodd's Diary, 1933–1938,* edited by W. E. Dodd, Jr., and Martha Dodd (New York: Harcourt Brace Jovanovich, Inc., 1941). Sketches of Dodd and of American Ambassadors William C. Bullitt and Joseph P. Kennedy are included, with numerous European contemporaries, in *The Diplomats, 1919–1939,* edited by Gordon A. Craig and Felix Gilbert (Princeton: Princeton University Press, 1953), which also contains an interesting essay, "The Department of State and American Public Opinion," by Dexter Perkins. See also Robert Dallek, *Democrat and Diplomat: The Life of William E. Dodd* (New York: Oxford University Press, Inc., 1968). Douglas Miller, who, like Dodd, had early warned Washington of Hitler's purposes, recorded his Berlin experiences and impressions in *You Can't Do Business with Hitler* (Boston: Little, Brown and Company, 1941). What the policy of a victorious Nazi Germany would have been toward Latin America is described by Alton Frye in *Nazi Germany and the American Hemisphere, 1933–1941* (New Haven: Yale University Press, 1967).

The gradual drift of the United States from isolation to alignment with the European democracies is related in several of the books cited earlier in this section, especially those of Adler, Nevins, and Pratt. Two more extended treatments are D. F. Drummond, *The Passing of American Neutrality, 1937–1941* (Ann Arbor: University of Michigan Press, 1955), and R. A. Divine, *The Reluctant Belligerent: American Entry into World War II* (New York: John Wiley & Sons, Inc., 1965). But the most comprehensive narrative of this development, including relations in the Far East as well as Europe, is found in two massive volumes by W. L. Langer and S. E. Gleason, *The Challenge to Isolation, 1937–1940,* and *The Undeclared War, 1940–1941* (New York:

Harper & Row, Publishers, 1952, 1953). These volumes, while sympathetic to the Roosevelt foreign policy, are, in the main, objective. Outspokenly pro-Roosevelt is Basil Rauch, *Roosevelt from Munich to Pearl Harbor* (New York: Farrar, Straus & Giroux, Inc., Creative Age Press, 1950). The lend-lease policy, initially designed to sustain England in the war against Germany, is described by its first administrator, Edward R. Stettinius, Jr., in *LEND-LEASE: Weapon for Victory* (New York: The Macmillan Company, 1944).

Of American historians who have argued that Roosevelt unnecessarily and dishonestly led the United States into World War II, the most distinguished is the late Charles A. Beard. His two books, *American Foreign Policy in the Making, 1932–1940* (New Haven: Yale University Press, 1946), and *President Roosevelt and the Coming of the War, 1941* (New Haven: Yale University Press, 1948), portray a President who disregarded constitutional limitations on his power to pursue a course which the author believes contrary to the true national interest. C. C. Tansill in *Back Door to War: The Roosevelt Foreign Policy* (Chicago: Henry Regnery Co., 1952), is a heavily documented study which largely agrees with Beard. Unable to get into the war with Hitler directly, Tansill holds, FDR used Japan to enter by the "back door." W. H. Chamberlin, *America's Second Crusade* (Chicago: Henry Regnery Co., 1950), finds Roosevelt's policy during the war as misguided as that which led into it.

The operation of private groups in the United States which tried to sway public opinion in favor of or against aid to England (and possible participation in the war) are described respectively in Walter Johnson, *The Battle against Isolation* (Chicago: University of Chicago Press, 1944), and W. S. Cole, *America First: The Battle Against Intervention* (Madison: University of Wisconsin Press, 1953). A leading advocate of America First, Col. Charles A. Lindbergh, has published his illuminating diaries of the period in *The Wartime Journals of Charles A. Lindbergh* (New York: Harcourt Brace Jovanovich, Inc., 1970).

For a view of American policy as seen by one of the great European belligerents, the outstanding work, needless to say, is Winston S. Churchill's six-volume masterpiece, *The Second World War* (Boston: Houghton Mifflin Company, 1948–1953). Relevant to the period of neutrality are Volumes 2, *Their Finest Hour,* and 3, *The Grand Alliance.*

Hitler's reaction to the unneutral behavior of the United States during its period of "nonbelligerence" is explained in H. L. Trefousse, *Germany and American Neutrality, 1939–1941* (New York: Twayne Publishers, Inc., Bookman Associates, Inc., 1951).

American relations with Japan from 1933 to Pearl Harbor are covered in several of the works cited for relations with Europe, namely, those of Adler, Pratt, Drummond, Divine (*The Reluctant Belligerent*), and the two Langer and Gleason volumes. Dorothy Borg, *The United States and the Far Eastern Crisis of 1933–1938* (Cambridge: Harvard University Press, 1964), shows, unlike some other accounts, that the State Department during these years was giving highest priority to avoiding war with Japan. Herbert Feis, *The Road to Pearl Harbor: The Coming of War Between the United States and Japan* (Princeton: Princeton University Press, 1950), writes with the advantage of unusual freedom of access to official records. Joseph C. Grew, U.S. Ambassador to Japan, 1932–1941, has left a detailed record of a long diplomatic career, with special attention to the experience in Tokyo, in *Turbulent Era: A Diplomatic Record of Forty Years, 1904–1945* (cited under II), and a much briefer narrative in *Ten Years in Japan* (New York: Simon & Schuster, Inc., 1944). A favorable appraisal of his career is Waldo H. Heinrichs, *American Ambassador: Joseph C. Grew and the Development of the U. S. Diplomatic Tradition* (Boston: Little, Brown and Company, 1967). F. C. Jones, *Japan's New Order in East Asia: Its Rise and Fall, 1937–1945* (New York: Oxford University Press, Inc., 1954), is a competent description of Japan's expansionist policy by an English writer. The American reaction to the New Order is described in an earlier work, W. C. Johnstone, *The United States and Japan's New Order* (New York: Oxford University Press, Inc., 1941). Paul W. Schroeder, *The Axis Alliance and Japanese-American Relations, 1941* (Ithaca, N.Y.: Cornell University Press, 1958), argues that a more flexible policy in Washington might have reached an acceptable accommodation with Japan.

The Japanese surprise attack at Pearl Harbor has produced a vast amount of literature, much of it controversial. The books by Adler, Pratt, Feis, Langer and Gleason (*The Undeclared War*), Jones, Johnstone, Schroeder, and Grew cited earlier, cover this event. One of the earliest accounts, and still one of the best in spite of subsequent revelations, is Walter Millis, *This Is*

Pearl!: The United States and Japan, 1941 (New York: William Morrow & Co., Inc., 1947). Also recommended for brilliant narrative is the account in S. E. Morison, *The Rising Sun in the Pacific, 1931–April 1942*, Vol. 3 of *History of United States Naval Operations in World War II* (Boston: Little, Brown and Company, 1948). The chief problems facing historians who have written later have been two: why did Japan attack an adversary so far her superior in resources and potential military might? Why was the United States caught by surprise? Two accounts by Japanese participants are important. Shigenori Togo, Japanese Foreign Minister, 1941–1945, in *The Cause of Japan* (New York: Simon & Schuster, Inc., 1956), places responsibility for Japan's decision squarely on the military High Command. Toshikazu Kase, a lesser Foreign Office official, in *Journal to the Missouri* (New Haven: Yale University Press, 1950), describes the maneuvers between different groups in the "establishment" which brought about the naming of General Tojo as Premier and the final decision for war. Nobutake Ike, in *Japan's Decision for War: Records of the 1941 Policy Conferences* (Stanford: Stanford University Press, 1967), has translated and edited the crucial documents indicated by the title. The fullest American analysis of Japan's fateful decision is in R. J. C. Butow, *Tojo and the Coming of the War* (Princeton: Princeton University Press, 1961). A judicious but much briefer treatment is Louis Morton, "Japan's Decision for War," in Kent R. Greenfield, ed., *Command Decisions* (New York: Harcourt Brace Jovanocich, Inc., 1959).

The real reason for the American blind spot at Pearl Harbor—the failure of American Intelligence to sift the grain from the chaff in its bewildering intake—is convincingly explained by Roberta Wohlstetter in *Pearl Harbor: Warning and Decision* (Stanford: Stanford University Press, 1962). The various mistakes and mischances that contributed to the disaster are interestingly detailed in M. S. Watson, *Chief of Staff: Pre-War Plans and Preparations* (Washington: Department of the Army, Historical Division, 1950), especially pp. 518–19. The theory, now thoroughly discredited, that Roosevelt deliberately enticed the Japanese to attack Pearl Harbor in order to bring the United States into the war against Hitler is most ambitiously presented in the books by C. C. Tansill and Charles A. Beard, cited earlier in this section. The first book in this genre to make much impression was *Pearl Harbor: The Story of the Secret War* (Old Greenwich, Conn.: The Devin-Adair Co., 1947), by George Morgenstern, a *Chicago Tribune* reporter. It was followed in 1950 by W. H. Chamberlin's *America's Second Crusade*, previously mentioned, and by F. R. Sanborn, *Design for War: A Study of Secret Power Politics, 1937–1941* (Old Greenwich, Conn.: The Devin-Adair Co., 1951). H. E. Barnes edited a collection of essays, generally of the same tenor, by several of these writers and others, under the ironic title, *Perpetual War for Perpetual Peace* (Caldwell, Idaho: The Caxton Printers, Ltd., 1953). Two objective surveys of the earlier Pearl Harbor literature are Louis Morton, "Pearl Harbor in Perspective: A Bibliographical Survey," *U. S. Naval Institute Proceedings*, 81 (April 1955), 461–68, and R. H. Ferrell, "Pearl Harbor and the Revisionists," *Historian*, 17 (Spring 1955), 215–33. H. L. Trefousse, *What Happened at Pearl Harbor?* (New York: Twayne Publishers, Inc., 1958), is for the most part a collection of statements by participants.

XIX. The Diplomacy of World War II (Chapters 39, 40)

An excellent summary with a useful bibliography is Gaddis Smith, *American Diplomacy During the Second World War, 1941–1945* (New York: John Wiley & Sons, Inc., 1965), in paperback. The following works, cited in the preceding section, are also useful for this period: Pratt, *Cordell Hull* (through 1944); Hull, *Memoirs;* Sherwood, *Roosevelt and Hopkins;* Welles, *The Time for Decision;* and Churchill, *The Second World War*, Volumes 3 (*The Grand Alliance*), 4 (*The Hinge of Fate*), 5 (*Closing the Ring*), and 6 (*Triumph and Tragedy*). On military decisions having important diplomatic implications, see Greenfield, ed., *Command Decisions* (cited under XVIII), and Trumbull Higgins, *Winston Churchill and the Second Front, 1940–1943* (New York: Oxford University Press, Inc., 1957); also Dwight D. Eisenhower, *Crusade in Europe* (Garden City, N.Y.: Doubleday & Company, Inc., 1948). The relationship of the "Big Three" heads of government is described in some detail by Herbert Feis in *Churchill—Roosevelt—Stalin: The War They Waged and the Peace They Sought* (Princeton: Princeton University Press, 1957). Two recent writers take the United States to task for holding back in its war effort with unfortunate postwar results. James McG. Burns, in *Roosevelt: The*

Soldier of Freedom (New York: Harcourt Brace Jovanovich, Inc., 1970), blames the two-year delay in opening the second front in Europe for Russian distrust that helped produce the cold war. William L. Neumann, in *After Victory: Churchill, Roosevelt, Stalin and the Making of the Peace* (New York: Harper & Row, Publishers, 1969), holds the Anglo-American determination to keep down casualties responsible for Soviet domination of Eastern Europe. John L. Snell, *Wartime Origins of the East-West Dilemma over Germany* (New Orleans, La.: Hauser Press, 1959), throws light on one source of the cold war. Gabriel Kolko, in *The Politics of War: The World and United States Foreign Policy, 1943–1945* (New York: Random House, Inc., 1969), finds economic motives behind virtually every American wartime policy.

For United States-Soviet bilateral relations, see Bailey, *America Faces Russia,* Dulles, *The Road to Teheran* (cited under XI), and Kennan, *Russia and the West under Lenin and Stalin* (cited under XV); also William A. Williams, *American-Russian Relations, 1781–1947* (New York: Holt, Rinehart & Winston, Inc., 1962), and R. P. Browder, *The Origins of Soviet American Diplomacy* (Princeton: Princeton University Press, 1953). R. H. Dawson, *The Decision to Aid Russia, 1941* (Chapel Hill: University of North Carolina Press, 1959), is revealing on the caution observed in reaching that crucial decision. J. R. Deane, *The Strange Alliance* (New York: The Viking Press, Inc., 1947), and Raymond Dennett and J. E. Johnson, eds., *Negotiating with the Russians* (Boston: World Peace Foundation, 1951), reveal the difficulties of negotiating with a suspicious and secretive ally.

On wartime relations with China, Herbert Feis, *The China Tangle: The American Effort in China from Pearl Harbor to the Marshall Mission* (Princeton: Princeton University Press, 1953), should be supplemented by Tsou Tang, *American Failure in China, 1941–1950* (Chicago: University of Chicago Press, 1963) and by the stories of two rival American generals in China: C. L. Chennault, *Way of a Fighter: The Memoirs of Claire Lee Chennault,* edited by Robert Hotz (New York: G. P. Putnam's Sons, 1949), and J. W. Stilwell, *The Stilwell Papers,* arranged and edited by T. H. White (New York: Wm. Sloane Associates, Inc., 1948). See also Barbara W. Tuchman, *Stilwell and the American Experience in China, 1911–45* (New York: The Macmillan Company, 1971).

The justification of Washington's controversial relations with the government of France at Vichy is set forth by W. L. Langer in *Our Vichy Gamble* (New York: Alfred A. Knopf, Inc., 1947). The same subject is treated in Langer and Gleason, *The Undeclared War* (cited under XVIII), in D. C. McKay, *The United States and France* (Cambridge: Harvard University Press, 1951), and by the American ambassador to Vichy, Admiral W. D. Leahy, in *I Was There* (New York: McGraw-Hill Book Company, Whittlesey House, 1950). The very prickly relations with General de Gaulle's Free French, touched upon in Pratt, *Cordell Hull,* are treated at more length in A. L. Funk, *Charles de Gaulle: The Crucial Years, 1943–1944* (Norman: University of Oklahoma Press, 1959), and in *The War Memoirs of Charles de Gaulle,* translations, Volumes 1 (New York: The Viking Press, Inc., 1955), and 2 (New York: Simon & Schuster, Inc., 1959).

Historian Carlton J. H. Hayes has recorded his experiences as ambassador to Franco's Spain in *Wartime Mission in Spain, 1942–1945* (New York: The Macmillan Company, 1945). The story is told from the point of view of Washington in Herbert Feis, *The Spanish Story: Franco and the Nations at War* (New York: Alfred A. Knopf, Inc., 1948).

Relations with Latin America to early 1942 are described in Bemis, *Latin American Policy.* For accounts covering the entire war period, see Dozer, *Are We Good Neighbors?* (cited under XVIII); J. L. Mecham, *The United States and Inter-American Security, 1889–1960* (Austin: University of Texas Press, 1961); Stetson Conn and Byron Fairchild, *The Framework of Hemisphere Defense* (Washington: Office of the Chief of Military History, Department of the Army, 1960). Hemisphere cooperation to prevent European colonies in America from falling into Axis hands is treated in J. A. Logan, Jr., *No Transfer: An American Security Principle* (cited under VI).

On the closing phases of the war, including conferences of the heads of governments at Casablanca, Teheran, and Yalta, two excellent accounts are Feis, *Churchill—Roosevelt—Stalin* (mentioned earlier) and William H. McNeill, *America, Britain and Russia: Their Cooperation and Conflict, 1941–1946* (London: Oxford University Press, 1953). Feis has added to the work just cited two other books on the ending of the war: *Between War and Peace: The Potsdam Conference* (Princeton: Princeton University Press, 1960), and *The Atomic Bomb and the End of World War II* (Princeton: Princeton University Press, 1966, a revised edition of *Japan Subdued,* same publisher, 1961). The last three volumes of Churchill's *The Second World War (The Hinge of Fate, Closing the Ring, Triumph and Tragedy)* all have important material. Roosevelt's "unconditional surrender" formula at Casablanca and the publicizing of the Morgenthau Plan for Germany—incidents that may have prolonged the war—are discussed briefly in H. W. Baldwin, *Great Mistakes of the War* (New York: Harper & Row, Publishers, 1950). Anne Armstrong, *Unconditional Surrender: The Impact of the Casablanca Policy on World War II* (New Brunswick: Rutgers University Press, 1961), tries ambitiously to evaluate the effect of the formula. The Morgenthau Plan was presented in *Germany Is Our Problem* by Henry Morgenthau, Jr. (New York: Harper & Row, Publishers, 1945). There is interesting comment on it in Hull, *Memoirs*, Vol. 2, and in H. L. Stimson and McGeorge Bundy, *On Active Service in Peace and War* (cited under XVII). John L. Snell, ed., *The Meaning of Yalta* (Baton Rouge: Louisiana State University Press, 1956), provides probably the best evaluation of the work of the controversial Yalta Conference. Accounts of the Yalta Conference by American participants are found in E. R. Stettinius, Jr., *Roosevelt and the Russians: The Yalta Conference* (Garden City, N.Y.: Doubleday & Company, Inc., 1949); James F. Byrnes, *Speaking Frankly* (New York: Harper & Row, Publishers, 1947), and *All in a Lifetime* (same publishers, 1958); and in Leahy, *I Was There,* and Sherwood, *Roosevelt and Hopkins* (both cited above).

On the surrender of Japan, see, in addition to Feis's book, cited above, R. J. C. Butow, *Japan's Decision to Surrender* (Stanford: Stanford University Press, 1954); Toshikazu Kase, *Journey to the Missouri,* and J. C. Grew, *Turbulent Era* (both cited under XVIII); and Stimson and Bundy, *On Active Service* (cited above).

The following official collections of the documents of several of the wartime conferences are published in the *Foreign Relations* series: *The Conferences at Cairo and Teheran, 1943* (1961); *The Conferences at Malta and Yalta, 1945* (1955); *The Conference of Berlin (Potsdam), 1945,* 2 vols. (1960).

XX. Postwar Foreign Policy in General (Chapters 41–49; see also sections XXI–XXVI)

There are a number of useful surveys of American foreign relations since 1945. Robert H. Ferrell, in *American Diplomacy: A History* (cited under I), devotes 225 pages, one fourth of the book, to this period, with excellent chapter bibliographies. Dexter Perkins, *The Diplomacy of a New Age: Major Issues in U. S. Policy since 1945* (Bloomington: Indiana University Press, 1967), is concise, fair-minded, and readable; it treats events up to the middle 1960's. Seyom Brown, *The Faces of Power: Constancy and Change in the United States Foreign Policy from Truman to Johnson* (New York: Columbia University Press, 1968), finds constancy in purpose (maintenance of a balance of power) but change in emphasis (from Europe to the Third World). C. L. Robertson, *International Politics since World War II: A Short History* (New York: John Wiley & Sons, Inc., 1966), is a general survey ending with 1966. John W. Spanier, *American Foreign Policy since World War II,* 3rd ed. (New York: Praeger Publishers, Inc., 1968) and William G. Carleton, *The Revolution in American Foreign Policy: Its Global Range* (New York: Random House, Inc., 1965), are also useful. Lawrence S. Kaplan, *Recent American Foreign Policy: Conflicting Interpretations* (Homewood, Ill.: Dorsey Press, 1968), gives essential documents and views of participants and observers on fifteen controversial topics, from the origins of the cold war to the war in Vietnam. Edward Weintal and Charles Bartlett, *Facing the Brink: An Intimate Study of Crisis Diplomacy* (New York: Charles Scribner's Sons, 1967), gives the story of five international crises with sharp criticism of United States policy. *The American Secretaries of State* series continue with sketches of *E. R. Stettinius, Jr.,* by Richard L. Walker, and *James F. Byrnes* by George Curry in Volume 14 (1965); *George C. Marshall* by Robert H. Ferrell in Volume 15 (1966); *Dean Acheson* by Gaddis Smith in Volume 16 (1972); *John Foster Dulles* by Louis L. Gerson in Volume 17 (1967); *Christian A. Herter* by G. Bernard Noble in Volume 18 (1970). Two critical studies of Secretary Dulles are Richard Gould-Adams, *John Foster Dulles: A Reappraisal* (New York: Appleton-Century-Crofts, 1962) and Roscoe Drummond and Gaston Coblentz, *Duel at the Brink: John Foster Dulles' Command of American Power* (Garden City, N.Y.: Doubleday & Company, Inc., 1960). A. H. Berding, in *Dulles on Diplomacy* (New York: Van Nostrand Reinhold Company, 1965), gives much of Dulles' philosophy at first hand. Rowland Evans and Robert Novak, in *Lyndon B. Johnson: The Exercise of Power* (New York: The New American Library, Inc., 1966), have several chapters on President Johnson's foreign policy. Tom Wicker, a perspicacious journalist, treats the 1963 transition in the White

House in *JFK and LBJ: The Influence of Personality on Politics* (New York: William Morrow & Co., Inc., 1968).

Also to be recommended is the series *The United States in World Affairs,* one volume for 1945–1947 and annual volumes thereafter, published for the Council on Foreign Relations (New York: Harper & Row, Publishers, 1947–1967; Simon & Schuster, Inc., 1968); volumes for 1945–1947, 1947–1948, 1948–1949 by J. C. Campbell; 1949 to 1954, 1956 to 1963, 1965 to 1967 by R. P. Stebbins; 1955 by H. W. Barber; 1964 by Jules David.

Accounts by influential participants are Byrnes, *Speaking Frankly* and *All in a Lifetime* (cited under XIX), Dean Acheson, *Present at the Creation: My Years at the State Department* (New York: W. W. Norton & Company, Inc., 1969); *Memoirs by Harry S. Truman:* Volume 1, *Year of Decisions;* Volume 2, *Years of Trial and Hope* (Garden City, N.Y.: Doubleday & Company, Inc., 1955, 1956); Dwight D. Eisenhower, *The White House Years:* Volume 1, *Mandate for Change, 1953–1956;* Volume 2, *Waging Peace, 1956–1961* (Garden City, N.Y.: Doubleday & Company, Inc., 1963, 1965); John Foster Dulles, *War or Peace* (New York: The Macmillan Company, 1950); Robert Murphy, *Diplomat among Warriors* (cited under II); Averell Harriman, *America and Russia* (also cited under II). Of basic importance for the Kennedy period are Theodore C. Sorensen, *Kennedy* (New York: Harper & Row, Publishers, 1965), and especially Arthur M. Schlesinger, Jr., *A Thousand Days: John F. Kennedy in the White House* (Boston: Houghton Mifflin Company, 1965). Also rich in many insights for this period is Roger Hilsman, *To Move a Nation: The Politics of Foreign Policy in the Administration of John F. Kennedy* (Garden City, N.Y.: Doubleday & Company, Inc., 1967).

XXI. The United States and the United Nations (Chapter 41)

On the United Nations in general a very useful treatise is Clark M. Eichelberger, *UN: The First Twenty-five Years* (New York: Harper & Row, Publishers, 1970), successor to two earlier volumes at the 15- and 20-year birthdays. It is both a history and a critique of the U.N. and of America's policy toward it. The conversion of the United States to internationalism as exemplified in its role in preparing for the U.N. is the subject of R. A. Divine, *Second Chance: The Triumph of Internationalism in America during World War II* (New York: Atheneum Publishers, 1967). *A History of the United Nations Charter: The Role of the United States, 1940–1945,* by Ruth B. Russell and Jeanette E. Muther (Washington: The Brookings Institution, 1958), is authoritative. Its theme can be pursued further in B. V. Cohen, *The United Nations: Constitutional Development, Growth and Possibilities* (Cambridge: Harvard University Press, 1961). Ernest A. Gross, *The United Nations: Structure for Peace* (New York: Harper & Row, Publishers, 1962), is a standard work by a one-time Permanent Representative of the U.S. to the U.N. On the subject of the peacekeeping activities of the U.N., Leon Gordenker, in *The UN Secretary-General and the Maintenance of Peace* (New York: Columbia University Press, 1967), analyzes the ideas and practices of the three Secretaries-General who have served to date. Rosalyn Higgins, *United Nations Peacekeeping, 1946–1967: Documents and Commentary, I: The Middle East* (New York: Oxford University Press, Inc., 1969), is an important legal and political study, the first of three projected volumes. An earlier and overlapping study is A. L. Burns and Nina Heathcote, *Peace-Keeping by U.N. Forces: From Suez to the Congo* (New York: Praeger Publishers, Inc., 1963). Of a number of works on the relation of the United States to the U.N., the following are important: Lawrence D. Weiler and Anne P. Simons, *The United States and the United Nations* (New York: Manhattan Publishing Company, 1967), surveys U.S. peace and security policies in the U.N. from 1945 to 1955. Ruth B. Russell, *The United Nations and United States Security Policy* (Washington: The Brookings Institution, 1968), argues that the United States could make better use of the U.N. as a road to East-West détente. Arnold Beichman, *The "Other" State Department* (New York: Basic Books, Inc., Publishers, 1968), describes the work and problems of the U.S. mission to the U.N. Two personal accounts by former Permanent U.S. Representatives to the U.N. are Adlai E. Stevenson, *Looking Outward: Years of Crisis at the United Nations* (New York: Harper & Row, Publishers, 1963), and James J. Wadsworth, *The Glass House: The United Nations in Action* (New York: Praeger Publishers, Inc. 1966). *The Play within the Play: The Inside Story of the U.N.,* by Hermane Tavares de Sá (New York: Alfred A. Knopf, Inc., 1966), is an often humorous and at times satirical picture of the U.N. by a Brazilian journalist who served for five years as head of U.N. Information Services.

On American policy in sub-Saharan Africa, implemented largely through the U.N., see Chester Bowles, *Africa's Challenge to America* (Berkeley: University of California Press, 1956); Rupert Emerson, *Africa and United States Policy* (Englewood Cliffs, N.J.: Prentice-Hall, Inc., 1967); King Gordon, *The United Nations in the Congo: A Quest for Peace* (New York: Carnegie Endowment for International Peace, 1962). Vernon VanDyke, *Human Rights, the United States, and World Community* (New York: Oxford University Press, Inc., 1970), defines human rights and analyzes the international efforts to establish standards, with emphasis on the role of the United States.

XXII. Europe and the Cold War (Chapters 42, 43)

On American occupation policy in Germany, a first-hand account is Lucius D. Clay, *Decision in Germany* (Garden City, N.Y.: Doubleday & Company, Inc., 1950). Eugene Davidson, *The Death and Life of Germany: An Account of the American Occupation* (New York: Alfred A. Knopf, Inc., 1959), and J. D. Montgomery, *Forced to Be Free: The Artificial Revolution in Germany and Japan* (Chicago: University of Chicago Press, 1958), describe the effort of the United States to reshape defeated enemy countries after its own image. A crucial phase of the occupation is the subject of W. P. Davison, *The Berlin Blockade: A Study in Cold War Politics* (Princeton: Princeton University Press, 1958). The failure of American policy in Eastern Europe is described in a group of essays entitled *The Fate of East Central Europe: Hopes and Failures of American Foreign Policy*, edited by Stephen D. Kertesz (Notre Dame, Ind.: University of Notre Dame Press, 1956), and for Poland in particular by the postwar American ambassador, A. B. Lane, in *I Saw Poland Betrayed* (Indianapolis: The Bobbs-Merrill Company, Inc., 1948).

On the cold war there are a multitude of books and articles, of which only a few can be mentioned here. A good place to start is with Walter LaFeber, *America, Russia, and the Cold War, 1945–1966* (New York: John Wiley & Sons, Inc., 1967), which is concise and fair, though moderately revisionist, and has an extensive bibliography. William H. McNeill, *America, Britain, and Russia* (cited under XIX) is excellent for the opening rounds. John Lukacs, *A New History of the Cold War* (Garden City, N.Y.: Doubleday & Company, Inc., Anchor Books, 1966), is both factual and analytical. Herbert Feis, *From Trust to Terror: The Onset of the Cold War, 1945–1950* (New York: W. W. Norton and Company, Inc., 1970), is in the main favorable to American policy, though conceding errors on Truman's part. Historians who place the major blame on the aggressive economic and counterrevolutionary policies of the United States include David Horowitz, author of *The Free World Colossus* (New York: Hill & Wang, Inc., 1965) and editor of a group of essays published as *Containment and Revolution* (Boston: Beacon Press, 1967); W. A. Williams, author of *The Tragedy of American Diplomacy*, rev. ed. (New York: Dell Publishing Co., Inc., 1962); Gabriel Kolko, whose book, *The Politics of War*, was cited under XIX; and Lloyd C. Gardner, author of *Architects of Illusion: Men and Ideas in American Foreign Policy, 1941–1949* (Chicago: Quadrangle Books, Inc., 1970). These men write from the "new left" angle, as does Gar Alperovitz, whose *Atomic Diplomacy: Hiroshima and Potsdam, The Use of the Atomic Bomb and the American Confrontation with Soviet Power* (New York: Simon & Schuster, Inc., 1965), contends that Truman and Secretary Byrnes were obsessed with the bomb's potentiality as a diplomatic weapon against Russia. Alperovitz also touches on the bomb and other sources of friction with the Soviets in *Cold War Essays* (Garden City, N.Y.: Doubleday & Company, Inc., Anchor Books, 1970). No "new leftist" is D. F. Fleming, the veteran historian of America's failure to join the League of Nations and the first World Court. In *The Cold War and Its Origins, 1917–1960*, 2 vols. (Garden City, N.Y.: Doubleday & Company, Inc., 1961), he states frankly that he has "sought at every stage to present the other side, how it looks to 'the enemy,' " as a means, he hopes, of avoiding World War III. Martin F. Hertz, *Beginnings of the Cold War* (Bloomington: Indiana University Press, 1966), sees in Russia's need at the end of the war an opportunity for economic leverage that the United States failed to use. Barton J. Bernstein, ed., and the contributors to his volume, *Politics and Policies of the Truman Administration* (Chicago: Quadrangle Books, Inc., 1970), tax Truman and his advisers with disregard of legitimate Soviet interests. See Charles S. Maier, "Revisionism and the Interpretation of Cold War Origins," *Perspectives on American History*, 14 (1970), 313–47, for a judicious analysis of the "new left" approach.

The thesis that the cold war resulted less from aggressive policies of either party than from largely unjustified (though natural) fears aroused by measures that were basically defensive, is represented by Louis J. Halle, *The Cold War as History* (New York: Harper & Row, Publishers, 1967); Adam B. Ulam, *Expansion and Coexistence: The History of Soviet Foreign Policy, 1917–1967* (New York: Praeger Publishers, Inc., 1968); Robert D. Warth, *Soviet Russia in World Politics* (New York: Twayne Publishers, Inc., 1963), and Marshall D. Shulman, *Beyond the Cold War* (New Haven: Yale University Press, 1966). Three essays, presenting three conflicting interpretations, are brought together in Lloyd C. Gardner, Arthur Schlesinger, Jr., and Hans J. Morgenthau, *The Origins of the Cold War* (Waltham, Mass.: Ginn/Blaisdell, 1970).

The "containment" policy—the American strategy in the cold war—was announced in President Truman's message of March 12, 1947, proposing aid for Greece and Turkey and setting forth the Truman Doctrine. The evolution of that doctrine and the initiation of the Marshall Plan that followed it are described in Joseph M. Jones, *The Fifteen Weeks (February 21–June 5, 1947* (New York: The Viking Press, Inc., 1955). George Kennan's anonymous essay, "The Sources of Soviet Conduct," signed "X" and published in *Foreign Affairs* in July 1947, laid a theoretical basis for the containment policy, but Kennan in his *Memoirs, 1925–1950* (Boston: The Atlantic Monthly Press, 1967), maintained that it had been misunderstood and misapplied. Walter Lippmann, in *The Cold War* (New York: Harper & Row, Publishers, 1947), criticized the worldwide commitment implied in Truman's language. Dean Acheson, in *Present at the Creation* (cited under XX), relates his part, as Under Secretary and later Secretary of State, in launching the Truman Doctrine, the Marshall Plan, and NATO. The origin and early results of the Marshall Plan are described in H. B. Price, *The Marshall Plan and Its Meaning* (Ithaca, N.Y.: Cornell University Press, 1955).

Of the origins of NATO, in addition to the Acheson account just mentioned, *The Private Papers of Senator Vandenberg,* edited by Arthur H. Vandenberg, Jr. (Boston: Houghton Mifflin Company, 1952), give an interesting bit of background. Searching American and British appraisals, respectively, were given after NATO's first decade, in R. E. Osgood, *The Entangling Alliance* ◆

(Chicago: University of Chicago Press, 1962), and Alastair Buchan, *NATO in the 1960's* (New York: Praeger Publishers, Inc., 1960). W. T. R. and Annette B. Fox analyzed the process of American participation in *NATO and the Range of American Choice* (New York: Columbia University Press, 1967). Relations within NATO between the United States and its allies are described by Harlan Cleveland in *NATO: The Transatlantic Bargain* (New York: Harper & Row, Publishers, 1970), and with particular emphasis on Anglo-American frictions, by Richard E. Neustadt in *Alliance Politics* (New York: Columbia University Press, 1970). Frictions far more debilitating to NATO are the subject of John Newhouse, *De Gaulle and the Anglo-Saxons* (New York: The Viking Press, Inc., 1970). The problem of containing the competition in nuclear arms is well described in nontechnical terms by Chalmers M. Roberts in *The Nuclear Years: The Arms Race and Arms Control* (New York: Praeger Publishers, Inc., 1970).

The American attitude to the formation of the European Common Market and to proposals for further integration of Western Europe is treated in a number of studies: D. D. Humphrey, *The United States and the Common Market: A Background Study* (New York: Praeger Publishers, Inc., 1962); Walter Lippmann, *Western Unity and the Common Market* (Boston: Little, Brown and Company, 1962); Joseph Kraft, *The Grand Design: From Common Market to Atlantic Partnership* (New York: Harper & Row, Publishers, 1962); Christian Herter, *Toward an Atlantic Community* (New York: Harper & Row, Publishers, for Council on Foreign Relations, 1963). Ernest H. Preeg, *Traders and Diplomats* (Washington, D.C.: Brookings Institution, 1970), tells the story of the "Kennedy Round" of tariff negotiations with the Common Market countries.

American relations with one European state excluded from NATO and the Common Market but strategically important are described in A. P. Whitaker, *Spain and Defense of the West: Ally and Liability* (New York: Harper & Row, Publishers, for Council on Foreign Relations, 1961).

XXIII. The United States and Postwar East Asia: China, Japan, Korea (Chapters 44, 45)

On the controversial postwar relations of the United States with the Nationalist government of China, Feis, *The China Tangle* (cited under XIX), covers the beginning only. Tsou Tang, *American Failure in China, 1941–1950* (also cited under XIX), sees mistakes in American policy, while Anthony Kubek, *How the Far East Was Lost: American Policy and the Creation of Communist China, 1941–1949* (Chicago: Henry Regnery Co., 1963), claims to see conspiracy at work. The official account was set forth, in narrative and an impressive collection of documents, in *United States Relations with China, With Special Reference to the Period 1944–1949*, Department of State Publication 3573 (Washington: Department of State, 1949), republished as *The China White Paper (1949)* (Stanford: Stanford University Press, 1967). J. K. Fairbank, *The United States and China*, rev. ed. (Cambridge: Harvard University Press, 1962), is a concise account by a leading scholar in the field. On the Marshall mission, in addition to Ferrell's sketch of Secretary Marshall (cited under XX), John R. Beal, in *Marshall in China* (Garden City, N.Y.: Doubleday & Company, Inc., 1970), describes the mission as seen by an American journalist acting as adviser to the Nationalist government. On Communist China, R. L. Walker paints a grim picture of internal repression and external chauvinism (mostly verbal) in two studies: *China under Communism: The First Five Years* (New Haven: Yale University Press, 1955), and *The Continuing Struggle: Communist China and the Free World* (New York: Athene Press, 1959). Communist China as an international problem is highlighted by A. Doak Barnett in *Communist China and Asia: Challenge to American Policy* (New York: Harper & Row, Publishers, 1960). A more recent venture in constructive analysis of Sino-U.S. relations is *The United States and China in World Affairs*, by Robert Blum, edited by A. Doak Barnett (New York: McGraw-Hill Book Company, for Council on Foreign Relations, 1966). *Recognition of Communist China*, by R. P. Newman (New York: The Macmillan Company, 1961), is still a persuasive argument for the course suggested by the title. Later views are given in a number of excellent essays in A. Doak Barnett and E. O. Reischauer, eds., *The United States and China: The Next Decade* (New York: Praeger Publishers, Inc., 1970). Kenneth T. Young describes the difficulties of dealing with the Peking government in *Negotiating with the Chinese Communists: The United States Experience, 1953–1967* (New York: McGraw-Hill Book Company, for Council on Foreign Relations, 1968).

Of a number of books dealing with the break between China and the Soviet Union, two of the most useful are Donald S. Zagoria, *The Sino-Soviet Conflict, 1956–1961* (Princeton: Princeton University Press, 1962), for the earlier period, and Harrison E. Salisbury, *War Between Russia and China* (New York: W. W. Norton & Company, Inc., 1969), for later years.

On U.S. relations with Japan during the occupation and since, Edwin O. Reischauer, first-rank American authority and ambassador to Japan (1961–1969), has two brief and readable books: *The United States and Japan*, rev. ed. (Cambridge: Harvard University Press, 1965), and *Japan: The Story of a Nation* (New York: Alfred A. Knopf, Inc., 1970). Herbert Feis, in *Contest over Japan* (New York: W. W. Norton & Company, Inc., 1967), describes the contest between the United States and the Soviet Union for control over defeated Japan. The American occupation is described, from the American point of view, in H. E. Wildes, *Typhoon over Tokyo* (New York: The Macmillan Company, 1954), and in J. D. Montgomery, *Forced to Be Free* (cited under XXII). A fair but sometimes ironic view through Japanese eyes is given in Kazuo Kawai, *Japan's American Interlude* (Chicago: University of Chicago Press, 1960). Books on General Douglas MacArthur's regime in Japan have so far been either adulatory, like Courtney Whitney, *MacArthur: His Rendezvous with History* (New York: Alfred A. Knopf, Inc., 1956), or denigrative, like R. H. Rovere and A. M. Schlesinger, Jr., *The MacArthur Controversy and American Foreign Policy* (New York: Farrar, Straus & Giroux, Inc., 1965), a revision of the earlier *The General and the President*. A more objective treatment is promised by D. Clayton James, whose *The Years of MacArthur*, Vol. 1, 1880–1941 (Boston: Houghton Mifflin Company, 1970), stops with Pearl Harbor. The making of the peace treaty with Japan is described in F. S. Dunn, *Peace-Making and the Settlement with Japan* (Princeton: Princeton University Press, 1963). James Cary, *Japan Today: Reluctant Ally* (New York: Praeger Publishers, Inc., 1963), deals with post-treaty Japanese-American relations, and Robert Guillain, *The Japanese Challenge* (Philadelphia: J. B. Lippincott Co., 1970), is a translation of a sympathetic French work showing how a nation can achieve "greatness without the bomb." Shigeru Yoshida, Japanese Prime Minister during most of the postwar decade, gives his account of the occupation in *The Yoshida Memoirs: The Story of Japan in Crisis* (Boston: Houghton Mifflin Company, 1962).

For American occupation policy in Korea and the Korean War, a good introduction is George McCune, *Korea Today* (Cambridge: Harvard University Press, 1950). A careful study of American policy is L. M. Goodrich, *Korea: A Study of United States Policy in the United Nations* (New York: Council on Foreign Relations, Inc., 1956). The American occupation is described in E. G. Meade, *American Military Government in Korea* (New York: Columbia University, King's Crown Press, 1951). Glenn D. Paige, *The Korean Decision* (New York: The Free Press, 1968), is a fresh study of President Truman's decision to oppose North Korean aggression, for which one should also consult Truman's *Memoirs* and Acheson, *Present at the Creation* (both cited under XX). On President Truman's controversial recall of General MacArthur, one should consult the two works just named, the Rovere and Schlesinger volume cited in an earlier paragraph, and also the following: Trumbull Higgins, *Korea and the Fall of MacArthur: A Précis in Limited War* (New York: Oxford University Press, Inc., 1960), and J. W. Spanier, *The Truman-MacArthur Controversy and the Korean War* (Cambridge: Harvard University Press, 1959). Of the two American officers who in turn succeeded to MacArthur's command in Korea, General Ridgway approved, while General Clark subsequently criticized, the policy of limited war prescribed in Washington. See Matthew B. Ridgway, *The Korean War* (Garden City, N.Y.: Doubleday & Company, Inc., 1967); Mark W. Clark, *From the Danube to the Yalu* (New York: Harper & Row, Publishers, 1954). General J. Lawton Collins, Army Chief of Staff at the time, has told the story from the point of view of the Joint Chiefs of Staff (though with no startling revelations) in *War in Peacetime: The History and Lessons of Korea* (Boston: Houghton Mifflin Company, 1969).

The story of the capture of the U.S. intelligence ship *Pueblo* and its crew by the North Koreans is related by its commander, Lloyd M. Bucher, in *Bucher: My Story* (Garden City, N.Y.: Doubleday & Company, Inc., 1970), and placed in its military-bureaucratic context by Trevor Armbrister in *A Matter of Accountability: The True Story of the* Pueblo *Affair* (New York: Coward-McCann, Inc., 1970).

XXIV. The United States and Postwar Indochina, with Emphasis on the War in Vietnam (Chapter 46)

A useful background study is *Southeast Asia: Its Historical Development* by John F. Cady (New York: McGraw-Hill Book Company, 1964). Ellen J. Hammer, *The Struggle for Indochina* (Stanford: Stanford University Press, 1954), describes the rise of Communism and nationalism in Indochina and the struggle with France to the eve of the French defeat in 1954. Robert Shaplen, *Time Out of Hand: Revolution and Reaction in Southeast Asia* (New York: Harper & Row, Publishers, 1969), is a brilliant survey of the contending forces in the whole area, country by country, in the 1960's. Laos, the diminutive land which became a bone of contention in the cold war, is described by Oden Meeker in *The Little World of Laos* (New York: Charles Scribner's Sons, 1959). Its international significance is discussed by Hugh Toye in *Laos: Buffer State or Battleground* (New York: Oxford University Press, Inc., 1968). The late Bernard B. Fall analyzed a high point in the contest in *Anatomy of a Crisis: The Laotian Crisis of 1960–1961*, edited with an Epilogue by Roger M. Smith (Garden City, N.Y.: Doubleday & Company, Inc., 1969).

Of the flood of books on the war in Vietnam, there is space here for only a few. Books dealing primarily with military operations are omitted for lack of space, as are a number of serious books of argumentative rather than factual content. The manner of the American involvement and the efforts to conclude the war will receive chief emphasis. A useful introductory study is Ellen Hammer, *Vietnam: Yesterday and Today* (New York: Holt, Rinehart & Winston Inc., 1966). A more detailed and heavily documented history, severely critical of French colonial policy in Vietnam, is *Vietnam: A Dragon Embattled,* by Joseph Buttinger, 2 vols. (New York: Praeger Publishers, Inc., 1967). This work, which covers the period from 1900 to 1963, was issued in abridged form, with an additional chapter to 1968, as *Vietnam: A Political History* (New York: Praeger Publishers, Inc., 1968). It followed a study of the earlier period entitled *The Smaller Dragon: A Political History of Vietnam* (New York: Praeger Publishers, Inc., 1958). How French repressive policy enabled the Communist Viet Minh to dominate Vietnamese nationalism is brilliantly set forth by the American scholar, John T. McAlister, Jr., in

Viet Nam: The Origins of Revolution (New York: Alfred A. Knopf, Inc., 1969). Jean Lacouture, a French specialist, has told the life story of the founder of Vietnamese Communism in *Ho Chi Minh: A Political Biography* (New York: Random House, Inc., 1968). A detailed description of the organization and mode of operation of the Viet Cong (South Vietnamese Communists) is given by Douglas Pike in *Viet Cong: The Organization and Techniques of the National Liberation Front of South Vietnam* (Cambridge, Mass.: The M.I.T. Press, 1966). This study was brought up to 1969 in the same author's *War, Peace and the Viet Cong* (Cambridge, Mass.: The M.I.T. Press, 1969). *New York Times* journalist Harrison E. Salisbury was permitted, late in 1966, to spend two weeks in the North Vietnamese capital. His dispatches from there, giving his impressions of the results of American bombing and the morale of the people, were published in revised form in *Behind the Lines—Hanoi, December 23, 1966–January 7, 1967* (New York: Harper & Row, Publishers, 1967).

Probably the leading authority on the end of the French regime and the transition to American dominance in Vietnam was the French-born Bernard B. Fall, who was killed by a Viet Cong mine in February 1967. One of his most important books, *The Two Viet-Nams: A Political and Military Analysis* (New York: Praeger Publishers, Inc., 1963), describes developments in both North and South from the Japanese occupation in World War II to the death of Ngo Dinh Diem in 1963. The little known origins of American policy toward Vietnam in the war years are explored by Edward R. Drachman in *United States Policy Toward Vietnam, 1940–1945* (Rutherford, N.J.: Fairleigh Dickinson University Press, 1970). Melvin Gurtov, *The First Vietnam Crisis: Chinese Communist Strategy and United States Involvement, 1953–1954* (New York: Columbia University Press, 1967), recounts American vacillations over the Dienbienphu crisis and the Geneva Conference. Victor Bator, in *Vietnam: A Diplomatic Tragedy* (Dobbs Ferry, N.Y.: Oceana Publications, Inc., 1965), blames largely the hard line followed by American Secretary of State John Foster Dulles for America's isolation from its European allies in assuming responsibility for Vietnam. Robert Shaplen, in *The Lost Revolution: The U. S. in Vietnam, 1946–1966*, rev. ed. (New York: Harper & Row, Publishers, 1966), takes the United States to task on its failure to head off

Communism by sponsoring non-Communist revolution in Indochina. He pursues the same theme in recounting later events in *The Road from War: Vietnam 1965–1970* (New York: Harper & Row, Publishers, 1970). Two Cornell University professors, George McT. Kahin and John W. Lewis, in *The United States in Vietnam* (New York: The Dial Press, Inc., 1967), find no justification, legal or otherwise, for American policy. Their argument is in some instances based on questionable assumptions. The legal basis for American policy is examined from varied angles in a collection of readings and documents entitled *The Vietnam War and International Law,* edited by Richard A. Falk (Princeton: Princeton University Press, 1968).

The charge that the Johnson administration, by inadvertence or design, overlooked or disregarded a number of hints that Hanoi was willing to negotiate, developed in David Kraslow and S. H. Loury, *The Secret Search for Peace in Vietnam* (New York: Random House, Inc., 1968), loses much of its significance in view of the negative results when negotiations actually began. Joseph C. Goulden, in *Truth Is the First Casualty: The Gulf of Tonkin Affair—Illusion and Reality* (Chicago: Rand McNally & Co., 1969), shows that there was much doubt about the aggressive character of the alleged attack that led to the President's requesting and getting a free hand from Congress to make war in Vietnam. To this list of books critical of the war should be added a well-written and persuasive small volume by Arthur M. Schlesinger, Jr., *The Bitter Heritage: Vietnam and American Democracy, 1941–1966* (Boston: Houghton Mifflin Company, 1967), and a group of lectures by Senator J. William Fulbright, published as *The Arrogance of Power* (New York: Random House, Inc., 1967). Schlesinger aims his sharpest barbs at President Johnson and Secretary of State Dean Rusk. Fulbright denounces American interventionist policy, in Latin America as well as Asia, and calls for cutting back U.S. commitments abroad.

In contrast with the literally dozens of books critical of American policy in Vietnam, there are only two of real significance that defend it. General Maxwell D. Taylor, one of the architects of the policy, supports it in *Responsibility and Response* (New York: Harper & Row, Publishers, 1967). The other, *Why Vietnam?* by Frank N. Trager (New York: Praeger Publishers, Inc.,

1966), includes a survey of the Vietnamese historical background and finds hope for success in the premiership of Nguyen Cao Ky (1965). With these should be taken the State Department White Paper, *Aggression from the North,* Department of State Publication 7839 (Washington: Government Printing Office, 1965). A late entry to the lists and an important one, which perhaps can be regarded as neutral, is *The Lost Crusade: America in Vietnam,* by Chester L. Cooper (New York: Dodd, Mead & Co., 1970). Cooper served in the U.S. "foreign-policy bureaucracy" from the Geneva Conference of 1954 to the deadlock in the peace negotiations in Paris. He describes the decision-making process from inside and apparently without intent to assign either praise or blame. In this respect his book is probably the most revealing one that has appeared.

Two useful documentary volumes, both in paperback (their value limited by their dates), are *The Viet-Nam Reader: Articles and Documents on American Foreign Policy and the Viet-Nam Crisis,* edited by Marcus G. Raskin and Bernard B. Fall (New York: Random House, Inc., Vintage Books, 1965), and *The Vietnam Hearings,* with an Introduction by J. William Fulbright (New York: Random House, Inc., Vintage Books, 1966), selections from hearings before the Senate Committee on Foreign Relations in January and February 1966.

Finally, a firsthand account of President Johnson's decision to stop the bombing of North Vietnam as a prelude to negotiations is Townsend Hoopes, *The Limits of Intervention* (New York: David McKay Co., Inc. 1969).

XXV. American Policy in the Middle East (Chapter 47)

American concern with the Middle East since 1948 has been irresistibly drawn to the Israeli-Arab conflict. Here two books in Harvard's American Foreign Policy Library series are of special importance: William R. Polk, *The United States and the Arab World,* rev. ed. (Cambridge: Harvard University Press, 1969), and Nadav Safran, *The United States and Israel* (same publisher, 1963). Another useful study, based like Polk's on long experience in the area, is John S. Badeau, *The American Approach to the Arab World* (New York: Harper & Row, Publishers, for Council on Foreign Relations, 1968). American material interests in the area and resulting policies prior to

World War II are ably expounded by John A. DeNovo, in *American Interests and Policies in the Middle East, 1900–1939* (Minneapolis: University of Minnesota Press, 1963), which should be supplemented by Benjamin Shwadran, *The Middle East, Oil, and the Great Powers* (New York: Praeger Publishers, Inc., 1957). Leonard Stein, *The Balfour Declaration* (New York: Simon & Schuster, Inc., 1961), explains in detail the origin of the British commitment to "a national home for the Jewish people" in Palestine. M. A. Fitzsimons, *Empire by Treaty: Britain and the Middle East in the Twentieth Century* (Notre Dame, Ind.: University of Notre Dame Press, 1964), summarizes British policy in the area, up to and including the Suez crisis of 1956. A forthcoming study by Selig Adler on "Franklin D. Roosevelt and the Problem of Palestine" will show divergences within the administration as to the American attitude to the simmering conflict between Jew and Arab. Herbert Feis, *The Birth of Israel: The Tousled Diplomatic Bed* (New York: W. W. Norton & Company, Inc., 1969), illuminates Anglo-American differences over policy in Palestine just prior to independence. A. M. Lilienthal, *The Other Side of the Coin* (Old Greenwich, Conn.: The Devin-Adair Company, Publishers, 1965), is the most recent of several books by an author outspokenly disapproving of the creation of Israel as a Jewish state. Nadav Safran, *From War to War: The Arab-Israeli Confrontation, 1948–1967* (New York: Pegasus, 1969), is a comprehensive account of the varied conflicts and rivalries of the period. Fred J. Khouri, *The Arab-Israeli Dilemma* (Syracuse, N.Y.: Syracuse University Press, 1968), is discreetly sympathetic to the Arab cause.

On the Suez crisis of 1956, revelations of Anglo-French connivance with Israel, publicized by Hugh Thomas in *Suez* (New York: Harper & Row, Publishers, 1967), are authoritatively confirmed by a former British Minister of State, Anthony Nutting, in *No End of a Lesson: The Story of Suez* (New York: Clarkson N. Potter, Inc., 1967). *The Memoirs of Anthony Eden: Full Cycle* (Boston: Houghton Mifflin Company, 1960), tells much but not all. On the role of the United States, see the books on Dulles cited under XX; Herman Finer, *Dulles over Suez: The Theory and Practice of His Diplomacy* (Chicago: Quadrangle Books, Inc., 1964), a work very critical of Dulles; Eisenhower, *Waging Peace* (cited under XX). The United Nations' part in peacekeeping is related by Rosalyn Higgins in *United Nations Peacekeeping,*

1946–1967 (cited under XXI). A spirited account of the origins of the Six-Day War of 1967 is Theodore Draper, *Israel and World Politics: Roots of the Third Arab Israeli War* (New York: The Viking Press, Inc., 1968). A useful compilation is *The Israeli-Arab Reader: A Documentary of the Middle East Conflict,* edited by Walter Laqueur (New York: Citadel Press, Inc., 1969).

The early American attempts to prevent Russian intrusion into the area were described by John C. Campbell in *Defense of the Middle East* (New York: Harper & Row, Publishers, for Council on Foreign Relations, 1958). Soviet pressure and American response are described in two books by Walter Laqueur, *The Soviet Union and the Middle East* (New York: Praeger Publishers, Inc., 1959), and *The Struggle for the Middle East: The Soviet Union in the Mediterranean, 1958–1968* (New York: The Macmillan Company, 1969). J. C. Hurewitz, ed., *Soviet American Rivalry in the Middle East* (New York: Praeger Publishers, Inc., 1969), brings together essays by a dozen authors on the current state of the cold war in the area, including the military balance.

An experienced journalist's account of the civil war in Yemen, critical of the American attitude, is Dana Adams Schmidt, *Yemen: The Unknown War* (New York: Holt, Rinehart & Winston, Inc., 1968). Volumes in Harvard's American Foreign Policy Library series on relations with Middle Eastern states peripheral to the Arab-Israel conflict are L. V. Thomas and R. N. Frye, *The United States and Turkey and Iran* (Cambridge: Harvard University Press, 1952), and C. F. Gallagher, *The United States and North Africa: Morocco, Algeria, and Tunisia* (same publisher, 1963).

XXVI. American Postwar Policy in the Western Hemisphere (Chapters 48, 49)

United States relations with Latin America in the years after 1945 are put in proper perspective by the veteran specialist J. Fred Rippy in *Globe and Hemisphere: Latin America's Place in the Postwar Foreign Relations of the United States* (Chicago: Henry Regnery Co., 1958). Some general problems facing the United States are discussed, with the advantage of long experience, by Adolf A. Berle, in *Latin America: Diplomacy and Reality* (New York: Harper & Row, Publishers, for Council on Foreign Relations, 1962). The background, formation, and early functioning of the

Organization of American States (OAS) are carefully described in *The Organization of American States,* by Ann Van Wynen Thomas and A. J. Thomas, Jr. (Dallas, Tex.: Southern Methodist University Press, 1963), which may be supplemented with John C. Dreier, *The Organization of American States and the Hemisphere Crisis* (New York: Harper & Row, Publishers, for Council on Foreign Relations, 1962). Jerome Slater, *The OAS and United States Foreign Policy* (Columbus: Ohio State University Press, 1967), finds serious divergences between the aims of the United States and those of its Latin American allies. Gordon Connell-Smith, *The Inter-American System* (New York: Oxford University Press, Inc., 1966), gives a British critic's assessment of both the OAS and the Alliance for Progress. *The OAS in Transition,* by Margaret Ball (Durham, N.C.: Duke University Press, 1969), is the most comprehensive and scholarly treatment of the subject.

The deterioration of U.S. relations with its southern neighbors after World War II is described by Donald M. Dozer in *Are We Good Neighbors?* (cited under XVIII) and by Milton S. Eisenhower (who made two surveys for his brother the President), in *The Wine Is Bitter: The United States and Latin America* (Garden City, N.Y.: Doubleday & Company, Inc., 1963). President Kennedy's attempt to recapture the good will of Latin America through the Alliance for Progress was described briefly and idealistically in lectures by Lincoln Gordon, U.S. ambassador to Brazil, published as *A New Deal for Latin America: The Alliance for Progress* (Cambridge: Harvard University Press, 1963). Subsequent assessments have tended to be critical. Simon G. Hanson, *Five Years of the Alliance for Progress* (Washington, D.C.: Inter-American Affairs Press, 1967), finds that the program has been used "to reward rather than to penalize resistance to change." The same author, in *Dollar Diplomacy, Modern Style: Chapters in the Failure of the Alliance for Progress* (Washington, D.C.: Inter-American Affairs Press, 1970), finds that too much Alliance activity has been diverted to serve the interests of U.S. business. William D. Rogers, *The Twilight Struggle: The Alliance for Progress and the Politics of Development in Latin America* (New York: Random House, Inc., 1967), while not wholly pessimistic, stresses obstacles to the success of the program, both in the United States and in Latin America. Herbert K. May, *Problems and Prospects of the Alliance for*

Progress: A Critical Examination (New York: Praeger Publishers, Inc., 1969), places responsibility for success or failure of the program primarily upon the Latin Americans themselves. A more hopeful note is struck by Harvey S. Perloff in *Alliance for Progress: A Social Invention in the Making* (Baltimore: The Johns Hopkins Press, 1969), but Jerome Levinson and Juan de Onis, in *The Alliance That Lost Its Way: A Critical Report on the Alliance for Progress* (Chicago: Quadrangle Books, Inc., 1971), find little evidence of progress of any kind. George C. Lodge, *Engines of Change: United States Interests and Revolution in Latin America* (New York: Alfred A. Knopf, Inc., 1970), is a plea for United States support for non-Communist revolutionary change in Latin America. But the basic difficulty of instituting peaceful social and economic change in Latin America is analyzed and illustrated by John Mander in *The Unrevolutionary Society: The Power of Latin American Conservatism in a Changing World* (New York: Alfred A. Knopf, Inc., 1969).

An early assessment of the Communist threat in the area was *Communism in Latin America* by R. J. Alexander (New Brunswick, N.J.: Rutgers University Press, 1957). The brief blossoming of Communism in Guatemala and its extinction by indirect U.S. intervention are recounted by Daniel James in *Red Design for the Americas: Guatemalan Interlude* (New York: The John Day Company, Inc., 1954), and Ronald M. Schneider, *Communism in Guatemala, 1944–1954* (New York: Praeger Publishers, Inc., 1959). President Eisenhower in *Mandate for Change* (cited under XX) tells frankly of the U.S. role.

On Communism in Cuba, Robert F. Smith, *The United States and Cuba: Business and Diplomacy 1917–1960* (New York: Twayne Publishers, Inc., Bookman Associates, Inc., 1960), shows how American policy in Cuba produced conditions that invited revolution. Earl E. T. Smith, last U.S. ambassador to Cuba before Castro's triumph, in *The Fourth Floor: An Account of the Castro Communist Revolution* (New York: Random House, Inc., 1962), blamed lower echelons ("the fourth floor") in the State Department for Castro's success. Theodore Draper, in *Castro's Revolution: Myths and Realities* (New York: Praeger Publishers, Inc., 1962), describes vividly how the bearded hero turned what began as a liberal revolution into a Communist one, but James O'Connor in *The Origins of Socialism in Cuba* (Ithaca,

N.Y.: Cornell University Press, 1970), argues that Castro planned from the beginning to destroy the monopolization of Cuban agriculture and industry by United States capital, which he believed to be the cause of the island's economic stagnation. *Castro, the Kremlin, and Communism in Latin America*, edited by D. Bruce Jackson (Baltimore: The Johns Hopkins Press, 1969), is a collection of essays exploring the hemispheric implications of Communism in Cuba. Probably the best account of the Bay of Pigs fiasco is *The Cuban Invasion: The Chronicle of a Disaster,* by K. E. Meyer and Tad Szulc (New York: Praeger Publishers, Inc., 1962), but for this and the missile crisis of 1962, one should also consult Schlesinger, *The Thousand Days;* Sorensen, *Kennedy;* and Hilsman, *To Move a Nation* (all cited under XX). On the missile crisis, in addition, see Robert F. Kennedy, *Thirteen Days: A Memoir of the Cuban Missile Crisis* (New York: W. W. Norton & Company, Inc., 1969), posthumously published; Elie Abel, *The Missile Crisis* (Philadelphia: J. B. Lippincott Co., 1966); and Weintal and Bartlett, *Facing the Brink* (cited under XX).

For background of revolt in the Dominican Republic in 1965 and American intervention, one should read Juan Bosch, *The Unfinished Experiment: Democracy in the Dominican Republic* (New York: Praeger Publishers, Inc., 1965), in which the author reviews the events of 1961–1964, including the brief period of his presidency. Eyewitness accounts by able newsmen are Tad Szulc, *Dominican Diary* (New York: The Delacorte Press, 1965), and Dan Kurzman, *Santo Domingo: Revolt of the Damned* (New York: G. P. Putnam's Sons, 1965). A former U.S. ambassador to the Republic and agent of President Johnson in the 1965 crisis was John Bartlow Martin. His account, *Overtaken by Events: The Dominican Crisis from the Fall of Trujillo to the Civil War* (Garden City, N.Y.: Doubleday & Company, Inc., 1966), defends U.S. policy as necessary. Quite the opposite position is taken by Theodore Draper in his lively volume, *The Dominican Revolt: A Case Study in American Policy* (New York: Commentary, 1968). A debate over the need for American intervention, with Adolf A. Berle and Wolfgang Friedmann as chief Theodore Draper in his lively volume, *The Dominican Republic Crisis, 1965* (Dobbs Ferry, N.Y.: Oceana Publications, Inc., 1967). A detailed and exceptionally objective account, explaining without judging, is Jerome Slater, *Intervention* and *Negotiation: The United States and the Dominican Republic* (New York: Harper & Row, Publishers, 1970).

Important recent books on relations with other Latin American nations are Frederick B. Pike, *Chile and the United States, 1880–1962: The Emergence of Chile's Social Crisis and the Challenge to United States Diplomacy* (Notre Dame, Ind.: University of Notre Dame Press, 1962), and Harold F. Peterson, *Argentina and the United States, 1810–1960* (Albany: State University of New York, 1964).

On United States relations with Canada, there are a number of good recent books. Best, perhaps, is Gerald M. Craig, *The United States and Canada* (Cambridge: Harvard University Press, 1968), a fair-minded account by a Canadian historian in Harvard's American Foreign Policy Library series. Joseph Barber, *Good Fences Make Good Neighbors: Why the U.S. Provokes Canadians* (Indianapolis: The Bobbs-Merrill Company, Inc., 1958), states the Canadian point of view persuasively. Blair Fraser, *The Search for Identity: Canada, 1945–1967* (Garden City, N.Y.: Doubleday & Company, Inc., 1968), has important sections on relations with the United States. In *Canada: The Uneasy Neighbor* (New York: David McKay Co., Inc., 1965), Gerald Clark, a Canadian journalist, analyzes modern Canada on the basis of "two dominant themes: English Canada vis-à-vis French Canada, and Canada as a whole vis-à-vis the United States." Paul Martin, former Canadian Minister for External Affairs, in *Canada and the Quest for Peace* (New York: Columbia University Press, 1967), presents lectures on three subjects: Canada's role in UN peacekeeping activities, Canada's contributions to foreign aid, and "Canada's approach to the Vietnam conflict." Finally, *Neighbors Taken for Granted: Canada and the United States,* edited by American diplomat Livingston T. Merchant (New York: Praeger Publishers, Inc., 1966), comprises contributions by eight distinguished personalities, four from each side of the border.

XXVII. Critiques of United States Foreign Policy (Chapter 50)

Criticism of American foreign policy since World War II has passed through two principal phases. The first, in the early 1950's, was characterized by such books as Robert E. Osgood, *Ideals and Self-Interest in American Foreign Relations: The Great Transformation of the Twentieth Century* (Chicago: The University of Chicago Press, 1953); Hans J. Morgenthau, *In Defense of the National Interest: A Critical Examination of American Foreign Policy* (New York: Alfred A. Knopf, Inc., 1951), and George F. Kennan, *American Diplomacy, 1900–1950* (cited under XIV). Such men, as "realists," argued that a wise foreign policy must aim at concrete and realizable goals rather than utopias, and be guided by a true concept of the "national interest" rather than by moralistic or legalistic formulas. The first two generations of American statesmen, they believed, had generally followed these principles; later generations, especially many of the men in command since 1898, had been diverted from them. Such early postwar policies as the Marshall Plan (or European Recovery Program) seemed, to Osgood at least, an indication that American foreign policy had matured, but the broadening of containment into a worldwide program with ideological criteria, implemented by military intervention in faraway places, brought second thoughts to these men and stimulated a new group of critics. While Osgood, in *Alliance and American Foreign Policy* (Baltimore: The Johns Hopkins Press, 1968), advocated an adjustment rather than a reversal of American policy, Kennan and Morgenthau went further. Kennan, in his *Memoirs, 1925–1950* (cited under XXII), repudiated the whole idea of military containment and lamented that his own blueprint for containment had been misunderstood and perverted. In hearings before the Senate Committee on Foreign Relations (*The Vietnam Hearings,* cited under XXIV), he called for an early withdrawal from Vietnam. Morgenthau, in *A New Foreign Policy for the United States* (New York: Praeger Publishers, Inc., for Council on Foreign Relations, 1969), deplored the policy of "embarking upon costly and futile interventions for the purpose of building nations and viable economies abroad."

The war in Indochina and the intervention in the Dominican Republic inspired not only numerous critiques of those specific interventions but a number of books sharply critical of the entire containment policy as applied beyond the borders of Europe. The chief lines of attack were three: first, containment in the "third world" was a counterrevolutionary policy, having the effect of maintaining the status quo, however unjust; second, the dissolution of the Communist monolith—the break between Russia and China and the growing independence of minor Communist states—had exorcised the specter of world revolution: third, a policy of worldwide containment, even were it justified, would strain the resources of the United States to the great detriment of domestic well-being. Historians of the "new left" (cited under XXII) were of course critical of the containment policy, but they were joined by many not in that category. Unqualified condemnation, especially of military intervention, is found in the following: J. William Fulbright, *The Arrogance of Power* (cited under XXIV); Richard J. Barnet, *Intervention and Revolution: The United States in the Third World* (New York: The World Publishing Company, 1968); Theodore Draper, *Abuse of Power* (New York: The Viking Press, Inc., 1967); Edmund Stillman and William Pfaff, *Power and Impotence: The Failure of America's Foreign Policy* (New York: Random House, Inc., 1966). In a different category are Ronald Steel, *Pax Americana* (New York: The Viking Press, Inc., 1967), who traces the growth of the postwar American empire and raises questions but offers no solutions, and George Liska, *Imperial America* (Baltimore: The Johns Hopkins Press, 1967), who finds fault with the United States less for having become an imperial power than for failing to adjust its thinking to the role. George W. Ball (Under Secretary of State for six years under Presidents Kennedy and Johnson) takes a well balanced view in *The Discipline of Power: Essentials of a Modern World Structure* (Boston: Little, Brown and Company, 1968). While holding that "the depressing conflict in Vietnam is the dead end" of a policy that disregards the limits of American power, he makes a strong case for continued American cooperation with Europe—preferably a united Europe. Finally, another former Under Secretary of State, Eugene V. Rostow, in *Law, Power, and the Pursuit of Peace* (Lincoln: University of Nebraska Press, 1968), finds justifications for all, or nearly all, U.S. interventions since World War II from Korea to Vietnam.

Index

Germany (*Cont.*):

67; precipitates World War II, 367–68; avoids break with U.S., 376; in Tripartite Pact, 378–79; declares war on U.S., 386; as Enemy Number One, 390; future of, debated at Teheran, 404–5; at Yalta, 406; surrender of, 409; Allied Control Committee for, 409; occupation zones, 434–35, 434n.; U.S. respects Russian zone, 435; Potsdam decisions, 435–38; East-West deadlock in, 438–39; divided, 442–43; state of war ended (1951), 476n.

Gerry, Elbridge, 45

Ghana, 426

Ghent, Treaty of (1814), 65–66, 69, 96; arbitrations under, 69

Giap, General Vo Nguyen, 512

Gibraltar, 21, 25

Gilbert, Prentiss, 332

Gillespie, Lieutenant Archibald H., 122, 127, 128n.

Ginn, Edward, 244

Ginseng, 138

Giraud, General Henri H., 398

Girondists, 39n.

Glass, Carter, 305

Godoy, Don Manuel, 44

Golan Heights, 525, 526

Goldberg, Arthur, 430, 505

Goldwater, Senator Barry, 501

Goluchowski, Count, 190, 191

Gomulka, Wladyslaw, 451, 452, 452n.

Good Neighbor Policy, and Buchanan, 148; begun under Hoover, 350, 350n.; under Franklin D. Roosevelt, 351–59; and Mexico, 355–59

Gore-McLemore resolutions, 261

Gran Chaco War, 354, 354n.

Grant, Ulysses S., 162, 165, 166, 167, 168, 196

Graves, General William S., 309

Gray, George, 207, 209

Gray, Captain Robert, 70, 101n.

Great Britain (*See also* Treaties of U.S. with; War of 1812; Anglo-Japanese Alliance), 13; disruption of Empire, 18; Parliament repeals offensive acts, 20; crisis of 1794, 40–41; impressment of American seamen, 59–61; charges against (1812), 59; naval limitation, 68; postwar arbitrations with, 69–71; and Quadruple Alliance, 79–80; and recognition of Spanish colonies, 80–82; and Monroe Doctrine, 82–84, 87–88; and Russia, 85; and Panama Congress, 87; Texas, 112, 116; California, 120, 121, 122; and opening of China, 138, 140, 142–43, 142n.; and Japan, 142; Central America, 150; Cuba, 151, 152; U.S. Civil War, 155–61; and *Alabama* claims, 161–63; Venezuelan boundary, 178–81; sphere of interest in China, 189–90; approves of U.S. policy in Cuba, 201; wishes U.S. to retain Philippines, 207; isthmian canal, 214–15; new spirit of accommodation, 214; Mexico, 227; in Russo-Japanese war, 236, 236n.; blockade in World War I, 257–59; and naval limitation, 310–12, 314–16; and Japanese aggression in Manchuria, 334; and Munich settlement, 365–66; and opening of World War II, 366–69; aided by U.S. nonbelligerency, 372–76; and U.S. in World War II, 390–92; and Vietnam,

Great Britain (*Cont.*):

492, 493, 497n.; policy in Middle East, 513, 516, 517; in Suez Canal crisis, 518–20

Greece, 83, 420, 440, 444, 458, 517

Greenland, occupied by U.S., 14, 374, 374n.

Greenville, Treaty of, 43

Greer, U.S.S., 375

Grenville, Lord, 42, 43, 43n.

Gresham, Walter Q., 178n., 179

Grew, Joseph C., 336, 361, 362, 364–65, 379, 380n., 382, 382n., 386, 387

Grey, Sir Edward (later Lord), 259, 262, 294

Greytown, 88

Grotius, Hugo, 36, 107

Guadalupe Hidalgo, treaty of (*See* Treaties of U.S., Mexico)

Guadeloupe, island, 57

Guam, 204, 205, 208, 208n., 210; Guam (Nixon) Doctrine, 474, 561

Guano islands, 146, 147; Guano Law (1856), 147

Guantanamo Bay, naval base, 213, 219, 353

Guatemala, 460n., 534, 535n., 558

Guevara, Ernesto (Ché), 536, 538

Guizot, François P. G., 122

Hague Peace Conferences, 244–45

Hague, Permanent Court of Arbitration, 243, 244, 245, 246–48, 300

Hainan island, 377

Haiti, 86, 223–24, 352

Hakodate, 141

Halifax, 89

Hamaguchi, Premier Yuko, 330

Hamilton, Alexander, 38, 39, 41, 41n., 42, 42n., 45, 46

Hammarskjöld, Dag, 422, 422n., 423, 424

Hammond, George, British minister, 42n.

Hanihara, Masanao, Ambassador, 329

Hanna, Mark, 196, 215

Hannegan, Edward A., 107

Hanoi (*See* Vietnam, North)

Harding, Warren G., 297–99, 312, 318, 321, 323, 348

Harmar, General Joseph, 40

Harper, John A., 63

Harriman, Edward H., 241

Harriman, W. Averell, 393, 407, 464, 505, 506

Harris, Townsend, 141, 143–44

Harrison, Benjamin, 170, 177, 196

Harrison, William Henry, 64

Harvey, George, 299

Havana, Act of, 397

Hawaii, 14; early interest in, 146–47, 167; proposed annexation, 147, 169, 170, 194, 196–97; annexation vs. reciprocity, 169–70; reciprocity treaty (1875), 169; revolution in, 170; President Cleveland blocks annexation, 171, 192; and Republican party, 193; new annexation treaty fails, 197; "yellow peril," in, 197; annexed by joint resolution, 210; free trade with, as territory, 322

Hawthorne, Nathaniel, 8

Hay, John, and Philippines, 207; and isthmian canal, 214–16; and China, 231–36, 235n.; and Japan, 238; arbitration treaties, 241

Hay-Bunau-Varilla Treaty (1904), 216
Hay-Herrán Treaty, 216
Hay-Pauncefote Treaty (1901), 214, 214n., 250
Hayes, Rutherford B., 167, 188
Hearst, William R., 198
Henlein, Konrad, 365
Herrán, Dr. Tomás, 216
Herrera, President José, 118n., 122, 123
Herter, Christian A., 454, 454n., 537
Hindenburg, President Paul von, 340
Hippisley, A. E., 232, 232n.
Hirohito, Emperor of Japan, 383, 384, 410–11, 464
Hiroshima, 410, 410n.
Hirota, Koki, 336
Hispaniola, 48n., 151
Hitchcock, Gilbert M., 293, 294
Hitler, Adolf, 271n., 353, 381; rise of, 339–40; foreign policy of, 339–42, 364–68; aims known in U.S., 341–42; accord with Mussolini, 360–61; answers Roosevelt, 367; precipitates war, 367–68; pact with Soviet Union, 368; threat of, to U.S., 369n.; and destroyer bases deal, 372; attacks Soviet Union, 374; wishes to avoid war with U.S., 376; meets Franco, 399; and "Jewish question," 403–4; death of, 409
Ho Chi Minh, 490, 491, 496, 497; death, 507
Ho Chi Minh Trail, 505, 511n.
Hoar, George F., 209, 210
Holy Alliance (See also Quadruple Alliance), 72n.
Honduras, 88, 546
Hong Kong, 138, 142, 204
Hoover, Herbert, 6, 11, 234, 294, 304, 321; and tariff, 323, 323n.; moratorium, 324; Stimson Doctrine, 332, 333–34; Good Neighbor Policy, 350, 350n., 351
Hoover Commission, 9–10
Hoover-Stimson Doctrine, 333–34, 335
Hope and Baring, 53n.
Hopkins, Harry, 12, 393, 413, 416, 435n., 464
Horseshoe Bend, battle of, 66
"Hot-line," agreement on, 449n.
Hotze, Henry, 160
House, Colonel Edward M., 12, 253, 255, 262–63, 272, 278, 286; House-Grey Memorandum, 262
Houston, Sam, 111, 115, 151
Hudson, Manley O., 302
Hudson's Bay Company, 42, 101, 102, 102n., 109, 120
Huerta, General Victoriano, 225, 227
Hughes, Charles Evans, 272, 299, 300–302, 302n., 309, 311–12, 319, 329, 350n., 356
Hull, Cordell (See also Reciprocity, tariff), Reciprocal trade agreements, 326–28; World Economic Conference, 326; policy in Far East, 336–37; Spanish Civil War, 346, 346n.; Montevideo Conference, 351–52; and Mexico, 358–59; neutrality law, 367; four principles for Japan, 380, 382; discourages Roosevelt-Konoye meeting, 382; final proposal to Japan, 385–86; and de Gaulle, 399, 399n.; at Moscow, 402–3; and international organization, 412–13
Human rights (See United Nations)
Hungary, 145, 284n., 422, 437, 451–52
Hurley, Patrick J., 464, 465

Hussein, King, 521, 522, 524, 527, 528, 529

Iberville River, 54, 71
ICBM (Intercontinental ballistic missile), 448, 457–58
Iceland, 14, 375, 444n.
Ignatiev, General Nikolay P., 143
Ikeda, Premier Hayato, 478
Imbert Barreras, Antonio, 546
Immigration, U.S. policy (See China; Japan)
Imperial Maritime Customs, 140, 232
Imperial preference, 91
Imperialism, 165, 166, 208–9, 211–12
Impressment of seamen, 40, 59–62, 64, 65, 66, 66n., 97
Indelible allegiance, 60, 66n.
Independence, of United States, Declaration of, 19; recognition of, 20, 27, 28; effect on trade, 30
India, 475; on armistice commissions, 492, 496
Indians (See also Mosquito Indians; Seminole War; Tecumseh), 31, 33, 40, 41, 43, 59, 63, 64, 66, 72, 105
Indochina (See also Cambodia, Laos, Vietnam), 490, 491, 511–12
Indonesia, 420, 463
"Inquiry, The" at Paris Peace Conference (1919), 272
Inter-American Conferences (See also International Conferences of American States), (1936) Buenos Aires, for Maintenance of Peace, 354–55; (1945) Mexico City, 416, 532; (1947) Rio de Janeiro, 532; (1961) Punta del Este, Economic and Social Conference, 538; (1965) Rio de Janeiro, 547
Inter-American Conferences of Foreign Ministers, (1939) Panama, 396–97; (1940) Havana, 397; (1942) Rio de Janeiro, 397; (1959, 1960) Santiago, San José, 536; (1962) Punta del Este, 540; (1965) Washington, 545–46
Inter-American Development Bank, 537
Inter-American Treaty of Reciprocal Assistance (See Rio Pact)
International Atomic Energy Agency, 419n., 431
International Bank for Reconstruction and Development, 417, 430
International Conferences of American States (See also Inter-American Conferences), 1st (1889) Washington, 177; 7th (1933) Montevideo, 327, 351, 353; 8th (1938) Lima, 355; 9th (1948) Bogotá, 532; 10th (1954) Caracas, 534
International Court of Justice (second World Court), 417, 418, 418n., 424, 430
International Development Association, 431
International Labor Organization (ILO), 287n., 300, 417
International Monetary Fund, 417
International Prize Court of Appeals, 245
Interoceanic Canal Commission, 167
Investments, U.S. foreign, 217, 221, 241–42, 317–18, 320–21, 321n.
Iran, 420, 513n., 516, 517; Declaration regarding, 405n.
Iraq, 280, 280n., 411n., 513n., 517, 521, 523, 525

Policy Planning Council, 6
Polignac, Prince de, 84–85
Polk, James K., 16; and Oregon, 104–9; low-tariff policy, 108; election, 113–14; and Texas, 114–15; and Mexico, 117–25, 126–27, 133; and California, 117, 119–22, 125; achievements of, 119n., 135; reasserts Monroe Doctrine, 122; "Polk Corollary," 122; war message, 125; and Mexican War, 126–35; and Trist, 129, 130, 133, 133n.; accepts treaty, 133; and Yucatan, 151; and Cuba, 151
Pompidou, Georges, President, 459n.
Port Arthur, 189, 237, 238
Porter, Peter B., 63, 96
Portsmouth, Treaty of, 238
Portugal, 86, 311, 428, 429, 429n., 444n.
Portuguese Guinea, 428
Potsdam Conference (1945), 435–36, 453n.
Potsdam Declaration, 410
Powers, Francis Gary, 454
Presidential elections (1796), 45; (1844), 113–14; (1900), 211–12; (1940), 372; (1944), 406; (1952), 452, 471; (1960), 483n.; (1964), 501; (1968), 506
Pribilof Islands (See Fur seal controversy)
Prince Edward Island, 146n.
Prince of Wales Island, 74n.
Privateering, 71, 81, 156, 157, 157n.
Proctor, Redfield, 200
Prussia, 28, 30, 37, 79, 84, 156
Puebla, Mexico, 129
Pueblo, U.S.S., 473
Puerto Rico, 74, 87; occupied by U.S., 204; cession to U.S., 208; under American tutelage, 222; free trade with, 322
Puget Sound, 104
Pulitzer, Joseph, 198

Quadruple Alliance, 79, 79n., 83, 86, 87; proposed interference in America, 79, 84–85
Quakers (society of Friends), 67, 206n.
"Quarantine" speech (F.D.R.), 362
Quebec: Act, 24; Conferences, 390n.; (1944), 402
Quemoy Islands, defense of, 482–83
Querétaro, 132, 134
Quitman, John A., 151, 152

Raccoon, H.M.S., 70
Radio Free Europe, 452
Railroads (See also Chinese Eastern; Trans-Siberian; South Manchurian; Chinese Changchun), transcontinental, 147, 164, 167; Southern Pacific, 148; proposed inter-American, 177; Central Pacific, 187
Randolph, Edmund, 38, 42
Rauch, Basil, 346–47n.
Reciprocity, tariff (See also Tariffs, U.S.), 30; (1854) with Canada, 146; (1875) with Hawaii, 169; (1889) proposed inter-American, 177; (1890) in McKinley tariff, 190; (1897) in Dingley tariff, 191; (1903) with Cuba, 322; (1911) proposed with Canada, 322; (1934) Hull reciprocal trade program, 13, 326–28

Recognition policy of U.S., 80–81, 81n.; changed by Woodrow Wilson, 225; return to de facto, 350, 350n.
Red Cross, 244
"Red line maps," 94n.
Red River, 73
Regional security organizations, 416–17, 422
Regular Army, 15
Reid Cabral, Donald, 545
Reid, Whitelaw, 207
Religion (See also Missions, Christian), and expansion, 206–7, 206n., 209, 212; and peace movement, 244
Reparations: Germany, basis for, 271; at Peace Conference, 282–83; under Dawes and Young Plans, 319–20; in Hoover moratorium, 324–25; World War II, 406, 407, 408, 436–37, 437n., 439
Reparations: Japan, 476
Republican party, and Canadian reciprocity, 146; and Monroe Doctrine, 176; and expansion, 164, 193, 196; defends Philippine policy, 211–12; condemns "containment," 447, 452
Republican party (Jeffersonian), 53, 65
Reston, James, 461
Reuben James, U.S.S., 375
Reynolds, Captain William, 166
Rhea letter, 72n.
Rhee, President Syngman, 467, 471
Rhineland, 282
Rhodesia, 428, 429, 430
Ribbentrop, Joachim von, 368, 393n.
Richardson, Admiral James O., 388
Ridgway, General Matthew B., 448n.
Right of deposit, 44, 47, 49, 50, 51
Right of search (See also Impressment), and slave trade, 96–98
Rio Bravo (See Rio Grande)
Rio Grande, 71, 111, 118, 123, 129, 133, 134, 135, 147, 148
Rio Pact (1947), 444, 532
Roatan, island, 88
Robinson, Joseph T., 357
Robles, President Marco A., 544
Rochambeau, General, 21, 22
Rockefeller, Nelson, 417, 547, 551–52
Rockhill, W. W., 232, 232n., 234n.
Rockingham, Marquis of, 22
Rocky (Stony) Mountains, 70, 71, 101, 102, 108
Rodriguez Hortalez et Compagnie, 19
Rogers, Secretary William P., 430, 488, 527
Rogers Act, 9
Roman Catholic Church, 206n., 228n.
Rome-Berlin-Tokyo Axis, 361
Roosevelt Corollary, 219–20, 222, 350
Roosevelt, Franklin D., 11, 12, 327, 336; Good Neighbor Policy, 230, 351–59; and World Court, 302; World Economic Conference, 325–26; offers cooperation with League, 340; Mexico, 357–59; "quarantine" speech, 362; Munich settlement, 366; proposes "methods short of war," 366–67; urges repeal of arms embargo, 367; view of war in Europe, 369–70; promises aid to opponents of force, 370; directs rearmament, 371; destroyer-

U-2 incident, 454
Ulam, Adam, 447
"Unconditional surrender," 401–2, 410
Underwood Tariff, 322
UNESCO (United Nations Educational, Scientific and Cultural Organization), 417
"Unguarded frontier," 68–69
Union of South Africa, 428, 429, 429n., 430
Union of Soviet Socialist Republics (U.S.S.R.) (*See* Soviet Union)
"United Action for Peace," 421–22, 469
United Arab Republic (U.A.R.) (*See also* Egypt), 513, 513n., 521–29 *passim*
United Nations, preliminary steps for, 412–13; Dumbarton Oaks draft, 413–14; Yalta decisions, 414–15; veto, 415, 416, 420, 421; Charter drawn at San Francisco, 415–16; Charter analyzed, 416–18; amended, 427; accepted by U.S., 418, 418n.; enforcement provisions not implemented, 418–19; disarmament provisions fail, 419; atomic energy, 419, 419n.; paralysis of Security Council, 420; deadlock over new members, 420; early work of General Assembly, 420–21; proposals for strengthening, 421–22; and Korea, 421–22, 467, 468–71; labels Communist China aggressor, 421; new activities—peacekeeping operations, 422–424, 422n., 423n.; and Suez Canal crisis, 422, 520; and Hungary, 422, 452; in Middle East crisis (1958), 422–23n., 522; U.N. Emergency Force (UNEF), 422, 520, 524; "Operation Congo" (ONUC), 423–24, 423n.; Financial crisis, 424–26, 424n.; U.S. share of Budget, 424n.; crisis over Cyprus, 426; states not members, 426n.; growth of African-Asian bloc, 426–27; problem of "ministates," 427; temper of new majorities, 427–28; anticolonial enthusiasm, 428; the problem of Africa, 428–30, 428n.; U.S. attitude, 428–30, 429n., 430n.; African Charter, 429n.; World Court and South West Africa, 430; U.S. casts its first veto, 430n.; U.S. and economic program, 430–31; U.S. and human rights treaties, 431; exclusion of Communist China, 484–85; and war in Vietnam, 505, 505n.; and Six-Day War, 524–26; importance to U.S., 561–62
United Nations Conference on Trade and Development (UNCTAD II), 551
United Nations Development Decade, 431
United Nations Disarmament Commission, 419
United Nations Emergency Force (UNEF), 422, 520, 524
United Provinces of Rio de la Plata (*See* Argentina)
U.N. Relief and Works Agency for Palestine Refugees (UNRWA), 514
Upshur, Abel P., **112**
Uruguay, 88, 546, 547
U.S. Information Agency (USIA), 7
U.S.S.R. (*See* Soviet Union)
Utrecht, Treaty of (1713), 37

Van Buren, Martin, 98, 111, 112
Vandenberg, Arthur H., 415, 415n.

Vandenberg Resolution, 444
Vanderbilt, Cornelius, 150
Vattel, Sir Emmeric de, 36, 107
Venezuela, 85, 192; boundary controversy, 178–81; Anglo-German intervention, 219, 219n.; Vice-President Nixon in, 535
Veracruz, 88, 126, 129, 227
Vergennes, Comte de, French Foreign Minister, 19, 20, 22, 24
Verona, Congress, 79
Versailles, Treaty of (1919), 13, 278–83; includes League Covenant, 278–79; and the Fourteen Points, 279–82; self-determination in, 281–82; reparations, 282–83; economic clauses, 283; "war guilt" clause, 283; accepted by Germany, 284; submitted to Senate, 289; opposition to in U.S., 289–91; Wilson's appeal for, 291; first defeat in Senate, 293; attempts at compromise, 294; final defeat, 295; responsibility for defeat, 295–96
Vest, George G., 208
Veto, in U.N. Charter (*See* United Nations)
Victor Emmanuel III, 366
Vienna, Congress of, 79
Viet Cong (*See also* National Liberation Front), 490, 497, 498, 499, 500, 501, 503, 504, 508
Viet Minh, 491, 492, 497
Vietnam (*See also* Vietnam, North; Vietnam, South), 490, 490n., 491, 492, 493
Vietnam, North (Democratic Republic of Vietnam), independence proclaimed, 491; at war with France, 491–92; at Geneva (1954), 492; determined to "liberate" South, 496; how far responsible for Viet Cong?, 497; bombed by U.S., 501, 501–2, 504–6; peace proposals, 504, in peace negotiations, 506–8
Vietnam, South (State—later Republic—of Vietnam), at Geneva, 492; eligible for SEATO benefits, 493; republic under Diem, 495; guerrilla war in, 496–97; refuses election, 496; receives U.S. support, 497–98; U.S. forces in, 498, 501, 502; Senator Mansfield's report, 498n., 499–500, 500n.; overthrow of Diem, 500; constitutional government in, 500; U.S. obligation to, 502–3, 503n.; at peace negotiations, 506–8; to take over U.S. role in war (Vietnamization), 508–9
Vietnam, war in (*See also* Indochina), origins of, 490, 491, 496–97; first U.S. military assistance in, 498; escalation of, 500–502; "hawks" vs. "doves" in U.S., 502–3; war a stalemate, 503–4; Tet offensive, 504; peace feelers, 504–5; halts in bombing, 505, 506; peace negotiations, 506–8; Nixon's offers, 507, 508; NLF proposals, 507, 508; Vietnamizing the war, 508–9; extension of war to Cambodia, 509–12; effect on NATO, 560
Villa, Francisco, 227, 228
Virgin Islands (*See* Danish West Indies)
Vladivostok, 243, 529
Voice of America, 7, 452

Wakatsuki, Premier, 330, 331
Wake Island, 211

Walker, Robert J., 131
Walker, William, 150
Wall Street Journal, 200
Walsh, Bishop James E., 380
Wang Ching-wei, 364
Wanghia, Treaty of, 138–40
War Debts (*See* Debts, World War I)
"War guilt," German, 283
"War hawks," 63, 64
War Industries Board, 267
War of 1812, 16, 65, 71; causes of, 59–64; peace negotiations, 65–66; results of, 66, 67, 68
"War of the Pacific," 176n.
Warsaw Alliance, 447, 447n., 451, 460–61
Warsaw, U.S.-Chinese meetings, 483, 487, 488
Washington Conference (1921–1922), issues to be resolved, 306–10; invitations to, 311; Five-Power Naval Limitation Treaty, 311–12, 311n.; Nine-Power Treaty on China, 312; Four-Power Pacific treaty, 312–13; abrogation of Anglo-Japanese Alliance, 312; Senate action, 313; minor agreements, 313; appraisal of, 313–14
Washington, George, 5, 15, 22, 40, 45; consults cabinet on neutrality, 38–39; "Farewell Address," 45n., 77
Washington, Treaty of (*See* Treaties, U.S., Great Britain)
Watt, Alastair, 99n.
Wayne, Anthony, 40–41
Webster-Ashburton Treaty, 93–98; and slave trade, 96–98; and Oregon, 104
Webster, Daniel, 112, 138, 141; Webster-Ashburton Treaty (q.v.); and slave trade, 96–98; *Caroline* incident, 98–99; and Oregon, 104, 107; and California, 134; and Hungarian independence, 145; and Hawaii, 147; death, 152
Wedemeyer, General Albert C., 466n.
Welles, Sumner, 346n., 351, 353, 414
Wellington, Duke of, 67
Wessin y Wessin, Brig. General Elias, 545, 546
West Germany (*See* German Federal Republic)
West Indian trade (*See* British West Indies)
West Irian (Western New Guinea), 423n.
West (post-Revolution), problems of, 30–34; British policy in, 31, 40–41; Spanish policy, 33; settlements in, 47; and closing of deposit, 49; in favor of war (1812), 63
Western European Union (WEU), 446
Westmoreland, General William C., 503, 506
Weyler, Captain General Valeriano, 197, 199
Wheelus Field, 523n.
White, Andrew D., 207
White, Henry, 271, 289
"White Squadron," 196n.
White, William Allen, 370
Whitman, Dr. Marcus, 102
Whitney, Asa, 147
Wilhelm I, German Kaiser, 163n.
Wilhelm II, German Kaiser, 180, 252, 268, 270, 273
Wilkes, Charles, 120, 158, 159, 211
Wilkinson, General James, 33, 34, 53
Willamette Valley, 102, 104
Williams, G. Mennen, 429, 429n.

Willis, Albert S., 171
Willkie, Wendell L., 372
Wilson, Henry Lane, 227
Wilson, Woodrow, 11, 12, 76, 81n., 229n., 243; and Latin America, 222–30; Nicaragua, 222; Haiti, 223–24; Dominican Republic, 224; Mexico, 225–28, 250; consults "ABC" powers, 227, 229; and U.S. Catholics, 228n.; proposed Pan American treaty, 229–30; and China, 242; Panama Canal tolls, 250; neutrality World War I, 255–66; German submarine war, 259–61, 264–65; *Lusitania,* 261, 261n.; *Sussex,* 261–62; irritation at Great Britain, 262–63; peace proposals (1917), 263–64; reasons for entering war, 265, 265n.; war message, 265–66; Fourteen Points, 269–70, 273–75; relation to Bolshevik revolution, 269, 270; subsequent addresses, 270n.; the armistice, 270–71; decides to go to Paris, 271; choice of delegates, 271–72; appeal for Democratic Congress, 272; loss of election, 272, 272n., 273; problems at Paris, 272–73; secret treaties, 272–73; the Peace Conference and Russia, 276–77; Conference organized, 277–78; League Covenant adopted, 278; modified to appease Senate, 278–79, 279n.; the treaty and the Fourteen Points, 279–82; the mandate system, 280–81; Japan and Shantung, 280–81; self-determination, 281–82; tripartite treaty, 282; reparations, 282–83; Germany accepts, 283–84; praises Treaty, 284; part in writing League Covenant, 286; confers with senators, 290–91; speaking tour and illness, 291; and Hitchcock reservations, 293; rejects Lodge reservations, 293, 295; proposes League as election issue, 294, 294n.; responsibility for defeat, 295–96; vetoes resolution ending war, 297; hints at third term candidacy, 298; breaks ties with League, 299; and Yap, 309; and war debts, 318; vetoes tariff bill (1921), 322–23
Wohlstetter, Roberta, 387
Wood, General Leonard, 218
Wood, General Robert E., 370
Woodford, Stewart L., 201
World Court (Permanent Court of International Justice). (*See also* International Court of Justice), organization and jurisdiction, 300–301; and U.S., 301–2; end of, 417
World Economic Conference (1933), 325–26
World Food Program, 431
World Health Organization (WHO), 417, 430–31
World Peace Foundation, 244
World War I, 16, 254–66, 267–68; U.S. opinion, 254–56; belligerent propaganda, 256; neutrality problems, 255, 257–63; U.S. economy, 256–57; submarine in, 259–63; U.S. enters, 265–66; U.S. part in 267–68; armistice, terms of, 270–71; Allied reservations, 270–71; state of war ended in U.S., 297
World War II, 17, 368; U.S. neutrality, 369ff.; U.S. as nonbelligerent, 369–76; U.S. opinion of, 370, 375; joint planning with British, 372–73; joint defense with Canada, 373; U.S. patrols Atlantic, 374–75; U.S. reclaims "freedom of seas," 375; U.S. participation in, 386, 389–90; wartime con-